THE
BOOK
OF THE
STATES

2007 EDITION
VOLUME 39

ISBN 978-0-87292-838-1

The Council of State Governments
Lexington, Kentucky

Headquarters: (859) 244-8000
Fax: (859) 244-8001
Internet: www.csg.org

Sharing capitol ideas.

Headquarters:
Daniel M. Sprague, Executive Director
2760 Research Park Drive, P.O. Box 11910
Lexington, KY 40578-1910
Phone: (859) 244-8000
Internet: www.csg.org

Southern:
Colleen Cousineau, Director
P.O. Box 98129
Atlanta, GA 30359
Phone: (404) 633-1866
Internet: www.slcatlanta.org

Eastern:
Alan V. Sokolow, Director
100 Wall Street, 20th Floor
New York, NY 10004
Phone: (212) 482-2320
Internet: www.csgeast.org

Western:
Kent Briggs, Director
1107 9th Street, Suite 650
Sacramento, CA 95814
Phone: (916) 553-4423
Internet: www.csgwest.org

Midwestern:
Michael H. McCabe, Director
701 E. 22nd Street, Suite 110
Lombard, IL 60148
Phone: (630) 925-1922
Internet: www.csgmidwest.org

Washington, D.C.:
Jim Brown, General Counsel & Director
444 N. Capitol Street, NW, Suite 401
Washington, D.C. 20001
Phone: (202) 624-5460
Internet: www.csg.org

Publication Sales Department
1(800) 800-1910

Paperback Price: $99.00
ISBN # 978-0-87292-839-8

Hard Cover Price: $125.00
ISBN # 978-0-87292-838-1

Foreword

On behalf of The Council of State Governments, I am pleased to offer the 2007 edition of *The Book of the States*, a premier reference source for politics, policy and administration of the 50 states and U.S. territories. Published since 1935, *The Book of the States* is one of our core publications designed to assist state leaders and managers, as well as students of state government, in their policymaking with timely, accurate and reliable information and data.

This particular edition of the annual reference book contains a comprehensive analysis of the results of the 2006 elections for the three branches of state government, including legislators, governors and other elective executive officials and judges; current and future state finances; and trends and issues in selected policy areas: homeland security, education, health care, welfare, energy and economic development. In addition, the edition highlights steadily changing demographic characteristics in the states, foreign investment challenges and U.S. relations with Mexico.

We would like to take this opportunity to express our gratitude to all authors who have contributed timely articles and the many individuals who have participated in CSG's annual surveys for more than 200 tables in this volume. We know we could not have compiled all the most recent data without their help. We hope that readers will find the edition to be as informative and beneficial as the previous editions.

May 2007   Daniel M. Sprague
                                                 Executive Director
                                                 The Council of State Governments

The Book of the States 2007

Editor in Chief	Keon S. Chi
Project Manager	Audrey S. Wall
Associate Editor	Heather M. Perkins
Production Coordinator	Lisa K. Eads
Graphic Designer	Chris D. Pryor
Proofreader	Kasey Cooke

Acknowledgements

The editorial and production staff members wish to thank the article authors who graciously shared their expertise and insights, the hundreds of individuals in the states who responded to national surveys conducted by The Council of State Governments, national organizations of state officials, federal agencies and think tank organizations who made their most recent data and information available for this volume.

Table of Contents

CONTENTS

Chapter Four
STATE EXECUTIVE BRANCH 145

ARTICLES

The State of the States: Political Change Emboldens Governors

Gubernatorial Elections, Campaign Costs and Powers

TABLES

Governors

CONTENTS

Chapter Five
STATE JUDICIAL BRANCH 247

Chapter Six
ELECTIONS 275

CONTENTS

Chapter Seven
STATE FINANCE AND DEMOGRAPHICS **339**

Chapter Eight
STATE MANAGEMENT AND ADMINISTRATION...449

Chapter Nine
SELECTED STATE POLICIES AND PROGRAMS 471

CONTENTS

Emerging Trends and Issues in the States: 2007 and Beyond

By Keon S. Chi

This year appears to be a turning point in American politics. One of the most obvious changes in 2007 is the Democrats' newly-acquired control in Congress as well as a majority of state legislatures and governor's offices: last year's elections ended a decade-long Republican dominance. More women than ever before are serving as lawmakers, and the number of female governors remains a record high at nine. Campaigns for the 2008 presidential election are in full swing across the states, and several states have broken away from traditional election schedules by changing their primary election or convention dates.

Thanks to increased revenues, most, if not all, states seem to be in a much better fiscal condition than they were in the last two to three years. Consequently, this year's governors' state of the state addresses have not focused as much as they did before on belt-tightening measures; most chief executives are urging improvement in traditional policy areas, such as education, health care, taxation, energy/natural resources and economic development. Overall, state policymakers appear to have returned to routines, preparing for a few anticipated changes in areas such as the reauthorization of the No Child Left Behind Act, new welfare reform rules and Real ID issues that deal with homeland security.

A bright picture notwithstanding, state policymakers will need to address some serious issues they are likely to face this and future years. Among them are demographic and societal changes, such as continuous growth, aging and shifts of the population, and the related education and health care costs and public safety issues. In addition, economic changes, which include proposed cuts in federal aid to state and local governments and challenges from abroad, will pose challenges to states. Some governors, legislative leaders and chief justices are proposing to re-examine the way they govern and develop alternative approaches, if necessary, to better face emerging issues and meet expectations of their state's residents. Most people say state government should be more citizen-oriented and have plans for the future, but they likely will continue to resist tax hikes or demand tax relief and expect more and better services from government.

As in the previous editions, the 2007 edition of *The Book of the States* includes the usual 10 chapters,

each containing article(s) by national experts and tables with the most up-to-date data. In this introduction, we provide for readers an overview of emerging trends and issues from the 30 articles in this edition under four headings: state governance, finances, policies and challenges.

State Governance

The 2006 elections are regarded as among the most successful elections in recent decades. "It was a year when all new federal mandates contained in the Help America Vote Act of 2002 came due," the Election Center's Doug Lewis said. "Massive changes in virtually every part of the process were accomplished in this election cycle." In last year's elections, John Dinan reports, voters in many states also adopted the largest number of constitutional amendments either through constitutional initiative or legislative proposal. Citizen participation in the electoral process was record-breaking indeed. John Matsusaka, in his analysis of 2006 initiatives and referendums, reports that the number of citizen-initiated ballot measures was the third highest in U.S. History. The two most popular issues were bans on same-sex marriage and increases in the minimum wage. However, as Kay Stimson of the National Association of Secretaries of State notes, lack of confidence in electronic voting machines is a concern for state election officials and other election observers.

States' relations with the federal government are likely to change only if the Democratic majority in Congress reverses the trend of what John Kincaid calls "coercive federalism" by allowing more flexibility and waivers and by eliminating unfunded federal mandates and preemptions. It is doubtful, however, that the divided government in Washington will be able to change centralist approaches to federalism in the next couple of years. As states often criticize Uncle Sam about federal encroachment, they also are targets of complaints from local governments. According to a recent survey by Joseph Zimmerman, local officials are complaining about the continued imposition of state mandates and restraints.

As for state legislatures, new political party lineups in many states could change agenda-setting and policy-formulation at least on a short-term basis. In

2007, Democrats control 22 state legislatures and Republicans control 15, while in 12 states, control is divided with neither party holding both chambers. Democrats now have more legislative seats in the Eastern and Midwestern states. The overall turnover rate in 2006 was approximately 19 percent; states with term limits had higher turnover rates. Currently, term limits are in place in 15 states, but two—Louisiana and Nevada—have yet to implement the measure. Several states have considered increasing the number of terms or years legislators are allowed to serve, but it seems highly unlikely that more states will adopt term limits in the near future. Other than high turnover rates, many of proponents arguments supporting term limits have not materialized. A recent report, "Coping with Term Limits," suggests that state legislatures are making adjustments to respond to the challenges created by term limits.

As for the executive branch, voters in 36 states elected or re-elected governors last year, resulting in a Democratic majority for the first time since 1994. Currently, 28 states have Democratic governors and 22 states have Republican governors. In recent decades, governors have tended to expand their institutional powers, especially the veto power. However, governors' budgetary powers have not increased, according to Thad Beyle, who monitors formal powers of governors based on selected indices, such as the length of term of office, number of elected executives, veto, budget-making, appointment and reorganization powers. Legislators and their staffs in term-limited states tend to believe the legislative branch has lost power to the executive branch in part due to the loss of experienced lawmakers.

Lieutenant governors are more visible now, with many of them actively involved in policymaking and management roles. According to Julia Hurst of the National Lieutenant Governors Association, some lieutenant governors are now heading a department or division of state government, while many others are involved in a variety of statewide projects. Expanded roles of lieutenant governors have been featured in the media. When voters in New Jersey elect their lieutenant governor in 2009, we will have a total of 45 states with the second highest-ranking executive position.

Regarding other constitutional state officers, this year marks the 100 year anniversary of the National Association of Attorneys General, one of the oldest national organizations of state officials. Attorneys general, who serve as states' chief litigation officers, are involved in a number of multi-state issues, such as antitrust, bankruptcy, civil rights, consumer protection, criminal law, end-of-life health care, environment,

Medicaid fraud, tobacco and appellate advocacy. As noted earlier, the National Association of Secretaries of State is concerned about implementation of the HAVA of 2002 and the integrity of electronic voting. Two key undertakings of the National Association of State Auditors, Comptrollers and Treasurers are setting benchmarks to improve their performance and implementing the new requirements of the Government Accounting Standards Board. State treasurers, through the National Association of State Treasurers, continue to improve the way they handle debt management, investment of state funds and college savings plans.

In the judicial branch, reformers of state court systems were not successful with their ballot issues in 2006, but are likely to continue their reform agenda. As in previous elections, observers have noted problems with special interest groups' campaign contributions to judicial elections. Methods of electing judges will continue to be a hot issue. At the same time, the issue of performance management has dominated state courts. "The state judicial branches in 2006 made significant strides in refining and creating methods for measuring their performance and demonstrating their accountability to the other branches of government," said David Rottman of the National Center for State Courts. In fact, state courts have been working on "high-performing courts" with "CourTools" in recent years. CourTools consists of 10 evaluation criteria, including court-user ratings, fairness, time to disposition for cases, cost per case and effective use of juries. State policymakers in the executive and legislative branches might learn something from the judicial branch's experiences in performance management.

State Finances

The overall fiscal outlook for 2007 remains as positive as in 2006. The most recent fiscal survey conducted by the National Association of State Budget Officers (NASBO) shows strong revenue growth, surpassing budgeted estimates by nearly 6 percent in most states. When looking ahead, however, state policymakers need to be cautious with their spending plans. Brian Sigritz of NASBO warns:

"Areas such as health care and elementary and secondary education are expected to grow. States will also face increased costs in transportation construction and maintenance, pensions, higher education, and managing the myriad issues associated with the retirement of the baby boomers. Finally, as the federal debt continues to increase, states will face the possibility of slow growth of assistance from the federal government. All these factors taken together show that while the current state fiscal situation is bright, clouds may be on the horizon."

Sigritz's forecast is shared by Brian Stenson, formerly of the Rockefeller Institute, who wrote: "States are likely to face challenges from slowing tax collections, a resumption in Medicaid's traditional spending growth, pressures in K-12 education, and new accounting requirements for employee benefits."

Medicaid spending in 2006 did not grow much thanks to Medicare Part D, which transferred certain prescription drug costs for older recipients from Medicaid to Medicare. This was a one-time reduction in Medicaid spending. In some states, Medicaid is now the largest single expenditure area in budgets, according to Stenson. Medicaid spending is expected to continue to grow steadily.

Proposed cuts in federal financial aid to states are likely to add more pressures to state spending plans. "The president's $2.9 trillion FY 2008 budget proposal would eliminate or deeply cut 141 federal programs and increase discretionary spending outside of security by only 1 percent over 2007, below the inflation rate," said John Kincaid, who tracks trends in state-federal relations. "The new Democratic majority will certainly resist cuts; nonetheless, in the long term, federal aid for nonsocial welfare programs will slip downward, and even federal aid for social welfare, such as Medicaid, will barely keep pace with inflation. Alone, the rising costs of the federal government's three major entitlements—Social Security, Medicare and Medicaid—will crowd out federal discretionary spending, which includes most grants-in-aid. These three programs, plus other social welfare programs, constitute 54 percent of Bush's FY 2008 budget request."

In early 2007, governors, through their annual state of the state addresses, proposed a variety of plans to deal with short- and long-term fiscal problems. On a short-term basis, several governments have developed tax credits and financial incentive programs for economic development, energy conservation and alternative fuel use; property tax relief; plans to lengthen the terms of existing bonded indebtedness; and a relief package to cut taxes for the middle class. New Jersey's governor proposed initiatives to reduce the state's high property tax rate by instituting new ways of auditing, local government consolidations and shared services, collective bargaining on pension and health benefits and asset monetization to reduce state credit card payments. Other governors have addressed the problem of long-term structural imbalances. According to Katherine Willoughby, who analyzed the 2007 state

of the state addresses, "governors are concerned about the primary responsibilities of state government and how best to extend services to residents in need, yet mindful of the balancing act that must occur between revenues and expenditures in order for their governments to remain financially viable."

This year, most state financial officials will have to prepare themselves for the implementation of the Government Accounting Standards Board's Statement 45, which is scheduled to take effect during fiscal year 2008. GASB 45, issued in 2004, requires governments to disclose the true cost of retirees' health insurance and other post-employment benefits (OPEB) on their financial statements. Under GASB 45, as Stenson notes, states must disclose several pieces of information for their respective OPEB plans, such as the annual OPEB cost, actual contributions made and the funded status. Fully funding the annual OPEB cost would require setting aside money in a trust that would invest it, thus meeting OPEB expenses as they are due. Historically, states have accounted for OPEB liabilities on a pay-as-you-go basis. Now, states will account for those liabilities on an accrual basis, similar to pension liabilities. According to Robin Prunty and Parry Young of Standard & Poor's, "GASB 45 is a new way to account for and report on these liabilities, but there is no requirement to fund the liability at this time. GASB will bring greater transparency to the financial disclosure surrounding post-employment benefits."

State Policies

Among the hot issues affecting state policymakers in 2007 and beyond are the controversial funding formula for homeland security grants to states, reauthorization of the No Child Left Behind Act, preventive health care, renewable and sustainable energy sources, declining foreign investment and job creation, new rules of the welfare program and border problems with the Southern neighbors.

As in the federal government, homeland security remains a top priority for most states this year. State emergency management officials are concerned about the implementation of the 9/11 Commission Report recommendations, including a streamlined homeland security funding allocation formula. The issue here is whether funding levels should be based on risk and infrastructure vulnerability, a percentage plus population basis or population density, or the priority of international border states versus coastal states.

Another issue related to homeland security deals with the Real ID Act passed by Congress in 2005. This law sets minimum standards for issuing states' driver's licenses. Congress has appropriated only $40 million in state assistance funds even though initial estimates to implement the law exceeded $11 billion over a five-year period. For most states, this federal mandate, scheduled to take effect in 2008, requires additional state resources. Although the May 2008 deadline has been extended up to 19 months, states may not be able to locate and verify all the necessary records to issue new ID cards to meet the federal standards.

The debate on the controversial No Child Left Behind Act is likely to heat up since the Act, enacted in 2002, is scheduled for reauthorization this year. The Act requires states to annually test students to measure competency in the core subjects of reading and math. By 2013–14, all states are to ensure that 100 percent of students are proficient on state reading and math standards. The NCLB debates have centered around funding, mandatory testing and flexibility issues. While the federal government has insisted it has given sufficient funding to implement the act, many states consider the law another example of unfunded federal mandates.

In the health care field, states are not waiting for the federal government to act. Some states, including California and Massachusetts, are either implementing or considering universal health care for their residents. In the meantime, many states have passed laws to reduce cancer risk by focusing on smoke-free places, obesity prevention and various types of cancer—cervical, colorectal, ovarian, prostate and skin.

More state policymakers also are turning their attention to energy challenges. "While both health and education will continue to rank high and continue to challenge governors and legislators, the convergence of three other issues—climate change, peaking of world oil supply and water shortages—could be an even greater problem for these policymakers," reports former Wyoming Gov. Jim Geringer, now an energy consultant. Of those issues, the development of renewable energy sources poses a challenge. Currently, solar, biomass, geothermal, hydroelectric, and wind—all forms of renewable energy—provide 6 percent of total energy used. The question is this: Can states increase the proportion of such renewable energy and reduce consumption of imported petroleum?

The welfare caseload has been declining in recent years, and welfare is not among the top policy priorities for states. However, the Deficit Reduction Act of 2005, which reauthorized the Temporary Assistance to Needy Families program, poses a new challenge. The act requires states to comply with the new rules by the start of fiscal year 2008. States must maintain a 50 percent work requirement for all adults on welfare and 90 percent for two-parent families. All parents must participate in at least 20 hours of core activities, and parents with children age 6 or older must engage in an additional 10 hours of core activities. Each state's success will depend upon more effective programs to increase work participation, and 2007 work participation rates will be calculated under the new rules.

State policymakers need to be aware of trends in business incentives for economic development in light of recent Supreme Court decisions, such as *Cuno v. DaimlerChrysler*. The issue is this: Can states continue to offer development incentives to selected companies as in the past? Or, should states support the Economic Development Act of 2005, designed to affirm states' rights to offer incentives, pending in Congress? Another area of concern for state economic development officials is the declining trend in direct foreign investments in the states. According to Jeffrey Finkle of the International Economic Development Council, "the U.S. can no longer assume that foreign firms will continue to invest and employ people here at the same rate as in the past" because investors are going to other countries with a more favorable business climate, including China and India. Lastly, it is important for state leaders to pay particular attention to U.S.-Mexico relations as they address a hemispheric strategy for immigration, economic development and security problems.

Other Challenges

Challenges state policymakers face are not limited to the trends and issues highlighted above; there are several other trends to consider when re-examining current policies. Many states are beginning to address the aging issue from different policy perspectives. Policymakers should also pay attention to the increasing foreign-born population. While the majority of the racial/ethnic minority population still resides in what demographers call "gateway states" and metropolitan areas, as demographer William Frey reports, they are now moving into states and cities that did not have many minority populations until a decade ago. At the same time, as Mark Mather of the Population Reference Bureau said, "the foreign-born are increasingly settling in other parts of the United States—especially in the South—bringing new cultures, languages, racial and ethnic diversity, economic opportunity and challenges for policymakers." Are states ready to address policy implications of these fast changing demographic characteristics?

Finally, as briefly noted above, New Jersey's ongoing efforts to be more effective and efficient through restructuring and cooperation are likely to become an emerging trend at the state level. Structural and functional consolidations and shared services have been widely used in local government as described by Marc Holzer and his colleagues. States can certainly learn valuable lessons from local experiments and consider implementing some of the successful approaches. Today, collaboration seems to be a new buzz word in public management at all levels of government—formal and informal collaboration among agencies, with other states, other levels of government and other sectors. Collaborative efforts can help state governance transform itself to better address challenges of the 21st century.

Keon S. Chi is editor in chief of *The Book of the States*.

Chapter One

STATE CONSTITUTIONS

"After several years during which the number of state constitutional amendments had dropped from previous levels, amendment activity increased slightly... A significant number of constitutional amendments dealt with individual rights."

—John Dinan

State Constitutional Developments in 2006
By John Dinan

After several years during which the number of state constitutional amendments had dropped from previous levels, amendment activity increased slightly, in that the number of amendments proposed in 2006 equaled the number of amendments proposed in 2004 and 2005 combined, and the number of amendments adopted in 2006 exceeded the total for 2004–05. Eight states enacted amendments prohibiting legalization of same-sex marriage, and another eight states approved amendments restricting use of the eminent domain power for private purposes. Multiple states approved amendments increasing the minimum wage and regulating the use of tobacco settlement funds. Also of note were a Michigan amendment banning affirmative action, a Missouri amendment ensuring continuation of embryonic stem cell research, and a Florida amendment requiring future constitutional changes to obtain 60 percent of the popular vote.

Although the 2006 elections are likely to be most remembered as the occasion when Democrats regained control of the U.S. House and Senate and a majority of state governorships, voters also passed judgment on a sizable number of constitutional amendments (166 proposed and 125 adopted), which represented an increase not only from 2005, an off-year election in most states, but also from 2004, a presidential election year.

A significant number of constitutional amendments dealt with individual rights. Same-sex marriage bans continued to be proposed in response to the Massachusetts Supreme Judicial Court's legalization of same-sex marriage in *Goodridge v. Department of Public Health* (2003), and such bans were approved in eight states. However, voters in Arizona defeated a same-sex marriage ban, the first time such an amendment failed. Voters also approved eight constitutional amendments proposed in the aftermath of the U.S. Supreme Court's decision in *Kelo v. City of New London* (2005) for the purpose of disallowing use of the eminent domain power for economic development purposes; however, voters in California rejected a more expansive measure that would have also compensated property owners for regulatory takings. Meanwhile, Michigan voters approved a constitutional amendment banning affirmative action, following the lead of California voters a decade earlier.

Voters also passed judgment on numerous policy amendments. Constitutional amendments for minimum wage increases were approved in three states. Tax and expenditure limitation constitutional amendments were defeated in two states. Various tobacco-related amendments were also placed on the ballot, and although cigarette tax increases failed in two states, amendments regulating the use of tobacco set-

Table A: State Constitutional Changes by Method of Initiation: 2002–03, 2004–05 and 2006

Method of initiation	Number of states involved			Total proposals			Total adopted			Percentage adopted		
	2002–2003	2004–2005	2006	2002–2003	2004–2005	2006	2002–2003	2004–2005	2006	2002–2003	2004–2005	2006
All methods.............................	38	40	34	232	166	166(a)	164	112	125(a)(b)	70.6	67.5	75.3
Legislative proposal	36	38	32	208	127	133(a)	155	95	114(a)	74.5	74.8	85.7
Constitutional initiative........	11	13	12	24	39	33	9	17	11(b)	37.5	43.6	33.3
Constitutional convention.....	...	...	...	...	...	...	...	...	...	...	...	...
Constitutional commission ...	...	...	...	...	...	...	...	...	...	...	...	...

Source: Based on surveys conducted in previous years by Janice May and updated by John Dinan for the years 2005 and 2006.
Key:
. . . — Not applicable.
(a) Excludes one Alabama amendment that was proposed by the legislature and appeared on the ballot but was determined by the Governor's office prior to the vote not to have received enough votes in the legislature to properly appear on the ballot, and thus even though the amendment was approved by voters in November 2006 and the vote totals were certified by the state canvassing board, the governor did not proclaim the results for the amendment and so it has not received an official amendment number.
(b) These totals include one amendment approved in a first election, but not yet in a second election, in Nevada (where initiatives must be approved in two successive general elections).

tlement funds were approved in three states. Meanwhile, Missouri voters approved a constitutional amendment ensuring the continuation of all embryonic stem cell research permitted by federal law.

Also of note were several amendments dealing with governing institutions and the constitutional amendment process itself. Colorado and South Dakota voters rejected controversial amendments that targeted the judiciary, whether by imposing judicial term limits (in Colorado) or depriving judges of immunity from citizen lawsuits (in South Dakota). Colorado voters approved an ethics reform amendment that, among other things, prevents legislators from becoming lobbyists for two years after leaving office. And Florida voters approved an amendment requiring future constitutional changes to receive 60 percent of the popular vote, making Florida and New Hampshire the only states to require a popular supermajority to approve constitutional amendments.

Constitutional Amendment and Revision Methods

Constitutional amendments were proposed in 2006 in 34 states, far more than the 11 states that considered amendments in the off-year election of 2005 and slightly above the 33 states that considered amendments in 2004. All told in 2006, 166 amendments were proposed and 125 were approved. This compares with 2005, when 26 amendments were proposed and 14 were approved, and with 2004, when 140 amendments were proposed and 98 were approved.

Legislative Proposals and Constitutional Initiatives

The 166 constitutional amendments considered by voters in 2006 were all proposed by legislatures or through the initiative process. Legislatures proposed 133 amendments, and 113 of these legislature-initiated amendments were approved, for a passage rate of 85.7 percent.[1] Thirty-three amendments were proposed by constitutional initiative, a process available in 18 states, and 11 of these initiated amendments were approved, for a passage rate of 33.3 percent.[2]

Constitutional Conventions and Revision Commissions

Although no constitutional conventions were held in 2006, discussions continued from previous years in Alabama and New Jersey about whether to call a convention. In Alabama, the public interest group Alabama Citizens for Constitutional Reform (ACCR) has been trying for several years to build support for a convention to revise Alabama's 1901 Constitution,

the oldest in the nation. Although proponents of a convention were unable in 2006 to persuade the legislature to submit a convention call to the people, this measure did attract more legislative support than in recent years, with 10 senators voting to move the measure out of a senate committee and seven representatives offering their support in a house committee.[3]

In New Jersey, Gov. Jon Corzine has, since his election in November 2005, urged the legislature to find a way to reduce the state's property taxes, the highest in the country. He has also suggested that a constitutional convention might be necessary if the legislature fails to act. In late 2006, the governor and legislature agreed to hold a special legislative session to address the tax issue. As part of the process, the legislature established four special joint Senate/Assembly committees, including one committee charged with assessing the need for constitutional changes. This committee determined that a convention was not needed in order to bring about property tax reform, and that any constitutional changes would be minor and could be handled through the amendment process. But that does not eliminate the possibility a convention will be held. The two houses of the legislature were unable to reach agreement on a tax reform package by year's end, and the governor has continued to argue, including in his State of the State address in January 2007, that a convention remains an option in the event of legislative inaction.[4]

The one constitutional revision commission operating in 2006 was the Utah Constitutional Revision Commission, the only commission that has an ongoing charge to propose constitutional amendments that are then considered by the legislature. Commission members in 2006 debated constitutional changes regarding property tax exemptions, gubernatorial succession, the veto power and the judicial rulemaking power, among other issues.

Constitutional Changes

Voters in 2006 were not asked to approve any new constitutions or wholesale revisions of existing constitutions. The proposed changes all took the form of constitutional amendments. Of particular importance were numerous amendments pertaining to individual rights and various public policy issues. Several notable amendments also dealt with governing institutions and the amendment process itself.

Rights

As in the past two years, the Massachusetts Supreme Judicial Court's 2003 legalization of same-sex marriage continued to generate constitutional amend-

Table B: Substantive Changes in State Constitutions: Proposed and Adopted: 2002–03, 2004–05 and 2006

Subject matter	Total proposed			Total adopted			Percentage adopted		
	2002–03	2004–05	2006	2002–03	2004–05	2006	2002–03	2004–05	2006
Proposals of statewide applicability	191	138	141	128	94 (a)	104 (b)	67.0	68.1	73.7
Bill of Rights..........................	12	16	29 (c)	8	15	25 (b)(c)	66.6	93.8	86.2
Suffrage & elections.................	6	14	6	3	6	3	50.0	42.9	50.0
Legislative branch....................	24	14	11	17	6	6	70.8	42.8	54.5
Executive branch......................	8	5	1	4	4	1	50.0	80.0	100.0
Judicial branch........................	19	10	7	11	5	3	57.8	50.0	42.8
Local government.....................	5	4	1	5	3	0	100.0	75.0	0.0
Finance & taxation..................	65	33	55	39	23	44	60.0	69.7	80.0
State & local debt....................	10	7	4	5	6	3	50.0	85.7	75.0
State functions........................	16	14	3	13	8 (a)	2	81.2	57.1	66.7
Amendment & revision.............	3	1	1	3	1	1	100.0	100.0	100.0
General revision proposals.......	0	0	0	0	0	0	0.0	0.0	0.0
Miscellaneous proposals...........	23	20	23	20	17	16	86.0	85.0	69.5
Local amendments.....................	41	28	25 (d)	36	18	21 (d)	87.8	64.3	84.0

Source: Based on surveys conducted in previous years by Janice May and updated by John Dinan for the years 2005 and 2006.

Key:

(a) Includes Delaware, where amendments do not require popular approval.

(b) Includes one Nevada amendment that received approval in a first election, but not yet in a second election, as required for initiative amendments in that state.

(c) Includes amendments restricting the use of eminent domain, re-

gardless of whether these protections were actually inserted in the bill of rights or in other articles.

(d) Excludes one Alabama amendment that was proposed by the legislature and appeared on the ballot but was determined by the Governor's office prior to the vote not to have received enough votes in the legislature to properly appear on the ballot, and thus even though the amendment was approved by voters in November 2006 and the vote totals were certified by the state canvassing board, the governor did not proclaim the results for the amendment and so it has not received an official amendment number.

ments intended to forestall similar rulings by other state courts. Prior to 2006, 18 states had enacted constitutional provisions prohibiting same-sex marriage, and Hawaii had adopted a constitutional provision empowering the legislature to limit marriage to opposite-sex couples. Eight more states adopted same-sex marriage bans in 2006, including Alabama (in June) and Colorado, Idaho, South Carolina, South Dakota, Tennessee, Virginia and Wisconsin (all in November), bringing to 27 the number of states with constitutional provisions on the topic. Most of these 2006 measures passed easily, with Alabama and Tennessee voters providing the largest margins of victory, 81 percent to 19 percent in both states. However, South Dakota voters approved a ban by the narrowest margin to date, 52 percent to 48 percent. Moreover, Arizona voters rejected a same-sex marriage ban on a 52-48 percent vote, marking the first time that such a measure has been defeated at the polls.

Meanwhile, a constitutional amendment that would effectively overturn the Massachusetts Supreme Court's *Goodridge* decision and ban same-sex marriage in that state continued to move forward, but only after encountering significant difficulties that nearly derailed its passage. An earlier effort to submit such an amendment by legislative proposal was defeated in September 2005 when legislators failed to give the required second approval to a measure that had

received initial legislative approval in March 2004. Opponents of same-sex marriage then turned to the constitutional initiative process, which in Massachusetts requires gathering signatures from 3 percent of the voters in the last gubernatorial election and then receiving the approval of 25 percent of the members of the House and Senate convened as a constitutional convention, and in successive legislative sessions. The first of these requirements was met in December 2005 with the gathering of 170,000 signatures. The second step proved more difficult. Although it was clear that the amendment enjoyed the support of the requisite number of legislators, legislative leaders employed procedural tactics to recess a Nov. 9, 2006, constitutional convention without allowing a vote. With outgoing Republican Gov. Mitt Romney urging the legislature to bring the amendment to a vote on the grounds that it was constitutionally required to do so, and incoming Democratic Gov. Deval Patrick counseling against such a vote on the grounds that it would amount to supporting discrimination, the issue was brought to the Massachusetts Supreme Judicial Court. The justices determined on Dec. 27, 2006, that they lacked the power to compel the legislature to take a vote; but they made it clear that legislators would be disregarding their constitutional duty if they adjourned without bringing the amendment to a vote. Prodded to action by the court's ruling, the legislature assembled in constitutional convention on Jan. 2, 2007, the last day of the legislative session, and approved the amendment by the requisite 25 percent—62 members voted for it and 132 voted against it. The amendment still needs to be approved a second time, in the 2007–08 legislative session, again by 25 percent of legislators, before it can be placed on the November 2008 ballot.[5] Other states that could also see same-sex marriage bans on the 2008 ballot include Indiana, where legislators must give their second approval to a proposed amendment, and Florida, where proponents are working to place such an amendment on the ballot through the initiative process.[6]

Voters in 2006 also considered numerous constitutional amendments intended to respond to the U.S. Supreme Court's 2005 *Kelo* decision holding that the use of eminent domain for economic development purposes does not violate the federal constitution. A sizable number of state legislatures in 2005 and 2006 responded to public dissatisfaction with this ruling by making statutory changes to restrict use of the eminent domain power by state and local governments, generally by prohibiting use of the power to condemn private property for economic development purposes. However, property rights advocates also sought to accomplish this goal by amending state constitutions, and amendments were placed before the voters in nine states. Voters in Arizona, Idaho, Oregon and Washington also passed judgment on statutory measures seeking to restrict eminent domain and/or provide compensation for regulatory takings. Constitutional amendments restricting the use of eminent domain were approved in Louisiana (in September), and Florida, Georgia, Michigan, Nevada (where it received the first of two required approvals), New Hampshire, North Dakota and South Carolina (all in November). However, a more expansive amendment seeking to limit use of eminent domain and to compensate property owners for regulatory takings was rejected in California.

Assorted other amendments dealing with rights also appeared on the ballot in 2006. Michigan voters approved an initiated amendment prohibiting public institutions from giving preferential treatment based on race, gender, color, ethnicity or national origin, thereby following California (in 1996) in restricting affirmative action through the constitutional initiative process. Washington voters had approved a statutory measure of this sort in 1998. In fact, Ward Connerly, the principal backer of these measures, announced plans in the aftermath of the Michigan vote to consider organizing similar campaigns in other states

with the initiative procedure, including Arizona, Colorado, Missouri, Nebraska, Nevada, Oregon, South Dakota, Wyoming and Utah.[7] Meanwhile, Rhode Island voters approved a constitutional amendment expanding suffrage rights of ex-felons by eliminating a provision denying felons the vote while on probation or parole; felons will now be disenfranchised only while in prison. Additionally, California voters rejected for the second time in two years an initiated amendment that would have required parental notification 48 hours before a minor could obtain an abortion. Oregon voters rejected a similar measure placed on the ballot as a statutory initiative.

Policy

Voters in 2006 considered a wide range of constitutional amendments dealing with public policy issues, many of which had been blocked in the legislature and were placed on the ballot through the initiative process.

Constitutional amendments increasing the minimum wage were approved in three states—Colorado, Nevada and Ohio. Arizona, Missouri and Montana voters also approved statutory minimum wage increases.

Voters in two states—Nebraska and Oregon—considered tax-and-expenditure limitation amendments modeled after the Taxpayers' Bill of Rights (TABOR) that was added to the Colorado Constitution in 1992 but then partially suspended for five years in 2005. However, voters in both states rejected these measures. (A Maine initiative that was placed on the ballot as a statutory change was also defeated.)

Voters passed judgment on a number of constitutional amendments dealing with tobacco policy, regarding cigarette taxes, restrictions on smoking and the use of money from legal settlements between states and tobacco companies. Amendments to increase cigarette taxes were rejected in California (a $2.60 a pack increase) and Missouri (an 80 cents a pack increase). Statutory cigarette tax increases were approved in Arizona and South Dakota. Meanwhile, Ohio voters rejected an industry-supported amendment to restrict smoking in certain public places but permit smoking in other public places and also pre-empt local governments from banning smoking in these other places. The Ohio measure was placed on the ballot in an unsuccessful attempt to head off passage of a competing health organization-sponsored statutory measure that imposed much more stringent restrictions on smoking. Similar battles between health organization-sponsored smoking bans and industry-supported counter-measures were waged on a statutory basis in Arizona and Nevada, and in each case the health organization measure won and the industry measure failed. Additionally, voters in Florida, Idaho and Louisiana approved constitutional amendments regulating use of the settlement money that these states receive from tobacco companies. The Florida measure requires a portion of the settlement money to be spent on youth anti-smoking campaigns. The Idaho measure requires most of the settlement money to be spent on health-related purposes. And the Louisiana measure, approved in September, allows a portion of the settlement money to be used for coastal conservation.[8]

Education-spending amendments experienced mixed success in 2006. Voters in Colorado defeated an amendment that would have required at least 65 percent of school spending by local school districts to be dedicated to classroom instruction. But Nevada voters approved an Education First amendment requiring legislators to approve the education spending bill before approving any other spending bill. The intent was to prohibit advocates of higher spending and taxes from, in essence, holding hostage the education spending bill as a way of forcing legislators to support a tax increase, as was done in 2003 in a dispute that led to a controversial Nevada Supreme Court decision, *Guinn v. Legislature* (2003).[9]

Amendments were also placed on the ballot regarding a variety of controversial public policy questions including gambling, drugs, stem cell research and illegal immigration. In terms of gambling, Arizona voters approved an amendment permitting charities to run bingo games, while Ohio voters rejected an amendment that would have authorized slot machines, and Rhode Island voters defeated an amendment that would have permitted the operation of a privately run casino. Regarding drug policy, a proposal to amend the Colorado constitution to legalize possession of up to an ounce of marijuana was rejected. Meanwhile, Missouri voters narrowly approved a complex amendment that supporters said was intended to permit all forms of embryonic stem cell research authorized under federal law. Arizona and Colorado voters approved several immigration-related constitutional amendments. Arizonans passed amendments declaring English the official state language, denying bail to illegal immigrants charged with committing a serious felony, and prohibiting illegal immigrants from collecting punitive damage awards in civil suits. Colorado voters passed a constitutional amendment directing the state attorney general to sue the federal government to bring about enforcement of current immigration laws. Several statutory measures targeting illegal immigration were also approved in these states.

Governing Institutions

Judges were the target of several amendments, including measures in Colorado and South Dakota that generated a great deal of media attention but were ultimately defeated. Colorado voters rejected an amendment that would have limited state appellate judges to serving a single 10-year term and would have taken effect retroactively, thereby forcing the removal within two years of five supreme court judges and seven appellate court judges. The amendment would have made Colorado the first state to adopt term limits for appellate judges, but it was defeated, 57 percent to 43 percent. Meanwhile, South Dakota voters rejected by a much wider margin—89 percent to 11 percent—an even more controversial "Jail 4 Judges" amendment that would have established special grand juries to evaluate citizen lawsuits against judges and would have stripped judges of their immunity for acts that violated individual rights. Two other proposed amendments that received less national attention but would have had important political implications in Hawaii and Oregon were also defeated. Hawaii voters rejected an amendment that would have repealed the mandatory retirement age of 70 for state judges and thereby would have denied Republican Gov. Linda Lingle the opportunity to make two replacement appointments in the next few years. Oregon voters rejected an amendment intended to give increased representation to rural, more conservative regions of the state by requiring appellate judges to run for election in geographic districts and reside in those districts.[10]

Legislators were targeted in various ways by three notable amendments, two of which were approved. Colorado voters approved a wide-ranging ethics reform package that applies to legislators and other public officials. It prohibits them from accepting gifts from lobbyists and from becoming lobbyists themselves within two years after leaving office. A similar two-year lobbying ban, albeit on a statutory basis, was also approved by Montana voters. Meanwhile, Oklahoma voters approved an amendment prohibiting legislators from being paid their salary while in jail on a misdemeanor conviction, in reaction to a recent case where a legislator was paid while spending a month in jail. A felony conviction would already result in their removal from office. However, voters in Oregon rejected an amendment that would have restored legislative term limits—six years for representatives and eight years for senators—after they were originally adopted in 1992 and took effect after 2000 but were then invalidated by the state supreme court in 2002.

Amendment Process

In a development that will make it more difficult to secure future constitutional changes, Florida voters in 2006 approved an amendment, by a 58 percent to 42 percent vote, that requires constitutional amendments or revisions to receive 60 percent of the popular vote. An existing provision requiring amendments imposing new state taxes or fees to receive two-thirds of the vote was unchanged. The measure was backed by business groups and was opposed by liberal groups as well as by some conservatives who feared that the new requirement would make it more difficult to use the amendment process to overturn controversial state supreme court decisions, such as the Florida Supreme Court's *Bush v. Holmes* (2006) ruling striking down a school voucher program.[11] Florida becomes only the second state to require a supermajority of the people to approve constitutional amendments, joining New Hampshire, which requires a two-thirds vote. Five states require approval by a majority voting in the entire election, rather than on the particular question.

Trends

Several trends emerge from a review of state constitutional developments in 2006. Regarding the methods of state constitutional change, legislative-initiated and citizen-initiated amendments continue to be the dominant mechanisms, and were in fact the exclusive means by which constitutional changes were proposed this year, as was the case last year. Yet another year passed, therefore, without a constitutional convention, although momentum continued to build for calling a convention in Alabama, and discussion continued in New Jersey about a possible convention to reform the tax system.

Several types of amendments appeared on multiple state ballots in 2006 and are likely to reappear over the next several years. Judicial decisions such as the Massachusetts Supreme Judicial Court's *Goodridge* ruling and the U.S. Supreme Court's *Kelo* ruling are likely to generate continuing state constitutional responses in the form of bans on same-sex marriage and limits on use of eminent domain for economic development purposes. Public policy issues that are believed to be attracting insufficient attention in the legislative process are also likely to continue generating constitutional amendments, often through the initiative process. Judging from the results in 2006, amendments increasing the minimum wage, restricting illegal immigration and banning affirmative action were all successful and can be expected to return to state ballots in coming years. Although the success rate of tobacco-related amendments was mixed this year, there is good reason to expect more of these amendments to be proposed in future years, especially for the purpose of regulating the use of tobacco settlement funds, and if this year's results are a good indication, they will stand a good chance of passage. On the other hand, tax-and-expenditure limitation amendments are likely to continue to be proposed; but the partial suspension of Colorado's TABOR provision in 2005, followed by the defeat of similar amendments in 2006, could signal that these measures may encounter difficulty in coming years.

Notes

[1] Excluded from these totals is an Alabama amendment dealing with the selection of members of the Macon County Board of Education. After the amendment had been certified and placed on the ballot, the governor's office determined that it had not received a sufficient number of legislative votes to be properly placed on the ballot; therefore, although the state canvassing board certified after the November 2006 election that the amendment had been approved, the governor's office did not proclaim the results, and it has not been deemed a valid amendment.

[2] Included in these totals is a Nevada amendment restricting use of the eminent domain power for private purposes. This measure was approved by voters in November 2006, but because initiated amendments in Nevada are required to be approved by voters in two successive general elections, it must be approved again in November 2008 before it can take effect.

[3] David White, "Senate panel backs bill to allow vote on constitutional convention," *Birmingham News*, February 22, 2006, 1B.

[4] John P. McAlpin, "Corzine: Tax reform must stay top priority," *Bergen County Record*, January 10, 2007, A1.

[5] Frank Phillips and Lisa Wangsness, "Same sex marriage ban advances," *Boston Globe*, January 3, 2007, A1.

[6] Cheryl Wetzstein, "Gay 'marriage' ballot measures running their course," *The Washington Times*, January 7, 2007, A2.

[7] Leslie Fulbright, "Connerly gearing up for wider crusade," *San Francisco Chronicle*, December 14, 2006, A1.

[8] These tobacco-related amendments are discussed in Richard Craver, "Tobacco outcomes vary," *Winston-Salem Journal*, November 9, 2006, D1.

[9] Ed Vogel, "Question 1: Education First," *Las Vegas Review-Journal*, October 19, 2006, 43DD.

[10] These amendments are discussed in Valerie Richardson, "Ballot measures propose limits on judicial authority," *The Washington Times*, October 24, 2006, A4.

[11] Gary Fineout, "Constitution just got harder to tinker with," *Miami Herald*, November 8, 2006 (Netscape version).

About the Author

John Dinan is associate professor of political science at Wake Forest University. He is the author of *The American State Constitutional Tradition* and *The Virginia State Constitution: A Reference Guide*, among other books and articles on state constitutions.

Table 1.1
GENERAL INFORMATION ON STATE CONSTITUTIONS
(As of January 1, 2007)

State or other jurisdiction	Number of constitutions*	Dates of adoption	Effective date of present constitution	Estimated length (number of words)**	Number of amendments Submitted to voters	Adopted
Alabama	6	1819, 1861, 1865, 1868, 1875, 1901	Nov. 28, 1901	340,136 (a)(b)(c)	1,088	794
Alaska	1	1956	Jan. 3, 1959	15,988 (b)	41	29
Arizona	1	1911	Feb. 14, 1912	28,876	254	141
Arkansas	5	1836, 1861, 1864, 1868, 1874	Oct. 30, 1874	59,500 (b)	190	92 (d)
California	2	1849, 1879	July 4, 1879	54,645	870	514
Colorado	1	1876	Aug. 1, 1876	74,522 (b)	315	150
Connecticut	4	1818 (f), 1965	Dec. 30, 1965	17,256 (b)	30	29
Delaware	4	1776, 1792, 1831, 1897	June 10, 1897	19,000	(e)	138
Florida	6	1839, 1861, 1865, 1868, 1886, 1968	Jan. 7, 1969	51,456 (b)	141	110
Georgia	10	1777, 1789, 1798, 1861, 1865, 1868, 1877, 1945, 1976, 1982	July 1,1983	39,526 (b)	86 (g)	66 (g)
Hawaii	1 (h)	1950	Aug. 21, 1959	20,774 (b)	128	108
Idaho	1	1889	July 3, 1890	24,232 (b)	206	119
Illinois	4	1818, 1848, 1870, 1970	July 1, 1971	16,510 (b)	17	11
Indiana	2	1816, 1851	Nov. 1, 1851	10,379 (b)	78	46
Iowa	2	1846, 1857	Sept. 3, 1857	12,616 (b)	57	52 (i)
Kansas	1	1859	Jan. 29, 1861	12,296 (b)	123	93 (i)
Kentucky	4	1792, 1799, 1850, 1891	Sept. 28, 1891	23,911 (b)	75	41
Louisiana	11	1812, 1845, 1852, 1861, 1864, 1868, 1879, 1898, 1913, 1921, 1974	Jan. 1, 1975	54,112 (b)	210	150
Maine	1	1819	March 15, 1820	16,276 (b)	203	171 (j)
Maryland	4	1776, 1851, 1864, 1867	Oct. 5, 1867	46,600 (b)	257	221 (k)
Massachusetts	1	1780	Oct. 25, 1780	36,700 (l)	148	120
Michigan	4	1835, 1850, 1908, 1963	Jan. 1, 1964	34,659 (b)	66	28
Minnesota	1	1857	May 11, 1858	11,547 (b)	214	119
Mississippi	4	1817, 1832, 1869, 1890	Nov. 1, 1890	24,323 (b)	158	123
Missouri	4	1820, 1865, 1875, 1945	March 30,1945	42,600 (b)	170	109
Montana	2	1889, 1972	July 1, 1973	13,145 (b)	54	30
Nebraska	2	1866, 1875	Oct. 12, 1875	20,048	344 (m)	224 (m)
Nevada	1	1864	Oct. 31, 1864	31,377 (b)	226	134 (i)
New Hampshire	2	1776, 1784	June 2, 1784	9,200	287 (n)	145
New Jersey	3	1776, 1844, 1947	Jan. 1, 1948	22,956 (b)	74	41
New Mexico	1	1911	Jan. 6, 1912	27,200	284	155
New York	4	1777, 1822, 1846, 1894	Jan. 1, 1895	51,700	291	216
North Carolina	3	1776, 1868, 1970	July 1, 1971	16,532 (b)	42	34
North Dakota	1	1889	Nov. 2, 1889	19,130 (b)	262	149 (o)
Ohio	2	1802, 1851	Sept. 1, 1851	48,521 (b)	275	163
Oklahoma	1	1907	Nov. 16, 1907	74,075 (p)	340 (p)	175 (p)
Oregon	1	1857	Feb. 14, 1859	54,083 (b)	477 (q)	238 (q)
Pennsylvania	5	1776, 1790, 1838, 1873, 1968 (r)	1968 (r)	27,711 (b)	36 (r)	30 (r)
Rhode Island	3	1842 (f), 1986 (s)	Dec. 4, 1986	10,908 (b)	11 (s)	10 (s)
South Carolina	7	1776, 1778, 1790, 1861, 1865, 1868, 1895	Jan. 1, 1896	22,300	679 (t)	492 (t)
South Dakota	1	1889	Nov. 2, 1889	27,675 (b)	223	213
Tennessee	3	1796, 1835, 1870	Feb. 23, 1870	13,300	61	38
Texas	5 (u)	1845, 1861, 1866, 1869, 1876	Feb. 15, 1876	90,000	614 (v)	439
Utah	1	1895	Jan. 4, 1896	11,000	158	107
Vermont	3	1777, 1786, 1793	July 9, 1793	10,286 (b)	211	53
Virginia	6	1776, 1830, 1851, 1869, 1902, 1970	July 1, 1971	21,319 (b)	51	43
Washington	1	1889	Nov. 11, 1889	33,564 (b)	170	97
West Virginia	2	1863, 1872	April 9, 1872	26,000	121	71
Wisconsin	1	1848	May 29, 1848	14,392 (b)	193	144 (i)
Wyoming	1	1889	July 10, 1890	31,800	123	97
American Samoa	2	1960, 1967	July 1, 1967	6,000	14	7
No. Mariana Islands	1	1977	Jan. 9, 1978	11,000	55	51 (w)(x)
Puerto Rico	1	1952	July 25, 1952	9,281	6	6

See footnotes at end of table.

GENERAL INFORMATION ON STATE CONSTITUTIONS — Continued
(As of January 1, 2007)

Source: Based on surveys conducted in previous years by Janice May and updated by John Dinan in 2005 and 2006.

Key:

*The constitutions referred to in this table include those Civil War documents customarily listed by the individual states.

**Estimated word length is from the 2006 edition.

(a) The Alabama constitution includes numerous local amendments that apply to only one county. An estimated 70 percent of all amendments are local. A 1982 amendment provides that after proposal by the legislature to which special procedures apply, only a local vote (with exceptions) is necessary to add them to the constitution.

(b) Computer word count.

(c) The total number of Alabama amendments includes one that is commonly overlooked.

(d) Eight of the approved amendments have been superseded and are not printed in the current edition of the constitution. The total adopted does not include five amendments proposed and adopted since statehood.

(e) Proposed amendments are not submitted to the voters in Delaware.

(f) Colonial charters with some alterations served as the first constitutions in Connecticut (1638, 1662) and in Rhode Island (1663).

(g) The Georgia constitution requires amendments to be of "general and uniform application throughout the state," thus eliminating local amendments that accounted for most of the amendments before 1982.

(h) As a kingdom and republic, Hawaii had five constitutions.

(i) The figure includes amendments approved by the voters and later nullified by the state supreme court in Iowa (three), Kansas (one), Nevada (six) and Wisconsin (two).

(j) The figure does not include one amendment approved by the voters in 1967 that is inoperative until implemented by legislation.

(k) Two sets of identical amendments were on the ballot and adopted in the 1992 Maryland election. The four amendments are counted as two in the table.

(l) The printed constitution includes many provisions that have been annulled. The length of effective provisions is an estimated 24,122 words (12,400 annulled) in Massachusetts, and in Rhode Island before the "rewrite" of the constitution in 1986, it was 11,399 words (7,627 annulled).

(m) The 1998 and 2000 Nebraska ballots allowed the voters to vote separately on "parts" of propositions. In 1998, 10 of 18 separate propositions were adopted; in 2000, six of nine.

(n) The constitution of 1784 was extensively revised in 1792. Figure shows proposals and adoptions since the constitution was adopted in 1784.

(o) The figures do not include submission and approval of the constitution of 1889 itself and of Article XX; these are constitutional questions included in some counts of constitutional amendments and would add two to the figure in each column.

(p) The figures include five amendments submitted to and approved by the voters which were, by decisions of the Oklahoma or U.S. Supreme Courts, rendered inoperative or ruled invalid, unconstitutional, or illegally submitted.

(q) One Oregon amendment on the 2000 ballot was not counted as approved because canvassing was enjoined by the courts.

(r) Certain sections of the constitution were revised by the limited convention of 1967–68. Amendments proposed and adopted are since 1968.

(s) Following approval of the eight amendments and a "rewrite" of the Rhode Island Constitution in 1986, the constitution has been called the 1986 Constitution. Amendments since 1986 total 11 proposed and 10 adopted. Otherwise, the total is 106 proposals and 60 adopted.

(t) In 1981 approximately two-thirds of 626 proposed and four-fifths of the adopted amendments were local. Since then the amendments have been statewide propositions.

(u) The Constitution of the Republic of Texas preceded five state constitutions.

(v) The number of proposed amendments to the Texas Constitution excludes three proposed by the legislature but not placed on the ballot.

(w) By 1992, 49 amendments had been proposed and 47 adopted. Since then, one was proposed but rejected in 1994; all three proposals were ratified in 1996, and, in 1998, of two proposals one was adopted.

(x) The total excludes one amendment ruled void by a federal district court.

Table 1.2
CONSTITUTIONAL AMENDMENT PROCEDURE: BY THE LEGISLATURE
Constitutional Provisions

State or other jurisdiction	Legislative vote required for proposal (a)	Consideration by two sessions required	Vote required for ratification	Limitation on the number of amendments submitted at one election
Alabama	3/5	No	Majority vote on amendment	None
Alaska	2/3	No	Majority vote on amendment	None
Arizona	Majority	No	Majority vote on amendment	None
Arkansas	Majority	No	Majority vote on amendment	3
California	2/3	No	Majority vote on amendment	None
Colorado	2/3	No	Majority vote on amendment	None (b)
Connecticut	(c)	(c)	Majority vote on amendment	None
Delaware	2/3	Yes	Not required	No referendum
Florida	3/5	No	3/5 vote on amendment (d)	None
Georgia	2/3	No	Majority vote on amendment	None
Hawaii	(e)	(e)	Majority vote on amendment (f)	None
Idaho	2/3	No	Majority vote on amendment	None
Illinois	3/5	No	(g)	3 articles
Indiana	Majority	Yes	Majority vote on amendment	None
Iowa	Majority	Yes	Majority vote on amendment	None
Kansas	2/3	No	Majority vote on amendment	5
Kentucky	3/5	No	Majority vote on amendment	4
Louisiana	2/3	No	Majority vote on amendment (h)	None
Maine	2/3 (i)	No	Majority vote on amendment	None
Maryland	3/5	No	Majority vote on amendment	None
Massachusetts	Majority (j)	Yes	Majority vote on amendment	None
Michigan	2/3	No	Majority vote on amendment	None
Minnesota	Majority	No	Majority vote in election	None
Mississippi	2/3 (k)	No	Majority vote on amendment	None
Missouri	Majority	No	Majority vote on amendment	None
Montana	2/3 (i)	No	Majority vote on amendment	None
Nebraska	3/5	No	Majority vote on amendment (f)	None
Nevada	Majority	Yes	Majority vote on amendment	None
New Hampshire	3/5	No	2/3 vote on amendment	None
New Jersey	(l)	(l)	Majority vote on amendment	None (m)
New Mexico	Majority (n)	No	Majority vote on amendment (n)	None
New York	Majority	Yes	Majority vote on amendment	None
North Carolina	3/5	No	Majority vote on amendment	None
North Dakota	Majority	No	Majority vote on amendment	None
Ohio	3/5	No	Majority vote on amendment	None
Oklahoma	Majority	No	Majority vote on amendment	None
Oregon	(o)	No	Majority vote on amendment (p)	None
Pennsylvania	Majority (p)	Yes (p)	Majority vote on amendment	None
Rhode Island	Majority	No	Majority vote on amendment	None
South Carolina	2/3 (q)	Yes (q)	Majority vote on amendment	None
South Dakota	Majority	No	Majority vote on amendment	None
Tennessee	(r)	Yes (r)	Majority vote in election (s)	None
Texas	2/3	No	Majority vote on amendment	None
Utah	2/3	No	Majority vote on amendment	None
Vermont	(t)	Yes	Majority vote on amendment	None
Virginia	Majority	Yes	Majority vote on amendment	None
Washington	2/3	No	Majority vote on amendment	None
West Virginia	2/3	No	Majority vote on amendment	None
Wisconsin	Majority	Yes	Majority vote on amendment	None
Wyoming	2/3	No	Majority vote in election	None
American Samoa	2/3	No	Majority vote on amendment (u)	None
No. Mariana Islands	3/4	No	Majority vote on amendment	None
Puerto Rico	2/3 (v)	No	Majority vote on amendment	3

See footnotes at end of table.

CONSTITUTIONAL AMENDMENT PROCEDURE: BY THE LEGISLATURE—Continued
Constitutional Provisions

Source: Surveys conducted in previous years by Janice May and updated by John Dinan in 2005 and 2006.

Key:

(a) In all states not otherwise noted, the figure shown in the column refers to the proportion of elected members in each house required for approval of proposed constitutional amendments.

(b) Legislature may not propose amendments to more than six articles of the constitution in the same legislative session.

(c) Three-fourths vote in each house at one session, or majority vote in each house in two sessions between which an election has intervened.

(d) Three-fifths vote on amendment, except amendment for "new state tax or fee" not in effect on Nov. 7, 1994, requires two-thirds of voters in the election.

(e) Two-thirds vote in each house at one session, or majority vote in each house in two sessions.

(f) Majority vote on amendment must be at least 50 percent of the total votes cast at the election (at least 35 percent in Nebraska); or, at a special election, a majority of the votes tallied which must be at least 30 percent of the total number of registered voters.

(g) Majority voting in election or three-fifths voting on amendment.

(h) If five or fewer political subdivisions of the state are affected, majority in state as a whole (and also in effected subdivisions) is required.

(i) Two-thirds of both houses.

(j) Majority of members elected sitting in joint session.

(k) The two-thirds must include not less than a majority elected to each house.

(l) Three-fifths of all members of each house at one session, or majority of all members of each house for two successive sessions.

(m) If a proposed amendment is not approved at the election when submitted, neither the same amendment nor one which would make substantially the same change for the constitution may be again submitted to the people before the third general election thereafter.

(n) Amendments concerning certain elective franchise and education matters require three-fourths vote of members elected and approval by three-fourths of electors voting in state and two-thirds of those voting in each county.

(o) Majority vote to amend constitution, two-thirds to revise ("revise" includes all or a part of the constitution).

(p) Emergency amendments may be passed by two-thirds vote of each house, followed by ratification by majority vote of electors in election held at least one month after legislative approval. There is an exception for an amendment containing a supermajority voting requirement, which must be ratified by an equal supermajority.

(q) Two-thirds of members of each house, first passage; majority of members of each house after popular ratification.

(r) Majority of members elected to both houses, first passage; two-thirds of members elected to both houses, second passage.

(s) Majority of all citizens voting for governor.

(t) Two-thirds vote senate, majority vote house, first passage; majority both houses, second passage. As of 1974, amendments may be submitted only every four years.

(u) Within 30 days after voter approval, governor must submit amendment(s) to U.S. Secretary of the Interior for approval.

(v) If approved by two-thirds of members of each house, amendment(s) submitted to voters at special referendum; if approved by not less than three-fourths of total members of each house, referendum may be held at next general election.

Table 1.3
CONSTITUTIONAL AMENDMENT PROCEDURE: BY INITIATIVE
Constitutional Provisions

State or other jurisdiction	Number of signatures required on initiative petition	Distribution of signatures	Referendum vote
Arizona	15% of total votes cast for all candidates for governor at last election.	None specified.	Majority vote on amendment.
Arkansas	10% of voters for governor at last election.	Must include 5% of voters for governor in each of 15 counties.	Majority vote on amendment.
California	8% of total voters for all candidates for governor at last election.	None specified.	Majority vote on amendment.
Colorado	5% of total legal votes for all candidates for secretary of state at last general election.	None specified.	Majority vote on amendment.
Florida	8% of total votes cast in the state in the last election for presidential electors.	8% of total votes cast in each of 1/2 of the congressional districts.	Three-fifths vote on amendment except amendment for "new state tax or fee" not in effect Nov. 7, 1994, requires 2/3 of voters voting in election.
Illinois (a)	8% of total votes cast for candidates for governor at last election.	None specified.	Majority voting in election or 3/5 voting on amendment.
Massachusetts (b)	3% of total votes cast for governor at preceding biennial state election (not less than 25,000 qualified voters).	No more than 1/4 from any one county.	Majority vote on amendment which must be 30% of total ballots cast at election.
Michigan	10% of total voters for all candidates at last gubernatorial election.	None specified.	Majority vote on amendment.
Mississippi	12% of total votes for all candidates for governor in last election.	No more than 20% from any one congressional district.	Majority vote on amendment and not less than 40% of total vote cast at election.
Missouri	8% of legal voters for all candidates for governor at last election.	The 8% must be in each of 2/3 of the congressional districts in the state.	Majority vote on amendment.
Montana	10% of qualified electors, the number of qualified voters to be determined by number of votes cast for governor in preceding election in each county and in the state.	The 10% to include at least 10% of qualified voters in 1/2 of the counties.	Majority vote on amendment.
Nebraska	10% of total votes for governor at last election.	The 10% must include 5% in each of 2/5 of the counties.	Majority vote on amendment which must be at least 35% of total vote at the election.
Nevada	10% of voters who voted in entire state in last general election.	10% of total voters who voted in each of 75% of the counties.	Majority vote on amendment in two consecutive general elections.
North Dakota	4% of population of the state.	None specified.	Majority vote on amendment.
Ohio	10% of total number of electors who voted for governor in last election.	At least 5% of qualified electors in each of 1/2 of counties in the state.	Majority vote on amendment.
Oklahoma	15% of legal voters for state office receiving highest number of voters at last general state election.	None specified.	Majority vote on amendment.
Oregon	8% of total votes for all candidates for governor at last election at which governor was elected for four-year term.	None specified.	Majority vote on amendment except for supermajority equal to supermajority voting requirement contained in proposed amendment.
South Dakota	10% of total votes for governor in last election.	None specified.	Majority vote on amendment.
No. Mariana Islands	50% of qualified voters of commonwealth.	In addition, 25% of qualified voters in each senatorial district.	Majority vote on amendment if legislature approved it by majority vote; if not, at least 2/3 vote in each of two senatorial districts in addition to a majority vote.

Source: Surveys conducted in previous years by Janice May and updated by John Dinan in 2005 and 2006.
  Key:
  (a) Only Article IV, the Legislature Article, may be amended by initiative petition.

(b) Before being submitted to the electorate for ratification, initiative measures must be approved at two sessions of a successively elected legislature by not less than one-fourth of all members elected, sitting in joint session.

Table 1.4
PROCEDURES FOR CALLING CONSTITUTIONAL CONVENTIONS
Constitutional Provisions

State or other jurisdiction	Provision for convention	Legislative vote for submission of convention question (a)	Popular vote to authorize convention	Periodic submission of convention question required (b)	Popular vote required for ratification of convention proposals
Alabama	Yes	Majority	ME	No	Not specified
Alaska	Yes	No provision (c)(d)	(c)	10 years (c)	Not specified (c)
Arizona	Yes	Majority	(e)	No	MP
Arkansas	No	No			
California	Yes	2/3	MP	No	MP
Colorado	Yes	2/3	MP	No	ME
Connecticut	Yes	2/3	MP	20 years (f)	MP
Delaware	Yes	2/3	MP	No	No provision
Florida	Yes	(g)	MP	No	3/5 voting on proposal
Georgia	Yes	(d)	No	No	MP
Hawaii	Yes	Not specified	MP	9 years	MP (h)
Idaho	Yes	2/3	MP	No	Not specified
Illinois	Yes	3/4	(i)	20 years; 1988	MP
Indiana	No	No			
Iowa	Yes	Majority	MP	10 years; 1970	MP
Kansas	Yes	2/3	MP	No	MP
Kentucky	Yes	Majority (j)	MP (k)	No	No provision
Louisiana	Yes	(d)	No	No	MP
Maine	Yes	(d)	No	No	No provision
Maryland	Yes	Majority	ME	20 years; 1970	MP
Massachusetts	No	No	No	Not specified	
Michigan	Yes	Majority	MP	16 years; 1978	MP
Minnesota	Yes	2/3	ME	No	3/5 voting on proposal
Mississippi	No	No			
Missouri	Yes	Majority	MP	20 years; 1962	Not specified (l)
Montana	Yes (m)	2/3	MP	20 years	MP
Nebraska	Yes	3/4	MP (o)	No	MP
Nevada	Yes	2/3	ME	No	No provision
New Hampshire	Yes	Majority	MP	10 years	2/3 voting on proposal
New Jersey	No	No			
New Mexico	Yes	2/3	MP	No	Not specified
New York	Yes	Majority	MP	20 years; 1957	MP
North Carolina	Yes	2/3	MP	No	MP
North Dakota	No	No			
Ohio	Yes	2/3	MP	20 years; 1932	MP
Oklahoma	Yes	Majority	(e)	20 years	MP
Oregon	Yes	Majority	(e)	No	No provision
Pennsylvania	No	No			
Rhode Island	Yes	Majority	MP	10 years	MP
South Carolina	Yes	(d)	ME	No	No provision
South Dakota	Yes	(d)	(d)	No	(p)
Tennessee	Yes (q)	Majority	MP	No	MP
Texas	No	No			
Utah	Yes	2/3	ME	No	MP
Vermont	No	No			
Virginia	Yes	(d)	No	No	MP
Washington	Yes	2/3	ME	No	Not specified
West Virginia	Yes	Majority	MP	No	Not specified
Wisconsin	Yes	Majority	MP	No	No provision
Wyoming	Yes	2/3	ME	No	Not specified
American Samoa	Yes	(r)	No	No	ME (s)
No. Mariana Islands	Yes	Majority (t)	2/3	No (u)	MP and at least 2/3 in each of 2 senatorial districts
Puerto Rico	Yes	2/3	MP	No	MP

See footnotes at end of table.

PROCEDURES FOR CALLING CONSTITUTIONAL CONVENTIONS — Continued
Constitutional Provisions

Source: Surveys conducted in previous years by Janice May and updated by John Dinan in 2005 and 2006.

Key:

MP — Majority voting on the proposal.

ME — Majority voting in the election.

(a) In all states not otherwise noted, the entries in this column refer to the proportion of members elected to each house required to submit to the electorate the question of calling a constitutional convention.

(b) The number listed is the interval between required submissions on the question of calling a constitutional convention; where given, the date is that of the first required submission of the convention question.

(c) Unless provided otherwise by law, convention calls are to conform as nearly as possible to the act calling the 1955 convention, which provided for a legislative vote of a majority of members elected to each house and ratification by a majority vote on the proposals. The legislature may call a constitutional convention at any time.

(d) In these states, the legislature may call a convention without submitting the question to the people. The legislative vote required is two-thirds of the members elected to each house in Georgia, Louisiana, South Carolina and Virginia; two-thirds concurrent vote of both branches in Maine; three-fourths of all members of each house in South Dakota; and not specified in Alaska, but bills require majority vote of membership in each house. In South Dakota, the question of calling a convention may be initiated by the people in the same manner as an amendment to the constitution (see Table 1.3) and requires a majority vote on the question for approval.

(e) The law calling a convention must be approved by the people.

(f) The legislature shall submit the question 20 years after the last convention, or 20 years after the last vote on the question of calling a convention, whichever date is last.

(g) The power to call a convention is reserved to the people by petition.

(h) The majority must be 50 percent of the total votes cast at a general election or at a special election, a majority of the votes tallied which must be at least 30 percent of the total number of registered voters.

(i) Majority voting in the election, or three-fifths voting on the question.

(j) Must be approved during two legislative sessions.

(k) Majority must equal one-fourth of qualified voters at last general election.

(l) Majority of those voting on the proposal is assumed.

(m) The question of calling a constitutional convention may be submitted either by the legislature or by initiative petition to the secretary of state in the same manner as provided for initiated amendments (see Table 1.3).

(n) Two-thirds of all members of the legislature.

(o) Majority must be 35 percent of total votes cast at the election.

(p) Convention proposals are submitted to the electorate at a special election in a manner to be determined by the convention. Ratification by a majority of votes cast.

(q) Conventions may not be held more often than once in six years.

(r) Five years after effective date of constitutions, governor shall call a constitutional convention to consider changes proposed by a constitutional committee appointed by the governor. Delegates to the convention are to be elected by their county councils. A convention was held in 1972.

(s) If proposed amendments are approved by the voters, they must be submitted to the U.S. Secretary of the Interior for approval.

(t) The initiative may also be used to place a referendum convention call on the ballot. The petition must be signed by 25 percent of the qualified voters or at least 75 percent in a senatorial district.

(u) The legislature was required to submit the referendum no later than seven years after the effective date of the constitution. The convention was held in 1985; 45 amendments were submitted to the voters.

Table 1.5
STATE CONSTITUTIONAL CHANGES BY LEGISLATIVE PROPOSAL
AND BY CONSTITUTIONAL INITIATIVE: 2006

	Legislative proposal			Constitutional initiative		
State	*Number of proposals*	*Number of adoptions*	*Percentage adopted*	*Number of proposals*	*Number of adoptions*	*Percentage adopted*
Alabama	25	21	84.0%	. . .	. . .	. . .
Arizona	6	5	83.3	2	0	0.0%
Arkansas.....................	1	1	100.0	. . .	. . .	. . .
California	1	1	100.0	6	0	0.0
Colorado	4	2	50.0	7	3	42.8
Florida	5	5	100.0	1	1	100.0
Georgia	3	3	100.0	. . .	. . .	. . .
Hawaii.........................	5	4	80.0	. . .	. . .	. . .
Idaho...........................	2	2	100.0	. . .	. . .	. . .
Louisiana	21	21	100.0	. . .	. . .	. . .
Maine	1	1	100.0	. . .	. . .	. . .
Maryland	3	3	100.0	. . .	. . .	. . .
Michigan......................	2	2	100.0	1	1	100.0
Minnesota	1	1	100.0	. . .	. . .	. . .
Missouri.......................	3	3	100.0	2	1	50.0
Montana	1	0	0.0	. . .	. . .	. . .
Nebraska......................	7	2	28.6	1	0	0.0
Nevada	3	0	0.0	3	3 (a)	100.0
New Hampshire............	2	2	100.0	. . .	. . .	. . .
New Jersey...................	3	3	100.0	. . .	. . .	. . .
New Mexico	4	4	100.0	. . .	. . .	. . .
North Dakota...............	3	3	100.0	1	1	100.0
Ohio	. . .	. . .	. . .	3	1	33.3
Oklahoma	4	4	100.0	. . .	. . .	. . .
Oregon	. . .	. . .	. . .	4	0	0.0
Rhode Island	3	2	66.7	. . .	. . .	. . .
South Carolina	7	7	100.0	. . .	. . .	. . .
South Dakota...............	2	1	50.0	2	0	0.0
Tennessee	2	2	100.0	. . .	. . .	. . .
Utah	1	1	100.0	. . .	. . .	. . .
Virginia........................	3	3	100.0	. . .	. . .	. . .
Washington...................	1	1	100.0	. . .	. . .	. . .
Wisconsin.....................	1	1	100.0	. . .	. . .	. . .
Wyoming......................	3	3	100.0	. . .	. . .	. . .
Totals...........................	133	114	85.7	33	11	33.3

Source: Survey conducted by John Dinan in January 2007.
(a) Includes one amendment that was approved by the people for the first time but has not yet received the required second approval.

Chapter Two

FEDERALISM AND INTERGOVERNMENTAL RELATIONS

Short-term changes in federal policymaking will be instituted by the new divided government in Washington, D.C., but the long-term trends in federalism will remain largely on course.

—John Kincaid

Trends include the creation of state control boards for local governments suffering fiscal distress, continued imposition of mandates and restraints, and increased use of joint powers authority.

—Joseph F. Zimmerman

State-Federal Relations: A Policy Tug of War

By John Kincaid

The new Democratic majority in Congress and the governorships will alter some federal poli-cies and frustrate some presidential policy initiatives, but the centralizing course of federalism will endure, and most facets of coercive federalism will persist. State policy activism will remain vigorous, but the Supreme Court is not likely to resuscitate its federalism revolution.

The Democrats' 2006 electoral victories, which gave them majority control of Congress and the governorships (28) for the first time since 1994, reflected not only public dissatisfaction with the Iraq war but also challenges to federal policies emanating from many states. For example, in the face of Congress' refusal to increase the national minimum wage, vot-ers in six states approved minimum wage increases in 2006, bringing to 29 the number of states having a minimum wage higher than the federal $5.15 per hour. Likewise, in health insurance, environmental protection, global warming, stem cell research and other policy fields, many states forged ahead of the federal government.

Although the Republican congressional majority that captured power in the 1994 midterm elections had genuflected toward federalism and states' rights, this majority, which held the Congress for 12 years, fell in line with the march of coercive federalism that began in the late 1960s. This majority contin-ued wresting policy power from the states through pre-emptions, mandates, conditions of aid and the like, this time to advance Republican rather than Democratic objectives. This drive accelerated when Republican George W. Bush won the White House in 2000.

As coercive federal policies weighed more heav-ily on the states and contradicted the policy prefer-ences of many Democratic states, state officials and voters sought to wrest control of important domestic policies from the federal government. A tug of war ensued as states reopened their shuttered laboratories of democracy in order "to try experiments in legisla-tion and administration"[1] and, thereby, also attract public support for new policies.

Consequently, "the common theme" of the National Governors Association's 2006 summer meeting "was one of utter disdain for Congress."[2] Examples of state contestants in this tug-of-war include Eliot Spitzer, former Democratic attorney general and now gov-ernor of New York, and the Republican governors of two Democratic states, Arnold Schwarzenegger of California and Mitt Romney of Massachusetts.

The Democratic gains in the states and Congress might produce more federal-state cooperation in policymaking, especially as Congress addresses such issues as the minimum wage, stem cell research, health insurance, consumer protection and global warming where many states have acted already. However, the combination of divided government, 44 fiscally conservative Blue Dog Democrats in Con-gress, federal deficits and debt, defense and security costs, and entitlement spending will limit Congress to marginal increases in federal grants-in-aid. Coer-cive federalism is not likely to be reversed either. The revenue-parched Congress will be tempted to advance Democratic policy objectives and national-ize pioneering state policies through mandates, pre-emptions and conditions of aid.

Whither Coercive Federalism?

Although American federalism remains cooperative in many ways, especially in most areas of intergov-ernmental administration, the predominant political, fiscal, statutory, regulatory and judicial trends feature federal dictates on state and local governments.

Grants-in-Aid

Congress' failure to complete FY 2007 appropriations in 2006, plus the turnover of Congress to Democrats, make it impossible to predict near-term levels of fed-eral aid. The president's $2.9 trillion FY 2008 budget proposal would eliminate or deeply cut 141 federal programs and increase discretionary spending outside of security by only 1 percent over 2007, below the rate of inflation. Bush proposed aid reductions for both FYs 2006 and 2007; however, even the Republi-can Congress refused to cut as deeply as the president requested in previous years. The new Democratic majority will certainly resist cuts; nevertheless, in the long term, federal aid for non-social-welfare pro-grams will slip downward, and even federal aid for social welfare, such as Medicaid, will barely keep pace with inflation. Alone, the rising costs of the fed-eral government's three major entitlements—Social Security, Medicare and Medicaid—will crowd out federal discretionary spending, which includes most grants-in-aid.[3] These three programs, plus other social welfare programs, constitute 54 percent of Bush's FY 2008 budget request.

Overall, federal aid under coercive federalism exhibits three characteristics.

First, aid has shifted substantially from places to persons; almost two-thirds of federal aid is dedicated for payments to individuals (i.e., social welfare).[4] Medicaid, which accounts for almost 45 percent of all aid, is the leading example. Among the long-term consequences of this shift are that place-based aid for infrastructure, economic development, education and the like has declined sharply; increased aid for social welfare has locked state budgets into programs ripe for escalating federal regulation and matching state costs; and local governments have experienced a steep decline in federal aid.

President Bill Clinton bucked this latter trend in some grant areas, such as the Community Oriented Policing Services program. However, funding for local policing has dropped precipitously since 2000. Federal aid now comprises about 1 percent of local police spending. Another example is the Community Development Block Grant, which experienced a 14-percent drop in formula funding during the last two fiscal years. Although the number of communities receiving CDBG funds directly from the federal government increased from 606 in FY 1975 to 1,128 in FY 2006, real per capita CDBG funding plunged from $48 in FY 1978 to $13 in FY 2006.

A second characteristic of federal aid under coercive federalism is increased use of conditions of aid to achieve federal objectives that lie outside Congress' constitutionally enumerated powers and to extract more state-local spending on federal objectives. Such conditions, now often mistakenly called unfunded or under-funded "mandates," are a powerful federal policy tool.

For example, the Child and Family Services Improvement Act of 2006, which directs $345 million annually to the Safe and Stable Families Program, caps states' child-welfare administration costs and requires states to provide foster children a monthly visit from a social worker. The Adam Walsh Child Protection and Safety Act of 2006 imposes a number of requirements on states, including establishment of a statewide registry of sex offenders that conforms to federal standards and is compatible with a new public National Sex Offender Web site. States that fail to comply by July 2009 will lose 10 percent of their funding under the 1968 Omnibus Crime Control and Safe Streets Act.

The No Child Left Behind Act (NCLB) of 2002 is the states' current *bete noir* because of the act's costly testing and performance requirements. Beginning with North Carolina and Tennessee in May 2006, however, the U.S. Department of Education opened the door slightly to state flexibility by allowing states to measure how individual students progress year by year in math and reading rather than measuring only whether larger proportions of students pass proficiency exams each year. Critics argue that this new measurement is weaker because it measures apparent progress toward proficiency rather than proficiency achievement. The Department of Education insists, though, that the NCLB's target that all students reach proficiency by 2014 remains in place. The NCLB is due for reauthorization in 2007; many states hope that Congress will increase both flexibility and funding.

The Deficit Reduction Act of 2005 reauthorized welfare reform—Temporary Assistance for Needy Families (TANF)—for another five years at the FY 2004 level of $16.5 billion. The original law, which expired in October 2002, had limped along on 12 temporary extensions. The law contains tougher work-participation rules, even though it keeps the prior 50-percent work-participation requirement. States also must implement work-verification procedures, and a penalty of up to 5 percent can be imposed on a state's family-assistance grant for non-compliance. The act increased funds for child care by $1 billion, but eliminated funds for some programs, such as reducing out-of-wedlock births.

However, this act, even while also cutting federal Medicaid spending by $4.8 billion, made a number of changes in the Medicaid program favorable to the states, especially by giving states more discretion to experiment with program design and cost-cutting without pursuing waivers from the U.S. Department of Health and Human Services.

The third notable federal aid change under coercive federalism has been congressional earmarking (i.e., state or local pork barrel projects). Earmarks in appropriations bills increased from 1,439 in 1995 to 13,997 in 2005 and then dropped to 9,963 in 2006, according to Citizens Against Government Waste. The total price of earmarks increased from $27.3 billion in 2005 to $29 billion in 2006. More than 50 bills, such as the Pork Barrel Reduction Act and Lobbying Transparency and Accountability Act, were introduced in Congress in 2005–06 to reform earmarking.

Some members of Congress defend earmarks, arguing that they keep spending decisions in the hands of Congress, which possesses the constitutional power of the purse, rather than awarding discretion to the president and federal agencies. Also, earmarks send money directly to state and local officials rather than consigning the money to the discretion of federal agencies. Indeed, state and local officials help proliferate earmarks by lobbying for them, perhaps out of necessity. With federal aid for places declining, earmarks for bridges, sewer systems, parks, museums and the like are attractive alternatives.

Many state officials, however, oppose earmarks. As a Colorado transportation department official remarked: "Why do we spend 18 months at public hearings, meetings and planning sessions to put together our statewide plan if Congress is going to earmark projects that displace our priorities?"[5]

Many efforts were made in 2006 to eliminate or reduce earmarks or make them transparent. One proposal is to create a database listing all federal grants, contracts and other payments. Some of this is already available on the Federal Assistance Award Data System.

Finally, an enduring characteristic of grants has been the unwillingness of Congress and presidents to funnel substantial amounts of aid through block grants. The lion's share of aid flows through categorical grants.

Mandates

Mandates characterize coercive federalism, too. However, the 1995 Unfunded Mandates Reform Act (UMRA) cut mandate enactments, though it did not eliminate standing mandates. Only seven intergovernmental mandates with costs above UMRA's threshold have been enacted since 1995.

The most recent mandate was a 2006 tax law requiring state and local governments that spend more than $100 million annually to withhold for federal taxes 3 percent of their payments to vendors and to pass that money on to the federal government. The law, which takes effect in 2011, was opposed by state and local officials. However, pursuant to the U.S. Supreme Court's ruling in *Printz v. United States* (1997), the law might be vulnerable to challenge as an unconstitutional commandeering of state and local governments.

A sizable new mandate is the REAL ID Act of 2005. States argue that it is underfunded and could cost them $11 billion to produce compliant driver's licenses. States, which must comply with the act by May 2008, can opt out of its rules, but then their residents' licenses will not be accepted for any federal government purpose, including boarding an airplane, riding Amtrak, purchasing a firearm, opening a bank account, applying for federal benefits and entering a federal building. In May 2006, the National Governors Association (NGA), National Conference of State Legislatures (NCSL) and American Association of Motor Vehicle Administrators (AAMVA) said that the states need more federal money and another eight years to implement REAL ID.

By wide margins, both houses of Congress reauthorized until 2032 the three temporary sections of the 1965 Voting Rights Act. Section 5 requires nine states and portions of seven other states having histories of voter discrimination to obtain clearance from the U.S. Department of Justice before making any changes related to voting. This section is vulnerable to challenge by the Supreme Court. Another section requires polling places to provide ballots in Spanish as well as Asian and American Indian languages when a sizable portion of their voters speak one of those languages and lack English fluency. Section 8 permits federal observers to look for discrimination at polling places.

Many state officials also regard costly conditions of federal aid as unfunded mandates, and they lobbied in 2006 to amend UMRA to include conditions of aid in the act's definition of unfunded mandates. By one estimate, federal programs cost state and local governments some $51 billion in FYs 2004 and 2005.[6] However, the likelihood of persuading Congress to add aid conditions to UMRA is slim. State and local governments are more likely to convince Congress to increase funding, though not fully, for such costly programs as No Child Left Behind and REAL ID.

Pre-emptions

Federal pre-emptions of state laws under the U.S. Constitution's supremacy clause are another characteristic of coercive federalism. U.S. Rep. Henry Waxman, D-Calif., reported in June 2006 that during the past five years, Congress voted at least 57 times to pre-empt state laws. Of these votes, 27 yielded pre-emption bills signed by President Bush.

For state officials, the most egregious 2006 pre-emption is the National Defense Authorization Act, which allows the president to federalize any state's National Guard without the consent of the governor in the case of "a serious natural or manmade disaster, accident or catastrophe" within the United States, Puerto Rico or U.S. territories. This law was hastened along by the relief disaster that followed Hurricane Katrina in 2005.

Congress also passed the Combat Meth Act, which pre-empts state laws that regulate the sale of pseudoephedrine, the main ingredient of methamphetamine. The act requires all drugs containing pseudoephedrine to be sold behind pharmacy counters.

It also became evident in 2006 that the president will use the executive rule-making process to advance pre-emption when Congress drags its feet.

For example, the Food and Drug Administration (FDA) issued a prescription-drug labeling regulation saying that FDA approval of manufacturers' labels "pre-empts conflicting or contrary state law." The rule's preamble includes language that pre-empts state liability laws. Manufacturers who comply with the federal standard cannot be sued in state courts by persons injured by their products. Many Democrats accused the FDA of abusing its power. The NCSL accused the FDA of inadequate consultation in formulating the rule, and other critics noted that the lawsuit-immunization provision was cleverly placed in the preamble, which is not usually subject to public comment. Ultimately, the federal courts will have to sort out this pre-emption issue, though meanwhile, some state courts might hold that they are not bound by the FDA's rule unless Congress explicitly affirms the pre-emption.

For the first time in its 33-year history, the Consumer Product Safety Commission issued a rule on mattress flammability that pre-empts state laws that set higher standards and includes language in the preamble to protect mattress manufacturers from state court lawsuits when their mattresses conform to the new federal standard.

After Congress failed to pass a pre-emptive telecommunications bill, the Federal Communications Commission issued a rule in December 2006 pre-empting some aspects of local control of cable television franchising. The rule, issued by a 3-2 party-line vote, requires states and localities to complete negotiations with prospective providers within 90 days and prohibits "unreasonable" build-out requirements.

Many state attorneys general and other critics argue that these and other pre-emptions disadvantage consumers to the benefit of corporations. A spokesman for the Office of Management and Budget replied: "State courts and juries often lack the information, expertise and staff that the federal agencies rely upon in performing their scientific, risk-based calculations ... having a single federal standard can be the best way to guarantee safety and protect consumers."[7]

Pre-emptions are frequently upheld by the Supreme Court. Indeed, the formerly "Federalism Five" justices (Kennedy, O'Connor, Rehnquist, Scalia and Thomas) most often voted against the states in pre-emption cases.

Taxation

Federal constraints on state taxation and borrowing are another facet of coercive federalism. Federal judicial and statutory prohibitions of state taxation of Internet services and mail-order sales are among the most prominent constraints. In response, a number of states negotiated the Streamlined Sales and Use Tax Agreement to collect sales taxes on interstate mail-order sales. The agreement was implemented voluntarily among consenting states in October 2005. Although several large retailers voluntarily comply with the agreement, Congress has not sanctioned the agreement and authorized states to require sales tax collections by out-of-state vendors. Obtaining congressional recognition of the agreement, even with the new Democratic majority, will be difficult.

In 2005, the President's Advisory Panel on Federal Tax Reform recommended eliminating deductions for state and local taxes. Most state and local officials oppose removing these deductions. This issue has a partisan electoral dimension because the average state-local tax payment in blue (Democratic) states was $7,487 in 2005 compared to $4,834 in red (Republican) states. State and local tax deductions equaled 5.9 percent of average income in the blue states and 3.7 percent in the red states.[8] Because most state income taxes are coupled to the federal tax code, state officials fear that changes in federal tax laws, especially tax cuts and retroactive changes, will reduce state tax revenues.

The NGA expressed concern in 2006 about the proposed Business Activity Tax Simplification Act (BATSA), which would pre-empt state laws by establishing a federal physical-presence rule to determine when a state can levy franchise taxes, business license taxes and other business-activity taxes on out-of-state businesses. The Congressional Budget Office concluded that BATSA would be an unfunded mandate under UMRA.

Federalization of Criminal Law

Another feature of coercive federalism is the federalization of criminal law. There are some 3,500 federal criminal offenses; more than half of them have been enacted since the mid-1960s. These laws cover a wide range of behavior from terrorism to carjacking, disrupting a rodeo, impersonating a 4-H Club member, and carrying unlicensed dentures across state lines. Generally, federal criminal laws are tougher, including capital punishment, than comparable state laws.

Another aspect of this federalization has been an effort by the Bush administration to enforce federal death penalty statutes in states lacking capital punishment. In 2006, for example, a federal jury in North Dakota imposed the death penalty in a murder case. North Dakota does not have the death penalty, and this case was the first death sentence in the state since 1914.

Demise of Intergovernmental Institutions

Coercive federalism has been marked, too, by the demise of executive and congressional intergovernmental institutions established during the era of cooperative federalism. Most notable was the death of the U.S. Advisory Commission on Intergovernmental Relations (ACIR) in 1996 after 37 years of operation.

Decline of Political Cooperation

There also has been a decline in federal-state cooperation in major intergovernmental programs such as Medicaid and surface transportation. Congress earmarks and alters programs more in response to national and regional interest groups than to elected state and local officials, who themselves are viewed as mere interest groups. A coalition led by Americans for Tax Reform (ATR) has petitioned Congress to terminate the exemption from federal lobbying rules of state and local government lobbyists. The ATR also wants to defund the NGA, labeling it "another liberal lobbying group."[9]

Presidential depletion of National Guard personnel and equipment for the Iraq war also reflects diminished cooperation. All 50 governors petitioned the president and the Pentagon for enhanced resources for the National Guard and for replacements of equipment left in Iraq. About one-third of the ground troops in Iraq belong to the Army National Guard.

The Supreme Court's Federalism-Lite

Since 2002, the Supreme Court has not advanced its state-friendly federalism jurisprudence initiated in 1991. This was reflected in two Eleventh Amendment sovereign-immunity cases in 2006, which held that states are not immune from suits brought under the Americans With Disabilities Act by disabled prisoners and from private lawsuits brought under federal bankruptcy law. The Court also ruled unanimously that the Eleventh Amendment does not protect local governments.[10]

In other cases, the Court upheld, by a 6-3 vote, Oregon's Death With Dignity Act, ruling that the 1970 federal Controlled Substances Act's prescription rule does not allow the U.S. attorney general "to bar dispensing controlled substances for assisted suicide in the face of a state medical regime permitting such conduct."[11] Justice Anthony Kennedy's majority opinion stated that "the structure and limitations of federalism … allow the states great latitude under their police powers to legislate for the protection of the lives, limbs, health, comfort and quiet of all persons." The new chief justice, John G. Roberts, participating in his first prominent federalism case, joined Antonin Scalia and Clarence Thomas in dissent.

The Court overturned a lower court's invalidation of New Hampshire's Parental Notification Prior to Abortion Act, opining that the act only needed a medical-emergencies provision to pass constitutional muster.

The Court unanimously rejected a taxpayer challenge to tax concessions given by Ohio to Daimler-Chrysler AG to expand its Ohio plant.[12] The plaintiffs argued that such corporate tax breaks violate the U.S. Constitution's commerce clause by advantaging in-state companies over out-of-state firms, thus hindering interstate commerce. Although the Court declined to address this issue because it ruled that the plaintiffs had no standing to sue Ohio, the decision seems to shield this type of interstate tax competition from federal judicial foreclosure.

In two important environmental cases, a fragmented Court slightly curtailed the Army Corps of Engineers' broad application of the Clean Water Act.[13] Four liberal justices upheld the broad application covering all of the country's waters, while four conservative justices narrowed the law to the nation's "permanent standing or continuously flowing" navigable waters. Justice Kennedy's prevailing middle position held that the Clean Water Act covers any wetlands having a "significant nexus to waters that are or were navigable in fact or that could reasonably be so made." Kennedy asserted that his significant-nexus test raises "no serious constitutional or federalism difficulty."

In a decision likely to exacerbate the political bloodletting associated with congressional redistricting, the Court upheld, by a 7-2 vote, the highly controversial 2003 redrawing of congressional districts by Texas' Republican legislature. The decision opens the door to mid-decade redistricting when a new party captures a legislature and governorship. However, the Court struck down, by a 6-3 vote, Vermont's low campaign contribution limits (e.g., a $400 limit on contributions to gubernatorial candidates in a two-year election cycle).

State Activism

A seemingly contrary development under coercive federalism has been state policy activism, especially since the early 1980s. However, this activism has been both a response to coercive federalism as states have bucked federal policies and filled federal policy voids and a stimulant of coercive federalism as interest groups have sought federal tranquilization of hyperactive state policymaking.

State officials have pursued litigation and regulation in many policy areas, especially environmental and consumer protection. Connecticut Attorney General Richard Blumenthal expressed a leading justification for such activism: "Our action is the result of federal inaction."[14] Also, in an effort to compete with the conservative American Legislative Exchange Council (ALEC), several hundred state legislators launched the Progressive Legislative Action Network (PLAN) in 2005.

State action on environmental protection garnered considerable attention in 2006, especially when California Gov. Arnold Schwarzenegger joined British Prime Minister Tony Blair to sign an accord on global warming in August 2006. In September, Schwarzenegger signed a bill to reduce California's greenhouse gas emissions by 25 percent by 2020. In 2004, California implemented rules on vehicular greenhouse gases that are stricter than the federal standards. Ten other states have adopted California's rules, which limit the amount of carbon dioxide and other gases that automobiles can expel into the atmosphere. In addition, California, New York and eight other states sued the U.S. Environmental Protection Agency for failing to regulate carbon dioxide emissions from power plants. Some 23 states have set standards requiring utilities to generate up to 33 percent of their energy from renewable sources by 2020.

In April 2006, Massachusetts became the first state to enact universal access to health care for its citizens. Many other states have sweeping health care plans under consideration.

Conclusion

Short-term changes in federal policymaking will be instituted by the new divided government in Washington, D.C., but the long-term trends in federalism will remain largely on course.

Notes

[1] James Bryce, *The American Commonwealth*, 3rd ed. (New York: Macmillan, 1907), I, p. 353.

[2] David Broder, "Governors seek relief from Congressional gridlock," *The Express-Times* (Easton), August 8, 2006, A7.

[3] See also, Rudolph G. Penner, "The Coming Federal Budget Squeeze and Its Impact on State and Local Government," *Proceedings: 98th Annual Conference on Taxation* (Washington, D.C.: National Tax Association, 2005), pp. 111–117.

[4] For explication, see John Kincaid, "The State of U.S. Federalism, 2000–2001," *Publius: The Journal of Federalism* 31 (Summer 2001): 1–69.

[5] Quoted in Brody Mullins, "As Earmarked Funding Swells, Some Recipients Don't Want It," *Wall Street Journal*, December 26, 2006, A10.

[6] William Wyatt, "Washington Watch: 10 Top Issues for States," *State Legislatures* 32 (January 2006): 15.

[7] Quoted in Stephen Labaton, "'Silent Tort Reform' Is Overriding States' Powers," *New York Times*, March 10, 2006, C5.

[8] John Maggs, "Limping Toward Tax Reform," *National Journal* 37 (October 22, 2005): 3280.

[9] Peter J. Ferrara, "The NGA Should Pay Its Own Way," *Policy Brief* (Washington, D.C.: Americans for Tax Reform, 2005).

[10] *Northern Insurance Company New York v. Chatham County*, 126 S.Ct. 1689 (2006).

[11] *Gonzales v. Oregon*, 546 U.S. 243 (2006).

[12] *DaimlerChrysler v. Cuno*, 547 U.S. ___ (2006).

[13] *Rapanos v. United States*, No. 547 U.S. ___ (2006) and *Carabell v. United States Army Corps of Engineers*, 547 U.S. ___ (2006).

[14] Quoted in Brooke A. Masters. "Who's Watching Out for the Consumer?" *Washington Post National Weekly Edition*, January 17, 2005, 30.

About the Author

John Kincaid is the Robert B. and Helen S. Meyner Professor of Government and Public Service and director of the Meyner Center for the Study of State and Local Government at Lafayette College, Easton, Pa. He is former editor of *Publius: The Journal of Federalism*; former executive director of the U.S. Advisory Commission on Intergovernmental Relations; and co-editor of *Constitutional Origins, Structure, and Change in Federal Countries* (2005).

Trends in State-Local Relations

By Joseph F. Zimmerman

State-local relations remain complex in 2007: Constitutional and statutory distribution of powers between states and general-purpose local governments differ in the various states. Trends include the creation of state control boards for local governments suffering fiscal distress, continued imposition of mandates and restraints, and increased use of joint powers authority.

The powers reserved to the states by the 10th Amendment to the U.S. Constitution can be placed in three broad spheres—a sphere most commonly controlled by local governments, a sphere generally controlled by state government, and a shared local and state sphere. Historically, the English common-law *Ultra Vires Rule* (Dillon's Rule) was followed in each state and the state legislature exercised plenary powers over its political subdivisions.

The legislature in many states in the 19th century enacted "ripper laws" changing the structure and powers of individual local governments. In response, voters in 41 states ratified constitutional provisions prohibiting the legislature from enacting a special law for a named local government unless its governing body requested its enactment. Legislative abuses, however, continued and led to constitutional amendments establishing an *Imperium in Imperio* (a federal system within a state) with the state constitution devolving authority to each general-purpose local government over its structure, property and local affairs.

Continuing resentment of legislative interference resulted in the development of a new constitutional amendment directing the legislature to devolve upon a municipality adopting a new charter all powers capable of devolution except civil relations, and the definition and punishment of a felony.[1]

State-Local Legal Relations

Such relations are exceptionally complex in a number of states. Constitutional provisions, statutes, state administrative rules and regulations, and court decisions determine the nature of state-local relations in various functional areas. An occasional state constitutional amendment devolves additional discretionary authority to local governments.

A Texas constitutional amendment allows voters to exempt the city from a state requirement that pension promises be kept, and Houston voters took advantage of this provision. State legislatures also grant additional discretionary authority to certain local governments. In Illinois, S.B. 2175 of 2004 allows the council in a city with a population under 50,000 and a managerial government to expand its membership from four to six. Chapter 209 of the Maine laws of 2005 allows water districts to form coalitions, and Chapter 48 of 2006 allows the island of Chebeague to secede from the town of Cumberland and become its own town.

The Georgia State Legislature during the Great Depression amalgamated three counties to form Fulton County, whose board created a single tax district for the unincorporated county area to pay for services. The affluent northern part of the county pays considerably more in county taxes than the southern part. Upon achieving power, the Republican-controlled state legislature decided upon a "municipalization" policy (Act 438 of 2006). One new city, Milton, has been created and voters on July 19, 2006, authorized the creation of two additional cities. When the new Milton mayor and council assumed office Dec. 1, 2006, they signed a contract with CH2M Hill-OmI, a management firm, to provide all city services.

The 2006 Illinois State Legislature may have initiated a new trend by enacting an Ambulance Revolving Loan Fund (Public Act 094-0829) to provide zero-interest loans up to $100,000 for 10 years to fire departments, fire protection districts and nonprofit ambulance services to purchase ambulances. The legislature also broadened the discretionary authority of municipalities by (1) authorizing them (Public Act 094-1007) to use eminent domain to take over privately owned waterworks and (2) allowing municipalities (Public Act 094-0740) to charge a driver with a misdemeanor for violating an ordinance prohibiting driving under the influence of alcohol in the event the state's attorney refuses to file state felony charges.

The 2006 New York State Legislature enacted Chapter 109 establishing a Restore New York Communities Program by authorizing $300 million in grants over a three-year period to support urban revitalization efforts. Chapter 22 authorizes the state Common Retirement Fund to increase from 15 percent to 25 percent the amount of assets that may be invested in accordance with the prudent investment standard.

Chapter 190 allows municipalities to issue bonds to finance repair or reconstruction of privately owned buildings posing a threat to public health or safety, and Chapter 654 adds strokes to the list of health problems deemed line-of-duty disabilities, which allows police officers and firefighters to receive tax-free pensions equal to 75 percent of their final salaries.

The 2006 South Carolina State Legislature enacted Act 388 authorizing an additional local option sales tax, in increments up to 1 percent, in addition to existing local option sales taxes, and Act 290 pre-empting local government regulation of agriculture facilities and operations.

The 2006 Vermont State Legislature removed the sunset clause from Act 60 that authorizes 76 municipalities to levy a 1-percent rooms and meals tax and/ or sales tax. New restraints continue to be enacted by state legislatures. In 2005, Gov. James Doyle of Wisconsin signed a bill forbidding Milwaukee and other local governments to establish minimum wage rates. The 2006 Rhode Island State Legislature established a new cap on local government property taxes (Chapter 253). Arizona reduced its income tax rate and thereby decreased state revenues significantly. The result for local government was less state aid with Phoenix suffering a $10 million decline in 2006.

Local governments increasingly are using their joint powers authority. Nearly 100 New Hampshire cities and towns, for example, are enrolled in the New Hampshire Public Works Mutual Aid Program, modeled on fire and police mutual aid programs. The program allows member municipalities to borrow equipment and personnel from other member municipalities to cope with natural disasters, such as floods.

Court Decisions

The United States Supreme Court in 2005 in *Kelo v. City of New London* (545 U.S. 469) opined the city's exercise of its eminent domain power to implement an economic development plan met the constitutional public use requirement. This decision generated citizen fears over the potential loss of their homes and led to introduction of bills in state legislatures restricting use of eminent domain power. Five state legislatures enacted eminent domain laws in 2005 and the number increased to 30 by October 2006 with voters in 12 states casting ballots on restrictive referendum propositions.

The 2006 Florida State Legislature enacted Chapter 11, which dramatically reduced a city's ability to engage in economic development activities. The law stipulates that property taken by eminent domain proceedings may be transferred without restriction

only under narrow circumstances involving a public infrastructure, right of way, road or utility services. All other properties acquired by a government by eminent domain must be held for a minimum of 10 years before the property may be transferred to a non-public body.

In 2005, the U.S. District Court for the District of New Hampshire in *Smith et al. v. Ayotte et al.* (356 F.Supp.2d 9) addressed the issues raised by plaintiff property taxpayers in Hollis and Hudson who challenged a state law authorizing local assessing officers to seek administrative inspection warrants when property owners refuse to allow them to enter their property to obtain information. The state law also states that those refusing consent lose their right to appeal tax abatement and exemption decisions. The court dismissed the lawsuit by holding the federal *Tax Injunction Act of 1948* (28 U.S.C. §1341) "operates to divest the court of subject matter jurisdiction over all actions within its statutory ambit."

The Washington Supreme Court in *Parkland Light & Water Company v. Tacoma-Pierce County Board of Health* (90 P.3d 37) in 2004 held a state law specifically grants water districts—not local boards of health—the authority to decide whether to fluoridate the water. This came on the heels of a 2002 decision by the County Board of Health to fluoridate the water, which they justified on the grounds it would save millions of dollars in medical costs and prevent dental problems in children. The Vermont Supreme Court in *Vermont Alliance of Nonprofit Organizations v. City of Burlington* (857 A2d 305) in 2004 upheld the decision of the Chittenden Superior Court that said the city lacked authority to tax the business personal property of a nonprofit organization. The court in 2005 in *Our Lady of Ephesus House of Prayer v. Town of Jamaica* (869 A2d 145) ruled apartments occasionally used by visiting clergy did not qualify as a parsonage. In 2005, the Washington Supreme Court in *Entertainment Industry Coalition v. Tacoma-Pierce County Health Department* (105 P.3d 985) invalidated a Tacoma-Pierce County resolution banning smoking in all public establishments by holding it conflicted with a state law (RCWA §70.160.040(1)) allowing smoking in a bar, tavern, bowling alley, tobacco shop or restaurant.

The New Hampshire Supreme Court in *Verizon New England, Incorporated v. City of Rochester* (855 A.2d 497) in 2004 decided the city may levy a real estate tax on the company regarding licenses concerning the placement of utility poles and related equipment along public ways. The court specifically held "the legislature intended for leases and other agreements that permit the use or occupation of public property to include a provision requiring payment of properly assessed real estate taxes."

The Wisconsin Supreme Court in 2004 issued two decisions—*State ex rel. Ziervoge v. Washington County Board of Adjustment* and *State v. Waushara County Board of Adjustment* (679 N.W.2d 514)—holding a variance applicant must prove all the statutory elements for any proposed variance; i.e., a zoning board cannot grant a variance unless the application proves the (1) proposed variance is not contrary to the public interest, (2) property has a special or unique condition, and (3) a special condition of the property creates an unnecessary hardship.

Fiscal Distress

One unfortunate trend is the fiscal distress of several large cities and urban counties. State legislatures respond to the problem by establishing a state-controlled finance board for each of these units. The 2004 Pennsylvania State Legislature established a financial control board termed the Intergovernmental Cooperation Authority for the City of Pittsburgh (Act 11). The 2004 Massachusetts General Court (state legislature) created a fiscal control board for Springfield, the third largest city, and authorized a $52 million loan (Chapter 169).

The New York State Legislature established a financial control board for New York City in 1975 (Chapter 868-70) and the board continues to function. A similar board (Chapter 871) was established in the same year for the City of Yonkers, but the board was dissolved Dec. 31, 1978, when the city's fiscal condition improved. Nevertheless, the state comptroller since 1976 bears the responsibility for annually certifying the city's budget. In 1995, the state legislature created a financial control board for the City of Troy that subsequently was disbanded as the city's fiscal health improved. And in 2005, the legislature enacted Chapter 18 establishing the Erie County Fiscal Stability Authority.

Functional Transfers

The inability of local governments to solve problems transcending local boundary lines persuaded several state legislatures to create public authorities. The Massachusetts General Court, concerned about problems in the greater Boston area, established the Metropolitan Sewage Commission in 1889, Metropolitan Parks Commission in 1893, and Metropolitan Water Commission in 1895. The sewer and water commissions were merged in 1901 and the merged body was consolidated with the parks commission

in 1919 to form the Metropolitan District Commission. The General Court in 2003 enacted Chapter 41 terminating the commission and transferring its functions to state departments.

The poor academic achievement of students in Detroit public schools led to Michigan assuming responsibility for the city's schools in 2004. Gov. Kathleen Blanco of Louisiana in 2005 made the transfer of control of the New Orleans public school system from the Orleans Parish School Board to the State Education Department a legislative priority. The state legislature responded favorably to her recommendation by enacting a law transferring to the department and the Board of Elementary and Secondary Education responsibility for 102 schools whose performance scores were below the state average.

The Maryland School Board on March 29, 2006, cited the federal No Child Left Behind Law and voted to transfer control of four high schools with poor achievement scores from the Baltimore City School District to the state, and to convert seven middle schools into charter schools. The next day, the Maryland State Legislature enacted a bill forbidding the state superintendent of schools to remove the concerned schools from local control.

On Sept. 18, 2006, California Gov. Arnold Schwarzenegger signed into law a bill nominally transferring powers over Los Angeles public schools, which have a low graduation rate and low test scores, to the Mayor Antonio R. Villaraigosa. In contrast to New York City where a 2002 law placed public schools under the direct control of the mayor, the powers over the Los Angeles public schools have been dispersed with the mayor sharing powers with a council of mayors representing 26 additional cities served by the schools. The seven-member elected school board continues to have jurisdiction over curricula questions and authority to select the superintendent, which is subject to a potential veto by the council of mayors. The superintendent controls the district's $7.4 billion operating budget and oversight of financial contracts. The Los Angeles School District announced it will challenge the constitutionality of the law on the ground the constitution prohibits cities and their officers to operate public schools. It should be noted the 2002 New York law has a 2009 sunset clause and New York City Mayor Michael R. Bloomberg is lobbying to convince the state legislature to make the law permanent.

In Nebraska, Douglas County District Court Judge Michael Coffey on Sept. 18, 2006, issued a temporary injunction blocking implementation of a 2006 state law that would divide the Omaha school district into a district with predominantly black students, a district with mostly Hispanic students, and a district with largely white students, effective in 2008. The purpose of the proposed statute is to end a dispute arising from the Omaha district's attempt to acquire jurisdiction over several suburban schools. The Chicano Awareness Center and five parents of Omaha students filed the suit. Judge Coffey opined the voting structure established by the law is "grossly disproportionate" and violates the Nebraska Constitution. Earlier, the National Association for the Advancement of Colored People challenged the law on the ground it would segregate Omaha's schools in violation of the U.S. Supreme Court's 1954 decision in *Brown v. Board of Education* (347 U.S. 483).

State-Local Government Irritants

State governments provide financial and other types of assistance to local governments that are welcomed by local government officers who may complain about conditions attached to some aid. Nevertheless, major irritants exist in state-local relations. These include state mandates and state restraints contained in statutes and administrative rules and regulations. The reader should be aware that a number of mandates termed state mandates are "pass-through mandates" under provisions of congressional minimum standards pre-emption statutes dating to the post-1964 period.[2] These acts authorize the federal administrator to establish minimum regulatory standards and authorize each state to continue regulating provided it develops a plan with standards at least as high as the national standards and demonstrates it has the personnel and equipment to enforce them.

As a result, what appears to be a state mandate has its origin in minimum national standards.

Local government complaints led to the amendment of constitutions in 16 states and enactment of statutes in 19 states providing prospective relief against future mandates; however, these statutes offer no retroactive relief. In various states, the relief provided varies from minor to major. California Proposition 4 of 1979 and New Hampshire (Part I, Art. 27a) constitutional relief provisions are the most effective in that they require 100 percent reimbursement of mandated costs. New Hampshire lacks a broad base tax and resulting revenue to fund mandated costs. In consequence, the General Court does not enact mandate bills other than an occasional minor one, and few administrative rules contain even a minor mandate. The New Hampshire Department of Environmental Services in 2006, however, promulgated regulations applicable to public beaches and bathing areas requiring restrooms, emergency radios and telephones within 200 feet of the water, and rescue equipment. A city or town can avoid these mandates by simply posting signs that none of the above is available.

Survey Responses

Questionnaires were sent in 2006 to each state municipal association and county association. Table A contains the responses of associations in 30 states.

Not surprisingly, 24 associations and 20 associations rated state financial assistance to local governments as inadequate. In Connecticut, for example, state aid decreased from 20 percent of total state appropriations in 1994 to 16 percent in 2006.

Table A: State-Local Government Relations

Problem area	Major problem	Minor problem	Not a problem
Special laws	4	10	19
State mandates	25	12	4
State administrative supervision	4	23	13
Compulsory binding arbitration	10	8	22
New special districts	2	11	25
State tax limits	17	9	15
State debt limits	3	17	17
Adequacy of state municipal/ county financial aid	24	12	3
Adequacy of state education aid	20	4	9
State-mandated functional transfers	9	20	8
Adequacy of home rule powers	15	15	6
Use of initiative to put a lid on spending	12	8	17

Source: Based on responses to questionnaires sent in 2006 to each state municipal association and county association. This table contains the repsonses of associations in 30 states.

Summary

Relatively little change in the discretionary authority of local governments has occurred since 2003 although state legislatures continue to impose mandates and restraints on local governments including financial control boards on Erie County, New York, Pittsburgh, and Springfield, Mass. Associations of local governments rate mandates, inadequate state financial aid and tax limits as major problems. U.S. and state court decisions have had a mixed impact on the authority of local governments.

Notes

[1] Jefferson B. Fordham, *Model Constitutional Provisions for Municipal Home Rule* (Chicago: American Municipal Association, 1953).

[2] Joseph F. Zimmerman, *Congressional Preemption: Regulatory Federalism* (Albany: State University of New York Press, 2005).

About the Author

Joseph F. Zimmerman is a professor of political science at Rockefeller College of the State University of New York at Albany. He is the author of more than 30 books and numerous articles.

Table 2.1
SUMMARY OF STATE INTERGOVERNMENTAL EXPENDITURES: 1944–2005
(Amounts are in thousands of dollars and per capitas are in dollars)

Fiscal year	Total Amount	Total Per capita	To Federal government (a)	To local governments Total	For general local government support	Education	Public welfare	Highways	Health	Miscellaneous and combined
1944	$1,842,000	$13.95	…	$1,842,000	$274,000	$861,000	$368,000	$298,000	…	$41,000
1946	2,092,000	15.03	…	2,092,000	357,000	953,000	376,000	339,000	…	67,000
1948	3,283,000	22.60	…	3,283,000	428,000	1,554,000	648,000	507,000	…	146,000
1950	4,217,000	28.13	…	4,217,000	482,000	2,054,000	792,000	610,000	…	279,000
1952	5,044,000	32.57	…	5,044,000	549,000	2,523,000	976,000	728,000	…	268,000
1953	5,384,000	34.20	…	5,384,000	592,000	2,737,000	981,000	803,000	…	271,000
1954	5,679,000	35.41	…	5,679,000	600,000	2,930,000	1,004,000	871,000	…	274,000
1955	5,986,000	36.61	…	5,986,000	591,000	3,150,000	1,046,000	911,000	…	288,000
1956	6,538,000	39.26	…	6,538,000	631,000	3,541,000	1,069,000	984,000	…	313,000
1957	7,440,000	43.87	…	7,440,000	668,000	4,212,000	1,136,000	1,082,000	…	342,000
1958	8,089,000	46.65	…	8,089,000	687,000	4,598,000	1,247,000	1,167,000	…	390,000
1959	8,689,000	49.26	…	8,689,000	725,000	4,957,000	1,409,000	1,207,000	…	391,000
1960	9,443,000	52.88	…	9,443,000	806,000	5,461,000	1,483,000	1,247,000	…	446,000
1962	10,906,000	58.97	…	10,906,000	839,000	6,474,000	1,777,000	1,327,000	…	489,000
1963	11,885,000	63.34	…	11,885,000	1,012,000	6,993,000	1,919,000	1,416,000	…	545,000
1964	12,968,000	68.15	…	12,968,000	1,053,000	7,664,000	2,108,000	1,524,000	…	619,000
1965	14,174,000	73.57	…	14,174,000	1,102,000	8,351,000	2,436,000	1,630,000	…	655,000
1966	16,928,000	86.94	…	16,928,000	1,361,000	10,177,000	2,882,000	1,725,000	…	783,000
1967	19,056,000	96.94	…	19,056,000	1,585,000	11,845,000	2,897,000	1,861,000	…	868,000
1968	21,950,000	110.56	…	21,950,000	1,993,000	13,321,000	3,527,000	2,029,000	…	1,080,000
1969	24,779,000	123.56	…	24,779,000	2,135,000	14,858,000	4,402,000	2,109,000	…	1,275,000
1970	28,892,000	142.64	…	28,892,000	2,958,000	17,085,000	5,003,000	2,439,000	…	1,407,000
1971	32,640,000	158.39	…	32,640,000	3,258,000	19,292,000	5,760,000	2,507,000	…	1,823,000
1972	36,759,246	176.27	…	36,759,246	3,752,327	21,195,345	6,943,634	2,633,417	…	2,234,523
1973	40,822,135	193.81	…	40,822,135	4,279,646	23,315,651	7,531,738	2,953,424	…	2,741,676
1974	45,941,111	216.07	$341,194	45,599,917	4,803,875	27,106,812	7,028,750	3,211,455	…	3,449,025
1975	51,978,324	242.03	974,780	51,003,544	5,129,333	31,110,237	7,136,104	3,224,861	…	4,403,009
1976	57,858,242	266.79	1,179,580	56,678,662	5,673,843	34,083,711	8,307,411	3,240,806	…	5,372,891
1977	62,459,903	285.10	1,386,237	61,073,666	6,372,543	36,964,306	8,756,717	3,631,108	…	5,348,992
1978	67,287,260	303.88	1,472,378	65,814,882	6,819,438	40,125,488	8,585,558	3,821,135	…	6,463,263
1979	75,962,980	339.25	1,493,215	74,469,765	8,224,338	46,195,698	8,675,473	4,148,573	…	7,225,683
1980	84,504,451	374.07	1,746,301	82,758,150	8,643,789	52,688,101	9,241,551	4,382,716	…	7,801,993
1981	93,179,549	406.89	1,872,980	91,306,569	9,570,248	57,257,373	11,025,445	4,751,449	…	8,702,054
1982	98,742,976	426.78	1,793,284	96,949,692	10,044,372	60,683,583	11,965,123	5,028,072	…	9,228,542
1983	100,886,902	431.77	1,764,821	99,122,081	10,364,144	63,118,351	10,919,847	5,277,447	…	9,442,292
1984	108,373,188	459.49	1,722,115	106,651,073	10,744,740	67,484,926	11,923,430	5,686,834	…	10,811,143
1985	121,571,151	510.56	1,963,468	119,607,683	12,319,623	74,936,970	12,673,123	6,019,069	…	13,658,898
1986	131,966,258	548.76	2,105,831	129,860,427	13,383,912	81,929,467	14,214,613	6,470,049	…	13,862,386
1987	141,278,672	581.88	2,455,362	138,823,310	14,245,089	88,253,298	14,753,727	6,784,699	…	14,786,497
1988	151,661,866	618.55	2,652,981	149,008,885	14,896,991	95,390,536	15,032,315	6,949,190	…	16,739,853
1989	165,415,415	667.98	2,929,622	162,485,793	15,749,681	104,601,291	16,697,915	7,376,173	…	18,060,733

See footnotes at end of table.

SUMMARY OF STATE INTERGOVERNMENTAL EXPENDITURES: 1944–2005—Continued
(Amounts are in thousands of dollars and per capitas are in dollars)

Fiscal year	Total		To Federal government (a)	To local governments		For specified purposes				
	Amount	Per capita		Total	For general local government support	Education	Public welfare	Highways	Health	Miscellaneous and combined
1990	175,027,632	705.46	3,243,634	171,783,998	16,565,106	109,438,131	18,403,149	7,784,316	…	19,593,296
1991	186,398,234	740.91	3,464,364	182,933,870	16,977,032	116,179,860	20,903,400	8,126,477	…	20,747,101
1992	201,313,434	791.04	3,608,911	197,704,523	16,368,139	124,919,686	25,942,234	8,480,871	…	21,993,593
1993	214,094,882	832.00	3,625,051	210,469,831	17,690,986	131,179,517	31,339,777	9,298,624	…	20,960,927
1994	225,635,410	868.50	3,603,447	222,031,963	18,044,015	135,861,024	30,624,514	9,622,849	…	27,879,561
1995	240,978,128	919.10	3,616,831	237,361,297	18,996,435	148,160,436	30,772,525	10,481,616	…	28,926,886
1996	252,079,335	952.30	3,896,667	248,182,668	20,019,771	156,954,115	31,180,345	10,707,338	10,790,396	18,530,703
1997	264,207,209	989.10	3,839,942	260,367,267	21,808,828	164,147,715	35,754,024	11,431,270	11,772,189	15,453,241
1998	278,853,409	1,031.60	3,515,734	275,337,675	22,693,158	176,250,998	32,327,325	11,648,853	12,379,498	20,037,843
1999	308,734,917	1,120.40	3,801,667	304,933,250	25,495,396	192,416,987	35,161,151	12,075,195	13,611,228	26,173,293
2000	327,069,829	1,164.57	4,021,471	323,048,358	27,475,363	208,135,537	40,206,513	12,473,052	15,067,156	19,690,737
2001	350,326,546	1,230.32	4,290,764	346,035,782	31,693,016	222,092,587	41,926,990	12,350,136	16,518,461	21,454,592
2002	364,789,480	1,269.25	4,370,330	360,419,150	28,927,053	227,336,087	47,112,496	12,949,850	20,816,777	23,276,887
2003	382,781,397	1,318.89	4,391,095	378,390,302	30,766,480	240,788,692	49,302,737	13,337,114	20,241,742	23,953,537
2004	389,706,202	1,327.17	4,720,728	384,985,474	31,027,535	248,356,196	42,802,564	13,972,060	20,366,508	28,460,611
2005	408,955,959	1,379.25	4,675,517	404,280,442	28,284,852	263,171,516	46,859,165	14,486,020	18,083,659	33,395,230

Source: U.S. Department of Commerce, Bureau of the Census, 2005.
2005 Population Source: Table NST-EST2006-01—Annual State Population Estimates: July 1, 2005. Population Division, U.S. Census Bureau, released December 22, 2006.
Notes:
Detail may not add to totals due to rounding.
Table previously titled "SUMMARY OF STATE INTERGOVERNMENTAL PAYMENTS." Change is for name only, data are unaffected.

Key:
… — Not available
(a) Represents primarily state reimbursements for the supplemental security July income program. This column also duplicates some funds listed under "Public welfare" and "Miscellaneous and combined" columns.

FEDERAL AID

Table 2.2
STATE INTERGOVERNMENTAL EXPENDITURES, BY STATE: 1999–2005
(Amounts are in thousands of dollars and per capitas are in dollars)

State	Expenditure amounts (in thousands)							Per capita amounts						
	2005	2004	2003	2002	2001	2000	1999	1999	2000	2001	2002	2003	2004	2005
United States	$403,467,210	$389,706,202	$382,781,397	$364,789,480	$350,326,546	$327,069,829	$304,933,250	$1,120.4	$1,164.6	$1,269.3	$1,269.3	$1,318.9	$1,329.6	$1,360.73
Alabama	4,494,345	4,164,719	4,074,005	4,095,562	3,892,653	3,908,350	3,631,426	831.0	878.9	914.4	914.4	904.5	920.4	988.13
Alaska	1,145,159	1,049,706	1,091,391	1,055,596	986,921	1,026,962	1,028,890	1,659.5	1,637.9	1,646.8	1,646.8	1,684.2	1,595.3	1,726.58
Arizona	8,069,461	7,544,080	6,936,753	6,968,635	6,439,144	5,940,651	5,944,003	1,244.0	1,157.8	1,280.8	1,280.8	1,243.4	1,314.3	1,355.53
Arkansas	3,869,400	3,233,499	3,210,582	3,071,214	2,941,918	2,725,242	2,649,550	1,038.6	1,019.5	1,135.0	1,135.0	1,176.9	1,175.8	1,394.02
California	80,948,431	80,132,150	84,468,847	74,687,370	69,747,365	65,389,054	58,350,134	1,760.5	1,930.5	2,133.8	2,133.8	2,381.9	2,235.7	2,238.98
Colorado	5,187,799	4,860,577	4,666,350	4,295,239	3,909,362	3,702,849	3,519,783	867.8	860.9	954.3	954.3	1,026.0	1,056.2	1,112.47
Connecticut	3,513,039	3,396,810	3,030,485	3,734,962	3,252,917	3,362,551	2,810,990	856.5	987.2	1,079.8	1,079.8	869.1	970.8	1,003.52
Delaware	945,950	922,710	903,476	822,544	788,160	856,008	720,975	956.2	1,091.8	1,020.5	1,020.5	1,104.5	1,111.7	1,123.80
Florida	17,328,518	16,473,396	14,460,722	14,053,858	15,010,631	14,073,445	13,437,789	889.3	880.6	842.0	842.0	850.7	947.6	975.26
Georgia	9,521,119	9,335,405	9,016,458	8,644,827	8,383,261	7,179,698	6,677,041	857.3	877.1	1,011.8	1,011.8	1,039.2	1,046.8	1,042.55
Hawaii	147,201	134,452	125,434	130,387	124,448	157,902	153,220	129.3	130.3	105.1	105.1	100.4	106.5	115.61
Idaho	1,519,654	1,496,785	1,449,076	1,407,058	1,363,445	1,277,688	1,213,378	969.2	987.4	1,047.7	1,047.7	1,060.0	1,073.0	1,063.17
Illinois	14,212,799	13,303,609	13,369,662	13,090,976	12,770,065	12,050,100	10,802,562	890.7	970.3	1,040.1	1,040.1	1,057.0	1,046.5	1,113.38
Indiana	7,993,289	7,963,397	6,760,945	6,556,774	7,052,415	6,735,704	6,247,767	1,051.3	1,107.8	1,064.9	1,064.9	1,090.5	1,278.8	1,275.66
Iowa	3,642,335	3,529,971	3,442,552	3,326,499	3,284,057	3,211,878	2,872,879	1,001.4	1,097.7	1,133.0	1,133.0	1,170.1	1,195.4	1,228.23
Kansas	3,281,217	2,878,801	2,925,220	2,971,413	2,953,527	2,853,333	2,806,135	1,057.1	1,061.5	1,095.7	1,095.7	1,073.5	1,053.0	1,193.96
Kentucky	3,915,278	3,967,334	3,693,634	3,559,669	3,620,278	3,280,144	3,249,308	820.3	811.5	870.3	870.3	896.9	957.8	938.33
Louisiana	4,588,748	4,410,251	4,329,053	4,168,290	3,800,785	3,721,576	3,644,823	833.7	832.8	931.3	931.3	963.3	978.5	1,018.06
Maine	1,093,027	1,049,160	1,051,164	1,009,582	976,233	912,376	858,131	684.9	715.6	779.6	779.6	803.0	797.8	829.17
Maryland	5,801,050	5,632,520	5,358,342	5,235,506	5,003,670	4,355,724	4,063,814	785.7	822.5	960.5	960.5	972.1	1,012.9	1,037.83
Massachusetts	6,475,520	6,202,583	6,435,841	6,283,972	6,886,054	6,240,692	6,751,995	1,093.4	982.9	978.5	978.5	1,002.5	968.1	1,006.55
Michigan	18,679,748	19,035,055	19,851,778	19,067,058	18,145,167	17,201,031	16,030,447	1,625.1	1,730.8	1,898.5	1,898.5	1,969.0	1,883.9	1,849.33
Minnesota	10,108,813	9,638,153	9,618,471	8,271,462	8,196,532	7,610,072	7,004,803	1,466.7	1,547.1	1,646.1	1,646.1	1,899.4	1,890.9	1,971.78
Mississippi	4,005,786	3,880,446	3,665,580	3,456,588	3,354,226	3,248,019	3,018,675	1,090.2	1,141.7	1,205.6	1,205.6	1,271.4	1,337.6	1,377.27
Missouri	5,485,698	5,260,101	5,159,094	5,073,185	4,802,371	4,528,746	4,441,636	812.3	809.4	894.7	894.7	902.1	913.2	946.18
Montana	1,005,091	955,378	938,000	910,845	863,553	760,511	708,248	802.1	843.1	1,000.9	1,000.9	1,021.8	1,030.6	1,075.27
Nebraska	1,770,897	1,695,613	1,784,749	1,820,137	1,684,159	1,585,847	1,487,295	892.7	926.9	1,053.3	1,053.3	1,027.5	970.0	1,007.24
Nevada	3,272,860	2,948,274	2,648,660	2,432,909	2,271,654	2,250,330	2,088,730	1,154.6	1,126.3	1,122.7	1,122.7	1,181.4	1,263.7	1,356.74
New Hampshire	1,245,235	1,278,988	1,283,091	1,178,642	1,040,566	1,053,267	477,913	397.9	852.2	925.2	925.2	995.4	984.6	952.87
New Jersey	11,394,615	9,813,688	8,997,417	9,320,357	9,081,634	8,639,491	7,798,959	957.8	1,026.8	1,086.9	1,086.9	1,041.1	1,130.0	1,309.25
New Mexico	3,608,081	3,031,473	2,951,328	2,768,420	2,561,979	2,447,354	2,366,077	1,359.8	1,345.4	1,494.8	1,494.8	1,570.7	1,593.0	1,873.37
New York	43,731,212	44,112,115	40,874,514	38,982,251	34,712,660	31,273,000	30,383,315	1,669.7	1,648.0	2,037.3	2,037.3	2,127.6	2,287.9	2,264.02
North Carolina	10,675,563	10,326,743	10,356,152	9,450,766	9,309,537	9,301,095	8,542,460	1,116.5	1,155.6	1,137.8	1,137.8	1,229.8	1,209.2	1,230.97
North Dakota	701,125	613,513	1,190,923	585,521	569,034	589,807	557,238	878.9	918.7	923.5	923.5	1,881.4	964.6	1,104.82
Ohio	16,368,355	15,730,201	15,249,395	15,052,078	14,594,220	12,932,081	12,015,358	1,067.4	1,139.1	1,319.3	1,319.3	1,333.2	1,373.8	1,426.97

See footnotes at end of table.

STATE INTERGOVERNMENTAL EXPENDITURES, BY STATE: 1999–2005—Continued
(Amounts are in thousands of dollars and per capitas are in dollars)

State	Expenditure amounts (in thousands)							Per capita amounts						
	2005	2004	2003	2002	2001	2000	1999	2005	2004	2003	2002	2001	2000	1999
Oklahoma	3,748,031	3,715,417	3,395,494	3,377,045	3,486,043	3,089,257	2,981,699	1,057.74	1,054.3	968.5	967.6	967.6	895.2	887.9
Oregon	4,764,615	4,637,052	4,071,501	4,212,673	4,027,505	3,919,771	3,672,493	1,309.37	1,291.3	1,142.4	1,196.8	1,196.8	1,145.8	1,107.5
Pennsylvania	13,307,866	12,156,969	11,943,470	12,787,590	13,120,752	11,369,795	10,947,652	1,072.75	980.9	965.4	1,037.2	1,037.2	925.8	912.8
Rhode Island	908,479	868,929	828,198	749,034	711,439	677,552	594,894	846.22	804.6	769.7	701.3	701.3	646.5	600.3
South Carolina	4,246,231	4,159,942	4,155,920	4,241,010	4,168,449	3,806,116	3,355,056	999.83	990.9	1,001.7	1,033.4	1,033.4	948.7	863.4
South Dakota	614,371	576,215	514,949	506,347	480,960	448,131	471,786	792.86	747.4	673.1	666.2	666.2	593.6	643.6
Tennessee	5,705,768	5,301,665	4,952,923	4,477,936	4,582,883	4,364,404	4,175,192	958.03	899.7	847.4	773.4	773.4	767.2	761.3
Texas	17,489,900	17,032,016	17,332,957	16,680,780	17,204,468	16,231,378	15,023,666	762.80	757.9	784.2	767.4	767.4	778.4	749.5
Utah	2,189,527	2,112,921	2,165,151	2,170,884	2,100,657	1,977,703	1,811,906	879.21	872.7	920.6	936.1	936.1	885.7	850.7
Vermont	1,266,715	981,307	938,085	918,858	919,865	931,604	699,231	2,035.25	1,580.2	1,515.5	1,491.7	1,491.7	1,529.7	1,177.2
Virginia	9,720,400	8,819,067	8,352,635	8,369,313	7,869,121	7,132,350	6,499,840	1,285.03	1,178.9	1,134.1	1,148.4	1,148.4	1,007.5	945.7
Washington	7,228,017	6,911,826	6,785,341	6,806,350	6,576,757	6,370,710	6,117,069	1,148.78	1,113.6	1,106.7	1,121.9	1,121.9	1,080.9	1,062.7
West Virginia	2,015,637	1,942,069	1,544,758	1,453,707	988,322	1,359,668	1,577,358	1,111.11	1,071.2	853.0	805.4	805.4	752.0	872.9
Wisconsin	9,200,766	9,285,137	9,478,166	9,523,191	8,895,941	8,170,504	7,887,652	1,664.50	1,687.0	1,731.5	1,750.6	1,750.6	1,523.2	1,502.4
Wyoming	1,314,469	1,204,014	952,705	974,608	818,841	838,308	762,009	2,583.48	2,379.5	1,897.8	1,953.1	1,953.1	1,697.0	1,587.5

Source: U.S. Department of Commerce, Bureau of the Census, January 2007.

Note: Includes payments to the federal government, primarily state reimbursements for the supplemental security income program.

Table 2.3
PER CAPITA STATE INTERGOVERNMENTAL EXPENDITURES, BY FUNCTION AND BY STATE: 2005
(Per capita amounts in dollars)

State	Total	General local government support	Specified functions				Miscellaneous and combined
			Education	Public welfare	Highways	Health	
United States	$1,379.2	$95.4	$887.6	$173.7	$48.9	$61.0	$112.7
Alabama	988.1	25.1	852.7	0.0	44.0	3.1	49.8
Alaska	1,726.6	33.7	1,225.7	74.5	15.1	73.1	302.8
Arizona	1,355.5	248.6	808.3	142.3	100.4	10.8	41.3
Arkansas.......................	1,394.0	97.8	1,182.4	0.0	57.6	0.0	55.5
California	2,238.0	159.6	1,255.1	622.6	67.3	195.9	72.6
Colorado	1,112.5	5.0	724.9	216.1	61.3	11.2	91.1
Connecticut	1,003.5	53.2	703.2	105.3	0.0	81.8	81.6
Delaware.......................	1,123.8	0.0	1,014.9	2.2	9.2	18.9	78.5
Florida	975.3	159.1	736.8	0.0	17.4	0.9	121.2
Georgia	1,042.5	43.4	840.4	74.6	0.0	46.1	35.4
Hawaii..........................	115.6	61.9	0.0	0.0	0.0	23.3	21.7
Idaho...........................	1,063.2	93.5	841.6	0.0	83.8	3.1	23.4
Illinois.........................	1,113.4	99.8	664.4	146.6	55.5	13.2	105.1
Indiana.........................	2,157.5	250.9	717.3	50.7	55.5	7.6	937.0
Iowa	1,228.2	44.9	862.7	58.9	146.2	33.8	84.0
Kansas	1,194.0	26.4	1,040.9	5.0	60.1	12.3	60.5
Kentucky	938.3	0.0	785.1	12.0	30.1	33.5	77.6
Louisiana	1,018.1	38.8	802.2	20.1	22.1	0.0	131.4
Maine...........................	829.2	97.3	669.8	13.9	17.7	0.0	39.3
Maryland	1,037.8	0.0	735.1	0.0	81.7	94.3	110.1
Massachusetts................	1,006.6	117.3	562.2	52.1	20.5	2.4	125.5
Michigan.......................	1,849.3	145.3	1,260.8	221.0	130.4	38.2	87.1
Minnesota	1,971.8	286.3	1,330.3	113.1	143.4	26.8	112.9
Mississippi	1,377.3	218.6	915.1	79.1	64.8	17.3	69.7
Missouri	946.2	0.8	781.5	17.3	49.5	0.9	97.1
Montana	1,075.3	143.9	749.0	20.8	24.0	22.3	90.6
Nebraska.......................	1,007.2	165.6	631.3	12.8	0.0	120.1	79.9
Nevada	1,356.7	345.2	825.5	26.5	35.5	5.6	28.5
New Hampshire.............	952.9	48.2	697.8	74.0	22.7	28.3	77.4
New Jersey....................	1,309.3	218.1	823.6	156.8	31.6	17.8	70.4
New Mexico	1,873.4	367.9	1,256.6	0.0	2.5	0.3	41.8
New York	2,264.0	56.7	1,182.0	518.1	0.8	207.9	288.6
North Carolina..............	1,231.0	76.2	870.6	155.3	24.2	39.7	70.5
North Dakota................	1,104.8	191.7	697.1	20.3	113.0	19.5	96.3
Ohio	1,427.0	155.1	869.9	143.4	79.3	92.8	68.2
Oklahoma	1,057.7	23.1	834.8	13.1	79.1	45.2	59.3
Oregon	1,309.4	38.3	834.2	82.6	200.2	39.0	117.8
Pennsylvania	1,072.8	2.1	645.4	180.6	33.6	99.6	111.8
Rhode Island	846.2	69.3	740.7	25.4	0.0	0.0	1.2
South Carolina	999.8	214.1	691.8	13.8	22.1	3.4	47.2
South Dakota................	792.9	17.1	611.0	3.7	42.6	1.4	89.4
Tennessee	958.0	66.1	617.3	134.8	62.2	0.2	73.5
Texas	762.8	4.8	681.5	29.3	8.1	8.5	29.1
Utah	879.2	0.0	814.1	11.4	11.9	14.4	27.4
Vermont	2,035.3	20.9	1,853.0	1.0	95.1	6.8	53.6
Virginia........................	1,285.0	118.0	818.7	83.3	48.7	34.5	178.8
Washington...................	1,148.8	14.0	923.1	8.0	92.7	26.4	88.5
West Virginia................	1,111.1	9.5	909.3	19.5	0.7	30.1	109.3
Wisconsin.....................	1,664.5	340.9	991.7	100.9	102.1	50.2	94.3
Wyoming.......................	2,583.5	347.9	1,524.6	2.2	14.3	21.1	312.8

Source: U.S. Department of Commerce, Bureau of the Census, February 2007.
Note: Includes payments to the federal government, primarily state reimbursements for the supplemental security income program (under "public welfare").

Table 2.4
STATE INTERGOVERNMENTAL EXPENDITURES, BY FUNCTION AND BY STATE: 2005
(In thousands of dollars)

State	Total	General local government support	Specified functions Education	Public welfare	Highways	Health	Miscellaneous and combined
United States	$408,955,959	$28,284,852	$263,171,516	$51,512,090	$14,486,020	$18,083,659	$33,417,822
Alabama	4,494,345	175,235	3,878,230	0	200,134	14,261	226,485
Alaska	1,145,159	23,454	812,934	49,439	9,999	48,492	200,841
Arizona	8,069,461	1,502,926	4,811,737	846,830	597,945	64,356	245,667
Arkansas	3,869,400	273,409	3,282,065	0	160,000	7	153,919
California	80,911,511	884,221	45,377,856	22,509,596	2,432,461	7,083,559	2,623,818
Colorado	5,187,799	36,702	3,380,268	1,007,682	285,814	52,390	424,943
Connecticut	3,513,039	110,720	2,461,619	368,739	9	286,195	285,757
Delaware	945,950	0	854,324	1,845	7,731	15,945	66,105
Florida	17,328,518	1,757,823	13,091,185	599	308,666	16,659	2,153,586
Georgia	9,521,119	420,437	7,675,441	681,249	0	420,615	323,377
Hawaii.........................	147,201	89,892	0	0	0	29,728	27,581
Idaho..........................	1,519,654	159,024	1,203,014	0	119,801	4,390	33,425
Illinois........................	14,212,799	1,639,996	8,481,967	1,872,020	708,101	168,759	1,341,956
Indiana........................	13,518,958	2,439,671	4,494,811	317,706	347,851	47,595	5,871,324
Iowa...........................	3,642,335	126,548	2,558,405	174,540	433,446	100,379	249,017
Kansas	3,281,217	41,371	2,860,688	13,620	165,295	33,924	166,319
Kentucky	3,915,278	0	3,276,083	50,037	125,656	139,778	323,724
Louisiana	4,588,748	190,453	3,615,809	90,745	99,662	39	592,040
Maine..........................	1,093,027	116,609	882,905	18,322	23,390	0	51,801
Maryland	5,801,050	93,519	4,108,649	116	456,589	526,972	615,205
Massachusetts...............	6,475,520	1,569,170	3,616,690	334,855	132,029	15,506	807,270
Michigan......................	18,679,748	1,130,294	12,734,713	2,231,842	1,317,460	385,613	879,826
Minnesota....................	10,108,813	1,257,663	6,820,240	579,669	735,262	137,217	578,762
Mississippi	4,005,786	672,606	2,661,518	230,094	188,540	50,370	202,658
Missouri......................	5,485,698	0	4,530,769	100,163	286,717	5,393	562,656
Montana	1,005,091	157,509	700,122	19,423	22,456	20,889	84,692
Nebraska......................	1,770,897	286,739	1,109,995	22,557	0	211,105	140,501
Nevada........................	3,272,860	1,049,598	1,991,378	63,967	85,620	13,493	68,804
New Hampshire.............	1,245,235	68,855	911,897	96,661	29,616	37,001	101,205
New Jersey...................	11,394,615	1,819,748	7,167,823	1,364,747	274,631	154,675	612,991
New Mexico	3,608,081	1,102,062	2,420,107	0	4,870	579	80,463
New York	43,731,212	1,288,931	22,830,248	10,007,517	14,623	4,015,997	5,573,896
North Carolina..............	10,675,563	613,093	7,549,832	1,347,003	209,551	344,656	611,428
North Dakota................	701,125	100,664	442,383	12,872	71,701	12,391	61,114
Ohio...........................	16,368,355	1,989,333	9,978,041	1,644,421	909,231	1,064,583	782,746
Oklahoma	3,748,031	92,829	2,958,234	46,352	280,272	160,218	210,126
Oregon	4,764,615	129,437	3,035,390	300,626	728,629	141,991	428,542
Pennsylvania	13,307,866	22,177	8,006,102	2,240,300	416,647	1,235,517	1,387,123
Rhode Island	908,479	84,688	795,218	27,314	0	0	1,259
South Carolina..............	4,246,231	940,719	2,938,033	58,584	94,048	14,435	200,412
South Dakota................	614,371	34,637	473,458	2,870	33,043	1,086	69,277
Tennessee	5,705,768	417,334	3,676,582	802,642	370,530	1,063	437,617
Texas	17,489,900	143,944	15,626,125	671,259	184,802	195,682	668,088
Utah	2,189,527	0	2,027,312	28,424	29,560	35,954	68,277
Vermont	1,266,715	16,027	1,153,270	628	59,215	4,234	33,341
Virginia.......................	9,720,400	915,837	6,192,928	629,746	368,240	261,294	1,352,355
Washington...................	7,228,017	63,396	5,808,093	50,463	583,150	165,801	557,114
West Virginia................	2,015,637	76,514	1,649,605	35,383	1,233	54,688	198,214
Wisconsin.....................	9,200,766	1,798,513	5,481,708	557,517	564,521	277,477	521,030
Wyoming......................	1,314,469	360,525	775,712	1,106	7,273	10,708	159,145

Source: U.S. Department of Commerce, Bureau of the Census, Governments Division, February 2007.
Note: Detail may not add to total due to rounding.

Table 2.5
STATE INTERGOVERNMENTAL EXPENDITURES, BY TYPE OF RECEIVING GOVERNMENT AND BY STATE: 2005
(In thousands of dollars)

State	Total intergovernmental expenditure	Federal	School districts	All other local governments
United States	$403,467,210	$4,768,438	$216,013,512	$182,740,181
Alabama	4,494,345	0	3,878,230	616,115
Alaska	1,145,159	0	0	1,145,159
Arizona	8,069,461	0	4,382,999	3,686,462
Arkansas...........................	3,869,400	565	3,282,014	586,821
California	80,948,431	3,447,852	42,720,290	34,780,289
Colorado	5,187,799	4,701	3,370,376	1,812,722
Connecticut	3,513,039	0	23,283	3,489,756
Delaware	945,950	1,080	850,489	94,381
Florida	17,328,518	0	12,702,490	4,626,028
Georgia	9,521,119	0	7,675,441	1,845,678
Hawaii	147,201	0	0	147,201
Idaho	1,519,654	30	1,203,014	316,610
Illinois	14,212,799	37	8,135,954	6,076,808
Indiana.............................	7,993,289	0	4,494,811	3,498,478
Iowa	3,642,335	57,100	2,554,758	1,030,477
Kansas	3,281,217	256	2,860,688	420,273
Kentucky	3,915,278	860	3,276,083	638,335
Louisiana	4,588,748	0	3,614,456	974,292
Maine	1,093,027	12,513	0	1,080,514
Maryland	5,801,050	0	0	5,801,050
Massachusetts....................	6,475,520	183,588	477,609	5,814,323
Michigan...........................	18,679,748	54,921	12,727,057	5,952,691
Minnesota	10,108,813	0	6,810,296	3,298,517
Mississippi........................	4,005,786	0	2,645,833	1,359,953
Missouri............................	5,485,698	4,429	4,530,769	950,500
Montana	1,005,091	0	700,122	304,969
Nebraska...........................	1,770,897	21,844	1,109,929	639,124
Nevada	3,272,860	1,351	1,991,378	1,280,131
New Hampshire..................	1,245,235	0	310	1,244,925
New Jersey........................	11,394,615	98,142	5,237,921	6,058,552
New Mexico	3,608,081	0	2,420,107	1,187,974
New York	43,731,212	629,000	11,808,627	31,293,585
North Carolina..................	10,675,563	0	0	10,675,563
North Dakota.....................	701,125	0	442,383	258,742
Ohio	16,368,355	3,024	9,978,041	6,387,290
Oklahoma	3,748,031	41,028	2,941,878	765,125
Oregon	4,764,615	0	3,033,728	1,730,887
Pennsylvania	13,307,866	161,782	8,006,102	5,139,982
Rhode Island	908,479	27,314	43,693	837,472
South Carolina	4,246,231	0	2,905,636	1,340,595
South Dakota.....................	614,371	0	473,458	140,913
Tennessee	5,705,768	0	219,389	5,486,379
Texas	17,489,900	0	15,610,105	1,879,795
Utah	2,189,527	29	2,027,312	162,186
Vermont............................	1,266,715	628	1,153,270	112,817
Virginia............................	9,720,400	1,615	0	9,718,785
Washington........................	7,228,017	3,974	5,790,159	1,433,884
West Virginia.....................	2,015,637	10,775	1,647,140	357,722
Wisconsin..........................	9,200,766	0	5,481,708	3,719,058
Wyoming...........................	1,314,469	0	774,176	540,293

Source: U.S. Department of Commerce, Bureau of the Census, January 2007.
Note: Detail may not add to total due to rounding.

Table 2.6
STATE INTERGOVERNMENTAL REVENUE FROM FEDERAL AND LOCAL GOVERNMENTS: 2005
(In thousands of dollars)

State	Total intergovernmental revenue	From federal government					From local governments				
		Total	Education	Public welfare	Health & hospitals	Highways	Total	Education	Public welfare	Health & hospitals	Highways
United States	$408,456,380	$386,034,095	$68,216,590	$221,932,568	$20,319,110	$32,735,017	$22,422,285	$2,259,493	$13,918,946	$725,791	$1,732,106
Alabama	7,460,913	6,848,479	1,435,662	3,670,094	340,786	536,582	612,434	15,362	497,697	32,677	32,950
Alaska	2,317,180	2,312,861	316,465	875,646	70,107	369,322	4,319	4,319	0	0	0
Arizona	7,566,075	7,101,844	1,278,477	4,591,981	254,494	509,134	464,231	19,276	302,178	53,792	38,326
Arkansas	4,113,478	4,088,711	671,322	2,281,954	88,496	413,967	24,767	13,014	0	768	0
California	51,163,273	47,145,771	10,107,729	25,399,633	2,309,824	2,368,940	4,017,502	2,089	2,652,806	7,005	587,283
Colorado	4,536,117	4,469,717	1,123,457	1,752,344	745,498	443,829	66,400	2,412	150	395	30,359
Connecticut	4,012,708	4,000,349	564,790	2,650,365	125,185	438,902	12,359	12,359	0	0	0
Delaware	1,157,400	1,122,606	141,820	606,868	87,147	118,422	34,794	34,590	0	0	0
Florida	18,287,697	18,162,543	3,369,957	8,994,239	1,389,000	1,937,399	125,154	11,448	0	77,130	0
Georgia	9,861,216	9,702,025	2,117,149	4,658,181	452,604	1,730,902	159,191	106,933	0	0	19,751
Hawaii	1,785,979	1,784,329	476,152	804,797	99,006	135,679	1,650		0	0	27
Idaho	1,749,617	1,739,865	311,131	842,135	152,447	244,305	9,752	679	6,378	0	2,594
Illinois	13,894,704	12,345,490	2,616,917	7,220,633	461,627	870,338	1,549,214	36,576	1,416,095	0	69,450
Indiana	6,949,410	6,763,534	1,249,767	3,940,615	263,410	645,346	185,876	24,144	88,984	9,098	30,407
Iowa	4,104,190	3,949,123	807,399	2,267,726	133,730	376,096	155,067	902	115,397	27,118	6,207
Kansas	3,219,968	3,162,459	662,367	1,618,037	103,942	365,322	57,509	10,000	0	0	15,586
Kentucky	5,840,378	5,822,316	1,065,266	3,483,342	217,898	458,526	18,062	11,809	0	0	0
Louisiana	7,087,581	7,045,166	1,232,513	4,486,427	301,887	509,265	42,415	3,322	0	3,326	7,218
Maine	2,528,819	2,519,505	243,054	1,670,922	68,370	185,798	9,314	0	0	0	0
Maryland	6,705,276	6,503,754	1,400,152	2,993,664	620,140	637,077	201,522	33,686	0	67,963	46,569
Massachusetts	8,423,035	7,891,583	991,543	4,678,410	798,697	455,287	531,452	7,665	13,994	8,297	80
Michigan	12,992,812	12,397,971	2,570,957	6,981,215	617,879	813,604	594,841	23,538	419,093	54,756	39,284
Minnesota	6,575,048	6,436,760	1,032,167	4,130,356	209,181	464,369	138,288	12,407	39,563	22,368	55,286
Mississippi	5,769,398	5,614,153	930,566	3,636,638	177,407	419,062	155,245	9,996	105,576	83	3,132
Missouri	7,904,419	7,755,530	1,179,141	4,543,198	709,881	828,493	148,889	1,229	88,675	9,284	41,572
Montana	1,813,841	1,800,360	301,105	753,689	98,155	307,898	13,481	306	7,145	52	5,544
Nebraska	2,502,664	2,471,549	167,601	1,714,094	90,487	286,416	31,115	13,940	919	1,194	14,054
Nevada	1,900,554	1,743,794	375,178	870,983	114,442	194,596	156,760	15,223	93,573	1,332	36,792
New Hampshire	1,738,974	1,491,056	224,928	730,541	28,487	145,660	247,918	2,115	227,528	0	8,108
New Jersey	10,258,349	9,693,544	1,556,069	5,114,981	519,720	1,212,684	564,805	211,469	5,237	24,288	198,268
New Mexico	3,978,116	3,879,935	775,483	2,427,049	164,777	276,958	98,181	28,411	0	67,771	0
New York	47,756,868	40,184,055	3,830,916	28,868,493	2,047,604	1,652,187	7,572,813	85,433	6,342,585	0	0
North Carolina	12,841,936	12,119,071	1,775,878	7,930,552	473,414	1,095,435	722,865	89,008	579,226	1,962	15,664
North Dakota	1,204,744	1,170,314	243,960	483,451	34,225	219,778	34,430	7	5,448	2,171	19,683
Ohio	15,745,517	15,377,452	2,264,010	9,890,466	771,193	1,027,090	368,065	21,954	110,670	20,412	58,398
Oklahoma	4,909,074	4,814,917	964,678	2,167,911	873,498	434,914	94,157	287	2,504	1,043	7,697
Oregon	4,474,091	4,444,968	918,466	2,377,520	165,504	333,713	29,123	8,332	0	0	16,635
Pennsylvania	16,656,455	16,292,777	2,497,701	10,970,590	498,147	1,235,018	363,678	331,463	0	4,690	16,051
Rhode Island	2,078,598	1,965,669	250,400	1,106,149	223,567	217,585	112,929	3,586	0	0	
South Carolina	7,180,316	6,766,302	1,004,908	4,121,350	270,526	820,606	414,014	53,559	298,586	7,356	9,936

See footnotes at end of table.

STATE INTERGOVERNMENTAL REVENUE FROM FEDERAL AND LOCAL GOVERNMENTS: 2005—Continued
(In thousands of dollars)

State	Total intergovernmental revenue	From federal government					From local governments				
		Total	Education	Public welfare	Health & hospitals	Highways	Total	Education	Public welfare	Health & hospitals	Highways
South Dakota............	1,235,882	1,218,131	188,723	499,821	65,981	216,865	17,751	7,104	0	4,243	5,724
Tennessee................	8,645,708	8,458,662	1,121,885	5,787,021	269,772	688,257	187,046	28,228	46,807	3,129	41,394
Texas	26,701,366	25,934,230	5,832,976	13,122,541	1,114,505	3,442,751	767,136	372,463	354,857	39,591	1
Utah	2,961,509	2,886,878	727,845	1,378,025	174,897	241,610	74,631	73,951	0	673	0
Vermont..................	1,260,499	1,260,002	203,599	649,297	117,504	129,776	497	0	0	0	497
Virginia..................	6,418,232	5,965,116	1,463,615	3,100,794	289,949	452,049	453,116	296,248	0	53,298	85,010
Washington..............	7,397,857	7,039,692	1,760,384	3,164,320	798,251	635,046	358,165	124,140	0	100,798	75,624
West Virginia..........	3,338,846	3,276,267	488,412	1,841,198	136,096	440,087	62,579	1,959	0	0	0
Wisconsin................	6,693,670	6,447,734	1,226,400	3,753,323	154,897	543,735	245,936	12,555	97,275	15,437	79,153
Wyoming................	2,756,023	2,645,176	155,550	328,989	25,459	208,337	110,847	91,688	0	2,291	11,792

Source: U.S. Department of Commerce, Bureau of the Census, June 2005. Released January 2007.

Note: Detail may not add to total due to rounding.

Table 2.7
SUMMARY OF FEDERAL GOVERNMENT EXPENDITURE, BY STATE AND OUTLYING AREA:
FISCAL YEAR 2004
(In millions of dollars)

State and outlying area	Total	Retirement and disability	Other direct payments	Grants	Procurement	Salaries and wages
United States	$2,161,948	$666,969	$469,544	$460,152	$339,681	$225,601
Alabama	39,047	12,930	8,017	7,008	7,600	3,492
Alaska	8,445	1,135	665	3,217	1,700	1,728
Arizona	41,979	12,942	7,269	8,364	9,797	3,608
Arkansas..............................	19,489	7,404	5,045	4,683	848	1,509
California	232,387	64,078	51,492	54,534	40,254	22,029
Colorado	30,060	8,918	5,295	5,643	5,747	4,457
Connecticut	30,304	7,809	5,828	5,556	9,509	1,602
Delaware.............................	5,253	2,085	1,168	1,241	265	494
Florida	121,934	48,050	32,432	19,610	11,447	10,395
Georgia	55,153	17,748	11,509	11,759	5,813	8,324
Hawaii..................................	12,187	3,202	1,607	2,158	2,066	3,154
Idaho...................................	8,968	3,053	1,649	1,995	1,373	898
Illinois.................................	76,828	25,597	21,111	16,531	6,583	7,007
Indiana................................	37,918	14,019	10,004	7,436	4,002	2,457
Iowa	19,218	6,971	5,359	4,039	1,599	1,249
Kansas	19,131	6,412	4,801	3,469	2,242	2,208
Kentucky	31,714	10,579	6,523	6,743	4,637	3,231
Louisiana	32,954	9,981	8,950	7,787	3,418	2,818
Maine	10,865	3,587	1,852	2,758	1,711	957
Maryland	64,726	14,190	10,372	8,837	20,804	10,523
Massachusetts.....................	53,120	14,186	12,374	13,876	9,127	3,557
Michigan..............................	60,488	22,916	16,616	13,227	4,119	3,610
Minnesota	28,791	10,059	6,891	7,209	2,329	2,302
Mississippi	22,338	7,297	5,196	5,379	2,372	2,094
Missouri	45,730	14,071	10,892	8,734	7,991	4,042
Montana	7,494	2,394	1,629	1,997	587	886
Nebraska..............................	11,795	4,070	3,199	2,531	697	1,298
Nevada	12,769	5,149	2,352	2,322	1,600	1,347
New Hampshire....................	7,959	3,028	1,412	1,879	985	654
New Jersey...........................	55,264	18,922	14,549	11,333	6,132	4,328
New Mexico	19,864	4,681	2,476	4,663	5,973	2,072
New York	143,903	41,209	34,726	50,009	8,889	9,070
North Carolina	55,233	20,131	11,398	12,574	3,933	7,197
North Dakota.......................	6,035	1,477	1,753	1,515	503	787
Ohio	73,195	26,251	17,918	16,514	6,936	5,576
Oklahoma	26,644	9,169	5,938	5,271	2,804	3,463
Oregon	21,871	8,452	5,048	5,185	1,283	1,903
Pennsylvania	94,900	33,147	25,917	19,916	9,311	6,609
Rhode Island	8,245	2,627	1,902	2,329	559	829
South Carolina	30,051	10,812	5,746	6,145	4,193	3,156
South Dakota.......................	6,602	1,842	1,937	1,620	438	765
Tennessee	45,441	14,517	9,467	9,863	8,118	3,476
Texas	141,858	41,765	30,642	27,792	26,969	14,690
Utah	13,684	4,123	2,158	2,948	2,304	2,150
Vermont...............................	4,633	1,417	847	1,423	541	405
Virginia................................	90,638	20,982	9,997	7,991	35,325	16,342
Washington..........................	44,841	14,472	8,282	9,083	6,946	6,058
West Virginia.......................	15,183	5,835	3,249	3,701	1,041	1,358
Wisconsin.............................	31,554	12,065	7,469	7,484	2,641	1,895
Wyoming..............................	4,393	1,192	641	1,636	403	521
Dist. of Columbia	37,630	1,882	2,670	4,205	13,347	15,526
American Samoa..............	262	44	14	178	17	9
Fed. States of Micronesia...	103	0		94	0	0
Guam	1,249	221	85	269	355	320
Marshall Islands..................	218	1		56	158	0
No. Mariana Islands	213	24	18	156	9	6
Palau	51	0		47		
Puerto Rico..........................	15,479	5,668	2,999	5,324	462	1,026
Virgin Islands......................	592	155	86	263	21	66
Undistributed	23,075	26	89	44	18,851	4,065

Source: U.S. Department of Commerce, Bureau of the Census, Consolidated
Federal Funds Report for Fiscal Year 2004, February 2006.

Table 2.8
FEDERAL GOVERNMENT EXPENDITURE FOR DIRECT PAYMENTS FOR INDIVIDUALS FOR RETIREMENT AND DISABILITY, FOR SELECTED PROGRAMS, BY STATE AND OUTLYING AREA: FISCAL YEAR 2004
(In thousands of dollars)

State and outlying area	Total	Social Security payments			Supplemental security income payments	Federal retirement and disability benefits		Veteran benefits		Other
		Retirement insurance payments	Survivors insurance payments	Disability insurance payments		Civilian	Military	Payments for service connected disability	Other benefit payments	
United States	$666,969,380	$315,780,113	$96,551,586	$80,439,028	$33,823,741	$53,358,037	$42,631,303	$22,145,959	$7,166,216	$15,073,398
Alabama	12,930,486	4,907,020	1,884,243	1,976,531	778,276	1,305,791	1,109,275	476,503	236,615	256,233
Alaska	1,135,323	371,558	126,327	118,864	46,223	172,624	174,285	99,197	9,268	16,977
Arizona	12,942,252	6,182,428	1,594,599	1,466,767	493,611	1,072,136	1,205,482	544,342	136,818	246,069
Arkansas	7,403,543	3,094,491	1,059,431	1,181,955	392,616	506,490	491,730	360,830	125,966	190,032
California	64,077,698	30,532,510	8,658,313	7,224,992	5,136,309	4,795,751	4,346,859	1,851,000	567,207	964,757
Colorado................	8,917,674	3,787,661	1,128,109	880,809	263,350	966,157	1,183,267	410,973	99,151	198,197
Connecticut	7,809,446	4,690,016	1,132,363	855,482	279,232	328,571	218,175	157,126	38,056	110,423
Delaware................	2,085,478	1,041,648	284,017	255,372	65,259	166,800	153,239	57,846	15,631	45,666
Florida...................	48,049,721	23,987,479	5,996,244	4,760,411	2,137,388	3,646,090	4,510,956	1,623,275	519,494	868,384
Georgia..................	17,747,906	7,179,098	2,435,158	2,385,352	937,443	1,653,185	1,780,211	711,101	273,155	393,202
Hawaii....................	3,202,245	1,449,376	315,726	239,702	110,650	544,952	357,679	124,352	26,297	33,510
Idaho.....................	3,052,909	1,427,554	414,504	340,844	101,666	272,335	239,682	134,890	31,458	89,977
Illinois	25,596,955	13,481,722	4,264,312	2,907,895	1,413,874	1,379,792	676,572	454,617	165,125	853,047
Indiana...................	14,018,979	7,385,676	2,326,265	1,755,426	490,581	735,566	404,468	336,900	97,724	486,372
Iowa	6,971,457	3,861,177	1,186,565	713,591	197,986	418,158	184,530	167,315	61,731	180,404
Kansas	6,411,819	3,180,694	961,944	639,288	188,612	501,725	426,287	193,574	64,749	254,944
Kentucky	10,578,704	4,084,327	1,660,539	1,932,208	885,312	686,837	474,420	376,826	136,684	341,551
Louisiana	9,980,931	3,854,113	1,978,726	1,500,633	836,365	560,852	540,510	357,950	173,321	178,460
Maine	3,586,700	1,574,198	463,211	518,995	149,026	302,599	228,866	230,614	49,333	69,857
Maryland	14,190,244	5,306,641	1,631,456	1,150,222	474,168	3,537,402	1,170,120	368,397	107,169	444,669
Massachusetts.........	14,186,357	7,377,584	1,981,480	1,920,008	772,958	942,166	374,757	467,299	120,742	229,364
Michigan.................	22,915,679	12,196,837	3,925,055	3,255,794	1,163,890	874,475	460,816	451,609	159,960	427,243
Minnesota	10,059,091	5,450,438	1,549,564	1,083,264	357,576	549,693	285,145	360,894	91,975	330,543
Mississippi	7,296,543	2,804,267	1,090,855	1,262,014	603,519	522,735	507,740	252,384	120,073	132,955
Missouri.................	14,070,928	6,691,848	2,125,701	1,914,728	565,702	1,103,398	677,635	424,964	160,446	406,455
Montana..................	2,393,731	1,071,128	337,076	251,115	66,828	253,356	153,211	118,220	27,743	115,055
Nebraska.................	4,069,531	1,985,447	604,240	380,293	105,570	267,411	285,366	197,684	47,951	195,569
Nevada...................	5,149,411	2,397,212	569,754	567,242	160,307	468,007	617,235	216,269	57,958	95,426
New Hampshire........	3,028,197	1,533,382	375,578	391,619	66,244	258,645	214,637	122,304	27,609	38,180
New Jersey..............	18,921,947	10,912,560	2,808,427	2,125,772	705,759	1,191,842	397,358	388,986	104,797	286,445

See footnotes at end of table.

FEDERAL GOVERNMENT EXPENDITURE FOR DIRECT PAYMENTS FOR INDIVIDUALS FOR RETIREMENT AND DISABILITY, FOR SELECTED PROGRAMS, BY STATE AND OUTLYING AREA: FISCAL YEAR 2004—Continued

| State and outlying area | Total | Social Security payments | | | Supplemental security income payments | Federal retirement and disability benefits | | Veteran benefits | | Other |
		Retirement insurance payments	Survivors insurance payments	Disability insurance payments		Civilian	Military	Payments for service connected disability	Other benefit payments	
New Mexico	4,680,750	1,790,396	580,951	515,307	245,398	579,176	484,927	310,452	65,883	108,260
New York	41,208,620	22,244,011	5,972,769	5,468,953	3,134,286	1,975,525	601,432	861,924	284,043	665,677
North Carolina	20,131,135	9,272,528	2,560,015	2,912,682	883,267	1,386,083	1,653,853	894,187	261,156	307,364
North Dakota	1,477,265	711,742	270,404	126,459	34,619	128,063	72,838	58,513	15,551	59,076
Ohio	26,251,410	13,072,842	4,731,633	2,937,551	1,332,197	1,558,668	827,999	636,565	251,530	902,425
Oklahoma	9,169,062	3,867,107	1,328,223	1,045,423	369,545	1,013,483	651,659	555,331	188,692	149,600
Oregon	8,452,069	4,285,328	1,156,601	921,560	292,481	687,089	434,335	389,510	108,621	176,543
Pennsylvania	33,146,850	16,987,377	5,370,410	3,666,130	1,607,229	2,231,626	911,518	751,174	287,795	1,333,593
Rhode Island	2,626,776	1,349,405	319,132	349,867	141,063	195,183	130,119	92,047	25,286	24,673
South Carolina	10,811,549	4,610,852	1,390,682	1,586,743	500,727	860,169	1,125,110	413,915	162,702	160,649
South Dakota	1,841,507	880,626	284,534	166,167	57,083	194,295	118,705	86,192	27,893	26,011
Tennessee	14,516,572	6,386,553	2,147,977	2,127,485	761,512	1,134,150	943,490	508,599	201,896	304,910
Texas	41,765,195	17,762,105	6,579,080	4,406,413	2,144,843	3,349,982	4,112,807	1,966,471	629,341	814,152
Utah	4,123,174	1,823,687	526,288	348,003	108,771	761,802	281,202	120,694	28,197	124,529
Vermont	1,416,964	736,134	203,693	182,185	53,849	87,007	64,734	52,523	13,707	23,131
Virginia	20,981,969	7,129,006	2,199,270	2,024,524	638,025	3,606,460	4,017,480	702,375	209,723	455,105
Washington	14,472,271	6,530,227	1,769,411	1,484,232	597,477	1,383,192	1,540,105	734,179	155,324	278,124
West Virginia	5,835,136	2,230,831	997,428	1,058,846	388,693	348,090	177,842	241,728	82,321	309,357
Wisconsin	12,064,717	6,816,175	1,901,050	1,355,653	445,116	535,352	303,702	374,460	101,168	232,042
Wyoming	1,192,428	555,200	162,105	115,814	25,623	120,542	91,612	49,775	10,635	61,122
Dist. of Columbia	1,882,456	419,234	132,172	129,962	111,566	934,262	69,280	37,971	18,301	29,708
American Samoa	43,973	11,191	11,580	9,905	0	1,756	4,022	4,376	1,076	66
Fed. States of Micronesia	475	136	52	22	0	170	0	89	5	0
Guam	221,055	69,584	29,500	15,796	0	56,249	35,393	11,384	2,195	954
Marshall Islands	1,162	741	291	91	0	21	0	9	7	2
No. Mariana Islands	24,090	5,750	4,558	1,310	4,073	5,812	1,890	606	82	8
Palau	450	167	87	13	0	143	0	8	32	0
Puerto Rico	5,667,797	2,341,320	1,028,104	1,506,016	0	223,124	110,554	250,964	178,185	29,530
U.S. Virgin Islands	155,075	89,762	23,803	18,678	0	14,908	4,824	1,698	659	744
Undistributed	25,546	0	0	0	0	112	9,358	0	0	16,076

Source: U.S. Department of Commerce, Bureau of the Census, Consolidated Federal Funds Report for Fiscal Year 2004, February 2006.

Table 2.9
FEDERAL GOVERNMENT EXPENDITURE FOR DIRECT PAYMENTS OTHER THAN FOR RETIREMENT AND DISABILITY, FOR SELECTED PROGRAMS, BY STATE AND OUTLYING AREA: FISCAL YEAR 2004
(In thousands of dollars)

State and outlying area	Total	Medicare benefits		Excess earned income tax credits	Unemployment compensation	Food stamp payments	Housing assistance	Agricultural assistance	Federal employees life and health insurance	Other
		Hospital insurance	Supplementary medical insurance							
United States	$469,544,433	$165,968,515	$134,120,136	$34,454,758	$38,214,521	$24,696,715	$4,472,029	$16,795,129	$19,149,309	$31,673,319
Alabama	8,016,960	3,108,922	2,181,182	891,981	267,296	512,604	118,739	175,541	327,866	432,829
Alaska	665,018	138,700	93,482	50,657	142,317	64,405	9,093	11,221	1,629	153,514
Arizona	7,268,771	2,395,722	2,180,176	637,207	301,514	577,868	28,051	108,719	213,980	825,534
Arkansas	5,045,499	1,658,308	1,228,044	474,388	273,045	346,881	33,372	636,001	111,628	283,833
California	51,492,139	18,165,171	16,548,507	3,739,113	5,545,644	1,989,214	229,569	664,910	1,482,647	3,127,364
Colorado	5,294,717	1,657,279	1,373,591	368,132	481,549	252,942	28,658	370,211	291,257	471,098
Connecticut	5,827,902	2,407,108	1,913,774	231,332	649,150	197,530	70,682	17,639	122,116	218,572
Delaware	1,167,621	422,307	342,301	88,207	111,564	56,542	13,042	19,542	40,111	74,005
Florida	32,432,424	12,536,415	12,413,462	2,434,876	1,113,007	1,268,549	128,092	179,589	827,046	1,531,387
Georgia	11,509,304	3,867,564	2,937,164	1,475,470	671,573	923,815	122,479	357,212	446,003	708,023
Hawaii	1,606,602	491,416	466,121	118,148	122,952	151,809	14,356	5,893	157,232	78,675
Idaho	1,649,444	478,188	385,797	149,369	154,603	90,972	1,622	186,190	61,578	141,124
Illinois	21,110,712	7,546,821	5,581,114	1,323,323	2,306,458	1,211,362	318,858	1,302,001	483,877	1,036,898
Indiana	10,003,603	3,386,007	2,497,223	646,620	581,386	549,501	49,559	532,489	205,157	1,555,661
Iowa	5,359,100	1,458,764	1,344,514	236,538	340,512	176,334	7,702	1,311,256	144,884	338,597
Kansas	4,800,691	1,455,262	1,256,451	262,871	305,206	158,017	18,869	1,033,016	92,383	218,617
Kentucky	6,523,441	2,403,473	1,743,294	522,773	450,755	542,744	56,002	162,247	166,285	475,869
Louisiana	8,949,939	3,526,466	2,222,089	1,021,656	296,173	753,905	102,121	360,416	195,250	471,863
Maine	1,851,541	691,840	528,138	113,635	122,736	139,619	9,989	34,947	77,463	133,174
Maryland	10,371,837	3,003,914	2,533,503	517,671	469,056	286,695	105,776	65,622	2,886,285	503,315
Massachusetts	12,373,615	5,383,438	3,526,783	403,016	1,640,955	304,436	140,342	14,780	329,439	630,426
Michigan	16,616,037	5,939,648	5,223,537	974,216	2,182,233	896,140	71,683	267,153	256,856	804,571
Minnesota	6,890,961	2,175,764	1,697,492	341,316	755,206	256,580	57,368	878,567	231,100	497,569
Mississippi	5,196,060	1,834,931	1,232,403	715,183	166,546	360,952	31,991	373,315	139,451	341,287
Missouri	10,892,183	3,625,433	2,782,389	670,007	551,712	663,426	63,703	594,931	1,385,515	555,067
Montana	1,629,390	418,672	345,493	104,105	73,222	79,197	4,346	394,142	62,967	147,245
Nebraska	3,198,934	761,281	658,999	159,359	127,677	108,691	12,971	863,665	91,805	414,485
Nevada	2,351,616	781,645	699,544	239,156	280,135	119,520	15,659	18,294	76,413	121,250
New Hampshire	1,411,826	569,322	414,069	77,498	88,935	43,549	9,869	8,576	93,986	106,024
New Jersey	14,549,149	5,519,432	4,706,812	729,942	2,130,180	377,526	211,409	14,320	294,718	564,810
New Mexico	2,475,868	690,711	613,224	322,464	130,158	217,424	15,016	91,637	144,285	250,949
New York	34,726,294	13,235,956	10,819,230	2,181,059	2,778,505	1,876,078	1,040,005	101,337	615,452	2,078,672
North Carolina	11,397,621	3,914,633	2,906,209	1,241,212	1,011,574	753,200	110,269	369,870	297,482	793,173
North Dakota	1,752,999	332,999	279,184	54,951	37,398	40,286	2,675	820,407	37,499	147,599
Ohio	17,918,392	6,947,442	5,516,066	1,202,261	1,345,432	1,027,772	206,583	389,779	416,055	867,001

See footnotes at end of table.

FEDERAL GOVERNMENT EXPENDITURE FOR DIRECT PAYMENTS OTHER THAN FOR RETIREMENT AND DISABILITY, FOR SELECTED PROGRAMS, BY STATE AND OUTLYING AREA: FISCAL YEAR 2004—Continued

State and outlying area	Total	Medicare benefits		Excess earned income tax credits	Unemployment compensation	Food stamp payments	Housing assistance	Agricultural assistance	Federal employees life and health insurance	Other
		Hospital insurance	Supplementary medical insurance							
Oklahoma	5,937,521	2,220,011	1,463,827	502,502	252,261	397,777	31,708	290,528	314,314	464,594
Oregon	5,048,156	1,513,218	1,338,760	315,176	784,582	430,542	19,157	131,498	200,244	314,979
Pennsylvania	25,917,388	10,401,546	7,994,982	1,118,578	2,557,152	933,274	288,690	143,691	1,170,610	1,308,866
Rhode Island	1,902,279	753,597	541,617	95,194	217,824	73,551	27,892	2,426	51,428	138,751
South Carolina	5,745,733	1,913,302	1,507,913	721,707	388,550	501,205	35,385	123,089	173,414	381,169
South Dakota	1,937,022	365,894	295,869	79,325	27,373	53,934	4,523	665,703	25,030	419,371
Tennessee	9,466,686	3,832,811	2,358,556	874,363	512,412	811,798	101,908	171,866	222,590	580,382
Texas	30,641,945	10,443,038	7,380,376	3,737,302	1,944,886	2,306,786	145,003	1,476,293	937,093	2,271,168
Utah	2,158,494	652,970	486,051	210,383	172,548	126,127	10,813	38,647	174,138	286,816
Vermont	846,747	296,254	207,162	46,362	82,274	47,076	3,160	16,927	23,608	123,923
Virginia	9,997,316	3,051,746	2,497,089	768,859	435,282	476,166	71,615	134,382	1,258,588	1,303,588
Washington	8,282,098	2,441,629	2,128,500	504,671	1,412,926	455,273	46,286	268,177	419,103	605,533
West Virginia	3,248,965	1,295,949	977,575	220,036	156,545	231,721	18,469	17,213	109,742	221,716
Wisconsin	7,469,165	2,544,911	2,097,250	408,958	894,421	269,439	28,233	393,016	192,614	640,323
Wyoming	641,467	216,041	161,534	48,410	40,803	24,981	1,023	47,756	35,083	65,835
Dist. of Columbia	2,669,812	461,260	382,698	79,580	93,126	97,508	49,459	86,467	942,721	476,993
American Samoa	14,073	0	0	0	0	5,600	0	24	0	8,449
Fed. States of Micronesia...	8,680	0	0	0	0		0	0	0	8,680
Guam	85,079	880	671	0	0	48,115	3,424	19	17,917	14,054
Marshall Islands	2,249	0	0	0	0	0	0	0	0	2,249
No. Mariana Islands	18,147	0	0	0	0	10,538	0	21	0	7,588
Palau	2,758	0	0	0	0	0	0	0	0	2,758
Puerto Rico	2,999,415	617,038	1,096,298	3,640	228,245		105,974	49,564	73,372	825,284
U.S. Virgin Islands	85,971	15,468	12,044	0	6,945	19,215	18,789	2,388	0	11,122
Undistributed	89,049	0	0	0	0	0	0	0	0	89,049

Source: U.S. Department of Commerce, Bureau of the Census, Consolidated Federal Funds Report for Fiscal Year 2004, February 2006.

Table 2.10
FEDERAL GOVERNMENT EXPENDITURE FOR GRANTS, BY AGENCY, BY STATE AND OUTLYING AREA: FISCAL YEAR 2004
(In thousands of dollars)

State and outlying area	Total	Department of Agriculture	Appalachian Regional Commission	Department of Commerce	Corporation for National and Community Service	Corporation for Public Broadcasting	Department of Defense	Department of Education
United States	$460,152,282	$24,921,811	$65,702	$1,574,605	$707,511	$411,970	$4,537,556	$38,757,134
Alabama	7,007,819	396,308	6,257	15,290	5,192	2,582	69,772	618,145
Alaska	3,216,865	135,264	0	118,446	6,227	8,898	70,716	336,167
Arizona	8,363,600	443,707	0	6,599	9,633	4,118	136,443	842,604
Arkansas	4,682,798	287,349	0	5,585	7,079	1,722	37,948	391,889
California	54,534,048	3,016,896	0	119,325	115,478	41,919	565,788	4,723,920
Colorado	5,643,498	318,235	0	64,831	6,314	4,724	80,854	478,121
Connecticut	5,555,683	169,217	0	19,817	4,852	2,459	77,737	373,606
Delaware	1,241,092	67,357	0	10,805	2,050	1	24,137	115,962
Florida	19,609,519	1,082,251	0	66,117	31,917	13,314	133,382	1,843,862
Georgia	11,758,731	791,014	4,821	16,329	15,351	5,342	51,984	1,059,737
Hawaii	2,158,313	124,896	0	40,919	3,106	2,177	57,236	249,624
Idaho	1,994,706	140,582	0	11,115	5,352	2,281	33,730	179,965
Illinois	16,531,175	824,666	0	24,553	17,133	12,481	106,418	1,524,116
Indiana	7,436,310	393,574	0	3,642	8,218	6,626	92,038	642,599
Iowa	4,038,677	229,681	0	4,969	6,477	3,922	64,620	328,767
Kansas	3,468,608	294,720	0	3,596	6,371	2,867	91,360	380,600
Kentucky	6,743,285	362,886	6,740	17,334	7,524	4,664	18,199	574,246
Louisiana	7,786,693	492,383	0	50,204	8,356	3,483	111,676	711,018
Maine	2,757,942	90,887	0	19,145	4,719	1,652	46,174	174,385
Maryland	8,836,910	303,989	2,401	44,365	20,521	5,074	168,512	586,581
Massachusetts	13,876,126	348,936	30	60,752	19,906	14,133	251,119	805,137
Michigan	13,227,411	690,364	17	35,366	11,962	8,652	81,021	1,187,632
Minnesota	7,208,781	397,391	0	9,986	10,472	13,700	91,873	538,856
Mississippi	5,378,932	369,931	3,928	26,312	5,486	2,101	44,898	474,736
Missouri	8,734,296	447,244	0	11,011	10,793	4,988	84,996	655,606
Montana	1,997,362	139,441	0	3,811	9,360	1,113	58,647	215,546
Nebraska	2,530,936	225,610	0	4,776	4,592	4,065	35,510	242,153
Nevada	2,321,630	124,513	0	3,814	4,248	2,357	22,297	221,173
New Hampshire	1,878,737	65,068	0	64,002	4,219	1,954	38,136	142,390
New Jersey	11,333,180	441,016	0	37,120	12,251	3,567	98,928	927,276
New Mexico	4,662,536	258,942	0	11,758	4,737	3,498	48,135	532,553
New York	50,008,574	1,467,457	3,537	69,040	72,381	37,777	210,427	2,754,077
North Carolina	12,574,492	694,641	4,188	31,594	8,627	82,720	116,236	975,830
North Dakota	1,515,253	208,635	0	4,187	2,117	1,211	38,007	155,718
Ohio	16,513,740	695,346	5,655	33,323	15,071	11,168	114,915	1,267,074
Oklahoma	5,270,581	389,263	0	14,018	9,337	2,634	19,271	556,138
Oregon	5,184,929	266,644	0	62,179	11,425	4,810	38,120	456,573
Pennsylvania	19,915,826	711,687	8,800	27,375	19,440	11,741	232,139	1,349,422
Rhode Island	2,329,088	65,849	0	10,119	4,554	710	25,310	157,668
South Carolina	6,145,106	343,856	2,504	84,882	5,897	3,311	76,770	548,713
South Dakota	1,620,407	162,994	0	1,683	2,496	1,426	34,508	182,710
Tennessee	9,863,362	445,153	6,206	11,114	8,622	5,062	54,845	712,885
Texas	27,792,386	2,313,836	0	47,561	25,430	13,115	192,055	3,177,815
Utah	2,947,857	194,704	0	3,164	5,780	5,556	45,656	296,455
Vermont	1,423,455	71,054	0	2,646	2,259	1,714	36,319	109,905
Virginia	7,991,079	436,014	4,342	46,576	22,517	8,650	105,144	821,824
Washington	9,082,685	428,573	106	86,840	23,839	6,621	90,720	713,947
West Virginia	3,700,592	167,967	5,376	13,227	7,709	1,347	70,638	274,228
Wisconsin	7,483,990	367,835	0	27,943	11,038	6,900	55,860	619,511
Wyoming	1,635,620	53,454	0	2,441	1,675	836	1,985	118,905
Dist. of Columbia	4,204,862	70,002	793	42,367	50,469	6,351	43,193	348,230
American Samoa	178,059	7,823	0	1,806	492	427	0	39,976
Fed. States of Micronesia	93,914	2,670	0	0	0	0	0	10,411
Guam	268,701	21,698	0	1,726	495	665	0	50,101
Marshall Islands	56,384	1,112	0	0	0	0	0	4,492
No. Mariana Islands	156,107	12,211	0	1,632	0	0	0	29,402
Palau	47,403	149	0	0	0	0	0	3,055
Puerto Rico	5,323,856	1,820,770	0	13,431	5,280	3,647	37,190	903,225
Virgin Islands	263,364	20,051	0	2,037	661	609	3,964	39,871
Undistributed	44,412	6,046	0	0	0	2,528	0	0

Source: U.S. Department of Commerce, Bureau of the Census, February 2006.

FEDERAL GOVERNMENT EXPENDITURE FOR GRANTS, BY AGENCY, BY STATE AND OUTLYING AREA: FISCAL YEAR 2004—Continued

State and outlying area	Election Assistance Commission	Department of Energy	Environmental Protection Agency	Equal Employment Opportunity Commission	Department of Health and Human Services	Department of Homeland Security	Department of Housing and Urban Development	Institute of Museum and Library Services
United States	$1,333,855	$1,847,718	$4,116,198	$30,959	$267,189,711	$3,644,351	$33,848,541	$238,922
Alabama	35,867	34,795	52,581	0	3,842,686	196,475	391,143	3,495
Alaska	0	6,214	85,441	156	1,268,933	13,536	147,376	1,372
Arizona	0	15,219	53,534	477	4,974,829	16,202	447,625	3,021
Arkansas............................	21,599	3,366	42,043	0	2,705,421	51,594	251,547	1,711
California	94,559	229,234	329,222	2,984	33,194,283	110,664	4,378,192	21,709
Colorado	34,545	59,023	67,278	329	2,667,061	17,478	398,556	3,336
Connecticut	27,720	45,230	65,752	796	3,346,103	21,105	580,480	3,480
Delaware............................	4,150	9,008	29,684	327	626,906	9,048	92,862	861
Florida	47,417	25,558	133,905	1,598	11,278,983	850,333	1,246,989	11,806
Georgia	64,748	43,440	80,824	184	6,962,809	20,550	759,810	5,447
Hawaii................................	0	4,320	29,475	144	1,006,912	3,816	141,756	2,186
Idaho	11,597	14,145	49,525	303	994,872	7,910	82,193	1,626
Illinois	0	61,430	157,069	1,491	9,318,522	37,803	1,778,448	11,634
Indiana...............................	48,545	37,327	71,274	546	4,321,705	45,671	527,817	6,181
Iowa	23,739	65,889	75,358	809	2,275,823	42,380	230,746	4,497
Kansas	7,662	11,537	42,449	327	1,770,890	20,711	199,849	2,025
Kentucky	32,899	13,834	59,971	202	4,053,926	68,730	450,887	3,370
Louisiana	35,068	9,852	58,652	38	4,790,508	38,236	486,638	3,230
Maine	4,150	5,793	37,581	225	1,806,184	14,378	187,212	1,799
Maryland	42,478	32,569	99,337	648	5,504,259	73,084	706,744	3,161
Massachusetts....................	52,222	141,440	128,340	1,674	8,582,655	35,191	1,685,156	8,100
Michigan............................	28,257	64,029	158,510	724	8,040,554	129,668	875,663	6,765
Minnesota	39,179	31,527	77,106	554	4,324,656	26,894	558,686	3,728
Mississippi	22,418	10,535	44,523	0	3,382,313	37,032	271,308	2,151
Missouri	44,915	13,114	88,676	766	5,481,317	27,759	542,818	4,261
Montana	4,150	6,632	36,197	267	831,614	8,108	108,635	1,468
Nebraska............................	4,920	5,738	31,482	567	1,355,822	22,172	143,383	1,623
Nevada...............................	5,785	48,151	27,720	1,078	976,594	8,094	157,350	1,523
New Hampshire..................	11,597	6,390	28,113	110	983,258	7,615	145,953	1,230
New Jersey.........................	24,358	38,732	82,368	531	6,381,963	71,943	1,292,431	6,222
New Mexico	14,280	62,227	47,761	287	2,540,713	19,981	167,670	2,118
New York	0	164,847	134,919	2,160	31,516,934	155,616	3,832,412	18,783
North Carolina...................	65,478	25,739	83,557	82	8,022,570	114,607	680,069	5,813
North Dakota.....................	4,150	15,731	28,740	165	555,679	17,121	104,802	704
Ohio	90,993	40,443	157,598	1,923	10,696,462	87,879	1,348,263	9,250
Oklahoma	0	9,681	65,391	362	2,906,542	35,493	429,291	3,682
Oregon	9,962	16,176	75,372	519	2,808,885	44,178	349,489	2,221
Pennsylvania	100,579	98,062	164,126	2,014	12,493,067	114,766	1,543,558	12,165
Rhode Island	4,150	4,590	36,894	226	1,448,237	3,118	228,872	1,207
South Carolina	32,421	22,495	34,888	661	3,740,808	24,887	329,424	2,314
South Dakota......................	0	4,863	34,155	181	633,066	5,615	117,246	890
Tennessee...........................	16,546	22,505	49,110	304	6,618,062	70,561	493,475	5,987
Texas	57,505	64,259	258,167	957	15,294,303	239,697	1,726,627	15,128
Utah	0	17,257	33,761	359	1,539,310	12,436	148,048	1,792
Vermont	11,597	5,645	30,340	60	799,357	7,509	79,660	775
Virginia..............................	20,573	39,084	109,857	246	3,708,084	234,418	652,819	5,348
Washington.........................	47,196	54,351	106,550	700	5,151,472	65,477	635,980	4,597
West Virginia......................	15,304	14,033	68,857	240	2,117,589	97,577	175,777	1,223
Wisconsin...........................	43,064	39,250	119,357	1,099	4,379,926	39,835	482,733	3,867
Wyoming............................	11,597	6,540	22,005	92	386,998	5,059	36,589	865
Dist. of Columbia	11,597	23,792	82,334	100	1,624,807	16,208	321,134	4,499
American Samoa	2,319	460	3,279	0	20,226	36,564	1,241	147
Fed. States of Micronesia......................	0	0	0	0	10,120	16,650	0	0
Guam	0	400	4,874	0	41,944	13,905	38,173	114
Marshall Islands.................	0	0	0	0	5,597	100	0	56
No. Mariana Islands	0	230	5,693	0	14,580	29,598	3,525	151
Palau	0	0	0	0	5,319	0	0	0
Puerto Rico........................	0	745	28,728	367	1,006,031	99,201	624,581	2,102
Virgin Islands.....................	0	248	5,896	8	50,660	2,117	27,604	104
Undistributed	0	0	0	0	0	0	1,226	0

See footnotes at end of table.

FEDERAL GOVERNMENT EXPENDITURE FOR GRANTS, BY AGENCY, BY STATE AND OUTLYING AREA: FISCAL YEAR 2004 — Continued

State and outlying area	Department of the Interior	Department of Justice	Department of Labor	National Aeronautics and Space Administration	National Archives and Records Administration	National Endowment for the Arts	National Endowment for the Humanities	National Science Foundation
United States	$4,021,625	$7,155,656	$8,561,568	$1,084,871	$9,704	$96,057	$121,739	$5,232,033
Alabama	38,744	97,762	122,708	41,048	0	861	1,087	49,985
Alaska	99,445	73,382	54,312	5,569	78	742	854	35,380
Arizona	99,829	139,047	156,348	17,667	53	1,154	977	107,783
Arkansas	13,357	62,476	71,760	1,911	0	630	578	12,786
California	262,112	912,192	670,354	193,641	829	8,517	7,208	798,740
Colorado	149,231	127,252	113,475	48,493	0	2,421	1,467	274,527
Connecticut	8,407	80,040	107,155	9,117	203	1,521	3,477	45,574
Delaware	7,283	35,937	27,633	2,271	361	637	853	18,432
Florida	39,462	345,577	390,984	28,744	10	1,546	2,310	147,153
Georgia	21,960	222,873	172,887	21,857	82	2,523	3,269	110,184
Hawaii	39,522	46,889	47,160	22,079	0	1,130	948	35,503
Idaho	57,687	48,470	55,188	3,515	10	809	628	10,684
Illinois	21,220	219,871	420,744	16,821	387	3,303	6,617	244,015
Indiana	14,782	100,256	139,572	6,885	22	941	1,670	90,939
Iowa	17,268	72,934	73,274	9,807	0	728	1,137	41,504
Kansas	15,765	63,827	61,055	6,281	20	981	677	29,775
Kentucky	46,420	107,194	125,919	2,783	99	994	811	32,130
Louisiana	60,400	117,022	105,195	6,215	0	1,264	769	39,932
Maine	19,313	49,389	54,097	5,160	199	1,040	1,492	19,002
Maryland	17,874	147,039	191,664	101,155	276	2,615	2,371	120,385
Massachusetts	23,110	167,504	205,894	54,180	719	4,192	9,591	393,836
Michigan	39,456	169,540	346,446	17,102	111	1,646	3,186	144,009
Minnesota	35,726	111,433	133,860	4,832	87	3,489	3,283	73,483
Mississippi	22,578	59,466	89,123	17,553	0	801	1,190	27,108
Missouri	24,122	123,103	150,157	9,438	163	2,457	2,709	46,694
Montana	107,611	44,713	40,201	7,517	9	875	811	23,485
Nebraska	14,042	65,415	36,901	2,248	56	712	802	27,872
Nevada	231,602	83,292	59,443	1,979	20	659	519	13,246
New Hampshire	14,716	69,358	31,113	12,631	0	800	757	16,683
New Jersey	13,329	188,682	239,348	12,977	445	1,303	2,381	108,354
New Mexico	435,457	91,174	61,602	4,972	71	1,449	1,538	39,720
New York	39,594	509,419	474,770	41,296	1,376	15,422	14,254	416,812
North Carolina	25,701	153,191	315,411	12,785	457	1,549	2,368	121,577
North Dakota	51,996	42,909	24,315	2,218	47	635	749	11,433
Ohio	32,934	199,047	315,626	42,593	0	1,661	3,468	90,292
Oklahoma	30,867	82,389	78,151	9,934	147	675	653	28,518
Oregon	176,013	81,110	165,473	6,284	0	1,098	1,125	60,983
Pennsylvania	25,623	225,797	430,203	20,509	296	3,359	7,406	239,945
Rhode Island	6,514	40,431	33,822	5,322	0	1,061	1,324	34,453
South Carolina	14,207	111,901	114,521	5,081	227	1,009	792	30,410
South Dakota	85,202	45,238	32,524	1,897	0	664	549	10,720
Tennessee	25,330	114,582	164,220	8,195	131	1,184	2,138	55,627
Texas	66,188	408,316	584,069	73,098	271	2,801	4,009	166,710
Utah	136,931	54,610	71,650	3,951	0	1,066	966	40,639
Vermont	10,409	40,844	22,719	1,233	0	862	799	8,214
Virginia	43,727	217,658	267,791	70,528	767	1,188	5,052	121,250
Washington	120,567	157,451	259,522	9,647	76	2,041	2,423	121,418
West Virginia	64,125	64,525	58,461	36,070	0	651	551	9,969
Wisconsin	27,709	113,030	191,842	11,301	316	1,006	1,788	136,483
Wyoming	668,915	29,339	21,255	1,637	20	606	516	10,170
Dist. of Columbia	26,416	123,272	211,972	20,130	1,262	3,116	3,049	320,656
American Samoa	34,925	7,760	644	0	0	247	305	0
Fed. States of Micronesia	52,358	0	1,705	0	0	0	0	0
Guam	62,884	9,548	2,056	0	0	240	296	0
Marshall Islands	44,192	0	836	0	0	0	0	0
No. Mariana Islands	15,232	7,288	1,540	0	0	241	289	0
Palau	38,609	0	269	0	0	0	0	0
Puerto Rico	7,394	63,036	153,376	4,563	0	654	608	15,366
Virgin Islands	69,452	9,857	7,451	150	0	281	296	1,483
Undistributed	5,783	0	0	0	0	0	0	0

See footnotes at end of table.

FEDERAL GOVERNMENT EXPENDITURE FOR GRANTS, BY AGENCY, BY STATE AND OUTLYING AREA: FISCAL YEAR 2004 — Continued

State and outlying area	Small Business Admin.	Social Security Admin.	Department of State	State Justice Institute	Tennessee Valley Authority (a)	Department of Transportation	Department of the Treasury (b)	Department of Veterans Affairs	Other
United States	$45,678	$11,016	$205,631	$1,767	$337,269	$48,496,756	$800,141	$654,107	$90,120
Alabama	2,085	0	805	2	80,958	887,492	151	13,231	312
Alaska	70	0	243	37	0	747,326	50	0	633
Arizona	372	0	3,199	6	0	873,747	2,738	5,853	815
Arkansas	38	0	803	0	0	706,796	80	2,381	349
California	1,162	0	26,080	39	0	4,638,913	2,900	48,519	18,666
Colorado	0	0	3,700	184	0	710,868	78	8,748	2,369
Connecticut	0	0	2,623	0	0	549,112	236	8,647	1,217
Delaware	0	0	850	1	0	149,234	52	3,729	659
Florida	1,153	0	5,908	2	0	1,860,100	5,001	11,751	2,386
Georgia	0	0	4,399	21	5,430	1,297,302	343	11,639	1,572
Hawaii	0	0	935	8	0	276,835	119	20,006	612
Idaho	117	0	575	47	0	270,150	72	10,966	593
Illinois	3,771	4,729	9,501	9	0	1,674,450	2,925	25,100	1,950
Indiana	1,220	0	2,801	6	0	863,239	452	6,600	1,161
Iowa	495	0	2,966	5	0	446,741	90	13,681	369
Kansas	307	0	1,327	6	0	438,043	58	14,829	694
Kentucky	0	0	1,575	20	27,193	711,514	319	10,554	350
Louisiana	235	0	2,455	0	0	623,269	100	30,395	99
Maine	1,531	0	562	0	0	203,945	85	7,618	226
Maryland	570	0	5,236	67	0	647,236	598	4,298	1,803
Massachusetts	44	3,449	12,205	1	0	834,230	1,388	25,933	5,061
Michigan	479	2,838	4,355	203	0	1,159,870	1,127	17,252	606
Minnesota	602	0	4,287	39	0	697,540	152	14,208	1,154
Mississippi	0	0	875	0	18,704	429,788	176	13,646	251
Missouri	1,327	0	3,662	0	0	924,927	349	25,717	1,204
Montana	3,386	0	1,127	0	0	338,929	32	3,318	361
Nebraska	300	0	1,999	0	0	285,606	374	11,889	307
Nevada	275	0	563	76	0	319,682	100	5,241	235
New Hampshire	0	0	795	6	0	225,632	81	4,943	1,185
New Jersey	433	0	3,189	19	0	1,323,741	2,937	16,578	755
New Mexico	981	0	1,759	20	0	305,088	44	3,127	873
New York	3,271	0	24,009	107	0	7,987,502	10,767	21,785	7,827
North Carolina	1,481	0	5,306	0	1,638	1,014,418	1,019	4,238	1,604
North Dakota	180	0	764	0	0	241,130	29	1,695	188
Ohio	553	0	5,090	16	0	1,224,484	1,880	16,732	3,999
Oklahoma	1,210	0	1,686	0	0	567,799	150	26,379	921
Oregon	1,647	0	3,223	0	0	536,715	731	2,915	1,060
Pennsylvania	4,321	0	8,319	22	0	2,028,265	406	31,198	1,214
Rhode Island	0	0	1,179	19	0	207,327	150	5,174	806
South Carolina	2,353	0	1,902	2	0	600,894	1,366	6,611	0
South Dakota	300	0	347	7	0	258,000	49	2,867	213
Tennessee	1,104	0	1,777	287	203,346	742,258	239	21,005	1,503
Texas	1,189	0	8,847	1	0	3,002,069	10,761	33,133	4,468
Utah	75	0	1,256	4	0	328,782	47	3,246	355
Vermont	0	0	986	26	0	173,083	167	3,187	2,085
Virginia	2,182	0	4,045	259	0	1,017,710	649	20,100	2,678
Washington	0	0	4,432	48	0	975,161	397	11,728	807
West Virginia	1,187	0	321	44	0	431,228	70	1,785	514
Wisconsin	1,520	0	2,787	32	0	760,754	197	36,092	1,112
Wyoming	28	0	253	0	0	252,575	43	1,159	64
Dist. of Columbia	1,825	0	17,635	69	0	417,963	408,133 (c)	1,417	2,071
American Samoa	300	0	0	0	0	19,119	0	0	0
Fed. States of Micronesia	0	0	0	0	0	0	0	0	0
Guam	0	0	0	0	0	19,583	0	0	0
Marshall Islands	0	0	0	0	0	0	0	0	0
No. Mariana Islands	0	0	0	0	0	34,496	0	0	0
Palau	0	0	0	0	0	0	0	0	0
Puerto Rico	0	0	107	0	0	191,962	339,634	1,265	593
Virgin Islands	0	0	0	0	0	20,516	50	0	0
Undistributed	0	0	0	0	0	21,619	0	0	7,210

Source: U.S. Department of Commerce, Bureau of the Census, Consolidated Federal Funds Report for Fiscal Year 2004, February 2006.

(a) Payments in lieu of taxes have been categorized as "grants."

(b) Includes distributions to state and local governments of seized cash and other assets.

(c) Also includes Treasury payments to recipients that are separate from the government of the District of Columbia and Washington Metropolitan Transit Authority (WMATA).

Table 2.11
FEDERAL GOVERNMENT EXPENDITURE FOR PROCUREMENT CONTRACTS, BY AGENCY, BY STATE AND OUTLYING AREA: FISCAL YEAR 2004
(In thousands of dollars)

State and outlying area	Total	Department of Defense Total	Army	Navy	Air Force	Army Corps of Engineers	Other defense	Nondefense agencies Total	Department of Agriculture	Department of Commerce
United States	$339,680,775	$211,538,185	$59,332,624	$59,586,122	$54,073,312	$3,304,576	$35,241,550	$128,142,590	$4,211,683	$1,678,062
Alabama	7,599,862	5,849,415	2,309,326	290,641	414,440	83,252	2,751,756	1,750,447	33,890	1,163
Alaska	1,699,744	1,262,270	659,026	52,142	355,224	46,938	148,941	437,474	44,841	42,809
Arizona	9,796,779	8,429,925	3,005,352	2,190,709	1,088,495	28,416	2,116,953	1,366,855	54,063	4,519
Arkansas....................	847,534	493,707	170,149	35,516	154,465	63,190	70,387	353,826	22,367	131
California	40,253,979	27,882,008	4,197,185	6,845,622	12,346,119	168,630	4,324,452	12,371,971	412,731	40,814
Colorado	5,747,033	3,151,275	622,817	143,424	1,919,786	26,066	439,182	2,595,759	113,034	38,542
Connecticut	9,508,964	8,958,624	1,673,515	5,068,128	1,926,510	5,756	284,715	550,340	8,576	3,409
Delaware	265,275	194,245	108,825	5,131	62,525	8,084	9,679	71,030	3,629	1,123
Florida	11,447,152	8,385,036	2,196,022	2,195,055	2,941,483	273,162	779,315	3,062,116	60,172	30,903
Georgia	5,812,510	3,905,793	1,413,601	388,941	1,750,770	103,051	249,430	1,906,717	47,980	12,703
Hawaii........................	2,066,038	1,713,256	521,089	584,529	223,409	7,978	376,250	352,783	22,649	11,499
Idaho	1,373,203	186,973	101,953	9,917	52,725	7,884	14,495	1,186,230	69,241	841
Illinois	6,582,810	3,007,055	1,014,867	492,774	743,968	170,374	585,072	3,575,755	164,636	8,957
Indiana.......................	4,002,129	3,172,722	1,772,598	535,314	207,080	35,630	622,100	829,407	24,399	4,169
Iowa	1,599,246	733,831	224,471	145,644	268,350	19,324	76,043	865,414	141,030	773
Kansas	2,241,633	1,411,996	532,875	26,856	744,804	19,294	88,168	829,637	114,255	2,210
Kentucky	4,636,868	2,890,584	665,024	214,841	119,479	105,997	1,785,244	1,746,284	27,878	556
Louisiana	3,418,393	2,543,966	476,013	1,295,327	42,820	244,456	485,350	874,427	86,640	15,459
Maine	1,711,354	1,555,527	173,553	1,319,121	12,189	7,799	42,865	155,827	5,848	2,680
Maryland	20,803,835	9,214,124	3,038,038	3,076,829	981,848	42,463	2,074,945	11,589,711	74,745	376,806
Massachusetts............	9,127,096	6,962,816	2,121,918	2,041,062	2,184,608	63,873	551,355	2,164,279	7,747	56,754
Michigan	4,119,315	2,611,013	1,863,717	139,946	175,169	35,215	396,976	1,508,302	55,904	1,761
Minnesota	2,329,461	1,337,805	465,718	514,206	135,222	34,518	188,140	991,656	298,651	23,755
Mississippi	2,372,436	1,866,646	390,157	1,013,813	244,960	126,000	91,716	505,790	21,444	26,848
Missouri	7,991,155	6,502,161	894,516	3,467,324	1,689,706	144,781	305,835	1,488,993	221,955	6,130
Montana	587,088	206,883	86,540	2,285	78,900	15,891	23,268	380,205	39,698	402
Nebraska....................	697,175	401,287	93,321	5,719	261,505	24,364	16,378	295,888	54,016	3,206
Nevada.......................	1,599,503	439,066	157,656	86,356	146,950	20,324	27,780	1,160,437	10,174	4,950
New Hampshire.........	985,478	715,932	290,102	161,972	205,226	3,797	54,834	269,546	1,341	5,899
New Jersey	6,132,289	4,196,890	1,472,425	1,594,947	299,101	208,613	621,805	1,935,399	45,590	8,161
New Mexico	5,972,835	1,070,390	478,057	37,714	424,382	40,578	89,659	4,902,445	17,345	919
New York	8,888,842	5,058,181	1,043,886	2,646,254	709,308	89,561	569,172	3,830,661	39,380	10,943
North Carolina	3,933,055	2,212,804	824,092	717,759	255,071	54,704	361,178	1,720,251	51,971	32,940
North Dakota..............	502,631	309,468	76,913	4,395	153,547	37,548	37,065	193,163	29,607	274
Ohio	6,935,685	4,636,529	1,551,633	327,210	1,657,398	61,451	1,038,838	2,299,156	77,350	2,515
Oklahoma	2,803,948	1,525,421	452,962	123,024	678,279	30,581	240,575	1,278,526	30,644	2,940
Oregon	1,282,768	529,634	282,292	103,529	19,801	80,029	43,983	753,135	176,852	9,216
Pennsylvania	9,311,177	6,202,651	3,072,896	1,425,830	542,202	66,197	1,095,526	3,108,526	50,702	86,217
Rhode Island	558,527	417,901	27,058	345,626	3,942	25,912	15,363	140,626		13,042
South Carolina	4,192,800	1,598,448	491,040	585,211	205,733	48,053	268,412	2,594,351	13,502	25,377
South Dakota..............	437,779	236,224	60,967	28,090	40,684	7,112	99,371	201,555	26,599	319
Tennessee	8,118,171	2,117,272	436,565	84,682	1,238,147	63,131	294,747	6,000,900	78,056	447
Texas	26,968,708	21,050,237	4,874,679	5,611,111	8,152,438	172,556	2,239,453	5,918,472	208,450	22,506
Utah	2,303,926	1,877,903	348,335	126,337	1,306,938	6,716	89,577	426,023	50,353	1,505
Vermont	540,709	452,362	308,659	36,097	11,675	11,511	84,420	88,347	2,893	656
Virginia	35,325,140	23,391,866	6,182,314	8,312,522	2,839,706	72,040	5,985,284	11,933,274	65,906	366,802
Washington................	6,945,805	3,324,631	532,916	853,479	1,174,905	100,775	662,555	3,621,174	120,040	42,483
West Virginia.............	1,040,791	279,595	51,905	45,511	30,782	89,162	62,236	761,196	19,524	844
Wisconsin	2,640,909	1,745,656	797,682	537,813	87,644	12,874	309,643	895,252	136,726	4,525
Wyoming....................	402,579	115,111	11,145	494	50,240	409	52,822	287,468	8,911	329
Dist. of Columbia	13,346,641	3,516,694	1,071,272	1,748,672	171,702	44,541	480,506	9,829,947	216,609	162,765
American Samoa.......	16,603	2,084	565	1,435	84	0	0	14,519	12,516	186
Fed. States of Micronesia	90	0	0	0	0	0	0	0	0	0
Guam	354,599	343,065	2,187	193,882	132,125	0	14,870	11,535	34	228
Marshall Islands........	158,014	158,014	158,014	0	0	0	0	0	0	0
No. Mariana Islands...	8,599	3,270	900	2,330	0	0	40	5,330	0	0
Palau	0	0	0	0	0	0	0	0	0	0
Puerto Rico................	461,613	285,001	65,000	44,591	394	39,898	135,120	176,612	6,394	608
Virgin Islands............	21,227	4,663	450	86	0	4,119	8	16,564	1,600	66
Undistributed (a).......	18,851,268	8,890,279	3,415,873	1,698,345	2,408,360	0	1,367,701	9,960,989	480,595	151,482

Source: U.S. Department of Commerce, Bureau of the Census, February 2006.

FEDERAL GOVERNMENT EXPENDITURE FOR PROCUREMENT CONTRACTS, BY AGENCY, BY STATE AND OUTLYING AREA: FISCAL YEAR 2004—Continued

State and outlying area					Nondefense agencies—continued					
	Department of Education	Department of Energy	Environmental Protection Agency	General Services Administration	Department of Health and Human Services	Department of Homeland Security	Department of Housing and Urban Development	Department of the Interior	Department of Justice	Department of Labor
United States	$1,528,756	$22,160,730	$1,000,582	$13,718,993	$7,679,801	$6,074,213	$1,060,807	$4,825,789	$4,417,977	$1,616,315
Alabama	26	1,907	1,759	258,893	101,604	29,228	3,256	26,482	49,607	18,460
Alaska	0	1,281	0	48,798	34,610	33,647	0	91,499	6,653	3,448
Arizona	6,300	58,804	751	132,602	69,168	106,051	12,629	209,777	218,862	34,090
Arkansas...................	0	641	70	74,098	46,855	647	379	9,863	19,508	5,766
California	81,187	2,372,323	43,025	826,906	372,400	482,296	36,578	386,070	360,924	83,072
Colorado	4,492	999,845	29,971	269,886	33,689	18,306	83,572	228,973	31,986	10,230
Connecticut	78,065	4,137	1,526	27,719	10,852	26,778	2,548	5,501	36,989	10,437
Delaware....................	2	0	2,461	8,930	1,755	709	77	969	2,877	902
Florida	23	32,572	12,062	510,079	19,624	237,284	45,212	66,092	108,347	70,403
Georgia	55,326	14,153	35,833	420,030	363,953	154,208	75,726	31,225	34,171	50,272
Hawaii.......................	4,237	37	0	92,121	6,402	52,112	31,569	25,138	4,003	10,547
Idaho........................	159	852,999	183	19,795	2,786	7,963	532	43,421	4,809	673
Illinois......................	28,348	921,760	32,425	183,918	95,260	10,196	34,796	32,979	54,580	19,544
Indiana......................	0	2,490	490	57,894	40,113	14,534	942	14,583	22,871	19,232
Iowa	87,681	34,611	0	40,765	160,519	10,387	899	3,587	6,114	26,563
Kansas	945	328	9,789	57,401	5,754	23,064	215	7,934	7,503	7,351
Kentucky	0	36,713	3,647	116,095	8,531	8,034	133	21,370	22,908	41,040
Louisiana	0	119,051	230	148,810	13,050	50,992	223	31,982	26,056	16,687
Maine	157	106	800	15,218	12,939	8,134	83	10,073	2,280	8,923
Maryland...................	572,584	258,139	82,873	1,028,718	3,168,554	455,485	92,622	263,054	255,867	129,854
Massachusetts............	9,600	9,905	96,771	255,129	211,559	51,690	4,386	53,745	25,810	34,088
Michigan	117	492	32,496	527,197	71,399	17,376	689	27,343	24,012	24,999
Minnesota	675	2,462	5,557	69,847	81,241	4,806	142	14,617	26,504	13,154
Mississippi	0	292	657	64,529	6,123	1,285	398	11,537	10,312	23,335
Missouri	876	482,104	23,192	187,676	26,619	5,209	286	22,467	22,305	29,163
Montana	316	18,285	367	23,928	126,247	1,518	97	42,507	7,397	7,158
Nebraska...................	1,042	779	0	66,431	17,018	189	0	5,984	4,566	455
Nevada	0	886,314	4,183	27,581	5,990	1,615	77	56,335	3,748	3,376
New Hampshire........	8,811	193	9,249	78,933	1,979	1,310	16,159	2,480	9,970	0
New Jersey................	26,394	97,119	57,169	299,770	64,042	102,793	1,114	53,497	68,990	17,669
New Mexico	1	4,362,582	1,393	36,820	55,785	16,996	367	137,326	10,795	20,607
New York	32,567	752,043	22,410	367,414	117,066	44,771	86,427	41,919	118,311	51,426
North Carolina	28,362	127,211	61,766	146,182	303,853	59,178	9,341	19,265	65,252	13,741
North Dakota.............	0	8,083	582	30,756	8,064	160	3,043	11,481	27,500	10,931
Ohio	4,939	666,789	100,702	307,330	111,227	42,737	-993	34,365	20,907	39,239
Oklahoma	2,082	12,955	7,342	573,460	51,801	3,122	41,986	56,267	43,364	44,371
Oregon	7,743	3,537	3,687	133,746	11,610	11,615	50	83,610	10,644	19,215
Pennsylvania	17,894	541,497	34,724	269,894	99,071	22,666	21,078	101,504	101,533	65,166
Rhode Island	5,271	1,200	6,453	19,326	5,701	2,222	245	4,916	2,208	4,812
South Carolina	314	1,627,730	273	63,824	54,858	26,639	224	5,757	39,218	12,728
South Dakota.............	0	3,758	0	10,513	22,545	274	195	59,762	4,864	1,403
Tennessee	0	2,971,752	456	116,279	51,940	20,048	642	9,628	38,291	23,328
Texas	14,004	465,500	8,810	486,384	136,423	670,106	143,819	71,820	137,452	97,157
Utah	5	3,096	574	72,404	35,887	1,745	152	77,287	8,809	23,594
Vermont	254	2,500	-200	18,023	1,400	675	0	2,891	1,535	6,958
Virginia.....................	81,316	710,633	179,664	2,657,744	501,944	2,003,312	51,948	958,545	471,696	214,692
Washington...............	1,033	2,445,903	16,031	177,872	83,947	91,205	774	76,067	14,173	21,326
West Virginia.............	5,291	46,194	0	48,357	7,001	21,952	50,173	20,541	53,390	22,677
Wisconsin..................	0	2,264	1,069	61,692	76,286	4,154	83	21,154	63,249	1,332
Wyoming...................	0	1,374	0	6,722	7,488	2,947	16	49,081	1,312	0
Dist. of Columbia	356,355	68,488	32,938	2,010,549	356,660	734,152	198,692	569,808	1,083,616	160,647
American Samoa.......	0	0	0	0	0	680	0	13	0	0
Fed. States of Micronesia	0	0	0	0	0	0	0	0	0	0
Guam	0	0	0	7,244	63	423	0	313	381	0
Marshall Islands........	0	0	0	0	0	0	0	0	0	0
No. Mariana Islands...	0	0	0	487	0	66	0	4,238	328	0
Palau	0	0	0	0	0	0	0	0	0	0
Puerto Rico...............	0	0	0	24,003	830	7,078	242	336	8,494	21,487
Virgin Islands	0	0	0	1,860	197	764	190	2,548	2,404	0
Undistributed (a).......	3,964	125,799	34,373	130,408	397,521	366,682	6,775	604,265	607,720	18,585

See footnotes at end of table.

FEDERAL GOVERNMENT EXPENDITURE FOR PROCUREMENT CONTRACTS, BY AGENCY, BY STATE AND OUTLYING AREA: FISCAL YEAR 2004—Continued

State and outlying area	NASA	National Archives & Records Admin.	National Science Foundation	Postal Service	Small Bus. Admin.	Social Security Admin.	Dept. of State	Dept. of Transportation	Dept. of the Treasury	Dept. of Veterans Affairs	Other nondefense
						Nondefense agencies—continued					
United States	$12,545,284	$140,524	$56,914	$14,140,419	$49,500	$530,929	$1,656,725	$5,166,807	$4,041,389	$12,912,531	$6,927,861
Alabama	624,421	0	25	171,723	65	4,528	49,650	8,206	1,251	51,816	312,486
Alaska	24,115	0	0	36,226	0	113	11,096	31,631	15,532	10,985	189
Arizona	148,982	0	10	218,816	0	679	7,327	16,903	1,578	62,712	2,231
Arkansas..................	1,355	210	0	110,965	0	60	27	1,495	1,087	58,175	127
California	3,848,597	1,312	1,291	1,488,099	1,499	9,545	68,020	323,985	371,321	736,640	23,334
Colorado...................	254,837	542	8,670	245,468	1,220	304	12,338	68,432	7,475	73,565	60,385
Connecticut	92,961	0	0	186,317	0	989	4,788	10,051	3,165	32,452	3,081
Delaware	2,540	0	0	38,280	0	55	195	102	1,160	4,667	599
Florida	635,025	0	0	741,573	487	832	24,285	204,154	29,705	199,239	34,044
Georgia	21,724	1,624	3	370,016	55	5,171	7,558	17,088	41,782	100,417	45,699
Hawaii......................	8,371	0	0	47,722	0	43	96	13,254	38	22,095	849
Idaho.......................	2,580	0	0	49,495	0	19	1,024	3,792	76,223	49,328	368
Illinois	16,808	37	492	688,567	1,203	9,329	11,877	236,857	98,075	862,290	62,819
Indiana.....................	208,685	0	3	264,269	0	75	689	34,326	5,689	81,625	32,328
Iowa	8,282	640	0	156,865	992	267	120	14,036	147,837	12,874	10,573
Kansas	5,444	3,735	0	146,960	0	29	502	27,826	1,539	405,623	1,230
Kentucky	1,966	26	0	167,334	0	473	556	5,954	15,039	75,324	1,192,708
Louisiana	92,034	0	0	177,985	36	1,014	38	19,605	560	63,937	10,038
Maine	5,066	0	0	73,778	0	9	0	1,787	3	7,670	274
Maryland	2,153,135	86,089	7,457	289,861	3,014	304,510	97,249	1,051,646	599,323	132,069	106,058
Massachusetts............	216,414	3,273	1,463	381,827	324	3,862	29,516	301,279	136,084	263,760	9,292
Michigan	18,449	1,787	0	482,787	1,000	6,299	1,747	15,417	101,870	91,415	3,747
Minnesota.................	10,958	0	0	280,668	906	268	8,166	22,808	2,528	95,072	28,872
Mississippi................	154,146	0	0	95,825	14	173	9	15,227	2,814	63,823	6,998
Missouri	12,381	2,553	175	328,456	303	12,403	15,464	46,697	8,111	32,112	2,355
Montana	10,586	0	0	45,751	0	151	805	43,264	5,023	6,437	269
Nebraska...................	1,631	0	0	97,680	0	28	411	2,622	89	28,104	11,637
Nevada.....................	5,280	0	0	88,172	0	99	33	8,738	1,832	51,358	581
New Hampshire.........	24,753	491	3	73,099	139	34	16,762	10,714	604	3,785	2,838
New Jersey................	97,218	0	131	536,141	0	6,501	7,285	334,213	34,939	50,572	26,092
New Mexico	117,579	0	0	71,045	260	312	0	21,085	380	30,280	568
New York	61,699	2,822	14	1,019,856	118	11,389	19,872	109,944	701,584	194,078	24,607
North Carolina..........	21,628	0	0	353,270	0	576	49,541	42,552	3,280	91,600	238,743
North Dakota............	1,023	0	0	37,535	375	31	0	787	6,867	15,821	245
Ohio	159,849	245	0	546,825	3	1,192	5,442	28,409	7,773	130,033	12,277
Oklahoma	7,247	0	0	145,220	0	130	543	198,821	8,253	42,582	5,398
Oregon	14,565	0	0	145,519	0	5	1,204	28,244	182	90,544	1,299
Pennsylvania.............	265,938	1,649	124	666,073	5,586	20,830	4,299	62,442	29,670	311,457	328,514
Rhode Island	2,979	0	0	57,280	0	120	4	446	3,831	10,313	257
South Carolina	4,621	0	0	140,251	24	54	11,114	69,049	192	478,335	20,268
South Dakota............	9,942	0	0	40,798	0	36	2,394	1,512	19	13,289	3,333
Tennessee	33,027	1,036	0	261,171	0	309	364	79,261	66,533	530,433	1,717,899
Texas	1,717,602	5,574	351	872,697	0	19,257	114,715	147,282	87,535	437,382	53,644
Utah	20,397	0	0	89,365	0	241	63	13,181	16,257	26,370	-15,261
Vermont	1,298	0	0	38,082	0	34	10	548	20	10,531	239
Virginia....................	848,285	5,484	31,277	354,860	5,742	32,039	508,801	679,689	370,347	387,546	445,000
Washington	30,812	1,266	0	262,844	1	1,162	1,320	66,458	3,528	157,162	5,768
West Virginia............	148,558	0	0	87,179	0	89	4,509	1,196	148,763	63,884	11,075
Wisconsin..................	22,578	0	0	253,204	0	308	1,087	13,112	851	224,410	7,169
Wyoming...................	1,146	0	0	22,842	0	33	0	27,918	4,666	11,965	140,716
Dist. of Columbia	262,874	6,323	1,311	103,263	20,192	18,188	482,494	460,528	741,938	283,678	1,497,881
American Samoa.......	0	0	0	166	0	0	0	959	0	0	0
Fed. States of Micronesia	0	0	0	0	0	0	90	0	0	0	0
Guam	20	0	0	2,004	0	0	0	825	0	0	0
Marshall Islands........	0	0	0	0	0	0	0	0	0	0	0
No. Mariana Islands...	0	0	0	182	0	0	0	23	5	0	0
Palau	0	0	0	0	0	0	0	0	0	0	0
Puerto Rico...............	2,242	0	0	59,582	0	181	5	2,061	615	42,012	442
Virgin Islands............	150	0	0	4,158	0	0	0	2,497	3	116	9
Undistributed (a).......	80,481	13,804	4,114	424,420	5,944	56,504	71,223	215,867	126,021	5,598,771	435,668

Source: U.S. Department of Commerce, Bureau of the Census, Consolidated Federal Funds Report for Fiscal Year 2004, February 2006.

(a) For all agencies, this line includes contract awards under $25,000 and procurement purchases made using government-issued purchase cards.

Table 2.12
FEDERAL GOVERNMENT EXPENDITURE FOR SALARIES AND WAGES, BY AGENCY, BY STATE AND OUTLYING AREA: FISCAL YEAR 2004
(In thousands of dollars)

State and outlying area	Total	Nondefense civilian (a)	Other defense Total	Other defense civilian (b)	Total	Active military	Inactive military	Civilian	Army Total	Army Active military
									Department of Defense	
							Military services			
United States	$225,601,344	$136,618,955	$88,982,389	$4,783,642	$84,198,747	$50,932,566	$10,561,834	$22,704,347	$32,284,066	$15,944,870
Alabama	3,492,347	1,795,899	1,696,448	70,479	1,625,969	506,833	387,172	731,964	1,206,712	233,720
Alaska	1,728,440	714,139	1,014,301	13,439	1,000,862	812,168	27,748	160,946	402,247	306,600
Arizona	3,607,900	2,244,582	1,363,318	55,016	1,308,302	933,896	84,303	290,103	400,708	214,840
Arkansas.......................	1,509,449	937,219	572,230	4,066	568,164	222,660	235,919	109,585	301,513	9,720
California	22,029,304	12,100,523	9,928,781	393,688	9,535,093	6,497,680	645,750	2,391,663	1,061,356	313,120
Colorado	4,457,406	2,690,899	1,766,507	142,156	1,624,351	1,166,830	134,080	323,441	774,076	583,440
Connecticut	1,601,990	1,121,872	480,118	45,574	434,544	273,491	92,589	68,464	90,736	1,200
Delaware.......................	493,682	235,890	257,792	2,451	255,341	166,830	37,559	50,952	38,845	280
Florida	10,394,686	6,005,001	4,389,685	139,963	4,249,722	2,845,392	361,003	1,043,327	501,784	124,040
Georgia	8,324,460	3,887,526	4,436,934	98,842	4,338,092	2,924,648	329,491	1,083,953	2,687,103	2,088,840
Hawaii..........................	3,153,871	509,979	2,643,892	41,552	2,602,340	1,865,382	108,850	628,108	898,482	684,200
Idaho	897,942	614,668	283,274	1,859	281,415	182,164	51,785	47,466	67,536	1,480
Illinois	7,006,708	4,878,485	2,128,223	77,026	2,051,197	1,286,383	315,437	449,377	528,364	24,560
Indiana.........................	2,457,431	1,661,645	795,786	161,265	634,521	55,673	327,960	250,888	369,879	19,120
Iowa	1,249,419	970,810	278,609	2,916	275,693	25,390	207,209	43,094	223,402	7,320
Kansas	2,207,926	1,189,624	1,018,302	14,678	1,003,624	675,828	152,876	174,920	777,917	521,640
Kentucky	3,231,244	1,482,706	1,748,538	43,259	1,705,279	1,417,239	129,109	158,931	1,649,920	1,388,560
Louisiana	2,818,104	1,581,530	1,236,574	17,668	1,218,906	746,384	252,348	220,174	706,404	382,240
Maine	957,014	490,845	466,169	15,135	451,034	137,016	65,853	248,165	69,740	7,680
Maryland	10,523,098	7,279,880	3,243,218	110,709	3,132,509	1,487,904	183,851	1,460,754	935,607	282,880
Massachusetts...............	3,557,251	2,906,164	651,087	76,337	574,750	153,443	178,293	243,014	243,409	10,200
Michigan	3,610,058	2,980,207	629,851	102,678	527,173	80,509	188,457	258,207	391,975	17,920
Minnesota	2,302,448	1,905,350	397,098	15,116	381,982	44,619	262,851	74,512	293,935	10,440
Mississippi	2,093,727	888,577	1,205,150	11,163	1,193,987	657,363	205,710	330,914	314,151	15,680
Missouri	4,041,576	2,721,617	1,319,959	99,842	1,220,117	619,075	378,522	222,520	872,450	367,880
Montana	885,996	646,948	239,048	1,514	237,534	140,182	55,616	41,736	65,642	1,080
Nebraska.......................	1,298,258	699,817	598,441	13,861	584,580	358,968	92,321	133,291	132,639	6,080
Nevada	1,347,252	814,126	533,126	6,496	526,630	407,761	44,353	74,516	51,126	3,880
New Hampshire.............	654,280	497,825	156,455	10,789	145,666	47,561	72,309	25,796	85,231	320
New Jersey....................	4,327,784	3,178,038	1,149,746	50,009	1,099,737	328,357	184,935	586,445	617,408	37,120
New Mexico	2,071,978	1,204,781	867,197	22,545	844,652	503,538	80,165	260,949	176,566	10,360
New York	9,070,246	7,385,357	1,684,889	85,757	1,599,132	860,036	416,633	322,463	1,202,644	630,920
North Carolina	7,197,116	2,500,687	4,696,429	77,604	4,618,825	3,761,793	358,097	498,935	2,213,901	1,714,400
North Dakota	786,652	374,453	412,199	2,873	409,326	280,630	69,429	59,267	73,571	880
Ohio	5,576,062	3,616,616	1,959,446	462,401	1,497,045	425,820	320,328	750,897	328,579	18,000
Oklahoma	3,462,800	1,380,544	2,082,256	57,630	2,024,626	988,368	196,481	839,777	784,311	484,600
Oregon	1,902,974	1,594,074	308,900	2,071	306,829	52,544	141,517	112,768	203,585	8,480
Pennsylvania	6,609,013	4,918,718	1,690,295	402,209	1,288,086	177,012	421,070	690,004	651,207	43,520
Rhode Island	828,541	379,795	448,746	4,667	444,079	149,145	59,856	235,078	60,436	4,120
South Carolina	3,155,983	1,074,994	2,080,989	47,686	2,033,303	1,489,952	242,593	300,758	716,266	428,200
South Dakota................	765,021	496,710	268,311	1,692	266,619	134,126	95,374	37,119	99,041	1,720
Tennessee	3,475,751	2,821,119	654,632	37,516	617,116	142,606	275,563	198,947	382,389	12,840
Texas	14,690,246	8,150,308	6,539,938	191,172	6,348,766	4,583,803	554,799	1,210,164	3,513,568	2,498,920
Utah	2,150,173	1,049,633	1,100,540	48,200	1,052,340	242,647	212,157	597,536	283,020	11,840
Vermont	405,058	335,487	69,571	2,642	66,929	8,738	41,914	16,277	48,491	800
Virginia........................	16,342,443	5,324,022	11,018,421	1,411,177	9,607,244	6,652,246	285,505	2,669,493	2,153,286	1,096,550
Washington...................	6,057,983	2,692,868	3,365,115	44,681	3,320,434	2,093,079	320,048	907,307	1,266,414	812,800
West Virginia	1,358,012	1,152,050	205,962	1,246	204,716	31,690	123,023	50,003	157,597	6,720
Wisconsin.....................	1,895,095	1,586,091	309,004	5,555	303,449	40,201	186,345	76,903	221,485	9,680
Wyoming......................	521,214	317,657	203,557	1,124	202,433	139,427	25,618	37,388	29,137	160
Dist. of Columbia	15,525,884	13,891,484	1,634,400	20,640	1,613,760	721,566	81,751	810,443	530,614	319,080
American Samoa..........	9,225	5,071	4,154	0	4,154	0	0	4,104	4,154	0
Micronesia	0	0	0	0	0	0	0	0	0	0
Guam	319,996	38,776	281,220	4,494	276,726	206,570	20,533	49,623	14,957	1,560
Marshall Islands............	0	0	0	0	0	0	0	0	0	0
No. Mariana Islands	6,264	6,253	11	0	11	0	0	11	11	0
Palau	0	0	0	0	0	0	0	0	0	0
Puerto Rico...................	1,025,908	726,455	299,453	8,514	290,939	22,818	225,045	43,076	242,357	7,440
Virgin Islands...............	66,108	53,278	12,830	0	12,830	1,382	9,563	1,885	10,982	0
Undistributed	4,064,549	3,909,285	155,264	0	155,264	155,200	64	0	155,200	155,200

Source: U.S. Department of Commerce, Bureau of the Census, February 2006.

FEDERAL GOVERNMENT EXPENDITURE FOR SALARIES AND WAGES, BY AGENCY, BY STATE AND OUTLYING AREA: FISCAL YEAR 2004—Continued

	Department of Defense—continued									
	Military services—continued									
	Army—continued		Navy				Air Force			
State and outlying area	Inactive military	Civilian	Total	Active military	Inactive military	Civilian	Total	Active military	Inactive military	Civilian
United States	$9,364,146	$6,975,050	$29,304,761	$20,236,155	$565,618	$8,502,988	$22,609,920	$14,751,541	$632,070	$7,226,309
Alabama	356,112	616,880	39,200	29,428	7,917	1,855	380,057	243,685	23,143	113,229
Alaska	20,215	75,432	7,325	5,848	696	781	591,290	499,720	6,837	84,733
Arizona	61,222	124,646	189,046	161,914	8,851	18,281	718,548	557,142	14,230	147,176
Arkansas	218,229	73,564	4,085	1,940	1,846	299	262,566	211,000	15,844	35,722
California	524,533	223,703	6,911,875	5,187,504	78,035	1,646,336	1,561,862	997,056	43,182	521,624
Colorado	115,693	74,943	54,951	45,303	7,565	2,083	795,324	538,087	10,822	246,415
Connecticut	79,644	9,892	316,808	264,911	4,442	47,455	27,000	7,380	8,503	11,117
Delaware	31,471	7,094	2,810	1,540	1,203	67	213,686	165,010	4,885	43,791
Florida	293,122	84,622	2,063,474	1,500,205	42,434	520,835	1,684,464	1,221,147	25,447	437,870
Georgia	284,049	314,214	500,436	328,791	17,587	154,058	1,150,553	507,017	27,855	615,681
Hawaii	91,263	123,019	1,318,332	900,434	5,169	412,729	385,526	280,748	12,418	92,360
Idaho	48,918	17,138	8,830	4,422	1,791	2,617	205,049	176,262	1,076	27,711
Illinois	278,141	225,663	1,012,586	928,084	20,712	63,790	510,247	333,739	16,584	159,924
Indiana	305,419	45,340	183,615	21,014	5,190	157,411	81,027	15,539	17,351	48,137
Iowa	194,899	21,183	11,555	7,670	3,722	163	40,736	10,400	8,588	21,748
Kansas	131,115	125,162	8,665	6,673	1,967	25	217,042	147,515	19,794	49,733
Kentucky	122,987	138,373	27,602	11,956	4,060	11,586	27,757	16,723	2,062	8,972
Louisiana	225,863	98,301	159,001	94,593	13,102	51,306	353,501	269,551	13,383	70,567
Maine	56,159	5,901	358,798	120,777	6,638	231,383	22,496	8,559	3,056	10,881
Maryland	174,552	478,175	1,617,463	738,561	4,674	874,228	579,439	466,463	4,625	108,351
Massachusetts	153,257	79,952	48,055	31,175	3,562	13,318	283,286	112,068	21,474	149,744
Michigan	170,178	203,877	46,446	38,222	7,325	899	88,752	24,367	10,954	53,431
Minnesota	240,904	42,591	27,849	18,812	8,406	631	60,198	15,367	13,541	31,290
Mississippi	194,676	103,795	428,625	312,401	4,898	111,326	451,211	329,282	6,136	115,793
Missouri	343,069	161,501	122,291	83,247	29,527	9,517	225,376	167,948	5,926	51,502
Montana	52,143	12,419	1,655	824	831	0	170,237	138,278	2,642	29,317
Nebraska	79,862	46,697	37,412	33,349	3,474	589	414,529	319,539	8,985	86,005
Nevada	38,281	8,965	64,739	49,734	3,246	11,759	410,765	354,147	2,826	53,792
New Hampshire	69,132	15,779	40,663	36,575	1,370	2,718	19,772	10,666	1,807	7,299
New Jersey	173,644	406,644	176,207	57,778	4,589	113,840	306,122	233,459	6,702	65,961
New Mexico	68,347	97,859	15,729	10,983	2,881	1,865	652,357	482,195	8,937	161,225
New York	365,371	206,353	179,580	150,431	22,382	6,767	216,908	78,685	28,880	109,343
North Carolina	333,055	166,446	1,915,892	1,623,465	11,257	281,170	489,032	423,928	13,785	51,319
North Dakota	60,909	11,782	1,500	809	590	101	334,255	278,941	7,930	47,384
Ohio	274,166	36,413	53,106	32,333	17,570	3,203	1,115,360	375,487	28,592	711,281
Oklahoma	177,752	121,959	97,219	87,658	5,754	3,807	1,143,096	416,110	12,975	714,011
Oregon	121,846	73,659	28,145	21,690	5,636	819	75,099	22,374	14,435	38,290
Pennsylvania	374,645	233,042	506,890	98,588	19,871	388,431	129,989	34,904	26,554	68,531
Rhode Island	50,116	6,200	359,499	132,886	6,630	219,983	24,144	12,139	3,110	8,895
South Carolina	217,710	70,356	818,587	646,795	8,076	163,716	498,450	414,957	16,807	66,686
South Dakota	86,826	10,495	950	243	677	30	166,628	132,163	7,871	26,594
Tennessee	251,449	118,100	151,448	99,871	10,977	40,600	83,279	29,895	13,137	40,247
Texas	494,005	520,643	525,971	429,860	39,208	56,903	2,309,227	1,655,023	21,586	632,618
Utah	206,087	65,093	15,807	11,192	3,400	1,215	753,513	219,615	2,670	531,228
Vermont	40,048	7,643	1,941	1,653	259	29	16,497	6,285	1,607	8,605
Virginia	238,188	818,548	6,187,056	4,574,966	34,127	1,577,963	1,266,902	980,730	13,190	272,982
Washington	282,977	170,637	1,626,286	950,771	19,259	656,256	427,734	329,508	17,812	80,414
West Virginia	117,402	33,475	19,467	14,221	2,104	3,142	27,652	10,749	3,517	13,386
Wisconsin	166,829	44,976	18,427	11,245	6,673	509	63,537	19,276	12,843	31,418
Wyoming	23,555	5,422	443	18	425	0	172,853	139,249	1,638	31,966
Dist. of Columbia	40,754	170,780	819,795	186,989	40,409	592,397	263,351	215,497	588	47,266
American Samoa	4,104	50	0	0	0	0	0	0	0	0
Micronesia	0	0	0	0	0	0	0	0	0	0
Guam	13,121	276	148,635	118,015	6	30,614	113,134	86,995	7,406	18,733
Marshall Islands	0	0	0	0	0	0	0	0	0	0
No. Mariana Islands	0	11	0	0	0	0	0	0	0	0
Palau	0	0	0	0	0	0	0	0	0	0
Puerto Rico	217,435	17,482	21,794	7,657	2,554	11,583	26,788	7,721	5,056	14,011
Virgin Islands	9,097	1,885	131	131	0	0	1,717	1,251	466	0
Undistributed	0	0	64	64	0	0	0	0	0	0

See footnotes at end of table.

FEDERAL GOVERNMENT EXPENDITURE FOR SALARIES AND WAGES, BY AGENCY, BY STATE AND OUTLYING AREA: FISCAL YEAR 2004 — Continued

State and outlying area	Total (a)	Dept. of Agriculture	Dept. of Commerce	Dept. of Education	Dept. of Energy	Environmental Protection Agency	Federal Deposit Insurance Corporation	General Services Admin.	Dept. of Health and Human Services
United States	$136,618,955	$5,707,828	$2,538,313	$364,676	$1,326,615	$1,494,644	$502,566	$936,686	$4,393,816
Alabama	1,795,899	71,131	6,105	84	0	3,199	2,537	3,415	3,477
Alaska	714,139	57,333	32,173	0	100	2,285	0	2,842	29,007
Arizona	2,244,582	107,299	9,867	0	16,869	421	1,902	3,894	192,144
Arkansas	937,219	114,410	2,932	0	2,432	0	1,975	1,350	25,195
California	12,100,523	467,971	60,915	14,478	41,679	77,689	29,026	68,299	85,623
Colorado	2,690,899	205,070	91,017	5,565	56,028	60,893	2,991	24,158	32,370
Connecticut	1,121,872	10,656	3,732	0	149	665	2,287	870	1,905
Delaware	235,890	12,899	457	0	0	0	978	188	670
Florida	6,005,001	101,044	54,213	335	109	6,875	5,546	6,958	17,235
Georgia	3,887,526	161,026	14,041	15,497	6,750	88,950	16,797	47,144	475,754
Hawaii.........................	509,979	29,128	16,377	0	182	492	0	2,900	1,329
Idaho...........................	614,668	148,557	7,224	0	32,554	1,837	0	1,162	2,532
Illinois	4,878,485	102,378	14,649	13,595	28,183	102,430	25,062	50,555	52,800
Indiana........................	1,661,645	51,912	57,167	107	0	123	3,237	2,423	2,339
Iowa	970,810	122,863	4,400	74	963	238	5,657	1,275	1,215
Kansas	1,189,624	63,122	10,167	0	0	41,636	6,876	979	11,339
Kentucky	1,482,706	66,825	6,547	0	2,008	220	4,537	1,073	1,085
Louisiana	1,581,530	170,432	9,737	0	6,686	1,056	3,972	2,870	11,553
Maine	490,845	17,189	5,061	0	0	0	0	457	1,392
Maryland	7,279,880	250,021	790,690	0	130,533	7,238	2,350	12,990	2,362,390
Massachusetts..............	2,906,164	25,884	35,739	7,157	1,542	60,117	17,686	18,699	39,636
Michigan	2,980,207	76,354	17,382	0	0	25,903	3,233	5,174	8,132
Minnesota	1,905,350	113,411	7,703	353	65	6,407	4,903	2,906	22,449
Mississippi	888,517	112,576	14,163	0	0	2,149	2,287	787	1,187
Missouri......................	2,721,617	261,736	30,525	7,680	8,274	821	15,930	56,799	29,739
Montana	646,948	172,933	7,187	0	9,918	2,716	1,041	1,259	49,678
Nebraska......................	699,817	90,441	5,403	0	1,319	92	3,181	1,066	4,599
Nevada........................	814,126	24,327	6,986	0	29,763	12,832	0	2,013	3,498
New Hampshire............	497,825	21,520	2,109	0	147	0	1,933	1,320	659
New Jersey...................	3,178,038	30,849	15,839	0	1,582	18,665	3,910	13,696	11,687
New Mexico	1,204,781	92,963	4,651	0	75,293	162	1,498	2,722	135,845
New York	7,385,357	65,114	23,033	7,111	13,090	61,620	18,027	49,194	62,836
North Carolina..............	2,500,687	118,710	29,831	0	125	99,028	3,785	3,336	63,840
North Dakota................	374,453	51,526	3,914	0	4,323	0	2,868	1,001	21,524
Ohio............................	3,616,616	57,267	9,361	2,364	10,627	45,361	2,374	7,353	39,914
Oklahoma	1,380,544	60,592	20,265	0	9,280	4,397	3,977	2,480	69,130
Oregon	1,594,074	253,399	20,239	0	108,883	9,728	1,505	2,691	11,302
Pennsylvania	4,918,718	99,905	14,527	8,034	30,926	70,964	5,471	40,531	64,717
Rhode Island	379,795	3,024	3,118	0	0	6,036	0	868	639
South Carolina	1,074,994	56,074	17,758	0	38,240	85	1,773	1,731	1,526
South Dakota................	496,710	54,782	5,614	0	12,202	73	2,131	877	56,056
Tennessee	2,821,119	71,643	8,097	183	52,793	417	11,736	2,588	6,761
Texas	8,150,308	218,466	38,245	9,395	13,633	72,169	70,364	71,759	51,761
Utah	1,049,633	105,240	7,941	0	1,528	139	3,511	1,843	2,710
Vermont	335,487	18,156	2,324	0	0	82	0	337	577
Virginia	5,324,022	147,817	603,144	0	1,153	109,610	787	117,601	3,393
Washington..................	2,692,868	130,170	85,055	5,761	178,796	43,327	4,230	31,431	48,528
West Virginia................	1,152,050	46,337	2,738	0	22,804	1,924	1,176	1,707	27,293
Wisconsin....................	1,586,091	103,695	7,030	0	59	153	5,670	1,769	3,553
Wyoming......................	317,657	49,338	3,680	0	4,577	0	0	810	4,537
Dist. of Columbia	13,891,484	606,268	281,857	266,492	370,448	439,650	191,070	252,608	227,312
American Samoa..........	5,071	384	1,068	0	0	0	0	0	0
Micronesia	0	0	0	0	0	0	0	0	0
Guam	38,776	3,453	1,889	0	0	59	0	0	0
Marshall Islands............	0	0	0	0	0	0	0	0	0
No. Mariana Islands	6,253	498	0	0	0	80	0	0	47
Palau	0	0	0	0	0	0	0	0	0
Puerto Rico..................	726,455	30,927	2,427	411	0	3,523	779	1,825	7,365
Virgin Islands...............	53,278	783	0	0	0	108	0	103	32
Undistributed	3,909,285	0	0	0	0	0	0	0	0

See footnotes at end of table.

FEDERAL GOVERNMENT EXPENDITURE FOR SALARIES AND WAGES, BY AGENCY, BY STATE AND OUTLYING AREA: FISCAL YEAR 2004 — Continued

State and outlying area	Dept. of Homeland Security	Dept. of Housing and Urban Development	Dept. of the Interior	Dept. of Justice (c)	Dept. of Labor	National Aeronautics and Space Administration	National Archives and Records	National Science Foundation	United States Postal Service
					Nondefense agencies—continued				
United States	$10,291,135	$812,386	$4,126,443	$10,133,630	$1,242,288	$1,659,774	$143,471	$109,882	$52,030,998
Alabama	81,174	5,882	8,521	69,752	9,837	228,313	59	0	651,425
Alaska........................	151,770	2,952	134,268	12,541	1,007	0	218	214	137,423
Arizona	291,432	8,740	238,333	124,501	3,596	284	0	0	830,069
Arkansas.....................	18,189	4,434	16,687	41,020	3,213	0	1,155	0	420,941
California	1,334,622	50,608	386,695	599,691	66,469	201,848	5,858	0	5,645,035
Colorado.....................	114,902	27,180	473,094	137,221	29,666	585	2,082	0	931,173
Connecticut	101,551	5,210	3,317	50,747	5,283	84	0	0	706,784
Delaware	3,655	265	2,310	11,005	762	0	0	0	145,215
Florida	799,892	20,076	79,963	388,134	31,933	155,463	0	0	2,813,123
Georgia	293,221	31,352	61,692	177,805	39,056	0	4,062	0	1,403,640
Hawaii........................	129,657	1,649	27,259	27,533	1,672	0	0	0	181,032
Idaho.........................	19,352	951	119,646	16,224	2,068	0	0	0	187,755
Illinois.......................	253,529	36,021	14,495	223,926	57,026	84	2,037	226	2,612,047
Indiana.......................	49,317	5,819	13,173	69,655	7,161	60	0	0	1,002,492
Iowa	16,399	2,489	7,224	19,095	2,364	0	933	0	595,061
Kansas	24,663	12,654	21,069	63,098	4,156	0	2,281	0	557,485
Kentucky	50,312	5,274	19,000	133,066	29,006	0	0	0	634,773
Louisiana....................	135,347	7,754	64,489	119,411	7,031	918	0	0	675,177
Maine	67,216	513	10,271	8,688	1,863	0	0	0	279,873
Maryland	241,642	9,911	45,054	295,056	6,653	263,401	59,370	0	1,099,574
Massachusetts..............	261,014	17,679	66,580	97,901	34,158	142	4,202	166	1,448,442
Michigan	228,370	12,566	21,548	110,601	7,935	114	1,365	0	1,831,430
Minnesota...................	93,218	7,324	45,700	88,788	4,054	0	0	0	1,064,700
Mississippi..................	30,325	3,888	23,474	43,152	3,419	23,553	0	0	363,509
Missouri.....................	94,404	9,184	46,033	98,981	28,723	77	26,673	0	1,245,983
Montana	37,513	701	109,713	13,023	1,901	107	0	0	173,554
Nebraska.....................	47,514	3,535	25,491	16,455	2,580	0	0	0	370,546
Nevada	70,955	2,238	108,924	37,697	2,013	0	0	0	334,478
New Hampshire.............	27,461	3,259	5,065	11,853	2,983	101	0	0	277,297
New Jersey	275,409	10,431	19,430	209,988	14,487	164	0	0	2,033,826
New Mexico	78,925	2,334	259,467	36,190	2,588	4,880	79	0	269,505
New York	626,711	40,932	52,414	371,252	51,056	2,565	2,009	0	3,868,775
North Carolina.............	177,219	8,169	30,754	114,249	5,294	0	0	61	1,340,112
North Dakota...............	28,764	503	44,272	7,048	1,330	0	0	0	142,387
Ohio	116,868	18,193	16,865	101,858	31,176	160,924	2,924	0	2,074,356
Oklahoma....................	35,158	10,054	55,203	82,508	3,585	0	0	0	550,887
Oregon	100,319	4,385	186,560	51,470	3,108	99	0	0	552,018
Pennsylvania	167,242	31,902	68,597	301,154	70,969	0	2,448	0	2,526,715
Rhode Island	47,738	2,163	3,282	9,716	1,808	0	0	0	217,288
South Carolina.............	72,844	5,538	11,735	74,306	2,886	0	0	0	532,036
South Dakota...............	7,268	458	75,105	17,110	1,024	0	0	0	154,766
Tennessee	57,405	11,107	34,718	80,042	7,752	0	0	0	990,742
Texas	1,107,185	45,343	63,035	575,352	58,234	275,633	5,485	0	3,310,536
Utah	32,184	1,916	105,601	29,406	8,681	674	0	0	339,002
Vermont	98,360	424	3,319	7,418	415	0	0	0	144,461
Virginia......................	724,953	7,419	285,449	758,468	37,397	211,938	0	109,183	1,346,144
Washington..................	271,630	14,926	134,896	74,242	19,365	0	1,469	32	997,088
West Virginia...............	21,616	1,853	43,951	216,473	33,822	3,005	0	0	330,708
Wisconsin....................	45,958	5,371	35,809	49,107	7,172	108	0	0	960,517
Wyoming.....................	4,711	318	91,182	8,219	1,227	0	0	0	86,651
Dist. of Columbia	955,969	282,113	291,230	1,630,167	478,703	124,650	18,762	0	391,722
American Samoa	884	0	888	0	0	0	0	0	628
Micronesia	0	0	0	0	0	0	0	0	0
Guam	14,006	64	1,110	5,468	53	0	0	0	7,603
Marshall Islands...........	0	0	0	0	0	0	0	0	0
No. Mariana Islands	2,731	0	764	944	104	0	0	0	691
Palau	0	0	0	0	0	0	0	0	0
Puerto Rico..................	128,491	6,362	6,958	63,614	2,464	0	0	0	226,023
Virgin Islands...............	19,877	0	4,761	8,474	0	0	0	0	15,772
Undistributed	2,094	0	0	2,142,770	0	0	0	0	0

See footnotes at end of table.

FEDERAL GOVERNMENT EXPENDITURE FOR SALARIES AND WAGES, BY AGENCY, BY STATE AND OUTLYING AREA: FISCAL YEAR 2004 — Continued

State and outlying area	Small Business Admin.	Social Security Admin.	Dept. of State	Dept. of Transportation	Dept. of the Treasury	Dept. of Veterans Affairs	All other nondefense (d)
				Nondefense agencies—continued			
United States	$255,926	$3,855,721	$1,111,956	$5,638,180	$6,835,610	$13,008,712	$8,097,699
Alabama	2,796	137,177	433	28,246	31,585	225,966	224,784
Alaska	1,204	2,823	66	113,384	6,857	24,796	875
Arizona	1,861	32,278	1,250	55,049	41,187	267,148	16,458
Arkansas......................	2,846	25,997	86	22,115	15,620	213,450	3,172
California	30,927	373,414	12,928	485,216	743,699	1,208,948	108,886
Colorado	9,258	42,051	632	135,992	105,429	167,999	35,543
Connecticut	1,679	23,453	1,201	22,741	46,922	128,269	4,366
Delaware......................	377	3,605	0	3,012	10,565	39,255	671
Florida	5,085	135,381	25,912	285,271	193,421	849,799	29,233
Georgia	12,610	96,708	1,583	246,382	318,410	316,288	58,758
Hawaii..........................	1,468	6,163	1,438	35,568	10,569	32,299	3,264
Idaho...........................	831	6,959	0	13,168	7,860	45,610	379
Illinois.........................	5,942	193,935	5,175	238,147	178,102	526,390	141,751
Indiana........................	1,427	44,621	0	111,145	55,839	173,731	9,897
Iowa	1,484	18,827	0	19,986	16,710	131,954	1,599
Kansas	1,161	19,553	126	100,616	100,339	143,104	5,200
Kentucky	2,147	45,602	189	39,445	213,366	158,892	69,339
Louisiana	1,566	47,796	4,528	34,210	41,104	227,168	8,725
Maine	1,291	10,709	72	17,322	8,873	59,325	729
Maryland	2,061	798,895	2,687	46,695	380,839	193,329	278,501
Massachusetts...............	3,315	70,045	3,443	123,750	212,979	319,422	36,466
Michigan......................	2,319	78,629	528	76,912	137,048	320,530	14,134
Minnesota	1,822	27,371	199	111,617	54,809	237,680	9,870
Mississippi	1,017	34,004	139	16,576	15,593	178,431	18,348
Missouri	5,025	140,700	46	107,427	192,381	302,553	11,923
Montana	842	6,738	179	15,037	7,129	34,697	1,082
Nebraska......................	1,020	10,271	142	15,941	17,673	81,106	1,442
Nevada	1,291	11,026	0	36,007	22,244	105,977	1,857
New Hampshire.............	1,146	7,940	4,919	78,882	13,323	35,185	723
New Jersey....................	2,770	60,098	1,152	162,592	95,622	186,126	9,716
New Mexico	1,068	41,733	509	71,269	11,618	109,006	2,476
New York	13,923	260,807	23,616	285,548	497,358	892,225	96,141
North Carolina.............	2,214	61,429	3,280	49,990	60,309	316,102	12,850
North Dakota................	1,136	5,599	0	12,884	5,967	39,026	381
Ohio............................	3,312	88,670	0	147,589	173,788	483,216	22,257
Oklahoma	1,064	28,116	142	251,382	36,677	153,127	2,521
Oregon	1,689	26,249	0	28,826	34,096	195,002	2,506
Pennsylvania	5,475	229,152	3,728	92,932	421,678	568,279	93,373
Rhode Island	945	9,010	645	9,750	11,398	51,426	940
South Carolina	939	34,252	13,760	26,413	17,236	161,837	4,026
South Dakota................	822	5,598	0	8,053	6,034	88,031	706
Tennessee.....................	1,582	57,051	0	111,961	223,699	348,057	742,785
Texas	19,475	165,915	16,475	427,997	565,983	899,284	68,583
Utah	1,526	10,846	0	71,527	232,674	89,376	3,307
Vermont	1,090	3,574	0	8,141	5,172	41,318	319
Virginia........................	5,774	120,995	4,260	242,388	116,404	273,677	96,068
Washington...................	3,819	81,323	3,443	191,938	79,019	277,519	14,861
West Virginia................	977	26,226	0	15,057	162,704	188,745	2,934
Wisconsin.....................	1,819	38,997	0	27,890	39,361	245,350	6,703
Wyoming......................	930	2,348	0	8,241	4,800	45,780	308
Dist. of Columbia	74,135	20,617	973,045	724,186	807,575	454,832	4,028,073
American Samoa..........	86	206	0	869	0	58	0
Micronesia	0	0	0	0	0	0	0
Guam	422	527	0	3,513	0	583	25
Marshall Islands...........	0	0	0	0	0	0	0
No. Mariana Islands	0	210	0	176	0	0	8
Palau	0	0	0	0	0	0	0
Puerto Rico..................	2,611	22,779	0	20,235	25,510	150,736	23,416
Virgin Islands...............	505	723	0	974	453	693	20
Undistributed	0	0	0	0	0	0	1,764,421

Source: U.S. Department of Commerce, Bureau of the Census, February 2006.

Note: Department of Defense data represent salaries, wages and compensation, such as housing allowances; distributions by state are based on duty station. State details for all other federal government agencies are estimates, based on place of employment.

(a) The "undistributed" amount includes the salary and wages data for the Federal Bureau of Investigation and for the Federal Judiciary that could not be geographically allocated.

(b) The "undistributed" amount represents Defense Logistics Agency salaries and wages that could not be geographically allocated.

(c) The "undistributed" amount includes the salaries and wages of the Federal Bureau of Investigation that could not be geographically allocated.

(d) The "undistributed" amount includes the salaries and wages for the Federal Judiciary that could not be geographically allocated.

Table 2.13
FEDERAL GOVERNMENT INSURANCE AND LOAN PROGRAMS, BY STATE AND OUTLYING AREA: FISCAL YEAR 2004
(In thousands of dollars)

	Direct loans by volume of assistance provided					Guaranteed loans by volume of coverage provided			
		Department of Agriculture						Federal	Veterans housing
State and outlying area	Total	Commodity loans— price supports	Other agriculture loans	Federal direct student loans	Other direct loans	Total	Mortgage insurance for homes	Family Education Loan program	guaranteed and insured loans— VA home loans
United States	$30,065,061	$2,771,370	$4,019,058	$22,072,946	$1,201,686	$228,779,115	$109,072,336	$45,097,174	$35,315,000
Alabama	934,471	360,805	66,273	501,604	5,789	2,909,379	1,245,827	669,600	603,665
Alaska	32,284	0	17,782	11,169	3,332	1,077,286	475,318	56,871	294,589
Arizona	547,083	3	35,775	509,431	1,875	8,775,014	3,693,177	2,724,189	1,642,498
Arkansas	169,253	0	113,189	54,786	1,277	1,990,458	819,609	414,438	277,770
California	2,924,512	458,900	219,615	2,025,121	220,876	16,012,010	5,938,035	3,648,825	1,966,460
Colorado	434,462	1,132	48,730	375,753	8,848	9,270,009	5,527,276	804,005	1,362,598
Connecticut	116,373	0	13,719	100,508	2,145	2,603,753	1,210,058	514,865	121,224
Delaware	68,232	0	19,871	44,267	4,094	636,702	289,724	83,656	156,278
Florida	659,440	0	69,887	457,756	131,796	12,632,586	5,621,421	2,497,149	2,742,847
Georgia	1,021,687	1	102,013	914,310	5,362	9,294,907	5,680,038	1,107,501	1,446,354
Hawaii	21,104	0	20,196	668	240	601,631	149,822	120,743	100,623
Idaho	375,563	342	67,576	307,645	0	1,309,290	697,050	78,203	269,705
Illinois	1,386,263	0	106,798	1,230,438	49,027	10,260,918	5,412,151	2,233,512	893,705
Indiana	814,887	0	90,478	694,007	30,403	5,686,585	3,178,849	1,318,671	583,738
Iowa	923,422	7	116,928	798,339	8,148	1,609,590	451,048	420,127	184,853
Kansas	248,461	4,912	57,770	182,142	3,636	1,873,109	747,025	479,112	340,416
Kentucky	429,142	80,415	148,121	174,075	26,532	2,660,966	1,138,111	516,830	374,301
Louisiana	166,606	0	102,129	48,437	16,040	2,725,259	1,169,642	848,312	319,279
Maine	82,975	0	50,960	31,135	881	787,375	234,422	206,913	90,094
Maryland	563,279	0	37,041	459,153	67,086	7,535,946	4,477,207	497,696	1,632,411
Massachusetts	928,697	0	33,000	891,098	4,598	3,495,177	1,477,336	1,158,566	153,766
Michigan	2,208,204	0	134,308	2,044,682	29,214	6,361,166	3,577,469	1,176,680	588,547
Minnesota	667,408	6	113,503	551,654	2,246	4,332,931	1,602,966	1,037,069	372,578
Mississippi	1,301,364	1,156,247	92,118	48,557	4,442	1,849,257	787,118	448,356	290,507
Missouri	479,863	0	94,907	346,382	38,574	4,688,908	2,038,865	1,183,176	680,196
Montana	117,980	486	41,407	71,642	4,445	835,926	310,042	171,711	103,863
Nebraska	246,220	433	77,985	154,190	13,612	1,602,579	603,997	319,790	383,323
Nevada	141,417	3	15,722	123,996	1,695	2,680,989	1,463,136	79,666	860,244
New Hampshire	63,249	0	32,097	28,587	2,565	836,850	271,281	272,621	93,140
New Jersey	451,765	0	37,749	375,201	38,815	6,291,918	4,308,482	582,567	385,130
New Mexico	169,734	0	34,617	134,773	343	1,623,561	907,831	155,561	419,865
New York	1,905,475	0	99,020	1,765,762	40,693	10,256,411	3,797,471	3,461,514	307,663
North Carolina	1,015,222	314,916	224,901	386,117	89,287	6,612,847	3,133,601	935,034	1,793,022
North Dakota	47,822	57	46,730	0	1,035	759,337	176,979	195,060	80,908
Ohio	1,881,693	0	105,443	1,724,026	52,224	8,028,767	4,143,894	1,605,874	1,058,209
Oklahoma	186,299	159	89,540	95,129	1,470	2,735,568	1,186,408	592,261	437,883
Oregon	821,413	0	78,209	742,177	1,027	2,714,452	1,325,005	473,524	544,238
Pennsylvania	254,313	0	122,494	93,564	38,255	7,402,576	2,489,193	3,311,412	759,797
Rhode Island	163,152	0	10,685	150,658	1,809	796,748	418,520	254,500	37,907
South Carolina	312,816	0	70,150	241,182	1,484	2,304,559	850,315	591,799	505,186
South Dakota	70,078	7	64,423	3,310	2,337	756,898	186,318	200,538	99,354
Tennessee	403,014	15,926	136,467	240,279	10,343	4,706,694	2,559,980	866,340	828,487
Texas	938,100	376,018	274,900	244,949	42,234	21,352,662	11,926,975	3,176,142	3,341,789
Utah	51,272	4	46,446	4,523	300	3,980,321	2,439,321	336,919	439,136
Vermont	36,377	0	21,241	15,136	0	422,363	47,878	203,584	32,420
Virginia	1,151,723	70	97,178	965,394	89,081	8,601,674	3,877,276	775,994	2,860,061
Washington	755,676	463	75,818	659,327	20,069	6,154,475	2,929,210	605,030	1,776,193
West Virginia	533,703	0	47,174	468,827	17,702	562,262	238,345	122,575	92,478
Wisconsin	378,183	53	104,212	263,063	10,855	2,937,769	830,160	659,309	449,260
Wyoming	8,653	6	8,429	13	205	478,865	176,857	112,723	82,682
District of Columbia ..	266,192	0	0	231,966	34,225	1,035,486	190,052	566,671	13,210
American Samoa	7,513	0	0	0	7,513	38	0	0	0
Fed. States of Micronesia	2,064	0	1,773	0	291	0	0	0	0
Guam	5,930	0	960	2,081	2,889	30,352	1,224	3,960	2,837
Marshall Islands	1,685	0	1,685	0	0	0	0	0	0
No. Mariana Islands ...	3,369	0	1,049	0	2,320	773	0	0	0
Palau	407	0	407	0	0	35,000	0	0	0
Puerto Rico	159,365	0	71,170	82,122	6,074	1,248,709	640,323	219,423	37,234
Virgin Islands	8,152	0	6,288	1,833	32	11,473	2,699	2	479
Undistributed	0	0	0	0	0	0	0	0	0

See footnotes at end of table.

FEDERAL GOVERNMENT INSURANCE AND LOAN PROGRAMS, BY STATE AND OUTLYING AREA: FISCAL YEAR 2004 — Continued

State and outlying area	Guaranteed loans by volume of coverage provided—continued			Insurance programs by volume of coverage provided					
	U.S.D.A. guaranteed loans	Small business loans	Other guaranteed loans	Total	Flood insurance	Crop insurance	Foreign Investment Insurance	Life Insurance for Veterans	Other insurance
United States	$12,303,320	$18,237,607	$1,634,451	$773,198,632	$722,811,352	$46,752,550	$1,279,824	$1,865,424	$489,481
Alabama	244,053	132,524	0	6,011,149	5,699,585	281,450	0	25,308	4,805
Alaska	134,101	23,056	0	408,402	399,394	546	0	2,560	5,902
Arizona	128,236	454,548	0	5,050,723	4,798,238	176,350	25,000	42,193	8,942
Arkansas.....................	380,178	95,900	0	1,815,360	1,280,109	517,423	0	15,925	1,903
California	259,589	3,526,058	35,000	50,435,096	46,968,582	3,160,344	34,090	193,721	78,359
Colorado	393,169	504,354	0	3,327,343	2,657,932	606,102	883	29,866	32,560
Connecticut	23,476	448,489	63,553	5,516,296	5,249,687	76,984	158,150	29,881	1,593
Delaware.....................	43,011	59,842	0	3,322,296	3,121,411	52,508	141,800	5,822	755
Florida	474,988	768,593	6	309,479,746	306,582,634	2,668,739	9,360	172,441	46,572
Georgia	515,464	420,591	0	13,448,971	12,576,633	793,509	72	41,776	36,982
Hawaii........................	70,441	40,778	0	6,436,137	6,321,889	93,867	0	15,979	4,402
Idaho.........................	152,253	109,171	0	1,509,403	931,489	508,485	60,000	8,138	1,292
Illinois.......................	294,229	743,594	0	9,341,948	5,290,450	3,942,722	21,000	77,571	10,205
Indiana.......................	370,093	181,297	0	4,892,213	2,831,007	2,028,611	0	28,083	4,512
Iowa	411,344	120,182	0	6,202,929	1,023,505	5,155,925	0	22,923	576
Kansas	187,966	112,901	0	3,090,385	1,016,179	2,034,337	10,782	18,523	10,564
Kentucky	431,834	152,040	0	2,445,375	1,987,898	436,858	0	18,352	2,267
Louisiana	290,907	81,647	0	52,929,954	52,451,732	410,144	20,060	22,126	25,891
Maine	75,808	172,607	0	1,119,854	1,055,671	54,031	0	9,994	158
Maryland	116,609	252,847	0	7,916,989	7,674,812	193,648	0	39,706	8,822
Massachusetts.............	37,701	517,041	0	7,101,746	6,996,266	46,969	7,200	50,114	1,197
Michigan.....................	468,728	361,643	0	4,066,748	3,113,725	898,124	0	50,882	4,017
Minnesota	613,295	408,788	0	4,828,383	1,138,473	3,649,111	0	38,287	2,511
Mississippi	217,723	104,301	0	5,553,703	5,049,874	484,623	360	13,323	5,523
Missouri	415,741	319,365	0	3,648,889	2,569,241	1,033,362	0	35,670	10,615
Montana	185,725	56,602	0	1,004,603	402,277	579,038	0	7,541	15,746
Nebraska.....................	212,682	81,097	0	4,632,969	1,461,707	3,155,584	0	13,814	1,864
Nevada	12,859	164,475	0	3,061,166	3,029,637	16,456	0	12,997	2,077
New Hampshire..........	29,885	117,003	0	747,841	727,970	10,069	0	9,802	0
New Jersey..................	16,492	571,238	1	32,225,292	32,078,618	71,795	2,519	64,600	7,760
New Mexico	65,173	62,331	0	1,469,257	1,372,734	80,476	0	14,018	2,029
New York	128,950	1,625,348	888,300	17,643,128	16,979,068	239,994	300,404	122,526	1,136
North Carolina............	346,478	256,555	47,700	19,903,402	18,749,168	1,092,552	0	47,476	14,207
North Dakota..............	239,828	61,085	0	2,975,191	681,253	2,283,923	0	4,765	5,250
Ohio	395,058	578,158	83,700	5,291,116	3,828,680	1,374,919	0	69,281	18,237
Oklahoma	369,265	134,690	3,800	1,924,022	1,469,526	430,329	270	20,843	3,054
Oregon	115,161	213,153	0	4,902,181	4,291,181	584,585	0	23,794	2,621
Pennsylvania	228,883	519,306	13,750	8,079,382	7,617,076	282,162	76,225	96,822	7,097
Rhode Island	980	69,807	0	2,017,662	2,008,537	1,297	0	7,828	0
South Carolina	245,969	100,766	0	28,273,688	27,907,290	314,404	19,098	25,839	7,057
South Dakota..............	225,145	44,889	0	2,254,999	352,630	1,894,950	0	5,999	1,420
Tennessee	227,776	158,930	0	3,084,921	2,378,758	670,947	0	27,895	7,321
Texas	965,718	1,518,620	325,000	84,451,335	81,791,204	2,178,582	355,514	106,955	19,079
Utah	240,539	315,012	0	469,977	426,211	18,938	1,126	11,642	12,060
Vermont	47,274	77,956	5,460	386,375	365,110	16,903	0	4,362	0
Virginia	155,103	330,189	100,685	14,015,983	13,588,841	339,890	14,951	54,650	17,651
Washington.................	140,318	396,382	0	5,388,072	4,474,312	860,955	1,180	41,151	10,474
West Virginia..............	80,058	28,578	0	1,740,278	1,714,766	14,539	0	10,265	707
Wisconsin...................	667,265	304,821	0	2,391,069	1,473,095	867,623	0	39,818	10,533
Wyoming.....................	71,611	34,517	0	365,558	292,967	66,869	0	3,536	2,187
District of Columbia...	0	176,650	67,497	141,558	114,336	0	19,780	3,444	3,999
American Samoa.......	0	38	0	868	868	0	0	0	0
Fed. States of Micronesia	0	0	0	0	0	0	0	0	0
Guam	15,204	7,043	0	31,807	31,807	0	0	0	0
Marshall Islands.........	0	0	0	0	0	0	0	0	0
No. Mariana Islands...	63	710	0	73	73	0	0	0	0
Palau	35,000	0	0	0	0	0	0	0	0
Puerto Rico.................	83,856	116,641	0	4,135,383	4,131,212	0	0	4,171	0
Virgin Islands.............	4,062	2,864	0	289,231	283,816	0	0	426	4,989
Undistributed	0	0	0	210	210	0	0	0	0

Source: U.S. Department of Commerce, Bureau of the Census, Consolidated Federal Funds Report for Fiscal Year 2004, February 2006.

Note: Amounts represent dollar volume of direct loans made during the fiscal year.

Table 2.14
PER CAPITA AMOUNTS OF FEDERAL GOVERNMENT EXPENDITURE, BY MAJOR OBJECT CATEGORY, BY STATE AND OUTLYING AREA: FISCAL YEAR 2004
(In dollars)

State and outlying area	United States resident population— July 1, 2004 (a)	Total	Retirement and disability	Other direct payments	Grants	Procurement	Salaries and wages
United States	293,655,404	$7,222	$2,250	$1,588	$1,545	$1,089	$750
Alabama	4,530,182	8,619	2,854	1,770	1,547	1,678	771
Alaska...................................	655,435	12,885	1,732	1,015	4,908	2,593	2,637
Arizona.................................	5,743,834	7,309	2,253	1,265	1,456	1,706	628
Arkansas...............................	2,752,629	7,080	2,690	1,833	1,701	308	548
California	35,893,799	6,474	1,785	1,435	1,519	1,121	614
Colorado	4,601,403	6,533	1,938	1,151	1,226	1,249	969
Connecticut	3,503,604	8,649	2,229	1,663	1,586	2,714	457
Delaware	830,364	6,326	2,512	1,406	1,495	319	595
Florida	17,397,161	7,009	2,762	1,864	1,127	658	597
Georgia	8,829,383	6,247	2,010	1,304	1,332	658	943
Hawaii...................................	1,262,840	9,651	2,536	1,272	1,709	1,636	2,497
Idaho.....................................	1,393,262	6,437	2,191	1,184	1,432	986	644
Illinois...................................	12,713,634	6,043	2,013	1,660	1,300	518	551
Indiana..................................	6,237,569	6,079	2,248	1,604	1,192	642	394
Iowa......................................	2,954,451	6,505	2,360	1,814	1,367	541	423
Kansas	2,735,502	6,993	2,344	1,755	1,268	819	807
Kentucky	4,145,922	7,649	2,552	1,573	1,626	1,118	779
Louisiana	4,515,770	7,298	2,210	1,982	1,724	757	624
Maine	1,317,253	8,248	2,723	1,406	2,094	1,299	727
Maryland	5,558,058	11,645	2,553	1,866	1,590	3,743	1,893
Massachusetts........................	6,416,505	8,279	2,211	1,928	2,163	1,422	554
Michigan	10,112,620	5,981	2,266	1,643	1,308	407	357
Minnesota	5,100,958	5,644	1,972	1,351	1,413	457	451
Mississippi	2,902,966	7,695	2,513	1,790	1,853	817	721
Missouri	5,754,618	7,947	2,445	1,893	1,518	1,389	702
Montana	926,865	8,085	2,583	1,758	2,155	633	956
Nebraska................................	1,747,214	6,751	2,329	1,831	1,449	399	743
Nevada...................................	2,334,771	5,469	2,206	1,007	994	685	577
New Hampshire.......................	1,299,500	6,124	2,330	1,086	1,446	758	503
New Jersey..............................	8,698,879	6,353	2,175	1,673	1,303	705	498
New Mexico	1,903,289	10,437	2,459	1,301	2,450	3,138	1,089
New York	19,227,088	7,484	2,143	1,806	2,601	462	472
North Carolina	8,541,221	6,467	2,357	1,334	1,472	460	843
North Dakota..........................	634,366	9,513	2,329	2,763	2,389	792	1,240
Ohio......................................	11,459,011	6,388	2,291	1,564	1,441	605	487
Oklahoma	3,523,553	7,562	2,602	1,685	1,496	796	983
Oregon	3,594,586	6,084	2,351	1,404	1,442	357	529
Pennsylvania	12,406,292	7,649	2,672	2,089	1,605	751	533
Rhode Island	1,080,632	7,630	2,431	1,760	2,155	517	767
South Carolina	4,198,068	7,158	2,575	1,369	1,464	999	752
South Dakota..........................	770,883	8,564	2,389	2,513	2,102	568	992
Tennessee	5,900,962	7,701	2,460	1,604	1,671	1,376	589
Texas	22,490,022	6,308	1,857	1,362	1,236	1,199	653
Utah	2,389,039	5,728	1,726	903	1,234	964	900
Vermont	621,394	7,456	2,280	1,363	2,291	870	652
Virginia..................................	7,459,827	12,150	2,813	1,340	1,071	4,735	2,191
Washington............................	6,203,788	7,228	2,333	1,335	1,464	1,120	976
West Virginia..........................	1,815,354	8,364	3,214	1,790	2,038	573	748
Wisconsin	5,509,026	5,728	2,190	1,356	1,358	479	344
Wyoming................................	506,529	8,673	2,354	1,266	3,229	795	1,029
District of Columbia	553,523	67,982	3,401	4,823	7,597	24,112	28,049
American Samoa.....................	57,844	4,528	760	243	3,078	287	159
Fed. States of Micronesia......	108,143	954	4	80	868	1	0
Guam	163,593	7,637	1,351	520	1,642	2,168	1,956
Marshall Islands.....................	56,429	3,860	21	40	999	2,800	0
No. Mariana Islands	76,129	2,801	316	238	2,051	113	82
Palau	19,717	2,567	23	140	2,404	0	0
Puerto Rico............................	3,878,532	3,991	1,461	773	1,373	119	265
Virgin Islands.........................	108,814	5,438	1,425	790	2,420	195	608

Source: U.S. Department of Commerce, Bureau of the Census, Consolidated Federal Funds Report for Fiscal Year 2004, February 2006.
Note: U.S. total population and per capita figures in the top row include only the 50 states and the District of Columbia; the U.S. Outlying Areas represented at the bottom of the table are excluded from this figure.
(a) All population figures represent resident population as of July 1, 2004.

Table 2.15
PERCENT DISTRIBUTION OF FEDERAL GOVERNMENT EXPENDITURE, BY MAJOR OBJECT CATEGORY, BY STATE AND OUTLYING AREA: FISCAL YEAR 2004
(In dollars)

State and outlying area	Percent distribution of United States resident population— July 1, 2004 (a)	Total	Retirement and disability	Other direct payments	Grants	Procurement	Salaries and wages
United States	100%	100%	100%	100%	100%	100%	100%
Alabama	1.5	1.8	1.9	1.7	1.5	2.2	1.5
Alaska	0.2	0.4	0.2	0.1	0.7	0.5	0.8
Arizona.............................	2.0	1.9	1.9	1.5	1.8	2.9	1.6
Arkansas...........................	0.9	0.9	1.1	1.1	1.0	0.2	0.7
California	12.2	10.7	9.6	11.0	11.9	11.9	9.8
Colorado...........................	1.6	1.4	1.3	1.1	1.2	1.7	2.0
Connecticut	1.2	1.4	1.2	1.2	1.2	2.8	0.7
Delaware...........................	0.3	0.2	0.3	0.2	0.3	0.1	0.2
Florida..............................	5.9	5.6	7.2	6.9	4.3	3.4	4.6
Georgia	3.0	2.6	2.7	2.5	2.6	1.7	3.7
Hawaii..............................	0.4	0.6	0.5	0.3	0.5	0.6	1.4
Idaho................................	0.5	0.4	0.5	0.4	0.4	0.4	0.4
Illinois..............................	4.3	3.6	3.8	4.5	3.6	1.9	3.1
Indiana.............................	2.1	1.8	2.1	2.1	1.6	1.2	1.1
Iowa.................................	1.0	0.9	1.1	1.1	0.9	0.5	0.6
Kansas	0.9	0.9	1.0	1.0	0.8	0.7	1.0
Kentucky	1.4	1.5	1.6	1.4	1.5	1.4	1.4
Louisiana	1.5	1.5	1.5	1.9	1.7	1.0	1.2
Maine...............................	0.4	0.5	0.5	0.4	0.6	0.5	0.4
Maryland...........................	1.9	3.0	2.1	2.2	1.9	6.1	4.7
Massachusetts....................	2.2	2.5	2.1	2.6	3.0	2.7	1.6
Michigan...........................	3.4	2.8	3.4	3.5	2.9	1.2	1.6
Minnesota	1.7	1.3	1.5	1.5	1.6	0.7	1.0
Mississippi	1.0	1.0	1.1	1.1	1.2	0.7	0.9
Missouri............................	2.0	2.1	2.1	2.3	1.9	2.4	1.8
Montana	0.3	0.3	0.4	0.3	0.4	0.2	0.4
Nebraska...........................	0.6	0.5	0.6	0.7	0.6	0.2	0.6
Nevada.............................	0.8	0.6	0.8	0.5	0.5	0.5	0.6
New Hampshire..................	0.4	0.4	0.5	0.3	0.4	0.3	0.3
New Jersey........................	3.0	2.6	2.8	3.1	2.5	1.8	1.9
New Mexico	0.6	0.9	0.7	0.5	1.0	1.8	0.9
New York	6.5	6.7	6.2	7.4	10.9	2.6	4.0
North Carolina...................	2.9	2.6	3.0	2.4	2.7	1.2	3.2
North Dakota.....................	0.2	0.3	0.2	0.4	0.3	0.1	0.3
Ohio	3.9	3.4	3.9	3.8	3.6	2.0	2.5
Oklahoma	1.2	1.2	1.4	1.3	1.1	0.8	1.5
Oregon	1.2	1.0	1.3	1.1	1.1	0.4	0.8
Pennsylvania	4.2	4.4	5.0	5.5	4.3	2.7	2.9
Rhode Island	0.4	0.4	0.4	0.4	0.5	0.2	0.4
South Carolina	1.4	1.4	1.6	1.2	1.3	1.2	1.4
South Dakota.....................	0.3	0.3	0.3	0.4	0.4	0.1	0.3
Tennessee	2.0	2.1	2.2	2.0	2.1	2.4	1.5
Texas	7.7	6.6	6.3	6.5	6.0	7.9	6.5
Utah	0.8	0.6	0.6	0.5	0.6	0.7	1.0
Vermont............................	0.2	0.2	0.2	0.2	0.3	0.2	0.2
Virginia.............................	2.5	4.2	3.1	2.1	1.7	10.4	7.2
Washington........................	2.1	2.1	2.2	1.8	2.0	2.0	2.7
West Virginia......................	0.6	0.7	0.9	0.7	0.8	0.3	0.6
Wisconsin..........................	1.9	1.5	1.8	1.6	1.6	0.8	0.8
Wyoming...........................	0.2	0.2	0.2	0.1	0.4	0.1	0.2
District of Columbia	0.2	1.7	0.3	0.6	0.9	3.9	6.9
American Samoa...............	0.0	0.0	0.0	0.0	0.0	0.0	0.0
Fed. States of Micronesia...	0.0	0.0	0.0	0.0	0.0	2.6	0.0
Guam	0.1	0.1	0.0	0.0	0.1	0.1	0.1
Marshall Islands................	0.0	0.0	0.0	0.0	0.0	0.1	0.0
No. Mariana Islands	0.0	0.0	0.0	0.0	0.0	0.0	0.0
Palau	0.0	0.0	0.0	0.0	0.0	0.0	0.0
Puerto Rico.......................	1.3	0.7	0.8	0.6	1.2	0.1	0.5
Virgin Islands....................	0.0	0.0	0.0	0.0	0.1	0.0	0.0
Undistributed	0.0	1.1	0.0	0.0	0.0	5.5	1.8

Source: U.S. Department of Commerce, Bureau of the Census, Consolidated Federal Funds Report for Fiscal Year 2004, February 2006.
Note: Values for the 50 states, the District of Columbia, and the U.S. Outlying Areas were used in calculating these distributions.

(a) All population figures represent resident population as of July 1, 2004.

Table 2.16
FEDERAL GOVERNMENT EXPENDITURE FOR DEFENSE DEPARTMENT AND ALL OTHER AGENCIES, BY STATE AND OUTLYING AREA: FISCAL YEAR 2004

State and outlying area	Federal expenditure (millions of dollars) Department of Defense	All other federal agencies	Per capita federal expenditure (dollars) (a) Department of Defense	All other federal agencies	Percent distribution of federal expenditure Department of Defense	All other federal agencies
United States	347,689	1,814,259	1,147.75	6,074.00	100%	100%
Alabama	8,725	30,323	1,925.95	6,693.45	2.5	1.7
Alaska	2,522	5,924	3,847.17	9,037.99	0.7	0.3
Arizona	11,135	30,844	1,938.63	5,369.96	3.2	1.7
Arkansas	1,596	17,893	579.67	6,500.41	0.5	1
California	42,723	189,664	1,190.27	5,284.03	12.3	10.5
Colorado	6,182	23,878	1,343.48	5,189.38	1.8	1.3
Connecticut	9,735	20,569	2,778.47	5,870.91	2.8	1.1
Delaware	629	4,624	758	5,568.32	0.2	0.3
Florida	17,419	104,514	1,001.26	6,007.56	5	5.8
Georgia	10,175	44,978	1,152.39	5,094.13	2.9	2.5
Hawaii	4,772	7,415	3,778.83	5,871.69	1.4	0.4
Idaho	744	8,225	533.75	5,903.09	0.2	0.5
Illinois	5,918	70,910	465.51	5,577.48	1.7	3.9
Indiana	4,465	33,453	715.83	5,363.22	1.3	1.8
Iowa	1,262	17,956	427.01	6,077.71	0.4	1
Kansas	2,948	16,183	1,077.66	5,915.82	0.8	0.9
Kentucky	5,132	26,582	1,237.78	6,411.55	1.5	1.5
Louisiana	4,433	28,521	981.61	6,315.94	1.3	1.6
Maine	2,297	8,568	1,743.58	6,504.30	0.7	0.5
Maryland	13,796	50,930	2,482.16	9,163.26	4	2.8
Massachusetts	8,240	44,881	1,284.15	6,994.57	2.4	2.5
Michigan	3,783	56,706	374.06	5,607.43	1.1	3.1
Minnesota	2,112	26,679	414.02	5,230.16	0.6	1.5
Mississippi	3,624	18,713	1,248.53	6,446.26	1	1
Missouri	8,585	37,145	1,491.80	6,454.88	2.5	2
Montana	658	6,836	709.69	7,375.16	0.2	0.4
Nebraska	1,321	10,474	755.83	5,994.82	0.4	0.6
Nevada	1,612	11,158	690.31	4,778.92	0.5	0.6
New Hampshire	1,125	6,833	865.84	5,258.45	0.3	0.4
New Jersey	5,843	49,421	671.69	5,681.36	1.7	2.7
New Mexico	2,471	17,393	1,298.09	9,138.56	0.7	1
New York	7,555	136,348	392.93	7,091.44	2.2	7.5
North Carolina	8,679	46,554	1,016.17	5,450.52	2.5	2.6
North Dakota	833	5,202	1,312.35	8,200.77	0.2	0.3
Ohio	7,539	65,656	657.9	5,729.67	2.2	3.6
Oklahoma	4,279	22,365	1,214.29	6,347.37	1.2	1.2
Oregon	1,311	20,560	364.71	5,719.69	0.4	1.1
Pennsylvania	9,037	85,864	728.39	6,920.98	2.6	4.7
Rhode Island	1,022	7,223	945.81	6,684.18	0.3	0.4
South Carolina	4,881	25,170	1,162.75	5,995.58	1.4	1.4
South Dakota	658	5,944	853.24	7,710.62	0.2	0.3
Tennessee	3,770	41,670	638.92	7,061.61	1.1	2.3
Texas	31,895	109,963	1,418.19	4,889.43	9.2	6.1
Utah	3,305	10,378	1,383.53	4,344.14	1	0.6
Vermont	623	4,010	1,002.56	6,453.15	0.2	0.2
Virginia	38,533	52,105	5,165.39	6,984.75	11.1	2.9
Washington	8,321	36,520	1,341.21	5,886.77	2.4	2
West Virginia	734	14,449	404.35	7,959.58	0.2	0.8
Wisconsin	2,414	29,140	438.23	5,289.44	0.7	1.6
Wyoming	412	3,981	813.9	7,859.46	0.1	0.2
District of Columbia	5,264	32,366	9,509.21	58,472.89	1.5	1.8
American Samoa	10	252	177.37	4,350.91	0	0
Fed. States of Micronesia	0	103	0	953.91	0	0
Guam	660	590	4,032.43	3,605.00	0.2	0
Marshall Islands	158	60	2,800.23	1,059.64	0	0
No. Mariana Islands	5	208	67.92	2,732.69	0	0
Palau	0	51	0	2,566.87	0	0
Puerto Rico	732	14,746	188.78	3,802.05	0.2	0.8
Virgin Islands	26	565	241.53	5,196.61	0	0
Undistributed	9,055	14,020	0	0	2.6	0.8

Source: U.S. Department of Commerce, Bureau of the Census, Consolidated Federal Funds Report for Fiscal Year 2004, February 2006.

(a) All population figures represent resident population as of July 1, 2004.

Table 2.17
STATE RANKINGS FOR PER CAPITA AMOUNTS OF FEDERAL GOVERNMENT EXPENDITURE: FISCAL YEAR 2004

State	Total	Retirement and disability	Other direct payments	Grants	Procurement	Salaries and wages
Alabama	9	2	15	22	7	18
Alaska	1	49	48	1	5	1
Arizona	24	33	44	30	6	29
Arkansas	28	6	9	16	50	38
California	34	48	28	23	15	31
Colorado	32	46	46	46	13	11
Connecticut	8	35	21	21	4	45
Delaware	39	15	29	26	49	33
Florida	29	4	8	48	33	32
Georgia	41	44	40	39	32	13
Hawaii	5	13	42	15	8	2
Idaho	36	39	45	35	19	28
Illinois	45	43	22	42	40	37
Indiana	44	34	25	47	34	48
Iowa	33	21	11	37	39	47
Kansas	30	25	18	43	22	16
Kentucky	19	12	26	18	17	17
Louisiana	25	37	4	14	28	30
Maine	13	5	30	11	12	23
Maryland	3	11	7	20	2	4
Massachusetts	12	36	5	7	9	36
Michigan	46	32	23	40	46	49
Minnesota	49	45	36	36	45	46
Mississippi	17	14	13	13	23	24
Missouri	15	18	6	24	10	25
Montana	14	9	17	9	35	12
Nebraska	31	28	10	31	47	22
Nevada	50	38	49	50	31	35
New Hampshire	42	27	47	32	27	41
New Jersey	38	41	20	41	30	42
New Mexico	4	17	41	4	3	6
New York	22	42	12	3	43	44
North Carolina	35	22	39	27	44	15
North Dakota	6	29	1	5	26	5
Ohio	37	30	27	34	36	43
Oklahoma	21	8	19	25	24	9
Oregon	43	24	31	33	48	40
Pennsylvania	18	7	3	19	29	39
Rhode Island	20	19	16	8	41	19
South Carolina	27	10	32	29	18	20
South Dakota	10	20	2	10	38	8
Tennessee	16	16	24	17	11	34
Texas	40	47	34	44	14	26
Utah	48	50	50	45	20	14
Vermont	23	31	33	6	21	27
Virginia	2	3	37	49	1	3
Washington	26	26	38	28	16	10
West Virginia	11	1	14	12	37	21
Wisconsin	47	40	35	38	42	50
Wyoming	7	23	43	2	25	7

Source: U.S. Department of Commerce, Bureau of the Census, Consolidated Federal Funds Report for Fiscal Year 2004, February 2006.
Note: States are ranked from largest per capita amount of federal funds (1) to smallest per capita amount of federal funds (50). Rankings are based upon per capita amounts shown in Table 2.10. Federal funds for loans and insurance coverage are excluded from consideration in this table. Also excluded are per capita amounts from the District of Columbia and the U.S. Outlying Areas.

Chapter Three

STATE LEGISLATIVE BRANCH

" *By almost every measure, the Democrats fared well in the 2006 election, achieving gains in both total seats and overall control of legislatures.* "

—Tim Storey

" *Term limits, at least for the present time, are here to stay and legislatures are making the best of them.* "

—Thomas H. Little, Jennifer Drage Bowser and Keon S. Chi

2006 Legislative Elections

By Tim Storey

In the November 2006 election, voters gave Democrats their biggest legislative victory in more than a decade, awarding them with a sizable majority of all legislative seats. Democrats now control more state legislatures (22) than they have since the 1994 Republican landslide marked the beginning of a 12-year stretch of political parity between the two parties in state legislatures.

After nearly three decades of watching their numerical dominance in state legislatures slip away, Democrats have now had two consecutive election cycles go their way. On the heels of nominal gains in 2004, Democrats scored a big win in 2006 and now enjoy the biggest majority of seats in the nation's legislatures than either party has held since 1994. That was when the GOP walloped Democrats and ushered in more than 10 years of remarkable political parity in legislatures.

By almost every measure, the Democrats fared well in the 2006 election, achieving gains in both total seats and overall control of legislatures. They seized control of 10 legislative chambers and lost only the Oklahoma Senate where Republicans managed a 24-24 tie prompting a bipartisan, power-sharing arrangement. The GOP gained control of one chamber, the Montana House, which was tied 50-50 headed into the election. And in a post-election development in early 2007, Republicans achieved numerical control of the Mississippi Senate when two Democratic senators switched party affiliation to the GOP. Another party switch by a Tennessee senator from Republican to independent took that chamber from the Republican control column and left it knotted at 16-16-1. All other party control shifts moved from the Republican column to the Democrats.

When the dust settled following numerous recounts to determine winners in an abundance of narrow contests, Democrats liked the look of the big picture. In 2007, Democrats control 22 state legislatures; Republicans have 15, and in 12 states, control is divided with neither party holding both chambers. The unicameral Nebraska Legislature is nonpartisan.

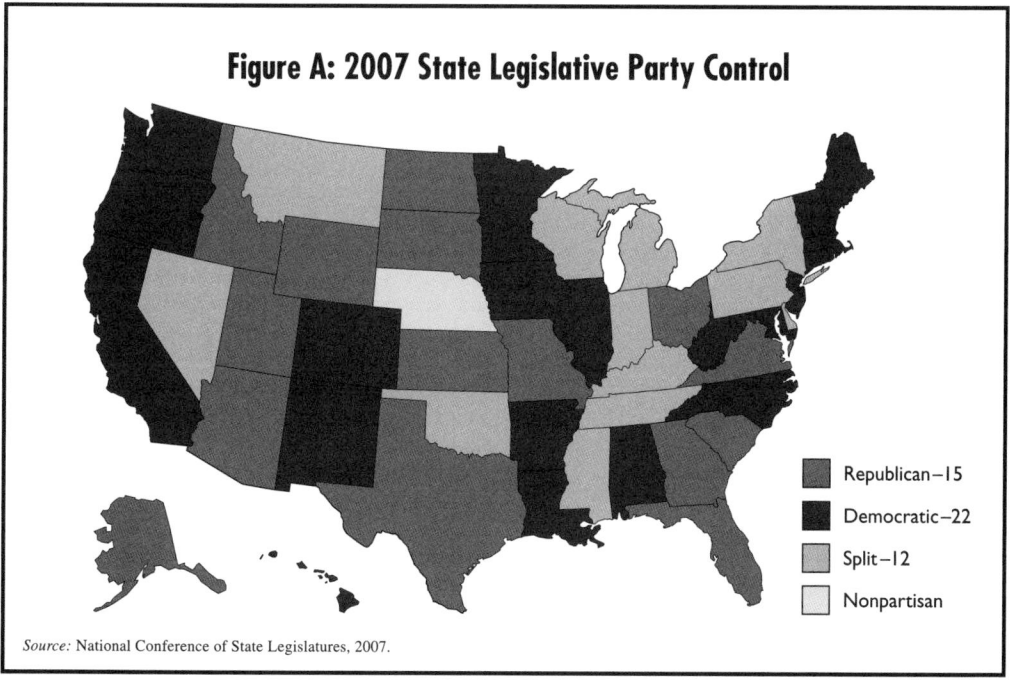

Figure A: 2007 State Legislative Party Control

Republican–15
Democratic–22
Split–12
Nonpartisan

Source: National Conference of State Legislatures, 2007.

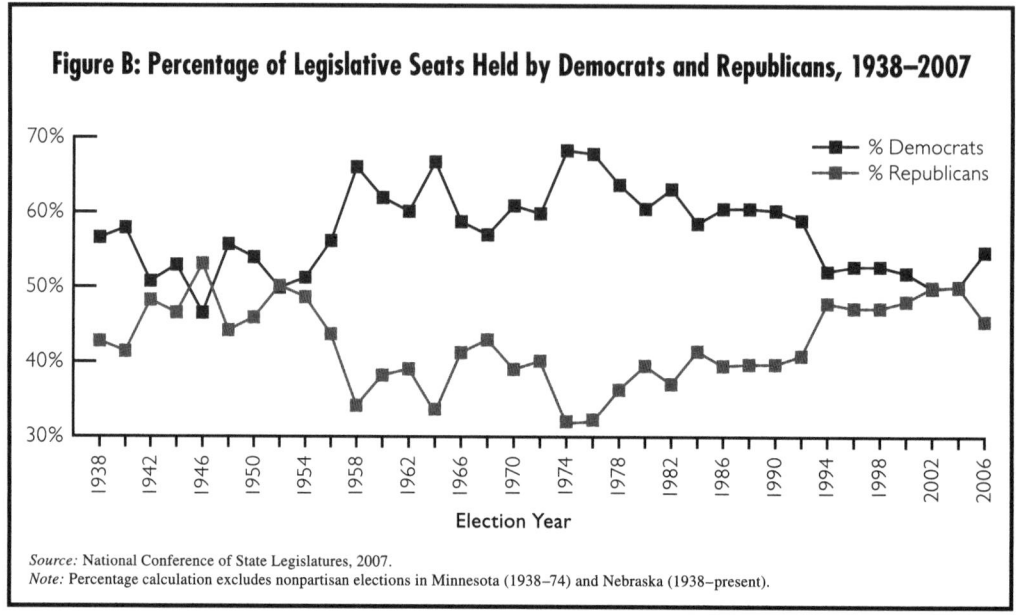

Figure B: Percentage of Legislative Seats Held by Democrats and Republicans, 1938–2007

Election Year

Source: National Conference of State Legislatures, 2007.
Note: Percentage calculation excludes nonpartisan elections in Minnesota (1938–74) and Nebraska (1938–present).

Those numbers reflect a pick-up of three states for Democrats who controlled 19 states before the election. Pre-election control stood at 20 Republican, 19 Democratic and 10 split.

Broken down by chamber, Democrats picked up 10 legislative bodies where the majority shifted. Republicans gained one—the Montana House that was tied heading into election night. Two legislative bodies are now tied after being in Democratic control before the election. The final count after early 2007 party affiliation switches by three legislators changed control in the Mississippi and Tennessee senates, shows the Democrats in control in 55 chambers and Republicans in control of 41, with the Tennessee and Oklahoma senates tied. It seems almost inevitable that at least a couple of legislative chambers will be numerically even between the two parties; prior to the 1984 election was the last time there was not a tied legislative chamber in the United States.

The scope of success for Democratic legislative candidates in 2006 might best be captured in one statistic. Republicans netted additional seats in only nine of the 87 chambers where seats were up for election. Democrats picked up seats in 58 chambers. That included the New Hampshire House where Democrats added a whopping 92 seats to their ranks to win control of that chamber for the first time since the 1800s. In the end, Democrats netted slightly more than 350 seats. For more than a decade, the two parties were locked in almost complete parity at the state legislative level. Now Democrats control 670 more seats than Republicans or just under 55 percent of all legislative seats. That is the biggest margin for either party since before the 1994 election. Democrats got wiped out in 1994 and saw their share of all legislative seats shrink from 59 percent to 52 percent, and it has been essentially even ever since.

The fact that Democrats performed well in the 2006 election cycle was consistent with the historic trend of the president's party losing seats in nearly every single mid-term election back to at least 1942. The only exception to that trend was in 2002 when Republicans gained 188 seats with George Bush in the White House. Figure B shows the historic, mid-term trend for the party in the White House with 1958 being the worst loss when Republicans lost more than 800 state legislative seats.

During a post-election briefing to state legislators and state government relations professionals, senior CNN political analyst Bill Schneider said that he believed voters treated the 2006 election as though it were a parliamentary election—where party preference trumps candidate preference. According to Schneider, most swing voters were determined to vote against Republicans and for Democrats all the way down the ticket, contrary to the typical American election where voters choose the candidate they know, and like, best. This emphasis on party by many voters led to the most successful night for Democratic legislative candidates in 12 years.

Every state except Louisiana, Mississippi, New Jersey and Virginia held regular legislative elections in 2006. In Kansas, New Mexico and South Carolina, only the House was up for election in 2006. There were 10,728 candidates running for the 6,120 legislative seats to be filled during the general election in November 2006. Slightly more than 35 percent of the general election races were not contested by candidates from the two major political parties.

Chamber Control Shifts

Ever-changing party control is a constant in state legislatures. In every election cycle, majority control changes from one party to the other in an average of 12 legislative chambers. 2006 hit right on the average with 12 chambers entering 2007 under new majority control. Only five states have not had at least one legislative chamber switch control in more than 100 years. In those five states (Alabama, Arkansas, Louisiana, Maryland and West Virginia), Democrats have held the legislature for decades. Were it not for two Democratic senators changing party early 2007 to switch the Mississippi Senate from Democratic to Republican, the Magnolia state would also be on that list.

Ten legislative chambers went from either being tied or held by the Republican party to a Democratic majority. The biggest surprise of the year had to be New Hampshire where Democrats netted a staggering 92 seats to win a solid majority in the 400-member House. Democrats, who also took the New Hampshire Senate and held the governor's office, have total control of the Granite State for the first time since the 1860s.

The results for the Oregon House also surprised some political observers when the Democrats won the House for the first time since losing it in 1990. Oregon is another state where Democrats now control all three levels of state policymaking—the house, senate and governor's office.

The most success for Democrats was in the Midwest. Democrats regained control of both chambers in Iowa, which was almost exactly even prior to the election. The Senate was tied, and Republicans held a narrow two-seat margin in the House. In the Indiana House, a chamber that has shifted party control in seven of the last ten elections, Democrats once again managed to score a majority albeit a narrow 51-49 advantage.

States on the Great Lakes proved fertile ground for the Dems. In Minnesota, Democrats gained 19 House seats to vault into control. Democrats won the Michigan House as well, taking control for the first time since 1998. They also picked up the Wisconsin Senate by an 18-15 margin. Pennsylvania added another surprise when the Democrats claimed a one-seat majority in the House, 102-101, after a protracted legal battle and a series of recounts awarded a contested seat to the Democrats just four days before Christmas—nearly six weeks after the election. The Democratic candidate finally won the pivotal seat by fewer than 30 votes.

There were a couple of bright spots for Republicans in the election returns. The Montana House was tied at 50-50 before the election, but one Democratic

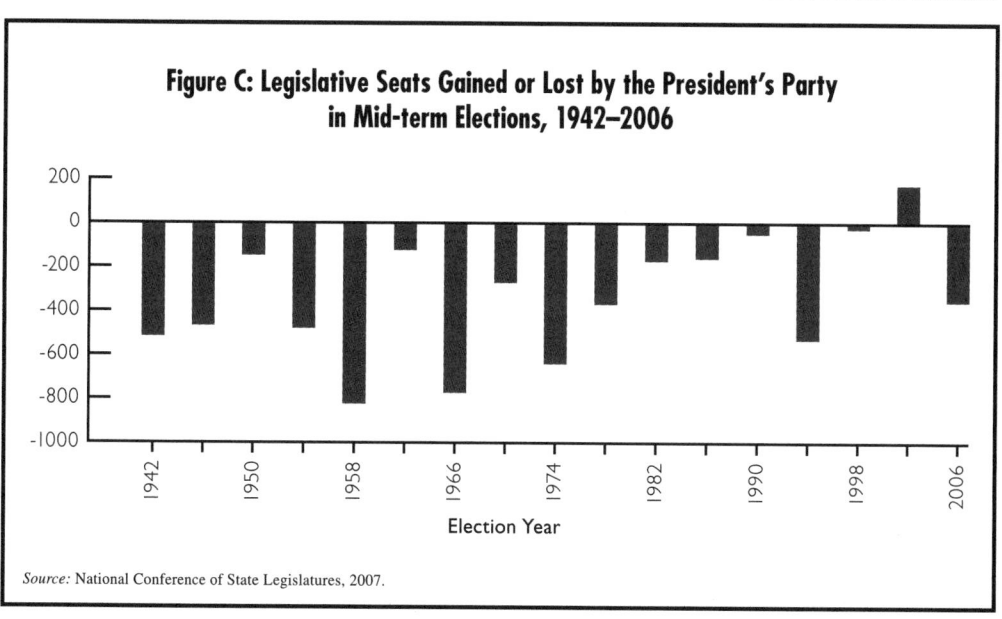

Figure C: Legislative Seats Gained or Lost by the President's Party in Mid-term Elections, 1942–2006

Election Year

Source: National Conference of State Legislatures, 2007.

incumbent lost to a member of the Constitution party, effectively giving the GOP a majority of 50-49-1 because the third party legislator, a former Republican, voted to organize the chamber along with the GOP legislators. The Montana representative is the only member of the Constitution Party in a state legislature. Of the 7,382 state legislative seats, only 18 are held by legislators from third parties or who are

Table A: Seat Changes by Region from 2004 to 2006

Region	Seat changes
East.....................	+148 Democrats
South	+24 Democrats
Midwest..............	+107 Democrats
West....................	+72 Democrats

Source: National Conference of State Legislatures, 2007.

independents. Eight of those third party legislators are Progressives in the Vermont House. In addition, the 49 senators in Nebraska do not run under a party banner, so the two major parties control 7,315 of all legislative seats—more than 99 percent.

Another victory for the GOP was in Oklahoma where Democrats lost majority control of the Senate in part due to the disparate, and negative, impact of term limits on incumbent Democratic members. The Oklahoma Senate is now tied 24-24.

Regional Reversal

Despite Republican gains in Oklahoma, Democrats actually realized a net gain in legislative seats in southern states for the first time since 1982. For well over two decades, Democrats have watched their dominance of southern legislatures slip away. In 1960, Democrats controlled 94 percent of all southern legislative seats, a figure that has fallen to 53 percent today even with slight gains in 2006. Prior to the 1992 election, Democrats controlled all 30 legislative chambers in the South, but they now hold less than half of those chambers.

Democrats gained seats in every region of the country in 2006 punctuated by a particularly strong showing in the East and Northeast. With the addition of both chambers in New Hampshire, Democrats control all legislative chambers in New England for the first time in more than 100 years. New England is also home to the most Democratic legislature in the country—the Massachusetts General Court. More than 88 percent of Massachusetts legislators are Democrats.

The strongest region for Republicans remains the Midwest, where they control 52 percent of all legislative seats. However, the most Republican legislature in the country is in the West. In Idaho, 75 percent of all legislative seats are held by the GOP.

Figure C shows the number of seats Democrats netted in each region in the 2006 election cycle. Four states—Louisiana, Mississippi, New Jersey and Virginia—conduct regular legislative elections in odd-numbered years. Seat changes in those states from 2005 elections are included in Table A.

Many Close Calls

Analysts have noted that despite the shift toward Democrats in 2006, the story would have been very different had Republicans gained only a small percentage of the overall vote in many close contests. An unusually high number of legislative races in 2006 were determined by narrow margins. For example, one Oklahoma House race was decided by only two votes, with the Republican earning 4,798 votes to beat his Democratic rival who garnered 4,796 votes. Montana House District 58 was tied after the initial vote tally, and a recount gave the GOP standard bearer a three-vote victory in the seat that determined control of the Montana House.

In this election, there were 77 legislative seats where the margin of victory was less than 100 votes. At least one seat in 25 different states fell into that "nail biter" category. In Maine, 16 House seats were decided by less than 100 votes.

Turnover and Term Limits

Maine was one of 13 states where legislative term limits prevented 266 incumbent legislators from seeking re-election in 2006. Nebraska was hardest hit by term limits because the law took effect for the first time in the 2006 election. Of the 49 Nebraska Senate seats, 24 were scheduled for election in 2006, and in 20 of those, the incumbent was termed out. So even before election day, turnover in the Nebraska Unicameral Legislature was 40 percent.

Overall, slightly more than 17 percent of all seats in states with 2006 elections were filled by new legislators for 2007 sessions. That election turnover was down slightly from 2004 when turnover was 19.2 percent. States with term limits for state legislators led the list of states with the highest turnover. Nine of the 10 states with the highest House turnover were term limits states. The New Hampshire House was the only chamber in the top 10 that was not fueled by term limits. The New Hampshire House turnover was 36 percent and ranked second only to the California Assembly, where term limits led to more than 43 percent turnover.

Term limits will take effect in Louisiana in 2007 when the Bayou State holds its regular elections. That will leave Nevada as the only state with term limits on the books where it has not taken effect. Nevada term limits take effect in 2010 elections.

Perhaps the most dramatic turnover resulting from the 2006 election was among legislative leaders. Nearly half, or 148, of the 311 top leaders in state legislatures are new to their posts in 2007. Turnover among legislative leaders is fairly common, but this year was particularly high. In any given 10-year period, more than 90 percent of legislative leaders typically change.

Conclusion

In some ways, 2006 was an average election year in state legislatures. The number of chambers switching was right on the average, and turnover was just about average. The number of seats lost by the party of the president was also about average. However, Democrats thought this election was anything but average, and their newfound strength in legislatures reflects their best position in years.

Campaign spending once again seemed extraordinary in 2006 with combined spending in many individual races topping $1 million in numerous states. That trend is likely to increase now that redistricting looms on the horizon. Aside from the fact that legislators are tackling the most difficult issues of the day including health care and immigration at a time when Washington remains gridlocked, control of legislatures becomes even more critical in the next election as they prepare for the decennial task of redistricting following the 2010 census.

About the Author

Tim Storey is a senior fellow in the Legislative Management Program of the Denver, Colo., based National Conference of State Legislatures. He specializes in the areas of elections and redistricting as well as legislative organization and management. He has staffed NCSL's Redistricting and Elections Committee since 1990 and authored numerous articles on the topics of elections and redistricting. Every two years, he leads NCSL's StateVote project to track and analyze legislative election results. He graduated from Mars Hill College in North Carolina and received his master's degree from the University of Colorado's Graduate School of Public Affairs.

Term Limits: Legislatures' Adaptation
By Thomas H. Little, Jennie Drage Bowser and Keon S. Chi

As the 2007 legislative sessions begin, term limits are in place in 15 states and fully affecting membership in 13. A recent study, "Coping with Term Limits," suggests that state legislatures are making adjustments to respond to the challenges created by term limits and that these legislatures are continuing to effectively make laws, implement budgets, represent constituents and balance the executive in spite of those challenges.

The implementation of legislative term limits can be viewed in three stages. The first stage occurred in the early and mid-1990s when a wave of term limit initiatives swept across the country. The second stage involved the period following passage when state legislators and legislatures began to experience the impact of those limits. Finally, the first part of the 21st century is defined by the third stage during which legislators respond to the consequences of term limits.

From 1990 to 2000, voters in 21 states approved legislative term limits. However, the limits in six states have either been repealed by the legislature (Idaho and Utah) or overturned by the courts (Massachusetts, Oregon, Washington and Wyoming), leaving 15 states with term limits on the books. The first term-limited class has yet to be removed in Louisiana and Nevada, leaving 13 states operating under term limits. Now that term limits have been in place for more than a decade in most states, legislators, scholars and journalists have moved beyond examining their impact to developing some strategies to deal with their impact and, perhaps, mitigate some of their negative consequences.

The Joint Project on Term Limits

The Joint Project on Term Limits (JPTL) was formed in 2000 in recognition of the fundamental effects that legislative term limits were expected to have on the politics, processes and policies of state legislatures. The JPTL is a unique coalition of organizations and academics, comprised of The National Conference of State Legislatures, The Council of State Governments, the State Legislative Leaders Foundation and a group of distinguished and knowledgeable legislative scholars from across the country.

JPTL's goal was twofold. First, it sought to identify the key effects that legislative term limits had on state legislatures where they were implemented. Second, the team was expected to recommend effective ways for legislatures and their leaders to respond to the effects of these term limits. While we will speak briefly of the effects of term limits here, our focus will be on the techniques that legislative leaders and legislators have developed in response to those effects.

Term Limits Challenges and Legislative Responses

While most legislators, especially those in leadership posts, may not like term limits, they remain a fact of life in 13 states (soon to be 15). State legislatures and the individuals who lead them have made significant efforts to adapt to the challenges noted above. Some of those efforts, along with the challenges they are designed to address, are discussed below.

Term Limits Challenge: High Turnover

Perhaps the most obvious impact of term limits relates to membership composition—turnover has increased and average years of service have decreased. The data in Table A indicates the extent of the changes. Interestingly, the demographic characteristics of legislators have not changed significantly under term limits, with relatively limited changes in the age, gender and ethnicity of legislators.[1] In the six states evaluated, the number of female legislators increased significantly in only one state and actually decreased in three.

Legislative Responses: Training, Mentoring and Written Rules

Legislative leaders have taken a variety of steps to minimize the negative consequences of high turnover, including improving new member orientations, offering ongoing training, sponsoring mentoring programs and compiling written copies of key rules and traditions. While all legislatures hold orientations for their new members, in term-limited states orientations have been significantly expanded, often including mock committee and floor sessions, budget process exercises and educational forums on policies. Many term-limited legislatures are even offering mini "refresher courses" during the session. Another

Table A:
Turnover in House Chambers in Select Term-Limited States

State	1981–90	1992	1994	1996	1998	2000	2002	2004	2006
Arizona	25%	48%	35%	32%	25%	45% (a)	58% (a)	33%	23%
Arkansas	14	19	31	20	57 (a)	34	32	39	27
California	16	40	41	46 (a)	35	39	43	30	41
Colorado	30	35	28	34	35 (a)	37	29	28	27
Maine	25	34	48	42 (a)	30	31	48	38	25
Ohio	17	21	21	14	20	55 (a)	29	16	34

Source: Data for 1981–2002: Gary Moncreif, Richard G. Neimi and Lynda Powell, "Time, Term Limits and Turnover." *Legislative Studies Quarterly XXIX* (August 2004): 357–81. 2004 and 2006 data from National Conference of State Legislatures.

Key:
(a) Indicates the first year of impact of legislative term limits.

approach is to establish mentoring programs where experienced members are paired with first-termers to help them "learn the ropes." Finally, given that rules and norms can no longer be maintained and passed on by the "old guard," legislative leaders are finding creative and permanent ways to make sure they are remembered. In Colorado, staff compiled a notebook of written and unwritten rules. In Missouri, the Senate minority leader recorded the chamber rules on CD and distributed them to all new members.

Term Limits Challenge: Leadership Instability

In term-limited states, the vast majority of legislative leaders serve two, or at most four, years in a single leadership post, leading to dramatic leadership turnover. No term-limited leader as of 2006 has served more than four years in one post.[2] Such inexperience would seem to put leaders at a disadvantage relative to counterparts as well as the executive, lobbyists and the media, all of whom generally have much more experience in their positions.

Legislative Responses: Leadership Ladders, Early Designation and Getting Personal

Term-limited legislatures have taken a variety of approaches to increase the stability of leadership, including establishing leadership ladders, identifying leaders early and building an early rapport between members and potential leaders. While leadership ladders (whip moves to floor leader and floor leader to speaker, for example) are common, they are rare in term-limited states. However, in the Maine House, most recent speakers served as majority leader and then moved up to speaker. This is also the case in Nevada where the impact of term limits is just now being felt. In a similar move, some term-limited states

are identifying the incoming leader very early in his or her legislative career, often in the leader's first or second term. In Arkansas, Florida and Oklahoma, speaker-designates are selected well before they take on their official duties, with a Florida sophomore already designated speaker for the 2009 legislative session. In the Michigan, Ohio and Colorado houses, leaders with just one or two legislative terms have been given the reigns of power.

Term Limits Challenge: Committee Inexperience

Traditionally, legislative committees have served in many capacities critical to the legislative process, including weeding out bad bills, improving good bills and building coalitions for bills that will go to the floor. The successful fulfillment of these functions, however, assumed a committee of people with a strong knowledge of the committee subject. However, under term limits, it is not safe to assume such knowledge exists with the committee chair, much less the members. In most term-limited states, it is inevitable that some committees will be chaired by legislators with limited legislative experience and many committees will be dominated by first-term legislators.

Legislative Responses: Training Chairs, Using Members and Developing Vice Chairs

There are several ways legislative leaders have tried to minimize the impact of term limits on their legislative committee. In a term-limited legislature, having inexperienced chairpersons is inevitable. The best one can hope for is to provide direction and guidance for them. Leaders in these states usually hold weekly (and sometimes daily) meetings with their committee chairs, especially early in the session. In Arkansas, the leader often sat beside a young

Table B:
Female Legislators in Select Term-Limited States
(percent of total members)

State	1993–94	1995–96	1997–98	1999–2000	2001–02	2003–04	2005–06	2007
Arizona	36%	30%	37%	36%	34%	27%	33%	34%
Arkansas	10	13	17	15	13	16	17	21
California	24	20	22	26	28	30	31	28
Colorado	34	31	35	34	34	33	32	34
Maine	32	26	26	28	30	27	26	31
Ohio	22	24	32	21	22	20	19	17

Source: Center for American Women and Politics.

committee chair, providing advice and support during particularly difficult sessions. Others even held practice committee sessions. The chairs aren't the only ones lacking experience; the members do too. One way to minimize the impact of inexperienced members is to take advantage of their non-legislative skills and knowledge in making committee assignments. For example, putting teachers on the education committee or bankers on the finance committee helps increase committee knowledge. Finally, while committee vice chairs have usually been honorary positions of little significance, a growing number of term-limited leaders are viewing them as training grounds for future chairs and encouraging the committee chairs to give them responsibilities and even occasionally turn the gavel over to them.

Term Limits Challenge: The Changing Role of Staff

Historically, professional, stable and nonpartisan staffs were a benchmark of an effective and autonomous legislature. They could assist the members and help the legislature hold its own with the powerful and professional executive branch. Under term limits, the role of legislative staff has changed, becoming less professional, less stable and more partisan. As new members come in, they find it difficult to trust the institutional and professional staff, turning instead to the more political partisan staff, many of whom they knew through their campaigns.

Legislative Responses: Better Training, Centralization and Building Relationships

Term-limited legislatures have taken significant steps to develop and retain high quality and professional staffs and to increase the willingness of skeptical

legislators to turn to them for information and direction. For example, staffers in the California Assembly must participate in extensive training about the budget process, the legislative process, management issues, effective scheduling and constituent casework. To take advantage of high quality professional staff, an increasing number of term-limited legislatures are establishing rules or norms that prohibit or limit staff changes with each change of leadership. For example, in Arkansas and Florida, the key leadership in the speaker's offices has remained intact across several new speakers. In order to minimize the instability among staff members, some term-limited legislatures are taking control of staff decisions out of the hands of individual legislators and centralizing them in the leadership offices where they can be more confident that they will not be terminated if their particular legislator is termed out. Finally, in order to build a bridge of trust between newly elected legislators and staff, leaders in Colorado and Ohio require their staffs to personally contact each legislator and ask how they can help.

Term Limits Challenge: The Loss of Civility and Collegiality

Historically, legislators have been able to vehemently disagree on the floor or in committee during the day and be friends over dinner or drinks that night because they had long-term relationships. However, term limits have ended such relationships and created institutions and debates that are much more partisan, personal and political. There is little time or opportunity to get to know each other beyond partisan or political contexts so political animosity builds into personal grudges and good legislation dies simply because of partisan anger and angst.

Legislative Responses: Bringing Together Republicans and Democrats, Junior and Senior Members

Much of the loss of civility comes from two factors. First, most term-limited legislators spend time with other legislators from their "class," with freshmen spending much time with other freshmen, etc. Therefore, they do not have relationships with members who might be able to help them be more effective. Second, with key decisions taking place in partisan caucuses and meetings, there is little interaction between Republicans and Democrats, so members of the other party become the enemy. In order to address these problems, leaders in term-limited states are providing opportunities for relationships to build across both partisan and generational lines. In Arkansas, legislative orientation includes several experienced and former legislators as "faculty" and the last two days of the Colorado legislative orientation are open to all legislators, not just freshmen. In Ohio, two days of the bipartisan orientation are held away from the statehouse, and families are invited so that members can build relationships that go beyond politics and stereotypes.

Term Limits Challenge: Loss of Influence to the Executive

One of the most critical impacts of legislative term limits appears to be a shift in the balance of power as more experienced and professional governors wield increased power. While term-limited legislative leaders and committee chairs are realistically limited to two to four years in their posts, all the governors they face can serve at least eight consecutive years. During that time, the governors, their administration and key staffers accrue experience, knowledge and influence not attainable by term-limited legislators. Further, the inexperienced legislators may be particularly susceptible to the persuasive powers of a seasoned chief executive. This seems particularly true when

it comes to budgets and complex policies, where the executive branch has an overwhelming advantage in experience, knowledge and professional staff.

Legislative Responses: Membership Education, Improved Oversight and Leadership Cooperation

Legislative leaders in term-limited states have worked hard to counter gubernatorial advantages by educating their members, increasing oversight and working together to present to the executive branch a united legislative front. In an effort to inoculate their new members against undue executive influence, California, Colorado, Ohio and Arkansas now include intense policy-oriented and budgetary sessions in their orientations. Further, these same orientations now also include intense discussions of the nature and significance of "separation of powers," emphasizing the importance of legislative autonomy. In an additional effort to counter this shift in power, some term-limited legislatures have created enhanced oversight mechanisms. In anticipation of term limits, the legislatures of both Florida and Maine created and empowered professional and autonomous oversight offices. These professional agencies provide the continuous oversight that the ever-changing membership cannot provide. Finally, legislative leaders are working together more closely to maintain legislative integrity and present a united front to the executive branch. Under term limits, budget control and negotiations have become significantly more concentrated in Ohio, California and Colorado as leaders try to halt executive efforts to "divide and conquer" the rank and file.

Term Limits Challenge: Increasing Influence of Lobbyists

One of the most significant concerns of term limits opponents revolved around the increased influence of lobbyists. New members, it was reasoned, would be more susceptible to the sometimes inaccurate infor-

Table C:
Leadership, Selected Leadership Positions, 2007

State	House leadership		Senate leadership	
Arizona	Speaker	2nd term	President	1st term
Arkansas	Speaker	1st term	President Pro Tempore	1st term
California	Speaker	1st term	President Pro Tempore	1st term
Colorado	Speaker	2nd term	President	2nd term
Maine	Speaker	1st term	President	1st term
Ohio	Speaker	2nd term	President/Majority Leader	1st term

Source: State Legislative Leaders Foundation, *The Handbook of State Legislative Leaders, 2006.*

mation and even unethical assistance provided by lobbyists. While some lobbyists suggest term limits have made their jobs more difficult, most acknowledge that their influence has increased as new legislators lack the institutional or policy knowledge to counter information provided by the professional, experienced and well-staffed lobbyists.

Legislative Responses: Informed Members and Ethical Lobbyists

In order to decrease the influence of lobbyists, legislative leaders in term-limited states have tried to better prepare their members and place statutory constraints on lobbyists. In order to achieve the former objective, legislative leaders and staff have stepped up their efforts to ensure that new members have a solid understanding of both the legislative processes and key policy positions before they are inundated by lobbyists trying to sway their votes. New member orientations in term-limited states now regularly include discussions of the proper (and improper) role of lobbyists and a thorough discussion of the rules and laws governing their interaction with legislators. An educated legislator is the best defense against an unethical lobbyist. Regarding efforts to alter or at least regulate the behavior of lobbyists, some term-limited states have put into statute or rules a "Code of Ethical Conduct for Lobbyists." For example, the Institute of Governmental Advocates in California has written "A Code of Ethics for Lobbyists" by which all its members will abide. The code establishes appropriate behaviors regarding confidentiality, honesty and respect.

Conclusion: Legislatures Adapt to the Challenges of Term Limits

Term limits, at least for the present time, are here to stay and legislatures are making the best of them. As noted above, legislative leaders in states with term limits have taken formal and informal steps to minimize the negative consequences of the limits and are still finding ways to effectively make policy, represent their constituents and balance the executive.

Editor's Note

This article is based mostly on Jennifer Drage Bowser, Keon S. Chi and Thomas H. Little, *Coping with Term Limits: A Practical Guide*, Denver, National Conference of State Legislatures, 2006.

Notes

[1] While the proportion of Hispanic members increased in Arizona and California, that is probably more a function of the changing demographic qualities of the two states than an effect of term limits.

[2] Jim Weirs, former speaker of the Arizona House (2000–2002) was re-elected speaker in 2004 after serving two years in the Senate (2004–2006). He is now eligible to serve an additional three terms as speaker if he is re-elected.

About the Authors

Thomas H. Little is the director of Curriculum Development and Research for the State Legislative Leaders Foundation. He is the author of several book chapters, articles and a book on state legislatures, legislative leadership and term limits. He has been on the steering committee for the Joint Project on Term Limits.

Jennifer Drage Bowser is a program principal in the Legislative Management Program at the National Conference of State Legislatures. Her work focuses on the areas of term limits, elections, campaign finance reform, and initiative and referendum. She has served as the project manager for the Joint Project on Term Limits.

Keon S. Chi is editor in chief of *The Book of the States* at The Council of State Governments. He has published extensively on state politics, policy and administration, and is coauthor of "State Legislative Term Limits" published by CSG in 1998. He has been on the steering committee for the Joint Project on Term Limits.

Table 3.1
NAMES OF STATE LEGISLATIVE BODIES AND CONVENING PLACES

State or other jurisdiction	Both bodies	Upper house	Lower house	Convening place
Alabama	Legislature	Senate	House of Representatives	State House
Alaska	Legislature	Senate	House of Representatives	State Capitol
Arizona	Legislature	Senate	House of Representatives	State Capitol
Arkansas	General Assembly	Senate	House of Representatives	State Capitol
California	Legislature	Senate	Assembly	State Capitol
Colorado	General Assembly	Senate	House of Representatives	State Capitol
Connecticut	General Assembly	Senate	House of Representatives	State Capitol
Delaware	General Assembly	Senate	House of Representatives	Legislative Hall
Florida	Legislature	Senate	House of Representatives	The Capitol
Georgia	General Assembly	Senate	House of Representatives	State Capitol
Hawaii	Legislature	Senate	House of Representatives	State Capitol
Idaho	Legislature	Senate	House of Representatives	State Capitol
Illinois	General Assembly	Senate	House of Representatives	State House
Indiana	General Assembly	Senate	House of Representatives	State House
Iowa	General Assembly	Senate	House of Representatives	State Capitol
Kansas	Legislature	Senate	House of Representatives	State Capitol
Kentucky	General Assembly	Senate	House of Representatives	State Capitol
Louisiana	Legislature	Senate	House of Representatives	State Capitol
Maine	Legislature	Senate	House of Representatives	State House
Maryland	General Assembly	Senate	House of Delegates	State House
Massachusetts	General Court	Senate	House of Representatives	State House
Michigan	Legislature	Senate	House of Representatives	State Capitol
Minnesota	Legislature	Senate	House of Representatives	State Capitol
Mississippi	Legislature	Senate	House of Representatives	State Capitol
Missouri	General Assembly	Senate	House of Representatives	State Capitol
Montana	Legislature	Senate	House of Representatives	State Capitol
Nebraska	Legislature	(a)		State Capitol
Nevada	Legislature	Senate	Assembly	Legislative Building
New Hampshire	General Court	Senate	House of Representatives	State House
New Jersey	Legislature	Senate	General Assembly	State House
New Mexico	Legislature	Senate	House of Representatives	State Capitol
New York	Legislature	Senate	Assembly	State Capitol
North Carolina	General Assembly	Senate	House of Representatives	State Legislative Building
North Dakota	Legislative Assembly	Senate	House of Representatives	State Capitol
Ohio	General Assembly	Senate	House of Representatives	State House
Oklahoma	Legislature	Senate	House of Representatives	State Capitol
Oregon	Legislative Assembly	Senate	House of Representatives	State Capitol
Pennsylvania	General Assembly	Senate	House of Representatives	Main Capitol Building
Rhode Island	General Assembly	Senate	House of Representatives	State House
South Carolina	General Assembly	Senate	House of Representatives	State House
South Dakota	Legislature	Senate	House of Representatives	State Capitol
Tennessee	General Assembly	Senate	House of Representatives	State Capitol
Texas	Legislature	Senate	House of Representatives	State Capitol
Utah	Legislature	Senate	House of Representatives	State Capitol
Vermont	General Assembly	Senate	House of Representatives	State House
Virginia	General Assembly	Senate	House of Delegates	State Capitol
Washington	Legislature	Senate	House of Representatives	State Capitol
West Virginia	Legislature	Senate	House of Delegates	State Capitol
Wisconsin	Legislature	Senate	Assembly (b)	State Capitol
Wyoming	Legislature	Senate	House of Representatives	State Capitol
Dist. of Columbia	Council of the District of Columbia	(a)		Council Chamber
American Samoa	Legislature	Senate	House of Representatives	Maota Fono
Guam	Legislature	(a)		Congress Building
No. Mariana Islands	Legislature	Senate	House of Representatives	Civic Center Building
Puerto Rico	Legislative Assembly	Senate	House of Representatives	The Capitol
U.S. Virgin Islands	Legislature	(a)		Capitol Building

Source: The Council of State Governments, *Directory I—Elective Officials 2006.*

Key:

(a) Unicameral legislature. Except in the District of Columbia, members go by the title Senator.

(b) Members of the lower house go by the title Representative.

Table 3.2
LEGISLATIVE SESSIONS: LEGAL PROVISIONS

State or other jurisdiction	Regular sessions				Special sessions		
	Legislature convenes			Limitation on length of session (a)	Legislature may call	Legislature may determine subject	Limitation on length of session
	Year	Month	Day				
Alabama	Annual	Jan. Mar. Feb.	2nd Tues. (b) 1st Tues. (c)(d) 1st Tues. (e)	30 L in 105 C	No	Yes (f)	12 L in 30 C
Alaska	Annual	Jan.	2nd Mon.	121 C	By petition, 2/3 members, each house	Yes	30 C
Arizona	Annual	Jan.	2nd Mon.	(i)	By petition, 2/3 members, each house	Yes	None
Arkansas	Biennial– odd year	Jan.	2nd Mon.	60 C (h)	No	No (j)	None
California	(l)	Jan.	1st Mon. (d)	None	No	No	None
Colorado	Annual	Jan.	No later than 2nd Wed.	120 C	By petition, 2/3 members, each house	Yes (g)	None
Connecticut	Annual	Jan. Feb.	Wed. after 1st Mon. (odd-years) Wed. after 1st Mon. (even-years)	(p)	By petition, 2/3 members, each house (q)	Yes	None
					Joint call, presiding officers, both houses		
Delaware	Annual	Jan.	2nd Tues.	June 30	Joint call, presiding officers, both houses	No	None
Florida	Annual	Mar.	1st Tues. after 1st Mon. (s)	60 C (h)	Joint call, presiding officers, both houses or by petition	Yes	20 C (h)
Georgia	Annual	Jan.	2nd Mon.	40 L	By petition, 3/5 members, each house	No	40 L
Hawaii	Annual	Jan.	3rd Wed.	60 L (h)	By petition, 2/3 members, each house	Yes	30 L (h)
Idaho	Annual	Jan.	Mon. on or nearest 9th day	None	No	No	20 C
Illinois	Annual	Jan.	2nd Wed.	None (ll)	Joint call, presiding officers, both houses	Yes (g)	None
Indiana	Annual	Jan.	2nd Mon. (d)(t)	odd–61 C or Apr. 29; even–30 C or Mar. 14	No	Yes	30 L or 40 C
Iowa	Annual	Jan.	2nd Mon.	None	By petition, 2/3 members, each house	Yes	None
Kansas	Annual	Jan.	2nd Mon.	odd–None; even–90 C (h)	Petition to governor of 2/3 members, each house	Yes	None
Kentucky	Annual	Jan.	1st Tues. after 1st Mon.	even–60 L; odd–30 L (pp)	No	No	None
Louisiana	Annual	Mar. (even-years) Apr. (odd-years)	last Mon. (even-years) last Mon. (odd-years)	even–60 L in 85 C; odd–45 L in 60 C	By petition, majority, each house	Yes	30 C
Maine	(l)(m)	Dec. Jan.	1st Wed. (b) Wed. after 1st Tues. (even-years)	3rd Wed. of June 3rd Wed. of April	By petition, majority, each house	Yes	None
Maryland	Annual	Jan.	2nd Wed.	90 C	By petition, majority, each house	Yes	30 C

See footnotes at end of table.

LEGISLATIVE SESSIONS: LEGAL PROVISIONS—Continued

State or other jurisdiction	Regular sessions				Special sessions		
	Legislature convenes			Limitation on length of session (a)	Legislature may call	Legislature may determine subject	Limitation on length of session
	Year	Month	Day				
Massachusetts.............	Biennium	Jan.	1st Wed.	(w)	By petition (x)	Yes	None
Michigan.......................	Annual	Jan.	2nd Wed.	None	No	No	None
Minnesota.....................	Biennium	Jan.	Wed., the 3rd 2007	120 L	No (qq)	Yes	None
Mississippi....................	Annual	Jan.	Tues. after 1st Mon.	125 C (z); 90 C (z)	No	No	None
Missouri........................	Annual	Jan.	Wed. after 1st Mon.	May 30	By petition, 3/4 members, each house	Yes (g)	30 C (aa)
Montana........................	Biennial–odd year	Jan.	1st Mon.	90 L	By petition, majority, each house	Yes	None
Nebraska.......................	Annual	Jan.	Wed. after 1st Mon.	odd–90 L; even–60 L	By petition, 2/3 members, each house	Yes	None
Nevada..........................	Biennial–odd year	Feb.	1st Mon.	120 C	No (oo)	No	None (k)
New Hampshire.............	Annual	Jan.	Wed. after 1st Tues.	45 L	By petition, 2/3 members, each house	Yes	15 L (r)
New Jersey.....................	Biennium	Jan.	2nd Tues. of even year	None	By petition, majority, each house (mn)	Yes	None
New Mexico...................	Annual	Jan.	3rd Tues.	odd–60 C; even–30 C	By petition, 3/5 members, each house (g)	Yes (g)	30 C
New York......................	Annual	Jan. (kk)	Wed. after 1st Mon.	None	By petition, 2/3 members, each house	Yes (g)	None
North Carolina.............	(y)	Jan.	3rd Wed. after 2nd Mon. (odd-years)	None	By petition, 3/5 members, each house	Yes	None
North Dakota................	Biennial–odd year	Jan.	Tues. after Jan. 3, but not later than Jan. 11	80 L in the biennium	Yes (ff)	Yes	None (ff)
Ohio..............................	Biennium	Jan.	1st Mon. (ee)	None	Joint call, presiding officers, both houses	Yes	None
Oklahoma......................	Annual	Feb.	1st Mon.	last Fri. in May	By petition, 2/3 members, each house	Yes	None
Oregon..........................	Biennial–odd year	Jan.	2nd Mon.	None	By petition, majority, each house	Yes	None
Pennsylvania.................	Biennium (dd)	Jan.	1st Tues.	None	Governor may call	No	None
Rhode Island.................	Annual	Jan.	1st Tues.	None	Joint call, presiding officers, both houses	Yes	None
South Carolina..............	Biennium	Jan.	2nd Tues.	(mm)	By vote, 2/3 members, each house	Yes	None
South Dakota................	Annual	Jan.	2nd Tues.	odd–40 L; even–35 L	By petition, 2/3 members, each house	Yes (o)	None
Tennessee......................	Biennium (bb)	Jan.	2nd Tues.	90 L (u)	By petition, 2/3 members, each house	Yes	30 L (u)
Texas.............................	Biennial–odd year	Jan.	2nd Tues.	140 C	No	No	30 C
Utah..............................	Annual	Jan.	3rd Mon.	45 C	No	No	30 C
Vermont........................	Annual	Jan.	Wed. after 1st Mon.	None	No	Yes	None

See footnotes at end of table.

LEGISLATIVE SESSIONS: LEGAL PROVISIONS — Continued

State or other jurisdiction	Regular sessions				Special sessions		
	Legislature convenes			Limitation on length of session (a)	Legislature may call	Legislature may determine subject	Limitation on length of session
	Year	Month	Day				
Virginia	Annual	Jan.	2nd Wed.	odd–30 C (h); even–60 C (h)	By petition, 2/3 members, each house	Yes	None (gg)
Washington	Annual	Jan.	2nd Mon.	odd–105 C; even–60 C	By vote, 2/3 members, each house	Yes	30 C
West Virginia	Annual	Jan.	2nd Wed.	60 C (h)	By petition, 3/5 members, each house	Yes (g)	None
Wisconsin	Biennium	Jan.	1st Mon.	None	(n)	No	None
Wyoming	Biennium	Jan. (odd-years) / Feb. (even-years)	2nd Tues. (odd-years) / 2nd Mon. (even-years)	odd–40 L; even–20 L; biennium–60 L	By petition, majority members, each house	Yes	20 L
Dist. of Columbia	(hh)	Jan.	2nd day	None			
American Samoa	Annual	Jan. / July	2nd Mon. / 2nd Mon.	45 L / 45 L	No	No	None
Guam	Annual	Jan.	2nd Mon. (ii)	None	No	No	None
No. Mariana Islands	Annual	(jj)	(d)(jj)	90 L (jj)	Upon request of presiding officers, both houses	Yes (g)	10 C
Puerto Rico	Annual (v)	Jan. / Aug.	2nd Mon. / 3rd Mon.	5 mo. / 4 mo.	No	No	20 C
U.S. Virgin Islands	Annual	Jan. (cc)	2nd Mon. (cc)	None	No, Governor calls	No	None

Source: The Council of State Governments' survey, December 2006.

Key:

Annual — holds legislative sessions every year.

Biennium – odd year — holds legislative sessions every other year.

Biennium — holds legislative sessions in a two-year term of activity.

C — Calendar day

L — Legislative day (in some states called a session day or workday; definition may vary slightly, however, generally refers to any day on which either house of legislature is in session).

(a) Applies to each year unless otherwise indicated.

(b) General election year (quadrennial election year).

(c) Year after quadrennial election.

(d) Legal provision for organizational session prior to stated convening date. Alabama—in the year after quadrennial election, second Tuesday in January for 10 C. California—in the even-numbered general election year, first Monday in December for an organizational session, recess until the first Monday in January of the odd-numbered year. Indiana—third Tuesday after first Monday in November. Northern Mariana Islands—in year after general election, second Monday in January.

(e) Other years.

(f) By 2/3 vote each house.

(g) Only if legislature convenes itself. In Illinois, legislative leaders determine subject if they convene special session; governor may call a special session and determine its subject. In New York, special sessions may also be called by the governor. Legislature may determine subject only if it has convened itself. In New Mexico, special sessions may only be called by the governor and subjects are limited to issues included in governor's proclamation; extraordinary sessions may only be called by the legislature and have no limitations on subject.

(h) Session may be extended by vote of members in both houses. Arkansas—2/3 vote. Florida—3/5 vote, session may be extended by vote of members in each house. Hawaii—petition of 2/3 membership for maximum 15-day extension. Kansas—2/3 vote. Virginia—2/3 vote for 30 C extension. West Virginia—may be extended by the governor.

(i) No constitutional or statutory provision; however, by legislative rule regular sessions shall be adjourned sine die no later than Saturday of the week during which the 100th day from the beginning of each regular session falls. The Speaker/President may by declaration authorize the extension of the session for a period not to exceed seven additional days. Thereafter the session can be extended only by a majority vote of the House/Senate.

(j) After governor's business has been disposed of, members may remain in session up to 15 C by a 2/3 vote of both houses.

(k) No limit; however legislators are only paid up to 20 calendar days during a special session. If Assembly Joint Resolution is approved by the voters, special sessions called by the Governor or the legislature will be limited to 20 calendar days.

(l) Regular sessions begin after general election, in December of even-numbered years. In California, legislature meets in December for an organizational session, recesses until the first Monday in January of the odd-numbered year and continues in session until November 30 of next even-numbered year. In Maine, session which begins in December of general election year runs into the following year (odd-numbered); second session begins in next even-numbered year.

(m) Second session limited to consideration of specific types of legislation. Maine—budgetary matters; legislation in the governor's call; emergency legislation; legislation referred to committees for study.

(n) The Legislature may call itself into Extraordinary Session on any subject by a majority vote of the organizing committees of each house, by joint resolution, or by a petition of a majority of each house.

(o) Legislators must address topic for which the special session was called.

LEGISLATIVE SESSIONS: LEGAL PROVISIONS — Continued

(p) Odd-numbered years—not later than Wednesday after first Monday in June; even-numbered years—not later than Wednesday after first Monday in May.

(q) Notice sent to secretary of state.

(r) Limitation is on legislative pay and mileage.

(s) A regular session of the legislature shall convene on the first Tuesday after the first Monday of each odd-numbered year, and on the first Tuesday after the first Monday in March, or such other date as may be fixed by law, of each even-numbered year.

(t) Legislators may reconvene at any time after organizational meeting; however, second Monday in January is the final date by which regular session must be in process.

(u) Ninety legislative days over a two-year period. During special sessions members will be paid up to 30 legislative days; further days will be without pay or per diem.

(v) Legislature meets twice a year. During general election years, the legislature only convenes on the January session.

(w) Legislative rules say formal business must be concluded by November 15 of the first session in the biennium, or by July 31 of the second session for the biennium.

(x) Joint rules provide for the submission of a written statement requesting special session by a specified number of members of each chamber.

(y) Legal provision for session in odd-numbered year; however, legislature may divide, and in practice has divided, to meet in even-numbered year as well.

(z) Ninety C sessions every year, except the first year of a gubernatorial administration during which the legislative session runs for 125 C.

(aa) Thirty C if called by legislature; 60 C if called by governor.

(bb) Each General Assembly convenes for a First and Second Regular Session over a two-year period.

(cc) The legislature convenes in January on the second Monday; March, June and September, the third Wednesday.

(dd) Sessions are two years and begin on the first Tuesday of January of the odd-numbered year. Session ends on November 30 of the even-numbered year. Each calendar year receives its own legislative number.

(ee) Unless Monday is a legal holiday; in second year, the General Assembly convenes on the same date.

(ff) Legislative Council may reconvene the Legislature assembly. However, a reconvened session may not exceed the number of days available (80) but not used by the last regular session.

(gg) No limitation, but the convening of the new General Assembly following an election would by operation end the special session.

(hh) Each Council period begins on January 2 of each odd-numbered year and ends on January 1 of the following odd-numbered year.

(ii) Legislature meets on the first Monday of each month following its initial session in January.

(jj) Sixty L before April 1 and 30 L after July 31.

(kk) Session officially begins on the first Wednesday following the first Monday of the new legislative term (commencing the first of the year), and lasts until the legislature completes its business and adjourns sine die. However, over the past several years, both houses have adopted the tactic of declaring a recess at the call of the leaders, in order to facilitate easy recall of the legislature to override vetoes, etc. Over time the custom has become to formally adjourn both houses just before the new session opens. This leads to the rather interesting convention that when the governor calls the legislature into session, it is considered "special" or "executive," even though the regular session is ongoing.

(ll) Constitution encourages adjournment by May 31.

(mm) The regular session ends the first Thursday in June (June 7, 2007); it can be extended with a 2/3 majority vote.

(nn) Or by joint call, presiding officers, both houses.

(oo) Assembly Joint Resolution No. 13 from the 72nd Session (2003) passed during the 2005 Session. Therefore, the question of whether the Legislature should be able to call itself into special session will be on the 2006 General Election ballot for approval. If the voters approve the measure, a signed petition of 2/3 of the elected members in both houses would allow the legislature to call itself into a special session for specific business (to be specified in the petition) and for no more than 20 calendar days.

(pp) During the odd-year session, the members convene for four days, then break until February.

(qq) Special session is called by the Governor.

Table 3.3
THE LEGISLATORS: NUMBERS, TERMS, AND PARTY AFFILIATIONS: 2007

State or other jurisdiction	Senate						House/Assembly						Senate and House/Assembly totals
	Democrats	Republicans	Other	Vacancies	Total	Term	Democrats	Republicans	Other	Vacancies	Total	Term	
State and territory totals	1,054	930	15	2	2,068*	...	3,005	2,447	25	3	5,500*	...	7,568*
State totals	1,010	909	3	0	1,971*	...	2,971	2,422	15	3	5,411*	...	7,382*
Alabama	23	12	...	...	35	4	62	43	...	...	105	4	140
Alaska	9	11	...	...	20	4	17	23	...	...	40	2	60
Arizona	13	17	...	...	30	2	27	33	...	...	60	2	90
Arkansas	27	8	...	...	35	4	75	25	...	...	100	2	135
California	25	15	...	...	40	4	48	32	...	...	80	2	120
Colorado	20	15	...	...	35	4	39	26	...	...	65	2	100
Connecticut	24	12	...	...	36	2	107	44	...	...	151	2	187
Delaware	13	8	...	...	21	4	18	23	...	...	41	2	62
Florida	14	26	...	...	40	4	41	79	...	...	120	2	160
Georgia	22	34	...	...	56	2	74	106	...	...	180	2	236
Hawaii	20	5	...	...	25	4	43	8	...	...	51	2	76
Idaho	7	28	...	...	35	2	19	51	...	...	70	2	105
Illinois	37	22	...	...	59	(a)	66	52	...	...	118	2	177
Indiana	17	33	...	...	50	4	51	49	...	...	100	2	150
Iowa	30	20	...	...	50	4	54	46	...	...	100	2	150
Kansas	10	30	...	...	40	4	47	78	...	...	125	2	165
Kentucky	16	21	1 (b)	...	38	4	61	39	...	...	100	2	138
Louisiana	24	15	...	...	39	4	59	43	1 (b)	2	105	4	144
Maine	18	17	...	...	35	2	89	60	2 (c)	...	151	2	186
Maryland	33	14	...	...	47	4	104	37	...	...	141	4	188
Massachusetts	35	5	...	...	40	2	141	19	...	...	160	2	200
Michigan	17	21	...	...	38	4	58	52	...	...	110	2	148
Minnesota	44 (d)	23	...	...	67	4	85 (d)	49	...	...	134	2	201
Mississippi	25	27	...	...	52	4	74	47	...	1	122	4	174
Missouri	13	21	...	...	34	4	71	92	...	...	163	2	197
Montana	26	24	...	...	50	4	49	50	1 (e)	...	100	2	150
Nebraska	········Nonpartisan election········				49	4	········Unicameral········						49
Nevada	10	11	...	...	21	4	27	15	...	...	42	2	63
New Hampshire	14	10	...	...	24	2	239	161	...	...	400	2	424
New Jersey	22	18	...	...	40	4 (f)	49	31	...	...	80	2	120
New Mexico	24	18	...	...	42	4	42	28	...	...	70	2	112
New York	29	33	...	...	62	2	105	45	...	...	150	2	212
North Carolina	31	19	...	...	50	2	68	52	...	...	120	2	170
North Dakota	21	26	...	...	47	4	33	61	...	...	94	4	141
Ohio	12	21	...	...	33	4	46	53	...	...	99	2	132
Oklahoma	24	24	...	...	48	4	44	57	...	...	101	2	149
Oregon	17	11	2 (b)	...	30	4	31	29	...	...	60	2	90
Pennsylvania	21	29	...	...	50	4	102	101	...	...	203	2	253
Rhode Island	33	5	...	...	38	2	62	13	...	...	75	2	113
South Carolina	20	26	...	...	46	4	51	73	...	...	124	2	170
South Dakota	15	20	...	...	35	2	20	50	...	...	70	2	105
Tennessee	16	17	...	...	33	4	53	46	...	...	99	2	132
Texas	11	20	...	...	31	4	69	81	...	...	150	2	181
Utah	8	21	...	...	29	4	20	55	...	...	75	2	104
Vermont	23	7	...	...	30	2	93	49	8 (g)	...	150	2	180
Virginia	17	23	...	...	40	4	40	57	3 (b)	...	100	2	140
Washington	32	17	...	...	49	4	62	36	...	...	98	2	147
West Virginia	23	11	...	...	34	4	72	28	...	...	100	2	134
Wisconsin	18	15	...	...	33 (h)	4	47	52	...	...	99 (h)	2	132
Wyoming	7	23	...	...	30	4	17	43	...	...	60	2	90
Dist. of Columbia (i)	9	1	1 (b)	2	13	4	········Unicameral········						13
American Samoa	········Nonpartisan election········				18	4	········Nonpartisan election········			20 (j)		2	38
Guam	7	8	...	...	15	2	········Unicameral········						15
No. Mariana Islands	2	3	4 (k)	...	9	4	2	7	9 (l)	...	18	2	27
Puerto Rico	17 (m)	9 (n)	1 (o)	...	27 (p)	4	32 (m)	18 (n)	1 (o)	...	51 (p)	4	78
U.S. Virgin Islands	9	...	6 (q)	...	15	2	········Unicameral········						15

See footnotes at end of table.

THE LEGISLATORS: NUMBERS, TERMS, AND PARTY AFFILIATIONS: 2007— Continued

Source: The Council of State Governments, March 2007.

*Note: Senate and combined body (Senate and House/Assembly) totals include Unicameral legislatures.

Key:

. . . — Does not apply

(a) The entire Senate is up for election every 10 years, beginning in 1972. Senate districts are divided into three groups. One group elects senators for terms of four years, four years and two years; the second group for terms of four years, two years and four years; the third group for terms of two years, four years and four years.

(b) Independent.

(c) Unenrolled (1); Green Independent Party (1).

(d) Democratic-Farmer-Labor.

(e) Constitution Party.

(f) All 40 Senate terms are on a 10-year cycle which is made up of a two-year term, followed by two consecutive four-year terms, beginning after the decennial census.

(g) Independent (2); Progressive (6).

(h) All House seats contested in even-numbered years; in the Senate 17 seats contested in gubernatorial years; 16 seats contested in presidential years.

(i) Council of the District of Columbia.

(j) Twenty-one seats; 20 are elected by popular vote and one is an appointed, nonvoting delegate from Swains Island.

(k) Independent (1); Covenant (3).

(l) Covenant (7); Independent (2).

(m) New Progressive Party.

(n) Popular Democratic Party.

(o) Puerto Rico Independent Party.

(p) An extra seat is granted to the opposition if necessary to limit any party's control to 2/3.

(q) Independent (2); Independent Citizens Movement (4).

Table 3.3A
THE LEGISLATORS: NUMBERS, TERMS, AND PARTY AFFILIATIONS BY REGION: 2007

State	Senate Democrats	Republicans	Other	Vacancies	Total	Term	House/Assembly Democrats	Republicans	Other	Vacancies	Total	Term	Senate and House/ Assembly totals
State totals.............	1,010	909	3	0	1,971*	...	2,971	2,422	15	3	5,411*	...	7,382*
Eastern Region													
Connecticut............	24	12	...	...	36	2	107	44	...	...	151	2	187
Delaware...............	13	8	...	...	21	4	18	23	...	...	41	2	62
Maine....................	18	17	...	...	35	2	89	60	2 (a)	...	151	2	186
Massachusetts.......	35	5	...	...	40	2	141	19	...	...	160	2	200
New Hampshire	14	10	...	...	24	2	239	161	...	...	400	2	424
New Jersey	22	18	...	...	40	4 (b)	49	31	...	...	80	2	120
New York..............	29	33	...	...	62	2	105	45	...	...	150	2	212
Pennsylvania.........	21	29	...	...	50	4	102	101	...	...	203	2	253
Rhode Island.........	33	5	...	...	38	2	62	13	...	...	75	2	113
Vermont	23	7	...	...	30	2	93	49	8 (c)	...	150	2	180
Regional total	232	144	0	0	376	...	1,005	546	10	0	1,561	...	1,937
Midwestern Region													
Illinois	37	22	...	...	59	(d)	66	52	...	...	118	2	177
Indiana..................	17	33	...	...	50	4	51	49	...	...	100	2	150
Iowa......................	30	20	...	...	50	4	54	46	...	...	100	2	150
Kansas..................	10	30	...	...	40	4	47	78	...	...	125	2	165
Michigan...............	17	21	...	...	38	4	58	52	...	...	110	2	148
Minnesota	44 (e)	23	...	...	67	4	85 (e)	49	...	...	134	2	201
Nebraska...............	--------- Nonpartisan election ---------				49	4	-------- Unicameral --------						49
North Dakota	21	26	...	...	47	4	33	61	...	...	94	4	141
Ohio......................	12	21	...	...	33	4	46	53	...	...	99	2	132
South Dakota	15	20	...	...	35	2	20	50	...	...	70	2	105
Wisconsin	18	15	...	...	33 (f)	4	47	52	...	...	99 (f)	2	132
Regional total	211	201	0	0	501	...	507	542	0	3	1,049	...	1,550
Southern Region													
Alabama................	23	12	...	...	35	4	62	43	...	...	105	4	140
Arkansas...............	27	8	...	...	35	4	75	25	...	...	100	2	135
Florida	14	26	...	...	40	4	41	79	...	...	120	2	160
Georgia	22	34	...	...	56	2	74	106	...	...	180	2	236
Kentucky	16	21	1 (g)	...	38	4	61	39	...	...	100	2	138
Louisiana	24	15	...	...	39	4	59	43	1 (g)	2	105	4	144
Maryland	33	14	...	...	47	4	104	37	...	...	141	4	188
Mississippi............	25	27	...	...	52	4	74	47	...	1	122	4	174
Missouri................	13	21	...	...	34	4	71	92	...	...	163	2	197
North Carolina	31	19	...	...	50	2	68	52	...	...	120	2	170
Oklahoma	24	24	...	...	48	4	44	57	...	...	101	2	149
South Carolina.......	20	26	...	...	46	4	51	73	...	...	124	2	170
Tennessee..............	16	17	...	...	33	4	53	46	...	...	99	2	132
Texas....................	11	20	...	...	31	4	69	81	...	...	150	2	181
Virginia.................	17	23	...	...	40	4	40	57	3 (g)	...	100	2	140
West Virginia	23	11	...	...	34	4	72	28	...	...	100	2	134
Regional total	341	316	1	0	658	...	1,018	903	4	5	1,930	...	2,588
Western Region													
Alaska...................	9	11	...	...	20	4	17	23	...	...	40	2	60
Arizona.................	13	17	...	...	30	2	27	33	...	...	60	2	90
California...............	25	15	...	...	40	4	48	32	...	...	80	2	120
Colorado	20	15	...	...	35	4	39	26	...	...	65	2	100
Hawaii	20	5	...	...	25	4	43	8	...	...	51	2	76
Idaho....................	7	28	...	...	35	2	19	51	...	...	70	2	105
Montana................	26	24	...	...	50	4	49	50	1 (h)	...	100	2	150
Nevada..................	10	11	...	...	21	4	27	15	...	...	42	2	63
New Mexico	24	18	...	...	42	4	42	28	...	...	70	2	112
Oregon..................	17	11	2 (g)	...	30	4	31	29	...	...	60	2	90
Utah.....................	8	21	...	...	29	4	20	55	...	...	75	2	104
Washington	32	17	...	...	49	4	62	36	...	...	98	2	147
Wyoming	7	23	...	...	30	4	17	43	...	...	60	2	90
Regional total	192	192	2	0	436	...	441	429	1	0	871	...	1,307

Source: The Council of State Governments, March 2007.

*Note: Senate and combined body (Senate and House/Assembly) totals include Unicameral legislatures.

Key:
... — Does not apply
(a) Unenrolled (1); Green Independent Party (1).
(b) All 40 Senate terms are on a 10-year cycle which is made up of a two-year term, followed by two consecutive four-year terms, beginning after the decennial census.

(c) Independent (2); Progressive (6).
(d) The entire Senate is up for election every 10 years, beginning in 1972. Senate districts are divided into three groups. One group elects senators for terms of four years, four years and two years; the second group for terms of four years, two years and four years; the third group for terms of two years, four years and four years.
(e) Democratic-Farmer-Labor.
(f) All House seats contested in even-numbered years; in the Senate 17 seats contested in gubernatorial years; 16 seats contested in presidential years.
(g) Independent.
(h) Constitution Party.

Table 3.4
MEMBERSHIP TURNOVER IN THE LEGISLATURES: 2006

State or other jurisdiction	Senate			House/Assembly		
	Total number of members	Number of membership changes	Percentage change of total	Total number of members	Number of membership changes	Percentage change of total
Alabama	35	8	23%	105	22	21%
Alaska	20	3	15	40	11	28
Arizona	30	9	30	60	20	33
Arkansas	35	4	11	100	34	34
California	40	13	33	80	34	43
Colorado	35	9	26	65	22	34
Connecticut	36	3	8	151	19	13
Delaware	21	0	0	41	7	17
Florida	40	6	15	120	37	31
Georgia	56	6	11	180	25	14
Hawaii	25	2	8	51	13	26
Idaho	35	8	23	70	18	26
Illinois	59	9	15	118	13	11
Indiana	50	4	8	100	13	13
Iowa	50	7	14	100	15	15
Kansas	40	1	3	125	28	22
Kentucky	38	2	5	100	18	18
Louisiana	39	1	3	105	3	3
Maine	35	8	23	151	56	37
Maryland	47	11	23	141	37	26
Massachusetts	40	2	5	160	18	11
Michigan	38	8	21	110	31	28
Minnesota	67	19	28	134	37	28
Mississippi	52	2	4	122	7	6
Missouri	34	7	21	163	32	20
Montana	50	9	18	100	32	32
Nebraska	49	22	45	·········· Unicameral ··········		
Nevada	21	1	5	42	9	21
New Hampshire	24	7	29	400	146	37
New Jersey	40	0	0	80	2	3
New Mexico	42	2	5	70	13	19
New York	62	7	11	150	19	13
North Carolina	50	5	10	120	18	15
North Dakota	47	12	26	94	15	16
Ohio	33	10	21	99	35	35
Oklahoma	48	9	19	101	28	28
Oregon	30	3	10	60	12	20
Pennsylvania	50	6	12	203	50	25
Rhode Island	38	4	11	75	10	13
South Carolina	46	1	2	124	20	16
South Dakota	35	12	34	70	21	30
Tennessee	33	8	24	99	19	19
Texas	31	5	16	150	27	18
Utah	29	7	24	75	17	23
Vermont	30	5	17	150	33	22
Virginia	40	3	8	100	3	3
Washington	49	9	18	98	11	11
West Virginia	34	5	15	100	17	17
Wisconsin	33	4	12	99	19	19
Wyoming	30	3	10	60	16	27
Dist. of Columbia	13	3	23	·········· Unicameral ··········		
American Samoa	18	3	17	21	12	57
Guam	15	7	47	·········· Unicameral ··········		
No. Mariana Islands	9	0	0	18	1	6
Puerto Rico	28	1	11	51	1	2
U.S. Virgin Islands	15	5	33	·········· Unicameral ··········		

Source: The Council of State Governments, February 2007.
Note: Turnover calculated after 2006 legislative elections.

Table 3.5
THE LEGISLATORS: QUALIFICATIONS FOR ELECTION

State or other jurisdiction	House/Assembly					Senate				
	Minimum age	U.S. citizen (years) (a)	State resident (years) (b)	District resident (years)	Qualified voter (years)	Minimum age	U.S. citizen (years) (a)	State resident (years) (b)	District resident (years)	Qualified voter (years)
Alabama	21	...	3 (c)	1	...	25	...	3 (c)	1	...
Alaska	21	★	3	1	★	25	★	3	1	★
Arizona	25	★	3	1	...	25	★	3	1	...
Arkansas	21	★	2	1	★	25	★	2	1	★
California	18	3	3	1	★	18	3	3	1	★
Colorado	25	★	1	1	★	25	★	1	1	★
Connecticut	18	★	★	★	★	18	★	★	★	★
Delaware	24	★	3	1	★	27	★	3 (c)	1	★
Florida	21	...	2	2	★	21	...	2	2	★
Georgia	21	...	2 (c)	1	★	25	...	2 (c)	1	★
Hawaii	18	★	3	1	★	18	★	3	1	★
Idaho	21	★	30 days	1	★	21	★	30 days	1	★
Illinois	21	★	2	2 (o)	...	21	★	2	2 (o)	...
Indiana	21	★	2	1	★	25	2	2	1	★
Iowa	21	★	1	60 days	...	25	2	1	...	3
Kansas	18	★	★ (c)	★	★	18	★	★ (c)	★	★
Kentucky	24	★	2 (c)	1	★	30	★	6 (c)	1	★
Louisiana	18	5	2	1	★	18	5	2	1	★
Maine	21	...	1	3 mo.	...	25	...	1	3 mo.	...
Maryland	21	...	1 (c)	6 mo. (f)	...	25	...	1 (c)	6 mo. (f)	...
Massachusetts	18	...	...	1	★	18	...	5	5	★
Michigan	21	★	★	(d)	★	21	★	★	(d)	★
Minnesota	18	...	1	6 mo.	★	21	...	1	6 mo.	★
Mississippi	21	...	4 (c)	2	★	25	...	4 (c)	2	★
Missouri	24	★	★	1	2	30	★	★	1	3
Montana	18	U	1	6 mo. (g)	...	18	...	1	6 mo. (g)	...
Nebraska	U	U	U	U	U	21	★	★ (c)	1	★
Nevada	21	★	1 (c)	30 days (l)	★	21	★	1 (c)	30 days (l)	★
New Hampshire	18	...	2 (c)	★	★	30	...	7 (c)	★	★
New Jersey	21	★	2 (c)	1	★	30	★	2 (c)	1	★
New Mexico	21	★	★	★	★	25	★	★ (c)	★	★
New York	18	★	5	1 (h)	★	18	★	5	1 (h)	★
North Carolina	21	...	1	1	★	25	...	2	1	★
North Dakota	18	...	1	★	★	18	...	1	★	★
Ohio	18	★	30 days	1	★	18	★	30 days	1	★
Oklahoma	21	★	★ (c)	★	★	25	★	★ (c)	★	★
Oregon	21	★	1	1	★	21	★	1	1	★
Pennsylvania	21	...	4 (c)	4	★	25	...	4 (c)	4	★
Rhode Island	18	★	30 days	30 days	★	18	★	30 days	30 days	★
South Carolina	21	...	...	★ (e)	...	25	...	...	★ (e)	...

See footnotes at end of table.

THE LEGISLATORS: QUALIFICATIONS FOR ELECTION — Continued

State or other jurisdiction	House/Assembly					Senate				
	Minimum age	U.S. citizen (years) (a)	State resident (years) (b)	District resident (years)	Qualified voter (years)	Minimum age	U.S. citizen (years) (a)	State resident (years) (b)	District resident (years)	Qualified voter (years)
South Dakota..............	21	★	2	★	★	21	★	2	★	★
Tennessee..............	21	★	(c)	1	★	30	★	3	1	★
Texas..............	21	★	2	1	★	26	★	5	1	★
Utah..............	25	★	3 (c)	6 mo.	...	25	★	3 (c)	6 mo.	...
Vermont..............	18	★	2	1	...	18	★	2	1	...
Virginia..............	21	★	1	★	★(m)	21	★	1	★	★f(m)
Washington..............	18	★	... (c)	...	★	18	★	... (c)	...	★
West Virginia..............	18	1	1 (c)	1	...	25	5	5 (c)	1	★
Wisconsin..............	18	★	1	★(n)	★(n)	18	★	1	★(n)	★(n)
Wyoming..............	21	★	★(c)	1	★	25	★	★(c)	1	★
Dist. of Columbia..............	U	U	U	U	U	18	...(i)	1	1	★
American Samoa..............	25	★(i)	5	1	...	30 (j)	★	5	1	...
Guam..............	U	U	U	U	U	25	...	5	...	★
No. Mariana Islands..............	21	...	3	(d)	★	25	★	5	(d)	...
Puerto Rico..............	25	...	2	1 (k)	...*	30	...	2	1 (k)	...
U.S. Virgin Islands..............	U	U	U	U	U	21	...	3 (c)	3	★

Source: The Council of State Governments' survey, December 2006.

Note: Many state constitutions have additional provisions disqualifying persons from holding office if they are convicted of a felony, bribery, perjury or other infamous crimes.

Key:

U — Unicameral legislature; members are called senators, except in District of Columbia.

★ — Formal provision; number of years not specified.

... — No formal provision.

(a) In some states candidate must be a U.S. citizen to be an elector, and must be an elector to run.

(b) In some states candidate must be a state resident to be an elector, and must be an elector to run.

(c) State citizenship requirement. In Tennessee—must be a citizen for three years.

(d) Must be a qualified voter of the district; number of years not specified.

(e) At the time of filing.

(f) If the district was established for less than six months, residency is length of establishment of district.

(g) Shall be a resident of the county if it contains one or more districts or if the district contains all or parts of more than one county.

(h) Must have been a resident of the county in which the district is contained for one year immediately preceding election.

(i) Or U.S. national.

(j) Must be registered matai.

(k) The district legislator must live in the municipality he/she represents.

(l) Thirty days prior to close of filing for declaration of candidacy.

(m) Qualified voters must be registered within 29 days of the election.

(n) Ten days prior to election.

(o) In the first election after a redistricting, a candidate may be elected from any district that contains a part of the district in which (s)he resided at the time of redistricting, and may be re-elected if a resident of the district (s)he represents for 18 months before re-election.

Table 3.6
SENATE LEADERSHIP POSITIONS: METHODS OF SELECTION

State or other jurisdiction	President	President pro tem	Majority leader	Assistant majority leader	Majority floor leader	Assistant majority floor leader	Majority whip	Majority caucus chair	Minority leader	Assistant minority leader	Minority floor leader	Assistant minority floor leader	Minority whip	Minority caucus chair
Alabama	(a)	ES	AT	...	(b)	...	...	...	EC	...	(b)	...	...	...
Alaska	ES	ES	EC	...	...	...	EC	...	EC	EC	...	...	EC	EC
Arizona	ES	AP	EC	...	...	...	EC	...	EC	EC	...	EC	EC	EC
Arkansas	(a)	ES	EC	...	...	...	EC	...	EC	EC	...	...	EC	EC
California	(a)	ES	EC	...	...	...	EC	...	EC	EC	...	EC	EC	EC
Colorado	ES	ES	EC	EC	...	...	AP	EC	EC	EC	...	AL	AL	EC
Connecticut (c)	(a)	ES	AP	AP	AP	AP	AP	AP	EC	AL	AL	AL	AL	AL
Delaware	ES	ES	EC	...	...	...	AP	AP	EC	EC	...	...	EC	EC
Florida	EC/ES	AP	AP	AL	AP or AL	AP or AL	AP or AL	AP or AL	EC	AL	AL	AL	AL	AL
Georgia	(a)	ES	EC	AL	...	...	EC	EC	EC	...	...	...	EC	EC
Hawaii	ES	ES (d)	EC	EC	EC	EC	...	EC (e)	EC	EC	...	...	EC	EC
Idaho	(a)	ES	EC	EC	EC	EC	...	EC	EC	EC	...	...	AL	AL
Illinois	(a)	...	AP	AP	...	...	AP	AP	EC	AL	EC	(f)	(f)	EC
Indiana	(a)	ES	EC	...	AT	AT	AT	EC	EC	EC	AT	...	...	EC
Iowa	ES	ES	EC	EC	...	...	EC	EC	EC	EC	...	EC	EC	EC
Kansas	ES	ES (d)	EC	EC	...	...	EC	EC	EC	EC	...	EC	EC	EC
Kentucky (g)	ES	ES	...	EC	EC	EC	EC	EC	EC	EC	EC	EC	EC	EC
Louisiana	ES	ES	...	...	EC	EC	AL/7	EC	EC	EC	...	...	EC/5	...
Maine	ES	AP	EC	EC	...	(h)	(i)	EC	EC	EC	(h)	(l)	(k)	...
Maryland	ES	ES	AP (l)	AP (l)	(l)	(l)	AP	EC	EC (m)	EC	(j) (m)	(j)	EC	EC
Massachusetts	EC	...	AP	AP	EC	EC	EC	(n)	EC	EC	ES	ES	ES	(n)
Michigan (o)	(a)	ES	EC	EC	EC	EC	EC	EC	EC	EC	EC	EC	EC	EC
Minnesota	ES	ES	EC	EC	EC	EC	AL/7	EC	EC	EC	EC	EC	EC/5	EC
Mississippi	(a)	ES	...	...	MA	MA	EC	EC	EC	EC	...	...	EC	EC
Missouri	(a)	ES	...	...	EC	EC	EC	EC	EC	EC	EC	EC	EC	EC
Montana	ES	ES	...	...	ES	...	ES	(n)	ES	...	ES	...	ES	...
Nebraska (U)	(a)	ES (p)	...	...	EC	...	EC	(n)	...	...	...	...	(n)	(n)
Nevada	(a)	ES	AP	...	EC	EC	EC	EC	EC	EC	EC	EC	EC	EC
New Hampshire	ES	AP	AP	AP	MA	MA	AP	AP	EC	AL	EC	AL	AL	AL
New Jersey	ES	ES	MA	MA	MA	MA	MA	MA	MI	MI	MI	MI	MI	MI
New Mexico	(a)	ES	EC (b)	...	EC (b)	...	EC	EC	EC (b)	EC	EC (b)	EC	EC	EC
New York (q)	(a)	ES (r)	(r)	AT (r)	AT (r)	AT (r)	AT	AT (r)	EC (b)	AT (r)	EC (b)	(r)	ES (u)	AL (r)
North Carolina	(a)	ES	EC	EC	ES	ES	EC	EC	EC	EC	EC	EC	EC	EC
North Dakota	(a)	ES	EC	...	EC	...	EC	EC	ES (n)	ES	ES	ES	EC	EC
Ohio (s)	ES (n)	ES	EC	EC	ES	ES	ES (t)	ES	ES (n)	ES	ES	ES	ES (u)	EC
Oklahoma	(a)	ES	EC	EC	EC	EC	EC	EC	EC	EC	EC	EC	EC	EC
Oregon	ES	ES	EC	EC	EC	EC	EC	EC	EC	EC	EC	EC	EC	EC
Pennsylvania	ES	ES	EC	EC	EC	EC	EC	EC	EC	EC	EC	EC	EC	EC
Rhode Island (v)	ES	ES	EC	AL	EC	EC	AL	EC	EC	AL	EC	EC	AL	EC
South Carolina	(a)	ES	EC	...	EC	...	AL	...	EC	AL	...	...	AL	...

See footnotes at end of table.

SENATE LEADERSHIP POSITIONS: METHODS OF SELECTION — Continued

State or other jurisdiction	President	President pro tem	Majority leader	Assistant majority leader	Majority floor leader	Assistant majority floor leader	Majority whip	Majority caucus chair	Minority leader	Assistant minority leader	Minority floor leader	Assistant minority floor leader	Minority whip	Minority caucus chair
South Dakota	(a)	ES	EC	EC	…	…	EC	…	EC	EC	EC	…	EC	EC
Tennessee	ES	AP	EC	…	…	EC	…	…	EC	…	EC	…	…	EC
Texas	(a)	ES	…	…	…	…	EC	…	EC	…	…	…	EC	…
Utah (w)	ES	…	EC	EC	EC (x)	EC (x)	EC (x)	EC (x)	EC	EC	EC (x)	EC (x)	EC (x)	EC (x)
Vermont	(a)	ES	EC	EC	EC	EC	…	…	EC	EC	EC	…	…	EC
Virginia	(a)	ES	EC (y)	EC	EC (y)	…	…	EC	EC	EC	EC (y)	…	…	EC
Washington	(a)	ES	EC	EC	EC	…	AP	EC	EC	EC	EC	EC	…	EC
West Virginia	ES (z)	AP	EC	…	EC	…	…	…	EC	EC	…	…	AL	EC
Wisconsin	ES	EC	EC	EC	…	…	EC	EC	EC	EC	…	…	…	EC
Wyoming	ES	ES (d)	…	…	EC	…	…	EC	EC	EC	…	…	…	EC
Dist. of Columbia (U)	(aa)	(bb)	…	…	…	…	…	…	…	…	…	…	…	…
American Samoa	ES	ES	…	EC	…	…	EC	…	EC	EC	…	…	…	…
Guam (U)	ES (p)	ES (d)	EC	EC	…	…	…	…	EC	EC	…	…	EC	…
No. Mariana Islands	ES (cc)	AS	(cc)	…	…	…	…	…	EC (n)	…	…	…	…	…
Puerto Rico	ES (n)	AS	AS	…	ES (dd)	…	…	(ff)	…	…	EC (ee)	…	…	(n)
U.S. Virgin Islands (U)	ES	AS	ES	…	EC (ee)	…	…	ES	ES	…	…	…	…	ES

Source: The Council of State Governments' survey, December 2006.

Note: In some states, the leadership positions in the Senate are not empowered by the law or by the rules of the chamber, but rather by the party members themselves. Entry following slash indicates number of individuals holding specified position.

Key:

ES — Elected or confirmed by all members of the Senate.
AP — Appointed by president.
AL — Appointed by minority leader.
MI — Elected by minority party.
… — Position does not exist or is not selected on a regular basis.

EC — Elected by party caucus.
AT — Appointed by president pro tempore.
MA — Elected by majority party.
(U) — Unicameral legislative body.

(a) Lieutenant governor is president of the Senate by virtue of the office.
(b) Majority leader also serves as majority floor leader. Minority leader also serves as minority floor leader.
(c) Position titles are as follows: chief deputy president pro tem, two deputy presidents pro tem, a chief assistant president pro tem, three assistant presidents pro tem, three deputy majority leaders (AP), a minority leader pro tem, two chief deputy minority leaders, a deputy minority leader-at-large, and three deputy minority leaders (AL).
(d) Official title is vice president. In Guam, vice speaker.
(e) Official title is majority caucus leader.
(f) Appointed by minority leader.
(g) In each chamber, the membership elects Chief Clerk; Assistant Clerk; Enrolling Clerk; Sergeant at Arms; Doorkeeper; Janitor; Cloakroom Keeper; and Pages.
(h) Same position as majority leader.
(i) Same position as assistant majority leader.
(j) Same position as minority leader.
(k) Same position as assistant minority leader.
(l) Majority leader also serves as majority floor leader; deputy majority leader is official title and serves as assistant majority floor leader. There is also an assistant deputy majority leader; there is also a deputy majority whip and assistant deputy majority whips; minority leader also serves as minority floor leader.
(m) Minority leader also serves as the minority floor leader.
(n) President and minority floor leader are also caucus chairs. In Ohio, president acts as majority leader and caucus chair. In Puerto Rico, president and minority leader are also caucus chairs. In Oregon, majority leader and minority leader.

(o) Additional positions include assistant president pro tempore (EC), associate president pro tempore (EC), assistant majority caucus whip (EC), assistant minority caucus whip (EC).
(p) Official title is the speaker. In Tennessee, official also has the statutory title of "lieutenant governor."
(q) Additional positions appointed by the majority leader: Senate Finance Comm. chair, vice president pro tem, Majority Program Development Comm. chair, Majority Steering Comm. chair, two assistant majority leaders, various deputies and assistants. Additional positions appointed by the minority leader: Senate Finance Comm. ranking member, Minority Policy Comm. chair, Minority Program Development chair, three (additional) assistant minority leaders, various deputies and assistants.
(r) President pro tempore is also majority leader by virtue of the office. The assistant majority leader bears the title of senior assistant majority leader; majority floor leader bears the title of deputy majority leader for legislative operations; majority caucus chair bears the title of majority conference chair; assistant minority leader bears the title deputy assistant minority leader; minority floor leader bears the title assistant minority leader for floor operations; minority caucus chair bears the title minority conference chair.
(s) While the entire membership actually votes on the election of leaders, selections generally have been made by the members of each party prior to the date of this formal election.
(t) Sixth ranking minority leadership position is assistant minority whip (ES).
(u) Fourth ranking minority leadership position is assistant minority whip (ES).
(v) Additional positions include deputy president pro tempore.
(w) Additional positions include majority whip (EC), assistant majority whip (EC), minority whip (EC), assistant minority whip (EC) and minority caucus leader (EC).
(x) Majority leader serves as majority floor leader and majority caucus chair. Assistant majority leader serves as assistant majority floor leader and majority whip. Minority leader serves as minority floor leader and minority caucus chair. Assistant minority leader serves as assistant minority floor leader and minority whip.
(y) Minority party in Senate elects caucus officers (vice-chair, secretary, and treasurer). The majority leader is also chair of the caucus. The majority floor leader is also vice-chair of the caucus.
(z) Caucus nominee elected by whole membership.
(aa) Chair of the Council, which is an elected position.
(bb) Appointed by the chair; official title is chair pro tem.
(cc) Speaker also serves as majority leader.
(dd) Official title is floor leader.
(ee) Official title is alternate floor leader.
(ff) Official title is caucus chairman.

Table 3.7
HOUSE/ASSEMBLY LEADERSHIP POSITIONS: METHODS OF SELECTION

State or other jurisdiction	Speaker	Speaker pro tem	Majority leader	Assistant majority leader	Majority floor leader	Assistant majority floor leader	Majority whip	Majority caucus chair	Minority leader	Assistant minority leader	Minority floor leader	Assistant minority floor leader	Minority whip	Minority caucus chair
Alabama	EH	EH	EC						EC					
Alaska	EH	AS	EC				EC		EC			EC	EC	EC
Arizona	EH	AS	EC				EC		EC	EC	EC	EC	EC	EC
Arkansas	EH	AS	EC	AS			AS		EC				EC	EC
California	EH	AS	AS	AS			AS	EC	EC		EC	EC	EC	EC
Colorado	EH	AS	EC	EC			EC	EC	EC	EC		EC	EC	EC
Connecticut	EH	AS/4 (b)	EC	EC/4 (b)		AS (b)	AS (b)	AS (b)	EC	AL (b)	AL (b)	AL (b)	AL (b)	AL (b)
Delaware	EH	EH	EC			AS	EC	EC	EC	EC	AL	AL	AL	AL (b)
Florida	EH	EH	AS	AS	AS	AS	AS	AS	EC	EC	AL	AL	AL	AL
Georgia	EH	EH	EC		EC	EC	EC	EC	EC	EC			EC	EC
Hawaii (d)	EH	EH (a)	EC		EC	EC	EC	EC	EC	EC	EC	EC	EC	EC
Idaho	EH		EC	EC			EC	EC	EC	EC	EC	EC	EC	EC
Illinois	EH	AL	AS (c)	AS (c)	EC		EC	AS (c)	EC	AL (c)	AL	AL	EC	AL (c)
Indiana	EH	AL	EC	AL	AL	AL	AL	AL	EC	AL	AL		AL	AL
Iowa	EH	EH	EC	EC			EC	AL	EC	EC	EC	EC	EC	EC
Kansas (e)	EH	EH	EC	EC			EC	EC	EC	EC	EC	EC	EC	EC
Kentucky (f)	EH	EH	EC	EC			EC	EC	EC	EC	EC	EC	EC	EC
Louisiana	EH	AS (g)			AL	AL	AL	AL	EC	AL	AL	AL	AL	EC
Maine	EH	EH (i)	EC (h)	EC (h)	(h)	(h)	(h)	(k)	EC (h)	EC (h)	(h)	(h)	(h)	(k)
Maryland	EH	EH (i)	AS (j)	AS (j)	(h)	AS	AS	(k)	ES (l)	AL	EC	EC	ES (l)	(m)
Massachusetts	EC	EH	AS	AS	EC	EC	EC	EC	EC (m)	EC	EC	EC	EC	EC
Michigan (n)	EH	AS	EC	EC			EC	EC	EC	AL	EC	EC	EC	(m)
Minnesota	EH	EH	EC	EC	EC	EC	EC	EC	EC	EC	EC	EC	EC	EC
Mississippi	EH	EH	EC	EC			EC	EC	EC	AL	EC	EC	EC	EC
Missouri	EH	EH			EC	EC	EC	EC	EC	EC	EC	EC	EC	EC
Montana		EH			EH	EH	EH	(o)	EH	EH	EH	EH	EH	
Nebraska														
Nevada	EH	EH			EC	EC	EC	EC	AS	AL	EC	EC	EC	EC
New Hampshire	EH	AS (a)	AS	AS	MA	MA	AS	AS	MI	MI	MI	MI	AL	MI
New Jersey	EH	EH	MA	MA	MA	MA	MA	MA	MI	MI	MI	MI	MI	MI
New Mexico	EH	EH	EC	EC	EC (m)	EC	EC	EC	EC	AL	EC (m)	EC	EC	EC
New York (p)	EH	AS	AS	AS (q)	AS	(q)	AS	AS (q)	EC (q)	EC	AL		EC	AL (q)
North Carolina	EH	EH	EC	EC	AS		EC	EC	EC	EC	EC	EC	EC	EC
North Dakota	EH	EH	EC	EC	EH	EH	EC	EC	EH (k)	EH	EH	EH	EH	EC
Ohio (r)	EH (k)	EH		EC	EH	EH	EH	EC	EC	EC	EH	EC	EH	
Oklahoma	EH	EH	AS	AS	AS	AS	AS	AS	EC	EC	EC	EC	EC	EC
Oregon	EH	EH	EC	EC	EC	EC	EC	EC	EC	EC	EC	EC	EC	EC
Pennsylvania	EH	EH	EC	EC	EC	EC	EC	EC	EC	EC	EC	EC	EC	EC
Rhode Island	EH	EH	EC	AL	EC	EC	AL	EC	EC	AL	EC	EC	EC	EC
South Carolina	EH	EH	EC						EC	AL			AL	

See footnotes at end of table.

HOUSE/ASSEMBLY LEADERSHIP POSITIONS: METHODS OF SELECTION — Continued

State or other jurisdiction	Speaker	Speaker pro tem	Majority leader	Assistant majority leader	Majority floor leader	Assistant majority floor leader	Majority whip	Majority caucus chair	Minority leader	Assistant minority leader	Minority floor leader	Assistant minority floor leader	Minority whip	Minority caucus chair
South Dakota	EH	EH	EC	EC	...	...	EC	...	EC	EC	EC	...	EC	EC
Tennessee	EH	EH	EC	EC	EC	...	EC	...	EC	EC	EC	EC	EC	EC
Texas	EH	AS	EC	EC (s)	...	...	EC	...	EC	EC (s)	EC	...	...	...
Utah	EH	AS	EC	EC	...	...	EC	...	EC	EC	EC	...	...	...
Vermont	EH	...	EC	EC	(h)	(h)	(h)	(h)	EC	EC	(h)	(h)	(h)	(h)
Virginia (t)	EH	...	EC (m)	...	(u)	EC	EC	EC	EC	EC	EC	...	AL	EC
Washington	EH	EH	EC	EC	EC	EC	EC	EC	EC	EC	EC	EC	EC	EC
West Virginia	EH	AS	AS	AS	...	...	AS	AS	EC	EC	...	...	...	AS
Wisconsin	EH (v)	EH (v)	EC	EC	...	...	EC	EC	EC	EC	EC	...	EC	EC
Wyoming	EH	EH	...	...	EC	EC	EC	EC	EC	EC	EC	...	EC	EC
Dist. of Columbia	EH	EH (a)	...	...	...	...	...	(o)	...	...	...	...	...	(o)
American Samoa	EH (a)	...	...	...	...	...	...	...	...	...	...	...	...	...
Guam	...	...	(w)	...	...	...	...	(o)	EC	...	EC (y)	...	...	(o)
No. Mariana Islands	EH (w)	...	(w)	...	EH (x)	...	...	...	EC (k)	...	...	...	...	...
Puerto Rico	EH (k)	EH (a)	EC	...	EC (y)	...	...	...	...	...	...	...	...	...
U.S. Virgin Islands	...	...	...	...	...	...	...	(o)	...	...	...	...	...	(k)

Source: The Council of State Governments' survey, December 2006.

Note: In some states, the leadership positions in the House are not empowered by the law or by the rules of the chamber, but rather by the party members themselves. Entry following slash indicates number of individuals holding specified position.

Key:
EH — Elected or confirmed by all members of the House.
EC — Elected by party caucus.
AS — Appointed by speaker.
AL — Appointed by party caucus.
MA — Elected by majority party.
MI — Elected by minority party.
... — Position does not exist or is not selected on a regular basis.

(a) Official title is deputy speaker. In Hawaii, American Samoa and Puerto Rico, vice speaker.
(b) Official titles: speaker pro tem—deputy speaker; assistant majority leader—deputy majority leader.
(c) The two deputy majority leaders appointed by the speaker are among eight assistant majority leaders; and the two deputy Republican (minority) leaders appointed by the Republican (minority) leader are among the leadership of the Republican (Minority) party. (The term "Minority" is in the state constitution, but has not been recently used by the eight assistant leaders.
(d) Other positions in Hawaii include speaker emeritus and minority policy/legislative management (EC) and minority policy chair (EC).
(e) Additional positions in Hawaii include minority agenda chair (EC) and minority policy chair (EC).
(f) In each chamber, the membership elects Chief Clerk; Assistant Chief Clerk; Enrolling Clerk; Sergeant at Arms; Doorkeeper; Janitor; Cloakroom Keeper; and Pages.
(g) Each occurrence.
(h) Majority leader also serves as majority floor leader; assistant majority leader also serves as assistant majority floor leader and majority whip; minority leader also serves as minority floor leader; assistant minority leader also serves as assistant minority floor leader and minority whip.
(i) There is also a deputy speaker pro tem.
(j) Majority leader also serves as majority floor leader. Official title of assistant majority leader is deputy majority leader. There are also an assistant majority whip, chief deputy majority whips, and deputy majority whips.
(k) Speaker and minority leader are also caucus chairs.

(l) Minority leader also serves as the minority floor leader. There are also an assistant minority floor leader, a chief deputy minority whip, an assistant minority whip, and several deputy minority whips.
(m) Majority leader also serves as majority floor leader; minority leader; minority leader also serves as minority floor leader.
(n) Other positions include: two associate speakers pro tempore (EH); majority caucus chair (EC); assistant majority whip (EC); assistant associate minority leader (EC); assistant associate minority floor leader; minority assistant caucus chair (EC); assistant minority whip (EC).
(o) Unicameral legislature; see entries in Table 3.6, "Senate Leadership Positions: Methods of Selection."
(p) Additional majority positions appointed by the speaker: deputy speaker (AS), deputy majority leader, Ways and Means Committee chair, Democratic Program Committee chair, Democratic Steering Committee chair, various deputies and assistants. Additional minority positions appointed by the minority leader: deputy minority leader, Ways and Means Committee ranking member, Republican Steering Committee chair, Republican Program Committee chair, various deputies and assistants.
(q) Official titles: the assistant majority leader assists in floor debate and so could also be considered the assistant majority floor leader; the majority caucus chair is majority conference chair; minority floor leader is the minority leader pro tem (this person is second to the minority leader); minority caucus chair is Republican conference chair.
(r) While the entire membership actually votes on the election of leaders, selections generally have been made by the members of each party prior to the date of this formal election. Additional positions include assistant majority whip, the sixth ranking majority leadership position (EH), and assistant minority whip, the fourth ranking minority leadership position (EH).
(s) Assistant majority floor leader is known as assistant majority whip; assistant minority floor leader is known as assistant minority whip.
(t) The majority caucus also has a secretary, who is appointed by the speaker; the minority caucus has two vice-chairs, one vice-chair/treasurer and an interim sergeant at arms.
(u) Selected by the minority leader with the approval of the Speaker.
(v) Caucus nominee elected by whole membership.
(w) Speaker also serves as majority leader.
(x) Official title is floor leader.
(y) Official title is alternate floor leader.

Table 3.8
METHOD OF SETTING LEGISLATIVE COMPENSATION

State or other jurisdiction	Constitution	Statute	Compensation commission	Legislators' salaries tied or related to state employees' salaries
Alabama	★	...	...	...
Alaska	...	★	★	...
Arizona	...	...	★(a)	...
Arkansas	★	★	...	...
California	★	...	★	...
Colorado	...	★	...	...
Connecticut	...	...	★(b)	...
Delaware	...	★	★(c)	...
Florida	...	★	...	Statute provides members same percentage increase as state employees.
Georgia	...	★	...	...
Hawaii	...	...	★(d)	...
Idaho	...	...	★	...
Illinois	...	★	★	Salaries are tied to employment cost index, wages and salaries for state and local government workers.
Indiana	...	★	...	...
Iowa	...	★	★	...
Kansas	...	★	...	...
Kentucky	...	...	★(e)	...
Louisiana	...	★	...	...
Maine	★	★(f)	★	...
Maryland	...	...	★(g)	...
Massachusetts	...	★(h)	...	...
Michigan	...	...	★(i)	...
Minnesota	...	★	★(j)	...
Mississippi	...	★	...	...
Missouri	★	★(k)	...	...
Montana	...	★	...	Tied to executive branch pay matrix.
Nebraska	★	★	...	...
Nevada	...	★	...	...
New Hampshire	★	...	...	...
New Jersey	★	★	★	...
New Mexico	★	★	...	...
New York	★	★	...	...
North Carolina	...	★	...	...
North Dakota	...	★	★	...
Ohio	★	★	...	...
Oklahoma	...	★	★	...
Oregon	...	★	...	...
Pennsylvania	...	★(l)	...	...
Rhode Island	★	...	...	...
South Carolina	...	★	...	...
South Dakota	★	★	...	...
Tennessee	★	★	...	...
Texas	★(m)	...	...	...
Utah	...	...	★	...
Vermont	...	★	...	...
Virginia	★	★(n)	...	...
Washington	★	★	★(o)	...
West Virginia	...	...	★(p)	...
Wisconsin	...	★	...	The Commission plan is approved by Joint Committee on Employment Relations and the governor. It is tied to state employer compensation.
Wyoming	...	★	...	...
Dist. of Columbia	...	★	...	...
U.S. Virgin Islands	...	★	...	...

See footnotes at end of table.

METHOD OF SETTING LEGISLATIVE COMPENSATION — Continued

Source: National Conference of State Legislatures, December 2005.

Key:

★ — Method used to set compensation.

. . . — Method not used to set compensation.

(a) Arizona commission recommendations are put on ballot for a vote of the people.

(b) The Connecticut General Assembly takes independent action pursuant to recommendations of a Compensation Committee.

(c) Are implemented automatically if not rejected by resolution.

(d) Commission recommendations take effect unless rejected by concurrent resolution or the governor. Any change in salary that becomes effective does not apply to the legislature to which the recommendation was submitted.

(e) The Kentucky committee has not met since 1995. The most recent pay raise was initiated and passed by the General Assembly.

(f) Presented to the legislature in the form of legislation, the legislature must enact and the governor must sign into law.

(g) Maryland commission meets before each four-year term of office and presents recommendations to the General Assembly for action. Recommendations may be reduced or rejected.

(h) In 1998, the voters passed a legislative referendum starting with the 2001 session; members will receive an automatic increase or decrease according to the median household income for the commonwealth for the preceding two-year period.

(i) If resolution is offered, it is put to legislative vote; if legislature does not vote recommendations down, the new salaries take effect January 1 of the new year.

(j) By May 1 in odd-numbered years, the Council submits salary recommendations to the presiding officers.

(k) Recommendations are adjusted by legislature or governor if necessary.

(l) Each chamber receives a cost-of-living increase that is tied to the Consumer Price Index.

(m) In 1991 a constitutional amendment was approved by voters to allow the Ethics Commission to recommend the salaries of members. Any recommendations must be approved by voters to be effective. This provision has yet to be used.

(n) In 1998 the Joint Rules Committee created a Legislative Compensation Commission. It was composed of two former governors and citizens that made recommendations regarding salary, per diem and office expenses.

(o) Salary commission sets salaries of legislature and other state officials based on market study and input from citizens.

(p) Submits, by resolution and must be concurred by at least four members of the commission. The Legislature must enact the resolution into law and may reduce, but shall not increase, any item established in such resolution.

Table 3.9
LEGISLATIVE COMPENSATION: REGULAR SESSIONS

State or other jurisdiction	Salaries			Mileage cents per mile	Per diem living expenses
	Regular sessions				
	Per diem salary	Limit on days	Annual salary		
Alabama	$10 C	...	...	10/mile for a single round-trip per session. 48.5/mile interim committee attendance.	$2,280/m plus $50/d for three days during each week that the legislature actually meets during any session (U).
Alaska	...	...	$24,012	40.5/mile for approved travel.	$163 or $218/d (depending on the time of year) tied to federal rate. Legislators who reside in the capitol area receive 75% of federal rate.
Arizona	...	...	$24,000	34.5/mile on actual miles.	$35/d for the 1st 120 days of regular session and for special session and $10/d thereafter. Members residing outside Maricopa County receive an additional $25/d for the 1st 120 days of regular session and for special session and an additional $10/d thereafter (V). Set by statute.
Arkansas	...	...	$14,765	48.5/mile until Dec. 31, 2005.	$130/d (V) plus mileage tied to federal rate.
California	...	...	$113,098	Members are provided a vehicle. Mileage is not reimbursed.	$162/d for each day they are in session.
Colorado	...	...	$30,000	28/mile or 32/mile for 4wd. Actual miles paid.	$45/d for members living in the Denver metro area. $99/d for members living outside Denver (V).
Connecticut	...	...	$28,000	40.5/mile.	No per diem is paid.
Delaware	...	...	$42,000	30/mile set by statute.	No per diem is paid.
Florida	...	...	$30,996	29/mile for business travel.	$126/d (V) tied to the federal rate. Earned based on the number of days in session. Travel vouchers are filed to substantiate.
Georgia	...	...	$17,342	28/mile – set by legislature.	$173/d (U) set by the Legislative Services Committee.
Hawaii	...	...	$35,900	...	$120/d for members living outside Oahu; $10/d for members living on Oahu (V). Set by the legislature.
Idaho	...	...	$16,116	One round-trip per week at state rate.	$122/d for members establishing second residence in Boise; $49/d if no second residence is established and up to $25/d travel (V) set by Compensation Commission.
Illinois	...	...	$57,619	40.5/mile, tied to federal rate.	$125 per session day.
Indiana	...	...	$11,600	40.5/mile.	$137/d (U) tied to federal rate.
Iowa	...	...	$25,000	29/mile.	$118/d (U). $88.50/d for Polk County legislators (U). Set by the legislature to coincide with federal rate. State mileage rates apply.
Kansas	$84.80 C	...	...	40/mile, set by Dept. of Administration.	$99/d (U) tied to federal rate.
Kentucky	$180.54 C	...	...	40.5/mile.	$108.90/d (U) tied to federal rate. (110% federal per diem rate.)
Louisiana	...	...	$16,800	44.5/mile, tied to federal rate.	$138/d (U) tied to federal rate. Additional $6,000/y (U) expense allowance.
Maine	...	...	$12,713	34/mile.	$38/d housing or reimbursement for mileage and tolls in lieu of housing at the rate of .36/mile up to $38/d. Per diem limits are set by statute.
Maryland	...	...	$43,500	34/mile, $500 allowance for in-district travel as taxable income, members may decline.	Lodging $116/d; meals $41/d maximum.

See footnotes at end of table.

LEGISLATIVE COMPENSATION: REGULAR SESSIONS — Continued

State or other jurisdiction	Salaries			Mileage cents per mile	Per diem living expenses
	Regular sessions		Annual salary		
	Per diem salary	Limit on days			
Massachusetts.............	...	...	$58,237.15	Between $10 and $100, determined by distance from Statehouse.	From $10/d – $100/d, depending on distance from Statehouse (V) set by the legislature.
Michigan........................	...	...	$79,650	41.5/mile.	$12,000 yearly expense allowance for session and interim (V) set by compensation commission.
Minnesota.....................	...	...	$31,140.90	Senate: a reasonable allowance. House: $75 – $650 for in-district mileage.	Senators receive $96/d and Representatives receive $77/L (U) set by the legislature.
Mississippi....................	...	...	$10,000	40.5/mile, set by federal rate and legislature.	$91/d (U) tied to federal rate.
Missouri........................	...	...	$31,351	37.5/mile.	$79.20/d tied to federal rate. Verification of per diem is by roll call.
Montana	$82.67 L	...	...	36/mile, rate is based on IRS rate. Reimbursement for actual mileage in connection with legislative business.	$98.75/d (U).
Nebraska.......................	...	...	$12,000	36/mile, tied to federal rate.	$99/d outside 50-mile radius from capitol; $39/d if member resides within 50 miles of capitol (V) tied to federal rate.
Nevada..........................	$137.90/d	60 days	...	34.5/mile.	Federal rate for capitol area (U). Legislators who live more than 50 miles from the capitol, if requiring lodging, will be paid HUD single room rate for Carson City area for each month of session.
New Hampshire.............	...	2-yr. term	$200	Round-trip home to State-house at 38/mile for first 45 miles and 19/mile there-after; or members will be reimbursed for actual expenses and mileage will be paid at the IRS mileage rate.	No per diem is paid.
New Jersey....................	...	...	$49,000	...	No per diem is paid.
New Mexico	...	...	...	40.5/mile, tied to federal rate.	$142/d (V) tied to federal rate and the constitution.
New York	...	...	$79,500	34.5/mile.	Varies (V) tied to federal rate.
North Carolina..............	...	...	$13,951	29/mile, 1 round-trip/w during session; 1 round-trip for interim committee meetings.	$104/d (U) set by statute. $559/m expense allowance.
North Dakota................	$125 C	...	...	37.5/mile, 1 round-trip/w during session.	Lodging reimbursement up to $900/m (V).
Ohio	...	...	$58,934	30/mile, 1 round-trip/w from home to Statehouse for legis-lators outside Franklin Co.	No per diem is paid.
Oklahoma	...	...	$38,400	40.5/mile, tied to federal rate.	$122/d (U) tied to federal rate.
Oregon	...	...	$18,408	40.5/mile.	$99/d (U) tied to federal rate.
Pennsylvania	...	...	$73,613	40.5/mile, tied to federal rate.	$129/d (V) tied to federal rate. Can receive actual expenses or per diem.
Rhode Island	...	...	$13,089	40.5/mile to and from session.	No per diem is paid.
South Carolina	...	...	$10,400	34.5/mile.	$119/d for meals and housing, for each session day and committee meeting tied to federal rate.

See footnotes at end of table.

LEGISLATIVE COMPENSATION: REGULAR SESSIONS — Continued

State or other jurisdiction	Salaries			Mileage cents per mile	Per diem living expenses
	Regular sessions		Annual salary		
	Per diem salary	Limit on days			
South Dakota...............	. . .	2-yr. term	$12,000	32/mile for 1 round-trip from Pierre to home each weekend. One trip is paid at 5/mile. 32/mile for interim committee meetings.	$110/L (U) set by the legislature.
Tennessee	. . .	. . .	$18,123	35/mile.	$153/L (U) tied to the federal rate.
Texas	. . .	. . .	$7,200	35/mile set by General Approp. bill; an allowance for single, twin and turbo engines from 40/mile to $1/mile is given.	$139/d (U) set by Ethics Commission.
Utah	$130 C	. . .	. . .	40.5/mile, round-trip from home to capitol.	$90/d (U) lodging allotment for each calendar day, tied to federal rate. $54/d (U) meals.
Vermont	. . .	. . .	$600.78/w during session.	40.5/mile, tied to federal rate and state employee reimbursement rate.	Federal per diem rate for Montpelier ($88/d for lodging and $51/d for meals for non-commuters; commuters receive $51/d for meals plus mileage.
Virginia..........................	. . .	. . .	Senate – $18,000 House – $17,640	32.5/mile.	Senate: $140/d (U) tied to federal rate. House: $135/d (U) tied to federal rate.
Washington...................	. . .	. . .	$36,311	40.5/mile.	$90/d tied to federal rate.
West Virginia................	. . .	. . .	$15,000	48.5/mile based on Dept. of Administration travel regs.	$115/d (U) during session set by compensation commission.
Wisconsin......................	. . .	. . .	$47,413	32.5/mile, 1 round-trip/w to capitol.	$88/d maximum (U) set by compensation commission (90% of federal rate).
Wyoming........................	$150 L	. . .	. . .	35/mile.	$85/d (V) set by the legislature, includes travel days for those outside of Cheyenne.

Source: National Conference of State Legislatures, March 2007.
Key:
C — Calendar day
L — Legislative day
(U) — Unvouchered
(V) — Vouchered
d — day
w — week
m — month
y — year
. . . — Not applicable
N.R. — Not reported

Table 3.10
LEGISLATIVE COMPENSATION: INTERIM PAYMENTS AND OTHER DIRECT PAYMENTS

State or other jurisdiction	Per diem compensation and living expenses for committee or official business during interim (2005)	Other direct payments or services to legislators (2005)
Alabama	$2,280/m (U); $50/d for committee meetings and $75/d attendance other legislative business. Not restricted to meals and lodging.	None.
Alaska	$150/d (V).	Senators receive $10,000/y and Representatives receive $8,000/y for postage, stationery and other legislative expenses. Staffing allowance determined by rules and presiding officers, depending on time of year.
Arizona	$35/d with prior approval of presiding officer (V) set by statute. Additional $25/d for those outside Maricopa County.	None.
Arkansas	$125/d plus mileage (V) tied to federal rate.	Legislators are entitled to receive a maximum reimbursement of $9,600/y for legislative expenses.
California	$138/d (V) tied to federal rate.	Senators are allowed staff according to the size of their districts. Assemblymen receive $264,000/y to cover non-specified salary expenses, travel costs, publications, printing, postage, etc.
Colorado	$99/d per diem plus actual expenses (V).	None.
Connecticut	None.	Senators receive $5,500/y and Representatives receive $4,500/y.
Delaware	None.	$6,728/y for office expenses.
Florida	$103/d.	$1,872/m for office expenses.
Georgia	$128/d (V) set by the Legislature. A committee roster is submitted with the members who attended the meeting. Those that did not attend do not get paid.	$7,000/y reimbursable expense account. If the member requests and provides receipts, the member is reimbursed for personal services, office equipment, rent, supplies, transportation, telecommunications, etc.
Hawaii	$10/d for official business on island of legal residence; $80/d for business on another island (V) set by the legislature.	House $5,000–$7,500/m for Jan.–April staffing. Senate varies between $350–$500/d for staffing allowance.
Idaho	Members are reimbursed for actual expenses (V).	$1,700/y for unvouchered constituent expense. No staffing allowance.
Illinois	No per diem is paid.	Senators receive $73,000/y and Representatives $66,483/y for office expenses, including district offices and staffing.
Indiana	$134/d (V) tied to federal rate.	40% of per diem for district offices during interim only. No staffing allowance.
Iowa	$86/d (U) set by the legislature. In addition, legislators may request reimbursement for meals, hotel/motel and air fare. State mileage rates apply.	$200/m to cover district constituency postage, travel, telephone and other expenses. No staffing allowance.
Kansas	During interim committee meetings, members receive $91/d tied to federal rate, plus round-trip tolls and mileage reimbursement at 40¢. All legislators receive $328.05 (U) for 20 pay periods ($6,561) considered taxable income.	$6,561/y which is taxable income to the legislators. Staffing allowances vary for leadership who have their own budget. Legislators provided with secretaries during the session only. This amount will increase to $332.10 in April 2006 (20 payments).
Kentucky	Vouchered only.	$1,617.09 for district expenses during interim.
Louisiana	$113/d (U) tied to federal rate.	$500/m. Senators and Representatives receive an additional $1,500 supplemental allowance for vouchered office expenses, rent, travel mileage in-district. Senators and Representatives staff allowance $2,000/m starting salary up to $3,000 with annual increases paid directly to staff person.
Maine	Actual attendance reimbursed at: $55 per diem; actual meals and mileage/housing expense. Upon approval of committee chair or presiding officer.	None. Supplies for staff offices are provided and paid out of general legislative account.
Maryland	$96/d lodging; $39/d meals related to official business (V) tied to federal rate and compensation commission.	Members, $18,265/y for normal expenses of an office with limits on postage, telephone and publications. Members must document expenses. Legislators must use $5,800 for clerical services. Senators receive one administrative assistant and session secretary.

See footnotes at end of table.

LEGISLATIVE COMPENSATION: INTERIM PAYMENTS AND OTHER DIRECT PAYMENTS—Continued

State or other jurisdiction	Per diem compensation and living expenses for committee or official business during interim (2005)	Other direct payments or services to legislators (2005)
Massachusetts	None.	$7,200/y for office expenses.
Michigan	None.	$58,425/y majority senator for office budget; $58,425/y for minority senator for office budget.
Minnesota	Senators receive $66/d and Representatives receive $56/d per approval of committee chair or leadership (U) set by the legislature.	None.
Mississippi	$85/d for committee meetings (U) tied to federal rate. $1,500 allowance (U).	A total of $1,500 per month out of session.
Missouri	None.	$800/m to cover all reasonable and necessary business expenses.
Montana	In state rate for meals, receipt not required . In state rate for lodging and mileage, receipt required (V). Claim form required.	None.
Nebraska	None. Actual expense reimbursed with expense vouchers provided.	No allowance; however, each member is provided with two full-time capitol staff year-round.
Nevada	Statutory amount (V) maximum allowable per diem is paid regardless of actual expenses.	None.
New Hampshire	None.	None.
New Jersey	None.	$750 for supplies, equipment and furnishings supplied through a district office program. $110,000/y for district office personnel. State provides stationery for each legislator and 12,500 postage stamps.
New Mexico	$181/d (V) tied to federal rate.	None.
New York	Varies (V) tied to federal rate.	Staff allowance set by majority leader for majority members and by minority leader for minority members. Staff allowance covers both district and capitol; geographic location; seniority and leadership responsibilities will cause variations.
North Carolina	$104/d (V) set by statute.	Non-leaders receive $6,708/y for any legislative expenses not otherwise provided. Full-time secretarial assistance is provided during session.
North Dakota	During interim committee meetings, members receive $100/d, $25/d meals (U); $50 plus tax/d lodging (V) plus round-trip mileage reimbursement at 37.5¢. All members receive a $350/m allowance for expenses during their term in office.	None.
Ohio	None.	$350/y for unvouchered office supplies plus five rolls of stamps.
Oklahoma	$25/d (U) set by the legislature.	None.
Oregon	$91/d committee and task force meetings (U) tied to federal rate.	$2,635/session; interim allowance is $400–$750/m depending on geographic size of district. Staffing allowance of $4,134/m during session; $1,846/m during interim.
Pennsylvania	$128 (V) tied to federal rate. Can receive actual expenses or per diem.	Staffing is determined by leadership.
Rhode Island	None.	None.
South Carolina	Member attending official meetings is eligible for $95/d subsistence and $35/d per diem (V) tied to the federal rate.	Senate $3,400/y for postage, stationery and telephone. House $1,800/y for telephone and $1,100/y for postage. Legislators also receive $1,000/m for in-district expenses that are treated as income.
South Dakota	$110 per diem for each day of a committee meeting (U). Meals and lodging expenses are paid at state rate.	None.
Tennessee	$141/d (U) tied to federal rate.	$1,000/m for expenses in-district and staff intrastate travel (U).
Texas	$128/d.	Approved allowance for staff salaries, supplies, stationery, postage, district office rental, telephone expense, etc.

See footnotes at end of table.

LEGISLATIVE COMPENSATION: INTERIM PAYMENTS AND OTHER DIRECT PAYMENTS — Continued

State or other jurisdiction	Per diem compensation and living expenses for committee or official business during interim (2005)	Other direct payments or services to legislators (2005)
Utah	$39/d.	None.
Vermont	Actual cost plus mileage (U) set by the legislature.	None.
Virginia	$200/d additional compensation for committee meeting attendance. No per diem is paid.	Legislators receive $1,250/m; leadership receives $1,750/m office expense allowance. Legislators receive a staffing allowance of $33,537/y; leadership receives $50,305/y.
Washington	$90/d (V) tied to federal rate (80% Olympia area). Maximum allowable per diem is paid regardless of actual expenses.	$1,950/quarter for legislative expenses, for which the legislator has not been otherwise entitled to reimbursement. No staffing allowance.
West Virginia	$115/d (U) set by compensation commission.	None.
Wisconsin	Per diem is paid year-round up to $88/d (U) set by compensation commission (90% of federal rate).	$45,000 for two-year period for office expenses. $191,700 for two-year period for staffing allowance.
Wyoming	$80/d (V) set by the legislature. Includes travel for those where meetings are not in "hometown."	Up to $750 per quarter through constituent service allowance.
Puerto Rico	$93/d within 35 miles of the capitol; $103/d beyond the 35 miles limit (U) tied to CPI.	Senate receives $10,833/m for staffing. House members receive $17,000/m for staffing.

Key:
(U) — Unvouchered
(V) — Vouchered
d — day
m — month
w — week
y — year
N.R. — Not reported

Source: National Conference of State Legislatures, December 2005.

Notes:

(i) For more information on legislative compensation, see the Chapter 3 table entitled "Legislative Compensation: Regular Sessions."

(ii) Although the official definition of "per diem" is daily expense allowance, it is also used in some states to refer to an interim salary that is taxed and reported as separate income from the annual salary.

Table 3.11
ADDITIONAL COMPENSATION FOR SENATE LEADERS

State	Presiding officer	Majority leader	Minority leader	Other leaders
Alabama	$2/day plus $1,500/mo expense allowance	None	None	None
Alaska	$500	None	None	None
Arizona	None	None	None	None
Arkansas	$15,400 (a)	None	None	None
California	$113,850 (a)	$106,425 (a)	$106,425 (a)	None
Colorado	All leaders receive $99/day salary during interim when in attendance at committee or leadership meetings.			
Connecticut	$10,689	$8,835	$8,835	Dep. min. and maj. ldrs., $6,446/yr; asst. maj. and min. ldrs. and maj. and min. whips, $4,241/yr
Delaware	$19,983	$12,376	$12,376	Maj. and min. whips, $7,794
Florida	$11,568	None	None	None
Georgia	None	$200/mo	$200/mo	Pres. pro tem, $400/mo; admin. flr. ldr., $200/mo; asst. admin. flr. ldr., $100/mo
Hawaii	$7,500	None	None	None
Idaho	$3,000	None	None	None
Illinois	$23,388	$17,539	$23,388	Asst. maj. and min. ldr., $17,539; maj. and min. caucus chair, $17,539
Indiana	$6,500	$5,000	$5,500	Asst. pres. pro tem, $2,500; asst. maj. flr. ldr. and maj. caucus chair, $1,000; maj. caucus chair, $5,000; min. asst. flr. ldr. and min. caucus chair, $4,500; maj. and min. whips, $1,500; asst. min. caucus chair, $500
Iowa	$11,593	$11,593	$11,593	Pres. pro tem, $1,243
Kansas	$13,004.16/yr	$11,731.98/yr	$11,731.98/yr	Asst. maj., min. ldrs., vice pres., $6,637.28/yr
Kentucky	$42.82/day	$33.82/day	$33.82/day	Maj., min. caucus chairs and whips, $25.92/day
Louisiana	$32,000	None	None	Pres. pro tem, $24,500
Maine	150% of base salary	125% of base salary	112.5% of base salary	None
Maryland	$13,000/yr	None	None	None
Massachusetts	$35,000	$22,500	$22,500	Asst. maj. and min. ldr. (and 2nd and 3rd asst.), pres. pro tem, each $15,000
Michigan	$5,513	$26,000	$22,000	Maj. flr. ldr., $12,000; min. flr. ldr., $10,000
Minnesota	None	$43,596 (a)	$43,596 (a)	Asst. maj. ldr., $35,291 (a)
Mississippi	Lt. gov. – $60,000	None	None	Pres. pro tem, $15,000
Missouri	None	None	None	None
Montana	$5/day during session	None	None	None
Nebraska	None	None	None	None
Nevada	$900	$900	$900	Pres. pro tem, $900
New Hampshire	$50/two-yr term	None	None	None
New Jersey	1/3 above annual salary	None	None	None
New Mexico	None	None	None	None
New York	$41,500	None	$34,500	22 other ldrs. with compensation ranging from $13,000 to $34,000
North Carolina	$38,151 (a) and $16,956 expense allowance	$17,048 (a) and $7,992 expense allowance	$17,048 (a) and $7,992 expense allowance	Dep. pro tem: $21,739 (a) and $10,032 expense allowance

See footnotes at end of table.

ADDITIONAL COMPENSATION FOR SENATE LEADERS — Continued

State	Presiding officer	Majority leader	Minority leader	Other leaders
North Dakota (b)	None	$10/day during session; $250/mo during term of office	$10/day during session; $250/mo during term of office	Asst. ldrs., $5/day during session
Ohio	$87,698 (a)	Pres. pro tem $80,016 (a)	$80,016 (a)	Compensation for cmte. leadership; maj.flr. ldr., $75,371; asst. maj. flr. ldr., $70,733; maj. whip, $66,094; asst. maj. whip, $61,452
Oklahoma	$17,932	$12,364	$12,364	None
Oregon	$16,284	None	None	None
Pennsylvania	$39, 076	$31,263	$31,263	Maj. and min. whip, $23,726; maj. and min. caucus chair, $14,793; maj. and min. caucus secretaries, $9,770; maj. and min. caucus admin., $9,770
Rhode Island	Double the base salary	None	None	None
South Carolina	Lt. gov. holds this position	None	None	Pres. pro tem, $11,000 (a)
South Dakota	None	None	None	None
Tennessee	$49,500 (a)	None	None	None
Texas	None	None	None	None
Utah	$2,500	$1,500	$1,500	Maj. whip, asst. maj. whip, min. whip and asst. min. whip, $1,500
Vermont	$593/wk during session. No add'l salary	None	None	None
Virginia	None	$200/day for interim business	$200/day for interim business	Pres. pro tem, $200/d for interim business
Washington	Lt. gov. holds this position	$42,227 (a)	$42,227 (a)	None
West Virginia	$50/day during session	$25/day during session	$25/day during session	Up to four add'l people named by presiding officer receive $150 for a maximum of 30 days
Wisconsin	None	None	None	None
Wyoming	$3/day	None	None	None

Source: National Conference of State Legislatures, December 2005.
(a) Total annual salary for this leadership position.
(b) House and Senate majority and minority leaders each receive additional compensation of $250/mo during their term of office, pursuant to NDCC Section 54-03-20, in addition to other compensation amounts provided by law during legislative sessions.

Table 3.12
ADDITIONAL COMPENSATION FOR HOUSE/ASSEMBLY LEADERS

State	Presiding officer	Majority leader	Minority leader	Other leaders
Alabama	$2/day plus $1,500/mo expense allowance	None	None	None
Alaska	$500	None	None	None
Arizona	None	None	None	None
Arkansas	$15,754 (a)	None	None	$2,400 spkr. designate
California	$113,850 (a)	$106,425 (a)	$106,425 (a)	None
Colorado	All leaders receive $99/day salary during interim when in attendance at committee or leadership matters.			
Connecticut	$10,689	$8,835	$8,835	Dep. spkr., dep. maj. and min. ldrs., $6,446/yr; asst. maj. and min. ldrs. and maj. and min. whips, $4,241/yr
Delaware	$16,893	$12,376	$12,376	Maj. and min. whips, $7,794
Florida	$11,568	None	None	None
Georgia	$6,462.32/mo	$200/mo	$200/mo	Governor's flr. ldr., $200/mo; asst. flr. ldr., $100/mo; spkr. pro tem, $400/mo
Hawaii	$7,500	None	None	None
Idaho	$3,000	None	None	None
Illinois	$23,388	$19,731	$23,388	Dep. maj. and min. ldr., $16,810; asst. maj. and asst. min. ldr., $15,346
Indiana	$6,500	$5,000	$5,500	Spkr. pro tem, $5,000; maj. caucus chair, $5,000; min. caucus chair, $4,500; asst. min. flr. ldr., $3,500; asst. maj. flr. ldr., $1,000; maj. whip, $3,500; min. whip, $1,500
Iowa	$11,593	$11,593	$11,593	Spkr. pro tem, $1,243
Kansas	$13,004.16/yr	$11,713.98/yr	$11,713.98/yr	Asst. maj. and min. ldrs., spkr. pro tem, $6,637.28/yr
Kentucky	$42.82/day	$33.82/day	$33.82/day	Maj. and min. caucus chairs and whips, $25.92/day
Louisiana	$32,000 (a)	None	None	Spkr. pro tem, $24,500 (a)
Maine	150% of base salary	125% of base salary	112.5% of base salary	None
Maryland	$13,000/yr	None	None	None
Massachusetts	$35,000	$22,500	$15,000	Asst. maj. and min. ldr. (and 2nd and 3rd asst.), and spkr. pro tem, $15,000
Michigan	$27,000	None	$22,000	Spkr. pro tem, $5,513; min. flr. ldr., $10,000; maj. flr. ldr., $12,000
Minnesota	140% of base salary	140% of base salary	140% of base salary	None
Mississippi	$60,000 (a)	None	None	Spkr. pro tem, $15,000
Missouri	$208.34/mo	$125/mo	$125/mo	None
Montana	$5/day during session	None	None	None
Nebraska	None	None	None	None
Nevada	$900	$900	$900	Spkr. pro tem, $900
New Hampshire	$50/two-year term	None	None	None
New Jersey	133% of base salary	None	None	None
New Mexico	None	None	None	None
New York	$41,500	$34,500	$34,500	31 ldrs. with compensation ranging from $9,000 to $25,000
North Carolina	$38,151 (a) and $16,956 expense allowance	$17,048 (a) and $7,992 expense allowance	$17,048 (a) and $7,992 expense allowance	Spkr. pro tem, $21,739 and $10,032 expense allowance
North Dakota (b)	$10/day during legislative session	$10/day during legislative session, $250/mo during term of office	$10/day during legislative session, $250/mo during term of office	Asst. ldrs., $5/day during legislative sessions

See footnotes at end of table.

ADDITIONAL COMPENSATION FOR HOUSE/ASSEMBLY LEADERS — Continued

State	Presiding officer	Majority leader	Minority leader	Other leaders
Ohio	$87,698.58 (a)	None	$80,016 (a)	Spkr. pro tem, $80,016 (a); maj. flr. ldr., $75,371 (a); asst. maj. flr. ldr., $70,733 (a); maj. whip, $66,094 (a); asst. maj. whip, $61,452 (a)
Oklahoma	$17,932	$12,364	$12,364	Spkr. pro tem, $12,364
Oregon	$16,284	None	None	None
Pennsylvania	$39,076	$31,263	$31,263	Maj. and min. whips, $23,726; maj. and min. caucus chairs, $14,793; maj. and min. policy chairs, $9,770; maj. and min. caucus admin., $9,770; maj. and min. caucus secretaries, $9,770
Rhode Island	200% of base salary	None	None	None
South Carolina	$11,000/yr	None	None	Spkr. pro tem, $3,600/yr
South Dakota	None	None	None	None
Tennessee	$49,500 (a)	None	None	None
Texas	None	None	None	None
Utah	$2,500	$1,500	$1,500	Whips and asst. whips, $1,500
Vermont	$652/wk during session plus an additional $10,080 in salary	None	None	None
Virginia	$18,681	None	None	None
Washington	$42,227 (a)	None	$38,227 (a)	None
West Virginia	$50/day during session	$25/day during session	$25/day during session	Up to four add'l people named by presiding officer receive $150 for a maximum of 30 days
Wisconsin	$25/mo	None	None	None
Wyoming	$3/day	None	None	None

Source: National Conference of State Legislatures, December 2005.
(a) Total annual salary for this leadership position.
(b) House and Senate majority and minority leaders each receive additional compensation of $250/mo during their term of office, pursuant to NDCC Section 54-03-20, in addition to other compensation amounts provided by law during legislative sessions.

Table 3.13
STATE LEGISLATIVE RETIREMENT BENEFITS

State or other jurisdiction	Participation	Plan name	Requirements for regular retirement	Employee contribution rate	Benefit formula
Alabama	None available.				
Alaska	Optional	Public Employees Retirement System	Age 60 with 10 yrs.	Employee 6.75%	2% (first 10 yrs.); or 2.25% (second 10 yrs.); or 2.5% over 20 x average over 5 highest consecutive yrs. x yrs. of service.
Arizona	Mandatory – except that officials subject to term limits may opt out for a term of office.	Elected Officials Retirement System	Age 65, 5+ yrs. service; age 62, 10+ yrs. service; or 20 yrs. service; earlier retirement with an actuarial reduction of benefits. Vesting at 5 yrs.	Employee 7%	4% x yrs. of credited service x highest 3-yr. average in the past 10 yrs. The benefit is capped at 80% of FAS. An elected official may purchase service credit in the plan for service earned in a non-elected position by buying it at an actuarially-determined amount.
Arkansas	Optional. Those elected before 7/1/99 may have service covered as a regular state employee but must have 5 yrs. of regular service to do so.	Arkansas Public Employees Retirement System	Age 65, 10 yrs. service; or age 55, 12 yrs. service; or any age, 28 yrs. service; any age if serving in the General Assembly on 7/1/79; any age if in elected office on 7/1/79 with 17 and 1/2 yrs. of service. As a regular employee, age 65, 5 yrs. service, or any age and 28 yrs. Members of the contributory plan established in 2005 must have a minimum of 10 yrs. legislative service if they have only legislative state employment.	Non-contributory plan in effect for those elected before 2006. For those elected then and thereafter, a contributory plan that requires 5% of salary.	For service that began after 7/1/99: 2.07% x FAS x yrs. of service. FAS based on 3 highest consecutive yrs. of service. For service that began after 7/1/91, $35 x yrs. of service = monthly benefit. For contributory plan, 2% x FAS x yrs. of service.
California	Legislators elected after 1990 are not eligible for retirement benefits for legislative service.				
Colorado	Mandatory	Either Public Employees' Retirement Association or State Defined Contribution Plan. A choice is not irrevocable.	PERA: age 65, 5 yrs. service; age 50, 30 yrs. service; when age + service equals 80 or more (min. age of 55). DCP: no age requirement and vested immediately.	Employee: 8%	PERA: 2.5% x FAS x yrs. of service, capped at 100% of FAS. DCP benefit depends upon contributions and investment returns.
Connecticut	Mandatory	State Employees Retirement System Tier IIA	Age 60, 25 yrs. credited service; age 62, 10–25 yrs. credited service. age 62, 5 yrs. actual state service. Reduced benefit available with earlier retirement ages.	2%	(.0133 x avg. annual salary) + (.005 x avg. annual salary in excess of "breakpoint" x credited service up to 35 yrs.). 2003 – $36,400 2007 – $46,000 2004 – $38,600 2008 – $48,800 2005 – $40,900 2009 – $51,700 2006 – $43,400 After 2009 – increase breakpoint by 6% per year rounded to nearest $100.

See footnotes at end of table.

STATE LEGISLATIVE RETIREMENT BENEFITS—Continued

State or other jurisdiction	Participation	Plan name	Requirements for regular retirement	Employee contribution rate	Benefit formula
Delaware	Mandatory	State Employees Pension Plan	Age 60, 5 yrs. credited service.	3% of total monthly compensation in excess of $6,000.	2% x FAS x yrs. of service before 1997 + 1.85% x FAS x yrs. of service from 1997 on. FAS = average of highest 3 yrs.
Florida	Optional. Elected officials may opt out and may choose between DB and DC plans.	Florida Retirement System	Vesting in DB plan, 6 yrs.; in DC plan, 1 yr. DB plan: age 62 with 6 yrs.; 30 yrs. at any age. DC plan: any age.	No employee contribution. Employer contribution for 2004–2005 for legislators is 12.49% of salary.	DB plan: 3% x yrs. of creditable service x average final compensation (average of highest 5 yrs.). DC plan: dependent upon investment experience.
Georgia	Optional. Choice when first elected.	Georgia Legislative Retirement System	Vested after 8 yrs.; age 62, with 8 yrs. of service; age 60 with reduction for early retirement.	Employee rate 3.75% + $7/month	$36/month for each year of service.
Hawaii	Mandatory	Public Employees Retirement System; elected officials' plan	Age 55 with 5 yrs. of service; any age with 10 yrs. of service. Vesting at 5 yrs.	Main plan is non-contributory; 7.8% for elected officials' plan for annuity.	3.5 x yrs. of service as elected official x highest average salary + annuity based on contributions as an elected official. Highest average salary = average of 3 highest 12-month periods as elected official.
Idaho	Mandatory		Age 65 with 5 yrs. service; reduced benefit at age 55 with 5 yrs. of service.	6.97%	Avg. monthly salary for highest 42 consecutive months x 2% x months of credited service.
Illinois	Optional	General Assembly Retirement System	Age 55, 8 yrs. service; or age 62, 4 yrs. service	8.5% for retirement; 2% for survivors; 1% for automatic increases; 11.5% total.	3% of each of first 4 yrs.; 3.5% for each of next 2 yrs.; 4% for each of next 2 yrs.; 4.5% for each of the next 4 yrs.; 5% for each yr. above 12.
Indiana	DB plan is optional for those serving on 4/30/89. Defined contribution plan is optional for those serving on 4/30/89 and mandatory for those elected or appointed since 4/30/89.	Legislator's Retirement System and Defined Benefit (DB) Plan and Defined Contribution (DC) Plan	DB plan: vesting at 10 yrs. Age 65 with 10 yrs. of legislative service; or if no longer in the legislature, these options apply: at least 10 yrs. service; no state salary; at age 55+ Rule of 85 applies; or age 60 with 15 yrs. of service. Early retirement with reduced benefit. Immediate vesting in the DC plan.	DC plan: 5% employee, 20% state (of taxable income). DB plan and employer contributions funded by appropriation.	DB benefit plan monthly benefit: lesser of (a) $40 x yrs. of General Assembly service completed before 11/8/89 or (b) 1/12 of the average of the 3 highest consecutive yrs. of General Assembly service salary. DC plan: numerous options for withdrawing accumulations in accord with IRS regulations. Loans are available. A participant in both plans may receive a benefit from both plans.
Iowa	Optional	Public Employees Retirement System	Age 65; age 62 with 20 yrs. service Rule of 88; reduced benefit at 55 with at least 4 yrs. of service.	3.7% individual	2% x FAS x yrs. of service for first 30 yrs., + 1% x FAS x yrs. in excess of 30 but no more than 5 in excess of 30. FAS is average of 3 highest yrs.
Kansas	Optional	Public Employees Retirement System	Age 65, age 62 with 10 yrs. of service or age plus yrs. of service equals 85 pts.	4% of salary, (4% annualized salary for Legislators)	3 highest yrs. x 1.75% x yrs. service ÷ 12.

See footnotes at end of table.

STATE LEGISLATIVE RETIREMENT BENEFITS—Continued

State or other jurisdiction	Participation	Plan name	Requirements for regular retirement	Employee contribution rate	Benefit formula
Kentucky	Optional. Those who opt out are covered by the state employees' plan.	Kentucky Legislator's Retirement Plan	Age 65 with 5 yrs. of service; any age with 30 yrs. of service, and intermediate provisions. Early retirement with reduced benefits.	5% of creditable compensation, set by law at $27,500; not the same as actual salary. Revised to be payable on compensation reported on W-2 forms beginning in 2005.	2.75% of FAS (based on creditable compensation) x yrs. of service. FAS is the average monthly earnings for the 60 months preceding retirement.
Louisiana	None available.				
Maine	Mandatory	Maine State Retirement Plan	Age 60 (if 10 yrs. of service on 7/1/93) and age 62 (if less than 10 yrs. of service on 7/1/93). Reduced benefit available for earlier retirement.	7.65% legislators; employer contribution is actuarially determined.	2% of average final compensation (the average of the 3 high-salary yrs.) x yrs. of service.
Maryland	Optional	State Legislator's Pension Plan	Age 60, with 8 yrs.; age 50, 8+ yrs creditable service (early reduced retirement).	5% of annual salary	3% of legislative salary for each yr. of service up to a maximum of 22 yrs. 3 months. Benefits are recalculated when legislative salaries are changed.
Massachusetts	Optional after each election or re-election to the General Court.	State Retirement System Legislator's Plan	Age 55 with 6 yrs. service; unreduced benefits at 65. Vesting at 6 yrs. Reduced benefits for retirement before age 65.	9%. Some legislators are grandfathered at lower rates.	2.5 x yrs. of service x FAS. FAS = average of highest 36 months. Service credit is allowed for membership in other Massachusetts retirement plans.
Michigan	Optional	Legislative Retirement System (DB) for legislators elected before 3/31/97. Others may join the state defined contribution plan.	Age 55, 5 yrs. or age plus service equals 70.	7% –13% for DB plan. For the DC plan, the state contributes 4% of salary. Members may contribute up to 3% of salary. The state will match the member's contribution in addition to the state's 4% contribution.	For DB plans, various provisions, depending on when service started. For the DC plan, benefits depend upon contributions and earnings.
Minnesota	Mandatory	Legislators Retirement Plan before 7/1/97; Defined Contribution Plan (DCP) since then.	LRP: age 62, 6 yrs. service and fully vested. DCP: age 55 and vested immediately. LRP members do not have Social Security coverage. DCP members have Social Security coverage.	LRP: 9% DCP: 4% from member, 6% from state.	2.7% x high 5-yr. avg. salary x length of service (yrs.) DCP benefit depends upon contributions and investment return.
Mississippi	Mandatory	Legislators' plan within the Public Employees' Retirement System	Age 60 with 4 or more yrs. of service, or 25 yrs. of service.	Regular: 7.25% state 9.75% to 10.75% effective 7/1/05. Supplement for legislative service: 3%/6.33%.	Legislators who qualify for regular state retirement benefits also automatically qualify for the legislators' supplemental benefits. Regular: 2% x FAS x yrs. of service up to and including 25 yrs. of service + 2.5% x FAS x service in excess of 25 yrs. FAS is based on the high 4 yrs. Supplement: 1% x FAS x yrs. of legislative service through 25 yrs.. + 1.25% x FAS x yrs. of service in excess of 25.

See footnotes at end of table.

STATE LEGISLATIVE RETIREMENT BENEFITS—Continued

State or other jurisdiction	Participation	Plan name	Requirements for regular retirement	Employee contribution rate	Benefit formula
Missouri...........	Mandatory	Missouri State Employee Retirement System	Age 55; three full biennial assemblies (6 yrs.) or Rule of 80. Vesting at 6 yrs. of service.	Non-contributory	Monthly pay ÷ 24 x yrs. of creditable service, capped at 100% of salary. Benefit is adjusted by the percentage increase in pay for an active legislator.
Montana	Optional	Public Employees Retirement System Either a DB or a DC plan is available.	Vesting at 5 yrs. Age 60 with at least 5 yrs. service; age 65 regardless of yrs. service; or 30 yrs. of service regardless of age.	6.9% for DB plan. Employer contribution of 4.19% plus employee contribution of 6.9% for DC plan.	DB plan: 1/56 x yrs. of service x FAS. Early retirement with reduced benefits is available. DC plan: Employee contributions and earnings are immediately vested. Employer contributions and earnings are vested after 5 yrs.
Nebraska...........	None available.				
Nevada	Mandatory; but Chapter 380, Laws of 2005, allows legislators to withdraw from the system at will. The decision is final.	Legislator's Retirement System	Age 60, 10 yrs. service.	15% of session salary	Number of yrs. x $25 = monthly allowance.
New Hampshire...........	None available.				
New Jersey...........	Mandatory	Public Employees' Retirement System	Age 60: no minimum service requirement. Early retirement with no benefit reduction with 25 yrs. of service. Vesting at 8 yrs.	5% of salary	3% x Final Average Salary x yrs. of service. FAS = higher of 3 highest yrs. or 3 final yrs. Benefit is capped at 2/3 of FAS. Other formulas apply if a legislator also has other service covered by the Public Employees' Retirement System.
New Mexico...........	Optional	Legislative Retirement Plan	Plans 1A and 1B: Age 65 with 5 yrs. of service; 64/8; 63/11; 60/12; or any age with 14 yrs. of service. Plan 2: 65 with 5 yrs. of service or any age with 10 yrs. of service.	Plan 1A: $100 per year for service after 1959. Plan 1B: $200 per year (now closed to new enrollments). Plan 2: $500 per year.	Plan 1A: $250 per year of service. Plan 1B: $500 per year of service after 1959. Plan 2: 11% of the IRS per diem rate in effect on December 31 of the year a legislator retires x 60 x the yrs. of credited service. For a legislator who retired in 2003 the benefit would be $957 per year of credited service. Annual 3% COLA.
New York...........	Mandatory	New York State and Local Retirement System	Age 62 with 5 yrs. of service; 55 with 30 yrs.; reduced benefit available at 55/5. Vesting at 5 yrs.	3% for first 10 yrs. of membership (Tier 4 provisions).	Tier 4: 2% x final average salary (average of 3 highest consecutive yrs.) x yrs. of service to 30 yrs.; multiplier of 1.5% after 30 yrs. For members who retire with fewer than 20 yrs. of service, the multiplier is 1.67%.
North Carolina...........	Mandatory	Legislative Retirement System	Age 65 with 5 yrs. of service; reduced benefit available at earlier ages.	7%	Highest annual compensation x 4.02% x yrs. of service.
North Dakota...........	None available.				
Ohio...........	Optional	Public Employees Retirement System	Age 60 with 5 yrs. service or 55 with 25 yrs. service or at any age with 30 yrs. service.	8.5% of gross salary. A 10% contribution rate for legislators will be phased in over 3 yrs. starting in 2006.	2.2% of final average salary x yrs. of service up to and through 30 yrs. of service. 2.5% starting with the 31st year of service and every year thereafter.

See footnotes at end of table.

STATE LEGISLATIVE RETIREMENT BENEFITS — Continued

State or other jurisdiction	Participation	Plan name	Requirements for regular retirement	Employee contribution rate	Benefit formula
Oklahoma	Legislators may retain membership as regular public employees if they have that status when elected; one-time option to join Elected Officials' Plan.	Public Employee Retirement System, as regular member or elected official member. [Information here is for the Elected Officials' Plan.]	Elected Officials' Plan: Age 60 with 6 yrs. service, vesting at 6 yrs.	Optional contribution of 4.5%, 6%, 7.5%, 8.5%, 9%, or 10% of total compensation.	Avg. participating salary x length of service x computation factor depending on optional contributions ranging from 1.9% for a 4.5% contribution to 4% for a 10% contribution.
Oregon	Optional	Public Employee Retirement System legislator plan	Age 55, 30+ yrs. service, 5 yrs. vesting.	16.317% of subject wages	1.67% x yrs. service and final avg. monthly salary.
Pennsylvania	Optional	State Employees' Retirement System	Age 50, 3 yrs. service; any age with 35 yrs. of service; early retirement with reduced benefit.	7.5%	3% x final avg. salary x credited yrs. of service (x withdrawal factor if under regular retirement age – 50 for legislators).
Rhode Island	Legislators elected after January 1995 are ineligible for retirement benefits based on legislative service. (a)				
South Carolina	Mandatory, but members may opt out 6 months after being sworn into office.	South Carolina Retirement System	Age 60, 8 yrs. service; 30 yrs. of service regardless of age.	10%	4.82% of annual compensation x yrs. service.
South Dakota	None available.				
Tennessee	Optional		Age 55, 4 yrs. service.	5.43%	$70 per month x yrs. service with a $1,375 monthly cap.
Texas	Optional	Employee Retirement System: Elected Class Members	Age 60, 8 yrs. service; age 50, 12 yrs. service. Vesting at 8 yrs.	8%	2.3% x district judge's salary x length of service, with the monthly benefit capped at the level of a district judge's salary, and adjusted when such salaries are increased. Various annuity options are available. Military service credit may be purchased to add to elective class service membership. In July 2005, a district judge's salary was set at $125,000 a year.
Utah	Mandatory	Governors' and Legislators' Retirement Plan	Age 62 with 10 yrs. and an actuarial reduction; age 65 with 4 yrs. of service for full benefits.	Non-contributory	$24.80/month (as of July 2004) x yrs. of service; adjusted semi-annually according to consumer price index up to a maximum increase of 2%.
Vermont	None available. Deferred compensation plan available.				
Virginia	Mandatory		Age 50, 30 yrs. service (unreduced); age 55, 5 yrs. service; age 50, 10 yrs. service (reduced).	8.91% of creditable compensation	1.7% of average final compensation x yrs. of service.

See footnotes at end of table.

STATE LEGISLATIVE RETIREMENT BENEFITS — Continued

State or other jurisdiction	Participation	Plan name	Requirements for regular retirement	Employee contribution rate	Benefit formula
Washington	Optional. If before an election the legislator belonged to a state public retirement plan, he or she may continue in that by making contributions. Otherwise the new legislator may join PERS Plan 2 or Plan 3.	See column to left. PERS Plan 2 is a DB plan. PERS Plan 3 is a hybrid DB/DC plan.	PERS Plan 2: age 65 with 5 yrs. of service credit. Plan 3: Age 65 with 10 yrs. of service credit for the DB side of the plan; immediate benefits (subject to federal restrictions) on the DC side of the plan. The member may choose various options for investment of contributions to the DC plan.	PERS Plan 2: employee contribution of 2.43% for 2002. Estimated at 3.33% for 2005–2007. Plan 3: No required member contribution for the DB component. The member may contribute from 5% to 15% of salary to the DC component.	PERS Plan 2: 2% x yrs. of service credit x average final compensation. Plan 3: DB is 1% x service credit yrs. x average final compensation. DC benefit depends upon the value of accumulations.
West Virginia	Optional		Age 55, if yrs. of service + age equal 80.	4.5% gross income	2% of final avg. salary x yrs. service. Final avg. salary is based on 3 highest yrs. out of last 10 yrs.
Wisconsin	Mandatory		Age 62, normal; age 57 with 30 yrs. of service.	2.6% of salary in 2003, adjusted annually	Higher benefit of formula (2.165% x yrs. of service x salary for service before 2000; 2% x yrs. of service x salary for service 2000 and after) or money-purchase calculation.
Wyoming	None available.				
Dist. of Columbia	Mandatory		Age 62, 5 yrs. service; age 55, 30 yrs. service; age 60, 20 yrs. service.	Before 10/1/87, 7%; after 10/1/87, 5%	Multiply high 3 yrs. average pay by indicator under applicable yrs. or months of service.
Puerto Rico	Optional	Retirement System of the Employees of the Government of Puerto Rico	After 1990, age 65 with 30 yrs. of service.	8.28%	1.5% of average earnings multiplied by the number of yrs. of accredited service.
Guam	Optional		Age 60, 30 yrs. service; age 55, 15 yrs. service.	5% or 8.5%	An amount equal to 2% of avg. annual salary for each of the first 10 yrs. of credited service and 2.5% of avg. annual salary for each yr. or part thereof of credited service over 10 yrs.
U.S. Virgin Islands	Optional		Age 60, 10 yrs. service.	8%	At age 60 with at least 10 yrs. of service, at 2.5% for each yr. of service, or at any time with at least 30 yrs. service.

Source: National Conference of State Legislatures, January 2006.

Notes:
This table shows the retirement plans effective for state legislators elected in 2003, 2004 and thereafter. In general the table does not include information on closed plans, plans that continue in force for some legislators who entered the plans in previous years, but which have been closed to additional members.
The information in this table was updated for all states and Puerto Rico in 2004 and updated for 2005 state legislation. Information for the District of Columbia, Guam and the Virgin Islands dates from 2002.

Key:
N.A. — Information not available.
None available. — No retirement benefit provided.
(a) Constitution has been amended effective 1/95. Any legislator elected after this date is not eligible to join the State Retirement System, but will be compensated for $10,000/yr. with cost-of-living increases to be adjusted annually.

Table 3.14
BILL PRE-FILING, REFERENCE AND CARRYOVER

State or other jurisdiction	Pre-filing of bills allowed (b)	Bills referred to committee by:		Bill referral restricted by rule (a)		Bill carryover allowed (c)
		Senate	House/Assembly	Senate	House/Assembly	
Alabama	★(d)	(e)(f)	Speaker (f)	L, M	L, M	...
Alaska	★	President	Speaker	L, M	L, M	★
Arizona	★	President	Speaker	L	L	...
Arkansas	★	President	Speaker	L	L	...
California	★(g)	Rules Cmte.	Rules Cmte.	L	L	★(h)
Colorado	★	President	Speaker	L, M (i)	L (i)	...
Connecticut	★	Pres. Pro Tempore	Speaker	M	M	...
Delaware	★	Pres. Pro Tempore	Speaker	L	L	★
Florida	★	President	Speaker	L, M	M	...
Georgia	★	President (f)	Speaker	...	...	★
Hawaii	(j)	President	Speaker	...	...	★
Idaho	...	President (e)	Speaker	L	L	...
Illinois	★	Rules Cmte.	Rules Cmte.	(k)	(k)	★
Indiana	★(l)	Pres. Pro Tempore	Speaker	(m)	...	...
Iowa	★	President	Speaker	M	M	★
Kansas	★	President	Speaker	L (n)	L (n)	★
Kentucky	★	Cmte. on Cmtes.	Cmte. on Cmtes.	L, M	L, M	...
Louisiana	★	President (o)	Speaker (o)	L	L	...
Maine	★	Secy. of Senate and Clerk of House		(p)	(p)	★(p)
Maryland	★	President	Speaker	L	L	...
Massachusetts	★	Clerk	Clerk	M	M	★
Michigan	...	Majority Leader	Speaker	...	...	★
Minnesota	★(q)	President	Speaker	L, M	L, M	★(r)
Mississippi	★	President (e)	Speaker	L	L	...
Missouri	★	Pres. Pro Tempore	Speaker	L	L	...
Montana	★	President	Speaker	...	...	...
Nebraska	★	Reference Cmte. (s)	U	L	U	★(t)
Nevada	★	(u)	(u)	L (v)	...	...
New Hampshire	★	President	Speaker	L	M	★
New Jersey	★	President	Speaker	L, M	L, M	★
New Mexico	★	(w)	Speaker	L, M	M (x)	...
New York	★	Pres. Pro Tempore	Speaker	L	L	★
North Carolina	...	Rules Chair	Speaker	M	M	★
North Dakota	★	President	Speaker	L	L	...
Ohio	★(y)	Reference Cmte.	Rules & Reference Cmte.	L (z)	L, M (aa)	★(bb)
Oklahoma	★	Majority Leader	Speaker	L	L	★(cc)
Oregon	★	President	Speaker	(dd)	(ee)	...
Pennsylvania	★	Pres. Pro Tempore	Chief Clerk	M	M	...
Rhode Island	★	President	Speaker	M	M	...
South Carolina	★	President	Speaker	M	M	★(ff)
South Dakota	★	Pres. Pro Tempore	Speaker	L	L	...
Tennessee	★	Speaker	Speaker	L, M	L, M	★(gg)
Texas	★	President	Speaker	L	L	...
Utah	★	President	Speaker	L	L	...
Vermont	(hh)	President	Speaker	M	M	★
Virginia	★	Clerk	Clerk (ii)	L, M (jj)	(kk)	★(ll)
Washington	★	(mm)	Speaker	L	L	★
West Virginia	★	President	Speaker	L, M	L, M	★(j)
Wisconsin	...	President	Speaker	...	...	★(nn)
Wyoming	★	President	Speaker	M	M	...
Puerto Rico	...	President	Secretary	M	M	...
U.S. Virgin Islands	...	Senate President in Pro-Forma Meeting	U	L	U	★

See footnotes at end of table.

Source: The Council of State Governments' survey, December 2006.

Key:

★ — Yes

. . . — No

L — Rules generally require all bills be referred to the appropriate committee of jurisdiction.

M — Rules require specific types of bills be referred to specific committees (e.g., appropriations, local bills).

U — Unicameral legislature

(a) Legislative rules specify all or certain bills go to committees of jurisdiction.

(b) Unless otherwise indicated by footnote, bills may be introduced prior to convening each session of the legislature. In this column only: ★ — pre- filing is allowed in both chambers (or in the case of Nebraska, in the unicameral legislature); . . . — pre-filing is not allowed in either chamber.

(c) Bills carry over from the first year of the legislature to the second (does not apply in Alabama, Arkansas, Montana, Nevada, North Dakota, Oregon and Texas, where legislatures meet biennially). Bills generally do not carry over after an intervening legislative election.

(d) Except between the end of the last regular session of the legislature in any quadrennium and the organizational session following the general election and special sessions.

(e) Lieutenant governor is the president of the Senate.

(f) Senate bills by president with concurrence of president pro tem, if no concurrence by rules committee. House bills by president pro tem with concurrence of president; if no concurrence, referred to rules committee for assignment.

(g) Bills drafted prior to session. Introduction on the first day.

(h) Bills introduced in the first year of the regular session and passed by the house of origin on or before the January 31 constitutional deadline are carryover bills.

(i) In either house, state law requires any bill which affects the sentencing of criminal offenders and which would result in a net increase of imprisonment in state correctional facilities must be assigned to the appropriations committee of the house in which it was introduced. In the Senate, a bill must be referred to the Appropriations Committee if it contains an appropriation from the state treasury or the increase of any salary. Each bill which provides that any state revenue be devoted to any purpose other than that to which is devoted under existing law must be referred to the Finance Committee.

(j) Prefiling allowed only in the house in even-numbered years.

(k) In even-numbered years, the Rules Committee is to refer to substantive committees only appropriation bills implementing the budget, and bills deemed by the Rules Committee to be of an emergency nature or of substantial importance to the operation of government.

(l) Only in the Senate.

(m) At the discretion of President Pro Tempore.

(n) Appropriation bills are the only "specific type" mentioned in the rules to be referred to either House Appropriation Committee or Senate Ways and Means.

(o) Subject to approval or disapproval. Louisiana—majority members present.

(p) Maine Joint Rule 308 sections 1, 2, 3, "All bills and resolves must be referred to committee, except that this provision may be suspended by a majority vote in each chamber."

(q) Allow pre-filing of bill prior to the convening of the second year of the biennium.

(r) Bill carryover allowed if in second year of a two-year session.

(s) The Nebraska Legislature's Executive Board serves as the Reference Committee.

(t) Bills can be carried over from the 90-day session beginning in the odd-numbered year to the 60-day session, which begins every even-numbered year. Bills not passing on the last day of the 60-day session are all indefinitely postponed by motion on the last day of the session. The odd-numbered year shall be carried forward to the even-numbered year.

(u) Motion for referral can be made by any member, but committee referrals are under the control of the majority floor leader.

(v) Rules do not require specific types of bills to be referred to specific committees.

(w) Sponsor and members.

(x) Speaker has discretion.

(y) Senate Rule 33: Between the general election and the time for the next convening session, a holdover member or member-elect may file bills for introduction in the next session with the Clerk's office. Those bills shall be treated as if they were bills introduced on the first day of the session. House Rule 61: Bills introduced prior to the convening of the session shall be treated as if they were bills introduced on the first day of the session. Between the general election and the time for the next convening session, a member-elect may file bills for introduction in the next session with the Clerk's office. The Clerk shall number such bills consecutively, in the order in which they are filed, beginning with the number "1."

(z) Senate Rule 35: Unless a motion or order to the contrary, bills are referred to the proper standing committee. All Senate bills and resolutions referred by the Committee on Reference on or before the first day of April in an even-numbered year shall be scheduled for a minimum of one public hearing.

(aa) House Rule 37: All House bills and resolutions introduced, in compliance with House Rules, on or before the fifteenth day of May in an even-numbered year shall be referred to a standing select, or special committee, and shall be scheduled for a minimum of one public hearing. House Rule 65: All bills carrying an appropriation shall be referred to the Finance and Appropriations Committee for consideration and report before being considered the third time.

(bb) Bills carry over between the first and second year of each regular annual session, but not to the next biennial two-year General Assembly.

(cc) A legislature consists of two years. Bills from the first session can carry over to the second session only. 2007 will begin a new Legislature, the 51st, and no bills will carry over to 2007.

(dd) The President can refer bills to any standing or special committee and may also attach subsequent referrals to other committees following action by the first committee.

(ee) Rules specify bills shall be referred by the Speaker to any standing or special committee and may also attach subsequent referrals to other committees following action by the first committee.

(ff) Allowed during the first year of the two-year session.

(gg) Bills and resolutions introduced in the First Regular Session may carry over to the Second Regular Session (odd-numbered year to even-numbered year) only.

(hh) Bills are drafted prior to session but released starting first day of session.

(ii) Under the direction of the speaker.

(jj) Jurisdiction of the committees by subject matter is listed in the Rules.

(kk) The House Rules establish jurisdictional committees. The Speaker refers legislation to those committees as he deems appropriate.

(ll) Even-numbered year session to odd-numbered year session.

(mm) By the floor leader.

(nn) From odd-year to even-year, but not between biennial sessions.

Table 3.15
TIME LIMITS ON BILL INTRODUCTION

State or other jurisdiction	Time limit on introduction of bills	Procedures for granting exception to time limits
Alabama	House: No limit. Senate: 22nd L day of regular session (a).	Unanimous vote to suspend rules.
Alaska	35th C day of 2nd regular session.	Introduction by committee or by suspension of operation of limiting rule.
Arizona	House: 29th day of regular session; 10th day of special session. Senate: 22nd day of regular session; 10th day of special session.	House: Permission of rules committee. Senate: Permission of rules committee.
Arkansas.......................	55th day of regular session (50th day for appropriations bills).	2/3 vote of membership of each house.
California	Deadlines established by rules committee.	House: Rules commitee grants exception with 3/4 vote of House. Senate: Approval of rules committee and 3/4 vote of membership.
Colorado.......................	House: 22nd C day of regular session. Senate: 17th C day of regular session.	Committees on delayed bills may extend deadline.
Connecticut	10 days into session in odd-numbered years, 3 days into session in even-numbered years (c).	2/3 vote of members present.
Delaware.......................	House: No limit. Senate: No limit.	
Florida	House: Noon of the 1st day of regular session. Senate: Noon of the 1st day of regular session (b)(e).	Existence of an emergency reasonably compelling consideration notwithstanding the deadline.
Georgia	Only for specific types of bills.	
Hawaii...........................	Actual dates established during session.	Majority vote of membership.
Idaho.............................	House: 20th day of session for personal bills; 36th day of session for all committees; beyond that only privileged cmtes. Senate: 12th day of session for personal bills; 36th day of session for all committees; beyond that only privileged cmtes.	House and Senate: Speaker/President Pro Tempore may designate any standing committee to serve as a privileged committee temporarily.
Illinois...........................	House: Determined by speaker. Senate: Determined by senate president.	House: The Speaker may set deadlines for any action on any category of legislative measure, including deadlines for introduction of bills. Senate: At any time, the President may set alternative deadlines for any legislative action with written notice filed with the Secretary.
Indiana..........................	House: Mid-January. Senate: Date specific—set in rules, different for long and short sessions. Mid-January.	House: 2/3 vote. Senate: If date falls on weekend/Holiday—extended to next day. Sine die deadline set by statute, does not change.
Iowa	House: Friday of 6th week of 1st regular session; Friday of 2nd week of 2nd regular session. Senate: Friday of 7th week of 1st regular session; Friday of 2nd week of 2nd regular session.	Constitutional majority.
Kansas	Actual dates established in the Joint Rules of the House and Senate every two years when the joint rules are adopted.	Resolution adopted by majority of members of either house may make specific exceptions to deadlines.
Kentucky	House: No introductions during the last 14 L days of odd-year session, during last 22 L days of even-year session. Senate: No introductions during the last 14 L days of odd-year session, during last 20 L days of even-year session.	None.
Louisiana	House: 10th C day of odd-year sessions and 23rd C day of even-year sessions. Senate: 10th C day of odd-year sessions and 23rd C day of even-year sessions.	None.
Maine	Cloture dates established by the Legislative Council. Cloture for 2nd session of 122nd legislature was October 7.	Approval by Rules Committee. Senate: Appeals heard by Legislative Council. Six votes required to allow introduction of legislation.
Maryland......................	No introductions during last 35 C days of regular session.	2/3 vote of elected members of each house.

See footnotes at end of table.

TIME LIMITS ON BILL INTRODUCTION—Continued

State or other jurisdiction	Time limit on introduction of bills	Procedures for granting exception to time limits
Massachusetts	1st Wednesday in December of even-numbered years, 1st Wednesday in November of odd-numbered years.	2/3 vote of members present and voting.
Michigan	No limit.	
Minnesota	No limit.	
Mississippi	14th C day in 90-day session; 49th C day in 125-day session (h).	2/3 vote of members present and voting.
Missouri	House: 60th L day of regular session. Senate: March 1.	Majority vote of elected members each house; governor's request for consideration of bill by special message.
Montana	General bills and resolutions: 10th L day; revenue bills: 17th L day; committee bills and resolutions: 36th L day; committee bills implementing provisions of a general appropriation act: 75th L day; committee revenue bills: 62nd L day; interim study resolutions: 75th L day (b)(i).	2/3 vote of members.
Nebraska	10th L day of any session (g).	3/5 vote of elected membership.
Nevada	Actual dates established at start of session.	Waiver granted by Majority Leader of the Senate and Speaker of the Assembly acting jointly.
New Hampshire	Determined by rules.	2/3 vote of members present.
New Jersey	None.	
New Mexico	House: 15 days in short session/even years, 30 days in long session/odd years. Senate: 15 days in short session/even years, 30 days in long session/odd years.	None. Statutory limit for legislators; governor not limited and can send bill with message.
New York	Assembly: For unlimited introduction of bills, 1st Tuesday in May; for introduction of 10 or fewer bills, last Tuesday in May. Senate: 1st Tuesday in March.	House: By unanimous consent or if introduced by Rules Cmte. Senate: President pro tem may designate a later date, or date may be exceeded if bill introduced by Rules Cmte.
North Carolina	Actual dates established during session.	Senate: 2/3 vote of membership present and voting shall be required.
North Dakota	Proposed limits for 2007 session; House: January 15. Senate: January 22.	2/3 vote of the floor or by approval of Delayed Bills Committee.
Ohio	No limit.	
Oklahoma	Time limit set in rules.	2/3 vote of membership.
Oregon	House: 50th C day of session. Senate: 36th C day of session. Rules adopted every 2 years.	House: Bills approved by the Speaker; appropriation of fiscal measures sponsored by the Cmte. on Ways and Means; measures drated by the Legislative Counsel and introduced as members' priority drafting requests. Senate: Senate Rules Cmte. and each senator has 2 priority bills that can be drafted and introduced at any time as permitted by Senate Rules.
Pennsylvania	No limit.	
Rhode Island	2nd week of February for Public Bills.	
South Carolina	House: Prior to April 15 of the 2nd year of a two-year legislative session; May 1 for bills first introduced in Senate. Rule 5.12. Senate: May 1 of regular session for bills originating in House. Rule 47.	Sponsor must give one legislative day's notice. House: 2/3 vote of members present and voting. Senate: 2/3 vote of membership.
South Dakota	Individual bills: 40-day session: 15th L day; 35-day session: 10th L day. Committee bills: 40-day session: 16th L day; 35-day session: 11th L day.	2/3 approval of members-elect.

See footnotes at end of table.

TIME LIMITS ON BILL INTRODUCTION — Continued

State or other jurisdiction	Time limit on introduction of bills	Procedures for granting exception to time limits
Tennessee	General bills, 10th L day of regular session (j).	Unanimous approval by Delayed Bills Committee.
Texas	60th C day of regular session.	4/5 vote of members present and voting.
Utah	12:00 p.m. on 11th day of general session.	Motion for request must be approved by 2/3 vote of members.
Vermont	House: 1st session—last day of February; 2nd session—last day of January. Senate: 1st session—53rd C day; 2nd session—25 C days before start of session.	Approval by Rules Committee.
Virginia	Set by joint procedural resolution adopted at the beginning of the session (usually the 2nd Friday of the session is the last day to introduce legislation that does not have any earlier deadline).	As provided in the joint procedural resolution (usually unanimous consent or at written request of the Governor).
Washington	Until 10 days before the end of session unless 2/3 vote of elected members of each house.	2/3 vote of elected members of each house.
West Virginia	House: 45th C day. Senate: 41st C day.	2/3 vote of members present.
Wisconsin	No limit.	
Wyoming	House: 15th L day of session. Senate: 12th L day of session.	2/3 vote of elected members.
Puerto Rico	1st session—within first 125 days; 2nd session—within first 60 days.	None.
U.S. Virgin Islands	None.	. . .

Source: The Council of State Governments' survey, December 2006.
Key:
C — Calendar
L — Legislative
(a) Not applicable to local bills, advertised or otherwise.
(b) Not applicable to appropriations bills. In West Virginia, supplementary appropriations bills or budget bills.
(c) Specific dates set in Joint Rules.
(d) Not applicable to standing committee bills.
(e) Not applicable to local bills and joint resolutions. Florida: Not applicable to local bills (which have no deadline) or claim bills (deadline is August 1 of the year preceding consideration or within 60 days of a senator's election).
(f) Beyond 36th day for Privileged Committees only. Privileged Committees—House: Appropriation, Education, Revenue and Tax, State Affairs, Ways and Means. Senate: Finance, Judiciary and Rules, State Affairs.

(g) Except appropriation bills and bills introduced at the request of the governor, bills can be introduced during the first 10 legislative days of the session. Appropriation bills and bills introduced at the request of the governor can be introduced at any time during the session.
(h) Except Appropriation and Revenue bills (51st/86th C day) and Local and Private bills (83rd/118th C day).
(i) Only certain measures may be considered in the Short Session—primarily those relating to appropriations, finance, pensions and retirement and localities; certain legislation from the 2001 Session; and legislation proposed by study commissions.
(j) Local bills have no cutoff.
(k) Not applicable to measures approved by Committee on Legislative Rules and Reorganization or by speaker; appropriation or fiscal measures sponsored by committees on Appropriations; true substitute measures sponsored by standing, special or joint committees; or measures drafted by legislative counsel.

Table 3.16
ENACTING LEGISLATION: VETO, VETO OVERRIDE AND EFFECTIVE DATE

State or other jurisdiction	Governor may item veto appropriation bills — Amount	Other (b)	Days allowed governor to consider bill (a) — During session: Bill becomes law unless vetoed	After session: Bill becomes law unless vetoed	After session: Bill dies unless signed	Votes required in each house to pass bills or items over veto (c)	Effective date of enacted legislation (d)
Alabama			6 (e)		10A	Majority of elected body	Date signed by governor, unless otherwise specified.
Alaska	★		15	20P		2/3 elected (f)	90 days after enactment.
Arizona	★	★	5	10A		2/3 elected (g)	90 days after adjournment.
Arkansas	★		5	20A		Majority elected	91st day after adjournment.
California	(h)		12	30A		2/3 elected	(i)
Colorado	★(j)		10 (k)	30A (k)		2/3 elected	90 days after adjournment (l).
Connecticut	★		5	15P		2/3 elected	Oct. 1, unless otherwise specified.
Delaware	★		10	10P	(m)	3/5 elected	Immediately.
Florida		★	7 (k)(n)	15P (k)	30A	2/3 present	60 days after adjournment.
Georgia	★	★	6	40A		2/3 elected	July 1 for generals, date signed by governor for locals.
Hawaii (o)	★(p)		10 (q)	45A (q)(n)	(n)	2/3 elected	Immediately.
Idaho			5	10P		2/3 present	July 1
Illinois	★(p)		60 (k)	60 (k)		3/5 elected (f)	Usually Jan. 1 of next year (r).
Indiana		★	7	7P		Majority elected	(s)
Iowa	★	★	3		30A	2/3 elected	July 1 (r)
Kansas	★	★	10 (k)	90A		2/3 membership	Upon publication or specified date after publication.
Kentucky	★	★	10			Majority elected	90 days after adjournment sine die. Unless the bill contains an emergency clause or special effective date.
Louisiana (o)	★	★	10 (k)	20P (k)		2/3 elected	Aug. 15
Maine	★	★	10	10P	(t)	2/3 elected	90 days after adjournment unless enacted as an emergency.
Maryland	★		6	30P (u)		3/5 elected	June 1 (v)
Massachusetts	★	★	10	10P	10A	2/3 present	90 days after enactment.
Michigan	★	★	14	10P	14P	2/3 elected and serving	90 days after adjournment.
Minnesota	★	(h)	3P	14A, 3P	3A, 14P	2/3 elected – 90 House; 45 Senate	Aug. 1 (w)
Mississippi	★		5	15P (u)		2/3 present	July 1 unless specified otherwise.
Missouri	★	★	15	45A		2/3 elected	Aug. 28 (x)
Montana (o)	★	★	10 (k)	25A (k)		2/3 present	Oct. 1 (w)
Nebraska	★		5	5A, 5P		3/5 elected	90 days following adjournment sine die.
Nevada			5 (y)	10A (y)		2/3 elected	Oct. 1, unless measure stipulates a different date.
New Hampshire		★	5	5P		2/3 present	60 days after enactment, unless otherwise noted.
New Jersey	★		45			2/3 elected	Dates usually specified.
New Mexico	★	★	3 (z)	(aa)	20A	2/3 present	90 days after adjournment unless other date specified.
New York	★		10 (aa)	30A	30A	2/3 elected	20 days after enactment.
North Carolina			10	30A		3/5 elected	60 days after adjournment.
North Dakota	★		3	15A		2/3 elected	(bb)
Ohio	★	★	10	10P	10A	3/5 elected (cc)	91st day after filing with secretary of state (dd).

See footnotes at end of table.

ENACTING LEGISLATION: VETO, VETO OVERRIDE AND EFFECTIVE DATE—Continued

State or other jurisdiction	Governor may item veto appropriation bills		Days allowed governor to consider bill (a)			Votes required in each house to pass bills or items over veto (c)	Effective date of enacted legislation (d)
	Amount	Other (b)	During session: Bill becomes law unless vetoed	After session: Bill becomes law unless vetoed	After session: Bill dies unless signed		
Oklahoma	★	...	5 (ee)		15A (ee)	2/3 elected	90 days after adjournment unless specified in the bill.
Oregon	★	...	5	30A (q)		2/3 present	Jan. 1st of following year (ff).
Pennsylvania	★	★	30	30A, 10P		Majority	60 days after signed by governor.
Rhode Island	...	...	6	10P (gg)	(gg)	3/5 present	Immediately (hh).
South Carolina	★	...	5	(u)		2/3 elected	Date of signature.
South Dakota	★	...	5 (ii)	15P (ii)		2/3 elected	July 1
Tennessee	★	...	10	(jj)		Constitutional majority	40 days after enactment unless otherwise specified.
Texas	★	...	10	20A		2/3 elected	90 days after adjournment.
Utah	★	...	...	60A		2/3 elected	60 days after adjournment.
Vermont	...	...	5		3A	2/3 present	July 1
Virginia	★	★(kk)	7		30A	2/3 present (ll)	July 1 (mm)
Washington	★	★	5	20A		2/3 present	90 days after adjournment.
West Virginia	...	(h)	5	15A (nm)		Majority elected	90 days after enactment.
Wisconsin	★	...	6	6P		2/3 present	Day after publication date unless otherwise specified.
Wyoming	★	★	3	15A		2/3 elected	Specified in act.
American Samoa	★	...	10	30A		2/3 elected	60 days after adjournment (oo).
Guam	★	★	10	30P		2/3 elected	Immediately (qq).
No. Mariana Islands	★	...	40 (k)(pp)			2/3 elected	Immediately.
Puerto Rico	★	...	10	30P		2/3 elected	Specified in act.
U.S. Virgin Islands	★(rr)	★(rr)	10	10P	30A	2/3 elected	Immediately.

See footnotes at end of table.

ENACTING LEGISLATION: VETO, VETO OVERRIDE AND EFFECTIVE DATE—Continued

Source: The Council of State Governments' survey, December 2006.

Key:

★ — Yes

. . . — No

A — Days after adjournment of legislature.

P — Days after presentation to governor.

(a) Sundays excluded, unless otherwise indicated.

(b) Includes language in appropriations bill.

(c) Bill returned to house of origin with governor's objections.

(d) Effective date may be established by the law itself or may be otherwise changed by vote of the legislature. Special or emergency acts are usually effective immediately.

(e) Except bills presented within five days of final adjournment, Sundays are included.

(f) Different number of votes required for revenue and appropriations bills. Alaska—3/4 elected. Illinois—3/5 members elected to override any gubernatorial change except for a reduction in an item, which a majority of the members elected to each house can restore to its original amount.

(g) Several specific requirements of 3/4 majority.

(h) Line-item veto.

(i) For legislation enacted in regular sessions: January of the following year. Urgency legislation: immediately upon chaptering by Secretary of State. Legislation enacted in Special Session: 91st day after adjournment of the special session at which the bill was passed.

(j) Must veto entire amount of any item; an item is an indivisible sum of money dedicated to a stated purpose.

(k) Sundays included.

(l) An act takes effect on the date stated in the act, or if no date is stated in the act, then on its passage.

(m) Bill enacted if not signed/vetoed within time frames.

(n) The governor must notify the legislature 10 days before the 45th day of his intent to veto a measure on that day. The legislature may convene on the 45th day after adjournment to consider the vetoed measures. If the legislature fails to reconvene, the bill does not become law. If the legislature reconvenes, it may pass the measure over the governor's veto or it may amend the law to meet the governor's objections. If the law is amended, the governor must sign the bill within 10 days after it is presented to him in order for it to become law.

(o) Constitution withholds right to veto constitutional amendments.

(p) Governor can also reduce amounts in appropriations bills. In Hawaii, governor can reduce items in executive appropriations measures, but cannot reduce nor item veto amounts appropriated for the judicial or legislative branches.

(q) Except Sundays and legal holidays. In Hawaii, except Saturdays, Sundays, holidays and any days in which the legislature is in recess prior to its adjournment. In Oregon, if the governor does not sign the bill within 30 days after adjournment, it becomes law without the governor's signature; Saturdays and Sundays are excluded.

(r) Effective date for bills which become law on or after July 1. Illinois—unless specified in the act. Exception: An act enacted by a bill passed after May 31 cannot take effect before June 1 of the following year unless it was passed by 3/5 of the members elected to each house.

(s) Varies with date of the veto.

(t) Bill becomes law unless the legislature by their adjournment prevents its return, in which case it shall have such force and effect, unless returned within three days after the next meeting of the same legislature which enacted the bill or resolution, the bill or resolution shall not be a law.

(u) Bills vetoed after adjournment are returned to the legislature for reconsideration. Maryland—reconsidered at the next meeting of the same General Assembly. Mississippi—returned within three days after the beginning of the next session. South Carolina—within two days after the next meeting.

(v) Unless otherwise provided, June 1 is the effective date for bond bills, July 1 for budget, tax and revenue bills. By custom October 1 is the usual effective date for legislation. For vetoed legislation 30 days after the veto is overridden or on the date specified in the bill, whichever is later. If the bill is an emergency measure it takes effect when enacted.

(w) Different date for fiscal legislation. Minnesota—July 1.

(x) If bill has an emergency clause, it becomes effective upon governor's signature.

(y) The day of delivery and Sundays are not counted for purposes of calculating these periods.

(z) Except bills going up in the last three days of session, for which the governor has 20 days.

(aa) If the legislature adjourns during the Governor's consideration of a 10-day bill, the bill shall not become law without the Governor's approval.

(bb) August 1 after filing with the secretary of state. Appropriations and tax bills, July 1 after filing with secretary of state, or date set in legislation by Legislative Assembly, or by date established by emergency clause.

(cc) The exception covers such matters as emergency measures and court bills that originally required a 2/3 majority for passage. In those cases, the same extraordinary majority vote is required to override a veto.

(dd) Emergency, current appropriation, and tax legislation effective immediately. The General Assembly may also enact an uncodified section of law specifying a desired effective date that is after the constitutionally established effective date.

(ee) During session the governor has five days (except Sunday) to sign or veto a bill or it becomes law automatically. After Session a bill becomes a pocket veto if not signed 15 days after Sine Die.

(ff) Unless emergency declared or date specific in text of measure.

(gg) Bills become effective without signature if not signed or vetoed.

(hh) Date signed, date received by Secretary of State if effective without signature, date that veto is overridden, or other specified date.

(ii) During a session, a bill becomes law if a governor signs it or does not act on it within five days. If the legislature has adjourned or recessed or is within five days of a recess or an adjournment, the governor has 15 days to act on the bill. If he does not act, the bill becomes law.

(jj) Adjournment of the legislature is irrelevant; the governor has 10 days to act on a bill after it is presented to him or it becomes law without his signature.

(kk) If part of the item.

(ll) Must include majority of elected members.

(mm) Special sessions—first day of fourth month after adjournment.

(nn) Five days for supplemental appropriation bills.

(oo) Laws required to be approved only by the governor. An act required to be approved by the U.S. Secretary of the Interior only after it is vetoed by the governor and so approved takes effect 40 days after it is returned to the governor by the secretary.

(pp) Twenty days for appropriations bills.

(qq) U.S. Congress may annul.

(rr) May item veto language or amounts in a bill that contains two or more appropriations.

Table 3.17
LEGISLATIVE APPROPRIATIONS PROCESS: BUDGET DOCUMENTS AND BILLS

State or other jurisdiction	Budget document submission							Budget bill introduction		
	Legal source of deadline		Submission date relative to convening					Same time as budget document	Another time	Not until committee review of budget document
	Constitutional	Statutory	Prior to session	Within one week	Within two weeks	Within one month	Over one month			
Alabama	★	★	(a)	...	...	...	...	★	...	...
Alaska	★	★	...	(a)	...	...	...	★	...	...
Arizona	...	★	★	...	...	...	...	...	...	★
Arkansas	...	★	★	...	...	...	...	...	...	★
California	★	...	...	...	...	...	...	★	...	...
Colorado	...	★	★(b)	...	...	...	...	...	76th day by rule	...
Connecticut	...	★	...	...	...	(a)	...	★	...	...
Delaware	...	...	...	...	...	...	...	...	...	★
Florida	★	★	★	...	...	...	...	★	...	...
Georgia	★	...	...	(a)	...	...	...	★	...	...
Hawaii	...	★	30 days	...	...	...	...	...	★	...
Idaho	...	★	...	★	...	...	...	...	...	★
Illinois	...	★	...	...	...	...	★(c)	...	★(d)	...
Indiana	...	★	...	...	...	...	...	...	★	...
Iowa	...	★	...	...	...	(a)	...	...	...	★(e)
Kansas	...	★	...	...	★(f)	...	...	...	★	...
Kentucky	★	...	...	(a)	...	...	...	★	...	...
Louisiana	...	★	(g)	(g)	...	...	...	(h)	...	...
Maine	...	★	...	(a)	...	...	...	★	...	...
Maryland	★	...	...	★(f)	...	...	...	★(i)	...	...
Massachusetts	...	★	...	...	...	★	...	★	...	...
Michigan	...	★	...	...	...	★	...	★	...	...
Minnesota	...	★	...	...	...	(a)	...	...	...	★
Mississippi	...	★	★	...	...	...	...	...	★	...
Missouri	★	...	...	...	...	★	...	...	...	★
Montana	...	★	★	...	...	...	...	...	★	...
Nebraska	...	★	★	...	...	...	...	★(j)	...	...
Nevada	★	...	(a)	...	...	...	...	...	...	★
New Hampshire	...	★	...	...	...	...	(a)	★	...	...
New Jersey	...	★	...	...	...	...	...	...	...	...
New Mexico	...	★	...	...	...	(a)	...	...	★	...
New York	★(l)	...	...	...	★(k)	...	...	...	★(m)	...
North Carolina	...	...	...	...	...	...	...	★	...	...
North Dakota	...	★	(n)	...	...	...	...	★	...	...
Ohio	...	★	...	...	...	...	★(e)(f)	★	...	...
Oklahoma	...	★	★	★	...	...	...	★	...	...
Oregon	...	★	...	...	...	...	★(o)	★(p)	...	...
Pennsylvania	★	...	...	...	...	...	★	...	...	★
Rhode Island	...	★	...	...	...	...	★	...	★	...
South Carolina	...	★	...	★	...	...	...	...	...	★(q)
South Dakota	...	★	...	...	...	...	★(r)	...	★(s)	...
Tennessee	...	★	...	...	★(a)(f)	★(a)(f)	...	★	...	...
Texas	...	★	...	6th day	...	...	...	...	★(t)	...
Utah	...	★	...	★(u)	...	...	...	...	★(v)	...
Vermont	...	...	...	(w)	...	...	...	...	...	★
Virginia	...	★	Dec. 20	...	...	...	...	★	...	...
Washington	★(x)	...	Dec. 20 (y)	...	...	...	...	★	...	...
West Virginia	★	...	...	★	...	...	...	★	...	...
Wisconsin	...	★	...	...	...	...	★(z)	★	...	...
Wyoming	...	★	Dec. 1	...	...	...	...	...	...	★
No. Mariana Islands	...	★	(a)	...	...	...	...	...	(z)	★
Puerto Rico	...	★	...	...	...	★	...	...	...	★
U.S. Virgin Islands	...	★	May 30	...	...	...	...	...	★	...

See footnotes at end of table.

LEGISLATIVE APPROPRIATIONS PROCESS: BUDGET DOCUMENTS AND BILLS — Continued

Source: The Council of State Governments' survey, December 2006.
Key:
★ — Yes
. . . — No

(a) Specific time limitations: Alabama—five days; Alaska—December 15, fourth legislative day; Connecticut—not later than the first session day following the third day in February, in each odd-numbered year; Georgia—first five days of session; Iowa—no later than February 1; Kentucky—10th legislative day; Maine—by Friday following the first Monday in January; Minnesota—by the fourth Tuesday in January each odd-numbered year; Nevada—no later than 14 days before commencement of regular session; New Hampshire—by February 15; New Mexico—by January 1 each year; Tennessee—on or before February 1 for sitting governor; No. Mariana Islands—no later than six months before the beginning of the fiscal year.

(b) Presented by November 1 to the Joint Budget Committee.

(c) Third Wednesday in February.

(d) Deadlines for introducing bills in general are set by senate president and house speaker.

(e) Executive budget bill is introduced and used as a working tool for committee.

(f) Later for first session of a new governor; Kansas—21 days; Maryland—10 days after; New Jersey—February 15; Ohio—by March 15; Tennessee—March 1.

(g) The governor shall submit his executive budget to the Joint Legislative Committee on the budget no later than 45 days prior to each regular session; except that in the first year of each term, the executive budget shall be submitted no later than 30 days prior to the regular session. Copies shall be made available to the entire legislature on the first day of each regular session.

(h) Bills appropriating monies for the general operating budget and ancillary appropriations, bills appropriating funds for the expenses of the legislature and the judiciary must be submitted to the legislature for introduction no later than 45 days prior to each regular session, except that in the first year of each term, such appropriation bills shall be submitted no later than 30 days prior to the regular session.

(i) Appropriations bills other than the budget bill (supplementary) may be introduced at any time. They must provide their own tax source and may not be enacted until the budget bill is enacted.

(j) Governor's budget bill is introduced and serves as a working document for the Appropriations Committee. The Governor must submit the budget proposal by January 15 of each odd-numbered year (Neb.Rev.Stat. sec.81-125). The statute extends this deadline to February 1 for a governor who is in his first year of office.

(k) The executive budget must be submitted by the governor to the legislature by the second Tuesday following the opening of session (or February 1 for the first session following a gubernatorial election).

(l) The legislature must transmit to the Governor itemized estimates of its financial needs no later than December 1.

(m) Submission of the Governor's budget bills to the legislature occurs with submission of the executive budget.

(n) Legislative Council's Budget Section hears the executive budget recommendations during legislature's December organizational session.

(o) By December 1 of even-numbered year unless new governor is elected; if new governor is elected, then February 1 of odd-numbered year.

(p) Legislature often introduces other budget bills during legislative session that are not part of the governor's recommended budget.

(q) The Ways and Means Committee introduces the Budget Bill within five days after the beginning of the session (S.C. Code 11-11-70).

(r) It is usually over a month. The budget must be delivered to the Legislature not later than the first Tuesday after the first Monday in December.

(s) It must be introduced no later than the 16th legislative day.

(t) Within first 30 days of session.

(u) Must submit to the legislature no later than three days after session begins.

(v) Legislative rules require budget bills to be introduced by the 43rd day of the session.

(w) No official submission dates. Occurs by custom early in the session.

(x) And Rules.

(y) For fiscal period other than biennium, 20 days prior to first day of session.

(z) Last Tuesday in January. A later submission date may be requested by the governor.

Table 3.18
FISCAL NOTES: CONTENT AND DISTRIBUTION

State or other jurisdiction	Intent or purpose of bill	Cost involved	Projected future cost	Proposed source of revenue	Fiscal impact on local government	Other	All	Available on request	Bill sponsor	Members	Chair only	Fiscal staff	Executive budget staff
	Content						Distribution — Legislators — Appropriations Committee						
Alabama	★	★	...	★	★	★(a)	...	★	★	...	...	...	...
Alaska	...	★	★	★	...	...	★	★	★	...	...	★	★
Arizona	★	★	★	★	★	★	★	★	★	★	...	★	★
Arkansas (b)	...	★	★	...	★	★	★	...	...	...	...	...	...
California	★	★	★	★	★	...	★	★	★	...	...	★	★
Colorado	★	★	★	★	★	...	★	...	...	...	...	...	...
Connecticut	★	★	★	★	★	...	(c)	...	...	...	...	...	...
Delaware	...	★	...	...	...	...	★	...	...	...	...	...	...
Florida	★	★	★	★	★	★	★	...	...	...	...	★	...
Georgia	...	★	★	...	★	...	★	★	...	...	...	...	...
Hawaii	...	...	...	...	...	★	...	...	...	...	★	★	★
Idaho	★	★	★	★	★	★(d)	★	...	...	...	...	(e)	(e)
Illinois	...	★	★	★	★	...	(f)	★	★	...	...	...	...
Indiana	★	★	★	★	★	...	★	...	...	...	...	★	★
Iowa	★	★	★	★	★	...	.... (g)						
Kansas	★	★	★	★	★	...	★	★	★	...	★	★	★
Kentucky	★	★	★	★	★	★	...	★	★	★	...	★	...
Louisiana	...	★	★	...	★	...	★	★	...	...	★(h)	...	...
Maine	...	★	★	...	★	...	...	★	★	★	...	★	★
Maryland	...	★	★	★	★	★	...	★(i)	...	...	...	...	...
Massachusetts	...	★(j)	★	...	...	★	★	...	...	...	★	...	...
Michigan	★	★	★	★	★	★(k)	★(l)	...	★	...	★	★	★
Minnesota	★	★	★	★	★	...	...	...	...	★	...	★	★
Mississippi	...	★	★	★	...	...	...	...	★(m)	...	...	...	...
Missouri	★	★	★	★	★	...	...	★	★	...	...	...	★
Montana	...	★	★	...	★	★(n)	★	...	...	...	...	★	★
Nebraska	...	★	★	★	★	...	★	...	...	...	...	★	...
Nevada	...	★	★	★	★	★	★	...	...	...	...	...	...
New Hampshire	★	★	...	★	★	...	...	★	...	★	...	★	★
New Jersey	...	★	...	★	★	...	★	...	...	...	...	★	★
New Mexico	★	★	★	★	★	...	...	★	★	★	...	(o)	(o)
New York	...	★	...	★	★	...	★	...	...	...	...	...	...
North Carolina	...	★	★	...	★	★	(p)	...	...	...	...	...	...
North Dakota	...	...	★	★	★	★(q)	(r)	★	...	...	...	★	★
Ohio	★	★	★	★	★	...	(s)	...	...	...	...	...	...
Oklahoma	★	★	★	★	...	...	...	★	★	...	★	★	...
Oregon	★	★	★	★	★	★	★	...	...	...	...	★	★
Pennsylvania	...	★	★	★	★	...	...	...	...	★	★	★	★
Rhode Island	★	★	★	★	★	...	...	★	...	...	★	★	★
South Carolina	★	★	★	★	★	...	...	★	...	...	(t)	★	★
South Dakota	...	★	★	★	★	...	...	★	...	...	...	...	...
Tennessee	★	★	★	...	★	...	★	★	★	...	...	...	...
Texas	...	★	★	★	★	★(u)	★	★	★	★	...	...	★
Utah	...	★	★	★	★	★(v)	★	★	★	...	...	★	★
Vermont	.... (w)						...	★	...	★	...	...	...
Virginia	★	★	★	★	★	★(x)	(y)	...	★	...	★	★(z)	...
Washington	...	★	★	★	★	★(aa)	★	★	★	★	★	★	...
West Virginia	...	★	★	★	★	...	...	...	...	★	...	...	...
Wisconsin	...	★	★	★	★	...	(bb)	...	...	...	...	(bb)	...
Wyoming	...	★	★	★	...	...	★	...	...	...	...	...	...
No. Mariana Islands	★	★	★	★	★	★	...	...	...	...	...	★	★
Puerto Rico	.... (cc)												
U.S. Virgin Islands	★	★	...	★	...	...	★	...	...	...	...	...	...

See footnotes at end of table.

FISCAL NOTES: CONTENT AND DISTRIBUTION — Continued

Source: The Council of State Governments' survey, December 2006.

Note: A fiscal note is a summary of the fiscal effects of a bill on government revenues, expenditures and liabilities.

Key:

★ — Yes

. . . — No

(a) Fiscal notes included on final passage calendar.

(b) Only retirement, corrections and local government bills require fiscal notes.

(c) The fiscal notes are printed with the bills favorably reported by the committees.

(d) Statement of purpose.

(e) Attached to bill, so available to both fiscal and executive budget staff.

(f) A summary of each fiscal note is attached to the summary of its bill in the printed Legislative Synopsis and Digest, and on the General Assembly's Web site. Fiscal notes are prepared for the sponsor and attached to the bill on file with the House Clerk or Senate Secretary.

(g) Fiscal notes are available to everyone.

(h) Prepared by the Legislative Fiscal Office when a state agency is involved and prepared by Legislative Auditor's office when a local board or commission is involved; copies sent to House and Senate staff offices respectively.

(i) And to the committee to which referred. After initial hard copy distribution to sponsor and committee, note is released to member computer system and thereafter to the legislative Web site.

(j) Fiscal notes are prepared only if cost exceeds $100,000 or matter has not been acted upon by the Joint Committee on Ways and Means.

(k) Other relevant data.

(l) At present, fiscal information is part of the bill analysis on the legislative Web site.

(m) And committee to which bill referred.

(n) Mechanical defects in bill.

(o) Fiscal impact statements prepared by Legislative Finance Committee staff are available to anyone on request and on the legislature's Web site.

(p) Fiscal notes are posted on the Internet and available to all members.

(q) Notes required only if impact is $5,000 or more. Bills impacting workforce safety and insurance benefits or premiums have actuarial statements as do bills proposing changes in state and local retirement systems.

(r) Fiscal notes are available online to anyone from the legislative branch Web site.

(s) Fiscal notes are prepared for bills before being voted on in any standing committee or floor session. Upon distribution to the legislators preparing to vote, the fiscal notes are made public.

(t) Fiscal impact statements on proposed legislation are prepared by the Office of State Budget and sent to the House or Senate standing committee that requested the impact. All fiscal impacts are posted on the OSB Web page.

(u) Equalized education funding impact statement and criminal justice policy impact statement.

(v) Fiscal notes are to include cost estimates on all proposed bills that anticipate direct expenditures by any Utah resident and the cost to the overall Utah resident population.

(w) Fiscal notes are not mandatory and their content will vary.

(x) Technical amendments, if needed.

(y) Fiscal impact statements are widely available because they are also posted on the Internet shortly after they are distributed. The Joint Legislative Audit Review Commission (JLARC) also prepares a review of the fiscal impact statement if requested by a standing committee chair. The review statement is also available on the Internet.

(z) Legislative budget directors.

(aa) Impact on private sector.

(bb) The fiscal estimate is printed as an appendix to the bill; anyone that has a copy of the bill has a copy of the fiscal estimate.

(cc) The Legislature of Puerto Rico does not prepare fiscal notes, but upon request the economics unit could prepare one. The Department of Treasury has the duty to analyze and prepare fiscal notes.

Table 3.19
BILL AND RESOLUTION INTRODUCTIONS AND ENACTMENTS:
2006 REGULAR SESSIONS

State or other jurisdiction	Duration of session**	Introductions		Enactments		Measures vetoed by governor	Length of session
		Bills	Resolutions*	Bills	Resolutions*		
Alabama	Jan. 10–April 18, 2006	1,432	978	365	290	7	30L
Alaska	Jan. 9–May 9, 2006	308	74	113	32	0 (c)	121C
Arizona	Jan. 9–Jun. 22, 2006	1,453	134	395	25	43 (c)	164C
Arkansas	No session in 2006						
California	Dec. 6, 2004–Nov. 30, 2006	1,853	169	632	122	179 (c)	237L (b)
Colorado	Jan. 11–May 10, 2006	651	22	440	2	44 (c)	120C
Connecticut	Feb. 8–May 3, 2006	1,550	257	206	157	3	85C
Delaware	Jan. 10–June 30, 2006	392	78	214	0	3	40L
Florida	Mar. 7–May 5, 2006	2,096	127	440	69	23 (c)	60C
Georgia	Jan. 9–March 30, 2006	1,937	2,290	509	1,883	19	40L
Hawaii	Jan. 18–May 4, 2006	2,758	1,030	354	374	32	60L
Idaho	Jan. 9–Apr. 11, 2006	737	99	459	65	0	93C
Illinois	Jan. 11–May 26, 2006	2,547	1,071	346	N.A.	7	(b)
Indiana	Nov. 22, 2005–Mar. 14, 2006 (d)	834	159	193	N.A.	0	(d)
Iowa	Jan. 9–May 3, 2006	1,211	270	191	N.A.	3 (a)(c)	108C
Kansas	Jan. 9–May 25, 2006	774	40	219	12	5 (a)(c)	93C
Kentucky	Jan. 3–Apr. 12, 2006	1,012	133	223	37	3 (c)	60L
Louisiana	Mar. 27–June 19, 2006	2,149	470	873	428	9 (c)	48L
Maine	Jan. 4–May 24, 2006	658	19	351	19	1	48L
Maryland	Jan. 11–Apr. 12, 2006	2,856	26	636	5	204	90C
Massachusetts	Jan. 4, 2006–July, 2006 (e)	N.A.	N.A.	448 (g)	N.A.	(g)	(f)
Michigan	Jan. 11–Dec. 29, 2006	1,752	17	682	1	N.A.	(b)
Minnesota	Mar. 1–May 21, 2006	3,139	0	113	0	1 (c)	46L
Mississippi	Jan. 3–Apr. 5, 2006 (h)	2,819	267	435	169	4 (c)	(h)
Missouri	Jan. 4–May 30, 2006	1,879	115 (i)	165 (i)	3 (i)	(c)	75L
Montana	No session in 2006						
Nebraska	Jan. 4–Apr. 13, 2006	500 (j)	210	135	73	2 (j)	60L
Nevada	No session in 2006						
New Hampshire	Jan. 4–June 28, 2006	1029	27	328	3	4	19L
New Jersey	Jan. 10, 2006–Jan. 8, 2007	6,430	683	237	240 (k)	3 (c)	(b)
New Mexico	Jan. 17–Feb. 16, 2006	1,623	28	112	4	13 (c)	30C
New York	Jan. 4, 2006–Jan. 3, 2007	17,700	(l)	750	4,783	210	365C
North Carolina	May 9–July 28, 2006	1,905	71	264	24	1	81C
North Dakota	No session in 2006						
Ohio	Jan. 3, 2006–(m)	403	45	134	9	1 (a)(c)(n)	(b)
Oklahoma	Feb. 6–May 26, 2006	2,133	142	327	48	6	62L
Oregon	No session in 2006						
Pennsylvania	Jan. 3–Nov. 22, 2006 (o)	4,450	1,310 (p)	365 (q)	(p)	15 (c)	(b)
Rhode Island	Jan. 3–Jun. 23, 2006	2,812	N.A.	704	389	37 (a)	(b)
South Carolina	Jan. 10–June 1, 2006	721	828	203	704	36 (a)(c)	63L
South Dakota	Jan. 10–Mar. 2, 2006	458	24	270	16	4 (a)	35L
Tennessee	Feb. 7–May 27, 2006	3,330	1,606	514	1,500 (r)	0	(b)
Texas	No session in 2006						
Utah	Jan. 16–Mar. 1, 2006	663	56 (s)	367	28	4 (c)	45C
Vermont	Jan. 3–June 1, 2006	485	299	157	267	4	(t)
Virginia	Jan. 11–Mar. 11, 2006	2,346	941	958	791	15	45L
Washington	Jan. 9–Mar. 8, 2006	929	20	155	N.A.	5 (c)	59C
West Virginia	Jan. 11–Mar. 11, 2006	2,105	100	370	15	6 (c)	59C
Wisconsin	Jan. 3–July 12, 2006 (u)	1,967	272	491	150	47 (c)	63L
Wyoming	Feb 13–Mar. 11, 2006	213	7	121	4	1 (a)	21L

See footnotes at end of table.

BILL AND RESOLUTION INTRODUCTIONS AND ENACTMENTS:
2006 REGULAR SESSIONS — Continued

Source: The Council of State Governments' survey of legislative agencies, March 2007.

* Includes Joint and Concurrent resolutions.

**Actual adjournment dates are listed regardless of constitutional or statutory limitations. For more information on provisions, see Table 3.2, "Legislative Sessions: Legal Provisions."

Key:

C — Calendar day.

L — Legislative day (in some states, called a session or workday; definition may vary slightly; however, it generally refers to any day on which either chamber of the legislature is in session.)

N.A. — Not available.

(a) Number of vetoes overridden: Iowa – 1; Kansas – 1; Ohio – 1;Rhode Island – 6; South Carolina – 25; South Dakota – 2; Wyoming – 1

(b) Length of session: California – 123L for first year of session, 2005, 114 L for second year of session 2006, total of 237 legislative days and 725 calendar days; Illinois – Senate 45L and House 55L; Michigan – Senate 97L and House 97L; New Jersey – Senate 45L and Assembly 40L; Ohio – Senate 119L and House 122L; Pennsylvania – Senate 67 session days and House, 71 session days; Rhode Island – Senate 58L and House 70L; Tennessee – Senate 41L and House 40L.

(c) Line item or partial vetoes. Alaska – 1partial or line item veto; Arizona – 1, subsequently overturned by the Arizona Supreme Court; California – 4 line item vetoes; Colorado – 4 line item vetoes; Florida – 3 line item vetoes; Iowa – 10 partial or line item vetoes; Kansas – 4 partial or line item vetoes; Kentucky – 39 line items; Louisiana – 7 line item vetoes;Minnesota – 1 line item or partial veto; Mississippi – 6; Missouri – 4 line item appropriations; New Jersey – 4 line item vetoes; New Mexico – 6 partial or line item vetoes; Ohio – 2 line item vetoes; Pennsylvania – 15; South Carolina – 7 partial or line item vetoes, all were overridden by the legislature; South Dakota – 1 partial or line item veto; Utah – 2 line item vetoes; Washington – 17 partial vetoes; Wisconsin – 2 partial vetoes

(d) The November 22, 2005, convening date was the annual one day "Organizational Day". The House reconvened on January 4, 2006, and the Senate reconvened on January 9, 2006. Both adjourned March 14, 2006. The House convened on 30 days and the Senate convened on 33 days (this does not include intervening days when they held committee meetings, etc.).

(e) The Massachusetts legislative session convened January 4, 2006 and adjourned July 31, 2006. Informal session will occur after July 31, 2006 until the end of 2006.

(f) 38 formal and 95 informal session days.

(g) In Massachusetts 421 approved by the governor, 5 approved in part, 19 passed over veto, 8 became law without executive approval.

(h) House convening date of January 7, 2006. House: 90C; Senate 93C.

(i) This includes the following bill enactments: 94 Senate, 55 House and 1 House Concurrent Resolution; resolution introductions include: 28 HJR, 49 HCR, 23 SJR and 15 SCR; resolutions passed: 1 HJR, 1 SJR and 1 HCR.

(j) Bill introduction total does not include appropriation bills. The two vetoes were of appropriation bills; of 6 partial or line item vetoes 5 were appropriation bills; of 4 vetoes overridden by the legislature 1 was an appropriation bill.

(k) 3 Joint and 237 other.

(l) There are no official statistics for resolution introductions.

(m) House adjournment: December 21, 2006; Senate adjournment: December 26, 2006.

(n) There is one other bill (Am.Sub.S.B. 117) not included in the numbers presented here – Governor Taft filed the act with the Secretary of State without his signature on January 5, 2007; Governor Strickland brought the bill back and vetoed it on January 8, 2007; procedures subject to a lawsuit and the outcome is uncertain.

(o) Pennsylvania meets in 2 – year sessions. The statistics reported are for the second year of the 2005–2006 biennium. See the 2006 edition for 2005 statistics.

(p) Pennsylvania does not track the number of resolutions that have been passed. Generally if a resolution is introduced it is passed.

(q) This number includes 285 general bills, 1 special bill and 79 appropriations bills.

(r) Estimated. Tennessee does not track number of enacted resolutions.

(s) Includes simple resolutions.

(t) Senate – 74 actual days, 151 calendar days; House – 79 actual days, 151 calendar days.

(u) All action carries over to even year.

Table 3.20
BILL AND RESOLUTION INTRODUCTIONS AND ENACTMENTS:
2006 SPECIAL SESSIONS

State or other jurisdiction	Duration of session**	Introductions		Enactments		Measures vetoed by governor	Length of session
		Bills	Resolutions*	Bills	Resolutions*		
Alabama	No special session in 2006						
Alaska	May 10–June 8, 2006	8	3	0	2	0	30C
	July 12–Aug. 10, 2006	12	1	2	0	0	30C
	Nov. 14–Nov. 20, 2006	4	1	1	1	1	7C
Arizona	Jan. 24 -Mar. 2, 2006	5	0	0	0	0	41C
Arkansas....................	Apr. 3–Apr. 21, 2006	75	44	39	44	0	6C
California	Jan. 5, 2005–Nov. 30, 2006	13	1	0	0	0	71L (a)
	June 27–Nov 30, 2006	12	1	0	1	0	12L (b)
Colorado	July 6–July 10, 2006	36	10	13	6	0	5C
Connecticut	No special session in 2006						
Delaware.....................	Sept. 6, 2006	0	0	1	0	0	1L
Florida	No special session in 2006						
Georgia	No special session in 2006						
Hawaii........................	No special session in 2006						
Idaho..........................	Aug. 25, 2006	1	0	1	0	0	1C
Illinois.......................	No special session in 2006						
Indiana.......................	No special session in 2006						
Iowa	July 14, 2006	0	0	0	0	(c)	1C
Kansas	No special session in 2006						
Kentucky	June 22–June 28, 2006	4	1 (d)	2	0	0	5L
Louisiana	Feb. 6–Feb. 17, 2006	157	101	43	94	0	11L
Maine	No special session in 2006						
Maryland....................	June 14–June 23, 2006	25	0	5	0	1 (e)	10C
Massachusetts.............	No special session in 2006						
Michigan.....................	No special session in 2006						
Minnesota	No special session in 2006						
Mississippi	Aug. 24–Aug 26, 2006	47	33	20	28	0	3C
	Oct. 5, 2006	10	3	1	3	0	1C
Missouri......................	No special session in 2006						
Montana	No special session in 2006						
Nebraska.....................	No special session in 2006						
Nevada	No special session in 2006						
New Hampshire..........	Sept. 26–Sept. 26, 2006	1	0	1	0	0	1L
New Jersey..................	July 4–July 28, 2006	84	16	1	2	1	4L
New Mexico	No special session in 2006						
New York	No special session in 2006 (k)						
North Carolina	No special session in 2006						
North Dakota..............	No special session in 2006						
Ohio	No special session in 2006						
Oklahoma	May 25–June 23, 2006	363	8	85	0	0	5L
Oregon	Apr. 20, 2006	5	2	5	1	0	1L
Pennsylvania	(f)	116	7	1	(g)	0	(f)
Rhode Island	No special session in 2006						
South Carolina	No special session in 2006						
South Dakota..............	No special session in 2006						
Tennessee	Jan. 10–Feb. 6, 2006	36	115	3	100 (h)	0	(i)
Texas	Apr. 17–May 16, 2006	213	91 (j)	11	39 (j)	0	30C
Utah	May 24, 2006	12	3	9	3	0	1C
	Sept. 19, 2006	3	0	2	0	0	1C
	Dec. 4, 2006	3	1	3	0	0	1C
Vermont	No special session in 2006						
Virginia......................	Mar. 27–Sept. 28, 2006	127	264	10	251	0	16L
Washington.................	No special session in 2006						
West Virginia	June 13–June 14, 2006	41	N.A.	22	N.A.	0	6C
	Nov. 9–Nov. 14, 2006	23	N.A.	21	N.A.	0	6C
Wisconsin....................	Feb. 14–Mar. 7, 2006	2	0	1	0	0	7L
Wyoming.....................	No special session in 2006						

See footnotes at end of table.

BILL AND RESOLUTION INTRODUCTIONS AND ENACTMENTS:
2006 SPECIAL SESSIONS — Continued

Source: The Council of State Governments' survey of state legislative agencies, March 2007.

* Includes Joint and Concurrrent resolutions.

** Actual adjournment dates are listed regardless of constitutional or statutory limitations. For more information on provisions, see Table 3.2, "Legislative Sessions: Legal Provisions."

Key:

N.A. — Not available

C — Calendar day.

L — Legislative day (in some states, called a session or workday; definition may vary slightly; however, it generally refers to any day on which either chamber of the legislature is in session).

(a) 694 calendar days in First Extraordinary Session.

(b) 159 calendar days in Second Extraordinary Session.

(c) 1 veto override by the legislature.

(d) Concurrent.

(e) 4 vetoes overiridden by legislature.

(f) House convened Jan. 23–Sept. 25, 2006; Senate convened January 4–September 21, 2006. House 25 session days and Senate 34 session days.

(g) Pennsylvania does not track the number of resolutions that have been passed. Generally, if a resolution is introduced it is passed.

(h) Estimated

(i) Senate 10L, House 13L.

(j) Concurrent resolutions introduced 56, passed 39; Joint resolutions introduced 35, passed 0.

(k) New York has a year round session. A special session, or extraordinary session is a session called by the governor.

Table 3.21
STAFF FOR INDIVIDUAL LEGISLATORS

State or other jurisdiction	Senate			House/Assembly		
	Capitol			Capitol		
	Personal	Shared	District	Personal	Shared	District
Alabama	...	YR/2	(a)	...	YR/10	(a)
Alaska	YR/SO	...	YR	YR/SO	...	YR
Arizona	YR (b)	...	...	...	YR (b)	...
Arkansas	...	YR	...	...	YR	...
California	YR	...	YR	YR	...	YR
Colorado	(c)	(c)	...	(c)	(c)	...
Connecticut (d)	YR/36	...	...	...	YR/38	...
Delaware	....(e)..					
Florida	YR (f)	...	YR (f)	YR (f)	...	YR (f)
Georgia	...	YR/3, SO/68	...	...	YR/25, SO/113	...
Hawaii	YR	...	...	YR	...	...
Idaho	...	SO, YR (g)	...	...	SO, YR (g)	...
Illinois	...	YR/1 (h)	YR (h)	YR	YR/2 (h)	YR (h)
Indiana	...	YR/2 (i)	...	...	YR	...
Iowa	SO	...	...	SO	...	...
Kansas	SO/1	...	...	(j)	SO/3	...
Kentucky	...	YR (k)	...	...	YR (k)	...
Louisiana	(l)	YR (m)	YR (l)	(l)	YR (m)	YR (l)
Maine	YR, SO (n)	YR/27, SO/7	...	...	(o)	...
Maryland	YR, SO (p)	...	YR (p)	YR (p)	SO (p)	YR (p)
Massachusetts	YR	...	...	YR	...	...
Michigan	YR (q)	...	...	YR/2 (q)	...	...
Minnesota	YR (r)	Varies	...	YR/3	Varies	...
Mississippi	...	YR	...	...	YR	...
Missouri	YR	YR	...	YR	YR	...
Montana	...	SO	...	...	SO	...
Nebraska	YR	...	...	.........................Unicameral.........................		
Nevada	SO (s)	YR	...	SO (s)	YR	...
New Hampshire	...	YR	...	...	YR	...
New Jersey	YR (f)	...	(f)	YR (f)	...	(f)
New Mexico	SO (t)	...	...	...	SO/2	...
New York	YR (u)	...	YR (u)	YR (u)	...	YR (u)
North Carolina	YR (v)	YR	...	YR (v)	YR	...
North Dakota	...	SO (s)	...	...	SO (s)	...
Ohio	YR/2	...	(w)	YR/1 (x)	...	(w)
Oklahoma	YR/1 (y)	YR (y)	...	YR (y)	YR/1 (y)	...
Oregon	SO/2	...	(z)	SO/2	...	(z)
Pennsylvania	YR	...	YR	YR	...	YR
Rhode Island	...	YR (aa)	...	...	YR (aa)	...
South Carolina	...	YR/2	...	YR/4	...	...
South Dakota	(bb)	(bb)	...	(bb)	(bb)	...
Tennessee	YR/1	...	...	(ii)	YR/1	...
Texas	YR/6 (cc)	...	...	YR/3 (cc)	...	...
Utah	(dd)	SO	...	(dd)	SO	...
Vermont	YR/1 (ee)	...	...	YR/1 (ee)	...	...
Virginia	SO (ff)	...	(ff)	SO (ff)	SO/2	(ff)
Washington	YR/1	...	YR/1	YR/1	...	YR/1
West Virginia	SO	...	...	...	SO/17	...
Wisconsin	(gg)	...	(gg)	(gg)	...	(gg)
Wyoming	...	...	...	...	...	...
No. Mariana Islands	YR (hh)	(hh)	...	YR (hh)	(hh)	(gg)
Puerto Rico	YR (hh)	...	...	YR (hh)	...	...
U.S. Virgin Islands	YR (hh)	...	...	.........................Unicameral.........................		

See footnotes at end of table.

STAFF FOR INDIVIDUAL LEGISLATORS — Continued

Source: The Council of State Governments' survey, December 2006.

Note: For entries under column heading "Shared," figures after slash indicate approximate number of legislators per staff person, where available.

Key:

... — Staff not provided for individual legislators.

YR — Year-round.

SO — Session only.

IO — Interim only.

(a) Six counties have local delegation offices with shared staff.

(b) Representatives share a secretary with another legislator; however, House leadership and committee chairs usually have their own secretarial staff. All legislators share professional research staff.

(c) Senate: has 17 session only staff and 18 year-round staff. There are no district staffers, and since the entire staff works for multiple senators, they are not listed as shared. There are five session only staff in the bill room who are jointly managed by the Colorado Senate and House. House: year-round staff consists of five majority caucus staff; four minority caucus staff; six chief clerk nonpartisan staff. The Colorado session only staff consists of three majority caucus staff; two minority caucus staff; 23 chief clerk nonpartisan staff. The Colorado House of Representatives may have up to 65 legislative aides who serve as the legislator's personal staff. The legislative aides are employed for a total of 330 hours per legislator during the session only and they can work only in the capitol, and not in the district office. Some of the legislators may hire an aide.

(d) The numbers are for staff assigned to specific legislators. There is additional staff working in the leadership offices that also support the rank-and-file members.

(e) Staffers are a combination of full-time, part-time, shared, personal, etc. and their assignments change throughout the year.

(f) Personal and district staff are the same. In Florida, two out of the three district employees may travel to the capitol for sessions.

(g) Idaho has two year-round full-time, three year-round part-time employees and 32 session only employees in the Senate. The House has two full-time and one part-time person(s) year-round and 37 additional people during session.

(h) The only staff working for individual rank-and-file legislators are one (1) secretary in the Capitol complex for each two members and (1–2) district staff, whom legislators select and pay from a separate allowance for that purpose. Partisan staffers help individual legislators with many issues in addition to staffing committees.

(i) Leadership has one legislative assistant. During session, college interns are hired to provide additional staff—one for every two members. Leadership has one intern.

(j) One clerical staff person for three individual House members is the norm. Chairpersons are provided their own individual clerical staff person.

(k) The General Assembly is provided professional and clerical staff services by a centralized, nonpartisan staff, with the exception of House and Senate leadership which employ partisan staff. No district staff provided.

(l) Each legislator may hire as many assistants as desired, but pay from public funds ranges from $2,000 to $3,000 per month per legislator. Assistant(s) generally work in the district office but may also work at the capitol during the session.

(m) The six caucuses are assigned one full-time position each (potentially 24 legislators per one staff person).

(n) President's office: six year-round; Majority office: seven year-round, one session only; Minority office: five year-round, one session only; Secretary's office: nine year-round, five session only.

(o) The House members do not have individual staff. There are 20 people who work year-round in the three partisan offices, 12 of whom are legislative aides who primarily work directly with legislators.

(p) Senators have one year-round administrative aide and one session only secretary. Delegates have one part-time year-round administrative aide and a shared session only secretary. Legislators may increase staff and also hire student interns if their district office funds are used.

(q) Senate—majority, five staff per legislator; minority, three staff per legislator. House—two staff per legislator.

(r) One to two staff persons per legislator.

(s) Secretarial staff; in North Dakota, leadership only.

(t) One plus; clerical plus attendant or analyst.

(u) House/party leaders determine allowances/funds for members once allocations are made. Members have considerable independence in hiring personal and committee staffs.

(v) Part-time during interim.

(w) Some legislators maintain district offices at their own expense.

(x) Some leadership offices have more.

(y) Senate: Pro Tem—five staff persons. House: year-round one to five, majority party only; minority party, one staff person per legislator. Committee, fiscal and legal staffs are available to legislators year-round.

(z) One staff person during interim.

(aa) The General Assembly has a total of 280 full-time positions, 267 full-time shared staff and additional 13 full-time positions for the House.

(bb) The nonpartisan Legislative Research Council serves all members of both houses year-round. Committee secretaries and legislative interns and pages provide support during the sessions, but that is for staff.

(cc) Average staff numbers from staff member totals from each chamber.

(dd) Legislators are provided student interns during session.

(ee) No personal staff except one administrative assistant for the Speaker and one for the Senate Pro Tempore.

(ff) Applies to secretarial staff provided to the members during the session by the Clerk's offices. Members also receive a set dollar allowance to hire additional staff (secretarial or legislative assistants) who may serve year-round.

(gg) Staffing levels vary according to majority/minority status and leadership or committee responsibilities. Members may assign personal staff to work in the district office.

(hh) Individual staffing and staff pool arrangements are at the discretion of the individual legislator.

(ii) Several House members have year-round personal staff. It depends on seniority, duties (such as committee chairs), and committee assignments.

Table 3.22
STAFF FOR LEGISLATIVE STANDING COMMITTEES

| State or other jurisdiction | Committee staff assistance | | | | Source of staff services ** | | | | | | | |
| | Senate | | House/Assembly | | Joint central agency (a) | | Chamber agency (b) | | Caucus or leadership | | Committee or committee chair | |
	Prof.	Cler.	Prof.	Cler.	Prof.	Cler.	Prof.	Cler.	Prof.	Cler.	Prof.	Cler.
Alabama	●	★	●	★	B	B	B	B	...	...	...	...
Alaska	★	★	★	★	B	B	...	...	...	...	B	B
Arizona	★	★	★	★	B	B	B	B	B	B	B	B
Arkansas	★	★	★	★	B	B	...	...	...	...	...	...
California	★	★	★	★	B	B	B	B	B	B	B	B
Colorado	★	...	★	...	B	...	B	B	B	B	...	...
Connecticut	...	★	...	★	B	...	...	...	...	B	...	B
Delaware	●	★	●	★	B	...	B	...	B	...	...	B
Florida	★	★	★	★	B	B	B	B	B	B	B	B
Georgia	●	★	●	★	B	B	B	B	B	B	B	...
Hawaii	●	★	★	★	B	B	B	B	B	B	B	B
Idaho	...	★	...	★	B (c)	B (c)	...	...	...	B (d)	...	...
Illinois	★	★	★	★	...	...	B	B	B	B	...	...
Indiana	★	...	●	...	...	...	S	...	S	...	...	...
Iowa	★	...	★	...	B	...	(e)	...	...	...	...	...
Kansas	★	★	★	★	B	B (f)	B	B	B	B	B	B
Kentucky	★	★	★	★	B	B	...	...	B (g)	B (g)	...	...
Louisiana	★(h)	★	★(h)	★	B	B	B	B	B	B	B (i)	B (i)
Maine	★(j)	★(j)	★(j)	★(j)	B	B	B	B	B	B	...	B
Maryland	★(k)	★(k)	★(k)	★(k)	B	B	...	...	...	...	...	...
Massachusetts	★	★	★	★	...	...	...	...	...	...	...	...
Michigan	★	★	★	★	B	...	...	H	B	...	...	S
Minnesota	★	★	★	★	...	...	B	S	B	S	B	B
Mississippi	●	★	●	★	...	...	B	B	B	...	B	B
Missouri	★	...	★	...	B	...	B	...	S	S	B	...
Montana	★	★	★	★	B	...	...	B	...	...	...	...
Nebraska	★	★	U	U	(l)	...	(l)	...	(l)	...	(l)	...
Nevada	★	★	★	★	B	...	...	B	...	...	...	...
New Hampshire	●	★	★	★	B	B	B	B	...	...	...	H
New Jersey	★	★	★	★	B	B	B	B	...	...	...	...
New Mexico	★	★	★	★	...	...	B	B	...	...	...	...
New York	★	★	★	★	B	...	B	B	B	B	B	...
North Carolina	★	★(m)	★	★(m)	B	...	...	...	...	...	...	B (m)
North Dakota	●	★	●	★	B	B	...	...	...	...	...	...
Ohio	★	★	★	★	B	...	...	...	B	...	B	B
Oklahoma	★	★	★	★	...	...	B	B	...	...	B	B
Oregon	★	★	★	★	B	B	B	B	B	B	B	B
Pennsylvania	★	★	★	★	B	B	B	B	B	B	B	B
Rhode Island	●	★	★	★	B	B	...	B	...	...	B	...
South Carolina	★	★	★	★	B	B	B	B	B	B	B	B
South Dakota	★	★	★	★	B	...	...	...	...	...	(k)	(k)
Tennessee	★	★	★	★	B	...	B	B	...	...	...	B
Texas	★	★	★	★	B	B	...	B	...	...	B	B
Utah	★	★	★	★	B	...	...	B	...	...	...	...
Vermont	★	●	★	●	B	B	...	...	...	...	...	...
Virginia	★	★	★	★	B	...	B	B	...	...	(o)	(o)
Washington	★	★	★	★	...	...	B	B	B	B	B	B
West Virginia	★	★	★	★	B	B	B	B	B	B	B	B
Wisconsin	★	★	★	★	B	...	...	...	...	...	(p)	B
Wyoming	...	★	...	★	...	...	B	...	...	...	...	...
No. Mariana Islands	★	★	★	★	B (n)	B (n)	B (n)	B (n)	B (n)	B (n)	B (n)	B (n)
Puerto Rico	★	★	★	★	B (n)	B (n)	B (n)	B (n)	B (n)	B (n)	B (n)	B (n)
U.S. Virgin Islands	★	★	U	U	S (n)	S (n)	S (n)	S (n)	S (n)	S (n)	S (n)	S (n)

See footnotes at end of table.

Source: The Council of State Governments' survey, December 2006.

** — Multiple entries reflect a combination of organizations and location of services.

Key:

★ — All committees

● — Some committees

. . . — Services not provided

B — Both chambers

H — House

S — Senate

U — Unicameral

(a) Includes legislative council or service agency or central management agency.

(b) Includes chamber management agency, office of clerk or secretary and House or Senate research office.

(c) Professional staff and clerical support are provided via the Legislative Services Office, a nonpartisan office serving all members on a year-round basis.

(d) Leadership in each party hire their respective support staff.

(e) The Senate secretary and House clerk maintain supervision of committee clerks.

(f) Senators and house chairpersons select their secretaries and notify the central administrative services agency; all administrative employee matters are handled by the agency.

(g) Leadership employs partisan staff to provide professional and clerical services. However, all members, including leadership are also served by the centralized, nonpartisan staff.

(h) House Appropriations and Senate Finance Committees have Legislative Fiscal Office staff at their hearings.

(i) Staff are assigned to each committee but work under the direction of the chair.

(j) Standing committees are joint House and Senate committees.

(k) Committees hire additional staff, not a part of the central agency, on a contractual basis during session only under direction of chair.

(l) Services not provided, except that the staff of the Legislative Fiscal Office serves the Appropriations Committee.

(m) Member's personal secretary serves as a clerk to the committee or subcommittee that the member chairs.

(n) In general, the legislative service agency provides legal and staff assistance for legislative meetings and provides associated materials. Individual legislators hire personal or committee staff as their budgets provide and at their own discretion.

(o) The House Appropriations Committee and the Senate Finance Committees have their own staff. The staff members work under the direction of the chair.

(p) Standing committees are staffed by subject specialist from the Joint Legislative Council.

Table 3.23
STANDING COMMITTEES: APPOINTMENT AND NUMBER

State or other jurisdiction	Committee members appointed by:		Committee chairpersons appointed by:		Number of standing committees during regular 2006 session	
	Senate	House/Assembly	Senate	House/Assembly	Senate	House/Assembly
Alabama	CC	S	CC	S	25	24
Alaska	CC	CC	CC	CC	9	9
Arizona	P	S	P	S	13	18
Arkansas	(a)	(b)	(a)	S	10	10
California	CR	S	CR	S	23	29
Colorado	MjL	S	MjL	S	10	11
Connecticut	CC	CC	CC	CC	(c)	(c)
Delaware	PT	S	PT	S	26	27
Florida	P	S	P	S	20	18
Georgia	CC	S	CC	S	25	34
Hawaii	P (d)	(e)	P (d)	(e)	15	19
Idaho	PT (f)	S	PT	S	10	14
Illinois	P, MnL	S, MnL	P	S	22	37
Indiana	PT	S	PT	S	20	20
Iowa	MjL, MnL	S	MjL	S	16	17
Kansas	(g)	S	(g)	S	17	21
Kentucky	P	S	P	S	14	19
Louisiana	P	S (h)	P	S	17	17
Maine	P	S	P	S	17	6
Maryland	P	S	P	S	8	9
Massachusetts	P	S	P	S	5 (c)	8 (c)
Michigan	MjL	S	MjL	S	17	23
Minnesota	CR	S	MjL	S	14	27
Mississippi	P	S	P	S	39	47
Missouri	PT (i)	S	PT	S	35	35
Montana	CC	S	CC	S	17	17
Nebraska	CC	U	E	U	14	U
Nevada	MjL	S	MjL	S	(j)	(j)
New Hampshire	P (k)	S (k)	P (k)	S (k)	14	21
New Jersey	CC	CC	CC	CC	13	23
New Mexico	CC	S	CC	S	9 (l)	15 (l)
New York	PT	S	PT	S	31	37
North Carolina	CC	CC	CC	CC	22	33
North Dakota	CC	CC	MjL	MjL	11	12
Ohio	P (m)	S (m)	P (m)	S (m)	14	19
Oklahoma	PT	S	PT	S	18	25
Oregon	P	S	P	S	(j)	(j)
Pennsylvania	PT	S	PT	S	21	23
Rhode Island	P	S	P	S	11	9
South Carolina	(n)	S	(o)	E	15	11
South Dakota	PT	S	PT	S	13	13
Tennessee	S	S	S	S	13	16
Texas	P	S (p)	P	S	20	40
Utah	P	S	P	S	11	15
Vermont	CC	S	CC	S	11	14
Virginia	E	S	(q)	S	11	14
Washington	P (r)	S	E (s)	S	14	21
West Virginia	P	S	P	S	18	15
Wisconsin	MjL	S	MjL	S	17	40
Wyoming	P	S	P	S	12	12
Dist. of Columbia	(t)	U	(t)	U	9	U
No. Mariana Islands	P	S	P	S	8	7
Puerto Rico	P	S	P	S	22	32
U.S. Virgin Islands	E	U	E	U	9	U

See footnotes at end of table.

STANDING COMMITTEES: APPOINTMENT AND NUMBER — Continued

Source: The Council of State Governments' survey, December 2006.
Key:
CC — Committee on Committees
CR — Committee on Rules
E — Election
MjL — Majority Leader
MnL — Minority Leader
P — President
PT — President Pro Tempore
S — Speaker
U — Unicameral legislature
(a) Selection process based on seniority.
(b) Members of the standing committees shall be selected by House District Caucuses with each caucus selecting five members for each "A" standing committee and five members for each "B" standing committee.
(c) Substantive standing committees are joint committees. Connecticut, 18 (there are also three statutory and four select committees for the House and the Senate); Massachusetts, 26.
(d) President appoints committee members and chairs; minority members on committees are nominated by minority party caucus.
(e) By resolution, with members of majority party designating the chair, vice-chairs and majority party members of committees, and members of minority party designating minority party members.
(f) Committee members appointed by the senate leadership under the direction of the president pro tempore, by and with the senate's consent.

(g) Committee on Organization, Calendar and Rules.
(h) Speaker appoints only 12 of the 19 members of the Committee on Appropriations.
(i) Senate minority committee members chosen by minority caucus, but appointed by president pro tempore.
(j) No session in 2006.
(k) Senate president and house speaker consult with minority leaders.
(l) Senate: includes eight substantive committees and one procedural committee. House: includes 12 substantive committees and three procedural committees.
(m) The minority leader may recommend for consideration minority party members for each committee.
(n) Appointment based on seniority (Senate Rule 19D).
(o) Appointed by seniority which is determined by tenure within the committee rather than tenure within the Senate. Also, chair is based on the majority party within the committee (Senate Rule 19E).
(p) For each standing substantive committee of the house, except for the appropriations committee, a maximum of one-half of the membership, exclusive of chair and vice-chair, is determined by seniority; the remaining membership of the committee is determined by the speaker.
(q) Senior member of the majority party on the committee is the chair.
(r) Lieutenant governor is president of the senate.
(s) Recommended by the Committee on Committees, approved by the president, then confirmed by the senate.
(t) Chair of the Council.

Table 3.24
RULES ADOPTION AND STANDING COMMITTEES: PROCEDURE

State or other jurisdiction	Constitution permits each legislative body to determine its own rules	Committee meetings open to public*		Specific, advance notice provisions for committee meetings or hearings	Voting/roll call provisions to report a bill to floor
		Senate	House/ Assembly		
Alabama	★	★	★	Senate: 4 hours, if possible. House: 24 hours, except Rules and Local Legislations committees.	Senate: final vote on a bill is recorded. House: recorded vote if requested by member of committee and sustained by one additional committee member.
Alaska	. . .	★	★	For meetings, by 4:00 p.m. on the preceding Thursday; for first hearings on bills, 5 days.	Roll call vote on any measure taken upon request by any member of either house.
Arizona	★	★	★	Senate: written agenda for each regular and special meeting containing all bills, memorials and resolutions to be considered shall be distributed to each member of the committee and to the Secretary of the Senate at least 5 days prior to the committee meeting. House: the committee chair shall prepare an agenda and distribute copies to committee members, the Information Desk and the Chief Clerk's Office by 4 p.m. each Wednesday for all standing committees meeting on Monday of the following week and 4 p.m. each Thursday for all standing committees meeting on any day except Monday of the following week.	Senate: roll call vote. House: roll call vote.
Arkansas	★	★	★	Senate: 2 days. House: 24 hours.	Senate: roll call votes are recorded. House: report of committee recommendation signed by committee chair.
California	★	★	★	Senate: advance notice provisions exist. House: advance notice provisions exist.	Senate: roll call. House: roll call.
Colorado	★	★	★	Senate: final action on a measure is prohibited unless notice is posted 1 calendar day prior to its consideration. The prohibition does not apply if the action receives a majority vote of the committee. House: none.	Senate: final action by recorded roll call vote. House: final action by recorded roll call vote.
Connecticut	★	★	★	Senate: 1 day notice for meetings, 5 days notice for hearings. House: 1 day notice for meetings, 5 days notice for hearings.	Senate: roll call required. House: roll call required.
Delaware	★	★	★	Senate: agenda released 1 day before meetings. House: agenda released 4 days before meetings.	Senate: results of all committee reports are recorded. House: results of all committee reports are recorded.
Florida	★	★	★	Senate: during session—3 hours notice for first 50 days, 4 hours thereafter. House: 2 days.	Senate: vote on final passage is recorded. House: vote on final passage is recorded.
Georgia	★	★	★	Senate: a list of committee meetings shall be posted by 10:00 a.m. the preceding Friday. House: none.	Senate: recorded roll call taken if one-third members sustain the call for yeas and nays. House: recorded roll call taken if one-fifth members sustain the call for yeas and nays.
Hawaii	★	★(a)	★(a)	Senate: 72 hours before first referral committee meetings, 48 hours before subsequent referral committee. House: 48 hours.	Senate: final vote is recorded. House: a record is made of a committee quorum and votes to report a bill out.
Idaho	★	★(a)	★(a)	Senate: none. House: per rule; chair provides notice of next meeting dates and times to clerk to be read prior to adjournment each day of session.	Senate: bills can be voted out by voice vote or roll call. House: bills can be voted out by voice vote or roll call.

See footnotes at end of table.

RULES ADOPTION AND STANDING COMMITTEES: PROCEDURE — Continued

State or other jurisdiction	Constitution permits each legislative body to determine its own rules	Committee meetings open to public*		Specific, advance notice provisions for committee meetings or hearings	Voting/roll call provisions to report a bill to floor
		Senate	House/ Assembly		
Illinois	★	★(b)	★(b)	Senate: 6 days. House: 6 days.	Senate: votes on all legislative measures acted upon are recorded. House: votes on all legislative matters acted upon are recorded.
Indiana	★	★	★	Senate: 48 hours. House: prior to adjournment or the meeting day next preceding the meeting or announced during session.	Senate: committee reports—do pass; do pass amended; reported out without recommendation. House: majority of quorum; vote can be by roll call or consent.
Iowa	★	★	★	Senate: none. House: none.	Senate: final action by roll call. House: committee reports include roll call on final disposition.
Kansas	★	★	★	Senate: none. House: none.	Senate: vote recorded upon request of member. House: total for and against actions recorded.
Kentucky	★	★	★	Senate: none. House: none.	Senate: each member's vote recorded on each bill. House: each member's vote recorded on each bill.
Louisiana	★	★(a)	★(a)	Senate: no later than 1:00 p.m. the preceding day. House: no later than 4:00 p.m. the preceding day.	Senate: any motion to report an instrument is decided by a roll call vote. House: any motion to report an instrument is decided by a roll call vote.
Maine	★	★	★	Senate: must be advertised 2 weekends in advance. House: must be advertised 2 weekends in advance.	Senate: recorded vote is required to report a bill out of committee. House: recorded vote is required to report a bill out of committee.
Maryland	★	★	★	Senate: none (c). House: none (c).	Senate: the final vote on any bill is recorded. House: the final vote on any bill is recorded.
Massachusetts	★	★	★	Senate: 48 hours for public hearings. House: 48 hours for public hearings.	Senate: voice vote or recorded roll call vote at the request of 2 committee members. House: recorded vote upon request by a member.
Michigan	★	★	★	Senate and House: notice shall be published in the journal in advance of a hearing. Notice of a special meeting shall be posted at least 18 hours before a meeting. Special provisions for conference committees.	Senate: committee reports include the vote of each member on any bill. House: the daily journal reports the roll call on all motions to report bills.
Minnesota	★	★	★	Senate: 3 days. House: 3 days.	Senate: not needed. House: not needed. Recorded roll call vote upon request by a member.
Mississippi	★	★	★	Senate: none. House: none.	Senate: bills are reported out by voice vote or recorded roll call vote. House: bills are reported out by voice vote or recorded roll call vote.
Missouri	★	★	★	Senate: 24 hours. House: 24 hours.	Senate: yeas and nays are reported in journal. House: bills are reported out by a recorded roll call vote.
Montana	★	★	★	Senate: 3 legislative days. House: none.	Senate: every vote of each member is recorded and made public. House: every vote of each member is recorded and made public.
Nebraska	★	★	U	7 calendar days notice before hearing a bill.	In executive session, majority of the committee must vote in favor of the motion made.
Nevada	★	★	★	Senate: by rule—"adequate notice" shall be provided. (d) House: by rule—"adequate notice" shall be provided. (d)	Senate: recorded vote is taken upon final committee action on bills. House: recorded vote is taken upon final committee action on bills.

See footnotes at end of table.

RULES ADOPTION AND STANDING COMMITTEES: PROCEDURE — Continued

State or other jurisdiction	Constitution permits each legislative body to determine its own rules	Committee meetings open to public*		Specific, advance notice provisions for committee meetings or hearings	Voting/roll call provisions to report a bill to floor
		Senate	House/ Assembly		
New Hampshire.......	★	★	★	Senate: 4 days. House: no less than 4 days.	Senate: committees may report a bill out by voice or recorded roll call vote. House: committees may report a bill out by voice or recorded roll call vote.
New Jersey..............	★	★	★	Senate: 5 days. House: 5 days.	Senate: the chair reports the vote of each member present on a motion to report a bill. House: the chair reports the vote of each member present on motions with respect to bills.
New Mexico	★	★	★	Senate: none. House: none.	Senate: vote on the final report of the committee taken by yeas and nays. Roll call vote upon request. House: vote on the final report of the committee taken by yeas and nays. Roll call vote upon request.
New York	★	★	★	Senate: 1 week. House: 1 week for hearings, Thursday of prior week for meetings.	Senate: majority vote required. House: majority vote required.
North Carolina........	(f)	★	★	Senate: none (e). House: none (e).	Senate: no roll call vote may be taken in any committee. House: roll call vote taken on any question when requested by member and sustained by one-fifth of members present.
North Dakota...........	★	★	★	Senate: hearing schedule printed Friday mornings. House: hearing schedule printed Friday mornings.	Senate: included with minutes from standing committee. House: included with minutes from standing committee.
Ohio	★	★	★	Senate: 2 days. In a case of necessity, the notice of hearing may be given in a shorter period by such reasonable method as prescribed by the Committee on Rules. House: 5 days. If an emergency requires consideration of a matter at a meeting not announced on notice, the chair may revise or supplement the notice at any time before or during the meeting to include the matter.	Senate: the affirmative votes of a majority of all members of a committee shall be necessary to report or to postpone further consideration of bills or resolutions. Every member present shall vote, unless excused by the chair. At discretion of chair the roll call may be continued for a vote by any member who was present at the prior meeting, but no later than 10:00 a.m. of next calendar day. House: the affirmative votes of a majority of all members of a committee shall be necessary to report or to postpone further consideration of bills or resolutions. Every member present shall vote, unless excused by the chair. At discretion of chair the roll call may be continued for a vote by any member who was present at the prior meeting, but no later than 12:00 noon 1 day following the meeting. Members must be present in order to vote on amendment.
Oklahoma	★	★	★	Senate: 3 days notice. House: 3 days notice.	Senate: roll call vote. House: roll call vote.
Oregon	★	★	★	Senate: at least 48 hours notice except at the end of session when President invokes 1 hour notice when adjournment sine die is imminent. House: at least 48 hours notice except in case of emergency or Speaker determines adjournment sine die is imminent.	Senate: affirmative roll call vote of majority of members of committee and recorded in committee minutes. House: affirmative roll call vote of majority of members of committee and recorded in committee minutes.
Pennsylvania	★	★	★	Senate: written notice to members containing date, time, place and agenda. House: written notice to members containing date, time, place and agenda.	Senate: a majority vote of committee members. House: a majority vote of committee members.
Rhode Island	★	★	★	Senate: notice required. House: notice required.	Senate: majority vote of the members present. House: majority vote of the members present.

See footnotes at end of table.

RULES ADOPTION AND STANDING COMMITTEES: PROCEDURE — Continued

State or other jurisdiction	Constitution permits each legislative body to determine its own rules	Committee meetings open to public*		Specific, advance notice provisions for committee meetings or hearings	Voting/roll call provisions to report a bill to floor
		Senate	House/ Assembly		
South Carolina	★	★	★	Senate: 24 hours. House: 24 hours.	Senate: before the expiration of 5 days from the date of reference, any bill may be recalled from committee by the vote of three-fourths of the Senators present and voting. House: favorable report out of committee (majority of committee members voting in favor).
South Dakota...........	★	★	★	Senate and House: at least 1 legislative day must intervene between the date of posting and the date of consideration in both houses.	Senate and House: a majority vote of the members-elect taken by roll call is needed for final disposition on a bill. This applies to both houses.
Tennessee	★	★	★	Senate: 6 days. House: 72 hours.	Senate: majority referral to Calendar and Rules Committee, majority of Calendar and Rules Committee referral to floor. House: majority referral to Calendar and Rules Committee, majority of Calendar and Rules Committee referral to floor.
Texas	★	★	★	Senate: 24 hours. House: the House requires 5 calendar days notice before a public hearing at which testimony will be taken, and 2 hours notice or an announcement from the floor before a formal meeting (testimony cannot be taken at a formal meeting). 24 hour advance notice is required during special session.	Senate: bills are reported by recorded roll call vote. House: committee reports include the record vote by which the report was adopted, including the vote of each member.
Utah	★	★	★	Senate: 24 hours. House: 24 hours.	Senate: each member present votes on every question and all votes are recorded. House: each member present votes on every question and all votes are recorded.
Vermont	★	★	★	Senate: none. House: none.	Senate: vote is recorded for each committee member for every bill considered. House: vote is recorded for each committee member for every bill considered.
Virginia	★	★(a)	★(a)	Senate: none. House: none.	Senate: recorded vote, except resolutions that do not have a specific vote requirement under the Rules. In these cases, a voice vote is sufficient. House: vote of each member is taken and recorded for each measure.
Washington	★	★	★	Senate: 5 days. House: 5 days.	Senate: bills reported from a committee carry a majority report which must be signed by a majority of the committee. House: every vote to report a bill out of committee is by yeas and nays; the names of the members voting are recorded in the report.
West Virginia...........	★	★	★	Senate: none. House: none.	Senate: majority of committee members voting. House: majority of committee members voting.
Wisconsin.................	★	★	★	Senate: Monday noon of the preceding week. House: Monday noon of the preceding week.	Senate: number of ayes and noes, and members absent or not voting are reported. House: number of ayes and noes are recorded.
Wyoming..................	★	★	★	Senate: by 3:00 p.m. of previous day. House: by 3:00 p.m. of previous day.	Senate: bills are reported out by recorded roll call vote. House: bills are reported out by recorded roll call vote.
Puerto Rico..............	★	★	★	Senate: must be notified every Thursday, 1 week in advance. House: 24 hours advance notice, no later than 4:00 p.m. of previous day.	Senate: bills reported from a committee carry a majority vote. House: bills reported from a committee carry a majority vote by referendum or in an ordinary meeting.
U.S. Virgin Islands...	★	★	U	7 calendar days.	Bills must be reported to floor by Rules Committee.

See footnotes at end of table.

RULES ADOPTION AND STANDING COMMITTEES: PROCEDURE—Continued

Source: The Council of State Governments' survey, December 2006.

Key:

★ — Yes

* — Notice of committee meetings may also be subject to state open meetings laws; in some cases, listed times may be subject to suspension or enforceable only to the extent "feasible" or "whenever possible."

U — Unicameral

(a) Certain matters may be discussed in executive session. (Other states permit meetings to be closed for various reasons, but their rules do not specifically mention "executive session.")

(b) A session of a house or one of its committees can be closed to the public if two-thirds of the members elected to that house determine that the public interest so requires. A meeting of a joint committee or commission can be closed if two-thirds of the members of both houses so vote.

(c) General directive in the Senate and House rules to the Department of Legislative Services to compile a list of the meetings and to arrange for distribution which in practice is done on a regular basis.

(d) Senate: This rule may be suspended for emergencies by a two-thirds vote of appointed committee members. House: This rule may be suspended for emergencies by a two-thirds vote of appointed committee members. In the Assembly this rule does not apply to committee meetings held on the floor during recess or conference committee meetings.

(e) If public hearing, five calendar days.

(f) Not referenced specifically, but each body publishes rules.

Table 3.25
LEGISLATIVE REVIEW OF ADMINISTRATIVE REGULATIONS: STRUCTURES AND PROCEDURES

State or other jurisdiction	Type of reviewing committee	Rules reviewed	Time limits in review process
Alabama	Joint bipartisan, standing committee	P	If not approved or disapproved within 35 days of filing, rule is approved. If disapproved by committee, rule suspended until adjournment, next regular session or until legislature by resolution revokes suspension. Rule takes effect upon final adjournment unless committee's disapproval is sustained by legislature.
Alaska	Joint bipartisan, standing committee	P, E	. . .
Arizona	Joint bipartisan	P, E	. . .
Arkansas	Joint bipartisan	P, E	. . .
California		P, E	Regulation review conducted by independent executive branch agency.
Colorado	Joint bipartisan	E	Rules continue unless the annual legislative rule review bill discontinues a rule. The rule review bill is effective upon the Governor's signature.
Connecticut	Joint bipartisan, standing committee	P	Submittal of proposed regulation shall be on the first Tuesday of month; after first submittal, committee has 65 days after date of submission. Second submittal: 35 days for committee to review/take action on revised regulation.
Delaware	Attorney General review	P	The Attorney General shall review any rule or regulation promulgated by any state agency and inform the issuing agency in writing as to the potential of the rule or regulation to result in a taking of private property before the rule or regulation may become effective.
Florida	Joint bipartisan	P, E	. . .
Georgia	Standing committee	P	The agency notifies the Legislative Counsel 30 days prior to the effective dates of proposed rules.
Hawaii	Legislative agency	P, E	In Hawaii, the legislative reference bureau assists agencies to comply with a uniform format of style. This does not affect the status of rules.
Idaho	Germane joint subcommittees	P	Germane joint subcommittees vote to object or not object to a rule. They cannot reject a proposed rule directly, only advise an agency which may choose to adopt a rule subject to review by the full legislature. The legislature as a whole reviews rules during the first three weeks of session to determine if they comport with state law. The Senate and House may reject rules via resolution adopted by both. Rules imposing fees must be approved or are deemed approved unless rejected. Temporary rules expire at the end of session unless extended by concurrent resolution.
Illinois	Joint bipartisan	P, E	An agency proposing nonemergency regulations must allow 45 days for public comment. At least five days after any public hearing on the proposal, the agency must give notice of the proposal to the Joint Committee on Administrative Rules, and allow it 45 days to approve or object to the proposed regulations.
Indiana	Joint bipartisan	P	. . .
Iowa	Joint bipartisan	P, E	. . .
Kansas	Joint bipartisan	P	Agencies must give a 60-day notice to the public and the Joint Committee of their intent to adopt or amend specific rules and regulations, a copy of which must be provided to the committee. Within the 60-day comment period, the Joint Committee must review and comment, if it feels necessary, on the proposals. Final rules and regulations are resubmitted to the committee to determine whether further expression of concern is necessary.
Kentucky	Joint bipartisan statutory committee	P, E	45 days.
Louisiana (b)	Standing committee	P	All proposed rules and fees are submitted to designated standing committees of the legislature. If a rule or fee is unacceptable, the committee sends a written report to the governor. The governor has 10 days to disapprove the committee report. If both Senate and House committees fail to find the rule unacceptable, or if the governor disapproves the action of a committee within 10 days, the agency may adopt the rule change. (d)

See footnotes at end of table.

LEGISLATIVE REVIEW OF ADMINISTRATIVE REGULATIONS: STRUCTURES AND PROCEDURES — Continued

State or other jurisdiction	Type of reviewing committee	Rules reviewed	Time limits in review process
Maine	Joint bipartisan, standing committee	P	One legislative session.
Maryland	Joint bipartisan	P, E	Proposed regulations are submitted for review at least 15 days before publication. Publication triggers 45-day review period which may be extended by the committee, but if agreement cannot be reached, the Governor may instruct the agency to modify or withdraw the regulation, or may approve its adoption.
Massachusetts (b)......	Public hearing by agency	P	In Massachusetts, the General Court (Legislature) may by statute authorize an administrative agency to promulgate regulations. The promulgation of such regulations are then governed by Chapter 30A of the Massachusetts General Laws. Chapter 30A requires 21-day notice to the public of a public hearing on a proposed regulation. After public hearing, the proposed regulation is filed with the State Secretary who approves it if it is in conformity with Chapter 30A. The State Secretary maintains a register entitled "Massachusetts Register" and the regulation does not become effective until published in the register. The agency may promulgate amendments to the regulations following the same process.
Michigan	Joint bipartisan	P	Joint Committee on Administrative Rules (JCAR) has 15 days in which to consider the rule and to object to the rule by filing a notice of objection. If no objection is made, the rules may be filed and go into effect. If JCAR does formally object, bills to block the rules are introduced in both houses of the legislature simultaneously by the committee chair and placed directly on the Senate and House calendars for action. If the bills are not enacted by the legislature and presented to the governor within 15 session days, the rules may go into effect. Between legislative sessions the committee can meet and suspend rules promulgated during the interim between sessions.
Minnesota	Joint bipartisan, standing committee	P, E	Minnesota Statute Sec. 3.842, subd. 4a.
Mississippi	....(a)..		
Missouri	Joint bipartisan, standing committee	P, E	The committee must disapprove a final order of rulemaking within 30 days upon receipt or the order of rulemaking is deemed approved.
Montana	Germane joint bipartisan committees	P	Prior to adoption.
Nebraska...................	Standing committee	P	If an agency proposes to repeal, adopt or amend a rule or regulation, it is required to provide the Executive Board Chair with the proposal at least 30 days prior to the Public Hearing, as required by law. The Executive Board Chair shall provide to the appropriate standing committee of the Legislature, the agency proposal for comment.
Nevada	Ongoing statutory committee (Legislative Commission)	P	Proposed regulations are either reviewed at the Legislative Commission's next regularly scheduled meeting (if the regulation is received more than three working days before the meeting), or they are referred to the Commission's Subcommittee to Review Regulations. If there is no objection to the regulation, then the Commission will "promptly" file the approved regulation with the Secretary of State. If the Commission or its subcommittee objects to a regulation, then the Commission will "promptly" return the regulation to the agency for revision. Within 60 days of receiving the written notice of objection to the regulation, the agency must revise the regulation and return it to the Legislative Counsel. If the Commission or its subcommittee objects to the revised regulation, the agency shall continue to revise and resubmit it to the Commission or subcommittee within 30 days after receiving the written notice of objection to the revised regulation.
New Hampshire.........	Joint bipartisan	P	Under APA, for regular rulemaking, the joint committee of administrative rules has 45 days to review a final proposed rule from an agency, Otherwise the rule is automatically approved. If JLCAR makes a preliminary or revised objection, the agency has 45 days to respond, and JLCAR has another 50 days to decide to vote to sponsor a joint resolution, which suspends the adoption process. JLCAR may also, or instead, make a final objection, which shifts the burden of proof in court to the agency. There is no time limit on making a final objection. If no JLCAR action in the 50 days to vote to sponsor a joint resolution, the agency may adopt the rule.

See footnotes at end of table.

LEGISLATIVE REVIEW OF ADMINISTRATIVE REGULATIONS: STRUCTURES AND PROCEDURES — Continued

State or other jurisdiction	Type of reviewing committee	Rules reviewed	Time limits in review process
New Jersey	Joint bipartisan	. . .	. . .
New Mexico	....(g)..		
New York	Joint bipartisan commission	P, E	Statute is silent as to time limits in review process.
North Carolina	Rules Review Commission; Public membership appointed by legislature	P, E	The Rules Review Commission must review a permanent rule submitted to it on or before the 20th of the month by the last day of the next month. The commission must review a permanent rule submitted to it after the 20th of the month by the last day of the second subsequent month.
North Dakota	Interim committee	E	The Administrative Rules Committee meets in each calendar quarter to consider rules filed in previous 90 days.
Ohio	Joint bipartisan	P, E (h)	The committee's jurisdiction is 65 days from date of original filing plus an additional 30 days from date of refiling. Rules filed with no changes, pursuant to the five-year review, are under a 90-day jurisdiction.
Oklahoma	Standing committee (c)	P, E	The legislature has 30 legislative days to review proposed rules.
Oregon	Office of Legislative Counsel	E	Agencies must copy Legislative Counsel within 10 days of rule adoption.
Pennsylvania	Joint bipartisan, standing committee	E	Time limits decided by the President Pro Tempore and Speaker of the House.
Rhode Island	....(a)..		
South Carolina	Standing committee (e)	P	General Assembly has 120 days to approve or disapprove. If not disapproved by joint resolution before 120 days, regulation is automatically approved. It can be approved during 120-day review period by joint resolution.
South Dakota	Joint bipartisan	P	Rules must be adopted within 75 days of the commencement of the public hearing; emergency rules must be adopted within 30 days of the date of the publication of the notice of intent. Many other deadlines exist; see SDCL 1-26-4 for further details.
Tennessee	Joint bipartisan	P	All permanent rules take effect 165 days after filing with the Secretary of State. Emergency rules take effect upon filing with the Secretary of State.
Texas	Standing committee	P	No time limit.
Utah	Joint bipartisan (f)	P, E	Each rule in effect on February 28 of each year expires May 1 of that year unless reauthorized by the legislature in annual legislation.
Vermont	Joint bipartisan	P	The Joint Legislative Committee Rules must review a proposed rule within 30 days of submission to the committee.
Virginia	Joint bipartisan, standing committee	P	Standing committees and the Joint Commission on Administrative Rules may object to a proposed or final adopted rule before it becomes effective. This delays the process for 21 days and the agency must respond to the objection.
Washington	Joint bipartisan	P, E	If the committee determines that a proposed rule does not comply with legislative intent, it notifies the agency, which must schedule a public hearing within 30 days of notification. The agency notifies the committee of its action within seven days after the hearing. If a hearing is not held or the agency does not amend the rule, the objection may be filed in the state register and referenced in the state code. The committee's powers, other than publication of its objections, are advisory.
West Virginia	Joint bipartisan		. . .
Wisconsin	Joint bipartisan, standing committee	P, E	The standing committee in each house has 30 days to conduct its review for a proposed rule. If either objects, the Joint Committee for the Review of Administrative Rules has 30 days to introduce legislation in each house overturning the rules. After 40 days, the bills are placed on the calendar. If either bill passes, the rules are overturned. If they fail to pass, the rules go into effect.

See footnotes at end of table.

LEGISLATIVE REVIEW OF ADMINISTRATIVE REGULATIONS: STRUCTURES AND PROCEDURES — Continued

State or other jurisdiction	Type of reviewing committee	Rules reviewed	Time limits in review process
Wyoming..................	Joint bipartisan	P, E	An agency shall submit copies of adopted, amended or repealed rules to the legislative service office for review within five days after the date of the agency's final action adopting, amending or repealing those rules. The legislature makes its recommendations to the governor who, within 15 days after receiving any recommendation, shall either order that the rule be amended or rescinded in accordance with the recommendation or file in writing his objections to the recommendation.
Puerto Rico..............	....(a)...		
U.S. Virgin Islands....	....(a)...		

Source: The Council of State Governments' survey, December 2006.

Key:

P — Proposed rules

E — Existing rules

. . . — No formal time limits

(a) No formal rule review is performed by both legislative and executive branches.

(b) Review of rules is performed by both legislative and executive branches.

(c) House has a standing committee to which all rules are generally sent for review. In the Senate rules are sent to standing committee which deals with that specific agency.

(d) If the committees of both houses fail to find a fee unacceptable, it can be adopted. Committee action on proposed rules must be taken within five to 30 days after the agency reports to the committee on its public hearing (if any) and whether it is making changes on proposed rules.

(e) Submitted by General Assembly for approval.

(f) Created by statute.

(g) No formal review is performed by legislature. Periodic review and report to legislative finance committee is required of certain agencies.

(h) The Committee reviews proposed new, amended, and rescinded rules. The Committee participates in a five-year review of every existing rule.

Table 3.26
LEGISLATIVE REVIEW OF ADMINISTRATIVE RULES/REGULATIONS: POWERS

State or other jurisdiction	Reviewing committee's powers			Legislative powers
	Advisory powers only (a)	*No objection constitutes approval of proposed rule*	*Committee may suspend rule*	*Method of legislative veto of rules*
Alabama	...	★	★	If not approved or disapproved within 35 days of filing, rule is approved. If disapproved by committee, rule suspended until adjournment, next regular session or until legislature by resolution revokes suspension. Rule takes effect upon final adjournment unless committee's disapproval is sustained by legislature. The committee may approve a rule.
Alaska	★	...	(b)	Statute
Arizona	★	N.A.	N.A.	N.A.
Arkansas	★	...	...	...
California	...	★	★	...
Colorado	...	★	...	Rules that the General Assembly has determined should not be continued are listed as exceptions to the continuation.
Connecticut	...	★	...	Statute CGS 4-170 (d) and 4-171; see footnote (c)
Delaware	N.A.	N.A.	N.A.	N.A.
Florida	★	...	...	Statute
Georgia	...	★	...	Resolution (d)
Hawaii	★	...	...	...
Idaho	...	★	...	Concurrent resolution. All rules are terminated one year after adoption unless the legislature reauthorizes the rule.
Illinois	...	(e)	★(f)	(f)
Indiana	★	...	...	(g)
Iowa	...	...	(h)	E-mail legislation
Kansas	★	...	...	Statute
Kentucky	...	★	★	Enacting legislation to void.
Louisiana	...	★	(i)	Concurrent resolution to suspend, amend or repeal adopted rules or fees. For proposed rules and emergency rules, see footnote (i).
Maine	...	★	...	(j)
Maryland	★(k)	...	...	...
Massachusetts	...	...	...	The legislature may pass a bill which would supersede a regulation if signed into law by the governor.
Michigan	...	...	(l)	Joint Committee on Rules has 15 days to approve the filing of a notice of objection. The filing of the notice of objection starts another 15-day session period that stays the rules and causes committee members to introduce legislation in both houses of the legislature for enactment and presentment to the governor. Any member of the legislature, pursuant to statute, can introduce a bill at a session, which in effect amends or rescinds a rule.
Minnesota	★	...	...	(m)
Mississippi	....(n)...			
Missouri	...	★	★	Concurrent resolution passed by both houses of the General Assembly.
Montana	...	...	★(o)	Statute
Nebraska	★(p)	★	...	(p)
Nevada	...	★	★	Proposed regulations are either reviewed at the Legislative Commission's next regularly scheduled meeting (if the regulation is received more than three working days before the meeting), or they are referred to the Commission's Subcommittee to Review Regulations. If there is no objection to the regulation, then the Commission will "promptly" file the approved regulation with the Secretary of State. If the Commission or its subcommittee objects to a regulation, then the Commission will "promptly" return the regulation to the agency for revision. Within 60 days of receiving the written notice of objection to the regulation, the agency must revise the regulation and return it to the Legislative Counsel. If the Commission or its subcommittee objects to the revised regulation, the agency shall continue to revise and resubmit it to the Commission or subcommittee within 30 days after receiving the written notice of objection to the revised regulation.

See footnotes at end of table.

LEGISLATIVE REVIEW OF ADMINISTRATIVE RULES/REGULATIONS: POWERS — Continued

	Reviewing committee's powers			Legislative powers
State or other jurisdiction	Advisory powers only (a)	No objection constitutes approval of proposed rule	Committee may suspend rule	Method of legislative veto of rules
New Hampshire.........	★	(q)	. . .	(r)
New Jersey.................	★	★	★	(s)
New Mexico	★	★	★	. . .
New York	. . .	. . .	. . .	The Commission may hold hearings, compel production of evidence, subpoena witnesses. The Commission may make recommendations to an agency based on its review. It must also report its recommendations to the legislature.
North Carolina	★	★	★	. . .
North Dakota.............	. . .	★(t)	. . .	The Administrative Rules Committee can void a rule.
Ohio	★	. . .	. . .	Concurrent resolution. Committee recommends to the General Assembly that a rule be invalidated. The General Assembly invalidates a rule through adoption of concurrent resolution.
Oklahoma	★	★(p)	★(p)	The legislature may disapprove (veto) proposed rules by concurrent or joint resolution. A concurrent resolution does not require the governor's signature. Existing rules may be disapproved by joint resolution. A committee may not disapprove; only the full legislature may do so. Failure of the legislature to disapprove constitutes approval.
Oregon	★	★	★	. . .
Pennsylvania	. . .	★	★	Written or oral
Rhode Island	....(n)...			. . .
South Carolina	. . .	★	. . .	. . .
South Dakota.............	. . .	★	★	The Interim Rules Review Committee may, by statute, suspend rules that have not become effective yet by an affirmative vote of the majority of the committee.
Tennessee	. . .	. . .	★	Bill approved by Constitutional majority of both houses declaring rule invalid.
Texas	★	. . .	. . .	N.A.
Utah	★	. . .	. . .	All rules must be reauthorized by the legislature annually.
Vermont	...............................(u)...............................			Statute
Virginia......................	. . .	. . .	(v)	The General Assembly must pass a bill enacted into law to directly negate the administrative rule.
Washington................	★	★	★	N.A.
West Virginia..............	★	. . .	. . .	(w)
Wisconsin...................	. . .	★	★	The standing committee in each house has 30 days to conduct its review for a proposed rule. If either objects, the Joint Committee for the Review of Administrative Rules has 30 days to introduce legislation in each house overturning the rules. After 40 days, the bills are placed on the calendar. If either bill passes, the rules are overturned. If they fail to pass, the rules go into effect.
Wyoming.....................	★	★	. . .	Action must be taken by legislative order adopted by both houses before the end of the next succeeding legislative session to nullify a rule.
U.S. Virgin Islands	....(n)...			

See footnotes at end of table.

LEGISLATIVE REVIEW OF ADMINISTRATIVE RULES/REGULATIONS: POWERS — Continued

Source: The Council of State Governments' survey, December 2006.

Key:

★ — Yes

. . . — No

N.A. — Not applicable

(a) This column is defined by those legislatures or legislative committees that can only recommend changes to rules but have no power to enforce a change.

(b) Authorized, although constitutionally questionable.

(c) Disapproval of proposed regulations may be sustained, or reversed by action of the General Assembly in the ensuing session. The General Assembly may by resolution sustain or reverse a vote of disapproval.

(d) The reviewing committee must introduce a resolution to override a rule within the first 30 days of the next regular session of the General Assembly. If the resolution passes by less than a two-thirds majority of either house, the governor has final authority to affirm or veto the resolution.

(e) The Administrative Procedure Act is not clear on this point, but implies that the Joint Committee should either object or issue a statement of no objections.

(f) Joint Committee on Administrative Rules can send objections to issuing agency. If it does, the agency has 90 days from then to withdraw, change, or refuse to change the proposed regulations. If the Joint Committee determines that proposed regulations would seriously threaten the public good, it can block their adoption. Within 180 days the Joint Committee, or both houses of the General Assembly, can "unblock" those regulations; if that does not happen, the regulations are dead.

(g) None—except by passing statute.

(h) Committee may delay rules.

(i) If the committee determines that a proposed rule is unacceptable, it submits a report to the governor who then has 10 days to accept or reject the report. If the governor rejects the report, the rule change may be adopted by the agency. If the governor accepts the report, the agency may not adopt the rule. Emergency rules become effective upon adoption or up to 60 days after adoption as provided in the rule, but a standing committee or governor may void the rule by finding it unacceptable within two to 61 days after adoption and reporting such finding to agency within four days.

(j) No veto allowed. Legislation must be enacted to prohibit agency from adopting objectionable rules.

(k) Except for emergency regulations which require committee approval for adoption.

(l) Committee can suspend rules during interim.

(m) The Legislative Commission to Review Administrative Rules (LCRAR) ceased operating, effective July 1, 1996. The Legislative Coordinating Commission (LCC) may review a proposed or adopted rule. Contact the LCC for more information. See Minn. Stat. 3.842, subd. 4a.

(n) No formal mechanism for legislative review of administrative rules. In Virginia, legislative review is optional.

(o) A rule disapproved by the reviewing committee is reinstated at the end of the next session if a joint resolution in the legislature fails to sustain committee action.

(p) Full legislature may suspend rules.

(q) Failure to object or approve within 45 days of agency filing of final proposal constitutes approval.

(r) The legislature may permanently block rules through legislation. The vote to sponsor a joint resolution suspends the adoption of a proposed rule for a limited time so that the full legislature may act on the resolution, which would then be subject to governor's veto and override.

(s) Article V, Section IV of the Constitution, as amended in 1992, says the legislature may review any rule or regulation to determine whether the rule or regulation is consistent with legislative intent. The legislature transmits its objections to existing or proposed rules or regulations to the governor and relevant agency via concurrent resolutions. The legislature may invalidate or prohibit an existing or proposed rule from taking effect by a majority vote of the authorized membership of each house.

(t) Unless formal objections are made or the rule is declared void, rules are considered approved.

(u) JLCAR may recommend that an agency amend or withdraw a proposal. A vote opposing rule does not prohibit its adoption but assigns the burden of proof in any legal challenge to the agency.

(v) With the concurrence of the governor. The Joint Commission on Administrative Rules may also suspend regulations with the concurrence of the rules.

(w) State agencies have no power to promulgate rules without first submitting proposed rules to the legislature which must enact a statute authorizing the agency to promulgate the rule. If the legislature during a regular session disapproves all or part of any legislative rule, the agency may not issue the rule nor take action to implement all or part of the rule unless authorized to do so. However, the agency may resubmit the same or a similar proposed rule to the committee.

Table 3.27
SUMMARY OF SUNSET LEGISLATION

State	Scope	Preliminary evaluation conducted by	Other legislative review	Other oversight mechanisms in law	Phase-out period	Life of each agency (in years)	Other provisions
Alabama	C	Dept. of Examiners of Public Accounts	Standing Cmte.	Perf. audit	No later than Oct. 1 of the year following the regular session or a time as may be specified in the Sunset bill.	(Usually 4)	Schedules of licensing boards and other enumerated agencies are repealed according to specified time tables.
Alaska	C	Budget & Audit Cmte.	...	...	1/y	...	...
Arizona	C	Legislative staff	Joint Cmte.	...	6/m	10	...
Arkansas	D	...	...	...	...	...	...
California	S	St. Legis. Sunset Review Cmte. (a)	...	...	...	Varies	...
Colorado	R	Dept. of Regulatory Agencies	Legis. Cmtes. of Reference	Bills need adoption by the legislature.	1/y	Up to 15	State law provides certain criteria that are used to determine whether a public need exists for an entity or function to continue and that its regulation is the least restrictive regulation consistent with the public interest.
Connecticut	S	Legis. Program Review & Investigations Cmte.	...	...	1/y (b)	5	...
Delaware	C	Agencies under review submit reports to Del. Sunset Comm. based on criteria for review and set forth in statute. Comm. staff conducts separate review.	...	Perf. audit	Dec. 31 of next succeeding calendar year	4	Yearly sunset review schedules must include at least nine agencies. If the number automatically scheduled for review or added by the General Assembly is less than a full schedule, additional agencies shall be added in order of their appearance in the Del. Code to complete the review schedule.
Florida	C	Cmte. charged with oversight of the subject area.	Jt. cmte. charged with oversight of the subject area.	...	4 – 6/y	10	...
Georgia	R	Dept. of Audits	Standing Cmtes.	Perf. audit	...	...	A performance audit of each regulatory agency must be conducted upon the request of the Senate or House standing committee to which an agency has been assigned for oversight and review. (c)
Hawaii	R	Legis. Auditor	Standing Cmtes.	Perf. eval.	None	Established by the legislature	Schedules various professional and vocational licensing programs for repeal. Proposed new regulatory measures must be referred to the Auditor for sunrise analysis.
Idaho	(d)	...	...	...	...	...	...
Illinois	R, S (e)	Governor's Office of Mgmt. & Budget	Cmte. charged with re-enacting law.	(f)	...	Usually 10	...
Indiana	S	Nonpartisan staff units	Interim cmte. formed to review.	...	...	...	Smaller program review process now in place after about a dozen years of formal sunset program.
Iowa				No program			
Kansas	(g)	...	...	...	...	...	...

See footnotes at end of table.

SUMMARY OF SUNSET LEGISLATION — Continued

State	Scope	Preliminary evaluation conducted by	Other legislative review	Other oversight mechanisms in law	Phase-out period	Life of each agency (in years)	Other provisions
Kentucky	R	Administrative Regulation Review Subcmte.	Joint cmte. with subject matter jurisdiction	...	...	...	...
Louisiana	C	Standing cmtes. of the two houses with subject matter jurisdiction	...	Perf. eval.	1/y	Up to 6	Act provides for termination of a department and all offices in a department. Also permits committees to select particular agencies or offices for more extensive evaluation. Provides for review by Jt. Legis. Cmte. on Budget of programs that were not funded during the prior fiscal year for possible repeal.
Maine	S	Joint standing cmte. of jurisdiction	Office of Program Evaluation & Government Accountability (not yet established)	...	...	Generally 10	...
Maryland	R	Dept. of Legislative Services	Standing Cmtes.	Perf. eval.	...	Varies (usually 10)	...
Massachusetts				.... No program			...
Michigan	(d)	...	...	...	...	...	...
Minnesota	S (d)	...	...	...	...	...	...
Mississippi	(h)	...	...	...	...	...	...
Missouri	R	Oversight Division of Cmte. on Legislative Research	...	...	...	6, not to exceed total of 12	...
Montana	(d)	...	...	...	...	...	...
Nebraska	D(d)(i)	...	...	...	...	...	...
Nevada	(d)	...	...	...	...	...	...
New Hampshire	(j)	...	...	...	...	...	...
New Jersey	(d)	...	...	...	...	...	...
New Mexico	S	Legis. Finance Cmte.	...	Public hearing before termination	1/y	6	...
New York	(d)	...	...	...	...	...	...
North Carolina	(k)	...	...	...	...	...	...
North Dakota				.... No program			...
Ohio	C (m)	Sunset Review Cmte.	...	Perf. eval.	(l)	4	...
Oklahoma	S, D	Jt. cmtes. with jurisdiction over sunset bills	Appropriations & Budget Cmte.	...	1/y	6	...
Oregon	D (n)	...	(n)	Perf. eval.	1/y	...	...
Pennsylvania	R	Leadership Cmte.	...	...	...	...	...
Rhode Island	(o)	...	...	...	...	Varies	...
South Carolina	(p)	...	...	...	...	...	...
South Dakota	(q)	...	...	...	...	...	...

See footnotes at end of table.

SUMMARY OF SUNSET LEGISLATION — Continued

State	Scope	Preliminary evaluation conducted by	Other legislative review	Other oversight mechanisms in law	Phase-out period	Life of each agency (in years)	Other provisions
Tennessee	C	Office of the Comptroller	Government Operations Committees	...	1/y	Up to 6	...
Texas	S	Sunset Advisory Commission staff	...	...	1/y	12	...
Utah	C	Legislative staff and committee members	Periodic interim committee review	...	...	...	...
Vermont	(r)	Legis. Council staff	Senate and House Government Operations Cmtes.	...	...	...	...
Virginia	S (d)	...	...	...	...	...	Sunset provisions vary in length. The only standard sunset required by law is on bills that create a new advisory board or commission in the executive branch of government. The legislation introduced for these boards and commissions must contain a sunset provision to expire the entity after three years.
Washington	D	...	...	Perf. eval.	1/y	...	...
West Virginia	S	Jt. Cmte. on Govt. Operations	Performance Evaluation and Research Division	Perf. audit	1/y	6	Jt. Cmte. on Govt. Operations composed of five House members, five Senate members and five citizens appointed by governor. Agencies may be reviewed more frequently.
Wisconsin	(d)	...	...	...	...	...	...
Wyoming	D (s)	Program evaluation staff who work for Management Audit Cmte.	...	Perf. eval. (t)	...	...	...

Source: The Council of State Governments' survey, December 2006.

Key:
C — Comprehensive
R — Regulatory
S — Selective
D — Discretionary
d — day
m — month
y — year
. . . — Not applicable

(a) Review by the Joint Legislative Sunset Review Committee of professional and vocational licensing boards terminates on January 1, 2004. Sunset clauses are included in other selected programs and legislation.

(b) Upon termination, a program shall continue for one year to conclude its affairs.

(c) The automatic sunsetting of an agency every six years was eliminated in 1992. The legislature must pass a bill in order to sunset a specific agency.

(d) While they have not enacted sunset legislation in the same sense as the other states with detailed information in this table, the legislatures in Idaho, Michigan, Minnesota, Montana, Nebraska, Nevada, New Jersey, New York, Virginia and Wisconsin have included sunset clauses in selected programs or legislation.

(e) Many tax laws provide that tax breaks enacted since 1994 will last only five years after taking effect unless the laws creating those breaks establish other sunset periods.

(f) Governor is to read GOMB report and make recommendations to the General Assembly every even-numbered year.

(g) Sunset legislation terminated July 1992. Legislative oversight of designated state agencies, consisting of audit, review and evaluation, continues.

(h) Sunset Act terminated December 31, 1984.

(i) Sunset legislation is discretionary, meaning that senators are free to offer sunset legislation or attach termination dates to legislative proposals. There is no formal sunset commission. Nebraska Revised Statutes section 50-1303 directs the Legislature's Government, Military and Veteran's Committee to conduct an evaluation of any board, commission, or similar state entity. The review must include, among other things, a recommendation as to whether the board, commission, or entity should be terminated, continued or modified.

(j) New Hampshire's Sunset Committee was repealed July 1, 1986.

(k) North Carolina's sunset law terminated on July 30, 1981. Successor vehicle, the Legislative Committee on Agency Review, operated until June 30, 1983.

(l) Authority for latest review (HB 548 of the 123rd General Assembly) expired December 31, 2004. HB 516 of the 125th General Assembly re-established the Sunset Review Committee, but postpones its operation until the 128th General Assembly. The bill terminates the Sunset Review Law on December 31, 2010.

(m) There are statutory exceptions.

(n) Sunset legislation was repealed in 1993. No general law sunsetting rules or agencies.

(o) No standing sunset statutes or procedures at this time.

(p) Law repealed by 1998 Act 419.

(q) South Dakota suspended sunset legislation in 1979. Under current law, the Executive Board of the Legislative Research Council is directed to establish one or more interim committees each year to review state agencies so that each state agency is reviewed once every 10 years.

(r) Sunsets are at the legislature's discretion. Their structure will vary on an individual basis.

(s) Wyoming repealed sunset legislation in 1988.

(t) The program evaluation process evolved out of the sunset process, but Wyoming currently does not have a scheduled sunset of programs.

Chapter Four

STATE EXECUTIVE BRANCH

" *In 2007, state chief executives seemed to extend discussions of state management that began in earnest last year.* "

—Katherine Willoughby

" *During the four and a half decades between 1960 and 2007, the overall institutional powers of the nation's governors increased by 13.6 percent.* "

—Thad Beyle

" *The office of lieutenant governor is a risen power, a fact demonstrated by research and anecdotal indicators as 2007 began.* "

—Julia Nienaber Hurst

" *The Internet age is transforming the office of secretary of state, both in terms of e-government innovations and policy challenges.* "

—Kay Stimson

" *Attorneys general are at the forefront of a number of crucial legal and law enforcement issues and play a vital leadership role as representatives of the public interest.* "

—Angelia Plemmer

" *State treasurers are integral to the fiscal health and prosperity of the states.* "

—National Association of State Treasurers

" *As state government finance and accountability stewards, state auditors and state comptrollers must face a variety of challenges each day.* "

—Jan I. Sylvis

The State of the States: Political Change Emboldens Governors
By Katherine Willoughby

Last year in their State of the State addresses, governors laid out measured approaches to fiscal management that emphasized a long-term perspective, budget balance and best practices to help strengthen states. Governors pushed tax cuts, and their spending initiatives were modest. State chief executives seemed hesitant to make grandiose promises even as the revenue situation eased. The 2006 elections and possibilities for dramatic political change help explain this hesitancy.

Today the fiscal situation continues to improve, although at a slower pace than last year. And, the 2006 elections brought the drama predicted; party control of governorships flipped and Democrats now hold the majority of these seats. Power shifted to Democrats in state legislatures as well. Examination of the governors' State of the State speeches this year indicates a "full speed ahead" attitude.[1] Still, governors remain focused on select areas of state government operation, as well as fully cognizant of the continued need for reasoned fiscal stewardship.

The Politics

Governors' seats in Arkansas, Colorado, Maryland, Massachusetts, Ohio and New York switched from Republican to Democrat in the 2006 elections, giving Democrats the stronghold on state chief executive seats. In the 2006 elections, the mix of 22 Democratic governors and 28 Republican governors flipped to 28 Democrats and 22 Republicans. Twelve Republican governors were re-elected to another term; 10 were newly elected or already completing a term. At the same time, 13 Democratic governors were re-elected while 15 were either newly elected or completing a term.

Legislatures changed politically as well, shifting power to Democrats. Today, 25 state senates are majority Democratic, 22 are majority Republican and two are split. Of state houses, 29 are majority Democratic and 20 are majority Republican. Nebraska has a unicameral, nonpartisan legislature. The shift to Democratic states is clear when the two branches of government are considered together. Fifteen states can be labeled Democratic having a Democratic gov-

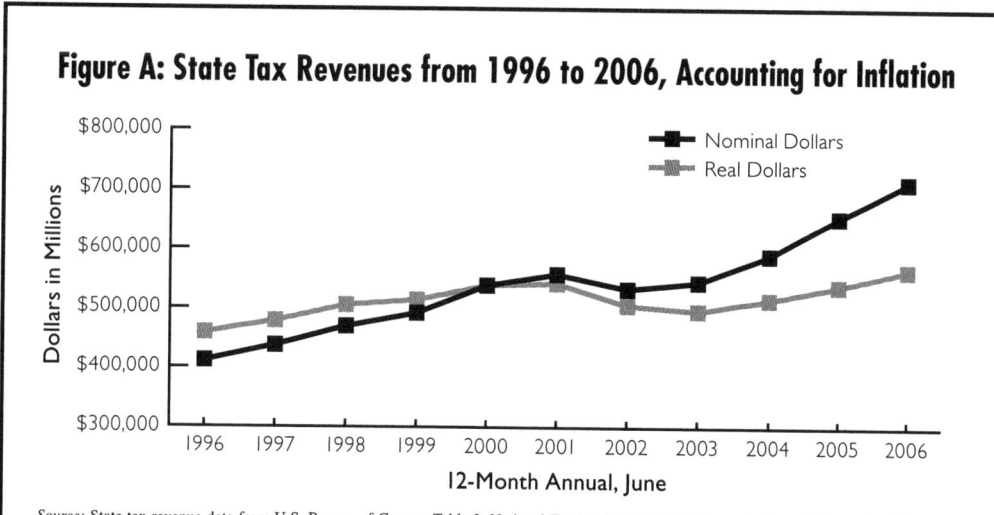

Figure A: State Tax Revenues from 1996 to 2006, Accounting for Inflation

Source: State tax revenue data from U.S. Bureau of Census, Table 2. National Totals of State Tax Revenue, by Type of Tax at *http://www.census.gov/govs/www/qtax.html.* Annual 12-month ending June figures used. Nominal and deflated dollars are provided; deflated dollars use the implicit price deflator for gross domestic product, state and local, Table 1.1.9 of NIPA tables available at the U.S. Bureau of Economic Analysis Web site at *http://www.bea.gov/national/nipaweb/SelectTable.asp?Selected=N* [Index numbers 2000=100]. IPD for fiscal year 2006 generated using three-year moving average of the rate of change of indices for fiscal years 2000 to 2005.

ernor and majority Democratic legislature; 10 states are Republican. The rest of the states break down in terms of party control accordingly:

- 1 with a Republican governor and a nonpartisan legislature
- 1 with a Republican governor, Republican house and split senate
- 3 with Republican governors and split legislatures
- 7 with Republican governors and Democratic legislatures
- 5 with Democratic governors and Republican legislatures
- 1 with a Democratic governor, a Republican house and a split senate
- 7 with Democratic governors and split legislatures

Revenues, Expenditures and Balance

No state missed its revenue target in 2006, according to the National Association of State Budget Officers (NASBO).[2] Revenues collected actually bested enacted budgets by almost 6 percent. Still, while states have done well to recover from the recent recession, fiscal confidence has not been fully restored. Figure A illustrates the revenue trend of state tax sources, considering both nominal and adjusted dollars. In real terms, state tax revenues have grown by 23.1 percent from 1996 to 2006. These revenues have grown by just 4.8 percent from 2000 to 2006, however.

Consideration of the tax sources upon which states depend helps to flesh out the revenue picture in the states. Table A shows tax types as a proportion of total tax sources used by the states in 1996 and 2006. Throughout this decade, states indicate stronger reliance on the individual income tax, tobacco product sales taxes and other taxes, but a declining reliance on all other tax sources. Sales and gross receipts taxes are second only to individual income taxes in importance as a state revenue source, but even this tax category has declined as a proportion of total taxes from 1996 to 2006. States have continued to erode corporate income tax as a significant source of revenue; similarly, states exhibit decreased reliance on property taxes.

Figure B provides general fund data from 2000 (actual) to 2007 (appropriated) and illustrates the improvements in revenues, expenditures and budget stabilization funds during this time. Certainly, states have done better in recent years. Still, if we consider that the bottom fell out of state revenues around 2002, there has not been a particularly strong resurgence in revenues. In fact, from 2000 to 2007, general fund expenditures outpaced revenues. General fund revenues increased in real terms by just 1.4 percent from 2000 to 2007, while expenditures increased by 5 percent during this same period. In real terms, budget stabilization funds declined by 23.9 percent during the period, although in 2007 these funds are expected to increase by more than 200 percent from 2002, when funds were lowest as a proportion of expenditures. In 2002, budget stabilization funds made up just 1.5 percent of expenditures; by 2007, these funds are expected to make up 4.2 percent of expenditures.

Finally, examination of the recent trend in states' total balances confirms the cautious optimism that should be used when assessing the current fiscal climate in the states. Total balances include budget stabilization funds and ending balances. While the rules differ across governments, these balances can help states manage through budget crises in any given fiscal year. In 2002, total balances equaled 3.7 percent of expenditures; by 2007, these balances are expected to reach 6.8 percent of expenditures, having dropped 3 percent from a high in fiscal 2006 of 9.8 percent.[3]

What's on the Agenda?

Table B summarizes agenda items as expressed by governors in their 2007 State of the State addresses. A content analysis on addresses given by governors as of March 6, 2007, looked for mention of the issues noted; issues mentioned specifically by a governor as

Table A: State Tax Sources as a Proportion of Total Tax Revenues, Ten-year Comparison

Type of tax	1996	2006
Individual income tax	32.0%	34.8%
General sales and gross receipts	33.3	32.1
All other taxes	13.1	13.8
Corporate income tax	7.0	6.8
Motor fuel sales	6.3	5.2
Motor vehicle and operators	3.5	2.9
Tobacco products sales	1.7	2.0
Property tax	2.2	1.7
Alcoholic beverages sales	0.9	0.7

Source: State tax revenue data from U.S. Bureau of Census, Table 2. "National Totals of State Tax Revenue, by Type of Tax," *http://www.census.gov/govs/www/qtax.html.*

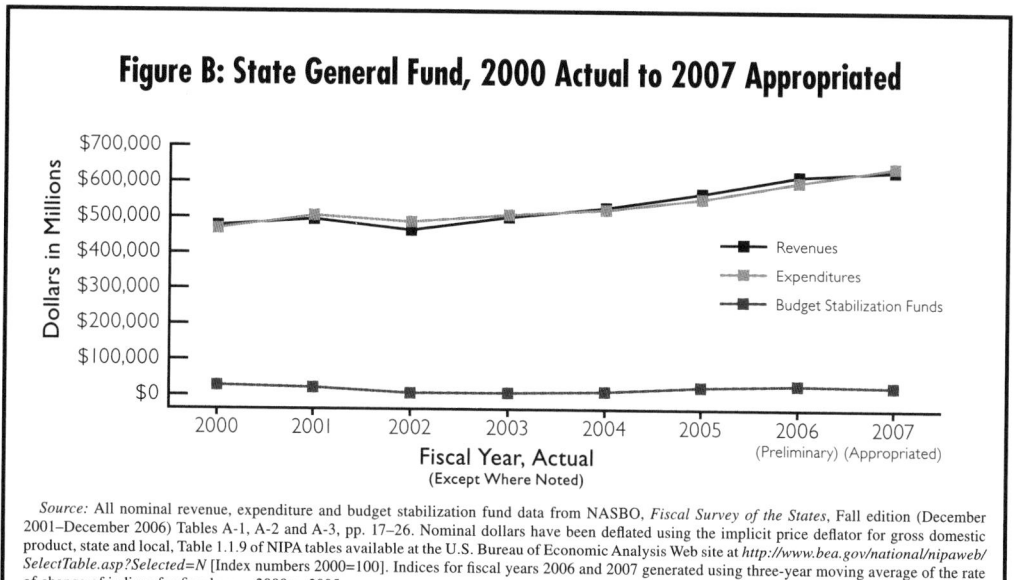

Figure B: State General Fund, 2000 Actual to 2007 Appropriated

Legend:
- ■ Revenues
- ■ Expenditures
- ■ Budget Stabilization Funds

Y-axis: Dollars in Millions — $0 to $700,000

X-axis: Fiscal Year, Actual (Except Where Noted) — 2000, 2001, 2002, 2003, 2004, 2005, 2006 (Preliminary), 2007 (Appropriated)

Source: All nominal revenue, expenditure and budget stabilization fund data from NASBO, *Fiscal Survey of the States*, Fall edition (December 2001–December 2006) Tables A-1, A-2 and A-3, pp. 17–26. Nominal dollars have been deflated using the implicit price deflator for gross domestic product, state and local, Table 1.1.9 of NIPA tables available at the U.S. Bureau of Economic Analysis Web site at *http://www.bea.gov/national/nipaweb/SelectTable.asp?Selected=N* [Index numbers 2000=100]. Indices for fiscal years 2006 and 2007 generated using three-year moving average of the rate of change of indices for fiscal years 2000 to 2005.

part of his or her budget agenda or of policy concern going forward were marked as expressed in a state. Issues governors mentioned as related to past work were not counted as agenda items in 2007. The number of states in which an issue was mentioned and the proportion of addresses in which an issue appears are provided in the table. Results show that, like last year, chief executives are primarily concerned with education and health care.

For example, Arkansas' Gov. Mike Beebe (D) presented a multi-pronged approach to education advancements in that state. His education agenda includes spending surplus dollars on education facilities; extra funding for school districts and special needs children; additional funding for the state's "Better Chance" programs regarding voluntary, preschool classes for poor families; scholarships for college students from families with $25,000 or less annual income; and increased support to community colleges and libraries. Perhaps most innovative, Beebe calls for state employees to receive one day off to attend parent-teacher conferences and gives them the opportunity to use paid leave to volunteer at schools. Other governors mentioned new funding formulas for local school districts; lottery funding reforms to reduce bureaucratic glitches; additional spending for classrooms and other educational facilities; additional specialists, counselors and mentors, and improved teachers' salaries to reduce class sizes and boost the classroom experience; college tuition freezes and additional funding for student financial aid, loan programs and scholarships.

Several governors discussed increased or universal access to education. Oklahoma's Gov. Brad Henry (D) pushed an option of early childhood education for all 3-year-olds and an "OK Promise" to provide college education to all who meet specified criteria. Similarly, Michigan Gov. Jennifer Granholm (D) asked for full-day kindergarten, an increase in the eligible dropout age to 18, scholarships for every student for two-year colleges, free tuition for three years for unemployed workers to attend community colleges, and the application of tobacco funds for college scholarships. Second-term Republican Gov. Mike Rounds of South Dakota spoke of the state's education programs in terms of "starting strong, finishing strong and staying strong." His education agenda calls for improvements in the graduation rates of American Indian students, better teacher salaries, a virtual high school, and advancement of a research consortium with neighboring states using a fiber optic network. A "Wisconsin Covenant" promoted by Gov. Jim Doyle (D) is a comprehensive agenda that includes a breakfast program, reduced class sizes and a performance-based incentive of a college education. Similarly, Nebraska Gov. Dave Heineman (R) calls for increased parental involvement in children's education and an increased tax deduction available to parents who take advantage of the state's college savings plan. Several governors also recommended state investment to increase the number of graduating doctors, nurses and/or dentists and/or to forgive the education debt of teachers who practice in rural areas.

Table B: Issues Expressed by Governors in 2007 State of the State Addresses

Issue expressed by governors	Number of governors mentioning issue	Percentage of governors mentioning issue
Education	44	100%
Health care	38	86.4
Tax/revenue initiative	37	84.1
Natural resources/energy	37	84.1
Economic development/tourism	35	79.5
Safety/corrections	33	75.0
Performance/accountability	32	72.7
Surplus/rainy day/reserves/balance	31	70.5
Military troops/Iraq recognition	30	68.2
Transportation	23	52.3
Local government	23	52.3
Pensions/OPEB	16	36.4
Transparency	9	20.5
Ethics reform	6	13.6
Debt reduction	6	13.6
Borders and illegal immigrants	5	11.4

Source: Content analysis of 2007 State of the State Addresses, Katherine Willoughby.

Democratic New Hampshire Gov. John Lynch's education agenda emphasizes gubernatorial focus this year—he asked for a constitutional amendment to renew the state's responsibility for education.

Governors' discussions of health care are equally extensive and substantive. Virginia Gov. Tim Kaine (D) lamented that the state does "well at treating the sick, but does not do well in keeping people healthy, combating obesity and advancing health education programs"—thus highlighting some of the initiatives that run through State of the State addresses. Similarly, Georgia's Republican Gov. Sonny Perdue asked for improved prevention strategies as well as a more transparent, businesslike approach to health care; one in which citizens can look up information about doctors and hospitals online and can choose health care services by cost and quality. Common themes of governors this year regarding health care include affordability, comprehensive and/or universal health care coverage, new or advanced choice of care and services, multistate drug purchasing pools, and/or the ability to purchase prescription drugs from Canada. For example, Connecticut's second-term Republican Gov. Jodi Rell is asking that state's Democratic legislature to support funding for premium assistance to help lower income residents enroll in the state's "Charter Oak" health care plan. Rell also asked for a "guarantee that every eligible newborn leaves the hospital with health insurance. Based on

income, parents might not even have to pay a premium. That is, if a premium is required but parents are unable to pay, the state will waive the premium for the first two months. This will be our gift to Connecticut's newborns." Likewise, Delaware Gov. Ruth Ann Minner (D) called for expansion of health care coverage to include additional cancer treatments for the uninsured.

Other governors pushed advancements in embryonic stem cell research, universal vaccine purchasing ability, free cervical cancer vaccines (Gardasil) to girls ages 11 to 18 years, and electronically based rather than paper-based health care systems. Nebraska's governor was the only one to talk about restructuring the state's health and human services department to advance health care services in that state. New Jersey Gov. Jon Corzine (D) was the only chief executive to mention health reform in terms of state employees' other post-employment benefits. Finally, Tennessee's second-term governor, Democrat Phil Bredesen, defended his reason for not discussing health care noting that, "health care spending has overshadowed everything else for so long."

Energy and natural resources initiatives span water, land, energy and wildlife issues. Common themes of state chief executives in 2007 include the development of alternative and/or renewable fuels (including wind, tidal, hydro and geothermal), coal conversion, water and land conservation, protection and redevelopment, and stricter emission standards. Several governors outlined very specific programs. For example, Georgia Gov. Perdue supported a $19 million "Go Fish" program to develop fishing facilities to draw tourists and fishing tournaments to the state in an effort that also could promote economic development. Alaska's newly elected Republican Gov. Sarah Palin sought to balance development of oil and energy supplies with conservation efforts. Palin asked for better oversight of current oil and gas pipelines and development of an area currently leased on the edge of the Arctic National Wildlife Refuge—"warehousing Alaska's resources is not an option anymore. We can't afford it!" Palin also promoted the Alaska Gasline Inducement Act or AGIA, which provides inducements to those companies building the pipeline, yet requires that those who compete for construction must support "gas

Table C: Enacted Revenue Actions by Type and Net Increase or Decrease (In millions)

					Revenue source				
FY enacted	Sales	Personal income	Corporate income	Cigarette/ tobacco	Motor fuel	Alcohol	Other taxes	Fees	Net
Ten year net.......	$3,635	($15,367)	($623)	$7,117	$737	$123	($5,188)	$4,765	($4,802)
2007....................	622.4	(2,321.9)	(239.7)	487.9	(115.2)	5.4	(772.8)	279.2	(2,054.7)
2006....................	994.5	(739.2)	119.6	1,249.1	81.1	36.4	141.7	685.6	2,568.8
2005....................	710.6	428.5	272.0	888.4	1.2	25.0	707.7	508.7	3,542.1
2004....................	2,569.7	2,461.4	601.0	751.1	132.9	46.5	1,178.2	1m809.5	9,550.3
2003....................	1,436.5	1,073.2	999.4	2,965.7	34.9	12.6	677.1	819.0	8,018.4
2002....................	186.1	(671.2)	381.6	98.7	. . .	. . .	126.4	182.2	303.8
2001....................	(926.7)	(2,594.4)	(708.9)	41.6	(104.1)	(41.3)	(1,426.9)	(56.1)	(5,816.8)
2000....................	(366.8)	(2,200.8)	(821.0)	218.8	212.5	42.9	(2,805.5)	524.7	(5,198.3)
1999....................	(582.2)	(4,442.6)	(395.6)	223.1	22.1	. . .	(1,267.3)	(584.3)	(7,026.8)
1998....................	(671.4)	(3,454.1)	(280.5)	118.7	462.0	(4.7)	(982.8)	231.4	(4,581.4)
1997....................	(337.5)	(2,906.3)	(551.2)	74.0	10.0	. . .	(760.9)	364.6	(4,107.3)

Source: NASBO, *Fiscal Survey of the States*, Fall Survey (December 1997–2006), Table 7.

for Alaskans, jobs for Alaskans, as well as project benchmarks." Among Gov. Rell's four-point "energy vision" in Connecticut is the creation of a new state Department of Energy that "will assume the policy and planning functions of our energy needs. And the DPUC will be restructured to focus its role on utility regulation." Rhode Island Gov. Don Carcieri (R) promoted the largest environmental bond in that state's history—$85 million to clean up the bay. Carcieri also asked to continue to strive for the generation of 20 percent of the state's electricity through renewable resources as well as the formation of a state power authority.

Two-thirds of the governors who addressed their residents by March 2007 promoted budget agendas that supported economic development, safety and corrections, performance and accountability measures, surplus and balance issues, and publicly recognized U.S. military service men and women. Major economic development concerns of governors included housing, work force development, responsible growth, incentives for filmmaking, refurbishment of historic sites to advance tourism, universal or advanced broadband connection in the state, and small business entrepreneurship incentives. New Mexico's Democratic Gov. Bill Richardson and South Dakota's Republican Gov. Rounds both pushed a higher minimum wage. Initiatives regarding safety and corrections included redeployment of current staff and/or spending for additional officers, increased salaries for prison staff, prison reforms and building additional facilities, reducing recidivism, combating drug abuse, particularly methamphetamine, and improving public safety communications systems. Other, less popular agenda items included

those of Missouri Gov. Matt Blunt (R) (to pass legislation allowing citizens to protect themselves from violent crime and protect second amendment rights), Richardson in New Mexico (to ban cockfighting) and Rounds in South Dakota (to ease requirements related to lethal injections).

Performance measurement and accountability suggestions by governors consider activities in education, economic development, technology, state purchasing and contracting, natural resources, health care and more. Some chief executives mentioned performance goals such as the reduction of greenhouse emissions by 2012 (Arizona), cutting the high school dropout rate in half in 10 years (Colorado), and bonuses for educational performance (Minnesota). Others were very specific. Connecticut's Rell suggested that local school districts that fail to make adequate progress "will be required to designate more money for intervention and will be in danger of losing their autonomy. For schools that continue to fail, the state Department of Education may replace personnel, replace school administrators or reconstitute schools entirely." Maryland Gov. Martin O'Malley (D), a former mayor, promoted StateStat (a knockoff of CitiStat) and BayStat, a performance application for the bay area restoration. New Jersey's governor called for stronger oversight of state spending through independent auditing and a new state comptroller. Gov. Corzine also pushed to "modernize archaic civil service laws." Other performance initiatives included those of Nevada Gov. Jim Gibbons (R), who pushed performance-based contracting, South Carolina Gov. Mark Sanford (R), who asked for a strengthened executive branch with department heads that work for the governor and are not independently elected, and Utah Gov. Jon Huntsman (R), who promoted greater flexibility for state managers regarding employee compensation.

Revenue Actions by Type, Fiscal Years 1997–2007

Table C illustrates enacted revenue actions by type in the states for the last decade. From 1997 through 2001, when revenues were fairly plentiful, states cut taxes involving this level's most predominant sources—sales and income taxes—as well as corporate income taxes. States realized a net decrease in revenues in millions of dollars in every one of these years. From 2002 through 2007, sales tax bases and rates are changed in order to generate additional revenue; from 2003 through 2005, personal income tax bases and rates are changed to generate increases as well. Net increases in revenues from all sources listed were realized from 2002 to 2006. The use of "sin" taxes to bring in revenues is a staple for states for all years noted. States realized approximately $7.1 billion (nominal) and $6.3 billion (actual; 2000=100) in new revenues from cigarette and tobacco taxes from 1997 to 2007.[4] Still, total net loss to states in revenues from tax changes for the 10-year period is $4.8 billion (nominal) and $8.3 billion (actual; 2000=100).

So what are governors' revenue considerations in 2007? Governors exhibit great awareness of the entire budgeting equation that stipulates balance between revenues and expenditures. For example, Maryland's O'Malley said his state is strong, but has "a huge looming structural deficit." Connecticut's governor talked of property tax relief and other tax cuts, but emphasized that "to pay for our historic and unprecedented investments, I am proposing a fractional increase across the board in the income tax rate—a quarter of a percent for this fiscal year, and a half of a percent in the following fiscal year. I am also calling for an increase in the cigarette tax of 49 cents per pack." She added, "Let me also be very clear about one more thing: I have had to make cuts I did not want to make and I have had to raise taxes I did not want to raise, in large part because we have a constitutional cap on spending. But, I respect that cap and I believe it acts to restrain runaway spending and taxes." New Jersey's Corzine also is looking for balance by instituting:

- cost-savings through independent auditing by a new nonpolitical state comptroller;
- consolidations and shared services;
- collective bargaining on pension and health benefits;
- asset monetization designed to reduce state credit card payments and provide for future capital investment; and

- a 4-percent cap on the increase in the property tax levy that is paid for with dedicated sales tax revenue, redirected homestead rebates and a number of efficiency measures

Mississippi Gov. Haley Barbour (R) explains the problem of structural balance directly:

> We know part of this surge in state tax revenue is one-time money ... the result of large sales tax increases caused by Katrina victims replacing ... durable goods. These purchases won't occur every year, and that sales tax revenue is not recurring revenue to the state. So we mustn't spend it on recurring expenditures. That would put us back in the same budget hole we were in when I was elected. We've dug out of the hole; and we have to stay out of it.

Montana Gov. Brian Schweitzer (D) outlined plans for that state's $1 billion surplus ("estimated if all goes well at the end of the biennium") that include spending for ongoing projects, for tax cuts and savings accounts, and on infrastructure. Schweitzer promoted a "Big Sky Savings Account" for the state. Nevada Gov. Gibbons spoke of presenting the state's first budget under a new spending cap and an effort to set aside money in the state's rainy day fund. In Wyoming, Gov. Dave Freudenthal (D) spoke of public misconception regarding the permanent mineral trust fund: "We become trust fund babies" when the trust fund becomes a significant portion of the general fund. "At its height, the trust fund accounted for 23 percent of the state's general fund," he said. Granholm talked of fixing Michigan's broken tax system noting that the "recent cut of business taxes needs replacement for the state to reach structural balance." Huntsman's effort to advance Utah's dual tax system allows that "citizens can pay under the old income tax structure or pay a flat 5.35 percent of income in taxes." The governor hopes to decrease the flat rate to 5 percent and impose a low-income tax credit along with a single statewide sales tax rate. Likewise in Virginia, where substantial tax reform has already occurred, Kaine called for increases in user fees, an increase in the personal income tax threshold and approval of a constitutional amendment to allow local governments to impose homestead exemptions up to 20 percent of the value of owner-occupied homes or farms.

Consistent themes regarding tax and revenue measures in the addresses this year include property tax relief; tax incentives for all sorts of behaviors—to lure filmmakers, for energy conservation and alternative fuel use; tax credits to producers of alternative energy and others in research and development; and tax exemptions for military and/or retirement income. As noted above, many new tax structures were discussed—Alaska's governor talked of the institution of a new oil and gas tax structure that taxes "oil companies' claimed expenses and profits" and called on the state's revenue commissioner to make sure that this petroleum profits tax "works as promised."

In Arizona, Gov. Janet Napolitano (D) asked legislators to allow the state to extend the terms of existing bonded indebtedness from 20 to 30 years and "free up" $400 million to go toward transportation projects. Heineman pointed to Nebraska's "high tax burden" as reason to promote a relief package to cut taxes for the middle class. Heineman's tax reform package included: elimination of the marriage penalty, reduction in the number of income tax brackets, a widening of the bracket impacting the largest number of middle class taxpayers, lowering tax rates across the board, indexing new brackets, repealing the remainder of the sales tax on construction labor, and eliminating the estate tax for family farmers and small business owners. In contrast, South Dakota's governor was one of a precious few not delving into tax issues because, as Rounds said, "we have the lowest state taxes per capita in the nation."

Finally, many governors couched revenue initiatives in terms of shoring up long-term funding of transportation projects. In Colorado, for example, Democratic Gov. Bill Ritter sought to "create a Transportation Finance and Implementation Panel to push forward a funded transportation policy. The panel will work with the state's Department of Transportation and the current Transportation Commission with a concentration on funding transportation projects, given declining dollars."

Conclusion

In 2007, state chief executives seemed to extend discussions of state management that began in earnest last year. That is, governors are concerned about the primary responsibilities of state government and how best to extend services to residents in need, yet mindful of the balancing act that must occur between revenues and expenditures in order for their governments to remain financially viable. Governors seem to be completely comfortable discussing intricate and comprehensive methods of taxing and service delivery; and capable of considering a variety of ways to further advance the work of these governments. Asset leveraging, multi-pronged taxing strategies and structures, and alternative delivery methods are all on the table as possibilities for getting the job done at this level of government. In fact, in some cases, states are not waiting for the federal government to act—the minimum wage, universal health care, global warming and illegal immigration were also mentioned by several governors. These are issues that undoubtedly will be further considered by state legislatures; inevitably state laws will be passed and these governments will continue to serve as laboratories of American government in action.

Notes

[1] Chief executives of state governments report annually or biennially to their legislatures regarding the fiscal condition of their state, commonwealth or territory. Governors often use their address to lay out their policy and budget agendas for their upcoming or continuing administration. The 2007 state of the state addresses were accessed from January through March 6, 2007 at *www.stateline.org*, *www.nga.org*, or at the state government home page. This research considers those 44 states with transcripts available at these sites as of March 6, 2007. Although Iowa's outgoing and newly elected governors gave speeches, only that of the newly elected Governor Chet Culver (D) is assessed here. Speeches not available by March 6, 2007, included those from Alabama, Illinois, Louisiana, Ohio, Oregon, and Texas. All quotes and data presented here are from the addresses accessed on these Web sites, unless otherwise noted.

[2] NASBO, *Fiscal Survey of the States* (December 2006): p. 8.

[3] NASBO, 2006, p. 12.

[4] Nominal dollars in Table C have been deflated using the implicit price deflator for gross domestic product, state and local, Table 1.1.9 of NIPA tables available at the U.S. Bureau of Economic Analysis Web site at *http://www.bea.gov/national/nipaweb/SelectTable.asp?Selected=N* [Index numbers 2000=100]. The IPD for fiscal year 2007 is generated using three-year moving average of the rate of change of indices for fiscal years 1997 to 2006. January 31, 2007 Next Release Date February 28, 2007.

About the Author

Katherine Willoughby is professor of Public Administration and Urban Studies in the Andrew Young School of Policy Studies at Georgia State University in Atlanta. Her research concentrates on state and local government budgeting and financial management, public policy development and public organization theory. She has conducted extensive research in the area of state budgeting practices, with a concentration on performance measurement applicability at this level of government in the United States.

Gubernatorial Elections, Campaign Costs and Powers
By Thad Beyle

The 2006 elections reversed a decade-long Republican trend as 20 Democrats and 16 Republicans won their races in 2006. This means that in 2007, the 50 states will be in a partisan split with 28 Democratic governors and 22 Republican governors—the exact reverse of the split going into the 2006 gubernatorial elections.

Governors continue to be in the forefront of activity as we move into the 21st century. With Republican governors across the states serving as his major supporters and guides, Texas Gov. George W. Bush sought and won the presidency in the 2000 election. He became the fourth of the last five presidents who had served as governor just prior to seeking and winning the presidency.[1] When George H.W. Bush, a non-governor, won the 1988 presidential election, he beat a governor, Michael Dukakis (D-Mass., 1975–1979 and 1983–1991). Clearly, presidential politics in the three decades following the Watergate scandal finds governors as major actors. In 2008, we will see if that trend continues.

Additionally, the demands on the governors to propose state budgets and then to keep them in balance during the two recessions of the early 1990s and in the early 2000s have made the governor's chair a "hot seat" in more ways than one.[2] In the most recent downturn, governors moved from the half-decade of economic boom of the late 1990s, in which they could propose tax cuts and program increases, to an economic downturn period in which there is increasing demand for program support while state tax revenues fell off significantly. Proposed and adopted budgets fell victim to severe revenue shortfalls in most states. Easy times had switched to hard times again. Now as we enter 2007, we have seen an upturn in the economy easing some of the budgetary problems that governors have been facing.

2006 Gubernatorial Politics

In the even years between presidential elections, 36 states hold their gubernatorial elections. Two states, New Hampshire and Vermont, have two-year gubernatorial terms, so they hold a gubernatorial election every other year. The 2006 elections reversed a decade-long Republican trend as 20 Democrats and 16 Republicans won their races in 2006. This means that in 2007, the 50 states will be in a partisan split with 28 Democratic governors and 22 Republican governors—the exact reverse of the split going into the 2006 gubernatorial elections.

There were changes in who was to be the governor in 2007 in 11 states. In five states—Arkansas, Colorado, Florida, Nevada and Ohio—the incumbent governor was term-limited so the races in those states were for an open seat. In three other states—Iowa, Massachusetts and New York—the incumbent governor decided to retire from being governor and did not seek re-election, again setting up an open seat race. Finally, in two other states, the incumbent governor sought re-election but was beaten in the party primary—Frank Murkowski, R-Alaska—or in the general election—Robert Ehrlich, R-Md. So, there were 11 new governors sworn in January, 2007. Seven were Democrats and four were Republicans.

One other new governor appeared in 2006. Republican Jim Risch was sworn in as the new governor of Idaho on May 26, 2006. As lieutenant governor, he ascended to the governorship upon the resignation of incumbent Republican Gov. Dirk Kempthorne, who was sworn in as U.S. Secretary of the Interior after being appointed to that position by President Bush and confirmed by the U.S. Senate. Risch became the 31st governor of Idaho.

Gubernatorial Elections

As seen in Table A, in the 519 gubernatorial elections held between 1970 and 2006, incumbents were eligible to seek another term in 399 (77 percent) of the contests. Seventy-eight percent (313) of the eligible incumbents sought re-election and 236 (75 percent) of them succeeded. Those who were defeated for re-election were more likely to lose in the general election than in their own party primary by a 2.8-to-1 ratio, although two of the four incumbent losses in 2004 and one of their losses in 2006 were tied to party primaries. Not since 1994 had an incumbent governor been defeated in a party primary.

Democratic candidates had a winning edge in elections held between 1970 and 2006 (56 percent). And in 201 races (39 percent) the results led to a party shift in which a candidate from a party other than the incumbent's party won. Yet these party shifts have evened out over the years so that neither of the

Table A: Gubernatorial Elections: 1970–2006

Number of incumbent governors

Year	Number of races	Democratic winner Number	Democratic winner Percent	Eligible to run Number	Eligible to run Percent	Actually ran Number	Actually ran Percent	Won Number	Won Percent	Lost Number	Lost Percent	Lost In primary	Lost In general election
1970	35	22	63	29	83	24	83	16	64	8	36	1 (a)	7 (b)
1971	3	3	100	0	. . .	. . .	. . .	. . .	. . .	. . .	. . .	. . .	. . .
1972	18	11	61	15	83	11	73	7	64	4	36	2 (c)	2 (d)
1973	2	1	50	1	50	1	100	. . .	. . .	1	100	1 (e)	. . .
1974	35	27 (f)	77	29	83	22	76	17	77	5	24	1 (g)	4 (h)
1975	3	3	100	2	66	2	100	2	100	. . .	. . .	. . .	. . .
1976	14	9	64	12	86	8	67	5	63	3	33	1 (i)	2 (j)
1977	2	1	50	1	50	1	100	1	100	. . .	. . .	. . .	. . .
1978	36	21	58	29	81	23	79	16	73	7	30	2 (k)	5 (l)
1979	3	2	67	0	. . .	. . .	. . .	. . .	. . .	. . .	. . .	. . .	. . .
1980	13	6	46	12	92	12	100	7	58	5	42	2 (m)	3 (n)
1981	2	1	50	0	. . .	. . .	. . .	. . .	. . .	. . .	. . .	. . .	. . .
1982	36	27	75	33	92	25	76	19	76	6	24	1 (o)	5 (p)
1983	3	3	100	1	33	1	100	. . .	. . .	1	100	1 (q)	. . .
1984	13	5	38	9	69	6	67	4	67	2	33	. . .	2 (r)
1985	2	1	50	1	50	1	100	1	100	. . .	. . .	. . .	. . .
1986	36	19	53	24	67	18	75	15	83	3	18	1 (s)	2 (t)
1987	3	3	100	2	67	1	50	. . .	. . .	1	100	1 (u)	. . .
1988	12	5	42	9	75	9	100	8	89	1	11	. . .	1 (v)
1989	2	2	100	0	. . .	. . .	. . .	. . .	. . .	. . .	. . .	. . .	. . .
1990	36	19 (w)	53	33	92	23	70	17	74	6	26	. . .	6 (x)
1991	3	2	67	2	67	2	100	. . .	. . .	2	100	1 (y)	1 (z)
1992	12	8	67	9	75	4	44	4	100	. . .	. . .	. . .	. . .
1993	2	0	0	1	50	1	100	. . .	. . .	1	100	. . .	1 (aa)
1994	36	11 (bb)	31	30	83	23	77	17	74	6	26	2 (cc)	4 (dd)
1995	3	1	33	2	67	1	50	1	100	. . .	. . .	. . .	. . .
1996	11	7	36	9	82	7	78	7	100	. . .	. . .	. . .	. . .
1997	2	0	0	1	50	1	100	1	100	. . .	. . .	. . .	. . .
1998	36	11 (ee)	31	27	75	25	93	23	92	2	8	. . .	2 (ff)
1999	3	2	67	2	67	2	100	2	100	. . .	. . .	. . .	. . .
2000	11	8	73	7	88	6	86	5	83	1	17	. . .	1 (gg)
2001	2	2	100	0	. . .	. . .	. . .	. . .	. . .	. . .	. . .	. . .	. . .
2002	36	14	39	22	61	16	73	12	75	4	25	. . .	4 (hh)
2003	4 (ii)	1	25	2	50	2	100	. . .	. . .	2	100	. . .	2 (jj)
2004	11	6	55	11	100	8	73	4	50	4	50	2 (kk)	2 (ll)
2005	2	2	100	1	50	. . .	. . .	. . .	. . .	. . .	. . .	. . .	. . .
2006	36	20	56	31	86	27	87	25	93	2	7	1 (mm)	1 (nn)
Totals:													
Number	519	286		399		313		236		77		20	57
Percent	100	55.1		76.9		78.4		75.4		24.6		26.0	74.0

Source: The Council of State Governments, *The Book of the States, 2006,* (Lexington, KY: The Council of State Governments, 2006), 144, updated.

Key:
(a) Albert Brewer, D-Ala.
(b) Keith Miller, R-Alaska; Winthrop Rockefeller, R-Ark.; Claude Kirk, R-Fla.; Don Samuelson, R-Idaho; Norbert Tieman, R-Neb.; Dewey Bartlett, R-Okla.; Frank Farrar, R-S.D.
(c) Walter Peterson, R-N.H.; Preston Smith, D-Texas.
(d) Russell Peterson, R-Del.; Richard Ogilvie, R-Ill.
(e) William Cahill, R-N.J.
(f) One independent candidate won: James Longley of Maine.
(g) David Hall, D-Okla.
(h) John Vanderhoof, R-Colo.; Francis Sargent, R-Mass.; Malcolm Wilson, R-N.Y.; John Gilligan, D-Ohio.
(i) Dan Walker, D-Ill.
(j) Sherman Tribbitt, D-Del.; Christopher "Kit" Bond, R-Mo.
(k) Michael Dukakis, D-Mass.; Dolph Briscoe, D-Texas.
(l) Robert F. Bennett, R-Kan.; Rudolph G. Perpich, D-Minn.; Meldrim Thompson, R-N.H.; Robert Straub, D-Oreg.; Martin J. Schreiber, D-Wis.
(m) Thomas L. Judge, D-Mont.; Dixy Lee Ray, D-Wash.
(n) Bill Clinton, D-Ark.; Joseph P. Teasdale, D-Mo.; Arthur A. Link, D-N.D.
(o) Edward J. King, D-Mass.
(p) Frank D. White, R-Ark.; Charles Thone, R-Neb.; Robert F. List, R-Nev.; Hugh J. Gallen, D-N.H.; William P. Clements, R-Texas.
(q) David Treen, R-La.
(r) Allen I. Olson, R-N.D.; John D. Spellman, R-Wash.
(s) Bill Sheffield, D-Alaska.
(t) Mark White, D-Texas; Anthony S. Earl, D-Wis.

(u) Edwin Edwards, D-La.
(v) Arch A. Moore, R-W.Va.
(w) Two Independent candidates won: Walter Hickel (Alaska) and Lowell Weiker (Conn.). Both were former statewide Republican office holders.
(x) Bob Martinez, R-Fla.; Mike Hayden, R-Kan.; James Blanchard, D-Mich.; Rudy Perpich, DFL-Minn.; Kay Orr, R-Neb.; Edward DiPrete, R-R.I.
(y) Buddy Roemer, R-La.
(z) Ray Mabus, D-Miss.
(aa) James Florio, D-N.J.
(bb) One Independent candidate won: Angus King of Maine.
(cc) Bruce Sundlun, D-R.I.; Walter Dean Miller, R-S.D.
(dd) James E. Folsom Jr., D-Ala.; Bruce King, D-N.M.; Mario Cuomo, D-N.Y.; Ann Richards, D-Texas.
(ee) Two Independent candidates won: Angus King of Maine and Jesse Ventura of Minnesota.
(ff) Fob James, R-Ala.; David Beasley, R-S.C.
(gg) Cecil Underwood, R-W.Va.
(hh) Don Siegelman, D-Ala.; Roy Barnes, D-Ga.; Jim Hodges, D-S.C.; and Scott McCallum, R-Wis.
(ii) The California recall election and replacement vote of 2003 is included in the 2003 election totals and as a general election for the last column.
(jj) Gray Davis, D-Calif.; Ronnie Musgrove, D-Miss.
(kk) Bob Holden, D-Mo.; Olene Walker, R-Utah, lost in the pre-primary convention.
(ll) Joe Kernan, D-Ind.; Craig Benson, R-N.H.
(mm) Frank Murkowski, R-Alaska.
(nn) Robert Ehrlich, R-Md.

two major parties has an edge in these party shifts. In three of the six party shifts in the 2006 elections, Democrats won the seat for the first time since the 1986 elections (Massachusetts, Ohio), and for the first time since the 1990 election (New York). But there have been some interesting patterns in these shifts over the past 36 years of gubernatorial elections.

Between 1970 and 1992, Democrats won 200 of the 324 races for governor (62 percent). Then beginning in 1993 to 2003, Republicans leveled the playing field by winning 85 of the 145 races for governor (59 percent). Despite this Republican trend, Democratic candidates did win eight of the 11 gubernatorial races in 2000, when Gov. Bush won the presidency in a very close race, and six of the 11 when Bush won his second term in 2004. And the Democrats have won 28 of the 49 most recent races in 2004 to 2006 (57 percent).

Another factor in determining how many governors have served in the states is how many of the newly elected governors are truly new to the office and how many are returning after complying with constitutional term limits or holding other positions. Looking at the number of actual new governors taking office over a decade, the average number of new governors elected in the states dropped from 2.3 new governors per state in the 1950s to 1.9 in the 1970s and to 1.1 in the 1980s. In the 1990s, the rate began to move up a bit to 1.4 new governors per state.

As we move through the first decade of the 21st century, we continue to find new faces in the governors' offices. New governors were elected in 56 of 102 elections held between 2000 and 2006 (55 percent). And, two other governors ascended to the office during 2004 and one each in both 2005 and 2006. So, in 2007, 24 incumbent governors will be serving in their first term (48 percent). The beginning of the 21st century has certainly proved to be a time of change in the governors' offices across the 50 states.

The New Governors

Over the 2003–2006 cycle of gubernatorial elections and resignations, there were several different routes to the governor's chair by the elected governors and by those governors who have ascended to the office. Twelve new governors have previously held statewide office. These include: five lieutenant governors—M. Jodi Rell (R-Conn.), Kathleen Blanco (D-La.), Dave Heineman (R-Neb.), Timothy Kaine (D-Va.) and James Risch (R-Idaho); four attorneys general— Christine Gregoire (D-Wash.), Mike Beebe (D-Ark.), Charlie Crist (R-Fla.) and Eliot Spitzer (D-N.Y.); and three secretaries of state—Matt Blunt (R-Mo.), Joe Manchin (D-W.V.) and Chet Culver (D-Iowa).

Five governors were members or former members of Congress who returned to work in their state. These included U.S. Sen. Jon Corzine (D-N.J.), and U.S. Congressmen Ernie Fletcher (R-Ky.), L.C. "Butch" Otter (R-Idaho), Jim Gibbons (R-Nev.) and Ted Strickland (D-Ohio). And Brian Schweitzer (D-Mont.), who had unsuccessfully sought a U.S. Senate seat in 2000 as the Democratic candidate, turned that around to win the governorship in 2004.

Two governors came from the business sector: John Lynch (D-N.H.) and John Huntsman Jr. (R-Utah). Two mayors or former mayors were elected in 2006: Sarah Palin (R-Wasilla, Alaska) and Martin O'Malley (D-Baltimore, Md.).

Five new governors followed a unique path compared to their counterparts: actor-businessman Arnold Schwarzenegger (R-Calif.), former head of the Federal Office of Management and Budget Mitch Daniels (R-Ind.), former Republican Party National Chairman Haley Barbour (R-Miss.), former Denver District Attorney Bill Ritter (D-Colo.) and Deval Patrick, former head of the Civil Rights Division of the U.S. Department of Justice in the Clinton Administration (D-Mass.).

In the 409 gubernatorial races between 1977 and 2006, among the candidates were 106 lieutenant governors (29 won), 90 attorneys general (24 won), 30 secretaries of state (eight won), 24 state treasurers (six won) and 16 state auditors, auditors general or comptrollers (three won). Looking at these numbers from a bettor's point of view, the odds of a lieutenant governor winning were 3.7-to-1, an attorney general 3.8-to-1, a secretary of state 3.8-to-1, a state treasurer 4.0-to-1 and a state auditor 5.3-to-1.

One other unique aspect about the current governors is that there will be nine women serving as governor in 2007—the same as in the last half of 2004 which was the all-time high for women serving at one time in the office. Seven women were elected in their own right: Sarah Palin (R-Alaska), Janet Napolitano (D-Ariz.), Ruth Ann Minner (D-Del.), Linda Lingle (R-Hawaii), Kathleen Sebelius (D-Kan.), Kathleen Blanco (D-La.), Jennifer Granholm (D-Mich.), Christine Gregoire (D-Wash.) and M. Jodi Rell (R-Conn.), who became governor upon the resignation of Gov. John Rowland in 2004 and was elected in her own bid in 2006 to continue serving as governor. While gubernatorial politics continues to be volatile, women are also continuing to hold their own in these races. In the 2003–2006 gubernatorial races, nine of the 15 women running either as the incumbent or as the candidate of a major party won—a 60 percent success rate.

Table B: Total Cost of Gubernatorial Elections: 1977–2005
(in thousands of dollars)

Year	Number of races	Total campaign costs		Average cost per state (2005$)	Percent change in similar elections (b)
		Actual $	2005$ (a)		
1977	2	12,312	39,717	19,859	N.A.
1978	36	102,342	306,412	8,511	N.A. (c)
1979	3	32,744	88,021	29,340	N.A.
1980	13	35,634	84,440	6,495	N.A.
1981	2	24,648	53,007	26,503	+33
1982	36	181,832	368,081	10,224	+20 (d)
1983	3	39,966	78,364	26,121	-11
1984	13	47,156	88,639	6,818	+5
1985	2	18,859	34,226	17,113	-35
1986	36	270,605	482,362	13,399	+31
1987	3	40,212	69,092	23,031	-12
1988	12 (e)	52,208	86,152	7,179	-3
1989	2	47,902	75,437	37,718	+120
1990	36	345,493	516,432	14,345	+7
1991	3	34,564	49,590	16,530	-28
1992	12	60,278	83,953	6,996	-3
1993	2	36,195	48,912	24,456	-35
1994	36	417,873	550,557	15,293	+7
1995	3	35,693	45,760	15,253	-8
1996	11 (f)	68,610	85,442	7,767	+2
1997	2	44,823	54,529	27,265	+11
1998	36	470,326	563,265	15,646	+2
1999	3	16,276	19,081	6,360	-58
2000	11	97,098	110,088	10,008	+29
2001	2	70,400	77,619	39,909	+42
2002	36	841,427	913,601	25,378	+62
2003	3	69,939	74,245	24,748	+289
2004	11	112,625	116,468	10,588	+6
2005	2	131,996	131,996	65,998	+70

Source: Thad Beyle.

Key:

(a) Developed from the Table, "Historical Consumer Price Index for All Urban Consumers (CPI-U)," Bureau of Labor Statistics, U.S. Department of Labor. Each year's actual expenditures are converted to the 2005$ value of the dollar to control for the effect of inflation over the period.

(b) This represents the percent increase or decrease in 2005$ over the last bank of similar elections, i.e., 1977 v. 1981, 1978 v. 1982, 1979 v. 1983, etc.

(c) The data for 1978 are a particular problem as the two sources compiling data on this year's elections did so in differing ways that excluded some candidates. The result is that the numbers for 1978 under-represent the actual costs of these elections by some unknown amount. The sources are: Rhodes Cook and Stacy West, "1978 Advantage," *CQ Weekly Report,* (1979): 1757–1758; and *The Great Louisiana Spendathon* (Baton Rouge: Public Affairs Research Council, March 1980).

(d) This particular comparison with 1978 is not what it would appear to be for the reasons given in note (c). The amount spent in 1978 was more than indicated here so the increase is really not as great as it appears.

(e) As of the 1986 election, Arkansas switched to a four-year term for the governor, hence the drop from 13 to 12 for this off-year.

(f) As of the 1994 election, Rhode Island switched to a four-year term for the governor, hence the drop from 12 to 11 for this off-year.

Timing of Gubernatorial Elections

The election cycle for governors has settled into a regular pattern. Over the past few decades, many states have moved their elections to the off-presidential years in order to decouple the state and national level campaigns. Now, only 11 states hold their gubernatorial elections in the same year as a presidential election. Two of these states—New Hampshire and Vermont—still have two-year terms for their governor so their elections alternate between presidential and the even non-presidential years.

As seen in Table A, the year following a presidential election has only two states with gubernatorial elections.[3] Then in the even years between presidential elections, 36 states hold their gubernatorial elections, and in the year before a presidential election, three Southern states hold their gubernatorial elections.[4]

Cost of Gubernatorial Elections

Table C presents data on the costs of the most recent elections. There is a great range in how much these races cost, from the all-time most expensive race recorded in New York in 2002 ($159.3 million in 2005 dollars) to the low-cost 2004 race in Vermont ($1,242,534 in 2005 dollars). Both the New York and the Vermont races saw an incumbent Republican governor successfully win re-election.

But if we look at how much all candidates spent per general election vote, a slightly different picture evolves. In 2004, the West Virginia governor's race was the most expensive at $16.05 per vote, followed by the Indiana race at $13.53 per vote. Both races were for an open seat. The most expensive governor's race per vote in the 2002–2005 cycle was in the New Hampshire 2002 race when the candidates spent $46.44 per vote in 2005 dollars. The least expensive race during the same cycle was in the Minnesota 2002 race when the candidates spent only $2.88 per vote.

In Figure A, by converting the actual dollars spent each year into the equivalent 2005 dollars, we see how the cost of these elections has increased over time. Since 1981, we have been able to compare the costs of each four-year cycle of elections with the previous cycle of elections.

In the 54 elections held between 1977 and 1980, the total expenditures were $519 million in equivalent 2005 dollars. In the 52 elections held between 2002 and 2005—just over two decades later—the total expenditures were a bit over $1,236 million in 2005 dollars, an increase of 138 percent. The greatest increase in campaign expenditures was between the 1997–2000 and 2002–2005 cycles when there was a 65.5-percent increase.

These increases reflect the new style of campaigning for governor—with the candidates developing their own personal party by using outside consultants, opinion polls, media ads and buys, and extensive fundraising efforts to pay for all of this. This style has now reached into most every state. Few states will be surprised by a high-price, high-tech campaign; they are commonplace now. The "air-war" campaigns have replaced the "ground-war" campaigns across the states.

Another factor has been the increasing number of candidates who are either wealthy or who have access to wealth and are willing to spend some of this money to become governor. For some, spending a lot of money leads to winning the governor's chair. In 2002, Gov. Gray Davis spent $69.7 million in 2005 dollars in his successful bid for re-election in California, while Gov. George Pataki spent $48 million in 2005 dollars to win his third term. However, spending that amount of money and winning

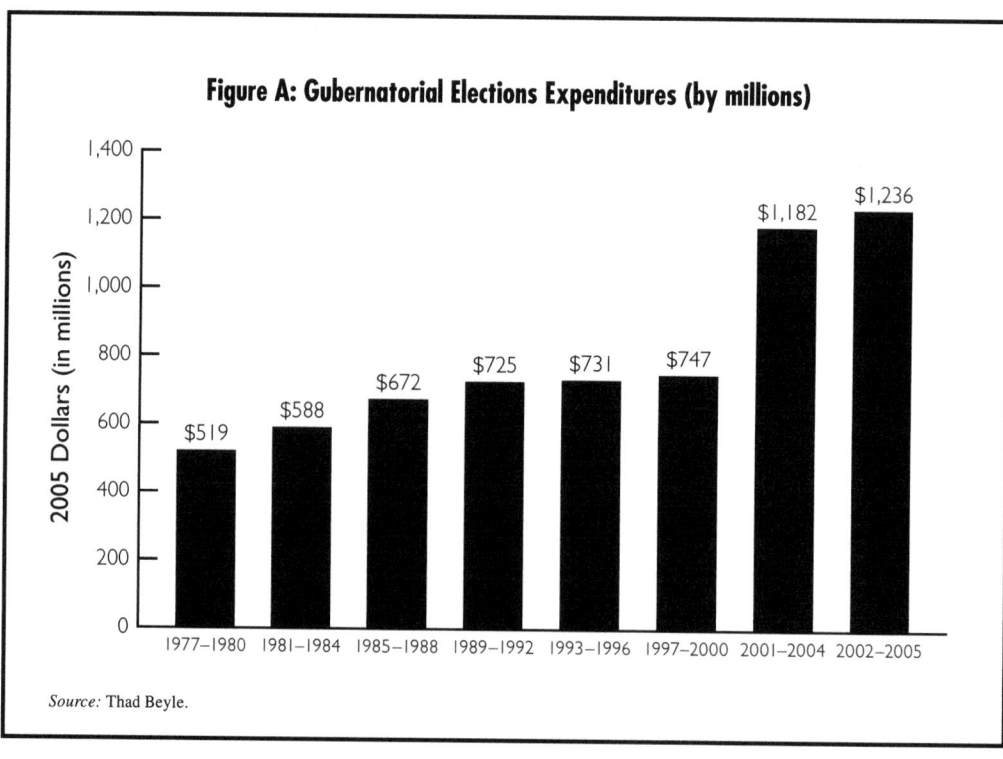

Figure A: Gubernatorial Elections Expenditures (by millions)

Source: Thad Beyle.

Table C: Cost of Gubernatorial Campaigns, Most Recent Elections, 2000–2005

State	Year	Winner	Point margin	All candidates (2005$)	Cost per vote (2005$)	Winner Spent (2005$)	Winner Percent of all expenditures	Winner Vote percent
Alabama	2002	R★★★	+0.3	$34,276,592	25.07	$15,035,805	43.9	49.2
Alaska	2002	R#	+15	5,801,363	25.58	1,877,435	32.4	55.9
Arizona	2002	D#	+1	8,269,772	6.74	2,495,093	30.2	46.2
Arkansas..............	2002	R★	+6	4,899,588	6.08	2,964,448	60.5	53.0
California	2002	D★	+4.9	118,967,033	15.92	69,723,350	58.6	47.3
Colorado..............	2002	R★	+29	6,573,049	4.66	5,232,764	79.6	62.6
Connecticut	2002	R★	+12	8,544,229	8.35	6,641,767	77.7	56.1
Delaware..............	2004	D★	+5.1	2,736,056	7.50	1,824,805	66.7	50.9
Florida	2002	R#	+13	18,631,452	3.65	8,278,899	44.4	56.0
Georgia	2002	R★★★	+5	26,339,492	12.99	3,968,732	15.1	51.4
Hawaii..................	2002	R#	+4	10,270,605	26.88	5,872,451	57.2	51.1
Idaho...................	2002	R★	+14	2,428,340	5.90	1,208,795	49.8	56.3
Illinois.................	2002	D#	+8	52,948,701	14.96	24,331,775	46.0	52.2
Indiana.................	2004	R★★★	+5.3	33,121,022	13.53	17,403,404	52.5	50.8
Iowa	2002	D★	+8	14,276,961	13.92	6,570,682	46.0	52.7
Kansas	2002	D#	+8	16,751,045	19.83	4,736,636	28.6	52.9
Kentucky	2003	R#	+10	12,137,530	11.20	6,049,179	49.8	55.0
Louisiana	2003	D#	+3.8	41,328,350	29.36	7,024,925	17.0	51.9
Maine	2002	D#	+5.6	4,700,459	9.30	1,720,282	36.6	47.1
Maryland..............	2002	R#	+3.9	5,576,868	3.27	2,751,178	49.3	51.6
Massachusetts.......	2002	R#	+5	33,226,827	14.97	10,163,955	30.6	49.8
Michigan...............	2002	D★★★	+4	17,620,847	5.55	9,650,701	54.8	51.4
Minnesota	2002	R#	+8	6,478,602	2.88	2,742,421	42.3	44.4
Mississippi	2003	R★★★	+7	20,779,410	23.23	11,982,403	57.7	52.6
Missouri................	2004	R★★	+2.9	16,056,590	5.90	4,992,482	31.1	50.8
Montana	2004	D#	+4.4	3,920,271	8.79	1,785,885	45.6	50.4
Nebraska...............	2002	R★	+41	1,736,127	3.61	1,317,215	75.9	68.7
Nevada	2002	R★	+46	2,949,722	5.85	2,870,828	97.3	68.1
New Hampshire....	2004	D★★★	+2.1	5,931,162	8.90	3,079,332	51.9	51.0
New Jersey............	2005	D#	+10.5	85,036,740	37.13	44,587,866	52.4	53.5
New Mexico	2002	D#	+16.5	10,881,913	22.47	7,954,937	73.1	55.5
New York	2002	R★	+15.5	159,339,374	33.97	47,979,478	30.1	48.2
North Carolina	2004	D★	+12.7	18,798,874	5.39	8,508,336	45.3	55.6
North Dakota........	2004	R★	+43.9	1,443,419	4.66	933,267	64.7	71.3
Ohio	2002	R★	+19.5	15,713,183	4.87	13,934,554	88.7	57.8
Oklahoma	2002	D#	+0.7	12,183,875	11.76	3,508,914	28.8	43.3
Oregon	2002	D#	+2.8	16,406,810	13.02	4,525,078	27.6	49.0
Pennsylvania	2002	D#	+9	70,728,345	19.75	42,522,878	60.1	53.4
Rhode Island	2002	R#	+10	7,517,619	22.65	2,651,130	35.3	54.8
South Carolina	2002	R★★★	+6	32,148,748	29.23	7,771,015	24.2	52.8
South Dakota........	2002	R#	+14.9	10,057,457	30.06	1,763,461	17.5	56.8
Tennessee..............	2002	D#	+3	18,671,319	11.29	10,600,807	56.8	50.6
Texas	2002	R★	+17.8	114,621,099	25.17	30,292,861	26.4	57.8
Utah	2004	R★★	+16.4	6,513,232	7.08	3,388,101	52.0	57.7
Vermont	2004	R★	+20.7	1,242,534	4.02	704,925	56.7	58.7
Virginia.................	2005	D#	+5.7	46,959,066	23.67	20,696,046	44.1	51.7
Washington...........	2004	D#	+0.005	14,757,740	5.25	6,422,148	43.5	48.9
West Virginia........	2004	D#	+29.5	11,947,552	16.05	3,661,550	30.6	63.5
Wisconsin..............	2002	D★★★	+3.7	18,572,054	10.46	6,000,339	32.3	45.1
Wyoming...............	2002	D#	+2.1	2,797,926	15.09	812,406	29.0	50.0

Source: Thad Beyle.

Note: 2005$ — Using the November 2005 CPI Index which was 1.953 of the 1982–84 Index = 1,000, the actual 2002 expenditures were based on a 1.799 value or .921 of the 2005$ index, the actual 2003 expenditures were based on a 1.840 index value or .942 of the 2005$ index, the actual 2004 expenditures were based on a 1.889 index value or .967 of the 2005$ index, and the 2005 expenditures were exact dollars spent in that election year. Then the actual expenditures of each state's governor's race were divided by the .9 value for that year to get the equivalent 2005$ value of those expenditures.

Key:
D — Democrat
I — Independent
R — Republican
— Open seat
★ — Incumbent ran and won.
★★ — Incumbent ran and lost in party primary.
★★★ — Incumbent ran and lost in general election.

Table D: Women Governors

Governor	State	Year elected or succeeded to office	How woman became governor	Tenure of service	Previous offices held	Last elected position held before governorship
Phase I—From initial statehood to adoption of the 19th Amendment to U.S. Constitution						
No women elected or served as governor						
Phase II—Wives of former governors elected governor, 1924–1966						
Nellie Tayloe Ross (D)	Wyoming	1924	E	1/1925–1/1927	F	...
Miriam "Ma" Ferguson (D)	Texas	1924	E	1/1925–1/1927 1/1933–1/1935	F	...
Lurleen Wallace (D)	Alabama	1966	E	1/1967–5/1968	F	...
Phase III—Women who became governor on their own merit, 1970 to date						
Ella Grasso (D)	Connecticut	1974	E	1/1975–12/1980	SH, SOS, (a)	(a)
Dixy Lee Ray (D)	Washington	1976	E	1/1977–1/1981	(b)	...
Vesta M. Roy (R)	New Hampshire	1982	S (c)	12/1982–1/1983	(d)	(d)
Martha Layne Collins (D)	Kentucky	1983	E	12/1983–12/1987	(e), LG	LG
Madeleine M. Kunin (D)	Vermont	1984	E	1/1985–1/1991	SH, LG	LG
Kay A. Orr (R)	Nebraska	1986	E	1/1987–1/1991	T	T
Rose Mofford (D)	Arizona	1988	S (f)	4/1988–1/1991	SOS	SOS
Joan Finney (D)	Kansas	1990	E	1/1991–1/1995	T	T
Barbara Roberts (D)	Oregon	1990	E	1/1991–1/1995	(g), C, SH, SOS	SOS
Ann Richards (D)	Texas	1990	E	1/1991–1/1995	C, T	T
Christy Whitman (R)	New Jersey	1993	E	1/1994–1/2001	(h)	(h)
Jeanne Shaheen (D)	New Hampshire	1996	E	1/1997–1/2003	(d)	(d)
Jane Dee Hull (R)	Arizona	1997	S (i)	9/1997–1/2003	(j), SOS	SOS
Nancy P. Hollister (R)	Ohio	1998	S (k)	12/1998–1/1999	LG	LG
Ruth Ann Minner (D)	Delaware	2000	E	1/2001–	SH, SS, LG	LG
Judy Martz (R)	Montana	2000	E	1/2001–1/2005	LG	LG
Sila Calderon (Pop D)	Puerto Rico	2000	E	1/2001–1/2005	M	M
Jane Swift (R)	Massachusetts	2001	S (l)	4/2001–1/2003	SS, LG	LG
Janet Napolitano (D)	Arizona	2002	E	1/2003–	(m), AG	AG
Linda Lingle (R)	Hawaii	2002	E	12/2002–	C, M (n)	M
Kathleen Sebelius (D)	Kansas	2002	E	1/2003–	SH, (o)	(o)
Jennifer Granholm (D)	Michigan	2002	E	1/2003–	(p), AG	AG
Olene Walker (R)	Utah	2003	S (q)	11/2003–1/2005	SH, LG	LG
Kathleen Blanco (D)	Louisiana	2003	E	1/2004–	SH, LG	LG
M. Jodi Rell (R)	Connecticut	2004	S (r)	7/2004–	SH, LG	LG
Christine Gregoire (D)	Washington	2004	E	1/2005–	AG	AG
Sarah Palin (R)	Alaska	2006	E	1/2007–	M (s)	M

Sources: National Governors Association Web site, www.nga.org, and individual state government Web sites.

Key:
S — Succeeded to office upon death, resignation or removal of the incumbent governor.
AG — Attorney general.   M — Mayor.
C — City council or   SH — State house member.
   county commission.
E — Elected governor.   SOS — Secretary of state.
F — Former first lady.   SS — State senate.
LG — Lieutenant governor.   T — State treasurer.
(a) Congresswoman.
(b) Ray served on the U.S. Atomic Energy Commission from 1972 to 1975 and was chair of the AEC from 1973 to 1975.
(c) Roy as state senate president succeeded to office upon the death of Gov. Hugh Gallen.
(d) State senate president.
(e) State supreme court clerk.
(f) Mofford as secretary of state became acting governor in February 1988 and governor in April 1988 upon the impeachment and removal of Gov. Evan Mecham.

(g) Local school board member.
(h) Whitman was a former state utilities official.
(i) Hull as secretary of state became acting governor when Gov. Fife Symington resigned. Elected to full term in 1998.
(j) Speaker of the state house.
(k) Hollister as lieutenant governor became governor when Gov. George Voinovich stepped down to serve in the U.S. Senate.
(l) Swift as lieutenant governor succeeded Gov. Paul Celluci who resigned after being appointed ambassador to Canada. Was the first governor to give birth while serving in office.
(m) U.S. attorney.
(n) Lingle was mayor of Maui for two terms, elected in 1990 and 1996.
(o) Insurance commissioner.
(p) Federal prosecutor.
(q) Walker as lieutenant governor succeeded to the governorship upon the resignation of Gov. Mike Leavitt in 2003.
(r) Rell as lieutenant governor succeeded to the governorship upon the resignation of Gov. John Rowland in 2004.
(s) Palin was a two-term Mayor of Wasilla, Alaska, and had unsuccessfully sought the lieutenant governor's office in 2002.

re-election did not deter those wanting to have Davis recalled from office less than a year later.

But spending a lot doesn't always lead to a win. For example, in the 2002 New York election, Thomas Golisano spent $82.8 million in 2005 dollars in his unsuccessful campaign for governor as an Independent candidate. And in Texas, Tony Sanchez also spent $82.8 million in 2005 dollars as the unsuccessful Democratic candidate. In California's 1998 gubernatorial election, three candidates spent $129.5 million in 2005 dollars in their campaigns. Two of these candidates won their party's nomination and faced off in November, with Democrat Gray Davis at $45.1 million in 2005 dollars the winner over Republican candidate Dan Lundgren at $37.8 million in 2005 dollars. The largest spender at $46.6 million in 2005 dollars, Al Checci, wasn't even able to win the Democratic nomination.

Gubernatorial Forced Exits[5]

The California 2003 gubernatorial recall and replacement votes highlighted the fact that some elected governors faced situations in which they could lose their office without being beaten by a challenger at the ballot box, becoming ill or dying. In 2004, two other governors resigned from office, John Rowland (R-Conn.) faced the threat of a potential impeachment move and Jim McGreevey (D-N.J.) due to personal reasons.

However, 2005 and 2006 were rather quiet on this type of situation and no governor was driven or recalled from office. Several governors have been facing some difficult times in terms of things that have happened while they served and their job approval ratings in state-level polls indicate many are not happy with their performance.

Gubernatorial Powers[6]

One way to view the changes that have been occurring in gubernatorial powers is to look at the "Index of Formal Powers of the Governorship" first developed by Joseph Schlesinger in the 1960s,[7] which this author has continued to update.[8] The index used here consists of six different indices of gubernatorial power as seen in 1960 and 2007. These indices include the number and importance of separately elected executive branch officials, the tenure potential of governors, the appointment powers of governors for administrative and board positions in the executive branch, the governor's budgetary power, the governor's veto power and the governor's party control in the legislature. Each of the individual indices is set in a five-point scale, with five being the most power and one being the least.

During the four and a half decades between 1960 and 2007, the overall institutional powers of the nation's governors increased by 13.6 percent. The greatest increase among the individual gubernatorial powers was in their veto power (plus 61 percent) as more governors gained an item veto, and in 1996 North Carolina voters were finally able to vote on a constitutional amendment giving their governor veto power. It was approved by a 3-to-1 ratio.

The indices measuring the governor's tenure potential (length of term and ability to seek an additional term or terms) also showed an increase in power (plus 26 percent) as did the number of separately elected

executive branch officials (plus 28 percent). However, the governor's appointment power over specific functional area executive branch officials increased by only 7 percent. In addition, the states continue to hold to the concept of the multiple executives in terms of the number of statewide elected officials. In 2006, there were 308 separately elected executive officials covering 12 major offices in the states.[9] This compares to 306 elected officials in 1972. Ten states also have multimember boards, commissions or councils with members selected by statewide or district election.

The gubernatorial budgetary power actually declined over the period (minus 14 percent). However, we must remember that during this same time period, state legislatures were also undergoing considerable reform, and gaining more power to work on the governor's proposed budget was one of those reforms sought. Hence, the increased legislative budgetary power more than balanced out any increases in gubernatorial budgetary power.

There has also been a drop in the gubernatorial party control in the state legislatures over the period (minus 11 percent). Much of this can be attributed to the major partisan shifts occurring in the Southern states as the region has been moving from one-party dominance to a very competitive two-party system.[10] In 1960, 13 of the 14 governors were Democrats, and all 28 state legislative chambers were under Democratic control. In 2007, Republicans and Democrats each control seven governorships, while the Democrats hold a 14-to-13 edge in control of the legislative chambers. Three Southern governors face a legislature completely controlled by the opposite party,[11] while three others face a legislature with split partisan control.[12] Four Democratic governors have legislative chambers controlled by their own party,[13] and four Republican governors also have legislative chambers controlled by their own party.[14]

Notes

[1] The former governors winning the presidency over the past three decades were Jimmy Carter (D-Ga., 1971–1975) in 1976, Ronald Reagan (R-Calif., 1967–1975) in 1980 and 1984, Bill Clinton (D-Ark., 1979–1981 and 1983–1992) in 1992 and 1996, and George W. Bush (R-Texas, 1995–2001) in 2000 and 2004.

[2] For an analysis of governors trying to handle the impact of the early 1990s economic downturn, see Thad Beyle, ed., *Governors in Hard Times* (Washington, D.C.: CQ Press, 1994).

[3] New Jersey and Virginia.

[4] Kentucky, Louisiana and Mississippi.

[5] For more detail on this topic check "Table E: Impeachments and Removals of Governors" and accompanying text

"Gubernatorial Forced Exits" in *The Book of the States*, 2005 (Lexington, KY: The Council of State Governments, 2005): 198–200.

[6] For more detail on this topic check Thad Beyle, "The Governors," in Virginia Gray and Russell L. Hanson, eds., *Politics in the American States: A Comparative Analysis*, 8th ed. (Washington, D.C.: CQ Press, 2004): 210–218.

[7] Joseph A. Schlesinger, "The Politics of the Executive," *Politics in the American States*, 1st and 2nd ed., Herbert Jacob and Kenneth N. Vines, eds., (Boston: Little Brown, 1965 and 1971).

[8] Thad L. Beyle, "The Governors," *Politics in the American States*, 8th ed., Virginia Gray and Russell L. Hanson, eds., (Washington, D.C.: CQ Press, 2003). Earlier versions of this index by the author appeared in the 4th edition (1983), the 5th edition (1990), the 6th edition (1996), and the 7th edition (1999).

[9] Kendra Hovey and Harold Hovey, "D-12—Number of Statewide Elected Officials, 2004," *CQ's State Fact Finder, 2006* (Washington, D.C.: CQ Press, 2007).

[10] The following states are included in this definition of the South: Alabama, Arkansas, Florida, Georgia, Kentucky, Louisiana, Mississippi, North Carolina, Oklahoma, South Carolina, Tennessee, Texas, Virginia and West Virginia.

[11] They are Republicans Bob Riley in Alabama and Haley Barbour in Mississippi, and Democrat Tim Kaine in Virginia.

[12] They are Republican Ernie Fletcher in Kentucky, and Democrats Brad Henry in Oklahoma and Phil Bredesen in Tennessee. In Oklahoma, the state senate is split with an equal number of Democrats and Republicans.

[13] They are Mike Beebe in Arkansas, Kathleen Blanco in Louisiana, Mike Easley in North Carolina and Joe Manchin in West Virginia.

[14] They are Charlie Crist in Florida, Sonny Perdue in Georgia, Mark Sanford in South Carolina, and Rick Perry in Texas.

About the Author

Thad Beyle is a professor of political science at the University of North Carolina at Chapel Hill. A Syracuse University A.B. and A.M., he received his Ph.D. at the University of Illinois. He spent a year in the North Carolina governor's office in the mid-1960s and has worked with the National Governors Association in several capacities on gubernatorial transitions.

Table 4.1
THE GOVERNORS, 2007

State or other jurisdiction	Name and party	Length of regular term in years	Date of first service	Present term ends	Number of previous terms	Maximum consecutive terms allowed by constitution	Joint election of governor and lieutenant governor (a)	Official who succeeds governor	Birthdate	Birthplace
Alabama	Bob Riley (R)	4	1/03	1/11	1	2	No	LG	10/3/1944	AL
Alaska	Sarah H. Palin (R)	4	12/06	12/10	…	2	Yes	LG	2/11/1964	ID
Arizona	Janet Napolitano (D)	4	1/03	1/11	1	2	(k)	SS	11/29/1957	NY
Arkansas	Mike Beebe (D)	4	1/07	1/11	…	2	No	LG	12/28/1946	AR
California	Arnold Schwarzenegger (R)	4	11/03 (c)	1/11	1 (c)	2	No	LG	7/30/1947	Aus.
Colorado	Bill Ritter (D)	4	1/07	1/11	…	2	Yes	LG	9/6/1956	CO
Connecticut	M. Jodi Rell (R)	4	7/04 (b)	1/11	1 (b)	…	Yes	LG	6/16/1946	VA
Delaware	Ruth Ann Minner (D)	4	1/01	1/09	1	2	No	LG	1/17/1935	DE
Florida	Charlie Crist (R)	4	1/07	1/11	…	2	Yes	LG	7/24/1956	PA
Georgia	Sonny Perdue (R)	4	1/03	1/11	1	2	No	LG	12/20/1946	GA
Hawaii	Linda Lingle (R)	4	12/02	12/10	1	2	Yes	LG	6/4/1953	MO
Idaho	C.L. "Butch" Otter (R)	4	1/07	1/11	…	…	No	LG	5/3/1942	ID
Illinois	Rod R. Blagojevich (D)	4	1/03	1/11	1	…	Yes	LG	12/10/1956	IL
Indiana	Mitch Daniels (R)	4	1/05	1/09	…	2 (f)	Yes	LG	4/7/1949	PA
Iowa	Chet Culver (D)	4	1/07	1/11	…	…	Yes	LG	1/25/1966	DC
Kansas	Kathleen Sebelius (D)	4	1/03	1/11	1	2	Yes	LG	5/15/1948	OH
Kentucky	Ernie Fletcher (R)	4	12/03	12/07	…	2	Yes	LG	11/12/1952	KY
Louisiana	Kathleen Babineaux Blanco (D)	4	1/04	1/08	…	2	No	LG	12/15/1942	LA
Maine	John Baldacci (D)	4	1/03	1/11	1	2	(k)	PS	1/30/1955	ME
Maryland	Martin O'Malley (D)	4	1/07	1/11	…	2	Yes	LG	1/18/1963	MD
Massachusetts	Deval L. Patrick (D)	4	1/07	1/11	…	…	Yes	LG	7/31/1956	IL
Michigan	Jennifer Granholm (D)	4	1/03	1/11	1	2	Yes	LG	2/5/1959	BC
Minnesota	Tim Pawlenty (R)	4	1/03	1/11	1	…	Yes	LG	11/27/1960	MN
Mississippi	Haley Barbour (R)	4	1/04	1/08	…	2	Yes	LG	10/22/1947	MS
Missouri	Matt Blunt (R)	4	1/05	1/09	…	2	No	LG	11/20/1970	MO
Montana	Brian Schweitzer (D)	4	1/05	1/09	…	2 (g)	Yes	LG	9/4/1955	MT
Nebraska	Dave Heineman (R)	4	1/05 (e)	1/11	1 (e)	2	Yes	LG	5/12/1948	NE
Nevada	James A. Gibbons (R)	4	1/07	1/11	…	2	No	LG	12/16/1944	NV
New Hampshire	John Lynch (D)	2	1/05	1/09	1	2	(k)	PS	11/25/1952	MA
New Jersey	Jon Corzine (D)	4	1/06	1/10	…	2	(i)	(i)	1/1/1947	IL
New Mexico	Bill Richardson (D)	4	1/03	1/11	1	2	Yes	LG	11/15/1947	CA
New York	Eliot Spitzer (D)	4	1/07	1/11	…	…	Yes	LG	6/10/1959	NY
North Carolina	Michael F. Easley (D)	4	1/01	1/09	1	2	No	LG	3/23/1950	NC
North Dakota	John Hoeven (R)	4	12/00	12/08	1	…	Yes	LG	3/13/1957	ND
Ohio	Ted Strickland (D)	4	1/07	1/11	…	2 (f)	Yes	LG	8/4/1941	OH
Oklahoma	Brad Henry (D)	4	1/03	1/11	1	2	No	LG	6/10/1963	OK
Oregon	Ted Kulongoski (D)	4	1/03	1/11	1	2	(k)	SS	11/5/1940	MO
Pennsylvania	Edward G. Rendell (D)	4	1/03	1/11	1	2	Yes	LG	1/5/1944	NY
Rhode Island	Don Carcieri (R)	4	1/03	1/11	1	2	No	LG	12/16/1942	RI
South Carolina	Mark Sanford (R)	4	1/03	1/11	1	2	No	LG	5/28/1960	FL

See footnotes at end of table.

THE GOVERNORS, 2007 — Continued

State or other jurisdiction	Name and party	Length of regular term in years	Date of first service	Present term ends	Number of previous terms	Maximum consecutive terms allowed by constitution	Joint election of governor and lieutenant governor (a)	Official who succeeds governor	Birthdate	Birthplace
South Dakota..............	Mike Rounds (R)	4	1/03	1/11	1	2	Yes	LG	10/24/1954	SD
Tennessee	Phil Bredesen (D)	4	1/03	1/11	1	2	No	SpS (1)	11/21/1943	NJ
Texas	Rick Perry (R)	4	12/00 (h)	1/11	2	...	No	LG	3/4/1950	TX
Utah	Jon M. Huntsman Jr. (R)	4	1/05	1/09	...	3	Yes	LG	3/26/1960	CA
Vermont	Jim Douglas (R)	2	1/03	1/09	2	...	No	LG	6/21/1951	MA
Virginia...................	Tim Kaine (D)	4	1/06	1/10	...	(j)	No	LG	2/26/1958	MN
Washington...............	Christine Gregoire (D)	4	1/05	1/09	...	...	No	LG	3/24/1957	WA
West Virginia............	Joe Manchin III (D)	4	1/05	1/09	...	2	(k)	PS (1)	8/24/1947	WV
Wisconsin.................	Jim Doyle (D)	4	1/03	1/11	1	...	Yes	LG	11/23/1945	DC
Wyoming..................	Dave Freudenthal (D)	4	1/03	1/11	1	2	(k)	SS	10/12/1950	WY
American Samoa.........	Togiola Tulafono (D)	4	4/03 (m)	1/09	1	2	Yes	LG	2/28/1947	AS
Guam	Felix P. Camacho (R)	4	1/03	1/11	1	2	Yes	LG	10/30/1957	Japan
No. Mariana Islands	Benigno Fitial (C)	4	1/06	1/10	...	2 (d)	Yes	LG	11/27/1945	CNMI
Puerto Rico...............	Anibal Acevedo-Vilá (PDP)	4	1/05	1/09	...	...	(k)	SS	2/13/1963	PR
U.S. Virgin Islands.........	John deJong Jr. (D)	4	1/07	1/11	...	(f)	Yes	LG	11/13/1957	USVI

Sources: The Council of State Governments, December 2006.

Key:
C — Covenant
D — Democrat
PDP — Popular Democratic Party
R — Republican
LG — Lieutenant Governor
SS — Secretary of State
PS — President of the Senate
SpS — Speaker of the Senate
... — Not applicable

(a) The following also choose candidates for governor and lieutenant governor through a joint nomination process: Florida, Kansas, Maryland, Minnesota, Montana, North Dakota, Ohio, Utah, American Samoa, Guam, No. Mariana Islands and U.S. Virgin Islands.
(b) Lieutenant Governor Rell was sworn in as governor on July 1, 2004 after Governor John Rowland resigned.
(c) Governor Schwarzenegger was sworn in on November 17, 2003, after winning the replacement election following the recall vote that removed Governor Gray Davis from office in the same election.

(d) Absolute two-term limitation, but terms need not be consecutive.
(e) Governor Heineman, as lieutenant governor, was sworn in as Nebraska's governor on Friday, January 21, 2005 after Governor Johanns resigned on January 20, 2005 upon being confirmed as the United States Secretary of Agriculture.
(f) After two consecutive terms as Governor, the candidate must wait four years before becoming eligible to run again.
(g) Absolute limit of eight years of service out of every 16 years.
(h) Lieutenant Governor Perry was sworn in on December 21, 2000 to complete President George W. Bush's term as governor of Texas.
(i) New Jersey will elect a lieutenant governor in 2009. The governor and lieutenant governor will be elected jointly. In the event of a permanent vacancy in the office before the inauguration date of the first lieutenant governor, the president of the senate, followed by the speaker of the assembly, would succeed the governor in the event of a permanent vacancy.
(j) Governor cannot serve immediate successive terms, but may be elected to non-consecutive terms.
(k) No lieutenant governor.
(l) Official bears the additional title of "lieutenant governor."
(m) Governor Tulafono, as lieutenant governor, became Governor in April 2003 after Governor Sunia's death.

Table 4.2
THE GOVERNORS: QUALIFICATIONS FOR OFFICE

State or other jurisdiction	Minimum age	State citizen (years)	U.S. citizen (years) (a)	State resident (years) (b)	Qualified voter (years)
Alabama	30	. . .	10	7	★
Alaska	30	★	7	7	★
Arizona	25	5	10	. . .	. . .
Arkansas	30	★	★	7	★
California	18	. . .	5	5	★
Colorado	30	. . .	★	2	. . .
Connecticut	30	. . .	★	★	. . .
Delaware	30	. . .	12	6	. . .
Florida	30	★	. . .	7	7
Georgia	30	. . .	15	6	. . .
Hawaii	30	. . .	5	5	★
Idaho	30	. . .	★	2	. . .
Illinois	25	3	★	3	★
Indiana	30	. . .	5	5	★
Iowa	30	2	2	2	★
Kansas	. . .	. . .	. . .	. . .	. . .
Kentucky	30	6	. . .	6	. . .
Louisiana	25	5	5	5	★
Maine	30	. . .	15	5	. . .
Maryland	30	. . .	(c)	5	5
Massachusetts	. . .	. . .	. . .	7	. . .
Michigan	30	. . .	★	★	4
Minnesota	25	. . .	★	1	★
Mississippi	30	★	20	5	★
Missouri	30	. . .	15	10	. . .
Montana	25	★	★	2	★
Nebraska	30	5	5	5	. . .
Nevada	25	2	2	2	★
New Hampshire	30	. . .	. . .	7	. . .
New Jersey	30	. . .	20	7	. . .
New Mexico	30	. . .	★	5	★
New York	25	★	★	1	. . .
North Carolina	30	. . .	5	2	★
North Dakota	30	. . .	★	5	★
Ohio	18	. . .	★	★	★
Oklahoma	31	. . .	10	10	10
Oregon	30	. . .	★	3	. . .
Pennsylvania	30	★	★	7	★
Rhode Island	18	30 days	30 days	30 days	30 days
South Carolina	30	5	5	5	. . .
South Dakota	18	★	★	★	★
Tennessee	30	7	★	. . .	. . .
Texas	30	. . .	★	5	. . .
Utah	30	5	★	5	★
Vermont	18	1	. . .	4	★
Virginia	30	★	★	★	5
Washington	18	. . .	★	★	★
West Virginia	30	5	★	1	★
Wisconsin	18	★	★	★	★
Wyoming	30	★	★	5	★
American Samoa	35	. . .	★	5	. . .
Guam	30	. . .	5	5	★
No. Mariana Islands	35	. . .	★	10	★
Puerto Rico	35	5	5	5	. . .
U.S. Virgin Islands	30	. . .	5	5	★

Source: The Council of State Governments' survey of governor's offices, November 2006.

Key:

★ — Formal provision; number of years not specified.

. . . — No formal provision.

(a) In some states you must be a U.S. citizen to be an elector, and must be an elector to run.

(b) In some states you must be a state resident to be an elector, and must be an elector to run.

(c) *Crosse v. Board of Supervisors of Elections* 243 Md. 555, 221A.2d431 (1966)—opinion rendered indicated that U.S. citizenship was, by necessity, a requirement for office.

Table 4.3
THE GOVERNORS: COMPENSATION, STAFF, TRAVEL AND RESIDENCE

State or other jurisdiction	Salary	Governor's office staff (a)	Access to state transportation			Receives travel allowance	Reimbursed for travel expenses	Official residence
			Automobile	Airplane	Helicopter			
Alabama	$112,895	60	★	★	★	...	...	★
Alaska	125,000	71	★	★	...	...	★(b)	★
Arizona	95,000	39	★	★	...	...	★(b)	...
Arkansas	80,848	67	★	★	...	...	★	★
California	206,500 (d)	185	★	...	...	(c)	(f)	(g)
Colorado	90,000	50	★	★	...	★	★	★
Connecticut	150,000	34	★	...	...	...	...	★
Delaware	132,500	32	★	...	...	...	...	★
Florida	132,932	293 (h)	★	★	...	...	★(b)	★
Georgia	135,281	42	★	★	★	...	★(b)	★
Hawaii	112,000	67	★	★	★	★	★	★
Idaho	105,560	24	★	★	...	★(e)	(f)	(i)
Illinois	155,600	130	★	★	★	★	(f)	★
Indiana	95,000	34	★	★	★	★(b)	★(b)	★
Iowa	130,000	32	★	...	...	...	★	★
Kansas	105,889	24	★	★	★	...	★	★
Kentucky	137,506	80	★	★	★	...	★(b)	★
Louisiana	95,000	93 (j)	★	★	★	...	★	★
Maine	70,000	21	★	...	...	★	★	★
Maryland	150,000	84	★	★	★	(e)	(f)	★
Massachusetts	140,535	70	★	...	★	★(b)	★(b)	...
Michigan	177,000	78	★	★	...	(k)	(k)	★
Minnesota	120,303	45	★	★	★	(e)	(f)	★
Mississippi	122,160	46	★	★	...	...	★	★
Missouri	120,087	38	★	★	...	(c)	(f)	★
Montana	96,462	61 (l)	★	★	★	★	★	★
Nebraska	105,000	9	★	★	...	★	★	★
Nevada	141,000	23 (m)	★	★	...	(c)	...	★
New Hampshire	108,990	23	★	...	...	(e)	(f)	★(n)
New Jersey	175,000 (o)	126	★	...	★	...	★(b)	★
New Mexico	110,000	39.3	★	★	★	...	...	★
New York	179,000	180	★	★	★	...	★	★
North Carolina	130,629	74	★	★	★	★	★	★
North Dakota	92,483	17	★	★	...	...	★	★
Ohio	144,830	60	★	★	★	(p)	(f)	★
Oklahoma	140,000	34	★	★	...	★(b)	★(b)	★
Oregon	93,600	65 (q)	★	...	...	★(b)	★(b)	★
Pennsylvania	164,396	68	★	★	...	...	★(b)	★
Rhode Island	117,817	46	★	...	★	...	★	...
South Carolina	106,078	22	★	★	...	★(b)	...	★
South Dakota	105,544	22.5	★	★	...	...	★(b)	★
Tennessee	85,000	36	★	★	★	(e)	(f)	★
Texas	115,345	266	★	★	★	...	★	★
Utah	104,100	19	★	★	★	...	★	★
Vermont	143,957	14	★	...	...	★	...	...
Virginia	175,000	44	★	★	★	...	★	★
Washington	150,995	36	★	★	...	(e)	(f)	★
West Virginia	95,000	56	★	★	★	(r)	(f)	★
Wisconsin	137,092	25	★	★	...	...	(f)	★
Wyoming	105,000	22	★	★	...	...	★(b)	★
American Samoa	50,000	23	★	...	...	(c)	...	★
Guam	90,000	42	★	...	...	$218/day	...	★
No. Mariana Islands	70,000	16	★	...	...	(e)(t)	...	★
Puerto Rico	70,000	28	★	(s)	(s)	...	★	★
U.S. Virgin Islands	80,000	86	★	...	...	...	★	★

See footnotes at end of table.

THE GOVERNORS: COMPENSATION, STAFF, TRAVEL AND RESIDENCE—Continued

Source: The Council of State Governments' survey, November 2006.
Key:
★ — Yes
. . . — No
N.A. — Not available.

(a) Definitions of "governor's office staff" vary across the states—from general office support to staffing for various operations within the executive office.

(b) Travel expenses.

Alaska—$42/day per diem plus actual lodging expenses.

Arizona—Receives up to $38/day for meals based on location; receives per diem for lodging out-of-state; default $28/day for meals and $50/day lodging in-state.

Florida—State can reimburse, however Gov. Bush chose not to be reimbursed. Reimbursed at same rate as other state officials: in-state, choice between $50 per diem or actual expenses; out-of-state, actual expenses.

Georgia—Governor has the statutory ability to be reimbursed for travel costs, including per diem for meals at $28 to $36 in state and federal per diem for out-of-state and actual reasonable lodging costs. This option is seldom used. The current governor does not file for any travel reimbursements.

Indiana—Statute allows $12,000 but due to budget cuts the amount has been reduced to $9,800 and reimbursed for actual expenses for travel/lodging.

Kentucky—Mileage at same rate as other state officials.

Massachusetts—As necessary.

New Jersey—Reimbursement may be provided for necessary expenses.

Oklahoma—Reimbursed for actual and necessary expenses.

Oregon—$1,000 a month for expenses, not specific to travel. Reimbursed for actual travel expenses.

Pennsylvania—Reimbursed for reasonable expenses.

South Dakota—Reimbursement rate varies.

Utah—Reimbursed for travel by state guidelines.

Wyoming—$99/day or actual.

U.S. Virgin Islands—Reimbursed 100 percent.

(c) Amount includes travel allowance for entire staff. American Samoa—$105,000. California—$145,000 in state; $36,000 out of state. Missouri amount not available. Nevada—these figures include travel expenses for governor and staff, $45,750 in state; $32,800 out of state, for the 2005–2007 biennium.

(d) Governor Schwarzenegger waives his salary.

(e) Travel allowance included in office budget.

(f) Information not provided.

(g) In California—provided by Governor's Residence Foundation, a non-profit organization which provides a residence for the governor of California. No rent is charged; maintenance and operational costs are provided by California Department of General Services.

(h) The Governor's office budget includes the following staff for the Executive Office: 119 Drug Control, 5 Office of Tourism, 21 Trade and Economic Dev., 43 System Design, 105 Office of Policy and Budget.

(i) J.R. and Esther Simplot donated their home to the state of Idaho in December 2004 for use as the future Governor's residence. Efforts are underway to raise private monies for renovation.

(j) Full-time employees—93, part-time (non-student)—21, students—25.

(k) The Governor is provided a $60,000 annual expense allowance, as determined by the State Officers Compensation Commission in 2000. "Expense allowance" is for normal, reimbursable personal expenses such as food, lodging, and travel costs incurred by an individual in carrying out the responsibilities of state office.

(l) Including 20 employees from the Office of Budget and Program Planning.

(m) For 2006 the number of authorized staff was 23; however, not all positions were filled as of September 10, 2006.

(n) The current governor does not occupy the official residence.

(o) Governor Corzine only accepts $1.

(p) Set administratively.

(q) Of this total, 45 are true Governor's staff and 20 are on loan for agency staff.

(r) Included in general expense account.

(s) The Governor's office pays for access to an airplane or helicopter with a corporate credit card and requests a refund of those expenses with the corresponding documentation to the Dept. of Treasury.

(t) Governor has a "contingency account" that can be used for travel expenses and expenses in other departments or other projects.

Table 4.4
THE GOVERNORS: POWERS

State or other jurisdiction	Budget making power — Full responsibility	Budget making power — Shares responsibility	Item veto power — Governor has item veto power on all bills	Item veto power — Governor has item veto power on appropriations only	Item veto power — Governor has no item veto power	Item veto — 2/3 legislators present or 3/5 elected to override	Item veto — majority legislators elected to override	Authorization for reorganization through executive order (a)
Alabama	★(b)		★				★	
Alaska	★		★			★		★
Arizona	★(b)			★		★		★
Arkansas		★		★		★	★	★(c)
California	★(b)		★			★		★(c)
Colorado		★		★		★		★
Connecticut		★		★		★		★
Delaware	★(b)		★			★		★
Florida		★	★			(d)		★
Georgia	★			★		★		★
Hawaii	★		★			★		★
Idaho	★		★			★		
Illinois		★	★			★		★
Indiana	★				★			★
Iowa	★		★			★		★
Kansas	★		★			★		★
Kentucky	★(b)			★		★(e)		★(f)
Louisiana		★		★		★		★
Maine		★			★		★	
Maryland	★		★			★		★
Massachusetts	★		★			★(e)		★(c)
Michigan	★(g)			★(h)		★(e)		★
Minnesota	★(b)			★		★(e)		★
Mississippi		★(i)	★			★(e)		★
Missouri	★(b)			★		★		★
Montana	★		★			★		★(k)
Nebraska		★		★		★(j)		
Nevada					★			
New Hampshire	★(b)				★			
New Jersey	★(b)		★			★(e)		
New Mexico	★			★		★		
New York	★		★			★		
North Carolina	★			★		★		★(k)
North Dakota	★			★		★		★
Ohio	★			★		★		★
Oklahoma				★			★(e)	
Oregon		★		★		★		★
Pennsylvania	★			★		★		★
Rhode Island		★			★			
South Carolina		★	★			★		

See footnotes at end of table.

THE GOVERNORS: POWERS — Continued

State or other jurisdiction	Budget making power		Item veto power					Authorization for reorganization through executive order (a)
	Full responsibility	Shares responsibility	Governor has item veto power on all bills	Governor has item veto power on appropriations only	Governor has no item veto power	Item veto— 2/3 legislators present or 3/5 elected to override	Item veto— 2/3 legislators present majority legislators elected to override	
South Dakota..................	★	…	…	★	…	★(l)	…	★
Tennessee......................	…	★	…	★	…	…	★	★
Texas	…	★	…	★	…	★	…	★
Utah	…	★	…	★	…	★	…	★
Vermont	★	…	…	…	★	…	…	…
Virginia.........................	★	…	…	★	…	★(l)	…	★
Washington....................	★	…	★(m)	…	…	★	…	…
West Virginia.................	★(b)	…	…	★(n)	…	★	…	…
Wisconsin......................	…	…	★	…	…	★	…	…
Wyoming.......................	…	★	★	…	…	…	…	…
American Samoa	…	★	…	…	…	…	…	★
Guam	★	…	…	★	…	★	…	★
No. Mariana Islands	…	★	…	★	…	★	…	★
Puerto Rico...................	…	★	…	★	…	★	…	★(o)
U.S. Virgin Islands........	★	…	…	★	…	★	…	★

Source: The Council of State Governments' survey of governor's offices, November 2006.

Key:

★ — Yes; provision for.

. . . — No; not applicable.

(a) For additional information on executive orders, see Table 4.5.

(b) Full responsibility to propose; legislature adopts or revises and governor signs or vetoes.

(c) Authorization for reorganization provided for in state constitution.

(d) Two-thirds of members to which each house is entitled required to override veto.

(e) Two-thirds of elected legislators of each house to override.

(f) Only for agencies and offices within the Governor's Office.

(g) Governor has sole authority to propose annual budget. No money may be paid out of state treasury except in pursuance of appropriations made by law.

(h) Governor may veto any distinct item or items appropriating money in any appropriations bill.

(i) Governor has the responsibility of presenting a balanced budget. The budget is based on revenue estimated by the Governor's office and the Legislative Budget Committee.

(j) Three-fifths majority required to override line-item veto.

(k) The office of the governor shall continuously study and evaluate the organizational structure, management practices, and functions of the executive branch and of each agency. The governor shall, by executive order or other means within the authority granted to him, take action to improve the manageability of the executive branch.

(l) Requires 2/3 of legislators present to override.

(m) Governor has veto power of selections for nonappropriations and item veto in appropriations.

(n) In Wisconsin, governor has "partial" veto over appropriation bills. The partial veto is broader than item veto.

(o) Only if it is not prohibited by law.

Table 4.5
GUBERNATORIAL EXECUTIVE ORDERS: AUTHORIZATION, PROVISIONS, PROCEDURES

State or other jurisdiction	Authorization for executive orders	Provisions								Procedures		
		Civil defense, public disasters, emergencies	Energy emergencies and conservation	Other emergencies	Executive branch reorganization plans and agency creation	Create advisory, coordinating, study or investigative committees/commissions	Respond to federal programs and requirements	State personnel administration	Other administration	Filing and publication procedures	Subject to administrative procedure act	Subject to legislative review
Alabama	S,I, Case Law	★	★	★	★	★				★		★
Alaska	C	···(a)						★		★		★
Arizona	I	★(a)	★(a)	★(a)	★			★		★(c)	★	
Arkansas	S,I, Common Law	★	★	★	★	★	★	★		★	★	
California	I	★	★	★	★	★	★	★	★	★	★	★
Colorado	C	★	★	★	★	★	★	★		★		
Connecticut	C,S	★	★	★	★	★	★	★		★	★	
Delaware	C	★	★	★	★	★	★	★		★	★	
Florida	C	★	★	★	★(b)	★	★	★		★	★(d)	★
Georgia	S,I (e)	★	★	★		★		★		★	★	
Hawaii	C	★	★	★	★	★	I	★		(f)	★	
Idaho	S		I	I		I	I					
Illinois	C,S	★	★	★	★	★	★	★		★	★	★
Indiana	C,S, Case Law	★	★	★	★(limited)	★	I	★	(h)	★	★	(i)
Iowa	(g)	★	★	★	★	★	★	★		★	★	★
Kansas	C,S	★	★	★(j)	★	★	★	★	★(k)(l)(m)	★(c)	★	★
Kentucky	C,S	★	★	★	★	★	★	★		★	★	★
Louisiana	C,S (n)	★	★	★	★	★	★	★		★	★	
Maine	I	★	★	★	★	★	★	★		★	★	
Maryland	C,S	★	★	★	★	★	★	★	★(o)	★	★	★(p)
Massachusetts	C,S	★	★	★	★	★	★	★	★	★		
Michigan	C,S,I	★	★(x)	★	★(v)	★(v)	★	★	(u)	★(c)(w)	★	★(p)
Minnesota	S	★	★	★	★	★	★	★		(y)	(y)	
Mississippi	C,S	★	I	I	★	★	★	★	★(p)	★(p)		★(p)(z)
Missouri	C,S. Common Law	★	★	★	★	★	★	★	★(q)	★	★	
Montana	S,I, Common Law	★	★	★	★	★	★	★		★	★	
Nebraska	C,S	★	★	★	★	★	★	★		★	★	
Nevada	S,I	★	★	★	★	★	★	★	I	★	★	
New Hampshire	S	★(a)	★(a)	I	★	★	I	★	★(l)	★		
New Jersey	C,S,I	★	★	★	★	★	★	★	★(q)	★	★	
New Mexico	C,S	★	★	★	★	★	★	★		★		
New York	C,S	★	★	★	★	★	★	★		★	★	
North Carolina	C,S	★	★	★	★	★	★	★		★		
North Dakota	S,I	★	★	★	★	★	★	★		★		★
Ohio	S,I (aa)	★	★	★	★	★	★		(m)(q)(r)(s)(t)(u)	★		

See footnotes at end of table.

GUBERNATORIAL EXECUTIVE ORDERS: AUTHORIZATION, PROVISIONS, PROCEDURES — Continued

State or other jurisdiction	Authorization for executive orders	Provisions								Procedures		
		Civil defense disasters, public emergencies	Energy emergencies and conservation	Other emergencies	Executive branch reorganization plans and agency creation	Create advisory, coordinating, study or investigative committees/commissions	Respond to federal programs and requirements	State personnel administration	Other administration	Filing and publication procedures	Subject to administrative procedure act	Subject to legislative review
Oklahoma.............	C	★	★	★	(cc)	★	★	★	…	★	…	…
Oregon...............	I	★	★	★	…	★	★	★	(dd)	★(c)(w)	…	…
Pennsylvania	C,S	★	…	★(o)(w)(bb)(dd)	…	★	★	…	…	…	…	…
Rhode Island	I, Case Law	•★	★	★	★	★	★	…	★	★	…	…
South Carolina	S	★	★	★	…	★	★	★	★	…	…	…
South Dakota........	C	★	★	★	★	★	★	★	★	…	…	…
Tennessee...........	S	★	★	★	★	★	★	★	★	★(c)	…	…
Texas	I	★	★	★	★	★	★	★	★	…	…	…
Utah	S,I	★	★	…	★	★	★	★	★	…	…	…
Vermont.............	S,I	★	★	★	★(ee)	★	★	★	…	…	…	★(ff)
Virginia.............	S	★	★	★	…	★	★	…	★	…	…	…
Washington..........	S	★	★	…	…	★	★	★	★	…	★	…
West Virginia........	C,S	★	I	★	…	★	★	★	★	…	…	★
Wisconsin...........	S,I	★	★	★	…	…	★	★	★	…	★	…
Wyoming............	(gg)	…	★	★	…	★	★	★	★	…	…	…
American Samoa	C,S	★	★	★	(ii)	★	★	★	★	★(hh)	★(hh)	…
Guam	C	★	I	…	…	S,I	S	★	★	S	I	…
No. Mariana Islands..	C	★	I	★	C	S,I	S	…	★	S	I	…
Puerto Rico..........	C,S,I, Case Law	★	★	★	★	★	★	★	★	(jj)	…	…
U.S. Virgin Islands	C	★	★	★	★	★	★	★	★	★	…	…

See footnotes at end of table.

GUBERNATORIAL EXECUTIVE ORDERS: AUTHORIZATION, PROVISIONS, PROCEDURES — Continued

Source: The Council of State Governments' survey of governor's offices, November 2006.

Key:

C — Constitutional

S — Statutory

I — Implied

★ — Formal provision.

. . . — No formal provision.

(a) Broad interpretation of gubernatorial authority.

(b) It could be debatable if the governor has the authority to create agencies by executive order, practically a governor certainly would not do so without support from the legislature as they must approve funding.

(c) Executive orders must be filed with secretary of state or other designated officer. In Idaho, must also be published in state general circulation newspaper.

(d) Under some circumstances the Cabinet must approve before an order becomes law. The Joint Administrative Procedure Committee must make sure agency rules have legislative authority to do so.

(e) Implied from Constitution.

(f) Some implied.

(g) Constitution, statute, implied, case law, common law.

(h) Executive clemency.

(i) Only for EROs. When an ERO is submitted, the legislature has 30 days to veto the ERO or it becomes law.

(j) To give immediate effect to state regulation in emergencies.

(k) To control administration of state contracts and procedures.

(l) To impound or freeze certain state matching funds.

(m) To reduce state expenditures in revenue shortfall.

(n) Inherent.

(o) To control procedures for dealing with public.

(p) Reorganization plans and agency creation.

(q) To administer and govern the armed forces of the state.

(r) To suspend certain officials and/or other civil actions.

(s) To designate game and wildlife areas or other public areas.

(t) Appointive powers.

(u) To assign duties to lieutenant governor, issue writ of special election.

(v) Executive reorganizations not effective if rejected by both houses of legislature within 60 days. Executive orders reducing appropriations not effective unless approved by appropriations committees of both houses of legislature.

(w) Filing.

(x) If an energy emergency is declared by the state's Executive Council or legislature.

(y) Governor is exempt from the Administrative Procedures Act and filing and administrative procedures Miss. Code Ann. § 25-43-102 (1972).

(z) Reorganization plans and agency creation and for meeting federal program requirements.

(aa) Executive authority implied except for emergencies which are established by statute.

(bb) For fire emergencies.

(cc) Limited authority in executive branch reorganization/agency creation.

(dd) To transfer funds in an emergency.

(ee) Subject to legislative approval.

(ff) Only if reorganization order filed with the legislature.

(gg) No specific authorization granted, general authority only.

(hh) If executive order fits definition of rule.

(ii) Can reorganize, but not create.

(jj) Executive Orders are filed in the Department of State.

Table 4.6
STATE CABINET SYSTEMS

State or other jurisdiction	Authorization for cabinet system				Criteria for membership			Number of members in cabinet (including governor)	Frequency of cabinet meetings	Open cabinet meetings
	State statute	State constitution	Governor created	Tradition in state	Appointed to specific office (a)	Elected to specified office (a)	Gubernatorial appointment regardless of office			
Alabama	★	...	★	★	★	...	...	26	Quarterly	...
Alaska	...	...	★	...	★	...	...	18	Gov.'s discretion	★(b)
Arizona	...	...	★	...	★	...	★	38	Monthly	...
Arkansas	...	...	★	...	★	...	...	47	Monthly	...
California	★	...	★	...	★	...	★	11	Every two weeks	...
Colorado	★	...	★	...	...	...	★	21	Monthly	...
Connecticut	★	...	...	...	...	...	★	27	Gov.'s discretion	...
Delaware	★	...	...	...	★	...	★	19	Gov.'s discretion	...
Florida	...	★	...	...	...	★	...	4	Monthly	...
Georgia					(d)					
Hawaii	...	★	...	...	★	...	★	22	Monthly	...
Idaho			(d)					22	Gov.'s discretion	...
Illinois	★	...	...	...	...	...	★	18	N.A.	...
Indiana	...	...	★	...	...	...	★	16	Bi-monthly	...
Iowa	★	...	★	★	★	...	...	30	(i)	...
Kansas	★	...	...	...	...	...	★	14	Bi-weekly	...
Kentucky	★	...	★	...	★	...	★	10	Weekly	...
Louisiana	★	...	★	★	★	...	...	16	Monthly	...
Maine	...	...	...	★	...	...	★	21	Weekly	...
Maryland	★	...	...	...	★	...	...	28	Every other week	...
Massachusetts	★	...	...	...	★	...	...	10	Bi-weekly	...
Michigan	...	...	★	★	...	...	(g)	24	Monthly and Gov.'s discretion	...
Minnesota	...	...	★	...	★	...	...	25	Regularly	...
Mississippi					(d)					
Missouri	...	★	...	★	★	...	...	17	Gov.'s discretion	...
Montana	★	★	...	...	★	...	...	22	Weekly	...
Nebraska	...	...	★	★	★	...	★	29	Monthly	...
Nevada			(d)					23	At call of the governor	...
New Hampshire					(d)					
New Jersey	★	★	...	...	★	...	...	24	Gov.'s discretion	...
New Mexico	★	...	...	★	★	...	...	25	Gov.'s discretion	...
New York	...	...	...	★	...	...	★	75	Gov.'s discretion	...
North Carolina (e)	★	★	★	...	...	...	★	10	Monthly	...
North Dakota	...	...	★	...	...	...	★	18	Monthly	★
Ohio	★	...	...	...	★	...	...	24	Gov.'s discretion	★
Oklahoma	★	...	...	...	...	...	★	10–15 (j)	Monthly	...
Oregon					(d)					
Pennsylvania	★	★	★	...	★(c)	...	★	28	Gov.'s discretion	★
Rhode Island	...	...	...	★	...	...	★	20	Bi-monthly	...
South Carolina	★	...	...	...	★(c)	...	...	15	Monthly	★
South Dakota	★	★	...	...	★	...	...	19	Monthly	...
Tennessee	★	...	...	...	★	...	...	28	Monthly	...
Texas					(d)					
Utah	★	...	★	...	★	...	...	21	Monthly, weekly during legislative session	...
Vermont	★	...	...	...	★	...	...	7	Gov.'s discretion	...
Virginia	★	...	...	...	...	...	★(f)	14	Weekly	...
Washington	...	...	★	...	★	...	...	28	Bi-weekly, weekly during legislative session	...
West Virginia	...	...	★	★	★	...	...	10	Weekly	...
Wisconsin	★	...	...	...	★	...	...	16	Gov.'s discretion	★
Wyoming	...	...	★	...	...	...	★	20	Monthly	...
American Samoa	★	★	...	...	★	...	★	16	Gov.'s discretion	★
Guam	...	...	★	...	★	...	...	55	Bi-monthly	...
No. Mariana Islands	...	★	...	...	★	...	...	16	Gov.'s discretion	★
Puerto Rico	★	★	...	...	...	...	★	10 (h)	Every 6 weeks	...
U.S. Virgin Islands	...	★	...	...	★	...	...	21	Monthly	★

See footnotes at end of table.

STATE CABINET SYSTEMS — Continued

Source: The Council of State Governments' survey, November 2006.
Key:
★ — Yes
. . . — No
N.A. — Not available

(a) Individual is a member by virtue of election or appointment to a cabinet-level position.

(b) Except when in executive session.

(c) With the consent of the senate.

(d) No formal cabinet system. In Idaho, however, sub-cabinets have been formed, by executive order; the chairs report to the governor.

(e) Constitution provides for a Council of State made up of elective state administrative officials, which makes policy decisions for the state while the cabinet acts more in an advisory capacity.

(f) Appointed by the governor and confirmed by each house.

(g) Membership determined by governor. Some officers formally designated as cabinet members by executive order.

(h) The Constitutional Cabinet has 10 members including the governor. There are other members of the Cabinet provided by statute.

(i) Every other month, and every month during session.

(j) Maximum of 16.

Table 4.7
THE GOVERNORS: PROVISIONS AND PROCEDURES FOR TRANSITION

State or other jurisdiction	Legislation pertaining to gubernatorial transition	Appropriation available to gov-elect ($)	Provision for: Gov-elect's participation in state budget for coming fiscal year	Gov-elect to hire staff to assist during transition	State personnel to be made available to assist gov-elect	Office space in buildings to be made available to gov-elect	Acquainting gov-elect staff with office procedures and routing office functions	Transfer of information (files,) (records, etc.)
Alabama	...	...	★	●	●	●	●	●
Alaska	●	★(a)	...	●	●	●	●	★
Arizona	...	...	★	...	●	●	●	●
Arkansas	●	10,000	...	...	...	...	...	...
California	★	450,000	★	★	★	★	●	●
Colorado	★	10,000	★	★	★	★	●	★
Connecticut	★	★	★	★	★	★	★	★
Delaware	★	15,000	●	★	●	●	●	●
Florida	★	2,500,000 (b)	●	★	●	★(b)	●	●
Georgia	★	50,000	●	★	★	★	●	★
Hawaii	★	50,000	★	★	●	★	●	●
Idaho	★	15,000	★	★	★	★	★	★
Illinois	...	...	...	★	...	★	★	★
Indiana	★	40,000	...	...	...	★	★	★
Iowa	●	100,000	★	●	●	●	●	★
Kansas	★	150,000 (c)	★	★	★	★	★	★
Kentucky	★	200,000	★	★	★	★	★	★
Louisiana	★	●65,000	★	★	...	★	...	●
Maine	●	5,000	★	●	●	●	●	●
Maryland	★	●	...	★	★	★	★	★
Massachusetts	●	●	●	...	●	●	●	★
Michigan	●	●	...	●	●	●	●	●
Minnesota	★	0	★	...	★	★	★	★
Mississippi	●	★(d)	★	★	★	★	★	★
Missouri	★	100,000	★	★	●	★	●	●(e)
Montana	★	★	★	★	★	★	★	★
Nebraska	★	70,000	●	★	★	★	●	★
Nevada	★	Reasonable amount	★	...	...	...	...	★(f)
New Hampshire	★	75,000	★	★	★	★	★	...
New Jersey	★	(g)	●	★	★	★	●	★
New Mexico	★	(h)	★	★	★	★	★	★
New York	...	...	...	...	★	★	★	★
North Carolina	★	★	●(i)	★	★	★	...	...
North Dakota	●	10,000	(j)	(k)	●	...	●	★
Ohio	★	Unspecified (l)	●	★	●	...	●	★
Oklahoma	●	●	★	●	●	★	●	●
Oregon	★	★	★	★	★	★	★	★
Pennsylvania	★	...	...	★	●	●	●	...
Rhode Island	★	500,000	...	★	★	★	●	●
South Carolina	...	●	●	●	●	●	●	●
South Dakota	★	...	...	...	...	...	...	...
Tennessee	★	★	●	★	★	★	●	●
Texas	●	●	●	●	●	●	●	●
Utah	★	★(m)	★	★	★	★	★	★
Vermont	...	(n)	★	●	●	●	●	...
Virginia	★	★(o)	★	★	★	★	★	★
Washington	★	★	●	★	●	★	●	●
West Virginia	...	●	...	●	...	●	●	●
Wisconsin	★	Unspecified	★	★	★	★	★	★
Wyoming	●	...	●	●	●	●	●	●
American Samoa	...	Unspecified	★(p)	★	●	●	★	●
Guam	★	(q)	...	...	★	★	★	...
No. Mariana Islands	★	Unspecified	...	★	★	★	★	★
Puerto Rico	★	...	★	★	★	★	★	★
U.S. Virgin Islands	★	100,000	...	★	★	★	★	★

See footnotes at end of table.

THE GOVERNORS: PROVISIONS AND PROCEDURES FOR TRANSITION — Continued

Source: The Council of State Governments' survey, December 2006.

Key:

. . . — No provisions or procedures.

★ — Formal provisions or procedures.

● — No formal provisions, occurs informally.

N.A. — Not applicable.

(a) Varies.

(b) There is a budget for the governor-elect to use during transition. Very specific procedures include legislative review to access the funds. Some of these funds may be shared with Cabinet transitions: CFO and Commissioner of Agriculture. Transition information is available with no formal provisions. Budget allows for space, etc., but actual office space is determined by availability at the time.

(c) Transition funds are used by both the incoming and the outgoing administrations.

(d) Miss. Code Ann.§ 7-1-101 provides as follows: the governor's office of general services shall provide a governor-elect with office space and office equipment for the period between the election and inauguration. A special appropriation to the governor's office of general services is hereby authorized to defray the expenses of providing necessary staff employees and for the operation of the office of governor-elect during the period between the election and inauguration. The state fiscal management board shall make available to a governor-elect and his designated representatives information on the following: (a) all information and reports used in the preparation of the budget report; and (b) all information and reports on projected income and revenue estimates for the state.

(e) Activity is traditional and routine, although there is no specific statutory provision.

(f) As determined in budget.

(g) No specific amount—necessary services and facilities.

(h) Legislature required to make appropriation; no dollar amount stated in legislation.

(i) New governor can submit supplemental budget.

(j) Responsible for submitting budget for coming biennium.

(k) Governor usually hires several incoming key staff during transition.

(l) Determined in budget.

(m) Appropriated by legislature at the time of transition.

(n) Governor-elect entitled to 70% of Governor's salary.

(o) Determined every four years.

(p) Can submit reprogramming or supplemental appropriation measure for current fiscal year.

(q) Appropriations given upon the request of governor-elect.

Table 4.8
IMPEACHMENT PROVISIONS IN THE STATES

State or other jurisdiction	Governor and other state executive and judicial officers subject to impeachment	Legislative body which holds power of impeachment	Vote required for impeachment	Legislative body which conducts impeachment trial	Chief justice presides at impeachment trial (a)	Vote required for conviction	Official who serves as acting governor if governor impeached (b)	Legislature may call special session for impeachment
Alabama	★	H	maj. mbrs.	S	★	majority of elected mbrs.	LG	...
Alaska	★	S	2/3 mbrs.	H	(c)	2/3 mbrs.	LG	★
Arizona	★(d)	H	maj. mbrs.	S	...	2/3 mbrs.	SS	★
Arkansas	★	H	maj. mbrs.	S	★(e)	2/3 mbrs.	LG	★
California	★	H	...	S	...	2/3 mbrs.	LG	...
Colorado	★	H	maj. mbrs.	S	★	2/3 mbrs.	LG	...
Connecticut	★	H	...	S	★	2/3 mbrs. must be present	LG	★
Delaware	★	H	2/3 mbrs.	S	★	2/3 mbrs.	LG	...
Florida	★	H	2/3 mbrs.	S	★(f)	2/3 mbrs. present (h)	LG (i)	...
Georgia	★	H	...	S	★(e)	2/3 mbrs.	LG (i)	★(g)
Hawaii	★	H	2/3 mbrs.	S	...	2/3 mbrs.	LG	★
Idaho	★	H	2/3 mbrs.	S	★	2/3 mbrs.	LG	...
Illinois	★	H	2/3 mbrs.	S	★	2/3 mbrs.	LG	★
Indiana	★(j)	H	2/3 mbrs.	S	...	2/3 mbrs.	LG	...
Iowa	★	H	maj. mbrs.	S	...	majority of elected mbrs.	LG	★
Kansas	★	H	(k)	S	...	2/3 mbrs.	LG	...
Kentucky	★	H	maj. mbrs.	S	★	2/3 mbrs. present	LG	...
Louisiana	★	H	(l)	S	...	(l)	LG	★
Maine	★	H	...	S	...	2/3 mbrs. present	PS	...
Maryland	★	H	maj. mbrs.	S	...	2/3 mbrs.	LG	...
Massachusetts	★	H	maj. mbrs.	S	...	...	LG	...
Michigan	★	H	maj. mbrs.	S	★(m)	2/3 mbrs.	LG	★
Minnesota	★	H	maj. mbrs.	S	...	2/3 mbrs. present	LG	...
Mississippi	★	H	2/3 mbrs. present	S	★(n)	2/3 mbrs.	LG	...
Missouri	★	H	...	(q)	(q)	2/3 mbrs. present (o)	LG	(p)
Montana	★	H	2/3 mbrs.	S	★	2/3 mbrs.	LG	★
Nebraska	★	S (r)	maj. mbrs.	(s)	(s)	(s)	LG	★
Nevada	★(d)	H	maj. mbrs.	S	★	2/3 mbrs.	LG	...
New Hampshire	★	H	...	S	★	...	LG	...
New Jersey	★	H	maj. mbrs.	S	★	2/3 mbrs. present	PS	...
New Mexico	★	H	maj. mbrs.	S	★(m)	2/3 mbrs.	PS (x)	★
New York	★	H	maj. mbrs.	S	★	2/3 mbrs. present	LG	★
North Carolina	★	H	2/3 maj. mbrs.	S	★	2/3 mbrs. present	LG	★
North Dakota	★(d)	H	maj. mbrs.	S	★	2/3 mbrs.	LG	★
Ohio	★	H	maj. mbrs.	S	...	2/3 mbrs. present	LG	...
Oklahoma	★	H	...	S	★	2/3 mbrs. present	LG	...
Oregon				.........(t).........			LG	★
Pennsylvania	★	H	...	S	...	2/3 maj. mbrs.	LG	★
Rhode Island	★	H	2/3 maj. mbrs.	S	★	2/3 maj. mbrs.	LG	★
South Carolina	★	H	2/3 mbrs.	S	★	2/3 mbrs.	LG	...

See footnotes at end of table.

IMPEACHMENT PROVISIONS IN THE STATES—Continued

State or other jurisdiction	Governor and other state executive and judicial officers subject to impeachment	Legislative body which holds power of impeachment	Vote required for impeachment	Legislative body which conducts impeachment trial	Chief justice presides at impeachment trial (a)	Vote required for conviction	Official who serves as acting governor if governor impeached (b)	Legislature may call special session for impeachment
South Dakota	★	H	maj. mbrs.	S	★	2/3 mbrs.	LG	★
Tennessee	★	H	maj. mbrs.	S	★	2/3 mbrs. (u)	PS	★
Texas	★	H	maj. mbrs.	S	★	2/3 mbrs. present	LG	...
Utah	★	H	2/3 mbrs.	S	...	2/3 mbrs.	LG	★
Vermont	★	H	2/3 mbrs.	S	...	2/3 mbrs.	LG	...
Virginia	★	H	maj. mbrs.	S	...	2/3 mbrs. present	LG	★
Washington	★(d)	H	maj. mbrs.	S	★	2/3 mbrs.	LG	★
West Virginia	★	H	...	S	★	2/3 mbrs.	PS	★
Wisconsin	★	H	maj. mbrs.	S	...	2/3 mbrs.	LG	...
Wyoming	★	H	maj. mbrs.	S	★	2/3 mbrs.	SS	★
Dist. of Columbia				(v)				...
American Samoa	(w)	H	2/3 mbrs.	S	★	2/3 mbrs.	...	...
Guam				(v)				...
No. Mariana Islands	★	H	2/3 mbrs.	S	...	2/3 mbrs.	LG	★
Puerto Rico	★	H	2/3 mbrs.	S	★	3/4 mbrs.	SS	...
U.S. Virgin Islands				(v)				

Source: The Council of State Governments' survey, January 2007.

Key:
★ — Yes; provision for.
. . . — Not specified, or no provision for.
H — House or Assembly (lower chamber)
S — Senate
LG — Lieutenant Governor
PS — President or Speaker of the Senate
SS — Secretary of State

(a) Presiding justice of state court of last resort. In many states, provision indicates that chief justice presides only on occasion of impeachment of governor.
(b) For provisions on official next in line of succession if governor is convicted and removed from office, refer to Chapter 4, "The Governors."
(c) An appointed Supreme Court justice presides.
(d) With exception of certain judicial officers. In Arizona and Washington—justices of courts not of record. In Nevada—justices of the peace. In North Dakota—county judges, justices of the peace, and police magistrates. In Oklahoma—all judicial officers not serving on the Supreme Court.
(e) Should the Chief Justice be on trial, or otherwise disqualified, the Senate shall elect a judge of the Supreme Court to preside.
(f) Except in a trial of the chief justice, in which case the governor shall preside.
(g) Special sessions of the General Assembly shall be limited to a period of 40 days unless extended by 3/5 vote of each house and approved by the Governor or unless at the expiration of such period an impeachment trial of some officer of state government is pending, in which event the House shall adjourn and the Senate shall remain in session until such trial is completed.
(h) An officer impeached by the house of representatives shall be disqualified from performing any official duties until acquitted by the senate, and, unless impeached, the governor may by appointment fill the office until completion of the trial.
(i) Governor may appoint someone to serve until the impeachment procedures are final.
(j) Judges not included.
(k) No statute, simple majority is the assumption.
(l) Concurrence of 2/3 of the elected senators.
(m) Only if governor or lieutenant governor is on trial.
(n) When the governor is tried; if Chief Justice is unable to preside, the next longest serving justice shall preside.
(o) No person shall be convicted without concurrence of 2/3 of all senators present. Miss Const. 1890 Art. IV § 52.
(p) It is implied but not addressed directly in Miss Const. 1890 Art. IV §§ 49–53.
(q) All impeachments are tried before the state Supreme Court, except that the governor or a member of the Supreme Court is tried by a special commission of seven eminent jurists to be elected by the Senate. A vote of 5/7 of the court of special commission is necessary to convict.
(r) Unicameral legislature; members use the title "senator."
(s) Court of impeachment is composed of chief justice and supreme court. A vote of 2/3 present of the court is necessary to convict.
(t) No provision for impeachment. Public officers may be tried for incompetence, corruption, malfeasance, or delinquency in office in same manner as criminal offenses.
(u) Vote of 2/3 of members sworn to try the officer impeached.
(v) Removal of elected officials by recall procedure only.
(w) Governor, lieutenant governor.
(x) Beginning in 2009, New Jersey will elect a lieutenant governor. Until the inauguration of the first lieutenant governor in 2010, the president of the senate would succeed the governor if necessary.

Table 4.9
CONSTITUTIONAL AND STATUTORY PROVISIONS FOR
NUMBER OF CONSECUTIVE TERMS OF ELECTED STATE OFFICIALS
(All terms last four years unless otherwise noted)

State or other jurisdiction	Governor	Lt. Governor	Secretary of state	Attorney general	Treasurer	Auditor	Comptroller	Education	Agriculture	Labor	Insurance
Alabama	2	2	2	2	2	...	...	...	2	...	...
Alaska	2	2	(b)	...	(w)	...	...	...	...	...	...
Arizona	2	(e)	2	2	2	...	...	2	...	...	...
Arkansas	2 (f)	2	2	2	2	...	...	...	...	...	...
California	2	2	2	2	2	...	2	2	...	...	...
Colorado	2	2	2	2	2	...	...	...	...	...	...
Connecticut	N	N	N	N	N	...	N	...	...	...	...
Delaware	2 (f)	2	...	N	N	N	...	...	...	...	N
Florida	2	2	...	2	2 (g)	...	2	N	N	...	(g)
Georgia	2 (a)	N	N	N	...	...	...	N	N	N	N
Hawaii	2	2	(b)	...	...	...	...	...	...	...	...
Idaho	N	N	N	N	N	...	2	N	...	...	...
Illinois	N	N	N	N	N	...	N	...	...	...	...
Indiana	(h)	2	2	...	(h)	...	2 (i)	...	...	...	...
Iowa	N	N	N	N	N	N	...	...	...	...	...
Kansas	2	N	N	N	...	...	...	...	...	...	...
Kentucky	2	2	2	2	2	2	...	...	2	2	...
Louisiana	2 (a)	N	N	N	N	...	...	N	N	...	N
Maine	2 (a)	(k)	...	(j)	...	...	...	...	...	...	...
Maryland	2 (a)	2	...	N	...	...	N	...	...	...	...
Massachusetts	N	N	N	2	N	N	...	...	...	...	...
Michigan	2	2	2	2	...	...	...	...	...	...	...
Minnesota	N	N	N	N	(l)	N	...	...	...	...	(m)
Mississippi	2	2 (a)	N	N	N	N	...	...	...	...	...
Missouri	2	N	N	N	2 (f)	N	...	...	...	...	...
Montana	2 (n)	2 (n)	2 (n)	2 (n)	...	N	...	2 (n)	...	...	...
Nebraska	2 (a)	2 (a)	N	N	2 (a)	N	...	...	...	...	...
Nevada	2	2	2	2	2	...	2	...	...	...	...
New Hampshire	(o)	(k)	...	...	...	...	...	...	...	...	...
New Jersey	2 (a)	(k)	...	...	...	...	...	...	...	...	...
New Mexico	2 (a)	2 (a)	2 (a)	2 (a)	2 (a)	2 (a)	...	...	...	...	...
New York	N	N	...	N	...	N (c)	N	...	...	...	...
North Carolina	2 (a)	2	N	N	N	N	...	N	N	N	N
North Dakota	N	N	N (q)	N (q)	N	N	...	N	N (q)(r)	N (q)	N
Ohio	2	2	2	2	2	2	...	...	...	...	...
Oklahoma	2 (a)	N	...	N	N	N	...	2 (a)	...	2 (a)	N
Oregon	(h)	(d)	(h)	N	(h)	...	...	...	...	...	...
Pennsylvania	2	2	...	2 (a)	2 (s)	2 (a)	...	...	...	...	...
Rhode Island	2	2 (a)	2 (a)	2 (a)	2 (a)	...	...	...	...	...	...
South Carolina	2 (a)	2	N	N	N	...	N	N	N	...	...
South Dakota	2 (a)	2 (a)	2 (a)	2 (a)	2 (a)	...	2	...	...	...	...
Tennessee	2 (a)	(k)	...	(y)	...	...	...	...	...	...	...
Texas	N	N	...	N	(c)	...	N	...	...	...	...
Utah	3	N	(b)	N	N	N	...	...	...	...	...
Vermont	(o)	(o)	(o)	(o)	(o)	(o)	...	...	...	...	...
Virginia	(t)	(u)	...	(u)	...	...	...	...	...	...	...
Washington	N	N	N	N	N	N	...	N	...	...	...
West Virginia	2	N (k)	N	N	N	...	N	...	N	...	...
Wisconsin	N	N	N	N	N	...	...	N	...	...	...
Wyoming	2 (n)	(d)	N	...	2	...	2	N	...	...	...
Dist. of Columbia	N (v)	2	...	...	...	...	...	...	...	...	...
American Samoa	2	2	(b)	...	...	...	(p)	...	...	...	...
Guam	2 (a)	2	(b)	...	...	2	(x)	...	...	...	...
No. Mariana Islands	(h)	N	...	...	...	...	(p)	...	...	...	(m)
Puerto Rico	(a)	(e)	...	...	...	1	...	...	...	...	...
U.S. Virgin Islands	2 (a)	2	(c)	...	(e)	...	(e)	...	...	...	(b)

See footnotes at end of table.

CONSTITUTIONAL AND STATUTORY PROVISIONS FOR
NUMBER OF CONSECUTIVE TERMS OF ELECTED STATE OFFICIALS — Continued
(All terms last four years unless otherwise noted)

Source: The Council of State Governments survey January 2007 and state constitutions and statutes, February 2007.

Note: All terms last four years unless otherwise noted. Footnotes specify if a position's functions are performed by an appointed official under a different title.

Key:

N — No provision specifying number of terms allowed.

. . . — Position is appointed or elected by governmental entity (not chosen by the electorate).

(a) After two consecutive terms, must wait four years and/or one full term before being eligible again.

(b) Lieutenant Governor performs this function.

(c) Comptroller performs this function.

(d) Secretary of State is next in line to the governorship.

(e) Finance Administrator performs function.

(f) Absolute two-term limitation, but not necessarily consecutive.

(g) Chief Financial Officer performs this function as of January 2003.

(h) Eligible for eight out of any period of twelve years.

(i) State auditor performs this function.

(j) Serves 2 year term and is eligible to serve 4 terms.

(k) President or Speaker of the Senate is next in line of succession to the governorship. In Tennessee, Speaker of the Senate has the statutory title "Lieutenant Governor".

(l) Office of the State Treasurer was abolished on the first Monday in January 2003.

(m) Commerce administrator performs this function.

(n) Eligible for eight out of sixteen years.

(o) Serves two-year term, no provision specifying the number of terms allowed.

(p) State treasurer performs this function.

(q) The terms of the office of the elected officials are four years, except that in 2004 the agricultural commissioner, attorney general, secretary of state and the tax commissioner are elected to a term of two years.

(r) Constitution provides for a secretary of agriculture and labor. However, the legislature was given constitutional authority to provide for (and has provided for) a department of labor distinct from agriculture, and a commissioner of labor distinct from the commissioner of agriculture.

(s) Treasurer must wait four years before being eligible for the office of auditor general.

(t) Cannot serve consecutive terms, but after 4 year respite can seek re-election.

(u) Provision specifying individual may hold office for an unlimited number of terms.

(v) Mayor.

(w) Deputy Commissioner of Department of Revenue performs function.

(x) General services administrator performs function.

(y) Term is for eight years and official is appointed by judges of the State Supreme Court.

Table 4.10
SELECTED STATE ADMINISTRATIVE OFFICIALS: METHODS OF SELECTION

State or other jurisdiction	Governor	Lieutenant governor	Secretary of state	Attorney general	Treasurer	Adjutant general	Administration	Agriculture	Auditor	Banking
Alabama	CE	CE	CE	CE	CE	GS	G	SE	CE	GS
Alaska	CE	CE	(a-1)	GB	AG	GB	GB	AG	L	AG
Arizona	CE	(a-2)	CE	CE	CE	GS	GS	GS	L	GS
Arkansas	CE	CE	CE	CE	CE	G	G	G	CE	GS
California	CE	CE	CE	CE	CE	GS	. . .	G	GB	GS
Colorado	CE	CE	CE	CE	CE	GS	GS	GS	L	CS
Connecticut	CE	CE	CE	CE	CE	GE	GE	GE	L	GE
Delaware	CE	CE	GS	CE	CE	GS	(c)	GS	CE	GS
Florida	CE	CE	GS	CE	CE (b)	G	GS	CE	L	CE (b)
Georgia	CE	CE	CE	CE	G	G	G	CE	(d)	G
Hawaii	CE	CE	(a-1)	GS	GS	GS	(e)	GS	CL	AG
Idaho	CE	CE	CE	CE	CE	GS	GS	GS	. . .	GS
Illinois	CE	CE	CE	CE	CE	GS	GS	GS	SL	B
Indiana	CE	CE	CE	SE	CE	G	G	LG	CE	G
Iowa	CE	CE	CE	CE	CE	GS	GS	CE	CE	GS
Kansas	CE	CE	CE	CE	SE	GS	GS	GS	N.A.	GS
Kentucky	CE	CE	CE	CE	CE	G	(f)	CE	CE	G
Louisiana	CE	CE	CE	CE	CE	GS	GS	CE	G	GLS
Maine	CE	(g)	CL	CL	CL	GLS	GLS	GLS	L	GLS
Maryland	CE	CE	GS	CE	CL	G	GS (a-26)	GS	. . .	AG
Massachusetts	CE	CE	CE	CE	CE	G	G	CG	CE	GS
Michigan	CE	CE	CE	CE	GS	GS	GS	B	CL	GS
Minnesota	CE	CE	CE	CE	(h)	GS	GS	GS	CE	A
Mississippi	CE	CE	CE	CE	CE	GE	GS	SE	CE	GS
Missouri	CE	CE	CE	CE	CE	G	GS	GS	CE	. . .
Montana	CE	CE	CE	CE	GS (a-5)	CE	GS	G	CE	A
Nebraska	CE	CE	CE	CE	CE	GS	GS	GS	CE	GS
Nevada	CE	CE	CE	CE	CE	G	G	BA	. . .	A
New Hampshire	CE	(g)	CL	GC	CL	GC	GC	GC	. . .	GC
New Jersey	CE	(g)	GS	GS	GS	GS	. . .	BG	(i)	GS
New Mexico	CE	CE	CE	CE	CE	G	GS (a-26)	B	CE	G
New York	CE	CE	GS	CE	A	G	. . .	GS	CE (a-14)	GS
North Carolina	CE	CE	SE	CE	CE	A	G	CE	CE	G
North Dakota	CE	CE	CE	CE	CE	G	. . .	CE	CE	GS
Ohio	CE	CE	CE	CE	CE	G	GS	GS	CE	A
Oklahoma	CE	CE	GS	CE	CE	GS	GS	GS	CE	GS
Oregon	CE	(a-2)	CE	SE	CE	G	GS	GS	SS	. . .
Pennsylvania	CE	CE	GS	CE	CE	GS	G	GS	CE	CS
Rhode Island	SE	SE	CE	SE	SE	GB	GB	CS	LS	CS
South Carolina	CE	CE	CE	CE	CE	CE	B	CE	B	A
South Dakota	CE	CE	CE	CE	CE	GS	GS	GS	L	A
Tennessee	CE	CL (g)	CL	CT	CL	G	G	G	SL (a-14)	G
Texas	CE	CE	G	CE	CE (a-14)	G	A	SE	(d)	B
Utah	CE	CE	CE (a-1)	CE	CE	GS	GS	GS	CE	GS
Vermont	CE	CE	CE	CE	CE	CL	GS	GS	CE	GS
Virginia	CE	CE	GB	CE	GB	GB	GB	GB	SL	SL
Washington	CE	CE	CE	CE	CE	GS	GS	GS	CE	GS
West Virginia	CE	(g)	CE	CE	CE	GS	GS	CE	CE	GS
Wisconsin	CE	CE	CE	CE	CE	G	GS	GS	LS	A
Wyoming	CE	(a-2)	CE	G	CE	G	GS	GS	CE	A
American Samoa	CE	CE	(a-1)	GB	GB	N.A.	GB	GB	N.A.	N.A.
Guam	CE	CE	. . .	CE	CS	GS	GS	GS	CE	GS
No. Mariana Islands	CE	CE	. . .	GS	CS	. . .	G	. . .	GB	C
U.S. Virgin Islands	SE	SE	SE (a-1)	GS	GS	GS	GS	GS	GS	LG

Sources: The Council of State Governments' survey of state personnel agencies, January 2007.

Note: The chief administrative officials responsible for each function were determined from information given by the states for the same function as listed in State Administrative Officials Classified by Function, 2006, published by The Council of State Governments.

Key:
N.A. — Not available.
. . . — No specific chief administrative official or agency in charge of function.
CE — Constitutional, elected by public.
CL — Constitutional, elected by legislature.
SE — Statutory, elected by public.
SL — Statutory, elected by legislature.
L — Selected by legislature or one of its organs
CT — Constitutional, elected by state court of last resort.
CP — Competitve process.

Appointed by:
G — Governor
GS — Governor
GB — Governor
GE — Governor
GC — Governor
GD — Governor
GLS — Governor
GOC — Governor &
Council or cabinet
LG — Lieutenant Governor
LGS — Lieutenant Governor
AT — Attorney General
SS — Secretary of State
C — Cabinet Secretary
CG — Cabinet Secretary

Approved by:

Senate (in Nebraska, unicameral legislature)
Both houses
Either house
Council
Departmental board
Appropriate legislative committee & Senate

Senate

Governor

SELECTED STATE ADMINISTRATIVE OFFICIALS: METHODS OF SELECTION — Continued

State or other jurisdiction	Budget	Civil rights	Commerce	Community affairs	Comptroller	Consumer affairs	Corrections	Economic development	Education	Election administration
Alabama	CS	...	G	G	CS	CS	G	G (a-13)	B	CS
Alaska	G	GB	GB	(a-12)	AG	(a-12)	GB	(a-12)	GD	AG
Arizona	L	AT	GS	AT	A	AT	GS	GS (a-12)	CE	CE (a-2)
Arkansas	A	...	GS	N.A.	G	A	B	GS	BG	CE (a-2)
California	G (a-24)	...	...	GS	CE	G	GS	...	CE	(j)
Colorado	G	CS	G	GS	C	CE	GS	G	AB	CS
Connecticut	CS	GE	GE	GE	CE	GE	GE	GE	BG	CS
Delaware	GS	CG	GS (a-2)	...	CG	AT	GS	GS	GS	GS
Florida	G	AB	G	GS	CE (b)	A	GS	G	GS	A
Georgia	G	G	BG	BG	CE	G	GD	N.A.	CE	A
Hawaii	GS	B	GS	...	GS	A	GS	GS	B	CL
Idaho	GS	B	GS	A	CE	CE (a-3)	B	A	CE	CE
Illinois	G	GS	GS	GS (a-12)	CE	CE (a-3)	GS	GS (a-12)	B	B
Indiana	G	G	G	G	CE (a-8)	AT	G	G	CE	(k)
Iowa	GS	GS	GS	GS	...	GS	GS	GS	GS	A
Kansas	G	GS	GS	A	C	AT	GS	(a-12)	B	(l)
Kentucky	G	B	G	G	CG	AT	G	GC	B	B
Louisiana	A	B	GS	G	GS	AG	GS	GS	BG	A
Maine	C	B	(a-17)	(a-17)	C	GLS	GLS	GLS	GLS	SS
Maryland	GS	G	GS	...	CE	A	AGS	GS	B	B
Massachusetts	CG	G	G	G	G	G	CG	G	B	CE
Michigan	GS	GS	GS	...	CS	...	GS	...	B	(m)
Minnesota	(h)	GS	GS	GS (a-17)	(h)	A	GS	GS	GS	CE (a-2)
Mississippi	GS	...	SE	A	GS	A	GS	GS	BS	A (n)
Missouri	AGS	AGS	GS (a-17)	(j)	A	CE (a-3)	GS	GS	BG	SS
Montana	G	CP	GS	CP	CP	CP	GS	G	CE	SS
Nebraska	A	B	GS	A	A	CE (a-3)	GS	GS	B	A
Nevada	(a-6)	G	G	...	CE	A	G	GD	B	(o)
New Hampshire	GC (a-6)	CS	GC	G	AGC	AGC	GC	AGC	B	CL (a-2)
New Jersey	GS	A	GS	GS	GS (a-10)	A	GS	G	GS	A
New Mexico	G	G	GS (a-17)	G	ALS	G	GS	GS	B	G
New York	G	GS	GS	GS (a-2)	CE	GS	GS	GS	B	B
North Carolina	G (a-24)	A	G	A	G	(j)	G	A	CE	G
North Dakota	A	G	G	...	A	AT	G	N.A.	CE	SS
Ohio	GS	B	GS	A	GS	A	GS	GS	B	CE (a-2)
Oklahoma	A	B	G	(j)	A	B	B	G	CE	L
Oregon	A	A	GS	G	A	GS	GS	GS	SE	A
Pennsylvania	G	B	GS	AG	G	AT	GS	GS	GS	C
Rhode Island	AG	B	G (a-17)	CS	CS	SE (a-3)	GB	G	B	F
South Carolina	A	B	GS	N.A.	CE	B	GS	GS (a-12)	CE	B
South Dakota	(a-24)	N.A.	(a-44)	(a-17)	(a-40)	N.A.	GS	(a-48)	GS	SS
Tennessee	A	G	G	G (a-17)	SL	A	G	G	G	A
Texas	G	B	G	G	CE	CE (a-3)	B	G (a-12)	B	(p)
Utah	G	A	GS	GS	AG	GS	GS	A	B	A
Vermont	AG	AT	GS	AG	AG	AT	AG	G	AG	BG
Virginia	GB	GB	GB	GB	GB	A	GB	B	GB	GB
Washington	N.A.	B	GS	GS	GS	CE	GS	GS	CE	A
West Virginia	CS	GS	GS	B	CE (a-8)	AT	GS	B (a-13)	B	CE (a-2)
Wisconsin	A	A	GS	...	A	A	GS	CS	CE	B
Wyoming	A	A	G	G	CE (a-8)	G	GS	G (a-12)	CE	A
American Samoa	GB	N.A.	GB	(a-12)	(a-4)	(a-3)	A	(a-12)	GB	G
Guam	GS	GS	GS	...	CS	CS	GS	B	GS	GS
No. Mariana Islands	G	A	GS	GS	C	GS	C	C	B	B
U.S. Virgin Islands	GS	GS	GS	GS	GS (a-24)	GS	GS	GS	GS	B

A — Agency head
AB — Agency head ... Board
AG — Agency head ... Governor
AGC — Agency head ... Governor & Council
AGS Agency head ... Senate
ALS — Agency head ... Appropriate legislative committee
ASH — Agency head ... Senate president & House speaker
B — Board or commission
BG — Board ... Governor
BGS — Board ... Governor & Senate
BS — Board or commission ... Senate
BA — Board or commission ... Agency head
CS — Civil Service
LS — Legislative Committee Senate
(a) Chief administrative official or agency in charge of function:
(a-1) Lieutenant governor.
(a-2) Secretary of state.

(a-3) Attorney general.
(a-4) Treasurer.
(a-5) Adjutant general
(a-6) Administration.
(a-7) Agriculture
(a-8) Auditor
(a-9) Banking
(a-10) Budget.
(a-11) Civil rights
(a-12) Commerce.
(a-13) Community affairs.
(a-14) Comptroller.
(a-15) Consumer affairs.
(a-16) Corrections
(a-17) Economic development.
(a-18) Education (chief state school officer).
(a-19) Election administration

SELECTED STATE ADMINISTRATIVE OFFICIALS: METHODS OF SELECTION — Continued

State or other jurisdiction	Emergency management	Employment services	Energy	Environmental protection	Finance	Fish & wildlife	General services	Health	Higher education	Highways
Alabama	G	CS	CS	B	G	CS	CS	B	B	G (a-49)
Alaska	AG	AG	B	GB	AG	GB	...	AG	B	GB
Arizona	G	A	...	GS	(a-14)	B	A	GS	B	A
Arkansas	GS	G	A	BG/BS	G	(j)	A	BG	BG	BS (a-49)
California	GS	GS	G	GS	G	G	GS	GS	B	GS (a-49)
Colorado	CS	GS	G	CS	CS	AB	GS	GS	GS	GS (a-49)
Connecticut	GE	A	A	GE	GE	CS (q)	GE	GE	BG	GE (a-49)
Delaware	CG	CG	A	GS (a-35)	GS	CG	CG	CG	B	GS (a-49)
Florida	A	GS	A	GS	CE (b)	GS	GS	GS	N.A.	GOC
Georgia	G	A	G	B	G	A	A	A	B	B (a-49)
Hawaii	A	CS	CS	CS	(r)	CS	GS (a-14)	GS	B	CS
Idaho	A	GS	A	GS	GS	B	...	GS	B	B (a-49)
Illinois	GS	GS	GS (a-12)	GS	G (a-10)	GS (a-35)	GS (a-6)	GS	B	GS (a-49)
Indiana	G	G	LG	G	G (a-10)	A	G (a-6)	G	G	G (a-49)
Iowa	GS	GS	...	A	A	A	A	GS	...	A
Kansas	(a-5) (s)	GS	B	C	...	CS	GS	C	B	GS (a-49)
Kentucky	AG	AG	AG	G	G	G	CG (a-6)	CG	B	CG
Louisiana	GS	A	CS	GS	GS	GS	GS	GS	B	GS (a-49)
Maine	C	C	(a-38)	GLS	(a-6)	GLS	C	C	N.A.	(a-49)
Maryland	AG	A	G	GS	GS	...	GS (a-6)	GS	G	AG
Massachusetts	G	CG	CG	CG	G (a-6)	CG	G	CG	B	G
Michigan	CS	CS	...	GS	GS (a-10)	(t)	...	GS	CS	GS (a-49)
Minnesota	GS	A	A	GS	(h)	A	GS (a-6)	GS (u)	B	CE (v)
Mississippi	GS	GS	A	GS	GS	GS	...	BS	BS	B (a-49)
Missouri	A	A	...	A	AGS	(w)	A	GS	B	B (a-49)
Montana	CP	CP	CP	GS	CP	GS	CP	GS (a-45)	CP	GS (a-49)
Nebraska	A	A	A	GS	(x)	(y)	A	GS	B	GS (a-49)
Nevada	A	A	A	A	...	A	...	AG	B	(a-49)
New Hampshire	G	GC	G	GC	GC (a-6)	BGC	GC	AGC	B	GC (a-49)
New Jersey	GS	A	A	GS	A	B	(z)	GS	B	A
New Mexico	G	GS (a-32)	GS	GS	GS	G	GS	GS	B	GS (a-49)
New York	G	GS (a-32)	B	GS	CE (a-14)	GS	G	GS	B (a-18)	GS (a-49)
North Carolina	G	G	A	G	G	G	G	G	B	A
North Dakota	A	G	A	A	A	G	G	G	B	G (a-49)
Ohio	AG	GS	A	GS	A (aa)	A	A	GS	B	GS
Oklahoma	GS	B	GS	B	GS	B	GS (a-6)	B	B	B (a-49)
Oregon	AG	GS	G	B	CE (a-4)	B	GS (a-6)	A	B	A
Pennsylvania	G	AG	AG	GS	G	B	GS	GS	AG	AG
Rhode Island	G	G	CS	GB	AG (a-10)	GB	GB	GB	B	GB (a-49)
South Carolina	A	B	A	B	B	B	A	GS	B	B (a-49)
South Dakota	A	(a-37)	(a-48)	(a-35)	GS	GS	(a-6)	GS	B	(a-47)
Tennessee	A	G	A	G	G	B	G	G	B	G (a-49)
Texas	A	B	...	B	CE (a-14)	B	B	BG	B	B (a-49)
Utah	A	GS	A	GS	AG	A	A	GS	B	GS (a-49)
Vermont	AG	GS	GS	AG	AG	AG	AG	AG	N.A.	GS (a-49)
Virginia	GB	GB	GB	GB	GB	B	GB	GB	B	GB
Washington	A	GS	N.A.	GS	GS	B	GS	GS	N.A.	B
West Virginia	GS	GS	GS	GS (a-22)	GS (a-6)	CS	C	GS	B (bb)	GS (a-49)
Wisconsin	A	GS	A	A	A	A	GS (a-6)	A	N.A.	A
Wyoming	G	GS	A	GS	CE (a-8)	CS	A	GS	B	GS (a-49)
American Samoa	G	A	GB	GB	(a-4)	GB	G	GB	(a-18)	GB (a-49)
Guam	GS	GS	G	GS	GS	GS	CS	GS	B	GS
No. Mariana Islands	G	C	C	G	GS	C	GS	GS	B	C
U.S. Virgin Islands	GS	GS	GS	GS	GS	GS	GS	GS	GS	GS

(a-20) Emergency management
(a-21) Employment Services
(a-22) Energy.
(a-23) Environmental protection.
(a-24) Finance.
(a-25) Fish and wildlife
(a-26) General services.
(a-27) Health
(a-28) Higher education
(a-29) Highways.
(a-30) Information systems
(a-31) Insurance
(a-32) Labor.
(a-33) Licensing
(a-34) Mental Health
(a-35) Natural resources.
(a-36) Parks and recreation.

(a-37) Personnel.
(a-38) Planning
(a-39) Post audit.
(a-40) Pre-audit.
(a-41) Public library development
(a-42) Public utility regulation.
(a-43) Purchasing.
(a-44) Revenue.
(a-45) Social services.
(a-46) Solid waste management
(a-47) State police
(a-48) Tourism.
(a-49) Transportation.
(a-50) Welfare.
(b) Effective Jan. 1, 2003 the positions of Commissioner & Treasurer and Comptroller merged into one Chief Financial Officer.

SELECTED STATE ADMINISTRATIVE OFFICIALS: METHODS OF SELECTION — Continued

State or other jurisdiction	Information systems	Insurance	Labor	Licensing	Mental health & retardation	Natural resources	Parks & recreation	Personnel	Planning	Post audit
Alabama	G	G	G	...	G	G	CS	B	G (a-13)	LS
Alaska	AG	AG	GB	AG	AG	GB	AG	AG	...	B
Arizona	A	GS	B	...	G	GS	B	A	L (a-10)	L
Arkansas	GS	GS	GS	...	A	A	GS	A	...	...
California	G	CE	AG	G	(cc)	GS	GS	GS	...	L
Colorado	G	GS	GS	GS	GS	GS	C	GS	G	L
Connecticut	GE	GE	GE	CS	GE (dd)	CS	CS	GE	A	(a-8)
Delaware	GS	CE	GS	CG	CG (ee)	GS	CG	CG	CG	CE (a-8)
Florida	A	CE (b)	N.A.	A	A (ff)	GS	A	A	GS	CE
Georgia	CE	CE	CE	A	A	B	A	GS	G	(d)
Hawaii	CS	AG	GS	CS	(gg)	GS	CS	GS	CS	CS
Idaho	GS (a-6)	GS	GS	GS	...	B	B	GS	...	CE (a-14)
Illinois	GS (a-6)	GS	GS	GS	GS (a-45)	GS	GS (a-35)	GS (a-6)	...	SL (a-8)
Indiana	G	G	G	G	A	G	A	G	...	G
Iowa	A	GS	GS	...	A	GS	A	A	...	...
Kansas	C	SE	GS	B	C (hh)	GS	CS	C	...	L
Kentucky	G	G	G	...	CG	G	CG	G	G	CE
Louisiana	A	CE	GS	...	GS	GS	LGS	B	CS	CL
Maine	C	GLS	GLS	C	(a-45)	GLS	(a-35)	C	G	N.A.
Maryland	A	GS	GS	A	A (ii)	GS	A	A	GS	CE
Massachusetts	C	G	G	G	CG (jj)	CG	CG	CG	G	CE
Michigan	GS	GS	GS (a-12)	CS	CS	GS	CS	GS	...	CL
Minnesota	GS	A	GS	A	GS (u)	GS	A	GS	N.A	CE (a-8)
Mississippi	BS	SE	...	...	B	GS (a-23)	GS	B	A	CE (a-8)
Missouri	A	GS	GS	A	A	GS	A	G	...	CE (a-8)
Montana	A	GS	GS	CP	CP	GS	CP	CP	G	L
Nebraska	A	GS	GS	A	A	GS	B	A	GS	CE (a-8)
Nevada	G	A	G	...	GD	G	...	G	...	...
New Hampshire	GC	GC	GC	...	AGC	GC	AGC	AGC	...	AGC (a-14)
New Jersey	A	GS	GS	A	A (kk)	A	A	GS	A	(i)
New Mexico	G	G	GS	G	G	GS	G	G	...	CE (a-8)
New York	G	GS	GS	(ll)	(mm)	GS (a-23)	GS	G	GS (a-17)	CE (a-14)
North Carolina	G	CE	CE	...	A	G	A	G	N.A.	CE (a-8)
North Dakota	G	CE	G	...	A	...	G	A	...	A(a-8)
Ohio	G	GS	A	...	(nn)	GS	A	A	LG	CE
Oklahoma	A	CE	CE	...	B	B (a-48)	B (a-48)	GS	...	...
Oregon	A	GS	SE	GS	A	GOC	B	A	...	SS
Pennsylvania	G	GS	GS	G	AG	GS	A	G	G	CE (a-8)
Rhode Island	CS	CS	AGS	CS	GB	GB	CS	CS	CS	CS
South Carolina	A	GS	GS	GS (a-32)	B (oo)	B	GS	A	AB	B
South Dakota	GS	A	GS	...	GS	GS	A	GS	...	(a-8)
Tennessee	A	G	G	A	G	G	A	G	A	SL (a-14)
Texas	B	G	B	B	B	B	B	A	G	L
Utah	GS	GS	GS	AG	AB	GS	AG	GS	CE (a-8)	CE (a-8)
Vermont	GS	GS	GS	SS	AG	GS	AG	AG	...	CE (a-8)
Virginia	GB	SL	GB	GB	GB	GB	GB	GB	GB (a-10)	SL (a-8)
Washington	GS	CE	GS	GS	N.A.	CE	B	GS	GS	N.A.
West Virginia	C	GS	GS	...	GS	GS	GS	C	GS (a-17)	LS
Wisconsin	A	GS	GS	GS	A	GS	A	GS	...	CE (a-8)
Wyoming	GS	G	A	A	A	G	GS	A	G	CE(a-8)
American Samoa	(a-49)	G	N.A.	N.A.	(a-45)	AG	GB	A	(a-12)	G
Guam	GS	GS	GS	GS	GS	GS	GS	GS	GS	CE
No. Mariana Islands	C	CS	C	B	C	GS	C	GS	G	GS
U.S. Virgin Islands	G	SE	GS	GS	GS	GS	GS	GS	G	L

(c) Department abolished 7/1/05; responsibilities transferred to office of Management and Budget, General Services and Department of State.

(d) The State Auditor is appointed by the House and approved by the Senate.

(e) Responsibilities shared between Director of Budget and Finance, (GS): Director of Human Resource Development, (GS) and the Comptroller, (GS).

(f) Vacant due to reorganization.

(g) In Maine, New Hampshire, New Jersey, Tennessee and West Virginia, the Presidents (or Speakers) of the Senate are next in line of succession to the Governorship.

In Tennessee and West Virginia, the Speaker of the Senate bears the statutory title of Lieutenant Governor. The office will be filled in New Jersey beginning with the Nov. 2009 General election.

(h) Effective January 6, 2003 the offices of State Treasurer, State Budget Director and Commerce were abolished and the duties were transferred to the Commissioner of Finance, (GS), in the Department of Finance.

(i) The auditor is a Constitutional office, but is appointed by the Senate and General Assembly in joint meeting as mandated in the New Jersey Constitution.

(j) Method not specified.

(k) Responsibilities shared between Co-Directors in Election Commission (G); appointed by the Governor, subject to approval by the Chairs of the State Republican/Democratic parties.

(l) Responsibilities shared between Secretary of the State (CE); and Deputy Assistant Secretary of State (SS).

(m) Responsibilities shared between Secretary of State (CE); and Director, Bureau of Elections (CS).

(n) Responsibilities shared between the Assistant Secretary of State (A) and the Senior Counsel for Elections (A).

(o) Responsibilities shared between Secretary of State (CE); Deputy Secretary of State for Elections, Office of Secretary of State (SS); and Chief Deputy Secretary of State, same office (A).

(p) Responsibilities shared between Secretary of State (G); and Division Director of Elections, Elections Division, Secretary of State (A).

SELECTED STATE ADMINISTRATIVE OFFICIALS: METHODS OF SELECTION — Continued

State or other jurisdiction	Pre-audit	Public library development	Public utility regulation	Purchasing	Revenue	Social services	Solid waste mgmt.	State police	Tourism	Transportation	Welfare
Alabama	CS (a-14)	B	SE	CS	G	B	CS	G	G	G	B (a-45)
Alaska	...	AG	GB	AG	GB	GB	AG	AG	AG	GB	AG
Arizona	A (a-14)	B	B	A	GS	GS	A	GS	GS	GS	GS
Arkansas	N.A.	B	A	A	A	GS	N.A.	G	GS	BS	GS
California	CE (a-14)	...	GS	(a-26)	BS	GS	G	GS	...	GS	AG
Colorado	C (a-14)	A	CS	CS	GS	GS	CS	CS	CS	GS	CS
Connecticut	CE (a-14)	CS	GB	CS	GE	GE	CS	GE	GE	GE	GE
Delaware	CE (a-8)	CG	CG	(a-26)	CG	GS (pp)	B	CG	CG	GS	CG
Florida	CE	A	L	A	GOC	GS	A	A	G	GS	A
Georgia	(d)	AB	CE	A	G	GD	A	B	A	B	A
Hawaii	CS	B	GS	GS	GS	GS	CS	...	B	GS	CS
Idaho	CE (a-14)	B	GS	A	GS	GS	...	GS	A	B	A
Illinois	CE (a-14)	SS	GS	GS (a-6)	GS	GS	GS (a-23)	GS	GS (a-12)	GS	GS
Indiana	CE	G	G	A	G	G	A	G	LG	G	G
Iowa	A	A	GS	A	GS	GS	A	A	A	GS	...
Kansas	A	GS	GS	C	GS	GS	C	GS	C	GS	C
Kentucky	G	G	G	G	G	G	AG	G	G	G	G (a-45)
Louisiana	CS	BGS	BS	CS	GS	GS	GS	GS	LGS	GS	GS
Maine	(a-14)	B	G	CS	C	GLS	CS	GLS	(a-17)	GLS	(a-45)
Maryland	A	A	GS	A	A	GS	A	GS	A	GS	GS (a-45)
Massachusetts	CE	B	G	CG	CG	CG	CG	CG	CG	G	CG
Michigan	...	CL	GS	CS	CS	GS	CS	GS	...	GS	GS (a-45)
Minnesota	CE (a-8)	N.A.	G (qq)	A	GS	GS	GS	A	A	CE (v)	GS (u)
Mississippi	CE (a-8)	B	A	A	GS	GS	A	GS	A	B	GS
Missouri	A	B	GS	A	GS	GS	A	GS	A	B	A
Montana	L	B	CE	CP	GS	GS	GS	A	CP	GS	GS (a-45)
Nebraska	A	B	B	A	GS	GS	A	GS	A	GS (a-29)	GS
Nevada	...	(rr)	G	A	G	G	...	A	GD	BG	AG
New Hampshire	AGC (a-14)	AGC	GC	CS	GC	GC	AGC	AGC	AGC	GC	AGC
New Jersey	...	...	GS	GS	A	GS	A	GS	A	GS	A
New Mexico	G (a-14)	G	CE	G	GS	...	(j)	GS	GS	GS	GS
New York	CE (a-14)	B (a-18)	GS	G (a-26)	GS	GS	GS (a-23)	G	GS (a-17)	GS	GS (a-45)
North Carolina	CE (a-8)	A	G	A	G	A	A	G	A	G	A
North Dakota	...	...	CE	A	CE	G	A	GS	G	G	GS
Ohio	GS	B	BG	A	GS	(ss)	A	GS	A	A	GS
Oklahoma	A (a-14)	B	(tt)	A	GS	GS	A	GS	A	B	GS
Oregon	A (a-10)	B	GS	A	GS	GS	B	GS	G	GS	GS
Pennsylvania	CE (a-4)	G	GS	A	GS	AG	A	GS	GB	GB	CS
Rhode Island	CS (a-14)	G	B	CS	CS	CS	CS	GB	A	B	GS
South Carolina	CE (a-14)	B	B	A	GS	GS	A	GS	GS	B	GS
South Dakota	CE	A	CE	A	GS	GS	A	A	GS	GS	(a-45)
Tennessee	A	A	SE	A	G	A	A	G	G	G	G
Texas	CE (a-14)	A	B	B	CE (a-14)	(j)	A	B	A	B	BG
Utah	AG	A	A	A	BS	GS	A	A	A	GS	AG
Vermont	AG (a-24)	AG	BG	AG	AG	AG	AG	AG	AG	GS	AG
Virginia	GB (a-14)	B	N.A.	A	GB	GB	GB (a-23)	GB	GB	GB	GB (a-45)
Washington	CE	A	GS	A	GS	GS	GS	GS	N.A.	B	GS
West Virginia	GS (a-8)	B	GS	CS	GS	C	B	GS	GS	GS (a-29)	GS
Wisconsin	A	A	GS	A	GS	A	A	A	GS	GS	A
Wyoming	CE (a-8)	A	G	A	G	GS	A	A	A	GS	GS (a-45)
American Samoa	(a-4)	(a-18)	N.A.	A	(a-4)	GB	GB	GB	(a-12)	GB (a-29)	N.A.
Guam	CE	(j)	N.A.	CS	GS	GS	GS	GS	CS	GS	GS
No. Mariana Islands	G	B	B	C	C	C	A	GS	GB	CS	A
U.S. Virgin Islands	GS	GS	G	GS	GS	GS	GS	GS	GS	GS	GS

(q) Responsibilities shared between Director of Wildlife, Director of Inland Fisheries and Director of Marine Fisheries (CS).

(r) Responsibilities shared between Director of Budget and Finance (GS) and the Comptroller (GS).

(s) Responsibilities shared between Adjutant General (GS) and Deputy Director (CS).

(t) Responsibilities shared between Director (GS), Chief of Fisheries (CS) and Chief of Wildlife (CS).

(u) Human/Social Services, Mental Health and Retardation and Welfare are under the Commissioner of Human Services (GS).

(v) The Lieutenant Governor currently serves as the agency head of the Department of Transportation.

(w) Responsibilities shared between Administrator, Division of Fisheries, Department of Conservation; Administrator, Division of Wildlife, same department (AB).

(x) Responsibilities shared between State Tax Commissioner, Department of Revenue (GS); Administrator, Budget Division (A) and the Auditor of Public Accounts (CE).

(y) Responsibilities shared between Director, Game and Parks Commission (B), Division Administrator, Wildlife Division, Game & Parks Commission (A) and Assistant Director of Fish and Wildlife (A).

(z) Responsibilities shared between Director, Division of Purchasing, Dept. of Treasury (GS), and Director, Division of Property and Management, Dept. of the Treasury (A).

(aa) Responsibilities shared between Assistant Director, Office of Budget and Management (A) and Deputy Director same office (A).

(bb) Responsibilities shared between Community and Technical (B) and Higher Education Policy Commission (B).

(cc) Responsibilities shared between Director of Mental Health (GS) and Director of Developmental Disabilities (GS).

(dd) Responsibilities shared between Commissioner of Mental Health (GE) and Commissioner of Retardation (GE).

SELECTED STATE ADMINISTRATIVE OFFICIALS: METHODS OF SELECTION — Continued

(ee) Responsibilities shared between Director, Division of Substance Abuse and Mental Health Department of Health and Social Services (CG); and Director , Division of Developmental Disabilities Services, same department (CG).

(ff) Responsibilities shared between Director, Mental Health, dept. of Children and Families (A) and Director, Substance Abuse, Dept of Children and Families (A).

(gg) Responsibilities shared between Deputy Director of Mental Health (G) and Deputy Director of Retardation (G).

(hh) Responsibilities shared between Director of Mental Health (C) and Director of Community Support (C).

(ii) Responsibilities shared between Director, Mental Hygiene Administration (A); and Director, Developmental Disabilities Administration, Department of Health and Mental Hygiene (A).

(jj) Responsibilities shared between Commissioner, Department of Mental Retardation (CG); and Commissioner, Department of Mental Health, Executive Office of Human Services (CG).

(kk) Responsibilities shared between Director, Division of Mental Health Services, Dept of Human Services (A) and Director, Division of Developmental Disabilities, Dept. of Human Services (A).

(ll) Responsibilities shared between Secretary of State (GS) and Commissioner of State Education Department (B).

(mm) Responsibilities shared between Acting Commissioner, Office of Mental Health, and Commissioner, Office of Mental Retardation and Developmental Disabilities, both (GS).

(nn) Responsibilities shared between Director, Dept. of Mental Retardation and Developmental Disabilities (GS) and Acting Director, Department of Mental Health (GS).

(oo) Responsibilities shared between Director of Disabilities and Special Needs (B) and Director of Mental Health (B).

(pp) Responsibilities shared between Secretary of Health and Social Services (GS) ; and Secretary , Department of Services of Children, Youth and their Families (GS).

(qq) Responsibilities shared between the five Public Utility Commissioners (G).

(rr) Responsibilities shared between Director, Dept. of Cultural Affairs (G) and Division Administrator of Library and Archives (A).

(ss) Responsibilities shared between Director, OH Dept. of Job and Family Services (GS), Superintendent of Dept. of Education (B), Executive Director of Rehabilitation Commission (B), Director of Depts. Aging (GS).

(tt) Responsibilities shared between General Administrator Public Utility Division, Corporation Commission (B); and 3 Commissioners, Corporation Commission (CE).

Table 4.11
SELECTED STATE ADMINISTRATIVE OFFICIALS: ANNUAL SALARIES BY REGION

State or other jurisdiction	Governor	Lieutenant governor	Secretary of state	Attorney general	Treasurer	Adjutant general	Administration	Agriculture	Auditor	Banking
Eastern Region										
Connecticut	$150,000	$110,000	$110,000	$110,000	$110,000	$153,281	$156,347	$113,300	(c)	$121,533
Delaware	132,500	75,500	123,100	140,200	109,300	117,500	...	114,800	104,600	107,400
Maine	70,000	(d)	71,302	90,438	71,032	100,672	100,672	96,803	83,845	94,661
Massachusetts	140,535	124,920	124,920	127,523	120,000	136,184	150,000	85,000	124,920	116,230
New Hampshire	108,990	(d)	94,584	105,396	94,584	94,584	105,396	89,388	...	94,584
New Jersey	175,000(e)	(d)	141,000	141,000	141,000	141,000	...	141,000	132,000	141,000
New York	179,000	151,500	120,800	151,500	124,811	120,800	...	120,800	151,500	127,000
Pennsylvania	164,396	138,091	118,366	136,778	136,778	118,366	142,358	118,366	136,778	118,366
Rhode Island	117,817	99,214	99,214	105,416	99,214	94,769	110,321	75,919	161,537	86,539
Vermont	143,957	61,110	91,291	109,283	91,291	84,573	130,291	110,469	91,291	97,000
Regional average	138,220	76,034	109,458	121,753	109,801	116,173	89,539	106,585	114,555	110,431
Midwestern Region										
Illinois	155,600	119,000	137,300	137,300	119,000	102,400	124,800	116,900	116,200	124,800
Indiana	95,000	76,000	66,000	79,400	66,000	106,723	96,915	102,004	66,000	93,210
Iowa	130,000	103,212	103,212	123,669	103,212	129,720	137,061	103,212	103,212	102,119
Kansas	105,889	29,950	82,260	94,597	82,260	96,917	104,027	98,385	...	84,909
Michigan	177,000	123,900	124,900	124,900	174,204	139,118	129,842	129,842	148,135	112,199
Minnesota	120,303	78,197	90,227	114,288	(f)	139,190	108,388	108,388	102,257	87,466
Nebraska	105,000	75,000	85,000	95,000	85,000	86,399	88,001	93,055	85,000	90,395
North Dakota	92,483	71,797	73,568	79,984	69,477	136,188	...	75,576	73,568	82,500
Ohio	144,830	142,500	106,990	106,990	106,990	108,929	125,000	111,972	106,990	100,484
South Dakota	105,544	16,343(g)	73,865	92,307	73,865	95,000	88,000	108,871	92,700	94,015
Wisconsin	137,092	72,394	65,079	133,033	65,079	100,769	130,000	113,318	115,788	98,088
Regional average	124,431	82,572	91,673	107,406	95,770	112,850	102,912	105,593	91,805	97,290
Southern Region										
Alabama	112,895	48,384	79,580	155,828	79,580	84,979	84,962	71,003	79,580	146,916
Arkansas	80,848	39,075	50,529	67,373	50,529	97,872	129,623	97,334	50,529	115,908
Florida	132,932	127,399	120,000	131,604	131,604	139,180	120,000	131,604	147,732	(a-4)
Georgia	135,281	88,941	120,036	133,778	126,500	153,616	140,000	118,016	146,726	128,700
Kentucky	137,506	101,596	101,596	101,596	101,596	131,105	(h)	101,596	101,596	94,500
Louisiana	95,000	85,008	85,000	85,000	85,000	159,266	193,170	85,000	124,800	108,057
Maryland	150,000	141,667	66,024(b)	125,000	125,000	95,767(b)	103,033(b)	103,033(b)	...	54,301(b)
Mississippi	122,160	60,000	90,000	108,960	90,000	121,201	128,845	90,000	90,000	128,679
Missouri	120,087	77,184	96,455	104,332	96,455	84,939	116,850	100,920	96,455	...
North Carolina	130,629	115,289	115,289	115,289	115,289	97,003	112,637	115,289	115,289	115,289
Oklahoma	140,000	109,250	94,500	126,500	94,839	146,228	80,451	78,100	109,250	137,239
South Carolina	106,078	46,545	92,007	92,007	92,007	92,007	150,458	92,007	N.A.	91,843
Tennessee	85,000	54,372(d)	143,292	150,000	143,292	100,944	143,292	100,944	143,292	100,956
Texas	115,345	115,345	117,516	125,000	(a-14)	105,000	N.A.	92,217	180,000	136,191
Virginia	175,000	36,321	146,916	150,000	128,371	126,830	146,916	N.A.	153,757	132,192
West Virginia	95,000	(d)	75,000	85,000	75,000	75,000	95,000	75,000	75,000	65,000
Regional average	120,860	76,857	99,296	116,079	103,754	113,184	110,685	90,754	100,875	105,461
Western Region										
Alaska	125,000	100,000	(a-1)	122,640	102,480	127,236	122,640	85,716	87,800	99,036
Arizona	95,000	(a-2)	70,000	90,000	70,000	104,825	141,650	99,282	124,732	110,650
California	206,500(i)	154,875	154,875	175,525	165,200	181,221	...	142,582	142,582	133,732
Colorado	90,000	68,500	68,500	80,000	68,500	139,092	140,000	140,004	119,064	105,588
Hawaii	112,000	100,000	(a-1)	109,242	(a-10)	181,525	(j)	93,636	104,040	88,587
Idaho	105,560	27,820	85,800	95,160	85,800	126,173	100,006	90,002	...	94,994
Montana	96,462	74,173	76,539	85,762	(a-10)	90,345	86,870	90,345	79,642	90,912
Nevada	141,000	60,000	97,000	133,000	97,000	110,323	120,401	101,306	...	92,290
New Mexico	110,000	85,000	85,000	95,000	85,000	106,038	103,938	131,560	85,000	84,999
Oregon	93,600	(a-2)	72,000	77,200	72,000	134,748	135,216	111,312	100,980	...
Utah	104,100	100,000	(a-1)	98,895	81,000	90,598	99,076	90,598	83,500	104,609
Washington	150,995	78,930	105,811	137,268	105,811	136,186	116,848	118,680	105,811	116,840
Wyoming	105,000	(a-2)	92,000	125,000	92,000	108,420	104,472	88,848	92,000	86,172
Regional Average	118,094	81,869	91,425	109,592	93,783	125,902	97,778	106,452	102,286	100,701
Regional Average without California	111,293	76,253	86,544	104,520	88,289	121,647	105,300	103,672	83,450	90,414
Guam	90,000	85,000	...	90,000	49,026	N.A.	88,915	60,850	100,000	74,096
No. Mariana Islands	70,000	65,000	...	80,000	40,800(b)	...	54,000	40,800(b)	80,000	40,800(b)
U.S. Virgin Islands	80,000	75,000	(a-1)	76,500	76,500	85,000	76,500	76,500	76,500	75,000

Sources: The Council of State Governments' survey of state personnel agencies, February 2007.

Note: The chief administrative officials responsible for each function were determined from information given by the states for the same function as listed in State

Administrative Officials Classified by Function, 2006, published by The Council of State Governments.

Key:
N.A. — Not available.
... — No specific chief administrative official or agency in charge of function.
(a) Chief administrative official or agency in charge of function:
(a-1) Lieutenant governor.
(a-2) Secretary of state.

SELECTED OFFICIALS: ANNUAL SALARIES — Continued

State or other jurisdiction	Budget	Civil rights	Commerce	Community affairs	Comptroller	Consumer affairs	Corrections	Economic development	Education	Election administration
Eastern Region										
Connecticut	$153,787	$120,000	$135,457	$154,500	$110,000	$120,000	$157,880	$135,457	$142,175	$125,179
Delaware	142,300	71,400	(a-2)	...	142,300	103,767	142,300	123,100	154,700	78,000
Maine	88,587	68,058	(a-17)	(a-17)	88,587	94,661	100,672	100,672	100,672	78,021
Massachusetts	125,000	103,560	150,000	140,000	148,720	125,000	140,064	150,000	191,857	124,920
New Hampshire	105,396	72,072	102,365	...	89,388	82,774	105,396	81,984	89,388	(a-2)
New Jersey	125,950	117,672	141,000	141,000	125,950	104,397(k)	141,000	160,000	141,000	96,329(k)
New York	175,680	109,800	120,800	120,800	151,500	101,600	136,000	120,800	170,165	154,511
Pennsylvania	158,514	117,223	124,940	110,377	128,627	104,548	131,517	124,940	131,517	82,367
Rhode Island	122,560	66,039	(a-17)	N.A.	106,551	(a-3)	118,914	101,598	135,516	78,727
Vermont	(a-24)	90,480	102,960	80,080	(a-24)	90,480	99,528	85,779	121,763	(a-2)
Regional average	128,834	93,630	120,289	84,743	118,219	103,264	127,327	118,433	137,875	100,393
Midwestern Region										
Illinois	110,000	101,400	124,800	(a-12)	119,000	(a-3)	131,700	(a-12)	142,500	113,616
Indiana	112,203	102,004	124,500	86,716	(a-8)	83,000	104,052	(a-12)	79,400	N.A.
Iowa	136,500	91,860	102,119	88,442	...	121,490	121,867	137,441	132,065	91,860
Kansas	(a-10)	73,148	97,148	86,307	81,600	74,500	113,512	(a-12)	150,000	(l)
Michigan	135,252	129,842	135,000	...	116,591	...	...	135,252	168,300	(m)
Minnesota	(f)	108,388	108,388	(a-17)	(f)	82,434	108,388	108,388	108,388	(a-2)
Nebraska	118,000	67,600	100,000	85,708	102,908	(a-3)	110,072	100,000	159,567	68,168
North Dakota	90,852	64,272	122,724	...	90,852	77,160	78,768	N.A.	83,748	29,328
Ohio	126,401	96,408	115,689	95,014	126,401	92,019	119,454	142,500	217,838	106,990
South Dakota	(a-24)	N.A.	(a-44)	(a-48)	(a-40)	60,000	105,000	(a-48)	151,868	52,000
Wisconsin	112,132	91,649	109,244	...	103,648	80,839	120,851	(n)	109,587	107,689
Regional average	115,796	84,234	112,965	72,852	89,932	82,158	113,538	93,263	136,660	77,691
Southern Region										
Alabama	165,480	...	144,690	84,962	132,358	76,793	115,500	(a-13)	178,553	56,938
Arkansas	107,088	...	(a-17)	N.A.	92,341	91,982	124,119	116,364	208,598	(a-2)
Florida	132,000	131,741	119,740	120,000	(a-4)	95,741	128,750	119,740	254,925	95,000
Georgia	132,600	102,138	150,000	141,831	N.A.	110,400	128,993	(a-12)	117,333	N.A.
Kentucky	155,000	97,000	130,038	115,500	103,260	84,415	101,530	225,000	175,000	107,230
Louisiana	145,600	73,902	232,544	N.A.	193,170	85,000	N.A.	232,544	214,386	100,000
Maryland	119,352(b)	82,814(b)	119,352(b)	...	125,000	75,195(b)	89,042(b)	119,352(b)	185,000	77,047(b)
Mississippi	(a-10)	...	90,000	69,458	(a-10)	77,000	119,428	5,000(o)	292,500	(p)
Missouri	95,747	70,999	100,913	N.A.	89,819	(a-3)	100,926	100,913	160,296	72,816
North Carolina	(a-24)	71,400	112,637	89,251	143,477	N.A.	112,637	110,300	115,289	104,630
Oklahoma	71,000	64,386	100,800	N.A.	87,885	61,337	126,009	100,800	118,450	79,860
South Carolina	119,515	91,947	152,000	N.A.	92,007	101,295	139,474	(a-12)	92,007	84,375
Tennessee	103512	80,892	107,436	(a-17)	143,292	67,752	111,240	107,436	107,436	105,700
Texas	156,646	80,674	...	117,516	125,000	102,267	165,000	...	164,748	(q)
Virginia	145,796	70,279	146,916	113,860	128,819	78,001	141,655	220,000	184,525	82,904
West Virginia	81,036	50,000	90,000	85,908	(a-8)	104,406	80,000	(a-13)	175,000	(a-2)
Regional average	125,977	66,761	119,589	65,358	111,992	82,245	111,519	118,555	170,603	81,722
Western Region										
Alaska	112,008	114,744	122,640	(a-12)	99,036	(a-12)	122,640	(a-12)	127,236	85,716
Arizona	109,541	116,199	126,741	116,199	106,000	116,199	139,962	(a-12)	85,000	(a-2)
California	(a-24)	...	...	117,997	165,200	133,732	225,000	...	148,750	118,404
Colorado	150,000	105,588	N.A.	131,988	118,800	(a-3)	140,004	N.A.	171,032	92,436
Hawaii	104,040	92,172	104,040	...	104,040	88,587	93,636	98,838	150,000	79,866
Idaho	94,307	67,704	99,653	62,400	85,800	95,160	122,450	62,400	85,800	85,800
Montana	95,264	65,521	90,345	77,035	79,830	62,192	91,701	96,461	89,472	51,667
Nevada	(a-10)	82,742	120,401	...	97,000	92,290	120,401	110,323	116,688	(r)
New Mexico	109,998	80,812	136,490	74,158	94,746	90,854	105,864	136,490	144,893	66,136
Oregon	100,980	79,176	122,592	N.A.	111,312	116,808	135,216	122,592	72,000	105,960
Utah	106,196	75,544	90,598	97,593	99,076	90,598	96,424	104,588	177,480	67,756
Washington	N.A.	108,000	137,160	137,160	158,000	(a-3)	137,160	137,160	107,978	88,392
Wyoming	101,904	63,108	151,716	151,716	(a-8)	151,716	118,584	(a-12)	92,000	72,444
Regional average	103,632	80,870	100,183	83,760	108,526	106,003	126,849	97,688	120,641	83,650
Regional average without California	100,387	87,609	108,531	80,907	103,803	103,693	118,670	105,829	118,298	80,754
Guam	88,915	88,915	75,208	...	75,576	51,662	67,150	74,096	125,000	61,939
No. Mariana Islands	54,000	49,000	52,000	52,000	40,800(b)	52,000	40,800(b)	45,000	80,000	53,000
U.S. Virgin Islands	76,500	60,000	76,500	(s)	76,500	76,500	76,500	85,000	76,500	76,500

(a-3) Attorney general.
(a-4) Treasurer.
(a-5) Adjutant general
(a-6) Administration.
(a-7) Agriculture
(a-8) Auditor
(a-9) Banking

(a-10) Budget.
(a-11) Civil rights
(a-12) Commerce.
(a-13) Community affairs.
(a-14) Comptroller.
(a-15) Consumer affairs.
(a-16) Corrections

SELECTED OFFICIALS: ANNUAL SALARIES — Continued

State or other jurisdiction	Emergency management	Employment services	Energy	Environmental protection	Finance	Fish & widlife	General services	Health	Higher education	Highways
Eastern Region										
Connecticut	$127,308	$121,200	$114,191	$131,068	$154,500	(t)	$156,347	$153,281	$164,800	$146,000
Delaware	79,300	92,500	55,040	(a-35)	142,300	94,900	82,600	158,200	90,293	(a-49)
Maine	N.A.	81,224	88,587	96,803	(a-10)	96,803	81,411	142,771	N.A.	(a-49)
Massachusetts	92,000	115,507	106,255	126,076	150,000	77,647	113,834	132,676	180,000	116,698
New Hampshire	75,857	94,584	75,857	102,365	(a-10)	89,388	(a-6)	81,984	70,867	(a-49)
New Jersey	132,300	120,000	110,556	141,000	120,000	94,442(k)	(u)	141,000	127,943	120,000
New York	128,570	127,000	120,800	136,000	151,500	136,000	136,000	136,000	170,165	136,000
Pennsylvania	117,321	118,886	117,634	131,517	158,514	112,157	124,940	131,517	115,013	126,240
Rhode Island	74,708	108,460	98,781	108,460	(a-10)	60,974	N.A.	131,975	134,639	(a-49)
Vermont	76,190	94,994	97,240	85,779	90,563	80,080	94,058	100,000	. . .	(a-49)
Regional average	90,355	107,436	98,494	118,217	129,601	96,324	100,382	130,940	105,372	122,377
Midwestern Region										
Illinois	101,400	124,800	(a-12)	116,900	(a-10)	(a-35)	(a-6)	131,700	191,100	(a-49)
Indiana	(v)	99,200	76,518	97,929	(a-10)	66,027	(a-6)	(v)	144,939	(a-49)
Iowa	97,028	98,430	. . .	110,968	110,968	110,968	110,968	122,065	. . .	141,773
Kansas	(w)	(a-32)	62,232	93,172	. . .	52,312	(a-6)	161,968	172,000	(a-49)
Michigan	119,802	110,531	. . .	140,452	(a-10)	(x)	. . .	135,252	103,655	(a-49)
Minnesota	108,388	97,906	108,388	108,388	108,388(f)	101,164	(a-6)	108,388	285,961	(a-1)
Nebraska	75,966	84,155	69,270	104,716	(y)	(z)	80,796	120,001	152,370	113,000
North Dakota	66,144	78,408	83,556	77,988	90,852	90,000	104,603	143,424	205,000	(a-49)
Ohio	97,489	141,980	83,678	125,008	(aa)	94,702	101,566	147,451(bb)	224,480(bb)	124,758
South Dakota	65,656	(a-37)	(a-48)	(a-35)	120,000	108,000	(a-6)	108,871	201,151	(cc)
Wisconsin	94,403	97,159	92,599	116,548	112,132	116,548	130,000	120,000	332,940	116,548
Regional average	82,930	102,843	75,185	109,176	101,104	95,731	95,460	118,102	183,054	111,990
Southern Region										
Alabama	139,125	91,265	91,265	134,609	84,962	105,934	80,647	217,412	167,904	84,962
Arkansas	81,088	122,594	95,110	108,486	(a-14)	110,552	110,101	183,232	131,310	(a-49)
Florida	116,220	120,000	65,729	123,295	(a-4)	129,430	120,000	120,000	N.A.	138,767
Georgia	N.A.	89,626	113,060	128,993	126,513	102,583	95,991	156,060	425,000	(a-49)
Kentucky	88,600	N.A.	95,000	N.A.	130,038	122,358	N.A.	151,878	297,150	120,555
Louisiana	N.A.	100,048	104,187	129,168	(a-6)	116,230	(a-6)	224,973	264,448	(a-49)
Maryland	82,814(b)	82,814(b)	70,492(b)	110,876(b)	119,352(b)	N.A.	(a-6)	119,352(b)	110,876(b)	153,650
Mississippi	93,581	117,505	87,811	109,293	(a-6)	108,114	. . .	213,313	325,000	(a-49)
Missouri	76,827	97,893	. . .	89,648	93,930	(dd)	85,675	107,353	135,000	(a-49)
North Carolina	91,038	133,161	86,699	96,482	133,943	108,416	112,637	160,477	425,000	145,000
Oklahoma	75,505	88,752	N.A.	93,922	98,000	116,536	80,451	191,205	367,00	(a-49)
South Carolina	93,524	125,330	99,444	151,942	150,458	121,380	105,000	136,441	N.A.	(a-49)
Tennessee	87,936	119,412	100,248	100,944	143,292	100,944	100,944	149,064	178,400	100,944
Texas	128,132	131,000	. . .	132,000	(a-14)	130,000	115,000	175,000	150,000	(a-49)
Virginia	110,240	119,943	78,241	144,440	146,916	103,289	135,799	168,983	184,525	182,000
West Virginia	65,000	75,000	90,000	(a-22)	(a-6)	74,304	75,000	95,000	(ee)	(a-49)
Regional average	83,102	100,896	73,580	109,006	126,915	102,691	94,591	160,609	195,598	128,336
Western Region										
Alaska	92,136	92,136	168,000	122,640	102,744	109,824	. . .	127,236	300,000	113,940
Arizona	88,044	106,798	. . .	129,284	(a-14)	140,438	111,650	128,775	160,000	117,500
California	117,997	133,732	127,308	142,582	142,582	133,732	133,732	133,732	(ff)	(a-49)
Colorado	124,800	127,200	120,000	N.A.	N.A.	130,188	140,000	139,992	130,008	N.A.
Hawaii	81,463	71,028(b)	77,640(b)	71,028(b)	(gg)	71,028(b)	(a-14)	104,040	360,000	77,640(b)
Idaho	59,966	99,653	73,798	90,002	94,994	117,000	. . .	130,000	108,713	(a-49)
Montana	73,683	88,378	83,718	90,345	79,830	90,345	82,982	(a-45)	196,778	(a-49)
Nevada	82,742	120,401	63,648	116,688	(a-14)	110,323	. . .	110,323	23,600(hh)	(a-49)
New Mexico	110,240	100,000	106,766	104,998	119,999	99,736	103,938	117,520	157,499	110,240
Oregon	75,504	122,592	100,980	105,960	(a-4)	103,884	(a-6)	145,332	219,504	100,980
Utah	59,174	115,278	79,762	105,361	99,076	104,609	99,076	178,649	113,838	(a-49)
Washington	119,892	137,160	N.A.	137,160	158,000	137,160	(a-6)	137,160	N.A.	(a-49)
Wyoming	79,000	102,000	65,256	105,000	(a-8)	130,000	76,000	181,224	113,736	(a-49)
Regional average	89,588	108,950	82,067	101,619	97,559	113,713	84,883	132,641	158,166	107,070
Regional average without California	87,220	106,885	78,297	98,206	93,807	112,045	80,813	132,550	156,973	104,848
Guam	68,152	73,020	55,303	60,850	88,915	60,850	54,475	74,096	174,787	88,915
No. Mariana Islands	45,000	40,800(b)	45,000	58,000	54,000	40,800(b)	54,000	80,000	80,000	40,800(b)
U.S. Virgin Islands	71,250	76,500	69,350	76,500	76,500	76,500	76,500	76,500	76,500	65,000

(a-17) Economic development.
(a-18) Education (chief state school officer).
(a-19) Election administration
(a-20) Emergency administration
(a-21) Employment Services
(a-22) Energy.
(a-23) Environmental protection.

(a-24) Finance.
(a-25) Fish and wildlife
(a-26) General services.
(a-27) Health
(a-28) Higher education
(a-29) Highways.
(a-30) Information systems

SELECTED OFFICIALS: ANNUAL SALARIES — Continued

State or other jurisdiction	Information systems	Insurance	Labor	Licensing	Mental health & retardation	Natural resources	Parks & recreation	Personnel	Planning	Post audit
Eastern Region										
Connecticut	$149,350	$124,836	$135,456	$98,929	(ii)	$130,194	$120,375	$156,347	$114,191	(a-8)
Delaware	154,700	104,600	114,800	94,100	(jj)	123,100	95,600	108,099	91,613	(a-8)
Maine	94,661	94,661	96,803	82,971	(a-45)	100,672	(a-35)	79,789	88,587	N.A.
Massachusetts	112,002	122,135	115,000	103,453	(kk)	150,000	102,677	121,087	150,000	124,920
New Hampshire	100,814	94,584	89,128	...	89,388	102,365	68,775	89,388	...	(a-14)
New Jersey	123,000	141,000	141,000	104,397(k)	(ll)	120,000	115,051	141,000	100,303	132,000
New York	149,350	127,000	127,000	145,482(mm)	136,000	136,000	127,000	120,800	120,800	151,500
Pennsylvania	126,045	118,366	131,517	105,018	117,516	124,940	109,751	128,979	134,964	(a-8)
Rhode Island	122,855	86,359	(a-21)	(nn)	126,582	75,919	(a-35)	106,551	98,543	N.A.
Vermont	85,093	97,000	94,994	74,963	100,000	104,000	80,080	86,320	...	(a-8)
Regional average	121,787	111,054	115,416	91,457	123,069	116,719	99,590	113,836	89,900	98,956
Midwestern Region										
Illinois	(a-6)	(a-9)	108,800	(a-9)	(a-45)	116,900	(a-35)	(a-6)	...	(a-8)
Indiana	102,004	90,129	94,867	84,162	96,915	94,000	73,456	91,806	...	90,792
Iowa	145,414	98,532	96,429	...	121,867	100,000	96,200	110,968	...	...
Kansas	102,829	82,260	98,372	71,437	(oo)	101,560	57,741	88,302	...	107,926
Michigan	146,017	112,199	135,000	116,591	122,198	135,252	109,315	146,143	...	148,135
Minnesota	122,400	91,183	108,388	82,079	(a-45)	108,388	108,367	108,388	N.A.	(a-8)
Nebraska	114,858	92,250	85,151	91,401	100,154	102,000	96,524	90,715	88,001	(a-8)
North Dakota	97,764	73,568	64,272	...	75,588	...	75,172	75,852	...	78,660
Ohio	125,008	128,564	97,468	(pp)	(qq)	128,033	97,177	106,953(bb)	124,009	106,990
South Dakota	129,192	78,250	105,965	N.A	97,580	108,871	78,231	100,328	N.A.	(a-8)
Wisconsin	99,314	112,000	95,413	94,158	103,980	116,548	69,948	97,152	...	(a-8)
Regional average	119,055	98,521	99,102	60,421	105,186	101,050	89,003	103,445	19,274	94,950
Southern Region										
Alabama	146,088	84,962	84,962	...	135,636	84,962	86,810	142,471	(a-13)	186,467
Arkansas	117,559	108,963	107,322	...	100,699	92,987	101,771	92,341	...	134,030
Florida	112,000	(a-4)	N.A.	104,030	(rr)	123,295	109,279	100,000	120,000	(a-4)
Georgia	N.A.	116,888	118,029	N.A.	124,431	128,993	108,175	145,000	132600	(a-8)
Kentucky	105,000	95,000	107,448	...	105,000	107,447	114,446	130,038	130,038	101,596
Louisiana	160,000	85,000	125,008	...	224,973	121,551	105,423	101,733	79,602	N.A.
Maryland	103,033(b)	103,033(b)	103,033(b)	82,814(b)	(b)	110,876(b)	66,024(b)	95,767(b)	103,033(b)	N.A.
Mississippi	157,162	90,000	...	...	147,643	109,293	108,114	105,160	78,885	(a-8)
Missouri	113,717	100,988	100,926	76,960	97,896	100,926	89,648	85,675	...	(a-8)
North Carolina	143,390	115,289	115,289	...	126,375	112,637	91,006	112,637	N.A.	(a-8)
Oklahoma	99,225	121,250	100,050	...	133,455	86,310	86,310	80,955	...	...
South Carolina	132,870	137,136	116,796	116,797	(ss)	121,380	112,504	108,651	N.A.	95,727
Tennessee	131,124	100,944	119,412	62,064	107,436	100,944	79,152	100,944	N.A.	(a-14)
Texas	N.A.	163,800	135,000	112,500	141,000	132,000	130,000	N.A.	156,646	180,000
Virginia	146,916	132,192	120,922	122,235	182,000	146,916	123,081	132,649	145,796	153,757
West Virginia	109,999	92,500	65,000	...	95,000	75,000	74,964	60,000	(a-13)	81,400
Regional average	111,130	111,222	94,950	42,338	131,096	109,720	99,169	106,268	69,842	103,584
Western Region										
Alaska	99,036	99,036	122,640	99,036	95,724	122,640	85,716	88,536	...	95,448
Arizona	111,677	115,650	142,440	...	91,440	116,100	124,703	111,486	109,541	...
California	127,572	165,200	142,582	133,732	(tt)	142,582	133,732	133,732	...	...
Colorado	120,000	105,000	127,200	140,004	105,588	N.A.	130,188	140,000	150,000	119,064
Hawaii	71,028(b)	90,931	98,838	67,656(b)	(uu)	98,838	71,028(b)	93,636	75,372(b)	71,028(b)
Idaho	100,006	90,002	99,653	65,000	...	93,288	91,915	86,008	...	(a-14)
Montana	104,000	79,642	90,345	75,442	94,835	90,345	63,003	79,445	96,461	123,615
Nevada	116,688	110,323	92,290	...	116,688	120,401	...	101,306	...	...
New Mexico	101,982	91,520	100,000	102,544	85,467	106,766	88,820	94,494	...	85,000
Oregon	N.A.	116,808	72,000	79,176	122,592	105,960	105,960	111,312	...	100,980
Utah	115,696	90,598	88,546	88,886	93,856	105,360	96,424	105,360	(a-10)	83,500
Washington	137,160	105,811	135,000	116,840	N.A.	107,978	116,840	137,160	(a-24)	N.A.
Wyoming	94,000	89,000	77,496	63,252	140,748	39,156	86,184	87,540	90,576	(a-8)
Regional average	99,911	103,809	106,848	79,351	90,491	96,109	91,886	105,386	60,471	65,880
Regional average without California	97,606	98,693	103,871	74,820	86,888	92,236	88,398	103,024	65,512	71,370
Guam	88,915	74,096	73,020	74,096	67,150	60,850	60,850	88,915	75,208	100,000
No. Mariana Islands	45,000	40,800(b)	45,000	45,360	40,800(b)	52,000	40,800(b)	60,000	45,000	80,000
U.S. Virgin Islands	71,250	75,000	76,500	76500	70,000	76,500	76,500	76,500	76,500	55,000

(a-31) Insurance
(a-32) Labor.
(a-33) Licensing
(a-34) Mental Health
(a-35) Natural resources.
(a-36) Parks and recreation.
(a-37) Personnel.

(a-38) Planning
(a-39) Post audit.
(a-40) Pre-audit.
(a-41) Public library development
(a-42) Public utility regulation.
(a-43) Purchasing.
(a-44) Revenue.

SELECTED OFFICIALS: ANNUAL SALARIES — Continued

State or other jurisdiction	Pre-audit	Public library development	Public utility regulation	Purchasing	Revenue	Social services	Solid waste management	State police	Tourism	Transportation	Welfare
Eastern Region											
Connecticut	(a-14)	$107,007	$153,787	$107,547	$157,880	$146,497	$116,565	$149,350	$93,843	$146,000	$146,497
Delaware	(a-8)	80,600	92,500	(a-26)	120,200	(vv)	155,000	145,000	62,118	133,200	110,900
Maine	(a-14)	85,467	109,949	70,054	79,934	102,024	70,054	94,661	(a-17)	100,672	(a-45)
Massachusetts	124,920	100,746	115,360	113,834	140,052	136,053	126,076	144,550	106,000	150,000	133,870
New Hampshire	(a-14)	81,984	99,778	62,712	105,396	108,990	89,388	94,584	81,984	105,396	94,024
New Jersey		...	141,000	101,325(k)	109,573	(ww)	100,554	132,300	98,615	141,000	120,000
New York	151,500	170,165	127,000	136,000	127,000	136,000	136,000	121,860	120,800	136,000	136,000
Pennsylvania	(a-4)	101,575	127,440	109,321	124,940	N.A.	100,421	124,940	110,377	131,517	131,517
Rhode Island	(a-14)	94,541	98,781	118,559	122,560	110,321	75,919	124,114	N.A.	(a-29)	86,768
Vermont	(a-24)	86,362	117,853	94,058	90,147	101,712	85,779	107,952	79,997	117,000	101,712
Regional average	100,289	81,845	118,345	99,601	117,768	111,780	105,576	123,931	85,441	128,335	116,331
Midwestern Region											
Illinois	(a-14)	89,292	117,500	(a-6)	124,000	131,700	N.A.	116,300	(a-12)	131,700	124,800
Indiana	66,000	85,000	104,500	56,101	97,929	110,175	85,254	120,179	78,546	102,189	110,175
Iowa	84,573	113,422	112,196	96,429	140,000	145,430	96,429	118,000	94,078	136,677	...
Kansas	73,611	89,913	87,437	80,000	98,372	102,701	83,179	98,372	79,351	98,372	71,639
Michigan	...	127,296	113,612	N.A.	116,591	130,050	122,198	129,842	...	140,000	(a-45)
Minnesota	(a-8)	N.A.	(xx)	97,906	108,388	108,388	108,388	100,057	108,388	(a-1)	(a-45)
Nebraska	102,908	85,981	101,080	80,796	126,506	120,001	61,248	97,839	67,113	113,000	120,001
North Dakota	...	...	75,576	61,080	79,845	115,248	62,340	75,000	78,408	102,000	115,248
Ohio	126,401	N.A.	109,595	101,566	126,401	(yy)	92,746	128,544	66,955	82,180	141,980
South Dakota	73,865	65,150	86,144	59,566	103,000	107,965	79,030	83,357	125,995	97,626	(a-45)
Wisconsin	(a-8)	104,404	112,000	88,606	115,000	120,000	101,468	99,278	(zz)	116,548	91,772
Regional average	78,582	69,133	100,735	76,986	112,367	111,736	81,116	106,070	82,409	108,954	102,002
Southern Region											
Alabama	(a-14)	95,785	96,609	122,880	84,962	155,052	98,395	84,962	84,962	(a-29)	(a-45)
Arkansas	N.A.	91,384	101,328	92,341	115,388	100,698	N.A.	98,940	79,222	139,620	(a-45)
Florida	(a-4)	95,545	132,464	97,531	132,393	134,680	92,700	129,760	119,940	(aaa)	113,300
Georgia	(a-8)	123,355	113,060	140,000	134,132	165,000	100,767	128,993	112,827	183,735	129,540
Kentucky	130,038	95,000	116,660	89,250	110,250	N.A.	103,267	100,494	115,093	134,520	N.A.
Louisiana	97,552	88,400	110,000	93,621	117,020	117,786	104,874	120,101	145,204	147,851	95,141
Maryland	89,042(b)	82,814(b)	185,000	77,047(b)	89,042(b)	110,876(b)	82,814(b)	110,876(b)	89,042(b)	119,352(b)	110,876(b)
Mississippi	(a-8)	96,000	126,100	72,317	122,561	136,798	73,042	117,384	88,922	141,087	136,798
Missouri	89,819	76,200	83,200	85,675	107,353	107,352	75,088	97,368	73,000	(a-29)	91,716
North Carolina	(a-8)	95,173	N.A.	102,595	112,637	109,669	98,130	109,869	95,173	112,637	N.A.
Oklahoma	(a-14)	77,805	(bbb)	75,285	104,055	155,000	92,793	101,030	86,310	117,705	155,000
South Carolina	(a-14)	N.A.	148,400	100,086	125,113	N.A.	151,942	112,068	112,504	N.A.	N.A.
Tennessee	102,516	105,696	107,472	67,496	100,944	100,944	84,348	107,436	100,944	100,944	100,944
Texas	(a-14)	88,500	105,000	81,808	(a-14)	160,000	N.A.	150,000	N.A.	175,000	200,000
Virginia	128,819	127,779	N.A.	123,507	131,544	137,933	144,440	140,180	160,000	146,916	137,933
West Virginia	(a-8)	72,000	80,000	94,836	92,500	69,960	74,784	80,000	70,000	92,500	95,000
Regional average	102,166	88,215	99,912	94,767	112,806	110,109	86,087	111,841	95,821	118,436	101,375
Western Region											
Alaska	...	99,036	85,716	95,724	127,236	127,236	99,036	122,640	65,220	122,640	88,824
Arizona	(a-14)	119,470	127,000	98,000	135,894	135,000	91,650	131,650	112,503	131,650	135,000
California	(a-14)	...	133,968	(a-26)	133,948	133,732	120,480	142,582	...	133,732	142,582
Colorado	(a-14)	72,000	105,588	99,876	140,000	140,391	105,588	128,388	76,000	N.A.	N.A.
Hawaii	71,028(b)	120,000	81,463	79,866	104,040	98,838	67,656(b)	...	240,000	104,040	71,028(b)
Idaho	(a-14)	87,152	85,222	N.A.	79,009	130,000	...	87,214	76,024	134,992	98,405
Montana	123,615	86,291	77,418	82,982	90,345	90,345	90,345	82,560	71,812	90,345	90,345
Nevada	...	(ccc)	116,688	92,290	120,401	120,401	(a-23)	120,401	110,323	120,401	110,323
New Mexico	94,744	70,033	N.A.	88,129	114,999	N.A.	80,926	110,240	104,998	110,240	129,085
Oregon	(a-10)	100,980	116,880	87,348	122,592	128,748	105,960	N.A.	N.A.	134,856	128,748
Utah	(a-24)	101,811	84,209	99,079	97,384	115,696	101,811	93,856	95,505	115,278	112,898
Washington	(a-4)	97,536	116,840	98,736	137,160	158,000	137,160	137,160	N.A.	162,560	(a-45)
Wyoming	(a-8)	85,644	98,256	68,316	101,448	91,464	94,260	98,256	97,908	114,300	(a-45)
Regional average	89,466	87,789	94,558	86,467	115,727	113,065	93,197	96,534	80,792	113,464	104,362
Regional average without California	83,155	95,105	91,273	82,529	114,209	111,343	90,923	92,697	87,524	111,775	101,177
Guam	100,000	55,303	N.A.	54,475	74,096	74,096	88,915	74,096	55,303	88,915	74,096
No. Mariana Islands	54,000	45,000	80,000	40,800(b)	45,000	40,800(b)	54,000	54,000	70,000	40,800(b)	52,000
U.S. Virgin Islands	76,500	53,350	54,500	76,500	76,500	76,500	76,500	76,500	76,500	65,000	76,500

(a-45) Social services.
(a-46) Solid waste management
(a-47) State police
(a-48) Tourism.
(a-49) Transportation.
(a-50) Welfare.

(b) Salary ranges, top figure in ranges follow: Hawaii: Employment Services, $105,096; Energy, $114,840, Environmental Protection, $105,096; Fish and Wildlife, $105,096; Highways, $114,840; Information Systems, $105,096; Licensing, $100,092; Parks and Recreation, $105,096; Planning, $111,504; Post-Audit, $105,096; Pre-Audit, $105,096; Solid Waste Management, $100,092; Welfare, $105,096.

SELECTED OFFICIALS: ANNUAL SALARIES — Continued

Maryland: Minimum figure in range: top of range follows: Interim Secretary of State, $106,013;Adjutant general, $127,942; Administration, $137,705; Agriculture, $137,705; Banking, $87,183; Budget, $159,632; Civil rights, $110,534; Commerce, $159,632; Consumer affairs, $120,859; Corrections, $118,903; Economic development, $159,632; Election administration, $102,787; Emergency management, $110,534; Employment services, $110,534; Energy, $113,178; Environmental protection, $148,245; Finance, $150,632; General Services, $137,705; Health, $159,632; Higher education, $148,245; Information systems, $137,705; Insurance, $137,705; Labor, $137,705; Licensing, $110,534; Mental Health, responsibilities shared between Executive director of Mental Hygiene Administration, range $138,184-$228,336 and Director of Developmental Disabilities Administration, range $89,042-$118,903;Natural resources, $148,245; Parks and recreation, $106,013; Personnel; $127,942; Planning, $137,705; Pre Audit, $118,903; Public library development, $110,534; Purchasing, $102,787; Revenue, $118,903; Social services, $148,245; Solid waste management, $110,534; Police, $148,245; Tourism, $118,903; Transportation, $159,632; Welfare, $148,245. Northern Mariana Islands: $49,266 top of range applies to the following positions: Treasurer, Banking, Comptroller, Corrections, Employment Services, Fish and Wildlife, Highways, Insurance, Mental Health and Retardation, Parks and Recreation, Purchasing, Social/Human Services, Transportation.

(c) Responsibilities shared between Kevin Johnston, $159,083 and Robert Jaekle, $159,083.

(d) In Maine, New Hampshire, New Jersey, Tennessee and West Virginia, the presidents (or speakers) of the Senate are next in line of succession to the governorship. In Tennessee and West Virginia, the speaker of the Senate bears the statutory title of lieutenant governor.

(e) Governor Corzine accepts $1 in salary.

(f) State Treasurer Position was abolished in January 2003. Functions now served by The Department of Finance, Commissioner, $108,388.

(g) Annual salary for duties as presiding officer of the Senate.

(h) Position is vacant due to reorganization.

(i) Governor Schwarzenegger waives his salary.

(j) There is no one single agency for Administration. The functions are divided amongst the Director of Budget and Finance, Director of Human Resources Development and the Comptroller.

(k) Acting salary.

(l) Responsibilities shared between Secretary of State, $82,260 and Deputy Secretary of State, $71,760.

(m) Responsibilities shared between Secretary of State, $124,900 and Bureau Director, $110,531.

(n) The salary range for this position is $65, 778 to $101,957. The person serving as acting administrator is paid $65,116

(o) Maximum salary available is $183,240; incumbent has requested a reduced salary.

(p) Responsibilities shared between Assistant Secretary of State, $81,500 and Senior Counsel for Elections, $81,500.

(q) Responsibilities shared between Secretary of State, $117,516; and Division Director, $107,796.

(r) Responsibilities shared between Secretary of State, $97,000; Deputy Secretary of State for Elections, $101,306 and Chief Deputy Secretary of State, $110,323.

(s) Responsibilities for St. Thomas, $74,400; St. Croix, $76,500; St. John, $74,400.

(t) Responsibilities shared between Director of Wildlife, $120,375, Director of Inland Fisheries, $117,329 and Director of Marine Fisheries, $124,849.

(u) Responsibilities shared between Director, Division of Purchasing, Dept. of the Treasury, $101,325 (acting salary) and Director, Division of Property and Management, Dept. of the Treasury, $117,133

(v) Contractual.

(w) Responsibilities shared between adjutant general, $96,917 and deputy director, $75,000.

(x) Responsibilities shared between Director, Dept. of Natural Resources, $135,200 and Chief, Fish, $110,531 and Chief, Wildlife, $99,606.

(y) Responsibilities shared between, State Auditor-$85,000; Director ofAdministration-$118,000 and State Tax Commissioner-$126,506.

(z) Responsibilities shared between Game & Parks Director-$96,524; Game & Parks Asst Dir-Fish & Wildlife-$76,4881; Wildlife Division Administrator-$70,533.

(aa) Responsibilities shared between Assistant Director of Budget, Payroll and Revenue Estimating, $95,014 and Deputy Director of Accounting, $110,011.

(bb) Salary of the last person in the position.

(cc) See state police, $83,357.

(dd) Responsibilities shared between Administrator, Department of Conservation, $89,424; Administration, Division of Protection, same department, $96,552.

(ee) Responsibilities shared between Community and Technical, $131,222 and Higher Education Policy Commission, $147,500.

(ff) Responsibilities shared between Chancellor of California Community Colleges, $191,976 and California Post Secondary Education Commission $153,000.

(gg) Responsibilities shared between Director of Budget and Finance, $104,040 and Comptroller, $104,040.

(hh) James Rogers, the Interim Chancellor only accepts the minimum amount of pay permitted through FLSA, $23,660.

(ii) Responsibilities shared between Commissioner Thomas Kirk, Mental Health: $157,880 and Commissioner Peter O'Meara, Retardation: $157,880.

(jj) Responsibilities shared between Director, Division of Substance Abuse and Mental Health, Department of Health and Social Services, $136,500 and Director, Division of Developmental Disabilities Service, same department, $110,800.

(kk) Responsibilities shared between Commissioners Gerald Morrissey, $136,235 and Elizabeth Child, $182,831.

(ll) Responsibilities shared between Director, Division of Mental Health Services, Dept. of Human Services, $118,559 and Director, Division of Developmental Disabilities, Dept. of Human Services, $117,666.

(mm) Responsibilities shared between Commissioner, State Education Department, $170,165; Secretary of State, Department of State, $120,800.

(nn) Responsibilities shared between Office of Health Professionals, $78,537 and Department of Health, $131,975.

(oo) Responsibilities shared between Director of Mental Health, $74,343 and Director of Community Support, $70,840.

(pp) Numerous licensing boards, no central agency.

(qq) Responsibilities shared between Director of Dept. of Mental Retardation and Developmental Disabilities, $126,089 and Acting Director of Dept. of Mental Health, $126,089 (this salary is for the person who previously held this position).

(rr) Responsibilities shared between, Director of Mental Health, Department of Children and Family Services, $105,641; and Director, Substance Abuse, same department, $105,575.

(ss) Responsibilities shared between Director for Disabilities and Special Needs, $157,765 and Director of Mental Health, $155,787.

(tt) Responsibilities shared between Director of Mental Health, $133,732 and Director of Developmental Services, $133,732.

(uu) Responsibilities shared between Deputy Director of Mental Health, $95,717 and Deputy Director of Retardation, $95,717.

(vv) Function split between two cabinet positions: Secretary, Dept. of Health and Social Services, $142,300 and Secretary, Dept. of Svcs. for Children, Youth and their Families, $128,099.

(ww) Responsibilities shared between Acting Commissioner, Department of Human Services, $141,000 and Commissioner, Department of Children and Families, $141,000.

(xx) Responsibilities shared between five commissioner's with salaries of $88,448 each.

(yy) Responsibilities shared between Director, Dept. of Job and Family Services, $141,980; Superintendent of Dept. of Education, $217,838; Executive Director of Rehabilitation Services Commission, $116,251 and Director of Dept. of Aging, $105,684.

(zz) This position is vacant at press time. The salary range is $82,864 to $128,441.

(aaa) Position is vacant at press time. Salary range is $68,135-$283,310.

(bbb) Responsibilities shared between three Commissioners, $87,875, $89,875 and $109,250 and General Administrator, $86,205.

(ccc) Responsibilities shared between Director, Department of Cultural Affairs, $110,323 and Division Administrator, Library and Archives, $92,290.

Lieutenant Governors: Quantified as Risen Powers

By Julia Nienaber Hurst

For an office traditionally understudied by academics, 2006 was a year which saw three new reports quantifying the office. Each shows that the office of lieutenant governor is a risen power. Data shows approximately one in every four governors in the nation for the past 100 years once served as lieutenant governor, and no office in the past 25 years had a better success rate of becoming governor. In addition, the office of lieutenant governor was the only statewide elected office to see an increase in real income in the 30-year period ending in 2005.

The office of lieutenant governor is a risen power, a fact demonstrated by research and anecdotal indicators as 2007 began. Three studies released in 2006 quantified the rise of the office of lieutenant governor in relationship to other state offices. A common question in regard to the office had been the success rate of those holding the office in reaching higher office. That question now has an answer. No other local, state or Congressional office has had more success in officeholders becoming governor in the past 25-year period. The use of the powers pursuant to the office in 2006 demonstrated the pivotal role the office can play in policy. And, in 2006, two former governors ran for and won the office of lieutenant governor in their states.

Research

Springboard

Nearly 25 percent of the nation's governors first served in the position of lieutenant governor, according to a June 2006 study commissioned by the National Lieutenant Governors Association (NLGA). A 50-state research project looked at the vitae of every governor in the states who served between January 1980 and June 2006. Each governor who once served as lieutenant governor or in the office first in line of gubernatorial succession was noted. In eight states, the official first in line of succession is the senate president or secretary of state and those individuals were treated as lieutenant governors in the study.

In combination with earlier research, this data established that for more than 100 years, about one in every four governors first served as lieutenant governor or first in line of succession. The 1996 publication "Lieutenant Governors: The Office and Its Powers" found that a "significant 23 percent of governors between the years of 1900–1980 served at one point as lieutenant governor." These studies include individuals who reached the office either through succession or election. Additional study would be required to determine the success rate of these officials in reaching the office through election only or in achieving other higher office such as Congress. As 2007 opens, seven governors will once have served as lieutenant governor, and one lieutenant governor, Mary Fallin of Oklahoma, will join Congress.

In December 2006, a second NLGA study showed the office of lieutenant governor has a greater success rate of its occupants becoming governor than any other local, state or Congressional office, according to researcher Morgan Mundell. In looking at the 25 total previous offices noted in all gubernatorial vitae of those who served between 1980 and 2006, the most prevalent offices previously held by governors were those of state representative, lieutenant governor, and state senator. Analysis showed that 56 of approximately 225 lieutenant governors in the period became governor, while 96 of more than 5,000 statehouse members, adjusted for turnover, became governor. Mundell concluded that for the period, approximately 25 percent of lieutenant governors became governor, while about 1 percent of statehouse members ascended to the office. In this study, only those individuals holding the title lieutenant governor were tallied as such. Additional study would be required to determine a pathway to governor, which included factors such as fundraising ability, name recognition and the like.

Salaries

State Legislator Compensation: A Trend Analysis, published by The Council of State Governments in 2006, showed lieutenant governor was the only statewide official whose real income increased as a national average between 1975 and 2005. The national average real income of governors, secretaries of state, attorneys general and treasurers decreased in the period. The report notes the increase is largely due to salaries in the east region, however other salary actions favorable to this trend in lieutenant governors' salary occurred outside the study window.

For example, in March 2006, the Utah governor signed House Bill 115 which set the salary of the lieutenant governor at 95 percent of the governor's salary, an increase in compensation. On Feb. 1, 2005, the Delaware lieutenant governor's salary increased 12 percent. It should be noted, however, that the Delaware Compensation Commission actually proposed a 36-percent pay raise, citing the need to pay the official as full-time and at least as much as the auditor and insurance commissioner. The proposed increase was reduced under political pressure. If one were to measure the value of the office by its compensation, these findings, too, would quantify the office of lieutenant governor as a risen power.

Powers

Twenty-five lieutenant governors have the power to preside over the state senate, and 25 have the power to cast tie-breaking roll call votes. While some question the real power of these roles, the result is a lieutenant governor often casts the deciding vote on a state's most controversial issues. Likewise, if one quantifies the effect of parliamentary rulings, the finding can be noteworthy. In 2006, South Carolina Lt. Gov. Andre Bauer campaigned that his Senate rulings had stopped more than $1.5 billion in proposed new taxes.

In 2007, the Oklahoma Senate is tied for party control. The power-sharing plan vests to Lt. Gov. Jari Askins the power to break a tie vote between the two party pro tems on legislation that comes to the floor for consideration. This is in addition to her usual tie-breaking authority. In Nevada, the Senate partisan split is 10-11. It is likely Lt. Gov. Brian Krolicki will have the opportunity to cast a number of tie-breaking votes. And, in Virginia, Lt. Gov. Bill Bolling cast two such votes last session. Having held no election in 2007, the Senate remains the same and an opportunity for further votes is possible.

Looking at recent history, South Carolina Lt. Gov. Andre Bauer cast tie-breaking votes in both 2005 and 2006 to keep tax reform alive in the Senate. In 2005, North Carolina Lt. Gov. Beverly Perdue cast the tie-breaking Senate vote to create a state lottery. In 2006, the National Conference of State Legislatures (NCSL) noted the states are in an era of party control tightening in record numbers. If the trend continues, these powers of lieutenant governor will grow in stature.

Whether a lieutenant governor has the above-named powers in a state, the role is or can be profound in the legislative and policy processes. In 2006, lieutenant governors provided legislative testimony on bills on energy, education, day care, ethics reform and more. Most initiate legislative packages handled by various legislators. Some, like Utah Lt. Gov. Gary Herbert, testify in Congress. Herbert testified in June 2006 regarding the energy plan and Utah's oil shale and tar sand.

These duties occur while the officeholders maintain their ceremonial and other leadership roles. At the end of 2006, eight of the 42 lieutenant governors led at least one division or department of state government. These included elections in Alaska, tourism in Louisiana and Nevada, transportation in Minnesota, aging in South Carolina, commerce in Ohio, and homeland security in Nebraska. In Indiana, the lieutenant governor holds 42 statutory duties and heads the departments of commerce and agriculture, as well as the divisions of tourism and homeland security.

In both Indiana and New Mexico, the lieutenant governor is tasked with a cross-departmental role which aims to make progress in a policy area deemed critical by the governor. In Indiana, Lt. Gov. Becky Skillman is head of rural affairs, a role which allows her to call meetings of directors of any department which may impact rural communities. For example, the heads of health, education and agriculture could be called together under her leadership to address the rural component of a shared issue. Likewise in New Mexico, Lt. Gov. Diane Denish chairs the Children's Cabinet. Created by the governor, it specifies the participation of 11 other cabinet secretaries to ensure progress in a myriad of measures regarding children.

As noted in the 2002 work of David Winder of Valdosta State University, lieutenant governors also derive policy power from their work on numerous commissions. Missouri Lt. Gov. Peter Kinder sat on or chaired 15 commissions in 2006, while Oklahoma Lt. Gov. Mary Fallin served on 10 commissions. Lieutenant governors in every region of the country partake in commission work ranging from Indian affairs and energy reliability to health care, economic development and emergency management. The president appointed Hawaii Lt. Gov. James Aiona to serve on the National Advisory Commission on Drug Free Communities.

Anecdotal
Pressworthy

In 2006, the press in many states opined on the key roles lieutenant governors now play. In September, the *Herald Tribune* wrote, "In recent years, the (Florida) lieutenant governors have played key policy roles in their administrations." *The Birmingham News* observed May 9, "As the presiding officer of the Alabama Senate, the lieutenant governor has a chance to use his or her official position to advocate for change." The *Dallas Morning News* in September 2006 reported that many feel the lieutenant governor is the most powerful elective office in the state. In Massachusetts, a September 2006 *Enterprise* headline read, "Pay Attention to Candidates for Lieutenant Governor," a sentiment echoed by the Ohio Associated Press the same month. Both outlets noted the critical role of the office as a successor to governor. As Greg Johnson of the *Knoxville News-Sentinel* put it Nov. 17, "It's almost impossible to overstate the power of the speaker of the Tennessee Senate. … Most importantly, the speaker serves as lieutenant governor and is one tick bite away from being governor."

Codification

New Jersey will elect its first lieutenant governor in 2009, a move voters approved in November 2005. That will bring to five the number of states without an official using the title lieutenant governor. In West Virginia and Tennessee, the senate president is empowered to use the title in recognition of the vital succession role. For the past two sessions, Arizona has passed bills to change the title of secretary of state to lieutenant governor. Various political pressures and implementation details have stopped the bill from becoming law, however, it seems reasonable to assume this state will continue to pursue that action.

Conclusion

The fact remains the office of lieutenant governor is the most diverse state office in state government. Wide disparities in duties and power exist from the 42 statutory duties given Indiana's lieutenant governor to the part-time nature of the office in South Dakota. That given, the trends and factors outlined here indicate the office of lieutenant governor will continue to grow in power, number and stature in state government on a national basis. The part-time or ceremonial nature of the office that may once have existed is now seen in a very few states. In July 2005, *USA Today* wrote, "Lieutenant governors, once the fifth wheel of U.S. politics, are playing an increasingly significant, visible and controversial role in state government."

As states face new challenges in the coming decade, such as the aging population and technology advances, it appears likely that lieutenant governors will be tapped to lead key efforts. The use of lieutenant governors may be innovative in coming years to address cross-cutting issues, such as in Indiana and New Mexico. It also appears likely that lieutenant governors will continue to grow in policy influence and activity.

About the Author

Julia Nienaber Hurst is executive director of the National Lieutenant Governors Association (www.nlga.us). Hurst's nearly 20 years of state government experience include time as chief operating officer of The Council of State Governments, four sessions as a legislative chief of staff, and time as a multistate lobbyist.

Table 4.12
THE LIEUTENANT GOVERNORS, 2007

State or other jurisdiction	Name and party	Method of selection	Length of regular term in years	Date of first service	Present term ends	Number of previous terms	Joint election of governor and lieutenant governor
Alabama	Jim Folsom Jr. (D) (b)	CE	4	1/86 (b)	1/11	1	No
Alaska	Sean R. Parnell (R)	CE	4	12/06	12/10	...	Yes
Arizona	.... (c)						
Arkansas...................	Bill Halter (D)	CE	4	1/07	1/11	...	No
California	John Garamendi (D)	CE	4	1/07	1/11	...	No
Colorado	Barbara O'Brien (D)	CE	4	1/07	1/11	...	Yes
Connecticut	Michael Fedele (R)	CE	4	1/07	1/11	...	Yes
Delaware...................	John Carney (D)	CE	4	1/01	1/09	1	No
Florida	Jeff Kottkamp (R)	CE	4	1/07	1/11	...	Yes
Georgia	Casey Cagle (R)	CE	4	1/07	1/11	...	No
Hawaii......................	James Aiona (R)	CE	4	12/02	12/10	1	Yes
Idaho........................	Jim Risch (R) (d)	CE	4	1/03	1/11	1 (d)	No
Illinois	Patrick Quinn (D)	CE	4	1/03	1/11	1	Yes
Indiana.....................	Becky Skillman (R)	CE	4	1/05	1/09	...	Yes
Iowa	Patty Judge (D)	CE	4	1/07	1/11	...	Yes
Kansas	Mark Parkinson (D)	CE	4	1/07	1/11	...	Yes
Kentucky	Stephen Pence (R)	CE	4	12/03	12/07	...	Yes
Louisiana	Mitch Landrieu (D)	CE	4	1/04	1/08	...	No
Maine	.... (c)						
Maryland	Anthony Brown (D)	CE	4	1/07	1/11	...	Yes
Massachusetts............	Tim Murray (D)	CE	4	1/07	1/11	...	Yes
Michigan...................	John D. Cherry (D)	CE	4	1/03	1/11	1	Yes
Minnesota	Carol Molnau (R)	CE	4	1/03	1/11	1	Yes
Mississippi	Amy Tuck (R)	CE	4	1/00	1/08	1	Yes
Missouri...................	Peter Kinder (R)	CE	4	1/05	1/09	...	No
Montana	John Bohlinger (R)	CE	4	1/05	1/09	...	Yes
Nebraska...................	Rick Sheehy (R)	CE	4	1/05 (e)	1/11	(e)	Yes
Nevada	Brian Krolicki (R)	CE	4	1/07	1/11	...	No
New Hampshire..........	.... (c)						
New Jersey.................	Beginning with the November 3, 2009 general election this office will be filled. (f)						
New Mexico	Diane Denish (D)	CE	4	1/03	1/11	1	Yes
New York	David A. Paterson (D)	CE	4	1/07	1/11	...	Yes
North Carolina	Beverly Purdue (D)	CE	4	1/01	1/09	1	No
North Dakota.............	Jack Dalrymple (R)	CE	4	12/00	12/08	1	Yes
Ohio	Lee Fisher (D)	SE	4	1/07	1/11	...	Yes
Oklahoma	Jari Askins (D)	CE	4	1/07	1/11	...	No
Oregon	.... (c)						
Pennsylvania	Catherine Baker Knoll (D)	CE	4	1/03	1/11	1	Yes
Rhode Island	Elizabeth H. Roberts (D)	SE	4	1/07	1/11	...	No
South Carolina	R. Andre Bauer (R)	CE	4	1/03	1/11	1	No
South Dakota.............	Dennis Daugaard (R)	CE	4	1/03	1/11	1	Yes
Tennessee	Ron Ramsey (R)	(g)	2	1/07	1/09	...	No
Texas	David Dewhurst (R)	CE	4	1/03	1/11	1	No
Utah	Gary Herbert (R)	CE	4	1/05	1/09	...	Yes
Vermont	Brian Dubie (R)	CE	2	1/03	1/09	2	No
Virginia	William T. Bolling (R)	CE	4	1/06	1/10	...	No
Washington................	Brad Owen (D)	CE	4	1/97	1/09	2	No
West Virginia	Earl Ray Tomblin (D)	(h)	2	1/95	1/09	7	No
Wisconsin..................	Barbara Lawton (D)	CE	4	1/03	1/11	1	Yes
Wyoming...................	.... (c)						
American Samoa.......	Ipulasi Aitofele Sunia (D)	CE	4	4/03 (i)	1/09	(i)	Yes
Guam	Michael W. Cruz (R)	CE	4	1/07	1/11	...	Yes
No. Mariana Islands...	Timothy Villagomez (j)	CE	4	1/06	1/10	...	Yes
Puerto Rico..............	.... (c)						
U.S. Virgin Islands	Greg Francis (D)	SE	4	1/07	1/11	...	Yes

See footnotes at end of table.

THE LIEUTENANT GOVERNORS, 2007 — Continued

Source: The Council of State Governments, January 2007.

Key:

CE — Constitutional, elected by public.

SE — Statutory, elected by public.

. . . — Not applicable.

(a) The following also choose candidates for governor and lieutenant governor through a joint nomination process: Florida, Kansas, Maryland, Minnesota, Montana, North Dakota, Ohio, Utah, American Samoa, Guam, No. Mariana Islands, and U.S. Virgin Islands. For additional information see The National Lieutenant Governors Association Web site at *http://www.nlga.us.*

(b) Previously served as lieutenant governor from 1986 to 1993. He assumed the office of governor when Guy Hunt was removed in 1993 and served until 1995 when Fob James was sworn in. He was elected to the office of lieutenant governor for another term in November 2006.

(c) No lieutenant governor.

(d) Jim Risch served as lieutenant governor from January 2003 until May 2006 when he assumed the duties of governor after Governor Kempthorne resigned to accept the position of Secretary of the Department of the Interior. Risch was re-elected as lieutenant governor in November 2006.

(e) Lieutenant Governor Sheehy was appointed to the position of lieutenant governor January 24, 2005, by Governor Heineman.

(f) New Jersey will elect a lieutenant governor in 2009. The governor and lieutenant governor will be elected jointly. In the event of a permanent vacancy in the office before the inauguration date of the first lieutenant governor, the president of the senate, followed by the speaker of the assembly, would succeed the governor.

(g) In Tennessee, the president of the senate and the lieutenant governor are one in the same. The legislature provided in statute the title of lieutenant governor upon the senate president. The senate president serves two-year terms, elected by the senate on the first day of the first session of each two-year legislative term.

(h) In West Virginia, the president of the senate and the lieutenant governor are one in the same. The legislature provided in statute the title of lieutenant governor upon the senate president. The senate president serves two-year terms, elected by the senate on the first day of the first session of each two-year legislative term.

(i) Lieutenant Governor Sunia was appointed to the position of lieutenant governor in April 2003 by Governor Togiola Tulafono.

(j) Covenant Party.

Table 4.13
LIEUTENANT GOVERNORS: QUALIFICATIONS AND TERMS

State or other jurisdiction	Minimum age	State citizen (years)	U.S. citizen (years) (a)	State resident (years) (b)	Qualified voter (years)	Length of term (years)	Maximum consecutive terms allowed
Alabama	30	7	10	7	...	4	2
Alaska	30	★	7	7	★	4	2
Arizona				(c)			
Arkansas	30	7	★	7	...	4	2
California	18	★	★	5	★	4	2
Colorado	30	...	★	2	...	4	2
Connecticut	30	...	...	★	★	4	...
Delaware	30	★	12	6	★	4	2
Florida	30	★	★	7	★	4	2
Georgia	30	★	15	6	★	4	...
Hawaii	30	5	★	5	★	4	2
Idaho	30	...	★	2	...	4	...
Illinois	25	...	★	3	...	4	...
Indiana	30	★	★	★	★	4	2
Iowa	30	...	2	2	...	4	...
Kansas	...	...	...	...	...	4	2
Kentucky	30	6	★	★	★	4	2
Louisiana	25	5	5	5	...	4	...
Maine				(c)			
Maryland	30	★	★	★	★	4	2
Massachusetts	...	★	★	★	★	4	...
Michigan	30	★	★	4	4	4	2 (h)
Minnesota	25	...	★	1	...	4	...
Mississippi	30	...	20	5	★	4	2
Missouri	30	10	15	10	...	4	...
Montana	25	2	★	2	...	4	2 (d)
Nebraska	30	5	★	5	★	4	2
Nevada	25	2	★	2	★	4	2
New Hampshire				(c)			
New Jersey	Beginning with the November 3, 2009 general election this office will be filled.						
New Mexico	30	★	★	5	★	4	2
New York	30	★	★	5	★	4	...
North Carolina	30	...	5	2	...	4	2
North Dakota	30	5	...	...	...	4	...
Ohio	18	...	★	★	★	4	2
Oklahoma	31	10	★	★	★	4	...
Oregon				(c)			
Pennsylvania	30	★	★	7	★	4	2
Rhode Island	18	★	★	★	★	4	2
South Carolina	30	5	5	5	★	4	2
South Dakota	21	2	★	2	★	4	2
Tennessee (e)	30	★	★	3	1	2	...
Texas	30	...	★	5	...	4	...
Utah	30	★	★	★	★	4	...
Vermont	18	4	★	4	★	2	...
Virginia	30	...	★	5	5	4	...
Washington	18	★	★	★	★	4	...
West Virginia (f)	25	1	1	1	★	2	...
Wisconsin	18	★	★	★	★	4	...
Wyoming				(c)			
American Samoa	35	(g)	★	5	★	4	2
Guam	30	...	5	5	★	4	2
No. Mariana Islands	35	★	★	★	★	4	2
Puerto Rico				(c)			
U.S. Virgin Islands	30	...	5	5	5	4	2

Source: The Council of State Governments' survey, January 2007.
Note: This table includes constitutional and statutory qualifications.
Key:
★ — Formal provision; number of years not specified.
. . . — No formal provision.
(a) In some states you must be a U.S. citizen to be an elector, and must be an elector to run.
(b) In some states you must be a state resident to be an elector, and must be an elector to run.
(c) No lieutenant governor.
(d) Eligible for eight out of 16 years.

(e) In Tennessee, the speaker of the senate, elected from senate membership, has statutory title of "lieutenant governor."
(f) In West Virginia, the president of the senate and the lieutenant governor are one in the same. The legislature provided in statute the title of lieutenant governor upon the senate president. The senate president serves two-year terms, elected by the senate on the first day of the first session of each two-year legislative term.
(g) Must be a U.S. national.
(h) In 1993 a constitutional limit of two lifetime terms in the office was enacted.

Table 4.14
LIEUTENANT GOVERNORS: POWERS AND DUTIES

State or other jurisdiction	Presides over Senate	Appoints committees	Breaks roll-call ties	Assigns bills	Authority for governor to assign duties	Member of governor's cabinet or advisory body	Serves as acting governor when governor out of state	Other duties
Alabama	★	★	★	★	...	...	★ (a)	...
Alaska	...	...	...	...	★	...	...	(b)
Arizona			·······(c)·······					
Arkansas	★	...	★	...	...	...	★	...
California	...	...	★	...	...	...	★	...
Colorado	...	...	...	...	...	...	★	...
Connecticut	★	...	★	...	★	★	★	(d)
Delaware	★	...	★	...	★	...	★	...
Florida	...	...	...	...	★	...	★	(e)
Georgia	★	★	...	★	★	...	...	...
Hawaii	...	...	...	...	★	...	...	...
Idaho	★	...	★	★	★	...	★	(f)
Illinois	...	...	...	...	★	...	★	...
Indiana	★	...	★	...	★	★	...	...
Iowa	...	(g)	...	...	★	(h)	(i)	...
Kansas	...	...	...	...	★	...	...	...
Kentucky	...	...	...	...	...	★	...	...
Louisiana	...	...	...	...	★	...	(j)	(k)
Maine			·······(l)·······					
Maryland	...	...	...	...	...	★	★	...
Massachusetts	...	★	...	...	★	★	★	(m)
Michigan	★	...	★	...	★	★	★ (n)	(o)
Minnesota	...	...	...	...	★	★	...	(p)
Mississippi	★	★	★	★	...	...	★	(q)
Missouri	★	...	★	...	★	...	★	(r)
Montana	...	...	...	...	★	★	★	...
Nebraska	★ (s)	...	...	...	...	★	★	...
Nevada	★	...	★ (t)	...	...	...	★	...
New Hampshire			·······(l)·······					
New Jersey			·······(l)·······					
New Mexico	★	...	★	...	...	...	★	...
New York	★	...	★ (u)	...	★	★	★	...
North Carolina	★	...	★	...	★	★	★	...
North Dakota	★	...	...	...	...	★	★	...
Ohio	...	...	...	...	★	★	...	...
Oklahoma	★ (v)	...	★	...	...	...	★	(w)
Oregon			·······(c)·······					
Pennsylvania	★	...	★	...	...	...	...	...
Rhode Island	...	...	...	...	...	...	...	...
South Carolina	★	★	★	★	...	...	...	(x)
South Dakota	★	...	★	...	...	★	★	(y)
Tennessee	★	★	★	...	★	...	...	(z)
Texas	★	★	★	★	...	...	★	...
Utah	...	...	...	...	...	★	...	(aa)
Vermont	★	★ (bb)	★	★ (cc)	...	...	★	...
Virginia	★	...	★	...	...	...	...	...
Washington	★	★	★	...	...	...	...	...
West Virginia	★	★	...	...	...	...	★	...
Wisconsin	...	...	...	...	★	...	...	(dd)
Wyoming			·······(c)·······					
American Samoa	(s)	...	...	...	...	...	★	...
Guam	...	...	...	...	...	...	★	...
No. Mariana Islands	...	...	...	...	★	★	★	...
Puerto Rico		·······(c)·······				★	★	(ee)
U.S. Virgin Islands	...	...	...	...	★ (h)	★	★	...

See footnotes at end of table.

LIEUTENANT GOVERNORS: POWERS AND DUTIES — Continued

Sources: The Council of State Governments' survey, January 2007 and state constitutions and statutes. For additional information on the powers and duties visit the National Lieutenant Governors Association website at http://www.nlga.us

Key:
★ — Provision for responsibility.
. . . — No provision for responsibility.

(a) The lieutenant governor performs the duties of the governor in the event of the governor's death, impeachment, disability, or absence from the state for more than 20 days

(b) The lieutenant governor bears these additional responsibilities: Alaska Historical Commission Chair; Alaska Workforce Investment Board; Division of Elections, Constitutional figurehead; State Seal Guardian, governor assigned; Clemency Advisory Committee; Denali Commission, State Co-chair; Faith Based and Community Initiatives Task Force, Figurehead; Aerospace States Association (ASA); Arctic Council; Arctic Winter Games; Experimental Program to Stimulate Competitive Research (EPSCoR), Chair; Project GRAD.

(c) No lieutenant governor; secretary of state is next in line of succession to governorship.

(d) Additional responsibilities include: Chair of the Colorado Commission of Indian Affairs (by statute); member of the Homeland Security and All-Hazards Senior Advisory Committee (Cabinet duty).

(e) Serves as President of the Board of Pardons.

(f) Serves as Secretary of State.

(g) Appoints all standing committees. Iowa – appoints some special committees.

(h) Presides over cabinet meetings in absence of governor.

(i) Only in emergency situations.

(j) The Kentucky Constitution specifically gives the lieutenant governor the power to act as governor, in the event he is unable to fulfill the duties of office.

(k) In addition to the duties set forth by the Kentucky Constitution, state law also gives the lieutenant governor the responsibility to act as chair, or serve as a member, on various boards and commissions. Some of these include: the State Property and Buildings Commission, Kentucky Turnpike Authority, Kentucky Council on Agriculture, Board of the Kentucky Housing Corporation and the Appalachian Development Council. The governor also has the power to give the Lieutenant governor other specific job duties. Under the Fletcher administration, the lieutenant governor served as Secretary of the Justice and Public Safety Cabinet.

(l) No lieutenant governor; senate president or speaker is next in line of succession to governorship.

(m) The lieutenant governor is a member of, and presides over, the Governor's Council, an elected body of 8 members which approves all judicial nominations.

(n) As defined in the state constitution, the lieutenant governor performs gubernatorial functions in the governor's absence. In the event of a vacancy in the office of governor, the lieutenant governor is first in line to succeed to the position.

(o) The lieutenant governor serves as a member of the State Administrative Board; and represents the governor and the state at selected local, state, and national meetings. In addition the governor may delegate additional responsibilities.

(p) Serves as the Chair of the Capitol Area Architectural and Planning Board Committee.

(q) The lieutenant governor also appoints chairs of standing committees, appoints conferees to committees and is a member of the Legislative Budget Committee, chair of this committee every other year.

(r) Other duties of the lieutenant governor include: Official Senior Advocate for State of Missouri and Advisor to Department of Elementary and Secondary Education on early childhood education and Parents-as-Teachers program. The lieutenant governor also serves on the following boards and commissions: Board of Fund Commissioners; Board of Public Buildings; Governor's Advisory Council for Veteran's (chair); Missouri Community Service Commission; Missouri Development Finance Board; Missouri Housing Development Commission; Missouri Rural Economic Development Council; Missouri Rural Economic Development Council; Missouri Senior Rx Program (chair); Missouri Tourism Commission (vice-chair); Personal Independence Commission (co-chair); Second State Capitol Commission; Statewide Safety Steering Committee; Veteran's Benefits Awareness Task Force (chair); Special Health, Psychological, and Social Needs of Minority Older Individuals Commission; Mental Health Task Force (chair); Missouri Energy Task Force.

(s) Unicameral legislative body. In Guam, that body elects own presiding officer.

(t) Except on final passage of bills and joint resolutions.

(u) With respect to procedural matters, not legislation.

(v) May preside over the Senate when desired.

(w) Lieutenant governor also serves on 10 boards and commissions including Tourism and School Land Commission.

(x) Serves as Chair of a number of Advisory Councils including issues related to Emergency Management, Long Term Care and Small Business. Each year submits a legislative package to the General Assembly.

(y) The lieutenant governor heads the State Office on Aging; appoints members and chairs the South Carolina Affordable Housing Commission.

(z) The lieutenant governor also serves as the Chair of the Workers Compensation Advisory Commission and as a member of the Constitutional Revision Commission.

(aa) The lieutenant governor serves as Secretary of State (Constitution); Chair of the Lieutenant Governor's Commission on Volunteers (statutory); Chair of the Lieutenant Governor's Commission on Civic and Character Education (statutory); Chair of the Utah Capitol Preservation Board (statutory); Chair (Governor's Cabinet). Direct cabinet oversight of following departments: 1. Utah Department of Public Safety and Homeland Security, 2. Utah Department of Transportation, 3. Utah Division of Water Rights, 4. Utah Division of Rural Affairs.

(bb) Appoints committees with the Pres. Pro Tem and one Senator on Committee on Committees.

(cc) Committee on Committees assigns bills.

(dd) In West Virginia, the President of the Senate and the Lieutenant Governor are one in the same. The legislature provided in statute the title of Lieutenant Governor upon the Senate President. The Senate President serves 2 year terms, elected by the Senate on the first day of the first session of each two year legislative term.

(ee) The Lieutenant Governor is charged with overseeing administrative functions.

Secretaries of State: Progress and Policymaking in Electronic Government

By Kay Stimson

The Internet age is transforming the office of secretary of state. States are expanding the content of their Web sites by adding public disclosure records and new transactions. At the same time, the availability of personal information on government sites and a lack of confidence in electronic voting machines are ongoing concerns.

Washington Secretary of State Sam Reed wants his state legislature to allow online voter registration in 2007. "Giving citizens the option to register to vote electronically would take our voter registration system into the digital age," he said.

Reed's secretary of state Web site already offers a sophisticated menu of e-government services: a database for checking voter registration status, a searchable digital archive, an online filing and payment system for corporate registrations, and even a searchable catalog linked to the state's public libraries. Adding electronic voter registration seems fitting.

Like most secretaries of state, Reed is on a mission to keep his state office in synch with the state of modern living. As a result, he and his peers increasingly are tackling their duties through electronic government.

Those who are familiar with the job generally associate it with election administration and business services, but the office of secretary of state varies from state to state.[1] Additional duties include keeping legislative records, managing state archives, handling international commerce, regulating securities, registering charities and serving as chief notary of the state. In a few instances, the job comes with unique assignments, such as serving as commissioner of the state boxing commission (Georgia) or heading up the state's office of diversity and multicultural affairs (New Jersey).

The e-government revolution has significantly affected business services and licensing. As secretaries of state work to develop Web sites and portals that can be used as tools for state commerce, they are adding more online filing options that allow for the completion of entire transactions in record time. Some officials say these new advances make it necessary to develop national standards for business services. Preventing fraud and abuse in business filings is another much-cited concern.

Meanwhile, secretaries of state who oversee elections are caught in a national controversy over paper trails for electronic voting machines. As the officials responsible for implementation of the Help America Vote Act (HAVA), a federal election reform law that went into full effect in 2006, secretaries of state are adopting e-voting safeguards along with rules on voter identification, absentee voting, and more. New federal policies aimed at increasing confidence in electronic voting may impact the outcome of this debate.

These issues highlight the fact that it's an interesting time to be serving as a secretary of state.[2] The e-government revolution is rapidly transforming the position, bringing with it both opportunities and challenges for officeholders. One only needs to follow the number of new options popping up on secretary of state Web sites in order to track their progress.

Digital Secretaries

Secretaries of state use their Web sites for a number of important purposes, including ensuring transparency of elections, simplifying business filings, supporting business expansion in the state, and providing open access to government documents. Since they are responsible for keeping a wide array of official government records, they are often compelled—by law or by public demand—to make a large amount of information available in electronic format.

One new twist involves showcasing history. To commemorate the 65th anniversary of the attack on Pearl Harbor, the Oregon secretary of state's office recently unveiled "Life on the Home Front: Oregon Responds to World War II," one of several online exhibits created by the state archives using historical documents, images and audio-video clips.

"We really want our state archives to be used as a tool," said Mary Conley, the spokesperson for Oregon's secretary of state. "It's part of our mission to increase accessibility to every state record for anyone who wants to read it or use it in research, and this is an exciting way to grab their attention."

As they convert stacks of old documents and microfilm to digital format for storage and retention, states are now aiming to increase their offerings on the Web. More than a half-dozen states already have searchable databases containing genealogical records, marriage licenses, land deeds and other historical documents, according to a joint report recently issued by the National Association of Secretaries of State (NASS) and the National Electronic Commerce Coordinating Council (eC3).[3]

"By placing government information and records that have traditionally been available in paper format online, people can learn about their family history or state history using their home computer," said Georgia Secretary of State Cathy Cox. "Plus, states reduce their costs and preserve important documents in a secure digital format that is more likely to hold up in the event of a terrorist attack or a natural disaster."

Cox points out that after Hurricane Katrina flooded much of the Gulf Coast, staffers from her office were able to assist Louisiana officials in preserving and recovering thousands of documents using electronic archiving techniques.

One of the fastest growing areas on secretary of state Web sites are the pages devoted to open records and disclosure reporting. By placing open meetings notices and other public information online, secretaries of state say they are enhancing access to government. For example, states such as Oklahoma and West Virginia post their meeting notices on the Web and update them in real time. Rhode Island e-mails these notices to subscribers.

Since all states require some level of public disclosure reporting for businesses and campaigns, placing this information online is the next logical step. Almost every state offers a searchable database that can tell users whether a company is in good standing and can identify the names and addresses of registered agents. Another common offering is Uniform Commercial Code (UCC) financing statements.

Meanwhile, candidate and campaign disclosures are slowly showing up online. Thirty-six states require candidates to file their reports electronically,[4] via a diskette or the Internet, and 49 states post the disclosure information on a public Web site. Two-thirds allow searches of campaign contribution reports (some also include lobbying disclosures), while states such as California and Michigan allow these documents to be filed electronically with the state.

California Secretary of State Debra Bowen, who as a state senator authored a bill that made her state the first in the country to give people electronic access to government records, wants to do more in this area. "It's easier to go on eBay and do a search for baseball memorabilia than it is to look online

and find out who's spending on campaigns and what the patterns are," she recently said in a *Los Angeles Times* article.[5]

As more information becomes available online, security is a growing issue. In March 2006, an Ohio man sued the secretary of state's office for listing Social Security numbers on state Web sites that are available for public searches.[6] The information is part of UCC filings that show retail purchases made using credit cards and bank loans. To date, the case has not been settled, but it has raised important policy implications for state officials.

Since many states do not allow for the alteration of public records, documents with signatures, Social Security numbers, and birthdates—including deeds, mortgages, tax liens, marriage licenses, and voter registrations—are accessible to anyone with a computer. While banks and other entities can use the data for verification purposes, unscrupulous users can do harm.

"States are looking at how to change their laws to catch up with technology," explains Leslie Reynolds, executive director of NASS. "To take advantage of open records laws, people used to have to go to a government office to look through files. Now all of those records are accessible with the click of a mouse, and in this age of identity theft, it's a real concern." Reynolds said some states are developing procedures to exclude sensitive personal data from public documents.

Secretaries of state point out that, in addition to privacy concerns, heightened national security, expansion of voter identification requirements and the impending federal ID mandates of the REAL ID Act are all expected to play a role in the continuing debate about public information and content on government Web sites.

Business and Legal Services

Nowhere is the impact of the e-government revolution more evident than in state business and legal services. Through Web portals and other Internet-based technologies, secretary of state offices are increasingly able to offer online transactions. With so many services going digital, some believe it is time to develop standard terms and procedures from state to state. They also cite the need to prevent fraud and abuse in online filings, particularly false corporate registrations that serve as shelters for potential tax cheats, money launderers and terrorist organizations.

According to NASS, roughly a third of all secretary of state Web sites offer interactive business features.[7] Thirty-one states allow businesses to register online, and 35 states plus the District of Columbia offer digital filing of UCC information. Users can renew a professional license online in 16 states and they can file complaints against licensees online in half of those states. North Carolina, Washington, Colorado and Pennsylvania are blazing the trail on digital signatures and seals, which are electronic authentication methods that allow for notarizations and other legal services to be conducted via the Internet.[8]

As online offerings continue to grow and diversify, there is a push to create more uniform standards for business and UCC filings. Secretaries of state involved in these efforts say it helps in the evaluation of different vendor services and adds some consistency to interstate or multi-state commerce.

"Standard setting is so absolutely vital to ensuring that states can effectively carry out these new services," said North Carolina Secretary of State Elaine Marshall, who served as chair of the first National e-Notarization Commission. "We must have definitions that are broad enough to evaluate each different system that's out there and similar enough that we can talk to one another on the same page." Marshall said before the national commission released its standards for e-notarizations in July 2006, states had different procedures for protecting signature credibility, avoiding identity fraud and promoting secure electronic commerce.

With an estimated 12 million new businesses filing in the states each year, secretaries of state must also find ways to prevent fraud and abuse. For example, some officials and experts contend that competition between states to lure new companies has resulted in the easing of reporting and information collection requirements on non-publicly traded companies.[9] They point out that most states do not require registered agents to verify company ownership information or check what is submitted against criminal watch lists, creating a transparency gap that allows the commitment of crimes such as money laundering, tax evasion and even terrorism.

Members of Congress say states will need to make these issues a priority this year. Delaware, Massachusetts and Nevada have already created task forces to issue recommendations on how states can work with federal agencies and law enforcement to address problems in the company formation process. The Internal Revenue Service and the Federal Bureau of Investigation also plan to issue recommendations in 2007.

Elections and Voting

The use of paperless electronic voting machines has commanded an enormous amount of public attention during the past two years. The 38 secretaries of state who serve as chief state election officials were responsible for vetting new voting machines as part of their oversight of the Help America Vote Act (HAVA), a sweeping new federal law passed in response to the presidential election recount of 2000. The act provided nearly $3 billion to states for, among other things, modernizing voting equipment, developing statewide voter registration databases, improving poll worker training and recruitment, and increasing voter education efforts. States had until 2006 to meet all of the law's mandates, including an optional provision to replace outdated punch card and lever voting systems.

The competitive atmosphere of the midterm election cycle raised the stakes for state election officials and new voting technologies. According to Stateline.org, 36 governors' races and 84 percent of state legislative posts across the country were up for grabs in November 2006.[10] The number of close congressional races whose outcomes could tip the balance of power in one or both chambers of Congress also heightened interest in the process. These forces, combined with HAVA implementation, led to a number of pre-emptive lawsuits.

High-profile legal cases included challenges to new photo ID laws in Georgia, Indiana and Missouri,[11] a challenge to new voter registration laws in Florida and Ohio, and a challenge in California regarding the accessibility of voting equipment for disabled voters. In Maryland, the state's Supreme Court rejected a new early voting law just 11 days before it was set to go into effect. Many of these lawsuits named secretaries of state as defendants and required considerable time and resources to deal with them.[12]

Of all the controversies, however, none garnered as much attention or generated as much debate as the issue of paper trails for electronic voting machines. Twenty-seven states have adopted voter verifiable paper audit trails (VVPAT) or paper-based balloting systems, with 15 of those states relying upon VVPATs as the vote of record in the event of a recount.[13] The remaining states were plagued with public concerns about the vulnerabilities of direct recording electronic (DRE) voting machines, including how they could be hacked and how votes could be altered without a paper trail.

State election officials now await the approval of new federal guidelines on electronic voting and anticipate the introduction of congressional legislation that could impact state preparations for the 2008 presidential election cycle. The U.S. Election Assistance Commission is likely to approve a new set of voluntary federal testing standards that require "software independent" audit capabilities for electronic voting equipment,[14] which could restrict or end the use of paperless electronic voting systems. The updated guidelines may also require new testing and inspection procedures for voting equipment software.

In Congress, U.S. Sen. Diane Feinstein, D-Calif., has submitted new federal legislation that would, among other things, require voter verifiable paper audit trails for machines and increase requirements for electronic voting machine security. Rep. Rush Holt, D-N.J., has also resubmitted a bill that would mandate voter verifiable paper audit trails for voting equipment.

With the national momentum shifting away from paperless voting machines, Kentucky Secretary of State Trey Grayson has asked his state legislature to require paper trails. "We haven't had the problems here yet, at least we don't feel it," Grayson said during a November 2006 state elections committee hearing. "Let's not wait for the problem and let's do it while people still trust the system."

Summary

The Internet age is transforming the office of secretary of state, both in terms of e-government innovations and policy challenges. From historical archives to notarizations, secretaries of state are expanding the digital content of their Web sites by adding public disclosure records and making their sites more transactional.

At the same time, secretaries of state must address new concerns regarding electronic government. The call for more uniform standards for business services and licensing is one issue; curbing fraud and abuse is another. States must deal with open records laws that allow the posting of personal information on government Web sites and lax requirements in the company formation process. Ensuring confidence and transparency in elections, especially those conducted using electronic voting machines, is also an ongoing concern.

Notes

[1] Of the nation's 47 secretaries of state (48 counting the District of Columbia's secretary of the district), 35 are directly elected, three are elected by the state legislature (Maine, New Hampshire and Tennessee), and nine are appointed by the governor (Delaware, Florida, Maryland, New Jersey, New York, Oklahoma, Pennsylvania, Texas and Virginia). Alaska, Hawaii and Utah, the three states that do not have a secretary of state position, assign administrative duties to their lieutenant governors. The U.S. territories of Puerto Rico, Guam and the U.S. Virgin Islands do the same.

[2] It's worth noting that a record number of former secretaries of state are now serving as governors and members of Congress. Current governors Chet Culver of Iowa, Matt Blunt of Missouri, Bob Taft of Ohio, Jim Douglas of Vermont and Joe Manchin of West Virginia are former secretaries of state. Former secretaries of state serving in Congress include: Missouri Rep. Roy Blunt, Oklahoma Rep. Tom Cole, Nevada

Rep. Dean Heller, Rhode Island Rep. Jim Langevin, Michigan Rep. Candice Miller, and Sens. Evan Bayh of Indiana and Sherrod Brown of Ohio.

[3] National Association of Secretaries of State and Electronic Commerce Coordinating Council, *Digital Archiving: From Fragmentation to Collaboration*, (December 2006), 10.

[4] Arkansas plans to add this function in 2007.

[5] Jenifer Warren, "Bowen Aims to Boost Voter Faith in Elections," *Los Angeles Times*, November 11, 2006.

[6] Todd Weiss, "Ohio Secretary of State Sued Over Information Posted Online," Computerworld, March 3, 2006, available at *http://www.computerworld.com/printthis/2006/0,4814,109213,00.html.*

[7] Research assistance provided by NASS Executive Assistant Rachel Becker.

[8] There is a difference between an "electronic signature" and a "digital signature," although they are sometimes used interchangeably. An "electronic signature" is a signature used to authenticate a written document. A "digital signature" is an electronically generated identifier that uses cryptography or other security measures to ensure the integrity or authenticity of the information to which it corresponds.

[9] Testimony before the U.S. Senate Subcommittee on Permanent Investigations, Stuart Nash, director of the U.S. Department of Justice Organized Crime Drug Enforcement Task Force, on November 14, 2006.

[10] Pamela Prah and Eric Keldermam, "Election '06—GOP Edge at Stake," Stateline.org, November 4, 2006, available at *http://www.stateline.org/live/details/story?contentId=154856.*

[11] According to the nonpartisan group Electiononline.org, 24 states and the District of Columbia currently have the minimum HAVA ID requirements in place. Eighteen states require some form of ID for all voters. Three states request that all voters present photo ID (Hawaii, Louisiana and South Dakota), while three others now require all voters to present photo ID at the polls (Florida, Indiana, Missouri). Georgia also passed a photo ID law in 2006, but a federal judge ruled that the requirement was unconstitutional.

[12] The Colorado Secretary of State's office reported spending more than $1 million in legal fees between 2002 and 2006 in dealing with election-related lawsuits, an amount that was three times the total annual budget for this office.

[13] Provided by Electiononline.org, *http://www.electionline.org/Default.aspx?tabid=290.*

[14] NIST Resolution #06-06, available at *http://vote.nist.gov/AdoptedResolutions12040506.pdf.* The EAC's Technical Guidelines Development Committee (TGDC) is using this resolution and others to draft updated Voluntary Voting Standards Guidelines that will tentatively be delivered to the EAC for approval in July 2007. After the draft is delivered to the EAC, it will be reviewed by the EAC Standards Board and EAC Board of Advisors. NIST will develop test suites for the new standards and deliver them to the EAC, so that testing will be more uniform and consistent regardless of which federally approved labs the states are using.

About the Author

Kay Stimson, an independent communications consultant, is currently representing the National Association of Secretaries of State (NASS) as director of communications and special projects. She was the organization's media spokesperson from 2000 through 2004, and previously spent several years as a television journalist.

Table 4.15
THE SECRETARIES OF STATE, 2007

State or other jurisdiction	Name and party	Method of selection	Length of regular term in years	Date of first service	Present term ends	Number of previous terms	Maximum consecutive terms allowed by constitution
Alabama	Beth Chapman (R)	E	4	1/07	1/11	. . .	2
Alaska	. . . . (a)						
Arizona	Jan Brewer (R)	E	4	1/03	1/11	1	2
Arkansas	Charlie Daniels (D)	E	4	12/02	12/10	1	2
California	Debra Bowen (D)	E	4	1/07	1/11	. . .	2
Colorado	Mike Coffman (R)	E	4	1/07	1/11	. . .	2
Connecticut	Susan Bysiewicz (D)	E	4	1/99	1/11	2	. . .
Delaware	Harriet Smith Windsor (D)	A	. . .	1/01	. . .	. . .	. . .
Florida	Kurt Browning (R)	A	. . .	12/06	. . .	. . .	. . .
Georgia	Karen Handel (R)	E	4	1/07	1/11	. . .	. . .
Hawaii	. . . . (a)						
Idaho	Ben Ysursa (R)	E	4	1/03	1/11	1	. . .
Illinois	Jesse White (D)	E	4	1/99	1/11	2	. . .
Indiana	Todd Rokita (R)	E	4	1/03	1/11	1	2
Iowa	Michael A. Mauro (D)	E	4	12/06	12/10	. . .	. . .
Kansas	Ron Thornburgh (R)	E	4	1/95	1/11	3	. . .
Kentucky	Trey Grayson (R)	E	4	12/03	12/07	. . .	2
Louisiana	Jay Dardenne (R)	E	4	11/06	12/07 (b)	. . .	. . .
Maine	Matthew Dunlap (D)	L	2	1/05	1/09	1	. . .
Maryland	Dennis Schnepfe (D)	A	. . .	2/07	. . .	. . .	. . .
Massachusetts	William Francis Galvin (D)	E	4	1/95	1/11	3	. . .
Michigan	Terri Lynn Land (R)	E	4	1/03	1/11	1	2
Minnesota	Mark Ritchie (DFL)	E	4	1/07	1/11	. . .	2
Mississippi	Eric Clark (D)	E	4	1/96	1/08	2	. . .
Missouri	Robin Carnahan (D)	E	4	1/05	1/09	. . .	. . .
Montana	Brad Johnson (R)	E	4	1/05	1/09	. . .	(c)
Nebraska	John Gale (R)	E	4	12/00 (d)	1/11	(d)	. . .
Nevada	Ross Miller (D)	E	4	1/07	1/11	. . .	2
New Hampshire	William Gardner (D)	L	2	12/76	12/10	16	. . .
New Jersey	Nina Mitchell Wells (D)	A	. . .	1/06	1/10	. . .	. . .
New Mexico	Mary E. Herrera (D)	E	4	1/07	12/10	. . .	2
New York	Lorraine A. Cortes-Vazquez (R)	A	. . .	1/07	. . .	. . .	. . .
North Carolina	Elaine Marshall (D)	E	4	1/97	1/09	2	. . .
North Dakota	Alvin Jaeger (R)	E	4 (e)	1/93	12/10	4	. . .
Ohio	Jennifer Brunner (D)	E	4	1/07	1/11	. . .	2
Oklahoma	M. Susan Savage (D)	A	4	1/03	1/11	1	. . .
Oregon	Bill Bradbury (D)	E	4	1/99 (f)	1/09	(f)	2
Pennsylvania	Pedro A. Cortes (D)	A	. . .	5/03	. . .	. . .	. . .
Rhode Island	Ralph Mollis (D)	E	4	1/07	1/11	. . .	2
South Carolina	Mark Hammond (R)	E	4	1/03	1/11	2	. . .
South Dakota	Chris Nelson (R)	E	4	1/03	1/11	1	2
Tennessee	Riley Darnell (D)	L	4	1/93	1/09	3	. . .
Texas	Roger Williams (R)	A	. . .	2/05	. . .	. . .	. . .
Utah	. . . . (a)						
Vermont	Deb Markowitz (D)	E	2	1/99	1/09	4	. . .
Virginia	Katherine K. Hanley (D)	A	. . .	3/06	. . .	. . .	. . .
Washington	Sam Reed (R)	E	4	1/01	1/09	1	. . .
West Virginia	Betty Ireland (R)	E	4	1/05	1/09	. . .	. . .
Wisconsin	Douglas LaFollette (D)	E	4	1/99	1/11	2	. . .
Wyoming	Max Maxfield (R)	E	4	1/07	1/11	. . .	. . .
American Samoa	. . . . (a)						
Guam	. . . . (a)						
No. Mariana Islands	. . . . (a)						
Puerto Rico	Fernando J. Bonilla	A	. . .	2005	. . .	. . .	. . .
U.S. Virgin Islands	. . . . (a)						

See footnotes at end of table.

THE SECRETARIES OF STATE, 2007 — Continued

Sources: The Council of State Governments' survey, January 2007.

Key:

E — Elected by voters.
A — Appointed by governor.
L — Elected by legislature.
. . . — No provision for.

(a) No secretary of state; lieutenant governor performs functions of this office. See Tables 4.12 through 4.14.

(b) Dardenne was elected in a special election September 20, 2006. After the death of W. Fox McKeithen in July 2005, First Deputy Secretary Al Ater assumed the duties of secretary of state until the special election could be held. Dardenne intends to run for secretary of state in the regular 2007 election.

(c) Eligible for eight out of 16 years.

(d) Secretary Gale was appointed by Governor Mike Johanns in December 2000 upon the resignation of Scott Moore. He was elected to a full four-year term in November 2002 and again in 2006.

(e) Because of a constitutional change approved by voters in 2000, the term for the secretary elected in 2004 was for two years. It will revert to a four-year term in 2007.

(f) Secretary Bradbury was appointed secretary of state in November 1999 and was elected to a four-year term in November 2000 and 2004.

Table 4.16
SECRETARIES OF STATE: QUALIFICATIONS FOR OFFICE

State or other jurisdiction	Minimum age	U.S. citizen (years) (a)	State resident (years) (b)	Qualified voter (years)	Method of selection to office
Alabama	25	7	5	★	E
Alaska			(c)		
Arizona	25	10	5	. . .	E
Arkansas	18	★	★	★	E
California	18	★	★	★	E
Colorado	25	★	2	. . .	E
Connecticut	18	★	★	★	E
Delaware	. . .	. . .	. . .	. . .	A
Florida			(d)		
Georgia	25	10	4	★	E
Hawaii			(c)		
Idaho	25	★	2	★	E
Illinois	25	★	3	. . .	E
Indiana	. . .	. . .	★	. . .	E
Iowa	18	★	. . .	. . .	E
Kansas	. . .	★	★	★	E
Kentucky	30	★	★	★	E
Louisiana	25	5	5	★	E
Maine	. . .	. . .	. . .	. . .	(e)
Maryland	. . .	. . .	. . .	. . .	A
Massachusetts	18	★	5	★	E
Michigan	18	★	★	★	E
Minnesota	21	★	30 days	★	E
Mississippi	25	★	5	★	E
Missouri	. . .	★	★	2	E
Montana	25	★	2	★	E
Nebraska	. . .	★	★	★	E
Nevada	25	2	2	. . .	E
New Hampshire	18	★	★	★	(e)
New Jersey	18	★	★	★	A
New Mexico	30	★	8	★	E
New York	18	★	★	. . .	A
North Carolina	21	. . .	. . .	★	E
North Dakota	25	★	5	★	E
Ohio	18	. . .	★	★	E
Oklahoma	31	★	★	10	A
Oregon	18	. . .	★	★	E
Pennsylvania	. . .	. . .	. . .	★	A
Rhode Island	18	★	30 days	★	E
South Carolina	. . .	★	★	★	E
South Dakota	. . .	. . .	. . .	. . .	E
Tennessee	. . .	. . .	. . .	. . .	(e)
Texas	18	★	. . .	. . .	A
Utah			(c)		
Vermont	18	★	★	★	E
Virginia	. . .	. . .	. . .	. . .	A
Washington	18	★	★	★	E
West Virginia	. . .	★	★	★	E
Wisconsin	18	★	★	★	E
Wyoming	25	★	1	★	E
American Samoa			(c)		
Guam			(c)		
No. Mariana Islands			(c)		
Puerto Rico	. . .	5	5	. . .	A
U.S. Virgin Islands			(c)		

Source: The Council of State Governments' survey of secretaries of state, January 2007.

Key:

★ — Formal provision; number of years not specified.

. . . — No formal provision.

A — Appointed by governor.

E — Elected by voters.

(a) In some states you must be a U.S. citizen to be an elector, and must be an elector to run.

(b) In some states you must be a state resident to be an elector, and must be an elector to run.

(c) No secretary of state.

(d) As of January 1, 2003, the office of Secretary of State shall be an appointed position (appointed by the governor). It will no longer be a cabinet position, but an agency head and the Department of State shall be an agency under the governor's office.

(e) Chosen by joint ballot of state senators and representatives. In Maine and New Hampshire, every two years. In Tennessee, every four years.

Table 4.17
SECRETARIES OF STATE: ELECTION AND REGISTRATION DUTIES

State or other jurisdiction	Election								Registration				
	Chief election officer	Determines ballot eligibility of political parties	Receives initiative and/or referendum petition	Files certificate of nomination or election	Supplies election ballots or materials to local officials	Files candidates' expense papers	Files other campaign reports	Conducts voter education programs	Registers charitable organizations	Registers corporations (a)	Processes and/or commissions notaries public	Registers securities	Registers trade names/marks
Alabama	★	★	...	★	★	★	★	★	★	★	★	...	★
Alaska (b)	★	★	★	★	★	...	...	★	...	...	★	...	...
Arizona	★	★	★	★	...	★	★	★	★	...	★	...	★
Arkansas	★	★	★	★	...	★	★	★	...	★	★	...	★
California	★(c)	★	★	★	...	★	★	★	★(d)	★	★	...	★
Colorado	★	★	★	★	...	★	★	★	★	★	★	...	★
Connecticut	★	★	...	★	★	★	★	★	★	★	★	...	★
Delaware	...	...	...	(e)	...	...	(f)	...	★(g)	★	★	...	★
Florida	★	★	★	★	...	★	★	...	★	★	...	...	★
Georgia	★	★	...	★	★	★	★	★	★	★	...	★	★
Hawaii (b)	...	...	...	...	...	...	...	...	★	★	★	...	★
Idaho	★	★	★	★	★	★	★	★	★	★	★	...	★
Illinois	...	...	★	(h)	...	...	...	...	★	★	★	★	★
Indiana	★	★	...	★	★	★	★	★	★	★	★	★	★
Iowa	★	★	...	★	★	...	...	★	★	★	★	...	★
Kansas	★	★	...	★	★	★	...	★	★	★	★	...	★
Kentucky	★	★	...	★	...	...	...	★	★	★	★	...	★
Louisiana	★	...	...	...	★	...	...	...	★	★	★	★	★
Maine	★	★	★	★	★	...	...	★	★	★	★	...	★
Maryland	...	★	★	★	...	...	...	★	★	★	★	...	★
Massachusetts	★	★	★	★	★	(f)	(f)	★	...	★	★	★	★
Michigan	★	★	★	★	...	★	★	★	...	...	★	...	...
Minnesota	★	★	★	★	...	...	...	★	★	★	★	...	★
Mississippi	★	★	★	★	★	★	★	★	★	★	★	★	★
Missouri	★	★	★	★	...	...	...	★	★	★	★	★	★
Montana	★	★	★	★	★	...	...	★	★	★	★	...	★
Nebraska	★	★	★	★	★	...	...	★	★	★	★	...	★
Nevada	★	★	★	★	★	★	★	★	...	★	★	★	★
New Hampshire	★	★	...	★	★	★	★	...	★	★	★	★	★
New Jersey	...	...	...	...	...	...	...	...	...	...	...	...	...
New Mexico	★	★	★	★	★	★	★	★	...	...	★	...	★
New York	...	...	...	...	...	...	...	...	★	★	★	...	★
North Carolina	...	...	...	...	...	...	...	...	★	★	★	★	★
North Dakota	★	★	★	★	★	★	★	★	★	★	★	...	★
Ohio	★	★	★	...	★	★	...	★	...	★	★	...	★
Oklahoma	...	...	★	★(i)	...	...	...	...	★	★(j)	★	...	★
Oregon	★	★	★	★	★	★	★	★	★	★	★	★	★
Pennsylvania	★	★	...	★	★	...	★	★	★	★	★	★	★
Rhode Island	★	★	...	★	★	...	...	★	...	★	★	...	★
South Carolina	...	...	...	...	...	...	...	...	★	★(k)	★	...	★
South Dakota	★	★	★	★	...	★	★	★	...	★	★	...	★
Tennessee (n)	...	★	...	★	★	...	...	★	★	★	★	...	★
Texas	★	★	...	★	★	...	...	★	★	★	★	...	★
Utah (b)	★	★	★	★	★	★	★	★	★	★	...	...	★
Vermont	★	...	...	★	★	★	...	★	★	★	★	...	★
Virginia	...	...	...	...	...	...	...	...	★	★	...	...	★
Washington	★	★	★	★	...	...	...	★	★	★	★	...	★
West Virginia	★	★	...	★	...	★	★	★	★	★	★	...	★
Wisconsin	...	...	...	...	...	...	...	...	...	★	...	...	★
Wyoming	★	★	★	★	(l)	★	★	★	★	★	★	★	★
American Samoa (b)	...	...	...	★	...	★	★	★	★	★	★	...	...
Guam (b)	...	...	...	...	...	...	...	...	...	★	...	...	...
Puerto Rico	...	...	...	...	...	...	...	...	★	★	★	★	★
U.S. Virgin Islands (b)	...	...	...	...	...	...	...	...	★	★(m)	★	...	★

See footnotes at end of table.

SECRETARIES OF STATE: ELECTION AND REGISTRATION DUTIES — Continued

Source: The Council of State Governments' survey of secretaries of state, January 2007.

Key:

★ — Responsible for activity.

. . . — Not responsible for activity.

(a) Unless otherwise indicated, office registers domestic, foreign and non-profit corporations.

(b) No secretary of state. Duties indicated are performed by lieutenant governor. In Hawaii, election-related responsibilities have been transferred to an independent Chief Election Officer.

(c) Other election duties include: tallying votes from all 58 counties, testing and certifying voting systems, maintaining statewide voter registration database, publishing Voter Information Guide/State Ballot Pamphlet.

(d) This office does not register charitable trusts, but does register charitable organizations as nonprofit corporations; also limited partnerships, limited liability corporations, and domestic partners.

(e) Files certificates of election for publication purposes only; does not file certificates of nomination.

(f) Federal candidates only.

(g) Incorporated organizations only.

(h) Office issues document, but does not receive it.

(i) Certifies U.S. Congressional election results to Washington, D.C.

(j) Also registers limited partnerships, limited liability companies and limited liability partnerships.

(k) Also registers the Cable Franchise Authority.

(l) Materials not ballots.

(m) Both domestic and foreign profit; but only domestic nonprofit.

(n) Appoints the Coordinator of Elections who performs the election duties indicated.

Table 4.18
SECRETARIES OF STATE: CUSTODIAL, PUBLICATION AND LEGISLATIVE DUTIES

State or other jurisdiction	Custodial				Publication					Legislative			
	Archives state records and regulations	Files state agency rules and regulations	Administers uniform commercial code provisions	Files other corporate documents	State manual or directory	Session laws	State constitution	Statutes	Administrative rules and regulations	Opens legislative sessions (a)	Enrolls or engrosses bills	Retains copies of bills	Registers lobbyists
Alabama	...	...	★	★	...	★	★	★	...	...	★	★	...
Alaska (b)	...	★	...	...	...	★	...	...	★	★	...	★	★
Arizona	★	★	★	...	...	★	...	...	★	...	...	★	★
Arkansas	★	★	★	★	...	★	...	...	★	...	...	★	★
California	★	...	★	★	★	...	...	...	...	...	(e)	...	★
Colorado	...	★	★	★	...	★	...	...	★	...	...	★	★
Connecticut	★(c)	★	★	★	★	...	...	...	...	S	...	★	...
Delaware	★	★	★	★	...	...	...	...	★	...	...	...	...
Florida	★	★	...	★	...	★	★	★	★	...	...	...	...
Georgia	★	★	...	...	★	...	★	...	★	...	...	...	...
Hawaii (b)	...	★	...	...	...	★	...	★	★	...	...	★	...
Idaho	...	...	★	...	★	★	★	...	...	...	...	★	★
Illinois	★	★	★	★	★	★	★	...	★	H	...	★	★
Indiana	★	★	★	★	...	...	★	...	...	...	...	★	...
Iowa	★	...	★	★	...	★	★	...	...	...	★	★	...
Kansas	...	★	★	★	★	...	...	★	★	...	...	...	★
Kentucky	★	...	★	★	...	...	...	...	...	...	★	★	...
Louisiana	★	...	★	★	★	...	...	★	...	...	...	★	...
Maine	★	★	★	★	...	...	★	★	★	...	...	...	...
Maryland	...	...	...	...	...	...	...	...	(d)	...	...	★	...
Massachusetts	★	★	★	★	★	★	★	★	★	...	...	★	★
Michigan	★	★	★	...	...	★	★	★	★	...	...	...	★
Minnesota	★	★	★	★	★	★	...	...	...	H	...	★	...
Mississippi	...	★	★	★	★	★	...	...	★	H	...	★	★
Missouri	★	★	★	★	★	...	...	...	★	H	★	★	...
Montana	★	★	★	★	...	...	★	...	★	H	...	★	...
Nebraska	★	★	★	★	...	...	...	...	...	...	...	★	...
Nevada	★	★	★	★	...	...	★	...	...	...	...	★	★
New Hampshire	★	...	★	★	★	...	★	...	...	...	...	★	★
New Jersey	★	...	...	...	...	...	★	...	...	...	...	★	...
New Mexico	...	★	★	...	...	★	★	★	...	H	...	★	★
New York	...	★	★	...	★	...	★	...	★	...	...	...	...
North Carolina	★	★	★	★	★	★	★	...	...	...	...	...	★
North Dakota	...	★	★	★	...	...	...	...	...	...	★	★	...
Ohio	...	★	★	★	★	★	★	...	...	...	★	★	...
Oklahoma	...	...	...	...	...	...	...	...	★	...	...	★	...
Oregon	★	★	★	★	★	...	★	...	...	...	...	★	...
Pennsylvania	...	...	★	★	...	...	...	...	...	...	★	★	...
Rhode Island (f)	★	★	★	★	...	...	★	...	★	...	...	★	★
South Carolina	★	...	★	★	...	...	...	...	...	...	...	★	...
South Dakota	★	★	★	★	★	...	★	...	...	★	...	★	★
Tennessee (g)	★	★	★	★	★	★	...	...	★	...	...	...	...
Texas	★	★	★	★	...	★	...	...	★	...	...	★	...
Utah (b)	...	...	...	...	...	...	...	...	...	...	...	★	★
Vermont	★	★	★	★	★	★	★	...	★	H	...	★	★
Virginia	...	...	...	...	★	...	...	...	...	...	...	...	★
Washington	★	...	...	★	★	...	...	...	...	...	...	★	...
West Virginia	★	★	★	★	...	...	...	...	★	...	...	★	...
Wisconsin	...	...	...	...	...	...	...	...	...	...	...	...	...
Wyoming	★	★	★	★	★	...	★	...	...	H	...	★	★
American Samoa (b)	...	★	...	★	...	★	★	★	★	...	...	...	...
Guam (b)	...	...	...	...	...	...	...	...	...	...	...	...	...
Puerto Rico	...	★	★	★	...	★	★	★	★	...	...	...	...
U.S. Virgin Islands (b)	...	★	★	★	...	...	...	★	...	...	★	★	...

Source: The Council of State Governments' survey of secretaries of state, January 2007.

Key:
★ — Responsible for activity.
. . . — Not responsible for activity.
(a) In this column only: ★ — Both houses; H — House; S — Senate.
(b) No secretary of state. Duties indicated are performed by the lieutenant governor.

(c) The secretary of state is keeper of public records, but the state archives is a department of the Connecticut State Library.
(d) Code of Maryland regulations.
(e) Office does not enroll or engross bills but does chapter them.
(f) Additional duties include administering oaths of office to general officers and legislators.
(g) Additional duties include the Tennessee State Library and Archives, administrative law judges, charitable gaming regulation, service of process/summons, sports agent registration and temporary liens.

Attorneys General: Working at the Forefront of National Issues

By Angelita Plemmer

The National Association of Attorneys General is celebrating its 100th anniversary, and continues to provide attorneys general with an opportunity to work collectively for the common good. Attorneys general are at the forefront of a number of critical legal and law enforcement issues and play a vital leadership role as representatives of the public interest.

The Work of Attorneys General

In October 1907, an historic event occurred that would change the landscape of law and public policy in the United States. For the first time in this nation's history, a group of state attorneys general met in St. Louis, Mo., to try to coordinate their law enforcement efforts. Their purpose was to discuss what role, if any, they could play in response to the anti-competitive practices of Standard Oil (1870–1911), the largest oil company in the country, based in Cleveland, Ohio. Standard Oil had created a powerful monopoly in the oil industry and consumers were paying the price.

The company began as an Ohio partnership formed by the well-known industrialist John D. Rockefeller, his brother William Rockefeller, Henry Flagler, chemist Samuel Andrews, and a silent partner, Stephen V. Harkness. Using highly effective and widely criticized tactics, Standard Oil absorbed or destroyed most of its competition in Cleveland, then throughout the northeastern United States, putting numerous small corporations out of business.[1]

State attorneys general, along with the U.S. Department of Justice, succeeded in breaking the monopoly and set the stage for what would evolve into one of the most effective associations of state officials in the country. This year, the National Association of Attorneys General (NAAG) celebrates its 100th anniversary. Today, under the auspices of NAAG, attorneys general meet three times a year to discuss a number of complex legal issues facing their states, including antitrust, consumer protection, public corruption and white collar crime, pharmaceutical pricing, victims' rights, civil rights, homeland security, cybercrime, pre-emption of state law, juvenile crime and gangs, tobacco enforcement, environmental protection, recent decisions by the U.S. Supreme Court, federal legislation and other critical legal areas of interest. During these gatherings, attorneys general also meet with the president and other leaders of the current administration, as well as members of Congress, to discuss federal policies and legislation that impact the states.

As attorneys general are often at the forefront of emerging legal issues, the role of the attorney general in protecting the public interest is becoming more complex with each passing year. And, as NAAG recognizes its 100th year in existence, the next century will continue to bring new opportunities for attorneys general to assume a leadership role in these critical areas of public life.

NAAG, and its related Mission Foundation, has a budget of $7.7 million and consists of the chief legal officers of the 50 states, the District of Columbia and the U.S. territories of American Samoa, Guam, the U.S. Virgin Islands and the commonwealths of Puerto Rico and the Northern Mariana Islands.

While the visibility of state attorneys general has increased in recent years, the far-reaching and critical role that attorneys general play in the operation of state government is often misunderstood by the public. Attorneys general serve as the chief civil litigator of the state, counseling and defending the state. Attorneys general also issue legal opinions to state officials and the public. Attorneys general also enforce a variety of civil laws, including consumer protection, antitrust, environment, securities, child support enforcement and labor. All that an attorney general must do is shaped by the ultimate charge to serve as guardian of the law and in so doing, to have the law serve the public interest.[2]

The myriad of responsibilities of attorneys general lend themselves to creative and innovative policymaking and law enforcement. Their 100 years of collective experience have shown that some solutions are best found by working together.[3] The following highlights some of these activities:

Antitrust

The NAAG Antitrust Committee and the Multistate Antitrust Task Force work to coordinate the exercise of powers of individual attorneys general in antitrust matters. The task force comprises antitrust attorneys from the 56 member states and jurisdictions and organizes the conduct of multistate investigations and the filing of multistate actions. A single attorney general or group of attorneys general will take the lead in an investigation, issuing administrative subpoenas or civil investigative demands. The parties agree that their responses will be shared with other interested attorneys general. The attorneys general have found that this process not only may reduce the burden on respondents, it also increases coordination among the states and allows the most efficient use of state resources. Attorneys general have investigated pharmaceutical pricing, mergers in the oil and airline industries, price-fixing by manufacturers of vitamins and computer hardware, and monopolization of computer software. The NAAG Antitrust Committee advocates competition through policy positions, comments on federal and state legislation, and amicus briefs in appropriate antitrust cases. Their goal today, as it was some 100 years ago, is to preserve competition, and accordingly, lower prices, to provide higher quality and a greater variety of innovative new products for residents of their states. NAAG's Antitrust Project supports these efforts by facilitating communication among attorney general offices, and monitors legislative and regulatory developments in antitrust.

Bankruptcy

Attorneys general established a NAAG Bankruptcy Project, initially, to assist their offices with presenting their property damage claims in several major asbestos bankruptcies. Today, it has been expanded to provide assistance to attorneys general with respect to all bankruptcy issues that might arise. Issues range from the impact of bankruptcy on state collection of taxes, student loans and domestic support obligations, to protection of states from bankruptcy's potential for interference with critical state police and regulatory enforcement activities in areas such as consumer protection, antitrust, environmental law, trade negotiations and tobacco enforcement.

Civil Rights

Attorneys general remain active on civil rights issues such as settlement agreements in housing, employment and mortgage lending discrimination. Many state attorneys general continue their active role in community education and outreach, which includes school harassment and disability rights. In addition, a number of attorneys general are considering the creation of "Cold Case" units to investigate unsolved homicides, with a focus on racial crimes dating back to the civil rights era. These units would investigate unsolved homicides using modern forensic and DNA techniques. NAAG's Civil Rights Project provides information and support to the states on affirmative civil rights issues developed and implemented largely through the efforts of task forces that work in virtually all areas of public life.

Consumer Protection

Attorneys general are using traditional enforcement tools in innovative ways, working together on multistate cases in both federal and state courts to protect consumers. These joint actions ensure consistent enforcement of state consumer protection laws. In some cases, state attorneys general have at their disposal a wider array of enforcement tools and remedies than are available to their federal counterparts. Joint state actions are widely recognized to be so effective that the Federal Trade Commission now routinely works with state attorneys general to seek coast-to-coast injunctions in instances of anti-consumer business practices. Recently, attorneys general have worked on predatory lending, consumer privacy and security breaches, and pharmaceutical marketing. NAAG's Consumer Protection Project encourages interstate cooperation by facilitating and funding multistate working group and litigation discussions and listserves, in addition to training opportunities.

Criminal Law

In most states, the attorney general's prosecutorial role is limited, focused on complex crimes such as Medicaid fraud, environmental crime or public corruption. In Delaware, Rhode Island and Alaska, however, the attorney general serves as the sole prosecutorial authority. Most attorneys general handle criminal appeals. Attorneys general use their offices to advance criminal justice initiatives within their own jurisdictions and nationwide. For example, many states have passed statutes restricting access to precursor chemicals for methamphetamine, based on a statute originally developed by Oklahoma. Other examples include initiatives related to sex offenders, cybercrime, gang violence and identity theft. Attorneys general also advocate for adequate state and local law enforcement assistance funding. NAAG's Criminal Law Project supports the work of attorneys general in criminal investigation and prosecution, and attendant policy issues, including legislative initiatives and programs; stays abreast of legal developments in the field; and coordinates and shares NAAG information with related associations, agencies and coalitions.

Cybercrime

There are approximately a dozen attorney general offices where cybercrime units are headquartered. However, the majority of attorney general offices work with cybercrime units through multidisciplinary task forces with other state entities, and the actual unit is housed in an alternative agency. Nonetheless, attorneys general are taking an active role in fighting cybercrime. Attorneys general across the country regularly propose state legislation to increase penalties for online predators who victimize children, the elderly or other unsuspecting consumers. Attorneys general are routinely involved in the education and outreach to all consumers to promote online safety, protect consumer privacy and implement proactive law enforcement strategies. NAAG has a Cybercrime Project that provides training to staff within attorney general offices on the most current information, technologies and approaches to combating computer-facilitated crimes. Through the project, attorneys general and their staffs further explore the legal complexities of spyware and Internet crimes against children, as well as develop an understanding of the basics of digital evidence. The project also provides information to state attorneys general on issues related to funding, equipment and manpower requirements, protocols and procedures.

End-of-Life Health Care

Attorneys general are charged with protecting constituents in matters affecting the public interest, including ensuring consumer protections for those who are dying. The focus for state attorneys general has been in three areas: ensuring the availability of appropriate pain management for citizens while aggressively pursuing prosecutions against those who illegally divert controlled substances; ensuring competent end-of-life care for citizens; and ensuring that state policies acknowledge and respect the wishes of those who are at the end of their lives. Many attorney general offices provide invaluable information to consumers to ensure that they are making informed health care decisions and that their wishes are clearly articulated to family members, caregivers and health care providers. NAAG's End of Life Health Care Project serves as an information clearinghouse for attorney general offices and provides invaluable links to various organizations involved in end-of-life issues.

Environment

State attorneys general have been at the forefront of environmental law developments during the last 30 years. As national legislation protecting the environ-ment was enacted, many states followed suit with parallel state statutes. Attorneys general made use of the new laws and built on existing common law to reduce pollution of the air, land and water. One area specific to state enforcement is environmental protection at federal facilities, and attorneys general have been diligent in working to safeguard the health and safety of their citizens by pushing the federal government to meet the same standards that private industry must follow. NAAG's Environment Project assists the attorneys general in activities to influence national and regional legal strategies on environmental matters and provides "capacity-building" assistance that allows the environmental sections of attorney general offices to function at a higher level of efficiency and knowledge through training, legal analysis and by providing forums for discussion.

Medicaid Fraud

Attorneys general, charged with the responsibility of protecting individuals and state programs from fraud, may rely on their Medicaid Fraud Control Unit (MFCU), an entity of state government, annually certified by the secretary of the U.S. Department of Health and Human Services. MFCUs are funded by the U. S. Department of Health and Human Services, with grant amounts matched by state funding. The unit has either statewide criminal prosecution authority or formal procedures for referring cases to local prosecutorial authorities with respect to the detection, investigation and prosecution of suspected criminal violations of the Medicaid program. Forty-two MFCUs are housed in attorney general offices, but all attorneys general are concerned with protecting the public, particularly its most vulnerable—those who may be the victims of abuse or neglect as residents of health care facilities that receive Medicaid funds. NAAG's MFCU Project provides a forum for the mutual exchange of views and experiences on subjects of importance to the state Medicaid Fraud Control Units and fosters interstate cooperation on legal and law enforcement issues affecting the unit.

Legislative

Frequently, attorneys general across the country are asked by Congress, the media, business organizations and constituents for their views on bills pending in Congress that affect the powers and duties of attorneys general. Often, such legislation seeks to pre-empt state law in the areas of consumer protection, environment, antitrust, bankruptcy, securities, criminal law and many other areas within the jurisdiction of attorneys general. NAAG's Legislative Project serves as the initial point of contact for information requests from attorney general offices, members of Congress/staff, and other interested associations and individuals about attorney general views on federal legislation. The Legislative Project remains current on federal legislation of interest to attorneys general, and the project assists in the development of policy positions on issues as directed by state attorneys general, ensuring that all perspectives are examined. Attorneys general are often at the front lines of emerging legal and law enforcement trends and can provide a unique and valuable perspective at the federal and state level.

Appellate Advocacy

Attorneys general will appear on behalf of their states or agencies in the U.S. Supreme Court. Attorneys general are second only to the United States Solicitor General, who represents the federal government, in frequency of appearance before the nation's highest court. The attorneys general will typically represent the state and many, if not all, state agencies. During the 1980s, attorneys general took a number of important steps to improve their individual and collective Supreme Court advocacy work. One step included creating NAAG's Supreme Court Project, which helps attorneys general present cases effectively before the Court, both as parties and collectively as *amici curiae*.[4]

The Project's Moot Court Program conducts moot courts for virtually every state attorney who argues in the Court. Moot court panelists are Supreme Court practitioners, including members of the U.S. Solicitor General's Office, former Supreme Court clerks and Supreme Court experts in academia and private practice. On the written advocacy side, project counsel edits about 40 merit briefs, *cert* petitions, briefs in opposition and *amicus* briefs filed in the Supreme Court each term. In addition to training and legal analysis, the project sponsors an intense Supreme Court Fellows Program, designed to give state lawyers an opportunity to obtain direct and intensive hands-on exposure to Supreme Court practice.

Tobacco

Since 1998, almost 50 tobacco manufacturing companies (known as Subsequent Participating Manufacturers under the agreement) have joined the 1998 landmark Tobacco Master Settlement Agreement. Attorneys general hope other tobacco companies that have not joined the agreement will join to make the coverage of the MSA close to universal. The MSA, enforced by attorneys general, contains a number of public health provisions designed to reduce youth smoking. It prohibits tobacco companies from targeting youth in advertising, promotions or marketing. It also bans industry actions aimed at initiating, maintaining or increasing youth smoking. Other provisions of the agreement ban all outdoor advertising, including billboards, signs and placards in arenas, stadiums, shopping malls and video game arcades; limit advertising signage outside of retail establishments to a size of 14 square feet; and ban transit advertising of tobacco products. Tobacco companies are also prohibited from attempting to suppress research about the health hazards from the use of their products or into the marketing or development of new products; and they are prohibited from making any material misrepresentations regarding the health consequence of smoking. NAAG's Tobacco Project helps attorneys general enforce the provision of the MSA by providing litigation support, technical assistance and legal analysis. As the chief legal officers of their respective jurisdictions, attorneys general have played a critical role in ensuring MSA compliance by tobacco companies and protecting the public health and safety.

Conclusion

Attorneys general serve as guardians of the law and ensure that these laws serve the public interest. Their cooperative efforts, born a century ago, have had a tremendous impact on public life. As individuals or working collectively through NAAG, attorneys general will continue to be at the forefront of emerging state and federal issues.

Notes

[1] Ralph W. Hidy and Muriel E. Hidy, *Pioneering in Big Business, 1882–1911: History of Standard Oil Company*, (New Jersey, 1955).

[2] Charles Burson, *State Attorneys General: Guardians of the Law*, (Washington, D.C.: National Association of Attorneys General, 1994–95).

[3] Ibid.

[4] Lynne Ross, editor, *State Attorneys General Powers and Responsibilities*, (Washington, D.C.: NAAG, 1990).

About the Author

This article was edited and compiled by **Angelita Plemmer**, director of communications for the National Association of Attorneys General. A former newspaper journalist, Plemmer joined the association staff in 2001. She formerly worked as the public information officer for the city of Roanoke, Va., and as the assistant city manager for public information for the city of Alexandria, Va. She holds a master's degree in journalism from Columbia University and a Bachelor of Arts degree in rhetoric and communications studies from the University of Virginia.

Table 4.19
THE ATTORNEYS GENERAL, 2007

State or other jurisdiction	Name and party	Method of selection	Length of regular term in years	Date of first service	Present term ends	Number of previous terms	Maximum consecutive terms allowed
Alabama	Troy King (R)	E	4	3/04 (a)	1/11	(a)	2
Alaska	Talis J. Colberg (R)	A	...	12/06	...	...	...
Arizona	Terry Goddard (D)	E	4	1/03	1/11	1	2
Arkansas	Dustin McDaniel (D)	E	4	1/07	1/11	...	2
California	Edmund Gerald Brown (D)	E	4	1/07	1/11	...	2
Colorado	John W. Suthers (R)	E	4	1/05 (b)	1/11	(b)	2
Connecticut	Richard Blumenthal (D)	E	4	1/91	1/11	4	★
Delaware	Joseph R. Biden III (D)	E	4	1/07	1/11	...	★
Florida	Bill McCollum (R)	E	4	1/07	1/11	...	2
Georgia	Thurbert E. Baker (D)	E	4	6/97 (c)	1/11	2 (c)	★
Hawaii	Mark J. Bennett (R)	A	4 (d)	1/03	12/10	1	...
Idaho	Lawrence Wasden (R)	E	4	1/03	1/11	1	★
Illinois	Lisa Madigan (D)	E	4	1/03	1/11	1	★
Indiana	Steve Carter (R)	E	4	1/01	1/09	1	★
Iowa	Tom Miller (D)	E	4	1/79 (e)	1/11	6 (e)	★
Kansas	Paul Morrison (D)	E	4	1/07	1/11	...	★
Kentucky	Greg Stumbo (D)	E	4	1/04	12/07	...	2
Louisiana	Charles C. Foti Jr. (D)	E	4	1/04	1/08	...	★
Maine	G. Steven Rowe (D)	L (f)	2	1/01	1/07	3	4
Maryland	Douglas F. Gansler (D)	E	4	1/07	1/11	...	★
Massachusetts	Martha Coakley (D)	E	4	1/07	1/11	...	2
Michigan	Mike Cox (R)	E	4	1/03	1/11	1	2
Minnesota	Lori Swanson (D)	E	4	1/07	1/11	...	★
Mississippi	Jim Hood (D)	E	4	1/04	1/08	...	★
Missouri	Jeremiah W. Nixon (D)	E	4	1/93	1/09	3	★
Montana	Mike McGrath (D)	E	4	1/01	1/09	1	2
Nebraska	Jon Bruning (R)	E	4	1/03	1/11	1	★
Nevada	Catherine Cortez Masto (D)	E	4	1/07	1/11	...	2
New Hampshire	Kelly Ayotte (R)	A	...	7/04	3/09	...	...
New Jersey	Stuart Rabner (D)	A	...	9/06	...	...	...
New Mexico	Gary King (D)	E	4	1/07	1/11	...	2 (g)
New York	Andrew Cuomo (D)	E	4	1/07	1/11	...	★
North Carolina	Roy Cooper (D)	E	4	1/01	1/09	1	★
North Dakota	Wayne Stenehjem (R)	E	4 (h)	1/01	12/06	2 (h)	★
Ohio	Marc Dann (D)	E	4	1/07	1/11	...	2
Oklahoma	W.A. Drew Edmondson (D)	E	4	1/95	1/11	3	★
Oregon	Hardy Myers (D)	E	4	1/97	1/09	2	★
Pennsylvania	Tom Corbett (R)	E	4	1/05	1/09	...	2
Rhode Island	Patrick Lynch (D)	E	4	1/03	1/11	1	2
South Carolina	Henry McMaster (R)	E	4	1/03	1/11	1	★
South Dakota	Larry Long (R)	E	4	1/03	1/11	1	2 (g)
Tennessee	Robert E. Cooper (D)	(i)	8	11/06	8/14	...	...
Texas	Greg Abbott (R)	E	4	1/03	1/11	1	★
Utah	Mark Shurtleff (R)	E	4	1/01	1/09	1	★
Vermont	William H. Sorrell (D)	E	2	5/97 (j)	1/09	4 (j)	★
Virginia	Robert F. McDonnell (R)	E	4	1/06	1/10	...	(k)
Washington	Rob McKenna (R)	E	4	1/05	1/09	...	★
West Virginia	Darrell Vivian McGraw Jr. (D)	E	4	1/93	1/09	3	★
Wisconsin	J.B. Van Hollen (R)	E	4	1/07	1/11	...	★
Wyoming	Pat Crank (D)	A (l)	...	1/03	1/11	...	...
Dist. of Columbia	Linda Singer (Acting) (D)	A	...	1/07	...	...	...
American Samoa	Frederick O'Brien (Acting)	A	4	1/07	1/09	...	...
Guam	Alicia G. Limtiaco	E	4	1/07	1/11	...	...
No. Mariana Islands	Matt Gregory	A	4	2006	N.A.	N.A.	...
Puerto Rico	Roberto J. Sanchez-Ramos	A	4	N.A.	...	...	...
U.S. Virgin Islands	Vincent Frazer (Acting)	A	4	1/07	...	...	...

See footnotes at end of table.

THE ATTORNEYS GENERAL, 2007 — Continued

Source: The Council of State Governments' survey of attorneys general, January 2007.

Key:

★ — No provision specifying number of terms allowed.

. . . — No formal provision; position is appointed or elected by governmental entity (not chosen by the electorate).

A — Appointed by the governor.

E — Elected by the voters.

L — Elected by the legislature.

N.A. — Not applicable.

(a) Appointed to fill unexpired term in March 2004 and elected to a full term in November 2006.

(b) Appointed to fill unexpired term in January 2005 and elected to a full term in November 2006.

(c) Appointed to fill unexpired term in June 1997. He was elected in 1998 to his first full term.

(d) Term runs concurrently with the governor.

(e) Attorney General Miller was elected in 1978, 1982, 1986, 1994, 1998, 2002 and in 2006.

(f) Chosen biennially by joint ballot of state senators and representatives.

(g) After two consecutive terms, must wait four years and/or one full term before being eligible again.

(h) The term of the office of the elected official is four years, except that in 2004 the attorney general was elected for a term of two years.

(i) Appointed by judges of state Supreme Court.

(j) Appointed to fill unexpired term in May 1997. He was elected in 1998 to his first full term.

(k) Provision specifying individual may hold office for an unlimited number of terms.

(l) Must be confirmed by the Senate.

Table 4.20
ATTORNEYS GENERAL: QUALIFICATIONS FOR OFFICE

State or other jurisdiction	Minimum age	U.S. citizen (years) (a)	State resident (years) (b)	Qualified voter (years)	Licensed attorney (years)	Membership in the state bar (years)	Method of selection to office
Alabama	25	7	5	★	...	...	E
Alaska	18	★	...	...	★	★	A
Arizona	25	10	5	...	5	5	E
Arkansas	...	...	★	★	...	...	E
California	18	★	★	★	(c)	(c)	E
Colorado	27	★	2	★	★	...	E
Connecticut	18	★	★	★	10	10	E
Delaware	...	...	...	...	...	...	E
Florida	30	★	7	★	★	5	E
Georgia	25	10	4	★	7	7	E
Hawaii	...	1	1	...	★	(d)	A
Idaho	30	★	2	...	★	★	E
Illinois	25	★	3	★	★	★	E
Indiana	...	2	2	★	5	...	E
Iowa	18	★	★	...	...	...	E
Kansas	...	...	...	...	...	...	E
Kentucky	30	...	2 (e)	...	8	2	E
Louisiana	25	★	5	★	★	★	E
Maine	...	...	...	...	★	★	(f)
Maryland	...	★(g)	★	★	★	10	E
Massachusetts	18	...	5	★	...	★	E
Michigan	18	★	★	...	★	★	E
Minnesota	21	★	30 days	★	...	...	E
Mississippi	26	★	5	★	5	★	E
Missouri	...	★	1	...	...	...	E
Montana	25	★	2	...	5	★	E
Nebraska	...	...	★	...	...	...	E
Nevada	25	★	2	★	...	...	E
New Hampshire	...	★	★	...	★	★	A (h)
New Jersey	18	...	★	...	...	...	A
New Mexico	30	★	5	★	★	...	E
New York	30	★	5	...	(i)	...	E
North Carolina	21	★	★	★	★	(i)	E
North Dakota	25	★	5	★	★	★	E
Ohio	18	★	★	★	...	...	E
Oklahoma	31	★	10	★	★	★	E
Oregon	18	★	★	★	...	...	E
Pennsylvania	21	★	...	...	★	...	E
Rhode Island	18	...	...	...	★	★	E
South Carolina	...	★	30 days	★	...	...	E
South Dakota	18	★	★	★	(i)	(i)	E
Tennessee	...	...	...	...	...	...	(j)
Texas	...	...	★	...	(i)	(i)	E
Utah	25	★	5 (e)	★	★	★	E
Vermont	18	★	★	★	...	...	E
Virginia	30	★	1 (k)	★	...	5 (k)	E
Washington	...	★	★	★	★	★	E
West Virginia	25	...	5	★	...	...	E
Wisconsin	...	★	★	...	...	...	E
Wyoming	...	★	★	★	4	4	A (l)
Dist. of Columbia	...	...	★	...	★	★	A
American Samoa	...	...	(c)	...	(i)	(i)	A
Guam	...	...	...	...	...	...	A
No. Mariana Islands	...	...	3	...	5	...	A
Puerto Rico	...	★	...	...	★	★	A
U.S. Virgin Islands	...	...	★	★	★	★	A

Sources: The Council of State Governments' survey of attorneys general, December 2006 and state constitutions and statutes, January 2007.

Key:

★ — Formal provision; number of years not specified.

... — No formal provision.

A — Appointed by governor.

E — Elected by voters.

(a) In some states you must be a U.S. citizen to be an elector, and must be an elector to run.

(b) In some states you must be a state resident to be an elector, and must be an elector to run.

(c) No statute specifically requires this, but the State Bar Act can be interpreted as making this a qualification.

(d) No period specified; all licensed attorneys are members of the state bar.

(e) State citizenship requirement.

(f) Chosen biennially by joint ballot of state senators and representatives.

(g) *Crosse v. Board of Supervisors of Elections* 243 Md. 555, 2221A.2d431 (1966)—opinion rendered indicated that U.S. citizenship was, by necessity, a requirement for office.

(h) Appointed by the Governor and confirmed by the Governor and the Executive Council.

(i) Implied.

(j) Appointed by state Supreme Court.

(k) Same as qualifications of a judge of a court of record.

(l) Must be confirmed by the Senate.

Table 4.21
ATTORNEYS GENERAL: PROSECUTORIAL AND ADVISORY DUTIES

State or other jurisdiction	Authority in local prosecutions:				Issues advisory opinions (a):				Reviews legislation (b):	
	Authority to initiate local prosecutions	May intervene in local prosecutions	May assist local prosecutor	May supersede local prosecutor	To state executive officials	To legislators	To local prosecutors	On the constitutionality of bills or ordinances	Prior to passage	Before signing
Alabama	A	A,D	A,D	A	★	★	★	...	★	...
Alaska	(c)	(c)	(c)	(c)	★	★	...	★	★	★
Arizona	A,B,C,D,F	B,D	B,D	B	★	★	★	...	...	...
Arkansas	...	...	D	...	★	★	★	★	...	...
California	A,B,C,D,E	A,B,C,D,E	A,B,C,D,E	A,B,C,D,E	★	★	★	...	...	...
Colorado	A,F	B	D,F	B	★	★	★	★	★	★
Connecticut	...	...	...	...	★	(d)	...	★	(e)	(e)
Delaware	A (f)	(f)	(f)	(f)	★	★	★	★	★(g)	★(g)
Florida	F	...	D	...	★	★	★	...	...	...
Georgia	B,D,F,G	...	A,D	...	★	★	★	...	...	...
Hawaii	A,B,C,D,E	A,B,C,D,E	A,B,C,D,E	A,B,C,D,E	★	★	...	★(h)	★	★
Idaho	B,D,F	...	D	...	★	★	★	...	★	★
Illinois	D,F	D,G	D	G	★	★	★	...	(i)	(i)
Indiana	F	...	D	...	★	★	★	★	...	...
Iowa	D,F	D,F	D,F	D,E,F	★	★	★	...	(j)	(j)
Kansas	A,B,C,D,F	A,D	D	A,F	★	★	★	★	...	...
Kentucky	D,F,G	B,D,G	D	B	★	★	★	★	...	...
Louisiana	D,E,G	D,E,G	D,E,G	E,G	★	★	★	...	★	★
Maine	A	A	A	A	★	★	...	...	...	...
Maryland	B,F	D	D	...	★	★	★	★	★	★
Massachusetts	A	A	A,D	A	★	★(k)	★	★	(l)	(l)
Michigan	A	A	A	A	★	★	★	★	...	...
Minnesota	B,F	B,D,G	A,B,D,G	B	★	★(k)	★	...	...	(l)
Mississippi	A,D,F	D,F	A,D,F	D,F	★	★	★	...	...	...
Missouri	B,F,G	F	B,F	G	★	★	★	...	(l)	(l)
Montana	D	E	E	E	★	★(m)	★	...	...	...
Nebraska	A	...	...	...	★	★	★	★	...	...
Nevada	D,F,G	D	...	...	★	...	★	★	...	...
New Hampshire	A,E,F	A,E,F	A,D,E,F	A,E,F	★	★	★	...	(n)	(n)
New Jersey	A,B,C,D	A,B,C,D	A,B,C,D	A,B,C,D	★	★	★	★	★	★
New Mexico	B,D,E,F	D,E,F	A,B,D,E,F	D,E,F,G	★	★	★	★	★	★
New York	B,F	B,D,F	D	B	★	★(k)	★	★	★	★
North Carolina	...	D	D	...	★	★	★	★	★	...
North Dakota	A,D,E,F,G	A,D,E,G	A,B,D,E,F,G	A,D,E,G	★	★	★	★	...	...
Ohio	F	D	D	F	★	(m)	★	...	...	...
Oklahoma	A,B,C,E,F	A,B,C,E,F	A,B,C,E	E	★	★	★	...	(o)	(o)
Oregon	B,D,F	B,D	B,D	...	★	★	★	...	...	★
Pennsylvania	A,D,F	D,F	D,F	...	★	...	...	...	...	...
Rhode Island	A	A	A	A	★	★	...	...	...	...
South Carolina	A,D,E,F (p)	A,B,C,D,E,F	A,D	A,E	★	(q)	★	★	★(r)	★(l)
South Dakota	A,B,D,E,F (p)	D,G (b)	A,B,D,E	D,F	★	★	★	...	★	...
Tennessee	D,F,G	D,G	D	...	★	★	★	★	...	...
Texas	...	...	...	...	...	...	...	...	...	...
Utah	A,B,D,E,F,G	E,G	D,E	E	★	★(q)	★	★	★(l)	★(l)
Vermont	A	A	A	G	★	★	★	★	★	★
Virginia	B,F	B,D,F	B,D,F	B	★	★	★	★	★	★
Washington	B,D	B,D	B,D	B,D	★	★	...	...	...	...
West Virginia	...	...	...	...	★	★	★	★	...	...
Wisconsin	B,C,F	B,C,D	D	B	★	★	★	★(h)	(e)	(e)
Wyoming	B,D,F	B,D	B,D	G	★	★	★	★(h)	★	★
Dist. of Columbia	F	D	D	F	★	★	(s)	★	★	★
American Samoa	A (t)	(t)	(t)	(t)	★	...	(t)	(e)	(l)	(l)
Guam	A	A	A	A	★	★	★	★	(l)	B
No. Mariana Islands	A (t)	(t)	(t)	(t)	★	★	★	★	...	...
Puerto Rico	A	(t)	(t)	(t)	★	★	...	...	★	★
U.S. Virgin Islands	A (t)	(t)	(t)	(t)	★	...	...	★	★	★

See footnotes at end of table.

Source: The Council of State Governments' survey of attorneys general, December 2006.

Key:

A — On own initiative.

B — On request of governor.

C — On request of legislature.

D — On request of local prosecutor.

E — When in state's interest.

F — Under certain statutes for specific crimes.

G — On authorization of court or other body.

★ — Has authority in area.

. . . — Does not have authority in area.

(a) Also issues advisory opinions to: Alabama—designated heads of state departments, agencies, boards, and commissions; local public officials; and political subdivisions. Hawaii—judges/judiciary as requested. Kansas—to counsel for local units of government. Montana—county and city attorneys, city commissioners.

(b) Also reviews legislation: Alabama—when requested by the governor. Alaska—after passage. Arizona—at the request of the legislature. Kansas—upon request of legislator, no formal authority.

(c) The attorney general functions as the local prosecutor.

(d) To legislative leadership.

(e) Informally reviews bills or does so upon request.

(f) The attorney general prosecutes all criminal offenses in Delaware.

(g) Also at the request of agency or legislature.

(h) Bills, not ordinances.

(i) Reviews and tracks legislation that relates to the office of attorney general and the office mission.

(j) No requirements for review.

(k) To legislature as a whole, not individual legislators.

(l) Only when requested by governor or legislature.

(m) To either house of legislature, not individual legislators.

(n) Provides information when requested by the legislature. Testifies for or against bills on the attorney general's own initiative.

(o) If required by legislature; may assist in drafting.

(p) Certain statutes provide for concurrent jurisdiction with local prosecutors.

(q) Only when requested by legislature.

(r) Has concurrent jurisdiction with state's attorneys.

(s) The office of attorney general prosecutes local crimes to an extent. The office's Legal Counsel Division may issue legal advice to the office's prosecutorial arm. Otherwise, the office does not usually advise the OUSA, the district's other local prosecutor.

(t) The attorney general functions as the local prosecutor.

Table 4.22
ATTORNEYS GENERAL: CONSUMER PROTECTION ACTIVITIES, SUBPOENA POWERS AND ANTITRUST DUTIES

State or other jurisdiction	May commence civil proceedings	May commence criminal proceedings	Represents the state before regulatory agencies (a)	Administers consumer protection programs	Handles consumer complaints	Subpoena powers (b)	Antitrust duties
Alabama	★	★	★	★	★	●	A,B,C
Alaska	★	★	★	★	★	★	A,B,C,D
Arizona	★	...	...	★	★	●	A,B,C,D
Arkansas	★	...	★	★	★	●	A,B
California	★	★	...	★	★	★	A,B,C
Colorado	★	★	★	★	★	●	A,C,D
Connecticut	★	(c)	★	★	★	●	A,B,D
Delaware	★	★	★	★	★	★	A,B,D
Florida	★	...	...	★	★	★	A,B,D
Georgia	★	★	★	...	...	●	...
Hawaii	★	★	★	★	★	★	A,B,C,D
Idaho	★	...	★	★	★	★	A,B,D
Illinois	★	...	★	★	★	★	A,B,C
Indiana	★	...	★	★	★	★	A,B
Iowa	★	★	★	★	★	★	B,C
Kansas	★	★	★	★	★	★	B,C,D
Kentucky	★	★	★	★	★	★	A,B,C,D
Louisiana	★	★	★	★	★	★	A,B,C
Maine	★	★	★	★	★	★	A,B,C
Maryland	★	★(d)	...	★	★	★	B,C,D
Massachusetts	★	★	★	★	★	★	A,B,C,D
Michigan	★	★	★	★	★	★	A,B,C,D
Minnesota	★	...	★	★	★	●	A,B,C
Mississippi	★	★	...	★	★	★	A,B,C,D
Missouri	★	★	★	★	★	★	A,B,C,D
Montana	★	★	...	★	★	...	A,B
Nebraska	★	★	★	★	★	...	A,B,C,D
Nevada	★	★	★	★	★	●	A,B,C,D
New Hampshire	★	★	★	★	★	★	A,B,C,D
New Jersey	★	★	★	★	★	★	A,B,C,D
New Mexico	★	★	★	★	★	★	A,B,C (f)
New York	★	★	★	★	★	★	A,B,C,D
North Carolina	★	★(e)	★	★	★	★	A,B,C,D
North Dakota	★	...	★	★	★	★	A,B,D
Ohio	★	★	★	★	★	★	A,B,C,D
Oklahoma	★	★	★	★	★	★	A,B,C,D
Oregon	★	★(e)	★	★	★	●	A,B,C
Pennsylvania	★	★	★	★	★	★	A,B
Rhode Island	★	★	...	★	★	★	A,B,C
South Carolina	★(a)	★(g)	★	...	★(h)	●	A,B,C,D
South Dakota	★	★	★	★	★	★	A,B,C
Tennessee	★	(d)(e)	(e)	...	...	★	B,C,D
Texas	★	★	★	★	★	★	A,B,C,D
Utah	★(i)	★	★(i)	...	★(j)	●	A (k),B,C,D (k)
Vermont	★	★	★	★	★	★	A,B,C
Virginia	★	(e)	★	★(j)	★(j)	●	A,B,C,D
Washington	★	...	(l)	★	★	●	A,B,D
West Virginia	★	...	★	★	★	★	A,B,D
Wisconsin	★	★	★	★	★	●	A,B,C (f)
Wyoming	★	...	★	★	★	●	A,B
Dist. of Columbia	★	★(m)	★	★	★	★	A,B,C,D
American Samoa	★	★	★	★	★	...	...
Guam	★	★	★	★	★	●	A,B,C,D
No. Mariana Islands	★	★	★	★	★	★	A,B
Puerto Rico	★	★	...	...	...	★	A,B,C,D
U.S. Virgin Islands	★	★	★	★	★	●	A

See footnotes at end of table.

ATTORNEYS GENERAL: CONSUMER PROTECTION ACTIVITIES, SUBPOENA POWERS AND ANTITRUST DUTIES — Continued

Source: The Council of State Governments' survey of attorneys general, December 2006.

Key:

A — Has parens patriae authority to commence suits on behalf of consumers in state antitrust damage actions in state courts.

B — May initiate damage actions on behalf of state in state courts.

C — May commence criminal proceedings.

D — May represent cities, counties and other governmental entities in recovering civil damages under federal or state law.

★ — Has authority in area.

. . . — Does not have authority in area.

(a) May represent state on behalf of: the "people" of the state; an agency of the state; or the state before a federal regulatory agency.

(b) In this column only: ★ — broad powers and ● — limited powers.

(c) In certain cases only.

(d) May commence criminal proceedings with local district attorney.

(e) To a limited extent.

(f) May represent other governmental entities in recovering civil damages under federal or state law.

(g) When permitted to intervene.

(h) On a limited basis because the state has a separate consumer affairs department.

(i) Attorney general has exclusive authority.

(j) Attorney general handles legal matters only with no administrative handling of complaints.

(k) Opinion only, since there are no controlling precedents.

(l) The Public Counsel Unit appears and represents the public before the Utilities and Transportation Commission.

(m) In antitrust not criminal proceedings.

Table 4.23
ATTORNEYS GENERAL: DUTIES TO ADMINISTRATIVE AGENCIES AND OTHER RESPONSIBILITIES

State or other jurisdiction	Serves as counsel for state	Appears for state in criminal appeals	Issues official advice	Interprets statutes or regulations	Conducts litigation: On behalf of agency	Conducts litigation: Against agency	Prepares or reviews legal documents	Represents the public before the agency	Involved in rule-making	Reviews rules for legality
Alabama	A,B,C (a)	★(a)	★	★	★	★	(b)	(b)	★	★
Alaska	A,B,C	★	★	★	★	★	★	★	★	★
Arizona	A,B,C	★	★	★	★	...	★	...	★	★
Arkansas	A,B,C	★	★	★	★	★	★	★	...	...
California	A,B,C	★	★	★	★	...	★	...	...	...
Colorado	A,B,C	★	★	★	★	★	★	★	★	★
Connecticut	A,B,C	(b)	★	★	★	★	★	★	★	★
Delaware (f)	A,B,C	★	★	★	★	★(g)	★	★	★	★
Florida	A,B,C	★	★	★	★	...	★	...	...	...
Georgia	A,B,C	★	★	★	★	...	★	...	...	★
Hawaii	A,B,C	★	★	★	★	★	★	★	★	★
Idaho	A,B,C	★(a)	★	★	★	★	★	★	★	★
Illinois	A,B,C	★	...	★	★	...	★	...	...	★
Indiana	A,B,C	★	★	★	★	...	★	...	★	★
Iowa	A,B,C	★	★	★	★	★	★	★	★	★
Kansas	A,B,C	★	★	★	★	★	★	...	★	★
Kentucky	A,B,C	★	★	★	★	...	...	★	...	...
Louisiana	A,B,C	...	★	★	★	...	★	★	★	★
Maine	A,B,C	★	★	★	★	...	★	...	★	★
Maryland	A,B,C	★	★	★	★	(b)	★	★	★	★
Massachusetts	A,B,C	(b)(c)(d)	★	★	★	★	★	★	★	★
Michigan	A,B,C	★	★	★	★	★	★	★	★	★
Minnesota	A,B,C	(c)(d)	★	★	(a)	★	★	★	★	★
Mississippi	A,B,C	...	★	★	★	...	★	...	...	...
Missouri	A,B,C	★	★	★	★	...	★	★	★	...
Montana (h)	A,B	...	★	★	★	★	★	...	...	...
Nebraska	A,B,C	★	★	★	★	★	★	...	★	★
Nevada	A,B,C	★	★	★	★	...	★	...	★	★
New Hampshire	A,B,C	★	★	★	★	...	★	★	★	★
New Jersey	A,B,C	★	★	★	★	...	★	...	★	★
New Mexico	A,B,C	★	★	★	★	★	★	★	★	★
New York	A,B,C	(b)	...	★	★	(b)	★	(b)	...	...
North Carolina	A,B,C	★	★	★	★	★	★	(b)	★	★
North Dakota	A,B,C	★	★	★	★	★	★	...	★	★
Ohio	A,B,C	★	★	...	★	...	★	...	...	...
Oklahoma	A,B,C	★	★	★	★	★	★	★	★	★
Oregon	A,B	★	★	★	★	...	★	...	★	★
Pennsylvania	A,B	...	...	...	★	...	★	...	...	★
Rhode Island	A,B,C	★	★	★	★	★	★	...	...	★
South Carolina	A,B,C	★(d)	(a)	★	★	(b)	★	...	★	★
South Dakota	A,B,C	★	★	★	★	★	★	...	...	...
Tennessee	A,B,C	★	★	★	★	...	★	(e)	(e)	★
Texas	A,B,C	★(i)	★	★	★	★	★	★	★	...
Utah	A,B,C	★(a)	★	★	★	★	★	(b)	★	★
Vermont	A,B,C	★	★	★	★	★	★	★	★	★
Virginia	A,B,C	★	★	★	★	★	★	★	★	★
Washington	A,B	★	★	★	★	★	★	★	★	★
West Virginia	A,B,C	★	★	★	★	★	★	...	...	...
Wisconsin	A,B,C	★	★	★	★	(b)	(b)	(b)	(b)	(b)
Wyoming	A,B,C	★	★	★	★	★	★	...	★	★
Dist. of Columbia	A,B	★(j)	★	★	★	...	★	...	★	★
American Samoa	A,B,C	★(a)	★	★	★	...	★	...	★	★
Guam	A,B,C	★	★	★	(d)	★	★	(b)	★	★
No. Mariana Islands	A,B,C	★	★	★	★	★	★	...	★	★
Puerto Rico	A,B,C	★	★	★	★	...	★	...	★	★
U.S. Virgin Islands	A,B	★	★	★	★	★	★	★	...	★

See footnotes at end of table.

ATTORNEYS GENERAL: DUTIES TO ADMINISTRATIVE AGENCIES AND OTHER RESPONSIBILITIES — Continued

Source: The Council of State Governments' survey of attorneys general, December 2006.

Key:

A — Defend state law when challenged on federal constitutional grounds.

B — Conduct litigation on behalf of state in federal and other states' courts.

C — Prosecute actions against another state in U.S. Supreme Court.

★ — Has authority in area.

. . . — Does not have authority in area.

(a) Attorney general has exclusive jurisdiction.

(b) In certain cases only.

(c) When assisting local prosecutor in the appeal.

(d) Can appear on own discretion.

(e) Consumer Advocate Division represents the public in utility rate-making hearings and rule-making proceedings.

(f) Except as otherwise provided by statute, the attorney general represents all state agencies and officials.

(g) Rarely.

(h) Most state agencies are represented by agency counsel who do not answer to the attorney general. The attorney general does provide representation for agencies in conflict situations and where the agency requires additional or specialized assistance.

(i) Primarily federal habeas corpus appeals only.

(j) However, OUSA handles felony cases and most major misdemeanors.

State Treasurers: Guardians of the Public Trust

By The National Association of State Treasurers

State treasurers are the chief financial officers of the states whose duties are to assure the absolute safety of all taxpayer dollars and to guarantee the prudent use of public resources that fund vital government programs. In several states, treasurers also improve the financial security of their residents by providing college savings opportunities and financial education, and returning unclaimed property.

State treasurers are integral to the fiscal health and prosperity of the states. Financial stewardship in the complex modern economy is significantly impacted by the status of the state budget, shaping the financial health of the state as a whole. Whether in times of budget shortfalls or times of budget surplus, state treasurers must provide states the necessary financial resources to fund vital public services and plan for long-term fiscal obligations.

Policy Leaders

State treasurers are key players in policymaking within their states but also on a national level. On issues ranging from corporate governance to accounting standards, state treasurers are at the forefront of policy discussions and initiatives that attempt to safeguard investments made by and on behalf of the residents of their states.

State treasurers commit substantial time and resources to proactive interactions with Congress, the federal government and other organizations representing state government. They have had a lasting and substantive impact on federal actions and activities that impact the investment and management of state and local government funds, debt management, financial education and a wide range of other fiscal issues. In this respect the treasurers are partners with the federal government so they can affect public policy that enhances the financial well-being of the states.

Through this fiscal oversight and policy setting, state treasurers work daily to protect and benefit their individual states and the nation as a whole.

Selection and Term of Service

State treasurers are elected by the people in 37 states, elected by the legislature in four states and appointed by the governor in nine states. Forty state treasurers serve four-year terms in office, while the state treasurers of Maine, New Hampshire, Tennessee and Vermont serve two-year terms. The remaining state treasurers serve at the discretion of the state official—usually the governor—who makes the appointment.

Responsibilities of State Treasurers

All state treasurers are responsible for cash management. All but three state treasurers are responsible for banking services and in 35 states, state treasurers are responsible for some aspect of debt management—issuance, service or both. Thirty-three state treasurers are administrators of unclaimed property programs.

All 50 state treasurers are involved in either the oversight or investment of their state's retirement or trust funds. Retirement funds for public employees are scattered in literally thousands of public pension plans. Sound investment of these funds is critical to the successful operation of public pension funds. Twenty-four state treasurers sit on the oversight board for their individual state's investment plan.

Several examples—though certainly not an exhaustive listing—are listed below and touch on the wide array of responsibilities held by state treasurers.

Cash Management and Banking Services

It is especially important for treasurers in every state to diligently allocate every state dollar for which they are responsible. Treasurers effectively employ innovative cash management practices to increase capital and contribute to a state's solid financial reputation in national and world markets. Although the public views the responsibility of managing revenue shortfalls as an issue for the state's governor and legislature, state treasurers are also key policymakers.

State treasurers are also responsible for managing states' short- and long-term investment portfolios; depositing public funds in financial institutions and protecting those funds; collecting various fees from all state agencies; and ensuring that the state's financial obligations are paid on a daily basis. These activities encompass, but are not limited to, lock boxes, wire transfers, bank drafts and zero balance accounts.

Twenty-three state treasurers host collection services of some type whether they are performed in-house or through a banking partner. Twenty-four states offer controlled disbursement programs, while all 50 states utilize an automated clearinghouse. All but nine states engage in account reconciliation services and 30 state treasuries conduct data transfer services.

Debt Management

Tax-exempt municipal bonds are the basic tool used by states and local governments to fund the capital improvements necessary to provide utilities, roads and bridges, airports, health care, education, housing and other public services. The ability to sell debt with interest exempt from federal income taxes has been a significant benefit to state and local government borrowers. The practical effect of this lower borrowing cost is a direct reduction of the tax burdens that citizens would otherwise have to shoulder to finance essential public services.

Debt management is a critical component of state financial operations. Many times the state treasury must borrow money by issuing state debt, usually in the form of bonds, to pay for a state's essential capital and public infrastructure needs. That money is often used to fund school and road improvements, airports, water and waste systems, housing, and other vital services. The most recently collected statistics show that state treasurers issued $13,285,296,405 in general obligation bonds and $5,111,065,053 in taxable bonds.

In the 46 states that issue debt, 46 state treasurers are involved in some capacity. State treasurers in two states are solely responsible for the authorization of a state's short-term debt. In seven states, the treasurer shares this responsibility, usually with a board, the legislature or the governor. Six state treasurers share the responsibility of issuing general obligation bonds, while four state treasurers share investment responsibility on the issuance of revenue bonds. However, only one state treasury, Michigan, shares authority to issue taxable bonds. Treasurers in Maine, Michigan, Montana and Oregon have the ability to authorize taxable debt. Only Florida, Kansas, Kentucky and Utah state treasurers have the authority to issue foreign currency as denominated debt.

Investment of State Funds

The management and oversight of state investment functions is a key responsibility of state treasurers. Earnings from investments are an important source of revenue for state governments. These earnings are used to fund vital public services, cover public employee retirement obligations, and fund economic development programs, among other uses. In contemporary financial markets, maximizing this source of revenue is a complex and time-consuming undertaking. To make the best use of investment-eligible public funds,

public investors like state treasurers must, within the constraints of applicable state and federal laws, try to maximize return while prudently managing risk.

While the task of investing available state funds may seem fairly straightforward to the public, the process is quite complex and requires specialized knowledge and skill. State treasurers' performance and record of investment income critically affects the bottom line of the states' fiscal fitness, which in turn can have a measurable effect on the well-being of the states' budgetary status in any given year.

The state treasurers, who collectively have fiduciary responsibility for more than $1 trillion in public funds, contend that greater corporate responsibility is vital, since the business practices of U.S. corporations have a profound effect on the public treasury, ranging from pension funds to state tax revenue investments. State treasurers, in particular, have fiduciary responsibility not only for pension plans, trust funds and general state funds, but also for other investment vehicles, such as state college savings plans.

Repurchase agreements and U.S. Treasury or agency obligations are the most common types of investments states are allowed to use. Forty-seven states choose to optimize their investment return with repurchase agreements, while 46 states invest with U.S. Treasury or agency obligations. Only seven states utilize real estate as an allowable investment, while nine states use derivatives in their investment portfolio. Eleven state treasurers invest in foreign corporate stocks, and three states opt to put their money into venture capital and private equity enterprises. All but five state treasurers invest in commercial paper. In comparison, 33 states invest in mortgage-backed securities.

Treasurers in Alabama, Alaska, Michigan, Mississippi, North Carolina, Vermont and West Virginia are the sole fiduciaries for their state's investments. Twenty-seven states have some type of investment board, committee or council that determines investment policy. Treasurers sit on 24 of these boards.

Fifteen state treasurers are considered administrators for their state's "Rainy Day" funds. While these funds come with a variety of titles, they all serve as a state's reserve or budget stabilization source. Treasurers, auditors and comptrollers are responsible for the safe investment and appropriate draw-down of these reserve funds, totaling more than $5 billion in assets.

College Savings Plans

State college savings plans offer many attractive benefits not found in other savings options. In establishing the first college savings plans in 1988, states leveraged their experience as major institutional investors to establish low-cost, low-fee college savings investment options for their residents. Thanks to the states' involvement, families now have access to a college savings strategy that does not require them to use a financial intermediary and does not charge a sale load or commission. These plans provide an easy, affordable and dedicated way for the average American family to save for college. Forty-nine states and the District of Columbia have state college savings plans.

College savings plans are often called 529 plans, in reference to the Internal Revenue Service Code Section 529 and the resulting federal tax break. Section 529 plans are offered in two forms, prepaid tuition programs and savings plans. The prepaid tuition program offers families a method to prepay tuition based on current college tuition rates and provides a guarantee to keep pace with tuition inflation. The savings plans offer dedicated college savings accounts, which provide families a variable rate of return in a tax-advantaged college savings account.

More than 9.2 million children across the country have been enrolled in state prepaid tuition or savings plans. Participants in both types of programs receive a federal tax exemption on the investment earnings of the accounts when the funds are used to pay for qualified higher education expenses, which include tuition, room and board, books and fees, and any other expenses that students are required to pay to attend any accredited college or university in the United States and in some foreign countries.

The state treasurer plays a vital role in the administration of the programs, including oversight of all program operations, serving as the board chair or board member, investment manager or board member.

Unclaimed Property

State treasurers are responsible for the administration of unclaimed property programs in 33 states and the District of Columbia. Unclaimed property refers to accounts in financial institutions and companies that have had no activity generated or contact with the owner for one year or more. Common forms of unclaimed property include savings or checking accounts, stocks, uncashed dividends or payroll checks, refunds, traveler's checks, trust distributions, unredeemed money orders or gift certificates, insurance payments and life insurance policies, annuities, certificates of deposit, customer overpayments, utility security deposits, mineral royalty payments and contents of safe deposit boxes.

Each state has enacted an unclaimed property statute that protects funds from reverting back to the company if it has lost contact with the owner. These laws instruct companies to turn forgotten funds over to state officials, who through public outreach return that property to rightful owners or heirs. In addition to searchable databases that are free of charge and available on the Internet, state officials utilize a variety of resources for promoting their return efforts, such as publishing extensive lists of missing owners in newspapers and employing staff to find and return lost accounts. Most states hold lost funds until owners are found, returning them at no cost or for a nominal handling fee upon filing a claim form and verification of identity.

State unclaimed property programs returned more than $1 billion to the nation's citizens last year alone and state treasurers are committed to increasing the amount of returned property in the future.

Financial Literacy Initiatives

Over the past few decades, state treasurers have taken an active role in promoting financial literacy to their states' residents. Drawing upon their substantial expertise in the financial management of both personal and public funds, state treasurers are committed to educating the citizens of the states on savings, from birth to retirement.

Thirty-five state treasurers presently offer educational opportunities ranging from "Bank at School" programs designed to teach students basic monetary concepts to women's conferences that help adults gain control of their personal finances.

Conclusion

State treasurers' responsibilities are many and critically important to states' fiscal well-being. Prudent and profitable investments made by state treasurers make it possible for budgets to be balanced, for taxpayer-supported programs to be maintained and grown, and for a positive and equitable level of investment growth for public funds to be achieved.

About the Author

The **National Association of State Treasurers**, an organization of state financial leaders, encourages the highest ethical standards, promotes education and the exchange of ideas, builds professional relationships, develops standards of excellence and influences public policy for the benefit of the citizens of the states. NAST is composed of all state treasurers, or state financial officials with comparable responsibilities from the United States, its commonwealths, territories and the District of Columbia.

Table 4.24
THE TREASURERS, 2007

State or other jurisdiction	Name and party	Method of selection	Length of regular term in years	Date of first service	Present term ends	Maximum consecutive terms allowed by constitution
Alabama	Kay Ivey (R)	E	4	1/03	1/11	2
Alaska (a)..................	Brian Andrews	A	Governor's Discretion	1/07	. . .	. . .
Arizona	Dean Martin (R)	E	4	1/07	1/11	2
Arkansas....................	Martha Shoffner (D)	E	4	1/07	1/11	2
California	Bill Lockyer (D)	E	4	1/07	1/11	2
Colorado	Cary Kennedy (D)	E	4	1/07	1/11	2
Connecticut	Denise Nappier (D)	E	4	1/99	1/11	★
Delaware....................	Jack Markell (D)	E	4	1/99	1/11	★
Florida (b)	Adelaide "Alex" Sink (D)	E	4	1/07	1/11	2
Georgia	W. Daniel Ebersole	A	Pleasure of the Board	11/97	. . .	. . .
Hawaii (c)	Georgina Kawamura	A	Governor's Discretion	12/02	. . .	. . .
Idaho..........................	Ron Crane (R)	E	4	1/99	1/11	★
Illinois.......................	Alexi Giannoulias (D)	E	4	1/07	1/11	★
Indiana.......................	Richard Mourdock (R)	E	4	2/07	2/11	(d)
Iowa	Michael Fitzgerald (D)	E	4	1/83	1/11	★
Kansas	Lynn Jenkins (R)	E	4	1/03	1/11	★
Kentucky	Jonathan Miller (D)	E	4	1/00	12/07	2
Louisiana	John Kennedy (D)	E	4	1/00	1/08	★
Maine	David Lemoine (D)	L	2	1/05	1/09	4
Maryland	Nancy Kopp (D)	L	4	2/02	1/11	★
Massachusetts............	Timothy Cahill (D)	E	4	1/03	1/11	★
Michigan....................	Robert J. Kleine	A	Governor's Discretion	5/06	. . .	. . .
Minnesota (e).............	Tom Hanson	A	Governor's Discretion	12/06	. . .	. . .
Mississippi	Tate Reeves (R)	E	4	1/04	1/08	★
Missouri	Sarah Steelman (R)	E	4	1/05	1/09	2
Montana	Janet Kelly	A	Governor's Discretion	1/05	. . .	. . .
Nebraska....................	Shane Osborn (R)	E	4	1/07	1/11	2
Nevada.......................	Kate Marshall (D)	E	4	1/07	1/11	2
New Hampshire.........	Catherine Provencher	L	2	1/07	12/08	★
New Jersey.................	Bradley I. Abelow	A	Governor's Discretion	1/06	. . .	. . .
New Mexico	James Lewis (D)	E	4	1/07	1/11	2
New York	Aida Brewer	A	Governor's Discretion	2/02	. . .	. . .
North Carolina	Richard Moore (D)	E	4	1/01	1/09	★
North Dakota.............	Kelly Schmidt (R)	E	4	1/05	1/09	★
Ohio	Richard Cordray (D)	E	4	1/07	1/11	2
Oklahoma	Scott Meacham (D)	E	4	6/05	1/11	★
Oregon	Randall Edwards (D)	E	4	1/01	1/09	2
Pennsylvania	Robin Wiessmann (f)	E	4	2/07 (f)	1/09	2
Rhode Island	Frank T. Caprio (D)	E	4	1/07	1/11	2
South Carolina	Thomas Ravenel (R)	E	4	1/07	1/11	★
South Dakota.............	Vernon L. Larson (R)	E	4	1/03	1/11	2
Tennessee	Dale Sims	L	2	10/03	1/09	. . .
Texas (g).....................	Susan Combs (R)	E	4	1/07	1/11	★
Utah	Edward Alter (R)	E	4	1/81	1/09	★
Vermont	Jeb Spaulding (D)	E	2	1/03	1/09	★
Virginia	Braxton Powell	A	Governor's Discretion	1/06	. . .	. . .
Washington................	Michael Murphy (D)	E	4	1/97	1/09	★
West Virginia.............	John Perdue (D)	E	4	1/97	1/09	★
Wisconsin..................	Dawn Sass (D)	E	4	1/07	1/11	★
Wyoming....................	Joe Meyer (R)	E	4	1/07	1/11	2
American Samoa.......	Velega Savali Jr.	A	4	N.A.	N.A.	. . .
Dist. of Columbia	Lasana Mack	A	Pleasure of CFO	8/05	N.A.	. . .
Guam	Yasela Pereira	CS	. . .	10/96	. . .	. . .
No. Mariana Islands...	Antoinette S. Calvo	A	4	N.A.	N.A.	. . .
Puerto Rico...............	Juan Carlos Mendez Torres	N.A.	4	N.A.	N.A.	. . .
U.S. Virgin Islands	Austin L. Nibbs (Acting)	A	4	N.A.	N.A.	. . .

Source: National Association of State Treasurers, March 2007.

Key:

★ — No provision specifying number of terms allowed.

. . . — No formal provision, position is appointed or elected by governmental entity (not chosen by the electorate).

A — Appointed by the governor. (In the District of Columbia, the Treasurer is appointed by the Chief Financial Officer. In Georgia, position is appointed by the State Depository Board.)

E — Elected by the voters.

L — Elected by the legislature.

CS — Civil Service.

N.A. — Not applicable.

(a) The Deputy Commissioner of Department of Revenue performs this function.

(b) The official title of the office of state treasurer is Chief Financial Officer.

(c) The Director of Finance performs this function.

(d) Eligible for eight out of any period of 12 years.

(e) The Commissioner of Finance performs this function.

(f) Governor Ed Rendell appointed Treasurer Robin Wiessmann in February 2007. Her confirmation by the state senate was pending at press time.

(g) The Comptroller of Public Accounts performs this function.

Table 4.25
TREASURERS: QUALIFICATIONS FOR OFFICE

State or other jurisdiction	Minimum age	U.S. citizen (years)	State resident (years)	Qualified voter (years)
Alabama	25	7	5	...
Alaska	...	...	★	...
Arizona	25	10	5	...
Arkansas	21	★	★	...
California	18	★	★	★
Colorado	25	★	★	★
Connecticut	...	★	★	★
Delaware	18	★	★	★
Florida	30	★	7	★
Georgia	...	...	...	...
Hawaii	...	★	5	...
Idaho	25	★	2	...
Illinois	25	★	★	...
Indiana	...	★	★	★
Iowa	18	...	...	...
Kansas	...	...	...	...
Kentucky	30	★	6	★
Louisiana	25	(a)	(c)	(c)
Maine	...	★	★	...
Maryland	...	...	...	...
Massachusetts	...	...	★	...
Michigan	...	...	...	...
Minnesota	...	...	...	...
Mississippi	25	★	5	(d)
Missouri	...	★	5	★
Montana	...	...	...	...
Nebraska	19	★	★	★
Nevada	25	★	★	★
New Hampshire	...	...	...	...
New Jersey	...	...	★	...
New Mexico	30	★	★	★
New York	...	★	★	N.A.
North Carolina	21	★	1	★
North Dakota	25	★	5	★
Ohio	18	★	★	★
Oklahoma	31	★	★	(e)
Oregon	18	...	★	...
Pennsylvania	...	...	...	...
Rhode Island	(d)	★	★	★
South Carolina	...	★	★	★
South Dakota	...	...	...	...
Tennessee	...	...	...	...
Texas	18	★	★	...
Utah	25	★	5	★
Vermont	...	★	2	...
Virginia	...	...	...	...
Washington	18	★	...	★
West Virginia	18	(b)	(b)	★
Wisconsin	18	★	★	★
Wyoming	25	★	1	★
Dist. of Columbia	...	...	...	...

Source: National Association of State Treasurers, March 2007.
Key:
★ — Formal provision; number of years not specified.
. . . — No formal provision.
N.A. — Not applicable.

(a) Five years immediately preceding the date of election.
(b) Five years prior to taking office.
(c) Five years immediately preceding the date of qualification for office.
(d) Must be qualified elector.
(e) Must be able to vote for at least 10 years immediately preceding election.

Table 4.26
RESPONSIBILITIES OF THE TREASURER'S OFFICE

State or other jurisdiction	Cash management	Investment of retirement funds	Investment of trust funds	Deferred compensation	Management of bonded debt	Bond issuance	Debt service	Arbitrage rebate	Banking services	Unclaimed property	Archives for disbursement of documents	College savings	Collateral programs	Local government investment pool	Other
Alabama	★	...	...	...	★	...	★	...	★	★	...	★	★	...	...
Alaska	★	★	★	...	★	★	★	★	★	★	...	...	...	...	(a)
Arizona	★	...	★	...	...	...	...	...	★	★	...	...	...	★	...
Arkansas	★	...	★	...	...	...	...	...	★	★	...	...	...	★	...
California	★	...	★	...	★	★	★	★	★	...	...	...	★	★	...
Colorado	★	...	...	...	...	...	...	...	★	★	...	...	...	...	...
Connecticut	★	★	★	...	★	★	★	★	★	★	...	★	...	★	(b)
Delaware	★	...	...	★	...	★	★	★	★	...	...	★	★	★	(c)
Florida	★	...	★	★	...	...	...	...	★	★	...	...	...	...	(d)
Georgia	★	...	...	...	...	...	★	...	★	...	...	★	★	★	...
Hawaii	★	★	...	...	★	★	★	★	★	★	...	★	★	...	...
Idaho	★	...	...	...	...	...	...	...	★	...	...	★	...	★	...
Illinois	★	...	★	...	...	...	★	★	★	★	...	★	...	★	...
Indiana	★	...	★	...	★	...	...	...	★	...	★	★	...	★	...
Iowa	★	★	...	...	★	★	★	★	★	★	...	★	★	...	...
Kansas	★	...	...	...	...	...	...	...	★	★	...	★	...	...	(e)
Kentucky	★	...	...	...	...	...	...	...	★	★	★	...	...	...	...
Louisiana	★	...	★	...	★	★	★	★	★	★	...	...	★	...	(f)
Maine	★	...	★	...	★	★	★	★	★	★	...	★	...	...	Municipal Revenue Sharing
Maryland	★	...	...	...	★	★	★	★	★	...	...	...	★	★	...
Massachusetts	★	★	★	★	★	★	★	★	★	★	...	...	...	★	(g)
Michigan	★	★	★	...	★	★	★	★	★	★	★	...	...	...	...
Minnesota	★	...	...	...	★	★	★	★	★	...	...	...	★	...	...
Mississippi	★	★	...	...	★	★	★	★	★	★	...	...	★	...	...
Missouri	★	...	...	...	...	...	...	...	★	★	...	...	★	...	(h)
Montana	★	...	...	...	★	★	★	★	★	...	...	...	...	...	...
Nebraska	★	...	...	...	...	...	...	...	★	★	...	★	...	...	(i)
Nevada	★	...	...	...	★	★	★	...	★	★	...	★	★	★	...
New Hampshire	★	...	★	...	★	★	★	★	★	★	...	★	...	...	...
New Jersey	★	★	...	★	★	★	★	...	★	★	...	...	...	★	...
New Mexico	★	...	...	...	★	...	...	...	★	★	★	...	...	★	...
New York	★	...	...	...	...	...	...	...	★	★	...	...	...	...	(j)
North Carolina	★	★	★	...	★	★	★	★	★	★	...	...	★	★	...
North Dakota	★	...	★	...	...	...	...	...	★	...	...	...	...	★	...
Ohio	★	...	★	...	★	★	★	...	★	...	...	...	...	★	...
Oklahoma	★	...	★	...	...	...	...	★	★	★	...	...	...	...	...
Oregon	★	★	★	★	★	★	★	★	★	★	...	★	★	★	(k)
Pennsylvania	★	★	...	...	★	...	★	★	★	★	...	★	...	★	...
Rhode Island	★	★	...	...	...	...	★	★	★	...	...	★	★	★	...
South Carolina	★	★	★	★	★	★	★	★	★	...	...	★	★	★	...
South Dakota	★	★	★	...	...	...	...	...	★	★	...	...	★	...	(l)
Tennessee	★	★	...	★	...	...	...	...	★	★	...	★	★	★	...
Texas	★	...	★	...	...	★	...	...	★	★	...	★	★	★	(m)
Utah	★	...	★	...	★	★	★	★	★	★	...	★	...	★	...
Vermont	★	★	★	★	★	★	★	★	★	★	...	...	...	...	...
Virginia	★	...	★	...	★	★	★	★	★	★	...	...	★	★	(n)
Washington	★	...	★	...	★	★	★	★	★	...	...	...	...	★	...
West Virginia	★	...	...	...	...	...	★	...	★	★	...	★	★	...	...
Wisconsin	...	...	...	...	...	...	...	...	...	★	...	★	...	★	...
Wyoming	★	...	★	...	★	★	★	★	★	★	...	★	★	★	...
Dist. of Columbia	★	★	★	★	★	★	★	★	★	★	...	...	★	...	...

Source: National Association of State Treasurers, March 2007.
Key:
★ — Responsible for activity.
. . . . — Not responsible for activity.
(a) Revenue collection including oil and gas royalties and corporate income taxes; child support enforcement; permanent fund dividend eligibility.
(b) Second Injury Fund.
(c) General Fund account reconcilement; disbursements.
(d) State Accounting Disbursement, Fire Marshall, Insurance and Banking Consumer Services, Insurance Rehabilitation and Liquidation, Risk Management, Workers' Compensation, Insurance Fraud, Insurance Agent and Agency Services.

(e) Municipal bond servicing.
(f) Social Security for Section 218 Agreements.
(g) Massachusetts Municipal Depository Trust Funds for Cities and Towns.
(h) Investment of all state funds.
(i) Nebraska Child Support Payment Center.
(j) Linked Deposit Program.
(k) Legislation pending to move Unclaimed Property program to Treasurer's office.
(l) Treasurer is a member of the trust and retirement investment programs.
(m) Tax Administration/Collection.
(n) Risk Management.

Table 4.27
STATE INVESTMENT BOARD MEMBERSHIP

State or other jurisdiction	Name of board	Board membership									
		Governor	Lt. Governor	Treasurer	Auditor	Comptroller	Attorney General	Secretary of State	Secretary/Director of Finance	Gubernatorial Appointments	Other
Alabama	No Board	...	...	...	...	...	...	...	...	...	...
Alaska	No Board	...	...	...	...	...	...	...	...	...	(a)
Arizona	Arizona State Board of Investment	...	...	★	...	...	...	...	...	...	(b)
Arkansas	Board of Finance	★	...	★	★	...	...	...	★	1	(c)
California	Pooled Money Investment Board	...	...	★	...	★	...	...	★	...	...
Colorado	Investment Advisory Board	...	...	★	...	...	...	...	...	...	(d)
Connecticut	No Board	...	...	...	...	...	...	...	...	...	...
Delaware	Cash Management Policy Board	...	...	★	...	★	...	...	★	5	(e)
Florida	No Board	...	...	...	...	...	...	...	...	...	...
Georgia	State Depository Board	★	...	★	★	...	...	...	...	...	(f)
Hawaii	No Board	...	...	...	...	...	...	...	...	...	...
Idaho	No Board	...	...	...	...	...	...	...	...	...	...
Illinois	No Board	...	...	...	...	...	...	...	...	...	(g)
Indiana	No Board	...	...	...	...	...	...	...	...	...	(h)
Iowa	Treasurer's Investment Committee	...	...	★	...	...	...	...	...	...	(g)
Kansas	Pooled Money Investment Board	...	...	★	...	...	...	...	...	4	...
Kentucky	Kentucky State Investment Commission	★	...	★	...	...	...	...	★	2	...
Louisiana	No Board	...	...	...	...	...	...	...	...	...	...
Maine	Trust Committee	...	...	★	...	...	★	...	★	...	(h)
Maryland	No Board	...	...	...	...	...	...	...	...	...	(h)
Massachusetts	Investment Advisory Council	...	...	★	...	...	...	...	...	2	(i)
Michigan	No Board	...	...	★	...	...	...	...	...	...	(a)
Minnesota	Minnesota State Board of Investment	★	...	...	★	...	★	★	...	...	...
Mississippi	No Board	...	...	...	...	...	...	...	...	...	...
Missouri	No Board	...	...	...	...	...	...	...	...	...	...
Montana	Montana Board of Investments	...	...	...	...	...	...	...	...	9	...
Nebraska	Nebraska Investment Council	...	...	★	...	...	...	...	...	5	(j)
Nevada	Board of Finance	★	...	★	...	★	...	...	...	2	...
New Hampshire	No Board	...	...	...	...	...	...	...	...	...	...
New Jersey	State Investment Council	...	...	★	...	...	...	...	...	6	(k)
New Mexico	Board of Finance	★	★	...	...	...	...	...	★	4 to 5	...
New York	No Board	...	...	...	...	...	...	...	...	...	(h)
North Carolina	No Board	...	...	...	...	...	...	...	...	...	(a)
North Dakota	State Investment Board	...	★	★	...	...	...	...	...	...	(l)
Ohio	No Board	...	...	...	...	...	...	...	...	...	...
Oklahoma	Cash Management and Investment Oversight Commission	...	...	...	...	...	...	...	★	1	(m)
Oregon	Oregon Investment Council	...	...	★	...	...	...	...	...	...	(j)
Pennsylvania	No Board	...	...	...	...	...	...	...	...	...	...
Rhode Island	State Investment Commission	...	...	★	...	...	...	...	...	3	...
South Carolina	No Board	...	...	...	...	...	...	...	...	...	...
South Dakota	South Dakota Investment Council	...	...	★	...	...	...	...	...	...	(n)
Tennessee	State Pooled Investment Fund	★	...	★	...	★	...	★	★	...	...
Texas	No Board	...	...	...	...	...	...	...	...	...	...
Utah	No Board	...	...	...	...	...	...	...	...	...	...
Vermont	No Board	...	...	...	...	...	...	...	...	...	(a)
Virginia	Commonwealth of Virginia Treasury Board	...	...	★	...	★	...	...	...	4	(o)
Washington	Office of the State Treasurer	...	...	★	...	...	...	...	...	...	...
West Virginia	West Virginia Investment Management Board	★	...	★	★	...	...	...	...	10	...
Wisconsin	State of Wisconsin Investment Board	...	...	...	...	...	...	...	...	5	...
Wyoming	Wyoming State Loan and Investment Board	★	...	★	★	...	...	...	★	...	(h)
Dist. of Columbia	No Board	...	...	...	...	...	...	...	...	...	(h)

See footnotes at end of table.

STATE INVESTMENT BOARD MEMBERSHIP — Continued

Source: National Association of State Treasurers, March 2007.
Key:
★ — Yes
. . . — No
(a) Treasurer/Commissioner is sole fiduciary.
(b) Director of the Department of Administration, State Banking Superintendent. Two individuals appointed by Treasurer.
(c) Bank Commissioner.
(d) Deputy Treasurer and a representative from the Land Board, Department of Labor. Three investment officers and nine public investment professionals from private sector.
(e) Secretary of Administration.
(f) Insurance Commissioner, Transportation Commissioner, Banking and Finance Commissioner, Revenue Commissioner.

(g) Deputy Treasurers and Chief Investment Officer.
(h) Commissioner of Education.
(i) Two Treasury appointees. Executive Director of both state and teacher's retirement system.
(j) Public Employees Retirement System Director.
(k) Five representatives of Pension Fund Boards.
(l) Commissioner of University and School Lands. Director of Workers' Compensation. Commissioner of Insurance.
(m) Senate appoint. President Pro Tempore appoint.
(n) Commissioners of School and Public Lands. State Retirement Director and five others appointed by state legislature.
(o) Tax Commissioner.

Trends and Issues for State Auditors and Comptrollers
By Jan I. Sylvis

It is an old cliché—the only given in life is change. Not all change is bad, however painful it may be. State auditors and state comptrollers are learning to accept and embrace change as they face an evolving professional landscape that includes a new, younger work force, a plethora of new accounting and auditing standards, fluctuations in funding and leadership, and a daunting array of innovative technologies and related security threats.

An Interesting Journey

State finance officials are living and working in interesting times. Old notions of government recently have given way to an unprecedented wave of creative and innovative thinking, employing advanced technologies and processes to more closely align citizen/government interactions with citizens' business and personal experiences. The average citizen wants to use the same processes and technologies to conduct business transactions, communicate on a personal level with family and friends, and interface with government. Never before have we been closer to realizing this vision.

As state government finance and accountability stewards, state auditors and state comptrollers must face a variety of challenges each day. However, we are also in a position to leverage technology and innovative business models to address these governing challenges.

Benchmarking and Best Practices

Benchmarking, a proven practice that has helped countless private sector organizations identify process improvements and drive down administrative costs, has been around for many years and enjoys widespread adoption in the private sector. However, the conventional wisdom for government has been that state governments are organized and funded in such different ways that benchmarking is not feasible.

For a variety of reasons, functions and processes may be organized differently within state governments to the point that separate organizations may call the same processes by different names. Often these variations are caused by differences in organizational structure. For example, in some states, the payroll and HR functions are handled by the state comptroller's office, while in other states HR is handled by completely separate administrative offices. Significant variations may also result from differences in funding strategies. For example, administrative operations are financed with general fund resources in some states, while in others, administrative agencies are allowed to charge other agencies to recover costs. To further complicate the matter, these functions are sometimes performed and accounted for by private sector consultants outside of government. The problem, simply stated, has been this: How does a state conduct a benchmarking study that can be compared to another state?

Comparability is crucial to supporting performance assessments. Comparability requires consistent definitions and methodology, including how data is defined, collected, cleansed, validated, analyzed and summarized into performance metrics. Discrepancies in definitions and methodology can cause fatal flaws in the capacity to accurately compare benchmark findings from one state to another.

The National Association of State Comptrollers (NASC) saw the need for a benchmarking strategy to overcome these challenges, allowing state governments to benefit from the obvious advantages benchmarking presents. In 2004, NASC developed a pilot project that examined four finance processes. Information garnered through this pilot was used to refine the concept. Ultimately, NASC recommended that its parent organization, the National Association of State Auditors, Comptrollers and Treasurers (NASACT), launch a national Benchmarking Project and serve as the primary contractor for states wishing to participate. The project was launched in the summer of 2005 and offers benchmarking services in four core back-office functions: finance, HR/payroll, procurement and IT.

Since that time, eight states have contracted for one or more of the benchmarks available through the program. Tennessee was the first to sign up for the project, and chose to benchmark in all four available areas. For Tennessee, it made sense to benchmark as it was poised to make some major operational changes. In the end, each state will probably choose to benchmark for seemingly different reasons. However, all states will have one ultimate goal—the improvement of government operations.

NASACT's project allows states to choose one or more of the four benchmarks and to use the comparative data for state-to-state, agency-to-agency and government-to-private sector comparisons. As more states participate in the program and the benchmark database for comparisons becomes more comprehensive and robust, the ability for states to compare and thus improve their administrative functions will be elevated to a level never before possible within state government.

NASACT's program was on the forefront of an emerging trend for the public sector, which has seen various federal and local organizations following the benchmarking path. It will be interesting in the months and years to come to see the comparative data that comes of these various initiatives.

Accounting and Financial Reporting

In the world of financial management and accounting, standards are king. There has been no shortage of new standards to consider during the past year.

Many state and local governments offer employees some sort of health care benefits after retirement. The basis for these programs may be statutory, contractual or little more than an informal understanding. In any case, government is building a liability to employees which will require substantial resources to fulfill sooner or later. In 2004, the Governmental Accounting Standards Board issued Statement No. 45, *Accounting and Financial Reporting by Employers for Post-employment Benefits Other Than Pensions*. This statement requires governments to measure, recognize and report their other post-employment benefits (OPEB) expenses, liabilities and assets, if they have been set aside to meet the OPEB liability. The provisions of Statement No. 45 are effective for state governments in fiscal year 2008.

Last year, measurement of this OPEB liability was a major focus for state governments. Data has been collected and actuaries engaged to produce preliminary valuations. Sometimes a set of valuations is requested, reflecting the impact of different benefits, funding provisions and discount rates. Several states have moved to establish irrevocable trusts that would be funded annually and used to increase the assets that will be necessary to meet the OPEB liability.

In April 2006, NASC established an OPEB Implementation Network to share questions and information through monthly conference calls. The group conducted a survey about the status of states with respect to OPEB in May 2006 and plans to update the survey early in 2007, when it is expected that many states will have received their preliminary valuation reports. At the end of 2006, 36 states were represented on the network by staff from the offices of state auditors and comptrollers, budget offices, state retirement systems and state universities. Although it is hard to say at this point what the ultimate result of OPEB requirements will be, this issue will undoubtedly continue to be a high priority for states in coming years.

The trickle-down from Sarbanes-Oxley and the establishment of the Public Company Accounting Oversight Board (PCAOB) also continue to indirectly affect state governments. The creation of the PCAOB increased the number of standards-setting organizations to three: PCAOB, the American Institute of Certified Public Accountants' Auditing Standards Board (ASB) and the U.S. Government Accountability Office (GAO).

To improve coordination between the three groups, U.S. Comptroller General David Walker established the U.S. Auditing Standards Coordinating Forum, which includes principals from the three organizations and meets several times a year to discuss and coordinate their agendas. The purpose of the forum is to maximize complementary standards-setting agendas, minimize duplicative or competing efforts, develop strategies for overcoming barriers to modernizing the audit profession, and assure consistency where appropriate for core auditing standards. PCAOB responded to the call to address private sector corporate scandals with a rash of standards to be followed by auditors of public companies. The ASB and GAO have responded in kind by issuing their own new standards and updates. The AICPA recently released a suite of eight risk assessment standards as well as a standard on communicating internal control-related matters identified in audits. GAO has issued a complete rewrite of *Government Auditing Standards*, which includes an increased emphasis on audit quality and ethics. These are significant changes that reflect major developments in the government accountability and audit environment. These changes will undoubtedly have an impact on the state audit community as it seeks to implement the standards and make changes based on the new audit requirements.

Technology and Government

It is hard to talk about any topic these days without considering it within the context of technology. The past half century has seen a complete reworking of the typical workday for most employees within both the public and private sectors. Not many of us can imagine a world without cell phones and the ability to instantly read and respond to e-mail messages. When networks go down, when technology fails us, we are immobilized at worst and lost at best.

Our reliance on technology quickly becomes apparent during times of disaster. Although it has been some time since the Gulf Coast was struck by hurricanes Katrina and Rita, our collective government psyche still shudders from the complexity of trying to operate a behemoth like state government after disasters of such proportion. After the hurricanes, government workers conducted business without basic necessities like clean water, food/ice and electricity, much less the conveniences of reliable modes of communication and computer networks. Some important lessons have been learned along the path to recovery and will go far to ensure that governments consider disaster planning and recovery issues well before they are ever needed.

Beyond the strategic concerns that technology issues bring to mind, the day-to-day logistics of managing an environment predicated on gathering and protecting sensitive information are daunting. Average citizens have become increasingly reliant upon and educated about available technologies. Not only do they expect to interact with government on a platform equal to those used for business and personal transactions, they are fully aware of the vulnerabilities and potential liabilities if governments do not respond to and adapt to technology changes and demands. In addition to higher citizen expectations, state finance officials must successfully navigate privacy and data management laws from their states and the federal government as well as payment card security standards from the major credit card companies.

The desire by citizens to conduct business with state governments online is a realistic and valid demand. Although government portals are able to address this desire to a certain extent, governments have unfortunately run into complications concerning the acceptance of electronic payments for services in some cases. In the private sector, when credit card interchange rates dramatically increase the cost of doing business, those costs are simply passed on to the consumer. However, many times legislative restrictions prevent governments from doing this. States are seeking to find electronic payment methods that will be comparable to the ease and convenience of using credit cards, but no reasonable alternative has yet emerged. Additionally, attempts to negotiate with the credit card industry to lower interchange rates for transactions conducted within the unique and low-risk government environment have to date proven fruitless. Enhancing citizen e-commerce experiences will continue to be a priority for state governments.

Government *must* invest in technology to survive. Such an important investment cannot be made lightly, however, so government finance and accounting officials must go about their daily business looking to the future and how technology will affect it. Data security and integrity, physical network security, the emergence of wireless technologies and cyberterrorism are just a few of the topics that must remain in clear view as we seek to hire and retain qualified IT professionals to help government keep pace with the private sector.

Fiscal Accountability

Doing more with less is a familiar plight for state and local governments. It is not difficult to foresee that in light of our country's troubling financial forecast, in the very near future there will be even less federal assistance coming to state and local governments than ever. The growing federal deficit will impact all levels of government, and accountability professionals realize that the public must not only be educated about the looming crisis facing the country but also on personal fiscal discipline.

With the impending retirement of the baby boom population, costs of programs such as Social Security, Medicare and Medicaid will continue to strain government budgets. Unfortunately, there is currently no realistic plan to fund these programs other than by continuing to increase the national debt. According to U.S. Comptroller General Walker, the current fiscal policy is on an unsustainable course, and steep tax increases and severe benefit cuts may be the only options to steer from this path.

The future of the national economy could well be dependent on actions our leaders choose to follow today. Changes in Congressional leadership mean changes in national spending priorities, translating in many cases to a reduction in funding for many benefit programs. State and local governments must review their own fiscal policies, keeping in mind that the cost of health care is projected to continue to increase at alarming rates, taking up a larger portion of state budgets. The growing national debt is an issue that will continue to dominate decisions and chart the course of not only state auditors, comptrollers and treasurers, but all public sector leaders who must make tough decisions in determining how to serve citizens with finite resources.

Last year, Congress passed the Tax Increase Prevention and Reconciliation Act, which includes a provision that raises approximately $7 billion in revenue by requiring governments to withhold 3 percent on certain payments to persons providing property or services. The provision was not a part of either the House or Senate version of the reconciliation bill and was added with little knowledge during conference negotiations.

In addition to raising $7 billion in revenue, the provision is the current administration's attempt to undermine misreporting by certain government vendors not currently subject to withholding. The U.S. Treasury has reasoned that information reporting and back-up withholding have improved compliance in other areas and should be imposed on government vendors to address this component of the tax gap.

Effective Jan. 1, 2011, the provision will require governments to withhold 3 percent regardless of whether the government making the payment is the recipient of the goods or services. Initial inquiries reveal that the provision could cause administrative burdens for some states, particularly those with older systems, by imposing record-keeping for reconciliation between the vendors billed and what states have paid to them and to the IRS on their behalf. Payments made via purchase cards may also prove problematic in obtaining proper information for record-keeping. Additionally, the imposition of such a requirement may put governments at a competitive disadvantage, as the withholding requirement is not imposed for private sector payment of goods and services, and government vendors may inflate their bids to compensate for the withholding.

The Congressional Budget Office reports that the new withholding requirement exceeds the annual threshold established in the Unfunded Mandates Reform Act, thereby constituting an unfunded mandate on state and local governments. In response to this unfunded mandate, NASACT and several other national organizations sent a joint letter to Congressional leaders in support of repealing the problematic provision of the act. NASACT hopes that federal leaders will respond to input from state officials on this important matter and move to make corrections to remedy the issue.

Government's Greatest Resource— the People

States continue to face significant challenges in hiring and retaining qualified work forces. With growing numbers of employees at or near retirement, states are struggling to hire qualified professionals with education and experience in accounting and finance. Governmental accounting classes are no longer being offered at many universities and more and more accounting degree candidates are turning to the private sector to secure successful careers. And unfortunately, state governments can no longer rely on the appeal of plush benefits packages to attain desirable workers, as pension and OPEB plans are under attack and being targeted for change in many states.

In addition to the challenge of finding employees who are qualified and interested enough to work in government, we are now faced with a new, young, digitally indoctrinated work force that is different from any previously encountered. Today's college graduates have workplace expectations and quality-of-life demands that are very different from those of many government managerial veterans. The challenge is to figure out how to adapt a workplace that has not historically been characterized by flexibility or innovation to be attractive to this new type of employee, who is well-versed in technology, adept at multi-tasking and expects the workplace to be customized to meet the needs of each individual.

Finding a way to reconcile the differences between public and private sector salaries/environments and attracting qualified, interested job candidates must be a priority for state governments. There is no easy solution to this problem, but it is a problem that must not be underemphasized in importance because a talented, qualified work force is essential to the continued improvement of state government.

Conclusions and Perspectives

In government, change management is our main business. It seems that every year things get more complex and more technical, and changes occur at an ever-accelerating pace. A change-laden environment is our reality.

To address today's challenges and those awaiting us in the future, state government leaders—comptrollers, auditors, treasurers, chief information officers, budget officials, strategy officials and others—must work together toward a common vision that will find states operating at new levels of efficiency and effectiveness and responding in real time to the needs of the citizens we serve.

About the Author

Jan I. Sylvis was appointed chief of accounts of Tennessee's Department of Finance and Administration in 1995. She is past president of the National Association of State Comptrollers and is currently president of NASACT. Sylvis received her B.B.A. from Memphis State University and is a certified public accountant and a certified government financial manager.

Table 4.28
THE STATE AUDITORS, 2007

State or other jurisdiction	State agency	Agency head	Title	Legal basis for office	Method of selection	Term of office	U.S. citizen	State resident	Maximum consecutive terms allowed
Alabama	Dept. of Examiners of Public Accounts	Ronald L. Jones	Chief Examiner	S	LC	7 yrs.	★	...	None
Alaska	Division of Legislative Audit	Pat Davidson	Legislative Auditor	C, S	L	(a)	...	...	None
Arizona	Auditor General	Debra K. Davenport	Auditor General	S	LC	5 yrs.	...	...	None
Arkansas	Legislative Auditor	Charles L. Robinson	Legislative Auditor	S	LC	Indefinite	...	...	None
California	Bureau of State Audits	Elaine Howle	State Auditor	S	G	4 yrs.	★	...	None
Colorado	State Auditor	Sally Symanski	Acting State Auditor	C, S	L	5 yrs.	★	★	None
Connecticut	Auditors of Public Accounts	Kevin P. Johnston, Robert G. Jaekle	State Auditors	C	L	4 yrs.	...	...	None
Delaware	Auditor of Accounts	R. Thomas Wagner Jr.	Auditor of Accounts	C	E	4 yrs.	★	★	None
Florida	Auditor General	William O. Monroe	Auditor General	C, S	L	(a)	...	...	None
Georgia	Dept. of Audits and Accounts	Russell W. Hinton	State Auditor	S	L	Indefinite	...	★	None
Hawaii	Office of the Auditor	Marion M. Higa	State Auditor	C, S	L	8 yrs.	...	★	None
Idaho	Legislative Services Office – Legislative Audits	Don Berg	Manager of Legislative Audits	S	LC	Indefinite	★	...	None
Illinois	Auditor General	William G. Holland	Auditor General	C, S	L	10 yrs.	...	...	None
Indiana	State Board of Accounts	Bruce Hartman	State Examiner	S	G	4 yrs.	...	...	None
Iowa	Auditor of State	David A. Vaudt	Auditor of State	C, S	E	4 yrs.	★	★	None
Kansas	Legislative Division of Post Audit	Barbara J. Hinton	Legislative Post Auditor	S	LC	(b)	...	...	None
Kentucky	Auditor of Public Accounts	Crit Luallen	Auditor of Public Accounts	C, S	E	4 yrs.	★	★	2
Louisiana	Legislative Auditor	Steve J. Theriot	Legislative Auditor	C, S	L	Indefinite	...	★	None
Maine	State Auditor	Neria Douglas	State Auditor	S	L	4 yrs.	★	★	2
Maryland	Office of Legislative Audits	Bruce A. Myers	Legislative Auditor	S	ED	Indefinite	...	...	None
Massachusetts	State Auditor	A. Joseph DeNucci	Auditor of the Commonwealth	C, S	E	4 yrs.	★	★	None
Michigan	Auditor General	Thomas H. McTavish	Auditor General	C	L	8 yrs.	...	★	None
Minnesota	Legislative Auditor	James R. Nobles	Legislative Auditor	S	LC	6 yrs.	...	★	None
	State Auditor	Rebecca Ott	State Auditor	C	E	4 yrs.	★	★	None
Mississippi	State Auditor	Phil Bryant	State Auditor	C, S	E	4 yrs.	★	★	None
Missouri	State Auditor	Susan Montee	State Auditor	C, S	E	4 yrs.	★	★	None
Montana	Legislative Audit Division, Legislative Branch	Scott A. Seacat	Legislative Auditor	C, S	LC	2 yrs.	...	...	None
Nebraska	Auditor of Public Accounts	Mike Foley	Auditor of Public Accounts	C, S	E	4 yrs.	★	★	None
Nevada	Legislative Auditor	Paul Townsend	Legislative Auditor	S	LC	Indefinite	...	...	None
New Hampshire	Legislative Budget Assistant	Michael L. Buckley	Legislative Budget Assistant	S	LC	2 yrs.	...	...	None
New Jersey	State Auditor	Richard L. Fair	State Auditor	C, S	L	5-yr. term and until successor is appointed	...	...	N.A.
New Mexico	State Auditor	Hector Balderas	State Auditor	C	E	4 yrs.	★	★	2
New York	Office of the State Comptroller, State Audit Bureau	Alan G. Hevesi	Deputy Comptroller – State Services	C, S	E	4 yrs.	★	★	None
North Carolina	State Auditor	Leslie W. Merritt Jr.	State Auditor	C, S	E	4 yrs.	★	★	None
North Dakota	State Auditor	Robert R. Peterson	State Auditor	C, S	E	4 yrs.	★	★	None
Ohio	Auditor of State	Mary Taylor	Auditor of State	C	E	4 yrs.	★	★	2

See footnotes at end of table.

THE STATE AUDITORS, 2007 — Continued

State or other jurisdiction	State agency	Agency head	Title	Legal basis for office	Method of selection	Term of office	U.S. citizen	State resident	Maximum consecutive terms allowed
Oklahoma	State Auditor and Inspector	Jeff McMahan	State Auditor and Inspector	C, S	E	4 yrs.	★	★	None
Oregon	Secretary of State, Audits Division	Charles Hibner	State Auditor	C	SS	(c)	…	…	N.A.
Pennsylvania	Auditor General	Jack Wagner	Auditor General	C	E	4 yrs.	…	…	2
Rhode Island	Legislative Budget and Finance Cmte.	Philip R. Durgin	Executive Director	S	LC	(b)	…	…	None
	Auditor General	Ernest A. Almonte	Auditor General	S	LC	(b)	…	…	None
South Carolina	Legislative Audit Council	George L. Schroeder	Director	S	LC	4 yrs.	…	…	None
	State Auditor	Richard Gilbert	Interim State Auditor	S	SB	Indefinite	…	…	N.A.
South Dakota	Dept. of Legislative Audit	Martin L. Guindon	Auditor General	S	L	8 yrs.	…	…	None
Tennessee	Comptroller of the Treasury, Dept. of Audit	John G. Morgan	Comptroller of the Treasury	C, S	L	2 yrs.	…	…	None
Texas	State Auditor	John Keel, CPA	State Auditor	S	LC	(b)	★	★	None
Utah	State Auditor	Auston G. Johnson	State Auditor	C, S	E	4 yrs.	★	★	None
Vermont	State Auditor	Thomas M. Salmon	State Auditor	C, S	E	2 yrs.	★	★	None
Virginia	Auditor of Public Accounts	Walter J. Kucharski	Auditor of Public Accounts	C, S	L	4 yrs.	…	…	None
Washington	Office of the State Auditor	Brian Sonntag	State Auditor	C, S	E	4 yrs.	★	★	None
West Virginia	Legislative Audit Bureau	Thedford L. Shanklin	Legislative Auditor		L		…	…	
Wisconsin	Legislative Audit Bureau	Janice Mueller	State Auditor	C, S	LC	(b)	…	…	None
Wyoming	Dept. of Audit	Michael Geesey	Director	S	GC	6 yrs.	…	…	None
Dist. of Columbia	Office of the D.C. Auditor	Deborah Kay Nichols	District of Columbia Auditor		L		…	…	
Guam	Office of the Public Auditor	Doris Flores Brooks	Public Auditor	S	E	4 yrs.	★	★	None
No. Mariana Islands	Office of the Public Auditor	Michael S. Sablan	Public Auditor	C, S	GL	6 yrs.	N.A.	N.A.	2
Puerto Rico	Office of the Comptroller of Puerto Rico	Manuel Diaz Saldana	Comptroller of Puerto Rico	C	GL	10 yrs.	★	★	1

Sources: Auditing in the States: A Summary, 2006 Edition, The National Association of State Auditors, Comptrollers and Treasurers, and state constitutions and statutes, January 2007.

Key:
★ — Provision for
. . . — No provision
E — Elected by the public.
L — Appointed by the legislature.
G — Appointed by the governor.
SS — Appointed by the secretary of state.
LC — Selected by legislative committee, commission or council.

ED — Appointed by the executive director of legislative services.
GC — Appointed by governor, secretary of state and treasurer.
GL — Appointed by the governor and confirmed by both chambers of the legislature.
SB — Appointed by state budget and control board.
C — Constitutional
S — Statutory
N.A. — Not applicable.
(a) Serves at the pleasure of the legislature.
(b) Serves at the pleasure of a legislative committee.
(c) Serves at the pleasure of the secretary of state.

Table 4.29
STATE AUDITORS: SCOPE OF AGENCY AUTHORITY

State or other jurisdiction	Authority to audit all state agencies	Authority to audit local governments	Authority to obtain information	Authority to issue subpoenas	Authority to specify accounting principles for local governments	Investigations Agency investigates fraud, waste, abuse, and/or illegal acts	Agency operates a hotline
Alabama	★	★	★	★	★(a)	★	...
Alaska	★	...	★	★	...	★	...
Arizona	★	★	★	...	★(b)	★	...
Arkansas	★	★	★	★	...	★	...
California	★	★	★	★	...	★	★
Colorado	★	★	★	★	★	★	...
Connecticut	★	...	★	...	...	★	★
Delaware	★	★	★	★	...	★	★
Florida	(c)	★	★	...	...	★	...
Georgia	★	★	★	★	★	★	...
Hawaii	(c)	★	★	★	...	★	...
Idaho	★	...	★	★	...	★	...
Illinois	★	★	★	★	...	★	...
Indiana	★	★	★	★	★	★	...
Iowa	★	★	★	★	...	★	...
Kansas	★	★	★	...	...	...	...
Kentucky	★	★	★	★	...	★	★
Louisiana	★	★(d)	★	★(e)	...	★	...
Maine	★	★	★	(f)	...	★	...
Maryland	(c)	★(g)	★	★	...	★	★
Massachusetts	★	★	★	...	...	★	★
Michigan	★	...	★	★	...	★	...
Minnesota							
Legislative Auditor	★	(h)	★	★	...	★	...
State Auditor	(i)	★	★	★	★	★	...
Mississippi	★	★(j)	★	...	★	★	★
Missouri	★	★(k)	★	★	...	★ ·	★
Montana	★	...	★	...	...	★	★
Nebraska	★	★	N.A.	...	★(l)	★	★
Nevada	★	★	★	...	...	★	...
New Hampshire	★	...	★	...	...	...	...
New Jersey	★	(m)	★	...	...	★	...
New Mexico	(n)	★	★	...	...	★	...
New York	★	★	★	★	★	★	★
North Carolina	★	...	★	★	...	★	★
North Dakota	(o)	★	★	...	★	★	★
Ohio	★	★	★	★	★	★	★
Oklahoma	★	★	★	★	...	★	...
Oregon	★	★	★	★	★	★	★
Pennsylvania							
Auditor General	(p)	...	★	★	...	★	★
Legislative Budget and Finance Cmte.	★	...	★	★	...	...	...
Rhode Island	★	(q)	★	★	★	★	...
South Carolina							
Legislative Audit Council	★	(r)	★	...	...	★	...
State Auditor	(s)	...	★	...	...	★	...
South Dakota	★	★	★	★	★	★	...
Tennessee	★	★	★	★	★	★	★
Texas	★	(t)	★	★	★(u)	★	★
Utah							
Legislative Auditor	★	★	★	★	...	★	...
State Auditor	(v)	★	★	★	★	★	★
Vermont	★	...	★	★	★(w)	★	...
Virginia	★	...	★	...	★	★	...
Washington	★	★	★	★	★	★	...
West Virginia	N.A.	N.A.	N.A.	N.A.	N.A.	N.A.	N.A.
Wisconsin	★	★	★	★	...	★	...
Wyoming	★	★	★	★	...	★	...
Guam	...	★	★	★	★	★	★
No. Mariana Islands	★	N.A.	★	★	★	★	N.A.
Puerto Rico	★	★	★	★	★	★	★

See footnotes at end of table.

STATE AUDITORS: SCOPE OF AGENCY AUTHORITY — Continued

Source: Auditing in the States, 2006 Edition, The National Association of State Auditors, Comptrollers and Treasurers.

Key:

★ — Provision for responsibility.

. . . — No provision for responsibility.

N.A. — Not available.

(a) Municipalities not covered.

(b) Except for cities and towns, and certain special taxing districts.

(c) The legislature or legislative branch is excluded from audit authority.

(d) Only under certain circumstances.

(e) Only through oversight council.

(f) Municipalities only.

(g) Local school systems.

(h) Financial audits of local governments are excluded from audit authority.

(i) State agencies are audited by the Office of Legislative Auditor.

(j) All local governments excluded but municipalities.

(k) Has audit authority for counties that do not elect a county auditor and other political subdivisions upon petition by the voters of those subdivisions.

(l) Only counties.

(m) Entities not receiving state aid or state grants and school districts receiving less than 80 percent state aid are excluded from audit authority.

(n) The Gaming Commission, Mortgage Finance Authority, State Lottery Commission, Student Loan Guarantee Corporation are excluded from audit authority.

(o) The Bank of North Dakota, State Fair Association, and a few others are excluded from audit authority.

(p) The legislative and judicial branches are excluded from audit authority.

(q) No local governments are specifically excluded, but the agency goes in on orders from the Joint Committee and Legislative Services.

(r) County, school districts, special purpose districts are excluded from audit authority.

(s) State Ports Authority, State Public Service Authority, Research Authority are excluded from audit authority.

(t) All local governments and special districts are excluded; however, if a state entity passes money or contracts with a non-state entity, the state auditor has the authority to follow the money and perform any related audit work deemed necessary.

(u) Comptroller prescribes guidelines but the State Auditor's Office has responsibility to review and comment.

(v) State Retirement and Workers' Compensation Fund are excluded from audit authority.

(w) Required for county sheriff's departments and at the request of town governments.

Table 4.30
STATE AUDITORS: TYPES OF AUDITS

State or other jurisdiction	Financial statement	Single audit	Attestation engagements	Compliance only	Economy and efficiency	Program	Sunset	Performance measures	IT	Accounting and review services	Other audits
Alabama	★	★	…	…	…	★	…	★	…	…	…
Alaska	★	★	★	★	★	★	★	…	★	…	…
Arizona	★	★	…	…	★	★	★	…	★	…	(a)
Arkansas	★	★	…	…	…	★	…	…	★	…	(b)
California	★	★	…	★	★	★	…	★	★	…	(c)
Colorado	★	★	…	★	★	★	…	★	★	…	…
Connecticut	★	★	★	★	★	★	…	★	★	…	(d)
Delaware	★	★	★	★	★	★	★	★	★	★	…
Florida	★	★	★	★	★	★	★	…	★	…	…
Georgia	★	★	★	★	★	★	★	…	★	★	(e)
Hawaii	…	…	…	…	★	★	★	★	★	…	(f)
Idaho	★	★	…	★	★	★	★	…	★	…	(g)
Illinois	★	★	★	★	★	★	…	…	★	…	(d)
Indiana	★	★	★	★	★	★	★	…	★	…	…
Iowa	★	★	★	★	★	★	…	★	★	…	…
Kansas	★	★	…	★	★	★	…	★	★	★	…
Kentucky	★	★	★	★	★	★	…	★	★	…	…
Louisiana	★	★	★	★	★	★	…	★	★	…	…
Maine	★	★	★	★	★	★	…	…	…	…	…
Maryland	…	…	…	★	★	★	…	★	★	…	(h)
Massachusetts	★	★	★	★	★	★	★	★	★	★	(i)
Michigan	★	★	★	…	★	★	…	★	★	…	…
Minnesota											
Legislative Auditor	★	★	…	…	…	★	…	★	★	…	(j)
State Auditor	★	★	…	…	…	…	…	…	…	…	(d)
Mississippi	★	★	…	★	★	★	…	★	★	★	(k)
Missouri	★	★	…	★	★	★	…	★	★	…	…
Montana	★	★	★	★	★	★	…	★	★	…	…
Nebraska	★	★	★	★	★	★	…	★	★	★	…
Nevada	…	…	…	★	★	★	…	★	★	…	…
New Hampshire	★	…	…	★	★	★	…	★	★	…	…
New Jersey	★	★	…	★	★	★	…	…	★	…	…
New Mexico	★	★	…	★	★	★	…	★	★	…	…
New York	★	…	★	★	★	★	…	★	★	★	(l)
North Carolina	★	★	★	★	★	★	…	★	★	…	(m)
North Dakota	★	★	★	…	★	★	…	…	★	…	…
Ohio	★	★	★	★	★	★	…	★	★	★	…

See footnotes at end of table.

STATE AUDITORS: TYPES OF AUDITS — Continued

State or other jurisdiction	Financial statement	Single audit	Attestation engagements	Compliance only	Economy and efficiency	Program	Sunset	Performance measures	IT	Accounting and review services	Other audits
Oklahoma	★	★	★	…	★	★	…	…	★	…	…
Oregon	…	★	★	★	★	★	…	…	★	★	(n)
Pennsylvania											
Auditor General	★	★	★	★	★	★	…	★	★	…	(o)
Legislative Budget and Finance Cmte.	…	…	…	…	…	★	…	★	…	…	…
Rhode Island	★	…	…	★	★	★	…	…	…	…	…
South Carolina											
Legislative Audit Council	…	…	…	…	…	★	…	…	★	…	…
State Auditor	★	★	★	…	★	…	…	…	…	…	…
South Dakota	★	★	★	…	…	…	…	…	…	…	…
Tennessee	★	★	★	★	★	★	★	★	★	★	(p)
Utah	★	★	★	★	★	★	…	★	★	…	(q)
Legislative Auditor	…	…	…	…	…	…	…	…	…	…	…
State Auditor	★	★	★	★	★	…	★	★	…	…	(r)
Vermont	★	★	★	…	★	★	…	★	★	★	…
Virginia	★	★	★	…	…	…	…	…	…	…	…
Washington	★	★	★	★	…	★	…	★	★	…	…
West Virginia	N.A.	★	N.A.	N.A.	★	N.A.	…	★	★	…	…
Wisconsin	★	★	…	★	★	★	…	N.A.	N.A.	N.A.	N.A.
Wyoming	…	…	…	…	…	★	…	★	…	…	…
Guam	★	★	★	…	★	★	…	…	…	…	…
No. Mariana Islands	★	★	★	…	★	★	…	…	…	★	(c)
Puerto Rico	…	…	…	★	★	…	…	…	★	…	…

Sources: Auditing in the States: A Summary, 2006 Edition, The National Association of State Auditors, Comptrollers and Treasurers, and state constitutions and statutes.

Note: Government audits are divided into two types, financial and performance audits. Financial audits include financial statement audits and financial-related audits. Performance audits include economy and efficiency audits and program audits. In addition, government auditors perform a number of other audit-related functions that do not fall into one of these categories. State audit agencies must make certain that audit coverage is broad enough to fulfill the needs of potential audit report users.

Key:

★ — Provision for responsibility.

… — No provision for responsibility.

N.A. — Not available.

(a) Fraud, special audits, studies, and program evaluations.
(b) Internal control and compliance reviews.
(c) Investigations.
(d) Agreed upon procedures.
(e) Financial related audits, desk reviews.
(f) Mandatory health insurance analyses, financial-related audits.
(g) Federal grant audits.
(h) Special requests and follow-up reviews.
(i) Referrals.
(j) Investigation.
(k) Performance reviews.
(l) Internal control reviews: studies.
(m) Fraud and abuse investigations, internal control audits.
(n) Investigations (reviews).
(o) Informational reports, including referrals or investigation of fraud.
(p) Special investigations.
(q) Special investigative audits, classification audits, internal control reviews, training and other educational services.
(r) Special projects, consulting, feasibility studies.

Table 4.31
THE STATE COMPTROLLERS, 2007

State	Agency or office	Name	Title	Legal basis for office	Method of selection	Approval or confirmation, if necessary	Date of first service	Present term ends	Consecutive time in office	Length of term	Elected comptroller's maximum consecutive terms	Civil service or merit system employee
Alabama	Office of the State Comptroller	Robert L. Childree	State Comptroller	S	(c)	AG	5/1987	(b)	20 yrs.	(b)	...	★
Alaska	Division of Finance	Kim J. Garnero	Director of Finance	S	(d)	AG	8/1999	(a)	7 yrs.	(a)	...	...
Arizona	Financial Services Division	D. Clark Partridge	State Comptroller	S	(d)	AG	4/2002	...	5 yrs.	...	...	...
Arkansas	Department of Finance and Administration	Richard A. Weiss	Director	S	G	...	5/2002	(a)	5 yrs.	(a)	...	...
California	Office of the State Controller	John Chiang (D)	State Controller	C	E	...	1/2007	1/2011	6 mos.	4 yrs.	2 terms	...
Colorado	Office of the State Controller	Leslie Shenefelt	State Controller	S	(d)	...	7/2004	(b)	2.5 yrs.	(b)	...	...
Connecticut	Office of the Comptroller	Nancy Wyman (D)	Comptroller	C	E	...	1/1995	1/2011	12 yrs.	4 yrs.	unlimited	★
Delaware	Department of Finance	Richard S. Cordrey	Secretary of Finance	C, S	G	AS	2/2005	(a)	2 yrs.	(a)	2 terms	...
Florida	Department of Financial Services	Alex Sink (D)	Chief Financial Officer	C	E	...	1/2007	1/2011	6 mos.	4 yrs.	2 terms	...
Georgia (I)	State Accounting Office	Lynn H. Vellinga	State Accounting Officer	S	G	...	10/2004	(a)	2 yrs.	(a)	...	...
Hawaii	Department of Accounting and General Services	Russ K. Satio	State Comptroller	S	G	AS	12/2002	12/2010	5 yrs.	(a)	...	...
Idaho	Office of the State Controller	Donna Jones (R)	State Controller	C, S	E	...	1/2007	1/2011	6 mos.	4 yrs.	2 terms	★
Illinois	Office of the Comptroller	Daniel W. Hynes (D)	State Comptroller	C	E	...	11/1999	1/2011	8 yrs.	4 yrs.	unlimited	...
Indiana	Office of the Auditor of State	Tim Berry (R)	Auditor of State	C	E	...	1/2007	1/2011	6 mos.	4 yrs.	2 terms	...
Iowa	State Accounting Enterprise	Calvin McKelvogue	Chief Operating Officer	S	G	AS	7/2004	N.A.	2 yrs.	N.A.	...	...
Kansas	Division of Accounts and Reports	Robert Mackey	Director	S	(d)	...	1/2006	(b)	1 yr.	(b)	...	★
Kentucky	Office of the Controller	Edgar C. Ross	Controller	S	(f)	AG	6/1975	N.A.	32 yrs.	(i)	...	...
Louisiana	Division of Administration	Jerry Luke LeBlanc	Commissioner of Administration	S	G	...	1/2004	1/2008	3 yrs.	(a)	...	...
Maine	Office of the State Controller	Edward Karass	State Controller	S	(f)	AG	4/2003	(i)	4 yrs.	(i)	...	...
Maryland	Office of the Comptroller of the Treasury	Peter Franchot (D)	State Comptroller	C, S	E	...	1/2007	1/2011	6 mos.	4 yrs.	unlimited	★
Massachusetts	Office of the Comptroller	Martin J. Benison	State Comptroller	S	G	...	1/1999	(j)	8 yrs.	(j)	...	...
Michigan	Office of Financial Management	Michael J. Moody	Director	S	SBD	SBD	8/2002	8/2008	5 yrs.	(k)	...	★
Minnesota	Department of Finance	Peggy Ingison	Commissioner	S	G	AS	2/2004	(a)	3 yrs.	(a)	...	...
Mississippi	Department of Finance and Administration	J.K. Stringer Jr.	State Fiscal Officer	S	G	AS	1/2004	1/2008	3 yrs.	(a)	...	...
Missouri	Division of Accounting	Thomas Sadowski	Director of Accounting	C, S	(d)	...	2/2005	(g)	2 yrs.	(g)	...	...
Montana	Administrative Financial Services Division	Paul Christofferson	Administrator	S	(m)	...	6/2004	(b)	3 yrs.	(b)	...	★
Nebraska	Accounting Division	Paul Carlson	State Accounting Administrator	S	(d)	...	11/2000	(g)	6 yrs.	(g)	...	...
Nevada	Office of the State Controller	Kim Wallin (D)	State Controller	C	E	...	1/2007	1/2011	6 mos.	4 yrs.	2 terms	...
New Hampshire	Division of Accounting Services	Sheri Rockburn	Comptroller	S	G	...	8/2004	6/2008	3 yrs.	4 yrs.	...	...
New Jersey	Office of Management and Budget	Charlene M. Holzbaur	Director/State Controller	S	G	AS	10/1999	(b)	7 yrs.	(a)	...	...

See footnotes at end of table.

THE STATE COMPTROLLERS, 2007 — Continued

State	Agency or office	Name	Title	Legal basis for office	Method of selection	Approval or confirmation, if necessary	Date of first service	Present term ends	Consecutive time in office	Length of term	Elected comptroller's maximum consecutive terms	Civil service or merit system employee
New Mexico	Department of Finance and Administration, Financial Control Division	Anthony I. Armijo	State Controller and Director	S	G	...	1/1991	(b)	16 yrs.	(a)	...	★
New York	Office of the State Comptroller	Alan G. Hevesi (D)	State Comptroller	C, S	E	...	1/2003	12/2010	4 yrs.	4 yrs.	unlimited	...
North Carolina	Office of the State Controller	Robert L. Powell	State Controller	S	G	GA	7/2001	7/2008	5.5 yrs.	7 yrs.	...	...
North Dakota	Office of Management and Budget	Pam Sharp	Director	S	G	...	1/2003	(a)	4 yrs.	(a)	...	...
Ohio	Office of Budget and Management	Timothy S. Keen	Director	S	G	AS	3/2006	(a)	1 yr.	(a)	...	...
Oklahoma	Office of State Finance	Brenda Bolander	State Comptroller	S	(e)	...	12/2001	(b)	5 yrs.	(h)	...	★
Oregon	State Controller's Division	John J. Radford	State Controller	S	(d)	AG	11/1989	(b)	17 yrs.	(g)	...	...
Pennsylvania	Comptroller Operations	Harvey C. Eckert	Commonwealth Comptroller	S	G	...	3/1983	(b)	24 yrs.	(a)	...	...
Rhode Island	Office of Accounts and Control	Lawrence C. Franklin Jr.	State Controller	S	CS	...	8/1986	(b)	20 yrs.	(b)	...	★
South Carolina	Office of the Comptroller General	Richard Eckstrom (R)	Comptroller General	C, S	E	...	1/2003	1/2011	4 yrs.	4 yrs.	unlimited	...
South Dakota	Office of the State Auditor	Richard L. Sattgast (R)	State Auditor	C	E	...	1/2003	1/2011	4 yrs.	4 yrs.	2 terms	...
Tennessee	Division of Accounts	Jan I. Sylvis	Chief of Accounts	C, S	(f)	...	12/1995	(b)	11 yrs.	(b)	...	...
Texas	Office of the Comptroller of Public Accounts	Susan Combs (R)	Comptroller of Public Accounts	C, S	E	...	1/2007	1/2011	6 mos.	4 yrs.	unlimited	...
Utah	Division of Finance	John Reidhead	Director	S	(d)	AG	7/2005	(g)	1.5 yrs.	(g)	...	★
Vermont	Department of Finance and Management	James Reardon	Commissioner	S	G	AS	2/2005	2/2007	2 yrs.	(a)	...	...
Virginia	Department of Accounts	David A. Von Moll	State Comptroller	S	G	GA	11/2001	(a)	5 yrs.	(a)	...	★
Washington	Office of Financial Management	Victor Moore	Director	C, S	G	...	1/2005	(a)	2 yrs.	(a)	...	...
West Virginia	Office of the State Auditor	Glen B. Gainier III (D)	State Auditor	C, S	E	...	1/1992	1/2008	15 yrs.	4 yrs.	unlimited	...
	Finance Division, Office of the State Comptroller	Ross Taylor	Acting State Comptroller and Finance Director	S	(d)	AG	10/2005	(a)	1.5 yrs.	(g)	...	...
Wisconsin	State Controller's Office	William J. Rafferty	State Controller	S	CS	...	12/1988	(b)	19 yrs.	(b)	...	★
Wyoming	Office of the State Auditor	Rita Meyer (R)	State Auditor	C, S	E	...	1/2007	1/2011	6 mos.	4 yrs.	2 terms	...

Source: Comptrollers: Technical Activities and Functions, 2006 Edition, The National Association of State Auditors, Comptrollers and Treasurers.

Key:
. . . — No provision for.
C — Constitutional
S — Statutory
N.A. — Not applicable.
E — Elected by the public.
G — Appointed by the Governor.
CS — Civil Service
AG — Approved by the Governor.
AS — Approved/confirmed by the Senate.
SBD — Approved by the State Budget Director.
GA — Approved by the General Assembly.
SDB — Confirmed by the State Depository Board.

(a) Serves at the pleasure of the governor.
(b) Indefinite.
(c) Appointed by the Director of the Department of Finance (merit system position).
(d) Appointed by the head of the department of administration or administrative services.
(e) Appointed by the head of finance department or agency.
(f) Appointed by the head of financial and administrative services.
(g) Serves at the pleasure of the head of the department of administration or administrative services.
(h) Serves at the pleasure of the head of the finance department or agency.
(i) Serves at the pleasure of the head of financial and administrative services.
(j) Two full terms coterminous with the governor.
(k) Two-year renewable contractual term; classified executive service.
(l) As of July 1, 2005, the responsibility for accounting and financial reporting in Georgia was transferred to the newly created State Accounting Office.
(m) Classified position.

Table 4.32
STATE COMPTROLLERS: QUALIFICATIONS FOR OFFICE

State	Minimum age	U.S. citizen (years)	State resident (years) (b)	Education years or degree	Professional experience and years	Professional certification and years	Other qualifications	No specific qualifications for office
Alabama	★	★	★	★, B.S.	★, 6 yrs.	...	...	...
Alaska	...	...	...	...	...	...	...	★
Arizona	...	★, 1 yr.	★, 1 yr.	★, B.S.	★, 7–10 yrs.	★(a)	...	...
Arkansas	30	...	...	...	★	...	...	...
California	★	...	...	...	...	...	(b)	...
Colorado	...	...	★	★(i)	★, 6 yrs.	★, CPA	...	...
Connecticut	...	...	★	...	...	...	...	...
Delaware	...	...	...	...	...	...	...	★
Florida	★	...	★, 7 yrs.	...	...	...	...	...
Georgia	...	...	...	...	...	...	...	★
Hawaii	...	...	...	...	...	...	...	★
Idaho	★	★(j)	★, 2 yrs.	...	...	...	...	...
Illinois	25	★	★, 3 yrs.	...	...	...	...	...
Indiana	...	...	★(j)	...	...	...	...	...
Iowa	...	...	...	...	...	...	...	★
Kansas	...	...	...	...	...	...	...	★
Kentucky	...	...	...	...	...	...	(c)	★
Louisiana	...	...	...	...	...	...	...	★
Maine	...	...	...	...	...	...	(d)	★
Maryland	18	★	★	...	...	...	...	...
Massachusetts	...	...	...	★(k)	★, 7 yrs.	...	...	...
Michigan	...	...	...	★(l)	★, 5 yrs.	(l)	(l)	...
Minnesota	...	...	...	...	...	...	...	★
Mississippi	...	...	...	★(k)	★, 10 yrs.	★, CPA	(e)	...
Missouri	...	...	...	...	...	...	...	★
Montana	...	...	...	★(p)	★, 5 yrs.	★, CPA	...	★
Nebraska	...	...	...	★(m)	★(n)	★, CPA	...	...
Nevada	25	★	★	...	...	...	...	...
New Hampshire	...	...	...	...	...	...	(f)	...
New Jersey	...	...	...	...	...	...	...	★
New Mexico	30	★	5	N.A.	N.A.	N.A.	N.A.	N.A.
New York	★	★	★, 5 yrs.	...	...	...	...	...
North Carolina	...	...	...	★	★	...	(g)	...
North Dakota	...	...	...	...	...	...	...	★
Ohio	...	...	...	...	...	...	...	...
Oklahoma	...	★	★	★(q)	★, 5 yrs.	...	...	★
Oregon	...	...	...	...	...	...	...	★
Pennsylvania	...	...	...	...	...	...	...	★
Rhode Island	...	★	★	★(h)	★, 5 yrs.	★, CPA	...	...
South Carolina	18	★	★	...	...	...	...	...
South Dakota	★	★	★, 1 yr.	...	...	...	...	...
Tennessee	...	...	...	★	★, 7 yrs.	★, CPA	...	...
Texas	18	★(j)	★, 1 yr.	...	...	...	...	...
Utah	...	...	...	★	★, 6 yrs.	★, CPA	...	...
Vermont	...	...	...	...	...	...	...	★
Virginia	...	...	...	...	...	...	...	★
Washington	★	★, Whole life	★	★(o)	★	★, J.D.	...	...
West Virginia								
Office of State Auditor	...	★	★	...	...	...	...	...
Finance Division, Office of State Comptroller	...	★	★	★, B.S.B.A.	★, 7 yrs.	...	...	...
Wisconsin	...	...	...	★(p)	...	★, CPA	...	...
Wyoming	...	...	...	...	...	...	...	...

Source: Comptrollers: Technical Activities and Functions, 2006 Edition, The National Association of State Auditors, Comptrollers and Treasurers.

Key:
★ — Formal provision.
. . . — No formal provision.
N.A. — Not applicable.
(a) Any of those mentioned or CFE, CPM, etc.
(b) Eighteen years. At time of election or appointment and a citizen of the state.
(c) The Kentucky Revised Statutes state that "The state controller shall be a person qualified by education and experience for the position and held in high esteem in the accounting community."
(d) There are no educational or professional mandates, yet the appointed official is generally qualified by a combination of experience and education.
(e) At least five years experience in high-level management.

(f) Education and relevant experience.
(g) Qualified by education and experience for the position.
(h) Master's degree in accounting, finance or business management or public administration.
(i) Five years or college degree.
(j) Years not specified.
(k) Master's degree.
(l) Bachelor's degree, no professional certification required, but CPA certification is considered desirable. Financial management experience, knowledge of GAAP and good communication skills are other qualifications.
(m) Four years with major in accounting.
(n) Three years directing the work of others.
(o) Seven years and law degree.
(p) Bachelor's degree in accounting.
(q) Bachelor's degree.

Table 4.33
STATE COMPTROLLERS: DUTIES AND RESPONSIBILITIES

State	Comprehensive annual financial report (CAFR)	Disbursement of state funds	Payroll processing	Pre-auditing of payments	Post-audit	Operation of statewide financial management system	Management of state travel policies
Alabama	★	★	★	★	...	★	★
Alaska	★	★	★	...	...	★	★
Arizona	★	★	★	★	★	★	★
Arkansas	★	★	★	★	...	...	...
California	★	★	★	★	★	★	...
Colorado	★	★	★	★	★	★	...
Connecticut	★	...	★	...	★	...	...
Delaware	★	★	★	★	★	★	★
Florida	★	★	★	★	★	★	★
Georgia	★	★	★	...	...	★	★
Hawaii	★	★	★	★	★	★	★
Idaho	★	★	★	...	...	★	...
Illinois	★	★	★	★	★	★	...
Indiana	★	★	★	★	...	★	...
Iowa	★	★	★	★	★	★	★
Kansas	★	★	★	★	★	★	★
Kentucky	★	★	...	★	...	★	★
Louisiana	★	★	★	★	★	★	...
Maine	★	★	★	★	★	★	★
Maryland	★	★	★	★	★	★	...
Massachusetts	★	★	★	★	★	★	...
Michigan	★	...	★	...	...	★	...
Minnesota	★	★	★	...	...	★	...
Mississippi	★	★	★	★	...	★	★
Missouri	★	★	★	...	...	★	★
Montana	★	★	...	...	...	★	★
Nebraska	★	★	★	★	...	★	★
Nevada	★	★	★	...	...	★	...
New Hampshire	★	...	★	★	...	★	...
New Jersey	★	★	★	...	★	★	★
New Mexico	★	★	★	★	★	★	★
New York	★	★	★	★	★	...	★
North Carolina	★	★	★	★	★	★	...
North Dakota	★	★	★	...	...	★	★
Ohio	★	★	...	★	...	★	★
Oklahoma	★	★	★	...	...	★	★
Oregon	★	...	★	...	...	★	★
Pennsylvania	★	★	★	★	★	★	★
Rhode Island	★	★	★	★	...	★	★
South Carolina	★	★	★	★	...	★	★
South Dakota	★	★	★	★	...	...	...
Tennessee	★	★	★	★	★	★	★
Texas	★	★	★	...	★	★	...
Utah	★	★	★	...	★	★	★
Vermont	★	★	...	...	★	★	★
Virginia	★	★	★	★	★	★	★
Washington	★	...	...	...	★	★	★
West Virginia							
Office of State Auditor	...	★	★	★	...	...	...
Finance Division, Office of State Comptroller	★	...	...	★	...	★	★
Wisconsin	★	★	★	...	★	★	★
Wyoming	★	...	★	★	★	★	★

Source: Comptrollers: Technical Activities and Functions, 2006 Edition, The National Association of State Auditors, Comptrollers and Treasurers.

Key:
★ — Formal provision.
... — No formal provision.

Chapter Five

STATE JUDICIAL BRANCH

"*A very public struggle to define how and to whom state judicial branches should be accountable dominated the news in 2006.*"

—David Rottman

The State Courts in 2006: Surviving Anti-Court Initiatives and Demonstrating High Performance

By David Rottman

Ballot initiatives in four states sought fundamental, and in one state revolutionary, change to their judicial branch of government. All four were defeated at the polls but similar efforts are expected in the same and other states for 2008. A number of states again featured costly and ugly judicial elections. Also, it was clear that judicial candidates overwhelmingly chose to campaign within traditional expectations of what is appropriate in a fair and impartial court system. The state judicial branches in 2006 made significant strides in refining and creating methods for measuring their performance and demonstrating their accountability to the other branches of government and to the public. "High-performing courts" is one label for these efforts.

The Year in Review

A very public struggle to define how and to whom state judicial branches should be accountable dominated the news in 2006. Ballot initiatives designed to uproot the foundations of the American legal system, judicial election campaigns rendered decidedly injudicious by national interest groups, and high stakes litigation over whether a judge can make promises or commitments to the electorate tell one part of the story.

The rest of the story, told with little fanfare, concerns steady improvements made to the quality of justice dispensed by the state courts. The most significant breakthrough came in the emergence of high-performing courts that demonstrate their accountability through continuous monitoring of their effectiveness and efficiency. Court reformers took other steps to strengthen court management and to objectively inform the public about judicial performance.

The State Courts at the Polls

Ballot Initiatives

Four ballot initiatives on judicial accountability drew national attention as the main events of 2006. All four initiatives sought to redefine judicial accountability to advance specific economic, social or political agendas. A few individuals and groups from outside the four states funded professional signature collection firms paid on a per signature basis to get measures on the ballot, and then advertising campaigns.

South Dakota's Judicial Accountability Initiative Law for Judges, unofficially "J.A.I.L. 4 Judges" and "Amendment E" on the ballot, headlined the news. The brainchild of a California resident, Amendment E sought to allow any disappointed civil litigant or convicted criminal to challenge the judge's decision before an extra-judicial Special Grand Jury. The Spe-

cial Grand Jury would hold the ruling judge accountable "for making decisions which break rules defined by the volunteers [special grand jurors]."[1] The amendment called for retroactive punishment for judges and would permit sentences combining actions against the judge's personal assets and imprisonment. The final results appeared decisive to most: Amendment E lost by 89 percent to 11 percent. This did not stop the amendment's backers, who alleged a government plot and vowed to fight again in South Dakota and other states.

In Colorado, Amendment 40 sought to limit appellate judges to a maximum term of 10 years on the bench. Although presented as a judicial reform, the measure was a thinly veiled attempt to change the political makeup of the state judiciary. If passed, the measure would have immediately removed five of the current Supreme Court justices. With 57 percent of voters opposed, Amendment 40 failed. One commentator observed of Amendment 40's proponents that "these troublemakers were egged on by cynical politicians who successfully pander to their base by labeling judges as anti-American (or worse) when they issue unpopular rulings."[2]

In Oregon, Measure 40 would have switched elections of appellate judges from statewide to district-specific, a move that would have changed the political composition of the appellate bench. Previously rejected by the electorate in 2002, this measure failed with 56 percent of the voters opposed.

In Montana, a citizens' initiative to permit recall of a judge "for any reason acknowledging electoral dissatisfaction" was struck from the ballot due to fraudulent practices used to collect the qualifying number of signatures.[3] Voters in nine other states considered changes to their courts. Some changes sought to reduce judicial discretion. North Dakota voters defeated a measure to end judicial discretion in family cases by requiring judges to grant joint legal and physical custody to both parents and to place limits on child support, regardless of the facts in a case. Other ballot initiatives defused traditional flashpoints between the legislative and judicial branches. Voters in Hawaii and in Missouri adopted changes that removed judicial pay from the political process.

Judicial Elections

Thirty-nine states use elections as one form of judicial accountability.[4] Contested elections filled 46 state supreme courts seats. In Alabama, Kentucky and Nevada, three of the 35 incumbents were defeated, and 18 ran unopposed. Two open seats were filled by candidates without an opponent. All 18 justices facing retention elections were retained. The post-2000 trend of "nastier, noisier and costlier" judicial elections continued.

Alabama, Georgia, Kentucky and Washington hosted truly nasty, noisy and high-cost races. The race for the chief justice of Alabama, where would-be judges compete for seats through partisan elections, exemplified the new politics of judicial elections. Preliminary figures put the total cost of the race at more than $6 million. The incumbent chief justice survived a primary challenge by another justice on his court, only to lose the general election by a narrow margin to a Democrat.[5]

Much of the venom and cash in 2006 elections can be attributed to continuous efforts by national special interest groups in pursuit of their policy agendas. A cover story in *BusinessWeek* documented the ways in which contention among large business interests have transformed judicial elections.[6] Many negative advertisements could be traced to one side in the decade-long struggle between large corporations and the plaintiffs' bar over tort reform. The U.S. Chamber of Commerce, in effect, declared victory, noting that 80 percent of the candidates they supported won.[7]

A Georgia race, in which a lawyer, supported by the business-funded Georgia Safety and Prosperity Coalition, challenged a sitting supreme court justice, exemplifies the bare-knuckle fights through television negative advertisements. Two weeks before the election, local television stations aired the following advertisement:

Announcer: On Georgia's Supreme Court, liberal Carol Hunstein has made a habit of ignoring laws she doesn't like. Hunstein substituted her preferences on capital punishment for those who made

the law. Carol Hunstein also voted to throw out evidence that convicted a cocaine trafficker; her colleagues overruled her. Hunstein even ignored extensive case law and overruled a jury to free a savage rapist. If liberal Carol Hunstein wants to make laws, she should run for the legislature instead of judge.

The Hunstein campaign responded:

Announcer: We expect only experienced judges to serve on Georgia's Supreme Court. But Mike Wiggins has never tried a case. We expect our Supreme Court to uphold Georgia values, but Mike Wiggins was sued by his own mother for taking her money. He sued his only sister. She said he threatened to kill her while she was eight months pregnant. A judge ordered Wiggins never to have contact with her again. Mike Wiggins. The wrong experience. The wrong values for the Supreme Court.[8]

Hunstein won 63 percent to 37 percent.

The elections took place in an atmosphere already poisoned by media frenzies set off by radio and television talk show hosts who attacked a judge based on a single decision. Ohio trial judge John Connor was attacked by a nationally syndicated television commentator as the "worst judge in America." This use of invective is unexceptional nowadays, but the haste with which the state's Governor and Speaker of the House called for the judge's impeachment is not. Reason prevailed and Judge Connor remained on the bench.[9]

In the federal courts, the fight focused on what judicial candidates can say to promote their election. The litigation stemmed from an increasingly common campaign survey technique. Groups, mainly but not exclusively from the religious right, sent out questionnaires requesting candidates to express their views on social, political and legal controversies and on previously decided cases. Most questions used a multiple choice answer format. Options included "refuse" or "decline." A lengthy footnote with citation to federal court opinions distinguished those options, linking them to the U.S. Supreme Court's 2002 decision in *Republican Party of Minnesota v. White* and more recent lower court rulings on what judicial candidates can say and do.[10] If a candidate "declines," a First Amendment lawsuit likely follows challenging the state's Code of Judicial Conduct as a restriction on a candidate's first amendment rights.

The Third, Seventh, Tenth, and Eleventh Circuit Courts of Appeal are currently hearing challenges to traditional limits on judicial candidates' conduct. United States District Court challenges are pending in Arizona, Kentucky and Wisconsin. Attorney James Bopp, who served as counsel to the groups distributing questionnaires in all of these cases, predicts that judges will be allowed to express opinions, endorse candidates and solicit donations.[11] The ultimate fate of the litigation may lie with the Supreme Court.

Thus far, most judicial candidates seem inclined to campaign on their records and not on their ideological credentials. For example, of 27 Tennessee appellate judges facing retention elections, all but one wrote to decline or simply never responded. One answered some but not all of the questions. Chief Justice William Barker of Tennessee replied to the questionnaire by letter, noting that "As did Justice Roberts, I do not wish to hint or signal that I am predisposed to rule on any matter that may come before me as a judge."[12] So far, the rate of response to litigation-linked questionnaires suggests that few judges want to become politicians rather than fair and impartial arbiters of the law.

Positive developments include the creation of six new judicial campaign oversight committees—in Alabama, Kentucky, Maryland, North Carolina, Minnesota and South Dakota. These bodies generally set voluntary standards for judicial campaigning by using persuasion and their members' own First Amendment rights to set the tone.

Demonstrating Accountability

Performance Measurement

In its Strategic Plan for 2006–12, the California Judicial Branch identified "measuring performance and demonstrating accountability" as one of its fundamental challenges. The plan noted that all public institutions, including the judicial branch, are increasingly challenged to evaluate and be accountable for their performance, and to ensure that they use public funds responsibly and effectively.

For the courts, this means developing meaningful and useful measures of performance, collecting and analyzing data on those measures, reporting the results to the public on a regular basis, and implementing changes to maximize efficiency.[13] "High Performing Courts" was the most common label for such activities, featured at national events such as the September 2006 Courts Solutions Conference[14] and a January 2007 National Summit on Performance Management for the Judiciary.

The most developed methodology for performance measurement is *CourTools* from the National Center for State Courts.[15] *CourTools* draws on concepts drawn from successful public- and private-sector per-

formance measurement systems and offers a balanced set of applicable measures that tell courts, legislatures and the public if courts are effectively and efficiently using public resources. The 10 evaluative criteria include court user ratings of court accessibility and of the fairness with which litigants and others perceive of their treatment, as well as more conventional measures like time to disposition for cases, cost per case and effective use of juries.[16]

CourTools and other measurement systems speak to the institutional accountability of courts. When deciding a case, an individual judge is accountable to the Constitution, law and the appellate process.

2006 saw a renewed interest in expanding judicial performance evaluation programs. Most notably in six retention election states, voters have received the results of evaluations based, in part, on confidential survey feedback from jurors, litigants, attorneys and others who come into contact with a judge.[17] Judicial performance evaluation programs do not focus on cases but on a judge's adherence to "neutral, process-oriented standards."[18] Relevant questions include: "Did the judge give each party the opportunity to make his case? Did he treat everyone in the courtroom with dignity? Did he clearly and accurately explain the facts relevant to his decision, or give clear and accurate instructions to the jury?"[19]

Kansas in 2006 became the seventh retention election state to implement a performance evaluation program for all trial judges.[20] The authorizing legislation stated: "The goals of the Commission would be to improve judicial performance, help voters make more informed decisions and promote public accountability of the Judiciary."[21] Increased docket fees will fund the new program.

Building a Court Management Team

Trial courts have evolved into complex organizations. Monitoring performance and accountability requires a strong leadership position at the state level and for individual trial courts. The managerial responsibilities of presiding or chief judges of trial courts are of recent vintage, and policies and procedures defining the presiding judge's role fail to reflect the realities of what is involved in managing a trial court. For example, the court in Hennepin County of Minneapolis, Minnesota, has 78 judicial officers and more than 500 employees.

Only 17 states provide their presiding judges with extra compensation, and only 14 states promise a reduced caseload.[22] To correct this misalignment of authority and responsibilities, a national working group of judges, court administrators and judicial educators identified key elements of a rule of court that would govern the responsibilities of presiding judges and developed the *Key Elements of an Effective Rule of Court on the Role of the Presiding Judge in the Trial Courts.*[23]

Sentencing

A 2006 national survey recorded significant changes to the public's view of judges' role in sentencing. In a reversal of survey findings from the early 1990s, the American public prefers that judges have discretion rather than be limited by mandatory sentencing laws. The image of the "lenient judge" also seems to be fading. Only one adult in five (18 percent) finds sentencing too lenient, and holds judges mostly to blame.[24] More blame is assigned to elected officials, including prosecutors. While lawmakers were viewed as having the essential role in sentencing reform, two-thirds of the public believe judges should play a major, not a limited, role in sentencing reform.[25] The judicial role is being pursued through, among other avenues, the development of "evidence-based practices that reduce recidivism."[26]

In 2004, the Supreme Court in *Blakely vs. Washington*[27] found the use of facts by judges not decided by a jury to increase the length of a sentence unconstitutional. The decision applies to cases with a jury verdict in states where judges follow mandatory sentencing guidelines. Both federal and state legislators sought ways to conform their guidelines to the Court's decision. That effort continues, as evidenced in the January 2007 decision striking down California's sentencing guidelines in *Cunningham vs. California.*[28]

Looking Forward

For the state judiciary, 2006 was a year of bullets dodged and significant steps taken to achieve high levels of performance and accountability. The public rejected limits on judicial discretion, tenure and immunity while courts took it upon themselves to increase their accessibility and efficiency through newly developed measurement processes and the creation of court management teams. Some elections got ugly, but public perception of the judiciary remains favorable and, in the case of sentencing, has improved.

The future threat to the state judiciary is the politicization of judicial elections. The stakes are high. California Chief Justice Ronald George looked back on the year, noting "if the judiciary becomes politicized, then the rule of law is in jeopardy."[29] The darkest cloud on the horizon is the extraordinary infusion of out-of-state money into trial court races and a resulting sense of intimidation from the threat of public ordeal in the media or electoral defeat. The money spent on bending the courts in one direction or another is massive, but as was observed during the year, "Lobbying for judicial selection reform is like romancing your date in a fast-food restaurant."[30] Too few individuals and groups are active in efforts to keep our courts fair and impartial.

Notes

[1] Quotations are from the South Dakota attorney general's official explanation of the Amendment. The proposed amendment sought to eliminate judicial immunity, permit civil actions against judges, create special grand juries with power to remove judicial immunity, issue criminal indictments, and appoint a special trial jury to hear subsequent criminal trials. J.A.I.L. 4 Judges, South Dakota, *http://www.sd-jail4judges.org/*.

[2] Andrew Cohen, "The legal year in review," *Washington Post*, December 29, 2006.

[3] The National Center for State Courts tracks legislation that affects the state courts and ballot initiatives in *Gavel to Gavel* (accessible at *http://www.ncsconline.org/D_Research /gaveltogavel/*).

[4] Thirty-nine states elect some or all of their appellate and general-jurisdiction (main) trial judges: 89 percent of the state judiciary faces elections. Most of these are contestable elections: 60 percent of appellate judges and 80 percent of trial judges potentially run against an opponent. Other judges face "retention" elections (where incumbent judge runs against her own record). This applies to 26 percent of all appellate and 9 percent of all trial judges. Other judges are appointed by the governor or state legislature. In non-elective states, judges often stand periodically for re-selection. Only three states follow the federal model of lifetime appointments. See D. Rottman, C. Bromage, M. Zose, and B. Thompson. "Judicial Selection 101: What Varies and What Matters," *Caseload Highlights* 13 (2) 2006. (*http://www.ncsconline. org/D_Research/csp/Highlights/Vol13No2.pdf*).

[5] M.J. Ellington, "Cobb: No Parties in Justice," *Decatur Daily*, December 24, 2006.

[6] M. Orey, "How Business Trounced the Trial Lawyers," *BusinessWeek*, January 8, 2007.

[7] Dee J. Hall, "Special Interests Eye High Court Race," *Wisconsin State Journal*, January 28, 2007, D1.

[8] The transcript of the ads and an analysis of their respective accuracy can be found at *http://www.factcheck.org/arti cle470.html*.

[9] B.J. Marrison, (ed.), "Furor over Judge Abates as Truth Emerges," *Columbus Dispatch*, March 19, 2006. The editor observed that, "Given the furor over this case, what will a judge think when he or she faces a controversial ruling? Will the judge ponder, 'What will Geraldo think?'"

[10] 536 U.S. 765 (2002).

[11] T. Goldman, "In Kentucky Supreme Court Race, Judges Get Out Their Soapboxes," *Legal Times*, November 6, 2006. See the sidebar for Mr. Bopp's statement: "The judicial es-

tablishment has failed to realize there's been a fundamental change in the law. … They thought all they had to do was repair a few windows when the foundations for their entire regulatory scheme—for all those speech codes—has been destroyed."

[12] M. Coyle, "Judicial Surveys Vex the Bench," *National Law Journal*, September 8, 2006.

[13] Judicial Council of California, Justice for All: The Strategic Plan for California's Judicial Branch, 2006–2012, adopted December 1, 2006.

[14] *www.courtsolutions.org.*

[15] B. Ostrom, R. Hanson, C. Ostrom, and M. Kleiman, "Court Cultures and their Consequences," *The Court Manager* 20 (1).

[16] For an overview, visit *http://www.ncsconline.org/D_Research/CourTools/tcmp_courttools.htm.*

[17] Public confidence in the courts is most strongly influenced by the perceived fairness of the procedures used by the courts to reach decisions. The implications of this conclusion for court improvement are drawn out in a 2006 study of the California courts. J. Doble, and A.M. Arumi, *Trust and Confidence in the California Courts. 2006: Public Court Users and Judicial Branch Members Talk About the California Courts*, Judicial Council of California, December 2006. (*http://www.courtinfo.ca.gov/reference/4_37pubtrust.htm*).

[18] *Shared Expectations: Judicial Accountability in Context*, published by the Institute for the Advancement of the American Legal System in Denver, 2006. (*www.du.edu/legal institute*), 7.

[19] For an example of the implementation of such an approach in a trial court, see the systematic efforts by Hennepin County (Minneapolis) to measure fairness. (*http://www.courts.state.mn.us/district/4/?page=1756*).

[20] Public confidence in the courts is most strongly influenced by the perceived fairness of the procedures used by the courts to reach decisions. The implications of this conclusion for court improvement are drawn out in a 2006 study of the California courts. J. Doble, and A.M. Arumi, *Trust and Confidence in the California Courts. 2006: Public Court Users and Judicial Branch Members Talk About the California Courts*, Judicial Council of California, December 2006. (*http://www.courtinfo.ca.gov/reference/4_37pubtrust.htm*).

[21] Kansas House Bill 2612 (accessible at *http://www.kslegislature.org/bills/2006/2612.pdf*). The bill became effective on July 1, 2006.

[22] In some states the availability of extra compensation or reduced caseloads are available in some areas but not others. See Table 28 in D. Rottman and S. Strickland, *State Court Organization 2004*, U.S. Government Printing Office, (2006).

[23] See *Key Elements of an Effective Rule of Court on the Role of the Presiding Judge in the Trial Court*, (National Center for State Courts, June 2006). The rule is intended for use at the state-level and is a part of a larger effort to promote a strong executive team that includes the presiding judge and trial court administrator. (*http://www.ncsconline.org/D_Research/Documents/Res_JudInd_ElementsofaRule_final2.pdf*).

[24] Figures are from Princeton Survey Research Associates International, *The NCSC Sentencing Attitudes Survey: A Report on the Findings*, July 2006. (*http://www.ncsconline.org/D_Research/Documents/NCSC_SentencingSurvey_Report_Final060720.pdf*).

[25] When asked to choose between the statements "Mandatory sentences are a good idea" and "Judges should have more leeway in sentencing, 57 percent preferred judicial discretion, 36 percent preferred mandatory sentencing, and seven percent were undecided.

[26] See, for example, Crime and Justice Institute, *Evidence-Based Practices: A Framework for Sentencing Policy*, Boston, November 2006 (a report to the State of Maine Corrections Alternative Advisory Committee, Sentencing Practices Subcommittee).

[27] 542 U.S. 296 (2004).

[28] 127 S.Ct. 856 (2007).

[29] Jessica Garrison, "As Politics Enters Races for Judicial Seats, Some Fear a Loss of Objectivity on the Bench," *LA Times*, October 25, 2006.

[30] Jason Boog, "Before the Flood," *Judicial Reports*, December 14, 2006. (*http://www.judicialreports.com/archives/2006/12/before_the_flood.php*).

About the Author

David Rottman is principal court research consultant at the National Center for State Courts, where he has worked since 1987. His research interests include judicial selection, judicial campaign oversight committees, public opinion on the courts, the evolution of court structure, and the pros and cons of problem-solving courts. He is the author of books on community courts, social inequality and modern Ireland. Rottman has a Ph.D. in sociology from the University of Illinois at Urbana, and previously worked at the Economic and Social Institute in Dublin, Ireland.

Table 5.1
STATE COURTS OF LAST RESORT

State or other jurisdiction	Name of court	Justices chosen (a) At large	Justices chosen (a) By district	No. of judges (b)	Term (in years) (c)	Chief justice Method of selection	Chief justice Term of office for chief justice
Alabama	S.C.	★		9	6	Non-partisan popular election	6 years
Alaska	S.C.	★		5	10	By court	3 years
Arizona	S.C.	★		5	6	By court	5 years
Arkansas	S.C.	★		7	8	Non-partisan popular election	8 years
California	S.C.	★		7	12	Appointed by governor	12 years
Colorado	S.C.	★		7	10	By court	Indefinite
Connecticut	S.C.	★		7	8	Gubernatorial appointment from judicial nominating commission with consent of legislature.	8 years
Delaware	S.C.	★		5	12	Appointed by governor	12 years
Florida	S.C.	(d)		7	6	By court	2 years
Georgia	S.C.	★		7	6	By court	2 years
Hawaii	S.C.	★		5	10	Gubernatorial appointment from judicial nominating commission with consent of legislature.	10 years
Idaho	S.C.	★		5	6	By court	4 years
Illinois	S.C.		★	7	10	By court	3 years
Indiana	S.C.	★	★	5	10 (e)	Judicial nominating commission appointment	5 years
Iowa	S.C.	★		7	8	By court	8 years
Kansas	S.C.	★		7	6	Rotation by seniority	Indefinite
Kentucky	S.C.		★	7	8	By court	4 years
Louisiana	S.C.		★	7	10	By seniority of service	Duration of service
Maine	S.J.C.	★		7	7	Appointed by governor	7 years
Maryland	C.A.		★	7	10	Appointed by governor	Indefinite
Massachusetts	S.J.C.	★		7	To age 70	Appointed by governor (f)	To age 70
Michigan	S.C.	★		7	8	By court	2 years
Minnesota	S.C.	★		7	6	Gubernatorial appointment	6 years
Mississippi	S.C.		★	9	8	By seniority of service	Duration of service
Missouri	S.C.	★		7	12	By court	2 years
Montana	S.C.	★		7	8	Non-partisan popular election	8 years
Nebraska	S.C.	★(g)	★(g)	7	6 (h)	Appointed by governor from Judicial Nomination Commission	Duration of service
Nevada	S.C.	★		7	6	Rotation	2 years (i)
New Hampshire	S.C.	★		5	5	Seniority	5 years
New Jersey	S.C.	★		7	7 (j)	Gubernatorial appointment with consent of the legislature	Duration of service
New Mexico	S.C.	★		5	8	By court	2 years
New York	C.A.	★		7	14	Appointed by governor from Judicial Nomination Commission	14 years
North Carolina	S.C.	★		7	8	Non-partisan popular election	8 years
North Dakota	S.C.	★		5	10	By Supreme and district court judges	5 years (k)
Ohio	S.C.	★		7	6	Popular election (l)	6 years
Oklahoma	S.C.		★	9	6	By court	Duration of service
	C.C.A.		★	5	6	By court	5 years
Oregon	S.C.	★		7	6	By court	6 years
Pennsylvania	S.C.	★		7	10	Seniority	Duration of term
Rhode Island	S.C.	★		5	Life	Appointed by governor from Judicial Nominating Commission	Life
South Carolina	S.C.	★		5	10	Legislative appointment	10 years

See footnotes at end of table.

STATE COURTS OF LAST RESORT — Continued

State or other jurisdiction	Justices chosen (a)		Name of court	No. of judges (b)	Term (in years) (c)	Chief justice	
	At large	By district				Method of selection	Term of office for chief justice
South Dakota..............	★(m)	★(m)	S.C.	5	8	By court	4 years
Tennessee	★		S.C.	5	8	By court	4 years
Texas	★		S.C.	9	6	Partisan election	6 years
	★		C.C.A.	9	6	Partisan election	6 years (n)
Utah	★		S.C.	5	10 (o)	By court	4 years
Vermont	★		S.C.	5	6	Appointed by governor from Judicial Nomination Commission, with consent of the legislature	6 years
Virginia	★		S.C.	7	12	Seniority	4 years
Washington	★		S.C.	9	6	By court	4 years
West Virginia	★		S.C.A.	5	12	Seniority	1 year
Wisconsin...................	★		S.C.	7	10	Seniority	Until declined
Wyoming.....................	★		S.C.	5	8	By court	4 years
Dist. of Columbia	★		C.A.	9	15	Judicial Nominating Commission appointment	4 years
Puerto Rico.................	★		S.C.	7	To age 70	Gubernatorial appointment with consent of the legislature	To age 70

Sources: State Court Organization, 2004, U.S. Department of Justice Statistics, National Center for State Courts, August 2006.

Key:
S.C. — Supreme Court
S.C.A. — Supreme Court of Appeals
S.J.C. — Supreme Judicial Court
C.A. — Court of Appeals
C.C.A. — Court of Criminal Appeals
H.C. — High Court

(a) See Chapter 5 table entitled, "Selection and Retention of Appellate Court Judges," for details.
(b) Number includes chief justice.
(c) The initial term may be shorter. See Chapter 5 table entitled, "Selection and Retention of Appellate Court Judges," for details.
(d) Regional (5), Statewide (2), Regional based on District of Appeal

(e) Initial term is two years; retention 10 years.
(f) Chief Justice, in the appellate courts, is a separate judicial office from that of an Associate Justice. Chief Justices are appointed, until age 70, by the Governor with the advice and consent of the Executive (Governor's) Council.
(g) Chief justice chosen statewide; associate judges chosen by district.
(h) More than three years for first election and every six years thereafter.
(i) The term may be split between eligible justices.
(j) Followed by tenure. All judges are subject to gubernatorial reappointment and consent by the Senate after and initial seven-year term; thereafter, they may serve until mandatory retirement at age 70.
(k) Or expiration of term, whichever is first.
(l) Party affiliation is not included on the ballot in the general election, but candidates are chosen through partisan primary nominations.
(m) Initially chosen by district; retention determined statewide.
(n) Presiding judge of Court of Criminal Appeals.
(o) The initial term of appointment is until the next general election immediately following the third year from the time of the initial appointment.

Table 5.2
STATE INTERMEDIATE APPELLATE COURTS AND GENERAL TRIAL COURTS: NUMBER OF JUDGES AND TERMS

State or other jurisdiction	Intermediate appellate court			General trial court		
	Name of court	No. of judges	Term (years)	Name of court	No. of judges	Term (years)
Alabama	Court of Criminal Appeals	5	6	Circuit Court	142	6
	Court of Civil Appeals	5	6			
Alaska	Court of Appeals	3	8	Superior Court	34	6 (a)
Arizona	Court of Appeals	22	6	Superior Court	162	4
Arkansas	Court of Appeals	12	8	Chancery/Probate Court and Circuit Court	115	6
California	Courts of Appeal	88	12	Superior Court	1,498	6
Colorado	Court of Appeals	16	8	District Court	132	6 (b)
Connecticut	Appellate Court	10	8	Superior Court	196	8
Delaware	. . .	. . .	. . .	Superior Court	19	12
				Court of Chancery	5	12
Florida	District Courts of Appeals	62	6	Circuit Court	526	6
Georgia	Court of Appeals	12	6	Superior Court	188	4
Hawaii	Intermediate Court of Appeals	6	10	Circuit Court	33	10
Idaho	Court of Appeals	3	6	District Court	39	4
Illinois	Appellate Court	53	10	Circuit Court	494	6
Indiana	Court of Appeals	15	12 (c)	Superior Court, Probate Court and Circuit Court	298	6
Iowa	Court of Appeals	9	6	District Court	335 (d)	6 (e)
Kansas	Court of Appeals	12	4	District Court	234 (f)	4
Kentucky	Court of Appeals	14	8	Circuit Court	127	8
Louisiana	Courts of Appeal	53 (g)	10	District Court	213	6
Maine	. . .	. . .	. . .	Superior Court	16	7
Maryland	Court of Special Appeals	13	10	Circuit Court	143	15
Massachusetts	Appeals Court	28 (h)	To age 70	Superior Court	73	To age 70
Michigan	Court of Appeals	28	6	Circuit Court	215	6
Minnesota	Court of Appeals	16	6	District Court	276	6
Mississippi	Court of Appeals	10	8	Circuit Court	49	4
Missouri	Court of Appeals	32	12	Circuit Court	322 (i)	6 (j)
Montana	. . .	. . .	. . .	District Court	39 (k)	6
Nebraska	Court of Appeals	6	3 (l)	District Court	55	6 (m)
Nevada	. . .	. . .	. . .	District Court	60	6
New Hampshire	. . .	. . .	. . .	Superior Court	26	To age 70
New Jersey	Appellate Division of Superior Court	35	7 (n)	Superior Court	377	7 (o)
New Mexico	Court of Appeals	10	8	District Court	75	6
New York	Appellate Division of Supreme Court	57	5 (p)	Supreme Court	498	14
	Appellate Terms of Supreme Court	(q)	. . .	County Court	111	10
North Carolina	Court of Appeals	15	8	Superior Court	105 (r)	8 (s)
North Dakota	. . .	. . .	. . .	District Court	42	6
Ohio	Courts of Appeal	68	6	Court of Common Pleas	384	6

See footnotes at end of table.

STATE INTERMEDIATE APPELLATE COURTS AND GENERAL TRIAL COURTS: NUMBER OF JUDGES AND TERMS

State or other jurisdiction	Intermediate appellate court			General trial court		
	Name of court	No. of judges	Term (years)	Name of court	No. of judges	Term (years)
Oklahoma	Court of Appeals	10	6	District Court	221 (t)	4 (u)
Oregon	Court of Appeals	10	6	Circuit Court	169	6
				Tax Court	1	6
Pennsylvania	Superior Court	23 (v)	10	Court of Common Pleas	493 (x)	10
	Commonwealth Court	9 (w)	10			
Rhode Island	...	...	...	Superior Court	26 (y)	Life
South Carolina	Court of Appeals	10 (z)	6	Circuit Court	45 (aa)	6
South Dakota	...	...	...	Circuit Court	38	8
Tennessee	Court of Appeals	12	8	Chancery Court	34	8
	Court of Criminal Appeals	12	8	Circuit Court	83	8
				Criminal Court	33	8
				Probate Court	2	8
Texas	Courts of Appeal	80	6	District Court	424	4
Utah	Court of Appeals	7	6 (bb)	District Court	70	6 (cc)
Vermont	...	...	...	Superior Court and District Court	31 (dd)	6
Virginia	Court of Appeals	11	8	Circuit Court	156	8
Washington	Courts of Appeal	22 (ee)	6	Superior Court	179	4
West Virginia	...	...	...	Circuit Court	65	8
Wisconsin	Court of Appeals	16	6	Circuit Court	240	6
Wyoming	...	...	...	District Court	21	6
Dist. of Columbia	...	...	...	Superior Court	59	15
Puerto Rico	Circuit Court of Appeals	39	16	Court of First Instance	328 (ff)	12 (gg)

Sources: State Court Organization, 2004, U.S. Department of Justice Statistics, National Center for State Courts, August 2006.

Key:

... — Court does not exist in jurisdiction or not applicable.

(a) The initial term for Superior Court judges is three years.

(b) The initial term for District Court, Denver Probate Court, Denver Juvenile Court and County Court judges is two years.

(c) Two years initial; 10 years retention.

(d) The number of District Court judges includes associate judges and magistrates.

(e) The initial term for District Court judges is at least one year. Associate judges serve a term of four years with an initial term of at least one year, and magistrate judges serve a term of four years.

(f) The number of District Court judges includes magistrates.

(g) The Courts of Appeal have 55 authorized judicial positions.

(h) The Appeals Court has 25 authorized judicial positions. The judges of the Appeals Court are assisted by the services on recall of several retired judges.

(i) The number of Circuit Court judges includes associate judges.

(j) Associate Circuit judges serve a term of four terms.

(k) There are actually 42 District Court judges Three of those judges serve the Water Court and are included in the data for that court.

(l) More than three years for first election and retention is every six years thereafter.

(m) The initial term is for three years but not more than five years.

(n) Followed by tenure. All judges are subject to gubernatorial reappointment and consent by the Senate after an initial seven-year term; thereafter, they may serve until mandatory retirement at age 70.

(o) After an initial seven-year term, the reapportionment term for Superior and Tax Court judges is open-ended until mandatory retirement age at age 70.

(p) Or duration.

(q) Appellate Terms of the Supreme Court have been established within the First and Second Departments of the Appellate Division. Data for the Appellate Terms are not included in the information presented here.

(r) The number of Superior Court judges includes special judges.

(s) Special judges serve a term of four years.

(t) The number of District Court judges includes associate judges and special judges.

(u) District and associate judges serve four year terms; special judges serve at pleasure.

(v) The Superior Court has 15 authorized judicial positions. The judges of the Superior Court are assisted by senior judges specially appointed by the Supreme Court..

(w) The judges of the Commonwealth Court are assisted by senior judges specially appointed by the Supreme Court. Also, senior Common Pleas Court judges occasionally serve on the Commonwealth Court.

(x) These numbers include both active and senior judges.

(y) The number of judges includes magistrates.

(z) The Court of Appeals has nine authorized judicial positions. The judges of the Court of Appeals are assisted by a retired Court of Appeals judge now on special appointment to the court.

(aa) Four to five judges are currently working as active retired judges.

(bb) The initial term of appointment is until the next general election immediately following the third year from the time of the initial appointment.

(cc) The initial term of appointment is until the next general election immediately following the third year from the time of the initial appointment.

(dd) Plus 5 magistrates for Family Court.

(ee) The Courts of Appeal have 23 authorized judicial positions.

(ff) The number of Court of First Instance judges includes Municipal Division judges.

(gg) Municipal judges serve a term of eight years.

Table 5.3
QUALIFICATIONS OF JUDGES OF STATE APPELLATE COURTS AND GENERAL TRIAL COURTS

State or other jurisdiction	Years of minimum residence				Minimum age		Legal credentials	
	In state		In district					
	A	T	A	T	A	T	A	T
Alabama	1 yr.	1 yr.	...	1 yr.	...	...	Licensed attorney	Licensed attorney
Alaska	5 yrs.	5 yrs.	...	...	...	...	8 years practice	5 years practice
Arizona	10 yrs. (a)	5 yrs.	(b)	1 yr.	(e)	30	(c)	(d)
Arkansas	2 yrs.	2 yrs.	(b)	...	30	28	8 years practice	6 years licensed in state
California	...	...	...	...	...	...	10 years state bar	10 years state bar
Colorado	★	★	...	★	...	...	5 years state bar	5 years state bar
Connecticut	★	★	...	...	...	...	Licensed attorney	Member of the bar
Delaware	★	★	...	★	...	...	"Learned in law"	"Learned in law"
Florida	★(f)	★	★(f)	★(g)	...	...	10 years state bar	5 years state bar
Georgia	★	3 yrs.	...	...	...	30	7 years state bar	7 years state bar
Hawaii	★	★	...	...	...	...	10 years state bar	10 years state bar
Idaho	2 yrs.	1 yr.	...	...	30	...	10 years state bar	10 years state bar
Illinois	★	★	★	★	...	...	Licensed attorney	...
Indiana	★	1 yr.	...	★	...	...	10 years state bar (h)	...
Iowa	★	★	...	★	...	...	Licensed attorney	Admitted to state bar
Kansas	...	...	...	...	30	...	10 years active and	5 years state bar continuous practice (i)
Kentucky	2 yrs.	2 yrs.	2 yrs.	2 yrs.	...	...	8 years state bar and	8 years state bar licensed attorney
Louisiana	2 yrs.	2 yrs.	2 yrs.	2 yrs.	...	...	5 years state bar	5 years state bar
Maine	...	...	...	...	...	...	"Learned in law"	"Learned in law"
Maryland	5 yrs.	5 yrs.	6 mos.	6 mos.	30	30	State bar member	State bar member
Massachusetts	...	...	...	...	...	...	...	...
Michigan	★	★	...	...	...	...	State bar member and	State bar member 5 years practice
Minnesota	...	...	...	...	...	...	Licensed attorney	Licensed attorney
Mississippi	5 yrs.	5 yrs.	★(j)	...	30	26	5 years state bar	5 years practice
Missouri	9 yrs. (k)	3 yrs. (k)	...	★(k)	30	30	State bar member	State bar member
Montana	2 yrs.	2 yrs.	...	...	...	...	5 years state bar	5 years state bar
Nebraska	3 yrs.	★	★	★	30	30	5 years practice	5 years practice
Nevada	2 yrs.	2 yrs.	...	...	25	25	State bar member (l)	2 years state bar member and 10 years practice
New Hampshire	...	...	...	...	...	...	...	...
New Jersey	...	(m)	...	(m)	...	...	Admitted to practice in	10 years practice of law state for at least 10 years
New Mexico	3 yrs.	3 yrs.	...	★	35	35	10 years practice and/or	6 years active practice current state judge
New York	★	★	...	...	...	18	10 years state bar	10 years state bar
North Carolina	...	★	...	(n)	...	...	State bar member	State bar member
North Dakota	★	★	...	★	...	...	License to practice law	State bar member
Ohio	★	★	...	★	...	...	6 years practice	6 years practice
Oklahoma	★	(o)	1 yr.	★	30	...	5 years state bar	(p)
Oregon	3 yrs.	3 yrs.	...	1 yr.	...	...	State bar member	State bar member
Pennsylvania	1 yr.	★	...	1 yr.	...	...	State bar member	State bar member
Rhode Island	...	...	...	...	21	...	License to practice law	State bar member
South Carolina	5 yrs.	5 yrs.	...	(q)	32	32	8 years state bar	8 years state bar
South Dakota	★	★	★	★	...	...	State bar member	State bar member
Tennessee	5 yrs.	5 yrs.	★(r)	1 yr.	35	30	Qualified to practice law	Qualified to practice law
Texas	★	...	...	2 yrs.	35	25	(s)	(t)
Utah	5 yrs.	3 yrs.	...	★	30	25	Admitted to practice law	Admitted to practice law
Vermont	...	...	...	...	...	...	5 years state bar	5 years state bar
Virginia	...	★	...	★	...	...	5 years state bar	5 years state bar
Washington	1 yr.	1 yr.	1 yr.	1 yr.	...	...	State bar member	State bar member
West Virginia	5 yrs.	★	...	★	30	30	10 years state bar	5 years state bar
Wisconsin	10 days	10 days	10 days	10 days	...	...	5 years state bar	5 years state bar
Wyoming	3 yrs.	2 yrs.	...	...	30	28	9 years state bar	...
Dist. of Columbia	★	★	90 days	90 days	...	...	5 years state bar	5 years state bar (u)
Puerto Rico	5 yrs.	...	...	...	...	...	10 years state bar	7 years state bar

See footnotes at end of table.

QUALIFICATIONS OF JUDGES — Continued

Sources: *State Court Organization, 2004*, U.S. Department of Justice Statistics, National Center for State Courts, August 2006.

Key:

A — Judges of courts of last resort and intermediate appellate courts.

T — Judges of general trial courts.

★ — Provision; length of time not specified.

. . . — No specific provision.

N.A.— Not applicable

(a) For court of appeals, five years.

(b) No local residency requirement stated for Supreme Court. Local residency required for Court of Appeals.

(c) Supreme Court- ten years state bar, Court of Appeals—five years state bar.

(d) Admitted to the practice of law in Arizona for five years.

(e) Court of Appeals minimum age is 30.

(f) The candidate must be a resident of the district at the time of the original appointment.

(g) Circuit court judge must reside within the territorial jurisdiction of the court.

(h) In the Supreme Court and the Court of Appeals, five years service as a general jurisdiction judge may be substituted.

(i) Relevant legal experience, such as being a member of a law faculty or sitting as a judge, may qualify under the 10 year requirement.

(j) Must reside within the district.

(k) At the appellate level must have been a state voter for nine years. At the general trial court level must have been a state voter for three years and resident of the circuit for 1 year.

(l) Minimum of two years state bar member and at least 15 years of legal practice.

(m) For Superior court: out of a total of 441 authorized judgeships there are 283 restricted Superior court judgeships that require

residence within the particular county of assignment at time of appointment and reappointment; there are 158 unrestricted judgeships for which assignment of county is made by the chief justice.

(n) Resident judges of the Superior Court are required to have local residency, but special judges are not.

(o) District and associate judges must be state residents for six months if elected, and associate judges must be county residents.

(p) District Court: judges must be a state bar member for four years or a judge of court record. Associate judges must be a state bar member for two years or a judge of a court of record.

(q) Circuit judges must be county electors and residents of the circuit.

(r) Supreme Court: One justice from each of three divisions and two seats at large; no more than two may be from any grand division. Court of Appeals and Court of Criminal Appeals: Must reside in the grand division served.

(s) Ten years practicing law or a lawyer and judge of a court of record at least 10 years.

(t) District Court: judges must have been a practicing lawyer or a judge of a court in this state, or both combined, for four years.

(u) Superior Court: Judge must also be an active member of the unified District of Columbia bar and have been engaged, during the five years immediately preceding the judicial nomination, in the active practice of law as an attorney in the District, been on the faculty of a law school in the District, or been employed by either the by the United States or District of Columbia government.

Table 5.4
COMPENSATION OF JUDGES OF APPELLATE COURTS AND GENERAL TRIAL COURTS

State or other jurisdiction	Appellate courts						General trial courts	Salary
	Court of last resort	Chief Justice salaries	Associate Justice salaries	Intermediate appellate court	Chief/Presiding salaries	Judges salaries		
Eastern Region								
Connecticut............	Supreme Court	$166,000	$154,000	Appellate Court	$152,000	$145,000	Superior courts	$139,000
Delaware...............	Supreme Court	194,000	184,000	...	...	...	Superior courts	168,000
Maine..................	Supreme Judicial Court	130,000	112,000	...	...	...	Superior courts	105,000
Massachusetts.........	Supreme Judicial Court	151,000	146,000	Appellate Court	140,000	135,000	Superior courts	130,000
New Hampshire........	Supreme Court	132,000	128,000	...	...	...	Superior courts	120,000
New Jersey.............	Supreme Court	164,000	159,000	Appellate division of	...	150,000	Superior courts	141,000
New York..............	Court of Appeals	156,000	151,000	Appellate divisions of	148,000	144,000	Supreme courts	137,000
Pennsylvania..........	Supreme Court	160,000	156,000	Superior Court	153,000	151,000	Courts of common pleas	135,000
Rhode Island..........	Supreme Court	163,000	148,000	...	...	...	Superior courts	133,000
Vermont...............	Supreme Court	130,000	124,000	...	...	...	Superior/District/Family	118,000
Regional average		154,600	146,200		143,750	145,000		132,600
Midwestern Region								
Illinois................	Supreme Court	183,000	183,000	Court of Appeals	172,000	172,000	Circuit courts	158,000
Indiana................	Supreme Court	139,000	139,000	Court of Appeals	135,000	135,000	Circuit courts	115,000
Iowa...................	Supreme Court	150,000	144,000	Court of Appeals	139,000	134,000	District courts	126,000
Kansas................	Supreme Court	127,000	124,000	Court of Appeals	124,000	121,000	District courts	115,000
Michigan..............	Supreme Court	165,000	165,000	Court of Appeals	151,000	151,000	Circuit courts	140,000
Minnesota.............	Supreme Court	151,000	138,000	Court of Appeals	136,000	130,000	District courts	122,000
Nebraska..............	Supreme Court	127,000	127,000	Court of Appeals	121,000	121,000	District courts	117,000
North Dakota..........	Supreme Court	110,000	107,000	...	...	...	District courts	98,000
Ohio...................	Supreme Court	147,000	138,000	Court of Appeals	128,000	128,000	Courts of common pleas	118,000
South Dakota..........	Supreme Court	113,000	111,000	...	...	...	Circuit courts	104,000
Wisconsin.............	Supreme Court	142,000	134,000	Court of Appeals	127,000	127,000	Circuit courts	119,000
Regional Average......		141,273	137,273		137,000	135,444		121,091
Southern Region								
Alabama...............	Supreme Court	153,000	152,000	Court of Criminal Appeals	152,000	151,000	Circuit courts	112,000
Arkansas..............	Supreme Court	145,000	134,000	Court of Appeals	132,000	130,000	Chancery courts	126,000
Florida................	Supreme Court	161,000	161,000	District Court of Appeals	153,000	153,000	Circuit courts	145,000
Georgia...............	Supreme Court	158,000	158,000	Court of Appeals	157,000	157,000	Superior courts	(a)
Kentucky	Supreme Court	137,000	132,000	Court of Appeals	130,000	127,000	Circuit courts	122,000
Louisiana	Supreme Court	130,000	124,00	Court of Appeals	123,000	117,000	District courts	111,000
Maryland..............	Court of Appeals	163,000	144,000	Court of Special Appeals	138,000	135,000	Circuit courts	128,000
Mississippi............	Supreme Court	115,000	113,000	Court of Appeals	108,000	105,000	Chancery courts	104,000
Missouri...............	Supreme Court	126,000	123,000	Court of Appeals	115,000	115,000	Circuit courts	108,000
North Carolina........	Supreme Court	131,000	127,000	Court of Appeals	124,000	122,000	Superior courts	115,000
Oklahoma	Supreme Court	140,000	131,000	Court of Appeals	127,000	124,000	District courts	118,000
South Carolina........	Supreme Court	138,000	132,000	Court of Appeals	131,000	129,000	Circuit courts	125,000
Tennessee.............	Supreme Court	134,000	134,000	Court of Appeals	128,000	128,000	Chancery courts	123,000
Texas..................	Supreme Court	153,000	150,000	Court of Appeals	140,000	(b)	District courts	(c)
Virginia...............	Supreme Court	165,000 (d)	155,000 (d)	Court of Appeals	150,000 (d)	147,000 (d)	Circuit courts	144,000
West Virginia..........	Supreme Court	121,000	121,000	...	...	...	Circuit courts	116,000
Regional averages......		141,875	136,938		133,867	131,429		121,214

See footnotes at end of table.

COMPENSATION OF JUDGES OF APPELLATE COURTS AND GENERAL TRIAL COURTS — Continued

State or other jurisdiction	Court of last resort	Appellate courts					General trial courts	Salary
		Chief Justice salaries	Associate Justice salaries	Intermediate appellate court	Chief/Presiding salaries	Judges salaries		
Western Region								
Alaska	Supreme Court	166,000	165,000	Court of Appeals	156,000	156,000	Superior courts	(e)
Arizona	Supreme Court	129,000	127,000	Court of Appeals	124,000	124,000	Superior courts	121,000
California	Supreme Court	218,000	210,000	Court of Appeals	196,000	196,000	Superior court	172,000
Colorado	Supreme Court	126,000	123,000	Court of Appeals	121,000	118,000	District courts	113,000
Hawaii	Supreme Court	145,000	140,000	Intermediate Court	135,000	129,000	Circuit courts	126,000
Idaho	Supreme Court	112,000	111,000	Court of Appeals	110,000	110,000	District courts	104,000
Montana	Supreme Court	102,000	101,000	...	...	...	District courts	94,000
Nevada	Supreme Court	(f)	(f)	...	...	...	District courts	(g)
New Mexico	Supreme Court	117,000	115,000	Court of Appeals	111,000	109,000	District courts	104,000
Oregon	Supreme Court	108,000	105,000	Court of Appeals	105,000	103,000	Circuit courts	96,000
Utah	Supreme Court	128,000	126,000	Court of Appeals	121,000	120,000	District courts	114,000
Washington	Supreme Court	141,000	141,000	Court of Appeals	135,000	135,000	Superior courts	128,000
Wyoming	Supreme Court	115,000	115,000	...	...	...	District courts	110,000
Regional averages		133,917	131,583		131,400	130,000		116,545
Regional averages w/o California		126,910	125,049		124,222	122,667		111,000
Dist. of Columbia	Court of Appeals	176,000	175,000	...	...	...	Superior courts	165,000
American Samoa	High Court	125,000	119,000	...	...	...	District courts	97,000
Guam	Superior Court	(h)	(i)	...	...	...	Superior courts	(i)
No. Mariana Islands	Commonwealth Supreme Court	130,000	126,000	...	...	...	Superior courts	120,000
Puerto Rico	Supreme Court	125,000	120,000	Appellate Court	105,000	105,000	Superior courts	90,000
U.S. Virgin Islands	Territorial Court	145,000	135,000	...	...	...	...	...

Source: Salary information was taken from National Center for State Courts, *Survey of Judicial Salaries* Vol. 31 No. 1 (as of July 2006). With updates February 2007 by the National Center for State Courts.

Note: Compensation is shown rounded to the nearest thousand, and is reported according to most recent legislation, even though laws may not yet have taken effect. There are other non-salary forms of judicial compensation that can be a significant part of a judge's compensation package. It should be noted that many of these can be important to judges or attorneys who might be interested in becoming judges or justices. These include retirement, disability, and death benefits, expense accounts, vacation, holiday, and sick leave and various forms of insurance coverage.

(a) Salary range is between $113,000 and $166,000.
(b) Salary range is between $138,000 and $145,000.

(c) Salary range is between $125,000 and $140,000.
(d) Plus $6,500 in lieu of travel, lodging and other expenses.
(e) Salary range is between $153,000 and $160,000, varies by location and cost of living.
(f) Salary range is between $140,000 and $171,000 and may include longevity pay.
(g) Salary range is between $130,000 and $159,000 and may include longevity pay and may be dependent on election cticle.
(h) Salary range is between $128,000 and $163,000.
(i) Salary range is between $126,000 and $156,000.
(j) Salary range is between $100,000 and 128,000.

Table 5.5
SELECTED DATA ON COURT ADMINISTRATIVE OFFICES

State or other jurisdiction	Title	Established	Appointed by (a)	Salary
Alabama	Administrative Director of Courts	1971	CJ (b)	$105,000
Alaska	Administrative Director	1959	CJ (b)	163,000
Arizona	Administrative Director of Courts	1960	SC	(g)
Arkansas	Director, Administrative Office of the Courts	1965	CJ (c)	100,000
California	Administrative Director of the Courts	1960	JC	(h)
Colorado	State Court Administrator	1959	SC	121,000
Connecticut	Chief Court Administrator (d)	1965	CJ	160,000
Delaware	Director, Administrative Office of the Courts	1971	CJ	126,000
Florida	State Courts Administrator	1972	SC	131,000
Georgia	Director, Administrative Office of the Courts	1973	JC	132,000
Hawaii	Administrative Director of the Courts	1959	CJ (b)	109,000
Idaho	Administrative Director of the Courts	1967	SC	105,000
Illinois	Administrative Director of the Courts	1959	SC	172,000
Indiana	Executive Director, Division of State Court Administration	1975	CJ	105,000
Iowa	Court Administrator	1971	SC	(i)
Kansas	Judicial Administrator	1965	CJ	115,000
Kentucky	Administrative Director of the Courts	1976	CJ	122,000
Louisiana	Judicial Administrator	1954	SC	117,000
Maine	Court Administrator	1975	CJ	105,000
Maryland	State Court Administrator	1955	CJ (b)	130,000
Massachusetts	Chief Justice for Administration & Management	1978	SC	140,000
Michigan	State Court Administrator	1952	SC	142,000
Minnesota	State Court Administrator	1963	SC	122,000
Mississippi	Court Administrator	1974	SC	69,000
Missouri	State Courts Administrator	1970	SC	115,000
Montana	State Court Administrator	1975	SC	90,000
Nebraska	State Court Administrator	1972	CJ	106,000
Nevada	Director, Office of Court Administration	1971	SC	117,000
New Hampshire	Director of the Administrative Office of the Court	1980	SC	98,000
New Jersey	Administrative Director of the Courts	1948	CJ	150,000
New Mexico	Director, Administrative Office of the Courts	1959	SC	107,000
New York	Chief Administrator of the Courts	1978	CJ	148,000
North Carolina	Director, Administrative Office of the Courts	1965	CJ	119,000
North Dakota	Court Administrator (h)	1971	CJ	89,000
Ohio	Administrative Director of the Courts	1955	SC	129,000
Oklahoma	Administrative Director of the Courts	1967	SC	124,000
Oregon	Court Administrator	1971	SC	119,000
Pennsylvania	Court Administrator	1968	SC	(l)
Rhode Island	State Court Administrator	1969	CJ	119,000
South Carolina	Director of Court Administration	1973	CJ	119,000
South Dakota	State Court Administrator	1974	SC	99,000
Tennessee	Director	1963	SC	124,000
Texas	Administrative Director of the Courts (i)	1977	SC	105,000
Utah	Court Administrator	1973	SC	114,000
Vermont	Court Administrator	1967	SC	124,000
Virginia	Executive Secretary to the Supreme Court	1952	SC	141,000
Washington	Administrator for the Courts	1957	SC (e)	122,000
West Virginia	Administrative Director of the Supreme Court of Appeals	1975	SC	111,000
Wisconsin	Director of State Courts	1978	SC	119,000
Wyoming	Court Coordinator	1974	SC	104,000
Dist. of Columbia	Executive Officer, Courts of D.C.	1971	(f)	165,000
American Samoa	Administrator/Comptroller	N.A.	N.A.	46,000 (j)
Guam	Administrative Director of Superior Court	N.A.	CJ (m)	120,000
No. Mariana Islands				70,000
Puerto Rico	Administrative Director of the Courts	1952	CJ	111,000
U.S. Virgin Islands	Court/Administrative Clerk	N.A.	N.A.	92,000

Source: Salary information was taken from National Center for State Courts, *Survey of Judicial Salaries* Vol. 31 No. 1 (as of July 2006). With updates February 2007 by the National Center for State Courts.

Note: Compensation shown is rounded to the nearest thousand, and is reported according to most recent legislation, even though laws may not yet have taken effect. Other information from State Court Administrator Web sites.

Key:
SC — State court of last resort.
CJ — Chief justice or chief judge of court of last resort.
JC — Judicial council.
N.A. — Not available.

(a) Term of office for all court administrators is at pleasure of appointing authority.
(b) With approval of Supreme Court.
(c) With approval of Judicial Council.
(d) Administrator is an associate judge of the Supreme Court.
(e) Appointed from list of five submitted by governor.
(f) Joint Committee on Judicial Administration.
(g) Salary range is between $104,000 and $166,000.
(h) Salary range is between $ 168,000 and $185,000.
(i) Salary range is between $95,000 and $145,000.
(j) Plus $1,170/yr. increment.
(k) Salary range is $120,000 and $147,000.
(l) Salary range is $89,000 and $119,000.

Table 5.6
SELECTION AND RETENTION OF APPELLATE COURT JUDGES

State or other jurisdiction	Name of Court	Types of court	Method of selection Unexpired term	Full term	Method of retention	Geographic basis for selection
Alabama	Supreme Court	SC	GU	PE	PE	SW
	Court of Civil Appeals	IA	GU	PE	PE	SW
	Court of Criminal Appeals	IA	GU	PE	PE	SW
Alaska	Supreme Court	SC	GN	GN	RE (a)	SW
	Court of Appeals	IA	GN	GN	RE (a)	SW
Arizona	Supreme Court	SC	GN	GN	RE	SW
	Court of Appeals	IA	GN	GN	RE	DS
Arkansas	Supreme Court	SC	GU	NP	NP	SW
	Court of Appeals	IA	GU	NP	NP	DS
California	Supreme Court	SC	GU	GU	RE	SW
	Courts of Appeal	IA	GU	GU	RE	DS
Colorado	Supreme Court	SC	GN	GN	RE	SW
	Court of Appeals	IA	GN	GN	RE	SW
Connecticut	Supreme Court	SC	GNL	GNL	GNL	SW
	Appellate Court	IA	GNL	GNL	GNL	SW
Delaware	Supreme Court	SC	GNL	GNL	GNL	SW
Florida	Supreme Court	SC	GN	GN	RE	DS and SW (b)
	District Courts of Appeal	IA	GN	GN	RE	DS
Georgia	Supreme Court	SC	GN	NP	NP	SW
	Court of Appeals	IA	GN	NP	NP	SW
Hawaii	Supreme Court	SC	GNL	GNL	JN	SW
	Intermediate Court of Appeals	IA	GNL	GNL	JN	SW
Idaho	Supreme Court	SC	GN	NP	NP	SW
	Court of Appeals	IA	GN	NP	NP	SW
Illinois	Supreme Court	SC	CS	PE	RE	DS
	Appellate Court	IA	SC	PE	RE	DS
Indiana	Supreme Court	SC	GN	GN	RE	SW
	Court of Appeals	IA	GN	GN	RE	DS
	Tax Court	IA	GN	GN	RE	SW
Iowa	Supreme Court	SC	GN	GN	RE	SW
	Court of Appeals	IA	GN	GN	RE	SW
Kansas	Supreme Court	SC	GN	GN	RE	SW
	Court of Appeals	IA	GN	GN	RE	SW
Kentucky	Supreme Court	SC	GN	NP	NP	DS
	Court of Appeals	IA	GN	NP	NP	DS
Louisiana	Supreme Court	SC	CS (c)	PE (d)	PE (d)	DS
	Courts of Appeal	IA	SC (c)	PE (d)	PE (d)	DS
Maine	Supreme Judicial Court	SC	GL	GL	GL	SW
Maryland	Court of Appeals	SC	GNL	GNL	RE	DS
	Court of Special Appeals	IA	GNL	GNL	RE	DS
Massachusetts	Supreme Judicial Court	SC	(e)	GNE (f)	(g)	SW
	Appeals Court	IA	(e)	GNE (f)	(g)	SW
Michigan	Supreme Court	SC	GU	NP (h)	NP (h)	SW
	Court of Appeals	IA	GU	NP (h)	NP (h)	DS
Minnesota	Supreme Court	SC	GU	NP	NP	SW
	Court of Appeals	IA	GU	NP	NP	SW
Mississippi	Supreme Court	SC	GU	NP	NP	DS
	Court of Appeals	IA	GU	NP	NP	DS
Missouri	Supreme Court	SC	GN	GN	RE	SW
	Court of Appeals	IA	GN	GN	RE	DS
Montana	Supreme Court	SC	GNL	NP	NP (i)	SW
Nebraska	Supreme Court	SC	GN	GN	RE	SW and DS (j)
	Court of Appeals	IA	GN	GN	RE	DS
Nevada	Supreme Court	SC	GN	NP	NP	SW
New Hampshire	Supreme Court	SC	GE	GE	(k)	SW

See footnotes at end of table.

SELECTION AND RETENTION OF APPELLATE COURT JUDGES — Continued

State or other jurisdiction	Name of Court	Types of court	Method of selection		Method of retention	Geographic basis for selection
			Unexpired term	Full term		
New Jersey	Supreme Court	SC	GL	GL	GL	SW
	Superior Court, Appellate Div.	IA	GL	GL (l)	GL (l)	SW
New Mexico	Supreme Court	SC	GN	PE	RE	SW
	Court of Appeals	IA	GN	PE	RE	SW
New York	Court of Appeals	SC	GNL	GNL	GNL	SW
	Supreme Ct., Appellate Div.	IA	GN	GN	GN	SW (m)
North Carolina	Supreme Court	SC	GU	NP	NP	SW
	Court of Appeals	IA	GU	NP	NP	SW
North Dakota	Supreme Court	SC	GN (n)	NP	NP	SW
Ohio	Supreme Court	SC	GU	PE (o)	PE (o)	SW
	Courts of Appeals	IA	GU	PE (o)	PE (o)	DS
Oklahoma	Supreme Court	SC	GN	GN	RE	DS
	Court of Criminal Appeals	SC	GN	GN	RE	DS
	Court of Civil Appeals	IA	GN	GN	RE	DS
Oregon	Supreme Court	SC	GU	NP	NP	SW
	Court of Appeals	IA	GU	NP	NP	SW
Pennsylvania	Supreme Court	SC	GL	PE	RE	SW
	Superior Court	IA	GL	PE	RE	SW
	Commonwealth Court	IA	GL	PE	RE	SW
Rhode Island	Supreme Court	SC	GN	GN	(p)	SW
South Carolina	Supreme Court	SC	LA	LA	LA	SW
	Court of Appeals	IA	LA	LA	LA	SW
South Dakota	Supreme Court	SC	GN	GN	RE	DS and SW (q)
Tennessee	Supreme Court	SC	GN	GN	RE	SW
	Court of Appeals	SC	GN	GN	RE	SW
	Court of Criminal Appeals	IA	GN	GN	RE	SW
Texas	Supreme Court	SC	GU	PE	PE	SW
	Court of Criminal Appeals	SC	GU	PE	PE	SW
	Courts of Appeals	IA	GU	PE	PE	DS
Utah	Supreme Court	SC	GNL	GNL	RE	SW
	Court of Appeals	IA	GNL	GNL	RE	SW
Vermont	Supreme Court	SC	GNL	GNL	LA	SW
Virginia	Supreme Court	SC	GU (r)	LA	LA	SW
	Court of Appeals	IA	GU (r)	LA	LA	SW
Washington	Supreme Court	SC	GU	NP	NP	SW
	Courts of Appeals	IA	GU	NP	NP	DS
West Virginia	Supreme Court of Appeals	SC	GU (s)	PE	PE	SW
Wisconsin	Supreme Court	SC	GN	NP	NP	SW
	Court of Appeals	IA	GN	NP	NP	DS
Wyoming	Supreme Court	SC	GN	GN	RE	SW
District of Columbia	Court of Appeals	SC	(t)	(t)	(t)	SW (u)
Puerto Rico	Supreme Court	SC	GL	GL	(v)	SW
	Court of Appeals	IA	GL	GL	GL	SW

See footnotes at end of table.

SELECTION AND RETENTION OF APPELLATE COURT JUDGES — Continued

Source: Bureau of Justice Statistics, *State Court Organization, 2004* NCJ 212351, August 15, 2006.

Key:

SC — Court of last resort
IA — Intermediate appellate court
N/S — Not stated
N.A. — Not applicable
AP — At pleasure
CS — Court selection
DS — District
DU — Duration of service
GE — Gubernatorial appointment with approval of elected executive council
GL — Gubernatorial appointment with consent of the legislature
GN — Gubernatorial appointment from judicial nominating commission
GNE — Gubernatorial appointment from judicial nominating commission with approval of elected executive council
GNL — Gubernatorial appointment from judicial nominating commission with consent of the legislature
GU — Gubernatorial appointment
ID — Indefinite
JN — Judicial nominating commission appoints
LA — Legislative appointment
NP — Non-partisan election
PE — Partisan election
RE — Retention election
SC — Court of last resort appoints
SCJ — Chief justice/judge of the court of last resort appoints
SN — Seniority
SW — Statewide

(a) A judge must run for a retention election at the next election, immediately following the third year from the time of initial appointment.

(b) Five justices are selected by region (based on the District Courts of Appeal) and two justices are selected statewide.

(c) The person selected by the Supreme Court is prohibited from running for that judgeship; an election is held within one year to serve the remainder of the term.

(d) Louisiana uses a blanket primary, in which all candidates appear with party labels on the primary ballot. The two top vote getters compete in the general election.

(e) There are no expired judicial terms. A judicial term expires upon the death, resignation, retirement, or removal of an incumbent.

(f) The Executive (Governor's) Council is made up of nine people elected by geographical area and presided over by the Lieutenant Governor.

(g) There is no retention process. Judges serve during good behavior to age 70.

(h) Candidates may be nominated by political parties and are elected on a nonpartisan ballot.

(i) If the justice/judge is unopposed, a retention election is held.

(j) Chief Justices are selected statewide while Associate Justices are selected by district.

(k) There is no retention process. Judges serve during good behavior to age 70.

(l) All Superior Court judges, including Appellate Division judges, are subject to gubernatorial reappointment and consent by the Senate after an initial seven-year term. Among all the judges, the Chief Justice designates the judges of the Appellate Division.

(m) The Presiding Judge of each Appellate Division must be a resident of the department.

(n) The Governor may appoint from a list of names or call a special election at his discretion.

(o) Party affiliation is not included on the ballot in the general election, but candidates are chosen through partisan primary nominations.

(p) There is no retention process. Judges serve during good behavior for a life tenure.

(q) Initial selection is by district, but retention selection is statewide.

(r) Gubernatorial appointment is for interim appointments.

(s) Appointment is effective only until the next election year; the appointee may run for election to any remaining portion of the unexpired term.

(t) Initial appointment is made by the President of the United States and confirmed by the Senate. Six months prior to the expiration of the term of office, the judge's performance is reviewed by the tenure commission. Those found "well qualified" are automatically reappointed. If a judge is found to be "qualified" the President may nominate the judge for an additional term (subject to Senate confirmation). If the President does not wish to reappoint the judge, the District of Columbia Nomination Commission compiles a new list of candidates.

(u) The geographic basis of selection is the District of Columbia.

(v) There is no retention process. Judges serve during good behavior to age 70.

Table 5.7
SELECTION AND RETENTION OF TRIAL COURT JUDGES

State or other jurisdiction	Name of Court	Types of court	Method of selection		Method of retention	Geographic basis for selection
			Unexpired term	Full term		
Alabama	Circuit	GJ	GU (a)	PE	PE	Circuit
	District	LJ	GU (a)	PE	PE	County
	Municipal	LJ	MU	MU	RA	Municipality
	Probate	LJ	GU	PE	PE	County
Alaska	Superior	GJ	GN	GN	RE (b)	State (c)
	District	LG	GN	GN	RE (d)	District
	Magistrate's Division	N.A.	PJ	PJ	PJ	District
Arizona	Superior	GJ	GN or VA (e)	GN or NP (f)	NP or RE (f)	County
	Justice of the Peace	LJ	CO	PE	PE	Precinct
	Municipal	LJ	CC (g)	CC (g)	CC (g)	Municipality
Arkansas	Circuit	GJ	GU (h)	NP	NP	Circuit
	District	LJ	GU	NP	NP	District
	City	LJ	LD	LD	LD	City
California	Superior	GJ	GU	NP	NP (i)	County
Colorado	District	GJ	GN	GN	RE	District
	Denver Probate	GJ	GN	GN	RE	District
	Denver Juvenile	GJ	GN	GN	RE	District
	Water	GJ	SC (j)	SC (j)	RE	District
	County	LJ	GN	GN (k)	RE	County
	Municipal	LJ	MU	MU	RA	Municipality
Connecticut	Superior	GJ	GNL	GNL	GNL	State
	Probate	LJ	PE	PE	PE	District
Delaware	Superior	GJ	GNL	GNL	GNL	State
	Chancery	LJ	GNL	GNL	GNL	State
	Justice of the Peace	LJ	GNL (l)	GNL (l)	GU	County
	Family	LJ	GNL	GNL	GNL	County
	Common Pleas	LJ	GNL	GNL	GNL	County
	Alderman's	LJ	LD	CC	LD	Town
Florida	Circuit	GJ	GN	NP	NP	Circuit
	County	LJ	GN	NP	NP	County
Georgia	Superior	GJ	GN	NP	NP	Circuit
	Juvenile	LJ	CS (m)	CS (m)	CS (m)	County/Circuit
	Civil	LJ	GU	PE	PE	County
	State	LJ	GU	NP	NP	County
	Probate	LJ	GU	PE (n)	PE (n)	County
	Magistrate	LJ	LD	LD (o)	LD (o)	County
	Municipal/of Columbus	LJ	MA	Elected	Elected	Municipality
	County Recorder's	LJ	LD	LD	LD	County
	Municipal/City of Atlanta	LJ	MU	MU	LD	Municipality
Hawaii	Circuit	GJ	GNL	GNL	JN	State
	District	LJ	SCJ (p)	SCJ (p)	JN	Circuit
Idaho	District	GJ	GN	NP	NP	District
	Magistrate's Division	LJ	JN (q)	JN (q)	RE	County
Illinois	Circuit	GJ	SC	PE	RE	Circuit/County (r)
	Associate Division	N.A.	SC	PE	RE	Circuit/County (r)
Indiana	Superior	GJ	GU	PE (s)	PE (s)	County
	Circuit	GJ	GU	PE (t)	PE (t)	County
	Probate	GJ	GU	PE	PE	County
	County	LJ	GU	PE	PE	County
	City	LJ	GU	PE	PE	Municipality
	Town	LJ	GU	PE	PE	Municipality
	Small Claims/Marion County	LJ	GU	PE	PE	Township
Iowa	District	GJ	GN (u)	GN (u)	RE (u)	District
Kansas	District	GJ	GN and PE(v)	GN and PE (v)	RE and PE (v)	District
	Municipal	LJ	MU	MU	MU	City
Kentucky	Circuit	GJ	GN	NP	NP	Circuit
	District	LJ	GN	NP	NP	District
Louisiana	District	GJ	SC (w)	PE	PE	District
	Juvenile & Family	GJ	SC (w)	PE	PE	District
	Justice of the Peace	LJ	SC (w)	PE(x)	PE	Ward
	Mayor's	LJ	MA	LD	LD	City
	City & Parish	LJ	SC (w)	PE	PE	Ward

See footnotes at end of table.

SELECTION AND RETENTION OF TRIAL COURT JUDGES — Continued

State or other jurisdiction	Name of Court	Types of court	Method of selection Unexpired term	Full term	Method of retention	Geographic basis for selection
Maine............................	Superior	GJ	GL	GL	GL	State
	District	GJ	GL	GL	GL	State and District (y)
	Probate	LJ	GU	PE	PE	County
Maryland	Circuit	GJ	GNL	GNL	NP	County
	District	LJ	GNL	GNL	RA	District
	Orphan's	LJ	GU	PE (z)	PE (z)	County
Massachusetts.............	Superior	GJ	(aa)	GNE (bb)	(cc)	State
	District	LJ	(aa)	GNE (bb)	(cc)	State
	Probate & Family	LJ	(aa)	GNE (bb)	(cc)	State
	Juvenile	LJ	(aa)	GNE (bb)	(cc)	State
	Housing	LJ	(aa)	GNE (bb)	(cc)	State
	Boston Municipal	LJ	(aa)	GNE (bb)	(cc)	State
	Land	LJ	(aa)	GNE (bb)	(cc)	State
Michigan	Circuit	GJ	GU	NP	NP	Circuit
	Claims	GJ	GU	NP	NP	Circuit
	District	LJ	GU	NP	NP	District
	Probate	LJ	GU	NP	NP	District and Circuit
	Municipal	LJ	LD	NP	NP	City
Minnesota....................	District	GJ	GN	NP	NP	District
Mississippi..................	Circuit	GJ	GU	NP	NP	District
	Chancery	LJ	GU	NP	NP	District
	County	LJ	GU	NP	NP	County
	Municipal	LJ	LD	LD	LD	Municipality
	Justice	LJ	LD	PE	PE	District in County
Missouri	Circuit	GJ	GU and GN (dd)	PE and GN (ee)	PE and RE (ff)	Circuit/County (gg)
	Municipal	LJ	LD	LD	LD	City
Montana	District	GJ	GN	NP	NP	District
	Workers' Compensation	GJ	GN	GN	RA	State
	Water	GJ	SCJ (hh)	SCJ (hh)	SCJ (ii)	State
	Justice of the Peace	LJ	CO	NP	NP	County
	Municipal	LJ	MU	NP	NP	City
	City	LJ	CC	NP	NP	City
Nebraska	District	GJ	GN	GN	RE	District
	Separate Juvenile	LJ	GN	GN	RE	District
	County	LJ	GN	GN	RE	District
	Workers' Compensation	LJ	GN	GN	RE	District
Nevada.........................	District	GJ	GN	NP	NP	District
	Justice	LJ	CO	NP	NP	Township
	Municipal	LJ	CC	NP	NP	City
New Hampshire...........	Superior	GJ	GE	GE	(jj)	State
	District	LJ	GE	GE	(jj)	District
	Probate	LJ	GE	GE	(jj)	County
New Jersey	Superior	GJ	GL	GL	GL	County
	Tax	LJ	GL	GL	GL	State
	Municipal	LJ	MA or MU (kk)	MA or MU (kk)	MU	Municipality
New Mexico.................	District	GJ	GN	PE	RE	District
	Magistrate	LJ	GU	PE	PE	County
	Metropolitan/Bernalillo County	LJ	GN	PE	RE	County
	Municipal	LJ	MU	PE	PE	City
	Probate	LJ	CO	PE	PE	County
New York......................	Supreme	GJ	GL	PE	PE	District
	County	GJ	GL	PE	PE	County
	Claims	GJ	GNL	GNL	GU	State
	Surrogates'	LJ	GNL	PE	PE	County
	Family	LJ	GNL and MU (ll)	PE and MU (ll)	PE and MU (ll)	County and NYC
	District	LJ	(mm)	PE	PE	District
	City	LJ	Elected	Elected	LD	City
	NYC Civil	LJ	MA (nn)	PE	PE	City
	NYC Criminal	LJ	MA	MA	MA	City
	Town & Village Justice	LJ	LD	LD	LD	Town or Village
North Carolina	Superior	GJ	GU	NP	NP	District
	District	LJ	GU	NP	NP	District

See footnotes at end of table.

SELECTION AND RETENTION OF TRIAL COURT JUDGES — Continued

State or other jurisdiction	Name of Court	Types of court	Method of selection		Method of retention	Geographic basis for selection
			Unexpired term	Full term		
North Dakota.............	District	GJ	GN	NP	NP	District
	Municipal	LJ	MA	NP	NP	City
Ohio	Common Pleas	GJ	GU	PE (oo)	PE (oo)	County
	Municipal	LJ	GU	PE (oo)	PE (oo)	County/City
	County	LJ	GU	PE (oo)	PE (oo)	County
	Claims	LJ	SCJ	SCJ	SCJ	N.A.
	Mayor's	LJ	Elected	PE	PE	City/Village
Oklahoma....................	District	GJ	GN (pp)	NP (pp)	NP (pp)	District
	Municipal Not of Record	LJ	MM	MM	MM	Municipality
	Municipal of Record	LJ	MU	MU	MU	Municipality
	Workers' Compensation	LJ	GN	GN	GN	State
	Tax Review	LJ	SCJ	SCJ	SCJ	District
Oregon.........................	Circuit	GJ	GU	NP	NP	District
	Tax	GJ	GU	NP	NP	State
	County	LJ	CO	NP	NP	County
	Justice	LJ	GU	NP	NP	County
	Municipal	LJ	CC	CC/Elected	CC/Elected	(qq)
Pennsylvania..............	Common Pleas	GJ	GL	PE	RE	District
	Philadelphia Municipal	LJ	GL	PE	RE	City/County
	Magisterial District Judges	LJ	GL	PE	PE	District
	Philadelphia Traffic	LJ	GL	PE	RE	City/County
Rhode Island..............	Superior	GJ	GN	GN	(rr)	State
	Workers' Compensation	LJ	GN	GN	(rr)	State
	District	LJ	GN	GN	(rr)	State
	Family	LJ	GN	GN	(rr)	State
	Probate	LJ	CC	CC or MA	RA	Town
	Municipal	LJ	CC	CC or MA	CC or MA	Town
	Traffic Tribunal	LJ	GN	GN	(rr)	State
South Carolina............	Circuit	GJ	LA and GN (ss)(tt)	LA and GN (tt)	LA and GL (tt)	Circuit and State (tt)
	Family	LJ	LA	LA	LA	Circuit
	Magistrate	LJ	GL	GL	GL	County
	Probate	LJ	GU	PE	PE	County
	Municipal	LJ	CC	CC	CC	District
South Dakota	Circuit	GJ	GN	NP	NP	Circuit
	Magistrate	LJ	PJS	PJS	PJS	Circuit
Tennessee....................	Circuit	GJ	GU	PE (uu)	PE	District
	Chancery	GJ	GU	PE (uu)	PE	District
	Criminal	GJ	GU	PE (uu)	PE	District
	Probate	GJ	(vv)	PE (uu)	PE	District
	Juvenile	LJ	(vv)	PE (uu)	PE	County
	Municipal	LJ	LD	LD (uu)	LD	Municipality
	General Sessions	LJ	MU	PE (uu)	PE	County
Texas	District	GJ	GL	PE	PE	District
	Constitutional County	LJ	CO	PE	PE	County
	Probate	LJ	CO	PE	PE	County
	County at Law	LJ	CO	PE	PE	County
	Justice of the Peace	LJ	CO	PE	PE	Precinct
	Municipal	LJ	CC	LD	LD	Municipality
Utah	District	GJ	(ww)	GNL	RE	District
	Justice	LJ	MM (xx)	MM (xx)	RE and RA (yy)	County/Municipality
	Juvenile	LJ	(ww)	GNL	RE	District
Vermont.......................	Superior	GJ	GNL	GNL	LA	State
	District	GJ	GNL	GNL	LA	State
	Family	GJ	(zz)	(zz)	(zz)	(zz)
	Probate	LJ	GU	PE	PE	District
	Environmental	LJ	GNL	GNL	LA	State
	Judicial Bureau	LJ	PJ	PJ	AP	State
Virginia	Circuit	GJ	GU	LA	LA	Circuit
	District	LJ	CS (aaa)	LA	LA	District
Washington	Superior	GJ	GU	NP	NP	County
	District	LJ	CO	NP	NP	District
	Municipal	LJ	CC	MA/CC	MA/CC (bbb)	Municipality

See footnotes at end of table.

SELECTION AND RETENTION OF TRIAL COURT JUDGES — Continued

State or other jurisdiction	Name of Court	Types of court	Method of selection		Method of retention	Geographic basis for selection
			Unexpired term	Full term		
West Virginia	Circuit	GJ	GU	PE	PE	Circuit
	Magistrate	LJ	PJ	PE	PE	County
	Municipal	LJ	LD	LD	LD	Municipality
	Family	LJ	GU	PE	PE	Circuit
Wisconsin	Circuit	GJ	GU	NP	NP	District
	Municipal	LJ	MU (ccc)	NP	NP	Municipality
Wyoming	District	GJ	GN	GN	RE	District
	Circuit	LJ	GN	GN	RE	Circuit
	Municipal	LJ	MA	MA	LD	Municipality
District of Columbia ..	Superior	GJ	(ddd)	(ddd)	(ddd)	State (eee)
Puerto Rico	First Instance	GJ	GL	GL	GL	State

Source: Bureau of Justice Statistics, *State Court Organization, 2004* NCJ 212351, August 15, 2006.

Key:
GJ — General jurisdiction court
LJ — Limited jurisdiction court
N/S — Not stated
N.A. — Not applicable
AP — At pleasure
CA — Court administrator appointment
CC — City or town council/commission appointment
CO — County board/commission appointment
CS — Court selection
DU — Duration of service
GE — Gubernatorial appointment with approval of elected executive council
GL — Gubernatorial appointment with consent of the legislature
GN — Gubernatorial appointment from judicial nominating commission
GNE — Gubernatorial appointment from judicial nominating commission with approval of elected executive council
GNL — Gubernatorial appointment from judicial nominating commission with consent of the legislature
GU — Gubernatorial appointment
JN — Judicial nominating commission appoints
LA — Legislative appointment
LD — Locally determined
MA — Mayoral appointment
MC — Mayoral appointment with consent of city council
MM — Mayoral appointment with consent of governing municipal body
MU — Governing municipal body appointment
NP — Non-partisan election
PE — Partisan election
PJ — Presiding judge of the general jurisdiction court appoints
PJS — Presiding judge of the general jurisdiction court appoints with approval of the court of last resort
RA — Reappointment
RE — Retention election
SC — Court of last resort appoints
SCJ — Chief justice/judge of the court of last resort appoints
(a) The counties of Baldwin, Jefferson, Madison, Mobile, and Tuscaloosa use gubernatorial appointment from the recommendations of the Judicial Nominating Commission.
(b) A judge must run for retention at the next election immediately following the third year from the time of the initial appointment.
(c) Judges are selected on a statewide basis, but run for retention on a district-wide basis.
(d) Judges must run for retention at the first general election held more than one year after appointment.
(e) Maricopa and Pima counties use the gubernatorial appointment from the Judicial Nominating Commission process. The method for submitting names for the other 13 counties varies.
(f) Maricopa and Pima counties use the gubernatorial appointment from the Judicial Nominating Commission process. The other 13 counties hold non-partisan elections.
(g) Municipal court judges are usually appointed by the city or town council except in Yuma, where judges are elected.
(h) The office can be held until December 31 following the next general election and then the judge must run in a non-partisan election for the

remainder of the term.
(i) If unopposed for reelection, incumbent's name does not appear on the ballot unless a petition was filed not less than 83 days before the election date indicating that a write-in campaign will be conducted for the office. An unopposed incumbent is not declared elected until the election date. This is for the general election; different timing may apply for the primary election (see Elec. Code §8203).
(j) Judges are chosen by the Supreme Court from among District Court judges.
(k) The mayor appoints Denver County Court judges.
(l) The Magistrate Screening Commission recommends candidates.
(m) Juvenile Court judges are appointed by Superior Court judges in all but one county, in which juvenile judges are elected. Associate judges (formerly referees) must be a member of the state bar or law school graduates. They serve at the pleasure of the judge(s).
(n) Probate judges are selected in non-partisan elections in 66 of 159 counties.
(o) Magistrate judges are selected in nonpartisan elections in 41 of 159 counties.
(p) Selection occurs by means of Chief Justice appointment from the Judicial Nominating Commission with consent of the Senate.
(q) The Magistrate Commission consists of the administrative judge, three mayors and two electors appointed by the governor, and two attorneys (nominated by the district bar and appointed by the state bar). There is one commission in each district.
(r) There exists a unit less than county in Cook County.
(s) Non-partisan elections are used in the Superior Courts in Allen and Vanderburgh counties. Nominating commissions are used in St. Joseph County and in some courts in Lake County. In those courts that use the nominating commission process for selection; retention elections are used as the method of retention.
(t) Non-partisan elections are used in the Circuit Courts in Vanderburgh County.
(u) This applies to district judges only. Associate judges are selected by the district judges and retention is by a retention election. Magistrates are selected and retained by appointment from the County Judicial Magistrate Nominating Commission. The County Judicial Magistrate Nominating Commission consists of three members appointed by the county board and two elected by the county bar, presided over by a District Court judge.
(v) Seventeen districts use gubernatorial appointment from the Judicial Nominating Commission for selection and retention elections for retention. Fourteen districts use partisan elections for selection and retention.
(w) Depending on the amount of time remaining, selection may be by election following a Supreme Court appointment.
(x) Louisiana uses a blanket primary in which all candidates appear with party labels on the primary ballot. The top two vote getters compete in the general election.
(y) At least one judge who is a resident of the county in which the district lies must be appointed from each of the 13 districts.
(z) Two exceptions are Hartford and Montgomery counties where Circuit Court judges are assigned.
(aa) There are no expired judicial terms. A judicial term expires upon the death, resignation, retirement, or removal of an incumbent.
(bb) The Executive (Governor's) Council is made up of eight people elected by geographical area and presided over by the lieutenant governor.
(cc) There is no retention process. Judges serve during good behavior to age 70.

SELECTION AND RETENTION OF TRIAL COURT JUDGES — Continued

(dd) Gubernatorial appointment occurs in 40 partisan circuits; gubernatorial appointment from Judicial Nominating Commission takes place in five non-partisan circuits.

(ee) Partisan elections occur in 40 circuits; gubernatorial appointment from the Judicial Nominating Commission with a non-partisan election takes place in five circuits.

(ff) Partisan elections take place in 40 circuits; retention elections occur in five metropolitan circuits.

(gg) Associate circuit judges are selected on a county basis.

(hh) Selection occurs through Chief Justice appointment from Judicial Nominating Commission.

(ii) Other judges are designated by the District Court judges.

(jj) There is no retention process. Judges serve during good behavior to age 70.

(kk) In multi-municipality, joint, or countywide municipal courts, selection is by gubernatorial appointment with consent of the senate.

(ll) Mayoral appointment occurs in New York City.

(mm) The appointment is made by the County Chief Executive Officer with confirmation by District Board of Supervisors.

(nn) Housing judges are appointed by the Chief Administrator of the courts.

(oo) Party affiliation is not included on the ballot in the general election, but candidates are chosen through partisan primary nominations.

(pp) This applies to district and associate judges; special judges are selected by the district judges.

(qq) The geographic basis for selection is the municipality for those judges that are elected. Judges that are either appointed or are under contract may be from other cities.

(rr) There is no retention process. Judges serve during good behavior for a life tenure.

(ss) The governor may appoint a candidate if the unexpired term is less than one year.

(tt) In addition to Circuit Court judges, the Circuit Court has masters-in-equity whose jurisdiction is in matters referred to them in the Circuit Court. Masters-in-equity are selected by gubernatorial appointment from the Judicial Merit Selection Commission, retained by gubernatorial appointment with the consent of the senate, and the geographic basis for selection is the state.

(uu) Each county legislative body has the discretion to require elections to be non-partisan.

(vv) The selection method used to fill an unexpired term is established by a special legislative act.

(ww) There are no expired terms; each new judge begins a new term.

(xx) Appointment is by the local government executive with confirmation by the local government legislative body (may be either county or municipal government).

(yy) County judges are retained by retention election; municipal judges are reappointed by the city executive.

(zz) Superior and District Court judges serve as Family Court judges.

(aaa) Circuit Court judges appoint.

(bbb) Full-time municipal judges must stand for non-partisan election.

(ccc) A permanent vacancy in the office of municipal judge may be filled by temporary appointment of the municipal governing body or jointly by the governing bodies of all municipalities served by the judge.

(ddd) The Judicial Nomination Commission nominates for Presidential appointment and Senate confirmation. Not less than six months prior to the expiration of the term of office, the judge's performance is reviewed by the Commission on Judicial Disabilities and Tenure. A judge found "well qualified" is automatically reappointed for a new term of 15 years; a judge found "qualified" may be renominated by the President (and subject to Senate confirmation). A judge found "unqualified" is ineligible for reappointment or if the President does not wish to reappoint a judge, the Nomination Commission compiles a new list of candidates.

(eee) The geographic basis for selection is the District of Columbia.

Table 5.8
JUDICIAL DISCIPLINE: INVESTIGATING AND ADJUDICATING BODIES

State of other jurisdiction	Investigating body	Adjudicating body	Appeals from adjudication are filed with:	Final disciplining body	Point at which reprimands are made public
Alabama	Judicial Inquiry Committee	Court of the Judiciary	Supreme Court	Court of the Judiciary	Filing of the complaint with the Court of the Judiciary
Alaska	Committee on Judicial Conduct	Supreme Court	N.A.	Supreme Court	Filing of recommendation with Supreme Court
Arizona	Commission on Judicial Conduct	Commission on Judicial Conduct	Discretionary with Supreme Court	Supreme Court	Commission on Judicial Conduct determines if there is probable cause to bring formal charges.
Arkansas	Judicial Discipline and Disability Committees	Commission	Supreme Court	Supreme Court	At disposition of case
California	Commission on Judicial Performance	Commission on Judicial Performance	Supreme Court has discretionary review	Commission on Judicial Performance	Upon commission determination (a)
Colorado	Committee on Judicial Discipline	Commission on Judicial Discipline	No appeal	Supreme Court	Adjudication
Connecticut	Judicial Review Council	Judicial Review Council; Supreme Court	Supreme Court	Supreme Court	Public censure is issued at between 10 and 30 days after notice to the judge, provided that if the judge appeals, there is an automatic stay of disclosure.
	Council on Probate Judicial Conduct	Council on Probate Judicial Conduct	Supreme Court	Supreme Court	
Delaware	Preliminary Committee of the Court on the Judiciary Investigatory Committee of the Court on the Judiciary	Court on the Judiciary	No appeal	Court on the Judiciary	Upon issuance of opinion and imposition of sanction
Florida	Judicial Qualifications Commission	Judicial Qualifications Commission (b)	No appeal	Supreme Court (c)	Filing of formal charges by Committee with Supreme Court Clerk
Georgia	Judicial Qualifications Commission	Supreme Court	No appeal	Supreme Court	Formal Hearing
Hawaii	Commission on Judicial Conduct	Commission on Judicial Conduct	No appeal	Supreme Court	Imposition of public discipline by Supreme Court
Idaho	Judicial Council	Supreme Court	Supreme Court	Supreme Court	Filing with Supreme Court
Illinois	Judicial Inquiry Board	Courts Commission	No appeal	Courts Commission	Filing of complaint by Judicial Inquiry Board to Courts Commission
Indiana	Judicial Qualifications Committee	Supreme Court	N.A.	Supreme Court	Institution of Formal Proceedings
Iowa	Judicial Qualifications Commission	Judicial Qualifications Commission	Supreme Court	Supreme Court	Application by the commission to the Supreme Court
Kansas	Commission on Judicial Qualifications Qualifications		Supreme Court	Supreme Court	Supreme Court Reprimand is published by Supreme Court if approved by Supreme Court.
Kentucky	Judicial Conduct Committee	Judicial Conduct Committee	Supreme Court	Judicial Conduct Committee	Application of judge under investigation
Louisiana	Judiciary Commission	Supreme Court	No appeal	Supreme Court	Filing of formal complaint by commission with Supreme Court
Maine	Committee on Judicial Responsibility and Disability	Supreme Judicial Court	No appeal	Supreme Judicial Court	Filing of report to Supreme Judicial Court
Maryland	Commission on Judicial Disabilities	Court of Appeals	N.A.	Court of Appeals	Filing of record by Committee to Court of Appeals
Massachusetts	Commission on Judicial Conduct	Supreme Judicial Court	N.A.	Supreme Judicial Court	After final of formal charges with the Supreme Judicial Court
Michigan	Judicial Tenure Commission	Supreme Court	Supreme Court	Supreme Court	Filing of formal complaint by commission with Supreme Court

See footnotes at end of table.

JUDICIAL DISCIPLINE: INVESTIGATING AND ADJUDICATING BODIES — Continued

State or other jurisdiction	Investigating body	Adjudicating body	Appeals from adjudication are filed with:	Final disciplining body	Point at which reprimands are made public
Minnesota	Board of Judicial Standards	Supreme Court	No appeal	Supreme Court	Filing of formal charges by Committee with Supreme Court
Mississippi	Commission on Judicial Performance	Supreme Court	N.A.	Supreme Court	Recommendation of Commission to Supreme Court
Missouri	Commission on Retirement, Removal and Discipline	Commission on Retirement, Removal and Discipline	Supreme Court	Supreme Court	Filing of recommendation by Committee to Supreme Court
Montana	Judicial Standards Commission	Supreme Court	No appeal	Supreme Court	Filing of record by Committee with Supreme Court
Nebraska	Commission on Judicial Qualifications	Supreme Court	No appeal	Supreme Court	Commission may issue a public reprimand
Nevada	Commission on Judicial Discipline	Commission on Judicial Discipline	Supreme Court	Commission on Judicial Discipline	Upon filing of report by Committee and service upon judge
New Hampshire	Supreme Court Committee on Judicial Conduct	Supreme Court	Supreme Court	On issuance of reprimand (d)	Filing of formal complaint
New Jersey	Advisory Committee on Judicial Conduct	Supreme Court	N.A.	Supreme Court	Filing of record by Commission with Supreme Court
New Mexico	Judicial Standards Commission	Supreme Court	N.A.	Supreme Court	Completion of service of record on respondent
New York	Commission on Judicial Conduct	Commission on Judicial Conduct	Court of Appeals	Commission on Judicial Conduct and Court of Appeals	Upon recommendation of Commission to Supreme Court
North Carolina	Judicial Standards Commission	Supreme Court	No appeals	Supreme Court	At formal hearing
North Dakota	Commission on Judicial Conduct	Supreme Court	N.A.	Supreme Court	Adjudication
Ohio	Board of Commissioners on Grievance and Discipline (e)	Board of Commissioners on Grievance and Discipline	Supreme Court	Supreme Court	Filing with clerk of the Appellate Court
Oklahoma	Court on the Judiciary Trial Division; Council on Judicial Complaints	Court on the Judiciary Trial Division; Council on Judicial Complaints	Court on the Judiciary Division; no appeal from Council on Judicial Complaints	Court on the Judiciary Appellate Division	
Oregon	Commission on Judicial Fitness and Disability (f)	Supreme Court	No appeal	Supreme Court	(g)
Pennsylvania	Judicial Conduct Board	Court of Judicial Discipline	Supreme Court	Supreme Court	Once a final decision has been made
Rhode Island	Commission on Judicial Tenure and Discipline	Supreme Court	No appeals	Supreme Court	When Supreme Court affirms a recommendation for reprimand or removal
South Carolina	Commissioners on Judicial Conduct	Supreme Court	N.A.	Supreme Court	Adjudication
South Dakota	Judicial Qualifications Commission	Supreme Court	No appeals	Supreme Court	Filing with the Supreme Court
Tennessee	Court of the Judiciary	Court of the Judiciary	Supreme Court, then Gen. Assembly	Supreme Court or Gen. Assembly	Filing of complaint in Appellate Court Clerk's office

See footnotes at end of table.

JUDICIAL DISCIPLINE: INVESTIGATING AND ADJUDICATING BODIES — Continued

State or other jurisdiction	Investigating body	Adjudicating body	Appeals from adjudication are filed with:	Final disciplining body	Point at which reprimands are made public
Texas	State Commission on Judicial Conduct	Supreme Court, Commission on Judicial Conduct, or review tribunal consisting of Justices of Courts of Appeals	Supreme Court	Supreme Court, Commission on Judicial Conduct, or review tribunal consisting of Justices of Courts of Appeals	Convening of formal hearing by the Commission on Judicial Conduct
Utah	Judicial Conduct Commission	Judicial Conduct Commission	Supreme Court	Supreme Court	10 days after filing appeal
Vermont	Judicial Conduct Board	Supreme Court	Supreme Court	Supreme Court	Filing of formal charges by Board with Supreme Court
Virginia	Judicial Inquiry and Review Commission	Supreme Court	Supreme Court	Supreme Court	Filing of formal complaint by Committee with Supreme Court
Washington	Commission on Judicial Conduct	Supreme Court	No appeal	Committee on Judicial Conduct or Supreme Court	Beginning of fact finding hearing by Committee
West Virginia	Judicial Investigation Committee and Judicial Hearing Board	Judicial Hearing Board (JHB)	JHB recommends to SCA (i)	Supreme Court of Appeals (h)	Upon decision by Supreme Court of Appeals
Wisconsin	Judicial Commission	Supreme Court (i)	No appeal	Supreme Court	Filing of petitioner formal complaint by Judicial Commission w/Supreme Court
Wyoming	Commission on Judicial Conduct and Ethics	Supreme Court	N.A.	Supreme Court	Filing with Supreme Court
Dist. of Columbia	Commission on Judicial Disabilities and Tenure	Commission on Judicial Disabilities and Tenure	Federal judge panel: 3 appointments by Chief Justice of Supreme Court	Commission on Judicial. Disabilities and Tenure	Filing of order with D.C. Court of Appeals (j)
Puerto Rico	Disciplinary and Removal from office for health reasons	Supreme Court	N.A.	Supreme Court	Filing of formal complaint to the Discipline Commission

Source: Bureau of Justice Statistics, *State Court Organization, 2004* NCJ 212351, August 15, 2006.

Key:
N.A. — Not applicable

(a) In cases involving more serious misconduct, the commission may issue a public admonishment or public censure. The nature and impact of the misconduct generally determine the level of discipline. Both public admonishments and public censures are notices sent to the judge describing the improper conduct and stating the findings made by the commission. These notices are also made available to the press and the general public.

(b) The Judicial Qualifications Commission investigates and makes recommendations to the Supreme Court for discipline or removal.

(c) The Supreme Court power of removal is alternative and cumulative to the power of impeachment and suspension by the Governor and Senate.

(d) The Supreme Court Committee on Judicial Conduct may admonish, reprimand or order conditions, and the Supreme Court may impose formal discipline.

(e) Initial review is carried out by a panel of three commissioners.

(f) Technically, the Commission of Judicial Fitness and Disability does not adjudicate disciplinary matters. It hears the evidence and makes recommendations to the Supreme Court, which must review the records, or any stipulation for discipline and can hear additional evidence. Technically, then, there is no appeal. The Supreme Court orders any discipline, including any stipulated sanction.

(g) In Oregon, the allegations become public when the Commission issues a notice of public hearing, generally 14 days in advance of the hearing (although it can be less in the public interest). The actual complaint is not made public then, but the notice includes the general nature of the allegations. In a disciplinary case (but not a disability case), the Commission hearing, the evidence received there, and the Commission's decisions and recommendations are public. The Supreme Court decision is public when the Court files its opinion. There is no reprimand or other sanction until the Supreme Court decision.

(h) The final disciplining body is the same for both the Commission and Judicial Hearing Board.

(i) The Judicial Conduct and Disability Panel, through an ad hoc three-judge panel (two must be Court of Appeals judges, one can be a retired, reserve judge or Court of Appeals judge appointed as a hearing examiner) makes a report to the Supreme Court.

(j) This only applies in cases of removal or involuntary retirement wherein the Chief Justice appoints a three-member federal judge panel to review commission's order of removal.

Chapter Six

ELECTIONS

"*Despite dire predictions that there would be major failures in 2006, state and local jurisdictions made the process come together exceedingly well.*"

—R. Doug Lewis

"*Propositions again were a prominent feature on ballots in 2006, with voters in 37 states deciding on 226 statewide measures.*"

—John G. Matsusaka

2006 Elections: Successful Implementation and Continuing Issues

By R. Doug Lewis

Despite dire predictions that there would be major failures in 2006, state and local jurisdictions made the process come together exceedingly well. Ordinarily when a major change is ordered by Congress or a state legislature, it takes three decent-size elections to make the policy and procedure adjustments necessary to make the process work smoothly. Massive changes in virtually every part of the process were accomplished in this election cycle.

Election 2006 will likely be considered a defining moment in American election history. It was a year when all new federal mandates contained in the Help America Vote Act of 2002 (HAVA) came due. Any single mandate would have been a major accomplishment in previous elections, but 2006 brought many changes, including:

- the full implementation of statewide voter databases;

- final deadlines for new voting equipment—disability mandates requiring that voting equipment had to allow blind and visually impaired voters to be able to vote secretly and independently;

- state definitions on what constitutes a vote for that state;

- new identification requirements for first-time voters; and

- provisional ballots in use for the second federal election.

This was accomplished in the face of continued allegations by some groups, organizations and news outlets that the election process was fatally flawed, that voting equipment could not be trusted, and that election officials needed to be closely monitored. The aftermath of the presidential election of 2000 sowed the seeds of distrust, and partisan political strategists used the elements of distrust to provide almost constant attacks during the intervening years.

Despite dire predictions that there would be major failures in 2006, state and local jurisdictions made the process come together exceedingly well. Ordinarily when a major change is ordered by Congress or a state legislature, it takes three decent-size elections to make the policy and procedure adjustments necessary to make the process work smoothly. Massive changes in virtually every part of the process were accomplished in this election cycle.

Faith Restored: Despite pockets of problems in a limited number of locations, state and local election jurisdictions were so successful that voters' confidence in the process returned to numbers seen prior to Election 2000. CNN (Cable News Network) conducted exit polls of voters during the 2006 election and asked: "How confident are you that your vote will be counted accurately...?" Voters responded with a whopping 88 percent very confident to only 11 percent who were not confident.

Perhaps as remarkable, state governments' significantly increased role in managing the election process was also tested. Prior to HAVA, election administration was almost the exclusive province of local jurisdictions. State governments had to learn to adapt to the increased federal requirements for more state oversight and more direct involvement and responsibility for administrative outcomes.

To say that Election 2006 was the most stressful election in generations would be an understatement. So many major changes had been instituted in such a short time that it is astonishing there were not more major problems. Primary elections during 2006 did indeed indicate some training issues and procedures adjustments were necessary. Jurisdictions large and small had some transitional difficulties. But 98 percent of the jurisdictions seemed to find the right elements to make the general election of 2006 successful for the voters and candidates.

Issues for States to Address

It is easy to let success in one election cycle lead to the false assumption that all is well for the foreseeable future, and prudent states will need to plan for additional requirements or face possible election problems in the near future.

States have to recognize that $3 billion was infused into elections all over the United States. In some instances states will be able to utilize the federal funds pumped into the process through HAVA for many more years with revolving accounts. In other states the funding from HAVA will expire soon because costs exceeded the funds allocated. No matter which situation exists in individual states, the mandates created by HAVA are leaving local jurisdictions with significantly increased costs for election administration. Unless states act to shore up funding and support services from the state level, local jurisdictions will be left with ongoing costs that greatly exceed pre-HAVA requirements.

Equipment: For instance, the necessity of having either optical scan or direct recording equipment (DRE or electronic voting) to replace punch cards or lever machines or hand-voted, hand-counted paper ballots adds extensive continuing costs to jurisdictions; these costs did not exist prior to HAVA. Lever machines and punch card voting devices were low-maintenance items. Neither of those types of voting equipment required special storage facilities, but DREs and, to a lesser degree, Optical Scan devices necessitate special storage facilities that are environmentally controlled and free from pests including insects and rodents. DREs need facilities where they can remain attached to electrical outlets so the batteries don't have to be replaced constantly. Both DREs and OpScan units have considerably higher day-to-day maintenance costs than previous voting methods.

Security Issues: Add to this the concerns about voting system security and the facilities in the overwhelming number of jurisdictions could never pass even simple security requirements of controlled access to voting equipment, voting software and ballots. States will need to consider legislation to set requirements for voting equipment security facilities and ballot security facilities. Some of this will require funds but much of it is changing behaviors and developing policies and procedures that focus on security.

Provisional Ballots: The HAVA requirement to offer provisional ballots to voters who are not on the voting registration rolls where they believe they should be means those ballots have to be investigated individually. On average, jurisdictions will invest almost one hour (and often more) to each provisional ballot to ensure the ballots of qualified voters are counted. This is a significant personnel cost for local jurisdictions.

Paper Trail: Since 28 states have also implemented requirements for a paper trail with DREs, states have to make sure they don't impose an unfunded mandate on local governments. Paper trail costs also add significantly to overall operating and maintenance costs. The impact of those costs on local funding cannot be ignored. It appears at this writing the U.S. Congress is likely to pass additional federal legisla-

tion that will require paper trails with any electronic voting equipment. If so, despite the indications that Congress may fund the initial year of increased costs, state and local jurisdictions will have to absorb the long-term costs.

If states opt out of DREs and choose OpScan, significant ballot printing costs drive up the cost of elections each and every election cycle. Since printing for OpScan is an exacting and mission-critical function that cannot be done by the local print shop, local jurisdictions are faced with significantly increased costs over the days of punch card units or lever machines. While OpScan is not more expensive than DREs in the early years, it is certainly more expensive than previous forms of voting.

Funding Source and Problems: The easy solution is to ask Congress to take on a continued funding role for elections in America. Like a lot of easy solutions, it will come with momentous effect—if the federal government is to continuously fund elections it will also want to place conditions and strings on the money.

States' Dilemma: If states ignore or delay assisting local jurisdictions with the ongoing high costs of compliance with HAVA mandates, a groundswell for federal funding develops. If federal funding becomes commonplace, states begin to lose the ability to set their own rules and conditions for the conduct of elections, and local jurisdictions begin reporting to and are responsible to the federal government rather than the state government.

Services Needed from State Level

Technology: Clearly, increased technology use requires technological support. Unfortunately only about 20 to 30 percent of election jurisdictions in the United States have the funding or the skilled employees who can provide technical support during both the election cycle and maintenance periods. States must strongly consider developing technical support services within the offices of the state's chief election official to train and support local personnel. This will need to include programming of units, ballot setup and ballot layout, routine maintenance, and assisting with election day technical problems. States that have done some work in this area include Oklahoma, Alaska, Rhode Island and Georgia, among others.

The nature of the election process has changed dramatically within the last five years, but the states' response to the ongoing needs is significantly lagging.

Training: State mandates for election administrator training (not polling place officials), both within the state and nationally, need to be considered. Without a state mandate for training, many local jurisdictions will never make the funds available for their local election administration staff to travel either within the state or to national certification programs. Noteworthy training is available now through a variety of organizations aimed at either state-level employees or local jurisdictions. Because of the stresses of election administration since Election 2000, up to 50 percent of the election officials in several states have retired or sought employment elsewhere. That means training is more necessary than ever before. States like Washington, North Carolina and Ohio (and others) have their own certification programs for election administrators. Many other states offer state training but have difficulty in getting local governments to send people. Others—like California, Virginia and Delaware—contract with The Election Center for state certification of local election officials. Professional education which leads to the national status of Certified Election/Registration Administrator (CERA) has helped more jurisdictions become better managed elections offices. States need to assure that their election officials have certification training and that they must have continuing education. Every state requires lawyers, doctors and accountants, among others, to receive and maintain certification in order to practice within the state. Should elections be less important?

Money is not the only solution to improved elections. Much can be done through training, policies and procedures. Legislatures and governors are all too often faced with too many needs chasing too few dollars to fund all the desired services. States that ignore the increased funding realities of modern elections risk losing responsibility for—and authority over—elections in their own states. The appropriate response for state and local governments is to assure they maintain autonomy over the elections process. If they become unwilling to do so, it is clear the federal government is likely to become that resource—and that authority.

About the Author

R. Doug Lewis, CERA (Certified Election/Registration Administrator), is executive director of The Election Center, a nonpartisan, nonprofit organization representing the nation's election officials. He has been called upon by Congress, the federal agencies, state legislatures, and national and worldwide news media for solutions to voting issues.

Table 6.1
STATE EXECUTIVE BRANCH OFFICIALS TO BE ELECTED: 2007–2011

State or other jurisdiction	2007	2008	2009	2010	2011
Alabama	…	…	…	G,LG,AG,AR,A,SS,T (a)	…
Alaska	…	…	…	G,LG	…
Arizona	…	…	…	G,AG,SS,SP,T (b)	…
Arkansas	…	…	…	G,LG,AG,A,SS,T (d)	…
California	…	…	…	G,LG,AG,SS,SP,T,C (c)	…
Colorado	…	…	…	G,LG,AG,SS,T	…
Connecticut	…	…	…	G,LG,AG,C,SS,T	…
Delaware	…	G,LG,CI	…	AG,A,T	…
Florida	…	…	…	G,LG,AG,AR,CFO	…
Georgia	…	…	…	G,LG,AG,AR,C,SS,SP (e)	…
Hawaii	…	…	…	G,LG	…
Idaho	…	…	…	G,LG,AG,C,SS,SP,T	…
Illinois	…	…	…	G,LG,AG,C,SS,T	…
Indiana	…	G,LG,AG,SP	…	A,SS,T	…
Iowa	…	…	…	G,LG,AG,AR,A,SS,T	…
Kansas	G,LG,AG,AR,A,SS,T	…	…	G,LG,AG,SS,T (f)	…
Kentucky	G,LG,AG,AR,SS,T,CI	…	…	…	G,LG,AG,AR,A,SS,T
Louisiana	…	…	…	…	G,LG,AG,AR,SS,T,CI
Maine (g)	…	…	…	G	…
Maryland	…	…	…	G,LG,AG,C	…
Massachusetts	…	…	…	G,LG,AG,A,SS,T	…
Michigan	…	(h)	…	G,LG,AG,SS (h)	…
Minnesota	…	…	…	G,LG,AG,A,SS	…
Mississippi	G,LG,AG,AR,A,SS,T,CI	…	…	…	G,LG,AG,AR,A,SS,T,CI
Missouri	…	G,LG,AG,SS,T	…	A	…
Montana	…	G,LG,AG,A,SS,SP	…	G,LG,AG,A,SS,T	…
Nebraska	…	…	…	G,LG,AG,A,SS,T	…
Nevada	…	…	…	G,LG,AG,SS,T,C	…
New Hampshire	…	G	…	G	…
New Jersey	…	…	G,LG	…	…
New Mexico	…	…	…	G,LG,AG,A,SS,T (i)	…
New York	…	…	…	G,LG,AG,C	…
North Carolina	…	G,LG,AG,AR,A,SS,SP,T (j)	…	…	…
North Dakota	…	G,LG,A,T,SP,CI (k)	…	SS,AG,AR (k) (l)	…
Ohio	…	…	…	G,LG,AG,A,SS,T	…
Oklahoma	…	(m)	…	G,LG,AG,A,SP,T (m)	…
Oregon	…	AG,SS,T,SP	…	G (n)	…
Pennsylvania	…	AG,A,T	…	G,LG	…
Rhode Island	…	…	…	G,LG,AG,SS,T	…
South Carolina	…	…	…	G,LG,AG,AR,C,SS,SP,T (o)	…

See footnotes at end of table.

STATE EXECUTIVE BRANCH OFFICIALS TO BE ELECTED: 2007–2011 — Continued

State or other jurisdiction	2007	2008	2009	2010	2011
South Dakota	...	(p)	...	G,LG,AG,A,SS,T (p)	...
Tennessee	...	...	...	G	...
Texas	...	(q)	...	G,LG,AG,AR,C (q)	...
Utah	...	G,LG,AG,A,T	...	...	...
Vermont	...	G,LG,AG,A,SS,T	...	G,LG,AG,A,SS,T	...
Virginia	...	...	G,LG,AG	...	...
Washington	...	G,LG,AG,A,SS,SPT (r)	...	...	...
West Virginia	...	G,AG,AR,A,SS,T	SP	...	...
Wisconsin	...	...	...	G,LG,AG,SS,T	...
Wyoming	...	...	...	G,A,SS,SPT	...
American Samoa	...	G,LG	...	G,LG,A,AG	...
Guam	...	...	G,LG	...	...
No. Mariana Islands	...	...	...	...	...
Puerto Rico	...	G (s)	...	...	...
U.S. Virgin Islands	...	...	...	G,LG	...
Totals for year:					
Governor	3	13	3	38	3
Lieutenant Governor	3	10	3	32	3
Attorney General	3	10	1	30	3
Agriculture	3	2	0	7	2
Auditor	2	8	0	16	0
Chief Financial Officer	0	0	0	1	0
Comptroller	0	0	0	9	0
Commissioner of Insurance	2	2	0	0	2
Secretary of State	3	7	0	26	3
Superintendent of Public Instruction (t)	0	6	1	7	0
Treasurer	3	9	0	24	3

Sources: The Council of State Governments' survey, January 2007 and state election administration offices and Web sites, January 2007.

Note: This table shows the executive branch officials up for election in a given year. Footnotes indicate other offices (e.g., commissioners of labor, insurance, public service, etc.) also up for election in a given year. The data contained in this table reflect information available at press time.

Key:
... — No regularly scheduled elections
G — Governor
LG — Lieutenant Governor
AG — Attorney General
AR — Agriculture
A — Auditor
C — Comptroller/Controller
CFO — Chief Financial Officer
CI — Commissioner of Insurance
SS — Secretary of State
SP — Superintendent of Public Instruction (t)
T — Treasurer

(a) Commissioner of Agriculture and Industries, 2010.
(b) Corporation commissioners (5)–4-year terms, 2008–2012–3 seats, 2010–2 seats. State Mine Inspector–4-year term, 2010 election.
(c) Insurance Commissioner and Board of Equalization.
(d) Commissioner of State Lands.
(e) Commissioner of Labor–4-year term, 2010 and 2014.
(f) Commissioner of Insurance.
(g) In Maine the legislature elects constitutional officers (AG,SS,T) in even-numbered years for 2-year terms; the auditor was elected by the legislature in 2004 and will serve a 4-year term.

(h) Michigan State University trustees (8)–8-year terms, 2008–2, 2010–2, 2012–2, 2014–2; University of Michigan regents (8)–8-year terms, 2008–2, 2010–2, 2012–2, 2014–2; Wayne State University governors (8)–8-year terms, 2008–2, 2010–2, 2012–2, 2014–2; State Board of Education (8)–8-year terms, 2008–2, 2010–2, 2012–2, 2014–2.
(i) Commissioner of Public Lands–4-year term, 2010.
(j) Commissioner of Labor; Commissioner of Insurance are elected in 2008.
(k) There are three Public Service Commissioners. One is up for election every two years. (3)–6-year terms, 2008–1, 2010–1, 2012–1.
(l) Tax Commissioner.
(m) Corporation Commissioners (3)–6-year terms, 2008–1, 2010–1, 2012–1; Commissioner of Insurance–4-year term, 2010; Commissioner of Labor–4-year term, 2010.
(n) Commissioner of the Bureau of Labor and Industries.
(o) Adjutant General–4-year term.
(p) Commissioner of School and Public Lands, 2008; Public Utility Commissioners (3)–6-year terms, 2008–1, 2010–1, 2012–1.
(q) Commissioner of General Land Office–4-year term, 2010; Railroad Commissioners (3)–6-year terms, 2008–1, 2010–1, 2012–1.
(r) Commissioner of Public Lands, 2008 and Insurance Commissioner, 2008.
(s) Resident Commissioner to the House of Representatives, 2008.
(t) Superintendent of Public Instruction or Commissioner of Education.

Table 6.2
STATE LEGISLATURE MEMBERS TO BE ELECTED: 2007–2011

State or other jurisdiction	Total legislators		2007		2008		2009		2010		2011	
	Senate	House/Assembly	Senate	House/Assembly	Senate	House/Assembly	Senate	House/Assembly	Senate	House/Assembly	Senate	House/Assembly
Alabama	35	105							35	105		
Alaska	20	40			10	40			10	40		
Arizona	30	60			30	60			30	60		
Arkansas	35	100			18	100			17	100		
California	40	80			20	80			20	80		
Colorado	35	65			17	65			18	65		
Connecticut	36	151			36	151			36	151		
Delaware	21	41			11	41						
Florida	40	120			20	120			20	120		
Georgia	56	180			56	180			56	180		
Hawaii	25	51		2	12	51			13	51		
Idaho	35	70			35	70			35	70		
Illinois	59 (a)	118	39		39	118			20	118		
Indiana	50	100			25	100			25	100		
Iowa	50	100			25 (b)	100			25 (c)	100		
Kansas	40	125			40	125						
Kentucky	38	100			19	100			19	100		
Louisiana	39	105	39	105							39	105
Maine	35	151			35	151			35	151		
Maryland	47	141							47	141		
Massachusetts	40	160			40	160			40	160		
Michigan	38	110				110			38	110		
Minnesota	67	134				134			67	134		
Mississippi	52	122	52	122							52	122
Missouri	34	163			17	163			17	163		
Montana	50	100			25	100			25	100		
Nebraska	49	U			25	U			24	U		
Nevada	21	42			10	42			11	42		
New Hampshire	24	400			24	400			24	400		
New Jersey	40	80	40	80				80			40	80
New Mexico	42	70			42	70				70		
New York	62	150			62	150			62	150		
North Carolina	50	120			50	120			50	120		
North Dakota	47	94			23 (b)	46			24 (c)	48		
Ohio	33	99			16	99			17	99		
Oklahoma	48	101			24	101			24	101		
Oregon	30	60			15	60			15	60		
Pennsylvania	50	203			25 (c)	203			25 (b)	203		
Rhode Island	38	75			38	75			38	75		
South Carolina	46	124			46	124				124		

See footnotes at end of table.

STATE LEGISLATURE MEMBERS TO BE ELECTED: 2007–2011 — Continued

State or other jurisdiction	Total legislators		2007		2008		2009		2010		2011	
	Senate	House/Assembly	Senate	House/Assembly	Senate	House/Assembly	Senate	House/Assembly	Senate	House/Assembly	Senate	House/Assembly
South Dakota.............	35	70	...	...	35	70	...	...	35	70	...	...
Tennessee.................	33	99	...	...	16	99	...	...	17	99	...	...
Texas	31	150	...	...	15	150	...	...	16	150	...	...
Utah	29	75	...	...	14	75	...	...	15	75	...	...
Vermont...................	30	150	...	...	30	150	...	...	30	150	...	...
Virginia....................	40	100	40	100	...	...	...	100	...	...	40	100
Washington (f)...........	49	98	...	...	25	98	...	...	24	98	...	...
West Virginia............	34	100	...	...	17	100	...	...	17	100	...	...
Wisconsin.................	33	99	...	...	16	99	...	...	17	99	...	...
Wyoming..................	30	60	...	...	15	60	...	...	15	60	...	...
American Samoa.........	18	20	...	...	(d)	20	...	18	(e)	20	...	...
No. Mariana Islands	9	18	3	18	...	...	6	18	...	...	3	18
Puerto Rico (e)	28	51	...	...	28	51	...	...	...	...	...	...
U.S. Virgin Islands......	15	U	...	...	15	U	...	...	15	U	...	...
State Totals...............	1,971	5,411	171	409	1,113	4,710	0	180	1,148	4,792	171	407
Totals......................	2,041	5,500	174	427	1,156	4,781	6	198	1,163	4,812	174	425

Source: The Council of State Governments' survey, January 2007.

Note: This table shows the number of legislative seats up for election in a given year. As a result of redistricting, states may adjust some elections. The data contained in this table reflect information available at press time. See the Chapter 3 table entitled, "The Legislators: Numbers, Terms, and Party Affiliations," for specific information on legislative terms.

Key:

. . . — No regularly scheduled elections

U — Unicameral legislature

(a) The Illinois Senate operates on a ten-year election cycle. All 59 senators are elected in each year ending in "2" (following the redistricting based upon the decennial census). Senate districts are then divided into three

groups. One group of senators is elected for terms of four years, four years and two years; two years, four years and four years; four years, two years and four years.

(b) Even-numbered senate districts.

(c) Odd-numbered senate districts.

(d) In American Samoa, senators are not elected by popular vote. They are selected by county councils of chiefs.

(e) If in the general election more than two-thirds of the members of either house are elected from one party or from a single ticket, as both are defined by law, the numbers shall be increased in accordance with Article III Section 7 of the Puerto Rico Constitution.

(f) There may be some races in the odd years if appointments are made to fill vacancies.

Table 6.3
METHODS OF NOMINATING CANDIDATES FOR STATE OFFICES

State or other jurisdiction	Methods of nominating candidates
Alabama	Primary election; however, the state executive committee or other governing body of any political party may choose instead to hold a state convention for the purpose of nominating candidates. Submitting a petition to run as an independent or third-party candidate or an independent nominating procedure.
Alaska	Primary election. Petition for no-party candidates.
Arizona	Candidates who are members of a recognized party are nominated by an open primary election. Candidates who are not members of a recognized political party may file petitions to appear on the general election ballot. A write-in option is also available.
Arkansas	Primary election, convention and petition.
California	Primary election or independent nomination procedure.
Colorado	Primary election, convention or by petition.
Connecticut	Convention/primary election. Major political parties hold state conventions (convening not earlier than the 68th day and closing not later than the 50th day before the date of the primary) for the purpose of endorsing candidates. If no one challenges the endorsed candidate, no primary election is held. However, if anyone (who received at least 15 percent of the delegate vote on any roll call at the convention) challenges the endorsed candidate, a primary election is held to determine the party nominee for the general election.
Delaware	Primary election for Democrats and primary election and convention for Republicans.
Florida	Primary election. Minor parties may nominate their candidate in any manner they deem proper.
Georgia	Primary election.
Hawaii	Primary election.
Idaho	Primary election and convention. New political parties hold a convention nominating candidates to be placed on a general election ballot.
Illinois	Primary election. The primary election nominates established party candidates. New political parties and independent candidates go directly to the general election file based on a petition process.
Indiana	Primary election, convention and petition. The governor is chosen by a primary. All other state officers are chosen at a state convention, unless the candidate is an independent. Any party that obtains between 2 percent and 8 percent of the vote for secretary of state may hold a convention to select a candidate.
Iowa	Primary election, convention and petition.
Kansas	Candidates for the two major parties are nominated by primary election. Candidates for minor parties are nominated for the general election at state party conventions. Independent candidates are nominated for the general election by petition.
Kentucky	Primary election. A slate of candidates for governor and lieutenant governor that receives the highest number of its party's votes but which number is less than 40 percent of the votes cast for all slates of candidates of that party, shall be required to participate in a runoff primary with the slate of candidates of the same party receiving the second highest number of votes.
Louisiana	Candidates may qualify for any office they wish, regardless of party affiliation, by completing the qualifying document and paying the appropriate qualifying fee; or a candidate may file a nominating petition.
Maine	Primary election or non-party petition.
Maryland	Primary election, convention and petition. Unaffiliated candidates or candidates affiliated with non-recognized political parties may run for elective office by collecting the requisite number of signatures on a petition. The required number equals 1 percent of the number of registered voters eligible to vote for office. Only recognized non-principal political parties may nominate their candidates by a convention in accordance with their bylaws (at this time, Maryland has four non-principal parties: Libertarian, Green, Constitution and Populist).
Massachusetts	Primary election.
Michigan	Governor, State House, State Senate use primary election. Lieutenant Governor runs as the running mate to gubernatorial candidate, not separately, and is selected through the convention process. Secretary of State and Attorney General candidates are chosen at convention. Nominees for State Board of Education, University of Michigan Regents, Michigan State University Trustees and Wayne State University Governors are nominated by convention. Minor parties nominate candidates to all partisan offices by convention.
Minnesota	Primary election. Candidates for minor parties or independent candidates are by petition. They must have the signatures of 2,000 people who will be eligible to vote in the next general election.
Mississippi	Primary election, petition (for independent candidates), independent nominating procedures (for third-party candidates).
Missouri	Primary election.
Montana	Primary election and independent nominating procedure.
Nebraska	Primary election.
Nevada	Primary election. Independent candidates are nominated by petition for the general election. Minor parties nominated by petition or by party.
New Hampshire	Primary election. Minor parties by petition.
New Jersey	Primary election. Independent candidates are nominated by petition for the general election.

See footnotes at end of table.

METHODS OF NOMINATING CANDIDATES FOR STATE OFFICES — Continued

State or other jurisdiction	Methods of nominating candidates
New Mexico	Statewide candidates petition to go to convention and are nominated in a primary election. District and legislative candidates petition for primary ballot access.
New York	Primary election/petition.
North Carolina	Primary election. Newly recognized parties just granted access submit their first nominees by convention. All established parties use primaries.
North Dakota	Convention/primary election. Political parties hold state conventions for the purpose of endorsing candidates. Endorsed candidates are automatically placed on the primary election ballot, but other candidates may also petition their name on the ballot.
Ohio	Primary election, petition and by declaration of intent to be a write-in candidate.
Oklahoma	Primary election.
Oregon	Primary election. Minor parties hold conventions.
Pennsylvania	Primary election, and petition. Nomination petitions filed by major party candidates to access primary ballot. Nomination papers filed by minor party and independent candidates to access November ballot.
Rhode Island	Primary election.
South Carolina	Primary election for Republicans and Democrats; party conventions held for minor parties. Candidates can have name on ballot via petition.
South Dakota	Convention, petition and independent nominating procedure.
Tennessee	Primary election/petition.
Texas	Primary election/convention. Minor parties without ballot access nominate candidates for the general election after qualifying for ballot access by petition.
Utah	Convention, primary election and petition.
Vermont	Primary election. Major parties by primary, minor parties by convention, independents by petition.
Virginia	Primary election, convention and petition.
Washington	Primary election.
West Virginia	Primary election, convention, petition and independent nominating procedure.
Wisconsin	Primary election/petition. Candidates must file nomination papers (petitions) containing the minimum number of signatures required by law. Candidates appear on the primary ballot for the party they represent. The candidate receiving the most votes in each party primary goes on to the November election.
Wyoming	Primary election.
Dist. of Columbia	Primary election. Independent and minor party candidates file by nominating petition.
American Samoa	Individual files petition for candidacy with the chief election officer. Petition must be signed by statutorily mandated number of qualified voters.
No. Mariana Islands	Candidates are all nominated by petition. Candidates seeking the endorsement of recognized political parties must also include in their petition submission a document signed by the recognized political parties' chairperson/president and secretary attesting to such nomination. Recognized political parties may, or may not, depending on their bylaws and party rules, conduct primaries separate from any state election agency participation.
Puerto Rico	Primary election and convention.
U.S. Virgin Islands	Primary election.

Source: The Council of State Governments' survey of state election administration offices, January 2007.

Note: The nominating methods described here are for state offices; procedures may vary for local candidates. Also, independent candidates may have to petition for nomination.

Table 6.4
ELECTION DATES FOR NATIONAL, STATE AND LOCAL ELECTIONS
(Formulas and dates of state elections)

State or other jurisdiction	Type of primary	National (a) Primary	National (a) Runoff	National (a) General	State (b) Primary	State (b) Runoff	State (b) General	Local Primary	Local Runoff	Local General
Alabama	O	Feb., 1st T (c) / Feb. 5, 2008 (c)	...	Nov.,★ / Nov. 4, 2008	June, 1st T (even yrs) / None in 2007	June, Last T (even yrs) / None in 2007	Nov.,★(even yrs) / None in 2007	Varies	Varies	Varies
Alaska	C	Aug., 4th T (in even yrs) / Aug. 26, 2008	...	Nov.,★ / Nov. 4, 2008	Aug., 4th T (even yrs) / None in 2007	...	Nov.,★(even yrs) / None in 2007	...	30 days after certification TBD	Oct., 1st T / Oct. 2, 2007
Arizona	C	Feb., 1st T / Feb. 5, 2008	...	Nov.,★ / Nov. 4, 2008	8th T Prior (even yrs) / None in 2007	...	Nov.,★(even yrs) / None in 2007	Mar., 2nd T / Mar. 13, 2007	May, 3rd T / May 15, 2007	8 T prior to Nat. or Nat. / Sept. 11., Nov. 6, 2007
Arkansas	O	Feb., 1st T / Feb. 5, 2008	...	Nov.,★ / Nov. 4, 2008	T, 3 wks prior to runoff / None in 2007	June, 2nd T / None in 2007	Nov.,★(even yrs) / None in 2007	T, 3 wks prior to runoff / None in 2007	June, 2nd T / None in 2007	Nov.,★(even yrs) / None in 2007
California	C	Feb., 1st T / Feb. 5, 2008	...	Nov.,★ / Nov. 4, 2008	June,★ / None in 2007	...	Nov.,★(even yrs) / Nov. 4, 2008	...	...	Nov.,★(even yrs) / None in 2007
Colorado	C	Feb., 1st T / Feb. 5, 2008	...	Nov.,★ / Nov. 4, 2008	Aug., 2nd T (even yrs) / None in 2007	...	Nat. / None in 2007	Varies	...	Varies
Connecticut	C	Feb., 1st T / Feb. 5, 2008	...	Nov.,★ / Nov. 4, 2008	Aug., 2nd T (even yrs) / None in 2007	...	Nov.,★(even yrs) / None in 2007	56th day before election	...	Nat. or May, 1st M (e)
Delaware	C	Feb., 1st T / Feb. 5, 2008	...	Nov.,★ / Nov. 4, 2008	Sept., 1st S after 1st M / None in 2007	...	Nov.,★(even yrs) / None in 2007	...	...	(d)
Florida	C	Feb., 1st T / Feb. 5, 2008	...	Nov.,★ / Nov. 4, 2008	9th T prior to General / None in 2007	...	Nov.,★(even yrs) / None in 2007	Varies	Varies	Varies
Georgia	C	Feb., 1st T / Feb. 5, 2008	...	Nov.,★ / Nov. 4, 2008	(f) / None in 2007	...	Nov.,★(biennial) / None in 2007	...	...	...
Hawaii	O	Caucus (g) / Feb. 26 and Mar. 2, 2008	...	Nov.,★ / Nov. 4, 2008	Sept., 2nd Last S / Sept. 20, 2008	...	Nov.,★(even yrs) / Nov. 4, 2008	Sept., 2nd Last S / Sept. 20, 2008	...	Nov.,★(even yrs) / Nov. 4, 2008
Idaho	O	May, 4th T / May 27, 2008	...	Nov.,★ / Nov. 4, 2008	May, 4th T / None in 2007	...	Nov.,★(even yrs) / None in 2007	May, 4th T	...	Nov.,★
Illinois	O	Feb., 1st T / Feb. 5, 2008	...	Nov.,★ / Nov. 4, 2008	Mar., 3rd T / None in 2007	...	Nov.,★(even yrs) / None in 2007	Feb., last T / Feb. 27, 2007	...	Apr., last T (h) / Apr. 17, 2007
Indiana	O	Mar.,★ / Mar. 4, 2008	...	Nov.,★ / Nov. 4, 2008	Mar.,★ / None in 2007	...	Nov.,★(even yrs) / None in 2007	May,★	...	Nov.,★(even yrs) / None in 2007
Iowa	C	Caucus (i) / Jan. 14, 2008	...	Nov.,★ / Nov. 4, 2008	June,★ / None in 2007	...	Nov.,★ / None in 2007	4 wks before reg city election / Oct. 9, 2007	4 wks after reg city election / Dec. 4, 2007	Nov.,★ / Nov. 6, 2007

See footnotes at end of table.

ELECTION DATES FOR NATIONAL, STATE AND LOCAL ELECTIONS—Continued
(Formulas and dates of state elections)

State or other jurisdiction	Type of primary	National (a)			State (b)			Local		
		Primary	Runoff	General	Primary	Runoff	General	Primary	Runoff	General
Kansas	C	Feb., 1st T Feb. 5, 2008	...	Nov.,★ Nov. 4, 2008	Aug., 1st T (d) None in 2007	...	Nov.,★(even yrs)(d) None in 2007	5 wks prior to General (odd yrs)	...	Apr., 1st T (odd yrs)
Kentucky	C	May, 1st T after 3rd M May 20, 2008	...	Nov.,★ Nov. 4, 2008	May, 1st T after 3rd M May 22, 2007	35 days AP	Nov.,★(odd yrs) Nov. 6, 2007	May, 1st T after 3rd M May 22, 2007	...	Nov.,★ Nov. 6, 2007
Louisiana	O (j)	(f) Feb. 9, 2008	...	Nov.,★ Nov. 4, 2008	(f) Oct. 20, 2007	(f) Nov. 17, 2007	(f) Nov. 17, 2007	Varies Mar. 31, 2007	...	Varies May 5, 2007
Maine	C	(f) (k)	...	Nov.,★ Nov. 4, 2008	June, 2nd T None in 2007	...	Nov.,★ None in 2007	...	...	Varies
Maryland	C	Feb., 2nd T Feb. 12, 2008	...	Nov.,★ Nov. 4, 2008	2nd T after 1st M in Sept. None in 2007	...	Nov.,★ None in 2007	2nd T after 1st M in Sept.	...	Nov.,★
Massachusetts	C	(f) Mar. 4, 2008	...	Nov.,★ Nov. 4, 2008	7th T Prior None in 2007	...	Nov.,★(even yrs) None in 2007	Varies	...	Varies
Michigan	O	Feb., 4th T Feb. 26, 2008	...	Nov.,★ Nov. 4, 2008	Aug.,★ None in 2007	...	Nov.,★(even yrs) None in 2007	Aug.,★(l) Aug. 7, 2007	...	Nov.,★(l) Nov. 6, 2007
Minnesota	O	(m) Mar. 4, 2008	...	Nov.,★ Nov. 4, 2008	(m) None in 2007	...	Nov.,★(even yrs) None in 2007	Sept., 1st T after 2nd M Sept. 11, 2007	...	Nov.,★ Nov. 6, 2007
Mississippi	SC	Mar., 2nd T (n) Mar. 11, 2008	3 wks after 1st Primary Apr. 1, 2008	Nov.,★ Nov. 4, 2008	Aug.,★(o) Aug. 7, 2007	3rd T AP Aug. 28, 2007	Nov.,★ Nov. 6, 2007	May, 1st T (d) None in 2007	2nd T AP None in 2007	June,★(d) None in 2007
Missouri	O	Feb.,★ Feb. 5, 2008	...	Nov.,★ Nov. 4, 2008	Aug.,★ None in 2007	...	Nov.,★(even yrs) None in 2007	Aug.,★	...	Nov.,★
Montana	O	Feb.,★ Feb. 5, 2008	...	Nov.,★ Nov. 4, 2008	June,★ None in 2007	...	Nov.,★(even yrs) None in 2007	Sept., T following 2nd M Sept. 11, 2007	...	Nov.,★(odd yrs) Nov. 6, 2007
Nebraska	C	May, 1st T after 2nd M (p) May 13, 2008 (p)	...	Nov.,★	May, 1st T after 2nd M None in 2007	...	Nov.,★(even yrs) None in 2007	May, 1st T after 2nd M	...	Nov.,★
Nevada	C	Caucus Jan. 19, 2008	...	Nov.,★ Nov. 4, 2008	Aug., 3rd T None in 2007	...	Nov.,★(even yrs) None in 2007	Aug., 3rd T	...	Nov.,★
New Hampshire	SO	Set by SS	...	Nov.,★ Nov. 4, 2008	(f) None in 2007	...	Nov.,★(even yrs) None in 2007	Varies	...	Varies
New Jersey	C	Feb.,★ Feb. 5, 2008	...	Nov.,★ Nov. 4, 2008	June,★ June 5, 2007	...	Nov.,★(odd yrs) Nov. 6, 2007	June,★ June 5, 2007	...	Nov.,★ Nov. 6, 2007
New Mexico	C	Feb.,★ Feb. 5, 2008	...	Nov.,★ Nov. 4, 2008	June, 1st T None in 2007	...	Nov.,★ None in 2007	June, 1st T	...	Nov.,★
New York	C	Feb.,★ Feb. 5, 2008	...	Nov.,★ Nov. 4, 2008	Sept.,★ Sept. 12, 2007	...	Nov.,★ Nov. 6, 2007	Sept.,★ Sept. 12, 2007	Sept., 2 wks AP (d)	Nov.,★ Nov. 6, 2007

See footnotes at end of table.

ELECTION DATES FOR NATIONAL, STATE AND LOCAL ELECTIONS—Continued
(Formulas and dates of state elections)

State or other jurisdiction	Type of primary	National (a) Primary	National (a) Runoff	National (a) General	State (b) Primary	State (b) Runoff	State (b) General	Local Primary	Local Runoff	Local General
North Carolina	C (q)	Feb.,★ Feb. 5, 2008	7 wks AP	Nov.,★ Nov. 4, 2008	May,★ None in 2007	7 wks AP None in 2007	Nov.,★(even yrs) None in 2007	May,★(r) None in 2007	7 wks AP None in 2007	Nov.,★(even yrs)(tr) None in 2007
North Dakota	O	(s) Date not set at press time.	...	Nov.,★ Nov. 4, 2008	June, 2nd T None in 2007	...	Nov.,★(even yrs) None in 2007	...	...	June, 2nd T (t)
Ohio	C	Mar.,★ Mar. 4, 2008	...	Nov.,★ Nov. 4, 2008	Mar.,★ None in 2007	...	Nov.,★(even yrs) None in 2007	May,★(u)	(u)	Nov.,★(u)
Oklahoma	C	Feb., 1st S Feb. 2, 2008	...	Nov.,★ Nov. 4, 2008	July, last T (v) None in 2007	Aug., 4th T None in 2007	Nov.,★(even yrs) None in 2007	July, last T (v)	Aug., 4th T	Nov. 6, 2007
Oregon	O	May, 3rd T May 20, 2008	...	Nov.,★ Nov. 4, 2008	May, 3rd T None in 2007	...	Nov.,★(even yrs) None in 2007	(w)	...	(w)
Pennsylvania	C	Apr., 4th T Apr. 22, 2008	...	Nov.,★ Nov. 4, 2008	May, 3rd T None in 2007	...	Nov.,★(even yrs) None in 2007	May, 3rd T None in 2007	...	Nov.,★(even yrs) None in 2007
Rhode Island	O	Sept., 2nd T after 1st M Sept. 9, 2008	...	Nov.,★ Nov. 4, 2008	Sept., 2nd T after 1st M None in 2007	...	Nov.,★(even yrs) None in 2007	Sept., 2nd T after 1st M (x)	...	Nov.,★(x)
South Carolina	O	June, 2nd T June 10, 2008	...	Nov.,★ Nov. 4, 2008	June, 2nd T None in 2007	2nd T AP None in 2007	Nov.,★(even yrs) None in 2007	(y)	(y)	(y)
South Dakota	O	June,★ June 3, 2008	2nd T AP June 17, 2008	Nov.,★ Nov. 4, 2008	June,★ None in 2007	2nd T AP None in 2007	Nov.,★(even yrs) None in 2007	(z)	...	(z)
Tennessee	O	Feb.,★ Feb. 5, 2008	...	Nov.,★ Nov. 4, 2008	Aug., 1st TH None in 2007	...	Nov.,★(even yrs) None in 2007	Feb., 2nd T May, 1st T	...	Aug., 1st TH
Texas	O	Feb.,★ Feb. 5, 2008	...	Nov.,★ Nov. 4, 2008	Mar., 1st T None in 2007	Apr., 2nd T None in 2007	Nov.,★(even yrs) None in 2007	Mar., 1st T	Apr., 2nd T	Nov.,★
Utah	C	Feb.,★ Feb. 5, 2008	...	Nov.,★ Nov. 4, 2008	June, 4th T None in 2007	...	Nov.,★(even yrs) None in 2007	Oct.,★ Oct. 2, 2007	...	Nov. 6, 2007
Vermont (aa)	O	Mar., 1st T Mar. 4, 2008	...	Nov.,★ Nov. 4, 2008	Sept., 2nd T None in 2007	...	Nov.,★(even yrs) None in 2007	...	...	(bb)
Virginia	O	Feb., 2nd T Feb. 12, 2008	...	Nov.,★ Nov. 4, 2008	June, 2nd T June 12, 2007	...	Nov.,★(odd yrs) Nov. 6, 2007	State or Feb., last T	...	Nat. or May., 1st T
Washington	PC	May, 4th T (cc) May 22, 2008 (cc)	...	Nov.,★ Nov. 4, 2008	Aug., 3rd T None in 2007	...	Nov.,★(even yrs) None in 2007	Aug., 3rd T	...	Nov.,★(even yrs)
West Virginia	C	May, 2nd T May 13, 2008	...	Nov.,★ Nov. 4, 2008	May, 2nd T None in 2007	...	Nov.,★ None in 2007	Varies	...	Varies
Wisconsin	O	(f) Feb. 19, 2008	...	Nov.,★ Nov. 4, 2008	Sept., 2nd T None in 2007	...	Nov.,★(even yrs) None in 2007	Feb., 3rd T	...	Apr., 1st T
Wyoming	C	Caucus (dd)	...	Nov.,★ Nov. 4, 2008	Aug., 1st T after 3rd M None in 2007	...	Nov.,★(even yrs) None in 2007	Aug., 1st T after 3rd M	...	Nov.,★(even yrs)

See footnotes at end of table.

ELECTION DATES FOR NATIONAL, STATE AND LOCAL ELECTIONS—Continued
(Formulas and dates of state elections)

State or other jurisdiction	Type of primary	National (a)			State (b)			Local		
		Primary	Runoff	General	Primary	Runoff	General	Primary	Runoff	General
Dist. of Columbia	C	(f) Jan. 8, 2008	...	Nov.★ Nov. 4, 2008	... None in 2007	...	Nov.★(even yrs) None in 2007	Sept., 1st T after 2nd M	...	Nov.★
American Samoa	N.A. (ee)	(ee)	14 days after General Nov. 21, 2008	Nov.★ Nov. 4, 2008	(ee)	14 days after General Nov. 18, 2008	Nov.★(even yrs) None in 2007	(ee)	...	(ff)
Puerto Rico............	N.A. ...	(f) Mar. 9, 2008	Mar. 9, 2008	...	(f) Mar. 9, 2008	...	Nov.★(even yrs) None in 2007	...	...	...
U.S. Virgin Islands..	N.A. ...	...	...	...	Sept., 2nd S None in 2007	14 days AP	Nov.★(even yrs) None in 2007	Sept., 2nd S	14 days AP	Nov., 1st T

Sources: The Council of State Governments' survey of state election offices, January 2007 and state Web sites, March 2007.

Note: This table describes the basic formulas for determining when national, state and local elections will be held. For specific information on a particular state, the reader is advised to contact the specific state election administration office. All dates provided are based on the state election formula and dates are subject to change.

Key:

★ — First Tuesday after first Monday
... — No provision
M — Monday
T — Tuesday
TH — Thursday
S — Saturday
Nat. — Same date as national elections
State — Same date as state elections
Prior — Prior to general election
AP — After primary
V — Varies

Key, Column 1:

C — Closed primary
O — Open primary
PC — Private choice primary
SC — Semi-closed primary
SO — Semi-open primary

(a) National refers to presidential elections.

(b) State refers to election in which a state executive official or U.S. senator is to be elected. See Table 6.2, State Officials to be Elected.

(c) The primary date has not been set. A bill was passed in 2006 by the legislature to separate the Presidential Primary from the June statewide primary. This bill moves the presidential primary to February, but the change has not yet been submitted to the DOJ for pre-clearance.

(d) In Delaware, elections are determined by city charter. In Iowa, partisan elections only. In Kansas, state and county elections. In Minnesota, county elections only. In Mississippi, state and county elections are held together; municipal elections are held in separate years. In Montana, municipalities only. In New York, runoff in New York City only. In Ohio, municipalities and towns in odd years and counties in even years. In South Carolina, school boards vary.

(e) Unless that date conflicts with Passover, then first Tuesday following last day of Passover.

(f) Formula not available at press time.

(g) Democratic caucus, February 26, 2008; Republican caucus, March 2, 2008.

(h) When the first Tuesday in April falls during Passover, then the election is conducted on the first Tuesday following the end of Passover.

(i) Iowa does not have a presidential primary. The Iowa Caucuses mark the beginning of the presidential candidate selection process by choosing delegates to the next level of political party conventions.

(j) Louisiana has an open primary which requires all candidates, regardless of party affiliation, to appear on a single ballot. If a candidate receives over 50 percent of the vote in the primary, that candidate is elected to the office. If no candidate receives a majority vote, then a single election is held between the two candidates receiving the most votes. For national elections, the first vote is held on the first Saturday in October or even-numbered years with the general election held on the first Tuesday after the first Monday in November. For state elections, the election is held on the second to last Saturday in November with the runoff being held on the fourth Saturday after first election. Local elections vary depending on the location and the year.

(k) Democratic caucus February 10, 2008; Republican caucus, March 21, 2008.

(l) Local and school elections can vary. A limited number of cities will hold a primary and a limited number of villages will hold an election on the first Tuesday after the second Monday in September (Sept. 11, 2007).

(m) On the first Tuesday of March in even-numbered years, major political parties have local caucuses at which a preference ballot is taken for candidates for president or governor. Party conventions nominate presidential electors.

(n) Parties must notify the Secretary of State's Office in writing prior to December 1 the year preceding the date of the election of their intentions to hold a preference primary election.

(o) These dates are for state elections only and do not reflect congressional races. Elections held in years in which a U.S. Congressional election and a Presidential election are held, the congressional race will be held on the same day as the Presidential Primary if the parties notified the Secretary of State's Office of their intent.

(p) Nebraska may change from a Presidential Preference Primary in May to a caucus held on the second Saturday in February (Feb. 9, 2008).

(q) Unaffiliated voters, by state statute and with permission of a party, may vote in a party primary. Currently both the Democratic and Republican parties allow this.

(r) No county elections are held in 2007. They will be held in 2008. Municipal elections are held in 2007 on various dates.

(s) On one designated day, following presidential nominating contests in the states of Iowa and New Hampshire and prior to the first Wednesday in March in every presidential election year, every political party entitled to a separate column may conduct a presidential preference caucus. Before August 15 of the odd-numbered year immediately preceding the presidential election year, the secretary of state shall designate the day after consulting with and taking recommendations from the two political parties casting the greatest vote for president of the United States at the most recent general elections when the office of president appeared on the ballot.

(t) Cities only.

(u) Cities and villages having a charter form of government may provide for different primary dates and may provide for runoff elections.

(v) The primary election is held on the fourth Tuesday in August in each even-numbered year, including presidential election years. The presidential preferential primary is held on the first Tuesday in February during presidential election years.

ELECTION DATES FOR NATIONAL, STATE AND LOCAL ELECTIONS — Continued

(w) Oregon has four scheduled local elections each year. Second Tuesday in March — March 13, 2007; third Tuesday in May — May 15, 2007; third Tuesday in September — September 18, 2007; first Tuesday after first Monday in November — November 6, 2007.

(x) Rhode Island has two communities with local elections held on the odd-numbered years; all other local elections are held at the same time as the General Election.

(y) Municipalities and School Boards set their own election dates.

(z) Municipal and School elections are held between the second Tuesday in April and the third Tuesday in June. Those jurisdictions set their own election date at their meeting no later than the first meeting in January.

(aa) In Vermont, if there is a tie in a primary or general election (and a recount does not resolve the tie) the appropriate superior could order a recessed election, among the tied candidates only, within three weeks of the recount. In state primary runoffs, the runoff election must be proclaimed within seven days after primary; after proclamation, election is held 15–22 days later. Local elections are held by annual town meetings which may vary depending on town charter.

(bb) Most local (i.e. town/municipal) officials in Vermont are elected at town meeting, either by traditional meeting or by Australian ballot. (County officials are elected in November of even-numbered years.)

(cc) Date will likely change.

(dd) Republican caucus tentatively scheduled for January 22, 2008; Democratic caucus tentatively scheduled for May 10, 2008.

(ee) American Samoa does not conduct primary elections. (In addition, elections are conducted for territory-wide offices. There are no local elections.)

(ff) Must be held on the third Tuesday of the preceding September or on the seventh Tuesday immediately preceding such general election, whichever occurs first.

Table 6.5
POLLING HOURS: GENERAL ELECTIONS

State or other jurisdiction	Polls open	Polls close	Notes on hours (a)
Alabama	7 a.m.	7 p.m.	
Alaska	7 a.m.	8 p.m.	
Arizona	6 a.m.	7 p.m.	
Arkansas	7:30 a.m.	7:30 p.m.	
California	7 a.m.	8 p.m.	
Colorado	7 a.m.	7 p.m.	
Connecticut	6 a.m.	8 p.m.	
Delaware	7 a.m.	8 p.m.	
Florida	7 a.m.	7 p.m.	
Georgia	7 a.m.	7 p.m.	
Hawaii	7 a.m.	6 p.m.	
Idaho	8 a.m.	8 p.m.	Clerk has the option of opening all polls at 7 a.m. Idaho is in two time zones—MST and PST.
Illinois	6 a.m.	7 p.m.	
Indiana	6 a.m.	6 p.m.	
Iowa	7 a.m.	9 p.m.	Hours for school and city elections: polls open at 7 a.m. or noon (depending upon choice of county auditor, with legal limitations on opening the polls at noon). Polls close at 8 p.m.
Kansas	7 a.m.	7 p.m.	Counties may choose to open polls as early as 6 a.m. and close as late as 8 p.m. Several western counties are on Mountain Time.
Kentucky	6 a.m.	6 p.m.	
Louisiana	6 a.m.	8 p.m.	
Maine	Between 6 and 10 a.m.	8 p.m.	Applicable opening time depends on variables related to the size of the precinct. Anyone in line at 8 p.m. will be allowed to vote.
Maryland	7 a.m.	8 p.m.	
Massachusetts	7 a.m.	8 p.m.	
Michigan	7 a.m.	8 p.m.	
Minnesota	7 a.m.	8 p.m.	Towns outside of the twin cities metro area with less than 500 inhabitants may have a later time for the polls to open as long as it is not later than 10 a.m.
Mississippi	7 a.m.	7 p.m.	
Missouri	6 a.m.	7 p.m.	Those individuals in line at 7 p.m. will be allowed to vote.
Montana	7 a.m.	8 p.m.	Polling places with fewer than 200 registered electors must be open from noon until 8 p.m. or until all registered electors in any precinct have voted.
Nebraska	7 a.m. MST/8 a.m. CST	7 p.m. MST/8 p.m. CST	
Nevada	7 a.m.	7 p.m.	
New Hampshire	No later than 11 a.m.	No earlier than 7 p.m.	Polling hours vary from town to town. The hours of 11 a.m. to 7 p.m. are by statute.
New Jersey	6 a.m.	8 p.m.	
New Mexico	7 a.m.	7 p.m.	
New York	6 a.m.	9 p.m.	
North Carolina	6:30 a.m.	7:30 p.m.	
North Dakota	Between 7 and 9 a.m.	Between 7 and 9 p.m.	Counties must have polls open by 9 a.m., but can choose to open as early as 7 a.m. Polls must remain open until 7 p.m., but can be open as late as 9 p.m. The majority of polls in the state are open from 8 a.m. to 7 p.m. in their respective time zones (CST and MST).
Ohio	6:30 a.m.	7:30 p.m.	
Oklahoma	7 a.m.	7 p.m.	
Oregon	6 a.m.	3 p.m.	Oregon's polls (County Clerk's office and drop sites) are open from 7 a.m. to 8 p.m.
Pennsylvania	7 a.m.	8 p.m.	
Rhode Island	6 a.m.	9 p.m.	
South Carolina	7 a.m.	7 p.m.	
South Dakota	7 a.m.	7 p.m.	Local time.
Tennessee	8 a.m.	7 p.m. CST/8 p.m. EST	Poll hours are set by each county election commission. Polling places shall be open a minimum of 10 hours but no more than 13 hours. All polling locations in the Eastern time zone shall close at 8 p.m. and those in the Central time zone shall close at 7 p.m.
Texas	7 a.m.	7 p.m.	
Utah	7 a.m.	8 p.m.	
Vermont	Between 7 and 10 a.m.	7 p.m.	The opening time for polls is set by local boards of civil authority.

See footnotes at end of table.

POLLING HOURS: GENERAL ELECTIONS — Continued

State or other jurisdiction	Polls open	Polls close	Notes on hours (a)
Virginia	6 a.m.	7 p.m.	
Washington	7 a.m.	8 p.m.	
West Virginia	6:30 a.m.	7:30 p.m.	
Wisconsin	Between 7 and 9 a.m.	8 p.m.	In cities with a population of 10,000 or more, the polls must open at 7:00 a.m. In cities, towns and villages with populations of 10,000, the polls may open anytime between 7:00 a.m. and 9:00 a.m.
Wyoming	7 a.m.	7 p.m.	
Dist. of Columbia	7 a.m.	8 p.m.	
American Samoa			Election proclamation issued by Chief Election Officer contains a statement of time and place for each territorial election.
Guam	8 a.m.	8 p.m.	
No. Mariana Islands	7 a.m.	7 p.m.	Elections are held on six separate islands. At the close of the polls, ballots are flown to Saipan where they are tabulated at election headquarters.
Puerto Rico	8 a.m.	3 p.m.	
U.S. Virgin Islands	7 a.m.	7 p.m.	

Sources: The Council of State Governments' survey, January 2007 and state election Web sites, February 2007.

Note: Hours for primary, municipal and special elections may differ from those noted.

(a) In all states, voters standing in line when the polls close are allowed to vote; however, provisions for handling those voters vary across jurisdictions.

Table 6.6
VOTER REGISTRATION INFORMATION

State or other jurisdiction	Closing date for registration before general election (days)	Persons eligible for absentee voting (a)	Cut-off for receiving absentee ballots	Absentee votes signed by witness or notary	Residency requirements	Registration in other places	Voting rights revoked	Method/process or provision for restoration	Mental competency
			Absentee voting				**Provision for felons**		
Alabama	10	B, D, O, P, S, T	May apply 5 days prior to the election	N or 2W	S, 1 day	★	★	★	★
Alaska	30	No excuse required	10 days prior to Election Day	N or 1W	S, D, 30	★	★	★	★
Arizona	29	A	7 p.m. Election Day	…	S, C, 29	★	★	…	★
Arkansas	30	No excuse required	7:30 p.m. Election Day	…	C, 30	★	★	★	★
California	15	No excuse required	8 p.m. Election Day	…	S	…	★	★	★
Colorado	29	No excuse required	7 p.m. Election Day	…	(b)	★	★	★	…
Connecticut	14	A	8 p.m. Election Day	…	S, T	…	★	★	…
Delaware	20	A	12 p.m. day before election	N or W	S (c)	…	★	★	★
Florida	29	No excuse required	7 p.m. Election Day	…	S, C, 29	…	★	★	★
Georgia	(d)	A	Close of polls	W (e)	S, C	…	★	★(f)	★
Hawaii	30	No excuse required	6 p.m. Election Day	…	S	★	★	★	★
Idaho	25	No excuse required	8 p.m. Election Day	…	S, C, 30	★	★	★	★
Illinois	28 (g)	M/O	Close of polls on Election Day (h)	…	S, P, 30	★	★	★	★
Indiana	29	No excuse required	12 p.m. day before election	…	P, 30	…	★	★	★
Iowa	10	No excuse required	Postmarked by day before election (i)	…	S (j)	★	★	★	★
Kansas	15	No excuse required	(k)	…	(l)	★	★	★	★
Kentucky	29	A	Close of polls	…	S, C, 28	★	★	★	★
Louisiana	30	B, D, O, P, S, T (m)	Election Day	N and 2W	S, 30 (n)	★	★	★	★
Maine	Election Day	No excuse required	Tuesday before election	N or W	S, M	…	…	★	★
Maryland	21	B, C, D, O, S, T (o)	Friday after election	…	S, 21 (p)	…	★	★	★
Massachusetts	20	A	10 days after election	…	S	★	★	★	★
Michigan	30	B, C, D, O, R, T	(q)	N or 1W	S, M, 30 (r)	…	★(s)	★	★
Minnesota	Election Day (t)	B, D, O, P, R, T	Election Day	W	S, 20	…	★	…	★
Mississippi	30	A	5 p.m. day before election	W	S, C, 30	…	★	★	★
Missouri	28	A	Close of polls	N	S	…	★	★	★
Montana	30	No excuse required	Close of polls	…	S, C, 30	★	★	★	★
Nebraska	(u)	No excuse required	10 a.m. 2 days after election	W	S	…	★	★	★
Nevada	(v)	No excuse required	Close of polls	…	S, C, 30; P, 10 (w)	★	…	★	★
New Hampshire	Election Day (t)	B, D, E, O, R, S, T	(x)	W or N	S	★	…	★	★
New Jersey	29	A	8 p.m. Election Day	W or N	S, C, 30 (y)	…	★	★	★
New Mexico	28	No excuse required	7 p.m. Election Day	N or W	S	…	★	★	★
New York	25	A	Postmarked day before election	W (e)	S, C, 30 (z)	★	★	★	★
North Carolina	25	No excuse required	5 p.m. day before election	2W	S, C, D, M, P, T, 30	★	★	★	…
North Dakota	(aa)	No excuse required	2 days after election	N or W	S, C, D, M, P, T, 30	(aa)	(aa)	★	(aa)
Ohio	30	No excuse required	Close of polls (bb)	…	S, 30	★	★	★	★
Oklahoma	25	A	7 p.m. Election Day	N or W	S	…	★	★	★
Oregon	21	No excuse required	8 p.m. Election Day	…	S, 20	…	★	★	★
Pennsylvania	30	B, C, D, O, P, R, S, T	5 p.m. Friday before election	…	S, 30	★	★	★	…
Rhode Island	30	B, D, O, R, S	21 days	N or 2W	S, P, T, 30	★	…	★	★
South Carolina	30	B, C, D, E, M/O, O, P, R, S, T	7 p.m. Election Day	N or 1W	S, C, M, T, 30	★	★	★	★

See footnotes at end of table.

VOTER REGISTRATION INFORMATION—Continued

State or other jurisdiction	Closing date for registration before general election (days)	Persons eligible for absentee voting (a)	Absentee voting: Cut-off for receiving absentee ballots	Absentee votes signed by witness or notary	Residency requirements	Registration in other places	Provision for felons: Voting rights revoked	Method/process or provision for restoration	Mental competency
South Dakota	15	No excuse required (cc)	Close of polls	(dd)	(ee)	...	★	★	★
Tennessee	30	A	Close of polls	W (e)	S	...	★	★	★
Texas	30	A	Before close of polls	(ff)	S, C	...	★	★	★
Utah	20	No excuse required	Noon on day of canvass	...	S, 30	★	★	★	★
Vermont	8 (gg)	No excuse required	7 p.m. Election Day	...	S, C (j)	...	...	...	...
Virginia	29	A	Close of polls	1W	...	★	★	★	★
Washington	30	No excuse required (hh)	(ii)	2W	S, 30	★	★	★	★
West Virginia	21	A	6 days prior to election	W	(jj)	★	★	...	★
Wisconsin	Election Day (kk)(ll)	No excuse required	Close of polls	W	S, 10	...	★	★	★
Wyoming	Election Day (t)	No excuse required	7 p.m. Election Day	...	S (mm)	...	★	★	★
Dist. of Columbia	30	A	10 days after election	...	D, 30	★	★	★	★
American Samoa	30	A	1:30 p.m. Election Day	...	S, 30	N.A.	N.A.	N.A.	N.A.
Guam	10	A	N.A.	N.A.	N.A.	N.A.	N.A.	N.A.	N.A.
No. Mariana Islands	50	B, D, E, O, R, S, T	14 days after election	N (nn)	(oo)	N.A.	★	N.A.	N.A.
Puerto Rico	40 or 60	A	30 or 45 days after election	N.A.	S (pp)	★	...	N.A.	★
U.S. Virgin Islands	30	A	14 days before election	Affidavit	(qq)	...	★	N.A.	★

Source: The Council of State Governments' survey, December 2006.

Key:

★ — State provision prohibiting registration or claiming the right to vote in another state or jurisdiction.

★ — Columns 7, 8 and 9: State provision regarding criminal status or mental competency.

... — No state provision.

N.A. – Information not available.

Column 4: N — Notary, W — Witness. Numbers indicated the number of signatures required.

Column 5: S — State, C — County, D — District, M — Municipality, P — Precinct, T — Town. Numbers represent the number of days before an election for which one must be a resident.

Note: Previous editions of this chart contained a column for "Automatic cancellation of registration for failure to vote for ____ years". However, the National Voter Registration Act requires a confirmation notice prior to any cancellation and thus effectively bans any automatic cancellation of voter registration. In addition, all states and territories except Puerto Rico and the U.S. Virgin Islands allow mail-in registration.

(a) In this column: A — All of these; B — Absent on business; C — Senior citizen; D — Disabled persons; E — Not absent, but prevented by employment from registering; M/O — No absentee registration except military and overseas citizens as required by federal law; O — Out of state; P — Out of precinct (or municipality in PA); R — Absent for religious reasons; S — Students; T — Temporarily out of jurisdiction, or no excuse required.

(b) Municipalities may change this requirement in their city charter; it is not known how many have made this provision.

(c) Must be a permanent state resident.

(d) The 5th Monday before a general primary, general election, or presidential preference primary; the 5th day after the date of the call for all other special primaries and special elections.

(e) The request deadline is six days before the election, to be mailed the next day; the receipt deadline is before canvass with election day postmark, the day after the election with no postmark, and before canvass for military and overseas regardless of postmark.

(f) Upon parole, pardon, or probation, felons are required to re-register to restore lost voting rights.

(g) Closing date for registration before general election is 28 days before. Illinois now has grace period registration which allows for registration of voters and change of address during a period from close of registration for a primary or election and until 14th day before the primary or election. If a voter who registers during this time period wishes to vote at that first election occurring after grace period, he/she must do so by grace period voting (at the discretion of the election authority a grace period registrant may vote by mail).

(h) Except that mailed absentee ballots which are postmarked prior to election may be received up to the 14th day after election day.

(i) An absentee ballot must be returned before the polls are closed on election day; or if the ballot is mailed, the envelope must be postmarked before election day. Timely postmarked ballots are considerd on time if the ballot is received before noon on Monday following the election day. However, if the canvass of votes for the election is required by law to be held earlier, the ballot must be received by the time set for the canvass of votes. The canvass of votes for the school election and some city elections will be held on Thursday or Friday after the election.

(j) Iowa does not have a residency length of time requirement; it does require that a person be a resident when registering to vote. One must be registerd at least 10 days before a primary and general elections; 11 days before all others. Vermont has no durational residency requirement.

(k) In person: 12 p.m. day before election. By mail: close of polls on election day.

(l) Date of registration.

(m) Must be in Handicapped Program.

(n) A voter must be registered to vote 30 days before an election, and must be a resident in order to register.

(o) Voter is eligible if they may be out of the county; students eligible if out of precinct.

(p) State election law does not apply to municipal elections. Therefore each municipality may have a separate requirement.

(q) If a voter wishes to have a ballot mailed, clerk must receive written request by 2 p.m. on the Saturday prior to the election. Voters can obtain an absentee ballot in person anytime through 4 p.m on the day prior to the election. If the voter qualifies for an emergency ballot, request can be submitted through 4 p.m. on the date of the election.

VOTER REGISTRATION INFORMATION — Continued

(r) Must register at least 30 days before election day.

(s) Only while confined, automaic restoration after release.

(t) Minnesota — delivered 21 days before an election or election day registration at polling precincts; New Hampshire — received by city or town clerk 10 days before election or election day registration at precincts; Wyoming — delivered 30 days before or election day registration at polling precincts.

(u) Received by the 2nd Friday before election or postmarked by the 3rd Friday before the election.

(v) By 9 p.m. on the 5th Saturday preceding any primary or general election.

(w) Must have continuously resided in the state and county at least 30 days and in precinct at least 10 days before election. Must claim no other place as legal residence.

(x) In person: day before election. By mail: day of election.

(y) Must be a resident of the state and county at your address for 30 days before election.

(z) Must be a resident of the county or the City of New York at least 30 days before election.

(aa) No voter registration.

(bb) Voted ballots on in-country electors must be received by close of polls; voted ballots returned from outside the United States must be received within 10 days of election day.

(cc) No excuse required. In South Dakota must submit the application for absentee ballot to the person in charge of the election.

(dd) Absentee ballot applications (not absentee ballots) are required to be notarized or submitted with a copy of the voter's photo identification.

(ee) Municipality: at least 30 days during the year preceding the election. Town: 30 consecutive days each year.

(ff) If unable to sign.

(gg) Second Monday preceding election.

(hh) There is a late registration date, 15 days prior, for in-person new registrations and the voter must vote an absentee ballot.

(ii) Fifteen days following a primary; 21 days following a general election.

(jj) A voter must be a resident for 30 days prior to the election. West Virginia poll books for each election require that the voters acknowledge that their address is current and that they have been at that location for 30 days prior to the election.

(kk) By mail: Washington, 30 days; Wisconsin, 13 days.

(ll) Registration may be completed in the local voter registration office one day before the election.

(mm) Must be "an actual and physically bona fide resident."

(nn) Notary public or commissioned officer authorized to administer oath for Armed Services personnel.

(oo) State/territory: 120 days; district, municipality, precinct: 50 days.

(pp) According to Electoral Law the voter must have a permanent residence in Puerto Rico to be a qualified elector.

(qq) Ninety days residency requirement; 30 days for district.

Table 6.7
VOTING STATISTICS FOR GUBERNATORIAL ELECTIONS BY REGION

State or other jurisdiction	Date of last election	Primary election					General election								
		Republican	Democrat	Independent	Other	Total votes	Republican	Percent	Democrat	Percent	Independent	Percent	Other	Percent	Total votes
Eastern Region															
Connecticut	2006	......	31,799	(b)	0	53,469	710,048	63.2	398,220	35.4	0	0.0	15,198	1.4	1,123,466
Delaware	2004	21,670	54,422	0	0		167,008	45.8	185,548	50.9	10,753	2.9	1,450	0.4	364,759
Maine	2006	68,574		0	0	120,996	166,425	30.2	209,927	38.1	118,715	21.5	55,798	10.1	550,865
Massachusetts	2006	71,430	912,348	0	0	983,778	784,342	35.0	1,234,984	55.0	154,628	7.0	69,881	3.1	2,243,835
New Hampshire	2006	(d)	(d)	0	0	(d)	105,370	26.0	298,206	74.0	0	0.0	0	0	403,576
New Jersey	2005	302,521	235,778	0	0	538,299	985,271	43.0	1,224,551	53.5	0	0.0	80,277	3.5	2,290,099
New York	2006	138,263	624,684	0	0	762,947	1,105,681	23.5	2,740,864	58.3	190,661(c)	4	660,661	14	4,697,867
Pennsylvania	2006	572,375(d)	644,444(d)	0	0	1,216,819	1,622,135	39.6	2,470,517	60.4	0	0.0	0	0	4,092,652
Rhode Island	2006	63,148	88,688	0	0	151,836	57,383	14.8	150,126	39.0	180,361	46.5	0	0.0	387,870
Vermont	2006	33,645	31,048	0	86	64,779	148,014	56.3	108,090	41.1	2,477	0.9	3,305	1.7	262,524
Regional total		1,271,626	1,978,767	0	86	3,892,923	5,851,677	35.6	9,021,033	55.0	657,595	4	886,570	5.4	16,417,513
Midwestern Region															
Illinois	2006	699,786	931,779	0	0	1,631,565	1,368,682	38.2	1,736,219	48.4	0	0.0	381,770	10.6	3,586,292
Indiana	2004	505,758	283,924	0	0	789,682	1,302,912	53.2	1,113,900	45.4	0	0.0	31,684	0.1	2,448,498
Iowa	2006	73,903(d)	148,000	0	0	221,903	467,425	44.1	569,021	53.7	0	0.0	22,618	2.1	1,059,064
Kansas	2006	194,295	76,046(d)	0	0	382,003	343,586	40.4	491,993	57.9	0	0.0	14,121	1.7	849,700
Michigan	2006	581,404	531,322	0	119	1,112,845	1,608,086	42.3	2,142,513	56.3	0	0.0	50,657	1.3	3,801,256
Minnesota	2006	166,112	316,470	11,689	0	514,373	1,028,568	46.4	1,007,460	45.4	141,735	6.4	25,174	1.1	2,217,719
Nebraska	2006	271,487	73,592	0	128	345,207	435,507	73.3	145,115	24.5	4,193	1.3	12,735	2.1	593,357
North Dakota	2004	42,135	35,597	0	0	77,732	220,803	71.3	84,877	27.4	0	0.0	0	0.0	309,873
Ohio	2006	812,388	783,044	0	0	1,816,916	1,470,708	35.2	2,428,013	58.0	112,742	2.7	0	0.0	4,184,072
South Dakota	2006	(d)	36,389	0	0	92,763	206,990	61.7	121,226	36.1	0	0.0	7,292	2.2	335,508
Wisconsin	2006	234,020	320,782	0	1,812	556,614	979,427	45.3	1,139,115	52.7	0	0.0	43,158	2.0	2,161,700
Regional total		3,581,288	3,536,945	11,689	2,059	7,541,603	9,432,694	43.8	10,979,452	51.0	258,670	1.2	589,209	2.7	21,547,039
Southern Region															
Alabama	2006	460,019	466,537	0	0	925,467	718,327	57.4	519,827	41.5	0	0.0	12,247	1.0	1,250,401
Arkansas	2006	....No primary in 2006 due to only one candidate per party.....					314,630	40.7	430,090	55.5	15,739	2.0	13,093	1.7	773,552
Florida	2006	985,986	857,814	0	0	1,843,800	2,519,845	52.2	2,178,289	45.1	92,595	1.9	38,541	0.8	4,829,270
Georgia	2006	419,254	482,117	0	0	901,371	1,229,724	57.9	811,049	38.2	0	0.0	81,412	3.8	2,122,185
Kentucky	2003	160,050	298,082	0	0	458,341	596,284	55.0	487,159	45.0	0	0.0	0	0.0	1,083,443
Louisiana (a)	2003	351,371	871,198	172,158	0	1,394,727	368,698	48.0	871,715	52.0	175,228		0	0.0	1,415,641
Maryland	2006	213,744	524,671	0	0	738,415	825,464	46.2	942,279	52.7	0	0.0	20,573	1.1	1,717,068
Mississippi	2003	177,122	504,319	0	0	681,441	470,404	52.6	409,787	45.8	0	0.0	14,296	1.6	894,487
Missouri	2004	604,757	847,748	0	3,755	1,456,260	1,382,419	50.8	1,301,442	47.9	0	0.0	35,678	1.1	2,719,599
North Carolina	2004	364,420	444,559	0	0	808,979	1,495,021	42.8	1,939,154	55.6	0	0.0	52,513	1.1	3,486,688
Oklahoma	2006	182,136	264,467	0	0	446,603	310,327	33.5	616,135	66.5	0	0.0	0	0.0	926,462
South Carolina	2006	247,281	138,343	0	0	395,905	601,868	55.1	489,076	44.8	0	0.0	1,008	0.1	1,091,952
Tennessee	2006	534,824	539,018	0	809	1,074,651	540,853	29.7	1,247,491	68.6	30,205	1.6	0	0.0	1,818,549
Texas	2006	655,919	508,602	0	0	1,164,521	1,716,792	39.0	1,310,337	29.8	1,344,525	30.5	27,462	0.7	4,399,116
Virginia	2005	175,170	(b)	(b)	(b)	175,170	912,327	46.0	1,025,942	52.0	43,953	2.0	1,556	0.1	1,983,778
West Virginia	2004	43,223	283,262	0	0	326,485	253,131	34.0	472,758	63.5	18,430	0.0	114	0.2	744,433
Regional total		5,575,276	7,030,737	172,158	4,564	12,792,136	14,256,114	45.6	15,052,530	48.2	1,720,675	5.4	298,493	0.8	31,256,624

See footnotes at end of table.

VOTING STATISTICS FOR GUBERNATORIAL ELECTIONS BY REGION—Continued

State or other jurisdiction	Date of last election	Primary election					General election								
		Republican	Democrat	Independent	Other	Total votes	Republican	Percent	Democrat	Percent	Independent	Percent	Other	Percent	Total votes
Western Region															
Alaska..........	2006	101,695	97,238	22,443	2,944	160,874	114,697	48.1	97,238	40.8	22,443	7.9	2,944	1.2	238,307
Arizona..........	2006	333,604	246,876	0	4,046	584,526	543,528	35.4	959,830	62.6	0	0.0	30,287	2.0	1,533,645
California..........	2006	1,809,189	2,360,529	27,195	49,693	4,246,606	4,850,157	55.9	3,376,732	39.0	61,901	0.7	390,258	4.4	8,679,048
Colorado..........	2006	193,804(d)	142,586(d)	0	0	336,390	625,886	40.2	888,096	57.0	0	0.0	44,405	2.8	1,558,387
Hawaii..........	2006	32,107	179,227	0	642	211,976	215,313	61.7	121,717	34.9	0	0.0	11,721	3.4	348,751
Idaho..........	2006	137,175	30,443	0	0	184,456	276,029	52.7	198,845	44.1	0	0.0	14,550	3.2	489,424
Montana..........	2004	110,198	94,795	0	0	204,993	205,313	46.0	225,016	50.4	0	0.0	15,817	3.5	456,096
Nevada..........	2006	140,515	119,046	0	0	259,561	279,003	47.9	255,684	43.9	0	0.0	47,471	8.2	582,158
New Mexico..........	2006	53,974	107,520	0	0	160,575	174,364	31.2	384,806	68.8	0	0.0	0	0.0	559,170
Oregon..........	2006	300,554	319,177	0	0	619,731	533,650	38.1	579,060	41.3	248,655	17.7	37,925	2.7	1,399,650
Utah..........	2004		......(b)......				524,816	57.8	373,670	41.2	0	0.0	8,220	0.9	906,706
Washington..........	2004	793,015	557,106	114,264	15,268	1,480,247	1,373,232	48.8	1,373,361	48.8	0	0.0	63,465	2.2	2,883,499
Wyoming..........	2006	69,401	29,612	0	0	99,013	58,100	29.9	135,516	69.8	0	0.0	276	0.1	193,892
Regional total..........		4,075,231	4,284,155	163,902	72,593	8,548,948	9,774,088	49.2	8,969,571	45.2	332,999	1.7	667,339	3.7	19,828,733
Regional total without California..........		2,266,042	1,923,626	136,707	22,900	4,302,342	4,923,931	44.1	5,592,839	50.2	271,098	2.4	277,081	2.5	11,149,685
U.S. Virgin Islands..........	2006	2,803	31,615	1,740	0	36,158	2,838	6.2	32,308	59.2	1,778	30.8	16,093	3.7	53,017
Puerto Rico..........	2004	N.A.	N.A.	N.A.	N.A.	N.A.	(e)	(e)	(e)	(e)	(e)	(e)	1,990,372	(e)	1,990,372

Sources: The Council of State Governments' survey of election administration offices, February 2007 and state elections Web sites.

Key:
N.A. — Not applicable
(a) Louisiana has an open primary which requires all candidates, regardless of party affiliation, to appear on a single ballot. If a candidate receives over 50 percent of the vote in the primary, he is elected to the office.

If no candidate receives a majority vote, then a single election is held between the two candidates receiving the most votes.
(b) Candidate nominated by convention.
(c) Governor Eliot Spitzer was also the Independence Party candidate.
(d) Candidate ran unopposed.
(e) Unavailable.

Table 6.8
VOTER TURNOUT FOR PRESIDENTIAL ELECTIONS BY REGION: 1996, 2000 AND 2004
(In thousands)

State or other jurisdiction	2004 Voting age population (a)	2004 Number registered	2004 Number voting (b)	2000 Voting age population (a)	2000 Number registered	2000 Number voting (b)	1996 Voting age population (a)	1996 Number registered	1996 Number voting (b)
U.S. Total	208,247	170,937	122,501	205,410	156,420	105,587	195,193	132,796	96,414
Eastern Region									
Connecticut........................	2,574	1,823	1,579	2,499	1,874	1,460	2,300	1,900	750
Delaware............................	594	554	376	582	505	328	547	(c)	271
Maine................................	1,042	957	741	968	882	652	934	1,001	606
Massachusetts	4,931	3,973	2,927	4,749	4,009	2,734	4,623	(c)	2,556
New Hampshire	991	856	684	911	857	569	860	755	514
New Jersey	6,669	5,009	3,612	6,245	4,711	3,187	6,124	(c)	3,076
New York...........................	14,206	11,837	7,448	13,805	11,263	6,960	13,564	9,161	6,439
Pennsylvania......................	9,404	8,367	5,770	9,155	7,782	4,912	9,197	6,806	4,506
Rhode Island......................	803	709	437	753	655	409	751	603	390
Vermont.............................	490	445	312	460	427	294	430	385	261
Regional total	41,704	34,530	23,886	40,127	32,965	21,505	39,330	20,611	19,369
Midwestern Region									
Illinois	9,519	7,499	5,274	8,983	7,129	4,742	11,431	6,663	4,418
Indiana...............................	4,420	4,163	2,468	4,448	4,001	2,180	4,146	3,500	2,135
Iowa...................................	2,212	2,107	1,522	2,165	1,841	1,314	2,138	1,776	1,252
Kansas...............................	2,038	1,694	1,188	1,983	1,624	1,072	1,823	1,257	1,129
Michigan............................	7,541	7,164	4,839	7,358	6,861	4,233	7,072	6,677	3,849
Minnesota	3,823	2,977	2,828	3,547	3,265	2,439	3,412	2,730	2,211
Nebraska............................	1,257	1,160	778	1,234	1,085	697	1,208	1,015	677
North Dakota......................	487	(d)	316	477	(c)	288	437	(c)	272
Ohio...................................	8,604	7,973	5,426	8,433	7,538	4,702	8,300	6,638	4,534
South Dakota......................	573	502	395	543	471	316	530	456	324
Wisconsin	4,119	2,957(d)	2,997	3,930	(d)	2,599	3,786	(d)	2,196
Regional total	44,593	38,196	28,031	43,101	33,815	24,582	44,283	30,712	22,997
Southern Region									
Alabama.............................	3,252	2,597	1,883	3,333	2,529	1,666	3,220	2,471	1,534
Arkansas............................	1,951	1,686	1,055	1,929	1,556	922	1,873	1,369	884
Florida	12,539	10,301	7,610	11,774	8,753	5,963	11,043	8,078	5,444
Georgia	6,080	4,249	3,285	5,893	3,860	2,583	5,396	3,811	2,299
Kentucky............................	3,012	2,819	1,796	2,993	2,557	1,544	2,928	2,391	1,388
Louisiana	3,249	2,923	1,957	3,255	2,730	1,766	3,137	(c)	1,784
Maryland............................	3,922	3,070	2,396	3,925	2,715	2,024	3,811	2,577	1,794
Mississippi.........................	2,014	1,865	1,140	2,047	1,740	994	1,961	1,826	894
Missouri.............................	4,297	4,194	2,731	4,105	3,861	2,360	3,902	3,343	2,158
North Carolina....................	6,453	5,527	3,501	5,797	5,122	2,915	5,800	4,300	2,515
Oklahoma...........................	2,515	2,143	1,464	2,531	2,234	1,234	2,419	1,823	1,206
South Carolina....................	3,214	2,315	1,618	2,977	2,157	1,386	2,872	1,814	1,203
Tennessee...........................	4,284	3,532	2,437	4,221	3,181	2,076	3,660	3,056	1,894
Texas.................................	16,071	13,098	7,411	14,479	12,365	6,408	13,698	10,541	5,612
Virginia..............................	5,194	4,528	3,195	5,263	3,770	2,790	5,089	3,323	2,417
West Virginia	1,406	1,169	744	1,416	1,068	648	1,414	(c)	636
Regional total	79,453	66,016	44,223	75,938	60,198	37,279	72,223	50,723	33,662
Western Region									
Alaska................................	460	472	313	436	474	286	410	415	245
Arizona..............................	3,800	2,643	2,038	3,625	2,173	1,532	3,233	2,245	1,404
California...........................	22,075	16,557	12,589	21,461	15,707	11,142	19,526	15,662	10,263
Colorado............................	3,246	2,890	2,130	3,067	2,274	1,741	2,843	2,285	1,551
Hawaii	873	647	429	909	637	368	882	545	370
Idaho.................................	996	798	613	921	728	502	858	700	492
Montana.............................	680	596	450	668	698	411	647	590	417
Nevada...............................	1,580	1,094	830	1,390	898	609	1,180	778	464
New Mexico	1,318	1,105	756	1,263	973	599	1,224	838	580
Oregon...............................	2,665	2,120	1,837	2,530	1,944	1,534	2,344	1,962	1,399
Utah...................................	1,522	1,278	928	1,465	1,123	771	1,322	1,050	691
Washington	4,596	3,508	2,883	4,368	3,336	2,487	4,122	3,078	2,294
Wyoming	370	246	244	358	220	214	343	241	216
Regional total	44,181	33,954	26,040	42,461	31,185	22,196	38,934	30,389	20,386
Regional total without California...........	22,106	17,397	13,451	21,000	15,478	11,054	19,408	14,727	10,123
Dist. of Columbia	435	384	228	411	354	202	422	361	186

Sources: 1996 data provided by Committee for the Study of the American Electorate, with update by the state election administration offices. U.S. Congress, Clerk of the House, Statistics of the Presidential and Congressional Election, 2004, U.S. Census Bureau, Current Population Survey, November 2002, released July 2004.

The Council of State Governments' survey of election officials, January 2007. 2000 data provided by the Federal Election Commission.

Key:
(a) Estimated population, 18 years old and over. Includes armed forces in each state, aliens, and institutional population.
(b) Number voting is number of ballots cast in presidential race.
(c) Information not available.
(d) No statewide registration required. Excluded from totals for persons registered.

2006 Initiatives and Referendums[1]

By John G. Matsusaka

Propositions again were a prominent feature on ballots in 2006, with voters in 37 states deciding on 226 statewide measures. The number of citizen-initiated measures, 79, was the third highest ever. The most common issues were eminent domain (12 states) and same-sex marriage (nine states). Michigan voters approved a measure to ban the use of racial preferences, and South Dakota voters repealed an abortion ban.

A total of 204 ballot propositions went before the voters in 37 states Nov. 7, 2006, up from 162 in November 2004 and 202 in November 2002. Voters approved 137 measures and rejected 67. The approval rate of 67 percent was identical to the 67 percent approval rate in November 2004. Of the measures, 76 were initiatives (new laws qualified by petition), four were referendums (proposals to repeal existing laws), one was placed on the ballot by a commission, and the rest were legislative measures.

For the year (counting propositions that appeared on primary and special election ballots), voters decided 226 propositions and approved 156 of them. The 79 initiatives for the year (including the three that were voted on in the summer) constitute the third largest total since the initiative process was first used in 1902 (behind 93 in 1996 and 90 in 1914), and show that the initiative wave set off by California's tax-cutting Proposition 13 in 1978 is still swelling.[2] Voters approved 32 initiatives during the year. The 41 percent approval rate is equal to the historical average.

Table A summarizes the number of propositions by state, and the number that were approved, for the entire year. Table B lists each proposition, provides a brief description of its subject and reports the election outcome.[3]

Multi-state Issues

As happens every year, several issues emerged on the ballot in multiple states. The two most common issues—eminent domain and same-sex marriage— were largely responses to court rulings.

▪ **Eminent domain.** Land use measures designed to restrict the power of eminent domain were the most common type of ballot proposition in 2006. To a large extent, these measures were reactions to the U. S. Supreme Court's *Kelo v. New London* decision in June 2005 that allowed governments to condemn property for use by a private developer. Legislatures in more than two dozen states took action to prevent such condemnations, and propositions were placed on the ballot in 12 states. Nine states—Arizona, Florida, Georgia, Michigan, Nevada, New Hampshire, North Dakota, Oregon and South Carolina—approved the measures in November, Louisiana approved a measure in September, and two states (California and Idaho) rejected them. Four states also voted on "regulatory takings" measures that required governments to compensate owners when their property values were reduced by land use regulations, following in the wake of Oregon's Measure 37 in 2004. In Arizona, California and Idaho, the regulatory takings language was combined with the anti-*Kelo* language. Arizona voters approved the package but voters in California and Idaho said no, most likely because of the regulatory takings language. In Washington, a measure concerned with regulatory takings alone was defeated. Many of the land use measures were apparently funded by Howie Rich, a New York developer with libertarian leanings.

▪ **Same-sex marriage.** The second most common subject for ballot propositions was same-sex marriage. Constitutional amendments to define marriage as solely between a man and a woman went before the voters in nine states. The amendments were approved in eight states—Colorado, Idaho, South Carolina, South Dakota, Tennessee, Virginia and Wisconsin in November, and Alabama in June—bringing the number of states that have approved such amendments to 23. Arizona became the first state to reject a constitutional amendment banning same-sex marriage, in part because the measure also included a provision that would have prevented the state from giving benefits to same-sex couples. Colorado voters rejected a measure that would have created "domestic partnerships" that gave same-sex couples the same legal rights as married couples.

▪ **Tobacco and smoking.** Health organizations qualified initiatives in several states to increase taxes on tobacco products and ban smoking in public places. Tobacco companies dedicated a reported $100 million to fight these measures, and were successful in

Table A: Initiatives and Referendums State-by-State Totals, 2006

State	Initiatives	Referendums	Legislative measures	Notable issues
Alabama	. . .	. . .	4 (3)	Same-sex marriage
Alaska	4 (3)	. . .	. . .	Campaign contribution limits
Arizona	10 (5)	. . .	9 (7) (a)	Eminent domain, marriage, immigrants, smoking
Arkansas	. . .	. . .	2 (2)	Bonds
California	9 (2)	. . .	6 (5)	Eminent domain, bonds, oil tax, abortion
Colorado	7 (3)	. . .	7 (4)	Marriage, minimum wage, legal marijuana
Florida	1 (1)	. . .	5 (5)	Eminent domain, amendment approval
Georgia	. . .	. . .	9 (9)	Eminent domain
Hawaii	. . .	. . .	5 (4)	Mandatory retirement for judges
Idaho	2 (0)	. . .	3 (3)	Land use, sales tax increase, marriage
Louisiana	. . .	. . .	21 (21)	New Orleans assessors, eminent domain
Maine	1 (0)	. . .	1 (1)	Tax and spending limits
Maryland	. . .	1 (1)	3 (3)	Sale of parklands
Massachusetts	3 (0)	. . .	. . .	Liquor sales by grocery stores, fusion ballots
Michigan	2 (1)	1 (0)	2 (2)	Racial preferences/affirmative action
Minnesota	. . .	. . .	1 (1)	Gas tax
Missouri	3 (2)	. . .	3 (3)	Stem cell, minimum wage, tobacco tax
Montana	2 (2)	. . .	1 (0)	Minimum wage, lobbying
Nebraska	2 (0)	1 (0)	7 (2)	Tax and spending limits, video keno
Nevada	6 (4)	. . .	4 (1)	Eminent domain, smoking ban, minimum wage
New Hampshire	. . .	. . .	2 (2)	Eminent domain
New Jersey	. . .	. . .	3 (3)	Property tax relief, alien land law
New Mexico	. . .	. . .	7 (7)	Bonds
North Dakota	2 (1)	. . .	3 (3)	Eminent domain
Ohio	4 (2)	. . .	. . .	Smoking ban, slot machines, minimum wage
Oklahoma	. . .	. . .	4 (4)	Liquor sales on election day
Oregon	10 (3)	. . .	. . .	Eminent domain, tax and spending limits, abortion
Pennsylvania	. . .	. . .	1 (1)	Bonds for veterans
Rhode Island	. . .	. . .	9 (7)	Casino gambling, bonds
South Carolina	. . .	. . .	7 (7)	Eminent domain, marriage, property tax limit
South Dakota	8 (2)	1 (0)	2 (1)	Abortion, lawsuits against judges
Tennessee	. . .	. . .	2 (2)	Same-sex marriage
Utah	. . .	. . .	1 (1)	Property tax exemption
Virginia	. . .	. . .	3 (3)	Same-sex marriage
Washington	3 (1)	. . .	1 (1)	Regulatory takings, estate tax
Wisconsin	. . .	. . .	2 (2)	Death penalty, same-sex marriage
Wyoming	. . .	. . .	3 (3)	Scholarships
Total	79 (32)	4 (1)	143 (123)	

Source: Initiative & Referendum Institute (www.iandrinstitute.org).
Note: The table reports the total number of propositions during 2006, including primary and special elections as well as the November general election. The number of measures that were approved is reported in parentheses. A referendum in which the original law is retained is considered to have been "approved."

Key:
(a) Includes proposition from commission in Arizona.

defeating tobacco tax increases in California and Missouri. Voters approved tobacco tax increases that were not heavily contested in Arizona and South Dakota. Smoking bans were approved in all three states where they were on the ballot—Arizona, Nevada and Ohio. Voters in each state rejected "counter-initiatives" offering less restrictive smoking bans that were placed on the ballot by pro-tobacco groups.

▪ **Minimum wage.** Initiatives to increase the minimum wage and index it to inflation appeared on the ballot in six states—Arizona, Colorado, Montana, Missouri, Nevada and Ohio—and all were approved.

These measures were placed on the ballot as part of a coordinated campaign to increase support for Democratic candidates and possibly tip the balance of power in the U.S. House and Senate, apparently the first national effort of this kind.

▪ **Government finances.** Voters seemed to be in a fiscally expansive mood. TABOR-style tax and spending limitations were rejected in three states—Maine, Nebraska and Oregon—and a property tax limit failed in South Dakota. Voters approved all 16 statewide bond issues across the states. Leading the way was California, where voters said yes to five bond

Table B: Complete List of Statewide Ballot Propositions in 2006

State	Type	Description	Result
Alabama			
Amendment (June 6)	L/CA	Ban on same-sex marriage.	Approved 81-19
Amendment 1	L/CA	Concerning city of Prichard.	Failed 49.8-50.2
Amendment 2	L/CA	Supplementary property tax for schools.	Approved 59-41
Amendment 3	L/CA	Concerning Macon County Board of Education.	Approved 61-39
Alaska			
Measure 1 (Aug. 22)	I/ST	Lowers campaign contribution limits.	Approved 73-27
Measure 2 (Aug. 22)	I/ST	Taxes commercial passenger ships visiting the state.	Approved 52-48
Measure 1	I/ST	Reduces legislature sessions from 4 to 3 months.	Approved 51-49
Measure 2	I/ST	Taxes natural gas leases.	Failed 35-65
Arizona			
Prop. 100	L/CA	Denies bail to illegal immigrants.	Approved 78-22
Prop. 101	L/CA	Lowers local property tax limits.	Approved 51-49
Prop. 102	L/CA	No punitive damages to illegal immigrants.	Approved 74-26
Prop. 103	L/CA	Makes English the official language of the state.	Approved 74-26
Prop. 104	L/CA	Authorizes cities to borrow more for streets and public safety.	Approved 59-41
Prop. 105	L/CA	Preserves 43,000 acres of state land (response to 106 by cattlemen).	Failed 29-71
Prop. 106	I/CA	Preserves 690,000 acres of state trust land.	Failed 49-51
Prop. 107	I/CA	Defines marriage as solely between a man and a woman.	Failed 48-52
Prop. 200	I/ST	Awards $1 million to a random voter after each general election.	Failed 33-67
Prop. 201	I/ST	Prohibits smoking in public places (health industry version).	Approved 55-45
Prop. 202	I/ST	Raises minimum wage and indexes it to inflation.	Approved 65-35
Prop. 203	I/ST	Increases tobacco tax to fund early childhood development.	Approved 53-47
Prop. 204	I/ST	Minimum living space for pregnant pigs and calves.	Approved 62-38
Prop. 205	I/ST	Requires absentee ballots to be mailed to all voters.	Failed 29-71
Prop. 206	I/ST	Prohibits smoking in public places except bars (industry version).	Failed 43-57
Prop. 207	I/ST	Eminent domain, regulatory takings.	Approved 65-35
Prop. 300	L/ST	Prohibits state subsidies to illegal aliens.	Approved 71-29
Prop. 301	L/ST	Limits probation for methamphetamine convicts.	Approved 58-42
Prop. 302	C/ST	Increases legislator salaries.	Failed 48-52
Arkansas			
Amendment 1	L/CA	Allows charities to run bingo games and raffles.	Approved 69-31
Referred Question 1	L/ST	Authorizes the state to borrow $250 million for education.	Approved 69-31
California			
Prop. 80 (June 6)	L/ST	$600 million bond issue for libraries.	Failed 47-53
Prop. 81 (June 6)	I/CA + ST	Tax increase, high-income individuals to fund universal preschool.	Failed 39-61
Prop. 1A	L/CA	Prevents diversion of gas tax revenue meant for roads.	Approved 77-23
Prop. 1B	L/ST	$19.925 billion bonds for road projects.	Approved 61-39
Prop. 1C	L/ST	$2.85 billion bonds for low-income housing.	Approved 58-42
Prop. 1D	L/ST	$10.416 billion bonds for public school facilities.	Approved 57-43
Prop. 1E	L/ST	$4.09 billion bonds for levee repairs and flood control projects.	Approved 64-36
Prop. 83	I/ST	Increases penalties for sex crimes.	Approved 70-30
Prop. 84	I/ST	$5.388 billion bonds for water and conservation projects.	Approved 54-46
Prop. 85	I/CA	Waiting period and parental notification for abortion by minor.	Failed 46-54
Prop. 86	I/CA + ST	$2.60 per pack cigarette surtax with funds for hospitals.	Failed 48-52
Prop. 87	I/CA + ST	$4 billion for alternative energy research, severance tax on oil.	Failed 45-55
Prop. 88	I/CA + ST	Establishes a $50 parcel tax for schools.	Failed 23-77
Prop. 89	I/ST	Public funding for candidates.	Failed 26-74
Prop. 90	I/CA	Eminent domain, for regulatory takings.	Failed 48-52
Colorado			
Amendment 38	I/CA	Extends initiative rights.	Failed 31-69
Amendment 39	I/CA	65% of school spending for classroom instruction (Republican).	Failed 38-62
Amendment 40	I/CA	Establishes term limits for appellate court judges.	Failed 43-57
Amendment 41	I/CA	Restricts lobbying and gifts.	Approved 63-37
Amendment 42	I/CA	Increases minimum wage and indexes it to inflation.	Approved 53-47
Amendment 43	I/CA	Defines marriage as between one man and one woman.	Approved 55-45
Amendment 44	I/CA	Legalizes possession of one ounce of marijuana.	Failed 41-59
Referendum E	L/CA	Reduces property taxes for disabled veterans.	Approved 79-21
Referendum F	L/CA	Extends time to contest recall petitions.	Failed 45-55
Referendum G	L/CA	Removes obsolete constitutional provisions.	Approved 76-24
Referendum H	L/ST	Prohibits tax deduction of wages paid to illegal aliens.	Approved 51-49
Referendum I	L/CA	Establishes "domestic partnerships."	Failed 48-52
Referendum J	L/ST	65% of school spending for classroom instruction (Democratic).	Failed 42-58
Referendum K	L/ST	To sue federal government to enforce immigration laws.	Approved 56-44

See footnotes at end of table.

Complete List of Statewide Ballot Propositions in 2006 — Continued

State	Type	Description	Result
Florida			
Amendment 1	L/CA	Limits use of nonrecurring revenue.	Approved 60-40
Amendment 3	L/CA	Requires 60% approval for constitutional amendments.	Approved 58-42
Amendment 4	I/CA	Tobacco settlement money only for tobacco education.	Approved 61-39
Amendment 6	L/CA	Increases homestead tax exemption for low-income seniors.	Approved 76-24
Amendment 7	L/CA	Reduces homestead tax for disabled veterans.	Approved 78-22
Amendment 8	L/CA	Restricts use of eminent domain for private projects.	Approved 69-31
Georgia			
Amendment 1	L/CA	Restricts use of eminent domain for private projects.	Approved 83-17
Amendment 2	L/CA	State must preserve the "tradition of fishing and hunting."	Approved 81-19
Amendment 3	L/CA	Allows state to issue special vehicle license plates.	Approved 67-33
Question A	L/ST	Sales tax exemption for farm equipment.	Approved 61-39
Question B	L/ST	Sales tax exemption for historic aircraft.	Approved 71-29
Question C	L/ST	Sales tax exemption for property of charitable organizations.	Approved 68-32
Question D	L/ST	Property tax exemption for people 65 and older.	Approved 89-11
Question E	L/ST	Homestead tax break for spouse of officers killed in line of duty.	Approved 85-15
Question F	L/ST	Property tax limit for spouse of peace officer killed in line of duty.	Approved 90-10
Hawaii			
Amendment 1	L/CA	Governor chooses regents from pool nominated by commission.	Approved 62-38
Amendment 2	L/CA	Creates commission to recommend state salaries.	Approved 59-41
Amendment 3	L/CA	Repeals mandatory retirement age of 70 for judges.	Failed 38-62
Amendment 4	L/CA	Legislature to set standard for conviction in sex crimes.	Approved 77-23
Amendment 5	L/CA	Authorizes state to issue bonds for agricultural enterprises.	Approved 71-29
Idaho			
Prop. 1	I/ST	Adds 1% sales tax with funds dedicated to K–12 education.	Failed 45-55
Prop. 2	I/ST	Eminent domain, regulatory takings.	Failed 24-76
HJR 2	L/CA	Defines marriage as solely between one man and one woman.	Approved 63-37
SJR 107	L/CA	Creates restricted endowment from tobacco settlement money.	Approved 58-42
Advisory	L/AD	Asks if state should retain 3 mill property tax relief program.	Approved 72-28
Louisiana			
No. 1 (Sept. 30)	L/CA	Dedicates federal money from oil drilling to coastal conservation.	Approved 82-18
No. 2 (Sept. 30)	L/CA	Dedicates 20% of tobacco settlement money to coastal conservation.	Approved 79-21
No. 3 (Sept. 30)	L/CA	Merges regional levee boards.	Approved 81-19
No. 4 (Sept. 30)	L/CA	Government may not pay more than market value for property.	Approved 61-39
No. 5 (Sept. 30)	L/CA	Restricts use of eminent domain for private projects.	Approved 55-45
No. 6 (Sept. 30)	L/CA	Original owner may buy back unused expropriated property.	Approved 50.1-49.9
No. 7 (Sept. 30)	L/CA	Allows 35% of Medicaid Trust Fund to be invested in stocks.	Approved 63-37
No. 8 (Sept. 30)	L/CA	Extends tax exemption for homes damaged by natural disasters.	Approved 79-21
No. 9 (Sept. 30)	L/CA	Legislative supermajority to require more spending by school districts.	Approved 51-49
No. 10 (Sept. 30)	L/CA	Allows 35% of state university funds to be invested in stocks.	Approved 59-41
No. 11 (Sept. 30)	L/CA	Extends homestead tax exemption to property owned by living trust.	Approved 66-34
No. 12 (Sept. 30)	L/CA	Requires election to fill vacant offices.	Approved 69-31
No. 13 (Sept. 30)	L/CA	Increases number of years of law practice required to be a judge.	Approved 70-30
No. 1	L/CA	Freezes property tax assessments for disabled veterans.	Approved 68-32
No. 2	L/CA	Increases share of severance taxes allocated to local governments.	Approved 59-41
No. 3	L/CA	Property tax exemption for medical equipment.	Approved 59-41
No. 4	L/CA	Exempts motor vehicles from municipal taxes.	Approved 61-39
No. 5	L/CA	Exempts consigned art from ad valorem taxes.	Approved 54-46
No. 6	L/CA	Authorizes legislature to create new district court judgeships.	Approved 61-39
No. 7	L/CA	Replaces seven New Orleans tax assessors with single office.	Approved 78-22
No. 8	L/CA	Expands financing authority of East Baton Rouge school district.	Approved 55-45
Maine			
Question 1	I/ST	Tax and spending limits (TABOR).	Failed 46-54
Question 2	L/CA	Requires initiative to be submitted by constitutional deadline.	Approved 54-46
Maryland			
Question 1	L/CA	Prohibits public works board from selling park lands.	Approved 85-15
Question 2	L/CA	Allows more appeals to Court of Special Appeals.	Approved 78-22
Question 3	L/CA	Limits jury trials for civil cases with less than $10,000 at stake.	Approved 67-33
Question 4	R/ST	Election board procedures.	Approved 71-29
Massachusetts			
Prop. 1	I/ST	Allows food stores to sell wine.	Failed 44-56
Prop. 2	I/ST	Allows fusion candidates (nominated by more than one party).	Failed 35-65
Prop. 3	I/ST	Allows child care providers to bargain collectively with state.	Failed 48-52

See footnotes at end of table.

Complete List of Statewide Ballot Propositions in 2006—Continued

State	Type	Description	Result
Michigan			
Proposal 1	L/CA	Prevents diversion of state conservation funds to other purposes.	Approved 80-20
Proposal 2	I/CA	Prohibits racial preferences/affirmative action.	Approved 58-42
Proposal 3	R/ST	Allows hunting of mourning doves.	Failed 31-69
Proposal 4	L/CA	Restricts use of eminent domain for private purposes.	Approved 80-20
Proposal 5	I/ST	Sets minimum spending levels for schools.	Failed 38-62
Minnesota			
Amendment	L/CA	Requiring car tax revenue to be used for transportation projects.	Approved 57-43
Missouri			
Amendment 1 (Aug. 8)	L/CA	Extends for 10 years a 1/10% sales tax surtax for parks.	Approved 71-29
Amendment 2	I/CA	Allows stem cell research.	Approved 51-49
Amendment 3	I/CA	Increases tobacco tax.	Failed 49-51
Amendment 6	L/CA	Property tax exemption for nonprofit veteran groups.	Approved 61-39
Amendment 7	L/CA	Strips pensions from government officials convicted of felonies.	Approved 84-16
Prop. B	I/ST	Increases minimum wage and indexes it to inflation.	Approved 76-24
Montana			
C-43	L/CA	Changes name of State Auditor to Insurance Commissioner.	Failed 36-64
I-151	I/ST	Raises minimum wage and indexes it to inflation.	Approved 73-27
I-153	I/ST	Prohibits lobbying by government officials 2 years after leaving office.	Approved 76-24
Nebraska			
Amendment 1 (May 9)	L/CA	Salary increase for legislators.	Failed 45-55
Measure 421	I/ST	Permits a limited number of video keno machines.	Failed 39-61
Measure 422	R/ST	School district consolidation law.	Failed 44-56
Measure 423	I/CA	Limits the growth of state spending and taxes (TABOR).	Failed 30-70
Amendment 1	L/CA	Allows local governments to acquire land for use by nonprofits.	Failed 47-53
Amendment 2	L/CA	Management of local government endowments.	Failed 43-57
Amendment 3	L/CA	Allocates $1 million for compulsive gamblers.	Failed 39-61
Amendment 4	L/CA	Allows executive and courts to supervise parolees.	Approved 56-44
Amendment 5	L/CA	Dedicates $40 million to early childhood development.	Approved 54-46
Amendment 6	L/CA	Allows public debt for property that is not blighted.	Failed 30-70
Nevada			
Question 1	I/CA	Legislature must appropriate education before other programs.	Approved 55-45
Question 2	I/CA	Restricts use of eminent domain for private purposes.	Approved 63-37
Question 4	I/ST	Bans smoking in public places except bars/restaurants (industry).	Failed 48-52
Question 5	I/ST	Bans smoking in public places with children (health orgs).	Approved 54-46
Question 6	I/CA	Increases minimum wage and indexes it to inflation.	Approved 69-31
Question 7	I/ST	Legalizes possession of one ounce of marijuana.	Failed 44-56
Question 8	L/ST	Removes sales tax on trade-in cars and farm equipment.	Approved 69-31
Question 9	L/CA	Reduces board of regents from 13 to 9 members.	Failed 49-51
Question 10	L/CA	Allows legislature to call special session.	Failed 48-52
Question 11	L/CA	Doubles legislator pay.	Failed 30-70
New Hampshire			
Amendment 1	L/CA	Restricts the use of eminent domain for private purposes.	Approved 86-14
Amendment 2	L/CA	Prohibits division of cities when drawing legislative districts.	Approved 71-29
New Jersey			
Public Question 1	L/CA	Dedicates state revenue to reduce property taxes.	Approved 67-33
Public Question 2	L/CA	Dedicates state environment funds to recreational areas.	Approved 60-40
Public Question 3	L/CA	Increases portion of gas tax that is dedicated to transportation.	Approved 60-40
New Mexico			
Amendment 1	L/CA	Repeals obsolete Alien Land law.	Approved 70-30
Amendment 2	L/CA	Removes debt limits/referendum rules for lease-purchases.	Approved 69-31
Amendment 3	L/CA	Creates but does not fund water trust fund.	Approved 66-34
Amendment 4	L/CA	Permits state to pay costs of affordable housing.	Approved 56-44
Bond Issue A	L/ST	$15.958 million bonds for senior citizen facilities.	Approved 62-38
Bond Issue B	L/ST	$118.36 million bonds for higher education capital.	Approved 55-45
Bond Issue C	L/ST	$9.09 million bonds for libraries.	Approved 57-43
North Dakota			
Measure 1 (June 13)	L/CA	Removes obsolete language.	Approved 73-27
Measure 2 (June 13)	L/CA	Removes obsolete language.	Approved 73-27
Measure 1	I/CA	Public universities may spend more than endowment interest.	Approved 67-33
Measure 2	I/CA	Prohibits use of eminent domain for private projects.	Approved 67-33
Measure 3	I/ST	Requires joint custody of children after divorce.	Failed 44-56

See footnotes at end of table.

Complete List of Statewide Ballot Propositions in 2006 — Continued

State	Type	Description	Result
Ohio			
Issue 2	I/CA	Increases the minimum wage and indexes it to inflation.	Approved 57-43
Issue 3	I/CA	Allows slot machines, dedicating the revenue for college scholarships.	Failed 43-57
Issue 4	I/CA	Bans smoking in many public places except bars (industry).	Failed 36-64
Issue 5	I/ST	Bans smoking in public places (health org).	Approved 59-51
Oklahoma			
Question 724	L/CA	Prohibits paying legislators who are in jail.	Approved 87-13
Question 725	L/CA	Allows use of rainy day funds to subsidize at-risk manufacturers.	Approved 54-46
Question 733	L/CA	Allows sale of alcohol on election day by package stores.	Approved 53-47
Question 734	L/CA	No property taxes on goods shipped through the state.	Approved 63-37
Oregon			
Measure 39	I/ST	Restricts use of eminent domain for private purposes.	Approved 67-33
Measure 40	I/CA	Requires appellate court judges to be elected by district.	Failed 43-57
Measure 41	I/ST	Increases state income tax deductions to federal level.	Failed 37-63
Measure 42	I/ST	No credit scores when calculating insurance premiums.	Failed 35-65
Measure 43	I/ST	Waiting period and parental notification for abortion by minor.	Failed 45-55
Measure 44	I/ST	Residents without drug coverage eligible for state program.	Approved 78-22
Measure 45	I/CA	Restores voter-approved term limits struck down by court.	Failed 41-59
Measure 46	I/CA	Limits on campaign contributions/expenditures.	Failed 40-60
Measure 47	I/ST	Limits on contributions, effective only if Measure 46 approved.	Approved 53-47
Measure 48	I/CA	Limits state spending growth and taxes (TABOR).	Failed 29-71
Pennsylvania			
Referendum	L/ST	$20 million bond issue for Gulf War (1990–91) veterans.	Approved 61-39
Rhode Island			
Question 1	L/CA	Authorizes privately run resort casino in state.	Rejected 37-63
Question 2	L/CA	Voting rights of felons.	Approved 52-48
Question 3	L/CA	Increases rainy day funds, restricts use.	Approved 59-41
Question 4	L/ST	$72.79 million bonds for buildings at state university and college.	Approved 62-38
Question 5	L/ST	$88.5 million bonds for transportation projects.	Approved 75-25
Question 6	L/ST	$11 million bonds for zoo improvements.	Approved 68-32
Question 7	L/ST	$4 million bonds for state park in Newport.	Rejected 49-51
Question 8	L/ST	$3 million bonds for recreation projects.	Approved 61-39
Question 9	L/ST	$50 million bonds for affordable housing.	Approved 66-34
South Carolina			
Amendment 1	L/CA	Defines marriage as solely between one man and one woman.	Approved 78-22
Amendment 2A	L/CA	Allows either house of legislature to adjourn by majority vote.	Approved 79-21
Amendment 2B	L/CA	Deletes constitutional provision contrary to 2A.	Approved 76-24
Amendment 3A	L/CA	State retirement systems may invest in foreign companies.	Approved 71-29
Amendment 3B	L/CA	Eliminates state investment advisory panel.	Approved 67-33
Amendment 4	L/CA	Limits property tax assessments to +15% every 5 years.	Approved 69-31
Amendment 5	L/CA	Prohibits use of eminent domain for private projects.	Approved 86-14
South Dakota			
Amendment C	L/CA	Defines marriage as solely between one man and one woman.	Approved 52-48
Amendment D	I/CA	Limits annual increase in property tax assessments to 3%.	Failed 20-80
Amendment E	I/CA	Establishes grand jury to evaluate civil lawsuits involving judges.	Failed 11-89
Amendment F	L/CA	Revises technical constitutional language regarding legislature.	Failed 32-68
Measure 2	I/ST	Increases tobacco tax, dedicates revenue to health services.	Approved 61-39
Measure 3	I/ST	Prohibits school year from beginning before September.	Failed 43-57
Measure 4	I/ST	Allows medical use of marijuana.	Failed 48-52
Measure 5	I/ST	State-owned aircraft to be used only for official business.	Approved 55-45
Measure 7	I/ST	Repeals video lottery.	Failed 33-67
Measure 8	I/ST	Repeals 4% tax on wireless phone service.	Failed 39-61
Referred Law 6	R/ST	Ban on abortion.	Failed 44-56
Tennessee			
Amendment 1	L/CA	Defines marriage as solely between one man and one woman.	Approved 81-19
Amendment 2	L/CA	Property tax relief for people 65 and older.	Approved 83-17
Utah			
Amendment 1	L/CA	Allows tax exemption of property producing no revenue.	Approved 62-38
Virginia			
Question 1	L/CA	Defines marriage as solely between one man and one woman.	Approved 57-43
Question 2	L/CA	Allows churches to incorporate.	Approved 65-35
Question 3	L/CA	Allows tax breaks for new structures in development areas.	Approved 65-35

See footnotes at end of table.

Complete List of Statewide Ballot Propositions in 2006 — Continued

State	Type	Description	Result
Washington			
I-920	I/ST	Repeals estate tax.	Failed 38-62
I-933	I/ST	Requires compensation for regulatory takings.	Failed 41-59
I-937	I/ST	Requires utilities to use minimum amounts of renewable fuels.	Approved 52-48
HJR 4233	L/CA	Authorizes increased property tax exemptions.	Approved 80-20
Wisconsin			
Amendment	L/CA	Defines marriage as between man and woman.	Approved 59-41
Advisory measure	L/AD	Reinstates death penalty.	Approved 56-44
Wyoming			
Amendment A	L/CA	Prohibits diversion of money in the state's Mineral Trust Fund.	Approved 74-26
Amendment B	L/CA	Repeals limits on redistribution of property taxes for schools.	Approved 58-42
Amendment C	L/CA	Creates a fund for higher education scholarships.	Approved 75-25

Source: Initiative & Referendum Institute (www.iandrinstitute.org).
Note: Unless another date is given, a proposition appeared on the November 7 ballot. For referendums, "approved" means the challenged law was upheld by the voters; "rejected" means it was repealed.
Key:
AD — Advisory (not binding)

C — Commission
CA — Constitutional amendment
I — Initiative
L — Legislative measure
R — Referendum
ST — Statute

measures authorizing a combined $43 billion of debt for a variety of purposes including roads, schools, water projects and low-income housing. Bond issues were also approved in Arkansas (1), New Mexico (3), Pennsylvania (1), and Rhode Island (6).

▪ **Abortion.** South Dakota's Referred Law 6 received national attention. In an effort to create a test case for the U. S. Supreme Court to reverse *Roe v. Wade*, the South Dakota legislature passed a law banning abortion in early 2006. Opponents of the abortion ban qualified Referred Law 6 for the ballot, and voters repealed the ban Nov. 7 by a 56-44 margin. One reason the ban was repealed in traditionally pro-life South Dakota was due to concern that it was too restrictive and lacked adequate exceptions for the health of the mother. Abortion rights activists were also able to defeat laws in California and Oregon that would have required notification of parents before a minor received an abortion.

▪ **Animal rights** activists continued to enjoy success at the ballot box. In Arizona, voters approved an initiative that guaranteed minimum living space for pregnant pigs and calves. Florida voters approved a similar measure in 2002. Michigan voters repealed a law passed by the legislature that would have allowed hunting mourning doves.

▪ **Initiative process.** Two measures concerned the initiative process, and initiative proponents were defeated in both cases. In Florida, voters approved Amendment 3 that requires future constitutional amendments to receive 60 percent approval to pass. Florida becomes the only initiative state with a supermajority requirement and one of only two states overall with such a requirement for constitutional amendments. Colorado voters rejected Amendment 38 that would have extended initiative rights to various governments throughout the state and made it harder for courts to disqualify initiatives from the ballot.

Notable Single-state Issues

▪ **Racial preferences/affirmative action.** Michigan voters approved Proposal 2 that prohibits public institutions such as the University of Michigan from giving preferential treatment on the basis of race. This endorsement by voters could give new life to the campaign to ban racial preferences that seemed to have stalled after early successes in California and Washington. Proposal 2 was opposed by state leaders of both parties, including both gubernatorial candidates, and its hefty 58-42 margin was something of a surprise after early polls showed it failing. The passage of measures in California and Washington, and now Michigan, in all cases against the recommendations of bipartisan coalitions of political leaders, suggests that political leaders may be out of step with voters on this issue.

▪ **Stem cell research.** A contentious campaign emerged in Missouri concerning Amendment 2, which proposed a constitutional right to use embryonic stem cells in research. The issue followed on the heels of a more extensive measure in California in 2004 that was approved by a large majority. The Missouri campaign attracted mostly local attention until a commercial featuring actor Michael J. Fox, who suffers from Parkinson's disease, was aired in the last month of the campaign. The commercial generated intense discussion nationally, and spilled over into a close U.S. Senate race in which the Democratic candidate supported Amendment 2 while the Republican candidate opposed it. The final vote on Amendment 2 was extremely close, with 51 percent of the voters in favor of it. The measure, highly technical in nature, appeared to lose some support in the waning weeks of the campaign in response to claims that it might create a constitutional right to human cloning.

- **California's Proposition 87.** This initiative, proposed to tax oil extraction and use the money for development of renewable fuels, failed in California. The proposal itself was not exceptional—a very similar measure was rejected in California in 1980—but the spending on it was. Combined spending by both sides exceeded $150 million, breaking the previous record for the most money ever spent on a single ballot proposition by more than 50 percent. The Yes-on-87 campaign was largely funded by Hollywood producer Steve Bing, whose $50 million in contributions set a record for an individual in a ballot proposition campaign. Much of the funding for the opposition came from the oil industry.

Trends

The most obvious trend is the continued use of ballot propositions to decide important state issues, and especially the growing popularity of initiatives that citizens place on the ballot. The modern initiative movement began in the late 1970s with California's tax-cutting Proposition 13. Each decade since the 1970s has seen more initiatives on the ballot and more initiatives approved than the previous decade, with a total of 379 in the 1990s, 167 of which were approved. In the current decade, 300 initiatives have been on the ballot through 2006, with 127 passing, on track to match the numbers for the 1990s. The current decade is already the second busiest in history, with more than an entire election cycle to go.

Another interesting development likely to become a trend was the systematic attempt this year to use ballot propositions to influence candidate elections. Proponents of this strategy hope that by placing their measures on the ballot, more of their supporters will be drawn to the polls by the measure and then end up supporting a favored candidate. The idea is not new—California Gov. Pete Wilson is widely believed to have benefited from spillovers associated with Prop. 187, a proposal to deny government services

to illegal aliens, during his re-election campaign in 1994. What was new this year was the attempt by Democratic groups to use ballot propositions as part of a national strategy to tip the balance of power in Washington, D.C.[4] Liberal groups initially attempted to qualify minimum wage measures in 11 states, ending up with initiatives on the ballot in six states, some of which featured close Senate races (including Missouri and Montana). They also leaned heavily on the stem cell measure in Missouri, and even attempted to generate spillovers in states without such a measure on the ballot, such as Maryland. Whether the strategy ultimately made the difference for the Democrats remains to be seen after scholars have sifted through the election returns, but regardless, groups on both sides of the political spectrum are likely to attempt to exploit ballot proposition spillovers in 2008.

Notes

[1] This article uses referend*ums* instead of referend*a* as the plural of referendum following the *Oxford English Dictionary* and common practice.

[2] For an overview of initiative use since 1904 including year-by-year counts of the number of initiatives and the number that were approved, see *Initiative Use, 1904–2006*, published by the Initiative and Referendum Institute, November 2006, available at *www.iandrinstitute.org*.

[3] All current data provided by the Initiative and Referendum Institute at USC and available at *www.iandrinstitute. org*. Historical and legal information taken from *Initiative and Referendum Almanac*, by M. Dane Waters (Carolina Academic Publishers, 2003) and *For the Many or the Few: The Initiative, Public Policy, and Direct Democracy*, by John G. Matsusaka (University of Chicago Press, 2004).

[4] Same-sex marriage amendments in 2004 are often claimed to have put George W. Bush over the top in his re-election campaign, but the scholarly evidence suggests that they did not help him. See Alan Abromowitz, "Terrorism, Gay Marriage, and Incumbency: Explaining the Republican Victory in the 2004 Presidential Election," *FORUM*, December 2004; Stephen Ansolabehere and Charles Stewart III, "Truth in Numbers," *Boston Review*, February/March 2005; and Jeffrey R. Makin, "Are Ballot Propositions Spilling Over Onto Candidate Elections?," *IRI Report 2006-2*, October 2006, available at *www.iandrinstitute.org*. Also, the large number of marriage amendments in 2004 was not the result of a coordinated national campaign, but state-by-state responses to a perceived problem.

About the Author

John G. Matsusaka is a professor in the Marshall School of Business and School of Law, and president of the Initiative & Referendum Institute, all at the University of Southern California. He is the author of *For the Many or the Few: The Initiative, Public Policy, and American Democracy* (University of Chicago Press, 2004).

Table 6.9
STATE INITIATIVES & REFERENDUMS, 2006

State	Measure	Type of election	Type	Topics addressed by measure			Pass	Fail
Alabama (a)	Statewide Amendment 1	Primary Election, June 6, 2006	LR	Marriage	Constitutional Law	Civil Law	★	
	Statewide Amendment 1	General Election, Nov. 7, 2006	LR	Economic Development	Commerce	Government and Tax and Revenue	★	
	Statewide Amendment 2	General Election, Nov. 7, 2006	LR	Property Taxes	Education	Tax and Revenue	★	
	Statewide Amendment 3 (m)	General Election, Nov. 7, 2006	LR	Education	Elections	State and Local Government	★	
Alaska	Primary Ballot Measure 1	Primary Election, Aug. 22, 2006	I	Elections	Campaign Contributions		★	
	Primary Ballot Measure 2	Primary Election, Aug. 22, 2006	I	Tourism	Tax and Revenue		★	
	General Ballot Measure 1	General Election, Nov. 7, 2006	I	Legislature	Session Limits	State Government	★	
	General Ballot Measure 2	General Election, Nov. 7, 2006	I	Natural Resources	Tax and Revenue	Energy		★
Arizona	Proposition 100	General Election, Nov. 7, 2006	LR	Criminal Justice System	Bailable Offenses	Illegal Immigrants	★	
	Proposition 101	General Election, Nov. 7, 2006	LR	Tax and Revenue	Property Tax Levies		★	
	Proposition 102	General Election, Nov. 7, 2006	LR	Judicial System	Punitive Damages	Illegal Immigrants	★	
	Proposition 103	General Election, Nov. 7, 2006	LR	English Language	Immigration	Constitutional Law	★	
	Proposition 104	General Election, Nov. 7, 2006	LR	Local Government	Municipal Debt		★	
	Proposition 105	General Election, Nov. 7, 2006	LR	Public Lands	Natural Resources			★
	Proposition 106	General Election, Nov. 7, 2006	I	Conservation	Public Trust Lands	Natural Resources		★
	Proposition 107	General Election, Nov. 7, 2006	I	Marriage	Constitutional Law	Civil Law		★
	Proposition 200	General Election, Nov. 7, 2006	I	Voter Participation	Voter Reward	Elections		★
	Proposition 201	General Election, Nov. 7, 2006	I	Smoking	Public Health	Revenue	★	
	Proposition 202	General Election, Nov. 7, 2006	I	Minimum Wage	Labor		★	
	Proposition 203	General Election, Nov. 7, 2006	I	Education	Early Childhood Education	Health	★	
	Proposition 204	General Election, Nov. 7, 2006	I	Animal Rights	Agriculture	Criminal Justice	★	
	Proposition 205	General Election, Nov. 7, 2006	I	Election Reform	Vote by Mail			★
	Proposition 206	General Election, Nov. 7, 2006	I	Smoking	Public Health	Smoke-Free Arizona Act		★
	Proposition 207	General Election, Nov. 7, 2006	I	Eminent Domain	Economic Development	State and Local Government	★	
	Proposition 300	General Election, Nov. 7, 2006	LR	Illegal Immigrants	Education	Health and Human Services	★	
	Proposition 301	General Election, Nov. 7, 2006	LR	Methamphetamine Offenses	Criminal Justice		★	
	Proposition 302	General Election, Nov. 7, 2006	O	Legislators Salaries				★
Arkansas	Referred Amendment 1	General Election, Nov. 7, 2006	LR	Gaming	Charity		★	
	Referred Question 1	General Election, Nov. 7, 2006	LR	Education Bond	Revenue	Bond	★	
California	Proposition 81	Primary Election, June 6, 2006	LR	Public Libraries	Education	Bond		★
	Proposition 82	Primary Election, June 6, 2006	I	Education	Tax and Revenue	State Budget		★
	Proposition 1A	General Election, Nov. 7, 2006	LR	Transportation	Tax and Revenue	Tax and Revenue	★	
	Proposition 1B	General Election, Nov. 7, 2006	LR	Highway Safety	Transportation	Tax and Revenue	★	
	Proposition 1C	General Election, Nov. 7, 2006	LR	Emergency Shelter for Women	Human Services	Tax and Revenue	★	
	Proposition 1D	General Election, Nov. 7, 2006	LR	Education Facilities	Bond		★	
	Proposition 1E	General Election, Nov. 7, 2006	LR	Flood Prevention	Bond	Natural Resources	★	
	Proposition 83	General Election, Nov. 7, 2006	I	Sex Offenders	Criminal Justice		★	
	Proposition 84	General Election, Nov. 7, 2006	I	Water Quality	Flood Control	Natural Resources	★	
	Proposition 85	General Election, Nov. 7, 2006	I	Abortion	Parental Notification			★
	Proposition 86	General Election, Nov. 7, 2006	I	Cigarettes	Health	Tax and Revenue		★
	Proposition 87	General Election, Nov. 7, 2006	I	Alternative Energy	Tax and Revenue	Taxes		★
	Proposition 88	General Election, Nov. 7, 2006	I	Education Funding	Tax and Revenue			★
	Proposition 89	General Election, Nov. 7, 2006	I	Political Campaigns	Public Financing	Civil and Constitutional Law		★
	Proposition 90	General Election, Nov. 7, 2006	I	Eminent Domain	Economic Development	Public Health		★

See footnotes at end of table.

STATE INITIATIVES & REFERENDUMS, 2006—Continued

State	Measure	Type of election	Type	Topics addressed by measure			Pass	Fail
Colorado	Amendment 38	General Election, Nov. 7, 2006	I	Elections	Initiative Petitions			★
	Amendment 39	General Election, Nov. 7, 2006	I	School Expenditures	Education			★
	Amendment 40	General Election, Nov. 7, 2006	I	Judicial Term Limits	Elections			★
	Amendment 41	General Election, Nov. 7, 2006	I	Ethics	Elected Officials	State and Local Government	★	
	Amendment 42	General Election, Nov. 7, 2006	I	Minimum Wage	Labor		★	
	Amendment 43	General Election, Nov. 7, 2006	I	Marriage	Constitutional Law	Civil Law	★	
	Amendment 44	General Election, Nov. 7, 2006	I	Marijuana Decriminalization	Criminal Justice			★
	Referendum E	General Election, Nov. 7, 2006	LR	Property Taxes	Veterans		★	
	Referendum F	General Election, Nov. 7, 2006	LR	Recall Deadlines	Elections		★	
	Referendum G	General Election, Nov. 7, 2006	LR	Obsolete Constitutional Provisions			★	
	Referendum H	General Election, Nov. 7, 2006	LR	Business Taxes	Illegal Immigrants	Commerce	★	
	Referendum I	General Election, Nov. 7, 2006	LR	Domestic Partnerships	Constitutional Law	Civil Law		★
	Referendum J	General Election, Nov. 7, 2006	LR	School Expenditures	Education			★
	Referendum K	General Election, Nov. 7, 2006	LR	Immigration Lawsuit	Immigration Laws	Immigration Laws	★	
Connecticut (a)				(b)				
Delaware (a)								
Florida	Amendment 1	General Election, Nov. 7, 2006	LR	State Budget Process	General Revenue		★	
	Amendment 3	General Election, Nov. 7, 2006	LR	Constitutional Amendments	Voting Majorities		★	
	Amendment 4	General Election, Nov. 7, 2006	I	Health	Tobacco Use		★	
	Amendment 6	General Election, Nov. 7, 2006	LR	Homestead Exemption	Senior Citizens		★	
	Amendment 7	General Election, Nov. 7, 2006	LR	Homestead Tax	Disabled Veterans		★	
	Amendment 8	General Election, Nov. 7, 2006	LR	Eminent Domain	Economic Development	State and Local Government	★	
Georgia (a)	Amendment 1	General Election, Nov. 7, 2006	LR	Eminent Domain	Economic Development	State and Local Government	★	
	Amendment 2	General Election, Nov. 7, 2006	LR	Natural Resources	Fishing and Hunting		★	
	Amendment 3	General Election, Nov. 7, 2006	LR	License Plates	Budgets	Transportation	★	
	Referendum A	General Election, Nov. 7, 2006	LR	Ad Valorem Tax	Farm Equipment	Agriculture	★	
	Referendum B	General Election, Nov. 7, 2006	LR	Ad Valorem Tax	Historic Military Aircraft	Veterans Groups	★	
	Referendum C	General Election, Nov. 7, 2006	LR	Ad Valorem Tax	Charitable Institutions		★	
	Referendum D	General Election, Nov. 7, 2006	LR	Homestead Exemption	Homestead Exemption	Senior Citizens	★	
	Referendum E	General Election, Nov. 7, 2006	LR	Homestead Exemption	Law Enforcement	Surviving Spouse	★	
	Referendum F	General Election, Nov. 7, 2006	LR	Homestead Exemption	Assessed Value	Surviving Spouse	★	
Hawaii (a)	Amendment 1	General Election, Nov. 7, 2006	LR	Board of Regents Selection	Education		★	
	Amendment 2	General Election, Nov. 7, 2006	LR	Salary Commission	State Officials	State Government	★	
	Amendment 3	General Election, Nov. 7, 2006	LR	Judicial System	Retirement Age		★	
	Amendment 4	General Election, Nov. 7, 2006	LR	Sexual Assault	Minors	Criminal Justice		★
	Amendment 5	General Election, Nov. 7, 2006	LR	Agriculture	Bond	Tax and Revenue	★	
Idaho	Advisory Vote (e)	General Election, Nov. 7, 2006	O	Property Taxes	Property Taxes	Tax and Revenue	★	
	HJR 2	General Election, Nov. 7, 2006	LR	Marriage	Constitutional Law	Civil Law	★	
	Proposition 1	General Election, Nov. 7, 2006	I	Education Funding	Education Funding	Tax and Revenue		★
	Proposition 2	General Election, Nov. 7, 2006	I	Eminent Domain	Economic Development	State and Local Government		★
	SJR 107	General Election, Nov. 7, 2006	LR	Tobacco Settlement	Endowment Fund	State Budget	★	
Illinois (d)				(b)				

See footnotes at end of table.

STATE INITIATIVES & REFERENDUMS, 2006—Continued

State	Measure	Type of election	Type	Topics addressed by measure		Pass	Fail
Indiana (a)	....	....		...................(b)..................			
Iowa (a)	....	....		...................(b)..................			
Kansas (a)	....	....		...................(b)..................			
Kentucky (a)	....	....		...................(b)..................			
Louisiana (a).............	Amendment 1	Primary Election, Sept. 30, 2006	LR	Environmental Protection	State Budget	★	
	Amendment 2	Primary Election, Sept. 30, 2006	LR	Environmental Protection	Tobacco Funds	★	
	Amendment 3	Primary Election, Sept. 30, 2006	LR	Flood Protection	Environmental Protection	★	
	Amendment 4	Primary Election, Sept. 30, 2006	LR	Property Rights	Economic Development	Constitutional Law	★	
	Amendment 5	Primary Election, Sept. 30, 2006	LR	Eminent Domain	Economic Development	State and Local Government	★	
	Amendment 6	Primary Election, Sept. 30, 2006	LR	Expropriated Property	Economic Development	★	
	Amendment 7	Primary Election, Sept. 30, 2006	LR	Medicaid Trust Fund	Health and Human Services	★	
	Amendment 8	Primary Election, Sept. 30, 2006	LR	Homestead Election	Emergency or Disaster	★	
	Amendment 9	Primary Election, Sept. 30, 2006	LR	Local Financial Burdens	State and Local Government	★	
	Amendment 10	Primary Election, Sept. 30, 2006	LR	Higher Education Funds	Endowments	★	
	Amendment 11	Primary Election, Sept. 30, 2006	LR	Homestead Exemption		★	
	Amendment 12	Primary Election, Sept. 30, 2006	LR	Vacant Elective Offices	Statewide Officials	★	
	Amendment 13	Primary Election, Sept. 30, 2006	LR	Judicial System	Qualifications	★	
	Amendment 1	General Election, Nov. 7, 2006	LR	Homestead Exemption	Disabled Veterans	★	
	Amendment 2	General Election, Nov. 7, 2006	LR	Severance Tax	Natural Resources	Tax and Revenue	★	
	Amendment 3	General Election, Nov. 7, 2006	LR	Ad Valorem Tax	Medical Equipment	Health	★	
	Amendment 4	General Election, Nov. 7, 2006	LR	Motor Vehicle Taxes	Ad Valorem Taxes	Local Government	★	
	Amendment 5	General Election, Nov. 7, 2006	LR	Ad Valorem Tax	Arts	★	
	Amendment 6	General Election, Nov. 7, 2006	LR	Judicial System	Family Courts	Juvenile Courts	★	
	Amendment 7	General Election, Nov. 7, 2006	LR	Tax Assessor Election	Local Government	★	
	Amendment 8	General Election, Nov. 7, 2006	LR	Community School System	Education	Local Government	★	
Maine..................	Question 1	General Election, Nov. 7, 2006	I	Taxpayer Bill of Rights	Tax and Revenue	★	
	Question 2	General Election, Nov. 7, 2006	LR	Initiative Petition Deadlines	Elections		★
Maryland (a)	Question 1	General Election, Nov. 7, 2006	LR	State Parks	Natural Resources	★	
	Question 2	General Election, Nov. 7, 2006	LR	Judicial System	Court Decisions	★	
	Question 3	General Election, Nov. 7, 2006	LR	Judicial System	Civil Jury Trials	★	
	Question 4	General Election, Nov. 7, 2006	PR	Election Reform		★	
Massachusetts............	Question 1	General Election, Nov. 7, 2006	I	Wine Sales	Economic Development		★
	Question 2	General Election, Nov. 7, 2006	I	Nomination of Candidates	Public Office	Elections		★
	Question 3	General Election, Nov. 7, 2006	I	Family Child Care Providers	Labor	Employment		★
Michigan..............	Proposal 06-01	General Election, Nov. 7, 2006	LR	Natural Resources	State Budgets	★	
	Proposal 06-02	General Election, Nov. 7, 2006	I	Affirmative Action	Education	★	
	Proposal 06-03	General Election, Nov. 7, 2006	PR	Hunting Season	Natural Resources		★
	Proposal 06-04	General Election, Nov. 7, 2006	LR	Eminent Domain	Economic Development	★	
	Proposal 06-05	General Election, Nov. 7, 2006	I	School Funding Levels	Education		★
Minnesota (a)...........	Constitutional Amendment	General Election, Nov. 7, 2006	LR	Motor Vehicle Sales Tax	Transportation	Tax and Revenue	★	

See footnotes at end of table.

STATE INITIATIVES & REFERENDUMS, 2006 — Continued

State	Measure	Type of election	Type	Topics addressed by measure		Pass	Fail
Mississippi				(b)			
Missouri	Constitutional Amendment 1	Primary Election, Aug. 8, 2006	LR	Environmental Protection	Tax and Revenue	★	
	Constitutional Amendment 2	General Election, Nov. 7, 2006	I	Stem Cell Research	Health	★	
	Constitutional Amendment 3	General Election, Nov. 7, 2006	I	Tobacco Use	Health Trust Fund		★
	Constitutional Amendment 6	General Election, Nov. 7, 2006	LR	Property Tax Exemption	Nonprofit Organizations, Veteran's Organizations	★	
	Constitutional Amendment 7	General Election, Nov. 7, 2006	LR	Elected Official's Pensions	Criminal Justice, State Government	★	
	Proposition B	General Election, Nov. 7, 2006	I	Minimum Wage	Labor	★	
Montana	Constitutional Amendment 43	General Election, Nov. 7, 2006	LR	State Auditor	Insurance Commissioner, State Government		★
	Constitutional Amendment 97 (g)	General Election, Nov. 7, 2006	I	State Spending	State Budgets	⋮	⋮
	Constitutional Amendment 98 (g)(h)	General Election, Nov. 7, 2006	I	Recall by Petition	Judiciary	⋮	⋮
	Initiative 151	General Election, Nov. 7, 2006	I	Minimum Wage	Labor	★	
	Initiative 153	General Election, Nov. 7, 2006	I	Lobbyist	Revolving Door	★	
	Initiative 154 (g)	General Election, Nov. 7, 2006	I	Eminent Domain	Property Values	⋮	⋮
Nebraska	Constitutional Amendment 1	Primary Election, May 9, 2006	LR	Legislative Pay Increases		★	
	Initiative Measure 421	General Election, Nov. 7, 2006	I	Video Keno	Gambling		★
	Referendum Measure 422	General Election, Nov. 7, 2006	PR	School District Consolidation	Education		★
	Initiative Measure 423	General Election, Nov. 7, 2006	I	Limit on State Spending	Tax and Revenue		★
	Proposed Amendment 1	General Election, Nov. 7, 2006	LR	Revenue Bonds	Economic Development		★
	Proposed Amendment 2	General Election, Nov. 7, 2006	LR	Public Endowment Funds	Tax and Revenue		★
	Proposed Amendment 3	General Election, Nov. 7, 2006	LR	State Lottery Proceeds	Compulsive Gamblers Fund		★
	Proposed Amendment 4	General Election, Nov. 7, 2006	LR	Criminal Justice	Parole and Probation	★	
	Proposed Amendment 5	General Election, Nov. 7, 2006	LR	School Funding	Early Childhood Education	★	
	Proposed Amendment 6	General Election, Nov. 7, 2006	LR	Rehabilitating Property	Economic Development		★
Nevada	Ballot Question 1 (i)	General Election, Nov. 7, 2006	I	Education Funding	State Budget	★	
	Ballot Question 2	General Election, Nov. 7, 2006	I	Eminent Domain	Economic Development	★	
	Ballot Question 3	Removed from the General Election Ballot by the Nevada Supreme Court.					
	Ballot Question 4	General Election, Nov. 7, 2006	I	Smoking Ban	Health	★	
	Ballot Question 5	General Election, Nov. 7, 2006	I	Clean Indoor Air Act	Smoking		★
	Ballot Question 6 (i)	General Election, Nov. 7, 2006	I	Minimum Wage			
	Ballot Question 7	General Election, Nov. 7, 2006	LR	Regulation of Marijuana	Economic Development	★	
	Ballot Question 8	General Election, Nov. 7, 2006	LR	Sales and Use Tax	Tax and Revenue		★
	Ballot Question 9	General Election, Nov. 7, 2006	LR	Higher Education	Board of Regents	★	
	Ballot Question 10	General Election, Nov. 7, 2006	LR	Convening Special Sessions	Legislature	★	
	Ballot Question 11	General Election, Nov. 7, 2006	LR	Legislative Pay Raise			★
New Hampshire (a)(c)...	Question 1	General Election, Nov. 7, 2006	LR	Eminent Domain	Economic Development	★	
	Question 2	General Election, Nov. 7, 2006	LR	Elections	Redistricting	★	
New Jersey (a)	Public Question No. 1	General Election, Nov. 7, 2006	LR	Property Tax Reform	Tax and Revenue	★	
	Public Question No. 2	General Election, Nov. 7, 2006	LR	Environmental Protection	State Budget	★	
	Public Question No. 3	General Election, Nov. 7, 2006	LR	State Transportation System	State Budget	★	

See footnotes at end of table.

STATE INITIATIVES & REFERENDUMS, 2006 — Continued

State	Measure	Type of election	Type	Subject	Topics addressed by measure	Pass	Fail
New Mexico (a)	Bond Measure A	General Election, Nov. 7, 2006	LR	Capital Projects Bond	Tax and Revenue	★	
	Bond Measure B	General Election, Nov. 7, 2006	LR	Higher Education Bond	Capital Improvements	★	
	Bond Measure C	General Election, Nov. 7, 2006	LR	Library Acquisitions Bond	Tax and Revenue	★	
	Constitutional Amendment 1	General Election, Nov. 7, 2006	LR	Real Property Ownership		★	
	Constitutional Amendment 2	General Election, Nov. 7, 2006	LR	Education Funds	Building Lease Agreements	★	
	Constitutional Amendment 3	General Election, Nov. 7, 2006	LR	Water Trust Fund	Natural Resources	★	
	Constitutional Amendment 4	General Election, Nov. 7, 2006	LR	Affordable Housing	Human Services	★	
					State and Local Government		
New York (a)	...				(b)		
North Carolina (a)	...				(b)		
North Dakota	Constitutional Measure 1	Primary Election, June 13, 2006	LR	National Guard	Economic Development	★	
	Constitutional Measure 2	Primary Election, June 13, 2006	LR	Corporations, Regulation of	State and Local Government	★	
	Constitutional Measure 1	General Election, Nov. 7, 2006	LR	Education Funds	Economic Development	★	
	Constitutional Measure 2	General Election, Nov. 7, 2006	I	Eminent Domain	Human Services	★	
	Initiated Statutory Measure 3	General Election, Nov. 7, 2006	I	Child Custody			★
Ohio	Issue 1 (k)	General Election, Nov. 7, 2006	PR	Workers' Compensation Reform		...	...
	Issue 2	General Election, Nov. 7, 2006	I	Minimum Wage	Labor	★	
	Issue 3	General Election, Nov. 7, 2006	I	Education	Gambling		★
					Slot Machines		
	Issue 4 (j)	General Election, Nov. 7, 2006	I	Restricting Smoking			★
	Issue 5 (j)	General Election, Nov. 7, 2006	I	Prohibit Smoking		★	
Oklahoma	Question 724	General Election, Nov. 7, 2006	LR	Legislative Compensation		★	
	Question 725	General Election, Nov. 7, 2006	LR	Economic Development	State Budget	★	
	Question 733	General Election, Nov. 7, 2006	LR	Sale of Alcoholic Beverages	Property Taxes	★	
	Question 734	General Election, Nov. 7, 2006	LR	Freeport Exemption	Economic Development	★	
Oregon	Measure 39	General Election, Nov. 7, 2006	I	Eminent Domain	Private Property	★	
	Measure 40	General Election, Nov. 7, 2006	I	Judicial System	Elections		★
	Measure 41	General Election, Nov. 7, 2006	I	State Income Tax	Tax and Revenue		★
	Measure 42	General Election, Nov. 7, 2006	I	Insurance			★
	Measure 43	General Election, Nov. 7, 2006	I	Abortion	Parental Consent		★
	Measure 44	General Election, Nov. 7, 2006	I	Prescription Drug Coverage	Health	★	
	Measure 45	General Election, Nov. 7, 2006	I	Legislative Term Limits	Elections		★
	Measure 46	General Election, Nov. 7, 2006	I	Campaign Contributions	Campaign Expenditures		★
					Elections		
	Measure 47 (l)	General Election, Nov. 7, 2006	I	Campaign Finance Laws	Contributions and Expenditures	★	
					Elections		
	Measure 48	General Election, Nov. 7, 2006	I	State Budget	Tax and Revenue		★
Pennsylvania (a)	Referendum Question	General Election, Nov. 7, 2006	LR	Veterans' Compensation Fund		★	
Rhode Island (a)	Question 1	General Election, Nov. 7, 2006	LR	Casino	Gambling		★
	Question 2	General Election, Nov. 7, 2006	LR	Restoration of Felony Voting Rights	Criminal Justice	★	
	Question 3	General Election, Nov. 7, 2006	LR	Budget Reserve Account	Rainy Day Fund	★	
					State Budget		
	Question 4	General Election, Nov. 7, 2006	LR	Higher Education Bonds	Tax and Revenue	★	
	Question 5	General Election, Nov. 7, 2006	LR	Transportation Bonds	Tax and Revenue	★	
	Question 6	General Election, Nov. 7, 2006	LR	Zoo Bonds	Tax and Revenue	★	
	Question 7	General Election, Nov. 7, 2006	LR	Park Restoration Bonds	Tax and Revenue	★	
	Question 8	General Election, Nov. 7, 2006	LR	Environmental Bonds	Tax and Revenue	★	
	Question 9	General Election, Nov. 7, 2006	LR	Affordable Housing Bonds	Tax and Revenue	★	

See footnotes at end of table.

STATE INITIATIVES & REFERENDUMS, 2006—Continued

State	Measure	Type of election	Type	Topics addressed by measure		Pass	Fail
South Carolina (a)	Constitutional Amendment 1	General Election, Nov. 7, 2006	LR	Marriage		★	
	Constitutional Amendment 2a	General Election, Nov. 7, 2006	LR	Sessions of the General Assembly	Legislature	★	
	Constitutional Amendment 2b	General Election, Nov. 7, 2006	LR	Adjournment of the General Assembly	Legislature	★	
	Constitutional Amendment 3a	General Election, Nov. 7, 2006	LR	Retirement Systems	Labor — Economic Development	★	
	Constitutional Amendment 3b	General Election, Nov. 7, 2006	LR	Retirement Systems	Labor — Investment Panel	★	
	Constitutional Amendment 4	General Election, Nov. 7, 2006	LR	Property Taxes	Tax and Revenue	★	
	Constitutional Amendment 5	General Election, Nov. 7, 2006	LR	Eminent Domain	Economic Development	★	
South Dakota	Constitutional Amendment C	General Election, Nov. 7, 2006	LR	Marriage		★	
	Constitutional Amendment D	General Election, Nov. 7, 2006	I	Property Taxes	Property Taxes		★
	Constitutional Amendment E	General Election, Nov. 7, 2006	I	Judicial Decisions			★
	Constitutional Amendment F	General Election, Nov. 7, 2006	LR	Legislature	Expense Reimbursements — Private or Special Laws		★
	Initiated Measure 2	General Election, Nov. 7, 2006	I	Tobacco Products	Tax and Revenue	★	
	Initiated Measure 3	General Election, Nov. 7, 2006	I	School Terms	Education		★
	Initiated Measure 4	General Election, Nov. 7, 2006	I	Marijuana Decriminalization	Criminal Justice — Health		★
	Initiated Measure 5	General Election, Nov. 7, 2006	I	State Aircraft	State and Local Government	★	
	Initiated Measure 7	General Election, Nov. 7, 2006	I	Repeal Video Lottery	Gambling	★	
	Initiated Measure 8	General Election, Nov. 7, 2006	I	Repeal Wireless Services Tax	Tax and Revenue — Information Technology		★
	Referred Law 6	General Election, Nov. 7, 2006	PR	Repeals Ban on Abortion			★
Tennessee (a)	Amendment 1	General Election, Nov. 7, 2006	LR	Marriage		★	
	Amendment 2	General Election, Nov. 7, 2006	LR	Property Tax Relief	Senior Citizens	★	
Texas (a)	…………(b)…………						
Utah	Constitutional Amendment 1	General Election, Nov. 7, 2006	LR	Property Tax Exemption		★	
Vermont (a)	…………(b)…………						
Virginia (a)	Ballot Question 1	General Election, Nov. 7, 2006	LR	Marriage		★	
	Ballot Question 2	General Election, Nov. 7, 2006	LR	General Assembly Limitations	Obsolete Language	★	
	Ballot Question 3	General Election, Nov. 7, 2006	LR	Exempt Property	Tax and Revenue	★	
Washington	HJR 4223	General Election, Nov. 7, 2006	LR	Property Tax Exemption	Tax and Revenue	★	
	Initiative 920	General Election, Nov. 7, 2006	I	Estate Tax	Tax and Revenue		★
	Initiative 933	General Election, Nov. 7, 2006	I	Private Property Regulation	State and Local Government		★
	Initiative 937	General Election, Nov. 7, 2006	I	Electric Utilities	Energy Resource Use	★	
West Virginia (a)	…………(b)…………						
Wisconsin (a)	Question 1	General Election, Nov. 7, 2006	LR	Marriage		★	
	Question 2 (f)	General Election, Nov. 7, 2006	O	Death Penalty		★	
Wyoming	Constitutional Amendment A	General Election, Nov. 7, 2006	LR	Mineral Trust Fund	State Budget	★	
	Constitutional Amendment B	General Election, Nov. 7, 2006	LR	School Funding Equalization			★
	Constitutional Amendment C	General Election, Nov. 7, 2006	LR	Permanent Funds	Higher Education	★	
District of Columbia	…………(b)…………						

See footnotes at end of table.

STATE INITIATIVES & REFERENDUMS, 2006 — Continued

State	Measure	Type of election	Type	Topics addressed by measure	Pass	Fail
American Samoa				(b)	....	....
Guam	Proposal A—removed from ballot Nov. 6, 2006	General Election, Nov. 7, 2006	I	Minimum Wage / Alcohol Consumption	....	....
	Proposal B	General Election, Nov. 7, 2006	I	Gaming / Slot Machines		★
No. Mariana Islands				(b)		
Puerto Rico.................				(b)		
U.S. Virgin Islands				(b)		

Source: The Council of State Governments, December 2006.

Key:
LR — Legislative referendum
I — Initiative
PR — Popular referendum
O — Other

(a) State does not have an initiative process.
(b) State had no ballot measures in 2006.
(c) Requires 2/3 majority to pass.
(d) The state has an initiative process, but it is unusable.
(e) This is a non-binding advisory note on the issue of property tax relief in the state of Idaho.
(f) This is an Advisory Referendum. The legislature and the governor are not bound by the results of this referendum. A "yes" vote would advise members of the legislature that the voters want them to enact a change to the penalty for first-degree intentional homicide.
(g) In September 2006, Montana state courts held that Constitutional Amendments 97 and 98 and Initiative 154 were invalid. The questions will still appear on the ballot as it was too late to delete them, but votes may not be counted. The Montana Supreme Court will review the rulings.
(h) The Montana Constitution already provides for the recall of any public official. This is one of the ballot measures ruled to be invalid in September 2006 but it remains on the ballot.
(i) Constitutional amendments in the state of Nevada must be approved in consecutive general elections to take effect. This is the second time that this Question has appeared on the ballot (November 2004). If it passes at this election, it will become law.
(j) In Ohio, Issues 4 and 5 are similar; if both pass, Issue 4 will take effect because it is an amendment to the Constitution.
(k) Official results were not reported. Whether or not Issue 1 appears on the ballot or if any votes it receives count is still questionable. Ohio's no-fault absentee ballots have already been mailed and the resolution will probably contain this ballot issue. A resolution will not occur until after the election.
(l) This measure would only take effect if Measure 46 had been passed. Measure 46 was defeated.
(m) Although the state canvassing board certified the vote totals, the Governor did not proclaim the results for that amendment, thus there is no number assigned to the amendment.

Table 6.10
STATEWIDE INITIATIVE AND REFERENDUM

State or other jurisdiction	Changes to constitution			Changes to statutes			
	Initiative		Referendum	Initiative		Referendum	
	Direct (a)	Indirect (a)	Legislative (b)	Direct (c)	Indirect (c)	Legislative	Citizen petition (d)
Alabama	...	...	★	...	...	★	...
Alaska	...	...	★	★	...	...	...
Arizona	★	...	★	★	...	★	★
Arkansas	★	...	★	★	...	...	★
California	★	...	★	★	...	★	...
Colorado	★	...	★	★	...	★	...
Connecticut	...	...	★	...	...	...	...
Delaware	...	...	★	...	...	★	...
Florida	★	...	★	...	...	...	...
Georgia	...	...	★	...	...	★	...
Hawaii	...	...	★	...	...	...	...
Idaho	...	...	★	★	...	★	★
Illinois	★	...	★	...	...	★	...
Indiana	...	...	★	...	...	★	...
Iowa	...	...	★	...	...	...	...
Kansas	...	...	★	...	...	...	...
Kentucky	...	...	★	...	...	★	★
Louisiana	...	...	★	...	...	...	...
Maine	...	...	★	...	★	★	★
Maryland	...	...	★	...	...	...	★
Massachusetts	...	★	★	...	★	★	★
Michigan	★	...	★	...	★	★	★
Minnesota	...	...	★	...	...	...	...
Mississippi	...	★	★	...	★	...	...
Missouri	★	...	★	★	...	★	...
Montana	★	...	★	★	...	★	★
Nebraska	★	...	★	★	...	...	★
Nevada	★	...	★	★	★	...	★
New Hampshire	...	...	★	...	...	...	...
New Jersey	...	...	★	...	...	...	...
New Mexico	...	...	★	...	...	...	...
New York	...	...	★	...	...	★	...
North Carolina	...	...	★(f)	...	...	...	...
North Dakota	★	...	★	★	...	★	★
Ohio	★	...	...	...	★	...	★
Oklahoma	★	...	★	★	...	★	★
Oregon	★	...	★	★	...	★	★
Pennsylvania	...	...	★	...	...	★	★(e)
Rhode Island	...	...	★	...	...	...	...
South Carolina	...	...	★	...	...	...	...
South Dakota	★	...	★	★	...	★	★
Tennessee	...	...	★	...	...	★	...
Texas	...	...	...	...	...	...	...
Utah	...	...	★	...	★	★	★
Vermont	...	...	★	...	...	★(limited)	...
Virginia	...	...	★	...	...	...	...
Washington	...	...	...	★	★	★	★
West Virginia	...	...	★	...	...	★	...
Wisconsin	...	...	★	...	...	...	...
Wyoming	...	...	★	...	★	...	★
American Samoa	...	...	★	...	...	...	...
No. Mariana Islands	★	★	★	★	★	★	★
Puerto Rico	...	...	★	...	...	★	...
U.S. Virgin Islands	★	...	★	...	...	★	...

Sources: The Council of State Governments' survey of state election administration offices, January 2007 and state Web sites.

Note: This table summarizes state provisions for initiatives and referenda. Initiatives may propose constitutional amendments or develop state legislation and may be formed either directly or indirectly. The direct initiative allows a proposed measure to be placed on the ballot after a specific number of signatures has been secured on a citizen petition. The indirect initiative must be submitted to the legislature for a decision after the required number of signatures has been secured on a petition and prior to placing the proposed measure on the ballot. Referendum refers to the process whereby a state law or constitutional amendment passed by the legislature may be referred to the voters before it goes into effect. Three forms of referenda exist: (1) citizen petition, whereby the people may petition for a referendum on legislation which has been considered by the legislature; (2) submission by the legislature (designated in table as "Legisla-

tive"), whereby the legislature may voluntarily submit laws to the voters for their approval; and (3) constitutional requirement, whereby the state constitution may require that certain questions be submitted to the voters.

Key:
★ — State provision   . . . — No state provision
(a) See Table 1.3, "Constitutional Amendment Procedure: By Initiative," for more detail.
(b) See Table 1.2, "Constitutional Amendment Procedure: By the Legislature," for more detail.
(c) See Chapter 6 tables on State Initiatives, for more detail.
(d) See Chapter 6 tables on State Referendums, for more detail.
(e) No provision for statewide referenda initiated by citizen petition. There are several county/local referenda that can be initiated by citizen petition.
(f) Only the legislature can make statutory changes while in session. Proposed constitutional changes must be passed by the legislature and then are submitted to the citizens to be voted on.

Table 6.11
STATE INITIATIVES: REQUESTING PERMISSION TO CIRCULATE A PETITION

State or other jurisdiction	Applied to (a)		Signatures required to request a petition (b)		Request submitted to	Request form furnished by (c)	Restricted subject matter (d)	Individual responsible for petition		Financial contributions reported (e)	Deposits required (f)
	Const. amdt.	Statute	Const. amdt.	Statute				Title	Summary		
Alabama	...	...	...	...	...	...	...	...	...	...	...
Alaska	...	D	...	100	LG	SBE	Y	LG	LG	Y	$100
Arizona	D	D	15% (g)	10% (g)	SS	SS	N	(h)	(h)	Y	...
Arkansas....................	D	D	10%	8%	AG	SP	N	AG	AG	Y	...
California	D	D	...	...	AG	...	Y	AG	AG	N (i)	$200 (i)
Colorado	D	D	5% (j)	5% (j)	SS	SS	N	(k)	(k)	Y	N
Connecticut	...	...	...	...	...	...	...	...	...	...	...
Delaware....................	...	...	...	...	...	...	...	...	...	...	...
Florida	D	...	...	...	SS	SP	N	SP	SP	Y	N
Georgia	...	...	...	...	...	...	...	...	...	...	...
Hawaii........................	...	...	...	...	...	...	Y	...	...	...	...
Idaho.........................	...	D	...	20	SS	SP	N	AG	AG	Y	N
Illinois	D	...	...	...	...	...	Y	...	...	Y	N
Indiana......................	...	...	...	...	...	...	...	...	...	...	...
Iowa	...	...	...	...	...	...	...	...	...	...	...
Kansas	...	...	...	...	...	...	...	...	...	...	...
Kentucky	...	...	...	...	...	...	...	...	...	...	...
Louisiana	...	...	...	...	...	...	...	...	...	...	...
Maine	...	I	...	5 (l)	SS	SS	Y	P	SS	Y	...
Maryland	...	...	...	3% (m)	SS (n)	SBE	Y	...	...	Y	N
Massachusetts............	I	I	10	10	AG	SS	Y	AG	AG	Y	...
Michigan....................	...	...	...	...	...	...	Y	SP	SP	Y	N
Minnesota	...	...	...	...	...	...	...	...	...	...	...
Mississippi	I	...	12%	...	SS	SP	Y	AG	AG	Y	...
Missouri	D	D	...	...	SS	SP	Y	SS, AG	SS, AG	Y	N
Montana	D	D	...	...	(x)	SP	Y	AG	AG	Y	N
Nebraska....................	D	D	...	...	SS	SP	Y	SP	SP	Y	N
Nevada	...	...	...	...	SS	SS	Y	P, SP	P, SP	...	...
New Hampshire.........	...	...	...	...	...	...	...	...	...	...	...
New Jersey.................	...	...	...	...	...	...	...	...	...	...	...
New Mexico	...	...	...	...	...	...	...	...	...	...	...
New York	...	...	...	...	...	...	...	...	...	...	...
North Carolina..........	...	...	...	...	...	...	...	...	...	...	...
North Dakota.............	D	D	4% (o)	2% (o)	SS	SP	N	SS, AG	SS	Y (e)	N
Ohio	D	I	1,000	1,000	AG	(p)	N (q)	(p)	(p)	Y	N
Oklahoma	D	D	15%	8%	SS	O	N	P	P	Y	N
Oregon	D	D	8% (r)	6% (r)	SS	SS	N	AG	AG	Y	N
Pennsylvania	...	...	...	...	...	...	...	...	...	...	...
Rhode Island	...	...	...	...	...	...	...	...	...	...	...
South Carolina	...	...	...	...	...	...	...	...	...	...	...
South Dakota.............	D	D	(s)	5 EV	SS	SS	Y	SP	SP	Y	N
Tennessee	...	...	...	...	...	...	...	...	...	...	...
Texas	...	...	...	...	...	...	...	...	...	...	...
Utah	...	D, I	...	5 SP	LG	LG	N	SP	SP	Y	N
Vermont	...	...	...	...	...	...	...	...	...	...	...
Virginia......................	...	...	...	...	...	...	...	...	...	...	...
Washington................	...	D, I	...	(t)	SS	SP	N	AG	AG	N	$5
West Virginia..............	...	...	...	...	...	SS	...	...	...	...	...
Wisconsin..................	...	...	...	...	...	...	...	...	...	...	...
Wyoming....................	...	I	...	100	SS	SS	Y	SS	AG, SS	Y	$500
American Samoa	...	...	...	...	...	...	...	...	...	...	...
No. Mariana Islands...	D	I	50%	20%	AG	AG	Y	SP	SP	Y	N
Puerto Rico................	...	D	...	(u)	SBE	(v)	N	(v)	(v)	Y	$500
U.S. Virgin Islands	D	...	41% (w)	...	SBE	SBE	Y	SBE	SBE	Y	N

See footnotes at end of table.

STATE INITIATIVES: REQUESTING PERMISSION TO CIRCULATE A PETITION—Continued

Sources: The Council of State Governments' survey of state election administration offices, January 2007 and state Web sites.

Key:

. . . — Not applicable	AG — Attorney General
D — Direct initiative	O — Other
I — Indirect initiative	P — Proponent
EV — Eligible voters	ST — State
LG — Lieutenant Governor	SP — Sponsor
SS — Secretary of State	Y — Yes
SBE — State Board of Elections	N — No

(a) An initiative may provide a constitutional amendment or develop a new statute, and may be formed either directly or indirectly. The direct initiative allows a proposed measure to be placed on the ballot after a specific number of signatures has been secured on a petition. The indirect initiative must first be submitted to the legislature for decision after the required number of signatures has been secured on a petition, prior to placing the proposed measure on the ballot.

(b) Prior to circulating a statewide petition, a request for permission to do so must first be submitted to a specified state officer.

(c) The form on which the request for petition is submitted may be the responsibility of the sponsor or may be furnished by the state.

(d) Restrictions may exist regarding the subject matter to which an initiative may be applied. The majority of these restrictions pertain to the dedication of state revenues and appropriations, and laws that maintain the preservation of public peace, safety and health. In Illinois, amendments are restricted to "structural and procedural subjects contained in" the legislative article.

(e) In some states, a list of financial contributors and the amount of their contributions must be submitted to the specified state officer with whom the petition is filed. In North Dakota, must report any contributions and/or expenditures in excess of $100. Must also report the gross total of all contributions received and gross totals of all expenditures made. Must give total cash on hand in the filer's account at the start and close of a reporting period.

(f) A deposit may be required after permission to circulate a petition has been granted. This amount is refunded when the completed petition has been filed correctly.

(g) The number of signatures required to request permission to circulate a petition: constitutional amendment, 183,917; statute, 122,612.

(h) The proponent and sponsor are responsible for the title and summary.

(i) No report required at time of filing request, but later if any money is raised, $200 deposit required.

(j) Five percent of all votes cast for secretary of state at last election.

(k) Title Setting Board—secretary of state, attorney general, director of legislative legal services.

(l) The name and address of five voters.

(m) Three percent of last vote for governor—at this time 51,185.

(n) Secretary of state accepts and turns over to State Board of Elections.

(o) Percentage of resident population of the state at the last federal decennial census.

(p) Petitioners. Petitioners must prepare the summary and submit it to the Ohio Attorney General, who then must certify whether the summary fully and accurately describes the proposal.

(q) Such restrictions apply to referendums, but not initiatives.

(r) Constitutional amendment, 110,358; statute, 82,769.

(s) Number of signatures required to request a petition for a constitutional amendment, 10 percent of the total votes cast in the last gubernatorial election.

(t) Statute requires 224,880.

(u) Ten percent district and 41 percent territorial.

(v) Office of the Supervisor of Elections Titling Board.

(w) District-wide 10 percent, territory-wide 41 percent.

(x) Legislative Services Division.

Table 6.12
STATE INITIATIVES: CIRCULATING THE PETITION

State or other jurisdiction	Basis for signatures (see key below) — Const. amdt.	Basis for signatures — Statute	Maximum time period allowed for petition circulation (a)	Can signatures be removed from petition (b)	Completed petition filed with	Days prior to election — Const. amdt.	Days prior to election — Statute
Alabama							
Alaska	15% EV	10% TV from 3/4 ED		Y	LG		
Arizona	10% VG	10% EV	1 yr.	Y	SS	4 mos.	4 mos.
Arkansas	8% VG	8% VG	2 yrs.	N	SS	120 days	
California	8% VG	5% VG	120 days before election	Y	(c)	131 days	131 days
Colorado	5% VSS	5% VSS	6 mos. (3 mos. prior to election)	Y	SS	90 days	90 days
Connecticut							
Delaware							
Florida	8% VEP, 8% from 1/2 CD				SS	Feb. 1 (d)	
Georgia				N	SS		
Hawaii							
Idaho		6% EV	(e)	Y	SS		
Illinois	8% VG		24 mos. prior to election	Y	SBE	6 mos.	4 mos.
Indiana							
Iowa							
Kansas							
Kentucky							
Louisiana							
Maine		10% VG	1 yr.		SS		(f)
Maryland							
Massachusetts	3% VG, no more than 25% from 1 county	3% VG, no more than 25% from 1 county (g)	From 1st Wed. in Sept. to 1st Wed. in Dec. (i)	Y (h)	SS (i)	(g)	(j)
Michigan	10% VG	8% VG	180 days	N (k)	SS	120 days	160 days
Minnesota	12% VG						
Mississippi					(c)	90 days prior to LS	
Missouri	8% VG, 8% each from 2/3 CD	5% VG, 5% each from 2/3 CD	1 yr. / Approx. 18 mos.	Y	SS (c) / SS	6 mos.	6 mos.
Montana	10% VG and 10% in 40 of the SLD	5% VG and 5% in 34 of the SLD	(l)	Y	SS	(l)	(l)
Nebraska	10% EV	7% EV		Y	SS	4 mos.	4 mos.
Nevada	10% TV, 10% each from 3/4 counties	10% TV, 10% each from 3/4 counties	(m)	Y	SS	90 days	30 days prior to LS
New Hampshire							
New Jersey							
New Mexico							
New York							
North Carolina							
North Dakota	4% resident population	2% resident population	1 yr.	N	SS	90 days	90 days
Ohio	10% VG, 5% each from 1/2 counties	3% VG, 1.5% each from 1/2 counties		Y	SS	90 days	(n)

See footnotes at end of table.

STATE INITIATIVES: CIRCULATING THE PETITION — Continued

State or other jurisdiction	Basis for signatures (see key below)		Maximum time period allowed for petition circulation (a)	Can signatures be removed from petition (b)	Completed petition filed with	Days prior to election	
	Const. amdt.	Statute				Const. amdt.	Statute
Oklahoma	15% VH	8% VH	90 days	Y	SS	60 days	60 days
Oregon	8% VG	6% VG	Just under 2 yrs.	Y (o)	SS	4 mos.	4 mos.
Pennsylvania	...	...	...	...	...	...	...
Rhode Island	...	...	...	...	...	...	...
South Carolina	...	...	...	...	...	...	...
South Dakota	10% VG	5% VG	(p)	N	SS	...	...
Tennessee	...	...	...	...	...	...	...
Texas	...	...	...	...	...	...	...
Utah	...	10% VG, 10% each from 26 of 29 senate districts (q)	1 yr.	Y	LG	...	June 1
Vermont	...	...	...	...	...	...	...
Virginia	...	...	...	...	...	...	...
Washington	...	8% VG	6 to 9 mos.	N	SS	...	(r)
West Virginia	...	...	...	...	...	...	...
Wisconsin	...	...	...	...	...	...	...
Wyoming	15% TV, from 2/3 counties	15% TV, from 2/3 counties	18 mos.	Y	SS	...	120 days
American Samoa	...	...	(s)	Y	...	...	...
No. Mariana Islands	...	...	...	Y	...	...	...
Puerto Rico	...	...	...	...	...	...	...
U.S. Virgin Islands	...	10% ED	180 days	Y	SS	...	6 mos.

Sources: The Council of State Governments' survey of state election administration offices and state Web sites, January 2007.

Key:
... — Not applicable
VG — Total votes cast for the position of governor in the last election
EV — Eligible voters
VH — Total votes cast for the office receiving the highest number of votes in the last general election
TV — Total voters in last election
VSS — Total votes cast for all candidates for the office of secretary of state in the last general election
VEP — Total votes cast in the state as a whole in the last presidential election
ED — Election district
CD — Congressional district
SBE — State Board of Elections
SLD — State legislative district
LG — Lieutenant Governor
SS — Secretary of State
LS — Legislative session
Y — Yes
N — No
T — Tuesday

(a) The petition circulation period begins when petition forms have been approved and provided to sponsors. Sponsors are those individuals granted permission to circulate a petition, and are therefore responsible for the validity of each signature on a given petition.
(b) Should an individual wish to remove his/her name from a petition, a request to do so must be submitted in writing to the state officer with whom the petition is filed.
(c) County elections officials.

(d) February 1 of the general election year.
(e) Eighteen months from receipt of ballot title or April 30 of year of election on initiative, whichever occurs first.
(f) To be placed on November ballot, petitions must be submitted to secretary of state by 5:00 p.m. on 50th day after convening of legislature in first regular session, or by 5:00 p.m. on 25th day in second regular session.
(g) First Wednesday in December.
(h) Should an individual wish to remove his/her name from a petition, a request to do so must be submitted in writing to the local election official before the petition is submitted for certification of signatures.
(i) Petitions first must be submitted to local municipal clerks for signature certification.
(j) After legislative inaction, petitions must be filed no later than the first Wednesday in July, signed by not less than 1/2 of 1 percent of the last vote cast for governor.
(k) Not after petition has been filed.
(l) No maximum, but petitions must be submitted to the county election administrators at least four weeks before the third Friday in July. This is the deadline for county election administrators to file the petitions with the secretary of state after their review of signatures.
(m) Constitutional amendment—276 days; amend or create a statute—291 days.
(n) Ten days prior to commencement of General Assembly session for initial filing; second petition must be filed within 90 days after General Assembly takes no action, fails to enact or pass amended form; the petition is filed with the secretary of state.
(o) Only by the chief petitioners before submitting signatures for verification. Signatures may not be removed once the signatures have been submitted to the secretary of state.
(p) No more than 18 months preceding the election date specified on the petition.
(q) Five percent in both categories for indirect.
(r) Initiatives to the legislature must be turned in 10 days before the legislature convenes. If the legislature does not act, the initiative goes to the next general election ballot.
(s) Until 120 days before the date of the election.

Table 6.13
STATE INITIATIVES: PREPARING THE INITIATIVE TO BE PLACED ON THE BALLOT

State or other jurisdiction	Signatures verified by: (a)	Within how many days after filing	Number of days to amend/appeal a petition that is:		Penalty for falsifying petition (denotes fine, jail term)	Petition certified by: (d)
			Incomplete (b)	Not Accepted (c)		
Alabama	...	60 days	...	...	Class B misdemeanor	LG
Alaska	Division of Elections	10 days (e)	...	...	Class 1 misdemeanor	SS
Arizona	County recorder	30 days	30 days	...	...	SS
Arkansas	SS	30 days	...	30 days	Felony or misdemeanor (depending on severity)	SS
California	County clerk	...	...	...	...	SS
Colorado	SS	30 days	10 days	...	(f)	SS
Connecticut	...	...	...	...	...	...
Delaware	...	...	...	...	...	...
Florida	Supervisor of elections	N.A.	N.A.	N.A.	First degree misdemeanor	SS
Georgia	...	...	...	...	...	...
Hawaii	...	...	...	...	...	...
Idaho	County clerk	60 days	...	10 days	$5,000, 2 yrs.	SS
Illinois	SBE (g)	...	(h)	(h)	Class 3 felony	SBE
Indiana	...	...	...	...	...	...
Iowa	...	...	...	...	...	...
Kansas	...	...	...	...	...	...
Kentucky	...	...	...	...	...	...
Louisiana	...	...	...	...	...	...
Maine	Registrar of voters	...	...	...	...	SS
Maryland	...	...	...	...	...	...
Massachusetts	Local board of registrar	2 weeks	...	...	$1,000, 1 yr.	SS
Michigan	SS	Approx. 60 days	...	...	$500, 90 days	BSC
Minnesota	...	...	...	...	...	...
Mississippi	Circuit clerk	...	10 days	10 days	$1,000, 1 yr.	CC
Missouri	County clerk	63 days	...	10 days	Class A misdemeanor	SS
Montana	County election administrators	4 weeks	10 days	10 days	$500, 6 mos.	SS
Nebraska	County clerk	40 days	5 days (j)	...	...	SS
New Hampshire	County clerk	(i)	...	...	...	SS
New Jersey	...	...	...	...	...	...
New Mexico	...	...	...	...	...	...
New York	...	...	...	...	...	...
North Carolina	...	35 days	...	...	...	...
North Dakota	SS	10 days	...	20 days	(k)	SS
Ohio	County board of elections	...	10 days	...	5th degree felony	SS
Oklahoma	SS	...	10 days	...	$1,000, 1 yr.	SS
Oregon	County clerk	30 days	(l)	...	(m)	SS
Pennsylvania	...	...	...	...	...	...
Rhode Island	...	...	...	...	...	...
South Carolina	...	...	...	...	...	...

See footnotes at end of table.

STATE INITIATIVES: PREPARING THE INITIATIVE TO BE PLACED ON THE BALLOT — Continued

State or other jurisdiction	Signatures verified by: (a)	Within how many days after filing	Number of days to amend/appeal a petition that is:		Penalty for falsifying petition (denotes fine, jail term)	Petition certified by: (d)
			Incomplete (b)	Not Accepted (c)		
South Dakota...........	SS	...	...	...	Class 1 misdemeanor	SBE
Tennessee................	...	...	...	...	...	...
Texas......................	...	...	...	...	...	...
Utah........................	County clerk	30 days	...	14 days	Class A misdemeanor	LG
Vermont...................	...	...	...	...	...	...
Virginia...................	...	...	...	...	...	...
Washington..............	SS	(n)	5 days	5 days	Fine or imprisonment	SS
West Virginia...........	...	...	...	...	...	...
Wisconsin................	...	...	...	...	...	...
Wyoming..................	SS	60 days	30 days	30 days	$1,000, 1 yr.	SS
American Samoa........	...	...	...	...	...	...
No. Mariana Islands	Election Commission	(o)	30 days (p)	119 days	(q)	AG
Puerto Rico..............	Office of the Supervisor of Elections	15 days	3 days	...	...	SBE
U.S. Virgin Islands	Office of the Supervisor of Elections	15 days	7 days	...	...	Office of the Supervisor of Elections

Sources: The Council of State Governments' survey of state election administration offices, January 2007 and state Web sites.

Key:

... — Not applicable
CC — Circuit Clerk
SS — Secretary of State
LG — Lieutenant Governor
BSC — Board of State Canvassers
SBE — State Board of Elections

(a) The validity of the signatures, as well as the correct number of required signatures must be verified before the initiative is allowed on the ballot.

(b) If an insufficient number of signatures is submitted, sponsors may amend the original petition by filing additional signatures within a given number of days after filing. If the necessary number of signatures has not been submitted by this date, the petition is declared void.

(c) In some cases, the state officer will not accept a valid petition. In such a case, sponsors may appeal this decision to the Supreme Court, where the sufficiency of the petition will be determined. If the petition is determined to be sufficient, the initiative is required to be placed on the ballot.

(d) A petition is certified for the ballot when the required number of signatures has been submitted by the filing deadline, and are determined to be valid.

(e) Removal of petition and ineligible signatures by Secretary of State's office 15 days (A.R.S. § 19-121.01), certification by County Recorder 10 days after receipt from Secretary of State's office (A.R.S. § 19-121.02).

(f) Secretary conducts hearing, then turns over to the attorney general for investigation/possible criminal prosecution.

(g) State Board of Elections and County Clerks or Municipal Boards of Election Commissioners. Individual petition sheets must be from a single jurisdiction. The SBE verifies that all signatures are from a single jurisdiction and the County Clerks or Municipal Boards verify the signatures against their registration files.

(h) Amendments are not permitted. Judicial review must be sought within 10 days after determination by State Board of Elections.

(i) 1. Within four days, county clerk totals the number of signatures and forwards to the secretary of state. 2. The secretary of state immediately notifies county clerks if they are to proceed or not proceed with the signature verification. 3. If ordered by the secretary of state, the county clerks verify signatures within nine days (excluding weekends and holidays).

(j) In Nevada, appeal must be within five working days after secretary of state determines the petition is not sufficient.

(k) Any violations discovered will be reported to the attorney general for investigation and prosecution.

(l) Additional signatures may be submitted if signatures were turned in prior to deadline for submitting signatures.

(m) Whether a penalty is assessed would be based upon what information on the petition was falsified.

(n) Signatures must be verified by not later than the third Tuesday following the primary.

(o) Within 90 days before the date of election.

(p) Thirty days if submitted 150 days before the date of the election. No amendment/appeal if submitted 120 days before the date of election.

(q) Subject to statute governing fraud and perjury.

Table 6.14
STATE INITIATIVES: VOTING ON THE INITIATIVE

State or other jurisdiction	Ballot (a) Title by:	Ballot (a) Summary by:	Election where initiative voted on	Effective date of approved initiative (b) Const. amdt.	Effective date of approved initiative (b) Statute	Days to contest election results (c)	Can an approved initiative be: Amended?	Can an approved initiative be: Vetoed?	Can an approved initiative be: Repealed?	Can a defeated initiative be refiled?
Alabama	...	...	...	...	...	...	...	...	...	...
Alaska	LG	LG	GE, PR or SP	30 days (d)	90 days (d)	10	Y	N	Y	N
Arizona	SS, AG	LC	GE	...	IM (e)	5	(f)	N	N	Y
Arkansas	AG	AG	GE	30 days	30 days	20	Y	N	Y	Y
California	AG	AG	GE, PR or SP	1 day	IM	5 (d)	Y (g)	N	Y (g)	Y
Colorado	TB (h)	(h)	GE, Odd year	30 days	30 days	10	N (i)	N (i)	N (i)	...
Connecticut	...	...	...	...	...	...	...	...	...	...
Delaware	...	...	...	...	...	...	...	...	...	...
Florida	SP	SP	GE	(j)	...	10	Y (k)	N	Y (k)	Y
Georgia	...	...	...	...	...	...	...	...	...	...
Hawaii	...	...	...	...	...	...	...	...	...	...
Idaho	AG	AG	GE	...	30 days	20	Y	N	Y	Y
Illinois	...	SS (l)	GE	...	...	30	(m)	...	...	Y
Indiana	...	...	...	...	...	...	...	...	...	...
Iowa	...	...	...	...	...	...	...	...	...	...
Kansas	...	...	...	...	...	...	...	...	...	...
Kentucky	...	...	...	...	...	...	...	...	...	...
Louisiana	...	...	...	...	...	...	...	...	...	...
Maine	Sponsor, SS	(n)	REG or SP	...	30 days (e)	5	Y	N	Y	...
Maryland	...	...	...	...	...	...	...	...	...	...
Massachusetts	AG	AG	GE	30 days	30 days	10	Y	Y	Y	After 2 biennial elections
Michigan	BSC	BSC	GE	45 days	10 days	2 (o)	Y	N	Y	Y
Minnesota	...	...	...	...	...	...	...	...	...	...
Mississippi	AG	AG	GE	30 days	...	...	N	N	N	Y
Missouri	SS, AG	SS, AG	GE	30 days	IM	30 (o)	Y	N	Y	Y
Montana	AG	AG	GE	July 1	Oct. 1	1 yr.	Y	N	Y	Y
Nebraska	AG	AG	GE	10 days	10 days	40	Y	N	Y	N (p)
Nevada	SS, AG	SS, AG	GE	(q)	(q)	14	(r)	(r)	(r)	Y
New Hampshire	...	...	...	...	...	...	...	...	...	...
New Jersey	...	...	...	...	...	...	...	...	...	...
New Mexico	...	...	...	...	...	...	...	...	...	...
New York	...	...	...	...	...	...	...	...	...	...
North Carolina	...	...	...	...	...	...	...	...	...	...
North Dakota	SS, AG	SS	PR or GE	30 days	30 days	14	(s)	N	(s)	Y
Ohio	Ohio Ballot Board	(t)	GE	30 days	30 days	15	(u)	N	N	Y
Oklahoma	AG	P	GE or SP	IM	IM	...	Y	Y	Y	After 3 yrs.
Oregon	AG	AG	GE	30 days	30 days	40	Y	Y	Y	Y
Pennsylvania	...	...	...	...	...	...	...	...	...	...
Rhode Island	...	...	...	...	...	...	...	...	...	...
South Carolina	...	...	...	...	...	...	...	...	...	...
South Dakota	AG	AG	GE	1 day	1 day	...	Y	N	N	Y
Tennessee	...	...	...	...	...	...	...	...	...	...
Texas	...	...	...	...	...	...	...	...	...	...
Utah	LLS	LLS	GE	...	5 days (v)	40	Y	N	N	After 2 yrs.
Vermont	...	...	...	...	...	...	...	...	...	...
Virginia	...	...	...	...	...	...	...	...	...	...
Washington	AG	AG	GE	...	30 days	10	Y (w)	...	Y (w)	Y
West Virginia	...	...	...	...	...	...	...	...	...	...
Wisconsin	...	...	...	...	...	...	...	...	...	...
Wyoming	SS	SS, AG	GE 120 days after LS	...	90 days	15 after canvass	Y	N	After 2 yrs.	After 5 yrs.
American Samoa	...	...	...	...	...	...	...	...	...	...
No. Mariana Islands	AG	AG	GE	(x)	(x)	30	...	...	...	Y
Puerto Rico	LC	AG, LLS	GE	...	IM	...	Y	...	...	Y
U.S. Virgin Islands	Office of Supervisor of Elections	Office of Supervisor of Elections	Any election	IM	IM	7	(r)	...	(r)	Y

See footnotes at end of table.

STATE INITIATIVES: VOTING ON THE INITIATIVE — Continued

Sources: The Council of State Governments' survey of state election administration offices, January 2007 and state Web sites.

Key:

. . . — Not applicable	PR — Primary election
LG — Lieutenant Governor	GE — General election
SS — Secretary of State	REG — Regular election
AG — Attorney General	SP — Special election
P — Proponent	IM — Immediately
LC — Legislative Council	LS — Legislative session
LLS — Legislative Legal Services	TB — Title Board
BSC — Board of State Canvassers	Y — Yes
SBE — State Board of Elections	N — No

(a) In some states, the ballot title and summary will differ from those on the petition.

(b) A majority of the popular vote is required to enact a measure. In Massachusetts and Nebraska, apart from satisfying the requisite majority vote, the measure must receive, respectively, 30 percent and 35 percent of the total votes cast in favor. An initiative approved by the voters may be put into effect immediately after the approving votes have been canvassed. In California and Nebraska, the measure may specify an enacting date. In Colorado, measures take effect from the date of proclamation by governor, but no later than 30 days after votes have been canvassed and certified by secretary of state. In Nebraska, 10 days after completion of canvass by the State Board of Canvassers.

(c) Individuals may contest the results of a vote on an initiative within a certain number of days after the election including the measure proposed.

(d) After certification of election.

(e) Upon governor's proclamation.

(f) Initiative can be amended by three-fourths vote of the members of each house of the legislature (AZ Constitution Article 4, Part 1, Section 14).

(g) By vote only.

(h) Ballot title: Drafted by Legislative Council of the General Assembly, then finalized by three board members called the Title Board. Summary by: Legislative Council of the General Assembly.

(i) If it is statutory it can be changed by the legislature.

(j) It is effective the first Tuesday after the first Monday in January following election unless specified in the amendment.

(k) Amendments or repeals must be voted on by the voters.

(l) Subject to approval of the attorney general.

(m) Changing a constitutional amendment would require another constitutional amendment.

(n) Revisor of Statutes.

(o) After election is certified.

(p) Not on next ballot.

(q) Constitutional amendment—after passed twice by the voters it becomes effective upon the completion of the canvass of votes by the Supreme Court on the fourth Tuesday of November following the election. Statute—effective on the date approved by the governor or the canvass of the vote by the Supreme Court.

(r) It cannot be amended or repealed within three years from the date it takes effect.

(s) A measure approved by the electors may not be amended or repealed by the legislative assembly for seven years from its effective date, except by a two-thirds vote of the members elected to each house.

(t) No summary, but the Ohio Ballot Board prescribes the ballot language. Also, explanations and arguments for and against the proposal may be prepared by the petitioner and the person(s) appointed by the governor or, if appropriate, the General Assembly. The Ohio Ballot Board must prepare any missing explanation or argument.

(u) Initiated constitutional amendment proposed by petition cannot be vetoed, cannot be amended or repealed except by another constitutional amendment. Initiated statute cannot be vetoed by the governor, but may be amended or repealed after its effective date via legislation or another initiative.

(v) Effective date may be written in the initiative, otherwise it takes place within five days after governor's proclamation.

(w) An initiative may be challenged in court as to constitutionality. No act, law or bill approved by a majority of the electors voting thereon shall be amended or repealed by the legislature within a period of two years following such enactment. Such enactment may be amended or repealed at any general, regular or special election by direct vote of the people thereon.

(x) Effective upon approval by voters and certification of election result by Election Commission: usually 15 days after date of election or later if there is an election contest.

Table 6.15
STATE REFERENDUMS: REQUESTING PERMISSION TO CIRCULATE A CITIZEN PETITION

State or other jurisdiction	Citizen petition (a)	Signatures required to request a petition (b)	Request submitted to:	Request forms furnished by: (c)	Restricted subject matter (d)	Individual responsible for petition		Financial contributions reported (e)	Deposit required (f)
						Title	Summary		
Alabama	. . .	. . .	. . .	. . .	. . .	. . .	. . .	. . .	. . .
Alaska	Y	100	LG	DV	Y	LG	LG	Y	$100
Arizona	Y	5% VG	SS	SS	Y	P	P	Y	N
Arkansas	Y	8%	AG	SP	N	SP	AG	Y	N
California	Y	. . .	AG	. . .	Y	AG	AG	N	$200
Colorado	. . .	. . .	. . .	. . .	. . .	. . .	. . .	. . .	. . .
Connecticut	. . .	. . .	. . .	. . .	. . .	. . .	. . .	. . .	. . .
Delaware	. . .	. . .	. . .	. . .	. . .	. . .	. . .	. . .	. . .
Florida	. . .	. . .	. . .	. . .	. . .	. . .	. . .	. . .	. . .
Georgia	. . .	. . .	. . .	. . .	. . .	. . .	. . .	. . .	. . .
Hawaii	. . .	. . .	. . .	. . .	. . .	. . .	. . .	. . .	. . .
Idaho	Y	20	SS	SP	N	AG	AG	Y	N
Illinois	Y	. . .	. . .	. . .	Y	. . .	. . .	. . .	. . .
Indiana	(g)	Varies	SS	SS	Y	Varies	. . .	. . .	. . .
Iowa	. . .	. . .	. . .	. . .	. . .	. . .	. . .	. . .	. . .
Kansas	. . .	. . .	. . .	. . .	. . .	. . .	. . .	. . .	. . .
Kentucky	Y	. . .	SS	. . .	Y	. . .	. . .	. . .	. . .
Louisiana	. . .	. . .	. . .	. . .	. . .	. . .	. . .	. . .	. . .
Maine	Y	5 (h)	SS	SS	Y	SP, SS	SS (i)	Y	. . .
Maryland	Y	(j)	. . .	. . .	Y	SP	SP	Y	N
Massachusetts	Y	10	SS	SS	Y	AG	AG	Y	N
Michigan	Y	. . .	. . .	. . .	Y	SP	SP	Y	N
Minnesota	. . .	. . .	. . .	. . .	. . .	. . .	. . .	. . .	. . .
Mississippi	. . .	. . .	. . .	. . .	. . .	. . .	. . .	. . .	. . .
Missouri	Y	. . .	. . .	SP	Y	SS, AG	(l)	Y	N
Montana	Y	(k)	LS, SS, AG	SP	Y	AG	AG	Y	N
Nebraska	Y	. . .	SS	. . .	Y	SP	SP	Y	N
Nevada	Y	. . .	SS	SS	Y	P, SP	P, SP	Y	N
New Hampshire	. . .	. . .	. . .	. . .	. . .	. . .	. . .	. . .	. . .
New Jersey	. . .	. . .	. . .	. . .	. . .	. . .	. . .	. . .	. . .
New Mexico	. . .	. . .	. . .	. . .	. . .	. . .	. . .	. . .	. . .
New York	. . .	. . .	. . .	. . .	. . .	. . .	. . .	. . .	. . .
North Carolina	. . .	. . .	. . .	. . .	. . .	. . .	. . .	. . .	. . .
North Dakota	Y	(m)	SS	SP	N	SS, AG	SS	Y	N
Ohio	Y	. . .	SS, AG	PE	Y	PE	PE (n)	Y	N
Oklahoma	Y	(o)	SS	(j)	N	P	P	Y	N
Oregon	Y	4% or 55,179	SS	SS	Y (p)	AG	AG	Y	N
Pennsylvania	. . .	. . .	. . .	. . .	. . .	. . .	. . .	. . .	. . .
Rhode Island	. . .	. . .	. . .	. . .	. . .	. . .	. . .	. . .	. . .
South Carolina	. . .	. . .	. . .	. . .	. . .	. . .	. . .	. . .	. . .
South Dakota	Y	5% EV	SS (q)	SP	N	AG	AG	Y	N
Tennessee	. . .	. . .	. . .	. . .	. . .	. . .	. . .	. . .	. . .
Texas	. . .	. . .	. . .	. . .	. . .	. . .	. . .	. . .	. . .
Utah	Y	5 SP	LG	LG	Y (r)	SP	SP	Y	. . .
Vermont	. . .	. . .	. . .	. . .	. . .	. . .	. . .	. . .	. . .
Virginia	. . .	. . .	. . .	. . .	. . .	. . .	. . .	. . .	. . .
Washington	Y	112,440	SS	SS	Y (p)	AG	AG	N	$5.00
West Virginia	Y	Varies	. . .	SS	Y	. . .	. . .	N	N
Wisconsin	. . .	. . .	. . .	. . .	. . .	. . .	. . .	. . .	. . .
Wyoming	Y	100	SS	SS	Y	SS	SS	Y	$500
American Samoa	. . .	. . .	. . .	. . .	. . .	. . .	. . .	. . .	. . .
No. Mariana Islands	Y	. . .	. . .	. . .	Y	SP	AG	Y	N
Puerto Rico	Y	10% district/ 41% territorial	Other	SBE	N	SP	Other	Y	N
U.S. Virgin Islands	. . .	. . .	L	L	N	L	L	N	N

See footnotes at end of table.

STATE REFERENDUMS: REQUESTING PERMISSION TO CIRCULATE A CITIZEN PETITION — Continued

Sources: The Council of State Governments' survey of state election administration offices, January 2007 and state Web sites.

Key:

. . . — Not applicable	DV — Division of Elections
EV — Eligible voters	AG — Attorney General
VG — Total votes cast for the position of governor in the last election	P — Proponent
LG — Lieutenant Governor	PE — Petitioner
LS — Legislative Services	ST — State
L — Legislature	SP — Sponsor
SS — Secretary of State	Y — Yes
SBE — State Board of Elections	N — No

(a) Three forms of referenda exist: citizen petition, submission by the legislature, and constitutional requirement. This table outlines the steps necessary to enact a citizen's petition.

(b) Prior to circulating a statewide petition, a request for permission to do so must first be submitted to a specified state officer. Some states require such signatures to only be those of eligible voters.

(c) The form on which the request for petition is submitted may be the responsibility of the sponsor or may be furnished by the state.

(d) Restrictions may exist regarding the subject matter to which a referendum may be applied. The majority of these restrictions pertain to the dedication of state revenues and appropriations, and laws that maintain the preservation of public peace, safety and health. In Kentucky, referenda are only permitted for the establishment of soil and water and watershed conservation districts.

(e) In some states, a list of individuals who contribute financially to the referendum campaign must be submitted to the specified state officer with whom the petition is filed.

(f) A deposit may be required after permission to circulate a petition has been granted. This amount is refunded when the completed petition has been filed correctly.

(g) A referendum can only be placed on the ballot if authorized by a state law. As a result, a county or town election board cannot print any referendum on the ballot unless the legislature has already passed a law to permit the referendum. Therefore, each statute is different.

(h) The name and address of five voters.

(i) Revisor of statutes.

(j) Petition sponsor may submit proposed petition summary for approval to State Administrator of Elections but a formal request to circulate a petition is not required.

(k) No specific requirement to request a petition. Legislative Services receives the request and reviews it, and then the sponsor submits it to the secretary of state and attorney general for petition format review and legal and constitutional sufficiency review.

(l) State auditor writes the fiscal note.

(m) Two percent of resident population of state at the last federal decennial census.

(n) Petitioners must prepare the summary, and submit it to the Ohio Attorney General, who then must certify whether the summary fully and accurately describes the proposal.

(o) Five percent of legal voters based upon the total number of votes cast at the last general election for the state office receiving the highest number of votes at such election.

(p) No bills with an emergency clause.

(q) Do not have to request permission to circulate but must follow certain steps for this process.

(r) May not challenge laws passed by two-thirds of each house of the legislature.

Table 6.16
STATE REFERENDUMS: CIRCULATING THE CITIZEN PETITION

State or other jurisdiction	Basis for signatures	Maximum time period allowed for petition circulation (a)	Can signatures be removed from petition (b)	Completed petition filed:	
				With	Days after legislative session
Alabama	...	...	...	...	...
Alaska	10% TV, from 3/4 ED	w/i 90 days of LS	Y	...	90 days after LS
Arizona	5% VG	w/i 90 days after LS	Y	SS	90 days
Arkansas	6% VG	...	N	SS	90 days
California	5% VG	90 days	Y	(c)	...
Colorado	...	...	...	...	...
Connecticut	...	...	...	...	...
Delaware	...	...	...	...	...
Florida	...	...	...	...	...
Georgia	...	...	...	...	...
Hawaii	...	...	...	...	...
Idaho	6% EV	w/i 60 days after LS	Y	SS	60 days
Illinois	8% VG (d)	...	Y	SBE	...
Indiana	...	...	...	...	...
Iowa	...	...	...	...	...
Kansas	...	...	...	...	...
Kentucky	5% VG	...	...	SS	4 mos.
Louisiana	...	...	...	...	...
Maine	10% VG	90 days of LS (e)	...	SS	90 days
Maryland	3% VG	(f)	Y	SS	...
Massachusetts	1.5% VG for emergency 2% or immediate suspension	90 days	Y (g)	SS	90 days after signed by governor
Michigan	5% VG	90 days after LS	N	SS	90 days
Minnesota	...	...	...	...	...
Mississippi	...	...	...	...	...
Missouri	5% VG, from 2/3 ED	w/i 90 days after LS	Y	SS	90 days
Montana	5% EV and 5% from 34 of 100 ED	(h)	Y	SS	6 mos.
Nebraska	5% EV	...	Y	SS	90 days
Nevada	10% EV last GE	(i)	Y	SS	120 days prior to next GE
New Hampshire	...	...	...	...	...
New Jersey	...	...	...	...	...
New Mexico	...	...	...	...	...
New York	...	...	...	...	...
North Carolina	...	...	...	...	...
North Dakota	2% total population	90 days	N	SS	(j)
Ohio	6% VG, 3% each from 1/2 counties	90 days	Y	SS	90 days
Oklahoma	5% VH	w/i 90 days of LS	Y	SS	90 days
Oregon	4% VG	w/i 90 days of LS	Y (k)	SS	90 days
Pennsylvania	...	...	...	...	...
Rhode Island	...	...	...	...	...
South Carolina	...	...	...	...	...
South Dakota	5% VG	w/i 90 days of LS	N	SS	90 days
Tennessee	...	...	...	...	...
Texas	...	...	...	...	...
Utah	10% VG	40 days after LS	Y	CC	40 days
Vermont	...	...	...	...	...
Virginia	...	...	...	...	...
Washington	4% VG	Approx. 90 days	N	SS	90 days
West Virginia	...	...	...	...	...
Wisconsin	...	...	...	...	...
Wyoming	15% TV, from 2/3 county	18 mos.	N	SS	90 days
American Samoa	...	...	...	...	...
No. Mariana Islands	...	Up to 120 days before election	Y	AG	...
Puerto Rico	...	...	...	...	...
U.S. Virgin Islands	No. of registered voters	180 days	...	...	...

See footnotes at end of table.

STATE REFERENDUMS: CIRCULATING THE CITIZEN PETITION — Continued

---

Sources: The Council of State Governments' survey of state election administration offices and state Web sites, January 2007.

Key:

. . . — Not applicable

VG — Total votes cast for the position of governor in the last election

EV — Eligible voters

TV — Total voters in the last general election

VH — Total votes cast for the office receiving the highest number of votes in the last general election

VSS — Total votes cast for all candidates for the office of secretary of state at the previous general election

ED — Election district

GE — General election

LS — Legislative session

LG — Lieutenant Governor

SBE — State Board of Elections

SS — Secretary of State

AG — Attorney General

CC — County Clerk

Y — Yes

N — No

w/i — Within

(a) The petition circulation period begins when petition forms have been approved and provided to or by the sponsors. Sponsors are those individuals granted permission to circulate a petition, and are therefore responsible for the validity of each signature on a given petition.

(b) Should an individual wish to remove his/her name from a petition, a request to do so must first be submitted in writing to the state officer with whom the petition is filed.

(c) County elections office.

(d) Referenda are advisory only.

(e) Request for petition must be submitted within 10 days of adjournment of legislative session.

(f) No signature may be collected until the final action of the General Assembly. Session ends the second Monday in April. One-third of the signatures must be submitted not later than May 31. The remaining signatures are due no later than June 30.

(g) Should an individual wish to remove his/her name from a petition, a request to do so must first be submitted in writing to the local election official prior to the petition being submitted for certification of signatures.

(h) No specific beginning date for circulation of petitions, so there is no maximum time period. There is an ending deadline of six months after legislative session.

(i) Not later than the third Tuesday in May of even-numbered years.

(j) Within 90 days after the legislation is filed in the secretary of state's office.

(k) Only by the chief petitioners before submitting signatures for verification. Signatures may not be removed once the signatures have been submitted to the secretary of state for verification.

Table 6.17
STATE REFERENDUMS: PREPARING THE CITIZEN PETITION REFERENDUM TO BE PLACED ON THE BALLOT

State or other jurisdiction	Signatures verified by: (a)	Within how many days after filing	Number of days to amend/ appeal a petition that is:		Penalty for falsifying petition (denotes fine, jail term)	Petition certified by: (d)
			Incomplete (b)	Not Accepted (c)		
Alabama	. . .	. . .	. . .	. . .	. . .	. . .
Alaska	Division of Elections	60	10	10	Class B misdemeanor	LG
Arizona	County recorder	(e)	. . .	. . .	Class 1 misdemeanor	SS
Arkansas....................	SS	30	. . .	30	Class D felony	SS
California	County clerk	8	. . .	. . .	Felony or misdemeanor (depending on severity)	SS
Colorado.....................	. . .	. . .	. . .	. . .	. . .	. . .
Connecticut	. . .	. . .	. . .	. . .	. . .	. . .
Delaware.....................	. . .	. . .	. . .	. . .	. . .	. . .
Florida	. . .	. . .	. . .	. . .	. . .	. . .
Georgia	. . .	. . .	. . .	. . .	. . .	. . .
Hawaii........................	. . .	. . .	. . .	. . .	. . .	. . .
Idaho..........................	County clerk	. . .	. . .	. . .	$5,000, 2 yrs.	SS
Illinois........................	State Board of Elections	Varies	. . .	. . .	Class 3 felony	SBE
Indiana.......................	County clerk	. . .	. . .	. . .	. . .	. . .
Iowa	. . .	. . .	. . .	. . .	. . .	. . .
Kansas	. . .	. . .	. . .	. . .	. . .	. . .
Kentucky	. . .	. . .	. . .	. . .	. . .	. . .
Louisiana	. . .	. . .	. . .	. . .	. . .	. . .
Maine.........................	Registrars of voters	30	. . .	. . .	. . .	SS
Maryland	Local Board of Elections	20	. . .	. . .	Misdemeanor (f)	SS, SBE
Massachusetts............	Local boards of registrars	14	. . .	. . .	$1,000, 1 yr.	SS
Michigan	SS	Approx. 60	. . .	. . .	$500, 90 days	BSC
Minnesota	. . .	. . .	. . .	. . .	. . .	. . .
Mississippi	. . .	. . .	. . .	. . .	. . .	. . .
Missouri.....................	County clerk	(g)	. . .	10	Class A misdemeanor	SS
Montana	County election administrators	28	10	10	$500, 6 mos.	SS
Nebraska.....................	County clerk	40	. . .	. . .	. . .	SS
Nevada	County clerk	(h)	5	. . .	. . .	SS
New Hampshire..........	. . .	. . .	. . .	. . .	. . .	. . .
New Jersey.................	. . .	. . .	. . .	. . .	. . .	. . .
New Mexico	. . .	. . .	. . .	. . .	. . .	. . .
New York	. . .	. . .	. . .	. . .	. . .	. . .
North Carolina	. . .	. . .	. . .	. . .	. . .	. . .
North Dakota.............	SS	35	. . .	20	(i)	SS
Ohio...........................	County board of elections	10	10	. . .	5th degree felony	SS
Oklahoma	SS	. . .	10	. . .	$1,000, 1 yr.	SS
Oregon	SS, County clerk	. . .	. . .	. . .	(j)	SS
Pennsylvania	. . .	. . .	. . .	. . .	. . .	. . .
Rhode Island	. . .	. . .	. . .	. . .	. . .	. . .
South Carolina	. . .	. . .	. . .	. . .	. . .	. . .
South Dakota.............	SS	. . .	. . .	. . .	Class 1 misdemeanor	SS
Tennessee...................	. . .	. . .	. . .	. . .	. . .	. . .
Texas	. . .	. . .	. . .	. . .	. . .	. . .
Utah	County clerks	55 (k)	. . .	10	Class A misdemeanor	LG
Vermont.....................	. . .	. . .	. . .	. . .	. . .	. . .
Virginia	. . .	. . .	. . .	. . .	. . .	. . .
Washington................	SS	(l)	. . .	10	Class C felony (possible)	SS
West Virginia.............	. . .	. . .	. . .	. . .	. . .	. . .
Wisconsin...................	. . .	. . .	. . .	. . .	. . .	. . .
Wyoming....................	SS	60	60	60	$1,000, 1 yr.	SS
American Samoa........	. . .	. . .	. . .	. . .	. . .	. . .
No. Mariana Islands...	AG	. . .	(m)	(m)	(n)	AG
Puerto Rico...............	. . .	. . .	. . .	. . .	. . .	. . .
U.S. Virgin Islands	Supervisor of Elections	15	. . .	. . .	. . .	Supervisor of Elections

See footnotes at end of table.

STATE REFERENDUMS: PREPARING THE CITIZEN PETITION REFERENDUM TO BE PLACED ON THE BALLOT — Continued

Sources: The Council of State Governments' survey of state election administration offices, January 2007 and state Web sites.

Key:

. . . — Not applicable

SS — Secretary of State

LG — Lieutenant Governor

BSC — Board of State Canvassers

SBE — State Board of Elections

(a) The validity of the signatures, as well as the correct number of required signatures must be verified before the referendum is allowed on the ballot.

(b) If an insufficient number of signatures is submitted, sponsors may amend the original petition by filing additional signatures within a given number of days after filing. If the necessary number of signatures has not been submitted by this date, the petition is declared void.

(c) In some cases, the state officer will not accept a valid petition. In such cases, sponsors may appeal this decision to the Supreme Court, where the sufficiency of the petition will be determined. If the petition is determined to be sufficient, the referendum is required to be placed on the ballot.

(d) A petition is certified for the ballot when the required number of signatures has been submitted by the filing deadline, and are determined to be valid.

(e) In Arizona, the secretary of state has 15 days to count signatures and to complete random sample; the county recorder then has 10 days to verify signatures.

(f) Misdemeanor, punishable by a $10–$250 fine or 30 days–six months in jail, or both.

(g) In Missouri, must be certified as sufficient or insufficient by the 13th Tuesday prior to the general election.

(h) 1. Within four days, county clerks count total number of signatures and forward to the secretary of state. 2. The secretary of state immediately notifies county clerks if they are to proceed or not proceed with the signature verification. 3. If ordered by the secretary of state, the county clerks verify signatures within nine days (excluding weekends and holidays).

(i) Any violations discovered will be reported to the attorney general for investigation and prosecution.

(j) Whether a penalty is assessed would be based upon what information on the petition was falsified.

(k) After the end of the legislative session.

(l) Not later than the third Tuesday following the primary election.

(m) Incomplete: 30 or more days if submitted 150 days before date of the election; none if submitted 120 days before date of election. Not accepted: if submitted 119 days or less before the election.

(n) Subject to statute governing fraud or perjury.

Table 6.18
STATE REFERENDUMS: VOTING ON THE CITIZEN PETITION REFERENDUM

State or other jurisdiction	Ballot (a)		Election where referendum voted on	Effective date of approved referendum (b)	Days to contest election results (c)
	Title by:	Summary by:			
Alabama	...	...	...	...	...
Alaska	LG	LG	1st statewide election 180 days after LS	30 days	10
Arizona	SS, AG	LC	GE	(d)	5
Arkansas	AG	...	GE	...	20
California	AG	AG	GE or PR	1 day	5 (e)
Colorado	...	...	...	...	...
Connecticut	...	...	...	...	...
Delaware	...	...	...	...	...
Florida	...	...	...	...	...
Georgia	...	...	...	...	...
Hawaii	...	...	...	...	...
Idaho	AG	AG	GE	30 days	20 (e)
Illinois	...	...	GE	Advisory only	30
Indiana	...	...	...	...	...
Iowa	...	...	...	...	...
Kansas	...	...	...	...	...
Kentucky	...	...	GE or SP	IM	...
Louisiana	...	...	...	...	...
Maine	...	...	GE or statewide election more than 60 days after filing	30 days	5
Maryland	SS	LLS	GE	(f)	...
Massachusetts	SS, AG	AG	GE more than 60 days after filing	30 days	10
Michigan	BSC	BSC	GE	10 days	2 (e)
Minnesota	...	...	...	...	...
Mississippi	...	...	...	...	...
Missouri	SS, AG	SS	GE	IM	30
Montana	AG	AG	GE	(g)	1 yr.
Nebraska	AG	AG	GE	...	...
Nevada	SS, AG	SS, AG	GE	Nov., 4th Tues.	14
New Hampshire	...	...	...	...	...
New Jersey	...	...	...	...	...
New Mexico	...	...	...	...	...
New York	...	...	...	...	...
North Carolina	...	...	...	...	...
North Dakota	SS, AG	SS	PR	30 days	14 (e)
Ohio	...	...	GE more than 60 days after filing	IM	15 (h)
Oklahoma	LLS, AG	LLS	GE or SP	...	...
Oregon	AG	AG	GE (i)	30 days	40
Pennsylvania	...	...	...	...	...
Rhode Island	...	...	...	...	...
South Carolina	...	...	...	...	...
South Dakota	AG	AG	GE	1 day	...
Tennessee	...	...	...	...	...
Texas	...	...	...	...	...
Utah	LLS	LLS	GE	5 days	40
Vermont	...	...	...	...	...
Virginia	...	...	...	...	...
Washington	AG	AG	GE	30 days	10
West Virginia	...	...	...	...	...
Wisconsin	...	...	...	...	...
Wyoming	SS	SS, AG	GE more than 120 days after LS	90 days	15
American Samoa	...	...	...	...	...
No. Mariana Islands	AG	AG	GE or special election if specified	(j)	30
Puerto Rico	...	...	...	...	...
U.S. Virgin Islands	...	...	...	...	...

See footnotes at end of table.

STATE REFERENDUMS: VOTING ON THE CITIZEN PETITION REFERENDUM — Continued

Sources: The Council of State Governments' survey of state election administration offices, January 2007 and state Web sites.

Key:

. . . — Not applicable	SBE — State Board of Elections
LG — Lieutenant Governor	GE — General election
AG — Attorney General	PR — Primary election
SS — Secretary of State	REG — Regular election
BSC — Board of State Canvassers	SP — Special election
LC — Legislative Counsel	IM — Immediately
LLS — Legislative Legal Services	LS — Legislative session

(a) In some states, the ballot title and summary will differ from those on the petition.

(b) A majority of the popular vote is required to enact a measure in every state. In Arizona, a referendum approved by the voters becomes effective upon the governor's proclamation. In Nebraska, a referendum may be put into effect immediately after the approving votes have been canvassed by the Board of State Canvassers and upon the governor's proclamation. In Massachusetts, the measure must also receive at least 30 percent of the total ballots cast in the last election. In Oklahoma, put into effect upon certification of election results by state election board. In Utah, after proclamation by governor and date specified in petition.

(c) Individuals may contest the results of a vote on a referendum within a certain number of days after the election including this matter. In Alaska, five days to request recount with appeal to the court within five days after recount.

(d) Upon proclamation of the governor after the canvass. (AZ Const. Article 4, Part 1, Section 13.)

(e) After election is certified.

(f) After the certification of election results. Depends on date Board of State Canvassers meets. They must meet within 35 days after general election.

(g) Unless specifically provided by the legislature in an act referred by it to the people or until suspended by a petition signed by at least 15 percent of the qualified electors in a majority of the legislative representative districts, an act referred to the people is in effect as provided by law until it is approved or rejected at the election. An act that is rejected is repealed effective the date the result of the canvass is filed by the secretary of state under 13-27-503. An act referred to the people that was in effect at the time of the election and is approved by the people remains in effect. An act that was suspended by a petition and is approved by the people is effective the date the result of the canvass is filed by the secretary of state under 13-27-503. An act referred by the legislature that contains an effective date following the election becomes effective on that date if approved by the people. An act that provides no effective date and whose substantive provisions were delayed by the legislature pending approval at an election and that is approved is effective October 1 following the election.

(h) After election is certified or if recount conducted, 10 days after recount.

(i) Special election can be held at the request of the Legislative Assembly.

(j) Upon approval by voters and certification of election results by Election Commission, usually 15 days after date of election if no contest.

Table 6.19
STATE RECALL PROVISIONS

State or other jurisdiction	Provision for recall	Officials subject to recall	Constitutional and statutory citations for recall of state officials	Constitutional or statutory language
Alabama	No			
Alaska	Yes	All (a)	Const. Art., 11 § 8; AS § 15.45.470	All elected public officials in the State, except judicial officers, are subject to recall by the voters of the State or political subdivision from which elected. Procedures and grounds for recall shall be prescribed by the legislature.
Arizona	Yes	All	Const. Art. 8, § 1-6; ARS § 19-201–19-234	Every public officer in the state of Arizona, holding an elective office, either by election or appointment, is subject to recall from such office by the qualified electors of the electoral district from which candidates are elected to such office.
Arkansas	No			
California	Yes	All	Const. Art. 2, § 13–19; CA Election Code § 19-201–19-234	Recall is the power of the electors to remove an elective officer. Recall of a state officer is initiated by delivering to the Secretary of State a petition alleging reason for recall. Sufficiency of reason is not reviewable.
Colorado	Yes	All	Const. Art. 21, § 1; CRS § 1-12-101–1-12-122, 23-17-120.5, 31-4-501–505	Every elective public officer of the state of Colorado may be recalled from office at any time by the registered electors entitled to vote for a successor of such incumbent through the procedure and in the manner herein provided for, which procedure shall be known as the recall, and shall be in addition to and without excluding any other method of removal by law.
Connecticut	No			
Delaware	No			
Florida	No			
Georgia	Yes	All	Const. Art. 2, § 2.4; GA Code § 21-4-1 et seq.	The General Assembly is hereby authorized to provide by general law for the recall of public officials who hold elective office. The procedures, grounds, and all other matters relative to such recall shall be provided for in such law.
Hawaii	No			
Idaho	Yes	All (a)	Const. Art. 6, § 6; ID Code § 34-1701–34-1715	Every public officer in the state of Idaho, excepting the judicial officers, is subject to recall by the legal voters of the state or of the electoral district from which he is elected. The legislature shall pass the necessary laws to carry this provision into effect.
Illinois	No			
Indiana	No			
Iowa	No			
Kansas	Yes	All (a)	Const. Art. 4, § 3; KSA § 25-4301–25-4331	All elected public officials in the State, except judicial officers, shall be subject to recall by voters of the State or political subdivision from which elected. Procedures and grounds for recall shall be prescribed by law.
Kentucky	No			
Louisiana	Yes	All (a)	Const. Art. 10, § 26; LRS § 18:1300.1–18:1300.17	The legislature shall provide by general law for the recall by election of any state, district, parochial, ward, or municipal officer except judges of the courts of record. The sole issue at a recall election shall be whether the official shall be recalled.
Maine	No			

See footnotes at end of table.

STATE RECALL PROVISIONS — Continued

State or other jurisdiction	Provision for recall	Officials subject to recall	Constitutional and statutory citations for recall of state officials	Constitutional or statutory language
Maryland	No			
Massachusetts	No			
Michigan	Yes	All (a)	Const. Art. 2, § 8; MCL § 168.951–168.975	Laws shall be enacted to provide for the recall of all elective officers except judges of courts of record upon petition of electors equal in number to 25 percent of the number of persons voting in the last preceding election for the office of governor in the electoral district of the officer sought to be recalled. The sufficiency of any statement of reasons or grounds procedurally required shall be a political rather than a judicial question.
Minnesota	Yes	(b)	Const. Art. 8, § 6; MS § 211C.01 et seq.	A state officer other than a judge may be subject to recall for serious malfeasance or nonfeasance during the term of office in the performance of the duties of the office or conviction during the term of office for a serious crime.
Mississippi	No			
Missouri	No			
Montana	Yes	All	Mont. Code § 2-16-601–2-16-635	Every person holding a public office of the state or any of its political subdivisions, either by election or appointment, is subject to recall from such office.
Nebraska	No			
Nevada	Yes	All	Const. Art. 2, § 9; NRS § 294A.006	Every public officer in the State of Nevada is subject, as herein provided, to recall from office by the registered voters of the state, or of the county, district, or municipality which he represents.
New Hampshire	No			
New Jersey	Yes	All	Const. Art. 1, § 2; NJRS § 19:27A-1–19:27A-18	The people reserve unto themselves the power to recall, after at least one year of service, any elected official in this State or representing this State in the United States Congress.
New Mexico	No			
New York	No			
North Carolina	No			
North Dakota	Yes	All (c)	Const. Art. 3, § 1 and 10; ND Century Code § 16.1-01-09.1	Any elected official of the state, of any county or of any legislative or county commissioner district shall be subject to recall by petition of electors equal in number to twenty-five percent of those who voted at the preceding general election for the office of governor in the state, county, or district in which the official is to be recalled.
Ohio	No			
Oklahoma	No			
Oregon	Yes	All (c)	Const. Art. 2, § 18; ORS § 249.865–249.880	Every public official in Oregon is subject, as herein provided, to recall by the electors of the state or of the electoral district from which the public official is elected.
Pennsylvania	No			
Rhode Island	Yes	(d)	Const. Art. 4, § 1	Recall is authorized in the case of a general officer who has been indicted or informed against for a felony, convicted of a misdemeanor, or against whom a finding of probable cause of violation of the code of ethics has been made by the ethics commission.
South Carolina				

See footnotes at end of table.

STATE RECALL PROVISIONS — Continued

State or other jurisdiction	Provision for recall	Officials subject to recall	Constitutional and statutory citations for recall of state officials	Constitutional or statutory language
South Dakota............	No			
Tennessee	No			
Texas	No			
Utah	No			
Vermont	No			
Virginia..................	No			
Washington..............	Yes	All (a)	Const. Art. 1, Sec. 33-34; WRC § 29.82-010–29.82.220	Every elective public officer of the state of Washington except judges of courts of record is subject to recall and discharge by the legal voters of the state, or of the political subdivision of the state, from which he was elected whenever a petition demanding his recall, ... is filed with the officer with whom a petition for nomination, or certificate for nomination, to such office must be filed under the laws of this state, and the same officer shall call a special election as provided by the general election laws of this state. and the result determined as therein provided.
West Virginia............	No			
Wisconsin................	Yes	All	Const. Art. 13, § 12; Wisc. Stat. § 9.10	The qualified electors of the state, of any congressional, judicial or legislative district or of any county may petition for the recall of any incumbent elective officer after the first year of the term for which the incumbent was elected, by filing a petition with the filing officer with whom the nomination petition is filed, demanding the recall of the incumbent.
Wyoming.................	No			
No. Mariana Islands	Yes	All	N.A.	N.A.
Puerto Rico	Yes	All	N.A.	N.A.
U.S. Virgin Islands......	Yes	All	Constitutional and statutory citations exist.	N.A.

Sources: The Council of State Governments, state constitutions and statutes, January 2007.

Note: This table refers only to officials elected to statewide office.

N.A. — Not available

(a) Except judicial.

(b) State executive officers, legislators, and judicial officers.

(c) Except for U.S. Congress.

(d) Governor, Lieutenant Governor, Secretary of State, and Treasurer.

Table 6.20
STATE RECALL PROVISIONS: APPLICABILITY TO STATE OFFICIALS AND PETITION CIRCULATION

State or other jurisdiction	Officers to whom recall is applicable (a)	No. of times recall can be attempted	Recall may be initiated after official has been in office	Recall may not be initiated with days remaining in term	Basis for signatures (b) (see key below)		Maximum time allowed for petition circulation (c)
					Statewide officers	Others	
Alabama	...	...	...	...	...	...	...
Alaska	All state level officers	...	120 days	...	25% VO	25% VO	...
Arizona	All elected officials	1 (d)	6 mos./5 days legislators	180	25% VO (e)	25% VO (e)	120 days
Arkansas	...	...	...	...	...	...	...
California	All elected officials	(f)	90 days	6 mos.	12% VO, 1% from 5 counties	20% VO	160 days
Colorado	All elected officials	(g)	6 mos.	6 mos.	25% VO	25% VO	60 days
Connecticut	...	...	...	...	...	...	...
Delaware	...	...	...	...	...	...	...
Florida	...	...	...	...	...	...	...
Georgia	All state level officials, county and city elected officials	...	180 days	180	15% EV (b), 1/15 from each congressional district	30% EV (h)	(i)
Hawaii	...	...	...	...	...	...	...
Idaho	All but judicial officers	(d)	90 days	...	20% EVg	50% VO	60 days
Illinois	...	...	...	...	...	...	...
Indiana	...	...	...	...	...	...	...
Iowa	...	...	...	...	...	...	...
Kansas	All but judicial officers	1	120 days	180	40% VO	40% VO	90 days
Kentucky	...	...	...	...	...	...	...
Louisiana	All officers	(j)	1 day	6 mos.	33 1/3% EV (k)	33 1/3% EV (k)	180 days
Maine	...	...	...	...	...	...	...
Maryland	...	...	...	...	...	...	...
Massachusetts	...	...	...	...	...	...	...
Michigan	All but judicial officers	No limit	6 mos.	6 mos.	25% VG in district	25% VG in district	90 days
Minnesota	All state level officials	No limit	...	6 mos.	25% VO	25% VO	90 days
Mississippi	...	...	...	...	...	...	...
Missouri	...	...	...	...	...	...	...
Montana	All state level officers and elected officials	(l)	2 mos.	...	10% EV	(m)	3 mos.
Nebraska	Elected officials from political subdivisions	(n)	6 mos.	6 mos.	...	35–45% VO	...
Nevada	All officers	(d)	6 mos. (o)	...	25% VO in given jurisdiction	25% VO in given jurisdiction	90 days
New Hampshire	...	...	...	...	...	...	...
New Jersey	All elected officials	(p)	(q)	(r)	25% VO in given jurisdiction	25% VO in given jurisdiction	(s)
New Mexico	...	...	...	...	...	...	...
New York	...	...	...	...	...	...	...
North Carolina	All elected officials	1	...	...	...	...	...
North Dakota	All elected officials	1	...	...	25% EVg	25% EV	90 days
Ohio	...	...	...	190	...	...	...
Oklahoma	...	...	...	...	...	...	...
Oregon	All elected state officials	No limit	180 days	...	15% (u)	15% (u)	90 days
Pennsylvania	...	...	...	...	...	...	...
Rhode Island	Gov., lt. gov., atty. gen., sec. of state, treasurer	...	6 mos.	...	15% VO	15% VO	90 days
South Carolina	...	...	...	...	...	...	...

See footnotes at end of table.

STATE RECALL PROVISIONS: APPLICABILITY TO STATE OFFICIALS AND PETITION CIRCULATION — Continued

State or other jurisdiction	Officers to whom recall is applicable (a)	No. of times recall can be attempted	Recall may be initiated after official has been in office	Recall may not be initiated with days remaining in term	Basis for signatures (b) (see key below)		Maximum time allowed for petition circulation (c)
					Statewide officers	Others	
South Dakota.............	...	...	...	...	...	...	...
Tennessee	...	...	...	...	...	...	...
Texas	...	...	...	...	...	...	...
Utah	...	...	...	...	...	...	...
Vermont....................	...	...	...	...	...	...	...
Virginia....................	...	...	...	...	...	...	...
Washington...............	All but judges of courts of record	...	IM	180	25% VO	35% VO	(v)
West Virginia.............	...	...	...	...	...	...	...
Wisconsin..................	All elected officials	1	1 yr.	...	25% VG (w)	25% VG (w)	60 days
Wyoming...................	...	...	...	...	...	...	...
American Samoa.........	...	...	...	...	...	...	...
No. Mariana Islands....	All elected officials	(x)	180 days	...	40% EV (y)	...	(z)
Puerto Rico...............	...	...	...	...	...	...	...
U.S. Virgin Islands.....	All elected officials	No limit	1 yr.	365	Registered electors	...	180 days

Sources: The Council of State Governments' survey of state election administration offices, February 2007 and state Web sites.

Key:

... — Not applicable
All — All elective officials
VO — Number of votes cast in the last election for the office or official being recalled
EVg — Number of eligible voters in the last general election for governor
EV — Eligible voters
VG — Total votes cast for the position of governor in the last election
VP — Total votes cast for position of president in the last presidential election
IM — Immediately

(a) An elective official may be recalled by qualified voters entitled to vote for the recalled official's successor. An appointed official may be recalled by qualified voters entitled to vote for the successor(s) of the elective officer(s) authorized to appoint an individual to the position.
(b) Signature requirements for recall of those other than state elective officials are based on votes in the jurisdiction to which the said official has been elected.
(c) The petition circulation period begins when petition forms have been approved and provided to sponsors. Sponsors are those individuals granted permission to circulate a petition, and are therefore responsible for the validity of each signature on a given petition.
(d) Additional recall attempts can be made, provided that the state treasury is reimbursed the cost of the previous recall attempt(s). The specific reason for recalling on one petition cannot be the basis for a second recall petition during the current term of office.
(e) Twenty-five percent of the number of votes cast at the preceding general election for all candidates for the office held by the officer, even if the officer was not elected at that election, divided by the number of offices that were being filled at that election. (A.R.S. § 19-201.)
(f) Open ended.
(g) One attempt unless a second petition is circulated and valid signatures gathered are at least 50 percent of votes cast for all candidates in the last election.
(h) Eligible voters for office at last general election to fill office.

(i) For any statewide office, 90 days. Any officer holding an office other than statewide office and for whom no less than 5,000 signatures are required for the recall petition, 45 days. Any officer holding an office other than statewide office and for whom less than 5,000 are required, 30 days.
(j) Unlimited. Once every 18 months.
(k) Basis for signatures 33 1/3 percent if over 1,000 eligible voters; 40 percent if under 1,000 eligible voters.
(l) No recall petition may be filed against an officer for whom a recall election has been held for a period of two years during his term of office unless the state or political subdivisions financing such recall election is first reimbursed for all expenses of the preceding election.
(m) Fifteen percent to twenty percent of eligible voters, depending on the office.
(n) If voted on, no recall for one year.
(o) For legislators, anytime after 10 days from the beginning of the first legislative session after their election.
(p) An elected official sought to be recalled who is not recalled as the result of a recall election shall not again be subject to recall until after having served one year of a term calculated from the date of the recall election.
(q) The recall drive may not commence before the 50th day preceding the completion of the elected official's first year of the current term.
(r) No election to recall an elected official shall be held after the date occurring six months prior to the general election or regular election for that office, as appropriate, in the final year of the official's term.
(s) The maximum time allowed for petition circulation is 320 days for a governor or 160 days for other elected officials.
(t) Unless it is a state senator or representative and then it is anytime after fifth day from the beginning of legislative session or after election of legislator.
(u) Fifteen percent of the total number of votes cast in the public officer's electoral district for all candidates for governor at the last election at which a candidate for governor was elected to a full term.
(v) Statewide officials, 270 days; others, 180 days.
(w) At least 25 percent of the vote cast for the office of governor at the last election within the same district or territory as that of the officeholder being recalled.
(x) Not more than once a year or not during the first six months in office.
(y) Grounds for recall must be stated and must be signed by 40 percent of voters represented by the elected official.
(z) Until 120 days before the election.

Table 6.21
STATE RECALL PROVISIONS: PETITION REVIEW, APPEAL AND ELECTION

State or other jurisdiction	Signatures verified (a) by:	Days to amend/appeal a petition that is:		Penalty for falsifying petition (denotes fines, jail time)	Days allowed for petition to be certified (d)	Days to step down after certification (e)	Voting on the recall (f)		Days to contest election results (g)
		Incomplete (b)	Not Accepted (c)				Election held	Election type	
Alabama	…	…	…	…	…	…	…	…	…
Alaska	Division of elections	20	20	Class B misdemeanor	30	1	60–90 days after cert.	GE, PR, SP	10
Arizona	County recorder	…	…	Class 1 misdemeanor	70	5	(h)	(i)	5
Arkansas	…	…	…	…	…	…	…	…	…
California	County clerk/ Registrar of voters	10	10	…	10	(i)	60–80 days after cert.	GE	5
Colorado	SS	…	15 (k)	…	10	5	45–75 days after cert.	SP or GE	10
Connecticut	…	…	…	…	…	…	…	…	…
Delaware	…	…	…	…	…	…	…	…	…
Florida	Registrar of voters	…	…	Misdemeanor	…	…	30–45 days after cert.	SP	5
Georgia	…	…	…	…	30–45	…	…	…	…
Hawaii	…	…	…	…	…	…	…	…	…
Idaho	County clerk	30	…	$5,000, 2 yrs.	10	5	45+ days after cert. (l)	SP, PR, GE (l)	20 (m)
Illinois	…	…	…	…	…	…	…	…	…
Indiana	…	…	…	…	…	…	…	…	…
Iowa	…	…	…	…	…	…	…	…	…
Kansas	County clerk	…	…	Class B misdemeanor; up to $1,000, up to 1 yr. or both	30	Next day	60–90 days after cert.	SP	5 (m)
Kentucky	…	…	…	…	…	…	…	…	…
Louisiana	Registrar of voters	(n)	(n)	…	15–20	(o)	(p)	SP	(q)
Maine	…	…	…	…	…	…	…	…	…
Maryland	…	…	…	…	…	…	…	…	…
Massachusetts	…	…	…	…	…	…	…	…	…
Michigan	SS, local election officials (r)	…	…	$500, 90 days	35	…	(s)	SP	2 (m)
Minnesota	SS	90	…	Felony	10	…	(t)	GE	7
Mississippi	…	…	…	…	…	…	…	…	…
Missouri	…	…	…	…	…	…	…	…	…
Montana	County election administrators	10	10	$500 or 6 mos. in county jail or both	(u)	5	(v)	SP or GE (dd) (v)	12 mos.
Nebraska	County clerk	…	…	…	15	5	30–45 days after cert.	SP	40
Nevada	County clerk, Registrar of voters	5	…	Misdemeanor	(w)	5	(x)	SP	(v)
New Hampshire	…	…	…	…	…	…	…	…	…
New Jersey	Recall elections official	…	…	Crime of the 4th degree	10	5	(z)	SP or GE	(aa)
New Mexico	…	…	…	…	…	…	…	…	…
New York	…	…	…	…	…	…	…	…	…
North Carolina	…	…	…	…	…	…	…	…	…
North Dakota	SS	…	…	…	30	10	50–60 days	SP	14 (bb)
Ohio	…	…	…	…	…	…	…	…	…

See footnotes at end of table.

STATE RECALL PROVISIONS: PETITION REVIEW, APPEAL AND ELECTION — Continued

State or other jurisdiction	Signatures verified (a) by:	Days to amend/appeal a petition that is: Incomplete (b)	Not Accepted (c)	Penalty for falsifying petition (denotes fines, jail time)	Days allowed for petition to be certified (d)	Days to step down after certification (e)	Voting on the recall (f): Election held	Election type	Days to contest election results (g)
Oklahoma	...	...	...	...	...	...	...	...	...
Oregon	County clerk	(cc)	...	(dd)	10	5	w/i 35 days after resignation period	SP	40
Pennsylvania	...	...	...	...	...	...	...	...	...
Rhode Island	SBE	w/i 90 days	...	Misdemeanor and/or felony	90	...	...	SP	...
South Carolina	...	...	...	...	...	...	...	...	...
South Dakota.........	...	...	...	...	...	...	...	...	...
Tennessee..............	...	...	...	...	...	...	...	...	...
Texas....................	...	...	...	...	...	...	...	...	...
Utah.....................	...	...	...	...	...	...	...	...	...
Vermont................	...	...	...	...	...	...	...	...	...
Virginia................	SS	...	...	...	...	...	...	...	...
Washington...........	SS	30	...	Class B felony or misdemeanor	Not specified	...	45–60 days after cert. (ee)	SP	3
West Virginia.........	...	...	...	...	...	...	...	GE or PR	...
Wisconsin..............	SBE	...	...	Class 1 felony–$10,000, 3 yrs. prison or both	31	10	6 wks. after cert.	SP	3 (ff)
Wyoming...............	...	...	...	...	...	...	...	...	...
American Samoa......	AG	150	...	Statute governs fraud or perjury	15	...	...	...	...
No. Mariana Islands	...	...	...	...	...	...	(gg)	GE, SP	30
Puerto Rico............	...	...	...	...	...	...	...	...	...
U.S. Virgin Islands......	Office of the Supervisor of Elections	...	...	...	10	IM	...	GE	5

Sources: The Council of State Governments' survey of state election administration offices, January 2007 and state Web sites.

Key:

... — Not applicable

SBE — State Board of Elections

SS — Secretary of State

SP — Special election

GE — General election

PR — Primary election

IM — Immediate and automatic removal from office

w/i — Within

N.A. — Information not available

(a) The validity of the signatures, as well as the correct number of required signatures must be verified before the recall is allowed on the ballot.

(b) If an insufficient number of signatures is submitted, sponsors may amend the original petition by filing additional signatures within a given number of days. If the necessary number of signatures has not been submitted by this date, the petition is declared void.

(c) In some cases, the state officer will not accept a valid petition. In such a case, sponsors may appeal this decision to the Supreme Court, where the sufficiency of the petition will be determined. When this is declared, the recall is required to be placed on the ballot.

(d) A petition is certified for the ballot when the required number of signatures has been submitted by the filing deadline, and are determined to be valid.

(e) The official to whom a recall is proposed has a certain number of days to step down from his position before a recall election is initiated, if the desires to do so.

(f) A majority of the popular vote is required to recall an official in each state.

(g) Individuals may contest the results of a vote on a recall within a certain number of days after the results are certified. In Alaska, an appeal to courts must be filed within five days of the recount.

(h) The election order is issued within 15 days if the officer does not resign within five days after certification.

(i) To be held on the next consolidated election date pursuant to § 16-204 that is 90 days or more after the order calling the election (A.R.S. § 19-209(A)).

(j) Prior to election being called.

(k) After determination of sufficiency.

(l) In Idaho, the dates on which elections may be conducted are the first Tuesday in February, the fourth Tuesday in May, the first Tuesday in August, or the Tuesday following the first Monday in November. In addition, an emergency election may be called upon motion of the governing board of a political subdivision. Recall elections conducted by any political subdivision shall be held on the nearest of these dates which falls more than 45 days after the clerk of the political subdivision orders that the recall election shall be held.

(m) After election is certified. In Michigan, if a petition is filed against a local officer, a recount can be requested up to six days after certification of recall election.

(n) The Registrar of Voters shall honor the written request of any voter who either desires to have his handwritten signature stricken from or added to the petition at any time prior to certification of the petition, or within five days after receipt of such signed petition, whichever is earlier.

(o) Election returns are certified on the fifth day after the election, and the office is immediately vacant.

(p) The local registrar of voters sends the original certified recall petition to the governor, who issues, within 15 days, a proclamation calling a special election, placing the special election on the next regularly scheduled election date.

(q) Not later than 4:30 p.m. of the 30th day after the official promulgation of the results of the election. Promulgation is on or before the 12th day after the election.

(r) Secretary of state if filed on the state level; county or local clerks if filed on county level.

STATE RECALL PROVISIONS: PETITION REVIEW, APPEAL AND ELECTION — Continued

(s) Under Michigan's consolidated elections, the recall election is held on the next fixed election date that falls at least 95 days after the recall petition is filed.

(t) An election will not be held in the last six months of a term after certification.

(u) County election administrators have 30 days; sponsor has three months to submit the petition from the date of certification.

(v) A special election is called unless the filing is within 90 days of a general election.

(w) Within four days, county clerks count signature totals and forward to the Secretary of State. The Secretary of State immediately notifies the clerks if they are to proceed with signature verification.

(x) In Nevada, a recall election is held 10–20 days after the Secretary of State completes notification of the petition sufficiency unless a complaint is filed; the clerk shall issue a call for the election which is to be held within 30 days after the issuance of the call.

(y) Five days after recount is completed or 14 days after the election if no recount is demanded.

(z) New Jersey Permanent Statutes, 19:27A-13. In the case of an office which is ordinarily filled at the general election, a recall election shall be held at the next general election occurring at least 55 days following the fifth business day after service of certification, unless it was indicated in the notice of intention to recall that the recall election shall be held at a special election in which case the recall election official shall order and fix the date for holding the recall election to be the next Tuesday occurring during the period beginning with the 55th day and ending on the 61st day following the fifth business day after service of the certification of the petition.

(aa) New Jersey Permanent Statutes, 19:27A-16.

(bb) Fourteen days after the canvass board has certified the results.

(cc) Chief petitioners may submit additional signatures if the deadline for submitting signatures has not passed.

(dd) Whether a penalty is assessd would depend on what information on the petition was falsified.

(ee) If possible to be held on a regularly scheduled election; cannot be held between the primary and general.

(ff) Business days.

(gg) The election is held at the next regular general election or at a special election set forth in the recall petition.

Chapter Seven

STATE FINANCE AND DEMOGRAPHICS

" *While still positive, state officials are predicting that the fiscal 2007 outlook will be less lustrous.* "

—Brian Sigritz

" *Most observers of state finances have adopted a wary outlook where strong current indicators are tempered by factors that suggest a weakening revenue structure and spending pressures in several areas.* "

—Brian T. Stenson

" *Unfunded state pension liabilities continue to grow but should stabilize in the near term.* "

—Robin Prunty and Parry Young

" *At 36 million people, the number of foreign-born Americans is at its highest point in history.* "

—Mark Mather

" *Hispanic and Asian populations are spreading out from their traditional metropolitan centers, while blacks' shift towards the South is accelerating.* "

—William H. Frey

" *Efforts to actively recruit women for elected and appointed positions will be critical in determining what the future holds for women in state government.* "

—Susan J. Carroll

Emerging Trends in State Budgets: Revenue Growth Slows but Spending Pressures Remain
By Brian T. Stenson

Strong tax collections in recent years have bolstered state treasuries and paved the way for initiatives in health care and education reforms. However, states are likely to face challenges from slowing tax collections, a resumption in Medicaid's traditional spending growth, pressures in K-12 education, and new accounting requirements for employee health benefits.

Introduction

As 2007 began, states were poised to make significant advances on a broad range of issues. Some have been thrust on the states by the steady pullback from domestic policy initiatives by a federal government focused primarily on international and security priorities. It remains to be seen if the new Democratic Congress will reverse this trend and focus on domestic issues, or if gridlock in Washington leads to even greater dominance by state and local governments over domestic policies. Other issues have their roots at the state level. Pressure from citizens—either through the political process or the courts—has prompted states to find new ways to address old issues, including K-12 education and health care. Most observers of state finances have adopted a wary outlook where strong current indicators are tempered by factors that suggest a weakening revenue structure and spending pressures in several areas. This article surveys some of these emerging trends facing state governments.

Slowdown Looms in the Economy and Tax Collections

State tax collections have been extremely strong in recent years. The national economy continued its steady expansion and although many states experienced sluggish economic growth, strong gains in the western and southern states carried national indexes ever higher. Sustained job gains and robust corporate profits buoyed state coffers, and even states with strong revenue projections saw collections outpace expectations.

State tax collection growth registered above 5 percent for 11 consecutive quarters, on a year-over-year basis, according to the Nelson A. Rockefeller Institute of Government's quarterly reports on state tax collections.[1] However, in the July–September 2006 quarter, collection growth slowed to 4.6 percent, as illustrated in Figure A.

The corporate income tax was the stellar performer among state tax collections. An aberrant January–

March 2006 quarter aside, this source grew by double digits in 13 of the previous 14 quarters. Year-over-year growth exceeded 20 percent in nearly half those quarters. That tax collection performance appears to have slowed. Two recent quarters suggested the decline and state budget planners now have set their sights lower. According to the National Association of State Budget Officers (NASBO), overall state revenue projections for fiscal year 2007 show growth of only 3 percent, about one-third the prior year's growth.[2]

This more restrained state revenue outlook reflects two major factors. Last year, state lawmakers greeted this revenue surge enthusiastically and, among other things, enacted significant tax cuts. According to NASBO, these reductions amounted to $2.1 billion, and ended a five-year string of net tax increases.[3]

Another major determinant of state revenue forecasts is the economic outlook, and here too, indicators suggest leaner times for state budgets. The latest Congressional Budget Office (CBO) forecast calls for a slowing national economy. The most widely used measure, Gross Domestic Product (GDP), is predicted to grow 2.3 percent in real terms in 2007, fully 1 percent slower than 2006 growth, followed by a slight rebound to 3 percent in 2008, and an average growth of 2.9 percent in the subsequent four years. Other broad economic measures critical to tax collection performance, such as employment and inflation, also are expected to slow.[4] Corporate profits, a measure that has helped propel tax collections in the states where the corporate income tax is a major revenue source, can be expected to ease, as well. The Thompson Financial Corporation predicts that corporate profits will grow 7.9 percent in 2007, well below the double-digit growth seen during the last 13 quarters.[5]

Of course, the effects of any economic slowdown will vary across the states. The record of the past three years, 2004 through 2006, illustrates just how uneven economic performance has been in different regions. On a nationwide basis, nonfarm employment grew

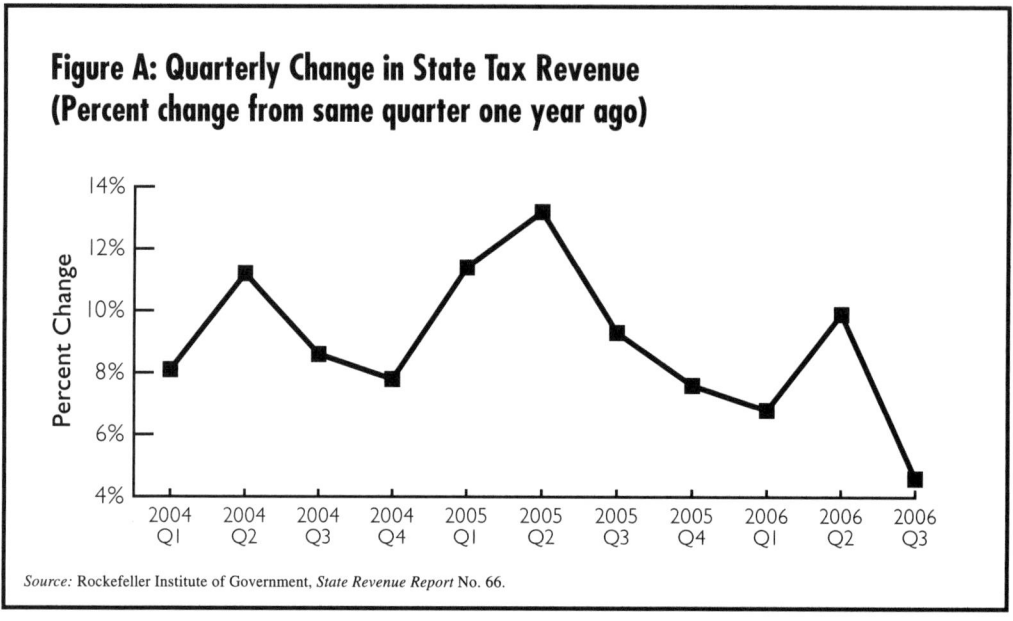

**Figure A: Quarterly Change in State Tax Revenue
(Percent change from same quarter one year ago)**

Source: Rockefeller Institute of Government, *State Revenue Report* No. 66.

3.3 percent during this period, but the states have exhibited wide extremes. Eighteen states—mainly concentrated in the West and South—notched growth of 4 percent or more, with six registering employment gains of at least 7 percent.[6] Such rapid economic growth carries significant implications for many aspects of a state's budget, including revenue collections, but also K-12 and higher education enrollment, police protection, transportation and other infrastructure, and other services demanded by new residents. At the other end of the scale, 13 states—primarily in the Northeast and Midwest—recorded growth of less than 2 percent, or actually lost jobs. The consequences of sluggish economic performance pose more difficult problems, with underutilized educational facilities, population losses in older communities, increasing concentrations of service-dependent residents, and accelerating outmigration of adults seeking better career opportunities.

Respite from Medicaid Spending Pressures Is Likely Short-lived

For several years, Medicaid has been a prime focus of state fiscal experts, as spending for this program for low-income citizens has spiraled ever higher. Medicaid is now the largest single expenditure area for state budgets.

After years during which national spending on Medicaid (including federal and state shares) routinely increased 7.5 percent or more each year, Medicaid cost projections slowed dramatically, at least for one year. According to the Centers for Medicare and Medicaid Services (CMS), national health expenditures for Medicaid were virtually flat in 2006 compared to annual growth rates of at least 7.2 percent in previous years. This sudden decline provided welcome relief for state budgets, and when coupled with the surge in tax collections, contributed to budget surpluses in many states.

Slowed Medicaid spending growth is widely attributed to the implementation of the new Medicare Part D prescription drug program. Effective Jan. 1, 2006, Part D transferred certain prescription drug costs for older recipients from Medicaid to Medicare. During the transition period in state fiscal year 2006, state budgets realized a substantial net benefit, taking a large element of spending off their Medicaid budgets. This provided a one-time cut in Medicaid spending and a smaller continuing offset to annual Medicaid growth. But once this short-term budget help is reflected, annual Medicaid spending growth should approximate traditional rates, as the historical drivers of program costs—increased utilization and more costly services—remain. Indeed, CMS projects Medicaid spending will grow 7.3 to 8.1 percent annually for the next five years, producing the unusual pattern shown in Figure B.[7]

Faced with mounting demands for universal access to health care, and Washington's resistance to a new federal program, states are increasingly looking to implement innovative solutions. Programs and proposals in Massachusetts, California, New York and elsewhere are designed to provide health care to uninsured children and streamline enrollment processes for Medicaid-eligible adults.

K-12 Education Is a Front-burner Issue

Elementary and secondary education has long been the largest element of state government spending from the general fund. According to NASBO, state spending on the K-12 grades accounted for 35.1 percent of all state general fund spending in fiscal year 2006, almost double the share devoted to Medicaid.[8]

Education is likely to stay at the top of the states' priority lists. First, demographics alone indicate that elementary and secondary education will demand considerable attention in the states, for different reasons depending on the state. According to the National Center for Education Statistics (NCES), enrollment is projected to grow 4 percent during the 2002 through 2014 period, with state-level patterns showing stark differences.[9] NCES projections indicate enrollment patterns closely linked to overall population growth, with sharp increases in the West, and declines in the Midwest and Northeast, as illustrated in Figure C.

Projections for 2002 through 2014 for individual states show major variations. Twenty-three states are predicted to experience enrollment growth, with double-digit increases in seven states, including Nevada's startling 28.4-percent increase. Enrollment growth of this magnitude will put severe strains on school budgets and state aid systems, as managers struggle to build or expand schools, add portable classrooms, increase class sizes and staff up. These states have already experienced significant enroll-

ment growth, which has strained capacity. A recent NCES study reported that in 2005, 22 percent of public school principals in western states considered their schools overcrowded already.[10]

At the other extreme, enrollment declines are projected for 27 states, with losses of 5 percent or more expected in 11 of these. K-12 enrollment in Vermont, Maine and North Dakota is predicted to decrease 10 percent or more. Retrenchment will likely be needed in many schools, especially if enrollment declines are concentrated in individual school districts, as school closings can have a wrenching effect on a community.

Perhaps an even more significant factor that will affect spending on schools is the combined impact of the movement to enhance accountability and performance in the nation's schools, and litigation brought by parents and advocacy groups to secure increased support and more equitable state and local funding distributions. Some states are rethinking the way they finance public education, expanding the level of reporting and increasing the expectations placed on education professionals. Several governors have advanced ambitious and expensive agendas to improve education and state assistance to local schools. An example of the scope of such plans and how expensive they can become is Gov. Eliot Spitzer's proposal for New York. He has proposed a major expansion in state education aid that is tied to greater transparency and better targeting in aid distribution formulas. The plan would help end successful litigation in this area. His plan would increase state education funding by $7 billion in the fourth year. Other sweeping propos-

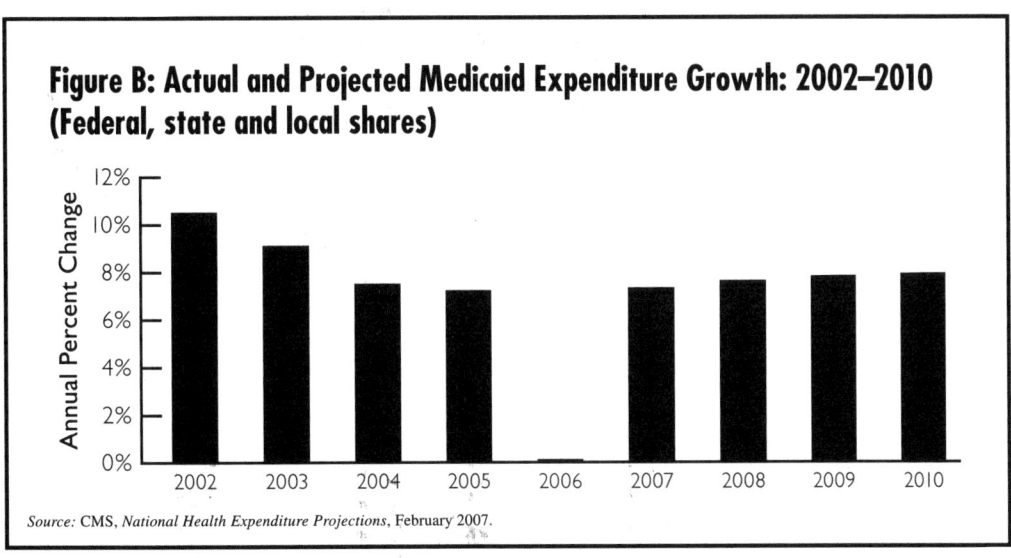

Figure B: Actual and Projected Medicaid Expenditure Growth: 2002–2010 (Federal, state and local shares)

Source: CMS, *National Health Expenditure Projections,* February 2007.

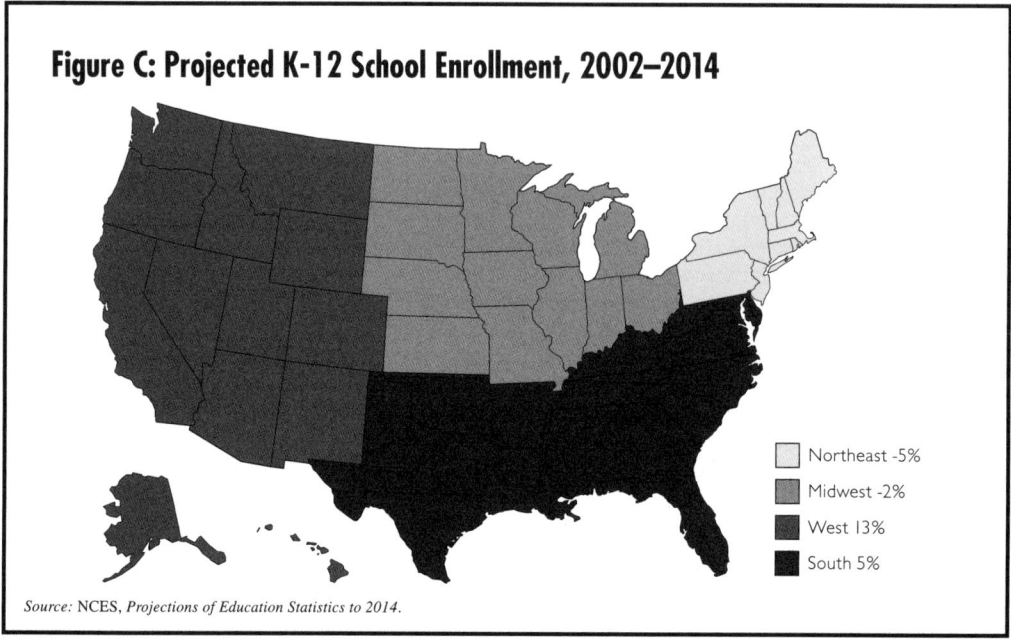

Figure C: Projected K-12 School Enrollment, 2002–2014

Northeast -5%

Midwest -2%

West 13%

South 5%

Source: NCES, *Projections of Education Statistics to 2014.*

als have been advanced by Govs. Jon Corzine of New Jersey and Jodi Rell of Connecticut, and many governors have proposed expanding preschool opportunities and increasing transparency and accountability.

Preparing for GASB 45

The arcane world of accounting standards leapt into the public spotlight when the Governmental Accounting Standards Board (GASB) released Statement 45 in 2004. GASB 45 requires that governments disclose the true cost of their retirees' health insurance and other post-employment benefits (OPEB) on financial statements. This requirement becomes effective with the fiscal year 2008 year-end financial statements for the largest governments, and later for smaller units. Competent fiscal managers and outside monitors have long understood that retirement benefits posed a growing and largely hidden financial obligation, much like unchecked borrowing. However, GASB 45 shed light on this practice and is likely to bring it into the public budgetary and labor relations debate.

Anecdotal evidence is starting to accumulate about the magnitude of this unfunded liability. Early estimates include: California ($40 billion to $70 billion); New York ($47 billion); Maryland ($20 billion); and Delaware ($3 billion). The impact of GASB 45 on all governments has been estimated at $1 trillion.

Under GASB 45, states must disclose several pieces of information for their respective OPEB plans: the annual OPEB cost, actual contributions made and the

funded status (the difference between the actuarial value of assets and accrued liabilities). Fully funding the annual OPEB cost would require setting aside money in a trust that would invest it, thus meeting OPEB expenses as they become due, much like pensions. A primary component of the annual OPEB cost is the "annual required contribution" (ARC) for such benefits, comprised of:

- A "normal cost" equaling the actuarial estimate of the employer's expenses attributable to current employees; and

- A portion of any unfunded actuarial accrued liability for retirees—the excess of accrued liabilities (stretching out decades in the future) over the actuarial value of assets. Governments may amortize an unfunded amount over a period of up to 30 years. For example, an unfunded OPEB liability of $25 billion, amortized over 30 years, would require posting a new expense (e.g., $3 billion to $4 billion) to the financial statement each year.

Over time, the accumulated amount of the amortized unfunded liability becomes enormous, annually boosted by any shortfalls between actual pay-as-you-go funding amounts and normal costs. This could well shift the government's financial position from a positive to a negative balance.

The big question is "So?" GASB 45 does not require governments to pre-fund OPEB liabilities. Rating agency pronouncements have reassured government managers that implementation of the new rules will not necessarily trigger immediate credit rating downgrades. Standard & Poor's, a leading rating agency noted, "OPEB liabilities are just one of many factors evaluated … and the overall effect of the liabilities will be realized over a long period."[11]

However, it is clear that the new accounting standard illuminates a part of state budgets that can be expected to grow significantly as baby boomers retire and health care costs continue to escalate. Retiree health coverage is very much a public sector phenomenon: One study estimated that in 2005, 92 percent of state governments offered health benefits to retirees under age 65, seven times the percentage of private sector employees.[12]

The potential impact of this new reporting requirement is illustrated by California's Legislative Analyst's Office (LAO). The LAO estimated California's actuarially required contribution at approximately $6 billion annually, with about one-third from the normal cost and two-thirds representing the annual amortization of that state's unfunded liability.[13] To put this in perspective, California will actually disburse approximately $1 billion this year in current funding for health insurance for its retirees. The $5 billion difference between the "required" contribution and actual funding represents a GAAP negative on California's financial statements. On a budgetary basis, the $6 billion required contribution reveals the budget pressure that California will face from retiree health coverage in years to come.

States have only two real options in addressing this issue. They can reduce retiree health coverage and thereby scale back their liabilities, or they can begin to accumulate assets to offset these costs. Assets can be accumulated primarily from either annual revenue deposited to a separate trust fund and/or from bond issue proceeds. These assets can be invested much like pension funds—by growing over time, they can balance at least part of these formerly hidden liabilities. However, both options present unpalatable budget choices for states already facing other real spending and revenue pressures.

Notes

[1] Brian T. Stenson and Nai-Ling Kuo, "State Tax Revenue Showing Signs of Slowdown," *State Revenue Report* No. 66, Rockefeller Institute of Government, (December 2006), 2.

[2] National Governors Association and National Association of State Budget Officers, *The Fiscal Survey of States*, (Washington, D.C., December 2006), 8, 20, 23, 26.

[3] The Fiscal Survey of States, (December 2006), 8.

[4] The Congressional Budget Office, *The Budget and Eco-*

nomic Outlook: Fiscal Years 2008 to 2017, (Washington, D.C., January 2007), Summary Table 2.

[5] Paul J. Lim, "Fundamentally, Tech Stocks Are Back With Caveats," *The New York Times*, January 28, 2007.

[6] Bureau of Labor Statistics, Local Area Unemployment Statistics.

[7] Centers for Medicare and Medicaid Services, *National Health Expenditure Projections*, (February 2007), Table 3.

[8] *The Fiscal Survey of States*, (December 2006), 1.

[9] U.S. Department of Education, National Center for Education Statistics, *Projections of Education Statistics to 2014*, (September 2005).

[10] U.S. Department of Education, National Center for Education Statistics, *Public School Principals Report on Their School Facilities: Fall 2005*, (January 2007), 24.

[11] Standard and Poor's, *OPEB Liabilities Pose Minimal Near-Term Rating Risk for Public Finance Credits*, December 4, 2006.

[12] Employee Benefit Research Institute, *The Impact of the Erosion of Retiree Health Benefits on Workers and Retirees*, (March 2005).

[13] California Legislative Analyst's Office, *Retiree Health Care: A Growing Cost for Government*, February 17, 2006.

About the Author

Brian Stenson is an investment banker with RBC Capital Markets. He was previously Deputy Director of the Rockefeller Institute of Government. Brian previously served as SUNY's Vice Chancellor for Finance and before that was Deputy for Fiscal Planning in the New York State Budget Division. Brian received his B.A. and M.P.A. from the University at Albany.

State Budgets in 2006 and 2007:
The Fiscal Situation is Strong, but Have the States Peaked?

By Brian Sigritz

In 2006 state fiscal conditions were very healthy. Tax collections either met or surpassed expectations in all 50 states; spending growth was above average; balances were at near record levels; and only two states were forced to make mid-year budget cuts. The overall outlook for fiscal 2007 remains positive, although there are signs that state fiscal conditions have peaked. States have budgeted for less expenditure growth, are anticipating a reduction in revenue growth, and are preparing for future spending demands.

Introduction

Overall, the state fiscal picture in fiscal year 2006 was extremely bright. States continued their recovery from the economic downturn of the early 2000s, and all 50 states either met or surpassed their revenue estimates. Corporate income tax collections were 20.5 percent higher than predicted; personal income tax collections exceeded expectations by 6.6 percent; and sales tax collections surpassed expectations by 2.3 percent. Along with strong revenue growth, states also experienced spending growth levels above the historical average. From fiscal 2005 to 2006, general fund expenditures grew by 8.7 percent, with the average historical growth rate standing at 6.4 percent. As a result of the positive fiscal picture in 2006, only two states made midyear budgets cuts, compared to 37 states that made midyear budget cuts in both fiscal 2002 and 2003. Additionally, states were able to replenish balances in budget stabilization and rainy day funds that had been diminished in fiscal 2002 and 2003. Ending balances in fiscal 2006 reached 9.8 percent of general fund expenditures, the highest level since fiscal 2000 and the second highest level in 28 years.

While still positive, state officials are predicting that the fiscal 2007 outlook will be less lustrous. Based on enacted fiscal 2007 budgets, states are expecting a 3-percent growth in revenue, compared to the 11-percent revenue growth in fiscal 2006. States are predicting slower revenue growth partly because of tax and fee decreases in fiscal 2007 budgets. States enacted overall tax and fee decreases of $2.1 billion in fiscal 2007. By comparison, states enacted tax and fee increases of $2.5 billion in fiscal 2006. States have also budgeted for less spending growth in 2007. Expenditure growth is expected to slow to 7 percent, above the historical average, but less than fiscal 2006. Lastly, states plan to dedicate fewer rev-

enues to budget stabilization and rainy day funds in 2007. States are estimating total balances will be 6.8 percent of general fund expenditures in fiscal 2007, less than the 9.8 percent of fiscal 2006.

The Current State Fiscal Condition

Revenues in Fiscal 2006

In fiscal 2006,[1] states continued to experience strong revenue growth. Collections of sales, personal income and corporate income taxes exceeded budgeted amounts in 46 states and were on target in four states. This marked the second consecutive fiscal year that all states have either met or surpassed budgeted estimates. By comparison, as recently as fiscal 2002, 42 states reported collecting less revenue than budgeted. This contrast illustrates both the cyclical nature of economic activity and the challenges of accurately projecting revenues.

Overall, fiscal 2006 revenue collections were 5.9 percent higher than anticipated in the enacted budgets. Most notably, in response to strong economic performance, corporate income taxes were 20.5 percent higher than original estimates. Personal income tax collections were 6.6 percent higher than anticipated in fiscal 2006, while sales taxes exceeded expectations by 2.3 percent.[2] Higher than anticipated revenue collections translated into states collecting $27.9 billion more than originally projected.

Revenues in Fiscal 2007

While states ended fiscal 2006 with higher than anticipated revenue collections, the latest information from the Nelson A. Rockefeller Institute of Government seems to point toward a slowing of state tax revenue growth. During the first quarter of fiscal 2007 (July–September 2006), state tax revenue grew by 4.6

percent compared to the same time the previous year. The 4.6 percent growth during the first quarter of fiscal 2007 is considerably less than the 9.9 percent growth from the last quarter of fiscal 2006. Furthermore, the nominal growth rate in the first quarter of fiscal 2007 was the lowest growth rate in three years.[3]

Similarly, states anticipated more modest revenue growth in 2007. Based on enacted fiscal 2007 budgets, states expect revenues will be 3 percent higher than those collected in fiscal 2006. States anticipate sales tax revenue will increase by 3.5 percent, personal income tax revenue will increase by 4 percent, and corporate income tax revenue will decrease by 4 percent.[4] According to enacted budgets, states are anticipating the revenue increase between fiscal 2006 and 2007 will be far less than the revenue increase between fiscal 2005 and 2006. States experienced an overall revenue increase of 11 percent in fiscal 2006, compared to the 3 percent revenue increase they are anticipating in fiscal 2007. The 11-percent revenue increase in fiscal 2006 consisted of a 6.7-percent revenue increase in sales tax, a 10.5-percent revenue increase in personal income tax, and a notable 38.2-percent revenue increase in corporate income tax.[5,6]

Tax and Fee Changes in Fiscal 2007

One reason states are anticipating slower revenue growth is because of overall tax and fee decreases enacted in fiscal 2007 budgets. States enacted net tax and fee decreases totaling $2.1 billion for fiscal 2007, which were made possible through higher than anticipated revenues and budget surpluses in fiscal 2006. By comparison, states enacted net tax and fee increases of $2.5 billion in fiscal 2006. In fiscal 2007, 24 states adopted net tax and fee decreases, while 15 states adopted net tax and fee increases.

The largest enacted tax and fee decrease for fiscal 2007 was seen in personal income taxes. Eighteen states enacted decreases in personal income taxes, while only two enacted increases. Ohio had the largest personal income tax reduction in fiscal 2007, with rates being cut by 4.2 percent. The 4.2-percent reduction was part of a 21-percent reduction evenly spread over five years. In addition to reductions in personal income taxes, states also enacted reductions in corporate income taxes ($239.7 million) and motor fuel taxes ($115.2 million).

In contrast to these reductions in personal income taxes, states enacted a net sales tax increase of $622 million in fiscal 2007 enacted budgets. The net increase of sales tax revenue can largely be attributed to New Jersey. New Jersey increased its sales tax rate from 6 to 7 percent, and also extended the base of the sales and use tax. These changes resulted in a revenue increase of $1.55 billion. Even though the overall totals across the states show a net increase in enacted sales tax changes, 15 states actually enacted net decreases in sales tax, while only six states enacted increases. In addition to the enacted net sales tax increases, states also enacted net increases of $493 million in cigarette, tobacco and alcohol taxes. The largest increase was seen in Texas, where the tax on a pack of cigarettes was raised from $1 to $1.41.[7]

State Spending in 2006

General funds serve as the primary source for financing a state's operations. General funds typically receive their revenue from broad-based state taxes such as sales taxes and personal income taxes. In fiscal 2006, state general fund expenditures were $602 billion (preliminary actual), an 8.7-percent increase compared to fiscal 2005. The 8.7-percent increase in fiscal 2006 was higher than the 28-year historical average of 6.4 percent. Fiscal 2006 marked the fourth consecutive year that state general fund expenditures grew at a higher rate than the previous year. Additionally, 13 states had general fund growth rates of 10 percent or higher, 26 states had growth rates from 5 percent to 9.9 percent, eight states had increases up to 4.9 percent, and three states experienced negative growth.[8]

According to estimated fiscal 2006 numbers from NASBO's *State Expenditure Report*, general funds accounted for 43.7 percent of total state expenditures. Federal funds accounted for 28.2 percent of total expenditures, bonds accounted for 2.8 percent, and other state funds were 25.3 percent.[9] General fund spending has decreased as a percentage of total state expenditures since fiscal 2000. In fiscal 2000 general fund spending accounted for 48.1 percent of total state expenditures, while in fiscal 2006 general fund spending decreased to 43.7 percent of total spending.[10] This is partly attributable to the increased use of other state funds, which includes funds that are restricted by law for specific governmental functions or activities.

Elementary and secondary education remained far and away the largest category of general fund expenditures in fiscal 2006, accounting for 35.1 percent of general fund expenditures. Medicaid represented 18.1 percent, and higher education accounted for 11.4 percent. Other categories included corrections at 7 percent, public assistance at 2.1 percent, transportation at 0.8 percent, and all other spending at 25.5 percent.

Medicaid accounted for only 14.4 percent of general fund expenditures in fiscal 2000, but has now risen to 18.1 percent. Medicaid has also increased as a percentage of total state expenditures. Medicaid accounted for 22.2 percent of total state expenditures in fiscal 2006, whereas in fiscal 2000 it stood at 19.5 percent of total expenditures.[11] Accordingly, Medicaid represents the largest share of total state expenditures, with elementary and secondary education second at 21.5 percent. For the first time in fiscal 2003, Medicaid surpassed elementary and secondary education as the largest share of total state expenditures. Other categories of total expenditures in fiscal 2006 included higher education representing 10.7 percent, transportation at 8.7 percent, corrections at 3.4 percent, public assistance at 1.9 percent, and all other spending at 31.6 percent.[12]

State Spending in 2007

Expenditure growth is expected to slow to 7 percent in fiscal 2007, according to appropriated budgets. While still slightly above the historical average growth rate of 6.4 percent, the 7-percent growth rate represents a decline from the 8.7-percent rate of fiscal 2006. Furthermore, four states are expected to have negative growth rates, 15 states are expected to have growth rates up to 4.9 percent, 17 states appropriated growth levels of 5 percent to 9.9 percent, and 14 states are expected to have growth rates of 10 percent or more.[13]

Budget Cuts

Fiscal 2006 continued the recent trend of a decline in the number of states forced to make midyear budget cuts. Only two states, Louisiana and Indiana, made budget cuts after their fiscal 2006 budgets passed, totaling $521 million. Louisiana suffered from Hurricanes Katrina and Rita, and Indiana has suffered from declines in its manufacturing sector. Significantly, no states in fiscal 2007 have yet had to make cuts to their enacted budgets. This marks a notable turnaround from fiscal 2002 and fiscal 2003 when 37 states in each year were forced to make midyear budget cuts that totaled nearly $15 billion and $11.8 billion, respectively.[14]

Balances

Fiscal 2006 was also noteworthy due to increases in state balances. Total balances include both ending balances and the amounts in states' budget stabilization funds; they reflect the funds states may use to respond to unforeseen circumstances after budget obligations have been met. Forty-seven states currently have budget stabilization funds, with about three-fifths of the states having limits on the size of these funds. Total balances in fiscal 2006 reached 9.8 percent of general fund expenditures, the highest level since fiscal 2000, when balances reached 10.3 percent of expenditures.

State balances and rainy day funds were depleted during the fiscal downturn of the early 2000s. States have since worked hard to replenish their balances to safeguard against a future economic slowdown. Whereas in fiscal 2003, balances were only 3.2 percent of total expenditures, fiscal 2004 saw a rise to 4.6 percent, fiscal 2005 balances were 8.4 percent of expenditures, and fiscal 2006 saw near record levels of balances at 9.8 percent of total expenditures. Total balances are estimated to decline in fiscal 2007 to 6.8 percent, although this level would still surpass the historical average of 5.5 percent.[15]

Looking Ahead

While overall state fiscal situations were very strong in 2006, and the outlook for 2007 is still mostly positive, the outlook for fiscal 2008 and beyond is much less clear. States are anticipating both lower revenue growth and lower expenditure growth in fiscal 2007 compared to fiscal 2006. Data from the first quarter of fiscal 2007 supports states' assessment that revenue growth in 2007 will not be as strong as 2006. Furthermore, it is possible that continued slowing revenue growth will cause some budget problems in the states. "Early indications are that tax collections are about as expected in the states, but more pronounced slowdowns could suggest some budget stress ahead," said Brian Stenson of the Nelson A. Rockefeller Institute of Government.[16]

In addition to slowing revenue growth, states are likely to face strong spending pressures in the near future. Areas such as health care and elementary and secondary education are expected to continue to grow. States will also face increased costs in transportation construction and maintenance, pensions, higher education, and managing the myriad issues associated with the retirement of the baby boomers. Finally, as the federal debt continues to increase, states will face the possibility of slowing growth of assistance from the federal government. All these factors taken together show that while the current state fiscal situation is bright, clouds may be on the horizon.

Notes

[1] The fiscal year in 46 states begins in July and ends in June. The exceptions are Alabama and Michigan, where the fiscal year runs October–September; New York, where it is April–March; and Texas, where the fiscal year runs September–August. Twenty states budget biennially.

[2] National Association of State Budget Officers, *The Fiscal Survey of States*, (December 2006), 8.

[3] Nelson A. Rockefeller Institute of Government, *State Revenue Report*, (December 2006), 1.

[4] See note 2 above.

[5] *The Fiscal Survey of States*, (December 2006), 36.

[6] National Association of State Budget Officers, *The Fiscal Survey of States*, (December 2005), 34.

[7] *The Fiscal Survey of States*, (NASBO, December 2006), 10.

[8] *The Fiscal Survey of States*, (NASBO, December 2006), 1–3.

[9] National Association of State Budget Officers, *2005 State Expenditure Report*, (Fall 2006), 4.

[10] National Association of State Budget Officers, *2000 State Expenditure Report*, (Summer 2001), 5.

[11] Ibid.

[12] *2005 State Expenditure Report*, (NASBO, Fall 2006), 8.

[13] *The Fiscal Survey of States*, (NASBO, December 2006), 2–3.

[14] *The Fiscal Survey of States*, (NASBO, December 2006), 1.

[15] *The Fiscal Survey of States*, (NASBO, December 2006), 12–15.

[16] Nelson A. Rockefeller Institute of Government, Press Release, December 19, 2006, "State Tax Revenue Off to Slow Start for Fiscal Year 2007."

About the Author

Brian Sigritz is a staff associate at the National Association of State Budget Officers. He received his M.P.A. from the George Washington University and his B.A. from St. Bonaventure University. Prior to working at NASBO, Sigritz worked for the Ohio Senate and the Ohio House of Representatives.

Table 7.1
FISCAL 2005 STATE GENERAL FUND, ACTUAL, BY REGION
(In millions of dollars)

State or other jurisdiction	Beginning balance	Revenues	Adjustments	Total resources	Expenditures	Adjustments	Ending balance	Budget stabilization fund
U.S. total	$23,823	$569,597	. . .	$598,404	$553,900	. . .	$38,488	$25,420
Eastern Region								
Connecticut (a)	0	14,063	. . .	14,063	13,699	. . .	364	666
Delaware*	646	2,878	0	3,524	2,822	0	701	148
Maine (b)	15	2,791	12	2,818	2,784	0	34	47
Massachusetts* (c)........	756	24,373	0	25,129	23,779	0	2,487	1,728
New Hampshire	15	1,392	0	1,407	1,325	0	82	17
New Jersey* (d).............	834	28,132	0	28,966	27,844	344	778	289
New York* (e)...............	2,302	43,863	0	46,165	43,619	0	2,546	872
Pennsylvania (f)............	77	23,309	98	23,483	23,054	64	365	329
Rhode Island (g)	35	3,005	-61	2,979	2,927	14	39	91
Vermont (h)..................	0	1,035	48	1,083	1,038	45	0	46
Regional totals..............	4,680	144,841	. . .	149,617	142,891	. . .	7,396	4,233
Midwestern Region								
Illinois (i).....................	182	23,647	2,513	26,342	22,184	3,661	497	276
Indiana (j)	0	11,488	158	11,647	11,800	-272	119	317
Iowa (k)	0	4,929	0	4,929	4,603	160	166	226
Kansas (l)......................	328	4,841	0	5,169	4,690	0	479	0
Michigan (m)................	0	8,163	701	8,865	8,644	0	221	2
Minnesota (n)................	1,269	14,653	0	15,922	14,529	0	1,393	1,340
Nebraska (o)	176	3,032	-84	3,124	2,720	0	403	177
North Dakota (p)..........	76	997	0	1,073	904	100	69	100
Ohio (q)........................	158	25,551	0	25,708	24,831	739	138	575
South Dakota (r)	0	958	33	991	989	2	0	134
Wisconsin (s)................	105	11,474	194	11,773	11,860	-91	4	0
Regional totals..............	2,294	109,733	. . .	115,543	107,754	. . .	3,489	3,147
Southern Region								
Alabama (t)....................	323	6,406	24	6,753	6,052	38	664	157
Arkansas	0	3,630	0	3,630	3,630	0	0	0
Florida	2,457	25,553	0	28,010	24,440	0	3,571	988
Georgia*	763	16,789	0	17,551	16,323	0	1,228	257
Kentucky (u).................	250	7,757	231	8,238	7,698	71	469	29
Louisiana (v).................	0	7,392	78	7,470	7,127	91	252	462
Maryland (w)................	453	11,548	438	12,438	11,264	0	1,174	521
Mississippi....................	3	3,727	0	3,730	3,678	0	52	20
Missouri (x)...................	489	6,933	0	7,421	7,121	0	300	232
North Carolina (y)	289	16,327	0	16,616	15,798	339	479	313
Oklahoma (z)................	67	5,374	-301	5,140	4,945	186	10	461
South Carolina* (aa)......	120	5,591	0	5,712	5,073	105	533	75
Texas (bb).....................	1,448	32,655	295	34,398	29,711	948	3,739	7
Tennessee (cc)...............	545	9,311	-60	9,796	9,113	221	462	275
Virginia........................	677	13,759	0	14,436	13,879	0	557	1,111
West Virginia (dd).........	291	3,505	8	3,803	3,410	32	361	79
Regional totals..............	8,175	176,256	. . .	185,141	169,261	. . .	13,850	4,987
Western Region								
Alaska (ee)....................	0	3,055	0	3,055	3,055	0	9	2,274
Arizona (ff)...................	360	7,799	25	8,184	7,545	0	639	161
California*....................	7,228	82,210	0	89,438	79,804	0	9,634	9,112
Colorado (gg)...............	224	6,475	-251	6,448	6,113	0	336	0
Hawaii	185	4,486	0	4,671	4,185	0	486	54
Idaho (hh)	100	2,268	-43	2,325	2,110	0	214	16
Montana.......................	135	1,531	-4	1,662	1,365	0	297	0
Nevada.........................	221	3,041	0	3,262	3,101	0	161	156
New Mexico*	327	4,982	473	5,782	4,727	367	688	688
Oregon (ii)	-716	5,516	0	4,801	4,492	0	309	0
Utah (jj)	54	4,092	-63	4,083	3,978	0	106	146
Washington (kk)............	500	12,067	522	13,089	12,220	0	870	0
Wyoming (ll)	58	1,246	0	1,304	1,299	0	5	446
Regional totals..............	8,676	138,768	. . .	148,104	133,993	. . .	13,752	13,053
Regional totals without California.......	1,448	56,558	. . .	58,666	54,189	. . .	4,118	3,941

See footnotes at end of table.

FISCAL 2005 STATE GENERAL FUND, APPROPRIATED, BY REGION — Continued
(In millions of dollars)

Source: National Association of State Budget Officers, The Fiscal Survey of the States (December 2006).

Note: For all states, unless otherwise noted, transfers into budget stabilization funds are counted as expenditures, and transfers from budget stabilization funds are counted as revenues.

Key:

* In these states, the ending balance includes the balance in the budget stabilization fund.

NA — Indicates data are not available.

(a) Includes the expenditure of $639.8 million of surplus funds.

(b) Revenue adjustments reflect $12.4 million in legislative and statutory authorized transfers.

(c) Includes Budgeted Operating Funds.

(d) Budget vs. GAAP Adjustments.

(e) The ending balance included $727 million to pay tax refunds and prior year obligations, $601 million in a spending stabilization reserve, $872 million in the tax stabilization reserve fund (rainy day fund), $325 million in the Community Projects Fund and $21 million in a reserve for litigation risks.

(f) Revenue adjustments include $97.2 million in prior year lapses and $.7 million in adjustments to the beginning balance. Expenditure adjustment reflects a statutory transfer to the budget stabilization (rainy day) fund.

(g) Revenue adjustments include Transfer to Budget Stabilization (Rainy Day) Fund. Expenditure adjustments include general revenue reappropriations.

(h) Revenue adjustments include $2 million for Vermont Economic Development Authority debt forgiveness, $20.6 in direct applications and transfers in, $13.8 million in additional property transfer tax to the General Fund, and $15.6 million in transfers from General Fund Surplus Reserve. Expenditure adjustments include transfers to the Transportation Fund of $4.8 million, transfers from the General Bond Fund of $1.7 million, transfers of $14.3 million to the Health Access Trust Fund, $3.7 million to Internal Service Funds, $3.1 million to miscellaneous other funds, $1.3 million to the Budget Stabilization Fund, and $19.6 million to the General Fund Surplus Reserve.

(i) Revenue adjustments include $2,513 million in transfers to general funds. Expenditure adjustments include transfers out of $3,163 million and $495 million to repay Pension Obligation Bond Debt Service.

(j) Revenue adjustments represent one-time transfers from dedicated funds and transfer to Rainy Day Fund. Expenditure Adjustments represent one-time capital reversions from prior biennium.

(k) $159.7 million was appropriated from the ending balance for the general fund to the Property Tax Credit fund to pay for property tax credits in Fiscal 2006.

(l) Kansas does not have a Rainy Day Fund. However, the balanced budget provision of the constitution requires revenues to finance the approved budget.

(m) Revenue adjustments include federal and state law changes of $98.4 million, revenue sharing law changes of $506.3 million, $15.6 million in property sales, a withdrawal from the Rainy Day Fund of $81.3 million, deposits from state restricted revenues of $21.5 million, and other revenue adjustments of -$21.7 million.

(n) Ending balance includes budget reserve of $653 million, cash flow account of $350 million and tax relief account of $336.7 million.

(o) Revenue adjustments are transfers between the General Fund and other funds. Per Nebraska law, includes a transfer to the Cash Reserve Fund (Rainy Day Fund) of the amount the prior year's net General Fund receipts exceeded the official forecast.

(p) Transfer to the budget stabilization fund.

(q) Federal reimbursements and other human services programs are included in the general revenue fund. Beginning balances are undesignated, unreserved fund balances. The actual cash balances would be higher by the amount reserved for encumbrances and designated transfers from the general revenue fund. Expenditures for fiscal 2005 do not include encumbrances outstanding at the end of the year. Ohio reports expenditures based on disbursements for the general revenue fund. Expenditure adjustments reflect a transfer to the Budget Stabilization Fund of $394.2 million and miscellaneous transfers-out of $193.5 million. These transfers-out are adjusted for a net change in encumbrances from fiscal 2004 levels of $151 million.

(r) Revenue adjustments include $7.4 million from one-time receipts, $24.6 million in transfers from the Property Tax Reduction Fund to cover the budget shortfall, and $1.2 million in obligated cash carried forward from Fiscal 2004. Expenditure adjustments include $1.2 million in transfers to the Budget Reserve Fund from the prior year's obligated cash, and $0.8 million in obligated cash to the Budget Reserve Fund.

(s) Revenue excludes $3.8 million of Tribal Gaming, $166.3 million in Transfers in to General Fund, $51.2 million in Unreserved designated balances, and a -$27.4 million adjustment to prior year tax collection accruals. These total $193.9, which also constitute the Revenue Adjustments. Expenditure Adjustments include $5.2 million designation for continuing appropriations, Interfund transfers of -$166.3 million, and a transfer to the MA Trust Fund of $70 million.

(t) Revenue adjustments reflect the release of prior year Debt Service Reserve. Expenditure Adjustments reflect reversions and reserves for General Obligation Debt Service Payments.

(u) Revenue includes $112.2 million in Tobacco Settlement funds. Revenue adjustments include $77.2 million that represents appropriation balances carried over from the prior fiscal year, and $154 million from fund transfers into the General Fund. Expenditure adjustments represent appropriation balances forwarded to the next fiscal year.

(v) Revenue adjustments include $22.8 million in general fund carry-forward, $32.9 million of prior year surplus, $2.7 million of fund balances, and $17.3 million of non-recurring revenue for capital outlays. Expenditure adjustments include $36.7 million in general fund carry-forward, $49.5 million in capital outlay carry-forward, and $4.6 million in carry-forward and prior appropriations for IEB.

(w) Adjustments reflect a $37 million reduction resulting from a multi-year reconciliation of cash, transfers from the Rainy Day Fund to the General Fund of $91 million, and $383.6 million from various special funds.

(x) Revenues are net of refunds. Refunds for Fiscal 2005 totaled $1,071.3 million. Revenues include $175.9 million transferred to the General Revenue Fund and $45.2 million from bond proceeds for capital improvement projects.

(y) $199.1 million increase to Rainy Day Fund, $125 million increase to Repair and Renovation Reserve, $14.9 million transferred from Unreserved Credit balance.

(z) The adjustment to the Revenues subtracts out the Rainy Day Fund deposit of $461 million and the increase in the deposit into the Cash Flow Reserve Fund from Fiscal 2005 to Fiscal 2006.

(aa) Correction of prior year's accounting errors.

(bb) The beginning balance is from the Comptroller's January 2005 Biennial Revenue Estimate. Revenues are from the Comptroller's April 2006 revised revenue estimate. Revenue adjustment is the actual increase in dedicated account balances. Total expenditures are 2005 budgeted, as reported by the Legislative Budget Board. Expenditure adjustment includes $905 million reserved for transfer to the Rainy Day Fund and other adjustments to reconcile the ending balance.

(cc) Revenue adjustments include $42.7 million in transfers from debt service fund unexpended appropriations, -$58.4 million in transfers to the Rainy Day Fund and -$44.5 million to the dedicated revenue appropriations reserve. Expenditure adjustments include a $36.3 million transfer to Transportation Equity Fund, an $81 million transfer to the capital outlay projects fund, $56 million in transfers to systems development projects, and $47.6 million in dedicated revenue appropriations.

(dd) Fiscal 2005 Actual General Fund beginning balance includes $203.3 million in Reappropriations, $21.2 million of Surplus Appropriations, and an Unappropriated Surplus balance of $66 million. Revenue adjustments include transfers from Special Revenue of $7.3 million, and prior year redeposits of $0.3 million. Total Expenditures include Regular Appropriations of $3,248.7 million, $118 million in Reappropriations, $20 million of Surplus Appropriations and 31 day prior year Expenditures of $23.7 million. Expenditure adjustments represent the amount transferred to the Rainy Day Fund.

(ee) Budget surplus.

(ff) Revenue adjustments represent enacted fund transfers, VLT transfer, and Ladewig lawsuit payments.

(gg) Revenue adjustments include diversions to the State Education Fund and the Older Coloradan's program, as well as transfers to the General Fund to mitigate revenue declines. Ending balance was $98 million above the 4 percent statutory reserve requirement. Colorado law requires monies in excess of the statutory reserve to be credited to the Highway User's Tax Fund and the Capital Construction Fund.

(hh) Revenue transfers include $21.3 million to the Revolving Development Fund and $21 million to the Budget Stabilization Fund.

(ii) Oregon budgets on a biennial basis. The constitution requires the state to be balanced at the end of each biennium.

(jj) Revenue adjustments include a $107.2 million reserve from prior fiscal year, $5 million lapsing balances from agencies, $2.2 million in transfers from various restricted accounts, $4.4 million in industrial assistance fund reserve from previous fiscal year, $2.1 million from other miscellaneous revenue sources, a $4.1 million surplus designated for debt service, $3.2 million in industrial assistance fund reserve for the following fiscal year, a $69.2 million transfer to the rainy day fund, and a $117.6 million Reserve for following fiscal year.

(kk) Transfers from other accounts to the General Fund and adjustments to balance to the official annual financial statement account for $522.4 million.

(ll) The state of Wyoming budgets on a biennial basis. To complete the survey using annual figures certain assumptions and estimates were required.

Table 7.2
FISCAL 2006 STATE GENERAL FUND, PRELIMINARY ACTUAL, BY REGION
(In millions of dollars)

State or other jurisdiction	Beginning balance	Revenues	Adjustments	Resources	Expenditures	Adjustments	Ending balance	Budget stabilization fund
U.S. total	$35,950	$618,473	$4,328	$658,751	$602,251	$7,426	$50,802	$31,193
Eastern Region								
Connecticut (a)	0	14,999	0	14,999	14,552	0	446	1,112
Delaware*	701	3,170	0	3,871	3,181	0	691	161
Maine (b)	34	2,858	93	2,984	2,872	98	15	80
Massachusetts* (c)........	759	26,306	0	27,064	25,585	0	3,208	2,160
New Hampshire (d).......	82	1,329	0	1,411	1,334	52	26	69
New Jersey * (e)	778	27,789	0	28,567	27,111	1	1,455	430
New York* (f)...............	2,546	47,206	0	49,752	46,495	0	3,257	944
Pennsylvania (g)	365	24,819	166	25,350	24,681	155	514	512
Rhode Island (h)	52	3,135	-64	3,124	3,100	0	24	95
Vermont (i)	0	1,112	45	1,157	1,114	43	0	52
Regional totals..............	5,317	152,723	240	158,279	150,025	349	9,634	5,615
Midwestern Region								
Illinois (j)......................	497	25,254	2,105	27,856	24,193	3,073	590	276
Indiana (k)	119	12,143	292	12,553	12,204	-62	411	328
Iowa (l)	0	5,382	0	5,382	5,021	213	149	392
Kansas (m).....................	479	5,394	0	5,873	5,139	0	734	0
Michigan (n)	221	8,315	606	9,141	9,032	0	110	2
Minnesota (o).................	1,393	15,314	0	16,707	15,806	0	901	1,095
Nebraska (p)	403	3,349	-271	3,482	2,916	0	566	274
North Dakota	69	1,094	0	1,163	966	0	197	100
Ohio (q)	139	25,846	0	25,985	24,866	486	632	1,011
South Dakota (r)	0	1,018	38	1,057	1,056	1	0	137
Wisconsin (s)	4	12,030	780	12,814	12,385	380	49	0
Regional totals..............	3,323	115,139	3,550	122,012	113,583	4,091	4,338	3,614
Southern Region								
Alabama (t)...................	730	7,155	9	7,894	6,962	26	907	419
Arkansas	0	3,825	0	3,825	3,825	0	0	0
Florida	3,571	27,141	0	30,712	27,140	0	3,572	1,068
Georgia*	1,228	18,485	0	19,713	17,851	0	1,863	904
Kentucky (u).................	469	8,479	346	9,294	8,436	177	681	119
Louisiana (v).................	0	8,305	300	8,605	7,740	37	827	682
Maryland (w)................	1,174	12,390	139	13,703	12,342	0	1,362	759
Mississippi (x)	52	3,980	0	4,032	4,037	-5	0	19
Missouri (y)	300	7,520	0	7,821	7,125	0	695	246
North Carolina (z).........	479	17,874	0	18,353	17,065	538	749	629
Oklahoma (aa)	10	6,201	-87	6,123	5,532	457	133	496
South Carolina* (bb)......	533	6,226	0	6,759	5,640	132	988	154
Tennessee (cc)..............	462	9,852	16	10,330	9,866	154	311	325
Texas (dd).....................	3,739	36,675	548	40,962	32,283	1,133	7,547	405
Virginia.........................	557	16,052	0	16,609	15,232	0	1,377	1,306
West Virginia (ee).........	361	3,661	54	4,076	3,562	45	469	124
Regional totals..............	13,664	193,822	1,325	208,811	184,636	2,694	21,481	7,654
Western Region								
Alaska (ff).....................	0	4,470	-1,223	3,247	3,247	NA	0	2,396
Arizona (gg)	639	9,270	-48	9,861	8,945	0	916	650
California* (hh)	9,634	92,749	-122	102,260	92,730	0	9,530	9,009
Colorado (ii)	237	7,322	227	7,786	7,097	0	689	0
Hawaii	486	4,925	0	5,411	4,679	0	732	54
Idaho (jj).......................	214	2,431	-126	2,520	2,218	0	302	109
Montana........................	297	1,708	-12	1,994	1,583	5	406	0
Nevada..........................	161	3,049	0	3,210	2,916	0	294	167
New Mexico*	688	5,510	287	6,485	5,417	287	781	781
Oregon (kk)	309	6,308	0	6,617	6,090	0	527	0
Utah (ll)	106	4,474	104	4,683	4,223	0	460	255
Washington (mm)	870	13,327	126	14,323	13,621	0	702	0
Wyoming (nn)................	5	1,247	0	1,252	1,242	0	10	892
Regional totals..............	13,646	156,790	-786	169,649	154,007	287	15,350	14,311
Regional totals without California......	4,012	64,040	-664	67,389	61,277	287	5,820	5,302

See footnotes at end of table.

FISCAL 2006 STATE GENERAL FUND, PRELIMINARY ACTUAL, BY REGION—Continued
(In millions of dollars)

Source: National Association of State Budget Officers, The Fiscal Survey of the States (December 2006).

Note: For all states unless otherwise noted, transfers into budget stabilization funds are counted as expenditures and transfers from budget stabilization funds are counted as revenue.

Key:

* — In these states, the ending balance includes the balance in the budget stabilization fund.

(a) Includes $485.5 million in surplus spending such as the expenditure of $85.5 million to pre-fund Economic Recovery Notes and the expenditure of $245.65 million for the Teachers' Retirement Fund.

(b) Revenue adjustments of $92.5 million and expenditure adjustments of $97.5 million are reflected in legislative and statutory authorized transfers.

(c) Includes Budgeted Operating Funds.

(d) Expenditure adjustment is a $51.7 million transfer to the Rainy Day Fund.

(e) Transfers to other funds.

(f) The ending balance includes over $2 billion in a spending stabilization reserve, $944 million in the tax stabilization reserve fund (Rainy Day Fund), $251 million in the Community Projects Fund and $21 million in reserve for litigation risks.

(g) Revenue adjustments include $165.9 million in prior year lapses. Expenditure adjustment reflects a statutory transfer to the budget stabilization (rainy day) fund and current year lapse of $15.9 million.

(h) Revenue Adjustments include Transfer to Budget Stabilization (Rainy Day) Fund.

(i) Revenue adjustments include $14.9 million in direct applications and transfers in, $10.3 million due to an increase in property transfer tax revenue estimate, $0.1 million from the liquidation of debt service and bond premium reserve, and transfers from General Fund Surplus Reserve of $19.6 million. Expenditure adjustments include $10.1 million in net transfers from the Human Services Caseload Reserve, $10 million in transfers to the Transportation Fund, a $0.7 million reserve for Fiscal 2006 bond insurance premium, $5.2 million from the Estate tax to the Higher Education Trust Fund, $9.3 million to Internal Service Funds, $0.6 million to miscellaneous other funds, $6.0 million to the Budget Stabilization Reserve, and $21.1 million to the General Fund Surplus Reserve.

(j) Revenue adjustments include $2,101 million of transfers into general funds. Expenditure adjustments include $427 million to repay Pension Obligation Bond Debt Service and transfers-out from general funds of $2,632 million.

(k) Revenue adjustments represent a one-time tax amnesty revenue (net of expenditures) of $228.8 million, and Quality Assessment Fees of $62.7 million. Expenditure adjustments include adjustments to the Property Tax Replacement Credit and Homestead Credit of $61.9 million.

(l) To pay for property tax credits in Fiscal 2007, $159.9 million was appropriated from the ending balance of the general fund to the Property Tax Credit fund. $2.8 million of the ending balance was appropriated to the Board of Regents to be spread among the Universities. $49.9 million of the ending balance was credited to the Senior Living Trust Fund.

(m) Kansas does not have a "Rainy Day" fund. However, the balanced budget provision of the constitution requires revenues to finance the approved budget.

(n) Revenue adjustments include federal and state law changes of -$33 million, $543 million in revenue sharing law changes, $47 million from several pending property sales, and deposits from state restricted revenues of $49 million.

(o) Ending balance includes budget reserve of $653 million, cash flow account of $350 million and tax relief account of $109.7 million.

(p) Revenue adjustments are transfers between the General Fund and other funds. Per Nebraska law, includes a transfer to the Cash Reserve Fund (Rainy Day Fund) of the amount the prior year's net General Fund receipts exceeded the official forecast.

(q) Federal reimbursements and other human services programs are included in the general revenue fund. Beginning balances are undesignated, unreserved fund balances. The actual cash balances would be higher by the amount reserved for encumbrances and designated transfers from the general revenue fund. Expenditures for Fiscal 2006 do not include encumbrances outstanding at the end of the year. Ohio reports expenditures based on disbursements for the general revenue fund. Expenditure adjustments reflect a transfer to the Budget Stabilization Fund of $434.1 million and miscellaneous transfers-out of $75.8 million. These transfers-out are adjusted for an anticipated net change in encumbrances from Fiscal 2005 levels of -$23.7 million.

(r) Revenue adjustments include $2.1 million from one-time receipts, $35.4 million in transfers from the Property Tax Reduction Fund to cover budget shortfall, and $0.8 million in obligated cash carried forward from Fiscal 2005. Expenditure adjustments include $0.8 million in transfers to the Budget Reserve Fund from the prior year's obligated cash, and $0.3 million in obligated cash to the Budget Reserve Fund.

(s) Revenue adjustments include $88.9 million of Tribal Gaming and $691.2 million of transfers from other funds. Expenditure Adjustments include a $43.2 designation for continuing appropriations, interfund transfers to MA of $341.8 million, and designated funds of $5.2 million.

(t) Revenue adjustment-release of prior year Debt Service Reserve. Expenditure Adjustment-Reversions and Reserve for General Obligation Debt Service Payment.

(u) Revenue includes $103 million in Tobacco Settlement funds. Revenue adjustments include $70.7 million that represents appropriation balances carried over from the prior fiscal year, and $275.7 million from fund transfers into the General Fund. Expenditure Adjustments represent appropriation balances forwarded to the next fiscal year.

(v) Revenue adjustments include $41.6 million of IEB and General Fund Carry-forward, $40.3 million of Bond Premium Dedication, and $217.9 million in transfers to the General Fund. Expenditure adjustments include $23 million of carry-forward balances, $13.1 million in capital outlay carry-forward, and $1.3 million of Carry-forward for IEB.

(w) Adjustments reflect transfers to the General Fund of $90 million from transfer tax revenues and $48.5 million from the local share of highway user revenues.

(x) Transfers, lapses & other adjustments.

(y) Revenues are net of refunds. Refunds for Fiscal 2006 totaled $1,128.9 million. Revenues include $188.1 million transferred to the General Revenue Fund.

(z) Includes a $222.2 million increase to Repair & Renovation Reserve and $316.1 million increase to Rainy Day Reserve.

(aa) Revenue adjustments subtracts out the Rainy Day Fund deposit of $34 million and the increase in the deposit into the Cash Flow Reserve Fund from Fiscal 2006 to Fiscal 2007.

(bb) Increased enforcement of Tax Collections.

(cc) Revenue adjustments include $65 million in transfers from debt service fund unexpended appropriations, and -$49.3 million in transfers to the Rainy Day Fund. Expenditure adjustments include transfers to Transportation Equity Fund of $32 million, transfers to capital outlay projects fund of $68.8 million, transfers to Highway Fund of $10 million, and dedicated revenue appropriations of $43 million.

(dd) The beginning balance is from the Comptroller's April 2006 revised revenue estimate. Revenues are from the Comptroller's monthly revenue collections report through August 2006. Revenue adjustment is the actual increase in dedicated account balances. Total expenditures are 2006 appropriated, as reported by the Legislative Budget Board. Expenditure adjustment is to reconcile appropriations to the preliminary estimated ending balance.

(ee) Fiscal 2006 Preliminary Actual General Fund beginning balance includes $243.5 million in Reappropriations and an Unappropriated Surplus Balance of $117.3 million. Revenue adjustments include $53.5 million in transfers from Special Revenue and $0.1 million in prior year redeposits. Total Expenditures include $3,342.8 million of Regular Appropriations, Reappropriations of $90.1 million, Surplus Appropriations of $101.5 million, and 31 day prior year Expenditures of $27.5 million. Expenditure adjustments represent the amount transferred to the Rainy Day Fund.

(ff) Budget surplus.

(gg) The revenue adjustments represent enacted fund transfers and Ladewig lawsuit payments.

(hh) The revenue adjustment is an adjustment to the Fiscal 2006 beginning fund balance.

(ii) Adjustments include diversions to the Older Coloradan's Program and State Education Fund. Ending balance includes $437.7 million above 4 percent statutory reserve requirement. Per Colorado Statute, these monies will be allocated for transportation and capital construction needs.

(jj) Revenue transfers include $92.7 million to the Budget Stabilization Fund, $11.5 million to the Economic Recovery Reserve Fund, $9.2 million to the Fire Suppression Fund, $5 million to the Public Education Stabilization Fund, $4.6 million to several endowment funds, and $3 million to the Revolving Development Fund.

(kk) Oregon budgets on a biennial basis. The constitution requires the state to be balanced at the end of each biennium.

(ll) Includes $117.6 million held in reserve from previous fiscal year, $25.0 million repayment of emergency loan to Washington County, a $7.0 million one-time revenue from implementing double weighted sales tax reform, $0.2 million from miscellaneous revenue sources, and a -$24.0 million transfer to the Rainy Day Fund.

(mm) The net amount for transfers from other accounts to the General Fund is $126 million.

(nn) The State of Wyoming budgets on a biennial basis. To complete the survey using annual figures certain assumptions and estimates were required.

Table 7.3
FISCAL 2007 STATE GENERAL FUND, APPROPRIATED, BY REGION
(In millions of dollars)

State or other jurisdiction	Beginning balance	Revenues	Adjustments	Resources	Expenditures	Adjustments	Ending balance	Budget stabilization fund
U.S. total	$46,825	$633,518	...	$682,549	$644,136	...	$28,367	$27,306
Eastern Region								
Connecticut...................	0	14,998	0	14,998	14,837	0	161	1,273
Delaware*	691	3,280	0	3,971	3,568	0	403	176
Maine (a)	15	2,934	126	3,075	2,918	157	0	110
Massachusetts (b)	1,048	26,941	0	27,989	27,989	0	0	2,160
New Hampshire	26	1,352	0	1,377	1,365	0	12	69
New Jersey* (c)	1,455	30,084	0	31,538	30,279	0	1,260	449
New York* (d)	3,257	50,860	0	54,117	50,843	0	3,274	944
Pennsylvania (e)	514	25,605	0	26,119	26,114	1	4	513
Rhode Island (f)............	24	3,264	-66	3,222	3,222	0	0	99
Vermont (g)...................	0	1,093	41	1,133	1,130	3	0	55
Regional totals	7,028	160,410	...	167,539	162,264	...	5,113	5,847
Midwestern Region								
Illinois (h).....................	590	26,035	2,295	28,920	25,235	3,091	594	276
Indiana (i)	411	12,414	-49	12,775	12,442	13	320	443
Iowa (j)	0	5,540	0	5,540	5,284	99	158	535
Kansas (k).....................	734	5,293	0	6,027	5,516	23	487	0
Michigan (l)...................	110	8,500	614	9,223	9,223	0	0	2
Minnesota (m)...............	901	16,018	0	16,919	15,807	0	1,113	1,095
Nebraska (n)..................	566	3,217	-253	3,530	3,181	162	187	516
North Dakota	197	978	0	1,174	1,024	0	151	100
Ohio (o)	632	25,997	0	26,629	26,074	291	264	1,012
South Dakota (p)..........	0	1,066	7	1,073	1,073	0	0	137
Wisconsin (q)................	49	12,491	591	13,131	13,035	25	70	0
Regional totals	4,189	117,548	...	124,940	117,893	...	3,343	4,116
Southern Region								
Alabama (r)...................	949	7,401	9	8,359	7,669	4	686	658
Arkansas	0	4,059	0	4,059	4,059	0	0	0
Florida	3,572	27,636	0	31,208	29,293	0	1,916	1,226
Georgia	1,863	18,655	0	20,517	18,655	0	1,863	904
Kentucky (s)	681	8,480	272	9,434	8,750	250	434	232
Louisiana (t)	0	7,293	29	7,322	7,321	0	1	683
Maryland (u).................	1,362	12,915	10	14,286	14,114	0	173	1,407
Mississippi (v)	0	4,479	-89	4,390	4,390	0	0	207
Missouri (w)	695	7,494	0	8,190	7,795	0	394	247
North Carolina	749	18,117	0	18,866	18,866	0	0	629
Oklahoma	133	6,219	0	6,352	6,057	0	296	NA
South Carolina*	988	6,108	0	7,096	6,771	0	325	168
Tennessee (x)	311	10,433	-172	10,572	10,451	120	1	497
Texas (y)......................	7,547	35,314	128	42,989	31,843	5,354	5,792	1,214
Virginia	1,377	16,427	0	17,804	17,570	0	234	1,388
West Virginia (z)..........	469	3,629	0	4,098	3,920	89	89	213
Regional totals	20,696	194,658	...	215,541	197,521	...	12,203	9,671
Western Region								
Alaska (aa)....................	0	5,761	-1,608	4,152	4,152	0	0	2,597
Arizona (bb)	916	9,537	-154	10,299	9,998	0	301	663
California* (cc).............	9,530	93,882	0	103,412	101,261	0	2,151	2,102
Colorado (dd)...............	252	7,439	33	7,724	7,457	0	267	0
Hawaii (ee)	732	5,178	0	5,911	5,428	0	483	61
Idaho (ff)......................	302	2,305	-57	2,550	2,343	0	207	109
Montana (gg)	406	1,597	0	2,004	1,659	0	345	0
Nevada	294	3,419	0	3,713	3,334	0	379	218
New Mexico*	781	5,537	381	6,699	5,204	363	1,132	1,132
Oregon (hh)	527	6,299	0	6,826	5,554	0	1,272	0
Utah (ii)	460	4,517	40	5,016	4,943	0	73	255
Washington (jj).............	702	13,990	80	14,771	13,677	0	1,094	0
Wyoming (kk)...............	10	1,443	0	1,453	1,448	0	5	536
Regional totals	14,912	160,903	...	174,529	166,458	...	7,709	7,673
Regional totals without California.......	5,382	67,021	...	71,117	65,197	...	5,558	5,571

See footnotes at end of table.

FISCAL 2007 STATE GENERAL FUND, APPROPRIATED, BY REGION — Continued
(In millions of dollars)

Source: National Association of State Budget Officers, The Fiscal Survey of the States (December 2006).

Note: For all states, unless otherwise noted, transfers into budget stabilization funds are counted as expenditures, and transfers from budget stabilization funds are counted as revenues.

Key:

* In these states, the ending balance includes the balance in the budget stabilization fund.

NA — Indicates data are not available.

(a) Revenue adjustments of $126.2 million and expenditure adjustments of $157.2 million are reflected in legislative and statutory authorized transfers.

(b) Includes Budgeted Operating Funds.

(c) Ending balance includes $600 million Property Tax Reserve Fund.

(d) The ending balance per the 2006-07 Enacted Budget includes over $1.8 billion in the spending stabilization reserve, $944 million in the tax stabilization reserve fund (rainy day fund), $276 million in the Community Projects Fund, $250 million in a debt reduction reserve, and $21 million in a reserve for litigation risks.

(e) Expenditure adjustments include a transfer of 25 percent of the ending balance to the budget stabilization (Rainy Day) fund.

(f) Revenue Adjustments include Transfer to Budget Stabilization (Rainy Day) Fund.

(g) Revenue adjustments include -$1.8 due to Streamlined Sales Tax, $17.1 million in direct applications and transfers, an $8.9 million increase in property transfer tax revenue estimates, -$1 million due to the downtown revitalization tax credit, and $17.5 million from the General Fund Surplus Reserve. Expenditure adjustments include $2.6 million to the Budget Stabilization Reserve and $0.3 million to the General Fund Surplus Reserve.

(h) Revenue adjustments include $2,056 million transfers into general funds. Expenditure adjustments include $432 million to repay Pension Obligation Bond Debt Service and transfers-out from general funds of $2,659 million.

(i) Revenue adjustments represents net enrolled acts in 2006 of $29.7, a transfer to the rainy day fund of -$100 million, Quality Assessment Fees of $19.9 million, and a transfer from dedicated funds of $1.2 million. Expenditure adjustments represent adjustments to the Property Tax Replacement Credit and Homestead Credit of $12.9 million.

(j) Revenues are based upon the October 16, 2006 Revenue Estimating Conference numbers. Expenditure adjustments include $4.8 million for Pandemic Flu vaccinations, $40.5 million for Medical Assistance payments and $53.5 million to the Senior Living Trust Fund.

(k) Kansas does not have a Rainy Day Fund. However, the balanced budget provision of the constitution requires revenues to finance the approved budget.

(l) Revenue adjustments include federal and state law changes of -$64.1 million, revenue sharing law changes totaling $585 million, several pending property sales totaling $28 million, deposits from state restricted revenues of $38.8 million, and other revenue adjustments of $26.3 million.

(m) Ending balance includes budget reserve of $653 million, cash flow account of $350 million and tax relief account of $109.7 million.

(n) Revenue adjustments are transfers between the General Fund and other funds. Per Nebraska law, includes a transfer to the Cash Reserve Fund (Rainy Day Fund) of the amount the prior year's net General Fund receipts are estimated to exceed the official forecast. Expenditure adjustments are reappropriations of unexpended balance of appropriations from the first fiscal year of the biennium and a small amount ($6.4 million) reserved for supplemental/deficit appropriations.

(o) Federal reimbursements and other human services programs are included in the general revenue fund. Beginning balances are undesignated, unreserved fund balances. The actual cash balances would be higher by the amount reserved for encumbrances and designated transfers from the general revenue fund. Expenditure adjustments reflect projected miscellaneous transfers out of $327.1 million.

(p) Revenue adjustments include $6.5 million projected from one time receipt

(q) Revenue adjustments include $92.7 million of Tribal Gaming and departmental revenues, including $497.8 million in transfers from other funds. Expenditure adjustments include $25.4million in transfer to MA.

(r) Revenue adjustments represent release of prior year Debt Service Reserve. Expenditure Adjustments represent reversions and reserve for General Obligation Debt Service Payment

(s) Revenue includes $88.8 million in Tobacco Settlement funds. Revenue adjustments include $139.5 million of appropriation balances carried over from the prior fiscal year, and $132.8 million from fund transfers into the General Fund. Expenditure Adjustments represent appropriation balances forwarded to the next fiscal year.

(t) Revenue adjustments include $23 million in general fund carry-forward, a transfer of $3 million from Incentive, and $3 million from the Mineral Resources Operating Fund.

(u) Adjustments reflect a $9.9 million reimbursement from the reserve for Heritage Tax Credits.

(v) Reinstated statutory 2 percent holdback.

(w) Revenues are net of refunds. Estimated refunds for Fiscal 2007 total $1,245.1 million. Revenues include $136.1 million transferred to the General Revenue Fund.

(x) Revenue adjustments include a -$172.2 million transfer to the Rainy Day Fund. Expenditure adjustments include a $32 million transfer to Transportation Equity Fund, a $74.3 million transfer to capital outlay projects fund, and dedicated revenue appropriations of $14 million.

(y) The beginning balance is a preliminary estimate. Revenues are from the Comptroller's April 2006 revised revenue estimate. Revenue adjustment is the Comptroller's estimated increase in dedicated account balances. Total expenditures are 2007 appropriated, as reported by the Legislative Budget Board. Expenditure adjustment includes nearly $3.9 billion in additional appropriations for public education/property tax relief made in the May 2006 special session, nearly $1.1 billion reserved for transfer to the Rainy Day Fund, and other adjustments needed to reconcile to the ending balance. An estimated $462.3 million in additional tax revenues from the cigarette tax and motor vehicle sales tax will be deposited in Fiscal 2007 to a new Property Tax Relief Fund outside the General Revenue Fund. These revenues are dedicated to property tax relief and are not included in the totals above.

(z) Fiscal 2007 Appropriated General Total Expenditures include $3,628.7 million of Regular Appropriations, Reappropriations of $266.4 million, and 31 day prior year expenditures of $25 million. Ending balances for Fiscal 2007 assume all appropriations will be expended and does not anticipate ending balances. However, some amounts will remain and be reappropriated to the next fiscal year.

(aa) Budget Surplus.

(bb) The revenue adjustments represent Ladewig lawsuit payments and one-time revenue shift due to recent legislation.

(cc) Of the $2,101.9 million, $471.8 million is in a separate Budget Stabilization Account and not included in the fund balance, but is included in the reserve for rainy day purposes.

(dd) Adjustments include diversions to the Older Coloradan's Program and State Education Fund.

(ee) Estimates do not reflect Governor's revenue and expenditure measures to be presented during the 2007 Legislative session.

(ff) Revenue transfers include $22.1 million from the Revolving Development Fund, $24.0 million to the Public School Facilities Cooperative Fund, $10.0 million to the Public Education Stabilization Fund, $23.9 million to the Economic Recovery Reserve Fund, and $21.0 million to the Permanent Building Fund.

(gg) Reported official general fund revenue projections for Fiscal 2007. Recent analysis shows significantly higher revenues for Fiscal 2007. Expenditures include $60 million potential supplementals.

(hh) Oregon budgets on a biennial basis. The constitution requires the state to be balanced at the end of each biennium.

(ii) $3.5 million from sales tax on food, $3.6 million from miscellaneous revenue sources.

(jj) The net amount for transfers from other accounts to the General Fund is $79.6.

(kk) The State of Wyoming budgets on a biennial basis. To complete the survey using annual figures certain assumptions and estimates were required.

Table 7.4
FISCAL 2006 STATE TAX COLLECTIONS COMPARED WITH PROJECTIONS
USED IN ADOPTING FISCAL 2006 BUDGETS, BY REGION
(In millions of dollars)

State or other jurisdiction	Sales tax		Personal income tax		Corporate income tax		Total revenue collection
	Original estimate	Current estimate	Original estimate	Current estimate	Original estimate	Current estimate	
U.S. total	$199,926	$204,566	$228,731	$243,795	$39,897	$48,062	...
Eastern Region							
Connecticut	$3,432	$3,414	$5,786	$6,170	$646	$781	H
Delaware	N.A.	N.A.	953	1,015	131	163	H
Maine	980	993	1,239	1,255	165	188	H
Massachusetts	4,037	4,004	9,728	10,483	2,043	2,256	H
New Hampshire	NA	NA	NA	NA	231	266	H
New Jersey	6,890	6,883	10,335	10,475	2,555	3,007	T
New York	10,611	10,593	30,345	30,813	4,283	5,084	H
Pennsylvania	8,269	8,334	9,182	9,524	2,059	2,302	H
Rhode Island	875	N.A.	994	N.A.	158	N.A.	T
Vermont	211	217	491	542	46	76	H
Regional totals	35,305	34,437	69,053	70,277	12,316	14,123	...
Midwestern Region							
Illinois	6,873	7,092	8,235	8,635	1,266	1,427	H
Indiana	5,187	5,226	4,371	4,322	757	925	H
Iowa	1,850	1,881	2,791	2,854	296	349	H
Kansas	1,995	2,005	2,310	2,371	330	350	H
Michigan (a)	6,905	6,710	6,176	6,255	1,914	1,853	T
Minnesota	4,468	4,467	6,604	6,875	956	1,062	H
Nebraska	1,264	1,264	1,500	1,545	245	262	H
North Dakota	432	456	227	273	42	112	H
Ohio	7,409	7,368	8,506	8,786	1,096	1,240	H
South Dakota	565	577	N.A.	N.A.	N.A.	N.A.	H
Wisconsin	4,182	4,128	6,145	6,144	683	780	H
Regional totals	41,130	41,174	46,866	48,061	7,585	8,360	...
Southern Region							
Alabama	1,873	2,002	2,405	2,689	314	484	H
Arkansas	1,999	2,087	1,879	2,013	271	350	H
Florida	18,642	19,378	N.A.	N.A.	1,841	2,405	H
Georgia	5,638	5,712	7,748	8,022	564	863	H
Kentucky	2,717	2,750	3,089	2,919	530	1,002	H
Louisiana	2,546	3,073	2,416	2,512	428	506	H
Maryland (b)	3,256	3,355	5,801	6,200	501	644	H
Mississippi	1,652	1,652	1,197	1,219	381	381	H
Missouri	1,948	1,962	4,184	4,579	342	405	H
North Carolina	4,693	4,894	8,840	9,400	906	1,204	H
Oklahoma	1,623	1,701	2,466	2,787	183	338	H
South Carolina	2,396	2,545	2,158	2,608	143	258	H
Tennessee (c)	6,346	6,516	162	194	1,358	1,492	H
Texas	16,558	18,201	N.A.	N.A.	N.A.	N.A.	H
Virginia	2,812	2,804	9,075	9,170	722	852	H
West Virginia	972	1,013	1,153	1,298	245	348	H
Regional totals	75,670	79,643	52,573	55,611	8,729	11,529	...
Western Region							
Alaska	N.A.	N.A.	N.A.	N.A.	329	694	H
Arizona	4,294	4,273	3,585	3,689	848	874	H
California	26,951	27,211	42,231	49,555	8,822	10,484	H
Colorado	1,846	1,957	3,484	4,376	313	448	H
Hawaii	2,144	2,355	1,400	1,551	71	130	H
Idaho	784	881	1,046	1,217	134	194	H
Montana	3	3	607	769	81	154	H
Nevada	925	1,005	N.A.	N.A.	N.A.	N.A.	H
New Mexico	2,025	2,150	1,012	1,127	210	382	T
Oregon	NA	NA	4,942	5,444	261	438	H
Utah	1,635	1,744	1,934	2,119	198	253	H
Washington	6,851	7,311	N.A.	N.A.	N.A.	N.A.	H
Wyoming	364	421	N.A.	N.A.	N.A.	N.A.	H
Regional totals	47,821	49,311	60,240	69,846	11,267	14,050	...
Regional totals without California	20,870	22,100	18,009	20,291	2,445	3,566	

See footnotes at end of table.

FISCAL 2006 STATE TAX COLLECTIONS COMPARED WITH PROJECTIONS USED IN ADOPTING FISCAL 2006 BUDGETS, BY REGION — Continued
(In millions of dollars)

Source: National Association of State Budget Officers, The Fiscal Survey of the States (December 2006).

Note: Unless otherwise noted, original estimates reflect the figures used when the fiscal 2006 budget was adopted, and current estimates reflect preliminary actual tax collections.

Key:

H — Revenues higher than estimates.

L — Revenues lower than estimates.

T — Revenues on target.

NA — Indicates data are not available because, in most cases, these states do not have this type of tax.

(a) The original Fiscal 2006 budget has been modified and is based on the May 2006 consensus estimates and is net of all enacted tax changes. Tax estimates represent total tax collections. Sales tax collections are for the Michigan sales tax only and do not include collections from Michigan use tax. Michigan does not have a Corporate Income tax; estimates are for Michigan's Single Business Tax. The Fiscal 2006 revenues are on target with the May 2006 consensus revenue estimates; final revenue figures will be available when the State of Michigan Comprehensive Annual Financial report is published in December 2006.

(b) Fiscal 2006 Actuals are final, not preliminary. Sales Tax Collections reflect the General Fund portion only; Personal Income Tax Collections estimates reflect proposed subtraction modifications; Corporate Income Tax Collections reflect the General Fund portion only, and Fiscal 2006 reflects an extraordinary item of $20.4 million (MCI settlement).

(c) Corporate Income Tax includes excise tax and franchise tax. Sales tax, personal income tax and corporate excise tax are shared with local governments.

Table 7.5
FISCAL 2006 STATE TAX COLLECTIONS COMPARED WITH PROJECTIONS
USED IN ADOPTING FISCAL 2007 BUDGETS, BY REGION
(In millions of dollars)

State or other jurisdiction	Sales tax Fiscal 2006	Sales tax Fiscal 2007	Personal income tax Fiscal 2006	Personal income tax Fiscal 2007	Corporate income tax Fiscal 2006	Corporate income tax Fiscal 2007
U.S. total	$204,566	$211,702	$243,795	$253,544	$48,062	$46,151
Eastern Region						
Connecticut...................	$3,414	$3,534	$6,170	$6,428	$781	$707
Delaware.......................	N.A.	N.A.	1,015	1,062	163	169
Maine...........................	993	1,026	1,255	1,277	188	168
Massachusetts...............	4,004	4,285	10,483	10,817	2,256	2,131
New Hampshire	N.A.	N.A.	N.A.	N.A.	266	246
New Jersey	6,883	8,722	10,475	11,475	3,007	2,727
New York......................	10,593	10,252	30,813	34,218	5,084	5,303
Pennsylvania.................	8,334	8,606	9,524	9,960	2,302	2,450
Rhode Island.................	N.A.	921	N.A.	1,052	N.A.	122
Vermont	217	228	542	533	76	54
Regional totals..............	34,437	37,573	70,277	76,823	14,123	14,078
Midwestern Region						
Illinois	7,092	7,280	8,635	8,888	1,427	1,707
Indiana.........................	5,226	5,472	4,322	4,523	925	804
Iowa.............................	1,881	1,946	2,854	2,918	349	320
Kansas	2,005	2,003	2,371	2,439	350	306
Michigan (a)	6,710	6,959	6,255	6,386	1,853	1,886
Minnesota	4,467	4,624	6,875	6,948	1,062	883
Nebraska.......................	1,264	1,266	1,545	1,517	262	219
North Dakota	456	467	273	237	112	42
Ohio.............................	7,368	7,610	8,786	8,650	1,240	895
South Dakota	577	605	N.A.	N.A.	N.A.	N.A.
Wisconsin	4,128	4,358	6,144	6,503	780	670
Regional totals..............	41,174	42,590	48,061	49,009	8,360	7,732
Southern Region						
Alabama........................	2,002	2,024	2,689	2,689	484	423
Arkansas.......................	2,087	2,137	2,013	2,064	350	314
Florida	19,378	20,022	N.A.	N.A.	2,405	2,439
Georgia.........................	5,712	5,926	8,022	8,193	863	829
Kentucky	2,750	2,778	2,919	3,161	1,002	759
Louisiana	3,073	2,719	2,512	2,124	506	425
Maryland	3,355	3,502	6,200	6,579	644	686
Mississippi....................	1,652	1,924	1,219	1,315	381	376
Missouri........................	1,962	1,985	4,579	4,677	405	393
North Carolina	4,894	5,033	9,400	9,635	1,204	1,053
Oklahoma	1,701	1,751	2,787	2,740	338	248
South Carolina	2,545	2,496	2,608	2,600	258	223
Tennessee (b)................	6,516	6,805	194	204	1,492	1,531
Texas............................	18,201	17,353	N.A.	N.A.	N.A.	N.A.
Virginia........................	2,804	3,148	9,170	9,650	852	788
West Virginia	1,013	1,018	1,298	1,318	348	296
Regional totals..............	79,643	80,620	55,611	56,948	11,529	10,779
Western Region						
Alaska..........................	N.A.	N.A.	N.A.	N.A.	694	552
Arizona.........................	4,273	4,629	3,689	3,879	874	902
California......................	27,211	28,114	49,555	50,885	10,484	10,507
Colorado.......................	1,957	1,944	4,376	3,976	448	435
Hawaii..........................	2,355	2,533	1,551	1,630	130	91
Idaho............................	881	842	1,217	1,164	194	173
Montana........................	3	3	769	713	154	97
Nevada..........................	1,005	1,007	N.A.	N.A.	N.A.	N.A.
New Mexico	2,150	2,160	1,127	1,065	382	325
Oregon..........................	NA	NA	5,444	5,182	438	239
Utah.............................	1,744	1,835	2,119	2,270	253	240
Washington	7,311	7,385	N.A.	N.A.	N.A.	N.A.
Wyoming	421	468	N.A.	N.A.	N.A.	N.A.
Regional totals..............	49,311	50,920	69,846	70,764	14,050	13,562
Regional totals without California.......	22,000	22,806	20,291	19,879	3,566	3,055

See footnotes at end of table.

FISCAL 2006 STATE TAX COLLECTIONS COMPARED WITH PROJECTIONS USED IN ADOPTING FISCAL 2007 BUDGETS, BY REGION — Continued
(In millions of dollars)

Source: National Association of State Budget Officers, The Fiscal Survey of the States (December 2006).

Note: Unless otherwise noted, fiscal 2006 figures reflect preliminary actual tax collections estimates as shown in Table A-7, and fiscal 2007 figures reflect the estimates used in enacted budgets.

Key:

N.A. — Indicates data are not available because, in most cases, these states do not have that type of tax.

(a) The Fiscal 2007 enacted budget is based on the May 2006 consensus estimates and is net of all enacted tax changes. Tax estimates represent total tax collections. Sales tax collections are for the Michigan sales tax only and do not include collections from Michigan use tax. Michigan does not have a Corporate Income tax; estimates are for Michigan's Single Business Tax. The Fiscal 2007 revenues are on target with the May 2006 consensus revenue estimates; updated Fiscal 2007 revenue figures will be released at the next regularly scheduled consensus revenue conference in January 2007.

(b) Corporate Income Tax includes excise tax and franchise tax. Sales tax, personal income tax and corporate excise tax are shared with local governments.

Table 7.6
TOTAL STATE EXPENDITURES: CAPITAL INCLUSIVE, BY REGION
(In millions of dollars)

State or other jurisdiction	Actual fiscal 2004					Actual fiscal 2005					Estimated fiscal 2006				
	General fund	Federal funds	Other state funds	Bonds	Total	General fund	Federal funds	Other state funds	Bonds	Total	General fund	Federal funds	Other state funds	Bonds	Total
U.S. total	$509,696	$343,561	$297,685	$30,388	$1,181,330	$540,954	$357,799	$310,379	$28,226	$1,237,358	$584,648	$377,662	$338,649	$37,180	$1,338,139
Eastern Region															
Connecticut (a)	12,547	1,982	3,194	1,741	19,464	13,814	1,951	3,658	1,746	21,169	14,681	1,952	3,759	1,945	22,337
Delaware	2,479	1,137	965	183	4,764	3,694	1,250	1,100	153	6,197	4,096	975	1,117	163	6,351
Maine	2,584	2,346	1,502	117	6,549	2,738	2,256	1,646	114	6,754	2,874	2,660	1,516	101	7,151
Massachusetts	18,311	4,710	1,126	717	24,864	20,337	4,517	293	1,175	26,322	21,431	5,189	298	1,186	28,104
New Hampshire	1,305	1,381	1,562	68	4,316	1,396	1,415	1,532	77	4,420	1,355	1,420	1,672	84	4,531
New Jersey (b)	24,364	8,006	3,937	908	37,215	27,844	7,985	4,456	1,218	41,503	27,578	9,239	4,689	1,149	42,655
New York ©	42,066	35,995	17,328	1,938	97,327	43,619	36,697	18,561	1,791	100,668	46,495	34,618	21,373	1,855	104,341
Pennsylvania	21,885	16,075	9,439	623	48,022	23,054	17,331	10,535	401	51,321	24,501	17,805	11,940	680	54,926
Rhode Island	2,726	1,835	1,215	73	5,849	2,927	1,858	1,174	79	6,038	3,124	2,049	1,464	170	6,807
Vermont	561	1,007	1,604	41	3,213	673	972	1,972	53	3,670	1,114	1,016	2,111	45	4,286
Regional totals	128,828	74,474	41,872	6,409	251,583	140,096	76,232	44,927	6,807	268,062	147,249	76,923	49,939	7,378	281,489
Midwestern Region															
Illinois	17,436	9,126	21,737	2,037	50,336	17,751	8,308	14,691	1,114	41,864	19,469	8,751	17,028	1,310	46,558
Indiana	11,386	7,041	7,048	496	25,971	11,689	6,700	6,824	254	25,467	11,912	6,769	6,373	307	25,361
Iowa	4,104	3,585	4,079	101	11,869	4,176	3,476	4,616	90	12,358	4,499	3,773	4,950	95	13,317
Kansas	4,316	2,945	2,714	222	10,197	4,690	3,410	2,288	197	10,585	5,163	3,212	3,226	226	11,827
Michigan	8,722	10,868	19,798	368	39,756	8,794	11,348	20,187	242	40,571	8,982	12,933	19,636	326	41,877
Minnesota	14,087	5,533	3,358	438	23,416	15,082	5,515	3,514	443	24,554	16,429	5,879	3,647	446	26,401
Nebraska (d)	2,576	2,252	2,280	0	7,108	2,721	2,351	2,400	0	7,472	3,072	2,936	3,113	0	9,121
North Dakota	894	1,164	832	35	2,925	904	1,217	980	81	3,182	979	1,320	1,358	85	3,742
Ohio (e)	23,839	7,294	15,621	1,399	48,153	24,830	8,002	16,479	1,354	50,665	25,363	9,192	18,529	2,309	55,393
South Dakota	877	1,191	1,069	2	3,139	987	1,179	1,232	5	3,403	1,090	1,364	834	25	3,313
Wisconsin (f)	10,660	6,408	15,842	0	32,910	11,859	6,977	13,032	0	31,868	12,385	7,166	13,931	0	33,482
Regional totals	98,897	57,407	94,378	5,098	255,780	103,483	58,483	86,243	3,780	251,989	109,343	63,295	92,625	5,129	270,392
Southern Region															
Alabama	5,512	5,954	4,179	384	16,029	6,008	6,503	4,610	285	17,406	6,919	7,517	5,119	124	19,679
Arkansas	3,505	4,234	5,869	66	13,674	3,596	4,243	6,386	65	14,290	3,810	5,739	8,275	61	17,885
Florida	21,118	15,366	13,400	1,954	51,838	24,180	19,053	13,808	1,291	58,332	26,475	20,411	16,794	1,756	65,436
Georgia	15,123	10,226	2,486	979	28,814	15,349	10,152	2,677	1,006	29,184	16,697	9,285	2,871	697	29,550
Kentucky	7,206	6,344	5,457	0	19,007	7,570	6,311	5,452	0	19,333	8,357	7,451	6,354	0	22,162
Louisiana	5,127	6,728	2,637	279	14,771	5,361	6,890	2,710	275	15,236	5,483	6,618	2,604	377	15,082
Maryland	10,262	5,845	6,440	751	23,298	11,275	5,878	6,892	663	24,708	12,356	6,420	7,783	679	27,238
Mississippi	3,166	4,445	3,319	378	11,308	3,363	4,471	3,892	221	11,947	3,613	4,909	3,880	160	12,562
Missouri (g)	6,660	5,061	5,870	364	17,955	7,126	5,491	6,437	56	19,110	7,209	6,122	6,167	414	19,912
North Carolina	14,705	9,506	6,224	712	31,147	16,592	10,224	7,482	1,260	35,558	17,256	9,972	6,198	370	33,796
Oklahoma	4,117	4,596	4,098	258	13,069	4,340	5,458	4,108	121	14,027	4,836	5,191	6,768	650	17,445
South Carolina	4,864	6,180	5,223	171	16,438	5,223	6,809	5,830	130	17,992	5,617	6,889	5,460	0	17,966
Tennessee (h)	8,432	8,796	4,257	210	21,695	9,424	9,394	4,732	469	24,019	10,273	9,933	4,966	430	25,602
Texas	28,930	21,260	8,536	1,936	60,662	29,832	22,361	10,649	2,122	64,964	32,646	24,699	10,808	1,973	70,126
Virginia	11,238	5,740	10,603	644	28,225	12,328	5,682	12,886	816	31,712	13,590	5,961	11,479	893	31,923
West Virginia	3,012	3,411	9,996	250	16,669	3,414	3,399	10,562	363	17,738	3,400	3,288	12,848	179	19,715
Regional totals	152,977	123,692	98,594	9,336	384,599	164,981	132,319	109,113	9,143	415,556	178,537	140,405	118,374	8,763	446,079

See footnotes at end of table.

TOTAL STATE EXPENDITURES: CAPITAL INCLUSIVE, BY REGION—Continued
(In millions of dollars)

State or other jurisdiction	Actual fiscal 2004					Actual fiscal 2005					Estimated fiscal 2006				
	General fund	Federal funds	Other state funds	Bonds	Total	General fund	Federal funds	Other state funds	Bonds	Total	General fund	Federal funds	Other state funds	Bonds	Total
Western Region															
Alaska..........	2,268	2,773	2,280	0	7,321	2,441	3,287	2,893	68	8,689	2,997	3,119	3,492	304	9,912
Arizona..........	7,589	6,857	6,684	599	21,729	7,509	7,737	6,993	569	22,808	8,353	7,411	7,388	479	23,631
California..........	78,345	52,420	18,892	6,986	156,643	79,804	52,122	22,192	5,595	159,713	90,294	56,945	25,400	11,790	184,429
Colorado..........	5,599	3,222	4,757	60	13,638	5,805	3,269	4,922	222	14,218	6,292	3,560	5,434	9	15,295
Hawaii..........	3,801	1,416	2,344	349	7,910	4,185	1,574	2,608	386	8,753	4,666	1,762	2,511	655	9,594
Idaho..........	1,987	1,719	873	4	4,583	2,110	1,769	913	9	4,801	2,224	2,034	1,219	0	5,486
Montana (i)..........	1,272	1,498	1,033	0	3,803	1,344	1,505	1,105	0	3,954	1,588	1,772	1,304	0	4,664
Nevada..........	2,091	1,566	2,497	323	6,477	2,324	1,677	2,758	296	7,055	2,691	2,037	3,371	308	8,407
New Mexico..........	4,117	3,545	1,961	349	9,972	4,387	3,608	2,052	375	10,422	4,691	3,835	2,383	562	11,471
Oregon..........	5,547	3,982	9,779	0	19,308	4,492	4,451	10,848	0	19,791	6,090	4,438	9,700	0	20,228
Utah..........	3,574	2,076	1,963	253	7,866	3,978	2,247	2,131	137	8,493	4,223	2,325	2,512	5	9,065
Washington..........	11,452	5,858	8,034	622	25,966	12,220	6,097	8,342	839	27,498	13,621	6,391	10,658	1,789	32,459
Wyoming..........	1,352	1,056	1,744	0	4,152	1,795	1,422	2,339	0	5,556	1,789	1,410	2,339	0	5,538
Regional totals..........	128,994	87,988	62,841	9,545	289,368	132,394	90,765	70,096	8,496	301,751	149,519	97,039	77,711	15,910	340,179
Regional totals without California......	50,649	35,568	43,949	2,559	132,725	52,590	38,643	47,904	2,901	142,038	59,225	40,094	52,311	4,120	155,750

Source: National Association of State Budget Officers, State Expenditure Report (2006).

Note: State funds refers to general funds plus other state fund spending. State spending from bonds is excluded. Total funds refers to funding from all sources–general fund, federal funds, other state funds and bonds.

Key:

(a) Fiscal 2004 and fiscal 2005 actual bond fund data is based on bond allocations by the Bond Commission, due to the unavailability of actual expenditure data as of April 27, 2006. In addition, actual fiscal 2005 total state expenditure data reflects estimates used due to the unavailability of certain actual expenditure data as of April 27, 2006.

(b) Figures include pension, post retirement medical, debt service on pension bonds, payroll taxes, and health benefits expenditures which total $1.13 billion in State General Fund in fiscal 2005 and $1.25 billion in State General Fund in fiscal 2006 spread across Education, Corrections, Transportation and All Other.

(c) New York budgets most employer contributions to employees' benefits and pensions centrally. The portion of employer contributions to employees' benefits not distributed to an expenditure category has been included in the All Other Expenditures category.

(d) Fiscal 2005-06 amounts shown are equal to appropriations for the year. It is assumed that some level of appropriations will not be expended this fiscal year.

(e) Certain federal reimbursements and block grants for certain human services programs (Medicaid, etc.) are deposited into the state's General Revenue Fund. Expenditures of these federal funds are contained in the General Fund number in this report to be consistent with other portrayals of Ohio's general fund. This amounts to $5,521.1 million in fiscal 2004 and $5,646.6 million in fiscal 2005, which includes a payment of $193.0 million made to the state as part of the Jobs and Growth Reconciliation Tax Package of 2003. This has an impact on percentage of total general fund expenditure calculations as well as on comparisons of Ohio's federal funding levels. Also, inherent in Ohio's budgetary accounting environment are significant overstatements of total spending due to two phenomena. First, fiduciary fund expenditures represent the distribution of funds collected by the state on behalf of other entities. These are not operating, program, or subsidy expenditures for the state. These expenditures total

$5,569.0 million in fiscal 2004 and $5,690.9 million in fiscal 2005. Second, "double counting" of revenue and expenditures related to intrastate transactions overstates overall state expenditure activity. The overstatement is primarily found in general services. Expenditure activity from these funds totals $1,295.2 million in fiscal 2004 and $1,404.7 million in fiscal 2005. This results in Ohio's "All Other" expenditures as a percentage of the total being overstated, and consequently other areas being understated. Ohio appropriates capital appropriations on a biennial basis rather than an annual basis, therefore, the amounts shown for fiscal 2006 are estimates.

(f) Funds for fiscal 2006 are updated to reflect preliminary actuals.

(g) Total expenditures exclude refunds. Fiscal 2004 expenditures exclude refunds of $1,118 million, including $1,071 million general revenue. Fiscal 2005 expenditures exclude refunds of $1,119 million, including $1,071 million general revenue. Fiscal 2006 estimates exclude refunds of $1,222 million, including $1,179 million general revenue. Other funds include federal reimbursements received by the Department of Highways and Transportation and the Department of Conservation which have constitutionally created funds. Federal and other funds for fiscal 2006 represent appropriations available to state agencies. These appropriations establish ceilings on what agencies may spend. The appropriations are often established at higher levels to provide agencies with appropriation authority in the event that revenues are available for various programs. Final expenditures will be lower.

(h) Tennessee collects personal income tax on income from dividends on stocks and interest on certain bonds. Tax revenue estimates do not include federal funds and other departmental revenues. However, federal funds and other departmental revenues are included in the budget as funding sources for the general fund, along with state tax revenues.

(i) Principal and interest payments on bonds are included in total expenditures. Fiscal 2006 appropriations include a one-time-only general fund transfer to state retirement programs of $125 million. Other one-time-only general fund appropriations for fiscal 2006 total approximately $43 million. Fire and emergency costs in fiscal 2004 were funded by using more than $35 million in federal funds received from the Jobs and Growth Tax Relief Reconciliation Act of 2003.

Table 7.7
ELEMENTARY AND SECONDARY EDUCATION EXPENDITURES, BY STATE AND REGION
(In millions of dollars)

State or other jurisdiction	Actual fiscal 2003					Actual fiscal 2004					Estimated fiscal 2006				
	General fund	Federal funds	Other state funds	Bonds	Total	General fund	Federal funds	Other state funds	Bonds	Total	General fund	Federal funds	Other state funds	Bonds	Total
U.S. total	$182,406	$38,947	$25,414	$6,358	$253,125	$193,693	$42,481	$26,620	$6,442	$269,236	$205,105	$44,477	$28,624	$10,023	$288,229
Eastern Region															
Connecticut	2,000	368	4	436	2,808	2,091	391	4	603	3,089	2,181	391	4	760	3,336
Delaware	857	121	402	135	1,515	916	135	446	152	1,649	966	0	490	163	1,619
Maine	925	168	12	10	1,115	977	176	11	8	1,172	1,048	179	3	14	1,244
Massachusetts	4,225	839	0	0	5,064	4,076	862	0	396	5,334	4,245	925	0	489	5,659
New Hampshire	63	140	848	9	1,060	63	153	748	6	970	0	159	847	3	1,009
New Jersey	8,299	770	16	0	9,085	8,963	822	20	0	9,805	9,475	837	18	3	10,330
New York	13,677	3,176	1,934	41	18,828	14,171	3,321	2,317	71	19,880	14,992	3,687	2,390	5	21,074
Pennsylvania	7,282	1,676	16	0	8,994	7,867	1,722	9	0	9,598	8,144	1,869	9	0	10,022
Rhode Island	776	152	2	0	930	794	183	3	0	980	835	180	4	0	1,019
Vermont	13	103	894	6	1,016	14	106	1,180	4	1,304	17	117	1,130	5	1,269
Regional totals	38,117	7,513	4,128	637	50,415	39,932	7,871	4,738	1,240	53,781	41,903	8,344	4,895	1,439	56,581
Midwestern Region															
Illinois (a)	6,288	1,710	40	474	8,512	6,758	1,895	19	288	8,960	6,794	1,996	40	247	9,077
Indiana	4,401	692	12	0	5,105	4,488	726	25	0	5,239	4,558	781	17	0	5,356
Iowa	2,108	363	286	1	2,758	2,215	371	287	4	2,877	2,342	399	322	6	3,069
Kansas	2,175	352	100	0	2,627	2,324	380	80	0	2,784	2,597	383	106	0	3,086
Michigan (b)	407	1,353	10,686	0	12,446	173	1,417	10,925	0	12,515	73	1,521	11,329	0	12,923
Minnesota (c)	5,714	557	29	17	6,317	6,319	612	29	5	6,965	6,881	611	32	8	7,532
Nebraska	819	222	4	0	1,045	807	240	3	0	1,050	912	518	2	0	1,432
North Dakota	309	118	36	0	463	317	112	37	0	466	324	114	37	0	475
Ohio (d)	6,523	1,354	981	465	9,323	6,736	1,525	912	477	9,650	6,934	1,684	1,225	601	10,444
South Dakota	274	50	0	0	324	333	0	0	0	333	342	0	4	0	346
Wisconsin	5,268	591	99	0	5,958	5,298	612	125	0	6,035	5,669	661	69	0	6,399
Regional totals	34,286	7,362	12,273	957	54,878	35,768	7,890	12,442	774	56,874	37,426	8,668	13,183	862	60,139
Southern Region															
Alabama (e)	2,901	712	143	0	3,756	3,148	778	140	0	4,066	3,513	1,000	138	0	4,651
Arkansas	1,627	384	222	0	2,233	1,628	429	707	0	2,764	1,701	578	764	0	3,043
Florida (f)	8,038	2,046	585	0	10,669	8,619	2,261	609	0	11,489	9,663	2,419	476	0	12,558
Georgia (g)	5,917	1,353	52	174	7,496	6,056	1,483	46	176	7,761	6,611	1,109	41	134	7,895
Kentucky	3,053	609	15	0	3,677	3,275	602	12	0	3,889	3,654	692	17	0	4,363
Louisiana	2,720	893	0	0	3,613	2,924	871	0	0	3,795	2,980	1,276	0	0	4,256
Maryland	3,417	760	8	0	4,185	3,736	813	8	0	4,557	4,141	878	9	0	5,028
Mississippi	1,502	469	352	0	2,323	1,687	572	387	0	2,646	1,842	571	396	0	2,809
Missouri	2,447	787	1,163	0	4,397	2,569	866	1,201	0	4,636	2,559	956	1,338	0	4,853
North Carolina	6,167	940	119	0	7,226	6,483	1,067	147	0	7,697	6,608	888	46	0	7,542
Oklahoma	1,427	484	1,082	0	2,993	1,586	1,019	423	0	3,028	1,566	576	1,207	0	3,349
South Carolina	1,738	579	702	74	3,093	1,835	618	752	0	3,205	2,005	585	667	0	3,257
Tennessee	2,799	722	11	0	3,532	3,012	816	16	0	3,844	3,160	854	47	0	4,061
Texas	12,101	3,584	1,453	0	17,138	11,783	3,858	2,062	0	17,703	12,692	4,017	1,892	0	18,601
Virginia	4,154	485	123	0	4,762	4,758	522	137	0	5,417	5,030	570	130	0	5,730
West Virginia	1,563	270	50	76	1,959	1,600	311	37	244	2,192	1,670	358	46	62	2,136
Regional totals	61,571	15,077	6,080	324	83,052	64,699	16,886	6,684	420	88,689	69,395	17,327	7,214	196	94,132

See footnotes at end of table.

ELEMENTARY AND SECONDARY EDUCATION EXPENDITURES, BY STATE AND REGION — Continued
(In millions of dollars)

State or other jurisdiction	Actual fiscal 2003					Actual fiscal 2004					Estimated fiscal 2006				
	General fund	Federal funds	Other state funds	Bonds	Total	General fund	Federal funds	Other state funds	Bonds	Total	General fund	Federal funds	Other state funds	Bonds	Total
Western Region															
Alaska	740	162	87	0	989	790	199	93	0	1,082	884	212	106	0	1,202
Arizona	2,959	680	446	0	4,085	3,184	769	524	0	4,477	3,380	865	696	0	4,941
California	27,283	5,388	56	4,152	36,879	31,434	5,925	36	3,717	41,112	32,936	6,151	63	6,926	46,076
Colorado	2,418	381	476	0	3,275	2,515	413	506	0	3,434	2,698	499	402	0	3,599
Hawaii	1,467	223	44	144	1,878	1,559	235	47	87	1,928	1,817	232	50	233	2,332
Idaho	966	172	64	0	1,202	988	180	51	0	1,219	1,019	192	54	0	1,265
Montana	518	135	49	0	702	513	139	61	0	713	563	146	52	0	761
Nevada	749	207	146	0	1,102	786	196	148	0	1,130	942	262	145	0	1,349
New Mexico	1,975	309	30	144	2,458	2,385	325	32	169	2,911	2,270	39	9	248	2,566
Oregon	2,254	408	517	0	3,479	2,112	438	376	0	2,926	2,525	528	266	0	3,319
Utah (h)	1,679	311	24	0	2,014	1,788	345	13	0	2,146	1,873	348	71	0	2,292
Washington	5,021	585	530	0	6,136	5,149	658	401	35	6,243	5,383	652	950	119	7,104
Wyoming	103	14	464	0	581	91	12	468	0	571	91	12	468	0	571
Regional totals	48,132	8,975	2,933	4,440	64,780	53,294	9,834	2,756	4,008	69,892	56,381	10,138	3,332	7,526	77,377
Regional totals without California	20,849	3,587	2,877	288	27,901	21,860	3,909	2,720	291	28,780	23,445	3,987	3,269	600	31,301

Source: National Association of State Budget Officers, State Expenditure Report (2006).

Key:

(a) Direct appropriations to the Illinois State Board of Education for Pre-Kindergarten through 12th grade education increased by $357 million from fiscal 2005 to fiscal 2006. Due to structural changes in the retirement system, contributions to the Teachers' Retirement System decreased by $322 million. The combination of these actions results in the General Fund net increase of $35.3 million. Thus, a third consecutive year of increasing direct appropriations for Pre-K through 12th grade education by more than $300 million is not readily apparent in the net reporting of education and retirement figures.

(b) Figures reflect K-12 education, the Michigan Department of Education, adult education, and pre-school. Employer contributions to current employees' pensions and health benefits are reported for Department of Education employees but excluded for employees of K-12 schools.

(c) School districts pay for Employer Contributions to Pensions, Employer Contributions to Health Benefits, and School Health Care/Immunization with their general operating funds, which are comprised of both state and local sources, depending on the district. Funding for these activities is marked as "excluded" because while state funds are often used to pay for these functions, state law does not require it or set aside specific amounts or funding streams for those purposes. Day care programs (subsidized child care) are funded in the budget base, but in the health and human services portion of the budget and not the elementary and secondary education numbers.

(d) See note (j) on Table 7.5 for Ohio for discussion of double counting issues that affect percentage of total expenditure amounts. In fiscal 2004, a new state special revenue fund was created to implement the Head Start Plus program. The new fund more appropriately reflects the funding sources for the program. Previously, funding was appropriated to the General Revenue Fund and was reimbursed by TANF dollars.

(e) Federal funds received directly at the local school system level are not reported at the state budget level.

(f) The increase in General Funds and Other State Funds is attributable to the implementation of a Constitutional amendment which limits the number of children per classroom. State appropriations to school districts for operational costs include funding intended to be expended by school districts for contributions to current employees' pensions, employee health benefits, and for operational costs of libraries.

(g) Expenditures for libraries are included in Higher Education.

(h) Included with General Fund is Education Fund (income tax revenue) which in Utah is restricted by the Utah state constitution for the sole use of public and higher education. Public Education in Utah is organized to include the Utah State Office of Rehabilitation (USOR). The numbers reflected in this report for Public Education include USOR. The USOR amounts are as follows: for fiscal 2004, $18 million in General Fund and Education Fund, $33 million in federal funds, and $1 million in other state funds; for fiscal 2005, $19 million in General Fund and Education Fund, $34 million in federal funds, and $1 million in other state funds; for fiscal 2006, $21 million in General Fund and Education Fund, $36 million in federal funds, and $1 million in other state funds.

Table 7.8
MEDICAID EXPENDITURES BY STATE AND REGION
(In millions of dollars)

State or other jurisdiction	Actual fiscal 2003				Actual fiscal 2004				Estimated fiscal 2006			
	General fund	Federal funds	Other state funds	Total	General fund	Federal funds	Other state funds	Total	General fund	Federal funds	Other state funds	Total
U.S. total	$85,986	$153,162	$22,024	$261,172	$96,750	$160,324	$25,887	$282,961	$105,667	$165,008	$26,382	$297,057
Eastern Region												
Connecticut (a)	2,849	0	692	3,541	2,995	0	721	3,716	3,290	0	760	4,050
Delaware	372	427	0	799	450	467	0	917	472	490	0	962
Maine	529	1,454	64	2,047	609	1,383	107	2,099	703	1,633	145	2,481
Massachusetts	2,908	2,908	0	5,816	2,999	2,999	0	5,998	3,449	3,449	0	6,898
New Hampshire	374	599	168	1,141	438	612	169	1,219	396	553	153	1,102
New Jersey	3,556	4,023	50	7,629	3,722	3,796	50	7,568	4,416	4,477	50	8,943
New York (b)	6,061	18,729	2,772	27,562	6,953	19,778	2,624	29,355	8,291	18,687	3,231	30,209
Pennsylvania	5,054	8,441	1,553	15,048	5,450	9,120	2,068	16,638	6,007	9,087	2,528	17,622
Rhode Island	607	902	0	1,509	746	916	0	1,662	798	922	0	1,720
Vermont	138	499	117	754	152	519	178	849	184	529	187	900
Regional totals	22,448	37,982	5,416	65,846	24,514	39,590	5,917	70,021	28,006	39,827	7,054	74,887
Midwestern Region												
Illinois	3,277	5,539	1,684	10,500	3,588	5,886	2,360	11,834	3,997	6,028	2,467	12,492
Indiana	1,485	2,808	10	4,303	1,667	2,833	10	4,510	1,680	2,899	14	4,593
Iowa	353	1,538	342	2,233	438	1,521	375	2,334	591	1,761	378	2,730
Kansas	549	1,103	80	1,732	767	1,294	101	2,162	812	1,368	85	2,265
Michigan (c)	1,960	4,803	1,492	8,255	1,892	4,944	1,851	8,687	2,234	4,854	1,478	8,566
Minnesota	2,283	2,831	0	5,114	2,533	2,779	0	5,312	2,703	2,845	0	5,548
Nebraska	457	895	25	1,377	539	847	18	1,431	611	968	20	1,599
North Dakota	136	356	0	492	162	351	0	513	174	355	0	529
Ohio (d)	9,858	1,702	934	12,494	9,731	1,792	1,041	12,564	9,991	1,987	1,461	13,439
South Dakota	175	423	0	598	204	424	0	628	224	471	0	695
Wisconsin	733	2,684	840	4,257	1,656	2,618	110	4,384	1,335	2,646	370	4,351
Regional totals	21,266	24,682	5,407	51,355	23,177	25,289	5,866	54,359	24,352	26,182	6,273	56,807
Southern Region												
Alabama (e)	326	2,731	716	3,773	443	2,871	748	4,062	515	2,905	767	4,187
Arkansas	459	2,101	150	2,710	540	2,236	231	3,007	553	2,466	321	3,340
Florida (f)	3,686	8,180	1,214	13,080	4,297	8,266	1,327	13,890	4,569	8,608	1,529	14,706
Georgia	1,806	3,635	607	6,048	1,938	3,846	686	6,470	2,112	4,194	620	6,926
Kentucky	740	3,003	377	4,120	836	2,969	444	4,249	973	3,091	403	4,467
Louisiana	723	3,614	541	4,878	723	3,816	527	5,066	791	1,710	265	4,766
Maryland (g)	2,097	2,579	174	4,850	2,442	2,606	119	5,167	2,597	2,811	165	5,573
Mississippi	223	2,618	353	3,194	205	2,644	788	3,637	292	2,797	533	3,622
Missouri (h)	1,097	3,691	957	5,745	1,352	4,029	1,180	6,561	1,232	3,712	1,066	6,010
North Carolina	1,983	5,163	235	7,381	2,351	5,608	530	8,489	2,510	5,897	628	9,035
Oklahoma	596	1,852	125	2,573	674	1,869	192	2,735	796	2,099	290	3,185
South Carolina	496	2,903	602	4,001	659	3,024	635	4,318	679	3,154	636	4,469
Tennessee (i)	2,108	4,857	666	7,631	2,539	5,196	865	8,570	2,649	5,024	626	8,299
Texas (j)	5,912	10,065	0	15,977	7,147	10,566		17,713	7,034	10,668	0	17,702
Virginia	1,812	1,977	37	3,826	2,147	2,091	71	4,309	2,085	2,377	311	4,773
West Virginia	228	1,554	211	1,993	295	1,561	232	2,088	349	1,662	273	2,284
Regional totals	24,292	60,523	6,965	91,780	28,588	63,198	8,575	100,331	29,736	63,175	8,433	103,344

See footnotes at end of table.

MEDICAID EXPENDITURES BY STATE AND REGION—Continued
(In millions of dollars)

State or other jurisdiction	Actual fiscal 2003 General fund	Federal funds	Other state funds	Total	Actual fiscal 2004 General fund	Federal funds	Other state funds	Total	Estimated fiscal 2006 General fund	Federal funds	Other state funds	Total
Western Region												
Alaska	230	669	83	982	276	688	63	1,027	280	710	80	1,070
Arizona	674	2,781	359	3,814	914	3,142	387	4,443	1,050	3,302	0	4,352
California	11,009	15,459	6,018	29,486	12,269	16,576	4,032	32,907	14,769	17,654	3,513	35,936
Colorado	1,095	1,270	41	2,406	1,193	1,225	90	2,508	1,247	1,321	129	2,697
Hawaii	322	530	8	860	361	548	3	912	401	583	10	994
Idaho	225	650	77	952	287	685	81	1,053	317	729	88	1,134
Montana	127	493	20	640	155	501	27	683	165	516	39	720
Nevada	429	626	109	1,164	344	683	116	1,143	393	708	114	1,215
New Mexico	404	1,856	96	2,356	469	1,798	134	2,401	547	1,829	151	2,527
Oregon	731	1,731	262	2,724	806	1,967	419	3,192	896	1,942	307	3,145
Utah	192	311	24	2,014	1,788	345	13	2,146	1,873	348	71	2,292
Washington	2,420	2,750	0	5,170	3,003	3,158	0	6,161	3,072	3,198	0	6,270
Wyoming	122	245	0	367	142	285	0	427	136	273	0	409
Regional totals	17,980	29,371	7,097	52,935	22,007	31,601	5,365	59,003	25,146	33,113	4,502	62,761
Regional totals without California	6,971	13,912	1,079	23,449	5,431	15,025	1,333	26,096	10,377	15,459	989	26,825

Source: National Association of State Budget Officers, State Expenditure Report (2006).

Note: States were asked to report Medicaid expenditures as follows: General funds: all general funds appropriated to the Medicaid agency and any other agency which are used for direct Medicaid matching purposes under Title XIX. Other state funds: other funds and revenue sources used as Medicaid match, such as local funds and provider taxes, fees, donations, assessments (as defined by the Health Care Finance Administration). Federal Funds: all federal matching funds provided pursuant to Title XIX. As noted above, the figures reported as Other State Funds reflect the amounts reported as provider taxes, fees, donations, assessments and local funds by states. State Medicaid agencies report these amounts to the Health Care Financing Administration (HCFA) on form 37, as defined by the Medicaid Voluntary Contribution and Provider-specific Tax Amendments of 1991 (P.L. 102–234). However, some state budget offices are unable to align their financial reporting to separate these costs for the NASBO State Expenditure Report. Thus, this report does not capture 100 percent of state provider taxes, fees, donations, assessments and local funds. Small dollar amounts, when rounded, cause an aberration in the percentage increase. In these instances, the actual dollar amounts should be consulted to determine the exact percentage increase. The states were asked to separately detail the amount of provider taxes, fees, donations, assessments and local funds reported as Other State Funds.

Key:

(a) Medicaid Appropriation is "gross funded"—Federal Funds are deposited directly to the State Treasury. The state's FMAP is currently at 50 percent of Medicaid benefit costs.

(b) Medicaid spending does not include administrative costs or local government shares.

(c) Other State Funds include local funds of $671.3 million, and provider taxes of $324.2 million for fiscal 2004; local funds of $432.3 million and provider taxes of $510.3 million for fiscal 2005; and local funds of $120.8 million and provider taxes of $627.3 million for fiscal 2006. Public health and community and institutional care for mentally and developmentally disabled persons are partially reported in the Medicaid totals.

(d) Federal funds deposited to the state General Fund and shown as General Fund expenditures for Medicaid amount to $5,275.5 million in fiscal 2004 and $5,593.7 million in fiscal 2005. See General Notes for Ohio on this issue. Local dollars may be used as state match for Medicaid services and administration. Dollars that are generated at the local level that are then used to draw down federal match are not included in Ohio's numbers for purposes of making the numbers reported here consistent with other reports for Ohio General Fund and All Fund spending in fiscal 2004 and 2005. Figures for fiscal 2004 and 2005 do not include Federal Fiscal Relief, Title IVE, or Foodstamp EBT contract.

(e) Fiscal 2004 through fiscal 2006 Other State Funds include provider taxes in the amount of $42 million, $54 million, and $59 million, respectively.

(f) For fiscal 2003–04, Other State Funds include provider assessments of $300 million, cigarette taxes of $110 million, tobacco settlement funds of $72 million, state drug rebates of $238 million, other non-general funds transferred as matching funds of $25 million, state fraud recoupments of $18 million, and local county funds of $451 million. For fiscal 2004–05, Other State Funds include provider assessments of $299 million, cigarette taxes of $109 million, tobacco settlement funds of $82 million, state drug rebates of $273 million, other non-general funds transferred as matching of $30 million, state fraud recoupments of $32 million, and local county funds of $502 million. For fiscal 2005–06, Other State Funds include provider assessments of $370 million, cigarette taxes of $136 million, tobacco settlement funds of $83 million, state drug rebates of $310 million, other non-general funds transferred as matching of $39 million, state fraud recoupments of $18 million, and local county funds of $572 million.

(g) 2004 Medicaid totals include $108.3 million in tobacco settlement funds and $65.9 million in local funds. 2005 Medicaid totals include $52.5 million in tobacco settlement funds, $3.5 million in funds from a provider tax on HMOs/MCOs, and $62.5 million in local funds. 2006 Medicaid totals include $66.8 million in tobacco settlement funds, $28.4 million in funds from a provider tax on HMOs/MCOs, and $69.3 million in local funds. All Medicaid totals are recorded on a cash basis, not an accrual basis.

(h) Medicaid and CHIP data are from the CMS 64 Report used for federal reporting of Medicaid expenditures. The split between the General Revenue Fund and Other Funds is an estimate. Medicaid does not track the General Revenue Fund versus Other State/Local Funds in its reporting. Other Funds include estimated local funds of $415 million for fiscal 2004, $418 million for fiscal 2005, and $404 million for fiscal 2006.

(i) Regarding premium revenue: fiscal 2004 totals $65 million, fiscal 2005 totals $58 million, and fiscal 2006 totals $60 million. Regarding Certified Public Expenditures – Local fund from Hospitals: fiscal 2004 totals $236 million, fiscal 2005 totals $204 million, and fiscal 2006 totals $197 million. Regarding Nursing Home Tax: fiscal 2004 totals $85 million, fiscal 2005 totals $85 million, and fiscal 2006 totals $85 million. Regarding the ICF/MR 6 percent Gross Receipts Tax: fiscal 2004 totals $15 million, fiscal 2005 totals $15 million, fiscal 2006 totals $15 million. Regarding Intergovernmental Transfers: fiscal 2004 totals $52 million, fiscal 2005 totals $0 million, and fiscal 2006 totals $0 million.

(j) Medicaid expenditures are reported from the Medicaid History Report (11/2004), which does not distinguish other funds from state funds.

Table 7.9
ALLOWABLE INVESTMENTS

State or other jurisdiction	CDs within state	CDs nationally	State and local government obligations	U.S. Treasury obligations	U.S. agency obligations	Other time deposits	Bankers' acceptances	Commercial paper	Corporate notes/bonds	Mortgage backed securities	Mutual/ Money Market funds	Eurodollars—CDs or TDs	Derivatives	Real estate	Repurchase agreements	Venture capital/ Private equity	Corporate stocks (foreign)	Corporate stocks (domestic)	Other
Alabama	★			★	★					★					★				
Alaska	★	★	★	★	★	★	★	★	★	★	★							★	
Arizona	★		★	★	★	★	★	★	★	★	★				★			★	
Arkansas	★	★	★	★	★	★	★	★	★	★					★				(a)
California	★	★	★	★	★		★	★	★						★			★	(b)
Colorado	★	★		★	★	★	★	★	★		★				★				
Connecticut	★	★	★	★	★	★	★	★	★	★	★				★				(c)
Delaware	★	★		★	★	★	★	★	★	★	★				★				(c)
Florida	★		★	★	★	★	★	★	★		★		★		★				
Georgia	★			★	★		★	★	★		★				★				
Hawaii	★		★	★	★			★			★				★				
Idaho	★			★	★		★	★	★	★	★				★	★			
Illinois	★	★	★	★	★	★	★	★	★	★	★		★		★				
Indiana	★			★	★		★	★		★	★				★				
Iowa	★			★	★	★	★	★	★		★				★				
Kansas	★		★	★	★	★	★	★	★	★	★				★			★	(d)
Kentucky	★	★	★	★	★		★	★	★	★	★				★				
Louisiana	★	★		★	★	★	★	★	★	★	★				★				
Maine	★	★	★	★	★	★	★	★		★	★				★				
Maryland	★			★	★	★	★	★			★				★				
Massachusetts	★	★	★	★	★	★	★	★	★	★	★			★	★		★	★	(e)
Michigan	★	★	★	★	★		★	★	★	★					★		★	★	(f)
Minnesota				★	★	★	★	★	★	★	★				★			★	
Mississippi	★			★	★	★		★											
Missouri	★			★	★			★	★	★	★				★				
Montana	★	★	★	★	★		★	★	★	★	★			★	★		★	★	
Nebraska	★	★		★	★	★	★	★	★	★	★				★			★	
Nevada	★	★	★	★	★	★	★	★	★	★	★	★	★	★	★		★	★	(g)
New Hampshire	★			★	★			★							★				
New Jersey	★			★	★			★		★					★				
New Mexico	★	★	★	★	★	★	★	★	★	★	★				★			★	
New York	★	★	★	★	★	★	★	★	★	★	★				★			★	
North Carolina	★		★	★	★	★	★	★		★	★				★				
North Dakota	★	★	★	★	★	★		★	★	★	★				★				
Ohio	★			★	★	★		★	★	★	★	★	★	★	★		★	★	

See footnotes at end of table.

ALLOWABLE INVESTMENTS—Continued

State or other jurisdiction	CDs within state	CDs nationally	State and local government obligations	U.S. Treasury obligations	U.S. agency obligations	Other time deposits	Bankers' acceptances	Commercial paper	Corporate notes/bonds	Mortgage backed securities	Mutual/Money Market funds	Eurodollars—CDs or TDs	Derivatives	Real estate	Repurchase agreements	Private equity/Venture capital	Corporate stocks (foreign)	Corporate stocks (domestic)	Other
Oklahoma	★	★	★	★	★		★	★			★				★				
Oregon	★		★	★	★	★	★	★	★	★			★		★				(h)
Pennsylvania	★	★	★	★	★	★	★	★	★	★					★				
Rhode Island	★	★		★	★	★		★	★					★	★	★			
South Carolina			★	★	★			★	★	★					★				
South Dakota	★	★		★	★	★	★	★	★		★		★	★	★		★	★	
Tennessee	★			★	★	★	★	★		★	★				★		★	★	(i)
Utah		★	★	★	★	★	★	★	★	★	★		★	★	★	★		★	
Vermont	★	★	★	★	★		★	★	★	★	★				★	★			
Virginia	★	★	★	★	★		★	★	★	★	★		★		★				(j)
Washington	★	★	★	★	★		★	★		★					★				
West Virginia	★	★	★	★	★			★	★	★					★		★	★	
Wisconsin	★	★	★	★					★		★		★		★		★	★	
Wyoming		★		★	★					★						★	★	★	(k)
Dist. of Columbia	★	★	★	★	★	★	★	★	★	★	★	★	★	★	★				

Source: National Association of State Treasurers, March 2007.

Key:
★—Yes, allowed
...— No, not allowed
(a) Small Business Administration guaranteed loans.
(b) Asset backed securities.
(c) Convertible Bonds.
(d) Collateralized Mortgage Obligation's & Other Mortgages; Assets Banking.
(e) Massachusetts Municipal Depository Trust; Chapter 29 Section 38A.
(f) Emergency loans to municipalities within the state.
(g) Time deposits within state.
(h) Reverse repurchase agreements.
(i) Private Equity.
(j) For certain non pension trust funds identified by statute, equities and corporate bonds/notes are permitted investments.
(k) Economic Development Loans.

Table 7.10
CASH FLOW MANAGEMENT: FORECASTING AND DISTRIBUTION OF DEMAND DEPOSITS

| | | Forecasting | | Distribution of demand deposits | | | |
| | | | | Used as depositories | | Number of | |
State or other jurisdiction	Development of cash flow forecasting method	Float analysis in collection and disbursement processes	Automated system for cash flow forecasting	Banks	Savings and loans	Banks in state	Savings and loans in state
Alabama	...	...	...	171	0	175	...
Alaska	In-house	...	★	4	0	3	0
Arizona	In-house	★	...	7	0	61	4
Arkansas	In-house	★	★	6	0	152	7
California	In-house	★	★	7	0	268	33
Colorado	In-house	...	...	3	0	...	...
Connecticut	In-house	★	★	9	...	91	8
Delaware	In-house	★	...	4	0	36	14
Florida	In-house	...	★	5	0	254	29
Georgia	In-house	★	...	(a)	0	340+	0
Hawaii	In-house	...	★	7	0	7	0
Idaho	In-house	★	...	11	0	30	5
Illinois	...	...	...	9	0	5	0
Indiana	In-house	★	...	232	37	300	55
Iowa	In-house	★	...	80	0	...	...
Kansas	In-house	...	...	2	0	354	16
Kentucky	In-house	★	★	(b)	(c)	...	...
Louisiana	In-house	★	...	15	0	120	9
Maine	...	...	...	14	0	...	...
Maryland	In-house	★	...	12	...	62	...
Massachusetts	In-house	★	...	19	0	270	...
Michigan	In-house	★	...	61	0	139	5
Minnesota	In-house	★	...	200	0	463	22
Mississippi	In-house	...	...	106	0	106	9
Missouri	In-house	...	...	80	2	300	6
Montana	In-house	★	...	62	...	267	...
Nebraska	In-house	★	...	46	0	332	16
Nevada	In-house	★	...	3	0	41	1
New Hampshire	In-house	★	...	5	...	42	...
New Jersey	In-house	★	...	45	4	110	74
New Mexico	In-house	★	...	44	6	48	9
New York	In-house	★	...	100+	NA	...	...
North Carolina	In-house	★	★	87	9	93	16
North Dakota	In-house	★	...	(d)	0	1	0
Ohio	In-house	...	...	137	...	...	...
Oklahoma	In-house	★	★	190	2	325	20
Oregon	In-house	...	...	20	0	55	4
Pennsylvania	Outsourced	★	★	96	15	96	15
Rhode Island	In-house	...	★	5	0	17	...
South Carolina	In-house	★	...	30	...	...	...
South Dakota	In-house	★	...	106	1	103	5
Tennessee	In-house	★	★	50	...	...	...
Texas	In-house	★	...	363	8	661	20
Utah	In-house	★	...	13	...	38	4
Vermont	In-house	★	...	13	0	24	1
Virginia	In-house	★	★	60	0	150	8
Washington	In-house	★	★	46	2	86	16
West Virginia	In-house	★	...	51	0	68	6
Wisconsin	In-house	★	...	70	8	273	37
Wyoming	In-house	★	...	1	...	47	3
Dist. of Columbia	In-house	★	★	10	4	21	6

Source: National Association of State Treasurers, March 2007.
Key:
★ — Yes
... — No
(a) 7 primary plus 100's of others.

(b) 1 Primary Depository.
(c) 0 — 100+Interest +Local Receipt Accounts.
(d) 1 State owned bank.

Table 7.11
UTILIZATION OF CASH MANAGEMENT

State or other jurisdiction	Collection services	Lock boxes	Wire transfers	Federal reserve wire transfer	Bank wire transfer	Depository transfer checks	Zero balance accounts	Bank drafts	Controlled disbursement programs	Information systems	Account reconciliation services	Data transfer services	Business services	Automated clearinghouse
Alabama	NU	B	B	B	I,B	B	B	I,B	NU	I	I	I,B	NU	I,B
Alaska	B	B	I	NU	B	I	B	I	I	I	NU	NU	NU	B
Arizona	NU	B	I,B	NU	B	NU	B	NU	NU	I,B	I	I,B	B	I,B
Arkansas	NU	NU	B	NU	B	NU	B	NU	NU	I	I	I	NU	B
California	I	B	I	I	I	NU	I	NU	NU	I	I,B	B	I,B	B
Colorado	NU	B	B	B	B	B	B	B	B	B	B	B	NU	B
Connecticut	I,B	B	I,B	I,B	I,B	NU	B	B	B	I,B	I,B	I,B	NU	I,B
Delaware	B	B	I,B	I,B	B	NU	B	NU	B	I,B	I	I,B	NU	I,B
Florida	NU	I,B	B	B	B	NU	NU	NU	NU	NU	NU	NU	NU	B
Georgia	NU	B	I	NU	I	NU	NU	I	I	I	I	NU	NU	I
Hawaii	NU	B	I	NU	B	NU	B	NU	NU	B	I,B	NU	B	I,B
Idaho	NU	NU	I	I	I	NU	I	NU	NU	NU	NU	NU	NU	B
Illinois	NU	B	I	Used	I	I	B	NU	NU	I,B	B	B	NU	I
Indiana	I	B	I	I	I	NU	B	NU	NU	NU	NU	NU	NU	I
Iowa	B	B	I	I	I	NU	B	I	I	I	I	NU	NU	I
Kansas	NU	B	B	B	B	NU	B	NU	NU	I	I	B	NU	I,B
Kentucky	B	NU	B	B	B	NU	B	NU	B	I	I	B	NU	B
Louisiana	I	Used	Used	Used	Used	Used	Used	NU	Used	Used	Used	Used	NU	Used
Maine	B	NU	I,B	NU	NU	NU	B	NU	NU	NU	I,B	I,B	NU	I,B
Maryland	NU	B	I	B	NU	NU	B	NU	B	I,B	I,B	I,B	NU	I,B
Massachusetts	Used	B	I,B	I,B	I,B	NU	B	NU	Used	I,B	I,B	I,B	NU	I,B
Michigan	NU	B	I,B	B	B	NU	B	NU	NU	NU	I,B	NU	NU	B
Minnesota	NU	NU	I	I	I	NU	B	NU	NU	I	I	NU	NU	I
Mississippi	NU	B	B	I	B	I	NU	NU	NU	NU	NU	NU	NU	B
Missouri	I	I,B	I,B	I	I	NU	B	NU	NU	I,B	I,B	I,B	NU	I,B
Montana	NU	NU	I,B	NU	NU	NU	NU	NU	NU	I	NU	NU	NU	I,B
Nebraska	I,B	B	B	B	B	NU	I,B	NU	I	I,B	I	I	NU	B
Nevada	I	B	I	I	I	NU	B	NU	I	B	I,B	I,B	NU	I
New Hampshire	NU	NU	B	NU	NU	NU	B	NU	B	I,B	I,B	NU	NU	I
New Jersey	B	B	I	I	I	NU	B	NU	B	B	I	I	NU	I
New Mexico	B	B	B	B	B	B	B	I	I	I,B	I	NU	NU	B
New York	NU	B	I,B	I,B	NU	NU	B	NU	B	I	I,B	I	NU	I,B
North Carolina	I	B	I	I	I	I	B	I	I,B	I	I	I,B	NU	I,B
North Dakota	NU	NU	B	I	B	NU	B	I	I	NU	I	NU	NU	B
Ohio	I	B	I,B	I,B	I,B	NU	I	NU	NU	B	I	I,B	NU	I,B

See footnotes at end of table.

UTILIZATION OF CASH MANAGEMENT — Continued

State or other jurisdiction	Collection services	Lock boxes	Wire transfers	Federal reserve wire transfer	Bank wire transfer	Depository transfer checks	Zero balance accounts	Bank drafts	Controlled disbursement programs	Information systems	Account reconciliation services	Data transfer services	Business services	Automated clearinghouse
Oklahoma	NU	B	B	NU	Used	I	B	NU	NU	NU	NU	NU	NU	B
Oregon	B	B	I	I	I	NU	I	I	B	I	I,B	I,B	NU	I
Pennsylvania	B	B	I,B	I,B	I,B	NU	B	NU	I,B	I,B	I,B	I,B	NU	I,B
Rhode Island	B	B	I,B	B	I,B	I,B	I,B	NU	B	I,B	I,B	NU	NU	I,B
South Carolina	NU	B	I,B	I,B	I,B	I	I,B	I	NU	I	I	I	NU	B
South Dakota	I	I	B	B	B	B	B	NU	I	NU	I	NU	NU	B
Tennessee	I	I	I,B	I,B	NU	NU	B	I	I	I	I	I	NU	B
Texas	NU	I,B	I	I	I	NU	B	NU	NU	I	I	NU	NU	I,B
Utah	NU	B	NU	B	NU	NU	B	NU	NU	I	NU	NU	NU	I
Vermont	I,B	B	I,B	B	B	B	B	NU	I,B	I,B	I,B	I	I,B	I,B
Virginia	NU	B	I	I	I	NU	B	NU	B	B	I	I	NU	B
Washington	NU	B	B	B	B	NU	B	NU	B	I	NU	I	NU	I,B
West Virginia	NU	I	NU	NU	B	NU	NU	NU	NU	I	I	NU	NU	I
Wisconsin	I,B	B	B	B	B	B	B	B	B	I,B	B	Used	NU	Used
Wyoming	NU	NU	Used	I	I	I	B	NU	B	I,B	I,B	I	NU	I
Dist. of Columbia	I	B	I	I	I	NU	B	NU	B	I	I,B	I	NU	I

Source: National Association of State Treasurers, March 2007.

Key:
B — Performed by bank
I — Performed in-house
NU — Not utilized

Table 7.12
BOND AUTHORIZATION

State or other jurisdiction	Central agency overseeing debt issuance	Party which holds issuance authority					Authority to issue foreign currency denominated debt
		General obligation bonds	Revenue bonds	Taxable bonds	Taxable debt	Short-term debt	
Alabama	No Central Agency	R, L, C	L, C	...	L, G, C	C	No
Alaska	Alaska State Bond Committee	R, L, G, C	L, G, C	L, G, C	...	...	No
Arizona	State does not issue debt	...	...	B	B	B	Yes
Arkansas	Development Finance Authority	R, L, G, B	L, G, B	...	...	...	No
California	California State Treasurer's Office	R (a)	B	...	...	(RANS)	
Colorado	No Central Agency	L, C, TR	L, G, C, TR	L, C, TR	L, C, TR	L, G, C, TR	No
Connecticut	Debt Management Division, Office of the Treasurer	L	L	...	...	L	No
Delaware	Department of Finance	L, B	L, B	L, B	L, B	L, B	No
Florida	Division of Bond Finance	L, C	L, C	L, C	L, B	L, B	Yes
Georgia	Georgia State Financing and Investment Commission	L, C	L, C	L, C	L, C	L, C	No
Hawaii	Department of Budget and Finance	L	L	L	L	L	
Idaho	No Central Agency	...	...	...	B	No	No
Illinois	No Central Agency	L, G	L, G, B	...	...	R, L, G	
Indiana	Public Finance Officer	(b)	(b)	(b)	(b)	(b)	No
Iowa	Treasury	R, L, G	L, G, B	L, G, B	...	G, TR	
Kansas	Kansas Development Finance Authority	R, B	R, B	R, B	Yes	R	Yes (c)
Kentucky	Office Of Financial Management	R	R	R	C	L, C	No
Louisiana	State Bond Commission	L, C	L, C	L, C	...	TR, Other	No
Maine	Office of the State Treasurer	R, L, G, TR	L, G	...	R, L, G, TR	B, TR	No
Maryland	General Obligation Debt - State Treasurer	L, B	L	L, B	...	...	
Massachusetts	Financial Advisory Board	L, G	L, G	L, G	L, G	L, G	No
Michigan	State Administrative Board	R, L, B, TR	L, B, TR	L, B, TR	L, B, TR	L, B, TR	No
Minnesota	Department of Finance (d)	L	L	L	L	L	No
Mississippi	State Treasury/OFA-Bond Advisory Division	L, C	L, C	L, C	L, C	L, C	No
Missouri	Office of Administration	R, L, B	L, B	...	...	...	
Montana	No Central Agency	L, B, TR	L, B, TR	L, B, TR	B, TR	No	
Nebraska	State does not issue debt	...	...	...	...	...	No
Nevada	No Central Agency	L, B	L, B	L, B	L, B	L, B	No
New Hampshire	Treasury	L	...	...	...	...	No
New Jersey	Treasury, Office of Public Finance	R, L	L, G, B	R	...	...	No
New Mexico	State Board of Finance	...	...	...	...	L, B, TR	No
New York	(e)	R, L, G (d) Comptroller issues	L, G (f)	L, G (f)	L, G (f)	L, G (f)	No
North Carolina	State and Local Government Finance Division, Dept. of State Treasurer	R, L	L	L	L	L	No
North Dakota	No Central Agency	...	...	...	...	...	No
Ohio	Office of Budget and Management	...	...	...	...	...	

See footnotes at end of table.

BOND AUTHORIZATION—Continued

State or other jurisdiction	Central agency overseeing debt issuance	Party which holds issuance authority					Authority to issue foreign currency denominated debt
		General obligation bonds	Revenue bonds	Taxable bonds	Taxable debt	Short-term debt	
Oklahoma	State Bond Advisor's Office	R	L, B, C	B, C	B, C	B, C	No
Oregon	Oregon State Treasury Debt Management Division	L, G, TR	L, G, TR	...	L, G, TR	L, G, TR	No
Pennsylvania	Office of Budget	R, L	L, B, C	...	L, G, TR	L	No
Rhode Island	Budget Office & Treasury	R, G	Not authorized	Not authorized	Not authorized	L	No
South Carolina	State Budget and Control Board	R, L, G, B, TR	L, G, B, C, TR	L,B, TR	L,B, TR	L,B, TR	No
South Dakota	State does not issue debt	...	...	...	...	...	...
Tennessee	Comptroller's Office—Division of Bond Finance	L, C	...	C	...	C	...
Texas	Texas Bond Review Board	R, L, B, C	L, B, C	L, B, C	L, B, C	L, B, C	No
Utah	Treasurer	L	L	L	TR	Yes (g)	No
Vermont	Office of the State Treasurer	L	L	L	...	TR	No
Virginia	Department of the Treasury	R, L, G	L, G, B, TR	...	...	...	No
Washington	Division of Debt Management	R, L	R, L	R, L	R, L	R, L	No
West Virginia	No Central Agency	R, L, G, TR, AG	L, B, C	L, G, B, C	L, G, B, C	L, G	No
Wisconsin	Capital Finance Office, Wisconsin Department of Administration	L	L	C	C	C	...
Wyoming	No Central Agency	Not authorized	L, C	L, C	Not authorized	L, G, C, TR	No
Dist. of Columbia	Office of the Chief Financial Officer	L, TR, A, (h)	L, (h)	N/A	N/A	L, TR, (h)	No

Source: National Association of State Treasurers, March 2007.

Key:
AG — Auditor General
B — Board
C — Commission
G — Governor
L — Legislation
R — Referendum
TR- Treasurer
(a) Committee.

(b) Indiana by statute cannot issue debt, so quasi-agencies are set up to do so.
(c) Requires legislative approval. Previously issued debt in Yen.
(d) Only for general obligation debt or for reporting purposes.
(e) No, the Office of the State Comptroller approves terms and conditions for certain negotiated bond deals of public authorities and local governments and issues State General Obligation bonds and LGAC bonds. Various State Public Authorities issue State-supported debt.
(f) Taxable debt may be issued for general obligation as well as revenue bonds. If general obligation, referendum is needed.
(g) Requires entering into a foreign exchange agreement with a AA or higher rated institution when bonds are issued to hedge the currency risk.
(h) Mayor.

Table 7.13
RESERVE FUNDS

State or other jurisdiction	Official title	Start year	Administrator	Limit on fund's size	Deposit requirements	Withdrawal rules	Replenishment requirement
Alabama	Education Trust Fund Rainy Day Account	2000	Board	$225,000,000	...	Proration	5 Years
Alaska	Constitutional Budget Reserve Fund	...	...	...	...	...	...
Arizona	Budget Stabilization Fund	1994	Treasurer	No	...	Supermajority vote of legislature.	No
Arkansas	None	...	...	...	...	...	...
California	None	...	...	...	...	...	...
Colorado	None	...	...	...	...	...	...
Connecticut	Budget Reserve Fund	1991	Treasurer	10% of current year's budget.	Statutory; No requirement/ Deposits made at will of legislature.	Revenue below forecast/budget. Controlled by state constitution and statute.	Inappropriate surplus goes to fund first.
Delaware	Reserve Cash Intermediate Account	...	Investment Manager	No	No requirement/Deposits made at will of legislature.	Cash Mgmt. Policy Board Guidelines	No
Florida	Budget Stabilization Fund	1994	Treasurer	10% of previous fiscal year year net revenue	Constitutional	Constitution and set guidelines.	5 Years
Georgia	Revenue Shortfall Reserve/ Midyear Adjust Reserve	1976	State Auditor	5% of net revenue collections	Statutory	Revenue below forecast/budget.	No
Hawaii	Emergency Budget and Reserve Fund	1999	Treasurer	No	Statutory	2/3 majority vote in each chamber of state legislature.	No
Idaho	Budget Stabilization Fund	1984	Dept. of Admin.	No	Statutory	Limit on amount withdrawn in a given year	No
Illinois	Budget Stabilization Fund	2000	Secretary/ Director of Revenue	...	...	...	End of Fiscal Year
Indiana	Indiana Rainy Day Fund	...	Treasurer	No	Deposits made when economic growth exceeds specified levels.	Revenue below forecast/budget.	No
Iowa	The Cash Reserve Fund and the Economic Emergency Fund	1992	Dept. of Mgmt.	(a)	Statutory	(b)	No
Kansas	None	...	...	...	...	...	...
Kentucky	Budget Reserve Trust Fund	1995	Office of Financial Mgmt. (Finance Cabinet)	No	NA	NA	NA
Louisiana	Budget Stabilization Fund	1998	Treasurer	Balance can not exceed 4% of state total revenue receipts for the previous year.	Constitutional	Revenue below budget. Supermajority vote of legislature. Limit on withdrawals.	No
Maine	Budget Stabilization Fund	...	Controller	...	Statutory	...	...

See footnotes at end of table.

RESERVE FUNDS—Continued

State or other jurisdiction	Official title	Start year	Administrator	Limit on fund's size	Deposit requirements	Withdrawal rules	Replenishment requirement
Maryland	State Reserve Fund—Revenue Stabilization Account	1986	Dept. of Budget and Mgmt.	No	Statutory	None	. . .
Massachusetts	Commonwealth Stabilization Fund	1986	Treasurer	15% of budgeted revenues.	Statutory	Vote of legislature.	No
Michigan	Budget Stabilization Fund	1985	Dept. of Mgmt. and Budget	No	Statutory	Revenue below forecast/budget. Formula in statute.	Depends on revenue growth.
Minnesota	None	. . .	. . .	. . .	. . .	. . .	No
Mississippi	Working Cash Stabilization Reserve Fund	. . .	Treasurer	. . .	Statutory	Statutory	. . .
Missouri	Budget Reserve Fund	1986	Office of Admin.	7 1/2% of general revenue collections of previous fiscal year.	Constitutional	(c)	. . .
Montana	None	. . .	. . .	. . .	. . .	. . .	. . .
Nebraska	Cash reserve fund	1983	Treasurer	No	Statutory	(d)	No
Nevada	The Fund to Stabilize the Operation of State Government	1991	Controller	Must not exceed total. appropriation of state.	Statutory; No requirement/ Deposits made at will of legislature.	(e)	Yearly, if revenue is sufficient.
New Hampshire	Revenue Stabilization Fund	1980s	Treasurer	10% of prior year's revenues.	Contingent upon financial performance.	No, funds may be used for any reason.	No
New Jersey	Surplus Revenue Fund	. . .	. . .	. . .	. . .	. . .	. . .
New Mexico	Emergency Fund	. . .	Treasurer	(f)	No requirement/Deposits made made at will of legislature.	Emergencies as ruled such by Board of Finance.	. . .
New York	Rainy Day Fund	Mid 1990s	Comptroller	. . .	Statutory	Revenue below forecast/ budget.	. . .
North Carolina	Rainy Day Fund	. . .	. . .	No	. . .	No, funds may be used for any any reason.	No
North Dakota	Budget Stabilization Fund	1987	State Investment Board	(g)	Statutory	Revenue below forecast/budget.	End of each biennium.
Ohio	Budget Stabilization Fund	. . .	. . .	. . .	. . .	. . .	. . .
Oklahoma	Rainy Day Fund	. . .	Secretary/Director of Revenue	. . .	Statutory	Limit on amount withdrawn in a given year	. . .
Oregon	Education Stability Fund	2002	(h)	5% of General Fund revenues of prior biennium	Statutory; Constitutional	(i)	No
Pennsylvania	Budget Stabilization Reserve Fund	(j)	Secretary of Budget and Admin.	(k)	Statutory	Supermajority vote of legislature.	(l)
Rhode Island	Budget Reserve and Cash Stabilization Account	. . .	. . .	. . .	. . .	. . .	. . .
South Carolina	General Reserve Fund	. . .	Treasurer	3% prior year revenues.	Statutory	To avoid year end deficit	3 Years
South Dakota	Budget Reserve Fund	. . .	. . .	. . .	. . .	. . .	. . .

See footnotes at end of table.

RESERVE FUNDS—Continued

State or other jurisdiction	Official title	Start year	Administrator	Limit on fund's size	Deposit requirements	Withdrawal rules	Replenishment requirement
Tennessee	Rainy Day Fund	...	Commissioner of Finance and Admin.	...	...	...	...
Texas	Economic Stabilization Fund	1989	Treasurer	(m)	Statutory	(n)	No
Utah	Budget Reserve Fund	1996	Treasurer	(o)	No requirement/Deposits made at will of legislature	Majority vote of legislature.	(p)
Vermont	(q)	1987	Commissioner of Finance and Mgmt.	(r)	Statutory	(s)	(t)
Virginia	Revenue Stabilization Fund	1993	(u)	(v)	Statutory	(w)	No
Washington	Emergency Reserve Fund	1993	Treasurer; Office of Financial Mgmt.	No	Statutory	Supermajority vote of legislature.	No
West Virginia	Revenue Shortfall Reserve Fund	1995	Budget	Aggregate amount—not to exceed 5% of total general revenue fund	Statutory	(x)	90 days for fiscal borrowing.
Wisconsin	Budget Reserve Fund	1992	Dept. of Admin.	No	No requirement/Deposits made at will of legislature.	No, funds may be used for any reason.	No
Wyoming	Budget Reserve Account	1984	State Auditor's Office	No	Statutory	Supermajority vote of legislature.	No
Dist. of Columbia	Emergency and Contingency Reserve Fund	2001	Treasurer	6% of local funds.	Statutory	Mayor and CFO declares.	By the end of the next fiscal year.

Source: National Association of State Treasurers, March 2007.

Key:
(a) CRF: 7.5% of general fund's estimated revenue. EEF: 5% of general fund's estimated revenue.
(b) Non-recurring emergencies. 3/5 majority required if balance of Cash Reserve Fund is below 3% of general fund revenues.
(c) 100% for cash flow loans with in fiscal year, must be repaid by May 15. Can appropriate 50% upon 2/3 approval of legislature to be repaid in 3 equal annual installments.
(d) Upon certification of DAS director that current cash balance of the general fund is inadequate to meet current obligations.
(e) Revenue below forecast/budget. Simple majority vote of legislature and governor if fiscal emergency exists.
(f) Zeros out at end of year.
(g) No activity since 1991.
(h) Treasurer Controlled by state constitution and statute.
(i) Revenue below forecast/budget; Supermajority vote of legislature. Funds to be used for education.
(j) July 2002–2003 replaced Tax Stabilization Reserve Fund.
(k) No, if the fund balance equals or exceeds 6% of the general fund revenues for the fiscal year in which the surplus occurs then the transfer is reduced to 10%.

(l) 25% of general funds fiscal year ending surplus.
(m) Amount not to exceed 10 % of General Revenue income during the previous biennium.
(n) Revenue below forecast/budget; Supermajority vote of legislature.
(o) 6% of the total of appropriations for the general fund and uniform school fund.
(p) No set time. Fund reserves one half of any year-end surplus.
(q) Various Budget Stabilization Reserves (not a separate fund, but a reserve in the general fund, transportation fund, and education fund).
(r) Generally 5% of the prior year appropriation for the fund (general, transportation, education).
(s) Certification of an undesignated fund deficit by the Commissioner of Finance and Management.
(t) Up to statutory levels in the next fiscal year or subsequent years as needed to reach the required level.
(u) The General Assembly appropriates funds pursuant to Article X, Section 8 of the Constitution of Virginia.
(v) 10% of average annual tax revenues derived from taxes on income and retail sales.
(w) Revenue below forecast/budget; Limit on amount withdrawn in a given year.
(x) Funds may be borrowed as defined in code, or withdrawn for emergency or fiscal needs by act of legislature.

Table 7.14
AGENCIES ADMINISTERING MAJOR STATE TAXES

State or other jurisdiction	Income	Sales	Gasoline	Motor vehicle
Alabama	Dept. of Revenue	Dept. of Revenue	Dept. of Revenue	Dept. of Revenue
Alaska	Dept. of Revenue	. . .	Dept. of Revenue	Dept. of Public Safety
Arizona	Dept. of Revenue	Dept. of Revenue	Dept. of Transportation	Dept. of Transportation
Arkansas	Dept. of Fin. & Admin.	Dept. of Fin. & Admin.	Dept. of Fin. & Admin.	Dept. of Fin. & Admin.
California	Franchise Tax Bd.	Bd. of Equalization	Bd. of Equalization	Dept. of Motor Vehicles
Colorado	Dept. of Revenue	Dept. of Revenue	Dept. of Revenue	Dept. of Revenue
Connecticut	Dept. of Revenue Serv.	Dept. of Revenue Serv.	Dept. of Revenue Serv.	Dept. of Motor Vehicles
Delaware	Div. of Revenue	. . .	Dept. of Transportation	Dept. of Public Safety
Florida	Dept. of Revenue	Dept. of Revenue	Dept. of Revenue	Dept. of Motor Vehicles
Georgia	Dept. of Revenue	Dept. of Revenue	Dept. of Revenue	Dept. of Revenue
Hawaii	Dept. of Taxation	Dept. of Taxation	Dept. of Taxation	County Treasurer
Idaho	Tax Comm.	Tax Comm.	Tax Comm.	Dept. of Transportation
Illinois	Dept. of Revenue	Dept. of Revenue	Dept. of Revenue	Secretary of State
Indiana	Dept. of Revenue	Dept. of Revenue	Dept. of Revenue	Bur. of Motor Vehicles
Iowa	Dept. of Revenue	Dept. of Revenue	Dept. of Revenue	Local
Kansas	Dept. of Revenue	Dept. of Revenue	Dept. of Revenue	Local (a)
Kentucky	Dept. of Revenue	Dept. of Revenue	Dept. of Revenue	Transportation Cabinet
Louisiana	Dept. of Revenue	Dept. of Revenue	Dept. of Revenue	Dept. of Public Safety
Maine	Revenue Services	Revenue Services	Revenue Services	Secretary of State
Maryland	Comptroller	Comptroller	Comptroller	Dept. of Transportation
Massachusetts	Dept. of Revenue	Dept. of Revenue	Dept. of Revenue	Reg. of Motor Vehicles
Michigan	Dept. of Treasury	Dept. of Treasury	Dept. of Treasury	Secretary of State
Minnesota	Dept. of Revenue	Dept. of Revenue	Dept. of Revenue	Dept. of Public Safety
Mississippi	Tax Comm.	Tax Comm.	Tax Comm.	Tax Comm.
Missouri	Dept. of Revenue	Dept. of Revenue	Dept. of Revenue	Dept. of Revenue
Montana	Dept. of Revenue	. . .	Dept. of Transportation	Local
Nebraska	Dept. of Revenue	Dept. of Revenue	Dept. of Revenue	Dept. of Motor Vehicles
Nevada	. . .	Dept. of Taxation	Dept. of Motor Vehicles	Dept. of Motor Vehicles
New Hampshire	Dept. of Revenue Admin.	. . .	Dept. of Safety	Dept. of Safety
New Jersey	Dept. of Treasury	Dept. of Treasury	Dept. of Treasury	Dept. of Law & Public Safety
New Mexico	Tax. & Revenue Dept.	Tax. & Revenue Dept.	Tax. & Revenue Dept.	Tax. & Revenue Dept.
New York	Dept. of Tax. & Finance	Dept. of Tax. & Finance	Dept. of Tax. & Finance	Dept. of Motor Vehicles
North Carolina	Dept. of Revenue	Dept. of Revenue	Dept. of Revenue	Dept. of Transportation
North Dakota	Tax Commr.	Tax Commr.	Tax Commr.	Dept. of Transportation
Ohio	Dept. of Taxation	Dept. of Taxation	Dept. of Taxation	Bur. of Motor Vehicles
Oklahoma	Tax Comm.	Tax Comm.	Tax Comm.	Tax Comm.
Oregon	Dept. of Revenue	. . .	Dept. of Transportation	Dept. of Transportation
Pennsylvania	Dept. of Revenue	Dept. of Revenue	Dept. of Revenue	Dept. of Transportation
Rhode Island	Dept. of Administration	Dept. of Administration	Dept. of Administration	Dept. of Administration
South Carolina	Dept. of Revenue	Dept. of Revenue	Dept. of Revenue	Dept. of Public Safety
South Dakota	. . .	Dept. of Revenue & Reg.	Dept. of Revenue & Reg.	Dept. of Revenue & Reg.
Tennessee	Dept. of Revenue	Dept. of Revenue	Dept. of Revenue	Dept. of Safety
Texas	. . .	Comptroller	Comptroller	Dept. of Transportation
Utah	Tax Comm.	Tax Comm.	Tax Comm.	Tax Comm.
Vermont	Dept. of Taxes	Dept. of Taxes	Commr. of Motor Vehicles	Commr. of Motor Vehicles
Virginia	Dept. of Taxation	Dept. of Taxation	Dept. of Motor Vehicles	Dept. of Motor Vehicles
Washington	. . .	Dept. of Revenue	Dept. of Licensing	Dept. of Licensing
West Virginia	Dept. of Revenue	Dept. of Revenue	Dept. of Revenue	Div. of Motor Vehicles
Wisconsin	Dept. of Revenue	Dept. of Revenue	Dept. of Revenue	Dept. of Transportation
Wyoming	. . .	Dept. of Revenue	Dept. of Revenue	Dept. of Transportation
Dist. of Columbia	Office of Tax & Rev.	Office of Tax & Rev.	Office of Tax & Rev.	Office of Tax & Rev.

See footnotes at end of table.

AGENCIES ADMINISTERING MAJOR STATE TAXES—Continued

State or other jurisdiction	Tobacco	Death	Alcoholic beverage	Number of agencies administering taxes
Alabama	Dept. of Revenue	Dept. of Revenue	Alcoh. Bev. Control Bd.	2
Alaska	Dept. of Revenue	Dept. of Revenue	Dept. of Revenue	2
Arizona	Dept. of Revenue	Dept. of Revenue	Dept. of Revenue	2
Arkansas	Dept. of Fin. & Admin.	Dept. of Fin. & Admin.	Dept. of Fin. & Admin.	1
California	Bd. of Equalization	Controller	Bd. of Equalization	4
Colorado	Dept. of Revenue	Dept. of Revenue	Dept. of Revenue	1
Connecticut	Dept. of Revenue Serv.	Dept. of Revenue Serv.	Dept. of Revenue Serv.	2
Delaware	Div. of Revenue	Div. of Revenue	Dept. of Public Safety	3
Florida	Dept. of Business Reg.	Dept. of Revenue	Dept. of Business Reg.	3
Georgia	Dept. of Revenue	Dept. of Revenue	Dept. of Revenue	1
Hawaii	Dept. of Taxation	Dept. of Taxation	Dept. of Taxation	2
Idaho	Tax Comm.	Tax Comm.	Tax Comm.	2
Illinois	Dept. of Revenue	Attorney General	Dept. of Revenue	3
Indiana	Dept. of Revenue	Dept. of Revenue	Dept. of Revenue	2
Iowa	Dept. of Revenue	Dept. of Revenue	Dept. of Revenue	2
Kansas	Dept. of Revenue	Dept. of Revenue	Dept. of Revenue	2
Kentucky	Dept. of Revenue	Dept. of Revenue	Dept. of Revenue	2
Louisiana	Dept. of Revenue	Dept. of Revenue	Dept. of Revenue	2
Maine	Revenue Services	Revenue Services	Bur. of Liquor Enf.	3
Maryland	Comptroller	Local	Comptroller	3
Massachusetts	Dept. of Revenue	Dept. of Revenue	Dept. of Revenue	2
Michigan	Dept. of Treasury	Dept. of Treasury	Liquor Control Comm.	3
Minnesota	Dept. of Revenue	Dept. of Revenue	Dept. of Revenue	2
Mississippi	Tax Comm.	Tax Comm.	Tax Comm.	1
Missouri	Dept. of Revenue	Dept. of Revenue	Dept. of Revenue	1
Montana	Dept. of Revenue	Dept. of Revenue	Dept. of Revenue	3
Nebraska	Dept. of Revenue	Dept. of Revenue	Liquor Control Comm.	3
Nevada	Dept. of Taxation	Dept. of Taxation	Dept. of Taxation	2
New Hampshire	Dept. of Revenue Admin.	Dept. of Revenue Admin.	Liquor Comm.	3
New Jersey	Dept. of Treasury	Dept. of Treasury	Dept. of Treasury	2
New Mexico	Tax. & Revenue Dept.	Tax. & Revenue Dept.	Tax. & Revenue Dept.	1
New York	Dept. of Tax. & Finance	Dept. of Tax. & Finance	Dept. of Tax. & Finance	2
North Carolina	Dept. of Revenue	Dept. of Revenue	Dept. of Revenue	2
North Dakota	Tax Commr.	Tax Commr.	Treasurer	3
Ohio	Dept. of Taxation	Dept. of Taxation	State Treasurer	3
Oklahoma	Tax Comm.	Tax Comm.	Tax Comm.	1
Oregon	Dept. of Revenue	Dept. of Revenue	Liquor Control Comm.	3
Pennsylvania	Dept. of Revenue	Dept. of Revenue	Dept. of Revenue	2
Rhode Island	Dept. of Administration	Dept. of Administration	Dept. of Administration	1
South Carolina	Dept. of Revenue	Dept. of Revenue	Dept. of Revenue	2
South Dakota	Dept. of Revenue & Reg.	Dept. of Revenue & Reg.	Dept. of Revenue & Reg.	1
Tennessee	Dept. of Revenue	Dept. of Revenue	Dept. of Revenue	2
Texas	Comptroller	Comptroller	Comptroller	2
Utah	Tax Comm.	Tax Comm.	Tax Comm.	1
Vermont	Dept. of Taxes	Dept. of Taxes	Dept. of Taxes	2
Virginia	Dept. of Taxation	Dept. of Taxation	Alcoh. Bev. Control	3
Washington	Dept. of Revenue	Dept. of Revenue	Liquor Control Bd.	3
West Virginia	Dept. of Revenue	Dept. of Revenue	Dept. of Revenue	2
Wisconsin	Dept. of Revenue	Dept. of Revenue	Dept. of Revenue	2
Wyoming	Dept. of Revenue	Dept. of Revenue	Dept. of Revenue	2
Dist. of Columbia	Office of Tax & Rev.	Office of Tax & Rev.	Office of Tax & Rev.	1

Source: The Federation of Tax Administrators, January 2006.
Key:
. . . — Not applicable
(a) Joint state and local administration. State-level functions are performed
by the Department of Revenue in Kansas.

Table 7.15
STATE TAX AMNESTY PROGRAMS
1982–2006

State or other jurisdiction	Amnesty period	Legislative authorization	Major taxes covered	Accounts receivable included	Collections ($millions) (a)	Installment arrangements permitted (b)
Alabama	1/20/84–4/1/84	No (c)	All	No	3.2	No
Arizona	11/22/82–1/20/83	No (c)	All	No	6.0	Yes
	1/1/02–2/28/02	Yes	Individual income	No	N.A.	No
	9/1/03–10/31/03	Yes	All (t)	N.A.	73.0	Yes
Arkansas......................	9/1/87–11/30/87	Yes	All	No	1.7	Yes
California	12/10/84–3/15/85	Yes	Individual income	Yes	154.0	Yes
		Yes	Sales	No	43.0	Yes
	2/1/05–3/31/05	Yes	Income, Franchise, Sales	N.A.	N.A.	Yes
Colorado	9/16/85–11/15/85	Yes	All	No	6.4	Yes
	6/1/03–6/30/03	N.A.	All	N.A.	18.4	Yes
Connecticut	9/1/90–11/30/90	Yes	All	Yes	54.0	Yes
	9/1/95–11/30/95	Yes	All	Yes	46.2	Yes
	9/1/02–12/2/02	N.A.	All	N.A.	109.0	N.A.
Florida	1/1/87–6/30/87	Yes	Intangibles	No	13.0	No
	1/1/88–6/30/88	Yes (d)	All	No	8.4 (d)	No
	7/1/03–10/31/03	Yes	All	N.A.	80.0	N.A.
Georgia	10/1/92–12/5/92	Yes	All	Yes	51.3	No
Idaho............................	5/20/83–8/30/83	No (c)	Individual income	No	0.3	No
Illinois.........................	10/1/84–11/30/84	Yes	All (u)	Yes	160.5	No
	10/1/03–11/17/03	Yes	All	N.A.	532.0	N.A.
Indiana........................	9/15/05–11/15/05	N.A.	All	N.A.	255.0	Yes
Iowa	9/2/86–10/31/86	Yes	All	Yes	35.1	N.A.
Kansas	7/1/84–9/30/84	Yes	All	No	0.6	No
	10/1/03–11/30/03	Yes	All	Yes	53.7	N.A.
Kentucky	9/15/88–9/30/88	Yes (c)	All	No	100.0	No
	8/1/02–9/30/02	Yes (c)	All	No	100.0	No
Louisiana	10/1/85–12/31/85	Yes	All	No	1.2	Yes (f)
	10/1/87–12/15/87	Yes	All	No	0.3	Yes (f)
	10/1/98–12/31/98	Yes	All	No (q)	1.3	No
	9/1/01–10/30/01	Yes	All	Yes	173.1	No
Maine	11/1/90–12/31/90	Yes	All	Yes	29.0	Yes
	9/1/03–11/30/03	Yes	All	N.A.	37.6	N.A.
Maryland	9/1/87–11/2/87	Yes	All	Yes	34.6 (g)	No
	9/1/01–10/31/01	Yes	All	Yes	39.2	No
Massachusetts...............	10/17/83–1/17/84	Yes	All	Yes	86.5	Yes (h)
	10/1/02–11/30/02	Yes	All	Yes	96.1	Yes
	1/1/03–2/28/03	Yes	All	Yes	N.A.	N.A.
Michigan.......................	5/12/86–6/30/86	Yes	All	Yes	109.8	No
	5/15/02–6/30/02	Yes	All	Yes	N.A.	N.A.
Minnesota	8/1/84–10/31/84	Yes	All	Yes	12.1	No
Mississippi	9/1/86–11/30/86	Yes	All	No	1.0	No
	9/1/04–12/31/04	Yes	All	No	7.9	No
Missouri........................	9/1/83–10/31/83	No (c)	All	No	0.9	No
	8/1/02–10/31/02	Yes	All	Yes	76.4	N.A.
	8/1/03–10/31/03	Yes	All	Yes	20.0	N.A.
Nebraska.......................	8/1/04–10/31/04	Yes	All	No	7.5	No
Nevada	2/1/02–6/30/02	N.A.	All	N.A.	7.3	N.A.
New Hampshire............	12/1/97–2/17/98	Yes	All	Yes	13.5	No
	12/1/01–2/15/02	Yes	All	Yes	13.5	N.A.
New Jersey....................	9/10/87–12/8/87	Yes	All	Yes	186.5	Yes
	3/15/96–6/1/96	Yes	All	Yes	359.0	No
	4/15/02–6/10/02	Yes	All	Yes	276.9	N.A.
New Mexico	8/15/85–11/13/85	Yes	All (i)	No	13.6	Yes
	8/16/99–11/12/99	Yes	All	Yes	45.0	Yes

See footnotes at end of table.

STATE TAX AMNESTY PROGRAMS — Continued
1982 – 2006

State or other jurisdiction	Amnesty period	Legislative authorization	Major taxes covered	Accounts receivable included	Collections ($millions) (a)	Installment arrangements permitted (b)
New York	11/1/85 – 1/31/86	Yes	All (j)	Yes	401.3	Yes
	11/1/96 – 1/31/97	Yes	All	Yes	253.4	Yes (o)
	11/18/02 – 1/31/03	Yes	All	Yes	582.7	Yes (s)
North Carolina	9/1/89 – 12/1/89	Yes	All (k)	Yes	37.6	No
North Dakota................	9/1/83 – 11/30/83	No (c)	All	No	0.2	Yes
	10/1/03 – 1/31/04	Yes	N.A.	N.A.	6.9	N.A.
Ohio	10/15/01 – 1/15/02	Yes	All	No	48.5	No
	1/1/06 – 2/15/06	Yes	All	No	N.A.	No
Oklahoma	7/1/84 – 12/31/84	Yes	Income, Sales	Yes	13.9	No (l)
	8/15/02 – 11/15/02	N.A.	All (r)	Yes	N.A.	N.A.
Pennsylvania	10/13/95 – 1/10/96	Yes	All	Yes	N.A.	No
Rhode Island	10/15/86 – 1/12/87	Yes	All	No	0.7	Yes
	4/15/96 – 6/28/96	Yes	All	Yes	7.9	Yes
South Carolina	9/1/85 – 11/30/85	Yes	All	Yes	7.1	Yes
	10/15/02 – 12/2/02	Yes	All	Yes	66.2	N.A.
South Dakota................	4/1/99 – 5/15/99	Yes	All	Yes	0.5	N.A.
Texas	2/1/84 – 2/29/84	No (c)	All (m)	No	0.5	No
	3/11/04 – 3/31/04	No (c)	All (m)	No	N.A.	No
Vermont	5/15/90 – 6/25/90	Yes	All	Yes	1.0 (e)	No
Virginia..........................	2/1/90 – 3/31/90	Yes	All	Yes	32.2	No
	9/2/03 – 11/3/03	Yes	All	Yes	98.3	N.A.
West Virginia................	10/1/86 – 12/31/86	Yes	All	Yes	15.9	Yes
	9/1/04 – 10/31/04	Yes	All	N.A.	10.4	Yes
Wisconsin......................	9/15/85 – 11/22/85	Yes	All	Yes (n)	27.3	Yes
	6/15/98 – 8/14/98	Yes	All	Yes	30.9	N.A.
Dist. of Columbia	7/1/87 – 9/30/87	Yes	All	Yes	24.3	Yes
	7/10/95 – 8/31/95	Yes	All (p)	Yes	19.5	Yes (p)

Source: The Federation of Tax Administrators, January 2006.

Key:

N.A. — Not available.

(a) Where applicable, figure indicates local portions of certain taxes collected under the state tax amnesty program.

(b) "No" indicates requirement of full payment by the expiration of the amnesty period. "Yes" indicates allowance of full payment after the expiration of the amnesty period.

(c) Authority for amnesty derived from pre-existing statutory powers permitting the waiver of tax penalties.

(d) Does not include intangibles tax and drug taxes. Gross collections totaled $22.1 million, with $13.7 million in penalties withdrawn.

(e) Preliminary figure.

(f) Amnesty taxpayers were billed for the interest owed, with payment due within 30 days of notification.

(g) Figure includes $1.1 million for the separate program conducted by the Department of Natural Resources for the boat excise tax.

(h) The amnesty statute was construed to extend the amnesty to those who applied to the department before the end of the amnesty period, and permitted them to file overdue returns and pay back taxes and interest at a later date.

(i) The severance taxes, including the six oil and gas severance taxes, the resources excise tax, the corporate franchise tax, and the special fuels tax were not subject to amnesty.

(j) Availability of amnesty for the corporation tax, the oil company taxes, the transportation and transmissions companies tax, the gross receipts oil tax and the unincorporated business tax restricted to entities with 500 or fewer employees in the United States on the date of application. In addition, a taxpayer principally engaged in aviation, or a utility subject to the supervision of the State Department of Public Service was also ineligible.

(k) Local taxes and real property taxes were not included.

(l) Full payment of tax liability required before the end of the amnesty period to avoid civil penalties.

(m) Texas does not impose a corporate or individual income tax. In practical effect, the amnesty was limited to the sales tax and other excises.

(n) Waiver terms varied depending upon the date the tax liability was assessed.

(o) Installment arrangements were permitted if applicant demonstrated that payment would present a severe financial hardship.

(p) Does not include real property taxes. All interest was waived on tax payments made before July 31, 1995. After this date, only 50 percent of the interest was waived.

(q) Exception for individuals who owed $500 or less.

(r) Except for property and motor fuel taxes.

(s) Multiple payments can be made so long as the required balance is paid in full no later than March 15, 2003.

(t) All taxes except property, estate and unclaimed property.

(u) Does not include the motor fuel use tax.

Table 7.16
STATE EXCISE TAX RATES
(As of January 1, 2007)

State or other jurisdiction	General sales and gross receipts tax (percent)	Cigarettes (cents per pack of 20)	Distilled spirits ($ per gallon)	Motor fuel excise tax rates (cents per gallon) (c)		
				Gasoline	Diesel	Gasohol
Alabama	4.0	42.5 (b)	(c)	18.0 (d)(e)	19.0 (d)(e)	18.0 (d)(e)
Alaska	. . .	180 (f)	12.80 (g)	8.0	8.0	. . .
Arizona	5.6	200	3.00	18.0 (h)	18.0 (h)	18.0 (h)
Arkansas	6	59	2.50 (g)	21.5	22.5	21.5
California	7.25 (i)(j)	87	3.30 (g)	18.0 (k)	18.0 (k)	18.0 (k)
Colorado	2.9	84	2.28	22.0	20.5	22.0
Connecticut	6.0	151	4.50 (g)	25.0	26.0	25.0
Delaware	. . .	55	5.46 (g)	23.0 (l)(m)	22.0 (l)(m)	23.0 (l)(m)
Florida	6.0	33.9	6.50 (n)	15.3 (o)(k)	28.4 (o)(k)	15.3 (o)(k)
Georgia	4.0	37	3.79 (g)	15.2 (k)	16.3 (k)	15.2 (k)
Hawaii	4.0	160 (f)	5.98	16.0 (d)(k)	16.0 (d)(k)	16.0 (d)(k)
Idaho	6.0	57	(c)	25.0 (p)	25.0 (p)	22.5 (p)
Illinois	6.25 (j)	98 (b)	4.50 (g)	20.1 (d)(h)(k)	22.6 (h)(k)	20.1 (h)(k)
Indiana	6.0	55.5	2.68 (g)	18.0 (h)(k)	16.0 (h)(k)	18.0 (h)(k)
Iowa	5.0	36	(c)	21.0	22.5	19.0
Kansas	5.3	79	2.50 (g)	24.0	26.0	24.0
Kentucky	6.0	30 (q)	1.92 (g)(n)	19.7 (h)(r)(k)	16.7 (h)(r)(k)	19.7 (h)(r)(k)
Louisiana	4.0	36	2.50 (g)	20.0	20.0	20.0
Maine	5.0	200	(c)	26.8 (m)	27.9 (m)	26.8 (m)
Maryland	5.0	100	1.50	23.5	24.25	23.5
Massachusetts	5.0	151	4.05 (n)(g)	21.0	21.0	21.0
Michigan	6.0	200	(c)	19.0 (k)	15.0 (k)	19.0 (k)
Minnesota	6.5	123 (s)	5.03 (g)	20.0	20.0	20.0
Mississippi	7.0	18	(c)	18.4 (k)	18.4 (k)	18.4 (k)
Missouri	4.225	17 (b)	2.00	17.55 (k)	17.55 (k)	17.55 (k)
Montana	. . .	170	(c)	27.0	27.75	27.0
Nebraska	5.5	64	3.75	28.0 (g)(m)	27.4 (g)(m)	28.0 (g)(m)
Nevada	6.5	80	3.60 (g)	24.805 (d)(k)	27.75 (d)(k)	24.805 (d)(k)
New Hampshire	. . .	80	(c)	19.625 (k)	19.625 (k)	19.625 (k)
New Jersey	7.0	257.5	4.40	14.5 (k)	17.5 (k)	14.5 (k)
New Mexico	5.0	91	6.06	18.875 (k)	22.875 (k)	18.875 (k)
New York	4.0	150 (b)	6.44 (g)	24.6 (k)	22.85 (k)	24.6 (k)
North Carolina	4.5 (t)	35	(c)(n)	30.15 (r)(k)	30.15 (r)(k)	30.15 (r)(k)
North Dakota	5.0	44	2.50 (g)	23.0	23.0	23.0
Ohio	5.5	125	(c)	28.0 (k)	28.0 (k)	28.0 (k)
Oklahoma	4.5	103	5.56 (g)	17.0 (k)	14.0 (k)	17.0 (k)
Oregon	. . .	118	(c)	24.0 (d)	24.0 (d)	24.0 (d)
Pennsylvania	6.0	135	(c)	31.2 (k)	38.1 (k)	31.2 (k)
Rhode Island	7.0	246	3.75	31.0 (k)	31.0 (k)	31.0 (k)
South Carolina	5.0 (u)	7	2.72 (g)	16.0	16.0	16.0
South Dakota	4.0	53	3.93(g)	22.0 (d)	22.0 (d)	20.0 (d)
Tennessee	7.0	20 (b)(q)	4.40 (g)	21.4 (d)(k)	18.4 (d)(k)	21.4 (d)(k)
Texas	6.25	141	2.40 (g)	20.0	20.0	20.0
Utah	4.75	69.5	(c)	24.5	24.5	24.5
Vermont	6.0	179	(c)(g)	20.0 (k)	26.0 (k)	20.0 (k)
Virginia	5.0 (j)	30 (b)	(c)	17.5 (d)(v)	16.0 (d)(v)	17.5 (d)(v)
Washington	6.5	202.5	(c)(n)	34.0 (k)(w)	34.0 (k)(w)	34.0 (k)(w)
West Virginia	6.0	55	(c)	31.5 (k)	31.5 (k)	31.5 (k)
Wisconsin	5.0	77	3.25	32.9 (k)(m)	32.9 (k)(m)	32.9 (k)(m)
Wyoming	4.0	60	(c)	14.0 (k)	14.0 (k)	14.0 (k)
Dist. of Columbia	5.75	100	1.50 (g)	20.0	20.0	20.0

See footnotes at end of table.

STATE EXCISE TAX RATES — Continued
(As of January 1, 2007)

Source: Compiled by The Federation of Tax Administrators from various sources, January 2007.

Key:

... — Tax is not applicable.

(a) The tax rates listed are fuel excise taxes collected by distributor/supplier/retailers in each state. Additional taxes may apply to motor carriers. Carrier taxes are coordinated by the International Fuel Tax Association.

(b) Counties and cities may impose an additional tax on a pack of cigarettes in Alabama 1¢ to 6¢; Illinois, 10¢ to 15¢; Missouri, 4¢ to 7¢; New York City $1.50; Tennessee 1¢; and Virginia 2¢ to 15¢.

(c) In 18 states, the government directly controls the sales of distilled spirits. Revenue in these states is generated from various taxes, fees and net liquor profits.

(d) Tax rates do not include local option taxes. In AL, 1 – 3 cents; HI, 8.8 to 18.0 cent; IL, 5 cents in Chicago and 6 cents in Cook county (gasoline only); NV, 4.0 to 9.0 cents; OR, 1 to 3 cents; SD and TN, one cent; and VA 2%.

(e) (Inspection fee

(f) Tax rate is scheduled to increase to $2.00 per pack on July 1, 2007 in AK and to $2.00 on Sept. 30, 2007 in HI.

(g) Other taxes in addition to excise taxes for the following states: Alaska, under 21 percent – $2.50/gallon; Arkansas, under 5 percent – $0.50/gallon, under 21 percent – $1.00/gallon, $0.20/case and 3 percent off – 14 percent on-premise retail taxes; California, over 50 percent – $6.60/gallon; Connecticut, under 7 percent – $2.05/gallon; Delaware, under 25 percent – $3.64/gallon, over 55.780%-$9.53/gallon 6.67 cents ounce; Georgia, $0.83/gallon local tax; Illinois, under 20 percent – $0.73/gallon, $1.845/gallon in Chicago and $2.00/gallon in Cook County; Indiana, under 15 percent – $0.47/gallon; Kansas, 8 percent off – and 10 percent on-premise retail tax; Kentucky, under 6 percent – $0.25/gallon, $0.05/case and 11 percent wholesale tax; Louisiana, under 6 percent – $0.32/gallon; Massachusetts, under 15 percent – $1.10/gallon, over 50 percent alcohol – $4.05/proof gallon, 0.57 percent on private club sales; Minnesota, $0.01/bottle (except miniatures) and 9 percent sales tax; Nevada, under 14 percent – $0.70/gallon and under 21 percent – $1.30/gallon; New York,no more than 24 percent – $2.54/gallon, $1.00/gallon New York City; North Dakota, 7 percent state sales tax; Oklahoma, 13.5 percent on-premise; South Carolina, $5.36/case and 9 percent surtax; South Dakota, under 14 percent – $0.93/gallon, 2 percent wholesale tax; Tennessee, $0.15/case and 15 percent on-premise, under 7 percent – $1.21/gallon; Texas, 14 percent on-premise and $0.05/drink on airline sales; Vermont, 10% on-premise sales tax and District of Columbia, 8 percent off – and 10 percent on-premise sales tax.

(h) Carriers pay an additional surcharge equal to Arizona, 8 cents; Illinois, 6.3 cents (gasoline) and 6.0 cents (diesel); Indiana, 11 cents; Kentucky, 2 percent (gasoline) and 4.7 percent (diesel).

(i) Tax rate may be adjusted annually according to a formula based on balances in the unappropriated general fund and the school foundation fund.

(j) Includes statewide local tax; in California and Virginia, 1.0 percent.

(k) Other taxes and fees; California-sales tax applicable; Florida – sales tax added to excise; Georgia – sales tax added to excise; Hawaii – sales tax applicable; Illinois – sales tax applicable, environmental fee and leaking underground storage tax (LUST); Indiana – sales tax applicable; Kentucky – environmental fee; Michigan – sales tax applicable; Mississippi – environmental fee; Missouri – inspection fee; Nebraska – petroleum fee; Nevada – Inspection and cleanup fee; New Hampshire – oil discharge cleanup fee; New Jersey – petroleum fee;New Mexico – Petroleum loading fee; New York – sales tax applicable and petroleum tax; North Carolina – Inspection tax; Ohio – plus 3 cents commercial; Oklahoma – environmental fee;Pennsylvania – oil franchise tax; Rhode Island – leaking underground storage tank tax (LUST);Tennessee – petroleum tax and environmental fee; Vermont – petroleum cleanup fee;Washington-$0.5 percent privilege tax; West Virginia – sales tax added to excise; Wisconsin – Petroleum inspection fee; Wyoming – license tax.

(l) Plus 0.5 percent GRT.

(m) A portion of the rate is adjustable based on maintenance costs, sales volume, or inflation.

(n) Sales tax is applied to on-premise sales only.

(o) Local taxes for gasoline and gasohol vary from 10.2 cents to 18.2 cents. Plus a 2.07 cents/gallon pollution tax.

(p) Tax rate is reduced by the percentage of ethanol used in blending (reported rate assumes the maximum 10 percent ethanol).

(q) Dealers pay an additional enforcement and administrative fee of 0.1¢ per pack in Kentucky and 0.05¢ in Tennessee.

(r) Tax rate is based on the average wholesale price and is adjusted quarterly. The actual rates are: Kentucky, 9 percent; and North Carolina, 17.5 cents plus 7 percent.

(s) Plus an additional 25.5 cent sales tax is added to the wholesale price of a tax stamp (total $1.485).

(t) Sales tax rate is scheduled to decrease to 4 percent on July 1, 2007.

(u) Sales tax rate is scheduled to increase to 6 percent on June 30, 2007.

(v) Large trucks pay an additional 3.5 cents.

(w) Tax rate scheduled to increase to 36 cents on July 1, 2007.

Table 7.17
FOOD AND DRUG SALES TAX EXEMPTIONS
(As of January 1, 2007)

State or other jurisdiction	Tax rate (percentage)	Exemptions		
		Food (a)	Prescription drugs	Nonprescription drugs
Alabama	4.0	...	★	...
Alaska	0.0	...	...	...
Arizona	5.6	★	★	...
Arkansas	6.0	...	★	...
California (c)	7.25 (b)	★	★	...
Colorado	2.9	★	★	...
Connecticut	6.0	★	★	★
Delaware	0.0	...	...	...
Florida	6.0	★	★	★
Georgia	4.0	★(d)	★	...
Hawaii	4.0	...	★	...
Idaho	6.0	...	★	...
Illinois (b)	6.25	1 percent	1 percent	1 percent
Indiana	6.0	★	★	...
Iowa	5.0	★	★	...
Kansas	5.3	...	★	...
Kentucky	6.0	★	★	...
Louisiana	4.0	★ (d)	★	...
Maine	5.0	★	★	...
Maryland	5.0	★	★	★
Massachusetts	5.0	★	★	...
Michigan	6.0	★	★	...
Minnesota	6.5	★	★	★
Mississippi	7.0	...	★	...
Missouri	4.225	1.225	★	...
Montana	0.0	...	...	...
Nebraska	5.5	★	★	...
Nevada	6.5	★	★	...
New Hampshire	0.0	...	...	...
New Jersey	7.0	★	★	★
New Mexico	5.0	★	★	...
New York	4.0	★	★	★
North Carolina (e)	4.5	★ (d)	★	...
North Dakota	5.0	★	★	...
Ohio	5.5	★	★	...
Oklahoma	4.5	...	★	...
Oregon	0.0	...	...	...
Pennsylvania	6.0	★	★	★
Rhode Island	7.0	★	★	★
South Carolina (f)	5.0	3 percent	★	...
South Dakota	4.0	...	★	...
Tennessee	7.0	6 percent	★	...
Texas	6.25	★	★	★
Utah	4.75	2.25	★	...
Vermont	6.0		★	★ ★
Virginia	5.0 (b)	2.5 (b)	★	★
Washington	6.5	★	★	...
West Virginia	6.0	5	★	...
Wisconsin	5.0	★	★	...
Wyoming	4.0	...	★(g)	...
Dist. of Columbia	5.75	★	★	★

Source: The Federation of Tax Administrators, January 2007.
Key:
★— Yes, exempt from tax.
. . . — Subject to general sales tax,
(a) Some states tax food, but allow an (income) tax credit to compensate poor households. They are: Hawaii, Idaho, Kansas, Oklahoma, South Dakota and Wyoming.
(b) Includes statewide local tax of 1.0 percent in California and 1 percent in Virginia.

(c) The tax rate may be adjusted annually according to a formula based on balances in the unappropriated general fund and the school foundation fund.
(d) Food sales are subject to local sales tax.
(e) Sales tax rate is scheduled to decrease to 4% on 7/1/2007.
(f) Sales tax rate is scheduled to increase to 6% on 6/30/2007.
(g) Food sales exempt through 6/30/2008.

Table 7.18
STATE INDIVIDUAL INCOME TAXES
(Tax rates for the tax year 2007—as of January 1, 2007)

State or other jurisdiction	Tax rate range (in percents) Low	Tax rate range (in percents) High	Number of brackets	Income brackets Low	Income brackets High	Personal exemptions Single	Personal exemptions Married	Personal exemptions Dependents	Federal income tax deductible
Alabama	2.0	– 5.0	3	500 (b) –	3,000 (b)	1,500	3,000	300	★
Alaska					(No state income tax)				...
Arizona	2.59	– 4.57	5	10,000 (b) –	150,000 (b)	2,100	4,200	2,300	...
Arkansas (a)	1.0	– 7.0 (e)	6	3,599 –	30,100	22 (c)	44 (c)	22 (c)	...
California (a)	1.0	– 9.3 (w)	6	6,622 (b) –	43,468 (b)	91 (c)	182 (c)	285 (c)	...
Colorado	4.63	1Flat rate	None	...					
Connecticut	3.0	– 5.0	2	10,000 (b) –	10,000 (b)	12,750 (f)	24,500 (f)	0	...
Delaware	2.2	– 5.95	6	5,000 –	60,000	110 (c)	220 (c)	110 (c)	...
Florida					(No state income tax)				...
Georgia	1.0	– 6.0	6	750 (g) –	7,000 (g)	2,700	5,400	3,000	...
Hawaii	1.4	– 8.25	9	2,400 (b) –	48,000 (b)	1,040	2,080	1,040	...
Idaho (a)	1.6	– 7.8	8	1,198 (h) –	23,964 (h)	3,400 (d)	6,800 (d)	3,400 (d)	...
Illinois	3.0		1	--------Flat rate --------		2,000	4,000	2,000	...
Indiana	3.4		1	--------Flat rate --------		1,000	2,000	1,000	...
Iowa (a)	0.36	– 8.98	9	1,343 –	60,436	40 (c)	80 (c)	40 (c)	★
Kansas	3.5	– 6.45	3	15,000 (b) –	30,000 (b)	2,250	4,500	2,250	...
Kentucky	2.0	– 6.0	6	3,000 –	75,000	20 (c)	40 (c)	20 (c)	...
Louisiana	2.0	– 6.0	3	12,500 (b) –	25,000 (b)	4,500 (i)	9,000 (i)	1,000 (i)	★
Maine (a)	2.0	– 8.5	4	4,550 (b) –	18,250 (b)	2,850	5,700	2,850	...
Maryland	2.0	– 4.75	4	1,000 –	3,000	2,400	4,800	2,400	...
Massachusetts (a)	5.3		1	--------Flat rate --------		4,100	8,250	1,000	...
Michigan (a)	3.9		1	--------Flat rate --------		3,300	6,600	3,300	...
Minnesota (a)	5.35	– 7.85	3	21,310 (j) –	69,991 (j)	3,400 (d)	6,800 (d)	3,400 (d)	...
Mississippi	3.0	– 5.0	3	5,000 –	10,000	6,000	12,000	1,500	...
Missouri	1.5	– 6.0	10	1,000 –	9,000	2,100	4,200	1,200	★(r)
Montana (a)	1.0	– 6.9	7	2,300 –	14,500	1,980	3,960	1,980	★(r)
Nebraska (a)	2.56	– 6.84	4	2,400 (k) –	27,001 (k)	106 (c)	212 (c)	106 (c)	...
Nevada					(No state income tax)				...
New Hampshire				(State income tax is limited to dividends and interest income only.)					...
New Jersey	1.4	– 8.97	6	20,000 (l) –	500,000 (l)	1,000	2,000	1,500	...
New Mexico	1.7	– 5.3	4	5,500 (m) –	16,000 (m)	3,400 (d)	6,800 (d)	3,400 (d)	...
New York	4.0	– 6.85	5	8,000 (b) –	20,000 (b)	0	0	1,000	...
North Carolina (n)	6.0	– 8	4	12,750 (n) –	120,000 (n)	3,400 (d)	6,800 (d)	3,400 (d)	...
North Dakota (a)	2.1	– 5.54 (o)	5	30,650 (o) –	336,550 (o)	3,400 (d)	6,800 (d)	3,400 (d)	...
Ohio (a)	0.712	– 7.185	9	5,000 –	200,000	1,400 (p)	2,800 (p)	1,400 (p)	...
Oklahoma	0.5	– 5.65 (q)	7	1,000 (b) –	10,000 (b)	1,000	2,000	1,000	★(q)
Oregon (a)	5.0	– 9.0	3	2,750 (b) –	6,851 (b)	159 (c)	318 (c)	159 (c)	★(r)
Pennsylvania	3.07	1Flat rate	None	...					
Rhode Island	25.0% Federal tax liability (s)			...					
South Carolina (a)	2.5	– 7.0	6	2,570 –	12,850	3,400 (d)	6,800 (d)	3,400 (d)	...
South Dakota				(No state income tax)					...
Tennessee				(State income tax is limited to dividends and interest income only.)					...
Texas				(No state income tax)					...
Utah	2.3	– 6.98 (t)	6	1,000 (b) –	5,501 (b)	2,550 (d)	5,100 (d)	2,550 (d)	★(t)
Vermont (a)	3.6	– 9.5	5	30,650 (u) –	336,551 (u)	3,400 (d)	6,800 (d)	3,400 (d)	...
Virginia	2.0	– 5.75	4	3,000 –	17,000	900	1,800	900	...
Washington				(No state income tax)					...
West Virginia	3.0	– 6.5	5	10,000 –	60,000	2,000	4,000	2,000	...
Wisconsin (a)	4.6	– 6.75	4	9,160 (v) –	137,411 (v)	700	1,400	400	...
Wyoming				(No state income tax)					...
Dist. of Columbia	4.5	– 8.7	3	10,000 –	40,000	2,400	4,800	2,400	...

See footnotes at end of table.

STATE INDIVIDUAL INCOME TAXES — Continued
(Tax rates for the tax year 2007 — as of January 1, 2007)

Source: The Federation of Tax Administrators from various sources, January 2007.

★ — Yes

... — No

(a) 17 states have statutory provision for automatic adjustment of tax brackets, personal exemption or standard deductions to the rate of inflation. Massachusetts, Michigan, Nebraska and Ohio indexes the personal exemption amounts only.

(b) For joint returns, the taxes are twice the tax imposed on half the income.

(c) Tax credits.

(d) These states allow personal exemption or standard deductions as provided in the IRC. Utah allows a personal exemption equal to three-fourths the federal exemptions.

(e) A special tax table is available for low income taxpayers reducing their tax payments.

(f) Combined personal exemptions and standard deduction. An additional tax credit is allowed ranging from 75% to 0% based on state adjusted gross income. Exemption amounts are phased out for higher income taxpayers until they are eliminated for households earning over $56,500.

(g) The tax brackets reported are for single individuals. For married households filing separately, the same rates apply to income brackets ranging from $500 to $5,000; and the income brackets range from $1,000 to $10,000 for joint filers.

(h) For joint returns, the tax is twice the tax imposed on half the income. A $10 filing tax is charge for each return and a $15 credit is allowed for each exemption.

(i) Combined personal exemption and standard deduction.

(j) The tax brackets reported are for single individual. For married couples filing jointly, the same rates apply for income under $31,150 to over $123,751. A 6.4% AMT rate is also applicable.

(k) The tax brackets reported are for single individual. For married couples filing jointly, the same rates apply for income under $4,000 to over $50,001.

(l) The tax brackets reported are for single individuals. For married couples filing jointly, the tax rates range from 1.4% to 8.97% (with 7 income brackets) applying to income brackets from $20,000 to over $500,000.

(m) The tax brackets reported are for single individuals. For married couples filing jointly, the same rates apply for income under $8,000 to over $24,000. Married households filing separately pay the tax imposed on half the income.

(n) The tax brackets reported are for single individuals. For married taxpayers, the same rates apply to income brackets ranging from $21,250 to $200,000. Lower exemption amounts allowed for high income taxpayers. Tax rate scheduled to decrease after tax year 2007.

(o) The tax brackets reported are for single individuals. For married taxpayers, the same rates apply to income brackets ranging from $12,000 to $336,551. An additional $300 personal exemption is allowed for joint returns or unmarried head of households.

(p) Plus an additional $20 per exemption tax credit.

(q) The rate range reported is for single persons not deducting federal income tax. For married persons filing jointly, the same rates apply to income brackets ranging from $2,000 to $15,000. Separate schedules, with rates ranging from 0.5% to 10%, apply to taxpayers deducting federal income taxes.

(r) Deduction is limited to $10,000 for joint returns and $5,000 for individuals in Missouri and to $5,000 in Oregon.

(s) Federal Tax Liability prior to the enactment of Economic Growth and Tax Relief Act of 2001.

(t) One half of the federal income taxes are deductible. Taxpayer has an option of using the standard brackets and rates with all deductions, or paying a flat 5.35% of income with limited deductions.

(u) The tax brackets reported are for single individuals. For married couples filing jointly, the same rates apply for income under $51,200 to over $336,551.

(v) The tax brackets reported are for single individuals. For married taxpayers, the same rates apply to income brackets ranging from $12,210 to $183,211. An additional $250 exemption is provided for each taxpayer or spouse age 65 or over.

(w) An additional 1% tax is imposed on taxable income over $1 million.

Table 7.19
STATE PERSONAL INCOME TAXES: FEDERAL STARTING POINTS
(As of January 1, 2007)

State or other jurisdiction	Relation to Internal Revenue Code	Tax base
Alabama	. . .	. . .
Alaska	No state income tax	
Arizona	1/2/2010	
Arkansas	. . .	Federal adjusted gross income
California	1/2/2009	. . .
		Federal adjusted gross income
Colorado	Current	Federal taxable income
Connecticut	Current	Federal adjusted gross income
Delaware	Current	Federal adjusted gross income
Florida	No state income tax	
Georgia	1/2/2010	Federal adjusted gross income
Hawaii	1/1/2010	Federal adjusted gross income
Idaho	1/2/2010	Federal taxable income
Illinois	Current	Federal adjusted gross income
Indiana	1/2/2010	Federal adjusted gross income
Iowa	2/1/2010	Federal adjusted gross income
Kansas	Current	Federal adjusted gross income
Kentucky	1/1/2009	Federal adjusted gross income
Louisiana	Current	Federal adjusted gross income
Maine	1/1/2010	Federal adjusted gross income
Maryland	Current	Federal adjusted gross income
Massachusetts	Current	Federal adjusted gross income
Michigan	Current (a)	Federal adjusted gross income
Minnesota	5/19/2010	Federal taxable income
Mississippi	. . .	. . .
Missouri	Current	Federal adjusted gross income
Montana	Current	Federal adjusted gross income
Nebraska	2/15/2011	Federal adjusted gross income
Nevada	No state income tax	
New Hampshire	On interest and dividends only	
New Jersey	. . .	. . .
New Mexico	Current	Federal adjusted gross income
New York	Current	Federal adjusted gross income
North Carolina	1/2/2010	Federal taxable income
North Dakota	Current	Federal taxable income
Ohio	Current	Federal adjusted gross income
Oklahoma	Current	Federal adjusted gross income
Oregon	Current	Federal taxable income
Pennsylvania	. . .	. . .
Rhode Island	6/4/2005	Federal adjusted gross income
South Carolina	1/1/2010	Federal taxable income
South Dakota	No state income tax	
Tennessee	On interest and dividends only	
Texas	No state income tax	
Utah	Current	Federal taxable income
Vermont	1/2/2009	Federal taxable income
Virginia	1/1/2010	Federal adjusted gross income
Washington	No state income tax	
West Virginia	1/2/2010	Federal adjusted gross income
Wisconsin	1/1/2009	Federal adjusted gross income
Wyoming	No state income tax	
Dist. of Columbia	Current	Federal adjusted gross income

Source: Compiled by the Federation of Tax Administrators from various sources, January 2006.

Key:
. . . — State does not employ a Federal starting point.

Current — Indicates state has adopted the Internal Revenue Code as currently in effect. Dates indicate state has adopted the IRC as amended to that date.
(a) Or 1/1/99, taxpayer's option.

Table 7.20
RANGE OF STATE CORPORATE INCOME TAX RATES
(For tax year 2007 — as of January 1, 2007)

State or other jurisdiction	Tax rate (percent)	Tax brackets		Number of brackets	Tax rate (a) (percent) financial institution	Federal income tax deductible
		Lowest	Highest			
Alabama	6.5	---------- Flat Rate ----------		1	6.5	★
Alaska	1.0–9.4	10,000	90,000	10	1.0–9.4	...
Arizona	6.968 (b)	---------- Flat Rate ----------		1	6.968	...
Arkansas	1.0–6.5	3,000	100,000	6	1.0–6.5	...
California	8.84 (c)	---------- Flat Rate ----------		1	10.84 (c)	...
Colorado	4.63	---------- Flat Rate ----------		1	4.63	...
Connecticut	7.5 (d)	---------- Flat Rate ----------		1	7.5 (d)	...
Delaware	8.7	---------- Flat Rate ----------		1	8.7–1.7 (e)	...
Florida	5.5 (f)	---------- Flat Rate ----------		1	5.5 (f)	...
Georgia	6.0	---------- Flat Rate ----------		1	6.0	...
Hawaii	4.4–6.4 (g)	25,000	100,000	3	7.92 (g)	...
Idaho	7.6 (h)	---------- Flat Rate ----------		1	7.6 (h)	...
Illinois	7.3 (i)	---------- Flat Rate ----------		1	7.3 (i)	...
Indiana	8.5	---------- Flat Rate ----------		1	8.5	...
Iowa	6.0–12.0	25,000	250,000	4	5.0	★(k)
Kansas	4.0 (l)	---------- Flat Rate ----------		1	2.25 (l)	...
Kentucky	4.0–7.0 (m)	50,000	100,000	3	(a)	...
Louisiana	4.0–8.0	25,000	200,000	5	(a)	★
Maine	3.5–8.93 (n)	25,000	250,000	4	1.0	...
Maryland	7.0	---------- Flat Rate ----------		1	7.0	...
Massachusetts	9.5 (o)	---------- Flat Rate ----------		1	10.5 (o)	...
Michigan		------------------------------ See Note ------------------------------				
Minnesota	9.8 (p)	---------- Flat Rate ----------		1	9.8 (p)	...
Mississippi	3.0–5.0	5,000	10,000	3	3.0–5.0	...
Missouri	6.25	---------- Flat Rate ----------		1	7.0	★(k)
Montana	6.75 (q)	---------- Flat Rate ----------		1	6.75 (q)	...
Nebraska	5.58–7.81	50,000		2	(a)	...
Nevada		------------------------------ See Note ------------------------------				
New Hampshire	8.5 (r)	---------- Flat Rate ----------		1	8.5 (r)	...
New Jersey	9.0 (s)	---------- Flat Rate ----------		1	9.0 (s)	...
New Mexico	4.8–7.6	500,000	1 million	3	4.8–7.6	...
New York	7.5 (t)	---------- Flat Rate ----------		1	7.5 (t)	...
North Carolina	6.9 (u)	---------- Flat Rate ----------		1	6.9 (u)	...
North Dakota	2.6–7.0	3,000	30,000	5	7.0 (b)	★
Ohio	5.1–8.5 (v)	50,000		2	(v)	...
Oklahoma	6.0	---------- Flat Rate ----------		1	6.0	...
Oregon	6.6 (b)	---------- Flat Rate ----------		1	6.6 (b)	...
Pennsylvania	9.99	---------- Flat Rate ----------		1	(a)	...
Rhode Island	9.0 (b)	---------- Flat Rate ----------		1	9.0 (w)	...
South Carolina	5.0	---------- Flat Rate ----------		1	4.5 (x)	...
South Dakota	...	...		...	6.0–0.25% (b)	...
Tennessee	6.5	---------- Flat Rate ----------		1	6.5	...
Texas		------------------------------ See Note ------------------------------				
Utah	5.0 (b)	---------- Flat Rate ----------		1	5.0 (b)	...
Vermont	6.0–8.5	10,000	250,000	3	(a)	...
Virginia	6.0	---------- Flat Rate ----------		1	6.0 (y)	...
Washington		------------------------------ See Note ------------------------------				
West Virginia	9.0	---------- Flat Rate ----------		1	9.0	...
Wisconsin	7.9	---------- Flat Rate ----------		1	7.9	...
Wyoming		------------------------------ See Note ------------------------------				
Dist. of Columbia	9.975 (z)	---------- Flat Rate ----------		...	9.975 (z)	...

See footnotes at end of table.

RANGE OF STATE CORPORATE INCOME TAX RATES — Continued
(For tax year 2007 — as of January 1, 2007)

Source: Compiled by the Federation of Tax Administrators from various sources January 2007.

Key:

★ — Yes

. . . — No

Note: Michigan imposes a single business tax (sometimes described as a business activities tax or value added tax) of 1.9% on the sum of federal taxable income of the business, compensation paid to employees, dividends, interest, royalties paid and other items. Similarly, Texas imposes a franchise tax of 4.5% of earned surplus or 2.5 mills of net worth. Nevada, Washington, and Wyoming do not have state

corporate income taxes.

(a) Rates listed include the corporate tax rate applied to financial institutions or excise taxes based on income. Some states have other taxes based upon the value of deposits or shares.

(b) Minimum tax is $50 in Arizona, $50 in North Dakota (banks), $10 in Oregon, $250 in Rhode Island, $500 per location in South Dakota (banks), $100 in Utah, $250 in Vermont.

(c) Minimum tax is $800. The tax rate on S-Corporations is 1.5% (3.5% for banks).

(d) Or 3.1 mills per dollar of capital stock and surplus (maximum tax $1 million) or $250.

(e) The marginal rate decreases over 4 brackets ranging from $20 to $650 million in taxable income. Building and loan associations are taxed at a flat 8.7%.

(f) Or 3.3% Alternative Minimum Tax. An exemption of $5,000 is allowed.

(g) Capital gains are taxed at 4%. There is also an alternative tax of 0.5% of gross annual sales.

(h) Minimum tax is $20. An additional tax of $10 is imposed on each return.

(i) Includes a 2.5% personal property replacement tax.

(k) Fifty percent of the federal income tax is deductible.

(l) Plus a surtax of 3.35% (2.125% for banks) taxable income in excess of $50,000 ($25,000).

(m) Minimum tax of $175. Or, the alternative minimum tax equal to 0.095% of gross sales in the state or 0.75% of state gross profits.

(n) Or the Maine Alternative Minimum Tax.

(o) Rate includes a 14% surtax, as does the following: an additional tax of $7.00 per $1,000 on taxable tangible property (or net worth allocable to state, for intangible property corporations); minimum tax of $456.

(p) Plus a 5.8% tax on any Alternative Minimum Taxable Income over the base tax.

(q) A 7% tax on taxpayers using water's edge combination. Minimum tax is $50.

(r) Plus a 0.50 percent tax on the enterprise base (total compensation, interest and dividends paid). Business profits tax imposed on both corporations and unincorporated associations.

(s) The rate reported in the table is the corporation business franchise tax rate. The minimum tax is $500. An Alternative Minimum Assessment based on Gross Receipts applies if greater than corporate franchise tax. Corporations not subject to the franchise tax are subject to a 7.25% income tax. Banking and financial corporations are subject to the franchise tax. Corporations with net income under $100,000 are taxed at 6.5%. The tax on S corporations at 0.67% is eliminated after June 30, 2007.

(t) Or 1.78 mills per dollar of capital (up to $350,000); or a 2.5% alternative minimum tax; or a minimum tax of $1,500 to $100 depending on payroll size; if any of these is greater than the tax computed on net income. Small corporations with income under $290,000 are subject to lower rates of tax on net income. An additional tax of 0.9 mills per dollar of subsidiary capital is imposed on corporations. For banks, the alternative bases of tax are 3% of alternative net income; or up to 1/50th mill of taxable assets; or a minimum tax of $250.

(u) Financial institutions are also subject to a tax equal to $30 per one million in assets.

(v) Rates shown are for the Franchise tax, which is being phased out through 2010. Current rates apply to 50% of the liability, or 50% of 4 mills time the value of the taxpayer's issued and outstanding share of stock with a maximum payment of $150,000; or $50 to $1,000 minimum tax, depending on worldwide gross receipts. The Commercial Activity Tax (CAT) equals $150 for gross receipts between $150,000 and $1 million, plus 0.26% of gross receipts over $1 million. The CAT applies to 40% of receipts through March 31, and 60% for the remainder of the year. Banks will pay the Franchise tax. An additional litter tax is imposed equal to 0.11% on the first $50,000 of taxable income, 0.22% on income over $50,000; or 0.14 mills on net worth.

(w) For banks, the alternative tax is $2.50 per $10,000 of capital stock ($100 minimum).

(x) Savings and Loans are taxed at a 6% rate.

(y) State and national banks subject to the state's franchise tax on net capital is exempt from the income tax.

(z) Minimum tax is $100. Includes surtax.

Table 7.21
STATE SEVERANCE TAXES: 2005–2006

State	Title and application of tax (a)	Rate
Alabama	Iron Ore Mining Tax	$.03/ton
	Forest Products Severance Tax	Varies by species and ultimate use.
	Oil and Gas Conservation & Regulation of Production Tax	2% of gross value at point of production, of all oil and gas produced. 1% of the gross value (for a 5-year period from the date production begins) for well, for which the initial permit issued by the Oil and Gas Board is dated on or after July 1, 1996 and before July 1, 2002, except a replacement well for which the initial permit was dated before July 1, 1996
	Oil and Gas Privilege Tax on Production	8% of gross value at point of production; 4% of gross value at point of incremental production resulting from a qualified enhanced recovery project; 4% if wells produce 25 bbl. or less oil per day or 200,000 cu. ft. or less gas per day; 6% of gross value at point of production for certain on-shore and off-shore wells. A 50% rate reduction for wells permitted by the oil and gas board on or after July 1, 1996 and before July 1, 2002 for 5 years from initial production, except for replacement wells for which the initial permit was dated before July 1, 1996. Under Act 2004-635 a temporary tax is levied (July 1, 2004 through June 30, 2005) of 1% of offshore production and 0.5% of onshore production.
	Coal Severance Tax	$.135/ton
	Coal and Lignite Severance Tax	$.20/ton in addition to coal severance tax.
Alaska	Fisheries Business Tax	1% to 5% of fish value based on type of fish and processing.
	Fishery Resource Landing Tax	3% of the value of the fishery resource at the place of landing for an established commercial fish species; 1% of the value of the of the fishery resource at the place of landing for a developing commercial fish species.
	Seafood Marketing Assessment	.03% on all commercial fish species.
	Oil and Gas Properties Production Tax	(Oil) The greater of either $0.80/bbl for old crude oil or 15% of gross value at the production point for oil fields in production more than 5 years and 12.25% for oil fields in production less than 5 years, multiplied by the Economic Limit Factor for oil; (Gas) The greater of either $0.64/1000 cu. ft. of gas or 10% of gross value at the production point, multiplied by the Economic Limit Factor for Gas; and conservation surcharges of $.03 cents per barrel, with an additional $.02 cents per barrel as needed to maintain a $50 million balance in the oil and hazardous substance response fund (when fund reaches $50 million cap, then additional $.02 cents is not charged).
	Salmon Marketing Tax	1% of the value of salmon that is removed or transferred.
Arizona	Severance Tax (b)	2.5% of net severance base for mining; $1.50/1000 board ft. ($2.13 for ponderosa pine) for timbering.
Arkansas	Natural Resources Severance Tax	Separate rate for each substance.
	Oil and Gas Conservation Tax	Natural gas 0.3 of $.01 cent per MCF; crude oil 4% to 5% depending on production levels.
	Oil and Gas Conservation Assessment	Maximum 43 mills/bbl. of oil and 9 mills per MCF produced of gas.
California	Oil and Gas Production Assessment	Rate determined annually by Department of Conservation. (d)
Colorado	Severance Tax (e)	Taxable years commencing prior to July 1, 1999, 2.25% of gross income exceeding $11 million for metallic minerals and taxable years commencing after July 1,1999, 2.25% of gross income exceeding $19 million for metallic minerals; on or after July 1,1999, $.05/ton for each ton exceeding 625,000 tons each quarter for molybdenum ore; 2% to 5% based on gross income for oil, gas, CO2, and coalbed methane; after July 1,1999, $.36/ton adjusted by the producers' prices index for each ton exceeding 300,000 tons each quarter for coal; and 4% of gross proceeds on production exceeding 15,000 tons per day for oil shale.
	Oil and Gas Conservation Levy	Maximum 1.5 mills/$1 of market value at wellhead. (f)
Florida	Oil, Gas and Sulfur Production Tax	5% of gross value for small well oil, and 8% of gross value for all other, and an additional 12.5% for escaped oil; the gas base rate times the gas base adjustment rate each fiscal year for gas; and the sulfur base rate times the sulfur base rate adjustment each fiscal year for sulfur.
	Solid Minerals Tax (g)	8% of the value of the minerals severed, except phosphate rock (rate computed annually at $1.69/ton times the changes in the producer price index) and heavy minerals (rate computed annually at a base rate of $2.93/ton times the base rate adjustment).
Idaho	Ore Severance Tax	1% of net value
	Oil and Gas Production Tax	Maximum of 5 mills/bbl. of oil and 5 mills/50,000 cu. ft. of gas. (c)
	Additional Oil and Gas Production Tax	2% of market value at site of production.

See footnotes at end of table.

STATE SEVERANCE TAXES — Continued

State	Title and application of tax (a)	Rate
Illinois	Timber Fee	4% of purchase price (h)
Indiana	Petroleum Production Tax (i)	1% of value or $.24 per barrel for oil or $.03 per 1000 cu. Ft. of gas, whichever is greater.
Kansas	Severance Tax (j)	8% of gross value of oil and gas, less property tax credit of 3.67%; $1/ton of coal.
	Oil and Gas Conservation Tax	54.70 mills/bbl. crude oil or petroleum marketed or used each month; 9.13 mills/1,000 cu. ft. of gas sold or marketed each month.
	Mined-Land Conservation & Reclamation Tax	$50, plus per ton fee of between $.03 and $.10.
Kentucky	Oil Production Tax	4.5% of market value
	Coal Severance Tax	4.5% of gross value, less transportation expenses
	Natural Resource Severance Tax (k)	4.5% of gross value, less transportation expenses
Louisiana	Natural Resources Severance Tax	Rate varies according to substance.
	Oil Field Site Restoration Fee	Rate varies according to type of well and production.
	Freshwater Mussel Tax	5% of revenues from the sale of whole freshwater mussels, at the point of first sale.
Maine	Mining Excise Tax	The greater of a tax on facilities and equipment or a tax on gross proceeds.
Maryland	Mine Reclamation Surcharge	$.17/ton of coal removed by open-pit, strip or deep mine methods. Of the $.15 , $.06 is remitted to the county from which the coal was removed.
Michigan	Gas and Oil Severance Tax	5% (gas), 6.6% (oil) and 4% (oil from stripper wells and marginal properties) of gross cash market value of the total production. Maximum additional fee of 1% of gross cash market value on all oil and gas produced in state in previous year.
Minnesota	Taconite and Iron Sulfides	$2.137 per ton of concentrates or pellets
	Direct Reduced Iron (l)	$2.137 per ton of concentrates plus an additional $.03 per ton for each 1% that the iron content exceeds 72%
Mississippi	Oil and Gas Severance Tax	6% of value at point of gas production; 3.5% of gross value of occluded natural gas from coal seams at point of production for well's first five years; also, maximum 35 mills/bbl. oil or 4 mills/1,000 cu. ft. gas (Oil and Gas Board maintenance tax). 6% of value at point of oil production; 3% of value at production when enhanced oil recovery method used.
	Timber Severance Tax	Varies depending on type of wood and ultimate use.
	Salt Severance Tax	3% of value of entire production in state.
Montana	Coal Severance Tax	Varies from 3% to 15% depending on quality of coal and type of mine.
	Metalliferous Mines License Tax (m)	Progressive rate, taxed on amounts in excess of $250,000. For concentrate shipped to smelter, mill or reduction work, 1.81%. Gold, silver or any platinum group metal shipped to refinery, 1.6%.
	Oil or Gas Conservation Tax	Maximum 0.3% on the market value of each barrel of crude petroleum oil or 10,000 cu. ft. of natural gas produced, saved and marketed or stored within or exported from the state. (n)
	Oil and Natural Gas Production Tax	Varies from 0.5% to 14.8% according to the type of well and type of production.
	Micaceous Minerals License Tax	$.05/ton
	Cement License Tax (o)	$.22/ton of cement, $.05/ton of cement, plaster, gypsum or gypsum products.
	Mineral Mining Tax	$25 plus 0.5% of gross value greater than $5,000. For talc, $25 plus 4% of gross value greater than $625. For coal, $25 plus 0.40% of gross value greater than $6,250. For vermiculite, $25 plus 2% of gross value greater than $1,250. For limestone, $25 plus 10% of gross value greater than $250. For industrial garnets, $25 plus 1% of gross value greater than $2,500.00
Nebraska	Oil and Gas Severance Tax	3% of value of nonstripper oil and natural gas; 2% of value of stripper oil.
	Oil and Gas Conservation Tax	Maximum 15 mills/$1 of value at wellhead, as of January 1, 2000 (c)
	Uranium Tax	2% of gross value over $5 million. The value of the uranium severed subject to tax is the gross value less transportation and processing costs.

See footnotes at end of table.

STATE SEVERANCE TAXES—Continued

State	Title and application of tax (a)	Rate
Nevada............................	Minerals Extraction Tax	Between 2% and 5% of net proceeds of each geographically separate extractive operation, based on ratio of net proceeds to gross proceeds of whole operation.
	Oil and Gas Conservation Tax	$50/mills/bbl. of oil and 50 mills/50,000 cu. ft. of gas.
New Hampshire..............	Refined Petroleum Products Tax	0.1% of fair market value
	Excavation Tax	$.02 per cubic yard of earth excavated.
	Timber Tax	10% of stumpage value at the time of cutting.
New Mexico.....................	Resources Excise Tax (p)	Potash .5%, molybdenum .125%, copper .25%, all others .75% of value.
	Severance Tax (p)	Potash 2.5%, copper .5%, timber .125% of value. Pumice, gypsum, sand, gravel, clay, fluospar and other non-metallic minerals, .125% of value. Gold, silver .20%; Lead, zinc, thorium, molybdenum, manganese, rare earth and other .125% of value.
	Oil and Gas Severance Tax	3.75% of value of oil, other liquid hydrocarbons, natural gas and carbon dioxide.
	Oil and Gas Emergency School Tax	3.15% of value of oil, other liquid hydrocarbons and carbon dioxide. 4% of value of natural gas.
	Natural Gas Processor's Tax	$0.0220/Mmbtu tax on volume.
	Oil and Gas Ad Valorem Production Tax	Varies, based on property tax in district of production.
	Oil and Gas Conservation Tax (q)	0.19% of value.
North Carolina	Oil and Gas Conservation Tax	Maximum 5 mills/barrel of oil and 0.5 mill/1,000 cu. ft. of gas.
	Primary Forest Product Assessment Tax	$.50/1,000 board ft. for softwood sawtimber, $.40/1,000 board ft. for hardwood sawtimber, $.20/cord for softwood pulpwood, $.12/cord hardwood pulpwood.
North Dakota..................	Oil Gross Production Tax	5% of gross value at well.
	Gas Gross Production Tax	$.04/1000 cu.ft. of gas produced (the rate is subject to a gas rate adjustment each fiscal year). For FY05, the rate was 10.37 cents per mcf.
	Coal Severance Tax	$.375/ton plus $.02/ton. (r)
	Oil Extraction Tax	6.5% of gross value at well (with exceptions due to production volumes and and production incentives for enhanced recovery projects).
Ohio	Resource Severance Tax	$.10/bbl. of oil; $.025/1,000 cu. ft. of natural gas; $.04/ton of salt; $.02/ ton of sand, gravel, limestone and dolomite; $.09/ton of coal; and $0.01/ton of clay, sandstone or conglomerate, shale, gypsum or quartzite.
Oklahoma........................	Oil, Gas and Mineral Gross Production Tax and Petroleum Excise Tax (s)	Rate: 0.75% levied on asphalt and metals. 7% (if greater than $2.10 mcf) 4% (if greater than $1.75 mcf, but less than $2.10 mcf) 1% (if less than $1.75 mcf) casinghead gas and natural gas as well as 0.95% being levied on crude oil, casinghead gas and natural gas. Oil Gross Production Tax is now a variable rate tax, beginning with January 1999 production, at the following rates based on the average price of Oklahoma oil: a) If the average price equals or exceeds $17/bbl, the tax shall be 7%; b) If the average price is less than $17/bbl, but is equal to or exceeds $14/bbl, the tax shall be 4%; c) If the average price is less than $14/bbl, the tax shall be 1%.
Oregon............................	Forest Products Harvest Tax	$2.85/1000 board ft. harvested from public and private land. (rate is for 2005 harvests)
	Oil and Gas Production Tax	6% of gross value at well.
	STF Severance Tax—Eastern Oregon Forestland Option	$3.12/1000 board ft. harvested from land under the Small Tract Forestland Option.
	STF Severance Tax—Western Oregon Forestland Option	$4.00.1000 board ft. harvested from land under the Small Tract Forestland Option.
South Carolina................	Forest Renewal Tax	Softwood products: 20 cents per 1,000 board feet or 25 cents per cord. Hardwood products: 25 cents per 1,000 board feet or 7 cents per cord.
South Dakota	Precious Metals Severance Tax	$4 per ounce of gold severed plus additional tax depending on price of gold; 10% on net profits or royalties from sale of precious metals, and 8% of royalty value.
	Energy Minerals Severance Tax (t)	4.5% of taxable value of any energy minerals.
	Conservation Tax	2.4 mills of taxable value of any energy minerals.
Tennessee.........................	Oil and Gas Severance Tax	3% of sales price.
	Coal Severance Tax (u)	$.20/ton

See footnotes at end of table.

STATE SEVERANCE TAXES — Continued

State	Title and application of tax (a)	Rate
Texas.............................	Gas Production Tax	7.5% of market value.
	Oil Production Tax	The greater of 4.6% of market value or $.046/bbl. 2.3% of market value for oil produced from qualified enhanced recovery projects.
	Sulphur Production Tax	$1.03/long ton or fraction thereof.
	Cement Production Tax	$.0275/100 lbs. or fraction thereof.
	Oil-Field Cleanup Regulatory Fees	5/8 of $.01/barrel; 1/15 of $.01/1000 cubic feet of gas. (v)
Utah	Mining Severance Tax	2.6% of taxable value for metals or metalliferous minerals sold or otherwise disposed of.
	Oil and Gas Severance Tax	3% of value for the first $13 per barrel of oil, 5% from $13.01 and above; 3% of value for first $1.50/mcf, 5% from $1.51 and above; and 4% of taxable value of natural gas liquids.
	Oil and Gas Conservation Fee	.2% of market value at wellhead.
Virginia	Forest Products Tax	Varies by species and ultimate use.
	Coal Surface Mining Reclamation Tax	Varies depending on balance of Coal Surface Mining Reclamation Fund.
Washington	Uranium and Thorium Milling Tax	$0.05/per pound.
	Enhanced Food Fish Tax	0.09% to 5.62% of value (depending on species) at point of landing.
	Timber Excise Tax	5% of stumpage value for harvests on public and private lands.
West Virginia	Natural Resource Severance Taxes	Coal: State rate is greater of 5% or $.75 per ton (4.65% for state purposes and .35% for distribution to local governments). Special state rates for coal from new low seam mines. For seams between 37" and 45" the rate is greater of 2% or $.75/ton (1.65% for state purposes and .35% for distribution to local governments). For seams less than 37" the rate is greater of 1% or $.75/ton (.65% for state purposes and .35% for distribution to local governments). For coal from gob, refuse piles, or other sources of waste coal, the rate is 2.5% (distributed to local governments). Additional tax for workers' compensation debt reduction is $.56/ton. Two special reclamation taxes at $.14/clean ton and $.02/clean ton. Limestone or sandstone, quarried or mined, and other natural resources: 5% of gross value. Natural gas: 5% of gross value (10% of net tax distributed to local governments), additional tax for workers' compensation debt reduction is $.047/mcf of natural gas produced. Oil: 5% of gross value (10% of net tax distributed to local governments). Timber: 3.22%, additional tax for workers' compensation debt reduction is 2.78%.
Wisconsin	Mining Net Proceeds Tax	Progressive net proceeds tax ranging from 3% to 15% is imposed on the net proceeds from mining metalliferous minerals. The tax brackets are annually adjusted for inflation based on the change in the GNP deflator.
	Oil and Gas Severance Tax	7% of market value of oil or gas at the mouth of the well. There are no wells in the state
Wyoming	Severance Tax	Severance Tax is defined as an excise tax imposed on the present and continuing privilege of removing, extracting, severing or producing any mineral in this state. Except as otherwise provided by W.S. 39-14-205 (Tax Exemptions), The total Severance Tax on crude oil, lease condensate or natural gas shall be six percent (6%), comprising one and one-half percent (1.5%) imposed by the Wyoming constitution article 15, section 19 and four and one-half percent (4.5%) imposed by Wyoming statute. The tax shall be distributed as provided in W.S. 39-14-211 and is imposed as follows: i. One and one-half percent (1.5%); plus ii. One-half percent (.5%); plus iii. Two percent (2%); plus iv. Two percent (2%). Severance Tax is applied to the taxable value of crude oil, lease condensate or natural gas. The taxable value is the gross sales value of the product less Federal, State or Tribal Royalties paid and less allowable transportation deductions. If the product produced is natural gas, an additional deduction is allowed for processing. Rates vary from 1.50% to 6.0% on different grades of oil. Taxes on coal and other minerals varies from 2% to 7%.

See footnotes at end of table.

STATE SEVERANCE TAXES — Continued

Sources: The Council of State Governments' survey, October 2005, and state Web sites, January 2006.

Key:

(a) Application of tax is same as that of title unless otherwise indicated by a footnote.

(b) Timber, metalliferous minerals.

(c) Actual rate set by administrative actions. Idaho – Current conservation rate is 5 mills (.005); Nebraska – Current conservation rate is 4 mills (.004).

(d) For 2005-06, $0.050898/bbl of oil or 10,000 cu. ft. of natural gas.

(e) Metallic minerals, molybdenum ore, coal, oil shale, oil, gas, CO2, and coalbed methane.

(f) As of July 1, 2004, set at .0005 mill/$1.

(g) Clay, gravel, phosphate rock, lime, shells, stone, sand, heavy minerals and rare earths.

(h) Buyer deducts amount from payment to grower; amount forwarded to Department of Conservation.

(i) Petroleum, oil, gas and other hydrocarbons.

(j) Coal, oil and gas.

(k) Coal and oil excepted.

(l) Production is considered commercial when it exceeds 50,000 tons annually. There is a six-year phase-in of the tax. In years one and two, the rate is zero. In year three, it is 25% of the statutory rate and 50% and 75% in years four and five respectively. An Aggregate Materials Tax is imposed by resoution of of county boards. It is not required that any county impose the tax, which is $.10/cubic yard or $.07/ton on materials produced in the county.

(m) Metals, precious and semi-precious stones and gems.

(n) The maxiumum rate of 0.3% is split between the Oil or Gas Conservation Tax and the Oil, Gas and Coal Natural Resource Account Fund. Currently the Oil or Gas Conservation Tax is .18% and the Oil, Gas and Coal Natural Resource Account fund tax rate is .08%.

(o) Cement and gypsum or allied products.

(p) Natural resources except oil, natural gas, liquid hydrocarbons or carbon dioxide.

(q) Oil, coal, gas, liquid hydrocarbons, geothermal energy, carbon dioxide and uranium.

(r) Rate reduced by 50 percent if burned in cogeneration facility using renewable resources as fuel to generate at least 10 percent of its energy output. Coal shipped out of state is subject to the $.02/ton tax and 30% of the $.375/ton tax. The coal may be subject to up to the $.375/ton tax at the option of the county in which the coal is mined.

(s) Asphalt and ores bearing lead, zinc, jack, gold, silver, copper or petroleum or other crude oil or other mineral oil, natural gas or casinghead gas and uranium ore.

(t) Any mineral fuel used in the production of energy, including coal, lignite, petroleum, oil, natural gas, uranium and thorium.

(u) Counties and municipalities also authorized to levy severance taxes on sand, gravel, sandstone, chert and limestone at a rate up to $.15/ton.

(v) Fees will not be collected when Oil-Field Cleanup Fund reaches $20 million, but will again be collected when fund falls below $10 million.

Table 7.22
STATE GOVERNMENT TAX REVENUE, BY TYPE OF TAX: 2005
(In thousands of dollars)

State	Total taxes	Sales and gross receipts	Licenses	Individual income	Corporation net income	Severance	Death and property taxes	Documentary and gift	Stock transfer	Other
United States	$647,886,410	$273,811,221	$35,863,173	$220,254,617	$38,691,026	$8,131,446	$10,470,510	$5,341,720	$10,049,250	$292,342
Alabama	7,799,948	3,988,617	438,447	2,536,521	397,308	144,813	231,136	14,462	48,644	N.A.
Alaska	1,858,311	198,797	100,670	N.A.	588,694	925,699	42,912	1,539	N.A.	N.A.
Arizona	11,008,428	6,699,014	325,931	2,848,450	701,859	26,338	374,024	32,812	N.A.	N.A.
Arkansas	6,552,449	3,457,887	312,280	1,875,065	277,311	18,565	556,561	13,802	38,834	2,144
California	98,434,685	37,673,127	6,707,940	42,992,007	8,670,065	14,251	2,164,259	213,036	N.A.	N.A.
Colorado	7,648,456	3,057,452	336,557	3,770,736	315,834	145,114	N.A.	22,763	N.A.	N.A.
Connecticut	11,584,728	5,128,163	377,130	5,033,442	574,984	N.A.	N.A.	264,795	206,214	N.A.
Delaware	2,725,095	397,264	1,063,543	882,472	248,869	N.A.	N.A.	6,180	123,560	3,207
Florida	33,894,971	6,430,205	1,894,180	N.A.	1,785,213	59,121	299,856	294,889	4,075,258	N.A.
Georgia	15,675,655	1,657,032	528,177	7,326,225	712,310	N.A.	67,019	42,657	670	31,444
Hawaii	4,434,356	2,748,613	143,109	1,381,481	124,125	N.A.	N.A.	12,712	24,316	N.A.
Idaho	2,934,459	1,501,302	238,132	1,040,512	140,585	2,488	N.A.	8,822	N.A.	N.A.
Illinois	26,411,689	13,355,555	2,471,210	7,936,884	2,183,066	448	56,131	301,423	106,972	N.A.
Indiana	12,853,976	7,195,173	467,002	4,213,480	824,802	695	8,874	143,950	N.A.	N.A.
Iowa	5,750,629	2,627,452	589,192	2,254,107	186,469	N.A.	N.A.	77,003	16,406	N.A.
Kansas	5,598,700	2,779,139	291,142	2,050,562	248,135	117,297	60,572	51,853	N.A.	N.A.
Kentucky	9,090,882	4,251,789	553,596	3,036,231	478,505	228,848	475,494	63,175	3,244	N.A.
Louisiana	8,638,674	4,585,883	520,360	2,392,727	352,136	711,766	45,401	30,401	N.A.	N.A.
Maine	3,071,161	1,362,192	520,360	1,299,252	135,863	N.A.	43,660	32,258	34,284	N.A.
Maryland	13,497,281	5,282,123	734,360	5,661,492	807,054	N.A.	528,638	183,084	239,071	61,459
Massachusetts	18,014,681	5,782,321	686,456	9,690,270	1,332,796	N.A.	70	255,127	267,641	N.A.
Michigan	23,525,187	11,534,044	1,339,931	6,108,924	1,907,190	68,055	2,152,022	101,473	313,548	N.A.
Minnesota	15,881,131	6,641,039	956,899	6,341,164	933,896	32,348	619,122	68,952	287,711	N.A.
Mississippi	5,432,152	3,523,388	329,526	1,174,065	283,231	66,275	44,070	11,597	N.A.	N.A.
Missouri	9,543,814	4,598,980	641,550	4,014,574	218,229	75	23,238	39,399	7,735	34
Montana	1,875,545	455,151	234,959	713,390	98,214	181,201	185,349	4,191	N.A.	3,090
Nebraska	3,796,551	1,973,117	203,197	1,393,897	198,380	2,560	2,400	13,566	9,434	N.A.
Nevada	5,010,443	4,596,795	703,961	N.A.	N.A.	39,691	149,008	20,516	160,198	N.A.
New Hampshire	2,022,146	705,116	204,718	67,686	476,489	N.A.	392,265	11,269	164,603	N.A.
New Jersey	22,933,999	10,171,999	1,289,107	8,224,290	2,224,633	N.A.	3,484	520,776	499,710	N.A.
New Mexico	4,471,477	2,170,521	209,907	1,086,015	242,462	712,539	40,756	4,925	N.A.	4,352
New York	50,190,396	16,161,717	1,277,135	28,100,047	2,784,721	N.A.	N.A.	898,483	968,293	N.A.
North Carolina	18,639,618	7,615,545	1,108,838	8,427,553	1,271,985	1,932	N.A.	154,108	59,657	N.A.
North Dakota	1,403,293	709,756	109,767	242,008	75,836	262,339	1,536	2,051	N.A.	N.A.
Ohio	24,006,560	11,146,285	1,992,880	9,434,452	1,327,484	7,920	37,158	60,381	N.A.	N.A.
Oklahoma	6,859,030	2,499,559	850,353	2,468,609	168,890	762,506	N.A.	75,708	14,001	19,404
Oregon	6,522,665	699,329	655,245	4,698,994	365,347	12,148	24,432	56,852	10,318	N.A.
Pennsylvania	27,262,969	13,227,212	2,725,459	8,275,589	1,703,295	N.A.	57,984	695,334	555,748	22,348
Rhode Island	2,628,747	1,378,034	90,999	998,042	113,326	N.A.	1,588	32,436	14,211	111
South Carolina	7,318,388	3,883,000	402,759	2,691,473	246,935	N.A.	9,633	19,135	65,453	N.A.

See footnotes at end of table.

STATE GOVERNMENT TAX REVENUE, BY TYPE OF TAX: 2005
(In thousands of dollars) — Continued

State	Total taxes	Sales and gross receipts	Licenses	Individual income	Corporation net income	Severance	Death and property taxes	Documentary and gift	Stock transfer	Other
South Dakota..............	1,110,035	903,929	149,523	N.A.	49,142	2,870	N.A.	4,442	129	N.A.
Tennessee	10,007,292	7,647,575	1,089,682	155,333	805,601	1,438	N.A.	85,597	188,594	33,472
Texas	32,784,942	25,850,841	4,484,915	N.A.	N.A.	2,347,512	N.A.	101,674	N.A.	N.A.
Utah	4,686,381	2,329,545	164,898	1,926,697	188,845	73,434	N.A.	2,962	N.A.	N.A.
Vermont....................	2,242,902	778,104	103,090	500,464	68,962	N.A.	744,535	18,863	22,831	6,053
Virginia....................	15,918,847	5,478,929	622,941	8,352,366	605,959	1,772	18,525	149,962	595,406	92,987
Washington................	14,839,634	11,642,308	726,406	N.A.	N.A.	43,034	1,590,722	N.A.	837,164	N.A.
West Virginia.............	4,301,156	2,154,087	183,962	1,171,987	463,249	307,265	3,638	4,797	12,171	N.A.
Wisconsin..................	13,452,250	5,790,733	798,872	5,465,082	782,742	3,476	112,159	112,346	77,221	9,619
Wyoming...................	1,739,646	641,657	108,373	N.A.	N.A.	805,613	180,821	3,182	N.A.	N.A.

Source: U.S. Department of Commerce, Bureau of the Census, February 2007.
Notes: "Other Taxes" include taxes that do not fall into other major categories. Because the table presents data on selected taxes, please be aware the total of all columns will not be equal to total taxes.

Key:
N.A. — Not applicable

Table 7.23
STATE GOVERNMENT SALES AND GROSS RECEIPTS TAX REVENUE: 2005
(In thousands of dollars)

State	Total	General sales or gross receipts	Total	Selective sales taxes							
				Motor fuels	Insurance premiums	Public utilities	Tobacco products	Alcoholic beverages	Amusements	Pari-mutuels	Other
United States	$311,074,039	$212,246,900	$98,827,139	$34,570,428	$14,842,349	$11,022,793	$13,216,670	$4,731,621	$5,241,621	$309,789	$14,891,868
Alabama	3,988,617	2,033,192	1,955,425	559,978	272,681	630,252	152,886	144,089	92	3,096	192,351
Alaska	198,797	N.A.	198,797	39,565	52,958	3,969	56,162	34,638	2,458	N.A.	9,047
Arizona	6,699,014	5,208,070	1,490,944	705,623	396,544	37,980	290,503	59,222	610	462	N.A.
Arkansas	3,457,887	2,573,503	884,384	437,097	124,954	N.A.	147,932	43,307	N.A.	4,783	126,311
California	37,673,127	29,967,136	7,705,991	3,366,141	2,232,955	569,116	1,096,224	314,252	N.A.	38,491	88,812
Colorado	3,057,452	2,003,066	1,054,386	588,869	191,941	8,952	130,106	31,593	99,092	3,833	N.A.
Connecticut	5,128,163	3,267,726	1,860,437	477,108	238,284	217,482	273,392	44,236	416,496	9,666	183,773
Delaware	397,264	N.A.	397,264	113,663	69,369	38,070	80,433	13,777	N.A.	169	81,783
Florida	25,486,454	19,056,249	6,430,205	2,093,900	764,559	1,840,560	465,772	622,635	N.A.	28,335	614,444
Georgia	6,967,153	5,310,121	1,657,032	926,494	331,612	N.A.	248,889	150,037	N.A.	N.A.	N.A.
Hawaii	2,748,613	2,136,604	612,009	86,426	87,285	108,686	85,244	43,717	N.A.	N.A.	200,651
Idaho	1,501,302	1,128,485	372,817	220,102	86,913	1,534	51,843	6,813	N.A.	N.A.	5,612
Illinois	13,355,555	7,195,445	6,160,110	1,419,883	366,584	1,726,498	656,473	147,238	826,426	11,654	1,005,354
Indiana	7,195,173	5,001,049	2,194,124	806,862	186,526	11,543	343,078	38,719	793,566	4,733	9,097
Iowa	2,627,452	1,721,763	905,689	438,322	131,183	N.A.	96,077	14,062	221,676	4,369	N.A.
Kansas	2,779,139	1,990,835	788,304	426,261	122,027	N.A.	123,746	90,244	585	3,216	22,225
Kentucky	4,251,789	2,594,976	1,656,813	496,340	357,504	N.A.	37,727	81,751	195	14,325	668,971
Louisiana	4,585,883	2,861,435	1,724,448	602,975	362,679	7,718	105,962	54,215	510,069	47,780	33,050
Maine	1,362,192	934,848	427,344	228,395	81,237	8,828	91,906	12,742	N.A.	4,236	N.A.
Maryland	5,282,123	2,889,952	2,392,126	752,809	268,912	263,677	275,795	27,352	10,929	2,002	790,650
Massachusetts	5,782,321	3,890,945	1,891,376	685,524	402,303	N.A.	423,637	69,251	4,607	4,677	301,377
Michigan	11,534,044	8,074,095	3,459,949	1,076,188	249,524	29,239	1,179,871	150,888	145,811	10,924	617,504
Minnesota	6,641,039	4,203,736	2,437,303	651,472	310,623	48	173,946	69,272	54,959	1,539	1,175,444
Mississippi	3,523,388	2,587,970	935,418	435,530	164,466	8,876	55,897	39,993	223,135	N.A.	7,521
Missouri	4,598,980	3,036,441	1,562,539	742,053	287,739	N.A.	110,282	28,307	327,385	N.A.	66,773
Montana	455,151	N.A.	455,151	191,912	61,290	29,071	61,217	21,737	53,126	90	36,708
Nebraska	1,973,117	1,516,705	456,412	305,058	38,600	3,683	71,451	24,087	5,937	270	7,326
Nevada	3,937,069	2,255,055	1,682,014	307,672	215,598	9,271	136,637	36,332	934,638	N.A.	41,866
New Hampshire	705,116	N.A.	705,116	132,137	80,315	69,376	101,735	12,227	381	3,606	305,339
New Jersey	10,171,999	6,552,200	3,619,799	525,027	454,450	981,399	800,142	99,359	475,661	N.A.	283,761
New Mexico	2,170,521	1,556,600	613,921	223,396	95,464	13,612	48,477	34,627	46,353	897	151,095
New York	16,161,717	11,003,520	5,158,197	532,687	987,438	769,410	975,949	184,610	731	31,505	1,675,867
North Carolina	7,615,545	4,602,082	3,013,463	1,338,403	442,228	327,798	42,981	220,546	11,157	N.A.	630,350
North Dakota	709,756	410,216	299,540	121,674	30,671	33,419	21,068	5,980	9,559	346	76,823
Ohio	11,146,285	8,194,419	2,951,866	1,671,915	440,475	155,842	579,111	89,920	N.A.	14,603	N.A.
Oklahoma	2,499,559	1,660,825	838,734	413,840	172,433	18,072	127,750	70,999	4,361	1,840	29,439
Oregon	699,329	N.A.	699,329	373,295	55,276	11,242	243,746	13,555	17	2,198	N.A.
Pennsylvania	13,227,212	8,064,868	5,162,344	1,907,673	677,098	1,131,296	1,030,512	237,405	521	26,041	151,798
Rhode Island	1,378,034	844,087	533,947	132,730	53,418	86,360	136,376	11,241	N.A.	3,990	109,832
South Carolina	3,883,000	2,903,274	979,726	484,981	128,821	49,651	29,610	141,827	36,145	N.A.	108,691

See footnotes at end of table.

STATE GOVERNMENT SALES AND GROSS RECEIPTS TAX REVENUE: 2005—Continued
(In thousands of dollars)

| State | Total | General sales or gross receipts | Total | Selective sales taxes | | | | | | | |
				Motor fuels	Insurance premiums	Public utilities	Tobacco products	Alcoholic beverages	Amusements	Pari-mutuels	Other
South Dakota.............	903,929	621,812	282,117	124,974	57,647	2,583	28,371	12,416	25	535	55,566
Tennessee...............	7,647,575	6,118,001	1,529,574	844,249	360,638	5,352	121,211	97,423	N.A.	N.A.	100,701
Texas	25,850,841	16,356,284	9,494,557	2,935,649	1,167,899	826,286	599,368	626,378	24,453	11,603	3,302,921
Utah	2,329,545	1,710,379	619,166	351,097	119,705	26,421	61,434	30,177	N.A.	N.A.	30,332
Vermont	778,104	310,805	467,299	85,980	52,463	10,721	48,360	17,878	N.A.	N.A.	251,897
Virginia..................	5,478,929	3,093,725	2,385,204	912,934	373,571	132,235	103,230	151,987	79	N.A.	711,168
Washington.............	11,642,308	9,147,303	2,495,005	930,975	357,381	373,835	354,014	199,426	61	1,836	277,477
West Virginia...........	2,154,087	1,095,341	1,058,746	319,671	113,426	155,741	102,825	8,646	N.A.	10,204	348,233
Wisconsin................	6,090,733	4,039,450	2,051,283	957,055	144,873	284,113	610,142	49,301	325	1,546	3,928
Wyoming.................	641,657	522,262	119,395	67,864	19,809	2,976	27,170	1,187	N.A.	389	N.A.

Source: U.S. Department of Commerce, Bureau of the Census, May 2006.

Key:
N.A. — Not applicable

Table 7.24
STATE GOVERNMENT LICENSE TAX REVENUE: 2005
(In thousands of dollars)

State	Total license revenue	Alcoholic beverages	Amusements	Corporation	Hunting and fishing	Motor vehicle operators	Motor vehicle	Public utility	Occupation and business, NEC	Other licenses
United States (a)..........	$42,702,918	$389,263	$242,023	$7,280,358	$1,263,309	$2,110,390	$18,220,765	$473,972	$12,068,439	$654,399
Alabama.........	438,447	2,468	N.A.	80,654	15,455	15,008	191,141	10,865	122,855	1
Alaska.........	100,670	1,768	1	1,019	25,155	N.A.	52,930	285	14,849	4,663
Arizona.........	325,931	4,799	29	12,212	18,019	16,588	170,473	N.A.	90,877	12,934
Arkansas.........	312,280	1,765	291	20,929	19,981	24,859	124,996	8,131	106,972	4,356
California.........	6,707,940	45,363	8,116	63,756	77,717	217,282	2,498,740	76,216	3,717,038	3,712
Colorado.........	336,557	5,670	942	4,363	63,543	14,694	204,520	231	42,068	757
Connecticut.........	377,130	6,346	53	16,917	3,920	45,710	205,546		93,905	4,502
Delaware.........	928,665	846	330	568,540	911	2,293	35,140	4,439	250,289	65,877
Florida.........	1,894,180	34,295	4,190	176,414	14,583	167,449	1,196,658	21,243	279,336	12
Georgia.........	528,177	1,699	N.A.	53,280	21,350	51,991	285,161	N.A.	114,682	14
Hawaii.........	143,109	N.A.	N.A.	2,017	365	531	99,735	16,871	22,117	1,473
Idaho.........	238,132	1,517	352	2,075	30,639	6,838	113,676	30,160	49,987	2,888
Illinois.........	2,471,210	11,424	2,127	191,156	29,546	85,908	1,400,405	N.A.	744,869	5,775
Indiana.........	467,002	9,920	4,029	5,418	19,575	209,393	177,324	N.A.	39,955	1,388
Iowa.........	589,192	9,376	20,379	37,536	25,809	13,742	382,374	13,462	81,884	4,630
Kansas.........	291,142	2,455	236	50,898	22,158	19,135	165,491	5,201	22,768	2,800
Kentucky.........	553,596	5,437	325	198,600	21,795	13,279	195,032	8,608	106,673	3,847
Louisiana.........	520,360	N.A.	N.A.	289,351	26,845	11,177	111,459	3,059	75,116	3,353
Maine.........	163,652	2,866	703	5,638	15,414	6,914	84,140	N.A.	47,714	263
Maryland.........	734,360	1,015	38	64,597	12,962	41,342	478,875	N.A.	133,373	2,158
Massachusetts.........	686,456	2,871	439	25,978	5,775	92,224	316,934	N.A.	144,893	97,342
Michigan.........	1,339,931	13,305	N.A.	20,258	49,421	51,345	903,103	16,326	144,200	141,973
Minnesota.........	956,899	1,058	852	7,096	57,990	41,654	521,114	N.A.	291,669	35,466
Mississippi.........	329,526	2,458	5,295	98,152	13,533	25,809	113,140	N.A.	67,328	3,811
Missouri.........	641,550	3,992	67	118,661	30,430	17,257	264,101	19,260	132,551	55,231
Montana.........	234,959	1,646	4,933	1,010	38,657	5,708	141,747	5	40,887	366
Nebraska.........	203,197	350	N.A.	6,752	14,175	8,270	89,200	N.A.	63,900	20,550
Nevada.........	703,961	N.A.	99,454	58,992	8,038	14,641	154,578	N.A.	362,948	5,310
New Hampshire.........	204,718	14,580	236	4,322	8,757	13,348	87,547	6,406	66,804	2,718
New Jersey.........	1,289,107	9,504	66,543	247,182	11,671	36,781	422,980	932	491,088	2,426
New Mexico.........	209,907	825	312	2,810	16,323	5,818	158,537	261	24,947	74
New York.........	1,277,135	42,400	48	68,772	4,637	225,714	739,061	24,276	156,851	15,376
North Carolina.........	1,108,838	14,093	N.A.	388,000	15,035	79,893	464,284	N.A.	144,173	3,360
North Dakota.........	109,767	264	307	N.A.	14,193	4,324	50,903	6	39,770	N.A.
Ohio.........	1,992,880	33,315	N.A.	418,324	34,697	83,432	716,048	3,933	697,782	5,349
Oklahoma.........	850,353	4,871	7,388	45,513	18,861	15,380	558,246	5	199,630	459
Oregon.........	655,245	2,694	2,233	9,003	40,799	25,701	419,807	13,516	130,894	10,598
Pennsylvania.........	2,725,459	14,538	45	845,455	67,351	60,110	824,017	50,844	847,330	15,769
Rhode Island.........	90,999	152	399	4,050	1,920	528	53,768	N.A.	29,387	795
South Carolina.........	402,759	9,572	2,399	68,397	20,008	38,715	130,873	N.A.	123,547	9,248

See footnotes at end of table.

STATE GOVERNMENT LICENSE TAX REVENUE: 2005—Continued
(In thousands of dollars)

State	Total license revenue	Alcoholic beverages	Amusements	Corporation	Hunting and fishing	Motor vehicle operators	Motor vehicle	Public utility	Occupation and business, NEC	Other licenses
South Dakota	149,523	305	121	2,836	24,041	2,366	43,829	891	63,978	11,156
Tennessee	1,089,682	1,033	350	516,956	27,282	42,670	261,728	6,136	228,855	4,672
Texas	4,484,915	32,001	7,316	2,233,551	86,019	112,464	1,282,551	17,876	678,564	34,573
Utah	164,898	1,227	N.A.	2,293	21,501	9,871	96,841	N.A.	29,411	3,754
Vermont	103,090	442	96	4,737	5,590	4,393	61,769	N.A.	23,602	2,461
Virginia	622,941	10,416	50	48,955	19,921	45,584	346,614	N.A.	146,691	4,710
Washington	726,406	10,175	434	20,677	29,487	48,630	355,171	23,487	202,710	35,635
West Virginia	183,962	11,616	13	9,106	15,618	154	89,263	18,425	39,540	227
Wisconsin	798,872	530	552	15,098	65,889	31,437	328,978	72,616	278,914	4,858
Wyoming	108,373	1	N.A.	7,174	29,948	2,036	50,217	N.A.	18,268	729

Source: U.S. Department of Commerce, Bureau of the Census, January 31, 2007.
Key:
N.A. — Not applicable
(a) U.S. Totals include the 50 state governments and do not include the District of Columbia or any local government.

Table 7.25
PER CAPITA PERSONAL INCOME, PERSONAL INCOME, AND POPULATION, BY STATE AND REGION, 2005–2006

State or other jurisdiction	Per capita personal income (dollars) 2005r	2006p	Rank in the U.S. 2005r	2006p	Percent of the U.S. 2005r	2006p	Percent change 2005–06	Rank of percent change 2005–06	Personal income (millions of dollars) 2005r	2006p	Percent change 2005–06	Rank of percent change 2005–06	Population (thousands of persons) 2005r	2006p	Percent change 2005–06	Rank of percent change 2005–06
United States	$34,471	$36,276	...	...	100	100	5.2	...	$10,220,942	$10,860,917	6.3	...	296,507	299,398	1.0	...
Alabama	29,623	31,295	40	40	86	86	5.6	12	134,736	143,925	6.8	13	4,548	4,599	1.1	18
Alaska	35,564	37,271	15	16	103	103	4.8	28	23,588	24,974	5.9	27	663	670	1.0	21
Arizona	30,019	31,458	38	39	87	87	4.8	29	178,706	193,983	8.5	5	5,953	6,166	3.6	1
Arkansas	26,681	27,935	47	48	77	77	4.7	32	74,059	78,521	6.0	22	2,776	2,811	1.3	16
California	36,936	38,956	12	11	107	107	5.5	16	1,335,386	1,420,245	6.4	16	36,154	36,458	0.8	25
Colorado	37,510	39,186	7	8	109	108	4.5	35	174,919	186,266	6.5	15	4,663	4,753	1.9	8
Connecticut	47,388	49,852	1	1	137	137	5.2	22	165,890	174,721	5.3	36	3,501	3,505	0.1	43
Delaware	37,088	39,022	11	10	108	108	5.2	21	31,218	33,304	6.7	14	842	853	1.4	15
Florida	34,001	35,798	20	20	99	99	5.3	19	604,131	647,583	7.2	11	17,768	18,090	1.8	9
Georgia	30,914	31,891	36	38	90	88	3.2	50	282,322	298,627	5.8	29	9,133	9,364	2.5	4
Hawaii	34,489	36,299	19	19	100	100	5.2	20	43,913	46,662	6.3	18	1,273	1,285	1.0	23
Idaho	28,478	29,952	42	43	83	83	5.2	23	40,706	43,924	7.9	8	1,429	1,466	2.6	3
Illinois	36,264	38,215	13	13	105	105	5.4	18	462,928	490,374	5.9	26	12,765	12,832	0.5	35
Indiana	31,173	32,526	33	33	90	90	4.3	38	195,332	205,355	5.1	41	6,266	6,314	0.8	29
Iowa	31,670	33,236	30	30	92	92	4.9	27	93,919	99,112	5.5	33	2,966	2,982	0.6	33
Kansas	32,866	34,743	23	21	95	96	5.7	11	90,320	96,031	6.3	17	2,748	2,764	0.6	31
Kentucky	28,272	29,352	44	46	82	81	3.8	45	117,967	123,458	4.7	47	4,173	4,206	0.8	26
Louisiana	24,664	30,952	50	41	72	85	25.5	1	111,167	132,715	19.4	1	4,507	4,288	-4.9	50
Maine	30,808	32,348	37	34	89	89	5.0	25	40,612	42,750	5.3	39	1,318	1,322	0.3	38
Maryland	41,972	44,077	4	4	122	122	5.0	24	234,609	247,526	5.5	35	5,590	5,616	0.5	36
Massachusetts	43,501	45,877	3	3	126	126	5.5	17	279,860	295,320	5.5	34	6,433	6,437	0.1	46
Michigan	32,804	33,847	24	27	95	93	3.2	49	331,349	341,710	3.1	50	10,101	10,096	-0.1	48
Minnesota	37,290	38,712	10	12	108	107	3.8	46	191,175	200,031	4.6	48	5,127	5,167	0.8	27
Mississippi	25,051	26,535	49	50	73	73	5.9	7	72,862	77,232	6.0	24	2,908	2,911	0.1	44
Missouri	31,231	32,705	32	31	91	90	4.7	31	181,066	191,086	5.5	32	5,798	5,843	0.8	28
Montana	29,015	30,688	41	42	84	85	5.8	9	27,122	28,989	6.9	12	935	945	1.1	19
Nebraska	32,923	34,397	22	23	96	95	4.5	34	57,885	60,826	5.1	42	1,758	1,768	0.6	32
Nevada	35,744	37,089	14	17	104	102	3.8	48	86,224	92,557	7.3	9	2,412	2,496	3.5	2
New Hampshire	37,768	39,311	6	7	110	108	4.1	43	49,356	51,690	4.7	45	1,307	1,315	0.6	30
New Jersey	35,324	37,388	17	15	102	103	5.8	8	365,453	382,658	5.3	40	8,717	8,725	0.1	49
New Mexico	27,889	29,673	45	44	81	82	6.4	5	53,714	57,998	8.0	7	1,926	1,955	1.5	13
New York	39,967	42,392	5	5	116	117	6.1	6	771,990	818,426	6.0	23	19,316	19,306	0.6	32
North Carolina	31,041	32,234	31	17	90	89	3.8	44	269,203	285,477	7.3	20	8,672	8,857	3.5	7
North Dakota	31,357	32,552	29	7	91	90	3.8	47	19,899	20,699	4.7	49	635	636	0.6	42
Ohio	31,860	33,338	29	15	92	92	4.6	33	365,453	382,658	5.3	46	11,471	11,478	-0.6	45
Oklahoma	27,889	32,210	45	44	81	82	7.6	3	106,119	115,288	8.6	4	3,543	3,579	1.5	13
Oregon	39,967	33,666	5	5	94	93	4.3	42	117,497	124,589	6.0	21	3,639	3,701	1.7	11
Pennsylvania	34,937	36,680	18	18	101	101	5.0	26	433,400	456,316	5.3	37	12,405	12,441	0.3	37
Rhode Island	35,324	37,388	17	15	102	103	5.8	8	37,923	39,916	5.3	40	1,074	1,068	-0.6	49
South Carolina	28,285	29,515	43	45	82	81	4.3	37	120,123	127,543	6.2	19	4,247	4,321	1.7	10

See footnotes at end of table.

PER CAPITA PERSONAL INCOME, PERSONAL INCOME, AND POPULATION, BY STATE AND REGION, 2005–2006—Continued

State or other jurisdiction	Per capita personal income (dollars)								Personal income (millions of dollars)				Population (thousands of persons)			
	2005r	2006p	Rank in the U.S.		Percent of the U.S.		Percent change 2005–06	Rank of percent change 2005–06	2005r	2006p	Percent change 2005–06	Rank of percent change 2005–06	2005r	2006p	Percent change 2005–06	Rank of percent change 2005–06
			2005r	2006p	2005r	2006p										
South Dakota.........	32,523	33,929	26	26	94	94	4.3	39	25,201	26,530	5.3	38	775	782	0.9	24
Tennessee...............	30,969	32,304	35	35	90	89	4.3	40	184,443	195,078	5.8	30	5,956	6,039	1.4	14
Texas	32,460	34,257	27	25	94	94	5.5	14	744,270	805,307	8.2	6	22,929	23,508	2.5	5
Utah	27,321	29,108	46	47	79	80	6.5	4	68,039	74,229	9.1	3	2,490	2,550	2.4	6
Vermont..................	32,717	34,264	25	24	95	94	4.7	30	20,362	21,377	5.0	43	622	624	0.2	40
Virginia...................	37,503	39,173	8	9	109	108	4.5	36	283,685	299,393	5.5	31	7,564	7,643	1.0	20
Washington.............	35,479	37,423	16	14	103	103	5.5	15	223,232	239,348	7.2	10	6,292	6,396	1.7	12
West Virginia..........	26,419	27,897	48	49	77	77	5.6	13	47,926	50,730	5.9	28	1,814	1,818	0.2	41
Wisconsin...............	33,278	34,701	21	22	97	96	4.3	41	183,948	192,818	4.8	44	5,528	5,557	0.5	34
Wyoming.................	37,305	40,676	9	6	108	112	9.0	2	18,981	20,948	10.4	2	509	515	1.2	17
District of Columbia.............	52,811	55,755	...	...	153	154	5.6	...	30,739	32,423	5.5	...	582	582	-0.1	...

Source: U.S. Bureau of Economic Analysis and Bureau of the Census.

Key:
r — revised
p — preliminary

Table 7.26
SUMMARY OF FINANCIAL AGGREGATES, BY STATE: 2005
(In millions of dollars)

State	Revenue				Expenditure				Total debt outstanding at end of fiscal year	Total cash and security holdings at end of fiscal year
	Total	General	Utilities and liquor store	Insurance trust	Total	General	Utilities and liquor store	Insurance trust		
United States	$1,637,821	$1,282,348	$19,840	$335,634	$1,470,463	$1,280,598	$26,867	$167,975	$798,355	$3,144,242
Alabama	22,538	19,152	178	3,209	21,047	19,111	183	1,753	6,262	34,273
Alaska	9,116	7,881	17	1,219	8,056	7,115	88	853	5,767	44,891
Arizona	25,311	21,492	27	3,793	23,957	21,623	31	2,304	8,037	41,753
Arkansas..................	14,935	12,851	0	2,084	13,634	12,666	0	969	4,298	20,824
California	249,057	170,566	5,664	72,828	209,771	176,705	5,893	27,210	107,373	465,301
Colorado..................	22,474	15,864	0	6,610	18,770	15,683	13	3,073	12,410	52,294
Connecticut	20,551	18,623	24	1,904	20,203	17,660	217	2,511	23,047	33,936
Delaware..................	6,166	5,470	10	686	5,904	5,484	88	402	4,351	11,896
Florida	77,078	62,085	20	14,973	70,418	62,411	66	8,006	25,880	175,349
Georgia	36,112	30,053	2	6,057	33,807	30,490	30	3,317	8,189	66,968
Hawaii......................	9,092	7,864	0	1,227	8,405	7,620	0	786	5,844	14,440
Idaho........................	7,204	5,679	86	1,440	6,138	5,481	63	594	2,386	13,034
Illinois......................	60,062	47,707	0	12,355	55,667	48,300	0	7,368	48,257	112,294
Indiana.....................	27,325	24,465	0	2,860	26,452	24,598	36	1,854	13,350	40,077
Iowa	15,677	12,573	150	2,955	14,143	12,735	102	1,306	4,931	29,172
Kansas	12,515	10,542	0	1,973	11,765	10,708	0	1,057	5,117	14,979
Kentucky	21,249	18,157	0	3,091	20,091	17,675	0	2,416	8,564	38,095
Louisiana	24,841	20,167	6	4,668	21,402	18,810	4	2,589	11,494	46,661
Maine........................	8,420	7,017	145	1,257	7,485	6,883	6	596	4,627	14,801
Maryland..................	28,890	24,673	106	4,110	26,803	24,032	631	2,546	13,723	50,544
Massachusetts..........	41,748	34,510	140	7,098	38,025	34,001	219	3,806	55,994	75,155
Michigan..................	55,726	45,960	689	9,078	51,408	45,665	557	5,186	26,168	85,405
Minnesota	31,724	25,790	0	5,934	30,169	26,969	99	3,197	7,265	53,334
Mississippi...............	15,518	12,817	203	2,498	14,705	13,172	165	1,368	4,328	24,771
Missouri....................	26,821	21,425	0	5,396	23,147	20,677	0	2,471	16,184	61,173
Montana	5,689	4,621	52	1,015	4,800	4,230	46	525	3,682	13,211
Nebraska...................	8,711	7,787	0	924	7,273	6,933	0	340	1,743	10,556
Nevada......................	11,535	8,774	103	2,659	9,158	8,076	109	973	3,911	25,156
New Hampshire........	6,151	5,041	396	713	5,784	5,050	351	387	6,864	10,895
New Jersey................	51,348	40,870	645	9,833	49,231	40,250	2,303	8,101	42,313	94,926
New Mexico	13,337	11,126	0	2,211	12,599	11,542	0	1,057	5,873	37,349
New York	140,223	110,985	6,321	22,916	136,786	114,139	10,935	13,982	101,992	274,733
North Carolina.........	44,892	36,303	0	8,589	39,482	35,750	126	3,712	15,773	80,366
North Dakota............	3,877	3,343	0	534	3,491	3,157	0	334	1,683	8,968
Ohio	72,203	49,037	618	22,549	60,554	49,491	387	10,676	23,124	173,817
Oklahoma	17,874	14,609	374	2,891	15,710	13,677	311	1,723	7,469	32,058
Oregon	22,589	14,769	311	7,510	19,217	15,516	169	3,546	11,265	61,326
Pennsylvania	69,760	54,095	1,171	14,494	62,833	53,869	1,133	7,882	27,691	113,364
Rhode Island	7,253	5,897	28	1,328	6,754	5,826	110	921	6,829	13,758
South Carolina.........	22,991	18,743	1,141	3,108	22,709	19,122	1,259	2,328	13,370	37,720
South Dakota.........	4,059	2,995	0	1,064	3,262	2,986	0	276	2,573	10,598
Tennessee	24,661	22,091	0	2,570	23,990	22,505	5	1,480	3,574	32,362
Texas	96,134	76,104	0	20,030	81,369	71,888	16	9,465	18,153	215,298
Utah	13,123	10,414	151	2,557	11,149	10,122	112	914	5,267	22,400
Vermont....................	4,599	4,222	38	340	4,436	4,206	56	192	2,800	5,718
Virginia....................	37,294	30,459	439	6,396	32,791	30,066	407	2,358	16,894	65,332
Washington..............	36,831	26,979	466	9,386	33,059	28,233	416	4,428	17,023	74,261
West Virginia...........	12,170	9,966	63	2,142	9,826	8,953	70	809	5,014	12,729
Wisconsin.................	34,438	24,611	0	9,827	28,828	25,168	3	3,657	18,763	82,128
Wyoming..................	5,933	5,125	60	748	4,000	3,570	52	377	868	13,797

Source: U.S. Department of Commerce, Bureau of the Census, January 2007.
Note: Detail may not add to total due to rounding. Data presented are statistical in nature and do not represent an accounting statement. Therefore, a difference between an individual government's total revenue and expenditure does not necessarily indicate a budget surplus or deficit.

Table 7.27
NATIONAL TOTALS OF STATE GOVERNMENT FINANCES FOR SELECTED YEARS: 2002–2005

Item	2005	2004	2003	2002	Per capita 2005	Per capita 2004	Per capita 2003	Per capita 2002
Population (in thousands)..................	296,507	293,638	290,231	287,405	N.A.	N.A.	N.A.	N.A.
Revenue total.......................................	$1,637,820,897	$1,586,718,729	$1,295,658,820	$1,096,347,277	$5,524	$5,404	$4,464	$3,820
General revenue................................	1,282,347,838	1,194,055,987	1,112,349,024	1,060,822,965	4,325	4,066	3,833	3,697
Taxes..	408,456,380	590,413,778	548,990,867	534,063,430	1,378	2,011	1,892	1,863
Intergovernmental revenue	408,456,380	394,613,110	361,617,049	335,422,978	1,378	1,344	1,246	1,167
From Federal Government..........	386,034,095	374,693,902	343,307,800	317,581,354	1,302	1,276	1,183	1,105
Public welfare......................	221,932,568	214,528,312	196,954,235	181,516,646	749	731	679	632
Education............................	68,216,590	64,913,198	56,361,735	51,103,376	230	221	194	178
Highways..............................	32,735,017	29,606,251	29,481,357	29,641,477	110	101	102	103
Employment security administration.....................	4,630,281	4,876,406	5,026,880	4,168,288	16	17	17	15
Other......................................	58,519,639	59,124,638	55,483,593	51,151,567	197	201	191	178
From local government...............	22,422,285	19,919,208	18,309,249	17,841,624	76	68	63	62
Charges and miscellaneous revenue	225,780,200	209,029,099	201,741,108	191,336,557	762	712	695	667
Liquor stores revenue	5,212,064	4,865,703	4,517,992	4,287,846	18	17	16	15
Utility revenue	14,627,471	12,954,913	12,517,945	11,935,400	49	44	43	42
Insurance trust revenue	335,633,524	374,842,126	166,273,859	19,301,066	1,132	1,277	573	67
Employee retirement..................	269,763,309	308,949,942	110,838,528	-25,244,197	910	1,052	382	-88
Unemployment compensation......	35,242,919	38,229,928	35,190,504	26,959,673	119	130	121	94
Worker compensation	23,018,659	21,757,876	16,122,680	13,624,173	78	74	56	47
Other...	7,608,637	5,904,380	4,122,147	3,961,417	26	20	14	14
Expenditure and debt redemption	1,551,947,283	1,497,114,170	1,426,714,871	1,335,230,625	5,234	5,099	4,916	4,645
Debt redemption	81,484,825	90,938,903	67,666,492	54,820,936	275	310	233	190
Expenditure total..............................	1,470,462,458	1,406,175,267	1,359,048,379	1,280,409,689	4,959	4,789	4,683	4,455
General expenditure..........................	91,532,787	1,209,435,776	1,163,968,202	1,109,346,913	309	4,119	4,011	3,860
Education...	455,104,018	429,340,569	411,093,625	389,390,099	1,535	1,462	1,416	1,355
Intergovernmental expenditure...............................	263,155,197	248,356,196	240,408,489	227,336,087	888	846	828	791
State institutions of higher education	152,556,732	152,783,448	145,941,224	139,745,935	515	520	503	486
Other education..........................	276,158,620	276,557,121	265,152,401	249,644,164	931	942	914	869
Public welfare.................................	368,806,663	339,408,778	314,406,504	287,015,523	1,244	1,156	1,083	999
Intergovernmental expenditure...............................	51,512,090	47,440,301	49,301,258	47,112,496	174	162	170	164
Cash assistance, categorical program	10,343,253	9,924,609	9,487,944	9,233,827	35	34	33	32
Cash assistance, other	2,474,923	2,358,980	1,993,148	1,417,080	8	8	7	5
Other public welfare	331,289,629	279,851,755	302,925,412	276,364,616	1,117	953	1,044	962
Highways......................................	90,273,738	86,165,985	85,726,099	84,197,951	305	293	295	293
Intergovernmental expenditure..............................	X	X	13,271,218	12,949,850	X	X	46	45
Regular state highway facilities..................................	83,854,936	78,751,658	78,142,687	77,295,568	283	268	269	269
State toll highways/facilities........	6,418,802	7,414,327	7,583,412	6,902,383	22	25	26	24
Health and hospitals.......................	91,532,787	89,985,045	88,615,522	87,685,190	309	306	305	305
State hospitals and institutions for handicapped......	42,751,419	39,851,464	37,874,685	36,864,020	144	136	131	128
Other (a)	N/A	858,584	520,199	528,621	X	3	2	2
Natural resources	18,360,179	18,651,542	18,576,793	17,821,117	62	64	64	62
Corrections	40,689,366	39,313,812	39,187,839	38,918,307	137	134	135	135
Financial administration	22,811,548	21,386,771	20,805,632	19,193,207	77	73	72	66
Employment security administration.............................	4,377,732	4,673,666	5,258,083	5,072,948	15	16	18	18
Police protection............................	11,362,668	9,471,421	11,144,395	10,705,936	38	32	38	37
Interest on general debt..................	34,362,180	32,953,170	31,294,763	31,426,313	116	112	108	109
Veterans' services...........................	1,349,107	1,503,741	1,016,563	361,190	5	5	4	1
Utility expenditure..........................	22,785,073	21,676,258	22,404,931	20,278,852	77	74	77	71
Insurance trust expenditure	167,974,677	171,139,160	168,978,731	147,285,899	567	583	582	513
Employee retirement.....................	118,332,771	111,375,680	103,048,619	91,971,465	399	379	355	320
Unemployment compensation........	29,776,222	43,173,792	51,410,604	42,016,889	100	147	177	146
Other..	19,865,684	16,589,688	14,519,508	13,297,545	67	57	50	46

See footnotes at end of table.

NATIONAL TOTALS OF STATE GOVERNMENT FINANCES FOR SELECTED YEARS: 2002–2005—Continued

Item	2005	2004	2003	2002	Per capita 2005	Per capita 2004	Per capita 2003	Per capita 2002
Total expenditure								
by character and object	1,470,462,458	1,406,175,267	1,359,048,379	1,280,409,689	4,959	4,789	4,683	4,455
Direct expenditure	1,066,995,248	1,016,469,065	976,851,809	915,620,209	3,599	3,462	3,366	3,186
Current operation	738,068,643	691,651,637	656,989,385	620,882,668	2,489	2,356	2,264	2,160
Capital outlay	94,550,657	90,950,079	91,942,748	89,918,425	319	310	317	313
Construction	72,609,708	73,372,464	72,374,446	71,034,814	245	250	249	247
Other capital outlay	21,940,949	17,577,615	19,568,302	18,883,611	74	60	67	66
Assistance and subsidies	30,307,592	28,104,471	25,900,969	24,313,447	102	96	89	85
Interest on debt	36,093,679	34,623,718	33,039,976	33,219,770	122	118	114	116
Insurance benefits								
and repayments	167,974,677	171,139,160	168,978,731	147,285,899	567	583	582	513
Intergovernmental expenditure	403,467,210	389,706,202	382,196,570	364,789,480	1,361	1,327	1,317	1,269
Cash and security holdings								
at end of fiscal year	3,144,241,774	2,930,126,017	2,594,215,994	2,534,028,608	10,604	9,979	8,939	8,818
Insurance trust	2,305,723,853	2,142,907,100	1,859,116,896	1,841,239,368	7,776	7,298	6,406	6,407
Unemployment fund balance	27,595,746	23,794,035	28,795,978	44,546,198	93	81	99	155
Debt offsets.......................................	349,347,741	328,219,839	315,588,433	305,728,839	1,178	1,118	1,087	1,064

Source: U.S. Department of Commerce, Bureau of the Census, January 2007.
2005 Population Sources: Table NST-EST2006-01 — Annual State Population Estimates: July 1, 2005, Population Division, U.S. Census Bureau, released December 22, 2006. Annual Estimates of the Population for the United States, Regions, and States and for Puerto Rico: April 1, 2000 to July 1, 2006 (NST-EST2006-01).

Key:
X — Not available
(a) Beginning in 2005 the "other" category for hospitals has been rolled up into the "state hospitals and institutions for the handicapped" category.

Table 7.28
STATE EXPENDITURE, BY CHARACTER AND OBJECT AND BY STATE: 2005 (In thousands of dollars)

State	Intergovernmental expenditures	Total	Direct expenditures								Exhibit: Total salaries and wages
			Current operation	Capital outlay			Assistance and subsidies	Interest on debt	Insurance benefits and repayments		
				Total	Construction	Other					
United States	$403,467,210	$1,066,995,248	$738,068,643	$94,550,657	$72,609,708	$21,940,949	$30,307,592	$36,093,679	$167,974,677		$196,220,683
Alabama	4,494,345	16,552,496	11,392,983	1,980,259	1,626,320	353,939	1,122,977	303,396	1,752,881		3,365,746
Alaska	1,145,159	6,910,816	4,696,216	896,979	756,464	140,515	166,335	298,532	852,754		1,308,627
Arizona	8,069,461	15,887,597	11,299,958	1,573,075	1,299,588	273,487	452,925	258,082	2,303,557		2,751,702
Arkansas	3,869,400	9,764,814	7,627,530	792,031	696,374	95,657	241,318	135,339	968,596		1,582,814
California	80,948,431	128,822,882	86,541,967	7,975,303	6,585,370	1,389,933	2,437,528	4,658,007	27,210,077		21,907,383
Colorado	5,187,799	13,581,771	8,858,655	964,449	813,958	150,491	172,214	513,522	3,072,931		2,930,371
Connecticut	3,513,039	16,690,131	11,199,210	1,165,687	1,021,279	144,408	455,406	1,359,158	2,510,670		3,587,753
Delaware	945,950	4,958,306	3,609,939	682,159	468,573	213,586	94,120	170,367	401,721		1,898,884
Florida	17,328,518	53,089,226	36,680,726	5,160,979	4,235,900	925,079	1,965,308	1,275,829	8,006,384		7,416,845
Georgia	9,521,119	24,285,463	18,153,321	1,501,309	1,358,085	143,224	858,467	455,725	3,316,641		3,906,032
Hawaii	147,201	8,258,243	6,441,970	520,397	393,293	127,104	110,963	399,345	785,568		2,089,721
Idaho	1,519,654	4,617,835	3,210,983	532,462	460,464	71,998	106,595	174,250	593,545		912,811
Illinois	14,212,799	41,454,190	27,947,446	2,623,459	2,196,022	427,437	1,131,135	2,384,643	7,367,507		7,556,632
Indiana	7,993,289	18,458,254	13,931,432	1,687,482	1,474,142	213,340	472,718	513,041	1,853,581		2,959,636
Iowa	3,642,335	10,500,341	7,540,752	1,185,582	1,027,622	157,960	272,444	196,066	1,305,497		2,188,308
Kansas	3,281,217	8,483,991	5,969,634	1,031,299	902,976	128,323	187,218	238,853	1,056,987		2,546,004
Kentucky	3,915,278	16,175,898	11,573,782	1,236,837	978,363	258,474	575,283	374,114	2,415,882		3,126,236
Louisiana	4,588,748	16,813,367	11,720,580	1,338,964	1,114,425	224,539	539,749	625,305	2,588,769		3,857,007
Maine	1,093,027	6,391,611	4,980,151	364,497	299,057	65,440	215,344	236,096	595,523		695,438
Maryland	5,801,050	21,002,232	15,231,981	1,808,545	1,424,680	383,865	681,864	733,598	2,546,244		4,162,077
Massachusetts	6,475,520	31,549,569	21,691,633	2,451,679	2,105,407	346,272	731,023	2,869,492	3,805,742		4,196,466
Michigan	18,679,748	32,728,673	23,431,476	2,101,266	1,824,755	276,511	1,044,284	965,597	5,186,050		5,572,330
Minnesota	10,108,813	20,060,635	14,369,919	1,254,816	934,823	319,993	849,541	389,004	3,197,355		3,165,931
Mississippi	4,005,786	10,698,977	8,041,738	938,957	751,515	187,442	154,876	195,003	1,368,403		1,896,243
Missouri	5,485,698	17,661,750	12,425,427	1,324,579	1,082,149	242,430	719,473	721,479	2,470,792		3,263,495
Montana	1,005,091	3,795,029	2,570,365	496,586	461,856	34,730	73,425	129,885	524,768		726,534
Nebraska	1,770,897	5,502,509	4,234,708	703,944	640,599	63,345	136,835	87,064	339,958		1,815,942
Nevada	3,272,860	5,885,413	3,863,023	711,280	613,187	98,093	139,089	199,257	972,764		1,288,293
New Hampshire	1,245,235	4,538,618	3,390,492	326,677	247,480	79,197	111,852	322,268	387,329		788,700
New Jersey	11,394,615	37,836,158	24,511,390	3,283,823	2,609,689	674,134	489,434	1,450,944	8,100,567		8,046,168
New Mexico	3,608,081	8,990,959	6,848,007	476,536	352,028	124,508	339,466	270,359	1,056,591		1,881,356
New York	43,731,212	93,055,189	63,267,105	9,919,203	7,706,134	2,213,069	1,530,935	4,355,815	13,982,131		14,336,257
North Carolina	10,675,563	28,806,687	20,024,533	3,421,528	2,748,497	673,031	1,183,314	465,183	3,712,129		6,461,958
North Dakota	701,125	2,789,779	1,979,072	349,149	321,527	27,622	41,084	86,458	334,016		703,394
Ohio	16,368,355	44,185,705	26,931,681	3,617,216	3,187,622	429,594	1,734,151	1,227,158	10,675,499		6,898,362

See footnotes at end of table.

STATE EXPENDITURE, BY CHARACTER AND OBJECT AND BY STATE: 2005 (In thousands of dollars)—Continued

State	Intergovernmental expenditures	Total	Current operation	Direct expenditures — Capital outlay Total	Construction	Other	Assistance and subsidies	Interest on debt	Insurance benefits and repayments	Exhibit: Total salaries and wages
Oklahoma	3,748,031	11,961,991	8,554,042	1,058,219	842,015	216,204	213,542	413,676	1,722,512	2,213,010
Oregon	4,764,615	14,451,939	8,867,218	1,206,070	978,518	227,552	359,858	473,125	3,545,668	3,209,234
Pennsylvania	13,307,866	49,525,392	34,746,650	4,121,923	3,679,371	442,552	1,558,877	1,216,316	7,881,626	7,560,623
Rhode Island	908,479	5,845,162	4,117,470	353,636	285,860	67,776	203,178	249,722	921,156	1,335,201
South Carolina	4,246,231	18,462,765	12,817,721	1,879,066	1,603,861	275,205	775,861	662,014	2,328,103	3,173,974
South Dakota	614,371	2,647,442	1,767,894	454,642	403,098	51,544	48,949	99,715	276,242	513,065
Tennessee	5,705,768	18,283,874	14,653,105	1,352,399	1,150,338	202,061	621,569	176,983	1,479,818	3,157,491
Texas	17,489,900	63,878,746	43,175,280	8,835,806	6,264,873	2,570,933	1,517,063	885,601	9,464,996	12,620,866
Utah	2,189,527	8,959,064	6,554,144	917,337	692,324	225,013	365,548	207,664	914,371	2,060,600
Vermont	1,266,715	3,169,059	2,517,826	210,757	181,035	29,722	114,982	133,557	191,937	618,075
Virginia	9,720,400	23,070,058	16,966,787	1,965,955	1,292,936	673,019	1,121,166	658,576	2,357,574	7,290,101
Washington	7,228,017	25,831,227	16,821,831	2,673,646	2,299,164	374,482	1,124,953	782,789	4,428,008	5,265,925
West Virginia	2,015,637	7,810,491	5,839,650	825,546	706,186	119,360	140,098	196,293	808,904	1,350,678
Wisconsin	9,200,766	19,627,568	12,688,230	1,856,671	1,654,307	202,364	570,276	855,163	3,657,228	3,547,388
Wyoming	1,314,469	2,685,356	1,791,010	439,991	401,402	38,589	32,979	44,251	377,125	512,996

Source: U.S. Department of Commerce, Bureau of the Census, January 2007.
Note: Detail may not add to total due to rounding.

Table 7.29
STATE GENERAL EXPENDITURE, BY FUNCTION AND BY STATE: 2005 (In thousands of dollars)

State	Total general expenditures (a)	Education	Public welfare	Hospitals	Health	Highways	Police	Corrections	Natural resources	Financial administration	Employment security administration
United States	$1,280,597,790	$455,104,018	$368,806,663	$42,751,419	$48,781,368	$90,273,738	$11,362,668	$40,689,366	$18,360,179	$21,044,260	$4,377,732
Alabama	19,110,685	7,950,050	4,972,897	1,313,980	878,991	1,247,394	140,111	422,780	237,518	192,549	99,940
Alaska	7,115,082	1,776,132	1,424,378	26,562	170,981	1,056,195	74,196	196,953	308,722	159,170	41,071
Arizona	21,622,931	7,835,788	6,179,132	62,077	1,270,421	1,738,776	205,139	852,183	278,157	270,712	55,072
Arkansas	12,665,618	5,352,240	3,286,417	572,661	319,624	955,472	99,450	348,766	224,796	322,010	48,902
California	176,704,508	64,791,455	52,582,821	5,372,029	9,146,757	8,939,844	1,242,628	6,020,393	2,856,903	4,019,843	351,766
Colorado	15,683,419	6,511,000	3,689,633	339,022	774,213	1,280,411	109,898	732,757	256,215	278,878	48,237
Connecticut	17,660,401	4,777,881	4,612,174	1,133,684	775,965	841,082	173,987	583,273	98,313	418,447	82,827
Delaware	5,484,231	1,828,920	1,124,234	57,976	304,274	502,562	86,186	218,016	93,378	188,765	14,046
Florida	62,411,360	19,410,331	16,260,738	247,938	2,942,651	5,636,396	479,317	2,307,216	1,680,204	1,048,460	96,386
Georgia	30,489,902	13,388,610	9,359,580	679,517	950,968	917,550	225,940	1,297,881	476,463	378,818	124,737
Hawaii	7,619,876	2,648,452	1,414,573	377,934	444,873	277,887	15,023	170,434	114,099	86,956	43,256
Idaho	5,480,890	2,083,213	1,371,096	41,289	125,138	563,206	43,352	186,581	198,903	135,145	36,195
Illinois	48,299,478	15,138,412	14,529,568	912,544	2,587,033	3,539,632	385,340	1,130,228	352,729	782,076	139,864
Indiana	24,597,962	9,470,593	6,160,681	281,297	624,826	1,901,154	235,532	678,587	265,346	349,109	140,505
Iowa	12,734,942	4,844,083	3,535,475	893,198	194,416	1,428,217	79,795	227,377	234,451	165,282	31,726
Kansas	10,708,221	4,770,153	2,709,078	113,079	185,726	1,220,276	100,289	307,630	183,914	137,370	44,943
Kentucky	17,675,294	6,570,798	5,426,285	743,349	519,203	1,391,479	174,319	432,359	377,876	219,690	54,602
Louisiana	18,809,752	6,725,095	4,531,619	1,622,753	541,726	1,276,992	273,865	637,139	447,673	282,794	124,119
Maine	6,882,857	1,715,308	2,318,631	52,105	489,275	522,015	63,136	123,645	161,376	129,035	31,897
Maryland	24,031,458	7,856,505	5,821,012	482,979	1,611,632	1,975,587	327,570	1,060,157	495,535	443,221	48,401
Massachusetts	34,000,844	8,658,969	11,058,215	426,053	713,527	1,772,974	449,717	978,756	279,886	499,125	62,777
Michigan	45,665,210	20,586,688	12,126,354	1,911,123	972,325	2,769,428	324,129	1,674,237	273,156	473,051	177,851
Minnesota	26,968,760	10,635,653	8,777,381	267,403	542,212	1,939,975	252,355	408,755	458,191	219,411	134,361
Mississippi	13,171,652	4,462,260	4,256,060	747,428	304,589	989,561	79,422	297,852	232,140	78,460	81,290
Missouri	20,676,629	7,262,960	6,315,288	1,182,344	700,460	1,737,885	155,192	632,552	317,359	251,146	39,321
Montana	4,229,665	1,405,749	797,105	38,854	265,455	531,417	53,440	124,632	200,415	147,013	13,983
Nebraska	6,933,448	2,412,456	1,967,208	205,669	340,447	616,226	73,314	194,709	185,367	89,738	55,512
Nevada	8,076,165	3,185,088	1,450,632	174,057	227,007	707,974	95,009	244,584	132,945	98,913	50,993
New Hampshire	5,050,029	1,672,685	1,540,334	52,642	138,832	381,823	39,326	123,618	61,392	60,238	25,308
New Jersey	40,250,422	13,788,329	9,561,576	1,673,764	707,789	2,240,664	510,984	1,383,350	361,596	684,122	64,511
New Mexico	11,542,449	4,077,625	3,067,798	536,201	323,199	672,335	134,753	291,444	182,691	174,881	17,882
New York	114,138,555	32,007,919	42,667,033	4,070,800	5,498,269	4,013,004	834,096	2,575,383	364,328	1,925,202	313,529
North Carolina	35,749,943	14,310,878	9,651,801	1,160,217	1,420,660	3,276,773	376,505	1,175,790	477,382	252,874	162,154
North Dakota	3,156,888	1,128,712	686,714	21,902	57,552	399,881	26,191	51,108	161,848	58,722	5,397
Ohio	49,491,254	17,907,503	14,371,145	1,904,118	2,379,303	3,268,580	260,181	1,538,207	400,742	1,279,181	262,220

See footnotes at end of table.

STATE GENERAL EXPENDITURE, BY FUNCTION AND BY STATE: 2005 (In thousands of dollars) —Continued

State	Total general expenditures (a)	Education	Public welfare	Hospitals	Health	Highways	Police	Corrections	Natural resources	Financial administration	Employment security administration
Oklahoma	13,676,939	5,794,702	3,773,228	148,501	552,638	1,074,227	132,634	520,801	215,400	164,351	43,908
Oregon	15,515,737	5,284,198	3,831,094	793,297	394,269	1,685,460	241,106	544,191	416,183	440,962	74,891
Pennsylvania	53,869,099	16,642,451	19,443,499	2,276,713	1,767,737	4,872,651	615,176	1,713,859	527,883	843,455	152,923
Rhode Island	5,826,068	1,704,258	2,062,958	107,815	183,008	283,239	53,225	165,827	45,676	130,737	6,454
South Carolina	19,121,686	6,478,166	5,244,386	1,051,425	814,337	1,440,673	167,731	403,758	212,574	606,272	81,097
South Dakota	2,985,571	932,993	735,142	49,545	102,468	459,039	29,862	74,141	111,003	63,034	20,185
Tennessee	22,504,710	6,968,027	9,307,577	387,123	981,832	1,631,873	152,976	619,807	291,622	240,626	101,249
Texas	71,887,759	29,349,306	19,728,003	2,940,405	928,865	7,307,878	491,572	3,127,702	1,029,200	598,944	293,605
Utah	10,122,327	4,436,054	2,170,004	669,048	296,852	676,976	127,206	288,684	173,799	229,102	19,190
Vermont	4,206,261	1,854,343	1,100,333	35,917	124,675	281,893	88,946	97,590	87,520	45,325	16,072
Virginia	30,066,152	11,617,866	6,098,229	2,236,882	749,046	2,671,324	587,606	1,285,925	190,761	450,187	162,481
Washington	28,233,163	11,474,257	6,717,693	1,438,941	1,380,246	2,209,778	271,573	901,258	668,704	380,021	132,029
West Virginia	8,953,047	3,170,690	2,370,536	72,699	299,834	967,521	53,005	200,802	163,728	247,662	25,395
Wisconsin	25,168,187	9,259,910	6,082,601	837,817	570,744	1,768,324	118,470	931,325	596,166	253,758	91,580
Wyoming	3,570,304	1,188,304	536,645	6,743	184,498	412,255	31,893	184,364	197,951	49,417	31,092

Source: U.S. Department of Commerce, Bureau of the Census, January 2007.

Note: Detail may not add to total due to rounding.

(a) Does not represent sum of state figures because total includes miscellaneous expenditures not shown.

Table 7.30
STATE DEBT OUTSTANDING AT END OF FISCAL YEAR, BY STATE: 2005
(In thousands of dollars, per capita in dollars)

State	Total	Per capita	Long-term total	Net long-term (a)	
				Short-term	Total
United States	509,384,911	1,718.0	502,752,485	6,632,426	442,375,031
Alabama	5,450,376	1,198.3	5,421,804	28,572	4,581,521
Alaska	1,795,688	2,707.4	1,657,313	138,375	1,616,835
Arizona	6,101,002	1,024.9	6,076,114	24,888	5,452,426
Arkansas..............................	2,229,800	803.3	2,221,235	8,565	2,134,824
California	79,295,644	2,193.3	79,256,644	39,000	78,082,466
Colorado	4,018,277	861.7	3,486,587	531,690	2,346,148
Connecticut	15,156,198	4,329.5	15,150,171	6,027	12,776,532
Delaware..............................	2,127,034	2,526.9	2,081,838	45,196	2,019,326
Florida	22,199,173	1,249.4	22,179,369	19,804	21,708,709
Georgia	6,456,196	706.9	6,456,196	0	6,343,519
Hawaii..................................	5,331,648	4,187.3	5,331,648	0	4,985,437
Idaho...................................	540,989	378.5	533,789	7,200	402,998
Illinois.................................	27,249,427	2,134.6	27,237,841	11,586	26,004,377
Indiana................................	6,896,619	1,100.6	6,876,359	20,260	5,372,113
Iowa	1,963,838	662.2	1,963,838	0	1,493,140
Kansas	4,361,729	1,587.1	4,351,437	10,292	4,169,545
Kentucky	4,038,360	967.8	3,999,164	39,196	3,869,641
Louisiana	7,562,679	1,677.9	7,558,260	4,419	5,493,750
Maine	2,087,073	1,583.3	2,087,073	0	958,008
Maryland	6,555,666	1,172.8	6,274,736	280,930	4,864,420
Massachusetts.....................	28,472,251	4,425.7	28,309,598	162,653	26,516,861
Michigan..............................	11,923,918	1,180.5	11,869,487	54,431	9,879,823
Minnesota	5,234,544	1,021.0	5,234,174	370	4,098,236
Mississippi	3,648,860	1,254.6	3,626,399	22,461	3,574,769
Missouri	7,463,444	1,287.3	7,444,217	19,227	3,022,202
Montana	750,953	803.4	747,925	3,028	688,423
Nebraska..............................	483,740	275.1	482,155	1,585	414,073
Nevada.................................	3,047,607	1,263.4	3,047,607	0	2,828,155
New Hampshire....................	2,722,166	2,083.1	2,715,656	6,510	1,677,999
New Jersey...........................	29,737,079	3,416.8	29,710,267	26,812	24,716,821
New Mexico	3,549,143	1,842.8	3,510,963	38,180	2,816,971
New York	76,966,776	3,984.7	75,989,807	976,969	61,370,337
North Carolina	9,207,808	1,061.7	9,064,667	143,141	8,995,386
North Dakota........................	921,694	1,452.4	818,290	103,404	739,245
Ohio	15,611,007	1,360.9	15,107,621	503,386	14,044,062
Oklahoma	5,987,288	1,689.7	5,967,633	19,655	4,167,042
Oregon	8,264,258	2,271.1	7,463,701	800,557	7,023,937
Pennsylvania	14,307,764	1,153.4	13,127,695	1,180,069	12,288,434
Rhode Island	2,665,391	2,482.7	2,658,713	6,678	2,646,599
South Carolina	11,758,583	2,768.7	11,555,921	202,662	11,315,034
South Dakota........................	595,527	768.5	595,527	0	447,932
Tennessee	2,130,463	357.7	1,720,942	409,521	1,612,882
Texas	13,430,296	585.7	12,810,068	620,228	9,548,811
Utah	2,384,848	957.6	2,357,831	27,017	2,285,805
Vermont	1,211,847	1,947.1	1,146,647	65,200	703,847
Virginia................................	11,379,682	1,504.4	11,357,613	22,069	7,126,366
Washington..........................	11,151,450	1,772.4	11,150,837	613	11,032,896
West Virginia........................	2,561,212	1,411.8	2,561,212	0	2,432,699
Wisconsin............................	10,292,973	1,862.1	10,292,973	0	9,586,233
Wyoming..............................	104,923	206.2	104,923	0	97,416

Source: U.S. Department of Commerce, Bureau of the Census, January 2007.
2005 Population Source: Table NST-EST2006-01 — Annual State Population Estimates: July 1, 2005, Population Division, U.S. Census Bureau, released December 22, 2006.

Note: Detail may not add to total due to rounding.
Key:
(a) Long-term debt outstanding minus long-term debt offsets.

Current Survey of State Pension Funds

By Robin Prunty and Parry Young

Unfunded state pension liabilities continue to grow but should stabilize in the near term. While pension fund performance may improve, states will now grapple with new disclosure requirements related to other post-employment benefits, which may be even larger. Post-retirement benefits will continue to be a factor in determining state credit ratings.

Editor's Note: The material in this article is reproduced with permission of Standard & Poor's, a division of The McGraw-Hill Companies, Inc.

Pension liabilities are a significant credit factor for state governments. Standard & Poor's has traditionally viewed unfunded pension liabilities as debt-like in nature because they represent future payments that usually have some legal basis for funding—whether constitutional, statutory or contract-based. However, a pension liability is subject to significant variation based on the actuarial methods and assumptions used to calculate the liability as well as the performance of any fund assets. There is no consistent funding method or set of assumptions for government pension accounting, which makes the liability difficult to compare across entities. This is an important differentiation from debt, where the obligation is fixed and the annual costs to service the debt are fixed. Fixed costs to service liabilities such as pensions and debt compete with other state funding requirements and budget priorities for limited state revenues. The annual funding burden of pensions as well as funding progress over time can impact state credit ratings.

It is important to consistently monitor the key variables of the issuer's retirement systems. Accordingly, Standard & Poor's reviews pension trends related to funding progress. This analysis includes changes in assets and liabilities, funded ratios, unfunded actuarial accrued liabilities (UAAL) and the relationship of the UAAL to payroll. Pension asset valuations can change, as can actuarial liabilities. The higher contribution requirements that result from unfunded liabilities could make any pre-existing fiscal stress more acute, especially if the increase was dramatic. Therefore, Standard & Poor's will evaluate the sponsor's pension funding strategy, and the current and projected cost implications on its financial profile. As part of this analysis, the track record in funding the actuarial required contributions (ARC) will be reviewed. The historical and forecast trends in pension funding are as important, if not more so, than the specific liability level at a single point in time.

Although U.S. state pension funding levels fell slightly in fiscal 2005, signs are pointing to a possible easing of pressures related to prior pension contribution increases. There is also reason to believe that funded ratios could stabilize and improve over the medium term if investment returns and liability growth meet expectations.

According to Standard & Poor's Ratings Services' current survey of fiscal 2005 data, the mean funded ratio for the principal state pensions was 81.8 percent, compared with 83.5 percent in fiscal 2004. The funded ratio, or actuarial value of assets divided by the actuarial accrued liabilities (AAL), is one measure of the health of a pension fund. For public pension funds, this measure has fallen dramatically from 2000, when average levels exceeded 100 percent. Above-average investment returns generated by pension funds over the past few years, however, could make this latest decline in funded ratios only a temporary setback.

The fiscal 2005 survey includes the principal state pension funds, which are generally composed of two major plans: (1) a public employees' retirement system, including employees from both the state and municipal jurisdictions, and (2) a teachers' retirement system. In some cases, a state could simply have one large plan covering all government workers; in other cases, it may sponsor a third significant plan. The pension liability statistics cited in this report are largely as of fiscal 2005, the latest year with substantially complete data available.

State Pension Funding History

State pension funding ratios made strong gains in the 1990s, averaging more than 100 percent by 2000 compared with roughly 80 percent a decade earlier. Above-average investment returns, particularly from equities, contributed to this rapid increase. From 1990–2000, the average annual increase of the S&P 500 Index of domestic equities was 15 percent compared with an average actuarial return assumption of about 8 percent. Public pension fund allocations to domestic equity rose to about 60 percent from 40 percent over the same time period. This combination of factors, coupled with strong fixed-income returns, enabled public funds to exceed their investment return assumptions and achieve the actuarial gains that led to the dramatically improved funded ratios.

In the first part of this decade, however, the funded ratio climate shifted quite rapidly when pension funds suffered a number of setbacks. In terms of investment yields, the S&P 500 fell 16 percent in fiscal 2001 and another 19 percent in fiscal 2002. In addition to falling asset values, a number of factors led to upward pressure on liabilities, including demographic changes such as members living longer and the phasing in of previously granted benefit enhancements. Not surprisingly, the combination of these negative effects on assets and liabilities resulted in average state pension funding levels falling to 83.5 percent as of June 30, 2004, from their previous high point four years earlier. The fiscal 2005 survey reports a further decline in funded ratios to 81.8 percent despite solid investment returns on a market value basis. One possible explanation for this occurrence is that in fiscal 2005, with the five-year smoothing of asset values used by most public funds, the earlier investment losses of 2001 and 2002 were still acting as a brake on the actuarial value of assets.

Contribution Rates are Easing

Another important measure related to public pension funds is reflected in the trend in employer contribution rates (employee rates tend to remain at a fixed level), which can cause budget pressures. A collection of U.S. Census data on public pension funds compiled by the National Association of State Retirement Administrators (NASRA) suggests that the rapid increase in employer rates experienced earlier in the decade may have been reversed in 2005. According to NASRA's findings, average employer contribution rates fell between fiscals 1998 and 2002, then subsequently rose by almost 50 percent in fiscal years 2003 and 2004 following the effectiveness of actuarial losses. Despite large investment losses in 2001 and 2002, employer contribution rates fell in those years due to the lags (such as asset smoothing and other factors) built into the actuarial models. The jump in rates in 2003 and 2004—even though investment returns improved—again reflected the effects of actuarial assumptions and methods. The NASRA data show employer rates easing again in 2005, however, declining by about 7 percent. This provides a degree of budgetary relief.

State Pension Liabilities and Debt

Table A displays selected pension and debt information for each state. The data are mainly as of fiscal 2005, which is the most recent year with substantially complete data available. The pension data are combined for the principal, state-sponsored, defined-benefit pension funds: generally the public employees' retirement system, including state and local employees in most cases, plus the teachers' retirement system. In some cases, a state may have just one combined system for all employees, while others may have a third significant system that is included in several cases. State sponsors have varying degrees of responsibility in relation to the funding of these pension plans. For example, in the case of multi-employer agent systems, the state would make contributions to plans that include its employees only, with local agencies contributing to their respective plans. For multi-employer cost-sharing systems, which can include a number of local jurisdictions like school districts with contributions from both employers and employees, the state may be a nonemployer contributor. Therefore, with some exceptions, states are generally not directly responsible for the full liabilities of these pension systems.

The pension information includes the systems' funded ratio for each state and the unfunded AAL (UAAL); the UAAL is also expressed on a per capita basis. Tax-supported debt is shown for each state in total as well as on a per capita basis. Pension and debt figures are combined on a per capita basis and then expressed as a percent of per capita income as a measure of resources to meet these obligations.

Compared with fiscal 2000, when an average state pension fund had little or no unfunded liabilities (with the exception of certain historically weak plans), the gross UAAL had increased to about $330 billion as of fiscal 2005 from $284 billion in 2004. On a state-by-state basis, the mean UAAL per capita equaled $1,378 in 2005, compared with $1,183 the prior year. State debt rose to $313.5 billion in 2005 from $288 billion in 2004, while 2005 mean state debt was $933 per capita, compared with $867 a year earlier. When evaluating the debt structure of state and local governments, Standard & Poor's does not add the UAAL in with other debt in its presentation of debt statistics. Because of its debt-like aspect, however, the UAAL factors into the analysis as an additional long-term liability. The total per capita UAAL and tax-supported debt mean for this survey was $2,310, up from the prior-year level of $2,050. In relation to the resources available to service these requirements, this measure divided by per capita income had a mean of 6.8 percent in 2005 compared with 6.3 percent in 2004.

Table A
STATE RETIREMENT SYSTEM AND DEBT STATISTICS: 2005

State	GO rating	Funded ratio (%)	UAAL (mil $)	UAAL PC ($)	Total debt (mil $)	Debt PC ($)	Debt PC + PCUL ($)	PC income ($)	(Debt PC + PCUL) ÷ PC income (%)
Alabama	AA	83.4%	$4,827	$1,059	$2,245	$493	$1,552	$29,136	5.3%
Alaska	AA	63.9	4,123	6,212	1,327	2,000	8,212	35,612	23.1
Arizona	AA (ICR)	85.2	4,251	716	2,975	501	1,217	30,267	4.0
Arkansas	AA	80.8	3,191	1,148	607	218	1,367	26,874	5.1
California	A+	86.7	46,932	1,299	53,212	1,473	2,772	37,036	7.5
Colorado	AA- (lease)	73.2	12,448	2,668	61	13	2,681	37,946	7.1
Connecticut	AA	58.3	14,801	4,217	9,900	2,820	7,037	47,819	14.7
Delaware	AAA	101.6	(87)	(104)	1,830	2,169	2,066	35,861	5.8
Florida	AAA	107.3	(7,614)	(428)	17,455	981	553	33,219	1.7
Georgia	AAA	100.1	(79)	(9)	6,882	759	750	31,121	2.4
Hawaii	AA	68.6	4,071	3,193	4,253	3,335	6,528	34,539	18.9
Idaho	AA- (lease)	93.5	570	399	212	148	547	28,158	1.9
Illinois	AA	58.4	31,340	2,455	25,566	2,003	4,459	36,120	12.3
Indiana	AA+ (ICR)	66.5	8,384	1,337	2,376	379	1,716	31,276	5.5
Iowa	AA+ (ICR)	88.7	2,289	772	359	121	893	32,315	2.8
Kansas	AA+ (ICR)	68.8	5,152	1,877	460	168	2,045	32,836	6.2
Kentucky	AA- (ICR)	78.9	7,239	1,735	3,423	820	2,555	28,513	9.0
Louisiana	A	63.5	10,791	2,385	3,311	732	3,117	24,820	12.6
Maine	AA-	76.0	2,802	2,120	753	570	2,690	31,252	8.6
Maryland	AAA	88.7	4,315	771	5,892	1,052	1,823	41,760	4.4
Massachusetts	AA	73.0	12,945	2,023	16,050	2,508	4,531	44,289	10.2
Michigan	AA	79.4	12,498	1,235	5,826	576	1,811	33,116	5.5
Minnesota	AAA	87.3	4,317	841	3,565	695	1,536	37,373	4.1
Mississippi	AA	72.4	6,546	2,241	3,099	1,061	3,302	25,318	13.0
Missouri	AAA	83.2	6,378	1,100	2,634	454	1,554	31,899	4.9
Montana	AA-	78.3	1,570	1,678	213	228	1,906	29,387	6.5
Nebraska	AA+ (ICR)	85.6	899	511	43	24	536	33,616	1.6
Nevada	AA+	75.6	5,722	2,370	975	404	2,773	35,883	7.7
New Hampshire	AA	66.4	2,011	1,535	532	406	1,941	38,408	5.1
New Jersey	AA	87.0	11,980	1,374	24,410	2,800	4,174	43,771	9.5
New Mexico	AA+	81.2	4,047	2,099	1,970	1,022	3,120	27,644	11.3
New York	AA	99.7	561	29	40,128	2,084	2,113	40,507	5.2
North Carolina	AAA	106.5	(3,046)	(351)	6,438	741	391	30,553	1.3
North Dakota	AA (ICR)	81.3	621	975	245	385	1,360	31,395	4.3
Ohio	AA+	79.7	29,793	2,599	8,470	739	3,338	32,478	10.3
Oklahoma	AA	56.9	9,933	2,800	1,031	291	3,090	29,330	10.5
Oregon	AA-	104.2	(2,089)	(574)	5,492	1,508	935	32,103	2.9
Pennsylvania	AA	86.6	12,065	971	10,102	813	1,783	34,897	5.1
Rhode Island	AA	59.4	3,786	3,518	1,601	1,488	5,005	36,153	13.8
South Carolina	AA+	80.3	5,115	1,202	2,631	618	1,820	28,352	6.4
South Dakota	AA (ICR)	96.6	191	246	189	244	489	31,614	1.5
Tennessee	AA+	98.7	366	61	1,213	203	265	31,107	0.9
Texas	AA	88.5	14,330	627	4,604	201	828	32,462	2.6
Utah	AAA	92.2	1,101	446	1,862	754	1,200	28,061	4.3
Vermont	AA+	93.8	164	263	489	785	1,048	33,327	3.1
Virginia	AAA	90.3	4,267	564	5,748	760	1,323	38,390	3.4
Washington	AA	73.8	6,441	1,012	10,583	1,663	2,676	35,409	7.6
West Virginia	AA-	47.1	5,660	3,115	1,542	849	3,964	27,215	14.6
Wisconsin	AA-	99.5	372	67	8,725	1,576	1,643	33,565	4.9
Wyoming	AA (ICR)	95.1	248	487	0	0	487	36,778	1.3
Mean		81.8	6,371	1,378	6,270	933	2,310	33,418	6.8
Median		82.3	4,259	1,124	2,633	740	1,822	32,657	5.4

Source: Standard & Poor's Ratings Services.
Note: The pension fund data for most states include the two principal state-sponsored retirement systems (i.e. public employees and teachers) or, in a few cases, a third large system. For 19 states, the data represent a single, all-inclusive system.

Key:
UAAL — Unfunded actuarial accrued liability.
UAAL PC — Unfunded actuarial accrued liability per capita.
Debt PC — Debt per capita.
PCUL — Per capita unfunded liability.
ICR — Issuer credit rating.

Other Post Employment Liabilities Will Be More Transparent

The funding of Other Post Employment Benefits (OPEB) has received a high profile due to the imminent implementation of new Governmental Accounting Standards Board (GASB) 45 accounting rules for OPEB reporting. OPEB liabilities are not new, and in fact have been a part of the state government cost structure for a long time, with the most significant cost being retiree health care. These benefits have traditionally been accounted for on a pay-as-you-go basis by states. Now, under GASB 45, they will be accounted for on an accrual basis, similar to pension liabilities. GASB 45 essentially is a new way to account for and report on these liabilities, but there is no requirement to fund the liability at this time.

GASB 45 will bring greater transparency to the financial disclosure surrounding post-employment benefits. Employers will be required to have an actuarial valuation completed to determine the OPEB liability and the annual required contribution. The new reporting will provide important information on future cash flow requirements for the employer. For governments with fiscal years that end in June, reporting under this statement will be required beginning in fiscal 2008.

OPEB liabilities are likely to be more volatile than pension liabilities over time. In addition to variation in actuarial methods and assumptions, OPEB liabilities factor in future health care cost inflation assumptions, which have varied over time. We've already seen wide ranges of liabilities for the same OPEB plan in subsequent actuarial valuations due to changes in assumptions. Further, there are wide spreads of estimated OPEB liabilities for a single employer, depending on the discount rate assumption used. The discount rate is based on the estimated long-term yield on the investments expected to be used to finance the payment of benefits. This rate will be based on the employer's method of funding OPEB liabilities, and whether there are assets available to fund them.

Disclosure on the future costs of these benefits can be viewed as a tool to better manage OPEBs over the long term. However, the rapidly increasing payment schedules (even on a pay-as-you-go basis) that almost all governments are facing—due not only to health care inflation but also to aging baby boomers—could strain budgets and balance sheets over the longer term. Failure to fund the actuarial required contribution or at least establish a plan to do so over time indicates that the benefit structure may be unaffordable. The two likely scenarios for managing the future cost pressure are either lowering liabilities through benefits modifications or boosting assets available to fund benefits. States are still in the development stages of determining what their exact OPEB liability is—as well as what their options are to mitigate its effects.

Pension Liability Outlook

If we look at prospective public pension funding levels from the standpoint of one key variable—investment return performance—recent investment results would suggest that the funding climate should improve. With actual market returns exceeding investment return assumptions, on average, for the past three fiscal years, we should see an increase in the actuarial value of assets in fiscal 2006. If the growth in benefit liabilities does not exceed expectations, the trend in funded ratios should stabilize or even begin to rise modestly. Because about 60 percent of large public funds use five-year smoothing to value assets, the investment losses from 2002 will continue to impact the June 30, 2006, actuarial valuations. It is only after fiscal 2006 that funds will be fully out of the woods from this drag on assets.

The risks to stabilization or improvement in pension funding in fiscal 2007 and beyond will depend on asset and liability performance. On the asset side, the uncertainty of future investment returns is the primary factor. Any shortfall compared with the assumed rate will create additional actuarial losses. Assets would also be adversely affected if less than the full annual required contributions are not made. Regarding investment returns, some systems have lowered their investment rate of return assumption, either toward or below 8 percent, with the effect of increasing liabilities. On the liability side, any benefit increases would increase liabilities. Demographic changes would impact liabilities to the extent that longevity continues to increase and as known or anticipated mortality experience is reflected in the actuarial models.

About the Authors

Robin Prunty is a director at Standard & Poor's Ratings Services. She is an analytic leader for state credit ratings and issues related to pension and other post-employment benefits. She holds a B.S. in economics from Siena College and an M.P.A. from the Rockefeller College of Public Affairs and Policy, University at Albany.

Parry Young is a director at Standard & Poor's Ratings Services. He is the sector leader for issues related to pension and other post-employment benefits, including pension fund ratings. He has been an adviser to the GFOA Committee on Retirement and Benefits Administration. He holds a B.A. from New York University and an M.B.A. from the City University of New York.

Table 7.31
NUMBER AND MEMBERSHIP OF STATE AND LOCAL GOVERNMENT EMPLOYEE-RETIREMENT SYSTEMS BY STATE: FISCAL YEAR 2004–05

State and type of government	Number of systems	Membership			Total beneficiaries receiving periodic benefit payments
		Total	Active members	Inactive members	
United States	2,656	17,931,572	14,116,352	3,815,220	6,903,407
State	222	16,207,122	12,569,872	3,637,250	5,846,393
Local..................................	2,434	1,724,450	1,546,480	177,970	1,057,014
Alabama	12	255,562	221,650	33,912	94,435
Alaska	5	69,425	47,402	22,023	30,882
Arizona	7	406,037	253,770	152,267	96,307
Arkansas............................	38	140,579	120,513	20,066	46,304
California	61	2,145,116	1,706,590	438,526	892,127
Colorado	64	330,627	209,893	120,734	88,282
Connecticut	63	140,012	126,406	13,606	81,029
Delaware	6	43,277	42,057	1,220	22,278
Florida	158	764,886	686,727	78,159	263,264
Georgia	31	556,429	385,450	170,979	129,824
Hawaii................................	1	67,948	63,010	4,938	33,300
Idaho..................................	4	72,913	64,445	8,468	27,372
Illinois	371	914,519	611,598	302,921	352,921
Indiana...............................	76	279,418	232,306	47,112	99,553
Iowa	9	231,513	165,708	65,805	83,835
Kansas	8	191,357	149,907	41,450	71,278
Kentucky	21	302,577	216,787	85,790	108,203
Louisiana	34	258,247	225,521	32,726	131,701
Maine	1	49,107	42,859	6,248	24,388
Maryland	13	278,924	228,953	49,971	130,920
Massachusetts.....................	100	371,910	298,449	73,461	169,298
Michigan............................	140	474,053	441,879	32,174	265,072
Minnesota	147	502,921	297,245	205,676	143,200
Mississippi	4	282,286	157,900	124,386	66,915
Missouri	62	313,855	267,078	46,777	124,570
Montana	9	73,607	51,905	21,702	28,300
Nebraska............................	13	78,990	60,452	18,538	19,843
Nevada	2	103,253	94,057	9,196	28,521
New Hampshire...................	3	53,346	52,660	686	19,539
New Jersey..........................	10	526,872	459,717	67,155	215,937
New Mexico	5	155,868	127,142	28,726	47,931
New York	14	1,286,501	1,153,311	133,190	732,861
North Carolina	10	537,774	466,943	70,831	178,595
North Dakota......................	12	35,006	28,971	6,035	12,436
Ohio	6	1,178,882	683,872	495,010	353,660
Oklahoma	12	172,322	152,024	20,298	79,937
Oregon	4	199,579	151,526	48,053	107,274
Pennsylvania	925	540,371	470,334	70,037	319,197
Rhode Island	14	46,923	40,795	6,128	26,324
South Carolina	6	372,147	215,760	156,387	104,201
South Dakota......................	5	50,352	36,792	13,560	18,355
Tennessee	14	251,487	230,296	21,191	109,740
Texas	48	1,338,073	1,214,532	123,541	392,912
Utah	6	124,020	97,404	26,616	34,577
Vermont	5	33,188	25,408	7,780	10,045
Virginia..............................	14	489,724	385,182	104,542	149,163
Washington.........................	27	301,468	265,558	35,910	124,745
West Virginia......................	41	68,463	56,976	11,487	47,160
Wisconsin...........................	3	414,885	281,754	133,131	144,206
Wyoming............................	6	43,170	37,306	5,864	17,479
Dist. of Columbia	6	11,803	11,572	231	3,211

Source: U.S. Department of Commerce, Bureau of the Census, September 2006.

Note: Caution should be used when comparing current year estimates to historic estimates prior to 2004. Estimates presented prior to 2004 were not based on a probability sample. Also, data users are warned that the change from book to market value-based reporting in the 2000 to 2003 timespan makes historic data comparisons invalid. As a result of this change in reporting, note that the imputation methodology was changed in 2002.

Table 7.32
FINANCES OF STATE-ADMINISTERED EMPLOYEE RETIREMENT SYSTEMS, BY STATE: FISCAL YEAR 2005
(In thousands of dollars)

State	Receipts during fiscal year					Payments during fiscal year			
			Government contributions						
	Total	Employee contributions	From states	From local governments	Earnings on investments	Total	Benefits	Withdrawals	Other
United States	$293,403,252	$26,787,379	$23,732,936	$21,980,850	$220,902,087	$126,790,593	$115,241,152	$3,120,814	$8,428,627
Alabama	3,321,021	425,559	410,238	84,443	2,400,781	1,572,199	1,468,160	71,383	32,656
Alaska	1,137,504	127,639	79,221	129,315	801,329	775,137	719,372	14,694	41,071
Arizona	3,213,206	509,799	86,318	356,081	2,261,008	1,887,194	1,744,163	68,547	74,484
Arkansas	1,946,728	96,126	151,629	306,652	1,392,321	831,644	721,618	6,123	103,903
California	57,760,279	5,523,623	3,696,855	5,513,812	43,025,989	19,221,005	15,594,861	315,172	3,310,972
Colorado	5,605,354	513,675	203,658	450,797	4,437,224	2,426,241	2,060,968	162,220	203,053
Connecticut	1,784,465	330,228	603,746	47,452	803,039	1,953,449	1,936,628	15,013	1,808
Delaware	725,762	42,921	129,010	8,708	545,123	326,959	300,693	2,819	23,447
Florida	13,166,727	30,556	518,488	1,669,084	10,948,599	4,622,810	4,305,857	0	316,953
Georgia	6,039,282	522,143	852,638	251,330	4,413,171	2,794,981	2,662,201	57,769	75,011
Hawaii..................	1,319,885	57,055	253,112	75,605	934,113	715,321	676,316	3,442	35,563
Idaho...................	1,190,400	145,906	79,011	157,418	808,065	399,478	359,611	0	39,867
Illinois	11,605,028	1,496,825	1,656,273	605,011	7,846,919	5,796,997	5,412,805	141,195	242,997
Indiana.................	2,940,915	290,610	656,769	179,515	1,814,021	1,326,590	1,168,988	47,003	110,599
Iowa	2,744,079	235,636	76,086	292,890	2,139,467	1,121,758	969,871	44,270	107,617
Kansas	1,814,257	227,157	195,034	98,918	1,293,148	875,300	799,116	46,774	29,410
Kentucky	3,111,093	559,922	550,064	0	2,001,107	2,027,958	1,939,031	34,888	54,039
Louisiana	5,306,743	598,709	991,564	255,271	3,461,199	2,484,696	2,172,687	95,222	216,787
Maine	1,434,799	138,623	291,615	0	1,004,561	557,774	470,218	15,975	71,581
Maryland	3,733,266	210,575	690,248	0	2,832,443	1,809,438	1,714,656	15,002	79,780
Massachusetts.......	6,589,680	963,548	1,136,535	113,632	4,375,965	2,591,205	2,361,353	68,613	161,239
Michigan..............	7,798,601	553,700	199,408	820,302	6,225,191	3,631,711	3,469,458	18,785	143,468
Minnesota	5,186,782	538,386	146,372	435,420	4,066,604	2,656,342	2,470,438	43,793	142,111
Mississippi	2,505,276	367,392	198,666	314,891	1,624,327	1,327,134	1,169,305	71,163	86,666
Missouri................	5,252,245	500,985	371,776	547,212	3,832,272	2,198,184	1,923,263	50,205	224,716
Montana	778,877	131,814	62,748	88,091	496,224	376,781	341,782	20,393	14,606
Nebraska..............	830,224	108,258	38,675	92,001	591,290	253,725	208,451	19,605	25,669
Nevada	2,488,595	66,930	149,043	726,674	1,545,948	814,736	740,208	14,499	60,029
New Hampshire....	643,454	145,706	33,176	58,455	406,117	355,916	296,353	22,002	37,561
New Jersey	7,623,968	1,348,126	81,376	219,914	5,974,552	5,740,742	5,593,462	100,210	47,070
New Mexico	2,396,495	330,610	285,241	151,462	1,629,182	997,105	892,948	52,862	51,295
New York	19,022,589	397,087	1,392,752	1,769,910	15,462,840	10,217,699	9,809,910	60,306	347,483
North Carolina......	7,687,268	947,633	177,474	214,067	6,348,094	2,992,219	2,816,677	160,918	14,624
North Dakota........	353,424	44,491	14,507	46,566	247,860	160,118	135,785	7,187	17,146
Ohio	20,126,673	2,380,629	1,777,117	1,713,240	14,255,687	8,055,599	7,322,045	364,403	369,151
Oklahoma	2,632,014	327,832	347,285	336,285	1,620,612	1,375,640	1,238,215	53,533	83,892
Oregon	6,800,940	9,590	785,754	9,590	5,996,006	2,769,781	2,364,401	60,242	345,138
Pennsylvania	11,865,429	1,114,054	331,112	224,452	10,195,811	5,858,745	5,571,214	29,466	258,065
Rhode Island	1,108,788	154,363	132,676	73,006	748,743	594,531	536,865	10,731	46,935
South Carolina	2,917,135	495,012	229,379	409,108	1,783,636	1,899,146	1,705,468	80,906	112,772
South Dakota........	1,071,911	89,159	29,034	48,441	905,277	243,689	219,923	20,840	2,926
Tennessee	2,710,917	215,606	629,250	0	1,866,061	1,081,173	1,028,917	30,816	21,440
Texas	18,830,943	2,312,366	1,589,529	934,282	13,994,766	8,054,437	7,467,998	414,876	171,563
Utah	2,471,783	34,738	446,182	0	1,990,863	611,309	578,711	7,045	25,553
Vermont	348,753	43,674	68,998	0	236,081	156,868	117,285	3,006	36,577
Virginia................	6,238,948	64,856	377,706	1,025,699	4,770,687	2,218,875	1,945,471	84,731	188,673
Washington...........	5,917,209	231,498	215,231	363	5,470,117	2,293,627	2,086,593	43,682	163,352
West Virginia........	1,361,294	107,987	149,397	572,993	530,917	598,761	556,577	12,439	29,745
Wisconsin.............	9,248,528	605,184	151,267	493,382	7,998,695	2,897,600	2,857,800	25,000	14,800
Wyoming..............	693,716	72,878	13,693	59,110	548,035	240,266	216,456	11,046	12,764

Source: U.S. Department of Commerce, Bureau of the Census, October 2006.
Note: Caution should be used when comparing current year estimates to historic estimates prior to 2004. Estimates presented prior to 2004 were not based on a probability sample. Also, data users are warned that the change from book to market value-based reporting in the 2000 to 2003 timespan makes historic data comparisons invalid. As a result of this change in reporting, note that the imputation methodology was changed in 2002.

Table 7.33
NATIONAL SUMMARY OF FINANCES OF STATE-ADMINISTERED EMPLOYEE RETIREMENT SYSTEMS:
SELECTED YEARS, 2002–2005

	Amount (in millions of dollars)			Percentage distribution		
	2004–05	2003–04	2002–03	2004–05	2003–04	2002–03
Total receipts	351,454,866	407,335,732	147,747,004	100.00	100.00	100.0
Employee contributions	31,324,625	30,785,801	28,843,747	8.91	7.56	19.5
Government contributions	59,197,693	60,995,984	46,212,289	16.84	14.97	31.3
From State Government	24,050,633	31,159,060	19,567,749	6.84	7.65	13.2
From Local Government	35,147,060	29,836,924	26,644,540	10.00	7.32	18.0
Earnings on investments	260,932,548	315,553,947	72,690,968	74.24	77.47	49.2
Total payments	155,325,508	145,449,071	134,844,916	100.00	100.00	100.0
Benefits paid	141,341,189	133,106,842	122,306,460	91.00	91.51	90.7
Withdrawals	3,777,732	4,430,593	4,891,041	2.43	3.05	3.6
Other payments	10,206,587	7,911,636	7,647,415	6.57	5.44	5.7
Total cash and investment holdings at end of fiscal year	2,657,525,869	2,495,352,487	2,172,001,788	100.00	100.00	100.0
Cash and short-term investments	89,741,655	84,811,257	99,812,059	3.38	3.40	4.6
Total securities	2,355,561,132	2,213,581,060	1,891,957,833	88.64	88.71	87.1
Government securities	231,482,987	223,412,871	222,534,967	8.71	8.95	10.3
Federal government	229,937,493	215,159,724	221,684,160	8.65	8.62	10.2
United States Treasury	169,551,462	134,943,113	161,289,726	6.38	5.41	7.4
Federal agency	60,386,031	80,216,611	60,394,434	2.27	3.21	2.8
State and local government	1,545,494	8,253,147	850,807	0.06	0.33	0.0
Nongovernment securities	2,124,078,145	1,990,168,189	1,669,422,866	79.93	79.75	76.9
Corporate bonds	390,101,290	421,340,923	317,074,720	14.68	16.89	14.6
Corporate stocks	1,033,302,329	930,524,635	811,107,881	38.88	37.29	37.3
Mortgages	11,674,518	17,754,616	22,795,540	0.44	0.71	1.1
Funds held in trust	79,922,026	52,227,528	67,250,825	3.01	2.09	3.1
Foreign and international	375,064,878	311,642,945	266,812,023	14.11	12.49	12.3
Other nongovernmental	234,013,104	256,677,542	184,381,877	8.81	10.29	8.5
Other investments	212,223,082	196,960,170	180,231,896	7.99	7.89	8.3
Real property	41,978,140	43,715,769	46,766,729	1.58	1.75	2.2
Miscellaneous investments	170,244,942	153,244,401	133,465,167	6.41	6.14	6.1

Source: U.S. Department of Commerce, Bureau of the Census, October 2006.
Note: Caution should be used when comparing current year estimates to historic estimates prior to 2004. Estimates presented prior to 2004 were not based on a probability sample. Also, data users are warned that the change from book to market value-based reporting in the 2000 to 2003 timespan makes historic data comparisons invalid. As a result of this change in reporting, note that the imputation methodology was changed in 2002.

Table 7.34
CUMULATIVE LOTTERY CONTRIBUTIONS TO BENEFICIARIES
(From start up to June 30, 2006) (In millions of dollars)

State or other jurisdiction	Start up year	Programs receiving funds	Cumulative total (in millions)
United States total..............			$229,571.53
Alabama		...............................(a)..............................	
Alaska		...............................(a)..............................	
Arizona	1982	Local Transportation Assistance Fund	$558.00
		County Assistance Fund	$152.64
		Heritage Fund	$298.53
		Economic Development Fund	$50.16
		Mass Transit	$62.35
		Healthy Arizona	$40.65
		General Fund (by Category)	
		Education	$445.64
		Health and Welfare	$178.27
		Protection and Safety	$82.12
		General Government	$46.13
		Inspection and Regulation	$7.79
		Natural Resources	$6.82
		Department of Gaming (Responsible Gaming Support)	$0.60
		Court Appointed Special Advocate Fund (Unclaimed prizes)	$28.76
		Clean Air Fund (Unclaimed prizes)	$0.50
		State General Fund (Unclaimed prizes)	$1.50
		Total	$1,960.46
Arkansas.............................		...............................(a)..............................	
California	1985	Education	$18,457.56
Colorado.............................	1983	Capital Construction Fund	$439.80
		Division of Parks and Outdoor Recreation	$161.50
		Conservation Trust Fund	$646.30
		Great Outdoors Colorado Trust Fund	$461.60
		General Fund	$1.30
		School Fund	$28.90
		Total	$1,739.40
Connecticut	1972	General Fund (to benefit education, roads, health and hospitals, public safety, etc.)	$5,847.68
Delaware..............................	1975	General Fund	$2,321.50
		Health & Social Services—Problem Gambler Programs	$13.18
		Total	$2,334.68
Florida	1987	Education Enhancement Trust Fund	$15,203.00
Georgia	1993	HOPE Scholarships	$3,580.43
		Pre-Kindergarten Program	$2,695.86
		Capital Outlay and Technology for Primary and Secondary Schools	$1,800.00
		Total	$8,076.29
Hawaii..................................		...............................(a)..............................	
Idaho....................................	1989	Public Schools (K-12)	$150.28
		Public Buildings	$150.28
		Total	$300.56
Illinois.................................	1974	Illinois Common School Fund (K-12)	$12,896.00
Indiana.................................	1989	Build Indiana Fund	$1,920.40
		Teachers' Retirement Fund	$462.60
		Police & Fire Pension Relief Fund	$276.30
		Help America Vote Act	$1.80
		Total	$2,661.10
Iowa	1985	Iowa Plan (economic development)	$170.32
		CLEAN Fund (environment and agriculture)	$35.89
		Gambler's Treatment Program	$12.08
		Special Appropriations	$13.77
		Sales Tax	$135.98
		General Fund	$647.23
		Total	$1,015.27
Kansas	1987	Economic Development Initiatives Fund	$646.99
		Correctional Institutions Building Fund	$76.28
		County Reappraisal Project (FY 88–90)	$17.20
		Juvenile Detention Facilities Fund	$25.19
		State General Fund (FY 1995–2004)	$121.99
		Problem Gambling Grant Fund	$0.48
		Total	$888.13

See footnotes at end of table.

CUMULATIVE LOTTERY CONTRIBUTIONS TO BENEFICIARIES — Continued
(From start up to June 30, 2006) (In millions of dollars)

State or other jurisdiction	Start up year	Programs receiving funds	Cumulative total (in millions)
Kentucky	1989	Education	$214.00
		Vietnam Veterans	$32.00
		General Fund	$1,387.60
		Post-Secondary & College Scholarships	$609.60
		Affordable Housing Trust Fund	$20.80
		Literacy Programs & Early Childhood Reading	$18.00
		Total	$2,282.00
Louisiana	1991	Various State Agencies	$147.30
		State General Fund	$69.20
		Minimum Foundation Program—	
		Funding elementary & secondary education in public schools	$1,512.25
		Problem Gambling	$5.50
		Total	$1,734.25
Maine	1974	General Fund	$732.00
		Outdoor Heritage Fund	$11.91
		Total	$743.91
Maryland	1973	General Fund	$9,270.87
		Subdivisions (for one year only FY 84–85)	$31.25
		Stadium Authority	$442.63
		Total	$9,744.75
Massachusetts	1972	Cities and Towns	$12,028.14
		Arts Council	$189.90
		General Fund	$2,991.44
		Compulsive Gamblers	$10.46
		Total	$15,219.94
Michigan	1972	Education (K-12)	$12,800.00
Minnesota	1989	General Fund	$866.49
		Environmental and Natural Resources Trust Fund	$381.40
		Game & Fish Fund	$61.47
		Natural Resources Fund	$61.47
		Other State Programs	$36.70
		Compulsive Gambling	$20.50
		Total	$1,428.03
Mississippi	............(a)............		
Missouri	1986	Public Education	$1,915.34
		General Revenue Fund (1986–1993)	$542.54
		Total	$2,457.88
Montana	1987	Property Tax Relief	$15.34
		Elementary and Secondary Schools	$34.09
		Juvenile Detention	$2.53
		General Fund	$78.20
		Study of Socioeconomic Impact on Gambling	$0.10
		Total	$130.26
Nebraska	1993	Compulsive Gamblers Assistance Fund	$5.51
		Education Innovation Fund	$106.37
		Environmental Trust Fund	$103.81
		Solid Waste Landfill Closure Assistance Fund	$18.46
		General Fund	$5.00
		State Fair Support & Improvement Fund	$3.79
		Nebraska Scholarship Fund	$15.90
		Total	$258.84
Nevada	............(a)............		
New Hampshire	1964	Education	$1,080.10
New Jersey	1970	Education and Institutions	$15,571.20
New Mexico	1996	Public School Capital Outlay	$66.55
		Lottery Tuition Fund	$217.24
		Total	$283.79
New York	1967	Education	$27,000.00
North Carolina	2006	Instant sales began March 2006, online sales October 2006	N.A.
North Dakota	2004	Compulsive Gambling Fund	$0.40
		State General Fund	$7.27
		Total	$7.67
Ohio	1974	Education	$14,300.00

See footnotes at end of table.

CUMULATIVE LOTTERY CONTRIBUTIONS TO BENEFICIARIES — Continued
(From start up to June 30, 2006) (In millions of dollars)

State or other jurisdiction	Start up year	Programs receiving funds	Cumulative total (in millions)
Oklahoma	2005	Education	$68.95
Oregon	1985	Economic Development	$1,570.00
		Public Education	$2,715.00
		Natural Resource Programs	$367.00
		Total	$4,652.00
Pennsylvania	1972	Older Pennsylvanians	$14,650.00
Rhode Island	1974	General Fund	$2,600.00
South Carolina	2002	Education Lottery Fund	$1,190.41
South Dakota	1989	General Fund	$376.35
		Capital Construction Fund	$20.98
		Property Tax Reduction Fund	$1,044.97
		Grant to Human Services	$1.92
		Total	$1,444.22
Tennessee	2004	Lottery for Education Account	$620.56
		After School Program	$16.32
		Total	$636.88
Texas	1992	General Revenue Fund	$4,997.82
		Foundation School Fund	$7,629.34
		Multicategorical Teaching Hospital	$100.00
		Tertiary Care Facility Account	$131.07
		Health and Human Services Commission's Graduate Medical Program	$40.00
		Total	$12,898.23
Utah		——————————(a)——————————	
Vermont	1978	General Fund	$212.46
		Education Fund	$128.70
		Total	$341.16
Virginia	1988	General Fund (FY 1989–1998)	$2,788.42
		Direct Aid to Public Education K-12 (FY 1999–present)	$3,003.89
		Literary Fund (primarily for school construction additions and renovations)	$155.63
		Debt set-off collection	$13.10
		Total	$5,961.04
Washington	1982	General Fund	$1,836.13
		Education Funds	$476.22
		Seattle Mariners Stadium (Safeco Field)	$42.43
		King County Stadium and Exhibition Center (Qwest Field)	$42.43
		Economic Devel. Strategic Reserve	$2.53
		Problem Gambling	$0.18
		Total	$2,399.92
West Virginia	1986	Education	$773.72
		Senior Citizens	$328.30
		Tourism	$318.33
		Bonds covering profit areas	$0.00
		General Fund	$457.74
		Other	$802.01
		Total	$2,680.10
Wisconsin	1988	Public Benefit such as Property Tax Relief	$2,368.00
Wyoming		——————————(a)——————————	
Dist. of Columbia	1982	General Fund	$1,340.00

Source: The National Association of State and Provincial Lotteries, March 2007.
Key:
N.A. — Not available
(a) State does not have lottery.

Table 7.35
LOTTERY PRODUCTS

State or other jurisdiction	Instant	Pulltab	3-Digit numbers	4-Digit numbers	5-Digit numbers	Lotto	Multistate	Keno	Video lottery terminals	Sports
Alabama					(a)					
Alaska					(a)					
Arizona	★		★			★	★			
Arkansas					(a)					
California	★		★			★	★	★		
Colorado	★					★	★			
Connecticut	★		★	★		★	★			
Delaware	★		★	★		★	★		★	
Florida	★		★	★	★	★				
Georgia	★		★	★		★	★	★		
Hawaii					(a)					
Idaho	★	★	★			★	★			
Illinois	★		★	★		★	★			
Indiana	★	★	★	★	★	★	★			
Iowa	★	★	★	★		★	★			
Kansas	★	★	★			★	★	★		
Kentucky	★	★	★	★		★	★			
Louisiana	★		★	★		★	★			
Maine	★		★	★		★	★			
Maryland	★		★	★	★	★	★	★		
Massachusetts	★	★		★	★	★	★	★		
Michigan	★	★	★	★	★	★	★	★		
Minnesota	★		★			★	★			
Mississippi					(a)					
Missouri	★	★	★	★	★	★	★	★		
Montana	★					★	★			
Nebraska	★		★			★	★			
Nevada					(a)					
New Hampshire	★		★	★			★			
New Jersey	★		★	★	★	★	★			
New Mexico	★		★	★	★		★			
New York	★		★	★		★	★	★	★	
North Carolina	★				★		★			
North Dakota							★			
Ohio	★		★	★	★	★	★			
Oklahoma	★		★		★		★			
Oregon	★	★		★		★	★	★	★	★
Pennsylvania	★		★	★		★	★			
Rhode Island	★	★		★		★	★	★	★	
South Carolina	★		★	★	★		★			
South Dakota	★					★	★		★	
Tennessee	★		★	★		★	★			
Texas	★		★		★	★	★			
Utah					(a)					
Vermont	★		★	★		★	★			
Virginia	★		★	★		★	★			
Washington	★		★	★	★	★	★	★		
West Virginia	★		★	★		★	★	★	★	
Wisconsin	★	★	★	★	★	★	★			
Wyoming					(a)					
Dist. of Columbia	★		★	★		★	★	★		
Puerto Rico		★	★			★	★			

Source: The National Association of State and Provincial Lotteries, March 2007.
Key:
(a) State does not have lottery.

Table 7.36
SALES AND PROFITS—FISCAL YEARS 2003–2006

Lottery jurisdiction	Population (millions) (a)	FY '03 sales (millions)	FY '03 profit (millions)	FY '04 sales (millions)	FY '04 profit (millions)	FY '05 sales (millions)	FY '05 profit (millions)	FY '06 sales (millions)	FY '06 profit (millions)	FY '06 sales per capita
United States total (U.S. dollars)............	277.35	$44,615.11	$13,854.71	$48,827.33	$14,943.22	$52,088.09	$16,267.98	$56,834.98	$16,912.82	$204.92
Alabama						(b)				
Alaska						(b)				
Arizona	5.83	$322.28	$96.29	$366.58	$108.31	$397.56	$116.80	$468.70	$141.12	$80.39
Arkansas........................						(b)				
California	35.89	2,781.57	976.10	2,973.98	1,044.06	3,333.60	1,795.30	3,585.00	1,240.57	99.89
Colorado	4.60	391.53	105.00	401.25	104.07	416.97	103.74	468.80	125.60	101.91
Connecticut	3.50	865.29	256.81	907.66	280.76	932.93	268.52	970.33	284.87	277.24
Delaware (c).................	0.83	628.06	213.00	640.92	222.00	689.29	234.00	727.99	248.80	877.01
Florida	18.40	2,867.98	1,035.18	3,070.96	1,051.00	3,537.00	1,103.63	4,030.00	1,230.00	219.02
Georgia	8.91	2,604.42	751.56	2,710.46	782.69	2,922.33	802.24	3,177.59	822.40	356.63
Hawaii...........................						(b)				
Idaho.............................	1.39	97.97	20.50	109.36	24.30	113.50	26.00	131.13	33.00	94.34
Illinois	12.71	1,585.62	540.30	1,709.19	570.10	1,806.75	614.00	1,964.83	637.67	154.59
Indiana..........................	6.08	664.42	175.60	734.87	199.32	739.63	189.04	816.40	218.00	134.28
Iowa	2.95	187.83	47.97	208.54	55.79	210.67	51.09	339.52	80.88	115.09
Kansas	2.74	210.83	63.80	224.20	71.20	206.72	62.28	236.05	67.09	86.15
Kentucky	4.15	673.49	180.76	725.25	193.48	707.26	158.19	742.30	204.30	178.87
Louisiana	4.52	311.46	111.05	340.09	121.60	307.01	108.92	332.12	118.76	73.48
Maine	1.32	164.63	40.25	185.87	42.53	209.29	50.33	229.69	51.70	174.01
Maryland	5.60	1,322.04	444.89	1,395.41	458.37	1,485.73	477.10	1,560.91	500.97	278.73
Massachusetts................	6.43	4,197.75	889.49	4,381.77	912.01	4,484.72	936.13	4,534.12	951.24	705.15
Michigan (d).................	10.11	1,681.55	586.04	1,973.90	644.88	2,069.49	667.58	2,212.37	688.02	218.83
Minnesota	5.14	351.82	79.40	386.90	100.70	408.57	106.18	450.00	121.30	87.55
Mississippi						(b)				
Missouri	5.75	708.57	193.90	791.52	230.32	785.59	218.64	913.52	260.67	158.87
Montana	0.93	34.68	7.45	36.74	8.12	33.81	6.22	39.92	9.11	42.92
Nebraska........................	1.75	80.92	19.97	92.61	19.80	100.66	23.86	113.11	30.32	64.63
Nevada...........................						(b)				
New Hampshire.............	1.30	221.23	66.57	237.00	73.74	227.98	69.30	262.74	80.32	202.11
New Jersey....................	8.70	2,074.07	764.21	2,187.00	795.00	2,273.81	804.42	2,406.57	849.25	276.62
New Mexico	1.90	137.33	33.10	148.70	35.94	139.27	32.23	154.71	36.86	81.43
New York (e)(c)	19.23	5,395.96	1,780.36	5,847.50	1,907.40	6,270.49	2,062.70	6,803.00	2,203.00	353.77
North Carolina (f)........	8.54	N.A.	N.A.	N.A.	N.A.	N.A.	N.A.	229.53	64.59	26.88
North Dakota (g)..........	0.63	N.A.	N.A.	5.84	1.67	19.15	6.46	22.33	6.92	35.44
Ohio	11.44	2,078.25	641.40	2,154.70	648.10	2,159.10	645.10	2,221.00	646.30	194.14
Oklahoma (h)	3.52	N.A.	N.A.	N.A.	N.A.	N.A.	N.A.	204.84	68.95	58.19
Oregon (c).....................	3.62	855.82	387.12	893.26	364.71	943.11	415.48	1,104.00	483.00	304.97
Pennsylvania	12.41	2,132.98	787.70	2,352.07	818.67	2,644.86	852.56	3,070.00	975.85	247.38
Rhode Island (i)............	1.08	1,290.41	249.04	1,480.63	281.14	1,636.84	307.55	1,731.47	323.90	1,603.21
South Carolina	4.20	724.31	219.29	950.00	290.10	956.95	277.50	1,144.60	319.40	272.52
South Dakota (i)..........	0.77	646.90	112.06	664.43	115.77	675.58	119.32	686.16	118.99	891.12
Tennessee (j).................	5.96	N.A.	N.A.	427.70	123.27	844.32	227.42	996.27	277.66	167.16
Texas (k)	22.91	3,130.69	955.20	3,487.92	1,044.13	3,662.46	1,076.82	3,774.69	1,036.11	164.76
Utah						(b)				
Vermont	0.62	79.40	16.20	92.38	19.58	92.59	20.35	104.88	22.88	169.16
Virginia.........................	7.46	1,135.73	375.20	1,262.36	408.05	1,333.94	423.52	1,365.00	454.90	182.98
Washington....................	6.20	460.36	98.52	481.44	117.58	457.62	115.60	477.89	116.95	77.08
West Virginia (c)	1.82	1,081.91	411.04	1,303.44	512.14	1,399.07	563.32	1,522.00	610.00	836.26
Wisconsin......................	5.51	435.05	122.39	482.93	140.82	451.87	128.54	508.90	150.60	92.36
Wyoming........................						(b)				
Dist. of Columbia (d) ...	0.55	237.24	72.05	240.63	73.50	233.43	71.05	266.20	73.40	484.00
Puerto Rico...................	4.00	337.30	113.00	337.30	70.90	317.90	79.00	334.50	115.90	83.62

Source: The National Association of State and Provincial Lotteries, March 2007.

Key:
N.A. — Not applicable
(a) — Population is from the U.S. Census Bureau July 1, 2004 estimated population.
(b) — State does not have lottery.
(c) — Includes net video lottery terminal sales. (Cash-in less cash-out)
(d) — Fiscal year ends September 30.

(e) — Fiscal year ends March 31.
(f) — Instant sales began March 30, 2006; online sales began October 2006.
(g) — Sales began March 25, 2004.
(h) — No sales for fiscal year 2005.
(i) — Includes gross video lottery terminal sales. (Cash-in)
(j) — Sales began January 20, 2004 and only reflect 5 months and 12 days of fiscal year 2004.
(k) — Fiscal year ends August 31.

The Foreign-Born Population in the United States
By Mark Mather

At 36 million people, the number of foreign-born Americans is at its highest point in history. Two-thirds of the foreign-born population reside in just six states—California, New York, Texas, Florida, Illinois and New Jersey. However, the foreign-born are increasingly settling in other parts of the United States—especially in the South—bringing new cultures, languages, racial and ethnic diversity, economic opportunities and challenges for policymakers.

As a country settled by immigrants, the United States has always had a large foreign-born population. In 2005, the number of U.S. foreign-born residents reached 36 million, an all-time high.[1] The foreign-born population currently accounts for about 12 percent of the U.S. population, and that proportion is expected to increase. In many states and cities across the country, especially in the South and Southwest, immigration has become a hot-button political issue. This article provides an overview of the foreign-born population in the United States, their demographic characteristics, emerging trends and some of the key implications for state policymakers.

Growth of the Foreign-Born Population in the United States

Although the number of foreign-born Americans is at its highest point in history, the foreign-born made up a larger proportion of the U.S. population in the early 1900s than it does today (Figure A). In 1910, almost 15 percent of the U.S. population was foreign-born, mostly immigrants from Europe. The immigration boom at the turn of the 20th century was followed by several decades of declining proportions of immigrants in the U.S. population, the result of two world wars, severe legal restrictions on immigration, the Great Depression and high U.S. fertility rates that boosted the size of the U.S.-born population.[2]

By 1970, less than 5 percent of the U.S. population was foreign-born, but the share more than doubled over the next 30 years. Based on the current rates of increase, the foreign-born population is projected to number more than 40 million by 2010.[3]

Who are these foreign-born residents and how did they come to live in the United States? Some came as legal, temporary migrants (e.g., students) and are expected to return to their home countries; these

---

The "Foreign-Born Population" vs. "Immigrants"

In this report, the terms "foreign-born" and "immigrants" are used interchangeably, but these are technically two different concepts. The U.S. Census Bureau collects information about the foreign-born population, which includes anyone who is not a U.S. citizen at birth, including immigrants, legal non-immigrants (temporary migrants), humanitarian migrants, and people illegally present in the United States (undocumented aliens). Immigrants are more narrowly defined as "aliens who are admitted to the United States for lawful permanent residence."

Census questionnaires do not ask about the legal status of people born outside the United States. In 2005, the foreign-born population in the United States numbered about 36 million, according to the American Community Survey. However, there were 1.1 million immigrants who obtained legal permanent resident status in the United States that year, according to the Office of Immigrant Statistics.

Reference

U.S. Department of Homeland Security, Office of Immigration Statistics, *Yearbook of Immigration Statistics: 2005* (2006): Table 1.

"nonimmigrants" may account for just 3 percent of all foreign residents. Roughly 7 percent are refugees who are unable or unwilling to return to their home countries. The remaining 90 percent is divided among three groups of roughly equal size: legal immigrants (28 percent), naturalized citizens (31 percent) and unauthorized migrants (30 percent).[4]

Most of the foreigners living in the United States arrived here fairly recently: More than one-fifth of the 2005 U.S. foreign-born population entered the country after 2000, and more than half came here since 1990. More than 90 percent of the foreign-born residents who arrived after 2000 lack U.S. citizenship. Southern states, which have not had historically high levels of immigration, had the highest proportions of recent immigrants. For example, in Alabama, North Carolina, South Carolina and Tennessee, more than one-third of the foreign-born population arrived in this country since 2000, while in New York, about one in six did.[5]

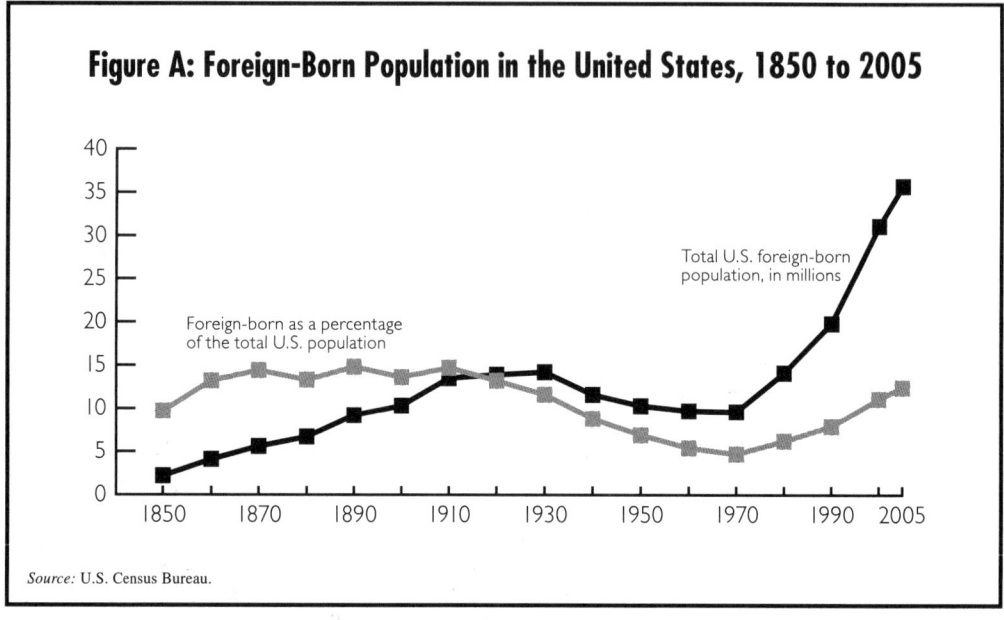

Figure A: Foreign-Born Population in the United States, 1850 to 2005

Total U.S. foreign-born population, in millions

Foreign-born as a percentage of the total U.S. population

Source: U.S. Census Bureau.

Immigration is the engine driving rapid population growth in the United States. Today about 40 percent of U.S. population growth each year is due to immigration, while 60 percent is due to natural increase (the excess of births over deaths). However, if the children born to immigrants after they enter the United States are factored in, immigration plays a much larger role in U.S. population growth.

In fact, immigration has created a population momentum in the United States that is unique among developed countries. In October 2006, the United States became only the third country—behind China and India—to pass the 300 million population threshold. Based on the current growth rate and immigration levels, the U.S. population is expected to reach 400 million by 2043.[6]

Geographic Distribution

Historically, most immigrants settled in a handful of "gateway" cities, mostly located on the east and west coasts. Although the foreign-born population is dispersing throughout the United States, two-thirds still reside in just six states—California, New York, Texas, Florida, Illinois and New Jersey (Figure B). These same six states are home to about two-fifths of the total U.S. population.

California has the highest proportion of residents born outside the United States, at 27 percent, followed by New York (21 percent) and New Jersey (20 percent). The states with the lowest shares of foreign-born residents are located in the South (Alabama, Kentucky, Louisiana, Mississippi, Missouri and West Virginia), in Maine, and in several states in the Great Plains (Montana, North Dakota, South Dakota and Wyoming). (Table A).

Country of Origin

Immigrants who have arrived in the United States since 1970—mostly from Latin America and Asia—look very different from those who came from Europe during earlier waves of immigration. In 2005, slightly more than one-half of the foreign-born population were born in Latin America, more than one-quarter were from Asia, about one-sixth were born in Europe or Canada, and most of the remainder were from African countries. About 31 percent of all foreign-born residents reported Mexico as their country of origin.

Immigrants from Latin America account for more than two-thirds of the foreign-born populations in six states: Arizona, Arkansas, Florida, Idaho, New Mexico and Texas (Table A). Alaska and Hawaii lead the nation in the proportions of foreign-born from Asia. And Montana and Vermont have the highest proportions of foreign-born from Europe. Many of these Europeans are elderly Americans who have lived in the United States for decades.

This shift in the country of origin has contributed to the changing racial and ethnic composition of the U.S. population. Between 2000 and 2005, the number of Hispanics increased from 35.6 million to 42.7 million, a 20-percent increase. During the 1990s, Hispanic population increased nearly fivefold in North

Carolina and at least doubled in 21 other states.[7] The majority of this growth is directly or indirectly linked to immigration, through new arrivals or through children born in the United States to foreign-born parents.

People arriving in the United States come here with a wide range of education levels and skills. Those who arrive from Latin America tend to have less education and lower skill levels. Many Latin American immigrants come here to work in farming, construction, manufacturing or service jobs. Those who come from Asia tend to be at the other end of the socioeconomic ladder. In fact, Asian immigrants are more highly educated, on average, than the U.S.-born population; many are recruited to work as scientists or engineers in the high-tech global economy. Both groups—those from Latin America and Asia—are filling important jobs in the U.S. labor force, but they have very different social and economic trajectories. In 2005, the average earnings for full-time, foreign-born workers from Asia were $57,000, nearly double the average earnings for full-time workers from Latin America ($30,000).[8]

English Language Ability

Country of origin is also important because many of the people arriving in the United States speak languages other than English. In 2005, about 84 percent of the foreign-born population spoke a language other than English at home. The number of Americans speaking a language at home other than English has more than doubled since 1980, reflecting the influx of millions of immigrants to the United States in recent decades, especially from Latin America. The Census Bureau estimates that about 32 million U.S. residents speak Spanish at home. With fewer migrants from Europe, several languages that were once spoken widely in the United States (French, German and Polish) are becoming less common.[9]

The majority of those who speak languages other than English at home report that they are very proficient in English. Fewer than 50 percent of people who speak Spanish or another non-English language at home have difficulty speaking English[10]—including 48 percent of those who speak Spanish.[11]

However, English language proficiency is a big issue in California, where one of every five residents 5 years and older has difficulty speaking English (Table A). The ability to speak English is closely linked to earnings and social and economic integration for new immigrants to the United States. Although many adults who arrive here have difficultly learning English, most young children of immigrants will grow up learning English as their primary language. These children are often called upon to act as translators for parents or older siblings.[12]

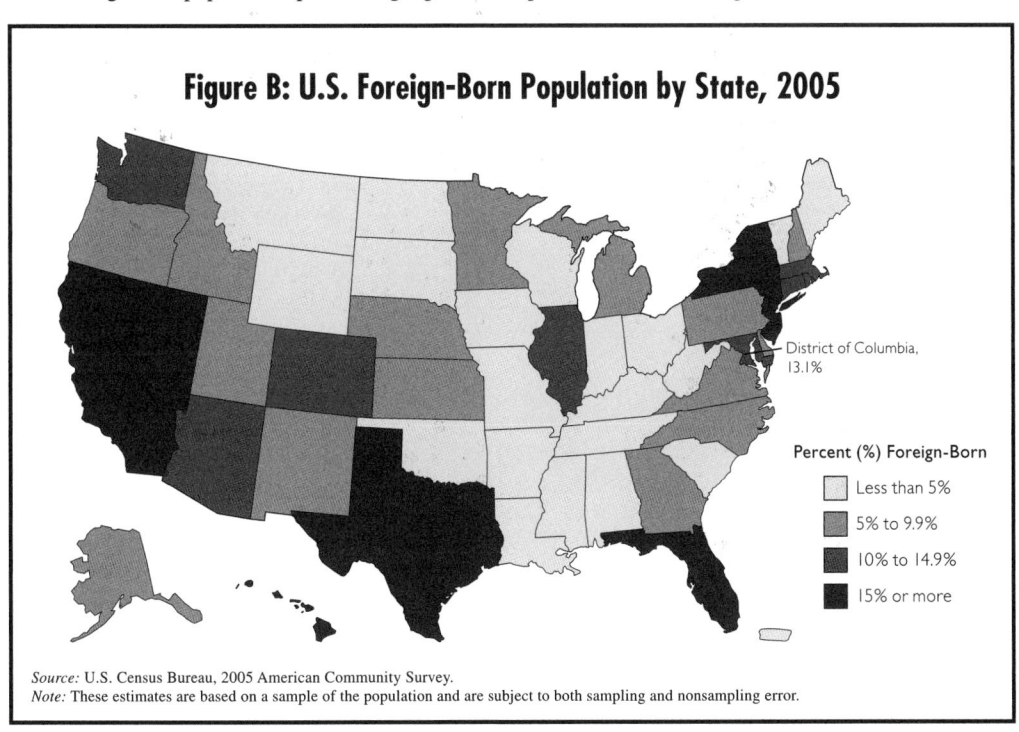

Figure B: U.S. Foreign-Born Population by State, 2005

District of Columbia, 13.1%

Percent (%) Foreign-Born

- Less than 5%
- 5% to 9.9%
- 10% to 14.9%
- 15% or more

Source: U.S. Census Bureau, 2005 American Community Survey.
Note: These estimates are based on a sample of the population and are subject to both sampling and nonsampling error.

Table A
CHARACTERISTICS OF THE U.S. FOREIGN-BORN POPULATION, BY STATE, 2005

State or other jurisdiction	Foreign-born population	Percent of total population that is foreign born	Place of birth for the foreign-born population			Percent of children in immigrant families (a)	Percent of people with difficulty speaking English (b)
			Latin America (%)	Asia (%)	Europe (%)		
United States	35,689,842	12.4%	53.0%	27.0%	14.0%	21.0%	9.0%
Eastern Region							
Connecticut....................	423,254	12.5	39.2	21.0	31.9	18.0	7.5
Delaware........................	62,867	7.7	41.5	27.1	19.2	13.0	4.9
Maine............................	38,727	3.0	10.0	20.9	26.4	5.0	2.0
Massachusetts...............	891,184	14.4	36.1	27.2	25.8	22.0	8.9
New Hampshire	72,480	5.7	18.6	27.0	30.5	9.0	2.5
New Jersey	1,662,857	19.5	43.5	30.0	20.4	30.0	11.5
New York......................	3,997,268	21.4	49.5	25.1	20.3	32.0	12.7
Pennsylvania.................	603,674	5.0	24.6	35.5	29.3	8.0	3.5
Rhode Island.................	130,517	12.6	43.8	14.8	27.1	25.0	8.9
Vermont	21,843	3.6	5.2	26.0	35.0	5.0	1.3
Midwestern Region							
Illinois	1,695,289	13.6	48.1	24.3	23.9	22.0	9.8
Indiana..........................	242,281	4.0	49.8	24.7	17.1	7.0	3.1
Iowa..............................	103,143	3.6	40.9	28.9	21.4	7.0	2.6
Kansas	153,535	5.8	55.6	27.8	9.6	11.0	4.3
Michigan.......................	605,656	6.1	19.8	42.4	24.5	11.0	3.5
Minnesota.....................	316,716	6.3	27.4	39.2	13.9	12.0	4.0
Nebraska.......................	96,127	5.6	56.5	23.2	11.0	11.0	4.5
North Dakota	11,968	2.0	15.1	30.3	20.7	4.0	1.4
Ohio..............................	387,216	3.5	19.0	36.9	29.4	5.0	2.2
South Dakota	17,269	2.3	25.2	27.7	29.5	5.0	2.1
Wisconsin	227,372	4.2	40.2	32.3	21.1	8.0	3.2
Southern Region							
Alabama........................	120,773	2.7	48.1	26.6	17.5	5.0	1.8
Arkansas.......................	101,169	3.7	65.7	19.4	9.3	7.0	2.8
Florida	3,212,955	18.5	73.4	9.3	11.9	29.0	11.4
Georgia.........................	795,419	9.0	55.3	23.6	11.3	15.0	5.8
Kentucky	98,798	2.4	35.8	30.7	22.6	4.0	1.7
Louisiana	121,590	2.8	42.7	37.0	14.6	4.0	2.5
Maryland	641,373	11.7	37.3	33.0	13.2	19.0	5.9
Mississippi	43,336	1.5	48.1	32.0	13.9	2.0	1.2
Missouri........................	193,735	3.4	31.9	33.0	24.9	6.0	2.0
North Carolina..............	560,753	6.7	58.4	20.0	11.9	12.0	4.7
Oklahoma	155,880	4.5	59.7	26.3	8.0	9.0	3.5
South Carolina..............	170,750	4.2	49.4	21.4	19.2	7.0	2.9
Tennessee......................	223,118	3.8	45.1	29.3	13.5	7.0	2.5
Texas............................	3,542,513	15.9	75.5	16.2	4.4	30.0	14.8
Virginia.........................	723,667	9.9	35.4	40.6	13.0	16.0	5.4
West Virginia	19,302	1.1	15.3	42.2	28.7	2.0	0.6
Western Region							
Alaska...........................	34,368	5.4	19.8	47.6	20.4	11.0	4.2
Arizona.........................	843,296	14.5	73.2	12.1	8.3	28.0	11.8
California......................	9,611,356	27.2	55.3	34.0	7.1	47.0	20.2
Colorado.......................	460,294	10.1	59.1	19.1	13.9	20.0	7.5
Hawaii	212,404	17.2	5.1	82.1	5.0	27.0	11.5
Idaho.............................	76,377	5.5	66.0	11.1	13.4	11.0	4.1
Montana........................	16,734	1.8	10.4	20.8	40.6	3.0	0.7
Nevada..........................	413,298	17.4	61.3	24.0	10.1	32.0	12.1
New Mexico	168,640	8.9	78.0	10.5	8.6	18.0	10.6
Oregon..........................	344,575	9.7	49.0	26.8	17.0	19.0	7.0
Utah..............................	192,916	7.9	60.4	17.9	12.4	14.0	5.7
Washington	750,258	12.2	30.0	39.0	19.1	21.0	7.5
Wyoming	11,235	2.3	45.4	16.0	23.6	4.0	1.7
District of Columbia	67,717	13.1	50.4	18.1	18.6	18.0	6.0
Puerto Rico...................	115,683	3.0	89.7	3.0	6.3	N.A.	80.2

Source: U.S. Census Bureau, 2005 American Community Survey.
Note: These estimates are based on a sample of the population and are subject to both sampling and nonsampling error. The 2005 American Community Survey excluded persons living in group quarters.

Key:
(a) The share of children who are foreign-born or residing with at least one foreign-born parent.
(b) People ages 5 and over who speak English less than "very well."

Emerging Trends

New Immigrant Hot Spots

Most of the states with the fastest-growing foreign-born populations between 2000 and 2005 are those that, historically, have had few immigrants: Arkansas, Delaware, Georgia, Kansas, Nebraska, Nevada, North Carolina, Mississippi, South Carolina and Tennessee.[13] Immigrants are also increasingly settling in small towns and rural areas across the United States. In the Southeast, new immigrants are attracted by opportunities for low-skilled work in manufacturing, food processing and agriculture. The Midwest is offering new jobs in meatpacking plants. And Western states provide employment in agriculture and, increasingly, tourism industries.[14]

In many cases, immigrants have revitalized and re-populated areas that have been in decline for decades. However, many longer-term residents in these areas are slow to adapt to the changing cultures, languages and racial and ethnic diversity of the new arrivals.[15]

The Debate Over Unauthorized Migrants

Most of the debate about immigration in the United States is focused on the estimated 12 million unauthorized migrants currently residing in the United States.[16] Unauthorized migrants include those who entered the United States illegally and those who entered the country legally but violated the terms of their admission (in most cases, by overstaying their visas). The Pew Hispanic Center estimates that between 2000 and 2005, the unauthorized migrant population increased by about 500,000 each year.[17]

About 56 percent of unauthorized immigrants are estimated to be Mexican, and another 22 percent are from elsewhere in Latin America. About 40 percent of the unauthorized population came to the United States since 2000.[18]

The growing number of unauthorized immigrants in the United States has gotten the attention of state policymakers and their constituents. Hundreds of pieces of legislation have been put before state legislatures around the country to deal with the issue. Most of these bills—but not all—are proposals to crack down on illegal workers and the businesses that hire them.[19]

The Children of Immigrants: Reshaping America

More often than not, children are left out of the immigration debate. An analysis of more than 9,000 articles on immigration published in the 20 largest newspapers in 2006 showed that fewer than 5 percent of articles covered issues related to immigrant children and families.[20] Most of the news coverage on immigration has focused on illegal immigration, border security, public sentiment or national and state policy issues.

However, the children of immigrants make up a large and growing segment of American society. In 2005, more than one in five children in the United States (15.7 million) were living in immigrant families. The vast majority of these children are U.S. citizens who were born in the United States to foreign-born parents. In 2005, nearly half of all children in California (47 percent) lived in immigrant families, and the state is home to nearly one-third of all children in immigrant families in the United States.[21]

Children are leading the way to a more diverse U.S. society, and not just in California. In 2005, nearly half of all children under age 5 were racial or ethnic minorities. As these children grow older, go to school, get jobs and start families of their own, they will lead a major shift in the racial and ethnic composition of the U.S. population and labor force.

Implications for State Governments

Immigrants play a vital role in both the U.S. and state economies, filling a broad range of positions ranging from low-wage agricultural workers to scientists and engineers working in high-tech industry. The federal government sets policies on migration across U.S. borders, but states can use a variety of mechanisms to meet the needs of the U.S. foreign-born population, including the following:

- Promoting English language instruction in schools, to ensure that all children have the resources they need to succeed in school and to become productive adults;
- Providing access to health care for the foreign-born population, including preventive medicine to reduce expenditures for emergency room care; and
- Providing financial services to help foreign-born populations buy homes, start businesses and send their children to college.

These programs can help integrate the foreign-born population, especially children, into American society to ensure a strong labor force for the future.

Notes

[1] Estimate from the Census Bureau's 2005 American Community Survey.

[2] Phillip Martin and Elizabeth Midgley, "Immigration: Shaping and Reshaping America," *Population Bulletin*, 6: 4 (2006).

[3] Projection by the Population Reference Bureau based on 2000–2005 trends.

[4] Jeffrey S. Passel, "Size and Characteristics of the Unau-

thorized Migrant Population in the U.S.: Estimates Based on the March 2005 Current Population Survey," (Pew Hispanic Center, 2006).

[5] Population Reference Bureau analysis of the 2005 American Community Survey.

[6] U.S. Census Bureau population projections.

[7] Mark Mather, Kerri L. Rivers, and Linda A. Jacobsen, "What the American Community Survey Tells Us About Immigration," (Population Reference Bureau, 2005).

[8] Population Reference Bureau analysis of the 2005 American Community Survey.

[9] Mary Kent and Robert Lalasz, "In the News: Speaking English in the United States," (Population Reference Bureau, 2006).

[10] Difficulty speaking English is defined here as those who speak English less than "very well."

[11] Mary Kent and Robert Lalasz, "In the News: Speaking English in the United States," (Population Reference Bureau, 2006).

[12] Jean D'Amico and Laura Beavers, "Children in Immigrant Families: U.S. and State-Level Findings from the Census 2000," *A Kids Count/PRB Report on Census 2000.* (Baltimore, MD: The Annie E. Casey Foundation and Washington, D.C.: Population Reference Bureau, 2005).

[13] Population Reference Bureau analysis of the Census 2000 Supplementary Survey and the 2005 American Community Survey.

[14] Leif Jensen, "New Immigrant Settlements in Rural America: Problems, Prospects, and Policies," A Carsey Institute Report on Rural America, (2006).

[15] Ibid.

[16] Jeffrey S. Passel, "Size and Characteristics of the Unauthorized Migrant Population in the U.S.: Estimates Based on the March 2005 Current Population Survey," (Pew Hispanic Center, 2006).

[17] Ibid.

[18] Ibid.

[19] T.R. Reid, "Hill Impasse Spurs States to Tackle Illegal Immigration," the *Washington Post*, Wednesday, May 3, 2006; Page A01.

[20] Population Reference Bureau analysis of Nexis.

[21] Population Reference Bureau analysis of the 2005 American Community Survey.

About the Author

Mark Mather is deputy director of Domestic Programs at the Population Reference Bureau, where he coordinates several projects that communicate population research to advocacy groups, educators, the media and the public. He holds Ph.D. and M.A. degrees in sociology/demography from the University of Maryland and has more than 10 years experience in demographic data analysis.

The New Race-Ethnic Dispersion of America's Population: Trends Since 2000

By William H. Frey

An analysis of Census Bureau population estimates detailing the distribution of racial and ethnic groups within and across metropolitan areas since Census 2000 reveals the following: Hispanic and Asian populations are spreading out from their traditional metropolitan centers, while blacks' shift towards the South is accelerating; the fastest growing metro areas for each minority group in 2000–2004 are no longer unique, but closely parallel the fastest growing areas in the nation; Of the nation's 361 metropolitan areas, 111 registered declines in white population from 2000 to 2004, with the largest absolute losses occurring in New York, San Francisco, and Los Angeles; and a strong multi-minority presence characterizes 18 large "melting pot" metro areas, and 27 large metro areas now have "majority minority" child populations.

Introduction

The idea of America as an ethnic "melting pot" gained currency at the turn of the 20th century amid an unprecedented wave of European immigrants to the United States. At the turn of the 21st century, the melting pot ideal persists, but envelops a more racially and ethnically diverse group of Americans, both native- and foreign-born. In particular, the recent growth advantages of the nation's minority populations over its white population animate this distinctly American concept.

This article examines continuing shifts in the nation's metropolitan areas by race and ethnicity during the first part of the current decade; examines the largest population centers for Hispanics, Asians and blacks, and how they have changed in the 1990-to-2004 period; reviews the fastest-growing areas for each minority group in order to assess future directions of minority dispersal, and contrasts their geographic shifts with those for whites; measures the degree to which minorities contribute to population increases in the fastest-growing metropolitan areas, and in inner and outer counties within metropolitan areas; examines the continued emergence of "melting pot" metropolitan areas and the rise of "majority minority" youth populations in many of these areas; and concludes with a discussion of the social and economic implications of these changing settlement patterns.

Methodology

This survey differs from most analyses conducted immediately after Census 2000 by utilizing new metropolitan area definitions announced by the Office of Management and Budget (OMB) in 2003.[a] These new definitions do not merely revise earlier classifi-

cations, but rather fundamentally reframe the metropolitan area concept.

The primary geographic units of analysis for this study are the 361 metropolitan statistical areas (MSAs) defined according to these standards. Different parts of this analysis will focus on the 88 "large metropolitan areas" that had populations exceeding 500,000 in 2000, "small metropolitan areas" (the remaining 273 MSAs), micropolitan areas and other nonmetropolitan territory.

The data for this study are drawn from county population estimates produced by the U.S. Census Bureau's Population Estimates Program for July 1990, July 2000 and July 2004 for race and ethnic groups.[b] They take into account the results of Census 2000 and information from a host of administrative data sources, including vital records, housing construction permits, tax returns and Medicare records, among others. The estimates for July 1990 come from the Census Bureau's archival estimate files and are based on the 1990 decennial enumeration.[c] For most of the analysis, county statistics are aggregated to form metropolitan areas, micropolitan areas and nonmetropolitan areas and other nonmetropolitan territory.

The Population Estimates Program provides annual estimates of basic demographic indicators for all U.S. counties, including population, race and ethnicity, age, and components of population change (births, deaths, internal migration and international migration). These estimates are intended to measure the total resident population in the United States, including undocumented immigrants and people in group quarters (e.g., dormitories, prisons, nursing homes).

The classification of racial and ethnic groups underlying this analysis differs slightly from that in Census 2000. This survey draws from the "modified race" classification in the Population Estimates Program. The modified race classification eliminates the "some other race" category used in the decennial census, and allocates its members to one of the other race groups.[d] Most of the study focuses on four main groups: whites, blacks, Asians and Hispanics.[e]

Findings

Hispanic and Asian populations are spreading out from their traditional metropolitan centers, while blacks shift toward the South at an accelerated pace.

An uneasy tension has long existed between notions of the American melting pot and the geographic clustering of its minority groups. For Hispanic and Asian groups, that clustering is explained by their initial settlement in a handful of "port of entry" metropolitan areas. For blacks, who have lived in the United States for several generations, that clustering reflects their initial forced settlement in the Old South, and their later migration to cities in the Northeast and Midwest, and on the West Coast.

Yet these longstanding concentration patterns show noticeable changes in the 2000s. This section reviews the changing metropolitan location of the nation's three largest minority groups—Hispanics, Asians and blacks.

Hispanics

As recently as the 1990 Census, taken 25 years after the 1965 Immigration Act paved the way for increased arrivals of Latin American Hispanics, this group was still relatively clustered within the United States. At that time, the 10 metropolitan areas with the largest Hispanic populations were home to fully 55 percent of all U.S. Hispanics. Although this group has since dispersed to different parts of the nation, about half of all Hispanics (49 percent) still live in these 10 areas.

Table A: Metro Areas with Largest 2004 Populations: Hispanics, Asians and Blacks

Rank 2004	Rank 2000	Rank 1990	Metro area	Population 2004	Share of metro area population (%)
			Hispanics		
1	1	1	Los Angeles-Long Beach-Santa Ana, CA	5,587,692	43.2%
2	2	2	New York-Northern New Jersey-Long Island, NY-NJ-PA	3,882,817	20.8
3	3	3	Miami-Fort Lauderdale-Miami Beach, FL	1,982,641	37.0
4	4	4	Chicago-Naperville-Joliet, IL-IN-WI	1,725,685	18.4
5	5	5	Houston-Baytown-Sugar Land, TX	1,637,992	31.6
6	6	6	Riverside-San Bernardino-Ontario, CA	1,580,457	41.7
7	7	8	Dallas-Fort Worth-Arlington, TX	1,423,020	25.0
8	9	12	Phoenix-Mesa-Scottsdale, AZ	1,056,145	28.4
9	8	7	San Antonio, TX	965,745	52.1
10	10	10	San Diego-Carlsbad-San Marcos, CA	849,771	29.0
			Asians		
1	1	1	Los Angeles-Long Beach-Santa Ana, CA	1,712,127	13.2
2	2	2	New York-Northern New Jersey-Long Island, NY-NJ-PA	1,616,489	8.6
3	3	3	San Francisco-Oakland-Fremont, CA	879,495	21.2
4	4	5	San Jose-Sunnyvale-Santa Clara, CA	491,876	28.2
5	6	6	Chicago-Naperville-Joliet, IL-IN-WI	454,300	4.8
6	5	4	Honolulu, HI	413,015	45.9
7	7	7	Washington-Arlington-Alexandria, DC-VA-MD-WV	405,859	7.9
8	8	9	Seattle-Tacoma-Bellevue, WA	308,600	9.7
9	9	8	San Diego-Carlsbad-San Marcos, CA	283,037	9.7
10	10	10	Houston-Baytown-Sugar Land, TX	281,894	5.4
			Blacks		
1	1	1	New York-Northern New Jersey-Long Island, NY-NJ-PA	3,202,808	17.1
2	2	2	Chicago-Naperville-Joliet, IL-IN-WI	1,694,518	18.0
3	4	7	Atlanta-Sandy Springs-Marietta, GA	1,406,290	29.9
4	3	3	Washington-Arlington-Alexandria, DC-VA-MD-WV	1,335,823	26.0
5	5	4	Philadelphia-Camden-Wilmington, PA-NJ-DE-MD	1,162,847	20.0
6	8	8	Miami-Fort Lauderdale-Miami Beach, FL	1,044,406	19.5
7	6	6	Detroit-Warren-Livonia, MI	1,026,048	22.8
8	7	5	Los Angeles-Long Beach-Santa Ana, CA	947,351	7.3
9	9	9	Houston-Baytown-Sugar Land, TX	848,221	16.4
10	10	11	Dallas-Fort Worth-Arlington, TX	789,807	13.9

Source: Author's analysis of Census Bureau Population Estimates and decennial census data.

Table B: Metro Areas with Largest Population Gains 2000–2004: Hispanics, Asians and Blacks

Rank			
2000–2004	1990–2000	Metro area	Population change 2000–2004
		Hispanics	
1	1	Los Angeles-Long Beach-Santa Ana, CA	435,674
2	7	Riverside-San Bernardino-Ontario, CA	333,527
3	4	Dallas-Fort Worth-Arlington, TX	290,590
4	2	New York-Northern New Jersey-Long Island, NY-NJ-PA	288,325
5	5	Houston-Baytown-Sugar Land, TX	268,834
6	6	Miami-Fort Lauderdale-Miami Beach, FL	261,354
7	8	Phoenix-Mesa-Scottsdale, AZ	226,472
8	3	Chicago-Naperville-Joliet, IL-IN-WI	217,047
9	14	Washington-Arlington-Alexandria, DC-VA-MD-WV	114,039
10	12	Atlanta-Sandy Springs-Marietta, GA	112,362
		Asians	
1	1	New York-Northern New Jersey-Long Island, NY-NJ-PA	201,543
2	2	Los Angeles-Long Beach-Santa Ana, CA	164,474
3	3	San Francisco-Oakland-Fremont, CA	71,326
4	6	Washington-Arlington-Alexandria, DC-VA-MD-WV	67,099
5	5	Chicago-Naperville-Joliet, IL-IN-WI	58,283
6	4	San Jose-Sunnyvale-Santa Clara, CA	54,218
7	8	Washington-Arlington-Alexandria, DC-VA-MD-WV	49,881
8	7	Houston-Baytown-Sugar Land, TX	46,557
9	9	Seattle-Tacoma-Bellevue, WA	43,738
10	18	Riverside-San Bernardino-Ontario, CA	42,515
		Blacks	
1	1	Atlanta-Sandy Springs-Marietta, GA	183,817
2	3	Miami-Fort Lauderdale-Miami Beach, FL	96,934
3	5	Dallas-Fort Worth-Arlington, TX	74,562
4	4	Washington-Arlington-Alexandria, DC-VA-MD-WV	64,439
5	7	Houston-Baytown-Sugar Land, TX	56,694
6	8	Philadelphia-Camden-Wilimington, PA-NJ-DE-MD	42,997
7	11	Orlando, FL	41,729
8	14	Charlotte-Gastonia-Concord, NC-SC	40,703
9	9	Baltimore-Towson, MD	38,579
10	15	Riverside-San Bernardino-Ontario, CA	35,292

Source: Author's analysis of Census Bureau Population Estimates and decennial census data.

degree than the Hispanic population. Indeed, the 10 metro areas with the largest Asian populations are the same in 2004 as in 1990 (Table 1). Led by Los Angeles, New York and San Francisco, these 10 metro areas were home to 57 percent of the nation's Asian population in 2004, down from 61 percent in 1990.

These areas' share of recent Asian population gains has dropped noticeably, however. From 2000 to 2004, they drew less than half (47 percent) of increased Asian population nationally, compared with 53 percent in the 1990s. Moreover, Dallas and Riverside, two metro areas that do not rank among those with the largest number of Asians, rank seventh and 10th respectively among the greatest gainers in 2000–2004 (Table B).

Blacks

In the 2000–2004 period, black movement toward the South not only continued, it expanded. The bottom chart in Figure 2 indicates a continued and gradual increase in the South's share of U.S. black population, from 54 percent in 1990 to 56 percent in 2004. More impressive still is the increased share of the nation's black population growth now occurring in the South, from 65 percent in the 1990s to 72 percent in the first four years of the 2000s. The New York and Chicago areas still count the largest African-American populations in the United States in absolute terms (Table A).

Overall, the New South dominates the list of metro areas with the largest recent gains in black population (Table B). Six of the top eight areas are located there, with Orlando and Charlotte emerging relatively recently. Philadelphia and Baltimore rank among the areas with the largest black gains due largely to natural increase (births minus deaths), rather than in-migration.

The fastest-growing metro areas for each minority group in 2000–04 are no longer unique, but closely parallel the fastest-growing areas in the nation.

Recent analyses of migration from Census 2000 show that metropolitan areas serving as new destinations for Hispanics and Asians are attracting not

Nonetheless, the original Hispanic settlement areas are slowly losing their grip on this population group. Although the 10 largest Hispanic destinations in 1990 today house about half of all Hispanics, they garnered only 43 percent of the increase in U.S. Hispanic population during the 1990s, and a somewhat lower share (41 percent) of growth in the first part of the 2000s.

While the top Hispanic-gaining metro areas overlap largely with the most populous ones, significant shifts occurred in the most recent period. The Riverside-San Bernardino area's rank moved up by five, reflecting the redistribution of Hispanics from the Los Angeles area to this more suburban metropolitan area (Table B).

Asians

The Asian population continues to cluster in traditional immigrant magnet areas to a somewhat greater only new immigrants, but also first- and second-generation domestic migrants leaving more traditional ports-of-entry. Similarly, over the 1990s, African-Americans exhibited high growth rates to new destinations that were off the beaten path. More recently, however, fast-growing areas for each minority group have begun to parallel those experiencing the fastest total population growth.

Hispanics

Overall the Hispanic population grew by 16 percent nationally during the 2000–2004 period. Well over half (53) of the 92 metropolitan areas with more than 50,000 Hispanics registered Hispanic population growth faster than this rate.

Among the 10 fastest-growing metropolitan areas for Hispanics over the 2000–2004 period, those in the Southeast—especially in Florida—dominate (Table C). The Cape Coral–Fort Myers, Fla., metro

area rose in rank from number eight in the 1990s to number one in 2000–2004. Also in Florida, the Lakeland area moved up a notch, while Naples and Sarasota advanced into the top 10.

Asians

Similar to the nation's Hispanic population, the U.S. Asian population has grown by 15 percent over the 2000–2004 period. Today, 30 metropolitan areas are home to more than 50,000 Asians, and 21 of those have seen their Asian populations grow faster than the national average.

Because Asians comprise a much smaller share of the U.S. population (4 percent) than Hispanics (14 percent), far fewer places nationwide exhibit relatively large Asian populations. Nonetheless, the 89 counties with Asian population shares of at least 5 percent in 2004—up from 44 in 1990—provide evidence that the population continues to spread out.

Table C: Metro Areas with Highest Growth Rates, 2000–2004 and 1990–2000: Hispanics, Asians and Blacks

Rank	Metro area	Population change 2000–2004 (%)	Rank	Metro area	Population change 1990–2000 (%)
	Hispanics: 2000–2004			**Hispanics: 1990–2000**	
1	Cape Coral-Fort Myers, FL	55.4%	1	Charlotte-Gastonia-Concord, NC-SC	605.9%
2	Charlotte-Gastonia-Concord, NC-SC	49.8	2	Raleigh-Cary, NC	541.7
3	Raleigh-Cary, NC	46.7	3	Nashville-Davidson-Murfreesboro, TN	422.5
4	Nashville-Davidson-Murfreesboro, TN	44.9	4	Atlanta-Sandy Springs-Marietta, GA	355.0
5	Indianapolis, IN	44.3	5	Indianapolis, IN	263.3
6	Atlanta-Sandy Springs-Marietta, GA	41.0	6	Las Vegas-Paradise, NV	259.1
7	Naples-Marco Island, FL	38.7	7	Portland-Vancouver-Beaverton, OR-WA	178.7
8	Lakeland, FL	38.3	8	Cape Coral-Fort Myers, FL	173.7
9	Sarasota-Bradenton-Venice, FL	38.0	9	Lakeland, FL	172.1
10	Las Vegas-Paradise, NV	35.1	10	Orlando, FL	165.3
	Asians: 2000–2004			**Asians: 1990–2000**	
1	Las Vegas-Paradise, NV	38.5	1	Las Vegas-Paradise, NV	191.2
2	Riverside-San Bernardino-Ontario, CA	31.1	2	Atlanta-Sandy Springs-Marietta, GA	169.4
3	Orlando, FL	30.2	3	Austin-Round Rock, TX	140.8
4	Atlanta-Sandy Springs-Marietta, GA	28.5	4	Orlando, FL	125.3
5	Stockton, CA	28.4	5	Dallas-Fort Worth-Arlington, TX	108.7
6	Tampa-St. Petersburg-Clearwater, FL	38.4	6	Tampa-St. Petersburg-Clearwater, FL	103.2
7	Austin-Round Rock, TX	28.2	7	Phoenix-Mesa-Scottsdale, AZ	93.4
8	Phoenix-Mesa-Scottsdale, AZ	27.0	8	Minneapolis-St. Paul-Bloomington, MN-WI	92.3
9	Sacramento-Arden-Arcade-Roseville, CA	25.6	9	Detroit-Warren-Livonia, MI	87.3
10	Dallas-Fort Worth-Arlington, TX	24.8	10	Houston-Bayton-Sugar Land, TX	81.9
	Blacks: 2000–2004			**Blacks: 1990–2000**	
1	Las Vegas-Paradise, NV	22.7	1	Minneapolis-St. Paul-Bloomington, MN-WI	80.3
2	Phoenix-Mesa-Scottsdale, AZ	19.2	2	Las Vegas-Paradise, NV	75.6
3	Orlando, FL	18.4	3	Atlanta-Sandy Springs-Marietta, GA	57.1
4	Minneapolis-St. Paul-Bloomington, MN-WI	16.2	4	Orlando, FL	55.2
5	Raleigh-Cary, NC	15.2	5	Phoenix-Mesa-Scottsdale, AZ	53.5
6	Atlanta-Sandy Springs-Marietta, GA	15.0	6	Miami-Fort Lauderdale-Miami Beach, FL	41.6
7	Providence-New Bedford-Fall River, RI-MA	14.4	7	Riverside-San Bernardino-Ontario, CA	41.3
8	Riverside-San Bernardino-Ontario, CA	14.3	8	Providence-New Bedford-Fall River, RI-MA	37.4
9	Tampa-St. Petersburg-Clearwater, FL	14.0	9	Raleigh-Cary, NC	35.7
10	Charlotte-Gastonia-Concord, NC-SC	13.7	10	Albany-Schenectady-Troy, NY	35.2

Source: Author's analysis of Census Bureau Population Estimates and decennial census data.
Note: Information is for metropolitan areas where end of period group population exceeds 50,000,

Table D: White Population Change in Metro Areas 2000–2004

Rank	Metro area	Population change 2000–2004
	Greatest white gains	**Change**
1	Phoenix-Mesa-Scottsdale, AZ	151,363
2	Riverside-San Bernardino-Ontario, CA	86,654
3	Atlanta-Sandy Springs-Marietta, GA	80,062
4	Las Vegas-Paradise, NV	79,909
5	Dallas-Fort Worth-Arlington, TX	76,069
6	Sacramento-Arden-Arcade-Roseville, CA	73,118
7	Portland-Vancouver-Beaverton, OR-WA	62,812
8	Houston-Baytown-Sugar Land, TX	59,172
9	Tampa-St. Petersburg-Clearwater, FL	58,123
10	Washington-Arlington-Alexandria, DC-VA-MD-WV	58,033
	Greatest white losses	**Change**
1	New York-Northern New Jersey-Long Island, NY-NJ-PA	-162,114
2	San Francisco-Oakland-Fremont, CA	-94,650
3	Los Angeles-Long Beach-Santa Ana, CA	-83,786
4	Boston-Cambridge-Quincy, MA-NH	-69,564
5	San Jose-Sunnyvale-Santa Clara, CA	-64,243
6	Miami-Fort Lauderdale-Miami Beach, FL	-50,205
7	Pittsburgh, PA	-39,648
8	Chicago-Naperville-Joliet, IL-IN-WI	-27,773
9	Cleveland-Elyria-Mentor, OH	-27,521
10	Philadelphia-Camden-Wilmington, PA-NJ-DE-MD	-27,191
	Highest white growth rates	**Change (%)**
1	St. George, UT	19.0
2	Greeley, CO	18.5
3	Bend, OR	13.7
4	Coeur d'Alene, ID	11.0
5	Prescott, AZ	10.5
6	Wilmington, NC	10.5
7	Boise City-Nampa, ID	10.4
8	Cape Coral-Fort Myers, FL	10.1
9	Naples-Marco Island, FL	9.9
10	Ocala, FL	9.9

Source: Author's analysis of Census Bureau Population Estimates and decennial census data.

Blacks

Unlike the other two minority groups, blacks grew only slightly faster (5 percent) than the U.S. population as a whole (4 percent) during the 2000–2004 period. Many of the areas that have registered the fastest growth in this group's population are located in the South, but they can also be found in other parts of the country that have experienced significant overall population increases.

The metro areas with the fastest-growing black populations from 2000 to 2004 are Las Vegas, Phoenix and Orlando. These are among the fastest-growing metro areas in the nation overall, and the jobs being created there—both low-skill and high-skill—appear to be attracting African-American in-migrants.[f] Still, the South retains a significant hold on black population increase, as the region contains five of the 10 metro areas experiencing the fastest black population growth in recent years.

Of the nation's 361 metropolitan areas, 111 registered declines in white population from 2000 to 2004, with the largest absolute losses occurring in New York, San Francisco and Los Angeles.

Though they make up two-thirds of U.S. population, 2,448 of the nation's 3,141 counties (78 percent) have a white population share exceeding the national average; and more than half (1,775) are at least 85 percent white. Those with the highest proportions are located largely in the Northeast and Midwest, regions that have not received as many immigrant minorities over the past several decades as the West and South.

Metropolitan areas showing the largest absolute gains in white population from 2000 to 2004 include growing "New Sunbelt" destinations in the South and West, including such staples as Phoenix, Atlanta, Las Vegas and Dallas (Table D). The ascendancy of interior California metro areas Riverside and Sacramento is also evident, as are increased flows to the Washington, D.C., area, an economically prosperous part of the country in recent years. These metropolitan areas contrast somewhat with those gaining the largest numbers of Hispanics and Asians in recent years (Table B); traditional immigrant gateways such as Los Angeles, New York, Chicago, Miami and San Francisco continue to stand out for growth in those groups. Indeed, the list of metropolitan areas sustaining the largest white population *losses* over the 2000–2004 period features these traditional gateways.

A strong multi-minority presence characterizes 18 large "melting pot" metro areas, and 27 large metro areas now have "majority minority" child populations.

Notwithstanding the popular narrative of America as a "melting pot" nation, a more precise rendering of its racial and ethnic landscape tends to confine melting pot status to a smaller part of the country. This section updates prior research to identify metropolitan areas that qualify statistically as melting pots in 2004.[g]

"Melting pot" metro areas

To identify these "melting pot metros," all 88 metropolitan areas with populations greater than one-half million are examined. A metro area in which more than one minority group is overrepresented—that is, the group's share of population in that metro area exceeds its share of population nationally—is considered to be a melting pot metro.[h] The metro area must also have a white population share lower than the national share of 67.4 percent.

Using this definition, 18 of the nation's 88 large metropolitan areas qualify as melting pots (Table E). They tilt heavily toward the West, especially California, which contains eight of the 18. Only Florida and Texas also contain more than one melting pot metro area, and the rest—outside of Chicago and New York—locate elsewhere in the South and West.

"Majority minority" child populations

Alongside the rise of multiethnic metro areas, an even larger number of areas have developed "majority-minority" populations among children. Immigrant minorities, who are typically younger and thus exhibit higher fertility rates, contribute significantly to this phenomenon. In nearly one-third of the nation's largest metropolitan areas, at least half of all people under age 15 are racial and ethnic minorities. They include the usual multi-immigrant magnet and West Coast polyglot metropolitan areas like Los Angeles, San Francisco and Miami, as well as a number of metropolitan areas that have typically been thought to be largely white, and which remain so in their overall populations.

Conclusion

No more than a decade ago, it could be reasonably argued that America was not really the racially and ethnically diverse melting pot (Frey, 1998) often portrayed in the media. That is, although the nation's demographic profile showed a significant share of blacks and growing numbers of Hispanics and Asians, the latter two groups, especially, were not spread evenly across the country. While clustering of these groups continues in select metro areas and regions, this survey makes plain that, especially since 2000, the spreading out of these minorities to large parts of the country is now well underway.

This is particularly the case for Hispanics, where 907 counties are at least 5 percent Hispanic in 2004, compared with just 538 in 1990. Twenty-eight states have reached the same threshold in 2004, up from 16 in 1990. These facts are not lost on national political parties, marketers and state/local governments. While movement away from the classic metropolitan magnets for Hispanics and Asians has not yet reached tidal wave proportions, the post-2000 trends show that these gateway areas are losing the strong grip they once had. Pull factors like strong employment opportunities, affordable housing and tolerance for fast growth have begun to tilt the migration balance toward new magnets in interior California, the interior West and the Southeast.

Table E: Large Melting Pot Metros: 2004

Rank	Metro area	Population 2004 (in thousands)	White	Black	Hispanic	Asian	AIAN	2+ races	Total
1	Honolulu, HI	876	20	3	7	46	8	16	100
2	Los Angeles-Long Beach-Santa Ana, CA	12,366	34	7	43	13	1	1	100
3	Fresno, CA	799	38	5	46	9	1	1	100
4	Miami-Fort Lauderdale-Miami Beach, FL	5,008	41	19	37	2	0	1	100
5	San Jose-Sunnyvale-Santa Clara, CA	1,736	41	2	25	28	1	2	100
6	Stockton, CA	564	42	7	34	13	1	3	100
7	Houston-Baytown-Sugar Land, TX	4,715	45	16	32	5	0	1	100
8	Albuquerque, NM	730	46	2	43	2	5	1	100
9	San Francisco-Oakland-Fremont, CA	4,124	47	9	19	21	1	3	100
10	New York-Northern New Jersey-Long Island, NY-NJ-PA	18,323	52	17	21	9	0	1	100
11	San Diego-Carlsbad-San Marcos, CA	2,814	53	5	29	10	1	2	100
12	Washington-Arlington-Alexandria, DC-VA-MD-WV	4,796	53	26	11	8	0	2	100
13	Oxnard-Thousand Oaks-Ventura, CA	753	54	2	35	6	1	2	100
14	Dallas-Fort Worth-Arlington, TX	5,162	55	14	25	4	0	1	100
15	Las Vegas-Paradise, NV	1,376	56	9	25	6	1	2	100
16	Chicago-Naperville-Joliet, IL-IN-WI	9,098	58	18	18	5	0	1	100
17	Orlando, FL	1,645	61	14	20	3	0	1	100
18	Sacramento-Arden-Arcade-Roseville, CA	1,797	61	7	17	10	1	3	100

Source: Author's analysis of Census Bureau Population Estimates and decennial census data.

Note: See text for definition of metros.

Key:
(a) "Overrepresented" minority groups are indicated in bold (see text).

The continued shift of the black population toward the South is also complemented by the group's movement to nontraditional areas outside the South. In fact, the two metro areas with the highest rates of black population growth are Las Vegas and Phoenix. Their growth rates from small initial black populations do not translate to the large numeric gains exhibited for southern metros like Atlanta, Dallas or Washington, D.C. Yet they indicate that some black movers, like their Hispanic and Asian counterparts, are increasingly part of broader economic migration trends.

These emerging dispersal patterns mean that the nation is not yet quite a melting pot with polyglot populations spreading from coast to coast. Among the 88 largest metropolitan areas, only 18 qualify as melting pot metro areas with overrepresentations of two or more minority groups.

The metropolitan trends observed in this survey portray the population dynamics of a nation in which racial and ethnic minorities have accounted for 82 percent of recent growth. The simultaneous concentration and dispersion of these minority groups has created a great deal of variation in the profiles of metropolitan areas across the United States. Indeed, it is between the extremes of 18 melting pot metro areas on the one hand, and the vast, mostly white interior of the county on the other, where challenges to the continued social integration and economic incorporation of the country's large and growing minority populations will assume great importance.

The metropolitan mosaic painted here suggests that private, government and nonprofit actors alike must be sensitive to the unique social and cultural contexts, and changes in those contexts, that characterize the communities they serve. The makeup of America's regions and communities are changing at a pace that the nation has not seen for many decades. How these changes will affect economics, politics and interethnic relations, from the national to the neighborhood scale, deserves our continued attention.

Notes

[a] William H. Frey and others, *Tracking Metropolitan America Into the 21st Century: A Field Guide to the New Metropolitan and Micropolitan Definitions* (Washington: Brookings Institution, 2004).

[b] U.S. Census Bureau, "Estimates and Projections Methodology: County Population Estimates by Age, Sex, Race and Hispanic Origin for July 1, 2004" (*www.census. gov/popest/topics/methodology/2004_co_char_meth.html* [March 2006]). Estimates for July 2004 were released in August 2005.

[c] U.S. Census Bureau, "Estimates of the Population of Counties by Age, Sex, Race and Hispanic Origin: 1990 to 1999" (*www.census.gov/popest/archives/methodology/90s-co-meth.txt* [March 2006]).

[d] In Census 2000, 5.5 percent of Americans indicated their only race as "some other race."

[e] The 1990 population estimates do not classify persons by more than one race, hence comparisons of whites, blacks and Asians between 1990 and 2000 or 2004 may overestimate the 1990 population if some members of that group would have identified themselves as being of more than one race, given the opportunity.

[f] On metropolitan growth, see Frey, "Metro America in the New Century."

[g] William H. Frey, "The Diversity Myth." *American Demographics*, June 1998; Frey, "Melting Pot Suburbs."

[h] For Hispanics and blacks, the national group shares are, respectively, 14.1 percent and 12.1 percent in 2004. For Asians, American Indian/Alaska Natives, and other race groups, this paper considers having at least 5 percent of population in a metro area as indicative of "over-representation."

About the Author

William H. Frey is a demographer known for his expertise on U.S. demographics, migration and urban and regional change. Frey is a fellow at the Brookings Institution, a research professor at the Population Studies Center, University of Michigan, a senior fellow at the Milken Institute and a contributing editor to *American Demographics* magazine.

Table F: Share of Population by Race/Ethnicity, Large Metropolitan Areas: 2004

Metro area	Population 2004 (in thousands)	White	Black	Hispanic	Asian	AIAN	2+ races	White share (%) 2000	1990
Northeast									
New York-Northern New Jersey-Long Island, NY-NJ-PA	18,710	52	17	21	9	0	1	54	62
Philadelphia-Camden-Wilmington, PA-NJ-DE-MD	5,801	69	20	6	4	0	1	71	76
Boston-Cambridge-Quincy, MA-NH	4,425	79	6	7	6	0	1	81	87
Pittsburgh, PA	2,402	89	8	1	1	0	1	89	91
Providence-New Bedford-Fall River, RI-MA	1,629	84	4	8	2	0	1	86	91
Hartford-West Hartford-East Hartford, CT	1,185	76	10	10	3	0	1	78	83
Buffalo-Niagara Falls, NY	1,154	82	12	3	2	1	1	83	86
Rochester, NY	1,041	81	11	5	2	0	1	82	86
Bridgeport-Stamford-Norwalk, CT	903	71	10	14	4	0	1	74	80
New Haven-Milford, CT	746	73	11	12	3	0	1	75	82
Albany-Schenectady-Troy, NY	745	87	7	3	3	0	1	88	92
Allentown-Bethlehem-Easton, PA-NJ	780	85	3	9	2	0	1	88	83
Worcester, MA	779	85	3	8	3	0	1	87	92
Springfield, MA	688	79	6	12	2	0	1	80	86
Poughkeepsie-Newburgh-Middletown, NY	664	76	9	11	2	0	1	79	85
Syracuse, NY	654	87	7	2	2	1	1	88	91
Scranton-Wilkes-Barre, PA	552	95	2	2	1	0	0	96	98
Harrisburg-Carlisle, PA	519	84	9	3	2	0	1	85	89
Northeast Total	**43,576**	**67**	**13**	**13**	**6**	**0**	**1**	**69**	**75**
Midwest									
Chicago-Naperville-Joliet, IL-IN-WI	9,392	58	18	18	5	0	1	60	67
Detroit-Warren-Livonia, MI	4,493	69	23	3	3	0	1	70	74
Minneapolis-St. Paul-Bloomington, MN-WI	3,116	83	6	4	5	1	2	85	92
St. Louis, MO-IL	2,764	77	18	2	2	0	1	78	81
Cleveland-Elyria-Mentor, OH	2,137	74	19	4	2	0	1	75	79
Cincinnati-Middletown, OH-KY-IN	2,058	84	12	1	1	0	1	85	88
Kansas City, MO-KS	1,925	78	12	6	2	1	1	79	83
Columbus, OH	1,694	79	14	2	3	0	2	81	86
Indianapolis, IN	1,622	79	14	4	2	0	1	81	85
Milwaukee-Waukesha-West Allis, WI	1,516	73	16	7	2	1	1	74	81
Dayton, OH	846	81	15	1	2	0	1	82	85
Omaha-Council Bluffs, NE-IA	804	82	8	7	2	1	1	84	89
Grand Rapids-Wyoming, MI	768	82	7	7	2	1	1	83	89
Akron, OH	702	85	11	1	2	0	1	86	88
Toledo, OH	658	80	12	5	1	0	1	81	85
Youngstown-Warren-Boardman, OH-PA	590	86	11	2	0	0	1	86	88
Wichita, KS	585	78	7	8	3	1	2	80	86
Madison, WI	532	87	4	4	4	0	1	89	94
Midwest Total	**36,201**	**73**	**15**	**8**	**3**	**0**	**1**	**74**	**79**
South									
Dallas-Fort Worth-Arlington, TX	5,700	55	14	25	4	0	1	59	70
Miami-Fort Lauderdale-Miami Beach, FL	5,362	41	19	37	2	0	1	44	54
Houston-Baytown-Sugar Land, TX	5,180	45	16	32	5	0	1	48	58
Washington-Arlington-Alexandria, DC-VA-MD-WV	5,140	53	26	11	8	0	2	56	64
Atlanta-Sandy Springs-Marietta, GA	4,708	57	30	8	4	0	1	61	71
Baltimore-Towson, MD	2,639	65	28	3	3	0	1	66	71
Tampa-St. Petersburg-Clearwater, FL	2,588	73	11	13	2	0	1	76	83
Orlando, FL	1,862	61	14	20	3	0	1	65	78
San Antonio, TX	1,854	39	6	52	1	0	1	41	46
Virginia Beach-Norfolk-Newport News, VA-NC	1,644	60	31	4	3	0	2	61	67
Charlotte-Gastonia-Concord, NC-SC	1,475	66	23	7	2	0	1	69	76
Austin-Round Rock, TX	1,412	58	7	29	4	0	1	61	67
Nashville-Davidson--Murfreesboro, TN	1,396	77	15	4	2	0	1	79	83
New Orleans-Metairie-Kenner, LA	1,320	54	38	5	2	0	1	55	60
Memphis, TN-MS-AR	1,250	50	45	3	2	0	1	52	57
Jacksonville, FL	1,225	69	22	5	3	0	1	71	76
Louisville, KY-IN	1,201	82	13	2	1	0	1	83	86
Richmond, VA	1,154	63	30	3	2	0	1	64	68
Oklahoma City, OK	1,144	72	11	8	3	4	3	73	80
Birmingham-Hoover, AL	1,082	68	28	2	1	0	1	69	73
Raleigh-Cary, NC	915	68	20	7	3	0	1	70	76
Tulsa, OK	882	73	9	6	1	7	4	74	82
Baton Rouge, LA	729	61	35	2	1	0	1	62	65
El Paso, TX	713	15	2	81	1	0	0	17	25

Table F: Share of Population by Race/Ethnicity, Large Metropolitan Areas: 2004, continued

Metro area	Population 2004 (in thousands)	White	Black	Hispanic	Asian	AIAN	2+ races	2000	1990
South, cont.									
El Paso, TX	713	15	2	81	1	0	0	17	25
Columbia, SC	679	61	33	3	1	0	1	62	66
Greensboro-High Point, NC	668	67	24	6	2	0	1	70	77
McAllen-Edinburg-Pharr, TX	658	10	0	89	1	0	0	10	14
Sarasota-Bradenton-Venice, FL	652	84	6	8	1	0	1	86	90
Knoxville, TN	647	89	6	2	1	0	1	90	92
Little Rock-North Little Rock, AR	637	73	22	3	1	0	1	74	79
Greenville, SC	584	76	17	4	1	0	1	78	81
Charleston-North Charleston, SC	583	64	30	3	1	0	1	64	67
South Total	**57,684**	**57**	**20**	**18**	**3**	**1**	**1**	**60**	**67**
West									
Los Angeles-Long Beach-Santa Ana, CA	12,925	34	7	43	13	1	1	36	46
San Francisco-Oakland-Fremont, CA	4,154	47	9	19	21	1	3	50	58
Riverside-San Bernardino-Ontario, CA	3,793	44	7	42	5	1	2	48	62
Phoenix-Mesa-Scottsdale, AZ	3,715	62	4	28	2	2	1	66	76
Seattle-Tacoma-Bellevue, WA	3,167	74	5	6	10	2	3	76	85
San Diego-Carlsbad-San Marcos, CA	2,932	53	5	29	10	1	2	55	65
Denver-Aurora, CO	2,330	68	5	21	3	1	2	71	79
Portland-Vancouver-Beaverton, OR-WA	2,064	80	3	9	5	1	2	82	90
Sacramento--Arden-Arcade--Roseville, CA	2,017	61	7	17	10	1	3	64	72
San Jose-Sunnyvale-Santa Clara, CA	1,741	41	2	25	28	1	2	45	58
Las Vegas-Paradise, NV	1,651	56	9	25	6	1	2	61	75
Salt Lake City, UT	1,019	79	1	14	3	2	1	82	90
Tucson, AZ	907	59	3	32	2	3	1	62	68
Honolulu, HI	900	20	3	7	46	8	16	20	30
Fresno, CA	867	38	5	46	9	1	1	40	51
Oxnard-Thousand Oaks-Ventura, CA	798	54	2	35	6	1	2	57	66
Albuquerque, NM	781	46	2	43	2	5	1	48	55
Bakersfield, CA	735	46	6	42	4	1	2	50	63
Stockton, CA	650	42	7	34	13	1	3	48	59
Colorado Springs, CO	576	76	6	12	3	1	3	77	82
West Total	**47,722**	**50**	**6**	**29**	**11**	**1**	**2**	**53**	**63**

Header spanning note: columns White/Black/Hispanic/Asian/AIAN/2+ races are under "Share of population, 2004 (%)"; columns 2000/1990 are under "White share (%)".

Source: Author's analysis of Census Bureau Population Estimates Program and decennial census data.

Table G: Black Population Change 1990–2004, Fifty Metro Areas with Largest Black Populations in 2004

Rank	Metro area	Black population 2004	Black population change 2000–2004	Black population change 1990–2000	Percent 2000–2004	Percent 1990–2000	Share of total (%) 2004	Share of total (%) 2000	Share of total (%) 1990
1	New York-Northern New Jersey-Long Island, NY-NJ-PA	3,202,808	-323	307,967	0.0	10.6	17.1	17.4	17.1
2	Chicago-Naperville-Joliet, IL-IN-WI	1,694,518	12,580	146,422	0.7	9.5	18.0	18.4	18.7
3	Atlanta-Sandy Springs-Marietta, GA	1,406,290	183,817	444,509	15.0	57.1	29.9	28.6	25.2
4	Washington-Arlington-Alexandria, DC-VA-MD-WV	1,335,823	64,439	218,544	5.1	20.8	26.0	26.4	25.4
5	Philadelphia-Camden-Wilmington, PA-NJ-DE-MD	1,162,847	42,997	116,209	3.8	11.6	20.0	19.7	18.4
6	Miami-Fort Lauderdale-Miami Beach, FL	1,044,406	96,934	278,583	10.2	41.6	19.5	18.8	16.4
7	Detroit-Warren-Livonia, MI	1,026,048	10,678	75,264	1.1	8.0	22.8	22.8	22.1
8	Los Angeles-Long Beach-Santa Ana, CA	947,351	-8,613	-26,588	-0.9	-2.7	7.3	7.7	8.7
9	Houston-Baytown-Sugar Land, TX	848,221	56,694	128,594	7.2	19.4	16.4	16.7	17.5
10	Dallas-Fort Worth-Arlington, TX	789,807	74,562	158,251	10.4	28.4	13.9	13.8	13.9
11	Baltimore-Towson, MD	738,760	38,759	85,632	5.5	13.9	28.0	27.4	25.7
12	Memphis, TN-MS-AR	558,959	34,890	84,134	6.7	19.1	44.7	43.4	41.1
13	Virginia Beach-Norfolk-Newport News, VA-NC	511,834	24,960	75,310	5.1	18.3	31.1	30.8	28.2
14	New Orleans-Metairie-Kenner, LA	498,420	9,459	55,852	1.9	12.9	37.8	37.2	34.3
15	St. Louis, MO-IL	498,302	19,095	53,365	4.0	12.5	18.0	17.7	16.5
16	Cleveland-Elyria-Mentor, OH	415,605	3,934	36,256	1.0	9.7	19.4	19.2	17.8
17	San Francisco-Oakland-Fremont, CA	368,803	-24,848	-34,253	-6.3	-8.0	8.9	9.5	11.5
18	Richmond, VA	348,672	15,241	50,445	4.6	17.8	30.2	30.3	29.7
19	Charlotte-Gastonia-Concord, NC-SC	337,348	40,703	74,252	13.7	33.4	22.9	22.1	21.6
20	Birmingham-Hoover, AL	302,290	12,615	36,344	4.4	14.3	27.9	27.5	26.4
21	Boston-Cambridge-Quincy, MA-NH	281,942	10,035	51,911	3.7	23.6	6.4	6.2	5.3
22	Riverside-San Bernardino-Ontario, CA	281,397	35,292	71,936	14.3	41.3	7.4	7.5	6.6
23	Tampa-St. Petersburg-Clearwater, FL	275,421	33,759	58,051	14.0	31.6	10.6	10.1	8.8
24	Jacksonville, FL	269,469	27,965	56,825	11.6	30.8	22.0	21.4	19.8
25	Orlando, FL	269,073	41,729	80,902	18.4	55.2	14.5	13.7	11.8
26	Baton Rouge, LA	251,509	10,589	39,518	4.4	19.6	34.5	34.1	32.2
27	Milwaukee-Waukesha-West Allis, WI	242,633	9,368	36,480	4.0	18.5	16.0	15.5	13.7
28	Cincinnati-Middletown, OH-KY-IN	240,238	8,692	27,050	3.8	13.2	11.7	11.5	11.1
29	Jackson, MS	238,521	13,903	34,890	6.2	18.4	46.1	45.1	42.3
30	Kansas City, MO-KS	234,905	7,451	26,799	3.3	13.4	12.2	12.3	12.2
31	Columbus, OH	234,726	24,445	45,380	11.6	27.5	13.9	13.0	11.7
32	Indianapolis, IN	233,327	18,340	41,516	8.5	23.9	14.4	14.0	13.3
33	Columbia, SC	226,451	13,951	36,836	6.6	21.0	33.3	32.7	31.8
34	Nashville-Davidson-Murfreesboro, TN	210,181	14,631	40,503	7.5	26.1	15.1	14.8	14.7
35	Pittsburgh, PA	194,821	3,074	11,388	1.6	6.3	8.1	7.9	7.3
36	Minneapolis-St. Paul-Bloomington, MN-WI	187,453	26,177	71,807	16.2	80.3	6.0	5.4	3.5
37	Augusta-Richmond County, GA-SC	182,942	8,240	31,161	4.7	21.7	35.5	34.9	32.7
38	Raleigh-Cary, NC	182,182	24,089	41,568	15.2	35.7	19.9	19.7	21.2
39	Charleston-North Charleston, SC	174,828	5,680	15,874	3.4	10.4	30.0	30.7	30.1
40	Seattle-Tacoma-Bellevue, WA	163,580	10,084	31,280	6.6	25.6	5.2	5.0	4.7
41	Greensboro-High Point, NC	158,314	9,389	32,686	6.3	28.1	23.7	23.1	21.4
42	Louisville, KY-IN	157,763	8,067	19,996	5.4	15.4	13.1	12.8	12.3
43	Las Vegas-Paradise, NV	152,103	28,182	53,360	22.7	75.6	9.2	8.9	9.3
44	San Diego-Carlsbad-San Marcos, CA	150,079	-8,066	6,175	-5.1	4.1	5.1	5.6	6.0
45	Shreveport-Bossier City, LA	148,005	4,669	15,696	3.3	12.3	38.8	38.1	35.5
46	Montgomery, AL	147,070	7,864	24,372	5.6	21.2	41.4	40.1	37.5
47	Sacramento-Arden-Arcade-Roseville, CA	140,727	15,048	19,798	12.0	18.7	7.0	6.9	7.0
48	Little Rock-North Little Rock, AR	138,225	9,625	25,655	7.5	24.9	21.7	21.0	19.2
49	Phoenix-Mesa-Scottsdale, AZ	137,824	22,224	40,273	19.2	53.5	3.7	3.5	3.3
50	Mobile, AL	137,082	3,701	15,576	2.8	13.2	34.2	33.3	31.1

Source: Author's analysis of Census Bureau Population Estimates and decennial census data.

Table H: Hispanic Population Change 1990–2004, Fifty Metro Areas with Largest Hispanic Populations in 2004

Rank	Metro area	Hispanic population 2004	Hispanic population change 2000–2004	1990–2000	Percent 2000–2004	1990–2000	Share of total (%) 2004	2000	1990
1	Los Angeles-Long Beach-Santa Ana, CA	5,587,692	435,674	1,212,240	8.5	30.8	43.2	41.5	34.9
2	New York-Northern New Jersey-Long Island, NY-NJ-PA	3,882,817	288,325	882,596	8.0	32.5	20.8	19.6	16.1
3	Miami-Fort Lauderdale-Miami Beach, FL	1,982,641	261,354	580,310	15.2	50.9	37.0	34.2	28.0
4	Chicago-Naperville-Joliet, IL-IN-WI	1,725,685	217,047	604,164	14.4	66.8	18.4	16.5	11.0
5	Houston-Baytown-Sugar Land, TX	1,637,992	268,834	580,929	19.6	73.7	31.6	28.9	20.8
6	Riverside-San Bernardino-Ontario, CA	1,580,457	333,527	543,084	26.7	77.2	41.7	38.0	26.8
7	Dallas-Fort Worth-Arlington, TX	1,423,020	290,590	597,214	25.7	111.6	25.0	21.8	13.3
8	Phoenix-Mesa-Scottsdale, AZ	1,056,145	226,472	443,839	27.3	115.0	28.4	25.3	17.2
9	San Antonio, TX	965,745	93,761	209,087	10.8	31.5	52.1	50.7	47.0
10	San Diego-Carlsbad-San Marcos, CA	849,771	91,208	241,572	12.0	45.7	29.0	26.9	20.6
11	San Francisco-Oakland-Fremont, CA	794,370	58,725	216,261	8.0	41.6	19.1	17.8	14.0
12	McAllen-Edinburg-Pharr, TX	586,221	78,128	177,688	15.4	53.8	89.1	88.5	85.3
13	El Paso, TX	575,515	40,798	119,092	7.6	28.7	80.7	78.5	69.8
14	Washington-Arlington-Alexandria, DC-VA-MD-WV	549,328	114,039	204,980	26.2	89.0	10.7	9.0	5.6
15	Denver-Aurora, CO	492,209	85,905	190,788	21.1	88.5	21.1	18.5	13.0
16	San Jose-Sunnyvale-Santa Clara, CA	443,968	13,893	97,492	3.2	29.3	25.5	24.7	21.7
17	Las Vegas-Paradise, NV	416,021	108,083	222,190	35.1	259.1	25.2	22.1	11.3
18	Austin-Round Rock, TX	405,256	71,014	155,176	21.2	86.7	28.7	26.4	21.0
19	Fresno, CA	399,708	44,901	115,295	12.7	48.1	46.1	44.2	35.6
20	Atlanta-Sandy Springs-Marietta, GA	386,741	112,362	214,074	41.0	355.0	8.2	6.4	2.0
21	Orlando, FL	372,756	95,973	172,441	34.7	165.3	20.0	16.7	8.4
22	Sacramento-Arden-Arcade--Roseville, CA	344,660	64,087	98,518	22.8	54.1	17.1	15.5	12.0
23	Albuquerque, NM	335,495	30,591	80,101	10.0	35.6	42.9	41.7	37.3
24	Philadelphia-Camden-Wilmington, PA-NJ-DE-MD	333,581	46,035	98,263	16.0	51.9	5.8	5.1	3.5
25	Tampa-St. Petersburg-Clearwater, FL	324,803	72,370	110,703	28.7	78.1	12.6	10.5	6.8
26	Boston-Cambridge-Quincy, MA-NH	324,356	40,192	93,089	14.1	48.7	7.3	6.5	4.6
27	Brownsville-Harlingen, TX	318,722	33,908	70,377	11.9	32.8	85.7	74.6	81.9
28	Bakersfield, CA	312,124	55,438	102,120	21.6	66.1	42.5	38.7	28.1
29	Tucson, AZ	287,920	37,295	85,822	14.9	52.1	31.7	29.5	24.6
30	Oxnard-Thousand Oaks-Ventura, CA	283,043	28,271	76,558	11.1	43.0	35.5	33.7	26.6
31	Corpus Christi, TX	224,712	10,721	28,055	5.0	15.1	54.8	53.1	50.5
32	Stockton, CA	220,034	46,316	59,602	26.7	52.2	33.9	30.6	23.6
33	Visalia-Porterville, CA	217,800	29,189	66,076	15.5	53.9	54.2	51.1	39.0
34	Laredo, TX	208,270	24,540	57,530	13.4	45.6	94.9	94.4	93.9
35	Salinas, CA	207,947	18,219	68,494	9.6	56.5	50.2	47.1	33.9
36	Seattle-Tacoma-Bellevue, WA	201,074	36,263	87,581	22.0	113.4	6.3	5.4	3.0
37	Portland-Vancouver-Beaverton, OR-WA	185,470	40,584	92,907	28.0	178.7	9.0	7.5	3.4
38	Modesto, CA	181,475	37,503	61,249	26.0	74.0	36.4	32.0	22.0
39	Detroit-Warren-Livonia, MI	148,607	20,453	44,332	16.0	52.9	3.3	2.9	2.0
40	Santa Barbara-Santa Maria-Goleta, CA	147,498	9,775	38,609	7.1	39.0	36.7	34.5	26.7
41	Salt Lake City, UT	141,842	26,827	67,303	23.3	141.1	13.9	11.8	6.2
42	Providence-New Bedford-Fall River, RI-MA	136,081	24,978	51,221	22.5	85.5	8.4	7.0	4.0
43	Minneapolis-St. Paul-Bloomington, MN-WI	127,807	27,340	62,015	27.2	161.3	4.1	3.4	1.5
44	Bridgeport-Stamford-Norwalk, CT	122,895	17,127	34,343	16.2	48.1	13.6	12.0	8.6
45	Hartford-West Hartford-East Hartford, CT	120,560	12,014	31,401	11.1	40.7	10.2	9.4	6.9
46	Las Cruces, NM	120,369	9,238	33,686	8.3	43.5	64.7	63.5	56.7
47	Merced, CA	119,061	22,636	37,368	23.5	63.3	50.2	45.6	32.8
48	Kansas City, MO-KS	118,938	23,591	48,921	24.7	105.4	6.2	5.2	2.8
49	El Centro, CA	113,796	10,385	30,304	10.0	41.5	74.6	72.6	66.0
50	Milwaukee-Waukesha-West Allis, WI	111,562	16,235	43,316	17.0	83.3	7.4	6.3	3.6

Source: Author's analysis of Census Bureau Population Estimates and decennial census data.

Table I: Asian Population Change 1990–2004, Fifty Metro Areas with Largest Asian Populations in 2004

		Asian population	Asian population change				Share of total (%)		
					Percent				
Rank	Metro area	2004	2000–2004	1990–2000	2000–2004	1990–2000	2004	2000	1990
1	Los Angeles-Long Beach-Santa Ana, CA	1,712,127	164,474	378,616	10.6	32.4	13.2	12.5	10.3
2	New York-Northern New Jersey-Long Island, NY-NJ-PA	1,616,489	201,543	579,747	14.2	69.4	8.6	7.7	4.9
3	San Francisco-Oakland-Fremont, CA	879,495	71,326	216,044	8.8	36.5	21.2	19.5	15.9
4	San Jose-Sunnyvale-Santa Clara, CA	491,876	54,218	180,291	12.4	70.1	28.2	25.2	16.8
5	Chicago-Naperville-Joliet, IL-IN-WI	454,300	58,283	142,837	14.7	56.4	4.8	4.3	3.1
6	Honolulu, HI	413,015	11,455	-104,563	2.9	-20.7	45.9	45.9	60.4
7	Washington-Arlington-Alexandria, DC-VA-MD-WV	405,859	67,099	135,722	19.8	66.8	7.9	7.0	4.9
8	Seattle-Tacoma-Bellevue, WA	308,600	43,738	101,625	16.5	62.3	9.7	8.7	6.3
9	San Diego-Carlsbad-San Marcos, CA	283,037	31,897	62,042	12.7	32.8	9.7	8.9	7.5
10	Houston-Baytown-Sugar Land, TX	281,894	46,557	105,980	19.8	81.9	5.4	5.0	3.4
11	Dallas-Fort Worth-Arlington, TX	250,875	49,881	104,673	24.8	108.7	4.4	3.9	2.4
12	Boston-Cambridge-Quincy, MA-NH	245,493	36,567	89,367	17.5	74.7	5.5	4.7	2.9
13	Philadelphia-Camden-Wilmington, PA-NJ-DE-MD	226,577	35,879	79,103	18.8	70.9	3.9	3.3	2.0
14	Sacramento--Arden-Arcade--Roseville, CA	207,816	42,377	49,046	25.6	42.1	10.3	9.1	7.7
15	Atlanta-Sandy Springs-Marietta, GA	181,066	40,181	88,585	28.5	169.4	3.8	3.3	1.7
16	Riverside-San Bernardino-Ontario, CA	179,431	42,515	40,129	31.1	41.5	4.7	4.2	3.7
17	Minneapolis-St. Paul-Bloomington, MN-WI	147,904	22,018	60,423	17.5	92.3	4.7	4.2	2.6
18	Detroit-Warren-Livonia, MI	130,221	23,833	49,583	22.4	87.3	2.9	2.4	1.3
19	Portland-Vancouver-Beaverton, OR-WA	105,165	15,096	37,659	16.8	71.9	5.1	4.7	3.4
20	Miami-Fort Lauderdale-Miami Beach, FL	104,501	16,839	37,445	19.2	74.6	1.9	1.7	1.2
21	Las Vegas-Paradise, NV	102,571	28,491	48,641	38.5	191.2	6.2	5.3	3.4
22	Baltimore-Towson, MD	87,102	16,580	27,928	23.5	65.6	3.3	2.8	1.8
23	Phoenix-Mesa-Scottsdale, AZ	86,414	18,368	32,858	27.0	93.4	2.3	2.1	1.6
24	Stockton, CA	83,345	18,430	8,056	28.4	14.2	12.8	11.4	11.7
25	Denver-Aurora, CO	75,352	10,339	28,842	15.9	79.7	3.2	3.0	2.2
26	Fresno, CA	74,149	8,917	9,910	13.7	17.9	8.6	8.1	8.2
27	Orlando, FL	60,655	14,055	25,914	30.2	125.3	3.3	2.8	1.7
28	Tampa-St. Petersburg-Clearwater, FL	59,339	13,107	23,482	28.4	103.2	2.3	1.9	1.1
29	Austin-Round Rock, TX	57,718	12,709	26,319	28.2	140.8	4.1	3.6	2.2
30	Vallejo-Fairfield, CA	55,546	4,746	9,419	9.3	22.8	13.5	12.8	12.0
31	Virginia Beach-Norfolk-Newport News, VA-NC	47,824	4,429	9,752	10.2	29.0	2.9	2.7	2.3
32	Oxnard-Thousand Oaks-Ventura, CA	47,233	6,965	7,133	17.3	21.5	5.9	5.3	4.9
33	Columbus, OH	46,346	8,565	16,782	22.7	79.9	2.7	2.3	1.5
34	St. Louis, MO-IL	45,526	7,401	14,348	19.4	60.3	1.6	1.4	0.9
35	Providence-New Bedford-Fall River, RI-MA	37,108	5,001	9,615	15.6	42.7	2.3	2.0	1.5
36	Milwaukee-Waukesha-West Allis, WI	36,619	4,778	13,142	15.0	70.3	2.4	2.1	1.3
37	Kansas City, MO-KS	36,118	6,555	12,304	22.2	71.3	1.9	1.6	1.1
38	Charlotte-Gastonia-Concord, NC-SC	35,857	7,607	17,574	26.9	164.6	2.4	2.1	1.0
39	Bridgeport-Stamford-Norwalk, CT	35,107	5,184	12,833	17.3	75.1	3.9	3.4	2.1
40	Cleveland-Elyria-Mentor, OH	34,428	3,677	8,857	12.0	40.5	1.6	1.4	1.0
41	Hartford-West Hartford-East Hartford, CT	34,139	6,948	10,109	25.6	59.2	2.9	2.4	1.5
42	Jacksonville, FL	31,813	5,617	11,483	21.4	78.0	2.6	2.3	1.6
43	Pittsburgh, PA	31,129	4,224	10,043	15.7	59.6	1.3	1.1	0.7
44	Oklahoma City, OK	31,069	3,614	10,125	13.2	58.4	2.7	2.5	1.8
45	New Orleans-Metairie-Kenner, LA	30,959	1,926	8,058	6.6	38.4	2.3	2.2	1.7
46	Raleigh-Cary, NC	30,678	8,096	14,024	35.9	163.9	3.4	2.8	1.6
47	Cincinnati-Middletown, OH-KY-IN	29,899	4,739	10,893	18.8	76.4	1.5	1.2	0.8
48	San Antonio, TX	27,325	4,231	8,307	18.3	56.2	1.5	1.3	1.0
49	Salt Lake City, UT	27,011	2,816	3,898	11.6	19.2	2.7	2.5	2.6
50	Richmond, VA	26,626	5,479	9,294	25.9	78.4	2.3	1.9	1.2

Source: Author's analysis of Census Bureau Population Estimates and decennial census data.

Table J: 2000–2005 Race-Ethnic and Growth Statistics for States

State or other jurisdiction	2005 size (1,000s)	Percent change 2000–05		Shares of total population 2005**			
		Total	Whites#	White#	Black#	Asian#	Hispanic#
Eastern Region							
Connecticut	3,412	2.9	-0.4	75.4	9.2	3.2	10.9
Delaware	786	7.3	2.8	69.6	20.2	2.7	6.0
Maine	1,277	3.5	2.8	96.0	0.7	0.8	1.0
Massachusetts	6,362	0.6	-2.3	80.3	5.8	4.7	7.9
New Hampshire	1,241	5.6	4.2	94.1	0.8	1.8	2.2
New Jersey	8,434	3.4	-1.7	63.2	13.2	7.2	15.2
New York	18,999	1.3	-1.2	60.9	15.0	6.6	16.1
Pennsylvania	12,286	1.2	-0.8	82.6	10.2	2.2	4.1
Rhode Island	1,051	2.4	-1.1	80.0	4.9	2.7	10.7
Vermont	610	2.1	1.7	95.9	0.6	1.0	1.1
Midwestern Region							
Illinois	12,440	2.6	-0.9	65.8	14.8	4.0	14.3
Indiana	6,092	3.0	1.0	84.3	8.7	1.2	4.5
Iowa	2,929	1.3	-0.1	91.5	2.2	1.5	3.7
Kansas	2,693	1.9	-0.1	81.6	5.7	2.1	8.3
Michigan	9,956	1.7	0.3	77.9	14.2	2.2	3.8
Minnesota	4,934	4.0	1.7	86.3	4.1	3.5	3.6
Nebraska	1,713	2.7	0.2	85.4	4.1	1.6	7.1
North Dakota	641	-0.7	-1.8	90.8	0.7	0.7	1.6
Ohio	11,364	0.9	-0.4	83.1	11.8	1.4	2.3
South Dakota	756	2.7	1.1	86.8	0.8	0.7	2.1
Wisconsin	5,374	3.0	1.3	86.0	5.8	2.0	4.5
Southern Region							
Alabama	4,452	2.4	0.8	69.3	26.2	0.8	2.3
Arkansas	2,679	3.8	1.5	77.0	15.6	1.0	4.7
Florida	16,049	10.8	5.0	62.1	15.0	2.1	19.5
Georgia	8,230	10.2	4.7	59.6	29.4	2.7	7.1
Kentucky	4,049	3.1	2.1	88.6	7.4	0.9	2.0
Louisiana	4,470	1.2	-0.5	61.6	32.9	1.4	2.8
Maryland	5,312	5.4	0.3	59.2	28.8	4.8	5.7
Mississippi	2,849	2.5	0.7	59.7	36.8	0.7	1.7
Missouri	5,606	3.5	2.2	82.9	11.4	1.4	2.7
North Carolina	8,078	7.5	4.5	68.3	21.4	1.8	6.4
Oklahoma	3,454	2.7	0.5	72.5	7.6	1.6	6.6
South Carolina	4,024	5.8	4.6	65.5	29.0	1.1	3.3
Tennessee	5,703	4.6	2.6	77.9	16.7	1.3	3.0
Texas	20,949	9.1	2.2	49.2	11.2	3.2	35.1
Virginia	7,104	6.5	3.3	68.2	19.5	4.6	6.0
West Virginia	1,807	0.5	0.2	94.4	3.2	0.6	0.9
Western Region							
Alaska	628	5.8	3.7	66.5	3.4	5.0	5.1
Arizona	5,166	15.0	8.7	60.4	3.2	2.2	28.5
California	34,003	6.3	-1.3	43.8	6.2	12.3	35.2
Colorado	4,327	7.8	4.1	72.1	3.7	2.6	19.5
Hawaii	1,212	5.2	7.1	23.5	2.1	49.0	8.0
Idaho	1,300	10.0	8.3	87.0	0.5	1.1	9.1
Montana	904	3.6	2.7	89.0	0.3	0.6	2.4
Nevada	2,018	19.7	9.7	60.0	7.2	6.0	23.5
New Mexico	1,822	5.9	1.6	43.1	1.8	1.2	43.4
Oregon	3,431	6.1	3.3	81.6	1.6	3.6	9.9
Utah	2,243	10.1	7.7	83.5	0.8	2.5	10.9
Washington	5,911	6.4	3.4	77.1	3.3	6.7	8.8
Wyoming	494	3.1	2.4	88.6	0.8	0.7	6.7
District of Columbia	571	-3.6	6.4	31.1	55.7	3.1	8.6

Source: William H. Frey analysis of US Census estimates.

** Race-ethnic Groups do not sum to 100% because of of omitted categories, native Americans and 2 or more races

Pertains to Non-Hispanic members of racial group

Women in State Government: Historical Overview and Current Trends

By Susan J. Carroll

In recent years the movement of women into state-level offices has slowed following several decades of gains. This pattern of stagnation did not change following the 2006 elections which produced only modest changes—most positive but some negative—in the numbers of women officials. Efforts to actively recruit women for elected and appointed positions will be critical in determining what the future holds for women in state government.

In the history of our nation, women are relative newcomers among state elected and appointed officials. Women first entered state-level offices in the 1920s following passage and ratification of the 19th Amendment to the U.S. Constitution which granted women suffrage. However, significant growth in the number of women in office occurred only after the emergence of the contemporary women's movement during the late-1960s and early-1970s. Since the mid-1970s, as data collected by the Center for American Women and Politics show,[1] women have greatly increased their numbers among elected and appointed officials in state government. Nevertheless, in recent years progress has slowed, and nationwide statistics show the numbers of women serving in state-level offices have leveled. The 2006 elections did little to alter the recent pattern of stagnation, with the numbers of women nationwide showing only small changes, most positive but some negative, following the elections.

Governors

Since the founding of our country, only 29 women (18D, 11R) have served as governors (Table A), and only one woman has served as governor of a U.S. territory (Puerto Rico).[2] A majority of the states, 28, have never had a woman chief executive. Arizona is the only state to have had three women governors as well as the only state where a woman succeeded another as governor. Connecticut, Texas, Kansas, Washington and New Hampshire have each had two women governors although one of the governors of New Hampshire, Vesta Roy, served for only seven days following the death of an incumbent.

The first woman governor, Nellie Tayloe Ross of Wyoming, was selected in a special election to succeed her deceased husband in 1925. Fifteen days later a second woman, Miriam "Ma" Ferguson, was inaugurated as governor of Texas, having been elected as a surrogate for her husband, a former governor who

had been impeached and consequently was barred constitutionally from running again. Ferguson's campaign slogan was "Two governors for the price of one."[3] The third woman to serve as a governor, Lurleen Wallace of Alabama, campaigned on the slogan, "Let George do it," and was similarly elected to replace a husband who was prohibited by term limits from seeking an additional term in office.[4]

The first woman elected in her own right (i.e., without following her husband) into the governorship was Ella Grasso, who presided over the state of Connecticut from 1975 to 1980. Nineteen of the women governors (including Grasso) who have served since the mid-1970s were elected in their own right. The other seven became governor through constitutional succession; only one of these seven was subsequently elected to a full term.

Nine women (6D, 3R) serve as governors in 2007, matching the record for the most women to serve simultaneously set in 2004. The number of women governors increased by one as a result of the 2006 elections as Sarah Palin (R) of Alaska was elected to her first term as governor. She joins five women—Janet Napolitano (D) of Arizona, M. Jodi Rell (R) of Connecticut, Linda Lingle (R) of Hawaii, Kathleen Sebelius (D) of Kansas, and Jennifer Granholm (D) of Michigan—who sought and won re-election, and three women—Ruth Ann Minner (D) of Delaware, Kathleen Blanco (D) of Louisiana, and Christine Gregoire (D) of Washington—whose seats were not up in 2006.

Other Statewide Elected and Appointed Officials in the Executive Branch

The states vary greatly in the number of statewide elected and appointed officials. For example, Maine, New Hampshire and New Jersey have only one statewide elected official, the governor, while North Dakota, at the other extreme, has 12.

The first woman to ever hold a major statewide office was Democrat Soledad C. Chacón, who was

Table A: Women Governors Throughout History

Name (party-state)	Dates served	Special circumstances
Nellie Tayloe Ross (D-WY)	1925–1927	Won special election to replace deceased husband.
Miriam "Ma" Ferguson (D-TX)	1925–1927, 1933–1935	Inaugurated 15 days after Ross; elected as surrogate for husband who could not succeed himself.
Lurleen Wallace (D-AL)	1967–1968	Elected as surrogate for husband who could not succeed himself.
Ella Grasso (D-CT)	1975–1980	First woman elected governor in her own right; resigned for health reasons.
Dixy Lee Ray (D-WA)	1977–1981	
Vesta Roy (R-NH)	1982–1983	Elected to state senate and chosen as senate president; served as governor for seven days when incumbent died.
Martha Layne Collins (D-KY)	1984–1987	
Madeleine Kunin (D-VT)	1985–1991	First woman to serve three terms as governor.
Kay Orr (R-NE)	1987–1991	First Republican woman governor and first woman to defeat another woman in a gubernatorial race.
Rose Mofford (D-AZ)	1988–1991	Elected as secretary of state, succeeded governor who was impeached and convicted.
Joan Finney (D-KS)	1991–1995	First woman to defeat an incumbent governor.
Ann Richards (D-TX)	1991–1995	
Barbara Roberts (D-OR)	1991–1995	
Christine Todd Whitman (R-NJ)	1994–2001	Resigned to take presidential appointment as commissioner of the Environmental Protection Agency.
Jeanne Shaheen (D-NH)	1997–2003	
Jane Dee Hull (R-AZ)	1997–2003	Elected as secretary of state, succeeded governor who resigned; later elected to a full term.
Nancy Hollister (R-OH)	1998–1999	Elected lieutenant governor; served as governor for 11 days when predecessor took U.S. Senate seat and successor had not yet been sworn in.
Jane Swift (R-MA)	2001–2003	Elected as lieutenant governor, succeeded governor who resigned for an ambassadorial appointment.
Judy Martz (R-MT)	2001–2005	
Olene Walker (R-UT)	2003–2005	Elected as lieutenant governor, succeeded governor who resigned to take a federal appointment.
Ruth Ann Minner (D-DE)	2001–present	
Jennifer M. Granholm (D-MI)	2003–present	
Linda Lingle (R-HI)	2003–present	
Janet Napolitano (D-AZ)	2003–present	First woman to succeed another woman as governor.
Kathleen Sebelius (D-KS)	2003–present	Father was governor of Ohio.
Kathleen Blanco (D-LA)	2004–present	
M. Jodi Rell (R-CT)	2004–present	Elected as lieutenant governor, succeeded governor who resigned.
Christine Gregoire (D-WA)	2005–present	
Sarah Palin (R-AK)	2007–present	

Source: Center for American Women and Politics, Eagleton Institute of Politics, Rutgers University

secretary of state in New Mexico from 1923–26.[5] Delaware, Kentucky, New York, South Dakota, and Texas also had women secretaries of state in the 1920s. The first woman treasurer, Grace B. Urbahns (R-Ind.), also served during this time period, from 1926–32.

Several more years passed before a woman became lieutenant governor. Republican Matilda R. Wilson served briefly as lieutenant governor of Michigan in 1940 when she was appointed to fill an expiring term. However, the first woman elected as a lieuten-ant governor was Consuelo N. Bailey (R-Vt.), who served from 1955–56. An additional three decades passed before a woman became attorney general of a state; the first was Arlene Violet (R-R.I.), who served from 1985–87.

As evident from Figure A, the proportion of women among statewide elective officials has grown substantially over the past three decades. From 1971 to 1985 the increases were small and incremental. Then, between 1983 and 1995, a period of significant growth, the number and proportion of women serv-

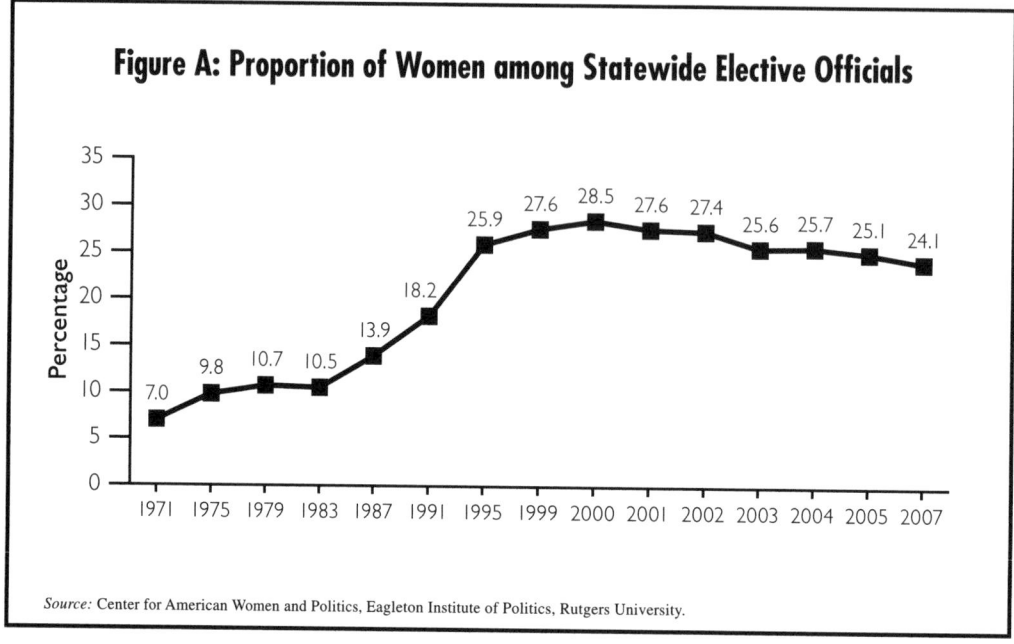

Figure A: Proportion of Women among Statewide Elective Officials

Source: Center for American Women and Politics, Eagleton Institute of Politics, Rutgers University.

ing in statewide office more than doubled. Since the mid-1990s, the number and proportion have leveled. Despite the addition of a new woman governor, the number of women serving in statewide elective offices actually decreased by two as a result of the 2006 elections, and fewer women, 76,[6] hold statewide offices in 2007 than in 1995 when there were 84 women.

In early 2007, women hold 24.1 percent of the 315 statewide elective positions. In addition to the nine women governors, 11 women (8D, 3R) serve as lieutenant governors in the 43 states that elect lieutenant governors in statewide elections. This is a notable decrease from the record high number of 19 women who served as lieutenant governors in 1995.

Other women statewide elected officials include 12 secretaries of state (7D, 5R), 10 state treasurers (6D, 4R), four attorney generals (4D), nine chief education officials (3D, 3R, 3 nonpartisan), six state auditors (3D, 3R), five public service commissioners (3D, 2R), four state comptroller/controllers (2D, 2R), two commissioners of insurance (1D, 1R), two corporation commissioners (2R), one commissioner of labor (R), and one railroad commissioner (R). The women serving in statewide elective office include one African-American (the state treasurer of Connecticut) as well as three Latinas (the secretary of state of New Mexico, the attorney general of Nevada, and the superintendent of public instruction for Oregon).

Women may be slightly better represented among top appointed officials in state government than among statewide elected officials although it is not possible to know for certain since the most recent data available are from 2004. According to nationwide data collected by the Center on Women in Government and Civil Society at SUNY-Albany, in 2004 women constituted 29.7 percent of department heads with major policymaking responsibilities (including heads of departments, agencies, offices, boards, commissions, and authorities) who were appointed by governors. Similarly, women were 41.1 percent of the top appointed advisers in governors' offices. These 2004 figures represented a slight increase over 2003 and a more notable increase over 1998 when women were 23.7 percent of department heads and 39.6 percent of governors' top advisers. Women of color were also slightly better represented among these appointed officials than among statewide elective officials,[7] with women of color in 2004 constituting 5.8 percent of all department heads and 7.7 percent of top advisers in governors' offices.[8]

Justices on Courts of Last Resort

The first woman to win election to a state court of last resort was Florence E. Allen, who was elected to the Ohio Supreme Court in 1922 and re-elected in 1928. Nevertheless, it was not until 1960 that a second woman, Lorna Lockwood of Arizona, was elected to a state supreme court. In 1965 Lockwood's colleagues on the Arizona Supreme Court selected her to be chief justice, thereby also making her the first woman in history to preside over a state court of last resort.[9] She was followed by Susie Sharp of North Carolina who in 1974 became the first woman to be elected by popular vote to be chief justice of a state court of last resort.[10]

In 2003, Petra Jiménez Maes of New Mexico, who currently serves as an associate justice, became the first Latina to serve as chief justice of a state supreme court. Similarly, in 2005 Leah Ward Sears of Georgia became the first African-American woman to preside over a state court of last resort.[11]

According to the National Center for State Courts, 106, or 30.5 percent, of the 348 justices on state courts of last resort in early 2007 are women.[12] Of the 53 chief justices of these courts, 17, or 32.1 percent, are women.

Women comprise a majority of justices on the courts of last resort in New York and the District of Columbia as well as 50 percent of the justices on the Supreme Court of Tennessee, which currently has one vacancy. Women constitute at least 40 percent of the justices, but less than a majority, on an additional 18 courts of last resort.

Legislators

Even before 1920 when women won the right to vote across the country, a few women had been elected to legislatures in states that granted the franchise to women. By 1971 the proportion of women serving in state legislatures across the country had grown to 4.5 percent, and over the years this proportion has increased more than fivefold. As Figure B illustrates, the proportion of women among legislators grew steadily throughout the 1970s and 1980s. However, the rate of growth slowed in the 1990s, and similar to the pattern for statewide elected officials, the number and proportion of women legislators nationally largely have leveled off since the late-1990s.

The 2006 elections did produce the largest increase in women legislators since the late-1990s, with the proportion of women among legislators growing from 22.8 percent in 2006 to 23.5 percent in January 2007. Women now hold 422, or 21.4 percent, of all state senate seats and 1,312, or 24.2 percent, of all state house seats across the country. Nevertheless, the record number of women, 1,734, who serve in state legislatures at the beginning of 2007 is only slightly greater than the 1,664 women legislators who served in 1999.

Great variation exists across the states in the proportion of legislators who are women (See Table C). Vermont ranks first among the states with 37.2 percent women in its legislature. Following closely behind Vermont are New Hampshire (36.3 percent), Minnesota (34.8 percent), Arizona (34.4 percent), and Colorado (34.0 percent). With the exception of Minnesota, all of the states ranked in the top 10 in the proportion of women in their legislatures are located in the west or the northeast. However, despite this geographic concentration, no easy explanation exists

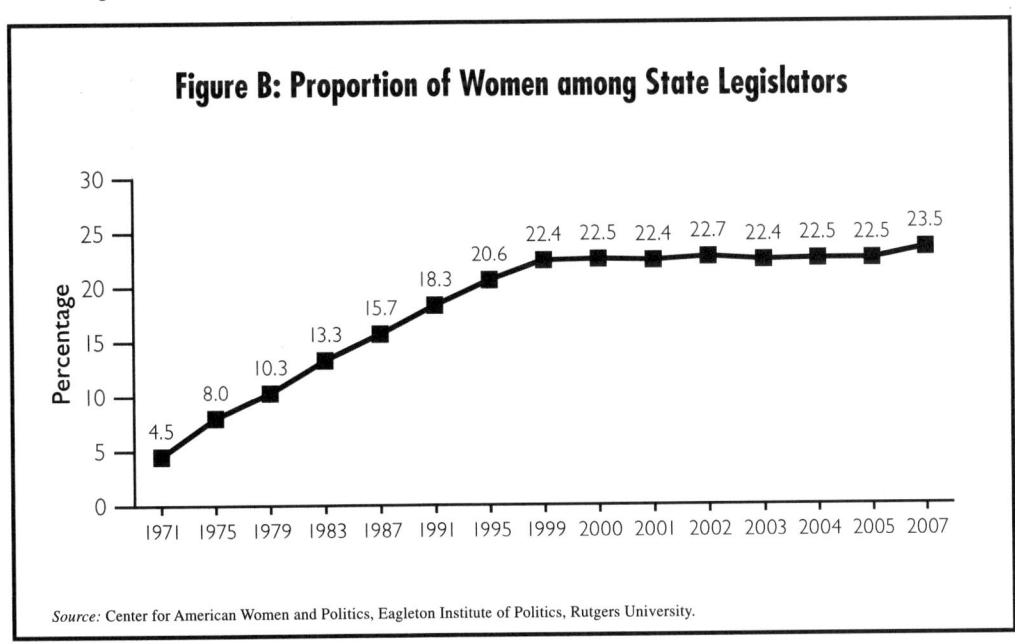

Figure B: Proportion of Women among State Legislators

Source: Center for American Women and Politics, Eagleton Institute of Politics, Rutgers University.

for why these states have risen to the top, and indeed scholars who have statistically examined the variation among the states in the representation of women in their legislatures have found no simple patterns.[13]

At the other extreme, South Carolina, with only 8.8 percent, ranks last among the 50 states in the representation of women among its legislators. Accompanying South Carolina in the bottom five states are Kentucky with 12.3 percent, Oklahoma with 12.8 percent, Alabama with 12.9 percent, and Mississippi with 13.8 percent. Eight of the 10 states with the lowest proportion of women are southern or border states. Only two southern states—North Carolina ranked 19th among the 50 states with 24.7 percent women and Florida ranked 21st with 23.8 percent women—are above the national average. As these rankings make clear, the South as a region lags behind the rest of the country in the representation of women in its legislatures.

Following gains in the 2006 elections, Democrats outnumber Republicans among state legislators nationwide, with 54.0 percent of all legislators Democrats and 45.0 percent Republicans.[14] However, the partisan gap is much larger among women legislators where Democrats outnumber Republicans by a ratio of about 2:1. Among women state senators nationwide, 69.0 percent are Democrats; among women state representatives, 68.2 percent are Democrats.

Almost one-fifth of women state legislators, 19.6 percent, are women of color. Of the 93 senators and 247 representatives serving in legislatures in early 2007, all but 22 are Democrats. African-American women hold 62 seats in state senates and 167 seats in state houses across 39 states. Latinas are concentrated in 22 states; they hold 20 senate and 50 house seats. Asian-American women count among their numbers seven senators and 22 representatives in eight states, while Native American women hold four senate and eight house seats in eight states.

Looking Toward the Future

Although women have made substantial progress over time in increasing their presence in state government, the leveling off of women's numbers among statewide elective officials and state legislators in recent years is a puzzling, and for many a troubling, development. At a minimum, the leveling off is evidence that increases over time are not inevi-

Table B: Women Statewide Elected Officials, 2007

State	Governor	Lieutenant governor	Attorney general	Secretary of state	Treasurer
Alabama	★	★	★	W	W
Alaska	W	★	★	...	...
Arizona	W	...	★	W	★
Arkansas	★	★	★	★	W
California	★	★	★	W	★
Colorado	★	W	★	★	W
Connecticut	W	★	★	W	W
Delaware	W	★	★	...	★
Florida	★	★	★	...	W
Georgia	★	★	★	W	...
Hawaii	W	★	...	...	...
Idaho	★	★	★	★	★
Illinois	★	★	W	★	★
Indiana	★	W	★	★	★
Iowa	★	W	★	★	★
Kansas	W	★	★	★	W
Kentucky	★	★	★	★	★
Louisiana	W	★	★	★	★
Maine	★	...	...	...	...
Maryland	★	★	★	...	...
Massachusetts	★	★	W	★	★
Michigan	W	★	★	W	...
Minnesota	★	W	W	★	...
Mississippi	★	W	★	★	★
Missouri	★	★	★	W	W
Montana	★	★	★	★	...
Nebraska	★	★	★	★	...
Nevada	★	★	W	★	W
New Hampshire	★	...	...	...	...
New Jersey	★	...	...	...	...
New Mexico	★	W	★	W	★
New York	★	★	★	...	...
North Carolina	★	W	★	W	★
North Dakota	★	★	★	★	W
Ohio	★	★	★	W	★
Oklahoma	★	W	★	...	★
Oregon	★	...	★	★	★
Pennsylvania	★	W	★	...	★
Rhode Island	★	W	★	★	★
South Carolina	★	★	★	★	★
South Dakota	★	★	★	★	★
Tennessee	★	...	...	...	...
Texas	★	★	★	...	...
Utah	★	★	★	...	★
Vermont	★	★	★	W	★
Virginia	★	★	★	...	...
Washington	W	★	★	★	★
West Virginia	★	...	★	W	★
Wisconsin	★	W	★	★	W
Wyoming	★	...	...	★	★

Source: Data for elected officials are current as of January 2007 and have been provided by the Center for American Women and Politics, Eagleton Institute of Politics, Rutgers University.

Key:

★ — Position is filled through a statewide election.

W — Position is filled through a statewide election and is held by a woman.

. . . — Position does not exist or is an appointed office.

Table C: Women in State Legislatures, 2007

	Senate			House			Legislature (both houses)	
State	Democrats	Republicans	% Women	Democrats	Republicans	% Women	% Women	State rank (a)
Alabama	3	1	11.4%	11	3	13.3%	12.9%	47
Alaska	1	2	15.0	6	4	25.0	21.7	27
Arizona	8	5	43.3	10	8	30.0	34.4	4
Arkansas	4	2	17.1	18	4	22.0	20.7	28
California	10	0	25.0	18	6	30.0	28.3	15
Colorado	10	1	31.4	19	4	35.4	34.0	5
Connecticut	7	1	22.2	30	15	29.8	28.3	15
Delaware	4	3	33.3	7	5	29.3	30.6	10
Florida	6	5	27.5	16	11	22.5	23.8	21
Georgia	6	2	14.3	28	10	21.1	19.5	32
Hawaii	7	0	28.0	11	7	35.3	32.9	7
Idaho	2	3	14.3	12	7	27.1	22.9	24
Illinois	10	3	22.0	24	12	30.5	27.7	17
Indiana	7	6	26.0	9	6	15.0	18.7	36
Iowa	3	3	12.0	19	9	28.0	22.7	25
Kansas	4	9	32.5	19	16	28.0	29.1	14
Kentucky	1	4	13.2	10	2	12.0	12.3	49
Louisiana	5	2	17.9	13	5	17.1	17.4	38
Maine	7	5	34.3	33	12	29.8	30.6	10
Maryland	9	2	23.4	41	10	36.2	33.0	6
Massachusetts	12	0	30.0	33	4	23.1	24.5	20
Michigan	6	3	23.7	16	4	18.2	19.6	31
Minnesota	18	9	40.3	35	8	32.1	34.8	3
Mississippi	4	1	9.6	15	4	15.6	13.8	46
Missouri	5	2	20.6	22	9	19.0	19.3	34
Montana	7	1	16.0	22	8	30.0	25.3	18
Nebraska (b)	··Nonpartisan··		20.4	················ Unicameral················			20.4	29
Nevada	5	1	28.6	10	3	31.0	30.2	12
New Hampshire	9	1	41.7	104	40	36.0	36.3	2
New Jersey	5	2	17.5	11	5	20.0	19.2	35
New Mexico	7	4	26.2	10	12	31.4	29.5	13
New York	8	3	17.7	34	5	26.0	23.6	22
North Carolina	7	1	16.0	22	12	28.3	24.7	19
North Dakota	4	2	12.8	7	12	20.2	17.7	37
Ohio	5	2	21.2	11	5	16.2	17.4	38
Oklahoma	6	1	14.6	3	9	11.9	12.8	48
Oregon	8	1	30.0	12	7	31.7	31.1	9
Pennsylvania	5	5	20.0	11	16	13.3	14.6	44
Rhode Island	6	1	18.4	13	2	20.0	19.5	32
South Carolina	1	0	2.2	8	6	11.3	8.8	50
South Dakota	4	1	14.3	3	10	18.6	17.1	41
Tennessee	4	3	21.2	9	5	14.1	15.9	43
Texas	2	2	12.9	18	15	22.0	20.4	29
Utah	1	2	10.3	8	7	20.0	17.3	40
Vermont	9	1	33.3	41	14	38.0 (c)	37.2	1
Virginia	7	1	20.0	9	6	16.0 (d)	17.1	41
Washington	15	5	40.8	21	7	28.6	32.7	8
West Virginia	0	2	5.9	12	5	17.0	14.2	45
Wisconsin	4	4	24.2	13	9	22.2	22.7	26
Wyoming	3	1	13.3	8	9	28.3	23.3	23

Source: Center for American Women and Politics, Eagleton Institute of Politics, Rutgers University. Figures are as of January 2007.

Key:
(a) States share the same rank if their proportions of women legislators are exactly equal or round off to be equal (CA, CT; DE, ME; GA, RI; LA, OH; NE, TX; SD, VA).

(b) Nebraska has a unicameral legislature with nonpartisan elections.
(c) Includes two members of the Progressive Party.
(d) Includes one Independent.

table; there is no invisible hand at work to insure that more women will seek and be elected to office with each subsequent election.

The leveling off has implications for women's representation not only among state legislators and nongubernatorial statewide officeholders, but also among governors and members of Congress. Probably the most striking positive development for women in state government in recent years has been the increase in women governors. Of the 29 women in the entire history of our country who have served as governors, more than half, 15, have served all or part of their terms during the first few years of the 21st century. Of the nine sitting governors, seven held statewide elective office before running for governor; three were lieutenant governors, three served as attorney generals, and one was her state's insurance commissioner. Four of the current women governors also served in their state legislatures. Similarly, many of the women who have run for Congress gained experience and visibility in state government before seeking federal office. Of the 71 women members of the U.S. House, 32 served in their state houses, 16 in their state senates, and three in statewide elective offices; of the 16 women U.S. senators, eight served in their state legislatures, three in statewide elective offices, and one in an appointed state cabinet post.

Activists who are interested in increasing the number of women serving in office often refer to a political "pipeline" through which potential women candidates for higher level office come forward from the pool of women who have gained experience at lower levels of office. Clearly, the pipeline has worked well for current women governors and members of Congress. But what if the pool of candidates in statewide and state legislative offices continues to stagnate or even decline? Then, the number of politically experienced women with the visibility and contacts necessary to run for governor or a seat in the U.S. House or Senate is also likely to stagnate or decline.

While several different factors may be responsible for the recent leveling off in the numbers of women in statewide elective and state legislative office, a lack of effective recruitment certainly is one of the most important. Statistics on the number of women candidates over time seem clearly to point to a problem with recruitment. For example, even though a record 2,429 women were general election candidates for the 6,127 seats up for election in state legislatures in 2006, this was only 54 more women than in 1992 when there were 2,375 women candidates![15] Clearly, then, a major factor contributing to the leveling off in the number of women officeholders is a lack of greater numbers of women candidates.

Research has found that women who run for office are less likely than their male counterparts to be self-starters. Women more often than men seek office only after receiving encouragement from others. For example, one recent study of major party candidates in state legislative races found that only 11 percent of women, compared with 37 percent of men, said that it was entirely their own idea to run for the legislature; in contrast, 37 percent of women, compared with 18 percent of men, reported that they had not seriously thought about running until someone else suggested it.[16] Another recent study of people in the professions from which political candidates are most likely to emerge (i.e., law, business, education and politics) found that notably fewer women (43 percent) than men (59 percent) had ever considered running for office.[17]

Findings such as these suggest the future for women in state government will depend, at least in part, upon the strength of efforts to actively recruit women for both elected and appointed positions. Legislative leaders, public officials, party leaders and advocacy organizations can help by renewing their commitment and augmenting efforts to identify and offer support to potential women candidates, especially in winnable races with open seats or vulnerable incumbents. Recruitment efforts may well be key to determining whether the numbers of women officials continue to stagnate or again begin to move steadily upward as they did in earlier decades.

Notes

[1] All statistical information in this essay, unless otherwise noted, has been provided by the Center for American Women and Politics (CAWP), Eagleton Institute of Politics, Rutgers University. Additional information is available at *www.cawp.rutgers.edu*. The author also thanks Judith Saidel of the Center on Women in Government and Civil Society at SUNY-Albany, Jennifer Norako and Joan Cochet from the National Center for State Courts, and especially her colleagues Gilda Morales and Linda Phillips from CAWP for their assistance with the data for this essay.

[2] Sila Calderón (Popular Democratic Party) served as governor of Puerto Rico from 2001 to 2004.

[3] Martin Gruberg, *Women in American Politics* (Oshkosh, WI: Academia Press, 1968), 189.

[4] Gruberg, 190.

[5] Women did serve as superintendents of public instruction in a few states earlier than this.

[6] These 76 women serving in statewide elective office include 46 Democrats, 27 Republicans and three nonpartisans.

[7] Women of color comprise 5.3 percent of all statewide elective officials.

[8] "Women's Leadership Profile 2004," A Report of the Center for Women in Government and Civil Society, University at Albany, State University of New York, Fall 2004. *http://www.cwig.albany.edu/2004leadershipprofile2004.pdf*.

[9] Gruberg, 190, 192.

[10] "Susie Sharp (1906–1996)," North Carolina History Project. *http://www.northcarolinahistory.org/encyclopedia/40/entry*.

[11] Information provided by the National Center for State Courts.

[12] Unlike all the other statistics in this essay, these numbers from the National Center for State Courts include the District of Columbia as well as the 50 states.

[13] See, for example, Barbara Norrander and Clyde Wilcox, "The Geography of Gender Power: Women in State Legislatures," in Sue Thomas and Clyde Wilcox, ed., *Women and Elective Office: Past, Present, and Future* (New York: Oxford University Press, 1998).

[14] These proportions are calculated from data available in a table entitled "2006 Post-Election Partisan Composition of State Legislatures" on the Web site of the National Conference of State Legislatures. *http://www.ncsl.org/state vote/partycomptable2007.htm.*

[15] There were 2,375 women candidates for state legislative seats in 1992; 2,285 in 1994; 2,277 in 1996; 2,280 in 1998; 2,228 in 2000; 2,348 in 2002; and 2,220 in 2004.

[16] Gary Moncrief, Peverill Squire, and Malcolm Jewell, *Who Runs for the Legislature?* (New York: Prentice-Hall, 2001), Table 5.5, 102; see also Susan J. Carroll and Wendy S. Strimling, *Women's Routes to Elective Office: A Comparison with Men's* (New Brunswick, NJ: Center for the American Woman and Politics, 1983).

[17] Jennifer L. Lawless and Richard L. Fox, *It Takes a Candidate: Why Women Don't Run for Office* (New York: Cambridge University Press, 2005), 44.

About the Author

Susan J. Carroll is professor of political science and women's and gender studies at Rutgers University and senior scholar at the Center for American Women and Politics (CAWP) of the Eagleton Institute of Politics. She has published numerous works on women public officials, women candidates and various aspects of women's participation in American politics.

Chapter Eight

STATE MANAGEMENT AND ADMINISTRATION

“*Internal services can be shared for functions where there is little interaction with the public.*”

—Marc Holzer, Leila Sadeghi and Richard W. Schwester

“*The burden of compliance with Real ID will prove challenging and costly for states.*”

—Bonnie Rutledge

State Shared Services and Regional Consolidation Efforts

By Marc Holzer, Leila Sadeghi and Richard W. Schwester

State governments are examining the prospect of interlocal shared service initiatives as a means of reducing service delivery costs and providing tax relief, as well as streamlining local services, eliminating duplicative services, and enhancing governmental responsiveness and transparency. In an effort to effectively encourage the development and implementation of shared services, states should: provide financial support or incentives; collect and disseminate concrete information regarding the benefits of shared service initiatives; establish shared service performance measures; develop a central point of information to field questions from communities who are in the process of developing, implementing, or sustaining shared services; and work to ensure that the long-term interests of the taxpayers are paramount.

Introduction

More recent calls for "doing more with less," promoting a public sector that is "efficient and effective," and bolstering public trust through greater governmental response have fostered interest in shared services at all levels of government. Several state governments are examining the prospect of interlocal shared service initiatives as a means of reducing service delivery costs and providing tax relief, as well as streamlining local services, eliminating duplicative services, and enhancing governmental responsiveness and transparency (see Figure A). The purpose of this article is to: provide an introduction to the possible array of shared services; highlight best state practices; discuss state funding mechanisms designed to encourage shared service agreements;

and provide recommendations to state and local government leaders seeking to develop, implement or improve existing shared service programs.

Types of Shared Services

Sharing Personnel

Sharing staff is a straightforward concept. Smaller municipalities, in particular, face the issue of some functions that must be performed but may not require a full-time employee. This may be resolved by having a staff member handle multiple functions, but this solution is not practical when the function requires technical or professional skills. Hence, part-time employees are common in positions such as a certified assessor, certi-

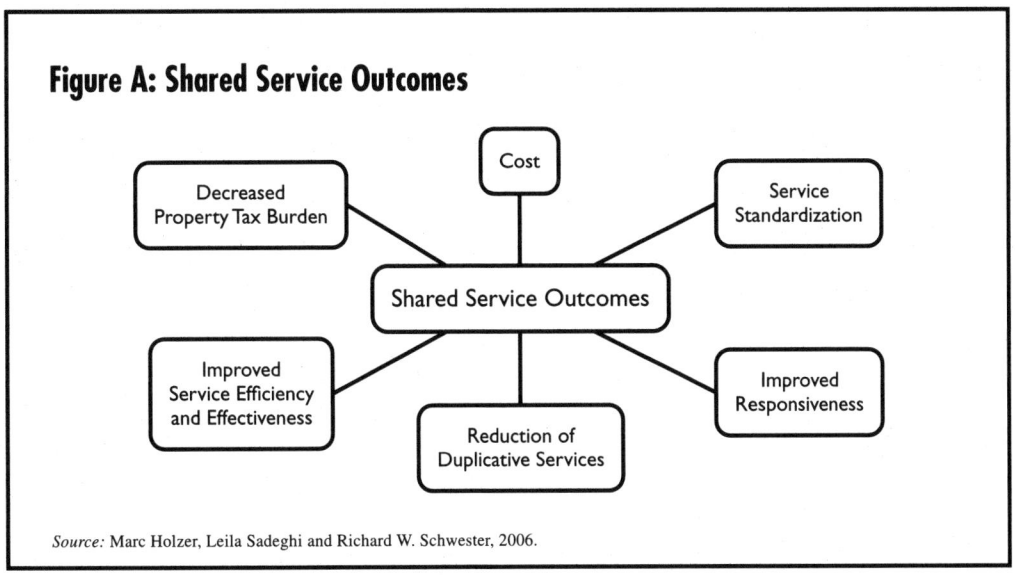

Figure A: Shared Service Outcomes

Cost

Decreased Property Tax Burden

Service Standardization

Shared Service Outcomes

Improved Service Efficiency and Effectiveness

Reduction of Duplicative Services

Improved Responsiveness

Source: Marc Holzer, Leila Sadeghi and Richard W. Schwester, 2006.

fied municipal finance officer, or zoning officer. The primary advantage of the part-time employee option is cost, but other problems arise around management control, availability to the public and accountability. Sharing personnel with other jurisdictions is usually a better solution, but requires planning and cooperation on the part of the jurisdictions involved, rather than leaving issues such as scheduling in the hands of the part-time employee. Sharing employees is preferable to the use of part-timers, due chiefly to increased accountability over a person employed and managed in concert by more than one municipality.

Sharing Equipment

Sharing equipment (or capital assets) assumes a partner model. Ownership is joint, or is shared by each community owning a separate part of the whole piece of equipment. In New Jersey, for example, an apparatus dubbed the "DitchMaster" is co-owned by the Townships of Franklin, Bridgewater and Montgomery in Somerset County; each has one-third ownership. The DitchMaster is used to clean roadside drain ditches. Franklin maintains and stores the equipment because it has a large garage and highly-trained mechanics, and Bridgewater maintains an escrow account of rental fees collected from other municipalities that are used to offset maintenance costs. The state dealt with the issue of scheduling simply by rotating the vehicle at the end of each month to the next municipality according to a pre-set schedule, but recognizing the need for flexibility in unanticipated situations.[1]

Sharing Internal Services

Internal services can be shared for functions where there is little interaction with the public. An example of this is the sharing of an animal shelter between municipalities, which is the case for the New Jersey municipalities of Maplewood and South Orange. The efficiency of this sharing arrangement is based on economies of scale and having one organization solely responsible for the performance. To the individual municipality, this is very much like a relationship with a vendor. The difference lies in the fact that it is in the interest of all the individual communities to have the relationship succeed, because it benefits all the participants acting as a group, and therefore a problem cannot be resolved by seeking another vendor.

Sharing External Services

"External services" refers to interlocal agreements whereby one municipality agrees to provide essential services to another municipality that no longer provides such services. Another alternative arrangement involves two or more municipalities consolidating services into one regional service delivery system. These types of shared service arrangements involve emergency services, such as police and fire, public works and waste disposal.

Shared Service Best Practices

States throughout the country are implementing shared service efforts in the interest of cutting costs, reducing property tax burdens and increasing governmental responsiveness by providing better services. The following examples highlight successful U.S. and international shared service efforts.

Established in 1999, the North Hudson Regional Fire and Rescue Department is a consolidated fire services initiative comprised of five New Jersey municipalities (Guttenberg, North Bergen, Union City, Weehawken and West New York). Serving nearly 200,000 residents, the North Hudson Regional Fire and Rescue Department is credited with saving each municipality roughly $5 million annually in fire service costs, while at the same time creating a more efficient and responsive fire department. Underscoring the point, shortly after the creation of this regional department, firefighters responded to a routine house fire in an enclave of West New York. However, the closest fire stations were in Weehawken and North Bergen, not West New York. In this case, eliminating jurisdictional boundaries proved valuable in terms of response time and therefore safety.[2]

The cities of Moreno Valley and Riverside, Calif., entered into a shared fire service agreement in 1996. Specifically, the cities agreed to construct a shared fire station, abandoning their original plans to construct separate stations roughly one mile apart. It was estimated that sharing a fire station saved $700,000 in capital costs and $50,000 annually in operating costs. Serving the western part of the Moreno Valley and the Canyon Crest and Canyon Springs areas of Riverside, the joint station has been credited with significantly reducing response times. For example, the response time to the Canyon Springs area of Riverside has decreased from roughly 15 to five minutes.[3]

The Pine-Marshall-Bradford Woods Joint Police Force is a model of service sharing. The small Pennsylvania communities of Pine, Marshall and Bradford Woods consolidated their police forces in 1969 in an effort to control costs and provide better services. Through consolidation, these communities support an 18-member police force, including a detective, a resource most small communities consider a luxury.[4]

Several other communities throughout the United States have followed the Pine-Marshall-Bradford

Woods model. The Illinois municipalities of Round Lake Park and Hainesville entered into a shared police agreement in 1999. The agreement proved mutually beneficial from a service coverage perspective, especially for Hainesville, which had a part-time police force prior to the consolidation.[5] In 2006, the New Jersey municipality of Woodlynne dissolved its eight-member police force, agreeing instead to pay the municipality of Collingswood $650,000 annually (annual cost saving of $150,000) for the services of its 37-member police force.[6] For Woodlynne, N.J., Hainesville, Ill., and many other communities, shared police services are particularly attractive from a safety and service quality perspective, the pros of which include: an enhanced police presence and officer coverage, better training, and opportunities for officer specialization.

In addition to shared fire and police services, solid waste and public works departments have emerged as focal points for interlocal service agreements. Most notably, three Wisconsin counties (Brown, Outagamie, and Winnebago) consolidated their waste disposal and recycling efforts in 2003. In terms of cost savings, this tri-county initiative is projected to save $35 million over 25 years for waste disposal, and $8 million over 12 years for recycling.[7]

The Chautauqua County, N.Y., bridge program is a cooperative effort to ensure bridge and roadway safety. The bridge program was established to address the problem that 62 percent of the county's 488 bridges were in need of repair, and 69 bridges alone were closed or weight restricted by the New York State Department of Transportation. By pooling municipal and county resources, bridge conditions within the county greatly improved. For example, when the bridge program was introduced in 1988, 55 percent of the county's bridges were deemed "deficient." This compares to 34 percent in 1996.[8]

Local communities are not limiting interlocal agreements to essential services. Several communities are pooling their resources in order to provide better parks and recreational opportunities. In particular, the Village and City of Pewaukee, Wis., consolidated their Parks and Recreation departments which proved mutually beneficial. Prior to consolidation, the Village of Pewaukee was only able to provide summer recreational services because of limited resources, and even though the City of Pewaukee was able to provide recreational services year-round, its recreation director was a part-time employee. The Pewaukee Joint Parks and Recreation Department was officially established in 1997, and it has been credited with improving the quality of the parks and recreational services for both

municipalities, as well as reducing operating costs. More recently, the Village and City are working on an effort to combine their water and sewer services.[9]

To provide better library services with limited resources, the municipality of Chula Vista, Calif., partnered with the Sweetwater Union High School District. The jointly supported East Lake Branch Library opened in 1993. For both students and Chula Vista residents, the pooled municipal and school district resources provide access to a more extensive book collection than could be provided without this shared service agreement.[10]

From an international perspective, Toronto, Ontario, and New Zealand are at the forefront of designing system-wide shared service models. In 2001, four local councils throughout the Southland region of New Zealand explored shared services with the hope of reducing costs. An initial investment of $60,000 yielded more than $1 million in cost savings over the first two years of implementation because of pooled resources and enhanced operational efficiency using the following strategies:

- Joint purchase of software operating systems.
- Creation of rural fire authority.
- Combination of economic tourism organizations.
- Adoption of protocol on shared planning policy.
- Establishment of regional landfill and joint waste management system.
- Combination of back-office services.[11]

The city of Toronto has reportedly achieved cost savings of more than $300 million from 1998 to 2000 by eliminating duplicative services and streamlining operations. This was accomplished, in part, by:

- Reducing staff positions and work force.
- Implementing one-time transition costs and reducing permit fees.
- Consolidating social and children's services with senior citizen services.
- Consolidating services in public health, library, shelter and housing support.[12]

State Support of Shared Services

The substantial anticipated cost savings and service efficiency gains over time have prompted some states to establish funding mechanisms that serve as a springboard for the development and implementation of intermunicipal and/or regional shared service initiatives. Most notably, the Department of Community Affairs for the State of New Jersey established a program known as Sharing Available Resources Efficiently (SHARE).[13]

The SHARE program provides municipal and county governments with grant money for the purposes of studying the feasibility of and implementing shared service programs. Feasibility study grants assist local governments with planning and developing shared service initiatives. These grants are typically $20,000 and require a 10-percent match. Implementation grants (up to $200,000) aid local governments with the start-up costs associated with shared service plans and/or the consolidation of local units (SHARE 2006).

The State of New York established a similar funding mechanism known as the Shared Municipal Service Incentive Program (SMSI). The SMSI program is a $25 million grant program that assists municipalities with their efforts to consolidate local government services. For example, grants of up to $1 million are available for municipalities seeking to merge into a single government unit, while awards of up to $300,000 are available for the development of county-wide shared service programs.[14]

The Pennsylvania Department of Community and Economic Development established the Shared Municipal Services Program (SMSP). This program provides grants ranging from $10,000 to $25,000 (50-percent match required) for cooperative municipal agreements, which typically include:

- Shared police records administration.

- Shared technology initiatives.

- Municipal insurance pooling.

- Shared public works operations.

- Consolidated recreation activities.

- Shared code enforcement operations.

- Shared motorized equipment.[15]

Recommendations

Leaders at all levels of government have come to understand the importance of devising ways to provide more and better services with fewer resources. Interlocal shared service initiatives have emerged as a viable means of providing efficient and quality services without imposing a heavier tax burden. The following recommendations are presented to assist public managers and elected officials with adoption and implementation of shared service initiatives.

Recommendation 1

In an effort to effectively encourage the development and implementation of shared services, states must provide financial support or incentives. Local governments and citizens may resist sharing services upon

reviewing the upfront costs of implementation. New Jersey's SHARE program, New York's SMSI program and Pennsylvania's SMSP program serve as noteworthy examples of state efforts to reduce such costs.

Recommendation 2

States need to collect and disseminate concrete information regarding the benefits realized from shared service initiatives, such as cost savings, cost effectiveness gains and tax burden implications. This information should be disseminated to both municipal and county government leaders to promote the development and implementation of additional shared service initiatives.

Recommendation 3

Finding appropriate ways to monitor government performance, to provide mechanisms for citizen feedback and complaints, and to document government responsiveness in terms of timeliness and service quality is imperative. Shared service performance measures should be established in an effort to ensure shared service quality to the citizenry and stakeholders. Performance measurement will further help drive down costs. It is important that performance measurement data be made public in the interest of accountability.

The National Center for Public Performance (NCPP) at Rutgers University is developing a measurement collection system that provides an easy mode of collecting key indicators of government performance. The technology used within this system will allow users the possibility of directly inputting data from larger databases or manually inputting appropriate data measures as they see fit. The data collected can easily be transformed into graphs and/or charts, allowing users to produce accessible reports for interested parties.

Recommendation 4

A central point of information is needed to field questions from communities that are in the process of developing, implementing or sustaining shared services. By providing a centrally informed point of contact, municipalities may be more inclined to pursue shared services initiatives. For example, states could provide local governments with a toolkit of best practices and templates that better enable them to replicate successful models of shared services. Often, as is the case with government reform efforts, adequate support and models of excellence are not offered, leaving participants feeling helpless or using the process itself as a learning experience. By providing such models, states can rest assured that instead of municipalities wasting grant money and time trying to figure out essentially "what to do," they can implement strategies immediately and effectively from the onset of the program.

Recommendation 5

One issue against the establishment of shared services is the fear that interlocal agreements may result in the termination of an employee. While laudable because of the loyalty to the staff, this may indicate a misplaced sense of purpose, particularly in an era when state and local resources are being stretched. The long-term interests of the taxpayer must come first. Indeed, some of those interests permit the enlightened view of maintaining employee morale and motivation for the best interests of the organization, but in the context of alternatives that are in the interests of citizens. Unless there are employee agreements to the contrary, looking for alternative work, even in another department, is an option that could be beneficial to all. The administration could also look for other employment opportunities for any staff that would be threatened in the communities they are trying to partner with or in other communities. Open communication is therefore essential when the agreement is being considered so the employee does not feel this is being done behind his or her back or that termination will result. A professional conversation with the employee, one that recognizes past contributions of that employee and discusses alternatives that demonstrate that recognition, may even uncover other options that would work for the individual as well as the municipality.

Conclusion

State and local governments throughout the U.S. have come to champion shared services as a means of "doing more with less." Communities in New Jersey, Pennsylvania, Illinois and California are sharing fire and police services in order to reduce costs and improve safety through better service coverage. Counties in Wisconsin have realized significant cost savings through regional consolidation of their waste disposal and recycling centers, while a small California municipality partnered with a school district in an effort to provide better library services. These are but a few examples of what shared services and interlocal cooperation are achieving.

Despite the potential benefits of shared service agreements, several obstacles remain. First, shared services are likely to draw opposition from union, civil service and tenured government employees. Sec-

ond, residents may resist shared services because of inadequate information regarding the potential benefits of such services. Third, many municipalities fear the loss of identity and control over their jurisdictions. The loss of "home rule" has proven a difficult obstacle to overcome psychologically for municipal leaders. This is particularly difficult for states that have many compartmentalized and autonomous governmental units, such as New Jersey, which has 566 municipalities, 611 school districts, 212 fire service districts and 21 counties. In order to overcome such obstacles, it is imperative that states take the lead in encouraging interlocal and regional service sharing by creating or expanding grant programs that support feasibility studies and help to offset start-up costs. Furthermore, measuring and disseminating cost savings and service delivery improvements attributable to shared service initiatives are key to winning over skeptics.

Notes

[1] T. Hester, "More towns reap what they sow through pooling of vital services," *The Star-Ledger*, August 8, 2000, 21.

[2] R. Smothers, "Regional fire service succeeds in its first test," *The New York Times*, January 12, 1999, B5.

[3] The U.S. Conference of Mayors, "Shared fire station saves money, improves service for Moreno Valley, Riverside residents," (November 24, 1997). *http://www.mayors.org/USCM/home.asp.*

[4] L. Barcousky, "One chief, two departments: Police chief for Pine-Marshall-Bradford Woods force also will lead Richland department under one-year agreement," *Pittsburgh Post-Gazette*, January 2, 2005, N6.

[5] L. Aucoin, "Round Lake Park, Hainesville to unite police departments," *Chicago Daily Herald*, June 3, 1999, L2.

[6] "Woodlynne votes to disband police," *Courier-Post*, April 14, 2006, 5B.

[7] P.A. Tom, "It takes three," *Waste Age*, Vol. 34, No. 10 (2003).

[8] M. Hattery, *Chautauqua County Bridge Program. Cooperative Highway Services Case Study Report: Number 2* (1996). *http://www.clgp.aem.cornell.edu/pdf/chat_co_bridge_prog.pdf.*

[9] M. Johnson, "Village open to merger, officials say Committee may form on consolidation issues for two Pewaukees," *Milwaukee Journal Sentinel*, July 20, 2006, B3.

[10] P. Repard, "City-school library is one for the books," *San Diego Union-Tribune*, August 3, 1993, B2.

[11] ICMA International Best Practices. Our way: Shared services forum, Southland, New Zealand (2004). *http://www.localgovt.co.nz/Resource/ViewFile.aspx?ID=591.*

[12] R. McInnis, "The Toronto amalgamation: Looking back, moving ahead," Speech delivered at the Greater Toronto Area (GTA) Forum, September 14, 2000. *http://www.toronto.ca/toronto_history/amalgamation/amal_speech.htm.*

[13] New Jersey Department of Community Affairs, SHARE (Sharing Available Resources Efficiently), Best practices handbook (2006). *http://www.nj.gov/dca/lgs/share/share_handbook.pdf.*

[14] NYSAC (New York State Association of Counties), The shared municipal incentive program: A policy primer (2006). *http://www.fredonia.edu/crrdg/docs/NYSACguide.pdf.*

[15] Pennsylvania Department of Community and Economic Development, SMSP (Shared Municipal Services Program). Program guidelines. (2005). *http://www.newpa.com/program Detail.aspx?id=101.*

About the Authors

Marc Holzer is dean of the School of Public Affairs and Administration, and Board of Governors Professor of Public Affairs and Administration, at Rutgers University's Newark campus. He is the editor-in-chief of the *Public Performance and Management Review*, and is a past president of the American Society for Public Administration, and is a fellow of the National Academy of Public Administration.

Leila Sadeghi is a project manager for the Public Performance Measurement and Reporting Network and a doctoral student in Urban Education Policy at Rutgers University's Newark campus. She recently participated in research on shared services and property tax reduction for the State of New Jersey.

Richard W. Schwester is assistant professor in the department of public management at John Jay College of Criminal Justice (CUNY). He serves on the editorial boards of *Public Performance and Management Review* and the *Journal of Public Management and Social Policy.*

Table 8.1
WORKFORCE COMPOSITION—CLASSIFIED EMPLOYEES
(Departments and agencies, excludes higher education and quasi-state agencies)

State	Employee headcount	FTE employees	Average age	Average years of state service	Average age of new hires
Alabama	30,382	(a)	44.56	12.35	35.09
Alaska	13,644	N.A.	44.66	8.85	37.75
Arizona	30,211	30,029.00	43.70	8.10	35.90
Arkansas	26,231	24,654.00	44.00	11.27	36.00
California	210,591	185,606.00	45.00	22.60	34.00
Colorado	22,087	N.A.	45.40	9.54	39.19
Connecticut	...	...	...	...	...
Delaware	11,920	11,792.00	44.00	11.00	...
Florida	84,554	83,714.00	43.74	11.50	36.00
Georgia	15,000	15,000.00	43.80	9.3	35.52
Hawaii	...	...	...	...	36.1
Idaho	11,649	11,623.00	44.00	11.00	...
Illinois	...	...	...	...	38.00
Indiana	35,951	31,836.00	46.60	12.20	...
Iowa	17,706	N.A.	46.98	14.26	35.80
Kansas	18,409	26,239.00	47.00	12.00	37.51
Kentucky	...	...	...	...	35.00
Louisiana	38,954	38,923.00	45.00	13.00	...
Maine	...	...	...	...	34.00
Maryland	51,507	50,928.08	46	14	N.A.
Massachusetts	27,597	27,419.00	45.90	14.60	...
Michigan	54,895	55,752.00	45.40	13.90	35.57
Minnesota	29,200	27,500.00	46.60	13.80	N.A.
Mississippi	25,730	25,730.00	43.61	9.99	36.10
Missouri	37,119	36,580.00	44	10.75	33.74
Montana	13,546	12,082.00	46.00	11.48	33
Nebraska	14,321	14,114.67	45.70	12.90	41.00
Nevada	15,345	14,748.00	38.20	N.A.	35.30
New Hampshire	...	...	...	...	N.A.
New Jersey (b)	63,684	61,709.00	45.00	13.00	...
New Mexico	...	...	...	...	36.00
New York	138,671	134,900.40	47.23	16.16	...
North Carolina	70,580	69,922.90	44.20	10.80	36.55
North Dakota	...	...	...	...	37.40
Ohio	...	...	...	...	...
Oklahoma	27,319	N.A.	45.40	11.10	...
Oregon	30,846	30,379.10	45.47	10.03	N.A.
Pennsylvania	54,297	54,809.06	46.00	13.00	37.54
Rhode Island	...	...	...	...	38.00
South Carolina	40,083	35,959.80	44.00	11.00	...
South Dakota	6,550	N.A.	43.4	11	37.00
Tennessee	39,910	N.A.	46.00	12.00	33.2
Texas (c)	144,935	142,621.00	43.00	10.00	39.00
Utah	16,411	15,814.00	43.34	9.91	N.A.
Vermont	7,699	7,584.30	45.90	12.30	32.47
Virginia	53,182	53,073.02	45.90	11.60	36.60
Washington	56,598	52,012.00	47.00	12.60	39.40
West Virginia (d)	20,334	N.A.	N.A.	12	N.A.
Wisconsin	39,629	38,112.11	46.30	14.80	35.57
Wyoming	7,919	7,797.00	45.50	11.30	37.20

Source: National Association of State Personnel Executives, February 2007.

Key:

... No response

N.A. — Not available

(a) Less than two percent of our workforce is part-time.

(b) New Jersey does not use the FTE concept. They have provided full-time employee count information instead.

(c) Headcount is "average number" for FY 2006, not the ending number on June 30, 2006. Classified employees include those employees that are subject to the state's position classification plan, excluding institutions of higher education. Texas state classified employees are not covered in a classified civil service with formal (legal) civil service protections covered by a merit system. Unclassified employees include those employees who are not subject to the state's position classification plan, excluding institutions of higher education. Texas state unclassified employees are not covered in a classified civil service with formal (legal) civil service protections covered by a merit system. Full-Time Equivalent employees not limited to classified or unclassified, but includes all types of state employees, both classified and unclassified.

(d) In distinguishing between classified and unclassified employees West Virginia only uses headcount. Average years of service includes classified and unclassified employees.

Table 8.2
WORKFORCE COMPOSITION—UNCLASSIFIED EMPLOYEES
(Departments and agencies, excludes higher education and quasi-state agencies)

State	Employee headcount	FTE employees	Average age	Average years of state service	Average age of new hires
Alabama	1,598	N.A.	N.A.	N.A.	N.A.
Alaska	1,285	N.A.	46.61	9.29	41.86
Arizona	6,903	6,767.60	46.00	7.60	39.30
Arkansas	1,367	836	51.00	13.40	43.00
California	1,030	1,030	45.00	N.A.	34.00
Colorado	5,212	N.A.	43.50	6.60	36.43
Connecticut	. . .	. . .	. . .	. . .	. . .
Delaware	1,045	1,028	46.00	11.00	35.00
Florida	22,463	22,416	48.47	15.43	41.09
Georgia	69,443	69,443	43.80	9.30	39.10
Hawaii	. . .	. . .	. . .	. . .	. . .
Idaho	1,117	1,098	46.00	11.00	43.00
Illinois	. . .	. . .	. . .	. . .	. . .
Indiana	15,207	12,850	46.00	12.80	36.50
Iowa	2,323	N.A.	44.75	12.46	32.81
Kansas	3,310		49.00	11.00	39.00
Kentucky	. . .	. . .	. . .	. . .	. . .
Louisiana	3,598	3,372	47.00	N.A.	N.A.
Maine	. . .	. . .	. . .	. . .	. . .
Maryland	N.A.	N.A.	N.A.	N.A.	N.A.
Massachusetts	16,501	15,779	45.80	13.30	35.84
Michigan	N.A.	N.A.	N.A.	N.A.	N.A.
Minnesota	2,600	2,400	43.10	8.60	36.40
Mississippi	5,701	5,000	43.80	7.44	36.01
Missouri	5,149	2,729	44.00	10.75	48.00
Montana	1,061	983	44.00	10.79	48.00
Nebraska	2,622	2,458.24	46.40	12.10	34.70
Nevada	965	951	N.A.	N.A.	N.A.
New Hampshire	. . .	. . .	. . .	. . .	. . .
New Jersey	10,070	9785	45.00	12.00	38.00
New Mexico	. . .	. . .	. . .	. . .	. . .
New York	N.A.	N.A.	N.A.	N.A.	N.A.
North Carolina	298	294.8	47.30	11.00	40.40
North Dakota	567	556	44.80	10.50	36.30
Ohio	. . .	. . .	. . .	. . .	. . .
Oklahoma	13,740	N.A.	45.40	9.80	N.A.
Oregon	1,803	1,774.33	46.75	12.04	38.43
Pennsylvania	24,145	24,530.22	43.00	12.00	39.00
Rhode Island	. . .	. . .	. . .	. . .	. . .
South Carolina	844	806.23	49.00	12.00	46.00
South Dakota	856	N.A.	45.60	13.10	37.50
Tennessee	2,626	N.A.	47.00	11.00	N.A.
Texas (a)	4,740	N.A.	N.A.	N.A.	N.A.
Utah	8,602	3,736	42.97	5.46	N.A.
Vermont	593	575.1	48.30	9.80	N.A.
Virginia	1,752	1,714.60	46.20	9.30	38.80
Washington	4,229	3,424	46.90	12.50	N.A.
West Virginia (b)	5,933	N.A.	N.A.	12.00	N.A.
Wisconsin	1,113	1,063.50	45.08	12.70	33.09
Wyoming	N.A.	N.A.	N.A.	N.A.	N.A.

Source: The National Association of State Personnel Executives, February 2007.

Key:
. . . — No response
N.A. — Not available
(a) Unclassified employees for the State of Texas include those employees who are not subject to the state's position classification plan, excluding institutions of higher education. Texas state unclassified employees are not covered in a classified civil service with formal (legal) civil service protections covered by a merit system.

(b) In distinguishing between classified and unclassified employees West Virginia only uses headcount. Average years of service includes classified and unclassified employees.

Table 8.3
EMPLOYEE COMPENSATION—CLASSIFIED EMPLOYEES
(Departments and agencies, excludes higher education and quasi-state agencies) (In dollars)

State	Average base salary of full-time employee	Average fringe benefit costs per full-time employee
Alabama	$37,124.45	$13,369.35
Alaska	47,570.00	29,125.00
Arizona (a)	35,220.00	10,560.00
Arkansas	31,418.17	3,690.00
California	69,123.48	20,737.04
Colorado	50,632.00	11,497.44
Connecticut	. . .	. . .
Delaware	37,873.00	16,486.00
Florida	34,834.45	12,193.00
Georgia	39,401.00	13,700.91
Hawaii	. . .	. . .
Idaho	38,436.00	21,419.00
Illinois	. . .	. . .
Indiana	32,646.26	15,079.23 (b)
Iowa	45,294.84	23,606.47
Kansas	35,074.00	5,675.00
Kentucky	. . .	. . .
Louisiana	36,990.00	13,316.00
Maine	. . .	. . .
Maryland	45,494.00	21,021.00
Massachusetts	51,014.00	16,670.12 (c)
Michigan	49,715.00	25,702.66
Minnesota	50,600.00	15,200.00
Mississippi	28,062.44	9,661.57
Missouri	29,370.00	16,535.31
Montana	34,876.00	8,991.00
Nebraska	36,607.00	25,918.00
Nevada	48,099.00	17,796.00
New Hampshire	. . .	. . .
New Jersey	53,282.07	14,439.44
New Mexico	. . .	. . .
New York	49,245.00	N.A.
North Carolina	35,958.00	15,627.00
North Dakota	34,158.00	14,889.00
Ohio	. . .	. . .
Oklahoma	32,527.90	16,831.38
Oregon	40,856.04	24,391.95
Pennsylvania	43,727.00	19,353.00
Rhode Island	. . .	. . .
South Carolina	34,696.00	9,714.00
South Dakota	31,790.00	9,754.00
Tennessee	28,107.00	N.A.
Texas	38,817.00	17,321.00
Utah	38,064.00	25,543.00
Vermont	43,882.00	17,795.00
Virginia	39,582.00	12,943.31
Washington	46,930.00	12,671.10
West Virginia	35,480.00	19,450.00
Wisconsin	47,464.00	9,231.75 (d)
Wyoming	39,384.00	14,292.00

Source: National Association of State Personnel Executives, February 2007.

Key:
. . . — No response
N.A. — Not available

(a) Average fringe benefit cost includes both classified and unclassified employees.

Figures derived from average salary and average percentage of personal service dollars.

(b) 18.79% in addition to the $8,945.00. The breakout is as follows: Life Insurance is 0.36%. Social Security is 7.65%. PERF-State Share is 5.50%. PERF-EE Share State Paid is 3.00%. Disability Insurance is 2.28% and Total FT fringe is 18.79%. The $8,945 is a blended value of health, dental, vision, and deferred comp employer paid benefits. This is a set amount rather than a percentage since we, as an employer, pay a set amount for these particular benefits, depending on whether you are single or family. The single value is estimated at $3,951. The family value is estimated at $10,518. Based on our demographics, that blends into $8291. Add on a Def Comp match and leave conversion estimate, and you arrive at the blended value of insurance benefits being $8,945.

(c) 32.62% (of salary) is the federally-approved rate fringe benefit rate for 2007.

(d) Information regarding the average fringe benefit cost per classified employee is not available. However, the total fringe benefit costs for both classified and unclassified employees working for the state is $4,698,255,095. If calculated on a percentage basis, the average fringe benefit cost per employee would be about 19.45% of the employee's salary.

Table 8.4
SUMMARY OF STATE GOVERNMENT EMPLOYMENT: 1953–2005

| | Employment (in thousands) | | | | | | Monthly payrolls (in millions of dollars) | | | Average monthly earnings of full-time employees | | |
| | Total, full-time and part-time | | | Full-time equivalent | | | | | | | | |
Year (October)	All	Education	Other	All	Education	Other	All	Education	Other	All	Education	Other
1953......................	1,082	294	788	966	211	755	$278.6	$73.5	$205.1	$289	$320	$278
1954......................	1,149	310	839	1,024	222	802	300.7	78.9	221.8	294	325	283
1955......................	1,199	333	866	1,081	244	837	325.9	88.5	237.4	302	334	290
1956......................	1,268	353	915	1,136	250	886	366.5	108.8	257.7	321	358	309
1957 (April)	1,300	375	925	1,153	257	896	372.5	106.1	266.4	320	355	309
1958......................	1,408	406	1,002	1,259	284	975	446.5	123.4	323.1	355	416	333
1959......................	1,454	443	1,011	1,302	318	984	485.4	136.0	349.4	373	427	352
1960......................	1,527	474	1,053	1,353	332	1,021	524.1	167.7	356.4	386	439	365
1961......................	1,625	518	1,107	1,435	367	1,068	586.2	192.4	393.8	409	482	383
1962......................	1,680	555	1,126	1,478	389	1,088	634.6	201.8	432.8	429	518	397
1963......................	1,775	602	1,173	1,558	422	1,136	696.4	230.1	466.3	447	545	410
1964......................	1,873	656	1,217	1,639	460	1,179	761.1	257.5	503.6	464	560	427
1965......................	2,028	739	1,289	1,751	508	1,243	849.2	290.1	559.1	484	571	450
1966......................	2,211	866	1,344	1,864	575	1,289	975.2	353.0	622.2	522	614	483
1967......................	2,335	940	1,395	1,946	620	1,326	1,105.5	406.3	699.3	567	666	526
1968......................	2,495	1,037	1,458	2,085	694	1,391	1,256.7	477.1	779.6	602	687	544
1969......................	2,614	1,112	1,501	2,179	746	1,433	1,430.5	554.5	876.1	655	743	597
1970......................	2,755	1,182	1,573	2,302	803	1,499	1,612.2	630.3	981.9	700	797	605
1971......................	2,832	1,223	1,609	2,384	841	1,544	1,741.7	681.5	1,060.2	731	826	686
1972......................	2,957	1,267	1,690	2,487	867	1,619	1,936.6	746.9	1,189.7	778	871	734
1973......................	3,013	1,280	1,733	2,547	887	1,660	2,158.2	822.2	1,336.0	843	952	805
1974......................	3,155	1,357	1,798	2,653	929	1,725	2,409.5	932.7	1,476.9	906	1,023	855
1975......................	3,271	1,400	1,870	2,744	952	1,792	2,652.7	1,021.7	1,631.1	964	1,080	909
1976......................	3,343	1,434	1,910	2,799	973	1,827	2,893.7	1,111.5	1,782.1	1,031	1,163	975
1977......................	3,491	1,484	2,007	2,903	1,005	1,898	3,194.6	1,234.4	1,960.1	1,096	1,237	1,031
1978......................	3,539	1,508	2,032	2,966	1,016	1,950	3,483.0	1,332.9	2,150.2	1,167	1,311	1,102
1979......................	3,699	1,577	2,122	3,072	1,046	2,026	3,869.3	1,451.4	2,417.9	1,257	1,399	1,193
1980......................	3,753	1,599	2,154	3,106	1,063	2,044	4,284.7	1,608.0	2,676.6	1,373	1,523	1,305
1981......................	3,726	1,603	2,123	3,087	1,063	2,024	4,667.5	1,768.0	2,899.5	1,507	1,671	1,432
1982......................	3,747	1,616	2,131	3,083	1,051	2,032	5,027.7	1,874.0	3,153.7	1,625	1,789	1,551
1983......................	3,816	1,666	2,150	3,116	1,072	2,044	5,345.5	1,989.0	3,357.0	1,711	1,850	1,640
1984......................	3,898	1,708	2,190	3,177	1,091	2,086	5,814.9	2,178.0	3,637.0	1,825	1,991	1,740
1985......................	3,984	1,764	2,220	2,990	945	2,046	6,328.6	2,433.7	3,884.9	1,935	2,155	1,834
1986......................	4,068	1,800	2,267	3,437	1,256	2,181	6,801.4	2,583.4	4,226.9	2,052	2,263	1,956
1987......................	4,115	1,804	2,310	3,491	1,264	2,227	7,297.8	2,758.3	4,539.5	2,161	2,396	2,056
1988......................	4,236	1,854	2,381	3,606	1,309	2,297	7,842.3	2,928.6	4,913.7	2,260	2,490	2,158
1989......................	4,365	1,925	2,440	3,709	1,360	2,349	8,443.1	3,175.0	5,268.1	2,372	2,627	2,259
1990......................	4,503	1,984	2,519	3,840	1,418	2,432	9,083.0	3,426.0	5,657.0	2,472	2,732	2,359
1991......................	4,521	1,999	2,522	3,829	1,375	2,454	9,437.0	3,550.0	5,887.0	2,479	2,530	2,433
1992......................	4,595	2,050	2,545	3,856	1,384	2,472	9,828.0	3,774.0	6,054.0	2,562	2,607	2,521
1993......................	4,673	2,112	2,562	3,891	1,436	2,455	10,288.2	3,999.3	6,288.9	2,722	3,034	2,578
1994......................	4694	2115	2579	3,917	1,442	2,475	10,666.3	4,176.8	6,489.3	2,776	3,073	2,640
1995......................	4,719	2,120	2,598	3,971	1,469	2,502	10,926.5	4,173.3	6,753.2	2,854	3,138	2,725
1996......................	(a)	(a)	(a)	(a)	(a)	(a)	(a)	(a)	(a)	(a)	(a)	(a)
1997 (March)	4,733	2,114	2,619	3,987	1,484	2,503	11,413.1	4,372.0	7,041.1	2,968	3,251	2,838
1998 (March)	4,758	2,173	2,585	3,985	1,511	2,474	11,845.2	4,632.1	7,213.1	3,088	3,382	2,947
1999 (March)	4,818	2,229	2,588	4,034	1,541	2,493	12,564.1	4,957.0	7,607.7	3,236	3,544	3,087
2000 (March)	4,877	2,259	2,618	4,083	1,563	2,520	13,279.1	5,255.3	8,023.8	3,374	3,692	3,219
2001 (March)	4,985	2,329	2,656	4,173	1,615	2,559	14,136.3	5,620.7	8,515.6	3,521	3,842	3,362
2002 (March)	5,072	2,414	2,658	4,223	1,659	2,564	14,837.8	5,996.6	8,841.2	3,657	4,007	3,479
2003 (March)	5,042	2,413	2,629	4,190	1,656	2,534	15,116.4	6,154.3	8,962.0	3,751	4,115	3,565
2004 (March)	5,041	2,432	2,608	4,187	1,672	2,514	15,477.5	6,411.7	9,065.7	3,845	4,256	3,631
2005 (March)	5,078	2,459	2,620	4,209	1,684	2,525	160,615.7	6,668.9	9,392.6	3,966	4,390	3,745

Source: U.S. Department of Commerce, Bureau of the Census, May 2006.
Note: Detail may not add to totals due to rounding.
Key:
(a) Due to a change in the reference period, from October to March, the October 1996 Annual Survey of Government Employment and Payroll was not concluded. This change in collection period was effective, beginning with the March 1997 survey.

Table 8.5
EMPLOYMENT AND PAYROLLS OF STATE AND LOCAL GOVERNMENTS BY FUNCTION: MARCH 2005

Functions	All employees, full-time and part-time (in thousands)			March payrolls (in millions of dollars)			Average March earnings of full-time employees
	Total	State government	Local government	Total	State government	Local government	
All functions	19,004	5,078	13,926	$58,123,288	$16,061,570	$42,061,717	$3,770
Education:							
Higher education.................................	2,861	2,303	558	7,395,870	6,132,873	1,262,996	4,404
Instructional personnel only	1,014	744	270	3,453,479	2,776,279	677,200	6,003
Elementary/Secondary schools.............	7,651	59	7,593	22,158,104	203,206	21,954,898	3,491
Instructional personnel only	5,169	41	5,128	17,491,809	167,199	17,324,610	3,935
Libraries...	184	1	184	361,255	1,645	359,611	3,194
Other Education..................................	97	97	0	332,842	332,842	0	3,742
Selected functions:							
Streets and Highways	568	242	326	1,929,979	885,886	1,044,093	3,563
Public Welfare	532	235	297	1,669,702	754,603	915,099	3,334
Hospitals...	998	423	574	3,368,785	1,411,251	1,957,534	3,679
Police protection................................	973	105	869	3,986,252	460,668	3,525,583	4,508
Police Officers	698	64	635	3,207,232	312,809	2,894,424	4,821
Fire protection....................................	450	N.A.	450	1,571,346	N.A.	1,571,346	5,034
Firefighters only	412	N.A.	412	1,466,345	N.A.	1,466,345	5,100
Natural Resources...............................	208	162	47	656,973	522,539	134,434	3,678
Correction	720	469	251	2,491,291	1,611,945	879,346	3,534
Social Insurance Admin.......................	87	87	N.A.	306,808	306,808	N.A.	3,669
Financial Admin..................................	431	173	258	1,428,891	624,556	804,335	3,716
Judicial and Legal..............................	441	169	272	1,714,204	735,532	978,672	4,205
Other Government Admin....................	470	61	409	1,071,999	217,272	854,727	3,862
Utilities..	530	8	522	1,946,703	44,774	1,901,929	3,999
Electric power	80	4	76	402,991	23,382	379,610	5,175
Gas supply	13	0	13	45,122	0	45,122	3,462
Sewerage..	137	2	136	495,720	9,149	486,571	3,916
Solid waste management	122	2	120	374,759	8,872	365,887	3,510
Water supply	178	1	177	628,111	3,371	624,740	3,854
State Liquor stores.............................	9	9	N.A.	19,647	19,647	N.A.	2,860
Other and unallocable	518	208	311	1,745,953	845,813	900,140	3,937

Source: U.S. Department of Commerce, Bureau of the Census, May 2006.
Note: Local government data are estimates subject to sampling variation;
see source. Detail may not add to total because of rounding.
Key:
0 — Represents zero or rounds to zero.
N.A. — Not applicable.

Table 8.6
STATE AND LOCAL GOVERNMENT EMPLOYMENT, BY STATE: MARCH 2005

State or other jurisdiction	All employees (full-time and part-time)			Full-time equivalent employment						2004 Population
				Number			Number per 10,000 population			
	Total	State	Local	Total	State	Local	Total	State	Local	
United States	19,004,053	5,078,268	13,925,785	15,923,650	4,208,522	11,715,128	537	142	395	296,507
Alabama	310,901	102,890	208,011	273,673	85,324	188,349	602	188	414	4,548
Alaska	62,013	28,004	34,009	51,720	24,553	27,167	780	370	410	663
Arizona	331,820	85,860	245,960	281,796	69,226	212,570	473	116	357	5,953
Arkansas..............	188,437	63,862	124,575	160,115	54,185	105,930	577	195	382	2,776
California	1,698,998	469,711	1,698,998	1,384,276	387,060	1,384,276	383	0	383	36,154
Colorado..............	304,417	85,495	218,922	250,068	66,035	184,033	536	142	395	4,663
Connecticut	223,541	72,719	150,822	185,219	59,827	125,392	529	171	358	3,501
Delaware..............	55,158	29,559	25,599	47,114	24,546	22,568	560	292	268	842
Florida	952,340	212,155	740,185	843,284	185,955	657,329	475	105	370	17,768
Georgia	562,523	145,444	417,079	498,781	120,843	377,938	546	132	414	9,133
Hawaii..................	82,237	66,929	15,308	68,630	54,286	14,344	539	426	113	1,273
Idaho...................	101,421	29,451	71,970	77,171	22,903	54,268	540	160	380	1,429
Illinois.................	783,110	159,398	623,712	637,313	132,934	504,379	499	104	395	12,765
Indiana.................	399,193	113,073	286,120	332,761	92,934	239,827	531	148	383	6,266
Iowa	237,142	65,543	171,599	185,874	52,946	132,928	627	179	448	2,966
Kansas.................	232,072	55,760	176,312	181,585	44,307	137,278	661	161	500	2,748
Kentucky	274,104	94,522	179,582	238,421	79,231	159,190	571	190	382	4,173
Louisiana	323,695	108,436	215,259	283,287	90,887	192,400	629	202	427	4,507
Maine	102,226	27,107	75,119	76,008	21,140	54,868	577	160	416	1,318
Maryland	320,437	96,819	223,618	278,497	90,542	187,955	498	162	336	5,590
Massachusetts.......	383,653	108,230	275,423	322,262	88,533	233,729	501	138	363	6,433
Michigan..............	649,366	168,292	481,074	495,030	131,254	363,776	490	130	360	10,101
Minnesota	354,010	91,493	262,517	269,273	74,278	194,995	525	145	380	5,127
Mississippi	217,383	64,558	152,825	188,707	56,568	132,139	649	195	454	2,909
Missouri...............	380,816	108,376	272,440	318,372	91,801	226,571	549	158	391	5,798
Montana	71,976	25,669	46,307	55,489	19,543	35,946	594	209	385	935
Nebraska..............	140,212	38,378	101,834	111,586	32,472	79,114	635	185	450	1,758
Nevada.................	120,989	33,443	87,546	100,408	25,766	74,642	416	107	309	2,412
New Hampshire....	84,507	24,495	60,012	69,186	19,477	49,709	529	149	380	1,307
New Jersey............	597,982	176,847	421,135	501,643	154,105	347,538	576	177	399	8,703
New Mexico	146,554	59,794	86,760	128,115	50,221	77,894	665	261	404	1,926
New York	1,350,345	274,750	1,075,595	1,184,190	245,437	938,753	613	127	486	19,316
North Carolina.....	199,299	159,747	39,552	158,378	135,285	23,093	183	156	27	8,673
North Dakota........	432,995	23,617	409,378	366,299	18,120	348,179	5,772	286	5,487	635
Ohio	768,651	178,316	590,335	620,466	136,370	484,096	541	119	422	11,471
Oklahoma	245,995	81,335	164,660	205,301	64,977	140,324	579	183	396	3,543
Oregon	235,345	75,241	160,104	182,390	57,932	124,458	501	159	342	3,639
Pennsylvania	679,211	190,799	488,412	576,511	159,682	416,829	465	129	336	12,405
Rhode Island	57,941	24,513	33,428	50,060	19,942	30,118	466	186	281	1,074
South Carolina	278,322	90,332	187,990	244,281	76,498	167,783	575	180	395	4,247
South Dakota........	62,341	16,558	45,783	43,626	13,477	30,149	563	174	389	775
Tennessee	369,813	98,998	270,815	321,954	82,786	239,168	541	139	402	5,956
Texas	1,435,257	319,581	1,115,676	1,290,828	274,352	1,016,476	563	120	443	22,929
Utah	165,666	61,610	104,056	127,713	49,164	78,549	513	197	315	2,490
Vermont	49,127	15,979	33,148	39,421	14,353	25,068	633	231	403	622
Virginia................	496,443	149,666	346,777	417,788	119,548	298,240	552	158	394	7,564
Washington...........	408,900	150,304	258,596	329,873	117,282	212,591	524	186	338	6,292
West Virginia........	113,518	44,329	69,189	98,422	37,710	60,712	543	208	335	1,814
Wisconsin.............	390,902	96,012	294,890	293,712	70,189	223,523	531	127	404	5,528
Wyoming..............	53,519	14,269	39,250	43,762	11,736	32,026	860	231	629	509
Dist. of Columbia...	47,519	N.A.	47,519	45,951	N.A.	45,951	790	N.A.	790	582

Source: U.S. Department of Commerce, Bureau of the Census, Governments Division, May 2006.

2005 Population Source: Table NST-EST2006-01—Annual State Population Estimates: July 1, 2005, Population Division, U.S. Census Bureau, released December 22, 2006.

Note: Statistics for local governments are estimates subject to sampling variation. Detail may not add to totals due to rounding.

Key:

N.A. — Not applicable

Table 8.7
STATE AND LOCAL GOVERNMENT PAYROLLS AND AVERAGE EARNINGS
OF FULL-TIME EMPLOYEES, BY STATE: MARCH 2005

State or other jurisdiction	Amount of payroll (in thousands of dollars)			Percentage of March payroll		Average earnings of full-time state and local government employees (dollars)		
	Total	State government	Local governments	State government	Local government	All	Education employees	Other
United States	58,123,287	16,061,570	42,061,717	27.6	72.4	3,770	3,664	3,882
Alabama	801,426	295,489	505,936	36.9	63.1	2,982	2,909	3,057
Alaska	209,472	100,915	108,556	48.2	51.8	4,186	3,906	4,439
Arizona	984,124	233,484	750,640	23.7	76.3	3,650	3,522	3,776
Arkansas...............	442,449	174,392	268,057	39.4	60.6	2,823	2,852	2,784
California	8,478,902	1,949,478	6,529,424	23	77	5,011	4,726	5,254
Colorado	942,057	279,364	662,693	29.7	70.3	3,924	3,742	4,112
Connecticut	825,653	286,979	538,674	34.8	65.2	4,639	4,521	4,789
Delaware..............	175,329	92,139	83,190	52.6	47.4	3,842	4,023	3,678
Florida	2,844,606	626,031	2,218,575	22	78	3,461	3,241	3,640
Georgia	1,540,617	398,386	1,142,231	25.9	74.1	3,151	3,227	3,057
Hawaii..................	253,077	195,763	57,314	77.4	22.6	3,758	3,743	3,769
Idaho....................	227,904	73,576	154,328	32.3	67.7	3,091	2,947	3,248
Illinois..................	2,395,059	519,883	1,875,176	21.7	78.3	3,931	3,698	4,202
Indiana.................	1,054,278	304,334	749,944	28.9	71.1	3,289	3,446	3,091
Iowa	593,524	215,338	378,186	36.3	63.7	3,362	3,181	3,598
Kansas..................	548,418	153,287	395,131	28	72	3,111	3,088	3,139
Kentucky	698,580	262,602	435,978	37.6	62.4	2,991	2,956	3,039
Louisiana..............	805,935	303,603	502,332	37.7	62.3	2,896	2,824	2,966
Maine	228,966	75,103	153,863	32.8	67.2	3,127	2,946	3,403
Maryland..............	1,160,138	366,234	793,904	31.6	68.4	4,254	4,470	4,026
Massachusetts.......	1,328,369	392,095	936,274	29.5	70.5	4,186	3,988	4,416
Michigan...............	1,882,486	538,633	1,343,853	28.6	71.4	4,086	4,160	3,986
Minnesota	1,025,461	316,920	708,541	30.9	69.1	4,053	3,943	4,178
Mississippi	513,116	168,304	344,812	32.8	67.2	2,770	2,882	2,648
Missouri................	934,623	273,100	661,522	29.2	70.8	3,004	2,979	3,031
Montana	159,745	61,521	98,224	38.5	61.5	2,988	2,929	3,055
Nebraska...............	358,280	98,020	260,260	27.4	72.6	3,338	3,240	3,430
Nevada..................	405,630	98,528	307,102	24.3	75.7	4,245	3,620	4,735
New Hampshire....	220,781	65,927	154,854	29.9	70.1	3,315	3,111	3,603
New Jersey............	2,278,593	725,708	1,552,885	31.8	68.2	4,707	4,814	4,589
New Mexico	369,591	155,310	214,281	42	58	2,925	2,737	3,140
New York	5,264,380	1,111,287	4,153,092	21.1	78.9	4,600	4,453	4,717
North Carolina	534,558	461,068	73,490	86.3	13.7	3,249	3,378	3,115
North Dakota.......	1,148,869	55,044	1,093,825	4.8	95.2	3,295	3,572	2,980
Ohio.....................	2,148,104	502,602	1,645,502	23.4	76.6	3,611	3,593	3,629
Oklahoma	559,135	203,489	355,646	36.4	63.6	2,793	2,657	2,964
Oregon	659,514	215,037	444,476	32.6	67.4	3,740	3,582	3,876
Pennsylvania	2,138,457	612,817	1,525,640	28.7	71.3	3,826	4,026	3,600
Rhode Island	213,628	84,170	129,458	39.4	60.6	4,410	4,472	4,346
South Carolina	718,014	235,125	482,888	32.7	67.3	3,007	3,010	3,004
South Dakota........	126,656	41,984	84,673	33.1	66.9	2,954	2,970	2,931
Tennessee..............	960,467	260,378	700,089	27.1	72.9	3,068	3,072	3,064
Texas	3,974,303	949,832	3,024,471	23.9	76.1	3,130	3,045	3,249
Utah	399,052	162,371	236,681	40.7	59.3	3,318	3,282	3,359
Vermont................	128,860	55,023	73,837	42.7	57.3	3,321	3,130	3,653
Virginia.................	1,399,970	424,369	975,601	30.3	69.7	3,456	3,404	3,522
Washington...........	1,348,345	457,092	891,253	33.9	66.1	4,333	4,285	4,365
West Virginia.......	279,204	114,000	165,205	40.8	59.2	2,866	3,068	2,634
Wisconsin.............	1,085,417	275,824	809,593	25.4	74.6	3,893	3,964	3,802
Wyoming..............	135,720	39,613	96,107	29.2	70.8	3,242	3,241	3,244
Dist. of Columbia	213,448	N.A.	213,448	N.A.	100.0	4,775	4,185	4,955

Source: U.S. Department of Commerce, Bureau of the Census, May 2006.
Note: Statistics for local governments are estimates subject to sampling variation. Detail may not add to totals due to rounding.

Table 8.8
STATE GOVERNMENT EMPLOYMENT (FULL-TIME EQUIVALENT) FOR SELECTED FUNCTIONS, BY STATE: MARCH 2005

State	All functions	Education		Highways	Public welfare	Hospitals	Corrections	Police protection	Natural resources	Financial and other governmental administration	Judicial and legal administration
		Higher education (a)	Other education (b)								
United States	4,208,522	1,545,379	138,503	238,061	231,038	398,696	464,701	102,713	146,161	224,377	164,595
Alabama	85,324	36,698	3,204	4,364	4,344	11,392	4,880	1,382	2,175	3,206	3,205
Alaska	24,553	4,910	3,392	2,889	1,740	212	1,719	446	2,301	1,591	1,262
Arizona	69,226	26,387	3,348	2,875	7,453	737	10,304	2,014	2,884	4,435	2,313
Arkansas...............	54,185	21,269	1,345	3,562	3,656	4,273	4,463	1,087	1,825	2,569	1,452
California	387,060	143,275	4,293	20,234	3,639	38,237	49,437	12,701	13,604	25,238	4,291
Colorado...............	66,035	37,017	1,311	3,123	1,928	3,547	6,522	1,170	1,407	2,632	3,505
Connecticut	59,827	15,783	2,538	2,912	4,366	10,363	7,727	1,984	804	3,553	4,568
Delaware...............	24,546	7,472	375	1,605	1,556	1,847	2,739	931	500	1,013	1,501
Florida	185,955	54,377	3,767	7,614	11,207	4,404	28,029	4,379	10,663	9,233	18,400
Georgia	120,843	47,962	3,093	5,845	8,647	7,955	19,524	2,028	3,759	5,471	3,090
Hawaii...................	54,286	8,512	24,937	860	937	3,998	2,278	0	1,071	1,300	2,252
Idaho....................	22,903	8,534	538	1,767	1,750	819	1,795	473	2,010	1,759	434
Illinois..................	132,934	56,630	2,233	7,571	10,058	11,693	14,045	3,907	3,662	7,415	3,067
Indiana.................	92,934	54,555	1,208	4,283	5,619	3,803	8,965	1,986	2,718	3,405	1,258
Iowa	52,946	25,351	1,164	2,488	2,823	6,895	3,138	891	1,720	1,954	2,263
Kansas	44,307	19,341	604	3,560	2,753	2,390	3,586	1,113	864	2,688	2,116
Kentucky	79,231	31,349	2,756	5,074	6,803	5,848	3,867	2,317	3,913	3,791	4,998
Louisiana	90,887	30,703	3,429	5,235	5,147	16,182	7,872	1,778	4,958	4,499	1,782
Maine	21,140	6,998	313	2,566	2,027	626	1,301	546	1,033	1,727	715
Maryland...............	90,542	26,388	2,127	4,702	6,754	5,024	11,985	2,514	2,052	5,093	4,675
Massachusetts.......	88,533	24,753	1,160	3,868	7,595	6,916	6,600	5,702	1,224	6,135	8,973
Michigan...............	131,254	62,614	2,029	2,874	10,251	12,892	17,379	2,743	4,554	6,056	1,511
Minnesota	74,278	33,518	3,565	4,749	2,725	4,774	3,839	911	3,254	3,834	2,731
Mississippi	56,568	18,860	1,546	3,364	2,536	12,457	3,701	1,183	3,272	1,643	660
Missouri................	91,801	28,054	1,879	6,816	8,386	12,130	12,942	2,263	2,732	3,668	4,139
Montana	19,543	7,137	431	2,134	1,579	566	1,104	422	1,399	1,570	467
Nebraska...............	32,472	12,241	549	2,150	2,502	4,267	2,480	724	2,172	877	702
Nevada..................	25,766	8,802	129	1,719	1,426	1,100	3,437	807	1,183	2,673	629
New Hampshire....	19,477	6,708	309	1,797	1,455	771	1,369	421	569	1,214	911
New Jersey............	154,105	30,986	22,461	7,380	7,478	18,523	10,269	4,463	2,473	8,108	14,812
New Mexico	50,221	17,522	1,150	2,301	1,580	10,388	4,236	633	1,812	2,355	2,839
New York	245,437	51,010	4,529	12,360	6,311	41,143	33,503	6,508	3,382	17,716	19,410
North Carolina.....	135,285	49,727	2,842	11,568	1,986	17,523	20,534	3,393	3,977	5,022	5,930
North Dakota........	18,120	8,083	281	997	465	984	676	179	1,644	1,001	524
Ohio......................	136,370	66,737	2,550	7,128	2,992	11,217	16,405	2,686	3,548	8,941	2,763
Oklahoma..............	64,977	26,239	1,907	2,892	5,827	2,488	5,570	1,850	2,007	2,650	2,580
Oregon	57,932	18,592	933	3,378	5,666	4,801	4,961	1,220	2,759	5,316	3,091
Pennsylvania	159,682	57,802	3,919	13,608	12,476	12,485	17,227	5,955	6,368	10,636	3,001
Rhode Island	19,942	5,530	1,184	865	1,484	1,063	1,739	309	500	1,650	1,258
South Carolina	76,498	28,690	2,717	4,940	4,437	7,862	7,363	1,858	1,956	3,915	687
South Dakota........	13,477	5,007	414	1,014	1,055	894	795	301	888	733	521
Tennessee	82,786	34,022	2,099	4,396	6,332	7,906	7,142	1,968	3,652	3,940	2,250
Texas	274,352	100,820	4,688	14,836	19,119	30,687	45,474	4,117	11,408	12,312	5,470
Utah	49,164	23,644	1,023	1,663	3,227	5,657	3,364	817	1,191	1,888	1,512
Vermont................	14,353	4,728	570	1,092	1,244	206	1,171	534	605	1,242	624
Virginia	119,548	50,085	2,800	9,475	2,348	12,945	14,224	2,748	3,177	4,881	3,686
Washington...........	117,282	51,098	2,059	7,022	9,914	9,726	9,095	2,213	4,921	4,197	1,891
West Virginia........	37,710	10,995	1,439	5,208	3,316	1,664	3,310	981	2,273	2,964	1,373
Wisconsin..............	70,189	34,711	1,120	1,708	1,336	3,621	9,700	895	2,515	3,951	1,981
Wyoming...............	11,736	3,153	246	1,630	783	795	916	262	823	717	522

Source: U.S. Department of Commerce, Bureau of the Census, May 2006.
(a) Includes instructional and other personnel.
(b) Includes instructional and other personnel in elementary and secondary schools.

Table 8.9
STATE GOVERNMENT PAYROLLS FOR SELECTED FUNCTIONS, BY STATE: MARCH 2005
(In thousands of dollars)

State	All functions	Education Higher education (a)	Other education (b)	Highways	Public welfare	Hospitals	Corrections	Police protection	Natural resources	Financial and other governmental administration	Judicial and legal administration
United States ...	$16,061,570,421	$6,132,873	$536,048	$885,886	$754,603	$1,411,251	$1,611,945	$460,668	$522,539	$841,828	$735,532
Alabama	$295,489,119	$138,912	$9,765	$11,801	$13,411	$39,250	$15,025	$5,233	$7,032	$11,137	$12,357
Alaska	100,915,433	20,514	11,949	12,762	5,972	861	7,161	2,173	9,342	6,568	5,612
Arizona	233,483,814	98,502	9,665	9,510	20,881	2,409	29,163	8,318	11,113	14,311	9,117
Arkansas............	174,391,908	74,974	4,453	11,168	10,382	12,763	11,713	3,717	5,341	8,530	4,615
California	1,949,478,056	694,063	19,190	120,496	15,938	192,975	259,288	70,494	62,206	106,902	25,675
Colorado.............	279,363,805	157,712	5,186	12,951	8,020	12,935	25,463	6,217	6,573	11,210	15,575
Connecticut	286,979,018	76,983	12,011	13,207	20,643	54,868	35,636	10,357	3,711	15,900	19,386
Delaware.............	92,138,617	30,954	1,818	5,126	4,933	5,806	9,587	4,843	1,742	3,744	5,320
Florida	626,030,538	227,529	10,683	27,874	29,420	11,672	80,230	15,365	30,553	32,303	66,930
Georgia	398,386,073	185,825	11,274	16,161	23,097	20,248	48,903	6,838	11,737	18,872	14,070
Hawaii..................	195,762,500	35,074	86,277	3,154	3,071	14,507	8,579	0	4,111	4,500	8,943
Idaho...................	73,576,144	27,322	1,683	5,424	5,253	2,359	4,986	1,706	6,511	5,772	2,406
Illinois................	519,883,496	194,627	8,952	32,209	41,995	44,680	58,321	19,451	12,467	31,237	20,655
Indiana................	304,334,385	185,717	3,922	12,910	15,185	10,108	25,334	7,701	8,908	11,375	6,615
Iowa	215,337,962	103,281	4,929	10,124	10,554	27,348	12,509	3,969	6,607	8,157	10,039
Kansas	153,286,977	77,708	2,033	10,550	7,714	6,241	9,727	4,121	2,873	8,128	7,415
Kentucky	262,602,063	114,288	10,053	15,485	19,506	18,113	9,808	8,041	11,650	14,332	15,909
Louisiana	303,603,103	110,618	11,495	16,036	15,723	50,176	22,813	7,675	16,238	14,980	7,600
Maine	75,103,205	24,831	1,078	9,256	6,321	2,266	4,434	2,395	3,942	5,868	2,912
Maryland.............	366,234,182	118,284	8,808	18,207	23,181	17,640	42,167	11,563	8,744	21,291	21,396
Massachusetts...	392,095,182	109,779	5,537	17,721	32,627	24,110	29,148	29,974	6,027	25,957	41,195
Michigan.............	538,633,186	264,270	7,884	12,302	39,845	45,553	72,771	10,276	17,838	25,768	9,659
Minnesota...........	316,919,528	147,475	15,218	20,084	9,096	17,671	14,614	4,425	13,144	15,628	13,821
Mississippi..........	168,303,805	67,645	4,377	8,521	5,625	31,449	9,143	3,524	8,664	5,352	3,445
Missouri..............	273,100,286	96,335	5,452	20,775	19,869	32,186	31,773	7,603	7,826	10,359	14,625
Montana	61,520,979	22,520	1,303	7,335	4,638	1,542	3,260	1,349	4,543	4,451	1,777
Nebraska.............	98,019,863	38,310	2,014	6,703	6,556	12,065	7,046	2,530	5,895	2,875	2,846
Nevada................	98,528,023	29,707	586	6,944	4,892	4,593	13,570	4,012	4,545	10,191	3,639
New Hampshire...	65,926,815	23,657	1,035	6,517	4,240	2,481	4,772	1,731	1,791	4,139	3,276
New Jersey..........	725,707,540	157,572	116,204	33,178	31,413	69,278	49,931	25,764	11,365	33,188	71,191
New Mexico	155,309,827	49,555	3,776	6,921	4,464	34,730	13,084	2,503	5,979	7,887	10,044
New York	1,111,287,360	225,317	19,319	52,927	26,429	165,576	143,670	38,423	14,803	69,863	110,061
North Carolina....	461,067,618	191,767	9,828	33,230	6,832	55,598	55,971	12,721	12,283	15,727	23,163
North Dakota.....	55,043,993	25,834	849	2,918	1,246	1,969	1,757	561	4,310	3,310	1,856
Ohio	502,602,088	231,815	11,087	29,869	13,540	33,446	59,866	11,798	12,192	38,429	12,337
Oklahoma	203,489,431	85,294	6,157	8,308	14,838	7,036	16,033	6,329	5,722	8,725	9,708
Oregon	215,037,283	73,419	3,348	13,412	19,115	18,762	17,314	4,789	9,025	17,977	11,206
Pennsylvania	612,816,983	245,126	14,851	43,716	43,604	37,390	61,185	28,825	26,883	38,280	14,892
Rhode Island	84,170,040	20,389	5,132	3,793	7,164	4,593	8,280	1,775	2,256	6,610	5,690
South Carolina ...	235,125,459	98,235	8,620	13,445	11,596	17,150	18,186	5,964	5,612	12,295	2,972
South Dakota......	41,983,617	17,093	1,165	3,113	2,747	2,296	2,116	1,010	2,580	2,369	1,771
Tennessee	260,377,964	115,550	6,669	12,179	15,966	22,490	19,748	6,814	10,837	13,870	9,727
Texas	949,831,999	421,028	16,114	44,957	50,324	103,304	109,839	13,425	42,270	41,547	23,311
Utah	162,370,679	82,552	3,208	5,784	9,708	16,675	9,816	2,790	3,874	6,206	5,397
Vermont..............	55,022,986	18,476	2,271	3,835	4,629	715	4,055	2,443	2,571	4,522	2,540
Virginia...............	424,369,364	194,815	10,635	33,513	8,138	39,681	38,837	10,755	10,528	17,397	15,184
Washington..........	457,901,617	193,017	8,161	30,353	39,495	43,313	31,346	10,552	19,163	16,521	9,802
West Virginia......	113,999,599	39,824	4,491	16,201	7,612	3,701	7,090	3,108	6,995	8,828	4,605
Wisconsin............	275,824,219	137,042	4,603	7,312	4,751	12,718	34,338	3,702	8,923	15,824	11,149
Wyoming.............	39,612,690	11,739	934	5,610	2,409	1,956	2,540	1,017	2,699	2,618	2,099

Source: U.S. Department of Commerce, Bureau of the Census, March 2007.
  (a) Includes instructional and other personnel.
  (b) Includes instructional and other personnel in elementary and secondary schools.

Implementation of the Real ID Act: States' Recommendations

By Bonnie Rutledge

On May 11, 2005, Congress passed the Real ID Act. The law sets minimum standards for the creation and issuance of state-issued driver's licenses and ID cards if they are to be accepted as valid identification for federal purposes. Initial estimates have shown Real ID implementation will exceed $11 billion over five years. The burden of compliance with Real ID will prove challenging and costly for states.

Due to the public's reliance on the driver's license as an identity document, the security of the credential—from point of issuance to card security features to the exchange of the license holder's information—is a growing public concern. In order for us to trust the holder is who they say they are, we must feel confident their license and the issuance process have passed a reasonable security litmus test.

The American Association of Motor Vehicle Administrators (AAMVA) and its members have long advocated the promotion of uniformity and interoperability of driver's licenses and ID cards (DL/IDs) nationwide. In layman's terms, this means: (1) all states should adhere to a minimum set of operating standards, security features and issuance requirements; (2) all licenses should contain security features that limit their susceptibility to fraud; and (3) there is a secure technological infrastructure that allows states to share driver information in real time within agreed upon guidelines to ensure individual privacy is protected. With this framework in place, both the security of the document and its trustworthiness to prove the holder's identity are greatly improved. These improvements will also close significant gaps that have led to vulnerabilities which are unacceptably easy to exploit today.

In a post-Sept. 11 business environment, balancing security concerns with customer service has been an ongoing challenge to motor vehicle agencies. Many of these challenges were described in an article included in the 2005 edition of this publication. Over the past five years, it is not surprising that political winds have continued to blow in a direction that emphasizes security over convenience. States have adapted by improving security features, restricting the identity documents used to obtain a license, or in some instances, tying residency requirements to eligibility. Against this backdrop has been a groundswell of federal legislative activity aimed at expediting standardization and

security processes, primarily through the passage of the Real ID Act of 2005.

The Real ID Act of 2005

Those concerns were brought to the forefront when, on May 11, 2005, Congress passed the Real ID Act (Real ID) as part of the Emergency Supplemental Appropriations Act for Defense, the Global War on Terror, and Tsunami Relief Act (P.L. 109-13). The legislation establishes certain standards, procedures and requirements that must be met by May 11, 2008, if state-issued DL/IDs are to be accepted as valid identification by the federal government (e.g., boarding an airplane, entering federal or nuclear facilities). It also sets minimum standards for the creation and issuance of the documents by motor vehicle agencies. A rulemaking process by the Department of Homeland Security will further define the minimum standards set in the act. These standards are likely to alter long-standing state laws, regulations and practices governing the qualifications for and the production and issuance of DL/IDs in every state.

To ensure Congress and the federal government understand the fiscal and operational impact of altering these complex and vital state systems, AAMVA in conjunction with the National Governors Association (NGA) and the National Conference of State Legislatures (NCSL) conducted a nationwide survey of state motor vehicle agencies (DMVs). Based on results of that survey, NGA, NCSL and AAMVA concluded, at a minimum, Real ID will cost more than $11 billion over five years. Clearly, this will have a major impact on customer services to the public and impose substantive burdens on states in order to comply with the act by the May 2008 deadline.

The three organizations also provided practical and cost-effective solutions for Congress and the Department of Homeland Security (DHS) to consider as a means to address shortcomings while still meeting the objectives of the act. A comprehensive version of the report is available on AAMVA's Web site (*http://www.aamva.org*). For the purposes of this article, related cost impacts, major findings and recommendations are summarized below.

Real ID Cost Impacts

Re-enrollment

The legislation requires *all* license and ID card holders to prove their identity. This means many of the identity documents gathering dust in forgotten lock boxes and file cabinets—such as birth certificates and social security cards—will need to be found and taken to the DMV. At that point, licensing officials will verify the authenticity of the documents with the relevant issuing agency (e.g., U.S. Citizenship and Immigration Services, Social Security Administration, etc.). Citizens who cannot provide the required identity documents are faced with the prospect of walking out without a license or ID card as the law currently states. This re-enrollment phase will take place over five years, beginning May 11, 2008, and is the most costly element of the projected $11 billion needed to implement Real ID.

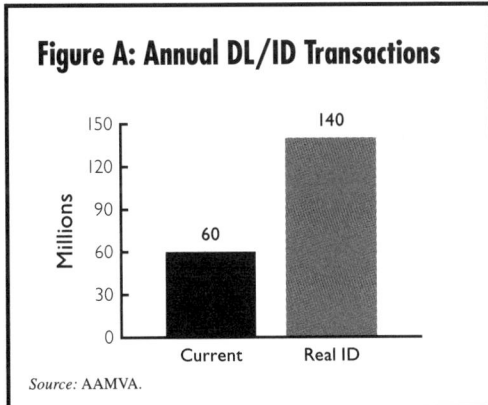

Figure A: Annual DL/ID Transactions

Source: AAMVA.

As is standard practice with new license issuances, DMV personnel must capture full legal name, process photos, signatures and most notably, determine the lawful presence of the applicant. Taking into account the current population of 245 million driver's license and ID card holders, and the number of documents required for authentication, states anticipate processing more than 1 billion verification transactions over the five-year period. It is important to note this does not include the typical duplicate, reinstatement and replacement transactions the DMV handles as part of its normal processing load. In addition, efficiencies

from alternative renewal processes (such as Internet and mail) will be lost during the re-enrollment period and states will face increased costs from the need to hire more employees and expand business hours. Total estimated cost: $8.48 billion.

New Verification Processes

Real ID supplants traditional DMV vetting processes by requiring states to independently verify each identification document with its issuing agency. While the act contemplates the use of five national electronic systems to facilitate verification, currently only one of these systems, Social Security Online Verification (SSOLV) is available on a nationwide basis. System development, programming, testing and training will take considerable time and investment that far exceed the deadlines or funds provided by the act or Congress. Total estimated cost: $1.42 billion.

DL/ID Design Requirements

The act calls for states to incorporate security features into DL/ID cards to prevent tampering and counterfeiting. Although most states have incorporated security features into their card designs, the contemplated regulations are likely to mandate the use of a single security configuration that will maximize cost by minimizing state flexibility in card design and production. State-issued licenses will still retain certain attributes that give them a unique appearance that distinguishes them from others. Depending on the technology DMVs choose , they could be forced to move away from "over-the-counter" issuance and toward central issuance systems. Total estimated cost: $1.11 billion.

Ancillary Support Requirements

Real ID contains several other requirements that will affect state business practices and budgets, including requirements to conduct security clearances on all employees involved in the production and issuance process and mandatory fraudulent document recognition training. Total estimated cost: $0.04 billion.

Key Findings and Recommendations

Despite the significance of the $11 billion estimated price tag, the findings gleaned from the survey likely *underestimate* the full impact of Real ID. Costs could escalate significantly if federal regulations differ substantially from the recommendations states used to form baseline assumptions. Lacking regulatory guidance, states were unable to estimate several elements of the act that will almost certainly contribute additional cost and administrative burdens to the compliance process, including:

- Facility security requirements;
- Development of federal verification systems and transaction costs;
- Consideration of a system that is adequate to support additional verification connectivity requirements;
- Law enforcement training and technology deployment;
- Expanded public education/data privacy protection; and
- Increased customer demand/care/advocacy.

Governors, state legislators and motor vehicle administrators are committed to improving the security and integrity of state DL/ID systems, but the timelines and requirements mandated by Real ID have to be realistic. In order to meet the objectives of the act, Congress and DHS should consider incorporating the following recommendations into the law and any final regulations:[1]

General Recommendations

- **Extend the compliance deadline:** It will be impossible for states to comply with every aspect of Real ID by the May 2008 deadline. DHS has yet to issue regulations and most of the major systems necessary to comply do not exist. A phased approach must be considered.
- **Provide funds necessary for states to comply with Real ID:** The projected cost of complying with the act far exceeds the Congressional Budget Office estimate and will require a more significant investment by Congress.
- **Grant the Secretary of Homeland Security the flexibility to recognize innovation at the state level:** Several states have updated their systems to meet objectives similar to those of Real ID. The secretary of Homeland Security should have the discretion to recognize state practices and innovations that accomplish the goals of the act.

Re-enrollment Recommendations

- **Implement a 10-year, progressive re-enrollment schedule:** It is impracticable for states to renew all 245 million DL/IDs in five years. States should be given the flexibility to delay re-verifying certain populations in order to maximize resources and avoid severe disruptions to customer service.
- **Allow reciprocity for persons already vetted by the federal government:** States could realize significant savings and reduced transaction time if individuals whose identities have already been verified for certain federal identification cards are considered pre-qualified for a Real ID compliant DL/ID.

Verification Recommendations

- **Provide the federal electronic verification systems necessary to comply with the law:** Only one of the five national electronic systems required to verify identification documents is fully operational. It will take considerable time, money and testing for the federal government to update its systems to meet the verification requirements of the act.
- **Require states to employ electronic verification systems only as they become available:** Until electronic systems are fully operational, states must be allowed to use existing verification processes to comply with the act.
- **Adopt uniform naming conventions to facilitate electronic verification between files:** An individual's name is a person's most common identifier. For electronic systems to work seamlessly, the federal government must adopt and universally apply common naming conventions to its systems.

DL/ID Design Requirements Recommendations

- **Establish card security criteria based on performance—not technology:** Limiting states to a single technology configuration increases risks and reduces innovation.

Conclusion

Governors, state legislators, motor vehicle administrators and federal officials share the goal of improving the security of state-issued DL/ID cards. However, the Real ID Act presents significant operational and fiscal challenges to states and the federal government. Moreover, it has become axiomatic that, in the public's eye, improvements to homeland security often generate less gratitude for what they achieve than they do resentment for the burdens of complying with them. Therefore, officials at all levels of government must recognize the personal impact Real ID will have on individual citizens.

The major findings described in this article represent the most critical challenges facing states and consumers as the act's implementation deadline approaches. However, even with full funding and aggressive state implementation plans, the difficulties of fully complying by the statutory deadline of May 2008 seem insurmountable. How these challenges continue to unfold will hinge upon a variety of sociopolitical factors that, at present, are difficult to gauge.

First, state governments are discovering reluctantly that they are in the identity business, as they maintain the public records that document the important legal events in their citizens' lives, and consequently their identities. States also issue most of the identity documents carried in this country. Except for the passport and the "green card" carried by legal immigrants, federal government agencies have generally done very little to authenticate identities, leaving the responsibility with the states. With an estimated 9 million U.S. residents each year reporting they are victims of identity theft or fraud, the implications are that state governments will be increasingly tasked to undertake conscientious identity management and improve the security of processes and systems.

Second, and perhaps one of the most intriguing unknown variables is the impact of the 2006 mid-term elections. At the time of this writing, voters propelled the Democrats to win back control of the U.S. Senate and House of Representatives for the first time since 1994. In addition, for the first time in 12 years, Democrats recaptured control of the majority of governorships, outpacing Republican ranks 28 to 20. What will the election results mean to Real ID implementation?

Gubernatorial changes will likely impact agendas at the state level as new administrations are established. Our primary members at AAMVA, the chief administrators in charge of each state's DMV, are by no means immune. Many are appointed by the governor and serve at their whim. At the very least, there will be a learning curve for new administrators and governors who must wrangle with the act's potential impacts and how they mesh with their state's political priorities.

Should Real ID prevail, our organizations strongly believe the recommendations presented here offer reasonable and workable solutions to help states meet the objectives of the legislation. It is our intention to work towards implementation of the act in a cost-effective and reasonable manner. Governors, state legislators and motor vehicle administrators encourage DHS to adopt regulations and Congress to pass legislation that incorporates the recommendations of this report. We also urge Congress to appropriate sufficient funds to allow states to implement the act. The objectives of Real ID are laudable, but only by working together will state and federal governments succeed in meeting the challenges the act presents.

Epilogue

On March 1, 2007, just prior to publication of this article, the Bush Administration released regulations for the implementation of REAL ID. The aforementioned concerns regarding the feasibility of the May 2008 deadline appear to have been heeded. Among the highlights of the report was an announcement by DHS Secretary Michael Chertoff that states unable to meet the original deadline could apply for a postponement. States would be granted up to nineteen months past the original deadline. In addition, Chertoff said states can use 20 percent of their homeland security grant money to offset costs. Currently, Congress has appropriated only $40 million in state assistance funds.

Though the deadline concession addressed one of the more vexing issues regarding REAL ID, it offered little solace to state and federal lawmakers who fear cost and privacy concerns surrounding the law will be difficult to surmount. Nonetheless, the extension did fend off at least one lawmaker's attempt to postpone the legislation. U.S. Senator Susan Collins (R-Maine) dropped a bill that would have forced a delay. However, other legislation may continue to loom as politicians wrangle with the burden of the act. For example, on the eve of the proposed rules, Senator Daniel Akaka (D-Hawaii) submitted a bill to jettison REAL ID and has called for hearings. At the state level, the Montana House voted overwhelmingly to refuse to comply with the federal license law.

The long-awaited draft regulations have by no means put the myriad issues surrounding REAL ID to rest. Indeed, they may usher in the next wave of debate and it will be interesting to see how various stakeholders involved in it can, or cannot, come to some level of consensus regarding its implementation.

Notes

[1] Additional recommendations are included in the Impact Analysis section of the full report and the February 2006 NGA, NCSL, AAMVA section-by-section report.

About the Author

Bonnie Rutledge has served as Commissioner of Motor Vehicles for the State of Vermont since 2000. Rutledge has over 35 years of distinguished public service with the State of Vermont and has provided leadership to the AAMVA community in various capacities, most recently as Chair of the association's Real ID Committee. She has also served the association as AAMVA Chair of the Board, and has worked closely with the organization on all issues relating to highway safety.

AAMVA provides advocacy on identification security and highway safety issues; professional development opportunities for motor vehicle agency professionals; programs that promote and facilitate uniformity and reciprocity; and services that enhance business operations in motor vehicle agencies. Find more information on AAMVA at *www.aamva.org.*

Chapter Nine

SELECTED STATE POLICIES AND PROGRAMS

“*Among states and emergency response disciplines, there is a common concern regarding long-term sustainable federal funding for homeland security.*”

—Beverly Bell

“*With public opinion mixed, the law scheduled for reauthorization in 2007, and its most ambitious demands still ahead, the long-term impact of NCLB is still very much up in the air.*”

—Frederick M. Hess

“*Until more effective cancer treatments are developed, legislation promoting lifestyle changes and supportive community environment offer the best hope of reducing cancer incidence and mortality.*”

—Martha M. McKinney

“*To meet these energy and environmental needs, we need transformational discoveries in basic science and truly disruptive technologies.*”

—Jim Geringer

“*Despite an impressive list of advantages, the U.S. can no longer assume that foreign firms will continue to invest and employ people here at the same rate as in the past.*”

—Jeffey A. Finkle

Chapter Nine—Continued

66 *What stands out about the incentive packages for their projects and, increasingly others on the radar, are noncash elements.* 99

—Adam Bruns

66 *New federal rules requiring states to increase work participation will change the shape of future caseloads.* 99

—Sheila Zedlewski

66 *The U.S.-Mexico relationship faces complex challenges that require practical solutions.* 99

—Edgar Ruiz

State Emergency Management and Homeland Security— More Changes Ahead
By Beverly Bell

More than a year has passed since the devastation of Hurricane Katrina, but the fallout continues. Three separate reports on the disaster from the U.S. House of Representatives, Senate and the White House have resulted in numerous criticisms, recommendations and requirements. Whether these reactive measures will result in a better prepared nation is yet to be determined. Underlying all of the challenges is the ongoing struggle between adequate funding and saving human life and property during a disaster. Given the recurring demands on state budgets as well as federal programs, this pressure shows no sign of abating.

Introduction

It's anticipated that the aftermath of Hurricane Katrina will continue to impact policy and operations in emergency management and homeland security for many years to come. The devastation caused by this hurricane revealed gaps on all levels of government in emergency preparedness, response and recovery. It illustrated the need for workable evacuation plans and sheltering; functioning interoperable communications; logistical support for catastrophes, and a fully qualified and staffed state and national disaster response system.

Of course, none of these capabilities is possible without sufficient money. Emergency management is a discipline that works from the bottom up. Local emergency managers are the first to respond to an event; state responders, then the federal government, join in when asked or when state resources are overwhelmed.

The 1950 Federal Civil Defense Act acknowledged that *the nation's ability to recover from an incident was dependent upon the coordination of an effective response at the lowest levels of government*. It recognized that national security was a shared responsibility and that the federal government had a vested interest in protecting citizens from hazards. The $3.1 billion act from more than 50 years ago mandated that preparedness was a joint federal-state-local responsibility, and it allowed for the use of federal funds as an incentive for state and local government participation. In recent years, however, this concept has either been ignored or forgotten. Key emergency management funding essentially has remained flat, while federal mandates on the states continue to grow.

Finally, the loss of experienced professionals is challenging the emergency management field. There has been a significant turnover in the ranks of the top state emergency management positions. Currently, 36 state emergency management directors have been in their jobs three years or less. Five of the most experienced directors have held their positions no longer than 11 years. Only one person has been state director between 12 and 15 years. Some of this change has been the result of the 2006 elections during which 36 states held gubernatorial contests. Most of it, however, was due to a maturation of the field. The question remains as to how emergency management can develop new talent as well as retain its knowledge base, so that lessons learned can be applied to better prepare for and manage future disasters.

Emergency Management and Homeland Security Structures

Emergency management is one of the most important functions of state government. It is the central coordination point for all resources and assistance provided during disasters and emergencies, including acts of terrorism. It also has the overarching responsibility of saving lives, protecting property and helping citizens recover once a disaster has occurred. Typically, emergency management comes to the forefront once an event has taken place. In reality, much of the critical work comes *before*—in the form of disaster drills and exercises, hazard mitigation programs, public warning tests and preparedness education.

Emergency management includes four main components, often referred to as the "Four Pillars":
- Mitigation—Activities that reduce or eliminate the degree of risk to human life and property.
- Preparedness—Pre-disaster activities to develop and maintain a capability to respond rapidly and effectively to emergencies and disasters. These include all facets of preparation such as develop-

ing emergency operation plans and procedures for disasters and emergencies; as well as conducting training, drills and exercises.

- Response—Activities to assess and contain the immediate effects of disasters, provide life support to victims and deliver emergency services. During a disaster, this means coordinating emergency response such as the facilitation of resources and supplemental assistance to local governments when events exceed their capabilities; managing transportation and evacuation; overseeing the emergency operation center and acting as the lead in incident management.

- Recovery—Activities to restore damaged facilities and equipment and support the economic and social revitalization of affected areas to their pre-emergency status. During and after a disaster, this includes assisting the governor's office by 1) providing accurate and realistic information for crisis communication, 2) activating mutual aid agreements, 3) providing damage assessments and estimates; coordinating public information and warnings, and 4) managing resources and logistics; facilitating sheltering and mass care; coordinating local volunteer organizations.

On the state level, these four parts encompass many different aspects, from planning and implementation to training and exercising. A state emergency manager will interact with all sectors of the population, including other state agencies, elected officials, local jurisdictions, all public safety personnel, the private sector and the general public.

How Emergency Management is Organized

The organization of state emergency management agencies varies widely. In 14 states,[1] the emergency management agency is located within the department of public safety; in 16 states, it is located within the military department under the auspices of the adjutant general; and in 11 states, it is located within the governor's office. Regardless of agencies' organizational structure for daily operations, emergency management ranks high among governors' priorities. In 34 states, the emergency management director is appointed by the governor. This is an increase from 32 in 2005 and 29 in 2004. The position is appointed by the adjutant general in eight states and by the secretary of public safety in seven states.

The 2007 operating budgets for these agencies range from a low of $270,000 to a high of more than $35 million. The average state agency budget is $4,169,149 and the median is $2,494,598. This compares to the 2006 operating budgets that spanned

from $454,000 to almost $38 million. In that year, the average state budget was $4,090,365 while the median was $2,065,250. Staffing levels at all of the state emergency management agencies include 4,675 personnel for 2007. In 2006, the total work force was almost 4,491.

Homeland Security Structures and Funding

Four and a half years after a National Strategy for Homeland Security was developed, many states still face the challenge of assimilating homeland security into their emergency management and response systems. This is apparent from the wide range of structures and responsibilities under which state homeland security offices operate. In some cases, state homeland security directors manage grants and budgets; in other cases, they have very limited roles. The inconsistent approach is a clear indication that the relationship between homeland security and emergency management is still being defined.

All states, in fact, have a designated homeland security point of contact and this position has become a critical component of a governor's staff. It has the enormous job of preparing citizens, businesses and governments for the next emergency or large-scale disaster.

Who takes on this responsibility varies from state to state. Currently, 22 states have established a unique position of homeland security advisor or homeland security director. In 11 states, either the emergency management director or a combined emergency management/homeland security director is the primary point of contact. Five states have the adjutant general serving in this capacity, which is a decrease from seven in 2005. Seven public safety secretaries/commissioners are in this role.

Many states are also modifying the structure of their homeland security office. Thirteen states house the day-to-day operations in the governor's office while six run it out of the adjutant general/military affairs department. Another six have it in a specific homeland security department. Nine states keep the homeland security function in their emergency management office, while nine operate out of their public safety department. The remaining have other structures in place.

The trend of the homeland security director becoming less of a political appointment in the governor's office and more institutionalized in the organizational structure of state government continues. Currently, 42 states have authorized their homeland security offices, departments or agencies through either executive order or state statute. This is up from 39 in 2005.

Table A: State Emergency Management: Agency Structure, Budget and Staffing

State or other jurisdiction	Position appointed	Appointed/ selected by	Organizational structure	Agency operating budget FY 2007	Full-time employee positions
Alabama	★	G	Governor's Office	$2,100,000	105
Alaska	★	G	Adjutant General/Military Affairs	2,742,000	44
Arizona	★	ADJ	Adjutant General/Military Affairs	1,300,000	62
Arkansas	★	G	Governor's Office	1,166,115	78
California	★	G	Governor's Office	35,374,000	538
Colorado	★	ED	Department of Local Affairs	540,000	30
Connecticut	. . .	HSEMC	Governor's Office	2,600,000	45
Delaware	★	G	Department of Safety & Homeland Security	1,300,000	45
Florida	★	G	Governor's Office	7,800,000	138
Georgia	★	G	Department of Homeland Security	1,950,000	100
Hawaii	★	ADJ	Department of Defense	1,500,000	45
Idaho	★	G	Adjutant General/Military Affairs	1,500,000	42 (a)
Illinois	★	G	Public Safety	35,000,000	257
Indiana	★	G	Department of Homeland Security	12,000,000	270 (a)
Iowa	★	G	Department of Public Defense	2,920,000	71 (a)
Kansas	. . .	ADJ	Adjutant General/Military Affairs	611,000	26
Kentucky	★	ADJ	Adjutant General/Military Affairs	3,137,200	83
Louisiana	★	G	Governor's Office	5,000,000	100
Maine	★	G	Adjutant General/Military Affairs	800,000	23
Maryland	★	G	Adjutant General/Military Affairs	2,558,816	68
Massachusetts	★	G	Public Safety	3,900,000	80
Michigan	★	G	State Police	4,754,400	67
Minnesota	★	PSS	Public Safety	4,674,000	66
Mississippi	★	G	Governor's Office	5,600,000	137
Missouri	★	G	Public Safety	3,000,000	70
Montana	. . .	CS	Adjutant General/Military Affairs	640,000	23
Nebraska	★	ADJ	Adjutant General/Military Affairs	1,317,129	34
Nevada	★	PSS	Public Safety	697,286	24
New Hampshire	★	G	Public Safety	4,300,000	44
New Jersey	★	G	State Police	3,400,000	300
New Mexico	★	G	Department of Homeland Security	1,540,000	47
New York	★	G	Governor's Office	5,400,000	123
North Carolina	★	G	Public Safety	9,077,073	178
North Dakota	★	ADJ	Adjutant General/Military Affairs	2,500,000	54
Ohio	★	PSS	Public Safety	5,500,000	101
Oklahoma	★	G	Governor's Office	760,000	32
Oregon	★	G	State Police	1,800,000	35
Pennsylvania	★	G	Governor's Office	8,000,000	158
Rhode Island	★	G	Adjutant General/Military Affairs	863,000	27
South Carolina	★	ADJ	Adjutant General/Military Affairs	1,870,000	63
South Dakota	★	PSS	Public Safety	584,384	16
Tennessee	★	G	Adjutant General/Military Affairs	3,500,000	107
Texas	. . .	PSS	Public Safety	1,300,000	176
Utah	★	PSS	Public Safety	797,500	65
Vermont	★	PSS	Public Safety	1,400,000	24
Virginia	★	G	Public Safety	10,150,000	113
Washington	. . .	ADJ	Adjutant General/Military Affairs	4,279,832	108
West Virginia	★	G	Public Safety	2,489,195	56
Wisconsin	★	G	Adjutant General/Military Affairs	2,996,089	49
Wyoming			.............(b).............		
American Samoa	★	G	Governor's Office	950,000	22
Dist. of Columbia	★	M	Mayor's Office	3,656,311	39
Guam	★	G	Department of Homeland Security	698,720	38
Micronesia	★	P	Territorial President's Office	270,000	12
U.S. Virgin Islands	★	G	Adjutant General/Military Affairs	569,970	17

Source: The National Emergency Management Association, November 2006.

Key:
★ — Yes
. . . — No
G — Governor
ADJ — Adjutant General
CS — Civil Service
ED — Executive Director, Dept. of Local Affairs

M — Mayor
P — Territory President
HSEMC — Homeland Security/Emergency Management Commissioner
PSS — Public Safety Secretary/Commissioner/Director
SPS — State Police Superintendent/Commissioner
(a) Homeland security and emergency management share positions.
(b) Wyoming is not a member of NEMA, and therefore is not represented in the survey data.

Funding for most of these state homeland security offices is still coming from the federal government in the form of grants. Forty-six states receive 60 percent or more of their homeland security funding from federal money. This compares to 39 states in 2005. Of these 46 states, 22 operate with 100 percent federal funding. Only three states—Georgia, New Hampshire and New Mexico—rely totally on state appropriations for their homeland security funding. This money helps support one of the most important components of homeland security—people. The number of state personnel dedicated to homeland security is now 2,399, ranging from one person in New Hampshire to more than 1,100 in New Jersey.

More Mandates, Less Money

States, as well as local emergency management, rely on federal funds to prepare for, respond to and recover from a disaster. The Emergency Management Performance Grant (EMPG) is the backbone of an all-hazards, ground-up approach to disaster preparedness, response and recovery. It is also the primary source of direct federal funding to state and local governments for building their emergency management capacity. As a pass-through program for states to distribute funds to local governments, EMPG enables local jurisdictions to develop and support their emergency management capabilities. This includes planning, training, exercises, public education and information, and many other day-to-day activities designed to prevent disaster loss. Because of its flexibility, EMPG allows states to make funding decisions based on identified needs and priorities. States are not required to pass through a set amount, but most allocate at least half of their funding to local jurisdictions.

Unfortunately, this program's shortfall is now an estimated $287 million, significantly higher than an earlier shortage of $260 million. The program did receive increases from 2002 to 2004, but this followed 10 years of flat funding. The fear is that as the gap grows, the nation's ability to respond to disasters of all types is seriously compromised.

Compounding the funding shortage is the fact that state emergency management agencies are being tasked with more homeland security responsibilities. Examples of this are three national priorities as identified by the U.S. Department of Homeland Security: the National Response Plan, the National Incident Management System (NIMS) and the National Preparedness Goal. In all three cases, these are assigned most frequently to emergency management—not the state homeland security agency—for implementation.

The National Response Plan is an all-hazards approach to domestic incident management, required by a presidential directive (HSPD-5). In 32 states, NRP implementation is handled by emergency management. The second priority, NIMS, is meant to be a consistent framework for a jurisdiction to manage any incident, regardless of the cause, size or complexity. Its implementation on the state level is similar to the NRP, with emergency management having the primary responsibility in 32 states.

The National Preparedness Goal provides priorities and targets in building, sustaining and improving this country's ability to manage any threat or hazard. Once more, this responsibility in 25 states is assigned to emergency management.

A final example of mandates without money occurred in 2006 when states were required under stringent time frames to complete comprehensive reviews of evacuation plans and other emergency plans—again with no federal support.

Other Unmet Needs

The issue of interoperability—the ability of various emergency responders to talk to each other through both voice and data systems—still has not been resolved. Over a five-year period, DHS has invested billions in grants to improve communications systems. Larger cities were able to take advantage of Urban Area Security Initiative Program (UASI) grants to enhance their systems. However, less populous states or those with smaller to mid-size communities that didn't qualify for these programs faced a distinct disadvantage.

Comprehensive interoperable communication is expensive and requires long-term financial investments. States now estimate that it will require more than $7 billion to either achieve statewide interoperability or reach levels required in each state's homeland security strategy. Of those states providing a dollar figure, this total averages in excess of $160 million per state.

In addition to interoperability, states continue to require more money to enhance state primary and alternate emergency operations centers (EOCs). During emergencies and disasters, EOCs serve as the nerve center for state and local coordination. Federal agencies also use these facilities as a central point for communication during response and recovery phases. After the 2001 terrorist attacks, Congress provided some funding to states to update their EOCs. However, it only allowed for limited planning and a needs-assessment.

It's estimated that almost $393 million would be needed to build, retrofit and upgrade the facilities.

Table B: Homeland Security Structures

State or other jurisdiction	State homeland security advisor		Homeland security organizations	
	Designated coordinator	Operates under authority of	Day-to-day operations under	Full-time employee positions
Alabama	Homeland Security Director	SS	Governor's Office	13
Alaska	Emergency Management Director	SS	Adjutant General / Military Affairs	8
Arizona	Homeland Security Director	SS	Homeland Security Department	20
Arkansas	Emergency Management Director	GA	Emergency Management	7
California	Homeland Security Director	EAO	Governor's Office	54
Colorado	Public Safety Secretary / Commissioner	EAO	Public Safety / Emergency Management	15
Connecticut	Commissioner of HS / EM	SS	Governor's Office	40
Delaware	Public Safety Secretary / Commissioner	SS	Various Agencies	50
Florida	Florida Dept. of Law Enforcement	SS	Florida Dept. of Law Enforcement	73
Georgia	Homeland Security Director	EAO	Governor's Office	5
Hawaii	Adj. General / Director of Civil Defense	GA	Department of Defense	5
Idaho	Adjutant General / HS Director	SS	Emergency Management / Homeland Security / Military Affairs	42 (d)
Illinois	Deputy Chief of Staff for Public Safety	GA	Emergency Management	8
Indiana	Homeland Security Director	SS	Homeland Security Department	270 (d)
Iowa	Administrator, HS & EM	GA	Department of Public Defense	71 (d)
Kansas	Adjutant General	SS	Adjutant General / Military Affairs	13
Kentucky	Homeland Security Director	SS	Governor's Office	20
Louisiana	Emergency Management Director	SS	Emergency Management	8
Maine	Emergency Management Director	SS	Emergency Management	2
Maryland	Homeland Security Director	EAO	Governor's Office	2
Massachusetts	Public Safety Secretary / Commissioner	EAO	Public Safety	9
Michigan	Commander, EM & HS Division	EAO	State Police	9
Minnesota	Director, Division of HS & EM	EAO	Emergency Management / Homeland Security	65.5
Mississippi	Homeland Security Director	EAO	Public Safety	15
Missouri	Public Safety Secretary / Commissioner	EAO	Public Safety	15
Montana	Emergency Management Director	EAO	Adjutant General / Military Affairs	3
Nebraska	Lieutenant Governor	SS	Emergency Management	9
Nevada	Homeland Security Director	GA	Public Safety	5
New Hampshire	Director of HS & EM	SS	Public Safety	1
New Jersey	Office of HS and Preparedness	EAO	Homeland Security Department	1,160
New Mexico	Homeland Security Director	EAO	Governor's Office	3
New York	Homeland Security Director	SS	Homeland Security Department	147
North Carolina	Public Safety Secretary / Commissioner	SS	Emergency Management	16
North Dakota	Homeland Security Director	EAO	Adjutant General / Military Affairs	5
Ohio	Public Safety Secretary / Commissioner	SS	Public Safety	20
Oklahoma	Homeland Security Director	SS	Governor's Office	18
Oregon	Emergency Management Director	GA	Emergency Management	0
Pennsylvania	Homeland Security Director	GA	Governor's Office	5
Rhode Island	Adjutant General	GA	Emergency Management	5
South Carolina	State Police Super / Commissioner	SS	State Police	10
South Dakota	Homeland Security Director	GA	Public Safety	3
Tennessee	Homeland Security Director	EAO	Homeland Security Department	29
Texas	Homeland Security Director	EAO	Governor's Office	3
Utah	Homeland Security Director	GA	Homeland Security Department	6
Vermont	Homeland Security Director	EAO	Public Safety	10
Virginia	Special Assistant to Governor	SS	Governor's Office	6
Washington	Adjutant General	EAO	Emergency Management	30
West Virginia	Public Safety Secretary / Commissioner	EAO	Public Safety	6
Wisconsin	Adjutant General	EAO	Adjutant General / Military Affairs	0
Wyoming	.... (a)			
American Samoa	Homeland Security Director	EAO	Governor's Office	0
Dist. of Columbia	Homeland Security Director	(b)	Mayor's Office	11
Guam	Homeland Security Director	EAO	Governor's Office	30
Micronesia	EM Director / Chief, National Police	(c)	President's Office	8
U.S. Virgin Islands	Adjutant General	EAO	Adjutant General / Military Affairs	2,118.5

Source: The National Emergency Management Association, November 2006.

Key:
GA — Governor's Verbal Authority
EAO — Executive/Administrative Order
SS — State Statute

(a) Wyoming is not a member of NEMA, and therefore is not represented in the survey data.
(b) Mayor's verbal authority.
(c) Other.
(d) Homeland security and emergency management share positions.

For local EOCs, that number increases to $1.1 billion, for a total of almost $1.5 billion. This includes the costs to upgrade equipment and software, train personnel, and conduct operations during emergency and non-emergency situations.

Components of Effective Emergency Management

Successful emergency management at the state level depends on many things: adequate funding, an all-hazards approach and competent professionals. It's also essential that other state and federal partners have strong systems in place so when an event is too large for one state to handle, the mechanisms exist for a sufficient response and recovery.

Mutual Aid Key in Disaster Response/Recovery

As demonstrated in the 2005 hurricane season, the mutual aid system in the U.S. continues to strengthen. The Emergency Management Assistance Compact (EMAC), a national mutual aid agreement that allows support across state lines when a disaster occurs, played a key role in the response to hurricanes Katrina and Rita. By spring 2006, the compact had deployed nearly 66,000 people from 48 states, at a cost of more than $830 million.

Thirty-five states now have established similar structures within their own borders. These intrastate agreements allow jurisdictions to help one another while having provisions in place to address reimbursement, liability and workers compensation issues. Thirty-six states have also created regional mutual aid mechanisms. This bodes well for faster, stronger and more efficient disaster response and recovery.

EMAC was formed in 1992 after the devastation of Hurricane Andrew. When it was signed into law (Public Law 104-321) in 1996, EMAC became the first national disaster-relief agreement ratified by Congress since the Civil Defense Compact of 1950. Fifty states, the District of Columbia, Puerto Rico and the U.S. Virgin Islands are members. Each member state is required to secure state legislative approval to become part of EMAC. Administered by the National Emergency Management Association, the compact includes key provisions on reimbursement, liability and workers' compensation

FEMA's Crucial Role

Mandated by law under the Robert T. Stafford Disaster Relief and Emergency Relief Act (42 U.S.C. 5121 et seq.), the Federal Emergency Management Agency (FEMA) is the only federal agency authorized to carry out disaster-relief duties on behalf of the president.

After Hurricane Katrina, FEMA was severely criticized and there were several Congressional proposals to either revamp or replace the agency with another structure. A compromise was reached and in October 2006, President Bush signed an appropriations bill, which included the Post-Katrina Emergency Management Reform Act of 2006, otherwise known as the FEMA Reform Act. While the agency remains within the U.S. Department of Homeland Security, its administrator will now serve as the principal adviser to the president in the event of a natural disaster, terrorist act or some other man-made incident. The link between emergency preparedness and response was also restored. All grants, programs and personnel in the DHS Directorate of Preparedness were transferred back to FEMA. The only exceptions were the Office of Infrastructure Protection, the National Communications System, the National Cybersecurity Division and the Office of the Chief Medical Officer. This re-linkage between funding and programs should help achieve what emergency management has been working toward—an effective and cost-efficient all-hazards approach.

In addition, the agency is attempting to address its staffing issues. A mandatory hiring freeze at the regional and federal levels in 2005 left FEMA understaffed. There is now a concerted effort to fully staff the regional offices, which serve as the direct line of communication for state and local governments to tap into federal resources when a disaster occurs. FEMA has also indicated that it will continue to beef up the federal offices with more personnel.

Change Is the One Constant

The various Hurricane Katrina reports as well as the implementation of the FEMA Reform Act are still having a ripple effect in disaster preparedness, response and recovery. For example, federal assistance programs for both individuals and public entities are being scrutinized, reviewed and, in some cases, revamped. There is a greater focus on reducing and eliminating fraudulent claims in these programs. Other areas, such as the unique requirements of special needs populations during a disaster and pet evacuations, are being evaluated.

In addition, the Democrats assumed control of both houses of Congress after the 2006 mid-term elections. They have indicated that implementing many of the 9/11 Commission Report recommendations is a priority. This will include streamlining emergency management and homeland security funding. There is a recurring discussion about revising the funding allocation formula for states to receive federal homeland security grants. This would be accomplished by placing greater emphasis on risk and critical infrastructure vulnerability as opposed to the current approach of allocating dollars on a percentage plus population basis. Other considerations, such as population density and the priority of international-border states versus coastal states, will also be taken into account.

If these funding changes take place, they will have a major impact on smaller rural states that cannot take the necessary terrorism-preparedness steps without federal support. The terrorism response equipment purchased by states and localities, along with the planning efforts and training conducted for thousands of state and local emergency response personnel, are characterized as a national security effort. These require long-term support from the federal government. Among states and emergency response disciplines, there is a common concern regarding long-term sustainable federal funding for homeland security.

Notes

[1] This data is based on an annual NEMA survey of state emergency management directors. There were at total of 54 responses which included 49 states, four territories and the District of Columbia.

About the Author

Beverly Bell is the policy analyst for the National Emergency Management Association, an affiliate of The Council of State Governments. In her position, she coordinates and conducts research, interacts with the states on changing federal policy and acts as an information clearinghouse for emergency management and homeland security issues.

No Child Left Behind: Trends and Issues
By Frederick M. Hess

The No Child Left Behind Act is the most ambitious piece of education legislation ever enacted by Congress. Designed to promote accountability and prod states to address educational inequities, NCLB includes significant provisions regarding assessment, sanctions for low-performing schools and districts, teacher quality and standards for educational research.

On Jan. 8, 2002, surrounded by members of both the Democratic and Republican congressional leadership, President George W. Bush signed No Child Left Behind (NCLB) into law. NCLB is the nation's most significant federal legislation on K–12 schooling since the Elementary and Secondary Education Act (ESEA) of 1965, and the most ambitious federal intervention in a domain long regarded as the preserve of state and local government.[1]

Enacted just months after the Sept. 11, 2001, terrorist attacks, Congress approved NCLB by large, bipartisan majorities. The U.S. Senate supported the new law 87-10, and the House of Representatives endorsed it 381-41.[2] Emerging from an exhaustive year of negotiations, NCLB refashioned federal education policy in the areas of testing, accountability and teacher quality. More than anything else, NCLB was a demand by Washington, D.C., policymakers that state and local officials do something about low-performing schools.

From ESEA to NCLB

Proposed in 1965 as a pillar of President Lyndon Johnson's "Great Society," the original ESEA included five titles. The heart of the law was a program of aid for the education of disadvantaged children. This provision, Title I, claimed the lion's share of ESEA funding. Over time, critics both left and right expressed concerns about the failure of Title I to improve achievement visibly among low-income students.[3]

By the early 1990s, Republican and Democratic leaders largely agreed that school improvement required more than targeted assistance, new texts and better curricula. The remedies urged by Presidents George H.W. Bush and Bill Clinton shared a commitment to higher standards, accountability, measured student achievement and increased school choice. The Clinton administration sought to use the 1994 ESEA reauthorization and the companion "Goals 2000" legislation to require every state to establish academic standards and assess whether students had met them.[4]

Sympathetic observers regarded the 1994 ESEA's call for all states to create performance-based accountability systems by 2000 as a radical advance. However, given the law's voluntary cast and the federal government's lack of enforcement authority, most states failed to comply.[5] That experience would color the 2001 deliberations over NCLB (which, technically, was the much-delayed reauthorization of the 1994 ESEA).

NCLB Standards and Assessment

The heart of NCLB is its language on standards and assessment, which aggressively supersized the tentative requirements of the 1994 ESEA. Eager to support a Republican president after two terms under a Democratic White House, conservatives on Capitol Hill accepted requirements regarding standards, testing and accountability that they had resisted as federal overreaching in 1994 and 1999.

The NCLB accountability system requires states to develop content standards for what students should know and be able to do, as well as complementary state assessments. It then requires states to annually test students to measure competency in the "core subjects" of reading and math. By 2013–14, all states are to ensure that 100 percent of students are "proficient" on state reading and math standards. The law leaves it to the states to determine the content and rigor of these standards and tests.[6]

NCLB requires states to set academic standards that define three levels of achievement: basic, proficient and advanced. For each assessment, each state must then develop corresponding tests in reading, math and eventually science. These assessments are to be administered every year in grades three through eight and at least once in high school. States also are required to design and administer a science assessment by 2007–08 and to test students at least once in elementary, middle and high school.

Adequate yearly progress (AYP) is the metric used to evaluate school and district performance under NCLB. The expectation is that all schools and districts will "make AYP." The concept of "making AYP" can be compared to schools and districts jumping over a bar. The bar is the percentage of children that must score "proficient" on the math and reading assessments. Over time, states must raise the bar so that, by 2013–14, it is set at 100 percent. For instance, a state could deem a school to be making AYP if 50 percent of its students were "proficient" in reading in 2007, so long as expectations were stepped up to 100 percent by 2013–14.

Calculating AYP is not as simple as measuring the percentage of students that meet the proficiency standard. Instead, NCLB requires that states hold schools accountable for various subpopulations by calculating AYP for each of a variety of subgroups. Each state is required to analyze the achievement of the following subgroups within each school: major racial/ethnic groups (white, African-American, Latino, Native American and so on); low-income students; students with disabilities; and students with limited English proficiency. In order for schools or districts to make AYP, each subgroup must clear the AYP bar in reading and in math. Obviously, some subgroups will be quite small. To protect student confidentiality and heighten statistical reliability, states are allowed to establish a minimum size for subgroups to be counted.

NCLB's testing requirements pose a number of challenges, and the legislation and subsequent guidance from the U.S. Department of Education have tried, with mixed success, to address these. The law stipulates schools must test 95 percent of their enrolled students in order to make AYP. It also includes a "safe harbor" provision that allows schools that miss the AYP bar to still make AYP if they increase the percentage of students who are proficient at a rapid enough rate and permits schools and districts to exclude from AYP calculations a small portion of special needs students.

NCLB Sanctions

The standards and testing provisions themselves constitute only the first two-thirds of the NCLB accountability system. NCLB links test results to consequences for schools and school districts. Under NCLB, schools that fail to make AYP are subject to a series of cascading remedies, sanctions and interventions that are designed to compel the schools to improve and to grant additional options to children in those schools. These interventions become increasingly intense if the school or district continues to fail for consecutive years, eventually resulting in major changes in school status, governance, staffing or all of the above.

If a school fails to make AYP two years in a row, it enters "in need of improvement" status. Once in improvement status, district and school officials must develop a school improvement plan, as well as explain to parents what the label signifies and what the school is doing to improve its rating. In addition to these school improvement activities, schools that fail to make AYP for two consecutive years must offer students the option of transferring to a district school that is making AYP. Schools that fail to improve for a third straight year must provide supplemental educational services, or free tutoring, to needy students. A fourth year of failure prompts what the law terms "corrective action," which could entail staffing changes, curriculum reform or the extension of the school day and year. Finally, if a school fails to make AYP for a fifth year, the district must restructure that school, either by converting it to a charter school, replacing the majority of the staff, hiring an educational management company, turning it over to the state, or through imposing another remedy of the state's choosing. The sanctions for districts are similar in intent to those for schools but different in the particulars. Districts that fail to make AYP for multiple years are eventually subject to restructuring, including the possibility of state takeover.[7]

Highly Qualified Teachers

Beyond its accountability and choice provisions, the other radical development adopted by NCLB was the federal mandate that all children be taught by a "highly qualified teacher" by the end of the 2005–06 school year (during 2005, the Department of Education pushed back the effective date to 2006–07). The rule applied to "core" academic subjects like mathematics, science and history. Unlike the testing and accountability provisions, the highly qualified teacher (HQT) language focuses less on outcomes than on "inputs"—it seeks to ensure that all schools have quality teachers who are knowledgeable about the content they teach.

To be deemed "highly qualified," a teacher must have attained a bachelor's degree, have passed the state teacher licensing examination or obtained a state teaching certification, and have demonstrated subject knowledge. Again, as with state standards and assessments, the law allows states to determine what all this means in practice.[8] That flexibility has yielded much concern that states have exploited loopholes to appease current teachers, improve apparent results, and reduce implementation headaches. Table A depicts the many ways in which some states allow teachers to obtain highly qualified status. In

Table A
OPTIONS PROVIDED BY STATES FOR ACHIEVING HIGHLY QUALIFIED STATUS

State	Student achievement	Course work in subject	In-service in subject	Portfolios	Professional service	Awards publications	Experience	Observation by administration	Mentoring	In-service not in subject	Course work not in subject	Option unique to state	Total number of options
Alabama	...	★	★	...	★	★	★	...	★	★	★	...	8
Alaska	...	★	★	...	★	★	★	...	★	...	...	1	7
Arizona	...	★	★	...	★	★	★	...	★	...	...	...	6
Arkansas	...	★	★	...	★	★	★	...	★	...	...	...	6
California	...	★	★	★	★	★	★	★	★	...	...	...	8
Colorado	★	★	★	...	...	...	...	...	...	...	...	1	4
Connecticut	...	★	...	...	...	...	...	★	...	...	...	...	2
Delaware	...	★	★	...	★	★	★	...	...	...	★	1	7
Florida	★	...	...	...	...	...	...	★	...	...	...	...	2
Georgia	...	★	★	...	★	★	★	...	★	...	...	...	6
Hawaii	...	★	★	...	★	★	★	...	★	...	...	...	6
Idaho	...	★	★	...	...	...	...	...	...	★	★	...	4
Illinois	...	★	★	...	...	...	★	...	★	...	...	2	5
Indiana	...	★	★	...	★	★	★	...	★	...	...	...	6
Iowa	...	★	★	...	...	...	...	★	...	★	★	1	6
Kansas	...	★	★	...	★	★	★	...	★	...	...	...	6
Kentucky	★	★	★	...	★	★	★	...	...	...	...	...	6
Louisiana	...	★	★	...	...	...	...	...	...	...	...	...	2
Maine	...	★	★	...	★	★	★	...	★	...	...	1	7
Maryland	...	★	★	...	★	★	★	...	★	★	★	...	8
Massachusetts	...	★	★	...	★	★	...	...	★	★	★	...	7
Michigan	...	★	★	★	★	...	★	★	★	...	...	...	7
Minnesota	★	★	★	...	★	★	★	...	...	...	...	...	6
Mississippi	...	★	★	...	...	...	...	...	...	...	...	1	3
Missouri	...	★	...	...	...	...	...	★	...	...	...	1	2
Montana	...	★	★	...	...	...	...	...	...	★	★	...	4
Nebraska	...	★	★	...	...	...	...	...	...	...	...	1	3
Nevada	...	★	★	...	...	...	★	...	...	★	★	...	5
New Hampshire	★	★	★	★	...	...	...	...	...	...	...	...	4
New Jersey	...	★	★	...	★	★	★	...	...	...	...	1	6
New Mexico	★	★	★	★	...	...	★	★	...	...	...	1	7
New York	...	★	★	...	★	...	★	...	★	...	...	5	10
North Carolina	★	★	★	...	★	★	★	★	★	...	...	...	8
North Dakota	...	★	★	...	★	★	★	...	★	...	★	...	7
Ohio	...	★	★	...	★	★	★	...	★	★	★	...	8
Oklahoma	★	★	★	...	★	★	★	...	★	...	...	...	7
Oregon	...	★	...	...	...	...	...	...	...	...	...	...	1
Pennsylvania	...	★	★	...	...	...	★	...	...	...	...	1	5
Rhode Island	...	★	★	...	★	★	★	...	★	...	...	...	6
South Carolina	...	...	...	...	...	...	...	★	...	...	...	...	1
South Dakota	...	★	...	...	...	...	...	...	...	...	★	1	3
Tennessee	★	★	★	...	★	★	★	★	★	...	★	...	9
Texas	...	★	★	...	...	...	★	...	...	...	...	...	3
Utah	...	★	★	...	...	...	★	...	...	...	...	...	3
Vermont	...	★	★	...	★	...	★	...	★	...	...	1	6
Virginia	...	...	...	...	...	...	...	...	...	...	...	...	
Washington	...	★	...	...	...	...	...	★	...	...	...	...	2
West Virginia	...	★	★	...	★	★	★	...	★	...	...	...	6
Wisconsin	...	★	★	★	...	...	...	★	...	...	★	...	4
Wyoming	...	★	★	...	★	★	★	...	★	...	...	...	6

Source: Kate Walsh and Emma Snyder, "How States are Responding to the Nation's Goal of Placing a Highly Qualified Teacher in Every Classroom," (National Council on Teacher Quality, December 2004), 33.

Key:
★ — Yes
. . . — No or not applicable

the 2004–05 school year, the most recent for which data are available, 47 states reported that at least 70 percent of their core academic classes were taught by highly qualified teachers and 33 states reported that the percentage of classrooms with highly qualified teachers was above 90 percent.[9]

Research and Reading First

Despite their import, NCLB's accountability and teacher quality provisions comprise only a small portion of the sprawling legislation. The law encompasses 10 separate titles authorizing more than 50 federal education programs. Noteworthy in NCLB is the emphasis on "scientifically based research" (SBR), a phrase that appears in reference to everything from reading programs, to teacher training, to school safety. SBR is defined as "the application of rigorous, systematic and objective procedures to obtain reliable and valid knowledge relevant to education activities and programs." The focus on scientifically based research has potentially far-reaching consequences for classrooms, policy and research.[10]

For good and ill, the import of SBR is illustrated by the law's Reading First program. Based on the conclusions of the National Reading Panel, convened in 1997 at Congress's request, Reading First requires schools seeking federal funds to implement a classroom-based reading program that includes the elements of "scientifically based" instruction. In 2006, the Reading First program was a source of controversy after the United States Department of Education Office of Inspector General report raised concerns about politicized implementation and potentially arbitrary use of scientific standards.[11]

Debating NCLB

NCLB has been a subject of fierce debate. Critics have attacked the system for encouraging states to engage in gamesmanship, promoting a fixation on testing, failing to acknowledge the different burdens borne by different schools, and setting unrealistic goals.[12] Meanwhile, supporters have applauded the focus on results and the attention AYP has brought to race- and class-based disparities in achievement.

This mixed assessment is reflected in public opinion. Like most pieces of sweeping and compromise-filled legislation, NCLB elicits mixed reactions. Parents and voters tend to endorse its goals while expressing concerns about its means. In fall 2006, the 38th Annual Phi Delta Kappa/Gallup Poll of the Public's Attitudes Toward the Public Schools reported that 45 percent of adults knew "a great deal" or "a fair amount" about NCLB, while 55 percent

knew "very little" or "nothing at all." When asked to rate the overall impact of NCLB on "the public schools in your community," 26 percent of respondents thought the effect was positive, and 21 percent thought it was negative.[13]

Emerging Trends

Perhaps the fiercest dispute over NCLB implementation has revolved around funding. Funding for the education programs in NCLB increased after the law's passage, with Title I funding rising 45 percent between 2001 and 2006.[14] The General Accounting Office ruled in 2004 that the federal aid fully covered the mandated expenses.[15] Meanwhile, critics like National Education Association President Reg Weaver have responded that, through 2006, the federal funds fell roughly $40 billion short of the amount promised by the law's authorization.[16] Many states have argued that the actions necessitated by NCLB cost billions more than the law provides.[17] What effect such pleas will have in a tight fiscal environment remains to be seen.

While the funding question may have yielded the fiercest rhetoric, the most substantive concern has been the degree to which NCLB gives states an incentive to "game" the NCLB accountability system by setting lax standards. Table B shows that states like Oklahoma, Rhode Island and Iowa claim that more than 90 percent of their schools are making adequate yearly progress, even though federal National Assessment of Educational Progress data report that no more than 33 percent of the fourth-graders in any of those states are "proficient" in reading. This phenomenon is a result of the latitude that NCLB gives states to select tests, set standards and determine passing rates, and has fueled interest in national standards or in replacing the 50 different states assessments with a national test. As two former U.S. secretaries of education, both Republicans, argued in September 2006, "We can now see that [NCLB] gives states entirely too much discretion over standards and tests while giving federal bureaucrats too much control over how schools operate. The remedy? … Washington should set sound national academic standards and administer a high-quality national test."[18]

State reaction to the law has been mixed, with press coverage highlighting vocal resistance to the law in states like Connecticut and Utah. This resistance has been newsworthy because states have the right to opt out of the law by forfeiting their federal NCLB funding.

Responding to state resistance, U.S. Department of Education officials have reaffirmed their commit-

Table B
INCONSISTENCY IN STATE STANDARDS

State or other jurisdiction	Percent of public school districts that made adequate yearly progress (AYP) 2004–2005	State or other jurisdiction	Percent of public schools that made adequate yearly progress (AYP) 2004–2005	State or other jurisdiction	Percent of students proficient or advanced in fourth grade reading 2004–2005	Percent of students proficient or advanced in fourth grade reading (NAEP)
Delaware	100%	Oklahoma	97%	Mississippi	89%	18%
Wisconsin	99.8	Rhode Island	95	Nebraska	88.5	33
Arkansas	98	Iowa	93.9	South Dakota	87.9	33
Maine	98	Montana	93.3	Tennessee	87.1	27
South Dakota	98	New Hampshire	92	Idaho	86.9	33
Michigan	96.3	Tennessee	91.9	Colorado	86.6	36
Iowa	94.2	Wisconsin	91.7	Georgia	85.4	26
Tennessee	94.1	Kansas	91.4	Alabama	83.2	22
Vermont	94.1	North Dakota	91.4	Oklahoma	83	26
Kansas	93.3	Vermont	90.8	North Carolina	82.4	30
Montana	92.9	Nebraska	89.7	New Jersey	81.6	38
Wyoming	91.7	Mississippi	89	West Virginia	81.2	26
Oklahoma	91	Michigan	88.5	Wisconsin	81	33
North Dakota	89.6	Utah	87.4	Maryland	80.9	32
Pennsylvania	89.6	Arizona	87	Washington	79.5	35
New York	88.4	Louisiana	83.8	Iowa	79.4	33
Texas	88.4	West Virginia	83.2	Texas	79	29
Indiana	87.7	Virginia	82.7	Utah	78	35
Connecticut	82	Washington	82.7	Alaska	76.9	26
Nevada	82	Minnesota	82	North Dakota	75.5	35
Minnesota	80.7	South Dakota	82	Montana	74.8	36
Nebraska	80.7	Georgia	81.8	Indiana	73	30
Mississippi	77	Pennsylvania	80.6	Florida	72	30
Arizona	76	New York	80.2	Michigan	69.4	31
Illinois	73	Connecticut	80	Kentucky	68	30
Washington	70.9	Wyoming	79.6	Louisiana	67.4	20
Alabama	67.9	Texas	78.5	Connecticut	67	39
Missouri	60.6	Maine	77	Arizona	62.6	24
California	60.2	Ohio	75.7	Hawaii	55.2	23
Colorado	59.3	Colorado	75.3	Maine	53	36
Utah	59.3	Delaware	74.3	New Mexico	51.8	21
Louisiana	58.8	Maryland	73.2	Arkansas	51	29
Ohio	55.8	Arkansas	73	Massachusetts	50	44
Virginia	50.7	Illinois	71	California	47.9	22
Georgia	45.3	Kentucky	70	Wyoming	47	34
Kentucky	44	Oregon	67.5	Nevada	41.5	21
Alaska	40.7	Missouri	65.2	South Carolina	35.3	26
Massachusetts	39.3	California	61.6	Virginia	N.A.	37
Idaho	38	Indiana	59.7	Delaware	N.A.	35
New Mexico	33.7	Alaska	59	District of Columbia	N.A.	11
Oregon	33.7	Massachusetts	56.9	Illinois	N.A.	30
District of Columbia	28	North Carolina	56.8	Kansas	N.A.	33
South Carolina	21.2	Alabama	53.3	Minnesota	N.A.	38
Maryland	16.6	Idaho	51	Missouri	N.A.	32
West Virginia	9.1	South Carolina	49.9	New Hampshire	N.A.	39
North Carolina	7	New Mexico	47.3	New York	N.A.	34
Florida	6.6	Nevada	44.4	Ohio	N.A.	35
Hawaii	N.A.	District of Columbia	40	Oregon	N.A.	30
New Hampshire	N.A.	Hawaii	34	Pennsylvania	N.A.	36
New Jersey	N.A.	Florida	28.2	Rhode Island	N.A.	30
Rhode Island	N.A.	New Jersey	N.A.	Vermont	N.A.	38

Sources: This table, with the exception of the rightmost column, was originally printed in Kevin Carey, "Hot Air: How States Inflate Their Educational Progress Under NCLB" (Education Sector, May 2006), 15. The rightmost column was added to show the official National Assessment of Education Progress (NAEP) scores as reported by the National Center for Education Statistics, *http://nces.ed.gov/nationsreportcard/nrc/reading_math_2005/s0006.asp?printver.*

ment to NCLB's accountability goals while accepting modifications regarding the testing, sanctions and teacher quality provisions. Department of Education officials and prominent Democratic leaders grade the new law differently; as Secretary Margaret Spellings has explained, "I like to talk about No Child Left Behind as Ivory soap. It's 99.9 percent pure. There's not much needed in the way of changes."[19] Rep. George Miller, perhaps the leading Democratic voice on education, has said, "I would give [NCLB] an A in terms of the goals that it has set ... in trying to develop a system to make sure that each and every child is proficient. I would give it an F for funding. ... And on implementation, I would give it a C."[20]

One widely discussed modification to NCLB accountability is the effort to focus it less on the level at which a school's students are performing and more on their rate of improvement.[21] State interest in such "value-added" accountability is motivated by the concern that many schools serving disadvantaged populations will otherwise be deemed "in need of improvement," even though students are making respectable achievement gains. In November 2005, Spellings allowed a handful of states to experiment with "value-added" approaches; in 2006–2007, two states began using value-added systems.[22]

NCLB has altered the American education landscape. It has focused attention on achievement and on racial and economic "achievement gaps" while nationalizing the education debate to an unprecedented degree. In the process, it has upended traditional education politics and created new federal-state tensions. With public opinion mixed, the law scheduled for reauthorization in 2007, and its most ambitious demands still ahead, the long-term impact of NCLB is still very much up in the air.

Notes

[1] Frederick M. Hess and Michael J. Petrilli, *No Child Left Behind Primer* (New York: Peter Lang, 2006), 3–26.

[2] Andrew Rudalevige, "No Child Left Behind: Forging a Congressional Compromise," in Paul E. Peterson and Martin R. West, eds., *No Child Left Behind? The Politics and Practice of School Accountability* (Washington, D.C.: Brookings Institution Press, 2003), 23–54.

[3] Diane Ravitch, "A Historical Perspective on a Historic Piece of Legislation," in John Chubb, ed., *Within Our Reach: How America Can Educate Every Child* (New York: Rowman & Littlefield, 2005), 35–51.

[4] Frederick M. Hess and Michael J. Petrilli, *No Child Left Behind Primer* (New York: Peter Lang, 2006), 3–26.

[5] See former United States Secretary of Education Richard W. Riley's statement before the United States House of Representatives Committee on Education and the Workforce on the Reauthorization of the Elementary and Secondary Education Act of 1965, 11 February 1999.

[6] Detailed information on the mechanics of No Child Left Behind is available at the United States Department of Education Web site, *http://www.ed.gov/nclb* (25 April 2007).

[7] See Education Commission of the States, "No Child Left Behind: State Requirements Under NCLB," June 2005, *http://www.ecs.org/clearinghouse/44/27/4427.pdf* (25 April 2007).

[8] Terry M. Moe, "A Highly Qualified Teacher in Every Classroom," in John E. Chubb, ed., *Within Our Reach: How America Can Educate Every Child* (Lanham, Md.: Rowman & Littlefield, 2005), 173–99.

[9] Kevin Carey, "Hot Air: How States Inflate Their Educational Progress Under NCLB" (Education Sector, May 2006), 18.

[10] Detailed information on what the scientifically based research language entails is available at the United States Department of Education Web site, *http://www.ed.gov/nclb* (25 April 2007).

[11] United States Department of Education Office of Inspector General, "The Reading First Program's Grant Application Process: Final Inspection Report," September 2006, ED-OIG/I13-F0017.

[12] Linda Darling-Hammond, "From 'Separate but Equal' to 'No Child Left Behind': The Collision of New Standards and Old Inequalities," in Deborah Meier and George Wood, eds., *Many Children Left Behind: How the No Child Left Behind Act Is Damaging Our Children and Our Schools* (Boston: Beacon Press, 2004), 3–32.

[13] Lowell C. Rose and Alec M. Gallup, "The 38th Annual Phi Delta Kappa/Gallup Poll Of the Public's Attitudes Toward the Public Schools" (Phi Delta Kappa/Gallup, September 2006), 50.

[14] House Committee on Education and the Workforce Issue Brief, "Education Funding: Setting the Record Straight on Education Spending Myths," June 2006, *http://www.house.gov/ed_workforce/issues/109th/education/funding/funding myths.htm* (25 April 2007).

[15] United States General Accounting Office, "Unfunded Mandates: Analysis of Reform Act Coverage," May 2004, *http://republicans.edlabor.house.gov/archive/issues/109th/education/funding/fundingmyths.htm* (25 April 2007).

[16] National Education Association News Release, "Schools Lack Funding to Comply with No Child Left Behind, According to New Report from Center on Education Policy," 29 March 2006, *http://www.nea.org/newsreleases/2006/nr060329.html* (25 April 2007).

[17] William J. Mathis, "The Cost of Implementing the Federal No Child Left Behind Act: Different Assumptions, Different Answers," *Peabody Journal of Education* 80, no. 2 (2005): 90–119.

[18] William J. Bennett and Rod Paige, "Why We Need a National School Test," *The Washington Post*, 21 September 2006, sec. A, p. 25.

[19] Lois Romano, "Tweaking of 'No Child' Seen," *The Washington Post*, 31 August 2006, sec. A, p. 4.

[20] Business Roundtable Speech Transcript, "The Fourth Annual No Child Left Behind Forum: Assessing Progress, Addressing Problems, Advancing Performance," 20 September 2006, *http://www.businessroundtable.org/newsroom/*

document.aspx?qs=5976BF807822B0F1ADD408422FB51 711FCF53CE (25 April 2007).

[21] John Chubb et al., "Do We Need to Repair the Monument? Debating the Future of No Child Left Behind," *Education Next* 5, no. 2 (Spring 2005): 8–19.

[22] United States Department of Education Press Release, "Secretary Spellings Announces Growth Model Pilot, Addresses Chief State School Officers' Annual Policy Forum in Richmond," 18 November 2005, *http://www.ed.gov/news/ pressreleases/2005/11/11182005.html* (25 April 2007).

About the Author

Frederick M. Hess is director of education policy studies at the American Enterprise Institute and executive editor of *Education Next*. His many books include *Common Sense School Reform, No Child Left Behind:A Primer* and *Spinning Wheels: The Politics of Urban School Reform*. A former high school teacher, he holds a Ph.D. in government from Harvard University.

Table 9.1
NUMBER OF PUBLIC ELEMENTARY AND SECONDARY SCHOOLS, BY TYPE OF SCHOOL AND STATE OR JURISDICTION: SCHOOL YEAR 2004–05

State or other jurisdiction	Total number of schools having membership (b)	Type of school				Charter schools		Magnet schools		Title I eligible schools		Title I schoolwide schools	
		Regular	Special education	Vocational education	Alternative education	Number of	Percent of all students in these schools	Number of	Percent of all students in these schools	Number of	Percent of all students in these schools	Number of	Percent of all students in these schools
Alabama	1,386	1,337	21	1	27	n/a	n/a	37	2.7	695	43.4	567	34.6
Alaska	497	471	4	1	21	21	3.1	16	3.1	298	36.0	116	17.6
Arizona	1,976	1,823	11	84	58	492	8.4	20	1.5	1,140	55.5	626	35.4
Arkansas	1,130	1,121	4	0	5	17	0.7	10	1.4	825	67.4	532	40.4
California	9,373	8,046	129	0	1,198	494	2.8	465	9.4	5,287	57.0	3,071	35.1
Colorado	1,679	1,598	8	4	69	110	4.8	5	0.2	873	43.3	348	17.3
Connecticut	1,095	1,011	31	17	36	14	0.5	34	2.3	497	40.8	140	11.9
Delaware	198	173	13	5	7	13	5.5	2	1.0	97	43.4	60	26.8
Florida	3,498	3,200	111	19	168	299	3.1	N.A.	N.A.	1,384	35.9	1,347	34.9
Georgia	2,069	2,037	8	0	24	49	1.7	59	3.6	1,150	45.9	954	37.6
Hawaii	285	281	3	0	1	27	2.8	n/a	n/a	196	63.9	176	59.4
Idaho	662	593	5	0	64	19	2.3	n/a	n/a	495	67.3	95	12.5
Illinois	4,245	3,888	229	0	128	26	0.7	356	12.1	2,392	57.4	1,015	25.9
Indiana	1,913	1,855	26	0	32	22	0.4	26	1.3	1,058	48.0	188	7.8
Iowa	1,524	1,440	10	0	74	2	…	n/a	n/a	684	37.3	129	8.0
Kansas	1,400	1,400	0	0	0	20	0.3	31	2.6	641	36.8	252	18.1
Kentucky	1,368	1,224	8	0	136	n/a	n/a	39	4.6	893	60.2	779	50.9
Louisiana	1,510	1,362	36	0	112	17	0.7	68	5.8	934	56.1	782	46.6
Maine	655	652	3	0	0	n/a	…	1	…	505	64.1	48	4.4
Maryland	1,372	1,267	44	10	51	1	…	N.A.	N.A.	384	20.4	313	16.3
Massachusetts	1,872	1,806	1	39	26	57	2.1	5	0.3	1,089	53.5	476	22.2
Michigan	3,901	3,495	168	13	225	239	4.7	(a)	(a)	1,141	27.3	1,141	27.3
Minnesota	2,214	1,623	246	1	344	123	2.1	66	3.4	953	39.9	241	8.4
Mississippi	896	896	0	0	0	1	0.1	6	0.5	687	70.2	639	65.1
Missouri	2,257	2,183	13	0	61	N.A.	N.A.	44	2.1	1,191	44.3	418	15.6
Montana	852	847	2	0	3	n/a	n/a	n/a	n/a	691	79.5	156	17.8
Nebraska	1,203	1,163	40	0	0	19	n/a	N.A.	N.A.	485	35.2	186	15.9
Nevada	556	516	5	1	34	3	1.0	1	…	124	18.7	123	18.6
New Hampshire	477	477	0	0	0	49	n/a	n/a	n/a	248	42.9	30	4.3
New Jersey	2,440	2,311	75	54	0	44	1.0	N.A.	N.A.	N.A.	N.A.	N.A.	N.A.
New Mexico	834	757	16	2	59	58	1.0	1	…	501	51.3	363	38.0
New York	4,470	4,290	65	25	90	97	0.6	33	0.7	3,186	65.2	1,241	29.4
North Carolina	2,283	2,190	21	1	71	n/a	1.8	139	7.3	1,144	38.2	902	29.5
North Dakota	511	511	0	0	0	n/a	n/a	n/a	n/a	351	54.3	63	10.3
Ohio	3,862	3,838	13	8	3	245	3.2	N.A.	N.A.	2,681	62.3	999	21.4
Oklahoma	1,787	1,787	0	0	0	12	0.6	n/a	n/a	1,289	64.3	960	44.4
Oregon	1,208	1,173	2	0	33	39	0.8	N.A.	N.A.	1,207	99.9	327	21.6
Pennsylvania	3,189	3,149	12	16	12	109	2.6	34	1.2	2,110	60.7	572	17.5
Rhode Island	334	320	4	3	7	11	1.4	N.A.	N.A.	147	38.8	62	18.4
South Carolina	1,101	1,079	10	0	12	22	0.5	60	6.5	555	40.7	507	36.6

See footnotes at end of table.

NUMBER OF PUBLIC ELEMENTARY AND SECONDARY SCHOOLS, BY TYPE OF SCHOOL AND STATE OR JURISDICTION: SCHOOL YEAR 2004–05 — Continued

State or other jurisdiction	Total number of schools having membership (b)	Type of school				Charter schools		Magnet schools		Title I eligible schools		Title I schoolwide schools	
		Regular	Special education	Vocational education	Alternative education	Number of	Percent of all students in these schools	Number of	Percent of all students in these schools	Number of	Percent of all students in these schools	Number of	Percent of all students in these schools
South Dakota............	713	688	2	0	23	n/a	n/a	n/a	n/a	344	44.0	129	14.9
Tennessee................	1,671	1,621	16	7	27	7	0.1	31	1.7	899	45.5	729	37.3
Texas......................	7,941	6,967	3	0	971	295	1.5	(a)	...	5,263	64.8	4,843	59.8
Utah.......................	915	767	41	2	105	27	1.3	8	0.3	227	18.9	179	14.7
Vermont..................	361	316	43	0	2	n/a	n/a	n/a	n/a	214	52.7	95	26.3
Virginia..................	1,861	1,827	11	0	23	4	...	172	12.7	779	28.0	779	28.0
Washington..............	2,203	1,854	97	7	245	n/a	n/a	N.A.	N.A.	1,224	52.0	510	20.8
West Virginia...........	752	721	7	3	21	n/a	n/a	n/a	n/a	412	40.8	354	33.3
Wisconsin...............	2,206	2,000	4	1	201	149	2.9	2	0.1	1,076	44.0	300	14.8
Wyoming.................	376	347	0	0	29	2	0.2	n/a	n/a	203	44.6	62	15.1
Dist. of Columbia	214	189	14	2	9	39	18.3	3	1.5	173	85.0	165	82.0
American Samoa........	31	29	1	1	0	n/a	n/a	n/a	n/a	N.A.	N.A.	N.A.	N.A.
Guam......................	36	36	0	0	0	n/a	n/a	n/a	n/a	N.A.	N.A.	N.A.	N.A.
No. Marianas Islands...	32	31	0	0	1	n/a	n/a	n/a	n/a	N.A.	N.A.	N.A.	N.A.
Puerto Rico..............	1,513	1,452	28	15	18	120	8.4	28	1.9	1,479	97.4	1420	93.2
U.S. Virgin Islands......	33	32	0	0	1	n/a	n/a	1	7.4	33	100	N.A.	N.A.

Source: Sable, J. and Hill, J. (2006). Overview of Public Elementary and Secondary Students, Staff, Schools, School Districts, Revenues and Expenditures: School Year 2004–05 and Fiscal Year 2004 (NCES 2007-309). U.S. Department of Education, Washington, DC: National Center for Education Statistics.

N.A. — Not available.

n/a — Not applicable.

... — Rounds to zero.

(a) Reporting standards not met, data was missing for more than 20 percent of the schools.

(b) Total number of schools with membership differs from the total number of operational schools, which includes schools that have no membership.

(c) Number of Title I eligible schools includes those with and without schoolwide Title I programs.

(d) Reporting states totals include the 50 states and the District of Columbia.

Table 9.2
TOTAL STUDENT MEMBERSHIP, STUDENT/TEACHER RATIO, AND NUMBER OF STAFF FOR PUBLIC SCHOOLS: SCHOOL YEAR 2004–05

State or other jurisdiction	Total student membership	Total student/ teacher ratio	Total staff	Teachers	Instructional aides	Instructional coordinators and supervisors	Guidance counselors	Librarians	Student/other support staff (a)	School administrators	School district administrators	Administrative support staff
United States (c)	48,794,911	15.8	6,053,465	3,030,513	707,028	47,688	101,842	54,145	1,397,236	165,693	64,092	425,228
Alabama	730,140	14.2	92,795	51,594	6,458	836	1,705	1,369	21,112	3,487	1,081	5,153
Alaska	132,970	17.1	17,632	7,756	2,200	173 (d)	270	146	3,635	707	445	2,300
Arizona	1,043,298	21.3	97,953	48,935	13,713	192	1,351	827	23,122	2,223	418	7,172
Arkansas	463,115	14.8	66,127	31,234	7,196	623	1,264	954	19,405	1,569	659	3,223
California	6,441,557 (e)	21.1 (e)	574,614	305,969 (e)	68,118	6,663	6,508	1,138	114,887 (f)(g)	13,752	2,723	54,856
Colorado	765,976	17	91,337	45,165	10,269	1,425	1,409	842	22,039	2,442	1,010	6,736
Connecticut	577,390	14.9	83,879	38,808	12,689	369	1,352	789	21,468	2,258	1,383	4,763
Delaware	119,091 (e)	15.2	14,966	7,856	1,693	206	268	132	3,381	374	297	759
Florida	2,639,336 (e)	17	311,853	154,864	31,517	677	5,942	2,800	76,484	7,242	1,892	30,435
Georgia	1,553,437	14.8	209,746	104,987	24,535	1,439	3,417	2,192	55,510	5,169	1,982	10,515
Hawaii	183,185	16.4	20,531	11,146	2,084	559	657	291	3,680	505	196	1,413
Idaho	256,084	17.9	25,533	14,269	2,736	264	590	171	5,333	716	115	1,339
Illinois	2,097,503	16	261,237	131,047	34,411 (d)	1,059	3,117	2,176	60,878 (d)	6,457	3,942	18,150 (d)
Indiana	1,021,348 (e)	16.9	133,375	60,563	19,355	1,720	1,827	996	36,911	3,023	1,045	7,935
Iowa	478,319	13.8	68,450	34,697	9,475	482	1,157	561	14,917	2,195	945	4,021
Kansas	469,136	14.2	64,114	32,932	7,108	110	1,112	924	16,023	1,717	1,260	2,928
Kentucky	674,796	16.3	95,920	41,463	13,634	887	1,425	1,115	26,310	2,208	836	8,042
Louisiana	724,281	14.7	101,381	49,192	11,149	1,446	3,317	1,259	26,028	2,731	301	5,958
Maine	198,820	11.9	34,899	16,656	5,974	320	650	266	7,407	947	610	2,069
Maryland	865,561	15.7	108,296	55,101	9,747	1,285	2,230	1,140	29,504	3,226	834	5,229
Massachusetts	975,574	13.3	137,613	73,399	19,652	908	2,117	949	25,176 (d)	3,892	1,603	9,917
Michigan	1,750,919	17.4	209,831	100,634	25,444	3,338	2,762	1,429	53,197	5,168	3,288	14,571
Minnesota	838,503	16.1	104,367	52,152	14,459	1,450	1,055	922	24,071	1,986	1,915	6,357
Mississippi	495,376	15.8 (e)	67,249	31,321 (e)	8,698	703	1,018	951	17,751	1,773	984	4,050
Missouri	905,449	13.8	125,868	65,481	11,575	981	2,562	1,622	30,358	3,066	1,316	8,907
Montana	146,705	14.3	18,762	10,224	1,917	188	433	362	3,726 (d)	503	140	1269 (d)
Nebraska	285,761	13.6	40,998	21,077	4,720	456	767 (e)	549	9,771	1,014	573	2,071 (f)(g)
Nevada	400,083 (e)	19.1	31,260	20,950	3,683	546 (h)	713 (e)	343	1,511	924	263 (h)	2,327 (h)
New Hampshire	206,852	13.5	31,408	15,298	6,429	201 (f)	823	302	6,062 (f)	543 (g)	521	1,229 (g)
New Jersey	1,393,347 (e)	12.1	213,418	114,875	25,878	2,701	2,382	1,553	45,432	4,013	1,488	15,096
New Mexico	326,102	15	46,531	21,730	5,400	907	772	296	12,265	1,014	580	3,567
New York	2,836,337 (e)	13.0 (e)(h)	399,089	218,612 (h)	54,938 (h)	2,172 (h)	6,551 (h)	3,329 (h)	71,122 (h)	7,911 (h)	2,839 (h)	31,615 (h)
North Carolina	1,385,754	15	177,308	92,550	28,598	962	3,514	2,337	32,701	4,901	1,650	10,095
North Dakota	100,513	12.5	15,157	8,070	1,638	104	277	203	3518	388	478	481
Ohio	1,840,032	15.6	239,988	118,060	17,321	601	3,828	1,642	55,278	4,792	7,991	30,475
Oklahoma	629,476	15.6	77,466	40,416	6,997	472	1,559	1,016	18,964	2,107	528	5,407
Oregon	552,322	20.1 (e)	56,637	27,431 (e)	9,585	495	1,221	431	10,719	1,592	639	4,524
Pennsylvania	1,828,089	15.1	237,122	121,167	26,510	1,457	4,409	2,225	58,667	4,686	1,709	16,292
Rhode Island	156,498	13.2 (e)	23,031	11,898 (e)	2,567 (d)	204 (d)	2,614	215 (d)	2,484	1,991	155	903
South Carolina	703,736	15	65,014	46,914	2,686	721	1,736	1,140	2,127	3,298	302	6,090 (d)

See footnotes at end of table.

TOTAL STUDENT MEMBERSHIP, STUENT/TEACHER RATIO, AND NUMBER OF STAFF FOR PUBLIC SCHOOLS: SCHOOL YEAR 2004–05 — Continued

State or other jurisdiction	Total student membership	Total student/ teacher ratio	Total staff	Teachers	Instructional aides	Instructional coordinators and supervisors	Guidance counselors	Librarians	Student/other support staff (a)	School administrators	School district administrators	Administrative support staff
South Dakota...........	122,798 (e)	13.5 (e)	18,106	9,064	3,383	377	289	148	3,202	397	441	805
Tennessee..............	941,091	15.7	111,891	60,022	14,181	778 (f)	1,936	1,566	24,183 (f)(g)	3,420	170	5,635 (g)
Texas..................	4,405,215	15	607,364	294,547	59,855	1,518	10,151	4,893	166,802 (f)(g)	30,737	7,863	30,998
Utah...................	503,607 (e)	22.6 (e)	44,499	22,287	6,954	732	675	262	9,123	1,060	375	3,031
Vermont................	98,352	11.3	18,899	8,720	4,339	296	426	220	3,255	432	148	1,063
Virginia...............	1,204,739	12.9	179,688	93,732	17,833	1,447	2,579	2,002	43,013	4,083	1,461	13,538
Washington	1,020,005	19.2	111,848	53,125	10,300	231	1,981 (e)	1,298	37,614	2,795	897	3,607
West Virginia	280,129	14	37,979	19,958	3,191	354	673	387	9,797	1,056	437	2,126
Wisconsin	864,757	14.3	104,018	60,521	10,951	1,395	1,963(e)	1,292	20,392	2,473	926	4,105
Wyoming	84,733	12.7	14,256	6,657	1,946	153	389(e)	132	3,340	332	308	999
Dist. of Columbia......	76,714	14.2	12,162	5,387	1,339	105	99	41	3,581	398	130	1,082
American Samoa.........	16,126	17.1	1,813	945	108	50	44	17	334	70	54	191
Guam..................	30,605	18.3	3,318	1,672	687	83	40	14	316	61	19	426
No. Marianas Islands...	11,601	20	1,166	579	263	11	18	1	144	33	6	111
Puerto Rico............	575,648	13.4	76,865	43,054	240	505	1,011	1,095	22,929	1,498	1,727	4,806
U.S. Virgin Islands......	16,429(e)	10.6	2,977	1,545	322	23	79	39	569	113	78	209

Source: Sable, J. and Hill, J. (2006). Overview of Public Elementary and Secondary Students, Staff, Schools, School Districts, Revenues and Expenditures: School Year 2004–05 and Fiscal Year 2004 (NCES 2007-309). U.S. Department of Education, Washington, DC: National Center for Education Statistics.

Note: All staff counts are full-time-equivalent (FTE) counts.

N.A.— Not available.

(a) Student/other support staff include library support staff, student support services staff, and all other nonadministrative support staff.

(b) Administrative support staff includes district- and school-level administrative support staff.

(c) U.S. totals include the 50 states and the District of Columbia.

(d) Data was imputed based on current-year (fall 2004) data.

(e) Data was totaled based on sum of internal or external detail.

(f) Data disaggregated from reported total.

(g) Adjusted. See appendix A, Imputed and adjusted data, for more information.

(h) Data imputed based on prior-year (fall 2003) data.

Table 9.3
PUBLIC SCHOOL GRADUATION RATE: SCHOOL YEAR 2003–04

State or or jurisdiction	Averaged freshman graduation rate (a)	Total (b)	Diplomas	Other high school completers	General Educational Development (GED) test passers (c)
Reporting states (d)...................	75.0	2,595,650	2,548,128	47,522	184,885
Alabama...............................	65.0	39,218	36,464	2,754	4,198
Alaska.................................	67.2	7,446	7,236	210	1,008
Arizona...............................	66.8	45,961	45,508	453	3,539
Arkansas.............................	76.8	27,253	27,181	72	3,386
California............................	73.9	343,480	343,480	n/a	9,452
Colorado..............................	78.7	45,535	44,777	758	4,012
Connecticut........................	80.7	34,618	34,573	45	1,140
Delaware	72.9	7,077	6,951	126	155
Florida................................	66.4	139,239	131,418	7,821	15,692
Georgia...............................	61.2	77,020	68,550	8,470	8,598
Hawaii.................................	72.6	10,501	10,324	177	790
Idaho...................................	81.5	15,659	15,547	112	1,615
Illinois................................	80.3	124,763	124,763	n/a	5,858
Indiana	73.5	57,636	56,008	1,628	4,589
Iowa....................................	85.8	34,403	34,339	64	1,716
Kansas................................	77.9	30,155	30,155	n/a	2,055
Kentucky.............................	73.0	38,144	37,787	357	3,657
Louisiana............................	69.4	38,723	37,019	1,704	4,179
Maine..................................	77.6	13,378	13,278	100	1,192
Maryland	79.5	53,545	52,870	675	2,762
Massachusetts.....................	79.3	59,192	58,326	866	3,927
Michigan	72.5	100,206	98,823	1,383	4,502
Minnesota...........................	84.7	59,096	59,096	n/a	2,574
Mississippi..........................	62.7	25,285	23,735	1,550	3,575
Missouri	80.4	57,983	57,983	n/a	3,731
Montana..............................	80.4	10,500	10,500	n/a	1,256
Nebraska.............................	87.6	20,506	20,309	197	1,043
Nevada................................	57.4	17,318	15,201	2,117	1,924
New Hampshire....................	78.7	13,428	13,309	119	721
New Jersey...........................	86.3	83,826	83,826	n/a	2,562
New Mexico..........................	67.0	18,307	17,892	415	2,403
New York.............................	N.A.	N.A.	N.A.	N.A.	11,567
North Carolina	71.4	73,055	72,126	929	4,697
North Dakota	86.1	7,888	7,888	n/a	527
Ohio....................................	81.3	119,029	119,029	n/a	4,932
Oklahoma............................	77.0	36,799	36,799	n/a	2,955
Oregon................................	74.2	36,826	32,958	3,868	3,729
Pennsylvania.......................	82.2	123,474	123,474	n/a	6,023
Rhode Island.......................	75.9	9,278	9,258	20	582
South Carolina.....................	60.6	35,962	33,235	2,727	1,979
South Dakota	83.7	9,001	9,001	n/a	672
Tennessee............................	66.1	50,203	46,096	4,107	5,360
Texas...................................	76.7	244,165	244,165	n/a	14,706
Utah....................................	83.0	30,423	30,252	171	2,324
Vermont...............................	85.4	7,127	7,100	27	374
Virginia...............................	79.3	75,101	72,042	3,059	5,861
Washington	74.6	61,394	61,274	120	5,336
West Virginia	76.9	17,339	17,339	0	1,665
Wisconsin	N.A.	N.A.	N.A.	N.A.	2,883
Wyoming..............................	76.0	5,878	5,833	45	703
Dist. of Columbia	68.2	3,307	3,031	276	199
American Samoa	80.2	852	852	n/a	6
Guam...................................	48.4	1,346	1,346	n/a	68
No. Marianas Islands.............	75.3	575	575	n/a	6
Puerto Rico	64.8	31,946	30,083	1,863	N.A
U.S. Virgin Islands	N.A.	816	816	n/a	33

See footnotes at end of table.

PUBLIC SCHOOL GRADUATION RATE: SCHOOL YEAR 2003–04 — Continued

Source: Sable, J. and Hill, J. (2006). Overview of Public Elementary and Secondary Students, Staff, Schools, School Disricts, Revenues and Expenditures: School Year 2004-05 and Fiscal Year 2004 (NCES 2007-309). U.S. Department of Education, Washington, DC: National Center for Education Statistics. GED data were acquired from the General Educational Development Testing Service.

Key:

N.A. — Not available.

n/a — Not applicable.

(a) Averaged freshman graduation rate (AFGR) is an estimate of the percentage of an entering freshman class graduating in 4 years. For 2003–04, it equals the total number of diploma recipients in 2003–04 divided by the average membership of the 8th grade class in 1999–2000, the 9th grade class in 2000–01, and the 10th grade class in 2001–02.

(b) Includes individuals who receive diplomas, certificates of attendance, or some other credential in lieu of diplomas.

(c) The number of individuals age 19 or younger who passed the GED test. Some of those individuals who passed the test may not have sought a high school credential. An individual may pass the GED test in a different state than where he or she last attended school.

(d) Reporting states totals include the 50 states and the District of Columbia. The reporting states estimate does not include data from two states with missing diploma counts: New York and Wisconsin. The adjusted national rate with estimates for these two states is 74.3 percent.

Table 9.4
TOTAL REVENUES, PERCENTAGE DISTRIBUTION, AND REVENUES PER PUPIL FOR PUBLIC ELEMENTARY AND SECONDARY SCHOOLS, BY SOURCE AND STATE OR JURISDICTION: FISCAL YEAR 2004

State or other jurisdiction	Total revenues (in thousands of dollars)				Percentage			Revenues per pupil			
	Total	Local	State	Federal	Local	State	Federal	Total	Local	State	Federal
United States (a)	$462,015,502 (b)	$202,711,210 (b)	$217,383,087	$41,921,206	43.9	47.1	9.1	$9,518 (c)	$4,176 (c)	$4,478 (c)	$864 (c)
Alabama	5,373,546	1,729,726	2,986,962	656,858	32.2	55.6	12.2	7,349	2,366	4,085	898
Alaska	1,550,365	384,049	879,186	287,130	24.8	56.7	18.5	11,576	2,867	6,564	2,144
Arizona	7,641,235 (b)	3,079,821 (b)	3,648,871	912,542	40.3	47.8	11.9	7,550	3,043	3,605	902
Arkansas	3,428,091	1,165,148	1,826,691	436,252	34.0	53.3	12.7	7,542	2,563	4,019	960
California	57,598,368	19,282,871	32,021,758	6,293,739	33.5	55.6	10.9	8,980 (c)	3,006 (c)	4,993 (c)	981 (c)
Colorado	6,545,403	3,267,217	2,834,721	443,466	49.9	43.3	6.8	8,639	4,312	3,741	585
Connecticut	7,396,816	4,330,876	2,686,572	379,368	58.6	36.3	5.1	12,815	7,503	4,654	657
Delaware	1,296,963	375,879	804,029	117,055	29.0	62.0	9.0	11,022	3,194	6,833	995
Florida	21,042,496	9,627,141	9,195,242	2,220,113	45.8	43.7	10.6	8,132	3,720	3,554	858
Georgia	13,828,817	6,244,838	6,349,957	1,234,022	45.2	45.9	8.9	9,082	4,101	4,170	810
Hawaii	2,141,931	50,929	1,854,533	236,469	2.4	86.6	11.0	11,666	277	10,100	1,288
Idaho	1,752,753	553,601	1,017,686	181,466	31.6	58.1	10.4	6,952	2,196	4,037	720
Illinois	20,713,607	12,055,001	6,915,271	1,743,335	58.2	33.4	8.4	9,859	5,738	3,291	830
Indiana	10,086,811	4,263,858	5,139,522	683,431	42.3	51.0	6.8	9,976	4,217	5,083	676
Iowa	4,256,454	1,938,572	1,953,414	364,467	45.5	45.9	8.6	8,845	4,028	4,059	757
Kansas	4,545,376	1,810,934	2,322,537	411,906	39.8	51.1	9.1	9,661	3,849	4,936	875
Kentucky	5,077,772	1,552,517	2,907,751	617,504	30.6	57.3	12.2	7,655	2,340	4,383	931
Louisiana	5,786,338	2,183,856	2,820,277	782,204	37.7	48.7	13.5	7,951	3,001	3,876	1,075
Maine	2,183,576	1,072,165	921,529	189,881	49.1	42.2	8.7	10,805	5,306	4,560	940
Maryland	9,004,475	4,988,384	3,435,060	581,031	55.4	38.1	6.5	10,361	5,740	3,952	669
Massachusetts	11,716,904	6,196,877	4,738,773	781,255	52.9	40.4	6.7	11,950	6,320	4,833	797
Michigan	18,032,874	5,435,547	11,146,466	1,450,861	30.1	61.8	8.0	10,260	3,093	6,342	825
Minnesota	8,565,550	2,082,220	5,956,037	527,293	24.3	69.5	6.2	10,163	2,470	7,067	626
Mississippi	3,483,210	1,038,807	1,907,470	536,933	29.8	54.8	15.4	7,058	2,105	3,865	1,088
Missouri	7,937,576	4,532,296	2,720,379	684,901	57.1	34.3	8.6	8,762	5,003	3,003	756
Montana	1,267,696	506,997	565,868	194,831	40.0	44.6	15.4	8,545	3,417	3,814	1,313
Nebraska	2,663,032	1,549,469	873,661	239,901	58.2	32.8	9.0	9,326	5,426	3,060	840
Nevada	3,075,673	1,939,217	910,143	226,312	63.1	29.6	7.4	7,980	5,032	2,362	587
New Hampshire	2,116,169	1,026,914	968,753	120,502	48.5	45.8	5.7	10,202	4,951	4,671	581
New Jersey	20,476,709	10,668,582	8,883,028	925,100	52.1	43.4	4.5	14,830	7,727	6,433	670
New Mexico	2,918,985	385,075	2,019,491	514,420	13.2	69.2	17.6	9,035	1,192	6,251	1,592
New York	40,610,043	19,942,026	17,561,566	3,106,451	49.1	43.2	7.6	14,176	6,961	6,130	1,084
North Carolina	9,877,454	2,633,074	6,211,941	1,032,439	26.7	62.9	10.5	7,262	1,936	4,567	759
North Dakota	877,701	408,425	334,525	134,751	46.5	38.1	15.4	8,585	3,995	3,272	1,318
Ohio	18,913,893	9,052,123	8,492,580	1,369,190	47.9	44.9	7.2	10,249	4,905	4,602	742
Oklahoma	4,363,285	1,427,328	2,372,609	563,347	32.7	54.4	12.9	6,968	2,279	3,789	900
Oregon	5,116,226	1,990,635	2,658,280	467,311	38.9	52.0	9.1	9,281	3,611	4,822	848
Pennsylvania	19,966,277	11,172,184	7,144,654	1,649,438	56.0	35.8	8.3	10,964	6,135	3,923	906
Rhode Island	1,863,135	957,222	767,153	138,760	51.4	41.2	7.4	11,690	6,006	4,814	871
South Carolina	5,978,578	2,588,862	2,753,882	635,833	43.3	46.1	10.6	8,551	3,703	3,939	909

See footnotes at end of table.

TOTAL REVENUES, PERCENTAGE DISTRIBUTION, AND REVENUES PER PUPIL FOR PUBLIC ELEMENTARY AND SECONDARY SCHOOLS, BY SOURCE AND STATE OR JURISDICTION: FISCAL YEAR 2004 — Continued

State or other jurisdiction	Total revenues (in thousands of dollars)				Percentage			Revenues per pupil			
	Total	Local	State	Federal	Local	State	Federal	Total	Local	State	Federal
South Dakota...........	1,015,552	507,317	348,909	159,327	50.0	34.4	15.7	8,090	4,041	2,779	1,269
Tennessee...............	6,478,661	3,006,049	2,776,513	696,099	46.4	42.9	10.7	6,917	3,209	2,964	743
Texas......................	35,409,121	17,901,943	13,678,202	3,828,976	50.6	38.6	10.8	8,174	4,133	3,158	884
Utah.......................	3,028,885	1,043,641	1,686,337	298,907	34.5	55.7	9.9	6,107	2,104	3,400	603
Vermont..................	1,208,241	312,538	801,161	94,542	25.9	66.3	7.8	12,192	3,154	8,084	954
Virginia...................	10,921,942	5,915,263	4,241,321	765,357	54.2	38.8	7.0	9,162	4,962	3,558	642
Washington..............	8,910,263	2,624,173	5,456,536	829,554	29.5	61.2	9.3	8,724	2,569	5,342	812
West Virginia...........	2,687,459	748,701	1,630,492	308,266	27.9	60.7	11.5	9,557	2,662	5,798	1,096
Wisconsin................	9,087,054	3,751,626	4,747,696	587,732	41.3	52.2	6.5	10,326	4,263	5,395	668
Wyoming.................	971,434	369,985	507,091	94,358	38.1	52.2	9.7	11,107	4,230	5,798	1,079
Dist. of Columbia......	1,224,730	1,038,712	N.A.	186,018	84.8	N.A.	15.2	15,690	13,307	N.A.	2,383
American Samoa.......	88,949	2,140	12,809	74,000	2.4	14.4	83.2	5,597	135	806	4,656
Guam......................	185,620	137,688	0	47,933	74.2	0.0	25.8	5,879	4,361	0	1,518
No. Marianas Islands	64,605	1,195	37,230	26,180	1.8	57.6	40.5	5,746	106	3,311	2,328
Puerto Rico..............	2,884,128	472	1,975,579	908,078	0.0	68.5	31.5	4,931	1	3,378	1,552
U.S. Virgin Islands....	185,139	145,909	0	39,231	78.8	0.0	21.2	10,450	8,236	0	2,214

Source: Sable, J. and Hill, J. (2006). Overview of Public Elementary and Secondary Students, Staff, Schools, School Districts, Revenues and Expenditures: School Year 2004–05 and Fiscal Year 2004 (NCES 2007-309). U.S. Department of Education, Washington, DC: National Center for Education Statistics.

Note: Detail may not sum to totals because of rounding.

Key:
N.A. — Not applicable.

(a) U.S. totals include the 50 states and the District of Columbia.
(b) Value affected by redistribution of reported values to correct for missing data items.
(c) Prekindergarten students were imputed, affecting total student count and per pupil expenditure calculation.

Table 9.5
TOTAL EXPENDITURES AND PER PUPIL EXPENDITURES FOR PUBLIC ELEMENTARY AND SECONDARY SCHOOLS: FISCAL YEAR 2004

State or other jurisdiction	Expenditures (in thousands of dollars)						Expenditures per pupil					
	Total (a)	Current for elementary/ secondary education (a)	Facilities acquisitions and construction	Replacement equipment	Other programs	Interest on debt	Total (a)	Current for elementary/ secondary education (a)	Facilities acquisitions and construction	Replacement equipment	Other programs	Interest on debt
United States (b)	$473,862,737	$403,376,186	$44,643,748	$5,832,318(c)	$6,929,952(c)	$13,080,534(c)	$9,762(d)	$8,310(d)	$920(d)	$120(d)	$143(d)	$269(d)
Alabama	5,482,123	4,812,479	403,885	48,974	104,624	112,161	7,497	6,581	552	67	143	153
Alaska	1,652,306	1,354,846	239,775	16,325	10,204	31,156	12,337	10,116	1,790	122	76	233
Arizona	7,115,562(c)(e)	6,063,009(c)	600,244	185,391(e)	48,505(e)	218,413	7,031	5,991	593	183	48	216
Arkansas	3,616,399	3,109,644	338,235	71,715	23,849	72,956	7,956	6,842	744	158	52	161
California	60,424,698	49,215,866	8,946,753	180,166	996,391	1,085,522	9,421(d)	7,673	1,395(d)	28(d)	155(d)	169(d)
Colorado	6,874,454	5,666,191	734,840	132,775	55,189	285,460	9,073	7,478	970	175	73	377
Connecticut	7,704,868(e)	6,600,767	768,293	74,543(e)	125,614(e)	135,650	13,349	11,436	1,331	129	218	235
Delaware	1,402,691(c)	1,201,631	154,819	10,150(e)	15,671(c)	20,420	11,921	10,212	1,316	86	133	174
Florida	21,877,780	17,578,884	3,147,155	213,909	433,791	504,042	8,455	6,793	1,216	83	168	195
Georgia	13,828,613	11,788,616	1,632,508	179,704	62,317	165,468	9,082	7,742	1,072	118	41	109
Hawaii	1,771,851	1,566,792	75,951	41,298	51,458	36,353	9,650	8,533	414	225	280	198
Idaho	1,782,485	1,555,006	158,198	29,564	4,227	35,489	7,070	6,168	627	117	17	141
Illinois	21,097,122	18,081,827	1,884,480	458,896	134,066	537,854	10,042	8,606	897	218	64	256
Indiana	9,862,544(c)	8,524,980	747,159	149,614	70,795	369,996(c)	9,754	8,431	739	148	70	366
Iowa	4,294,342	3,669,797	451,082	81,928	31,726	59,809	8,924	7,626	937	170	66	124
Kansas	4,070,677	3,658,421	121,319	151,034	6,399	133,504	8,652	7,776	258	321	14	284
Kentucky	4,851,132	4,551,648	25,285	107,461	65,587	101,152	7,313	6,861	38	162	99	152
Louisiana	5,819,589	5,290,964	290,333	81,291	51,576	105,425	7,997	7,271	399	112	71	145
Maine	2,214,924	1,969,497	146,804	32,258	22,494	43,871	10,960	9,746	726	160	111	217
Maryland	8,916,390	8,198,454	502,965	93,480	23,259	98,234	10,259	9,433	579	108	27	113
Massachusetts	11,489,116	10,799,765	143,261	62,181	170,580	313,329	11,718	11,015	146	63	174	320
Michigan	19,357,289	15,983,044	2,005,566	246,648	333,325	788,705	11,013	9,094	1,141	140	190	449
Minnesota	8,799,745	7,084,005	909,396	127,565	323,890	354,890	10,440	8,405	1,079	151	384	421
Mississippi	3,346,070	3,059,569	129,016	95,502	26,759	35,224	6,780	6,199	261	194	54	71
Missouri	7,961,108(c)	6,832,454(c)	538,235	201,713	153,389	235,318	8,788	7,542	594	223	169	260
Montana	1,234,592	1,160,838	38,321	17,312	6,528	11,593	8,322	7,825	258	117	44	78
Nebraska	2,749,830(c)	2,413,404	211,046	66,982(c)	4,205(c)	54,193	9,630	8,452	739	235	15	190
Nevada	3,223,659(e)	2,470,581	493,603	72,081(e)	17,721	169,672	8,364	6,410	1,281	187	46	440
New Hampshire	2,149,970	1,900,240	173,733	25,631	7,183	43,183	10,365	9,161	838	124	35	208
New Jersey	20,777,467(c)	18,416,695	1,778,239	92,054(c)	180,167(c)	310,313	15,048	13,338	1,288	67	130	225
New Mexico	2,959,048	2,446,115	413,706	26,128	26,329	46,770	9,159	7,572	1,281	81	81	145
New York	41,539,974	36,205,111	2,375,988	397,296	1,529,752	1,031,827	14,500	12,638	829	139	534	360
North Carolina	10,356,368	8,994,620	930,002	74,504	45,989	311,253	7,614	6,613	684	55	34	229
North Dakota	856,000	746,025	70,931	23,699	6,078	9,267	8,373	7,297	694	232	59	91
Ohio	19,584,115	16,662,985	1,722,069	395,625	429,127	374,309	10,612	9,029	933	214	233	203

See footnotes at end of table.

TOTAL EXPENDITURES AND PER PUPIL EXPENDITURES FOR PUBLIC ELEMENTARY AND SECONDARY SCHOOLS: FISCAL YEAR 2004 — Continued

State or other jurisdiction	Expenditures (in thousands of dollars)						Expenditures per pupil					
	Total (a)	Current for elementary/ secondary education (a)	Facilities acquisitions and construction	Replacement equipment	Other programs	Interest on debt	Total (a)	Current for elementary/ secondary education (a)	Facilities acquisitions and construction	Replacement equipment	Other programs	Interest on debt
Oklahoma	4,180,721	3,853,308	199,838	68,007	13,407	46,162	6,677	6,154	319	109	21	74
Oregon	4,919,701	4,199,485	446,282	40,523	19,366	214,045	8,924	7,618	810	74	35	388
Pennsylvania	20,877,878	17,680,332	1,734,329	222,066	417,619	823,531	11,464	9,708	952	122	229	452
Rhode Island	1,867,732	1,765,585	12,593	16,348	43,544	29,661	11,719	11,078	79	103	273	186
South Carolina	6,116,477	5,017,833	764,065	69,886	64,574	200,117	8,748	7,177	1,093	100	92	286
South Dakota	1,016,837	887,328	79,948	25,827	2,812	20,922	8,100	7,068	637	206	22	167
Tennessee	6,830,311(c)	6,056,657(c)	440,166	117,812	41,831	173,844	7,292(d)	6,466(d)	470(d)	126(d)	45(d)	186(d)
Texas	37,610,640	30,974,890	4,463,378	348,448	287,286	1,536,638	8,683	7,151	1,030	80	66	355
Utah	3,106,400	2,475,550	434,666	49,305	76,158	70,721	6,263	4,991	876	99	154	143
Vermont	1,206,127	1,111,029	59,767	17,577	3,156	14,597	12,170	11,211	603	177	32	147
Virginia	11,183,657	9,798,239	892,017	233,630	65,966	193,805	9,382	8,219	748	196	55	163
Washington	9,137,280	7,549,235	1,118,624	101,340	41,174	326,907	8,946	7,391	1,095	99	40	320
West Virginia	2,651,865	2,415,043	129,658	64,320	34,073	8,771	9,430	8,588	461	229	121	31
Wisconsin	9,988,217	8,131,276	342,608	142,849	198,096	1,173,389	11,350	9,240	389	162	225	1,333
Wyoming	946,819	814,092	94,939	30,807	2,339	4,642	10,825	9,308	1,085	352	27	53
Dist. of Columbia	1,177,174(c)	1,011,536(c)	127,679	18,175	19,785	0	15,081	12,959	1,636	233	253	0
American Samoa	65,117	55,519	4,350	1,661	3,587	0	4,097	3,493	274	104	226	0
Guam	185,401	182,506	0	2,265	105	525	5,872	5,781	0	72	3	17
No. Mariana Islands	48,530	47,681	350	411	87	0	4,316	4,241	31	37	8	0
Puerto Rico	2,582,216	2,425,372	10,188	58,530	70,166	17,960	4,415	4,147	17	100	120	31
U.S. Virgin Islands	147,675	128,250	16,405	1,261	1,759	0	8,336	7,239	926	71	99	0

Source: Sable, J. and Hill, J. (2006). *Overview of Public Elementary and Secondary Students, Staff, Schools, School Districts, Revenues and Expenditures: School Year 2004–05 and Fiscal Year 2004* (NCES 2007-309). U.S. Department of Education, Washington, D.C.: National Center for Education Statistics.

Note: Detail may not sum to totals because of rounding.

Key:
(a) Includes expenditures for individuals to attend private schools or schools in other states.
(b) U.S. totals include the 50 states and the District of Columbia.
(c) Value affected by redistribution of reported values to correct for missing data items.
(d) Prekindergarten students were imputed, affecting total student count and per pupil expenditure calculation.
(e) Value contains imputation for missing data.

Table 9.6
TOTAL CURRENT EXPENDITURES FOR PUBLIC ELEMENTARY AND SECONDARY SCHOOLS, PERCENTAGE DISTRIBUTION, AND EXPENDITURES PER PUPIL: FISCAL YEAR 2004

State or other jurisdiction	Current expenditures (in thousands of dollars)					Percentage				Current expenditures per pupil				
	Total (a)	Instruction and instruction related (a)	Student support	Admin.	Ops.	Instruction and instruction related (a)	Student support	Admin.	Ops.	Total (a)	Instruction and instruction related (a)	Student support	Admin.	Ops.
United States (b)	$403,376,186 (c)	$266,576,498 (c)	$20,839,154	$44,353,051(c)	$71,607,483	66.1	5.2	11.0	17.8	$8,310 (d)	$5,492 (d)	$429 (d)	$914 (d)	$1,475 (d)
Alabama	4,812,479	3,093,754	234,496	511,553	972,676	64.3	4.9	10.6	20.2	6,581	4,231	321	700	1,330
Alaska	1,354,846	846,109	89,319	148,629	270,789	62.5	6.6	11.0	20.0	10,116	6,317	667	1,110	2,022
Arizona	6,063,009 (c)	3,786,162	334,075	752,337(c)	1,190,435	62.4	5.5	12.4	19.6	5,991	3,741	330	743	1,176
Arkansas	3,109,644	2,049,358	142,810	353,991	563,484	65.9	4.6	11.4	18.1	6,842	4,509	314	779	1,240
California	49,215,866	33,032,977	2,201,000	6,086,169	7,895,720	67.1	4.5	12.4	16.0	7,673 (d)	5,150 (d)	343 (d)	949 (d)	1,231(d)
Colorado	5,666,191	3,527,790	253,380	971,459	913,562	62.3	4.5	17.1	16.1	7,478	4,656	334	1,282	1,206
Connecticut	6,600,767	4,431,057	373,317	654,872	1,141,521	67.1	5.7	9.9	17.3	11,436	7,677	647	1,135	1,978
Delaware	1,201,631	750,356	57,673	152,869	240,732	62.4	4.8	12.7	20.0	10,212	6,377	490	1,299	2,046
Florida	17,578,884	11,489,958	868,629	1,757,381	3,462,916	65.4	4.9	10.0	19.7	6,793	4,440	336	679	1,338
Georgia	11,788,616	8,116,312	544,176	1,209,186	1,918,941	68.8	4.6	10.3	16.3	7,742	5,331	357	794	1,260
Hawaii	1,566,792	1,027,246	173,309	147,914	218,323	65.6	11.1	9.4	13.9	8,533	5,595	944	806	1,189
Idaho	1,555,006	1,023,724	86,603	156,384	288,295	65.8	5.6	10.1	18.5	6,168	4,060	343	620	1,143
Illinois	18,081,827	11,549,751	1,124,763	2,194,653	3,212,660	63.9	6.2	12.1	17.8	8,606	5,497	535	1,045	1,529
Indiana	8,524,980	5,442,449	379,084	969,054	1,734,392	63.8	4.4	11.4	20.3	8,431	5,383	375	958	1,715
Iowa	3,669,797	2,420,430	229,115	408,300	611,953	66.0	6.2	11.1	16.7	7,626	5,030	476	848	1,272
Kansas	3,658,421	2,340,006	208,943	433,119	676,352	64.0	5.7	11.8	18.5	7,776	4,974	444	921	1,438
Kentucky	4,551,648	2,988,552	199,071(c)	479,232 (c)	884,793 (c)	65.7	4.4	10.5	19.4	6,861	4,505	300	722	1,334
Louisiana	5,290,964	3,448,897	232,567	530,294	1,079,206	65.2	4.4	10.0	20.4	7,271	4,739	320	729	1,483
Maine	1,969,497	1,383,484	65,690	181,450	338,873	70.2	3.3	9.2	17.2	9,746	6,846	325	898	1,677
Maryland	8,198,454	5,679,936	291,594	751,618	1,475,306	69.3	3.6	9.2	18.0	9,433	6,535	336	865	1,697
Massachusetts	10,799,765	7,492,665	599,451	968,972	1,738,677	69.4	5.6	9.0	16.1	11,015	7,642	611	988	1,773
Michigan	15,983,044	9,879,021	1,119,868	2,113,255	2,870,900	61.8	7.0	13.2	18.0	9,094	5,621	637	1,202	1,633
Minnesota	7,084,005	4,934,203	224,821	673,609	1,251,372	69.7	3.2	9.5	17.7	8,405	5,854	267	799	1,485
Mississippi	3,059,569	1,978,551	138,220	329,176	613,621	64.7	4.5	10.8	20.1	6,199	4,009	280	667	1,243
Missouri	6,832,454 (c)	4,451,064 (c)	338,244	745,429	1,297,716	65.1	5.0	10.9	19.0	7,542	4,913	373	823	1,432
Montana	1,160,838	754,745	59,397	129,855	216,841	65.0	5.1	11.2	18.7	7,825	5,087	400	875	1,462
Nebraska	2,413,404	1,622,253	97,847	254,971	438,334	67.2	4.1	10.6	18.2	8,452	5,681	343	893	1,535
Nevada	2,470,581	1,641,258	94,896	318,697	415,729	66.4	3.8	12.9	16.8	6,410	4,259	246	827	1,079
New Hampshire	1,900,240	1,292,293	127,383	183,271	297,293	68.0	6.7	9.6	15.6	9,161	6,230	614	884	1,433
New Jersey	18,416,695	11,527,074	1,657,198	1,820,745	3,411,679	62.6	9.0	9.9	18.5	13,338	8,348	1,200	1,319	2,471
New Mexico	2,446,115	1,488,498	242,223	264,424	450,970	60.9	9.9	10.8	18.4	7,572	4,607	750	818	1,396
New York	36,205,111	25,762,894	1,238,071	3,350,616	5,853,529	71.2	3.4	9.3	16.2	12,638	8,993	432	1,170	2,043
North Carolina	8,994,620	6,003,774	462,141	974,537	1,554,168	66.7	5.1	10.8	17.3	6,613	4,414	340	716	1,143
North Dakota	746,025	468,795	30,092	90,201	156,937	62.8	4.0	12.1	21.0	7,297	4,586	294	882	1,535
Ohio	16,662,985	10,602,966	996,604	2,234,468	2,828,946	63.6	6.0	13.4	17.0	9,029	5,746	540	1,211	1,533

See footnotes at end of table.

TOTAL CURRENT EXPENDITURES FOR PUBLIC ELEMENTARY AND SECONDARY SCHOOLS, PERCENTAGE DISTRIBUTION, AND EXPENDITURES PER PUPIL: FISCAL YEAR 2004—Continued

State or other jurisdiction	Current expenditures (in thousands of dollars)					Percentage				Current expenditures per pupil				
	Total (a)	Instruction and instruction related (a)	Student support	Admin.	Ops.	Instruction and instruction related (a)	Student support	Admin.	Ops.	Total (a)	Instruction and instruction related (a)	Student support	Admin.	Ops.
Oklahoma	3,853,308	2,329,604	251,383	435,115	837,205	60.5	6.5	11.3	21.7	6,154	3,720	401	695	1,337
Oregon	4,199,485	2,656,476	279,158	578,156	685,695	63.3	6.6	13.8	16.3	7,618	4,819	506	1,049	1,244
Pennsylvania	17,680,332	11,574,018	851,226	1,913,557	3,341,531	65.5	4.8	10.8	18.9	9,708	6,355	467	1,051	1,835
Rhode Island	1,765,585	1,216,956	141,672	153,810	253,147	68.9	8.0	8.7	14.3	11,078	7,636	889	965	1,588
South Carolina	5,017,833	3,308,438	339,628	489,942	879,825	65.9	6.8	9.8	17.5	7,177	4,732	486	701	1,258
South Dakota	887,328	560,598	48,469	110,995	167,266	63.2	5.5	12.5	18.9	7,068	4,466	386	884	1,332
Tennessee	6,056,657 (c)	4,206,901(c)	218,594	531,716	1,099,447	69.5	3.6	8.8	18.2	6,466 (d)	4,491(d)	233 (d)	568 (d)	1174 (d)
Texas	30,974,890	20,391,015	1,506,362	3,302,382	5,775,131	65.8	4.9	10.7	18.6	7,151	4,707	348	762	1,333
Utah	2,475,550	1,692,928	92,731	231,692	458,199	68.4	3.7	9.4	18.5	4,991	3,413	187	467	924
Vermont	1,111,029	752,475	80,691	125,632	152,231	67.7	7.3	11.3	13.7	11,211	7,593	814	1,268	1,536
Virginia	9,798,239	6,619,958	474,174	871,335	1,832,773	67.6	4.8	8.9	18.7	8,219	5,553	398	731	1,537
Washington	7,549,235 (c)	4,846,128 (c)	468,305	868,801	1,366,002	64.2	6.2	11.5	18.1	7,391	4,745	459	851	1,337
West Virginia	2,415,043	1,553,850	81,553	231,380	548,260	64.3	3.4	9.6	22.7	8,588	5,525	290	823	1,950
Wisconsin	8,131,276	5,396,077	375,947	1,005,032	1,354,221	66.4	4.6	12.4	16.7	9,240	6,132	427	1,142	1,539
Wyoming	814,092	524,810	48,230	93,774	147,279	64.5	5.9	11.5	18.1	9,308	6,000	551	1,072	1,684
Dist. of Columbia	1,011,536 (c)	617,902 (c)	64,960	107,043	221,630	61.1	6.4	10.6	21.9	12,959	7,916	832	1,371	2,839
American Samoa	55,519	32,166	2,456	4,439	16,458	57.9	4.4	8.0	29.6	3,493	2,024	155	279	1,036
Guam	182,506	108,122	20,503	22,506	31,375	59.2	11.2	12.3	17.2	5,781	3,425	649	713	994
No. Marianas Islands	47,681	41,078	612	3,758	2,234	86.2	1.3	7.9	4.7	4,241	3,653	54	334	199
Puerto Rico	2,425,372	1,827,728	57,500	69,190	470,953	75.4	2.4	2.9	19.4	4,147	3,125	98	118	805
U.S. Virgin Islands	128,250	87,958	7,175	15,867	17,249	68.6	5.6	12.4	13.4	7,239	4,965	405	896	974

Source: Sable, J. and Hill, J. (2006). Overview of Public Elementary and Secondary Students, Staff, Schools, School Districts, Revenues and Expenditures: School Year 2004-05 and Fiscal Year 2004 (NCES 2007-309). U.S. Department of Education, Washington, DC: National Center for Education Statistics.

Note: Detail may not sum to totals because of rounding.

(a) Includes expenditures for individuals to attend private schools or schools in other states.

(b) U.S. totals include the 50 states and the District of Columbia.

(c) Value affected by redistribution of reported values to correct for missing data items.

(d) Prekindergarten students were imputed, affecting total student count and per pupil expenditure calculation.

Table 9.7
INSTRUCTION-RELATED EXPENDITURES FOR PUBLIC ELEMENTARY AND SECONDARY SCHOOL DISTRICTS: 2004–05

State or other jurisdiction	Current instruction and instruction-related expenditures (in thousands of dollars)							Current instruction and instruction-related expenditures per pupil						
	Total (a)	Salaries	Employee benefits	Purchased services	Tuition to out-of-state schools	Supplies	Other	Total	Salaries	Employee benefits	Purchased services	Tuition to out-of-state schools	Supplies	Other
United States (a)	$266,576,498 (b)	$184,520,791	$53,200,984 (b)	$10,714,765 (b)	$3,327,600 (b)	$13,499,995	$1,312,362 (b)	$5,492 (c)	$3,801 (c)	$1,096 (c)	$221 (c)	$69 (c)	$278 (c)	$27 (c)
Alabama	3,093,754	2,110,482	626,905	107,053	1,814	232,840	14,659	4,231	2,886	857	146	2	318	20
Alaska	846,109	554,128	163,047	56,562	0	50,109	22,263	6,317	4,137	1,217	422	0	374	166
Arizona	3,786,162	2,980,667	553,242	76,303	9,890	145,289	20,772	3,741	2,945	547	75	10	144	21
Arkansas	2,049,358	1,444,135	324,180	75,982	3,217	180,396	21,448	4,509	3,177	713	167	7	397	47
California	33,032,977	22,578,345	6,397,570	1,568,830	660,685	1,823,294	4,252	5,150 (c)	3,520 (c)	997 (c)	245 (c)	103 (c)	284 (c)	1 (c)
Colorado	3,527,790	2,568,418	509,262	100,771	45,355	250,019	53,965	4,656	3,390	672	133	60	330	71
Connecticut	4,431,057	3,017,573	853,462	158,206	261,717	133,055	7,043	7,677	5,228	1,479	274	453	231	12
Delaware	750,356	499,782	183,399	16,463	7,481	34,121	9,110	6,377	4,247	1,559	140	64	290	77
Florida	11,489,958	7,513,716	2,051,654	1,168,993	431	624,420	130,744	4,440	2,904	793	452	...	241	51
Georgia	8,116,312	5,842,313	1,644,610	182,669	3,528	419,078	24,115	5,331	3,837	1,080	120	2	275	16
Hawaii	1,027,246	681,295	195,594	72,203	2,708	62,441	13,004	5,595	3,711	1,065	393	15	340	71
Idaho	1,023,724	709,237	218,644	39,191	725	55,621	307	4,060	2,813	867	155	3	221	1
Illinois	11,549,751	8,134,268	2,371,823	360,078	199,567	466,868	17,149	5,497	3,872	1,129	171	95	222	8
Indiana	5,442,449	3,469,420	1,645,725	107,329	11	184,735	35,229	5,383	3,431	1,628	106	...	183	35
Iowa	2,420,430	1,717,875	501,584	78,444	19,768	98,766	3,992	5,030	3,570	1,042	163	41	205	8
Kansas	2,340,006	1,705,486	380,069	91,541	1,339	140,988	20,583	4,974	3,625	808	195	3	300	44
Kentucky	2,988,552	2,207,577	579,012(b)	67,068	492	118,652	15,751	4,505	3,328	873	101	1	179	24
Louisiana	3,448,897	2,430,433	720,179	63,522	1,684	198,907	34,172	4,739	3,340	990	87	2	273	47
Maine	1,383,484	877,547	328,978	58,416	67,920	43,600	7,023	6,846	4,342	1,628	289	336	216	35
Maryland	5,679,936	3,861,165	1,262,825	117,469	217,898	204,846	15,734	6,535	4,443	1,453	135	251	236	18
Massachusetts	7,492,665	5,098,939	1,811,363	41,751	335,783	187,652	17,177	7,642	5,201	1,847	43	342	191	18
Michigan	9,879,021	6,443,458	2,552,649	466,842	100	381,779	34,193	5,621	3,666	1,452	266	...	217	19
Minnesota	4,934,203	3,454,713	969,529	256,227	39,199	196,212	18,322	5,854	4,099	1,150	304	47	233	22
Mississippi	1,978,551	1,398,596	362,920	67,468	4,230	136,247	9,090	4,009	2,834	735	137	9	276	18
Missouri	4,451,064 (c)	3,190,847	713,221	165,094 (b)	13,780 (b)	340,536	27,586 (b)	4,913	3,522	787	182	15	376	30
Montana	754,745	516,130	141,380	30,635	659	63,756	2,185	5,087	3,479	953	206	4	430	15
Nebraska	1,622,253	1,159,998	304,822	64,683	14,733	63,247	14,769	5,681	4,062	1,068	227	52	221	52
Nevada	1,641,258	1,066,784	351,116	37,820	245	113,281	72,012	4,259	2,768	911	98	1	294	187
New Hampshire	1,292,293	839,733	263,182	42,426	98,549	45,088	3,315	6,230	4,049	1,269	205	475	217	16
New Jersey	11,527,074	7,666,256	2,463,711	314,806	504,711	452,641	124,948	8,348	5,552	1,784	228	366	328	90
New Mexico	1,488,498	1,013,109	279,413	71,856	0	116,013	8,107	4,607	3,136	865	222	0	359	25
New York	25,762,894	17,563,521	5,847,903	1,238,231	215,980	893,490	3,769	8,993	6,131	2,041	432	75	312	1
North Carolina	6,003,774	4,552,085	945,950	161,813	0	336,641	7,284	4,414	3,347	695	119	0	247	5
North Dakota	468,795	336,311	89,448	14,744	2,390	24,004	1,898	4,586	3,290	875	144	23	235	19
Ohio	10,602,966	7,203,172	2,243,708	429,729	117,953	460,919	147,484	5,746	3,903	1,216	233	64	250	80
Oklahoma	2,329,604	1,680,046	402,144	48,469	0	187,078	11,866	3,720	2,683	642	77	0	299	19
Oregon	2,656,476	1,666,566	674,633	134,964	20,010	154,303	6,001	4,819	3,023	1,224	245	36	280	11
Pennsylvania	11,574,018	7,825,399	2,366,172	688,953	179,059	494,935	19,500	6,355	4,297	1,299	378	98	272	11
Rhode Island	1,216,956	812,062	286,906	19,367	62,348	32,194	4,079	7,636	5,095	1,800	122	391	202	26
South Carolina	3,308,438	2,313,170	638,751	123,314	236	206,220	26,748	4,732	3,308	914	176	...	295	38

See footnotes at end of table.

INSTRUCTION-RELATED EXPENDITURES FOR PUBLIC ELEMENTARY AND SECONDARY SCHOOL DISTRICTS—Continued

State or other jurisdiction	Current instruction and instruction-related expenditures (in thousands of dollars)							Current instruction and instruction-related expenditures per pupil						
	Total (a)	Salaries	Employee benefits	Purchased services	Tuition to out-of-state schools	Supplies	Other	Total	Salaries	Employee benefits	Purchased services	Tuition to out-of-state schools	Supplies	Other
South Dakota	560,598	380,666	100,760	29,417	5,947	41,896	1,911	4,466	3,032	803	234	47	334	15
Tennessee	4,206,901 (b)	2,967,778	692,054	107,550	183 (b)	422,404	16,931	4,491(c)	3,168 (c)	739 (c)	115 (c)	...	451 (c)	18 (c)
Texas	20,391,015	15,353,709	2,409,921	807,153	42,427	1,591,942	185,862	4,707	3,544	556	186	10	368	43
Utah	1,692,928	1,135,209	421,953	38,277	403	91,146	5,939	3,413	2,289	851	77	1	184	12
Vermont	752,475	472,475	151,136	46,273	56,043	24,626	1,922	7,593	4.768	1,525	467	565	248	19
Virginia	6,619,958	4,817,847	1,248,276	184,024	2,572	363,358	3,881	5,553	4,042	1,047	154	2	305	3
Washington	4,846,128 (b)	3,521,830	805,642	253,613	8,784 (b)	222,433	33,827	4,745	3,448	789	248	9	218	33
West Virginia	1,553,850	988,911	473,477	34,038	348	56,834	241	5,525	3,517	1,684	121	1	202	1
Wisconsin	5,396,077	3,446,113	1,518,705	130,633	67,477	214,923	18,226	6,132	3,916	1,726	148	77	244	21
Wyoming	524,810	349,217	114,908	27,569	495	31,709	912	6,000	3,993	1,314	315	6	363	10
Dist. of Columbia	617,902 (b)	382,279	43,464	69,931(b)	26,722	84,443	11,064 (b)	7,916	4,897	557	896	342	1,082	142
American Samoa	32,166	18,454	3,568	5,861	0	2,689	1,595	2,024	1,161	224	369	0	169	100
Guam	108,122	81,316	19,750	383	0	5,618	1,054	3,425	2,576	626	12	0	178	33
No. Mariana Islands	41,078	30,220	8,085	2,224	0	542	6	3,653	2,688	719	198	0	48	1
Puerto Rico	1,827,728	1,426,129	221,515	66,125	0	47,903	66,056	3,125	2,438	379	113	0	82	113
U.S. Virgin Islands	87,958	68,722	17,521	225	0	1,416	74	4,965	3,879	989	13	0	80	4

Source: Sable, J. and Hill, J. (2006). Overview of Public Elementary and Secondary Students, Staff, Schools, School Districts, Revenues and Expenditures: School Year 2004-05 and Fiscal Year 2004 (NCES 2007-309). U.S. Department of Education, Washington, DC: National Center for Education Statistics.

Note: Detail may not sum to totals due to rounding.

Key:
... — Rounds to zero
(a) U.S. totals include the 50 states and the District of Columbia.
(b) Value affected by redistribution of reported values to correct for missing data items.
(c) Prekindergarten students were imputed, affecting total student count and per pupil expenditure calculation.

Table 9.8
AVERAGE UNDERGRADUATE TUITION AND FEES AND ROOM AND BOARD RATES IN INSTITUTIONS OF HIGHER EDUCATION, BY CONTROL OF INSTITUTION AND STATE: 2003–2004 AND 2004–2005

State or other jurisdiction	Public 4-year 2003–2004		Public 4-year 2004–2005 (a)				Private 4-year 2003–2004		Private 4-year 2004–2005 (a)				Public 2-year tuition only (in-state)	
	Total	Tuition (in-state)	Total	Tuition (in-state)	Room	Board	Total	Tuition	Total	Tuition	Room	Board	2003–2004	2004–2005 (a)
United States	$10,674	$4,587	$11,441	$5,038	$3,418	$2,985	$25,083	$17,777	$26,489	$18,838	$4,166	$3,485	$1,702	$1,847
Eastern Region														
Connecticut	12,790	5,777	13,824	6,385	3,948	3,491	32,326	23,434	33,965	24,664	5,132	4,169	2,307	2,404
Delaware	12,502	6,183	13,353	6,671	3,765	2,917	16,294	9,680	17,368	10,458	3,499	3,411	1,992	2,088
Maine	10,994	5,001	11,826	5,565	3,186	3,075	26,813	19,627	28,371	20,711	3,779	3,881	2,781	2,802
Massachusetts	12,245	6,069	13,687	7,010	3,868	2,809	33,652	24,524	35,470	25,935	5,404	4,131	2,723	2,844
New Hampshire	13,843	7,615	14,651	8,086	3,998	2,567	28,320	20,499	29,728	21,452	4,796	3,480	4,821	5,338
New Jersey	15,088	7,255	16,349	7,989	5,286	3,073	28,210	19,710	29,751	20,910	4,750	4,092	2,443	2,569
New York	12,004	4,884	12,441	4,922	4,280	3,238	29,375	20,522	30,907	21,632	5,373	3,902	2,951	3,074
Pennsylvania	13,734	7,615	14,771	8,347	3,601	2,823	28,930	21,098	30,637	22,306	4,418	3,913	2,512	2,751
Rhode Island	12,767	5,391	13,541	5,866	4,112	3,563	29,295	21,110	30,907	22,394	4,663	3,850	2,120	2,310
Vermont	14,769	8,263	15,658	8,771	4,393	2,495	25,517	18,166	27,261	19,838	3,947	3,476	3,604	3,796
Regional average	13,074	6,405	14,010	6,961	4,044	3,005	27,873	19,437	29,437	21,030	4,576	3,831	2,825	2,998
Midwestern Region														
Illinois	11,795	5,642	12,803	6,497	3,152	3,154	25,543	18,049	26,966	18,996	4,743	3,226	1,782	1,952
Indiana	11,619	5,370	12,240	5,666	3,085	3,489	25,116	18,871	26,490	20,112	3,274	3,104	2,468	2,599
Iowa	10,876	4,991	11,541	5,407	3,017	3,118	21,774	16,394	23,012	17,339	2,658	3,015	2,688	2,876
Kansas	8,587	3,674	9,397	4,181	2,536	2,680	18,632	13,438	19,736	14,260	2,496	2,979	1,793	1,882
Michigan	12,187	5,994	12,658	6,189	3,268	3,202	18,147	12,434	19,286	13,253	3,066	2,967	1,865	1,936
Minnesota	10,826	5,728	11,958	6,478	3,054	2,426	24,498	18,559	25,946	19,510	3,433	3,003	3,416	3,839
Nebraska	9,611	4,238	10,704	4,679	2,889	3,137	19,000	13,750	19,725	14,412	2,778	2,535	1,673	1,772
North Dakota	8,035	3,837	9,011	4,549	1,803	2,659	13,511	9,501	12,525	8,571	1,647	2,306	2,421	2,850
Ohio	13,346	6,589	15,256	8,041	4,092	3,123	24,279	17,901	25,594	18,941	3,368	3,285	2,823	2,999
South Dakota	8,406	4,453	8,944	4,720	1,872	2,352	17,097	12,440	18,076	13,161	2,344	2,571	2,798	2,840
Wisconsin	9,061	4,676	9,872	5,290	2,688	1,894	23,318	17,386	24,574	18,380	3,148	3,046	2,589	2,796
Regional average	10,395	5,017	11,308	5,609	2,860	2,839	21,000	15,338	21,994	16,085	2,996	2,912	2,392	2,576
Southern Region														
Alabama	8,962	3,970	9,819	4,377	2,574	2,868	16,557	11,056	17,520	11,671	2,906	2,943	2,479	2,735
Arkansas	8,337	4,006	8,734	4,297	2,321	2,116	15,956	11,041	17,040	11,811	2,537	2,692	1,659	1,700
Florida	8,956	2,534	9,335	2,633	3,775	2,927	22,800	15,845	23,793	16,599	3,814	3,380	1,639	1,745
Georgia	9,052	3,192	9,439	3,392	3,629	2,418	23,241	16,090	24,734	17,146	4,313	3,275	1,421	1,470
Kentucky	8,515	3,859	9,400	4,502	2,703	2,195	18,197	12,684	19,262	13,577	2,790	2,895	2,266	2,562
Louisiana	7,460	3,185	7,973	3,526	2,355	2,093	25,543	18,262	26,583	19,312	4,144	3,126	1,228	1,429
Maryland	13,407	6,224	14,108	6,632	4,180	3,296	28,784	21,006	30,515	22,284	4,831	3,400	2,595	2,837
Mississippi	8,535	3,750	9,019	3,986	2,458	2,575	15,811	10,993	16,460	11,442	2,574	2,444	1,390	1,510
Missouri	10,355	5,396	11,356	5,833	3,196	2,327	20,462	14,322	21,431	15,045	3,281	3,105	1,941	2,128
North Carolina	8,780	3,239	9,450	3,563	3,190	2,697	23,186	16,982	24,600	18,139	3,248	3,214	1,166	1,248
Oklahoma	7,907	3,201	8,451	3,507	2,455	2,489	17,379	11,848	19,168	13,446	2,742	2,980	1,648	1,719
South Carolina	12,668	7,442	12,165	6,749	3,156	2,261	20,133	14,569	21,237	15,426	2,915	2,896	2,633	2,816
Tennessee	8,934	4,039	9,445	4,258	2,606	2,581	21,025	15,074	22,035	15,873	3,314	2,848	2,076	2,209
Texas	9,180	3,559	10,233	4,423	3,164	2,647	20,855	14,798	22,218	15,929	3,308	2,981	1,166	1,228
Virginia	10,903	5,068	11,616	5,556	3,243	2,817	22,248	16,162	23,277	17,010	3,165	3,101	1,802	1,929
West Virginia	8,764	3,170	9,450	3,572	3,003	2,876	18,373	12,685	19,067	13,284	2,823	2,960	2,920	3,105
Regional average	9,420	4,115	10,000	4,425	3,001	2,574	20,659	14,589	21,809	15,500	3,294	3,015	1,877	2,023

See footnotes at end of table.

AVERAGE UNDERGRADUATE TUITION AND FEES AND ROOM AND BOARD RATES IN INSTITUTIONS OF HIGHER EDUCATION, BY CONTROL OF INSTITUTION AND STATE: 2003–2004 AND 2004–2005 — Continued

State or other jurisdiction	Public 4-year 2003–2004		Public 4-year 2004–2005 (a)				Private 4-year 2003–2004		Private 4-year 2004–2005 (a)				Public 2-year tuition only (in-state)	
	Total	Tuition (in-state)	Total	Tuition (in-state)	Room	Board	Total	Tuition	Total	Tuition	Room	Board	2003–2004	2004–2005 (a)
Western Region														
Alaska	10,132	3,430	9,936	3,782	3,332	2,822	17,958	11,877	21,423	14,093	3,002	4,328	1,790	1,945
Arizona	10,149	3,587	10,863	4,076	3,854	2,934	19,147	12,466	19,448	13,197	2,922	3,329	1,141	1,226
California	12,288	3,800	13,356	4,323	4,578	4,456	28,337	19,749	30,186	21,046	5,082	4,058	486	721
Colorado	9,763	3,451	10,243	3,518	3,184	3,541	26,030	17,472	27,361	18,583	4,670	4,108	1,796	1,850
Hawaii	8,747	3,235	9,131	3,347	3,130	2,653	17,922	9,196	17,866	9,585	3,813	4,468	1,119	1,175
Idaho	8,082	3,321	9,066	3,589	2,459	3,018	10,905	5,155	11,388	5,502	2,315	3,571	1,657	1,817
Montana	9,347	4,155	9,867	4,511	2,437	2,920	16,740	11,458	17,918	12,172	2,688	3,058	2,569	2,558
Nevada	10,310	2,720	10,464	2,477	4,622	3,365	18,840	11,428	20,594	11,928	4,977	3,689	1,509	1,496
New Mexico	8,255	3,164	8,675	3,395	2,539	2,741	18,237	12,138	19,304	13,034	3,161	3,109	1,002	1,072
Oregon	11,632	4,667	12,177	5,151	3,469	3,556	26,059	19,531	27,493	20,593	3,493	3,407	2,427	2,558
Utah	7,878	2,896	8,348	3,177	2,134	3,036	10,069	4,537	10,521	4,767	2,864	2,889	1,954	2,089
Washington	11,335	4,626	11,902	4,926	3,334	3,642	24,671	17,983	26,021	19,031	3,746	3,245	2,228	2,390
Wyoming	8,485	3,090	8,514	2,721	2,590	3,203	…	…	…	…	…	…	1,614	1,680
Regional average	9,723	3,549	10,196	3,769	3,205	3,222	19,576	12,749	20,794	13,628	3,561	3,605	1,638	1,737
Regional average without California	9,510	3,529	9,932	3,723	3,090	3,119	18,780	12,113	19,940	12,953	3,423	3,564	1,734	1,821
Dist. of Columbia	…	2,070	…	2,070	3,090	…	29,236	20,312	31,594	22,240	6,020	3,334	…	…

Source: U.S. Department of Education, National Center for Education Statistics, 2003–2004 and 2004–2005; Integrated Postsecondary Education Data System (IPEDS), Fall 2003, Fall 2004 and Spring 2004. (This table was prepared August 2005.)

Note: Data are for the entire academic year and are average charges. Tuition and fees were weighted by the number of full-time equivalent undergraduates in 2003, but are not adjusted to reflect student residency. Room and board are based on full-time students. Some data revised from previously published figures. Detail may not sum to totals due to rounding.

Key:
… — Not applicable.
(a) Preliminary data based on fall 2003 enrollments.

Table 9.9
DEGREE GRANTING INSTITUTIONS AND BRANCHES, BY TYPE AND CONTROL OF INSTITUTION, 2004–2005

State or other jurisdiction	Total	All public institutions	Public 4-year					Public 2-year	All private institutions	Private 4-year					Private 2-year
			Total	Doctoral (a)	Master's (b)	Baccalaureate (c)	Other (d)			Total	Doctoral (a)	Master's (b)	Baccalaureate (c)	Other (d)	
United States	4,216	1,700	639	165	280	103	91	1,061	2,516	1,894	94	362	532	906	622
Eastern Region															
Connecticut...........	45	22	10	1	7	1	1	12	23	20	4	5	4	7	3
Delaware..............	10	5	2	1	1	0	0	3	5	4	1	0	1	2	1
Maine.................	30	15	8	1	1	5	1	7	15	12	0	3	5	4	3
Massachusetts.........	122	31	15	3	7	1	4	16	91	82	9	15	21	37	9
New Hampshire........	26	9	5	1	2	2	0	4	17	15	2	2	5	6	2
New Jersey	59	33	14	3	8	2	1	19	26	24	3	6	6	9	2
New York.............	307	78	43	6	20	7	10	35	229	177	16	32	34	95	52
Pennsylvania..........	260	65	44	4	17	20	3	21	195	105	6	28	34	37	90
Rhode Island..........	14	3	2	1	1	0	0	1	11	10	1	4	1	4	1
Vermont..............	25	6	5	1	2	1	1	1	19	17	0	6	7	4	2
Regional total	898	267	148	22	66	39	21	119	631	466	42	101	118	205	165
Midwestern Region															
Illinois...............	172	60	12	5	7	0	0	48	112	100	6	15	20	59	12
Indiana...............	99	29	14	5	6	3	0	15	70	47	1	8	20	18	23
Iowa.................	64	19	3	2	1	0	0	16	45	42	0	4	22	16	3
Kansas...............	63	36	9	3	4	0	2	27	27	23	0	8	10	5	4
Michigan..............	105	45	15	3	8	2	0	30	60	55	1	9	17	28	5
Minnesota............	105	42	12	7	7	3	1	30	63	52	3	6	13	30	11
Nebraska..............	39	15	7	1	5	0	1	8	24	20	0	4	8	8	4
North Dakota..........	21	14	7	2	1	0	1	7	5	5	0	1	1	3	2
Ohio..................	194	61	27	10	1	6	10	34	133	77	3	15	25	34	56
South Dakota..........	26	14	9	2	2	2	3	5	12	11	0	2	5	4	1
Wisconsin.............	67	31	13	2	11	0	0	18	36	34	1	8	10	15	2
Regional total	955	366	128	40	53	17	18	238	589	466	15	50	151	220	123
Southern Region															
Alabama..............	69	42	16	6	9	1	0	26	27	23	0	4	9	10	4
Arkansas..............	47	33	11	2	5	2	2	22	14	12	0	1	8	3	2
Florida...............	163	40	16	6	4	1	5	24	123	91	4	20	24	43	32
Georgia...............	128	74	21	3	13	1	4	53	54	44	0	4	15	23	10
Kentucky.............	76	31	8	2	6	0	0	23	45	30	2	4	16	10	15
Louisiana.............	90	59	17	4	9	0	4	42	31	13	0	4	3	5	18
Maryland.............	57	30	13	3	9	1	0	17	27	23	1	5	6	11	4
Mississippi............	40	25	9	4	3	1	1	16	15	11	0	2	5	4	4
Missouri..............	125	33	13	4	6	2	1	20	92	70	2	12	14	42	22
North Carolina........	127	75	16	4	8	3	1	59	52	46	2	7	25	12	6
Oklahoma............	54	29	16	2	7	3	4	13	25	19	1	5	7	6	6
South Carolina........	63	33	13	3	5	3	2	20	30	25	0	3	15	7	5
Tennessee............	97	22	9	5	4	0	0	13	75	55	1	11	16	27	20
Texas.................	208	109	42	12	20	2	8	67	99	62	4	14	20	24	37
Virginia..............	99	39	15	6	6	3	0	24	60	49	0	8	18	23	11
West Virginia.........	43	21	12	1	1	9	1	9	22	10	0	2	7	1	12
Regional total	1,486	695	247	67	115	32	33	448	791	583	18	106	208	251	208

See footnotes at end of table.

DEGREE GRANTING INSTITUTIONS AND BRANCHES, BY TYPE AND CONTROL OF INSTITUTION, 2004–2005—Continued

State or other jurisdiction	Total	All public institutions	Public 4-year					Public 2-year	All private institutions	Private 4-year					Private 2-year
			Total	Doctoral (a)	Master's (b)	Baccalaureate (c)	Other (d)			Total	Doctoral (a)	Master's (b)	Baccalaureate (c)	Other (d)	
Western Region															
Alaska	8	5	3	1	2	0	0	2	3	3	0	1	1	1	0
Arizona	77	25	5	3	1	0	1	20	52	31	1	6	1	23	21
California	399	144	34	10	20	2	2	110	255	192	11	30	25	126	63
Colorado	77	28	13	4	3	4	2	15	49	32	1	6	3	22	17
Hawaii	20	10	3	1	0	2	0	7	10	8	0	3	1	4	2
Idaho	14	7	4	2	1	1	0	3	7	6	0	1	1	4	1
Montana	23	18	6	2	2	1	1	12	5	4	0	1	2	1	1
Nevada	20	7	5	3	0	0	2	2	13	6	0	1	2	3	7
New Mexico	43	28	8	3	3	1	1	20	15	13	0	3	2	8	2
Oregon	59	26	9	3	3	1	2	17	33	30	0	6	9	15	3
Utah	27	13	7	2	2	2	1	6	14	9	1	2	3	3	5
Washington	81	46	11	2	8	1	0	35	35	32	0	11	4	17	3
Wyoming	9	8	1	1	0	0	0	7	1	0	0	0	0	0	1
Regional total	857	365	109	36	45	15	13	256	492	366	14	71	54	227	126
Regional total without California	458	221	75	26	25	13	11	146	237	174	3	41	29	101	63
Dist. of Columbia	15	2	2	0	1	0	1	0	13	13	5	4	1	3	0
U.S. Service Schools	5	5	5	0	0	0	5	0	0	0	0	0	0	0	0
American Samoa	1	1	0	0	0	0	0	1	0	0	0	0	0	0	0
Fed. States of Micronesia	4	4	0	0	0	0	0	4	0	0	0	0	0	0	0
Guam	3	2	1	0	1	0	0	1	1	1	0	0	0	1	0
Marshall Islands	1	1	0	0	0	0	0	1	0	0	0	0	0	0	0
No. Mariana Islands	1	1	0	0	0	0	0	1	0	0	0	0	0	0	0
Palau	1	1	0	0	0	0	0	1	0	0	0	0	0	0	0
Puerto Rico	77	17	14	1	1	7	5	3	60	43	0	7	19	17	17
Virgin Islands	2	2	2	0	0	2	0	0	0	0	0	0	0	0	0

Source: U.S. Department of Education, National Center for Education Statistics, 2004–05 Integrated Post-secondary Education Data System (IPEDS), Fall 2004. (This table was prepared August 2005.)

Note: New institutions which do not have sufficient data to report by detailed level are included under "Other" 4-year or 2-year depending on the level reported by the institution.

Key:

(a) Doctoral, extensive institutions are committed to graduate education through the doctorate, and award 50 or more doctor's degrees per year across at least 15 disciplines. Doctoral, intensive institutions are committed to education through the doctorate and award at least 10 doctor's degrees per year across 3 or more disciplines or at least 20 doctor's degrees overall.

(b) Master's institutions offer a full range of baccalaureate programs and are committed to education through the master's degree. They award at least 20 master's degrees per year.

(c) Baccalaureate institutions primarily emphasize undergraduate education.

(d) Other specialized 4-year institutions award degrees primarily in single fields of study, such as medicine, business, fine arts, theology and engineering. Includes some institutions which have 4-year programs, but have not reported sufficient data to identify program category. Also, includes institutions classified as 4-year under the IPEDS system, which had been classified as 2-year in the Carnegie classification system because they primarily award associate's degrees.

Emerging Legislative Approaches to Cancer Prevention

By Martha M. McKinney

Empirical studies provide strong evidence that most of the U.S. cancer burden can be attributed to tobacco use, physical inactivity, overweight and obesity, and failure to get screened for cancer at recommended intervals. This review of state legislation enacted between 2005 and 2006 suggests that legislators are becoming increasingly aware of the importance of policy interventions to reduce cancer risk.

In 2007, the American Cancer Society estimates that more than half a million Americans will die of cancer.[1] Tragically, 50 percent to 75 percent of these deaths could have been prevented through improved health behaviors and cancer screening practices.[2] Empirical studies provide strong evidence that most of the U.S. cancer burden can be attributed to tobacco use, physical inactivity, overweight and obesity, and failure to get screened for cancer at recommended intervals.[3] Because so many cancers are preventable, accelerated cancer prevention and early detection efforts could greatly reduce cancer incidence and mortality.[4]

Over the past decade, states have enacted numerous bills designed to promote healthier lifestyles. To identify new legislative initiatives as well as areas of continuing interest, this author researched 2005–2006 cancer prevention legislation in the Centers

Table A: Tobacco Use Prevention—Legislation Enacted 2005–2006

State or other jurisdiction	Clean indoor air	Excise taxes	Non-smoking incentives	Smokers' rights	Smoking cessation programs
Arizona	Prop 201[1]	Prop 201[1]	. . .	. . .	. . .
Arkansas	HB 1193; SB 19	. . .	. . .	. . .	. . .
Colorado	HB 1175	HB 1262	. . .	. . .	. . .
Florida	HB 317	. . .	SB 1324	. . .	. . .
Georgia	SB 90	. . .	. . .	. . .	. . .
Hawaii	SB 3262	SB 2961	. . .	. . .	. . .
Idaho	. . .	. . .	. . .	SB 1023	. . .
Illinois	HB 672; SB 2400	. . .	. . .	. . .	. . .
Indiana	. . .	. . .	. . .	. . .	HB 1314
Iowa	. . .	. . .	. . .	. . .	HB 841
Kentucky	HB 55	HB 272; 267; 403	. . .	. . .	HB 92
Louisiana	SB 742	. . .	. . .	. . .	. . .
Maine	SB 294	HB 1199	. . .	HB 1342	. . .
Massachusetts	. . .	. . .	HB 4850	. . .	HB 4479; 4850
Minnesota	HB 2480	HB 139	. . .	. . .	. . .
Mississippi	HB 123	. . .	. . .	. . .	. . .
Missouri	. . .	. . .	HB 596; SB 587	. . .	. . .
Montana	HB 643	. . .	. . .	. . .	. . .
Nevada	Question 5[2]	. . .	. . .	. . .	. . .
New Hampshire	. . .	HB 2	. . .	. . .	. . .
New Jersey	SB 1926	HB 4705	. . .	. . .	. . .
North Carolina	SB 1130; 1133	SB 622	. . .	SB 482	SB 1130
North Dakota	SB 2300	. . .	. . .	. . .	. . .
Ohio	Issue 5[3]	HB 66	. . .	. . .	. . .
Rhode Island	HB 6332	HB 7120	. . .	. . .	. . .
Tennessee	SB 3368	. . .	. . .	. . .	. . .
Texas	. . .	HB 5	. . .	. . .	. . .
Utah	SB 19	. . .	. . .	. . .	. . .
Vermont	HB 241	HB 843; 861	HB 861	. . .	. . .
Virginia	. . .	. . .	. . .	HB 2866	. . .
Washington	Initiative 901[4]	HB 2314; SB 6097	. . .	. . .	. . .
District of Columbia	LB 16-293	LB 16-117	. . .	. . .	. . .
Puerto Rico	PC 2073	. . .	. . .	. . .	. . .

Source: The Council of State Governments, December 2006
Key:
[1]Smoke-Free Arizona Act approved by voters on 11/7/06.
[2]Nevada Clean Indoor Act approved by voters on 11/7/06.
[3]Smokefree Workplace Act approved by voters on 11/7/06.
[4]Approved by voters on 11/8/05.

Table B: Youth Exposure and Access to Tobacco — Legislation Enacted 2005

State or other jurisdiction	Clean indoor air	School grant projects	Tobacco access by minors	Anti-tobacco education
Alabama	...	...	HB 781	...
Arkansas	HB 1046	...	...	...
Colorado	HB 1175	...	...	...
Florida	...	...	...	SB 772
Illinois	SB 2465	...	...	...
Kentucky	HB 55	...	HB 92	...
Louisiana	HB 1010	...	...	...
Maine	HB 799	...	HB 408; SB 293	...
Michigan	...	...	HB 5396	...
Mississippi	HB 123	...	...	SB 2602
Missouri	...	HB 568	...	...
Montana	HB 643	...	...	...
Nevada	HB 118; Q.5¹	...	...	...
New Jersey	HB 3659; SB 1926	...	SB 2783	...
North Carolina	HB 448	...	...	...
Rhode Island	...	...	SB 109; 585	...
South Carolina	...	...	SB 384	...
Utah	SB 19	...	...	HCR 3
Vermont	...	...	...	HB 862
Washington	...	...	SB 5048	...
Wisconsin	HB 443	...	...	...
Puerto Rico	PC 2073	...	...	...

Source: The Council of State Governments, December 2006
Key:
¹Nevada Clean Indoor Act approved by voters on 11/7/06.

for Disease Control and Prevention's Nutrition and Physical Activity Legislative Database (*http://apps. nccd.cdc.gov/DNPALeg/index.asp*), the National Cancer Institute's State Cancer Legislative Database (*http://www.scld-nci.net*), The Council of State Governments' Healthy States public health legislation database (*http://www.healthystates.csg.org*) and state legislation databases maintained by cancer advocacy organizations. Each enacted bill was reviewed to clarify the focus and key provisions.

Tobacco Use Legislation

Tobacco use is the single largest preventable cause of cancer. Each year, tobacco use accounts for an estimated 438,000 premature deaths among smokers, 38,000 deaths among nonsmokers exposed to secondhand smoke and $167 billion in health care expenditures and productivity losses.[5] In addition to causing most lung cancers, tobacco use increases the risk for cancer of the mouth, nasal cavities, larynx, pharynx, esophagus, stomach, liver, pancreas, kidney, bladder and uterine cervix.

Tobacco Use Legislation—General Population

Between 2005 and 2006, 19 states, the District of Columbia and Puerto Rico enacted legislation expanding the sites covered by state smoking restrictions, strengthening smoking prohibition enforcement

and/or allowing local governments to adopt stricter regulations (Table A). Voters in four additional states (Arizona, Ohio, Nevada and Washington) approved ballot measures prohibiting smoking in almost all public places and workplaces. In contrast to these efforts, three states (Idaho, Maine and North Carolina) passed laws relaxing smoking restrictions for certain facilities. Virginia prohibited postsecondary educational institutions from requiring current or prospective employees to abstain from tobacco use outside the workplace.

Various studies indicate that increases in tobacco excise taxes reduce smoking rates, particularly among children.[6] Fourteen states and the District of Columbia increased excise taxes on tobacco products between 2005 and 2006. Four states encouraged nonsmoking by including smoking cessation programs in health benefit plans, establishing smoking cessation programs or authorizing health insurance premium discounts for nonsmokers and people participating in smoking cessation programs. Five states authorized tobacco use studies or smoking cessation services for special populations.

Tobacco Legislation – Youth Exposure and Access

Thirteen states and Puerto Rico enacted bills mandating smokefree environments in day care facilities and/or other sites where youth might be exposed to environmental tobacco smoke (Table B). Eight states tightened restrictions on the sale and distribution of tobacco products to minors and/or increased penalties for tobacco possession by minors. Three states enacted bills or resolutions providing for school-based tobacco use prevention education, and one state funded a school-based tobacco prevention initiative. Vermont exempted home-schooled students ages 13 and older from studying the health effects of tobacco use.

Obesity Prevention Legislation

Next to tobacco avoidance, the behaviors most likely to reduce cancer risk include maintaining a healthy weight and exercising regularly. In the United States, obesity and physical inactivity account for 25 percent to 30 percent of some of the most common cancers, including breast, colon, endometrial, esophageal and kidney cancers.[7] Each year, about 14 percent of men and 20 percent of women die from cancers related to obesity.[8]

Almost one-third of U.S. adults are classified as obese.[9] As compared to 1995 when obesity prevalence in each state was less than 20 percent, 17 states now have obesity prevalence rates equal to or greater than 25 percent.[10] Obesity rates among children and teenagers have tripled since the 1960s and now exceed 17 percent for both groups.[11] Because overweight children tend to become overweight adults, this trend suggests that future adult populations will be at increased risk for cancer and other chronic illnesses.

Obesity Prevention Initiatives—Schools

Most of the obesity prevention legislation enacted between 2005 and 2006 focused on public schools (Table C). Twenty-two states enacted bills or resolutions relating to school physical education. Thirteen of these states (Florida, Illinois, Indiana, Kentucky,

Maryland, Missouri, Oklahoma, Pennsylvania, South Carolina, Tennessee, Texas, Virginia and West Virginia) required physical education for specified grade levels. Six additional states (Connecticut, Kansas, Louisiana, Montana, New York and Washington) authorized or encouraged school-based physical activity programs. Legislation in the remaining three states established task forces to recommend physical education policies (Arizona and Delaware), required student physical fitness assessments (Delaware) or exempted home-schooled students ages 13 and older from physical education requirements (Vermont).

Twenty-one states enacted legislation requiring nutritional standards for foods sold or distributed in schools and/or limiting the beverages and snack foods sold in school cafeterias and vending machines. To comply with the Child Nutrition and WIC Reauthorization Act of 2004, 13 states enacted bills requiring local school wellness policies. Nine states incorporated requirements for school nutrition education in these bills or in separate legislation.

Table C: Obesity Prevention (Schools) — Legislation Enacted 2005–2006

State	Nutrition education	Nutrition standards	Obesity screening	Physical activity	School wellness policies	Child wellness initiatives
Alabama	...	HR 818	...	...	...	...
Arizona	...	HB 2544	...	HB 2111	...	...
Arkansas	...	SB 965	...	...	...	...
California	HB 689	SB 12; 965	...	...	SB 567	SB 281
Colorado	SB 81	SB 81	...	...	SB 81	SB 127
Connecticut	...	SB 373	...	SB 204	...	...
Delaware	...	...	...	HCR 37; 372	...	SB 289
Florida	...	...	...	HB 7087; SB 772	SB 772	...
Illinois	HB 612	HB 612	...	HB 1540	SB 162	HB 612; 1541
Indiana	...	SB 111	...	SB 111	SB 111	...
Iowa	...	...	...	...	...	SB 2124; 2251
Kansas	...	SB 154	...	HR 6011-6	SB 154	SCR 1604
Kentucky	...	SB 172	...	SB 172	SB 172	...
Louisiana	...	SB 146	...	SB 146	...	...
Maine	SB 263	SB 263	...	...	...	SB 263
Maryland	...	SB 473	...	SB 473	...	...
Mississippi	SB 2602	SB 2602	...	...	HB 319	SB 2602
Missouri	...	...	HB 568	HCR 25	...	HB 568
Montana	...	...	...	HJR 17	...	...
Nevada	...	...	...	...	...	HB 231
New Hampshire	...	...	...	...	HB 151	...
New Mexico	...	HB 61	...	...	...	S.J.M. 2
New York	...	...	SB 3668	SB 3668	...	...
North Carolina	...	HB 855; SB 961	...	...	...	...
Oklahoma	...	SB 265	...	SB312	SB 1459	HB 2655
Pennsylvania	HB 185	...	...	HB 185	HB 185	HB 185
Rhode Island	...	HB 6968	...	...	HB 5563	...
South Carolina	HB 3499	HB 3499	...	HB 3499	HB 3499	HB 3499
Tennessee	...	...	HB 445	HB 3750	...	HJR 88; SB 2038
Texas	SB 42	SB 42	...	SB 42	...	SB 42
Vermont	...	...	...	HB 862	...	HB 456
Virginia	...	...	...	SB 1130	...	...
Washington	...	...	...	SB 5186	...	...
West Virginia	HB 2816	HB 2816	HB 2816; SB 785	HB 2816; SB 785	...	...

Source: The Council of State Governments, December 2006

Four states established obesity screening programs for children or required the collection of body mass index data to evaluate the effectiveness of school wellness programs. Seventeen states authorized child wellness initiatives, such as the development of school wellness curriculums (Mississippi, South Carolina, Tennessee, Texas), grants for youth obesity prevention programs (Iowa, Missouri) and farm-to-school programs (California, Colorado, Maine, Oklahoma, Vermont). Nevada addressed community design barriers to children's physical activity by requiring counties with 100,000 or more residents to study safe walking routes to schools.

Obesity Prevention Initiatives – General Population

Eight states enacted legislation relating to obesity prevention in the general population (Table D). Three of these states (Kentucky, Nevada, West Virginia) established state wellness programs or created new offices to coordinate wellness activities. Florida required state agencies to collaboratively develop obesity prevention strategies and included nutrition education, weight management and aerobic exercise in a schedule of minimum benefits for state employees participating in health maintenance organizations. Illinois and Maine established food policy councils to develop policies promoting balanced diets as well as food access and security. Vermont created a grant program to fund community health and wellness projects. Additional bills addressed community design issues, such as the adequacy of bicycle lanes and paths (Florida), opportunities to increase physical exercise through bicycling and walking (Kentucky) and pedestrian safety projects (Washington).

Breast Cancer Legislation

Excluding cancers of the skin, breast cancer is the most frequently diagnosed cancer among U.S. women. An estimated 178,480 women and 2,030 men will be diagnosed with breast cancer in 2007.[12] Breast cancer is the leading cause of death for U.S. women of Hispanic descent and the second leading cause of death for other U.S. women.

Numerous studies have shown that early detection of breast cancer saves lives and increases treatment options. Between 2005 and 2006, five states enacted bills to make breast cancer

screening programs more accessible to uninsured and underinsured low-income women (Table E). Two of these states—Pennsylvania and Washington—created new state-funded screening programs, and Texas established a five-year screening demonstration project.

Colorado appropriated a portion of the tax revenue from a voter-approved cigarette tax increase to expand breast and cervical cancer screening programs. Arizona, Georgia and Idaho authorized all or part of the revenues derived from breast cancer license plates to be used for breast cancer screening programs.

Six states enacted legislation requiring health insurance coverage of breast cancer screening. Oregon required health insurers to cover annual clinical breast examinations for women ages 18 and older. Idaho, Illinois, Minnesota and West Virginia required various health plans to cover mammograms.

Table D: Obesity Prevention (General) — Legislation Enacted 2005–2006

State	Community design projects	State wellness initiatives	Wellness health plan benefits
Florida	HB 1681	SB 1324	SB 1324
Illinois	. . .	HB 211	. . .
Kentucky	SCR 98	HB 646	. . .
Maine	. . .	HB 1497	. . .
Nevada	. . .	SB 197	. . .
Vermont	. . .	HB 881	. . .
Washington	SB 5186; 6241	. . .	. . .
West Virginia	. . .	HB 2816	. . .

Source: The Council of State Governments, December 2006

Table E: Breast Cancer Prevention — Legislation Enacted 2005–2006

State	Task forces & committees	Cosmetics safety	Designated screening funds	Screening programs	Screening coverage
Arizona	. . .	. . .	HB 2526	. . .	. . .
California	. . .	SB 484	. . .	. . .	. . .
Colorado	. . .	. . .	HB 1262	. . .	. . .
Connecticut	. . .	. . .	. . .	SB 317	SB 30; 422
Georgia	. . .	. . .	HB 1006	. . .	. . .
Idaho	. . .	. . .	HB 607	. . .	HB 825
Illinois	. . .	. . .	. . .	. . .	SB 12
Maryland	. . .	. . .	. . .	HB 1455	. . .
Minnesota	. . .	. . .	. . .	. . .	SB 3480
Oregon	. . .	. . .	. . .	. . .	HB 2498
Pennsylvania	. . .	. . .	. . .	HB 1606	. . .
Texas	. . .	. . .	. . .	SB 747	. . .
Washington	SB 5714	. . .	. . .	SB 5714	. . .
West Virginia	. . .	. . .	. . .	. . .	HB 4379

Source: The Council of State Governments, December 2006

Connecticut specified conditions under which health insurers must cover comprehensive ultrasound screening.

A California bill required cosmetics manufacturers to report product ingredients that studies have identified as carcinogens or reproductive toxins. Washington established a medical advisory committee to recommend breast and cervical cancer screening best practices.

Cervical Cancer Legislation

In 2007, an estimated 11,150 U.S. women will be diagnosed with cervical cancer, and 3,670 will die from this disease.[13] However, cervical cancer rates have decreased dramatically since the introduction of the Pap test in the 1950s. According to the American Social Health Association, virtually all cases of cervical cancer could be eliminated through regular Pap screening.

The most important risk factor for cervical cancer is infection with the human papillomavirus (HPV). Of the more than 100 types of HPV, types 16 and 18 account for about 70 percent of cervical cancers.[14] By performing an HPV test in conjunction with a Pap test, physicians can detect and treat early cell changes that may progress to cervical cancer. Because older women's immune systems are less likely to clear the HPV virus without treatment, the American College of Obstetricians and Gynecologists recommends that women ages 30 and older be offered an HPV test in addition to a Pap test and pelvic exam.

The U.S. Food and Drug Administration has given licensing approval to Gardasil,™ a vaccine shown to be nearly 100 percent effective in preventing pre-cancerous cervical changes caused by HPV 16 and 18. The CDC's Advisory Committee on Immunization Practices now recommends administering this vaccine to all girls ages 11–12 and as a "catch-up" for women ages 13–26. However, because the vaccine does not protect against all cancer-causing types of HPV, regular Pap tests are still required.

In January 2004, Women in Government, a bipartisan organization of women state legislators, launched a national campaign to eliminate cervical cancer. This campaign appears to have had a powerful effect on state legislation (Table F). Between 2005 and 2006, 10 states enacted bills creating cervical cancer

Table F: Cervical Cancer Prevention—Legislation Enacted 2005–2006

State	Prevention plan	Task force or advisory group	Screening financing	Screening programs	Screening coverage
Arizona	...	...	HB 2526	...	...
Arkansas	...	HB 2668	...	...	...
California	...	...	...	...	SB 1245
Colorado	...	...	HB 1262	...	...
Connecticut	...	...	...	SB 317	...
Georgia	...	SB 294	...	...	...
Maryland	...	...	...	HB 1455	SB 779
Minnesota	HB 139	...	...	...	SB 3480
Montana	...	SB 328	...	...	...
Nevada	...	SB 98	...	...	...
New Hampshire	...	HB 111	...	...	...
New Jersey	...	HB 4071	...	...	...
New Mexico	...	...	...	...	HB 477
New York	HB 8827	...	...	...	...
Pennsylvania	...	HB 801	...	HB 1606	...
Tennessee	...	SB 3678	...	...	...
Texas	HB 2475	...	...	SB 747	HB 1485
Vermont	...	HB 715	...	...	...
Washington	...	SB 5714	...	SB 5714	...
West Virginia	...	...	...	...	HB 3479

Source: The Council of State Governments, December 2006

advisory groups. Three additional states mandated the development of statewide cervical cancer prevention plans.

Five states enacted legislation expanding or strengthening cervical cancer screening programs for uninsured and underinsured low-income women. Six states enacted bills requiring health insurance coverage of cervical cancer screening. All of these states, except Minnesota, included HPV testing as a covered service.

Colorectal Cancer Legislation

Colorectal cancer is the third most common cancer among U.S. men and women. Although an estimated 112,340 cases of colon cancer and 41,420 cases of rectal cancer will be diagnosed in 2007, incidence rates have been declining since 1985.[15] Research-

Table G: Colorectal Cancer Prevention—Legislation Enacted 2005–2006

State	Prevention research	Public education	Screening programs	Screening coverage
Arkansas	HB 2781	...	HB 2323; 2781	HB 2781
Louisiana	...	...	...	HB 36
Minnesota	...	...	...	SB 3480
Oregon	...	...	...	SB 501

Source: The Council of State Governments, December 2006

Table H: Ovarian and Prostate Cancer Prevention— Legislation Enacted 2005–2006

State	Ovarian Cancer screening coverage	Prostate Cancer			
		Planning and research	Public education	Screening programs	Screening coverage
Arkansas	. . .	SB 14	. . .	. . .	. . .
Illinois	SB 521	. . .	. . .	. . .	. . .
Maryland	. . .	. . .	. . .	HB 1455	. . .
Minnesota	. . .	. . .	. . .	. . .	SB 3480
Oregon	. . .	. . .	. . .	. . .	SB 1026
Washington	. . .	SB 6197	SB 6188	. . .	SB 6188

Source: The Council of State Governments, December 2006

ers attribute this decline to increased screening and the removal of polyps that would have progressed to cancer.

The American Cancer Society recommends that people at average risk for colorectal cancer begin a screening regimen at age 50. Yet, almost 60 percent of Americans interviewed in a 2003 survey said they had not had a fecal occult blood test within the past year or a colorectal endoscopic procedure within the last five years.[16]

To address financial barriers to colorectal cancer screening, four states enacted bills requiring health insurance coverage of these screening tests (Table G). An additional Arkansas bill established a university-based colorectal cancer screening program.

Ovarian and Prostate Cancer Legislation

Ovarian cancer accounts for only 3 percent of all cancers among U.S. women but causes more deaths than any other cancer of the female reproductive system.[17] The screening tests developed to this point are not sensitive enough to detect ovarian cancer in women at average risk. However, for women at high risk of ovarian cancer, a thorough pelvic examination, transvaginal ultrasound and a blood test for the tumor marker CA-125 may help detect the disease. A 2005 Illinois bill required health benefit plans to cover these procedures for women who have a family history of ovarian, breast or nonpolyposis colorectal cancer or who have tested positive for certain cancer-related genes (Table H).

Prostate cancer is the most frequently diagnosed cancer among U.S. men and the second leading cause of male cancer-related deaths. In 2007, an estimated 218,890 American men will be diagnosed with prostate cancer, and 27,050 will die from this disease.[18] Although declining prostate cancer death rates sug-

gest a benefit from prostate cancer screening, researchers have not found sufficient evidence to recommend for or against the prostate-specific antigen blood test or the digital rectal examination.

Between 2005 and 2006, five states enacted legislation relating to prostate cancer prevention (Table H). These bills addressed prevention planning and research, prostate cancer awareness and guidelines for health insurance coverage of prostate cancer screening. A Maryland bill requiring cultural competency training for health professionals included increases in prostate cancer screening rates as an indicator of program effectiveness.

Skin Cancer Legislation

Each year, more than 1 million Americans develop basal cell or squamous cell cancers due to unprotected and excessive ultraviolet (UV) radiation exposure.[19] Sunburn during childhood and intense sun exposure increase the risk of skin cancers. The risk of skin cancer is particularly high for adolescents and young adults exposed to UV radiation in tanning beds.[20]

Between 2005 and 2006, five states enacted legislation relating to skin cancer prevention (Table I). New York required recreational and historic sites to provide information warning patrons of the dangers of sun overexposure. Arizona, Kentucky and Utah required or encouraged public schools to provide age-appropriate education on skin cancer prevention.

Three of the five states limited youth access to tanning facilities. New York established 18 as the minimum age for tanning facility use. New Jersey prohibited the use of tanning facilities by children younger than age 14 and required children ages 14–17 to have their parents' written authorization. Kentucky required children younger than 14 to be accompanied by a parent and children ages 14–18 to have their parents' written authorization.

Table I: Skin Cancer Prevention— Legislation Enacted 2005–2006

State	Public education	School-based education	Tanning facilities
Arizona	. . .	SB 1297	. . .
Kentucky	. . .	HB 589	HB 151
New Jersey	. . .	. . .	HB 2936
New York	HB 7422	. . .	SB 2602C
Utah	. . .	SR 2	. . .

Source: The Council of State Governments, December 2006

General Cancer Prevention Legislation

General cancer prevention legislation enacted between 2005 and 2006 most often dealt with genetic discrimination and the disclosure of genetic information (Table J). Idaho and New Mexico enacted legislation prohibiting health benefit plans from discriminating against an individual or a member of the individual's family on the basis of genetic information. These bills, along with New York legislation, prohibited the use of genetic information in employment decisions. Kentucky prohibited group health plans from imposing pre-existing condition exclusions based solely on genetic information. Minnesota required government entities to obtain written informed consent for the collection and use of an individual's genetic information.

What Lies Ahead?

The types of cancer prevention legislation enacted between 2005 and 2006 suggest that tobacco use prevention and obesity prevention will continue to be major foci of wellness-related legislation. Legislative deliberations also are likely to focus on the HPV vaccine. Should this vaccine be required for girls entering sixth grade and, if so, how will the $360 three-dose regimen be covered?

Tobacco Use Legislation

In recent years, numerous states have strengthened their smokefree air laws. Twenty states now have laws prohibiting smoking in almost all public places and workplaces.[21] With most Americans expressing support for these policies, comprehensive smokefree state air laws are likely to become more prevalent.[22] Recent trends suggest that state legislatures also will continue to increase tobacco excise taxes. Between 2001 and 2006, for example, the average state cigarette tax more than doubled ($0.42 to $0.90).[23] The American Lung Association expects youth access to tobacco to be an additional area of emphasis, with states considering bans on flavored cigarettes and ways of restricting cigarette sales over the Internet.

Obesity Prevention Legislation

Because eating and exercise habits tend to be set during childhood, schools are likely to remain the focus of obesity prevention legislation. However, as lawmakers explore ways of reducing obesity prevalence in their states, they may also consider taxes on soft drinks and snacks and/or restaurant menu labeling legislation. The New York City Board of Health's December 2006 decision to ban the use of trans fats in restaurant cooking has prompted at least 12 states to consider full or partial statewide bans. Legislators may also build upon 2005–06 initiatives by introducing more legislation to support walking and biking paths, safe routes to schools and access to parks and green space.

Cervical Cancer Legislation

In September 2006, Michigan became the first state to introduce legislation requiring the HPV vaccine for girls entering the sixth grade. Although the Michigan Senate unanimously approved this bill, the House of Representatives ended its 2005–06 session without acting on it. As of February 15, 2007, 23 states and the District of Columbia were considering similar legislation. Bills proposing to make the HPV vaccine compulsory are likely to generate debate about the long-term effects of the vaccine, financing mechanisms and infringements on parental autonomy.[24] As a result, states may be more likely to pass legislation requiring health insurance coverage of HPV tests.

Conclusion

This review of 2005–2006 legislation suggests that state legislators are becoming increasingly aware of the importance of policy interventions to reduce cancer risk. Further reductions in cancer incidence and mortality can be achieved by focusing legislation on evidence-based strategies for improving health habits and screening practices. Colorectal cancer is one of

Table J: General Cancer Prevention — Legislation Enacted 2005–2006

State	Genetics information	Prevention grants	Prevention task force	Wellness plans and programs
Colorado	. . .	HB 1262	. . .	. . .
Idaho	SB 1423	. . .	. . .	. . .
Kentucky	HB 418	. . .	. . .	. . .
Maryland	. . .	. . .	SB 824	. . .
Massachusetts	. . .	. . .	. . .	HB 4850
Minnesota	SB 3132	. . .	. . .	. . .
New Jersey	. . .	. . .	HB 4071	. . .
New Mexico	HB 183	. . .	. . .	. . .
New York	HB 3107	. . .	. . .	. . .
South Carolina	. . .	. . .	. . .	HB 4810
Texas	SB 53	. . .	. . .	. . .
Vermont	. . .	. . .	. . .	HB 861
Washington	. . .	. . .	SB 6197	. . .

Source: The Council of State Governments, December 2006

the few cancers that can be prevented through early detection. Yet, only 18 state laws require specified insurers to cover colorectal cancer screening tests.[25] Until more effective cancer treatments are developed, legislation promoting lifestyle changes and supportive community environments offer the best hope of reducing cancer incidence and mortality.

Notes

[1] American Cancer Society, *Cancer Facts & Figures 2007* (Atlanta: American Cancer Society, 2007), 2. *http://www.cancer.org/downloads/STT/CAFFR2007PWSecured.pdf.*

[2] National Cancer Institute, *Cancer Trends Progress Report—2005 Update* (Bethesda, MD: National Cancer Institute, 2005) *http://progressreport.cancer.gov.*

[3] Goodarz Danaei et al., "Causes of Cancer in the World: Comparative Risk Assessment of Nine Behavioural and Environmental Risk Factors," *Lancet* 366 (November 19, 2005): 1784–93.

[4] Susan J. Curry, Tim Byers, and Maria Hewitt, eds., *Fulfilling the Potential of Cancer Prevention and Early Detection* (Washington, D.C.: The National Academies Press, 2003), 30.

[5] American Cancer Society, *Cancer Prevention & Early Detection Facts & Figures 2006* (Atlanta: American Cancer Society, 2006), 17 *http://www.cancer.org/downloads/STT/CPED2006PWSecured.pdf.*

[6] American Cancer Society, *Cancer Prevention*, 20.

[7] National Cancer Institute, *Cancer Trends*.

[8] Eugenia Calle, Carmen Rodriguez, Kimberly Walker-Thurmond, and Michael Thun, "Overweight, Obesity and Mortality from Cancer in a Prospectively Studied Cohort of U.S. Adults," *The New England Journal of Medicine* 348 (April 24, 2003): 1625–38.

[9] National Cancer Institute, "Obesity and Cancer: Questions and Answers," undated, *http://www.cancer.gov/cancertopics/factsheet/Risk/obesity.* Researchers use body mass index—the ratio of weight (in kilograms) to height (in meters) squared—to measure overweight and obesity. Adults with a body mass index (BMI) of 25.0 to 29.9 are classified as overweight, and those with a BMI greater than 30.0 are classified as obese.

[10] Centers for Disease Control and Prevention, "Overweight and Obesity: Obesity Trends: U.S. Obesity Trends 1985–2005," 29 September 2006, *http://www.cdc.gov/nccdphp/dnpa/obesity/trend/maps.*

[11] Kathryn Foxhall, "Beginning to Begin: Reports from the Battle on Obesity," *American Journal of Public Health* 96 (December 2006): 2106–111.

[12] American Cancer Society, *Cancer Facts*, 9.

[13] American Cancer Society, *Cancer Facts*, 20.

[14] Catherine Lowndes and O. Noel Gill, "Cervical Cancer, Human Papillomavirus and Vaccination," *British Medical Journal* 331 (October 2005): 915–16.

[15] American Cancer Society, *Cancer Facts*, 12.

[16] American Cancer Society, *Cancer Prevention*, 39.

[17] American Cancer Society, *Cancer Facts*, 15.

[18] American Cancer Society, *Cancer Facts*, 17.

[19] American Cancer Society, *Cancer Facts*, 19.

[20] Ariel Whitworth, "Legislators Combat Melanoma, Restrict Teen Tanning," *Journal of the National Cancer Institute* 98 (November 15, 2006): 1594–96.

[21] American Nonsmokers' Rights Foundation, "Smokefree Air—America's New Year's Resolution," December 8, 2006, *http://www.no-smoke.org/pdf/2006_smokefreestatus.pdf.*

[22] Gallup News Service, "Increased Support for Smoking Bans in Public Places," July 20, 2005.

[23] Tax Policy Center, "Cigarette Rates 2001–2006," undated, *http://www.taxpolicycenter.org/TaxFacts/TFDB/Content/PDF/cigarette_rates.pdf.*

[24] James Colgrove, "The Ethics and Politics of Compulsory HPV Vaccination," *The New England Journal of Medicine* 355 (December 7, 2006): 2389–91.

[25] National Cancer Institute, "States with Laws Related to Third-Party Coverage for Colorectal Cancer Screening," June 30, 2005, *http://www.scld-nci.net/factsheets/pdf/colorectal_summer05_web.pdf.*

About the Author

Martha M. McKinney was the associate director for research for The Council of State Governments. She holds a Ph.D. from the School of Public Health, University of North Carolina, and has published extensively on health policy issues.

Table 9.10
HEALTH INSURANCE COVERAGE STATUS BY STATE FOR ALL PEOPLE: 2005
(In thousands)

State or other jurisdiction	Total	Covered and not covered by health insurance during the year			
		Covered	Percent	Not covered	Percent
United States	293,834	247,257	84.1%	46,577	15.9%
Eastern Region					
Connecticut...........................	3,487	3,093	88.7	394	11.3
Delaware.............................	844	734	87.0	110	13.0
Maine..................................	1,320	1,177	89.2	143	10.8
Massachusetts......................	6,328	5,710	90.2	618	9.8
New Hampshire	1,301	1,166	89.7	135	10.3
New Jersey	8,725	7,401	84.8	1,324	15.2
New York.............................	19,022	16,463	86.5	2,559	13.5
Pennsylvania........................	12,281	10,994	89.5	1,287	10.5
Rhode Island........................	1,054	929	88.2	125	11.8
Vermont	622	549	88.3	73	(a)
Regional total	54,984	48,216	87.7	6,768	12.3
Midwestern Region					
Illinois	12,608	10,806	85.7	1,802	14.3
Indiana...............................	6,141	5,270	85.8	871	14.2
Iowa...................................	2,909	2,657	91.4	251	8.6
Kansas	2,695	2,405	89.2	290	10.8
Michigan.............................	9,982	8,848	88.6	1,133	11.4
Minnesota	5,129	4,699	91.6	431	8.4
Nebraska	1,766	1,588	88.2	208	11.8
North Dakota	626	550	87.8	76	12.2
Ohio...................................	11,334	9,940	87.7	1,394	12.3
South Dakota	768	673	87.6	95	12.4
Wisconsin	5,447	4,913	90.2	534	9.8
Regional total	59,405	52,349	88.1	7,085	11.9
Southern Region					
Alabama..............................	4,524	3,828	84.6	696	15.4
Arkansas	2,760	2,266	82.1	494	17.9
Florida	17,886	14,183	79.3	3,703	20.7
Georgia	9,045	7,335	81.1	1,709	18.9
Kentucky	4,052	3,539	87.3	514	12.7
Louisiana	4,088	3,321	81.2	767	18.8
Maryland	5,569	4,781	85.8	788	14.2
Mississippi...........................	2,854	2,359	82.6	495	17.4
Missouri..............................	5,710	5,019	87.9	691	12.1
North Carolina	8,561	7,190	84.0	1,371	16.0
Oklahoma	3,505	2,859	81.6	647	18.4
South Carolina	4,181	3,439	82.3	741	17.7
Tennessee............................	5,867	5,031	85.8	836	14.2
Texas..................................	22,819	17,304	75.8	5,516	24.2
Virginia...............................	7,454	6,443	86.4	1,011	13.6
West Virginia	1,799	1,477	82.1	322	17.9
Regional total	110,674	90,374	81.6	20,301	18.3
Western Region					
Alaska.................................	659	542	82.3	117	17.7
Arizona...............................	6,047	4,828	79.8	1,219	20.2
California.............................	35,940	28,979	80.6	6,961	19.4
Colorado	4,641	3,853	83.0	788	17.0
Hawaii	1,279	1,163	90.9	116	9.1
Idaho..................................	1,442	1,221	84.6	222	15.4
Montana..............................	928	767	82.6	162	17.4
Nevada................................	2,448	2,023	82.6	425	17.4
New Mexico	1,938	1,542	79.6	396	20.4
Oregon................................	3,627	3,049	84.0	579	16.0
Utah...................................	2,524	2,104	83.4	420	16.6
Washington	6,250	5,384	86.2	866	13.8
Wyoming	511	428	83.9	82	16.1
Regional total	68,234	55,883	81.9	12,353	18.1
Regional total without California...........	32,294	26,904	83.3	5,392	16.7
Dist. of Columbia	540	467	86.5	73	(a)

Source: U.S. Census Bureau, Current Population Survey, 2006 Annual Social and Economic Supplement. URL: http://pubdb3.census.gov/macro/032006/health/ h06_000.htm. Revised August 29, 2006.
Key:
(a) Base less than 75,000.

Table 9.11
NUMBER AND PERCENT OF CHILDREN UNDER 19 YEARS OF AGE, AT OR BELOW
200 PERCENT OF POVERTY, BY HEALTH INSURANCE COVERAGE AND STATE: 2005
(In thousands)

State or other jurisdiction	Total children under 19 years, all income levels	At or below 200 percent of poverty		At or below 200 percent of poverty without health insurance	
		Number	Percent	Number	Percent
United States	77,210	29,891	38.7%	5,577	7.2%
Eastern Region					
Connecticut.........................	870	223	25.7	47	5.4
Delaware.............................	205	70	33.9	15	7.3
Maine..................................	298	115	38.4	16	5.3
Massachusetts.....................	1,587	431	27.2	34	2.1
New Hampshire	312	62	19.7	6	2.0
New Jersey	2,258	541	23.9	122	5.4
New York............................	4,793	1,969	41.1	243	5.1
Pennsylvania.......................	2,954	1,077	36.5	161	5.5
Rhode Island.......................	263	85	32.4	10	3.6
Vermont	144	38	26.0	3	2.2
Regional total	13,684	4,611	33.7	657	4.8
Midwestern Region					
Illinois	3,424	1,184	34.6	206	6.0
Indiana................................	1,664	685	41.2	88	5.3
Iowa....................................	722	226	31.3	18	2.6
Kansas................................	721	272	37.8	34	4.8
Michigan.............................	2,656	954	35.9	79	3.0
Minnesota...........................	1,289	306	23.7	39	3.0
Nebraska.............................	452	142	31.5	15	3.4
North Dakota	152	54	35.1	9	6.2
Ohio....................................	2,846	1,035	36.4	146	5.1
South Dakota	198	72	36.5	11	5.4
Wisconsin	1,379	458	33.3	62	4.5
Regional total	15,503	5,388	34.8	707	4.6
Southern Region					
Alabama...............................	1,127	497	44.1	42	3.7
Arkansas.............................	708	323	45.7	49	6.9
Florida	4,180	1,615	38.6	494	11.8
Georgia	2,467	1,028	41.7	181	7.3
Kentucky	1,044	433	41.5	54	5.2
Louisiana	1,119	509	45.5	60	5.4
Maryland	1,443	425	29.5	64	4.4
Mississippi..........................	801	434	54.1	72	9.0
Missouri..............................	1,456	561	38.5	77	5.3
North Carolina	2,296	929	40.5	199	8.7
Oklahoma	880	400	45.5	63	7.2
South Carolina	1,050	459	43.7	69	6.5
Tennessee............................	1,490	641	43.0	104	7.0
Texas...................................	6,731	3,203	47.6	899	13.4
Virginia...............................	1,907	606	31.8	107	5.6
West Virginia	406	181	44.7	16	4.0
Regional total	29,105	12,244	42.0	2,550	8.7
Western Region					
Alaska.................................	194	66	33.8	7	3.7
Arizona...............................	1,680	834	49.6	227	13.5
California............................	10,097	4,144	41.0	899	8.9
Colorado	1,230	395	32.1	105	8.5
Hawaii	315	86	27.4	7	2.1
Idaho...................................	413	162	39.1	28	6.7
Montana..............................	226	97	42.9	22	9.8
Nevada................................	679	247	36.4	55	8.1
New Mexico	527	279	53.0	85	16.2
Oregon................................	920	395	42.9	69	7.5
Utah....................................	800	281	35.1	60	7.5
Washington	1,593	557	34.9	85	5.4
Wyoming	123	38	31.2	8	6.6
Regional total	18,797	7,581	40.3	1,657	8.8
Regional total without California...........	8,700	3,437	39.5	758	8.7
Dist. of Columbia	117	65	56.0	6	5.1

Source: U.S. Census Bureau, Current Population Survey, 2006 Annual Social and Economic Supplement. URL: http://pubdb3.census.gov/macro/032006/health/ h06_000.htm. Revised August 29, 2006.

Renewable Energy—It's Never Too Early

By Jim Geringer

Governors and legislators should develop a suite of policy options that would recognize market demand with environmental sensitivity to cost-effectively increase energy efficiency and deliver sufficient and timely clean energy resources to citizens they serve.

"The best time to plant a tree was 20 years ago. The second best time is now."

"No shade tree? Blame not the sun but yourself."

Both these quotes are attributed to old Chinese proverbs. Trees are traditional symbols of long-term planning and renewal, and in today's world of energy policy, trees represent a cycle of carbon sequestration and renewable energy.

The top 10 priorities of governors and legislators typically include education, health, economy and energy. Education has been the most dominant state policy issue in recent years. Achievement, finance, graduation rate and competitiveness pepper policy discussions. Recently however, health care has replaced education in the top spot on many state prior-

ity lists. Quality, availability and cost of health care, the aging population and Medicaid dominate budget debates and legislative initiatives.

While both health and education will continue to rank high and continue to challenge governors and legislators, the convergence of three other issues— climate change, peaking of world oil supply and water shortages—could be an even greater problem for these policymakers. These three embody the overall challenge we face with energy access and consumption.

"We have a serious problem. America is addicted to oil, which is often imported from unstable parts of the world," President Bush declared in his 2006 State of the Union address. To break the addiction, Bush announced new research into and support for clean energy, and set a goal to replace more than 75 per-

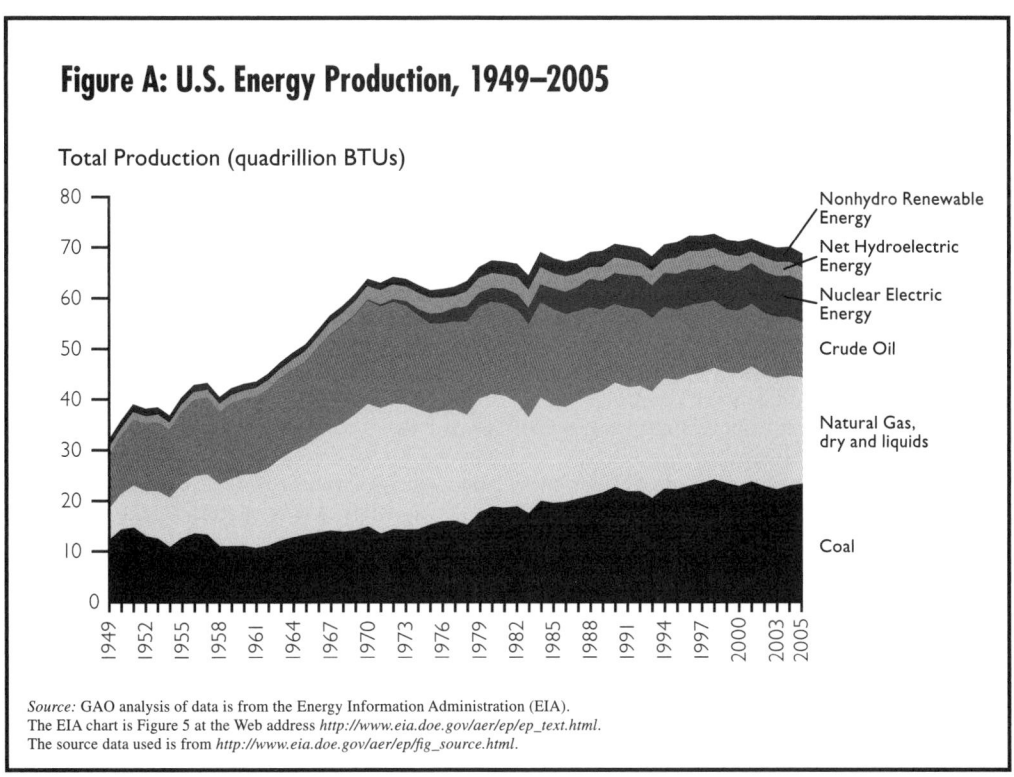

Figure A: U.S. Energy Production, 1949–2005

Total Production (quadrillion BTUs)

Nonhydro Renewable Energy

Net Hydroelectric Energy

Nuclear Electric Energy

Crude Oil

Natural Gas, dry and liquids

Coal

Source: GAO analysis of data is from the Energy Information Administration (EIA).
The EIA chart is Figure 5 at the Web address *http://www.eia.doe.gov/aer/ep/ep_text.html*.
The source data used is from *http://www.eia.doe.gov/aer/ep/fig_source.html*.

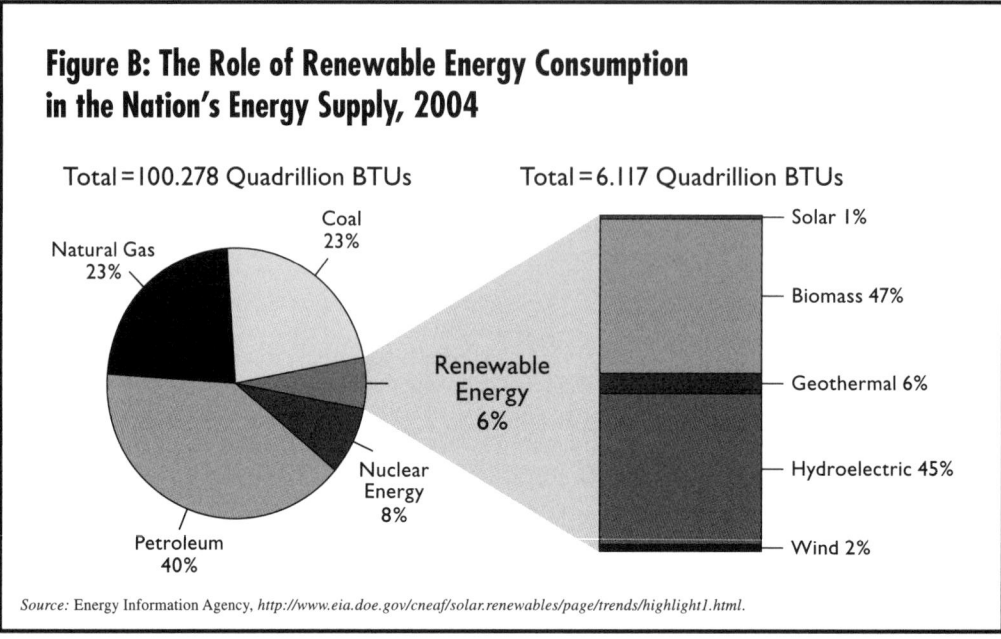

Figure B: The Role of Renewable Energy Consumption in the Nation's Energy Supply, 2004

Total = 100.278 Quadrillion BTUs

Coal 23%
Natural Gas 23%
Nuclear Energy 8%
Petroleum 40%
Renewable Energy 6%

Total = 6.117 Quadrillion BTUs

Solar 1%
Biomass 47%
Geothermal 6%
Hydroelectric 45%
Wind 2%

Source: Energy Information Agency, *http://www.eia.doe.gov/cneaf/solar.renewables/page/trends/highlight1.html.*

cent of our oil imports from the Middle East by 2025. President Bush upped the ante in his 2007 State of the Union Address by challenging us to meet the 75 percent goal within the next ten years and further advocated even greater use of clean coal technology, solar and wind energy, and clean, safe nuclear power.

Former Vice President Al Gore became an unlikely matinee movie idol with *An Inconvenient Truth*, prodding people about greenhouse gasses and the current state of energy production. He advocated clean and diversified energy sources.

That these two men, who often disagree, are drawing attention to energy security and sustainability reflects America's increasing awareness of energy policy and consumption. For many Americans, the new focus on energy issues is a wake-up call, prodding us with painful realities about our consumption. We as a country are ready to move toward alternative energy sources and lifestyles.

In 2006, the Western Governors Association said in a report, *Clean Energy, a Strong Economy and a Healthy Environment*, that it "recognizes that no organization, state or person is motivated by one single factor. Environmental issues including climate change, economics of energy, such as price spikes in electricity, natural gas and gasoline, along with personal choice, such as being unwilling or unable to change—each plays a role." The governors had asked a special committee, the Clean and Diversified Energy Advisory Committee (CDEAC), for recom-

mendations that would stress nonmandatory, incentive-based approaches that could be implemented by individual states, through action on a regional level, or through national policy.[1]

How hard would it be to reduce our oil imports from the Middle East by 75 percent? Not an easy task, considering the current known world oil and natural gas reserves and production capabilities. Although the United States accounts for only 5 percent of the world's population, we now consume about 25 percent of the energy used each year worldwide, yet America has only about 5 percent of the world's reserves of oil and gas. According to the Energy Information Administration, fossil fuels (coal, oil, and natural gas) provide about 86 percent of our total energy consumption, with the rest coming from non-fossil sources such as nuclear (8 percent) and renewables, such as hydroelectric energy and wind power (6 percent).[2] See the General Accounting Office figure (Figure A) on U.S. energy production history from 1949 through 2003.

Public policy is now pushing aggressively for us individually and collectively to pursue renewables and clean alternative fuels. At least 20 states have adopted mandatory renewable portfolio standards, or RPS, that would require up to 25 percent of energy for electricity to come from renewable sources. The question is how will states achieve the standards? Doug Larson of the Western State Energy Board observes that wind is generally the most economic renewable outside of hydro-electric, which generally doesn't count against RPS requirements. Federal Production Tax Credit subsidies were extended through 2008 just before Congress adjourned this past December. Further extensions are likely, but the fitful and costly stop and start on tax credits creates far too much uncertainty for investors. Solar costs are still high, but we will soon know if mass production can bring down the cost using Sterling Energy Systems dish technology based on the Southern California Edison work in the Mojave Desert.[3] Photovoltaics (PV) are extremely popular and expensive even though costs are dropping. When available, state and utility subsidies for PV installations are quickly exhausted.

Excluding hydropower, meeting a national goal of 25 percent would require as much as a sevenfold increase in renewables, certainly a daunting goal. However for one renewable energy source, the U.S. Department of Energy/Energy Information Agency estimates that if the federal tax credit were to remain predictable for several years, wind power generation in the United States could indeed grow nearly sevenfold over the next 20 years. The EIA summary of year 2004 renewable energy depicted in Figure B outlines the task ahead.[4] Hydropower, which doesn't count for RPS, constitutes nearly half of all renewables today followed by biomass. Wood-burning stoves and fireplaces make up most of biomass use today although ethanol made from high cellulose matter is

much cleaner and efficient. The apparent conclusion is that we have a significant but not impossible challenge to meet.

As we discuss the issues of climate change and energy security, we must discuss energy sources and our rate of consumption. How much energy do we consume? How much do we really need? While the issue of climate change is hotly debated, one thing is clear: Human activity is contributing to problems for our environment. The number of humans on the globe continues to increase, as will energy consumption. We can effect change even while the debate goes on.

There is broad agreement that the U.S. must act now to ensure it will have a diverse supply of secure, environmentally responsible and affordable energy well in the future. As traditional sources become more limited, could we quantify the difference and bring in alternative and renewable energy? If something needs to be done, who's in charge? Policy begins with governors and legislators. Our federal government plays a significant role but the policies should be nationally developed, not federally mandated. We are partners.

According to the U.S. Census Bureau analysis, world population from the dawn of mankind didn't reach 1 billion people until the turn of the 19th century, or roughly 8,000 years. It only took 100 years for human numbers, increasing at higher rates, to

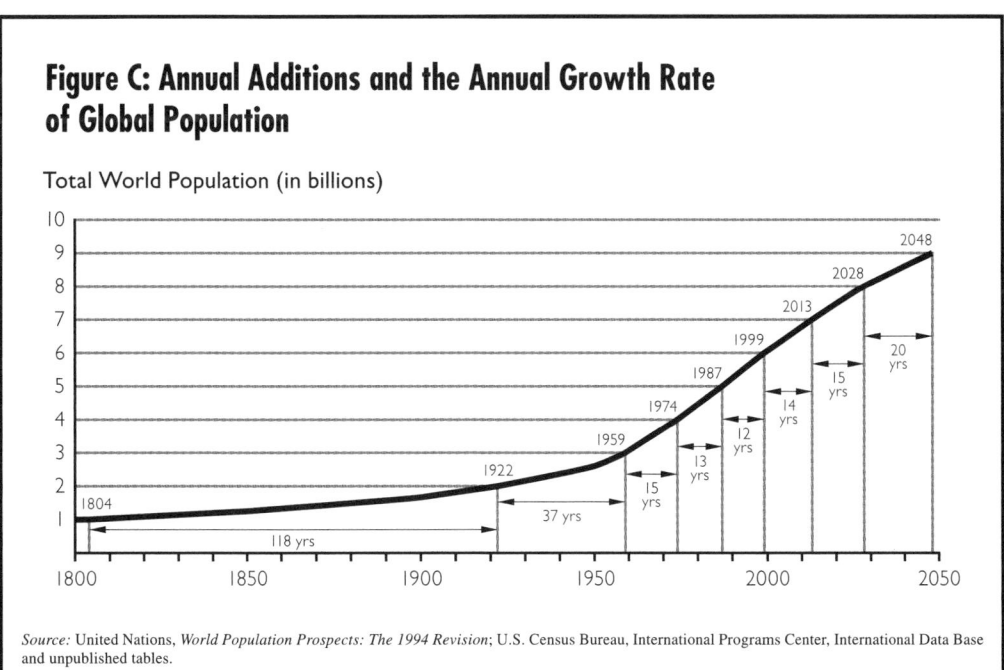

Figure C: Annual Additions and the Annual Growth Rate of Global Population

Total World Population (in billions)

Source: United Nations, *World Population Prospects: The 1994 Revision*; U.S. Census Bureau, International Programs Center, International Data Base and unpublished tables.

reach about 1.7 billion people by 1900. Even with declining birth rates and in spite of the toll taken by HIV/AIDS in most countries, world population quickly reached 6 billion by 2000. Check the comparison again—it took 8,000 years to reach 1 billion but only 12 years to increase from 5 billion to 6 billion from 1987 to 1999.

The Census Bureau projects world population will reach nearly 8 billion by 2025 and hit or exceed 9 billion just before 2050 as seen in Figure C.[5] The Census Bureau notes that the rate of growth has slowed to the point that it will take 20 years to go from 8 billion to 9 billion, whereas it only took 12 years for population to go from 5 billion to 6 billion. That change is small comfort as we contemplate what it might be like, having 50 percent more people in the world than we have today, clamoring for the energy they choose to use. Today's volatile competition for resources will pale by comparison to what our children will face when they reach retirement age.

Alternative energy sources are being evaluated today at a faster pace than ever. Every generation has the goal to pass along something better to their children than what the current generation received. That goal cannot be sustained without significant commitment.

Oil is used in the transportation sector as gasoline, diesel and jet fuel, with oil-based products accounting for more than 98 percent of the U.S. transportation sector's fuel consumption. The transportation sector—where there are currently no alternative fuels that compete widely with oil—accounts for about one-half of the total projected increase in oil use between 2003 and 2030. The International Energy Agency projects that the worldwide use of oil for transportation will nearly double between 2000 and 2030, with a commensurate increase in greenhouse gas emissions. Biofuels, such as ethanol, biodiesel and other liquid and gaseous fuels, could offer an important alternative to petroleum over this timeframe and help reduce atmospheric pollution.[6] However, the transportation sector relies on a complex network of pipelines to connect supply, processing, distribution and retailing. Not all biofuels, particularly ethanol, are as available or transportable as refined oil-based fuels.

Transportation may be the last sector to wean itself from the addiction to oil. In the meantime, we can devote considerable effort toward using alternative sources of energy in every other sector.

We can look at clean, alternative and renewable energy both as replacements for and as supplements to existing fossil fuels. Popular renewables today include solar collectors, photovoltaic, wind, fuel cells,

geothermal, biomass, biodiesel, wave action, hydropower and others. One indicator of public acceptance is the willingness of investors to participate in funding clean energy ventures. Economic advantage stimulates creativity, often toward positive outcomes.

According to Ron Pernick, co-founder of Clean Edge,[7] clean energy is going from niche to mainstream in at least four primary areas: biofuels, wind, solar and fuel cells. The amount of venture capital available for investment in these areas will increase fourfold in the next 10 years.

According to Pernick and others at Clean Edge, the tipping point is nigh: For the first time in modern history, clean-energy technologies are becoming cost-competitive with their "dirtier" counterparts. While oil and natural gas prices remain stubbornly high and frustratingly volatile across the globe, and as nuclear and coal-based energy remain dogged by environmental and safety concerns, the cost of renewable energy continues the steady downward trend. Public acceptance and expectations are higher than ever which will have a positive effect on entrepreneurs and market strategies.

As noted by Clean Edge however, turbulence remains in the clean-energy sector. The solar industry is experiencing growing problems, unable to gain access to enough silicon feedstock to keep pace with demand for photovoltaics (PV). But even with the pressure on upward pricing over the short term, new materials and manufacturing could dramatically reduce cost of PVs and increase availability. Biofuels, while showing great promise, face obstacles, not the least of which is how to quickly ramp up widespread distribution channels. Ethanol has the annoying habit of picking up water, particularly in pipelines, a habit that gasoline does not have. Biodiesel has great promise both in energy conversion efficiency and by having a variety of sources for the oils used. Growth of wind turbines, while currently expanding rapidly, could flag given short-term price increases due to high steel costs and shifting currency valuations. But new vertical axis turbine designs and use of composite materials could create a new positive tipping point. Mass adoption of fuel cells and hydrogen may be decades away absent research and development breakthroughs. Even though renewables appear to be constrained far below what we might like, we should not overlook the American knack for innovation and creativity. We recall the admonitions of two former presidents, Kennedy and Reagan, who called for actions that seemed impossible at the time.

In early 1961 President John F. Kennedy issued a challenge to Congress that he repeated to students

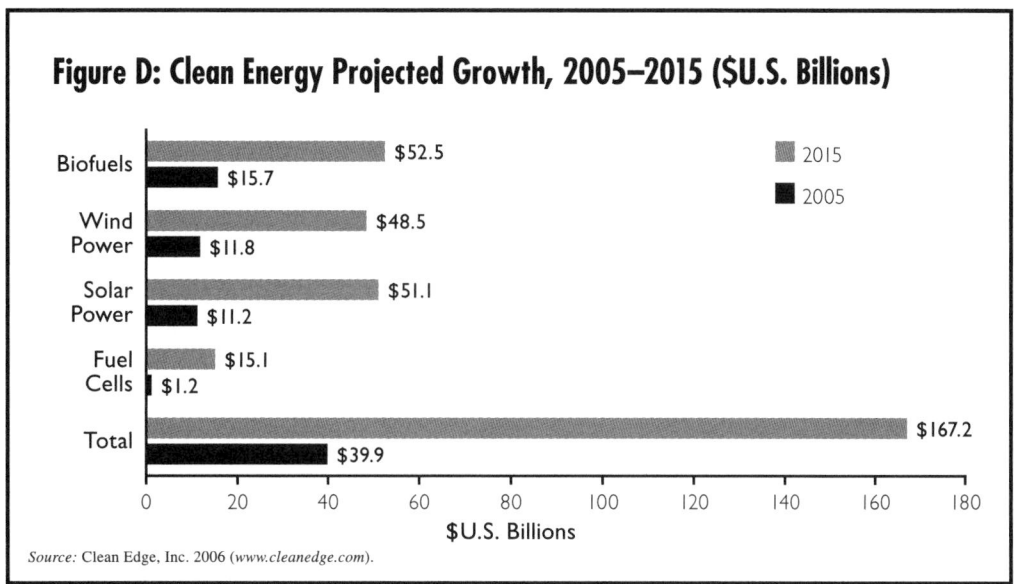

Figure D: Clean Energy Projected Growth, 2005–2015 ($U.S. Billions)

Biofuels: $52.5 (2015), $15.7 (2005)

Wind Power: $48.5 (2015), $11.8 (2005)

Solar Power: $51.1 (2015), $11.2 (2005)

Fuel Cells: $15.1 (2015), $1.2 (2005)

Total: $167.2 (2015), $39.9 (2005)

$U.S. Billions

Source: Clean Edge, Inc. 2006 (www.cleanedge.com).

at Rice University later that year. "We choose to go to the moon in this decade and do the other things, not because they are easy, but because they are hard, because that goal will serve to organize and measure the best of our energies and skills, because that challenge is one that we are willing to accept, one we are unwilling to postpone, and one which we intend to win," Kennedy said.

President Ronald Reagan stood at the Brandenburg Gate, West Berlin, Germany, June 12, 1987, and boldly said "Mr. Gorbachev. Tear down this wall!" The resulting rally of world opinion caused Gorbachev to yield, and the wall was torn down!

In times of national interest and in times of crisis, we as a country do respond and respond effectively. We can and should respond again with a national commitment to deal with energy concerns.

Meeting future energy needs will depend upon the extent that state, regional and federal policies promote energy efficiency, renewables and the development of advanced alternative energy generation. Tax credits, carbon trading opportunities and transmission lines are only three of the possible policy alternatives. Fossil fuel developments that are dramatically cleaner will aid transition to renewables in sufficient amounts to keep up with demand.

Connecting energy sources of any type to locations of consumption will require the necessary transmission infrastructure. If renewable energy sources are produced at smaller scales suitable for home and other modest applications, transmission lines won't be needed. However, any significant addition to elec-

tric energy will require large scale installations in close proximity to new or existing transmission lines. Coinciding with this issue are the serious strains on the North American power delivery system, which are beginning to surface due to the system's aging infrastructure. and the pending retirement of highly skilled technicians within the utility work force. Integration of large amounts of intermittent wind and solar into the grid will further challenge utility managers. While they may be slow to adapt, utility system operators will soon figure out a way to deal with intermittent generation just as they deal with today's fluctuations in load. New control technology and management processes will enable utility operators to consider wind and solar as base loads with traditional or clean fossil based generation making up the difference to match demand.

Doug Larson of the Western Interstate Energy board points out two big hurdles:

- First, determine how to virtually or physically consolidate control areas through shared generation reserves. Regional transmission organizations could have accomplished the task but they were pre-empted by federal and Congressional mandates over strong objection by the states. We now need immediate practical agreements among control areas to accommodate large amounts of intermittent generation. An interconnection-wide wind variability study would help determine how wind generation spread over large areas could generate a relatively firm and manageable output for consum-

Table A: Energy End-Use Sector Sources of U.S. Carbon Dioxide Emissions, 1990–2005

Sector	Million metric tons carbon dioxide		Percent change	
	1990	2005	1990–2005	2004–2005
Residential....................	953.7	1,253.8	31.5%	3.30%
Commercial..................	780.7	1,050.6	34.6	1.6
Industrial.....................	1,683.6	1,682.3	-0.1	-3.1
Transportation	1,566.8	1,958.6	25.0	1.0

Source: Energy Information Agency, November 2006.
http://www.eia.doe.gov/oiaf/1605/ggrpt/enduse_sector.html.
Note: Electric power sector emissions are distributed across sectors.

ers. This important building block would determine the benefits of consolidating control areas and what the transmission connections would have to be.

- Second, induce designers, developers and owners of fossil fuel plants to acquire fossil generation equipment that is capable of tracking the fluctuations in wind and solar output. That capability could have been achieved with recent gas-fired electric generation but several of the new natural gas combined-cycle power plants have sacrificed rapid ramping capability in order to achieve maximum thermal efficiency. In other words, near real-time reaction to fluctuating loads is possible with current technology but operators and designers have opted not to include that capability.

One possible option that Larson suggests is to combine wind generation with the most recent design of Integrated Gasification Combined Cycle (IGCC) clean-coal technology. IGCC power plants can turn coal or other fossil fuels into a clean-burning gas, which fires a gas turbine to generate electricity. This low emission technology also facilitates the cost-effective capture and sequestration of carbon dioxide, rather than releasing it into the atmosphere. The operating concept would have the gasification process running constantly so that when the collective wind generation in a given region is sufficient, gas would be put into storage. When wind generation falls below the demand, gas would be withdrawn from storage and put into a combined cycle plant. The result could be very low carbon-yield electric generation provided that the CO_2 from the gasification process be sequestered. This type of scenario recognizes that U.S. energy demand cannot be met just through conservation and renewables, that some

companion generation using fossil fuels will be necessary. In this case, new processes that are much more environmentally friendly would be applied.

Policies that encourage new approaches and ideas such as wind and IGCC could be accelerated with incentives such as carbon trading and tax credits. We will need that kind of thinking to avoid the magnitude of growth in carbon dioxide emissions summarized by the Energy Information Agency in Table A.[8]

Governors and legislators should develop a suite of policy options that would recognize market demand with environmental sensitivity to cost-effectively increase energy efficiency and deliver sufficient and timely clean energy resources to citizens they serve.

The policy options would result from analysis and balancing of affordability, environmental performance, resource diversity, domestic energy security and reliability implications. No single correct answer will suit every state's needs and priorities.

Choices that are developed regionally with cooperation among states will be more successful and effective so that partnerships with federal regulators and Congressional members recognize that the best solutions come from the states.

Two policy questions state leaders could ask:

- To what extent do state energy policies and incentive structures encourage appropriate energy development and usage over the long term?

- What is the appropriate balance between enhanced production of fossil fuels, alternative renewable energy sources and energy conservation?

Raymond L. Orbach, undersecretary for science at the U.S. Department of Energy, put it best: "The world therefore has a twofold problem: Where will this new energy come from, and how can we provide energy that is environmentally friendly? Solving this problem will—and should—challenge the scientific community. Current fossil energy sources, energy production methods and technology will be unable to meet this challenge, and incremental changes in technology will not suffice. To meet these energy and environmental needs, we need transformational discoveries in basic science and truly disruptive technologies. Electricity was not discovered by perfecting the candle."[9]

It's never too early to plant a tree. Or develop a renewable and clean energy source!

Notes

[1] *http://www.westgov.org/wga/initiatives/cdeac/index.htm.*

[2] *http://www.eia.doe.gov/cneaf/solar.renewables/page/trends/highlight1.html.*

[3] *http://www.renewableenergyaccess.com/rea/news/story?id=35263.*

[4] *http://www.eia.doe.gov/cneaf/solar.renewables/page/trends/highlight1.html.*

[5] *http://www.census.gov/ipc/prod/wp02/wp02-1.pdf,* 2002, Updated January 2006.

[6] *http://www.iea.org/textbase/publications/free_new_Desc.asp?PUBS_ID=1262.*

[7] Ron Pernick, Co-founder and Principal, Clean Edge, Inc., SRI In the Rockies, Oct. 30, 2006.

[8] *http://www.eia.doe.gov/oiaf/1605/ggrpt/enduse_sector.html.* Updated November 2006.

[9] Innovation: America's Journal of Technology Commercialization, December 2006–January 2007, *http://www.innovation-america.org/index.php?articleID=212.*

About the Author

Jim Geringer, former Wyoming governor, is director of Policy & Public Strategies at Environmental Systems Research Institute, Inc., headquartered in Redlands, California. Geringer is based in Wheatland, Wyoming.

Foreign Investments in the U.S.

By Jeffrey A. Finkle

Despite an impressive list of advantages, the U.S. can no longer assume that foreign firms will continue to invest and employ people here at the same rate as in the past. The effects of globalization and off-shoring trends have led to fluctuations in foreign investment, with the U.S. dropping to third place (from second) in 2005 as the most attractive future FDI location after China and India.

The effects of foreign direct investment (FDI) or the investment of foreign assets into domestic structures, equipment and organizations on the U.S. economy cannot be understated. Since the 1990s the U.S. trade balance has had a significant current account deficit and foreign investment has been essential to keeping the U.S. economy afloat. To put this in perspective: The U.S. imports more than it exports from its top trading partners (Figures A and B), and in 2005 the trade deficit increased more than 17 percent from the previous year, accounting for a $725.8 billion gap.

Foreign subsidiaries located in the U.S. contribute to one-fifth of U.S. exports and, in 2004 alone, the U.S. gained $96 billion from FDI. Those same foreign firms provide 5.1 million Americans with jobs, representing 4.5 percent of the private sector work force in the country. U.S. subsidiaries of firms headquartered overseas support an annual payroll of $324.5 billion. The average salary per worker being 32–34 percent higher than the average pay by U.S. companies, particularly in manufacturing.[1] Given that U.S. savings are not enough to finance domestic investment and the Bureau of Economic Analysis' latest report announced an increase in the current account deficit from $213.2 billion in the first quarter of 2006 to $218.4 billion in the second quarter,[2] it is undeniable that FDI in the U.S. must be sustained.

Historically, the U.S. has been successful in attracting FDI with the reputation of having the most sophisticated and efficient financial market in the world that provides easy access to capital, and a productive and flexible labor market. The U.S. pro-business environment, despite higher costs, has long been an asset, boasting the ease in starting a new business, the freedom in hiring and firing, a strong infrastructure, and the facility in purchasing property. A good transportation system, proximity to major markets, and high-speed Internet access have kept the U.S. attractiveness level high, and the legally protected intellectual property rights (IPR) in the U.S. has been a long-standing significant feature. Furthermore, the weakening of the dollar has actually improved U.S. cost competitiveness, lowering the entry cost for FDI. With U.S. investment opportunities producing higher yields than Japan and Europe, it is still advantageous to choose the U.S. over other developed countries.

Challenges on the Horizon

Despite an impressive list of advantages, the U.S. can no longer assume that foreign firms will continue to invest and employ people here at the same rate as in the past. The effects of globalization and off-shoring trends have led to fluctuations in foreign investment, with the U.S. dropping to third place (from second) in 2005 as the most attractive future FDI location after China and India. In manufacturing alone, the U.S. share of world trade fell to 10 percent in 2004 from 13 percent in the 1990s. A recent study conducted by the Council of Manufacturing Associations and the National Association of Manufacturers warned that failure to revitalize innovation in high-end manufacturing would result in a further migration of work overseas and risk further U.S. economic decline.

Global trends challenge some traditional U.S. strengths, notably intellectual capital, formerly one of its most important advantages. Today, it is not only low wages that attract companies to Asia; it's also the huge pool of skilled human capital available. And while challenges from China are largely from manufacturing, the challenge from India is linked to services, due to its strength as an English-speaking country. Competition is thus intensifying on both the low-wage, low-skill side and the high-wage, high-skill side.

And despite the strength of IPR in the U.S. today, countries that are considered to be lax IPR locations—like China, India and Brazil—are gaining in FDI in research and development (R&D). In an October 2006 report by the World Intellectual Property Organization, China ranked fifth in a global league of patent applications, well ahead of sixth place Germany. Why are these countries excelling despite their laxity in this area? With the cost factor aside, technology being worked on may be highly firm-specific and of limited value to others, so IPR

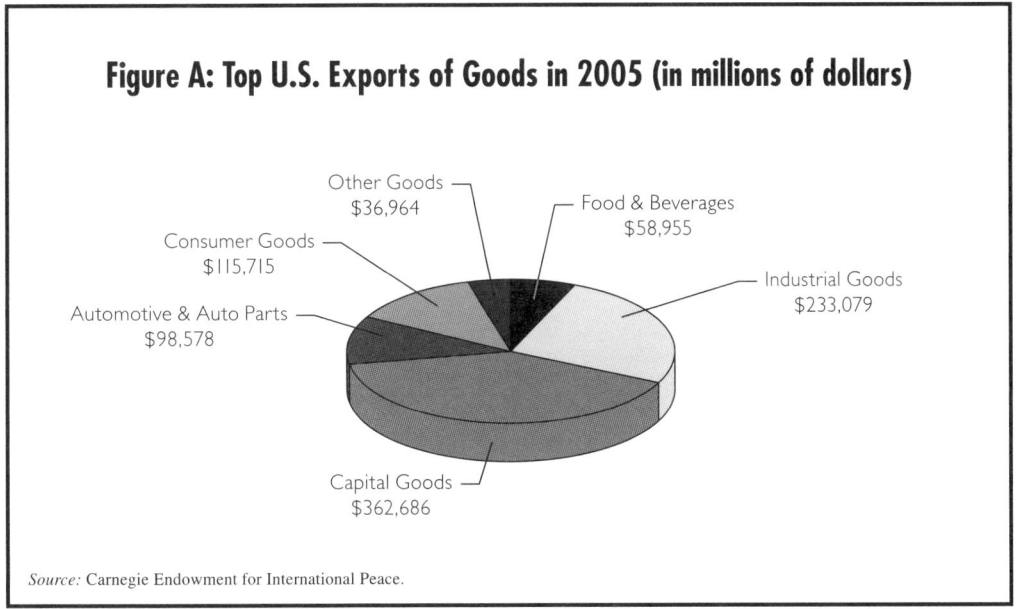

Figure A: Top U.S. Exports of Goods in 2005 (in millions of dollars)

Other Goods
$36,964

Food & Beverages
$58,955

Consumer Goods
$115,715

Industrial Goods
$233,079

Automotive & Auto Parts
$98,578

Capital Goods
$362,686

Source: Carnegie Endowment for International Peace.

risk is less important. Or, a firm may be involved in R&D that is far too technologically advanced for local competitors to be able to copy. Regardless of the reason, the fact that half the patents filed in China in 2004 were by foreign companies highlights the urgency for the U.S. to find ways to remain a competitive place for investment, and not overlook the fact that IPR strength might also be threatened.

Furthermore, not all challenges the U.S. is facing can be rationalized by globalization and the natural advancement of emerging nations. Some threats to FDI, though less tangible, cannot be ignored. For example, restrictions on visa requirements post-Sept. 11 have often blocked the best and the brightest scientific minds from being able to accept a job in the U.S., and corporate scandals have worn away any remaining trust of business leaders and in the financial integrity of public officials in the U.S. The widely viewed illustration of the federal government's weak and mismanaged response to the aftermath of Hurricane Katrina has contributed to a general lack of public confidence in the U.S. government, and no amount of rhetoric can erase those rueful images. In addition, for a wealthy nation, the U.S. infant mortality rates are higher than Japan, the Czech Republic and even Slovenia,[3] and spiraling costs for health care do not reflect the fact that Americans are receiving worse care than most other developed countries. This too is causing foreign investors to pause, and there's no doubt that U.S. health indicators are denting the country's overall competitiveness. As The Task Force

on the Future of American Innovation stated in a 2005 report, "The U.S. still leads the world in research and discovery, but our advantage is rapidly eroding, and global competitors may soon overtake us."[4]

With a current account deficit of more than $800 billion, or about 6.5 percent of GDP, and continued expenditures for national security skyrocketing, alarm bells should be ringing. Policymakers need to recognize the importance of maintaining the FDI flow and consider domestic conditions when seeking solutions to counter these challenges while maximizing the benefits for the U.S. economy. However, recent controversies involving foreign investment and national security have only burgeoned anxiety on this issue, causing politicians to wrangle over the question, while the trade balance continues to deteriorate.

FDI and National Security

In fairness, contention over foreign investment and national security is not new. In World War I, there were debates over foreign investment, especially from Germany, and in the 1980s there was much deliberation over Japanese investments in the country. In reaction to tension at the time, Congress passed the Exon-Florio Amendment in 1988[5] (or section 721 of the Defense Production Act of 1950), giving the president broad power to block acquisition of a U.S. company by a foreign entity if it threatened U.S. security. Globalization and Sept. 11 again brought the issue into the spotlight, and in 2005, furor rose over a bid by the Chinese National Off-

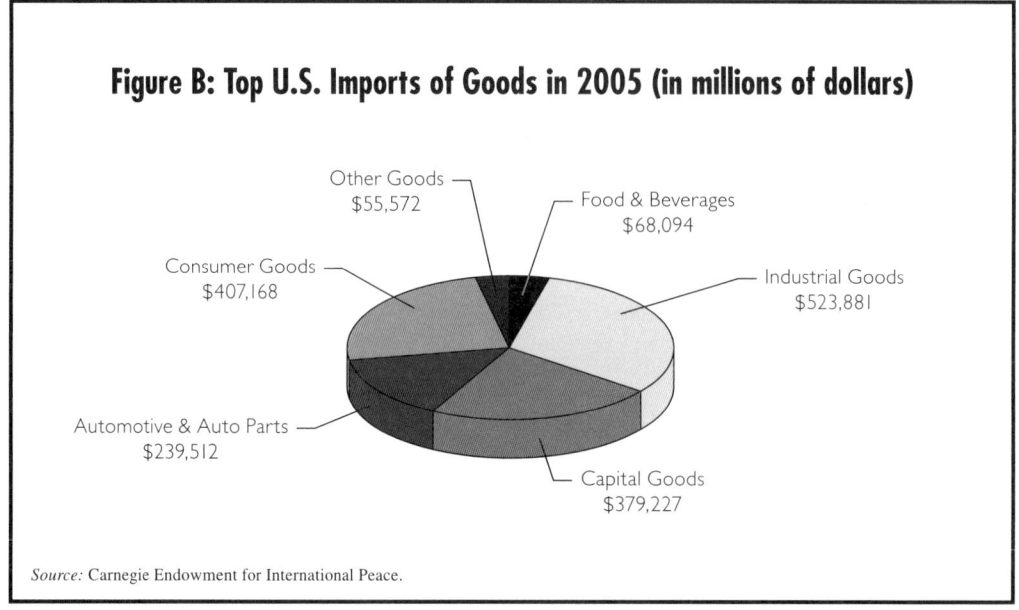

Figure B: Top U.S. Imports of Goods in 2005 (in millions of dollars)

Other Goods
$55,572

Food & Beverages
$68,094

Consumer Goods
$407,168

Industrial Goods
$523,881

Automotive & Auto Parts
$239,512

Capital Goods
$379,227

Source: Carnegie Endowment for International Peace.

shore Oil Corporation to buy the U.S. firm Unocal. The discussions escalated in 2006 when the Dubai Ports World almost took control of operations at six U.S. ports. Both companies withdrew their offers, but the CFIUS (Committee on Foreign Investment in the Unites States) process that is used to review such transactions came under heavy scrutiny, as did the question of what really defines a threat to national security, how this will (or will not) affect a firm's decision to invest in the U.S., and cast doubt on U.S. interest in encouraging foreign investment.

Moreover, several months later in May of this year, the Department of Transportation submitted a proposal allowing foreign investors increased equity in U.S. airlines, up 49 percent from the current 25 percent. While arguing that struggling U.S. airlines could benefit from further capital investment, Senate leaders expressed concerns over compromising U.S. national security.

Deputy Transportation Secretary Jeffrey Shanes disputed these concerns. "To the extent that an investment is attractive to a foreign citizen, it will be because there is the possibility of earning a return on that investment," he said.

Despite the provisions allowing for only 25 percent of voting shares, and this only for investors that have open-skies agreements with the U.S., this issue remains unresolved. However, perhaps as a sign that business lobbying is gaining some steam, in July of 2006, the CFIUS Reform Bill, the "National Security Foreign Investment Reform and Strengthened Transparency

Act of 2006," H.R. 5337, was passed in the House with provisions that are intended to protect U.S. jobs and opportunities for U.S. business abroad. Four leading U.S. business groups commended the House for passage of the bill that takes prudent steps to improve the vetting process for foreign investment without discouraging such investment from taking place.

Countering Threats

As politicians debate the national security issues, real or presumed, it is essential for the U.S. to maintain an open and friendly environment for FDI in order to sustain competitiveness and increase innovation, especially in light of the mounting U.S. account deficit. Economic developers and business leaders strive to attract investment and encourage business development through marketing and promotion at the state and local levels in order to attract FDI and to counter the threat of losing firms to overseas relocations.

R&D is a major source of knowledge creation and global R&D expenditure has grown rapidly over the past decade, and the U.S. accounts for more than 80 percent of the world's total.[6] R&D benefits to a local economy are formidable, with the spillover effects of a higher skilled work force and of knowledge sharing enhancing competition and accelerating economic growth. A recent study sponsored by the Ewing Marion Kauffman Foundation states that a majority of U.S. firms intend to keep their newest and most innovative research in the U.S., where IP protection is strongest and that only 22 percent of R&D work in developing countries is for cutting-edge research.[7] But, with Asian countries, particularly China, swiftly gaining their share of investments in this area, one does have to ask how much longer that will last without a conscious effort to counter these threats.

Advancing innovation, investment in education (particularly for advanced vocational training), and value-added services such as cluster development, and expanding business retention and expansion (BRE) efforts, will be key to both keeping businesses and to remaining competitive in attracting FDI. With so many jobs either shifted overseas or nonexistent today, mechanisms to assist displaced workers, by providing access for learning new skills and engaging in new industries is essential, and the educational system will need to be modified to prepare for more personal service type jobs that cannot be traded.

Encouraging universities to become more effective agents of regional development can be an effective strategy and examples of such collaboration can be witnessed in South Bend, Ind., where the city is working with the University of Notre Dame to establish a Research and Technology Park near the university's campus, and in Charlotte, N.C., where the Charlotte Research Institute (part of UNC-Charlotte) will open a new facility that will enable scientists to work on cutting-edge technology. Science parks are notorious for attracting R&D, and two-thirds of all parks are located in the U.S. and Europe, with the majority of science parks in emerging economies found in East Asia; therefore, focus in this area is critical.

Developing and promoting existing clusters is another key to retaining businesses, as well as attracting FDI. Michigan, for example, in 2004 launched an initiative to promote the state as an automotive Silicon Valley. Since then, the state has won investments from nine automotive companies from South Korea, Japan and Germany, creating some 3,000 engineering jobs. Asian automakers, from Toyota to Hyundai to Nissan Motor Co., are rushing to Michigan because the R&D centers of the Big Three and major U.S. suppliers are already located there, and in a region bestrewn with economic decay, the spillover from foreign investment in these automotive clusters is seen as a lifesaver. Honda's contribution to the U.S. economy reaches even further back in history, dating to the mid-1970s when it first entered the U.S. market, despite the groans of an "economic Pearl Harbor" arousing protectionist attitudes. Today, the company is no longer viewed derogatorily as a "Japanese company," but as an opportunity for a good job and economic advancement. This summer Honda announced its intention to open a $550 million plant in Greensburg, Ind., that will produce 200,000 cars a year and provide 2,000 jobs. Already in Ohio, Honda manufactures 680,000 cars a year and suppliers to Honda in the state benefit from its presence, countering the loss of jobs from Ford and GM with high paying blue-collar jobs.

Biotech clusters in the U.S. also continue to flourish precisely due to the value of intellectual property protection, the availability of venture capital, and the strong links between universities and research parks. Biotech in the U.S. generates sales of more than $50 billion per year, representing thousands of jobs and vigorous economic growth. These clusters also attract overseas investors and venture capitalists, as investors are pleased to put money into high-risk ventures in the hopes of high-level rewards in the U.S. Joint ventures and strategic alliances are common in the biotech industry. And to minimize the costs of keeping up with the more speculative areas of science, pharmaceutical companies are also partnering with smaller, more nimble companies that often lack the capital to see research through to the marketing stage.

In November 2005, Massachusetts Gov. Mitt Romney signed a partnership agreement with Italian officials to facilitate joint research projects and funding for Massachusetts biotechnology firms that want to do business overseas. Massachusetts is the first state to sign this type of agreement with the Lombardia region of Italy, where about 50 percent of the country's biotech firms are located. The agreement will foster R&D collaboration between the U.S. and Italy, establish joint research centers, and create technology transfer centers to commercialize new research, with an early emphasis on hematology and diabetes research. Through the Massachusetts Technology Transfer Center created in 2003, Massachusetts will gain access to European Union funding for research, and by tying the state's companies and universities to counterparts in Lombardia, the state is better positioned to secure future business partnerships with other nations.

Through BRE efforts, the U.S. can leverage its competitive advantage in order to slow the loss of R&D to Asia, as well as to Eastern Europe, by taking conscious steps to:

- maintain close links to universities, research labs, incubators and research parks;

- sustain an innovative business environment;

- promote the ease of commercialization of invention;

- provide support in areas of regulatory, tax issues and business assistance.

While the U.S. still has the largest market today, as Gene DePrez, America's leader for IBM's global location unit, recently said, "Companies looking to invest abroad have a lot more options." China and India are undeniably closing in on the U.S. and to retain a competitive advantage, U.S. policymakers and economic developers must actively work toward maintaining an environment that fosters a quality work force and collaborative relations between business and academia. Firms will need compelling reasons not only to retain facilities in the U.S., but also to expand within U.S. borders. Those who bristle over security issues will need to realize that upholding an amiable investment environment is in itself vital to the national security interests of the country and engaging in partnerships both at home and abroad, and learning to cooperate and adjust to global trends, will be crucial to maintaining a competitive advantage for the U.S.

Notes

[1] Office of International Investment, September 2006.

[2] *http://bea.gov/bea/newsrel/trans_highlights.pdf.*

[3] The World Economic Forum, *The Global Competitiveness Report 2006–2007*, 2006.

[4] The Task Force on the Future of American Innovation, *The Knowledge Economy: Is The United States Losing Its Competitive Edge?*, February 2005.

[5] Edward M. Graham and David M. Marchick, *U.S. National Security and Foreign Direct Investment, Institute for International Economics*, May 2006.

[6] United Nations Conference on Trade and Development (UNCTAD), World Investment Report 2005.

[7] Ewing Marion Kauffman Foundation, February 2006, Marie Thursby, Ph.D. and Jerry Thursby.

About the Author

Jeffrey A. Finkle, CEcD, is the president and CEO of the Washington, D.C.-based International Economic Development Council. He is a 20-year veteran in the world of economic development. Finkle, who earned a Bachelor of Science degree in communications from Ohio University and studied business administration at the graduate level at Ohio State University, also has a history in the public sector, having served as deputy assistant secretary of community planning and development for program management with the U.S. Department of Housing and Urban Development.

Economic Development Issues: Credits Where Credits Are Due
By Adam Bruns

The successful renewal of the research and development (R&D) tax credit in the nation's capital is just one of several economic development issues affecting states that continue to seek a head of steam in Congress, as supporters will try to convince the 110th Congress to make the Economic Development Act of 2005 into law. In the meantime, one state's experience with incentives demonstrates that not all that glitters is gold.

Two recent statements from big and stalwart midwestern industrial companies say it all about the importance of tax credits and other incentives to U.S. industry.

One came in an interview for *Site Selection* magazine in early December with Mark Gerstle, vice president-corporate quality and chief risk officer for Columbus, Indiana-based engine manufacturer Cummins, which reported net income of $550 million in 2005. When asked about the ongoing importance of both state and federal R&D tax credits to the company's growth, Gerstle said, "They're all critically important. Those credits are incredibly important not only to Cummins, but to the long-term competitiveness of America."

The second statement was more mundane, and probably similar to many others, coming in the third-quarter earnings statement of Milwaukee-based Harley-Davidson:

"The Company's third quarter effective income tax rate was 36.0 percent compared to 35.5 percent in the same quarter last year. This increase was due to the expiration of the federal research and development tax credit as of December 31, 2005. Assuming the retroactive reinstatement of this tax credit, the Company expects its full-year effective tax rate in 2006 will be 35.5 percent."

Doesn't seem like a lot, but for a company that's reporting $4.3 billion in revenue in the first nine months of 2006, half a percentage point can mean a lot. Thus it meant a lot to these two companies and others when, in early December 2006, the 109th Congress finally renewed the R&D tax credit, though only through 2007. Cummins and Harley-Davidson have even more in common. Both are pursuing major expansions in their home states (Indiana and Wisconsin, respectively) and both are receiving some measure of state incentives as part of the bargain.

What stands out about the incentive packages for their projects and, increasingly others on the radar, are noncash elements. At the same time, the phrase "economic development" has begun to appear in the titles of some corporate staff formerly labeled as "corporate real estate" or "planning." The PR value of corporations' economic development roles are being mined in ad campaigns from companies such as Toyota and Nucor. And organizations like the Ottumwa Economic Development Corporation are putting up billboards thanking Cargill and John Deere just for being there.

Is the cutthroat drive for the best project deal giving way to softhearted "we're all in this together" sentiment? Not completely. But corporations' sustainable development agendas are working their way into strategic planning and risk management departments.

True Partners

The fruit of that intermingling is a sense of community responsibility that goes well beyond a strict definition of incentives to cultivate a sense of partnership in more than name only.

That sense was evident in 2006 in Indiana Gov. Mitch Daniels' project negotiations with Toyota and Honda. Both companies announced major investments that together will create 3,000 automotive manufacturing jobs in the state. And both demurred on breaking the incentive bank to attain their goals.

"Toyota said an admirable thing to me," Daniels told *Site Selection*. "They said, 'Listen, more important to us than any incentives is that eventually you move to the single factor taxation, so we no longer have a disincentive to invest here.' At the time, I said we're working on that, but to my surprise we did get it through this legislature. And Toyota will forego some of the small package we had agreed to."

Similarly, though the overall package was substantial, the incentives for the $550 million Honda plant in Greensburg were not all cash, which fit with Daniels' goal of trying to "win every deal, but at the lowest possible number," and Honda's goal of not wanting to place an undue burden on the tax base of a community it's just entering.

Daniels said incentives were "the very last thing we talked about with Honda. Honda was very modest in its requests, and the only incentives they were interested in were funds for infrastructure. The accurate number for Indiana's investment is $80 million, and while we're at it we're going to build additional infrastructure that Honda doesn't need at all."

Apparently, some companies really *don't* want everything and the kitchen sink.

"We have the enterprise zone program, and we know that site could be encompassed if that were a perk necessary to finalize a deal," Vicki Haugen, president and CEO of eastern Illinois economic development agency Vermilion Advantage, said about her community's "mega-site" in Fithian, which was a finalist for the Honda project. "But with global clients, not every client of that magnitude wants to have a potentially burdensome impact on local tax rolls."

In fact, it often comes as a surprise to the general public that companies do the amount of homework they do, given the way corporate relocation is often portrayed in the mainstream media. Such was the eye-opening experience for an auditorium full of students last year at a session called "Site Selection and the Corporate Bottom Line—Where Will the Jobs Be?" hosted by Texas A&M University-Corpus Christi in partnership with the Industrial Asset Management Council, an association of industrial corporate real estate executives and their economic development and service provider partners. The IAMC had just held one of its semi-annual conferences in town, and among the presenters were corporate real estate and facilities directors from CSX, Weyerhaeuser, Pfizer and the former BOC Group (now part of Linde Co.).

Questions and issues ranged from the majors and minors in the IAMC members' own educational pedigree to the economic development promise of the Corpus Christi region. Students were given a candid look at how companies evaluate site selection decisions—and some expressed surprise that the process is more holistic, thorough and rational than they thought. The concept of a company applying analytical tools and even a conscience to its site selection processes served to rattle a few preconceptions about corporate, multinational America—and perhaps helped some younger minds begin to form their own understanding of what a partnership could entail.

Money Where Mouth Is

Back in Indiana, the selflessness extended beyond Honda to include what can sometimes be the most vicious antagonist: a neighboring jurisdiction. Combined state and local direct investment to support the

Table C: State Corporate Income Tax Revenue, FY 2006

Top 10 states	Revenue (in billions)
1. California	$12.433
2. New York	2.892
3. New Jersey	2.004
4. Pennsylvania	1.921
5. Michigan	1.917
6. Florida	1.73
7. Illinois	1.548
8. North Carolina	1.272
9. Massachusetts	1.063
10. Ohio	1.052

Bottom 10 states	Revenue (in millions)
1. Nevada	NA
1. South Dakota	NA
1. Texas	NA
1. Washington	NA
1. Wyoming	NA
6. Vermont	$60
7. Alaska	61
8. North Dakota	84
9. Rhode Island	84
10. Hawaii	86

Source: Nelson A. Rockefeller Institute of Government Revenue Report Database.
Note: Data from Michigan, New York and Texas was standardized to fit a July–June fiscal year.
Key:
NA — Not applicable (no corporate income tax)

Honda project includes tax credits, training assistance, and real and personal property tax abatements totaling up to $41.5 million. In addition, there will be infrastructure support for water, wastewater and road improvements of approximately $44 million. To accommodate future growth in the region, the state is expediting the long-sought interchange upgrade on Interstate 74, along with water, wastewater and other road upgrades totaling approximately $56 million. But key to making the project happen is a $10 million contribution from the City of Lawrenceburg, 50 minutes from Greensburg. Nestled on the Ohio River at the state line with Ohio, Lawrenceburg boasts a ski slope, but its real claim to fame is riverboat gambling. Having now caught up with the infrastructure deficit that the first wave of gaming tourism wrought, the forward-thinking leaders of Lawrenceburg decided some time ago to devote a significant portion of gaming money to helping their region at large.

Daniels believes this arrangement provides a new model for collaboration between two frequently warring sides of economic development, gambling and traditional industry. He called Lawrenceburg's commitment "very material" to the process.

"It's important in two dimensions," he said. "We would have found another way, but it made the transaction easier, and more balanced among state, local and regional entities. And it's a great model for regional cooperation, with the recognition two counties away that the whole area would benefit if Honda chose us. Before they knew anything about Honda, they were looking to invest something like $10 million in the region each year. Then this opportunity came, and this will be their Year One investment."

Daniels hopes Lawrenceburg officials might see the Honda-related development as a good target for Years Two and Three as well. But for now, the pace has been set. "I think it's a good model to be able to leverage those gaming receipts over a region," Don Schilling, CEO of Decatur County Rural Electric Member Cooperative and board president of the Greensburg-Decatur County Economic Development Corp., said. "Obviously a lot of those receipts are generated by people across the region, so it makes sense to return it to the region."

National Issues, Local Solutions

Even as states buoyed by the Supreme Court's dismissal of the *Cuno v. DaimlerChrysler* case on lack of standing move to enact innovative and more far-reaching incentive programs, the cost of manufacturing in the United States continues to rise.

So said "The Escalating Cost Crisis," a report issued in September 2006 by the National Association of Manufacturers, The Manufacturing Institute and Manufacturers Alliance/MAPI. Since 2003, the U.S. structural manufacturing cost gap vis-à-vis our major trading partners has increased by almost 40 percent, according to the report, mainly because the U.S. corporate tax rate stays the same while other nations' tax rates decline. According to the study, last conducted

in 2003, corporate tax rates, employee benefits, tort costs, natural gas prices and pollution abatement collectively add 31.7 percent to U.S. manufacturers' costs versus the nation's nine major competitors, an increase from 22.4 percent just three years ago.

While cheers resounded for the R&D credit renewal as well as the New Markets Tax Credit renewal, the Economic Development Act of 2005, which officially recognizes the power of states to offer tax incentives, continued to languish. In late September, a bipartisan coalition of senators supporting the act signed a letter that called on Senate Finance Committee members to take action.

"Traditionally, it has been the prerogative of each state to determine how to use its tax base, including the best ways to promote economic development within its borders," wrote the senators. "Congress generally has not interfered in that process. Before coming to the Senate, many of us were state and local officials who participated in these decisions and understand the important role that tax policy plays in maintaining strong states and communities."

One of those was Sen. George Voinovich, R-Ohio, who introduced the bill in 2005, and who has served as Ohio's governor and Cleveland's mayor. In a statement to *Site Selection*, he wrote:

"The support for *Cuno* remains significant because the Supreme Court's decision, which was procedural in nature, did not address the substantive issue of the constitutionality of state tax incentives. The substantive law in this area remains ambiguous. For example, in *Cuno* litigation, the federal trial court and the federal appellate court disagreed as to the appropriate application of the dormant Commerce Clause. The disagreement between these courts reflects the differences between two general, but conflicting, legal principles the Supreme Court has developed regarding state taxes. The first principle is that a state may not impose a tax that discriminates against interstate commerce by providing a direct commercial advantage to local business. The second principle is that a state may use its tax system to encourage intrastate commerce and may compete with other states for interstate commerce so long as the state does not discriminatorily tax the products manufactured or the business operations performed in any other state. The court does not appear to have ever completely reconciled these two principles. Consequently, the uncertainty for state and local governments remains, and the need for the Economic Development Act remains unchanged."

Capital Accumulation

A promising note for development finance was sounded in May 2006 on almost the exact same day as the *Cuno* decision. Included in the final version of the Tax Increase Prevention and Reconciliation Act of 2005 was an amendment accelerating an increase in the capital expenditure limit on small issue Industrial Development Bonds (IDBs) from Sept. 30, 2009, to Dec. 31, 2006. The increase raises the capital expenditure limit from $10 million to $20 million. The $10 million capital expenditure limitation was first established during the 1978–79 congressional session, but had not been adjusted for inflation. The $20 million cap was originally passed by Congress in 2004. Numerous economic developers testified to the acceleration's immediate benefits to industrial projects that had been hamstrung by the previous expenditure limit.

Seven months later, the Council of Development Finance Agencies, which had backed the accelerated schedule for IDBs, was seeking input from its membership on another front, as the IRS sought testimony on the subject of payment-in-lieu-of-taxes in its examination of whether to require PILOT payments to represent a fixed percentage of generally applicable taxes when issued for certain tax-exempt economic development bond deals.

Toyota Motor Manufacturing Kentucky Inc., which employs 7,000 people in central Kentucky, in early December 2006 presented a check for $1,213,532 to Scott County Schools, representing the company's 19th annual PILOT payment to the school system. As a company release explained, "TMMK financed portions of its original automobile manufacturing plant, the Powertrain facility, and the expanded manufacturing facility through Industrial Revenue Bonds. Since property financed through bonds is exempt from property taxation, the school system would usually not receive its share of property taxes on the financial property until the bonds mature in 2008. In 1988, Toyota agreed to make an annual payment to the Scott County Board of Education to make up for the loss of tax payments."

Six years later, the company accelerated a portion of the annual payments and made a lump-sum payment of $8 million in addition to its annual payment of more than $1 million, enabling the county to construct a new high school. The 2006 payment brings the total amount paid since 1988 to more than $27.4 million.

"Congressional action is needed in order to more thoroughly affirm states' right to compete, and give the markets the kind of predictability they require," said Jay Biggins, executive managing director of corporate advisory firm Stadtmauer Bailkin Biggins LLC, in a September advisory.

He said in an interview the Economic Development Act has lost some traction, but not its momentum. Meanwhile, "this risk is still out there, and the risk of uncertainty is almost as important as the risk of a result."

Stadtmauer Bailkin Biggins has developed a questionnaire for law firms with 100 attorneys or more asking whether they're aware of any cases challenging the same principles of the *Cuno* case in other circuits. Biggins said no legal information

services track this subject. And, he said, because of the misperception that the *Cuno* decision resolved the issue, "the anxiety level is clearly lower, and the guard is down."

One group whose guard is clearly up is The Council on State Taxation, whose officers and board include tax and finance executives from the likes of General Electric, Chevron, Johnson & Johnson, Alcoa and General Motors. In a July 2006 letter to Voinovich, COST wrote of the *Cuno* dismissal: "While the underlying case was dismissed on procedural grounds, the substantive issues remain unresolved. States that have looked to such incentives to encourage their economic growth and businesses that have reasonably relied upon such incentives in their investment decisions must now take a second look.

The risk for reduced future investment and lower U.S. economic growth will continue to exist until this issue is resolved. Moreover, the door is still open to additional expensive lawsuits targeting economic development incentives in almost every state.

"The Congress has the power to affirm States' right to use tax incentives to increase and enhance economic development within their borders," they continued. "Congress can establish needed certainty in this area by enacting the Economic Development Act of 2005. As currently drafted this legislation strikes the right balance between States' tax rights and long-established court protections against truly discriminatory practices."

A state-level case similar to *Cuno*, involving Dell in North Carolina, was also denied a hearing based on the technicality of standing. Joseph R. Crosby, COST legislative director, does not foresee another tax incentives challenge reaching the high court in the near future.

"The majority of challenges to tax incentives in the past have been from taxpayers (generally businesses) who *did not* qualify for an incentive (e.g., Northwest most recently), not from taxpayers (generally individuals) claiming harm because others *did* qualify for an incentive (e.g., *Cuno* and Dell)," Crosby wrote in an e-mail. "We expect that aggrieved business taxpayers, who can articulate a specific harm and are unaffected by the Supreme Court's ruling re: standing, will continue to file claims when they feel that an incentive discriminates against interstate commerce. The Supreme Court's decision certainly impacts the fortunes of those who had hoped to sue, like *Cuno*, under municipal taxpayer standing, but it is worth noting that the lead attorney in the *Cuno* case, Peter Enrich, has vowed to continue his crusade against tax incentives for economic development purposes."

Crusades like that are just one more reason for states to look at the creativity they can bring to noncash incentives. The linchpin of the Cummins decision, for example, was a unique educational partnership, designed to keep skilled employee candidates flowing to both Cummins and Honda. And Daniels said having its own fiscal house in order has also helped Indiana, something which has surprised even a former OMB director. As its debt ratings rise, the state has its first balanced budget in eight years, and is also setting things straight fiscally with its school systems.

"I probably underestimated the attention some would pay to this," said Daniels. "If people believe a balanced budget and a stronger fiscal position reduces the possibility of tax increases, they'd be exactly right as far as we're concerned."

In response to efforts by Voinovich and others to pass national legislation freeing states to offer economic development incentives as they choose, Daniels said it was a tough issue, but erring toward more freedom for the states is preferable.

"I do favor letting freedom reign here, and letting states make their own mistakes if they're dumb enough to make them," he said. "There's no question it's a risky thing to let politicians loose with money that's not their money. They go to the ribbon cuttings and if the deal goes bad in a few years, they're probably somewhere else. Our approach at IEDC is to try to replicate the rigor and caution that a business takes with its own money. I think the better side of the argument is to allow states to compete aggressively, and the competition on a net basis will be good just like global competition is. It makes businesses better. And those who tax too much or move too slowly will sooner or later see the error of their ways."

About the Author

Since early 2002, **Adam Bruns** has served as managing editor of *Site Selection*. Bruns' work has appeared in such publications as *American Libraries*, *Links*, *Golf Journal*, *Louisville*, *Golfweek* and *The Lane Report*, a regional business publication in central Kentucky. In 2001 he received first prize in magazine business reporting from the Louisville chapter of the Society of Professional Journalists.

Table A
FINANCIAL ASSISTANCE FOR INDUSTRY

State or other jurisdiction	State sponsored industrial development authority	Privately sponsored development credit corporation	State authority or agency revenue bond financing	State authority or agency general obligation bond financing	City and/or county revenue bond financing	City and/or County General obligation bond financing	State loans for building construction	State loans for equipment, machinery	City and/or county loans for building construction	City and/or county loans for equipment, machinery	State loan guarantees for building construction	State loan guarantees for equipment, machinery	City and/or county loan guarantees for building construction	City and/or county loan guarantees for equipment, machinery	State financing aid for existing plant expansion	State matching funds for city and/or county industrial financing programs	State incentive for establishing industrial plants in areas of high unemployment	City and/or county incentive for establishing industrial plants in areas of high unemployment
State totals	42	39	45	24	47	39	42	43	46	46	30	34	19	19	44	27	43	38
Alabama																		
Alaska																		
Arizona																		
Arkansas																		
California																		
Colorado																		
Connecticut																		
Delaware																		
Florida																		
Georgia																		
Hawaii																		
Idaho																		
Illinois																		
Indiana																		
Iowa																		
Kansas																		
Kentucky																		
Louisiana																		
Maine																		
Maryland																		
Massachusetts																		
Michigan																		
Minnesota																		
Mississippi																		
Missouri																		
Montana																		
Nebraska																		
Nevada																		
New Hampshire																		
New Jersey																		
New Mexico																		
New York																		
North Carolina																		
North Dakota																		
Ohio																		

See footnotes at end of table.

FINANCIAL ASSISTANCE FOR INDUSTRY — Continued

State or other jurisdiction	State sponsored industrial development authority	Privately sponsored development credit corporation	State authority or agency revenue bond financing	State authority or agency general obligation bond financing	City and/or county revenue bond financing	City and/or County General obligation bond financing	State loans for building construction	State loans for equipment, machinery	City and/or county loans for building construction	City and/or county loans for equipment, machinery	State loan guarantees for building construction	State loan guarantees for equipment, machinery	City and/or county loan guarantees for building construction	City and/or county loan guarantees for equipment, machinery	State financing aid for existing plant expansion	State matching funds for city and/or county industrial financing programs	State incentive for establishing industrial plants in areas of high unemployment	City and/or county incentive for establishing industrial plants in areas of high unemployment
Oklahoma	★	…	★	★	★	★	★	★	★	★	★	★	★	★	★	★	★	★
Oregon	★	★	★	★	★	★	★	★	★	★	★	★	★	★	★	★	★	★
Pennsylvania	★	★	★	★	★	★	★	★	★	★	★	★	★	★	★	★	★	★
Rhode Island	★	★	★	…	★	…	★	★	★	★	★	★	…	…	★	…	★	…
South Carolina	★	★	★	…	★	★	★	★	★	★	…	…	…	…	★	★	…	★
South Dakota	…	…	★	★	★	★	★	★	★	★	…	…	…	…	…	…	…	…
Tennessee	★	…	★	★	★	★	★	★	★	★	★	★	★	★	★	★	★	★
Texas	★	★	★	★	★	★	…	★	★	★	…	★	…	★	★	★	★	…
Utah	★	★	…	…	★	★	★	…	★	★	★	★	…	…	★	…	★	★
Vermont	…	★	…	…	★	★	…	★	★	★	…	★	…	…	★	★	★	…
Virginia	★	★	★	…	★	★	★	★	★	★	★	★	★	…	★	★	★	★
Washington	★	★	★	★	★	…	★	★	★	★	★	★	…	…	★	★	★	…
West Virginia	★	★	★	★	★	★	★	★	…	★	…	★	★	…	★	★	★	★
Wisconsin	★	★	★	…	★	★	★	★	★	★	★	★	…	…	★	★	…	…
Wyoming	★	★	…	…	★	★	★	★	★	★	…	★	…	…	★	★	…	…
Puerto Rico	★	★	★	★	★	★	★	★	…	…	★	★	★	★	★	★	★	★

Key:
★ — Yes
… — No; or state/jurisdiction did not respond to survey.

Source: *Site Selection*, November 2006.

Note: A significant number of footnotes are published with these charts in the November 2006 issue of *Site Selection* Magazine. For more information or to obtain a set of the footnotes, contact Editor Adam Bruns at adam.bruns@conway.com.

Table B
TAX INCENTIVES FOR INDUSTRY

State or other jurisdiction	Corporate income tax exemption	Personal income tax exemption	Excise tax exemption	Tax exemption or moratorium on land, capital improvements	Tax exemption or moratorium on equipment, machinery	Inventory tax exemption on goods in transit (freeport)	Tax exemption on manufacturers' inventories	Sales/use tax exemption on new equipment	Tax exemption on raw materials used in manufacturing	Tax incentive for creation of jobs	Tax incentive for industrial investment	Tax credits for use of specified state products	Tax stabilization agreements for specified industries	Tax exemption to encourage research and development	Accelerated depreciation of industrial equipment
State totals	41	37	28	40	44	49	47	49	50	45	45	8	12	42	41
Alabama	★	★	★	★	★	★	★	★	★	★	★			★	★
Alaska		★	★			★		★	★			★			★
Arizona	★			★	★	★	★	★	★	★	★	★		★	★
Arkansas	★		★	★	★	★	★	★	★	★	★			★	★
California	★	★		★	★	★	★	★	★	★	★			★	★
Colorado	★	★	★	★	★	★	★	★	★	★	★			★	★
Connecticut	★	★		★	★	★	★	★	★	★	★	★	★	★	★
Delaware	★	★	★	★	★	★	★	★	★	★	★			★	★
Florida	★	★		★	★	★	★	★	★	★	★			★	★
Georgia	★	★		★	★	★	★	★	★	★	★		★	★	★
Hawaii	★	★	★	★	★	★	★	★	★	★	★			★	★
Idaho	★	★	★	★	★	★	★	★	★	★	★			★	★
Illinois	★	★	★	★	★	★	★	★	★	★	★			★	★
Indiana	★	★		★	★	★	★	★	★	★	★			★	★
Iowa	★	★		★	★	★	★	★	★	★	★			★	★
Kansas	★	★	★	★	★	★	★	★	★	★	★			★	★
Kentucky	★	★		★	★	★	★	★	★	★	★	★		★	★
Louisiana	★	★	★	★	★	★	★	★	★	★	★		★	★	★
Maine	★	★	★	★	★	★	★	★	★	★	★		★	★	★
Maryland	★	★		★	★	★	★	★	★	★	★			★	★
Massachusetts	★	★		★	★	★	★	★	★	★	★			★	★
Michigan	★	★		★	★	★	★	★	★	★	★			★	★
Minnesota	★	★	★	★	★	★	★	★	★	★	★			★	★
Mississippi	★	★	★	★	★	★	★	★	★	★	★		★	★	★
Missouri	★	★	★	★	★	★	★	★	★	★	★			★	★
Montana	★	★		★	★	★	★	★	★	★	★			★	★
Nebraska	★	★	★	★	★	★	★	★	★	★	★	★	★	★	★
Nevada		★	★	★	★	★	★	★	★	★	★			★	★
New Hampshire	★			★	★	★	★	★	★	★	★			★	★
New Jersey	★	★	★	★	★	★	★	★	★	★	★			★	★
New Mexico	★	★	★	★	★	★	★	★	★	★	★			★	★
New York	★	★	★	★	★	★	★	★	★	★	★			★	★
North Carolina	★	★	★	★	★	★	★	★	★	★	★			★	★
North Dakota	★			★	★	★	★	★	★	★	★			★	
Ohio	★	★		★	★	★	★	★	★	★	★			★	★

See footnotes at end of table.

TAX INCENTIVES FOR INDUSTRY — Continued

State or other jurisdiction	Corporate income tax exemption	Personal income tax exemption	Excise tax exemption	Tax exemption or moratorium on land, capital improvements	Tax exemption or moratorium on equipment, machinery	Inventory tax exemption on goods in transit (freeport)	Tax exemption on manufacturers' inventories	Sales/use tax exemption on new equipment	Tax exemption on raw materials used in manufacturing	Tax incentive for creation of jobs	Tax incentive for industrial investment	Tax credits for use of specified state products	Tax stabilization agreements for specified industries	Tax exemption to encourage research and development	Accelerated depreciation of industrial equipment
Oklahoma	★	★	★	★	★	★	★	★	★	★	★	★	★	★	★
Oregon	.	.	★	★	★	★	★	★	★	.	★	.	.	★	★
Pennsylvania	.	★	★	★	★	★	★	★	★	★	★	★	★	★	★
Rhode Island	★	.	★	★	★	★	★	★	★	★	★	★	★	★	★
South Carolina	★	.	.	★	★	★	★	★	★	★	★	.	.	★	★
South Dakota	★	★	.	★	.	★	.	★	★	★	★	.	.	★	★
Tennessee	★	★	★	★	★	★	★	★	★	★	★	.	.	★	★
Texas	.	★	★	.	★	★	★	★	★	★	★	.	.	.	.
Utah	.	.	.	.	.	★	.	★	★	★	.	.	.	.	.
Vermont	.	.	.	.	.	★	★	★	★	★	★	.	★	★	★
Virginia	★	★	★	★	★	★	★	★	★	★	★	.	★	★	★
Washington	★	★	.	.	★	★	★	★	★	★	★	★	★	★	★
West Virginia	★	★	★	★	★	★	★	★	★	★	★	.	.	★	.
Wisconsin	★	★	.	.	.	★	.	★	★	★	★	★	.	★	★
Wyoming	★	★	.	.	★	★	★	★	★	.	★	.	.	★	.
Puerto Rico	★	★	★	★	★	★	★	★	★	★	★	★	★	★	★

Source: Site Selection, November 2006.

Note: A significant number of footnotes are published with these charts in the November 2006 issue of *Site Selection* Magazine. For more information or to obtain a set of the footnotes, contact Editor Adam Bruns at adam.bruns@conway.com.

Key:
★ — Yes
. . . — No; or state/jurisdiction did not respond to survey.

Table 9.12
STATE REVENUES USED FOR HIGHWAYS, BY REGION: 2005
(In thousands of dollars)

| State or other jurisdiction | Beginning balance total (a) | Highway-user revenues (b) | | | | Appropriations from general funds (c) | Other state imposts | Miscellaneous | Bond proceeds (d) | Payments from other governments | | | Total receipts |
| | | Motor-fuel taxes | Motor-vehicle and motor-carrier taxes | Road and crossing tolls | Total | | | | | Federal funds | | Local government | |
										Federal Hwy. Administration	Other agencies		
United States	$39,972,475	$31,032,149	$18,144,032	$6,355,728	$55,531,909	$3,383,776	$4,290,529	$2,896,340	$21,192,312	$29,933,989	$992,873	$2,151,125	$120,372,853
Eastern Region													
Connecticut............	310,046	297,686	173,846	167	471,699	112,772	82,724	82,527	309,831	316,907	7,827	2,994	1,387,281
Delaware.................	391,228	116,785	92,806	176,994	386,585	176,483	0	32,171	368,293	102,083	1,942	0	1,067,557
Maine.....................	82,515	208,152	52,708	84,580	345,440	0	0	11,531	76,715	178,342	1,008	0	613,036
Massachusetts.........	2,100,038	671,498	307,118	272,853	1,251,469	548,966	0	115,118	357,198	454,780	15,111	0	2,742,642
New Hampshire (f)...	130,950	146,426	92,147	64,987	303,560	0	0	8,850	5,281	127,389	1,614	3,335	450,029
New Jersey..............	2,093,288	253,542	325,209	886,553	1,465,304	0	0	124,795	4,864,237	687,254	7,350	0	7,148,940
New York................	-387,918	1,344,055	722,317	1,088,029	3,154,401	277,736	0	119,661	5,085,679	1,706,169	19,031	27,969	10,390,646
Pennsylvania...........	2,583,928	1,873,750	834,062	728,504	3,436,316	50,977	0	199,457	5,267,332	1,062,740	23,877	15,767	5,056,466
Rhode Island (e)......	40,637	66,286	29,872	12,181	108,339	0	1,495	49,036	33,350	218,549	2,691	0	411,965
Vermont..................	17,700	40,835	114,720	0	155,555	0	0	10,200	1,592	127,281	6,948	733	303,804
Regional average......	736,241	501,902	274,481	331,485	1,107,867	116,693	8,422	75,335	1,136,951	498,149	8,740	5,080	2,957,237
Midwestern Region													
Illinois...................	1,116,305	1,206,866	1,177,899	604,881	2,989,646	0	52	91,922	1,147,006	847,669	14,601	59,064	5,149,960
Indiana...................	361,624	879,038	131,678	89,023	1,099,739	71,374	0	147,772	0	578,482	19,927	182,147	2,099,441
Iowa.......................	153,896	418,344	362,342	0	780,686	40,338	289,054	7,411	0	319,452	8,870	0	1,445,811
Kansas....................	1,113,036	405,290	120,860	73,784	599,934	0	106,235	27,209	0	381,588	10,178	26,719	1,151,863
Michigan.................	1,156,397	916,116	785,105	31,394	1,732,615	335,529	37,338	138,323	319,990	805,330	18,572	50,944	3,438,641
Minnesota...............	908,642	652,031	527,235	0	1,179,266	16,797	190,886	55,707	123,169	442,145	17,750	32,060	2,057,780
Nebraska.................	108,280	301,469	84,366	0	385,835	28,579	145,196	10,525	0	282,188	3,316	37,787	893,426
North Dakota (e)......	49,801	113,418	49,177	0	162,595	0	6,284	262	0	215,364	9,453	20,967	414,925
Ohio.......................	1,155,727	1,696,753	702,880	182,449	2,582,082	0	0	44,184	149,274	1,050,601	32,070	64,783	3,922,994
South Dakota (e)......	101,066	121,940	2,676	0	124,616	0	58,583	28,069	0	221,111	1,893	14,980	449,252
Wisconsin................	482,671	861,706	369,407	0	1,231,113	0	0	31,648	364,789	533,770	8,538	134,915	2,304,773
Regional average......	609,768	688,452	392,148	89,230	1,169,830	44,783	75,784	53,003	191,293	516,155	13,197	56,761	2,120,806
Southern Region													
Alabama (e).............	304,179	477,558	221,154	0	698,712	62,630	50,107	7,699	59,446	577,109	44,037	34,448	1,534,188
Arkansas.................	193,811	430,923	115,009	0	545,932	88,912	1,356	10,865	0	411,958	8,809	4,914	1,072,746
Florida....................	1,834,717	1,807,525	740,004	910,573	3,458,102	234,835	106,737	137,654	1,872,806	1,868,942	18,679	293,300	7,991,055
Georgia...................	2,124,927	422,720	191,487	14,203	628,410	0	318,711	65,286	45,909	746,338	13,383	13,008	1,831,045
Kentucky.................	562,672	488,956	577,351	0	1,066,307	298,794	0	48,723	434,669	457,181	16,371	0	2,322,045
Louisiana (e)...........	146,041	577,102	42,763	34,834	654,699	154,651	0	39,973	0	474,887	8,024	0	1,332,234
Maryland.................	707,177	477,326	561,311	154,321	1,192,958	0	72,121	49,476	179,000	627,858	8,978	0	1,951,391
Mississippi..............	268,159	378,426	135,389	0	513,815	0	31,995	7,010	0	402,057	7,316	10,657	1,151,850
Missouri..................	441,752	707,665	251,060	0	958,725	7,255	218,227	15,772	0	776,723	8,812	7,007	1,992,521
North Carolina.........	624,554	1,237,025	440,996	2,298	1,680,319	0	420,103	62,496	324,601	1,085,537	38,333	11,458	3,622,847
Oklahoma...............	511,567	276,341	181,594	193,643	651,578	129	51,494	35,692	0	419,295	8,057	8,633	1,174,878
South Carolina.........	156,291	474,037	108,174	9,630	591,841	0	2,233	11,569	146,686	802,801	6,853	26,983	1,588,966
Tennessee...............	1,111,062	706,278	219,749	24	926,051	84,275	53,438	78,821	0	620,675	19,876	41,084	1,824,220
Texas......................	3,133,258	1,799,299	1,556,813	180,496	3,536,608	0	33,004	296,601	1,858,173	3,130,810	72,381	183,521	9,111,098
Virginia...................	1,484,871	861,724	717,716	117,287	1,696,727	286,086	511,474	82,598	349,167	431,485	27,817	85,002	3,470,356
West Virginia...........	155,744	289,092	262,749	55,727	607,568	13,618	0	26,666	351,405	439,964	18,286	0	1,457,507
Regional average......	860,049	713,250	395,207	104,565	1,213,022	76,949	116,938	61,056	351,366	829,601	20,376	45,001	2,714,309

See footnotes at end of table.

STATE REVENUES USED FOR HIGHWAYS, BY REGION: 2005—Continued
(In thousands of dollars)

State or other jurisdiction	Beginning balance total (a)	Highway-user revenues (b)				Appropriations from general funds (c)	Other state imposts	Miscellaneous	Bond proceeds (d)	Payments from other governments			Total receipts
										Federal funds			
		Motor-fuel taxes	Motor-vehicle and motor-carrier taxes	Road and crossing tolls	Total					Federal Hwy. Administration	Other agencies	Local government	
Western Region													
Alaska..............	52,771	31,473	39,648	21,751	92,872	87,558	0	26,569	0	384,419	7,882	0	599,300
Arizona.............	707,758	624,777	287,056	0	911,833	0	801,268	33,686	318,216	508,783	15,019	23,731	2,612,536
California...........	6,294,526	3,206,048	2,310,261	231,858	5,748,167	26,656	423,498	195,361	300,000	2,132,269	81,049	610,205	9,517,205
Colorado...........	1,461,813	500,621	693,880	0	1,194,501	81,212	0	142,391	0	365,959	4,233	24,660	1,812,956
Hawaii..............	376,473	71,118	54,219	0	125,337	10,625	43,950	14,918	55,087	158,204	2,165	0	546,369
Idaho...............	92,562	203,695	118,552	0	322,247	0	0	3,862	0	254,435	16,457	3,326	600,327
Montana............	105,886	121,376	79,888	0	201,264	0	6,590	2,318	130,750	300,396	17,792	5,843	664,953
Nevada	262,052	353,138	113,486	520	467,144	37,294	0	24,431	190,054	201,768	5,682	0	926,373
New Mexico	988,475	243,422	229,813	0	473,235	0	19,229	18,326	0	240,971	29,407	0	781,168
Oregon.............	740,395	378,823	346,446	0	725,269	34,766	10,220	29,875	430,741	361,212	116,022	0	1,708,105
Utah................	443,880	332,318	93,180	164	425,662	113,556	40,143	28,054	50,141	235,719	40,404	11,191	944,870
Washington.........	542,503	893,482	298,579	132,020	1,324,081	0	35,131	40,987	485,642	570,095	45,850	76,990	2,578,776
Wyoming...........	17,831	41,963	31,342	0	73,305	14,313	85,152	21,118	0	196,474	47,889	0	438,251
Regional average....	929,763	538,635	361,258	29,716	929,609	31,229	112,706	44,761	150,818	454,670	33,065	58,150	1,825,476
Regional average without California...	482,700	316,351	198,841	12,871	528,063	31,610	86,807	32,211	138,386	314,870	29,067	12,145	1,184,499
Dist. of Columbia	54,911	25,912	65,933	0	91,845	87,060	36,501	1,165	0	90,471	4,443	0	311,485

Source: U.S. Department of Transportation, Federal Highway Administration, *Highway Statistics, 2005,* (November 2006).

Note: Detail may not add to totals due to rounding. This table was compiled from reports of state authorities.

Key:

(a) Amount includes reserves for current highway work and reserves for debt service. Any differences between beginning balances and the closing balances on last year's information are the result of accounting adjustments, inclusion of funds not previously reported, etc.

(b) Amounts shown represent only those highway-user revenues that were expended on state or local roads.

(c) Amounts shown represent gross general fund appropriations for highways reduced by the amount of highway-user revenues placed in the State General Fund.

(d) Amount shown represents original and refunding issues.

(e) Preliminary data was used.

(f) 2004 data was used.

Table 9.13
STATE DISBURSEMENTS FOR HIGHWAYS, BY REGION: 2005
(In thousands of dollars)

State or other jurisdiction	Capital outlay		Total	Maintenance and highway service expenditures (a)	Administration, research and planning	Highway law enforcement and safety	Interest	Bond retirement (b)	Grants in-aid to local governments	Total disbursements	Total year-end balances (d)
	State administered highways (a)	Locally administered roads									
United States	$50,309,238	$4,378,538	$54,687,776	$16,094,629	$6,523,226	$7,521,740	$4,361,963	$14,863,373	$12,464,390	$116,517,007	$43,828,321
Eastern Region											
Connecticut.........	555,676	0	555,676	149,167	57,673	126,451	148,794	372,910	23,667	1,434,338	262,989
Delaware............	357,736	0	357,736	116,357	194,892	53,594	64,228	316,960	0	1,103,767	355,018
Maine (c)............	256,544	0	256,544	163,532	27,236	37,703	17,791	90,690	22,926	616,422	79,129
Massachusetts.....	1,151,518	115,314	1,266,832	171,900	198,049	189,779	426,619	813,084	130,223	3,196,486	1,646,194
New Hampshire (d)...	85,484	8,607	94,091	136,346	43,015	54,680	18,648	15,357	27,075	389,212	191,767
New Jersey	1,743,540	27,566	1,771,106	447,075	198,630	316,094	627,362	3,560,294	198,794	7,119,355	2,122,873
New York............	2,309,108	333,302	2,642,410	1,214,890	304,798	397,190	521,657	4,372,642	272,774	9,638,361	364,367
Pennsylvania......	2,122,168	0	2,122,168	1,214,509	314,245	440,981	176,257	84,313	214,210	4,566,683	3,073,711
Rhode Island (c)...	184,844	8,208	193,052	82,887	27,036	19,071	26,481	58,549	0	406,986	45,616
Vermont	124,562	24,179	148,741	53,982	34,315	45,061	689	2,241	25,111	310,140	11,364
Regional average ...	889,118	51,718	940,836	366,265	139,989	168,060	202,853	968,704	91,478	2,878,175	815,303
Midwestern Region											
Illinois	1,943,765	342,729	2,286,494	496,801	222,065	216,402	173,272	134,464	671,464	4,200,962	2,065,303
Indiana..............	832,250	0	832,250	423,659	60,806	121,202	81,768	29,492	685,403	2,234,580	226,485
Iowa.................	528,933	0	528,933	124,000	47,701	113,718	0	0	577,854	1,392,206	207,501
Kansas..............	707,018	111,585	818,603	145,911	66,725	64,595	86,919	55,825	155,691	1,394,269	870,630
Michigan (c)........	1,316,860	1,064,946	2,381,806	267,523	104,723	211,726	37,547	525,048	33,000	3,561,373	1,033,665
Minnesota (c).......	856,449	0	856,449	343,838	127,895	95,758	14,280	12,665	679,651	2,130,536	835,886
Nebraska............	386,604	86,842	473,446	101,442	51,608	72,802	0	0	176,629	875,927	125,779
North Dakota (c)...	284,581	39,093	323,674	37,593	14,710	17,710	0	0	61,863	455,550	9,176
Ohio.................	1,588,219	275,674	1,863,893	431,320	168,964	251,049	96,681	222,860	1,005,360	4,040,127	1,038,594
South Dakota (c)...	321,887	20,708	342,595	56,129	46,942	18,867	0	0	1,893	466,426	83,892
Wisconsin	946,906	157,770	1,104,676	166,946	157,055	73,032	80,176	390,190	390,872	2,362,947	424,497
Regional average ...	883,042	190,850	1,073,893	235,924	97,199	114,260	51,877	124,595	403,607	2,101,355	629,219
Southern Region											
Alabama (c).........	862,286	270,789	1,133,075	157,550	129,272	66,948	969	29,030	2,152	1,518,996	319,371
Arkansas............	638,894	0	638,894	165,961	29,674	51,402	29,039	0	163,063	1,078,033	188,524
Florida..............	4,063,856	84,291	4,148,147	1,088,539	193,956	334,773	344,214	843,555	416,268	7,369,452	2,456,320
Georgia.............	1,159,180	76,428	1,235,608	184,991	205,071	144,696	111,346	187,618	591	2,069,921	1,886,051
Kentucky............	847,748	36,170	883,918	286,904	114,047	61,502	52,814	182,405	141,074	1,722,664	1,162,053
Louisiana (c).......	962,512	0	962,512	355,945	47,367	13,808	3,620	3,530	350	1,387,132	91,143
Maryland............	983,356	42,863	1,026,219	269,822	54,921	126,438	30,994	84,328	456,586	2,049,308	609,260
Mississippi.........	560,562	136,254	696,816	92,558	45,705	57,836	18,788	44,250	125,190	1,081,143	338,866
Missouri............	940,764	97,507	1,038,271	465,315	64,580	155,863	43,785	32,500	268,593	2,068,907	365,366
North Carolina.....	2,075,266	0	2,075,266	792,408	347,764	278,077	32,011	36,965	135,302	3,697,793	549,608
Oklahoma...........	478,244	35,939	514,183	183,233	93,693	90,635	75,066	30,150	175,736	1,162,696	523,749
South Carolina.....	745,790	0	745,790	323,142	85,681	100,164	29,379	35,822	40,228	1,360,206	385,051
Tennessee..........	897,193	33,125	930,318	240,136	149,839	108,551	0	0	289,610	1,718,454	1,216,828
Texas................	5,691,657	0	5,691,657	1,406,398	250,642	583,895	180,167	347,870	457,338	8,917,967	3,326,389
Virginia.............	1,117,012	0	1,117,012	1,058,211	180,198	146,386	140,782	458,216	283,086	3,383,891	1,571,336
West Virginia.......	673,472	0	673,472	227,232	80,209	34,154	26,967	382,610	0	1,424,644	188,607
Regional average ...	1,418,612	50,835	1,469,447	456,147	129,539	147,196	69,996	168,678	184,698	2,625,700	948,658

See footnotes at end of table.

STATE DISBURSEMENTS FOR HIGHWAYS, BY REGION: 2005 — Continued
(In thousands of dollars)

State or other jurisdiction	Capital outlay			Maintenance and highway service expenditures (a)	Administration, research and planning	Highway law enforcement and safety	Interest	Bond retirement (b)	Grants in-aid to local governments	Total disbursements	Total year-end balances (d)
	State administered highways (a)	Locally administered roads	Total								
Western Region											
Alaska	378,618	0	378,618	163,784	46,045	30,017	9,606	12,766	2,060	642,896	9,175
Arizona	865,879	46,330	912,209	105,571	187,974	151,152	94,206	301,890	704,997	2,457,999	862,295
California	2,865,105	154,124	3,019,229	792,055	943,149	1,456,251	106,567	0	1,990,259	8,307,510	7,504,221
Colorado (c)	603,948	28,745	632,693	335,312	70,909	120,943	126,389	141,399	224,303	1,651,948	1,622,821
Hawaii	209,440	0	209,440	31,484	48,676	8,218	17,486	163,907	26,529	505,740	417,102
Idaho	321,519	38,052	359,571	57,888	25,452	29,803	0	0	135,544	608,258	84,631
Montana	360,763	53,755	414,518	89,293	42,534	36,916	2,337	0	78,893	664,491	106,348
Nevada	519,456	0	519,456	87,011	45,506	81,659	25,588	30,665	74,716	864,601	323,824
New Mexico	293,521	20,818	314,339	172,023	139,945	56,636	87,785	74,914	65,417	911,059	858,584
Oregon	723,430	391,564	1,114,994	118,316	76,257	49,014	23,520	132,555	113,052	1,627,708	820,792
Utah	478,668	0	478,668	101,345	89,997	38,396	53,295	72,535	152,001	986,237	402,513
Washington	1,118,922	45,095	1,164,017	359,072	114,021	140,925	89,361	173,392	584,262	2,625,050	496,229
Wyoming (c)	267,525	0	267,525	88,068	41,353	29,217	0	0	2,730	428,893	27,189
Regional average	692,830	59,883	752,714	192,402	143,986	171,473	48,934	84,925	319,597	1,714,030	1,041,210
Regional average without California	511,807	52,030	563,837	142,431	77,389	64,408	44,131	92,002	180,375	1,164,573	502,625
Dist. of Columbia	0	170,166	170,166	37,255	109,706	0	6,713	2,917	0	326,757	39,639

Source: U.S. Department of Transportation, Federal Highway Administration, *Highway Statistics, 2005,* (November 2006).

Note: This table is compiled from reports provided by state authorities.

(a) Includes expenditures for local roads and streets under state control. Most local roads are under state control in Delaware, North Carolina, Virginia and West Virginia.

(b) Bond retirement includes current revenues or sinking funds and refunding bonds.
(c) Preliminary data was used.
(d) 2004 data was used.

Table 9.14
TOTAL ROAD AND STREET MILEAGE: 2005
(Classified by jurisdiction)

State or other jurisdiction	Rural mileage Under state control	Under county control	Town, township & municipal control (a)	Other jurisdictions (b)	Under federal control (c)	Total rural roads	Urban mileage Under state control	Under county control	Town, township & municipal control (a)	Other jurisdictions (b)	Under federal control (c)	Total urban mileage	Total rural & urban mileage
United States	636,339	1,598,718	575,569	51,765	123,413	2,985,804	140,913	182,696	668,337	14,111	3,783	1,009,840	3,995,644
Eastern Region													
Connecticut..........	1,289	0	4,605	243	17	6,154	2,428	0	12,510	47	55	15,040	21,194
Delaware..............	3,038	0	98	0	73	3,209	2,205	0	634	0	46	2,885	6,094
Maine..................	7,557	0	11,975	136	168	19,836	991	0	1,955	21	4	2,971	22,807
Massachusetts.......	710	0	6,806	408	28	7,952	2,139	4	25,368	352	82	27,945	35,897
New Hampshire.....	3,216	0	7,467	29	133	10,845	759	1	3,960	1	0	4,721	15,566
New Jersey...........	454	1,951	3,904	585	425	7,319	1,867	4,454	24,398	425	89	31,233	38,552
New York (e).........	11,002	16,882	43,532	674	27	72,117	4,031	3,516	32,912	699	68	41,226	113,343
Pennsylvania.........	28,866	20	43,141	3,393	766	76,186	11,024	269	32,759	342	88	44,482	120,668
Rhode Island........	317	0	939	0	10	1,266	785	0	4,412	3	25	5,225	6,491
Vermont...............	2,454	0	10,175	210	163	13,002	180	0	1,192	0	25	1,397	14,399
Regional total.......	58,903	18,853	132,642	5,678	1,810	217,886	26,409	8,244	140,100	1,890	482	177,125	395,011
Midwestern Region													
Illinois................	11,323	14,286	74,102	418	229	100,358	4,780	2,123	31,285	263	24	38,475	138,833
Indiana (d)...........	9,532	61,312	3,501	0	0	74,345	1,651	5,683	13,896	0	0	21,230	95,575
Iowa...................	7,939	88,580	5,865	371	103	102,858	956	1,098	8,866	175	19	11,114	113,972
Kansas................	9,640	113,048	0	178	829	123,695	730	0	3,136	7,901	0	11,767	135,462
Michigan..............	7,088	74,150	2,908	37	1,850	86,033	2,610	14,890	17,923	0	0	35,423	121,456
Minnesota............	10,737	42,978	58,637	1,311	1,978	115,641	1,134	2,003	13,239	5	26	16,407	132,048
Nebraska.............	9,592	60,251	16,965	281	161	87,250	383	620	5,057	0	0	6,060	93,310
North Dakota........	7,167	10,029	66,188	23	1,540	84,947	215	0	1,631	0	0	1,846	86,793
Ohio...................	14,275	25,815	36,586	3,169	525	80,370	5,017	3,277	36,055	73	48	44,470	124,840
South Dakota........	7,636	35,947	35,496	165	2,042	81,286	237	293	2,029	65	1	2,625	83,911
Wisconsin............	9,754	19,197	62,408	12	839	92,210	2,028	1,501	18,346	57	0	21,932	114,142
Regional total.......	104,683	545,593	362,656	5,965	10,096	1,028,993	19,741	31,488	151,463	8,539	118	211,349	1,240,342
Southern Region													
Alabama..............	8,859	59,101	5,472	169	817	74,418	2,096	308	18,647	0	576	21,627	96,045
Arkansas.............	15,070	65,630	4,872	0	2,154	87,726	1,374	480	8,908	1	170	10,933	98,659
Florida................	5,969	29,278	2,392	0	1,829	39,468	6,071	41,917	32,953	0	148	81,089	120,557
Georgia...............	13,950	61,865	3,438	344	1,061	80,658	3,980	21,533	10,900	510	64	36,987	117,645
Kentucky.............	25,087	37,470	2,116	243	785	65,701	2,423	1,601	8,101	47	148	12,320	78,021
Louisiana.............	13,213	28,994	2,604	3	620	45,434	3,480	3,456	8,567	14	2	15,519	60,953
Maryland.............	3,095	10,306	387	137	39	13,964	2,045	10,502	4,214	125	112	16,998	30,962
Mississippi...........	9,565	50,605	2,545	52	783	63,550	1,331	2,210	7,047	5	38	10,631	74,181

See footnotes at end of table.

TOTAL ROAD AND STREET MILEAGE: 2005—Continued
(Classified by jurisdiction)

State or other jurisdiction	Rural mileage						Urban mileage						Total rural & urban mileage
	Under state control	Under county control	Town, township & municipal control (a)	Other jurisdictions (b)	Under federal control (c)	Total rural roads	Under state control	Under county control	Town, township & municipal control (a)	Other jurisdictions (b)	Under federal control (c)	Total urban mileage	
Southern Region, continued													
Missouri	30,524	69,331	5,591	0	1,027	106,473	1,940	3,209	14,200	0	0	19,349	125,822
North Carolina	62,515	0	4,673	748	3,079	71,015	16,516	0	15,455	0	142	32,113	103,128
Oklahoma	11,089	78,328	7,047	1,104	53	97,621	1,196	2,118	11,889	112	1	15,316	112,937
South Carolina	30,190	16,917	320	191	2,169	49,787	11,201	3,389	1,859	0	2	16,451	66,238
Tennessee	10,849	52,181	4,063	346	1,593	69,032	2,968	4,556	13,868	11	16	21,419	90,451
Texas	68,439	138,337	13,112	3	831	220,722	11,209	6,348	65,736	156	0	83,449	304,171
Virginia	48,151	28	626	24	1,645	50,474	9,709	1,610	9,941	15	212	21,487	71,961
West Virginia	31,516	0	644	64	621	32,845	2,471	0	1,689	23	0	4,183	37,028
Regional total	388,081	698,371	59,902	3,428	19,106	1,168,888	80,010	103,237	233,974	1,019	1,631	419,871	1,588,759
Western Region													
Alaska	5,084	2,311	1,690	761	2,268	12,114	575	1,169	205	5	301	2,255	14,369
Arizona	5,844	15,946	2,463	159	12,656	37,068	956	2,954	18,321	159	332	22,722	59,790
California	11,090	52,448	4,046	3,017	13,870	84,471	4,123	12,824	67,787	49	652	85,435	169,906
Colorado	7,694	50,724	2,269	1,237	6,855	68,779	1,412	4,622	12,713	25	47	18,819	87,598
Hawaii	567	1,319	0	47	101	2,034	361	1,897	0	12	17	2,287	4,321
Idaho	4,628	15,183	188	14,378	8,011	42,388	329	119	2,279	2,003	11	4,741	47,129
Montana	10,493	40,641	1,202	376	13,873	66,585	296	2	2,455	0	11	2,753	69,338
Nevada	4,694	20,240	419	523	1,820	27,696	705	2,405	3,818	0	0	6,928	34,624
New Mexico	11,023	35,936	1,359	215	7,252	55,785	967	3,525	3,481	0	0	7,973	63,758
Oregon	6,678	30,153	1,591	4,533	8,793	51,748	854	3,202	8,627	91	21	12,795	64,543
Utah	4,797	21,901	1,883	10	4,405	32,996	1,061	1,722	7,783	0	13	10,579	43,575
Washington	5,734	35,004	2,576	10,791	9,129	63,234	1,311	4,897	13,846	93	0	20,147	83,381
Wyoming	6,346	14,095	683	647	3,368	25,139	411	389	1,485	207	69	2,561	27,700
Regional total	84,672	335,901	20,369	36,694	92,401	570,037	13,361	39,727	142,800	2,644	1,463	199,995	770,032
Regional total without California	73,582	283,453	16,323	33,677	78,531	485,566	9,238	26,903	75,013	2,595	811	114,560	600,126
Dist. of Columbia	0	0	0	0	0	0	1,392	0	0	19	89	1,500	1,500
Puerto Rico	1,027	0	2,057	0	22	3,106	3,533	0	9,345	0	7	12,885	15,991

Source: U.S. Department of Transportation, Federal Highway Administration, *Highway Statistics, 2005,* (October 2006).

Key:

. . . — Not applicable.

(a) Prior to 1999, municipal was included with other jurisdictions.

(b) Includes state park, state toll, other state agency, other local agency and other roadways not identified by ownership.

(c) Roadways in federal parks, forests, and reservations that are not part of the state and local highway systems.

(d) Excludes 770 miles of federal agency-owned roads.

(e) 2004 data used.

Table 9.15
APPORTIONMENT OF FEDERAL-AID HIGHWAY FUNDS BY REGION: FISCAL YEAR 2006
(In thousands of dollars)

State or other jurisdiction	Interstate maintenance	National highway system	Surface transportation program	Bridge program	Congestion mitigation & air quality improvement	Appalachian development highway system	Recreation trails
United States	$4,635,352	$5,661,844	$5,966,119	$3,960,376	$1,616,774	$454,363	$68,468
Eastern Region							
Connecticut................	47,333	44,043	57,497	105,701	31,407	0	841
Delaware....................	7,700	43,786	29,831	15,138	8,084	0	734
Maine........................	26,574	30,669	32,548	31,855	8,084	0	1,020
Massachusetts	76,042	79,192	96,726	140,627	55,319	0	1,129
New Hampshire	18,669	32,817	29,831	23,436	8,084	0	918
New Jersey	89,771	134,494	132,072	164,838	75,123	0	1,147
New York....................	168,743	193,325	227,495	396,038	147,513	21,822	1,704
Pennsylvania..............	169,840	181,821	207,390	373,597	83,702	99,974	1,643
Rhode Island..............	10,657	40,829	29,831	57,081	8,573	0	731
Vermont	16,016	35,470	29,831	31,857	8,084	0	814
Regional average	63,135	81,645	87,305	134,017	42,397	12,180	1,068
Midwestern Region							
Illinois	199,854	171,380	218,697	121,356	71,571	0	1,805
Indiana......................	122,916	127,744	145,105	47,678	29,327	0	1,189
Iowa..........................	61,662	91,184	87,999	60,377	8,084	0	1,172
Kansas	59,588	81,658	92,164	55,975	8,084	0	1,109
Michigan....................	135,009	165,006	203,914	121,928	56,788	0	2,037
Minnesota..................	84,235	103,039	127,802	35,736	21,909	0	1,568
Nebraska....................	39,754	69,573	59,736	27,751	8,084	0	962
North Dakota	27,521	76,277	37,169	9,901	8,084	0	833
Ohio..........................	191,538	175,582	212,403	138,767	68,708	19,840	1,630
South Dakota	32,948	63,754	41,219	13,559	8,084	0	859
Wisconsin	76,203	124,010	124,053	27,985	16,669	0	1,520
Regional average	93,748	113,564	122,751	60,092	27,763	1,804	1,335
Southern Region							
Alabama.....................	88,264	98,378	116,301	78,178	8,084	28,263	1,414
Arkansas	62,447	77,748	81,180	44,862	8,084	0	1,104
Florida......................	186,852	262,712	287,569	74,200	8,084	0	2,713
Georgia	176,613	159,691	206,756	51,534	35,425	17,322	1,779
Kentucky	87,861	102,392	95,815	51,735	9,236	66,285	1,156
Louisiana	82,923	75,568	91,881	143,248	8,084	0	1,417
Maryland	79,083	89,499	96,913	69,313	43,101	6,200	994
Mississippi.................	61,136	88,002	85,568	44,797	8,084	5,126	1,247
Missouri.....................	121,578	139,075	149,040	131,359	15,722	0	1,329
North Carolina...........	118,691	143,956	163,305	86,226	33,222	36,964	1,578
Oklahoma	86,443	110,919	117,107	65,299	8,084	0	1,215
South Carolina...........	82,682	81,523	103,185	52,864	8,084	2,808	1,071
Tennessee..................	120,175	125,323	132,959	48,130	22,997	33,807	1,252
Texas........................	369,049	468,225	500,604	136,012	92,691	0	3,008
Virginia.....................	134,444	131,531	159,119	76,896	36,914	32,322	1,235
West Virginia	40,764	41,427	45,101	51,799	8,084	83,630	994
Regional average	118,688	137,248	152,025	75,403	22,124	19,545	1,469
Western Region							
Alaska........................	24,617	30,194	29,831	15,264	8,084	0	1,031
Arizona......................	95,689	104,868	106,202	13,371	31,844	0	1,439
California...................	416,102	532,351	581,191	347,005	341,541	0	5,049
Colorado	73,112	95,668	92,061	24,753	26,107	0	1,268
Hawaii	8,268	43,218	29,831	20,149	8,084	0	758
Idaho........................	35,478	47,407	36,069	15,322	8,084	0	1,131
Montana.....................	50,258	68,317	38,204	13,068	8,084	0	1,163
Nevada......................	40,137	45,741	42,387	9,901	17,031	0	932
New Mexico	64,052	77,413	53,472	16,054	8,084	0	1,170
Oregon......................	63,473	81,669	79,141	79,292	13,426	0	1,155
Utah..........................	64,908	44,902	49,138	9,901	8,084	0	1,215
Washington................	89,290	98,401	113,220	146,925	28,810	0	1,556
Wyoming	45,846	81,133	29,831	9,901	8,084	0	1,056
Regional average	82,402	103,945	98,506	55,454	39,642	0	1,456
Regional average without California...	54,594	68,244	58,282	31,158	14,484	0	1,156
Dist. of Columbia	2,544	48,942	29,831	31,836	8,084	0	671
American Samoa.........	0	1,945	0	0	0	0	0
Guam	0	7,921	0	0	0	0	0
No. Mariana Islands....	0	3,445	0	0	0	0	0
Puerto Rico (b)	0	0	0	0	0	0	0
U.S. Virgin Islands......	0	13,781	0	0	0	0	0

Source: U.S. Department of Transportation, Federal Highway Administration, *Highway Statistics, 2005,* (October 2006).

Note: Apportioned pursuant to the Safe, Accountable, Flexible, Efficient Transportation Act: A Legacy for Users (SAFETEA-LU) of 2005. Does not include funds from the Mass Transit Account of the Highway Trust Fund.

APPORTIONMENT OF FEDERAL-AID HIGHWAY FUNDS BY REGION: FISCAL YEAR 2006 — Continued
(In thousands of dollars)

State or other jurisdiction	Metropolitan planning	Coordinated border infrastructure	Safe routes to school	Equity bonus	Highway safety improvement program	Rail highway crossings program	Total (a)
United States	$286,896	$143,550	$96,030	$7,116,048	$1,005,652	$217,800	$31,229,272
Eastern Region							
Connecticut................	4,059	0	998	147,975	8,709	1,313	449,876
Delaware....................	1,434	0	990	10,116	5,028	1,089	123,930
Maine........................	1,434	9,056	990	0	5,346	1,192	148,767
Massachusetts............	8,030	0	1,753	77,091	14,316	2,342	552,566
New Hampshire	1,434	225	990	30,164	5,028	1,089	152,686
New Jersey	11,049	0	2,399	182,190	18,943	3,514	815,541
New York...................	22,093	19,656	5,115	269,820	32,425	6,266	1,512,013
Pennsylvania..............	11,700	0	3,345	334,309	33,015	7,254	1,507,589
Rhode Island..............	1,434	0	990	2,395	5,028	1,089	158,637
Vermont	1,434	6,071	990	0	5,028	1,089	136,684
Regional average	6,410	3,501	1,856	105,406	13,287	2,624	555,829
Midwestern Region							
Illinois	13,875	0	3,730	204,567	34,465	9,979	1,051,279
Indiana......................	4,860	0	1,798	272,859	19,038	6,941	779,456
Iowa..........................	1,588	0	990	1,733	15,248	4,850	334,887
Kansas.......................	1,721	0	990	14,417	18,137	6,113	339,954
Michigan....................	9,374	20,517	3,010	213,236	32,654	7,570	971,044
Minnesota	3,864	3,396	1,441	99,806	20,717	5,871	509,385
Nebraska....................	1,434	0	990	6,195	10,965	3,747	229,192
North Dakota	1,434	6,840	990	14,747	7,049	3,609	194,454
Ohio..........................	10,418	0	3,295	278,876	28,640	8,372	1,138,070
South Dakota	1,434	0	990	34,757	9,088	2,260	208,952
Wisconsin	4,050	0	1,554	211,479	21,021	5,274	613,820
Regional average	4,914	2,796	1,798	122,970	19,729	5,871	579,136
Southern Region							
Alabama.....................	2,766	0	1,314	178,372	22,753	4,544	628,631
Arkansas	1,434	0	990	99,170	15,737	3,655	396,411
Florida	19,194	0	4,494	619,669	50,661	8,079	1,524,226
Georgia	7,139	0	2,578	410,727	32,297	7,956	1,109,817
Kentucky	2,233	0	1,127	101,023	15,954	3,519	538,337
Louisiana	3,613	0	1,405	59,455	16,875	4,134	488,602
Maryland	6,127	0	1,577	79,750	14,061	2,258	488,878
Mississippi.................	1,434	0	990	58,547	13,168	3,244	371,342
Missouri.....................	4,404	0	1,621	139,050	28,813	6,038	738,030
North Carolina...........	5,359	0	2,334	265,131	25,048	6,215	888,030
Oklahoma	2,114	0	1,011	65,247	20,806	5,045	483,289
South Carolina...........	2,670	0	1,186	140,445	18,550	3,920	498,987
Tennessee...................	4,225	0	1,596	167,408	22,334	4,718	684,924
Texas.........................	21,083	36,346	7,009	824,215	95,709	16,640	2,570,591
Virginia.....................	6,716	0	2,025	224,984	24,415	4,378	834,979
West Virginia	1,434	0	990	53,004	8,552	1,985	337,764
Regional average	5,747	2,272	2,015	217,887	26,608	5,396	786,427
Western Region							
Alaska........................	1,434	952	990	163,270	5,028	1,089	281,784
Arizona......................	5,569	6,973	1,558	197,615	20,806	2,573	588,505
California...................	42,776	18,078	11,039	428,598	93,848	16,151	2,833,729
Colorado....................	4,578	0	1,254	54,709	18,396	3,020	394,927
Hawaii	1,434	0	990	22,149	5,028	1,089	140,998
Idaho.........................	1,434	895	990	76,439	7,812	1,592	232,653
Montana.....................	1,434	4,933	990	103,731	8,882	1,741	300,806
Nevada.......................	2,389	0	990	32,672	7,886	1,089	201,155
New Mexico	1,434	1,088	990	64,939	10,808	1,496	301,000
Oregon.......................	2,816	0	990	15,114	14,733	3,113	354,921
Utah..........................	2,491	0	990	30,488	8,368	1,543	222,028
Washington	6,133	8,524	1,695	4,681	17,534	3,977	520,746
Wyoming	1,434	0	990	28,715	5,872	1,089	213,950
Regional average	5,797	3,188	1,881	94,086	17,308	3,043	506,708
Regional average without California ...	2,715	1,947	1,118	66,210	10,929	1,951	312,789
Dist. of Columbia	1,434	0	990	0	5,028	1,089	130,450
American Samoa.........	0	0	0	0	0	0	1,945
Guam	0	0	0	0	0	0	7,921
No. Mariana Islands....	0	0	0	0	0	0	3,445
Puerto Rico (b)	0	0	0	0	0	0	0
U.S. Virgin Islands......	0	0	0	0	0	0	13,781

(a) Does not include funds from the following programs: emergency relief, federal lands highway programs, Commonwealth of Puerto Rico highway programs, high priority projects, Woodrow Wilson Bridge, National Byways, construction of ferry terminal facilities, and intelligent vehicle-system, among others. These funds are allocated from the Highway Trust Fund.

(b) Under SAFETY-LU, Puerto Rico received a stand-alone authorization of $82,768,218 for FY 2006.

Table 9.16
TRENDS IN STATE PRISON POPULATION BY REGION, 1995, 2004, and 2005

State or other jurisdiction	Total population December 31, 2005	Total population December 31, 2004	Total population December 31, 1995	Percent change 2004–2005	Average change 1995–2005 (a)	Incarceration rate 2005
United States	1,461,132	1,433,728	1,085,022	1.9%	3.0%	491
Federal..................................	166,173	159,137	83,663	4.4	7.1	56
State.......................................	1,294,959	1,274,591	1,001,359	1.6	2.6	435
Eastern Region						
Connecticut (b)	13,121	13,240	10,419	-0.9	2.3	373
Delaware...............................	3,972	4,087	3,014	-2.8	2.8	467
Maine......................................	1,905	1,961	1,326	-2.9	3.7	144
Massachusetts (c).................	9,081	8,688	10,427	4.5	-1.4	239
New Hampshire	2,520	2,448	2,015	2.9	2.3	192
New Jersey (d).......................	27,359	26,757	27,066	2.2	0.1	313
New York...............................	62,743	63,751	68,486	-1.6	-0.9	326
Pennsylvania..........................	42,345	40,931	32,410	3.5	2.7	340
Rhode Island (b)	2,025	1,894	1,833	6.9	1.0	189
Vermont (b)............................	1,542	1,451	1,048	6.3	3.9	247
Regional total	166,613	165,208	158,044	0.8	0.6	...
Midwestern Region						
Illinois (d).............................	44,919	44,054	37,658	2.0	1.8	351
Indiana....................................	24,416	23,939	16,046	2.0	4.3	388
Iowa (d)	8,737	8,525	5,906	2.5	4.0	294
Kansas (d)...............................	9,068	8,966	7,054	1.1	2.5	330
Michigan.................................	49,546	48,883	41,112	1.4	1.9	489
Minnesota	9,281	8,758	4,846	6.0	6.7	180
Nebraska.................................	4,330	4,038	3,006	7.2	3.7	245
North Dakota	1,327	1,238	544	7.2	9.3	208
Ohio (d)..................................	45,854	44,806	44,663	2.3	0.3	400
South Dakota	3,454	3,088	1,871	11.9	6.3	443
Wisconsin	21,110	22,189	10,337	-4.9	7.4	380
Regional total	222,042	218,484	173,043	1.6	3.1	...
Southern Region						
Alabama...................................	27,003	25,257	20,130	6.9	3.0	591
Arkansas.................................	13,383	13,668	8,520	-2.1	4.6	479
Florida	89,766	85,530	63,866	5.0	3.5	499
Georgia (e)..............................	48,741	51,089	34,168	-4.6	3.6	533
Kentucky	19,215	17,140	12,060	12.1	4.8	459
Louisiana	36,083	36,939	25,195	-2.3	3.7	797
Maryland	22,143	22,696	20,450	-2.4	0.8	394
Mississippi..............................	19,335	19,469	12,251	-0.7	4.7	660
Missouri (d)	30,803	31,061	19,134	-0.8	4.9	529
North Carolina	31,522	30,683	27,914	2.7	1.2	360
Oklahoma (d).........................	23,245	22,913	18,151	1.4	2.5	652
South Carolina	22,464	22,730	19,015	-1.2	1.7	525
Tennessee (d)	26,369	25,884	15,206	1.9	5.7	440
Texas.......................................	159,255	157,617	127,766	1.0	2.2	691
Virginia...................................	35,344	35,564	27,260	-0.6	2.6	464
West Virginia	5,292	5,026	2,483	5.3	7.9	291
Regional total	1,193,095	1,179,558	900,060	1.1	2.5	...
Western Region						
Alaska (b)	2,781	2,632	2,042	5.7	3.1	414
Arizona (e)..............................	31,411	31,106	20,291	1.0	4.5	521
California................................	168,982	164,933	131,745	2.5	2.5	466
Colorado (d)	21,456	20,293	11,063	5.7	6.8	457
Hawaii (b)...............................	4,422	4,174	2,590	5.9	5.5	340
Idaho......................................	6,818	6,375	3,328	6.9	7.4	472
Montana..................................	3,509	3,164	1,999	10.9	5.8	373
Nevada....................................	11,644	11,280	7,713	3.2	4.2	474
New Mexico	6,292	6,111	3,925	3.0	4.8	323
Oregon...................................	13,390	13,167	6,515	1.7	7.5	365
Utah..	6,269	5,915	3,447	6.0	6.2	252
Washington	17,320	16,503	11,608	5.0	4.1	273
Wyoming	2,047	1,980	1,395	3.4	3.9	400
Regional total	296,341	287,633	207,661	3.0	3.6	431
Regional total without California............	127,359	122,700	75,916	3.7	4.1	...

Source: U.S. Department of Justice, Bureau of Justice Statistics, *Prisoners in 2005*, (November 2006).

Key:

. . . — Not available.

(a) The average annual percentage increase from 1995 to 2004.

(b) Prisons and jails form one integrated system. Data include total jail and prison population.

(c) The incarceration rate includes an estimated 6,200 inmates sentenced to more than 1 year but held in local jails or houses of corrections.

(d) Includes some inmates sentenced to 1 year or less.

(e) Population based on custody counts.

Table 9.17
NUMBER OF SENTENCED PRISONERS ADMITTED AND RELEASED, BY REGION: 2000, and 2003—2004

State or other jurisdiction	Admissions (a)				Releases (a)			
	2004	2003	2000	Percent change 2000–2004	2004	2003	2000	Percent change 2000–2004
United States	697,066	686,437	625,219	11.5%	672,202	656,384	604,858	11.1%
Federal...............................	52,982	52,288	43,732	21.2	46,624	44,199	35,259	32.2
State..................................	644,084	634,149	581,487	10.8	625,578	612,185	569,599	9.8
Eastern Region								
Connecticut.........................	6,577	6,571	6,185	6.3	6,707	6,890	5,918	13.3
Delaware............................	1,648	2,212	2,709	. . .	2,013	2,129	2,260	. . .
Maine.................................	655	931	751	-12.8	636	782	677	-6.1
Massachusetts.....................	2,278	2,185	2,062	10.5	2,391	2,302	2,889	-17.2
New Hampshire	1,099	1,139	1,051	4.6	1,080	1,188	1,044	3.4
New Jersey	13,886	14,398	13,653	1.7	14,418	15,043	15,362	-6.1
New York	24,664	26,040	27,601	-10.6	26,043	27,467	28,828	-9.7
Pennsylvania.......................	14,319	14,039	11,777	21.6	14,396	13,268	11,759	22.4
Rhode Island (a).................	755	3,881	3,701	. . .	828	3,684	3,223	. . .
Vermont..............................	2,208	1,987	984	. . .	2,261	1,985	946	. . .
Regional total	68,089	73,383	70,474	-3.3	70,773	74,738	72,906	-2.9
Midwestern Region								
Illinois	39,293	36,063	29,344	33.9	38,646	35,372	28,876	33.8
Indiana..............................	16,029	15,615	11,876	35	15,100	14,146	11,053	36.6
Iowa..................................	4,364	5,545	4,656	-6.3	6,049	6,074	4,379	38.1
Kansas	4,519	4,605	5,002	-9.7	4,683	4,405	5,231	-10.5
Michigan............................	13,248	12,659	12,169	8.9	13,723	13,910	10,874	26.2
Minnesota...........................	6,604	5,914	4,406	49.9	5,849	5,437	4,244	37.8
Nebraska............................	2,085	1,959	1,688	23.5	2,029	1,953	1,503	35
North Dakota	1,008	992	605	66.6	917	870	598	53.3
Ohio..................................	28,196	26,506	23,780	18.6	28,170	27,369	24,793	13.6
South Dakota	2,304	1,915	1,400	64.6	2,428	1,980	1,327	83
Wisconsin...........................	8,071	8,000	8,396	-3.9	8,596	8,107	8,158	5.4
Regional total	125,721	119,773	103,322	21.6	126,190	119,623	101,036	24.9
Southern Region								
Alabama.............................	8,278	9,524	6,296	31.5	9,156	10,167	7,136	28.3
Arkansas	8,035	7,132	6,941	15.8	7,457	7,120	6,308	18.2
Florida	40,386	39,500	35,683	13.2	36,908	34,679	33,994	8.6
Georgia	20,140	17,575	17,373	15.9	18,211	17,333	14,797	23.1
Kentucky	13,009	9,595	8,116	60.3	10,740	9,208	7,733	38.9
Louisiana...........................	15,512	15,353	15,735	-1.4	15,009	13,841	14,536	3.3
Maryland	10,330	10,170	10,327	0	10,531	10,207	10,004	5.3
Mississippi.........................	9,187	8,421	5,796	58.5	8,607	7,679	4,940	74.2
Missouri.............................	18,281	17,151	14,454	26.5	17,307	16,967	13,346	29.7
North Carolina	10,411	9,494	9,848	5.7	9,315	9,116	9,687	-3.8
Oklahoma	9,003	8,139	7,426	21.2	8,432	8,164	6,628	27.2
South Carolina	9,850	9,934	8,460	16.4	10,060	9,829	8,676	16
Tennessee...........................	13,149	13,059	13,675	-3.8	13,295	13,768	13,893	-4.3
Texas.................................	66,883	69,921	58,197	14.9	65,800	65,169	59,776	10.1
Virginia.............................	11,645	11,700	9,791	18.9	11,148	11,606	9,148	21.9
West Virginia	2,267	2,097	1,577	43.8	1,946	1,881	1,261	54.3
Regional total	266,366	258,765	229,695	15.9	253,922	246,734	221,863	14.4
Western Region								
Alaska (b)	2,746	2,805	2,427	13.1	2,726	2,736	2,599	4.9
Arizona..............................	11,343	11,957	9,560	18.7	10,190	10,391	9,100	12
California...........................	123,537	125,312	129,640	-4.7	117,762	118,646	129,621	-9.1
Colorado............................	8,634	7,998	7,036	22.7	8,001	7,113	5,881	36
Hawaii	1,677	1,832	1,594	5.2	1,667	1,504	1,379	20.9
Idaho.................................	4,392	3,168	3,386	29.7	3,480	3,033	2,697	29
Montana.............................	2,182	1,910	1,202	81.5	1,897	1,642	1,031	84
Nevada...............................	6,548	4,865	4,929	32.8	4,715	4,800	4,374	7.8
New Mexico	4,279	4,160	3,161	35.4	4,090	3,943	3,383	20.9
Oregon...............................	5,378	5,095	4,059	32.5	4,910	4,483	3,371	45.7
Utah	3,275	3,301	3,270	0.2	3,050	3,088	2,897	5.3
Washington	11,894	9,034	7,094	. . .	11,547	9,067	6,764	. . .
Wyoming	769	791	638	20.5	658	644	697	-5.6
Regional total	186,654	182,228	177,996	4.8	174,693	171,090	173,794	0.5
Regional total without California...........	63,117	56,916	48,356	30.5	56,931	52,444	44,173	28.8

Source: U.S. Department of Justice, Bureau of Justice Statistics, *Bulletin, Prisoners and Jail Inmates at Midyear 2005,* (May 2006).
Note: Excludes escapes, AWOLs, and transfers to and from other jurisdictions.
. . . — Not calculated due to changes in reporting.

(a) Changed reporting in 2004 to include only prisoners sentenced to 1 year or more.
(b) Alaska data may include some escapes, AWOLs, and transfers.

Table 9.18
STATE PRISON CAPACITIES, BY REGION: 2005

State or other jurisdiction	Rated capacity	Operational capacity	Design capacity	Population as a percent of capacity: (a)	
				Highest capacity	Lowest capacity
Federal..................................	106,046	...	...	139%	139%
Eastern Region					
Connecticut (b)....................	...	...	...	...	...
Delaware..............................	6,679	6,665	5,475	102	124
Maine...................................	1,897	1,897	1,897	103	103
Massachusetts......................	...	...	7,778	133	133
New Hampshire	2,419	2,238	2,213	100	109
New Jersey	...	25,949	...	89	89
New York.............................	59,904	61,330	53,843	103	117
Pennsylvania........................	38,347	38,347	38,347	108	108
Rhode Island........................	3,861	3,861	4,054	84	88
Vermont...............................	1,716	1,716	1,355	94	120
Midwestern Region					
Illinois	33,801	33,801	29,861	133	150
Indiana................................	17,590	24,167	...	94	129
Iowa....................................	...	...	7,238	121	121
Kansas	9,357	...	...	97	97
Michigan..............................	...	49,837	...	99	99
Minnesota............................	...	8,203	...	97	97
Nebraska..............................	...	3,969	3,175	111	139
North Dakota	1,005	952	1,005	126	134
Ohio....................................	35,531	...	...	121	121
South Dakota	...	3,445	...	97	97
Wisconsin (c).......................	...	17,325	...	127	127
Southern Region					
Alabama (d).........................	...	25,206	12,444	95	193
Arkansas..............................	13,500	13,283	12,610	92	99
Florida	...	88,156	66,641	98	130
Georgia	...	47,542	...	103	103
Kentucky	12,301	12,301	12,301	103	103
Louisiana.............................	19,371	20,050	...	97	100
Maryland	...	22,647	...	100	100
Mississippi (e)	22,403	...	...	72	72
Missouri...............................	...	30,788	...	99	99
North Carolina (f)...............	...	...	31,500	116	116
Oklahoma (e).......................	24,145	24,145	24,145	95	95
South Carolina.....................	...	23,169	...	97	97
Tennessee.............................	20,122	19,670	...	96	98
Texas (c)	162,075	158,024	162,075	86	88
Virginia...............................	31,358	...	...	93	93
West Virginia	3,655	4,226	3,655	96	110
Western Region					
Alaska..................................	3,098	3,206	...	107	111
Arizona................................	28,077	33,938	30,051	84	102
California.............................	...	164,159	87,250	102	193
Colorado..............................	...	14,153	12,836	120	133
Hawaii	...	3,487	2,451	110	157
Idaho...................................	5,845	5,553	5,845	80	84
Montana (e)	...	1,591	...	121	121
Nevada (e)	11,063	20,895	7,766	56	150
New Mexico (e)....................	...	6,713	6,227	98	106
Oregon.................................	...	12,646	12,646	102	102
Utah	...	6,203	6,411	79	82
Washington	12,992	15,014	15,014	112	129
Wyoming	1,283	1,260	1,231	97	102

Source: U.S. Department of Justice, Bureau of Justice Statistics, *Prisoners in 2005* (November 2006).

Key:

... — Not available.

(a) Population counts are based on the number of inmates held in facilities operated by the jurisdiction. Excludes inmates held in local jails, in other states, or in private facilities.

(b) Connecticut no longer reports capacity because of a law passed in 1995.

(c) Excludes capacity of county facilities and inmates housed in them.

(d) Design capacity defined as the original design capacity.

(e) Includes capacity of private and contract facilities and inmates housed in them.

(f) Capacity figures refer to standard operating capacity, based on single occupancy per cell and 50 square feet per inmate in multiple occupancy units.

Table 9.19
ADULTS ON PROBATION BY REGION, 2005

State or other jurisdiction	1/1/05	Probation population 2005 Entries	Exits	12/31/05	Percent change during 2005	Number on probation on 12/31/05 per 100,000 adult residents
United States	4,143,466	2,228,300	2,209,700	4,162,536	0.5%	1,858
Federal................................	28,602	12,135	14,402	26,719	-6.6	12
State....................................	4,114,864	2,216,200	2,195,300	4,135,817	0.5	1,846
Eastern Region						
Connecticut (a)	54,067	28,250	26,245	56,072	3.7	2,092
Delaware..............................	18,725	14,643	14,906	18,462	-1.4	2,828
Maine...................................	8,907	4,890	5,677	8,120	-8.8	776
Massachusetts (a).................	163,719	84,343	82,697	165,365	1	3,350
New Hampshire	4,285	3,440	3,110	4,615	...	457
New Jersey	143,315	45,136	49,360	139,091	-2.9	2,117
New York.............................	124,853	34,644	40,472	119,025	-4.7	810
Pennsylvania (a)(b)..............	167,366	67,300	67,100	167,561	0.1	1,741
Rhode Island (a)...................	26,085	5,410	5,882	25,613	-1.8	3,091
Vermont (a)..........................	9,731	4,341	5,138	8,934	-8.2	1,820
Regional total	721,053	292,397	300,587	712,858	-1.1	...
Midwestern Region						
Illinois (a)	143,871	60,951	61,686	143,136	-0.5	1,500
Indiana (a)	121,675	98,681	99,342	121,014	-0.5	2,583
Iowa....................................	22,408	15,829	14,833	23,404	4.4	1,018
Kansas	14,439	19,755	19,184	15,010	4	723
Michigan (a)(b)....................	176,630	130,200	128,300	178,609	1.1	2,350
Minnesota	113,121	70,752	66,800	117,073	3.5	2,988
Nebraska..............................	17,994	15,330	14,856	18,468	2.6	1,387
North Dakota	3,749	2,808	2,597	3,960	5.6	791
Ohio (a)(b)..........................	230,758	141,300	133,000	239,036	3.6	2,745
South Dakota	5,372	3,196	3,260	5,308	-1.2	899
Wisconsin	53,865	25,505	24,195	55,175	2.4	1,298
Regional total	903,882	584,307	568,053	920,193	1.8	...
Southern Region						
Alabama (a)	36,799	14,039	11,843	38,995	6	1,121
Arkansas	28,771	8,435	6,958	30,248	5.1	1,431
Florida (a)(b)	278,606	240,000	240,800	277,831	-0.3	2,002
Georgia (a)(b)(c)..................	423,547	215,500	216,200	422,848	...	...
Kentucky	32,619	20,800	18,300	35,230	8	1,100
Louisiana	38,231	13,772	13,695	38,308	0.2	1,133
Maryland	76,676	38,282	39,365	75,593	-1.4	1,793
Mississippi..........................	20,375	8,124	4,635	23,864	17.1	1,096
Missouri..............................	54,848	25,179	26,413	53,614	-2.2	1,208
North Carolina.....................	111,537	62,157	62,068	111,626	0.1	1,693
Oklahoma (a)(b)	28,404	14,600	14,100	28,865	1.6	1,065
South Carolina	38,941	14,768	14,360	39,349	1	1,212
Tennessee (a)(b)...................	47,099	24,800	22,600	49,302	4.7	1,072
Texas...................................	428,836	181,333	179,857	430,312	0.3	2,580
Virginia (a)	43,470	27,078	24,959	45,589	4.9	788
West Virginia (b)..................	6,977	3,200	2,500	7,646	9.6	533
Regional total	1,695,736	912,067	898,653	1,709,220	0.8	...
Western Region						
Alaska..................................	5,547	1,022	878	5,680	2.4	1,182
Arizona (a)(b)......................	70,532	39,700	39,100	71,138	0.9	1,606
California (a)	384,852	195,343	191,935	388,260	0.9	1,462
Colorado (a)(b)	57,779	29,900	31,000	56,623	-2	1,613
Hawaii (d)...........................	16,113	6,236	5,524	16,825	4.4	1,693
Idaho (a)(e)..........................	44,579	35,717	36,584	43,712	...	...
Montana (a)(b).....................	7,634	4,500	3,900	8,233	7.8	1,121
Nevada................................	12,645	6,305	6,019	12,931	2.3	709
New Mexico (a)(b)	17,725	8,500	7,500	18,706	5.5	1,287
Oregon	43,324	17,852	16,323	44,853	3.5	1,597
Utah....................................	10,267	5,312	5,500	10,079	-1.8	578
Washington (a)(b)(d)............	111,193	66,900	73,800	104,293	-6.2	2,155
Wyoming	4,418	2,828	2,420	4,826	9.2	1,216
Regional total	786,608	420,100	420,500	786,159	-0.1	1,546
Regional total without California...........	401,756	224,772	228,548	397,899	-0.9	...
Dist. of Columbia (a)...........	7,585	7,216	7,414	7,387	-2.6	1,696

See footnotes at end of table.

ADULTS ON PROBATION BY REGION, 2005 — Continued

Source: U.S. Department of Justice, Bureau of Justice Statistics, *Probation and Parole in the United States, 2005,* (November 2006).

Note: Because of nonresponse or incomplete data, the probation population for some jurisdictions on December 31, 2005, does not equal the population on January 1, plus entries, minus exits.

Key:

. . . — Not calculated.

(a) Some or all data are estimated.

(b) Data for entries and exits were estimated for nonreporting agencies.

(c) Counts include private agency cases and may overstate the number under supervision.

(d) Due to a change in recordkeeping procedures, data are not comparable to previous reports.

(e) Counts include estimates for misdemeanors based on admissions.

Table 9.20
ADULTS ON PAROLE BY REGION, 2005

State or other jurisdiction	1/1/05	Parole population 2005 Entries	Parole population 2005 Exits	12/31/05	Percent change during 2005	Number on parole on 12/31/05 per 100,000 adult residents
United States	771,852	516,400	503,800	784,408	1.6%	350
Federal................................	89,589	36,121	34,549	91,211	1.8	41
State....................................	682,263	480,300	469,300	693,197	1.6	309
Eastern Region						
Connecticut.........................	2,552	2,813	2,794	2,571	0.7	96
Delaware.............................	539	361	300	600	11.3	92
Maine..................................	32	1	1	32	0	3
Massachusetts.....................	3,854	5,062	5,337	3,579	-7.1	73
New Hampshire	1,212	861	671	1,402	...	139
New Jersey	13,880	10,818	10,824	13,874	0	211
New York............................	54,524	23,340	24,331	53,533	-1.8	364
Pennsylvania (a)	76,989	26,300	27,500	75,732	-1.6	787
Rhode Island (b)	344	381	389	338	-1.7	41
Vermont (b)(c)	922	657	520	1,059	14.9	216
Regional total	154,848	70,594	72,667	152,720	-1.3	...
Midwestern Region						
Illinois	34,277	35,636	35,337	34,576	0.9	362
Indiana...............................	6,627	6,446	5,778	7,295	10.1	156
Iowa (b)	3,325	2,665	2,430	3,560	7.1	155
Kansas (b)...........................	4,525	4,500	4,359	4,666	3.1	225
Michigan.............................	20,924	10,429	11,375	19,978	-4.5	263
Minnesota...........................	3,676	5,035	4,745	3,966	7.9	101
Nebraska.............................	801	869	1,003	667	-16.7	50
North Dakota	246	728	687	287	16.7	57
Ohio...................................	18,882	9,956	9,326	19,512	3.3	224
South Dakota	2,217	1,848	1,621	2,444	10.2	414
Wisconsin	14,438	7,682	6,615	15,505	7.4	365
Regional total	109,938	85,794	83,276	112,456	2.2	...
Southern Region						
Alabama..............................	7,745	3,030	3,523	7,252	-6.4	208
Arkansas.............................	13,476	8,130	5,075	16,531	22.7	782
Florida	4,484	6,198	5,897	4,785	6.7	34
Georgia	23,344	11,366	11,859	22,851	-2.1	338
Kentucky	8,255	5,727	4,420	9,562	15.8	298
Louisiana	24,219	13,330	13,477	24,072	-0.6	712
Maryland	14,351	7,658	7,738	14,271	-0.6	339
Mississippi..........................	1,758	996	784	1,970	12.1	90
Missouri..............................	17,400	13,458	12,484	18,374	5.6	414
North Carolina	2,882	3,506	3,287	3,101	7.6	47
Oklahoma (c).......................	4,329	1,488	1,800	4,017	-7.2	148
South Carolina	3,237	1,050	1,132	3,155	-2.5	97
Tennessee (b)	8,223	3,748	3,126	8,721	6.1	190
Texas..................................	102,072	32,701	32,857	101,916	-0.2	611
Virginia	4,392	2,570	2,463	4,499	2.4	78
West Virginia	1,216	1,015	815	1,416	16.4	99
Regional total	241,383	115,971	110,737	246,493	2.1	...
Western Region						
Alaska (b)	949	645	621	973	2.5	202
Arizona...............................	5,728	11,782	11,402	6,108	6.6	138
California (b)	110,262	162,329	160,848	111,743	1.3	421
Colorado	7,383	6,880	6,067	8,196	11	234
Hawaii	2,296	632	722	2,119	-7.7	213
Idaho..................................	2,370	1,443	1,331	2,482	4.7	233
Montana (b)	810	570	545	835	3.1	114
Nevada...............................	3,610	2,612	2,257	3,965	9.8	217
New Mexico	2,469	1,439	1,042	2,866	16.1	197
Oregon...............................	20,515	9,037	8,053	21,499	4.8	766
Utah...................................	3,246	2,502	2,471	3,277	1	188
Washington (d)	10,640	5,668	4,740	11,568	8.7	239
Wyoming	563	327	281	609	8.2	153
Regional total	170,841	205,866	200,380	176,240	3.2	347
Regional total without California............	60,579	43,537	39,532	64,497	6.4	...
Dist. of Columbia (c)..........	5,253	2,112	2,180	5,288	0.7	1,214

Source: U.S. Department of Justice, Bureau of Justice Statistics, *Probation and Parole in the United States, 2005*, (November 2006).

Note: Because of nonresponse or incomplete data, the parole population for some jurisdictions on December 31, 2005, does not equal the population on January 1, plus entries, minus exits.

Key:
... — Number not calculated.

(a) Data for entries and exits were estimated for nonreporting county agencies.

(b) Excludes parolees in one of the following categories: absconder, out of state, or inactive.

(c) All data were estimated.

(d) Due to a change in recordkeeping procedures, data are not comparable to previous reports.

Table 9.21
CAPITAL PUNISHMENT (as of December 2005)

State or other jurisdiction	Capital offenses	Minimum age (a)	Prisoners under sentence of death	Method of execution
Alabama	Intentional murder with 18 aggravating factors.	16	193	Electrocution or lethal injection
Alaska	. . .	. . .	. . .	. . .
Arizona (b)	First degree murder accompanied by at least 1 of 14 aggravating factors.	(c)	105	Lethal gas or lethal injection (d)
Arkansas (b)	Capital murder with a finding of at least 1 of 10 aggravating circumstances; treason.	14 (e)	39	Lethal injection or electrocution (f)
California (b)	First-degree murder with special circumstances; train-wrecking; treason; perjury causing execution.	18	637	Lethal gas or lethal injection
Colorado (b)	First-degree murder with at least 1 of 17 aggravating factors; treason.	18	3	Lethal injection
Connecticut (b).............	Capital felony with 8 forms of aggravated homicide.	18	7	Lethal injection
Delaware (b)	First-degree murder with aggravating circumstances.	16	17	Hanging or lethal injection (g)
Florida (b)	First-degree murder; felony murder; capital drug-trafficking; capital sexual battery.	17	364	Electrocution or lethal injection
Georgia (b)	Murder; kidnapping with bodily injury or ransom when the victim dies; aircraft hijacking; treason.	17	109	Lethal injection
Hawaii............................	. . .	. . .	. . .	. . .
Idaho (b).......................	First-degree murder with aggravating factors; aggravated kidnapping; perjury resulting in death.	(c)	22	Firing squad or lethal injection
Illinois (b)	First-degree murder with 1 of 21 aggravating circumstances.	18	6	Lethal injection
Indiana (b)....................	Murder with 16 aggravating circumstances.	18	27	Lethal injection
Iowa	. . .	. . .	. . .	. . .
Kansas (b).....................	Capital murder with 8 aggravating circumstances.	18	0	Lethal injection
Kentucky (b).................	Murder with aggravating factors; kidnapping with aggravating factors.	16	34	Electrocution or lethal injection (h)
Louisiana (b)	First-degree murder; aggravated rape of victim under age 12; treason.	(c)	87	Lethal injection
Maine............................	. . .	. . .	. . .	. . .
Maryland (b)	First-degree murder, either premeditated or during the commission of a felony, provided that certain death eligibility requirements are satisfied.	18	9	Lethal injection
Massachusetts................	. . .	. . .	. . .	. . .
Michigan........................	. . .	. . .	. . .	. . .
Minnesota	. . .	. . .	. . .	. . .
Mississippi	Capital murder; aircraft piracy.	16	70	Lethal injection
Missouri (b)	First-degree murder.	16	52	Lethal injection or lethal gas
Montana	Capital murder with 1 of 9 aggravating circumstances; capital sexual assault.	(i)	4	Lethal injection
Nebraska (b).................	First-degree murder with a finding of at least 1 statutorily-defined aggravating circumstance.	18	8	Electrocution
Nevada (b)	First-degree murder with at least 1 of 15 aggravating circumstances.	18	83	Lethal injection
New Hampshire............	Six categories of capital murder.	17	0	Lethal injection or hanging (j)
New Jersey....................	Murder by one's own conduct, by solicitation, committed in furtherance of a narcotics conspiracy, or during the commission of a crime of terrorism.	18	11	Lethal injection
New Mexico (b)	First-degree murder with at least 1 of 7 statutorily-defined aggravating circumstances.	18	2	Lethal injection

See footnotes at end of table.

CAPITAL PUNISHMENT — Continued

State or other jurisdiction	Capital offenses	Minimum age (a)	Prisoners under sentence of death	Method of execution
New York (b)	First-degree murder with 1 of 13 aggravating factors.	18	2	Lethal injection
North Carolina (b)	First-degree murder.	17	181	Lethal injection
North Dakota................	. . .	. . .	. . .	. . .
Ohio	Aggravated murder with at least 1 of 10 aggravating circumstances.	18	201	Lethal injection
Oklahoma	First-degree murder in conjunction with a finding of at least 1 of 8 statutorily-defined aggravating circumstances.	13	91	Electrocution, lethal injection, or firing squad (k)
Oregon	Aggravated murder.	18	30	Lethal injection
Pennsylvania	First-degree murder with 18 aggravating circumstances.	(c)	222	Lethal injection
Rhode Island	. . .	. . .	. . .	. . .
South Carolina (b)	Murder with 1 of 11 aggravating circumstances.	(c)	71	Electrocution or lethal injection
South Dakota (b)..........	First-degree murder with 1 of 10 aggravating circumstances; aggravated kidnapping.	18	4	Lethal injection
Tennessee (b)	First-degree murder with 1 of 15 aggravating circumstances.	18	99	Lethal injection or electrocution (l)
Texas	Criminal homicide with 1 of 8 aggravating circumstances.	17	446	Lethal injection
Utah (b).........................	Aggravated murder.	14 (m)	10	Lethal injection or firing squad
Vermont	. . .	. . .	. . .	. . .
Virginia (b)	First-degree murder with 1 of 13 aggravating circumstances.	14 (m)	23	Electrocution or lethal injection
Washington (b).............	Aggravated first-degree murder.	18	10	Lethal injection or hanging
West Virginia................	. . .	. . .	. . .	. . .
Wisconsin......................	. . .	. . .	. . .	. . .
Wyoming.......................	First-degree murder.	18	2	Lethal injection or lethal gas (n)
Dist. of Columbia	. . .	. . .	. . .	. . .

Source: U.S. Department of Justice, Bureau of Statistics, *Capital Punishment, 2005*, (December 2006).

Key:

. . . — No capital punishment statute.

(a) Information reported in this table reflects the minimum age as defined by statute as of 12/31/05. The United States Supreme Court ruling in *Roper v. Simmons* (2005) declared unconstitutional imposition of the death penalty on persons under the age of 18.

(b) As of December 31, 2005, 27 states excluded mentally retarded persons from capital sentencing: Arizona, Arkansas, California, Colorado, Connecticut, Delaware, Florida, Georgia, Idaho, Illinois, Indiana, Kansas, Kentucky, Louisiana, Maryland, Missouri, Nebraska, Nevada, New Mexico, New York, North Carolina, Ohio, South Dakota, Tennessee, Utah, Virginia, and Washington. Mental retardation is a mitigating factor in South Carolina.

(c) No age specified.

(d) Arizona authorizes lethal injection for persons whose capital sentence was received after 11/15/92; for those sentenced before that date, the condemned may select lethal injection or lethal gas.

(e) See Arkansas Code Ann. 9-27-318(c)(2)(Supp. 2001).

(f) Arkansas authorizes lethal injection for those whose capital offense occurred on or after 7/4/83; for those whose offense occurred before that date, the condemned may select lethal injection or electrocution.

(g) Delaware authorizes lethal injection for those whose capital offense occurred after 6/13/86; for those whose offense occurred before that date, the condemned may select lethal injection or hanging.

(h) Kentucky authorizes lethal injection for persons whose capital sentence was received on or after 3/31/98; for those sentenced before that date, the condemned may select lethal injection or electrocution.

(i) Montana law specifies that offenders tried under the capital sexual assault statute be 18 or older. No statutory minimum age is specified for other capital offenses.

(j) New Hampshire authorizes hanging only if lethal injection cannot be given.

(k) Oklahoma authorizes electrocution if lethal injection is ever held to be unconstitutional, and firing squad if both lethal injection and electrocution are held unconstitutional.

(l) Tennessee authorizes lethal injection for those whose capital offense occurred after 12/31/98; those whose offense occurred before that date may select electrocution by written waiver.

(m) The minimum age for transfer to adult court by statute is 14.

(n) Wyoming authorizes lethal gas if lethal injection is ever held to be unconstitutional.

Trends in Welfare Programs
By Sheila R. Zedlewski

State welfare caseloads in 2006 reflected the maturation of policies adopted in response to federal TANF legislation passed 10 years earlier. Caseloads continued to shrink, and many families on welfare received benefits only for the children. Significant shares of adults on welfare were exempt from work requirements due to illness or disability. Some received welfare through a time limit extension, and others were denied assistance because of a sanction. New federal rules requiring states to increase work participation will change the shape of future caseloads. States with large shares of their caseloads exempt from work requirements face the greatest challenge.

Recent Caseload Experience

Nationwide, caseloads for Temporary Assistance for Needy Families (TANF) declined between 2005 and 2006, extending the trend started more than a decade ago (Table A). Caseloads declined by 7.8 percent between 2005 and 2006, contributing to the 128.6 percent drop in welfare caseloads since 1996. Caseloads declined between 2005 and 2006 in all but three states—Arkansas, Massachusetts and Michigan. Welfare caseloads in some states are now only one-quarter or less of pre-TANF levels. For example, caseloads have declined by more than 200 percent in Alaska, Florida, Georgia, Idaho, Illinois, Louisiana, Maryland, Mississippi, North Carolina, Oklahoma, Texas, West Virginia and Wyoming.

Recent trends in welfare caseloads generally correspond to declines in unemployment. Nationwide, the unemployment rate dropped from 5.1 to 4.6 percent between 2005 and 2006.[1] Nineteen states experienced significant unemployment rate declines, and only three states (Massachusetts, Nevada and Vermont) experienced significant increases.[2] Unemployment did not change significantly in more than half the states.

Welfare caseloads include traditional families with parents and children, "child only" families in which only the children receive cash assistance, and families in Separate State Programs (SSPs). Nationwide, 42 percent of welfare cases were classified as "child only," and 7.6 percent of cases were in SSPs. The most common reasons for child-only cases include families with parents on Supplemental Security Income, SSI (24 percent), partially sanctioned families in which the parent no longer receives a benefit because of noncompliance with participaton requirements (7 percent), families with an ineligible parent due to immigration status (19 percent), and families without a parent present (44 percent).[3] SSPs include two-parent families (44 percent), parents with dis-

abilities (25 percent), and other families (33 percent) that states exclude from federal work participation rate calculations.

New Program Requirements

The shape of states' welfare caseloads is likely to change in the future as a result of the Deficit Reduction Act (DRA) that reauthorized the TANF program.[4] The DRA maintained a 50-percent work requirement for all adults on the caseload and 90 percent for two-parent families, but it substantially expanded requirements for who must be counted toward the work participation requirement and made other adjustments to increase work participation. The DRA requires states to include most adults in their work participation rate calculations, including those funded through state maintenance of effort monies. Under the new rules, individuals assigned to SSPs must either be counted in the TANF caseload or states can fund their benefits through a Separate State Funded (SSF) program with monies that will not count toward their TANF maintenance of effort requirement. The DRA also requires states to include sanctioned parents in their rate calculations.

The DRA also narrowed the definitions of the activities that can count toward the work participation rates. All parents must engage in at least 20 hours of "core" activities, and parents with children age 6 or older have to engage in an additional 10 hours of core or noncore activities.[5] Core activities include unsubsidized employment, subsidized private sector or public sector employment, work experience, on-the-job training, job search and job readiness assistance (up to six weeks a year), community service, vocational educational training (up to 12 months total), and child care services to an individual who is participating in community service. Noncore activities include job skills training and education gener-

Table A: TANF Caseload 2006: Distribution and Trends

State or other jurisdiction	Total caseload (a)	Distribution by caseload status:			Percent change from:	
		TANF families: with parent(s)	TANF families: child only	SSP families	2005	1996
Alabama	19,385	52.1%	46.8%	1.1%	-6.9%	-110.0%
Alaska	3,348	69.2	30.8	0.0	-5.3	-268.0
Arizona	38,086	52.0	48.0	0.0	-11.7	-62.2
Arkansas	8,596	52.6	47.4	0.0	1.3	-157.2
California	477,441	46.2	46.2	7.3	-4.5	-82.3
Colorado	12,972	62.0	38.0	0.0	-17.3	-158.7
Connecticut	21,543	46.3	36.2	17.4	-7.7	-165.1
Delaware	5,462	51.9	46.5	1.6	-6.5	-91.8
Florida	50,289	22.5	76.2	1.2	-14.6	-298.3
Georgia	27,553	17.6	82.3	0.1	-38.1	-338.8
Hawaii	9,336	49.9	23.1	27.0	-6.3	-134.4
Idaho	1,767	19.2	80.8	0.0	-2.7	-375.0
Illinois	34,376	46.1	51.7	2.2	-12.9	-533.6
Indiana	42,835	53.8	42.0	4.2	-18.6	-16.1
Iowa	20,450	53.0	25.4	21.6	-8.3	-52.0
Kansas	16,974	74.3	25.7	0.0	-6.8	-37.8
Kentucky	32,436	46.9	53.1	0.0	-5.1	-117.2
Louisiana	11,183	31.4	68.6	0.0	-37.3	-495.0
Maine	11,000	60.9	23.3	15.8	-0.6	-79.5
Maryland	19,049	55.5	44.3	0.2	-30.4	-261.9
Massachusetts	49,034	62.6	34.6	2.8	0.1	-72.0
Michigan	89,806	70.2	29.8	0.0	10.3	-86.5
Minnesota	30,176	58.2	32.4	9.4	-2.0	-89.7
Mississippi	12,594	46.0	54.0	0.0	-17.7	-259.1
Missouri	43,520	63.1	24.6	12.3	-3.6	-81.8
Montana	3,487	62.5	37.5	0.0	-10.2	-181.4
Nebraska	12,653	52.2	27.4	20.4	-3.7	-13.6
Nevada	6,548	29.6	49.4	21.0	-12.3	-101.7
New Hampshire	6,251	65.6	32.7	1.8	-1.5	-42.6
New Jersey	41,363	67.9	27.8	4.3	-16.0	-143.7
New Mexico	16,175	65.0	35.0	0.0	-9.4	-103.9
New York	169,727	40.7	35.8	23.5	-9.2	-143.2
North Carolina	28,514	35.3	64.7	0.0	-11.3	-276.9
North Dakota	2,409	71.2	28.8	0.0	-20.0	-93.8
Ohio	77,746	45.0	55.0	0.0	-4.4	-159.7
Oklahoma	9,534	36.2	63.8	0.0	-17.9	-270.2
Oregon	18,045	53.6	46.4	0.0	-5.6	-58.1
Pennsylvania	89,967	67.7	32.3	0.0	-9.4	-100.2
Rhode Island	11,813	54.3	22.9	22.8	-8.7	-73.4
South Carolina	17,889	45.2	42.6	12.2	-5.5	-139.8
South Dakota	2,840	34.6	65.4	0.0	-0.5	-100.6
Tennessee	67,487	72.4	26.1	1.5	-5.3	-42.6
Texas	68,408	34.9	62.7	2.5	-20.2	-249.0
Utah	6,247	54.3	45.5	0.2	-38.1	-124.8
Vermont	4,792	69.9	23.2	6.8	-3.5	-81.1
Virginia	33,908	25.2	. . .	74.8	-7.9	-78.3
Washington	53,267	59.8	36.8	3.3	-8.2	-81.7
West Virginia	11,051	46.2	48.9	4.9	-11.4	-240.2
Wisconsin	17,910	34.2	64.4	1.4	-5.4	-178.8
Wyoming	305	20.0	74.4	5.6	-8.2	-1,323.9
Dist. of Columbia	15,871	54.3	42.5	3.2	-6.5	-58.4
United States	1,900,860	50.1	42.2	7.6	-7.8	-128.6

Source: U.S. Department of Health and Human Services, Administration of Children and Families, "Caseload Data" 2006, 2005 and 1996. Downloaded from *http://www.acf.dhhs.gov/programs/ofa/caseload/caseloadindex.htm, March 2007.*

Key:
(a) The toal caseload is determined by adding TANF families and SSP families.
(b) Change is assessed based on data from September in 2006, 2005 and 1996.

ally related to employment and restricted to those without a high school education. Employment barrier removal activities such as mental health treatment count as job readiness activities in this new system and will be limited to six weeks per year.

States must monitor and document these work activities. Unpaid activities must be supervised daily (through daily telephone contact), and unpaid work must be documented. Hours in paid work can be verified through pay stubs and projections of future hours of work.

The change in the "caseload reduction" credit implemented by the DRA also significantly increases states' work participation requirements relative to the original TANF program. The original credit allowed states to reduce their work participation rates by the percentage point decline in caseload after 1995. Given the rapid and steep caseload declines after 1995, many states had effective work participation rates of zero.[6] The DRA bases the credit on caseload decline after 2005, a time when most states' caseloads have been declining more slowly. States that do not meet their work participation rates face a financial penalty of 5 percent of their block grant for the first failure, increasing by 2 percentage points a year for continued failure up to a maximum of 21 percent. Penalized states must make up the federal penalty to maintain TANF resource levels.

The New Rules Present a Significant Challenge for Some States

The effects of these changes on TANF programs will depend on the share of states' caseloads already participating in work activities, and the share more difficult to move into work activities because of illness or disability, a demonstrated inability to find work or a sanction. Recent caseload data provide some indication of the variation in these factors across the states (Table B).

In 2004 (the latest data available) 32 percent of nonexempt TANF adults met federal all family work participation standards. Only five states—Iowa, Ohio, South Dakota, Wisconsin and Wyoming—had work participation rates of 50 percent or higher. Most states will have to increase work participation rates substantially to meet the new federal standards. States also will need to increase the number of hours in work activities and change allowable work activities for some of those already engaged. For example, 17 percent of adults counted as participating in TANF work activities in 2005 were in education and training programs, activities that will be substantially curtailed by the new legislation.[7]

States will have to look carefully at groups of adults in "hard to employ" categories. The share of the adult caseload exempt because of illness or disability varies significantly across the states (Table B). Five states (Michigan, Nebraska, New Hampshire, Oregon and South Carolina) had one quarter or more of adults in the disabled category in 2005. Nationwide, 5 percent of adult cases had extensions after reaching their time limit, including 21 percent of adult cases in the District of Columbia. On average, 9 percent of adults were sanctioned, but California, the District of Columbia, Hawaii, Massachusetts and Tennessee had sanction rates of 15 percent or higher.[8] More than one-quarter of states' caseloads fell into these hard-to-employ categories, but the hard to employ share exceeded one-third in the District of Columbia and eight states (Massachusetts, Michigan, Nebraska, New Hampshire, New York, Oregon, Pennsylvania and Rhode Island).

Some states will receive caseload reduction credits that will reduce the 50-percent work participation rate requirement. In 2007, for example, all but three states (Arkansas, Massachusetts and Michigan) will receive some credit because of caseload decline between 2005 (the new base year) and 2006 (Table A). Twelve states—Colorado, Florida, Georgia, Indiana, Louisiana, Maryland, Mississippi, New Jersey, North Dakota, Oklahoma, Texas and Utah—will have credits exceeding 15 percentage points, substantially reducing their required work participation rates.

Conclusions

Caseloads declined between 2005 and 2006, adding to the dramatic drop since the advent of the TANF program. The status of current welfare caseloads highlights the diversity of families on welfare across the states. Child-only families now comprise more than one in four of all families on TANF. More than one-quarter of adults on welfare fall into hard-to-employ categories, including those assessed as significantly ill or disabled, those who exceeded their time limit and those with sanctions. Only one-third of adults on welfare were in work participation activities that counted toward the 2006 federal standards.

In many ways 2006 represents a turning point in the TANF program. The DRA forces most states to increase work participation rates for their caseloads substantially. States also must comply with stricter rules about what counts as work participation. One bright note is that the general caseload decline between 2005 and 2006 means that most states will have a caseload reduction credit toward the required 50-percent work participation rate. States must be

Table B: Characteristics of Welfare Caseloads

State or other jurisdiction	Work participation FY 2004	Total adult caseload (a)	Adult caseload in at-risk groups:			
			TANF/SSP exempt: disability	Time limit extended (b)	TANF/SSP cases in sanction (c)	Total percent caseload
Alabama	37.9%	11,074	14.1%	1.1%	9.4%	24.6%
Alaska	43.6	3,301	10.5	3.5	2.9	17.0
Arizona	25.5	24,325	8.7	0.1	0.9	9.8
Arkansas	27.3	4,311	15.6	0.1	13.0	28.7
California	23.1	284,981	10.9	6.4	14.7	32.0
Colorado	34.7	10,282	16.5	0.7	1.0	18.2
Connecticut	2.3	15,915	18.9	0.4	1.8	21.2
Delaware	22.1	3,105	21.3	0.0	2.5	23.7
Florida	40.4	22,502	1.5	1.1	13.9	16.5
Georgia	24.8	16,773	1.2	1.3	1.6	4.1
Hawaii	70.5	8,691	0.0	0.0	27.6	27.6
Idaho	41.0	516	0.0	0.0	0.0	0.0
Illinois	46.1	20,293	0.0	0.0	2.1	2.1
Indiana	36.3	27,647	12.6	0.0	3.5	16.1
Iowa	50.0	16,747	0.6	1.3	4.8	6.7
Kansas	88.0	12,702	2.2	5.3	0.0	7.4
Kentucky	38.1	18,175	8.0	1.0	7.4	16.4
Louisiana	35.4	5,744	9.5	1.1	0.0	10.6
Maine	32.1	8,952	17.3	11.6	2.3	31.1
Maryland	16.0	16,370	16.0	11.6	1.1	28.7
Massachusetts	60.0	31,734	0.3	0.1	61.5	61.9
Michigan	24.5	53,048	30.5	17.4	0.0	47.9
Minnesota	26.8	23,186	6.8	10.3	4.9	22.0
Mississippi	21.0	8,651	7.8	0.6	0.8	9.2
Missouri	19.5	35,013	11.2	1.1	3.2	15.4
Montana	92.7	3,197	0.1	0.1	4.7	5.0
Nebraska	34.5	6,368	29.7	9.4	0.1	39.2
Nevada	34.5	4,222	4.0	0.2	0.0	4.2
New Hampshire	30.2	4,402	27.0	4.0	7.4	38.3
New Jersey	34.6	32,510	13.3	11.2	5.8	30.4
New Mexico	46.2	12,020	18.0	0.0	6.1	24.1
New York	37.8	131,895	17.2	4.9	11.4	33.5
North Carolina	31.4	14,637	14.3	0.2	2.3	16.8
North Dakota	25.3	2,221	4.3	0.2	3.3	7.8
Ohio	65.2	39,450	1.0	0.7	0.1	1.8
Oklahoma	33.2	5,392	1.1	1.9	0.0	3.0
Oregon	32.1	10,852	29.7	0.0	4.7	34.4
Pennsylvania	7.1	70,824	19.4	13.5	3.8	36.6
Rhode Island	23.7	10,426	13.8	16.4	3.7	33.8
South Carolina	53.7	10,369	29.6	0.0	2.2	31.7
South Dakota	54.8	1,006	0.0	0.4	0.9	1.3
Tennessee	50.6	53,389	4.4	0.0	15.9	20.2
Texas	34.2	41,434	24.1	0.0	0.3	24.4
Utah	26.2	6,019	0.2	1.8	2.8	4.8
Vermont	24.9	3,936	21.7	0.0	4.8	26.5
Virginia	50.1	36,682	21.9	0.0	0.0	21.9
Washington	35.4	37,534	5.9	12.1	5.7	23.8
West Virginia	11.7	7,567	19.7	0.0	5.5	25.2
Wisconsin	61.3	9,532	1.0	4.3	13.6	18.9
Wyoming	77.8	69	8.8	0.0	13.6	22.4
Dist. of Columbia	18.2	13,828	5.9	21.2	23.2	50.3
United States	32.2	1,267,379	12.5	5.3	9.2	26.8

Source: U.S. Department of Health and Human Services, Administration of Children and Families, "Characteristics and Financial Circumstances of TANF Recipients," FY 2004 and FY 2005, downloaded from *http://www. acf.hhs.gov/programs/ofa/character/indexchar.htm*, September 2006 and February 2007.

Key:

(a) The total caseload is calculated as the sum of all families on TANF and in Separate State Programs, minus families with no adult, plus families with a parent in the household but not included in the unit that are in sanction status. Note that sanction data for child-only units are not available for Colorado, Hawaii, Maryland, Montana, Nebraska, Oklahoma or Wyoming.

(b) Percent of heads of household or spouses with over 60 months countable toward the federal time limit.

(c) This column includes child-only units in sanction and adult recipients in sanction/waiver status. Note that sanction data for child-only units are not available for Colorado, Hawaii, Maryland, Montana, Nebraska, Oklahoma or Wyoming.

fully compliant with the new rules by the start of the 2008 federal fiscal year, and 2007 work participation rates will be calculated using the new rules. States' success will depend on more effective programs to increase work participation, and the ability of local labor markets to absorb more adults leaving welfare. It will be important to monitor the effects of the DRA on future welfare caseloads.

Notes

[1] From the *Economic Report of the President*, 2007, (Council of Economic Advisers, Washington, D.C.: U.S. GPO), the civilian unemployment rate, Table B-42, 280.

[2] State unemployment data from "Regional and State Employment and Unemployment: January 2007," The Bureau of Labor Statistics, the U.S. Department of Labor, (March 2007).

[3] Reasons for child only cases represent the average for the national caseload in 2006, from the *TANF Seventh Annual Report to Congress*, 2006, (Washington, D.C.: USDHHS).

[4] See "Implementing the TANF Changes in the Deficit Reduction Act: 'Win-Win' Solutions for Families and States," Second Edition, the Center on Budget and Policy Priorities and the Center for Law and Social Policy, February, 2007 for a thorough discussion of the DRA.

[5] Two parents must participate more hours and the number depends on whether or not they receive subsidized child care.

[6] The average effective work participation rate for all families was 3.9 percent in 2005, *TANF Seventh Annual Report to Congress*, (Washington, D.C.: U.S. Department of Heath and Human Services, 2006).

[7] *TANF Seventh Annual Report to Congress*, (USDHHS, 2006).

[8] These statistics do not include cases closed due to full family sanctions.

About the Author

Sheila R. Zedlewski is the director of the Income and Benefits Policy Center at the Urban Institute, a nonpartisan think tank in Washington, D.C. Her recent work focuses on the safety net for hard to employ parents, food stamp program participation, and trends in work support spending. She has written extensively about the TANF program with a focus on families unable to move from welfare to work.

U.S.-Mexico Relationship: Tough Challenges Ahead

By Edgar Ruiz

While enjoying an unprecedented level of cooperation in recent years on numerous cross-border policy issues, the United States and Mexico face important challenges that will affect the long-term prosperity of North America. These challenges include the need for both countries to address the contentious issue of immigration, promote a shared vision for competitiveness in the 21st century and give government the tools to manage binational concerns along the U.S.-Mexico border.

Introduction

While enjoying an unprecedented level of cooperation in recent years on numerous cross-border policy issues, the United States and Mexico face important challenges that will affect the long-term prosperity of North America. These challenges include the need for both countries to address the contentious issue of immigration, promote a shared vision for competitiveness in the 21st century and give government the tools to manage binational concerns along the U.S.-Mexico border.

Changing Political Environment in Mexico

As newly elected President Felipe Calderon takes the reigns of Mexico's executive branch, the country continues to be embroiled in the aftermath of the closest presidential election in its history. While Calderon is moving forward after his razor thin victory over challenger Andres Manuel Lopez Obrador, he does so with great caution and uncertainty in a politically divided country. The election results display a great divide between northern and southern Mexican states. Northern Mexico states have benefited from cross-border trade and greater economic exchange as a result of the North American Free Trade Agreement (NAFTA). Southern states have not benefited from such trade integration and historically have seen a decline in economic competitiveness, an increase in unemployment and a high exodus of migrants.

Both Calderon of the National Action Party (PAN) and Andres Manuel Lopez Obrador of the Democratic Revolutionary Party (PRD) hail from political alliances that, until most recently, did not have a strong political voice during the 70-plus years of the Institutional Revolutionary Party's (PRI) one-party rule. The newly established Mexican Federal Congress is comprised of nine political parties with the PAN holding only a slim majority.[1] Any reform or major initiative will require broad consensus among the different political parties and a strong political will for change.

As Mexico moves forward from this important election cycle that tested the validity of critical government institutions such as the independent Federal Elections Institute and the Federal Elections Tribunal, Calderon must deal with poverty, work force and economic development, justice and energy reform, public safety and education. His administration will need to hammer out a new bilateral agenda with the U.S. to address border security, immigration and economic integration that goes beyond NAFTA.

Immigration Reform

Early in the terms of both President George W. Bush and former Mexican President Vicente Fox a great sense of optimism loomed as an agreement on immigration reform seemed within reach. However, the Sept. 11, 2001, terrorist attacks dramatically altered those prospects as the United States shifted its focus to the global war on terror and border security. Since then, the U.S.-Mexico relationship has been dominated by immigration, primarily from a security perspective. The U.S. Congress and the American public have had an intense debate over immigration, focusing on border security, the estimated 11.5 million to 12 million undocumented immigrants already in the United States, and unmet U.S. labor needs, particularly in agriculture.[2]

In 2004, President Bush proposed a temporary worker program to match willing foreign workers with willing U.S. employers when no Americans can be found to fill the jobs. The president also asked Congress to work with him to achieve immigration reform that controls the border, offers incentives for temporary workers to return to their home countries and protects the rights of legal immigrants while not unfairly rewarding those who entered unlawfully.

Immigration came to the forefront of the 2006 U.S. Congress as it debated several measures, including passage of Border Fence Act, which authorizes 700 miles of additional fencing, barriers, checkpoints

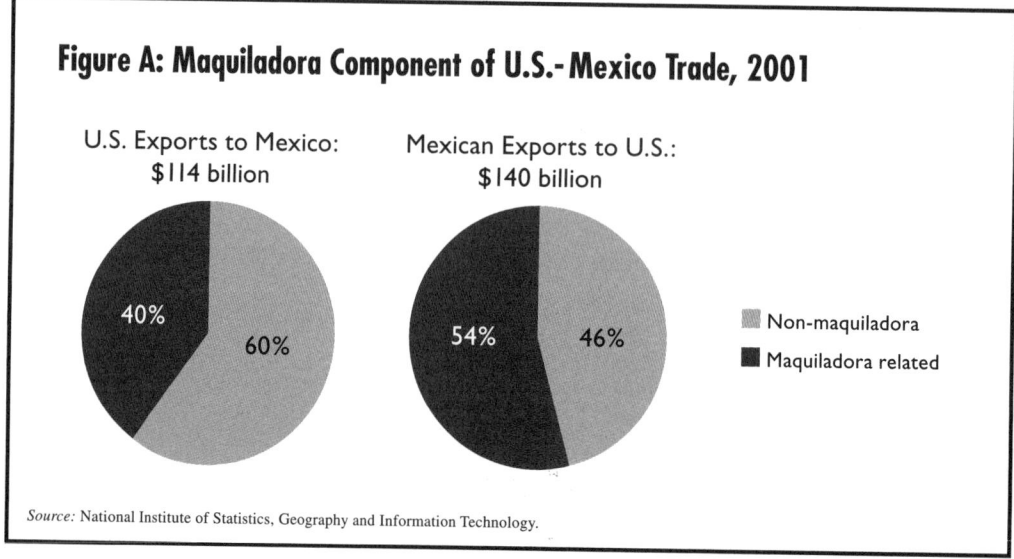

Figure A: Maquiladora Component of U.S.-Mexico Trade, 2001

U.S. Exports to Mexico: $114 billion

Mexican Exports to U.S.: $140 billion

40% | 60%

54% | 46%

Non-maquiladora
Maquiladora related

Source: National Institute of Statistics, Geography and Information Technology.

and lighting along the southern border. The act also increases the use of advanced technology such as cameras, satellites and unmanned aerial vehicles to reinforce security.[3] Many criticized this measure as an "enforcement only" approach that did not address the root of the problem. Passage of this bill sparked criticism in the U.S. and Mexico about the negative symbolism of a border fence and compared it to past Cold War efforts to contain fears and enemies with walls.

The U.S. Congress also considered immigration reform legislation, including a bill co-sponsored by Sens. John McCain and Edward Kennedy that included temporary worker and earned legalization provisions. While such reform efforts were not passed in the last session, it is likely that similar versions will be reintroduced in 2007.

In addition to federal legislation, several states and local governments have attempted to curb illegal immigration using a series of laws and ordinances. In addition to English-only laws, these measures included ordinances denying public services to undocumented immigrants, giving local law enforcement authority to detain undocumented immigrants, and punishing home owners who rent to undocumented immigrants.

Although the immigration debate has become polarized, pragmatic solutions need to prevail. Both countries share a responsibility to secure the border. Both must pass laws to promote secure, safe, legal and humane immigration patterns.

Enforcement-only approaches have been ineffective in reducing undocumented immigration. For instance, operations along the California and Texas

borders in the 1990s provided more border patrol agents and illegal immigration control operations. While initially successful, these efforts eventually led to rerouting migration flows overland through dangerous desert and mountain areas such as Arizona and New Mexico, as well as underground through sophisticated tunnel systems.[4] Since then, the federal government has continued to increase border enforcement with little success in stopping undocumented immigration as demonstrated by the presence of 11 million unauthorized residents in the United States.[5]

Moreover, enforcement-only measures have had the unintended consequence of increasing criminal smuggling networks. The harder it is for undocumented immigrants to cross the border, the more they rely on professional smugglers and organized criminals to help them enter the country.[6] An Associated Press analysis of a recent survey found the use of smugglers on the rise among illegal border crossers, up to 55 percent in 2005 from 18 percent in 2000.[7] Border enforcement tragically has increased immigrants' exposure to greater physical risks and deaths.

Mexico, which loses a significant number of young and productive employees to migration, must create an environment that promotes job opportunities and investments, particularly in rural areas and southern states. In the long run, such approaches will stem migration. Moreover, Mexico must invest heavily on education to prepare its labor force for the jobs of the future. However, promoting economic growth in Mexico will not reduce undocumented immigration overnight, and it will not address the legal status of undocumented immigrants already in the United

States. As such, the president and the U.S. Senate must seek legal solutions, like a temporary guest worker program.[8]

A New Vision to Meet Competitiveness Challenge of the 21st Century

As the world has become more interconnected, U.S. and Mexico stakeholders have begun discussions to enhance regional, continental competitiveness. The issue has captured considerable attention in North America as numerous manufacturing jobs continue to be lost to overseas competition.

The Maquiladora industry, which is the most visible demonstration of the U.S.-Mexico trade relationship, has been impacted by global competition and outsourcing. Maquiladoras are manufacturing plants that process and assemble components imported into Mexico that are, in turn, exported, usually to the U.S. The industry uses relatively inexpensive Mexican labor to perform a range of manufacturing operations, including assembly and processing. In recent years, these types of operations have moved to lower cost locales in Central America, Southeast Asia and China. Plants with the simplest production practices—such as textile, clothing and furniture manufacturing—are among the first to leave. The continued exodus of industries in these sectors to lower-cost countries such as China have made it clear that Mexico can no longer compete on the basis of cheap labor.

However, Mexico's proximity to the United States, the world's largest consumer market, gives it a unique advantage over other countries. Its location is ideal for designing and producing items for which proximity to the end user matters. The long-term prosperity of Mexico's manufacturing sector will depend on its ability to capitalize on this advantage with rapid-fire turnaround that Asia and other countries can't match. Meanwhile, this sector, along with the support of government from both countries, must seek to produce more complex, value-added products that are not as dependent on low-end manufacturing skills.

Regional partnerships can promote collaboration and joint marketing of assets in both countries. For example, in 2004 Texas and the four Mexican Northeastern states of Nuevo Leon, Tamaulipas, Coahuila and Chihuahua signed the historic Agreement for Regional Progress to create new jobs and economic opportunities along the border.[9] Under the agreement, states in the Northeast Mexico-Texas region agreed to establish technical cooperation programs. The agreement offers an integrated vision on how the region can take advantage of the region's 30 million inhabitants, its dynamic growth and border crossings which account for more than 50 percent of the total crossings between Mexico and the United States.

In a similar fashion, government and the private sector along the Arizona-Sonora and California-Baja California border have been working to enhance economic growth through a series of projects such as the CANAMEX Corridor Project and the proposed Silicon Border project.

The CANAMEX Corridor Project extends from central Mexico to Alberta, Canada, and promotes tourism, communications, transportation investments and streamlined international clearance at land

---

Table A: United States v. Mexico, at a Glance

General information	United States	Mexico
Population	290,809,777 in 2003 (U.S. Census Bureau, 2003)	101,000,000 in 2002 (World Bank, "World Development Report 2004")
Population growth	0.92% per year (2001 est.—CIA World Factbook)	1.5% per year (World Bank, "World Development Indicators 2003")
Nominal GDP 2003	$10,987.9 billion (Bureau of Economic Analysis, 2001)	$637.2 billion (World Bank, "World Development Indicators")
GDP per capita 2002	$35,060 (World Bank, "World Development Report 2004")	$5,910 (2001) (World Bank, "World Development Report 2004")
Area	3,717,792 square miles	758,445.2 square miles

Source: U.S. Embassy in Mexico, http://mexico.usembassy.gov.

border ports of entry. The Silicon Border proposal was conceived by semiconductor industry executives concerned about the overdependence and concentration in Asia. It would create a 10,000 acre high-tech science park along the border between Baja California and California.[10]

Enticing and maintaining valued-added manufacturing operations in North America not only increases the standard of living for both countries, but also offers unique advantages. A case in point is Motorola, which transferred its manufacturing operations to China because of low labor costs. Now the company is moving those operations back to the Arizona-Sonora border region. In China, late deliveries, decreased product quality and high manufacturing turnover rates, as well as cultural and language differences, were resulting in rising production costs. Now relocated to Nogales, Sonora, Motorola has established a close working relationship with engineering centers and manufacturing sites, and production is closer to customers and within the same trade zone.

Need for a Seamless Border

Most recently, the Border Legislative Conference, a CSG binational program of state legislators comprising the 10 U.S.-Mexico border states, convened a series of regional border economic development forums. These forums brought together border stakeholders to identify ways to promote economic competitiveness. One of the biggest priorities is to create a seamless border that integrates the concepts of "fast, secure and smart" to expedite the crossing of legitimate people and commerce at U.S.-Mexico ports of entry. In addition, the program recommended tax incentives for defense-related manufacturing, high-priority transportation corridors, high technology systems at ports of entry and work force training investments to prepare for high-skilled jobs.

Governance Reforms

Today, as a result of recent government reforms and increased political plurality, Mexico's federal Congress and individual states wield greater influence in politics than ever before. Ongoing efforts to decentralize authority in specified policy areas have given legislatures, governors and other agencies greater standing in the policymaking process. Further reforms will be needed to continue Mexico's continued democratic advancement.

State executive and legislative branches remain challenged and limited due to the primacy of the federal government over domestic policy issues in Mexico. As a result of the federal government's dom-

inance over public revenues, state and local governments continue to be dependent on federal resources to meet their citizens' basic needs and deliver public services. State institutions in Mexico need to be strengthened so they can be effective change agents.

Differences in governmental structures, as well as very restrictive term limits, challenge the continuity of binational cooperation. In Mexico, state legislators, mayors, city councils and federal representatives in Mexico's Chamber of Deputies are allowed to serve a single three-year term. Governors, federal senators and the president serve a single, six-year term.

These challenges are compounded by the minimal coordination between governments and the private sector on both sides of the border. However, the long-term health of the U.S.-Mexico relationship and their shared border region will depend on finding common goals and benefits.

Legislatures Increased Level of Engagement

Over the last decade, the legislatures of the southern border region have increased their level of engagement in U.S.-Mexico relations. They have developed links with their regional border counterparts through the creation of border affairs committees. Of the six Mexican states bordering the United States, five—Baja California, Sonora, Chihuahua, Coahuila and Tamaulipas—have active border affairs committees.

Likewise, in the U.S. border states of California, Arizona and Texas, legislative committees have been established to address cross-border issues and promote greater collaboration with Mexico. While their influence is limited by the purview of the federal government, these committees have had success in voicing local concerns in the areas of the environment, health, regional transportation planning and public safety. Additionally, through their oversight and budget functions, the committees have been successful in promoting funding for border specific projects.

U.S. and Mexican border state legislatures continue to expand their cooperative relationships. Because of their unique understanding of the complex issues affecting the border region, border legislators can provide community-based approaches to benefit the region. Border lawmakers can serve as effective critics and advocates of federal proposals in Washington, D.C., and Mexico City so national strategies correlate to practical realities. As Mexico continues to change politically, state legislatures are becoming breeding grounds for new political leadership. State legislatures will be the innovators in public education, regional planning and fiscal reform, among other things.

Conclusion

The U.S.-Mexico relationship faces complex challenges that require practical solutions. As the relationship between the United States and Mexico evolves from friends to strategic allies, leaders from both countries must work on a hemispheric strategy that fosters economic prosperity and security.

Notes

[1] Congreso de la Union, Camara de Diputados, *http://www.diputados.gob.mx.*

[2] Pew Hispanic Center Web site, "Estimates of the Unauthorized Migrant Population for States Based on the March 2005 CPS."

[3] White House Fact Sheet: The Secure Fence Act of 2005, *www.whitehouse.gov/news/releases/2006.*

[4] *Newsweek*, interview with border expert David Shirk, October 12, 2006.

[5] *Newsweek*, interview with border expert David Shirk, October 12, 2006.

[6] *Newsweek*, interview with border expert David Shirk, October 12, 2006.

[7] "U.S. crackdown is lucrative for guides," *Sacramento Bee*, January 3, 2007.

[8] *Newsweek*, interview with border expert David Shirk, October 12, 2006.

[9] Texas Secretary of State's Web site, *http://www.sos.state.tx.us/border/arr.shtml.*

[10] Presentation by Daniel Hill, "Silicon Border" at the 2nd Regional Border Economic Development Forum in San Diego, California, February 24, 2006.

About the Author

Edgar Ruiz is the program director of the Border Legislative Conference in The Council of State Governments' Western Regional Office. He holds a master's degree in public administration and a bachelor of arts degree in political science from State Diego State University.

Chapter Ten

STATE PAGES

If you are concerned with the apparently irresistible rush toward federal centralization, read about The Council of State Governments.

—Henry Toll

TABLE 10.1
OFFICIAL NAMES OF STATES AND JURISDICTIONS, CAPITALS, ZIP CODES AND CENTRAL SWITCHBOARDS

State or other jurisdiction	Name of state capitol (a)	Capital	Zip code	Area code	Central switchboard
Alabama, State of	State House	Montgomery	36130	334	242-7000
Alaska, State of	State Capitol	Juneau	99801	907	465-4648
Arizona, State of	State Capitol	Phoenix	85007	602	926-4900
Arkansas, State of	State Capitol	Little Rock	72201	501	682-3000
California, State of	State Capitol	Sacramento	95814	916	322-9900
Colorado, State of	State Capitol	Denver	80203	303	866-5000
Connecticut, State of	State Capitol	Hartford	06106	860	240-0100
Delaware, State of	Legislative Hall	Dover	19903	302	744-4114
Florida, State of	The Capitol	Tallahassee	32399	850	488-4441
Georgia, State of	State Capitol	Atlanta	30334	404	656-2000
Hawaii, State of	State Capitol	Honolulu	96813	808	586-0221
Idaho, State of	State Capitol	Boise	83720	208	332-1000
Illinois, State of	State House	Springfield	62706	217	782-2000
Indiana, State of	State House	Indianapolis	46204	317	232-1000
Iowa, State of	State Capitol	Des Moines	50319	515	281-5011
Kansas, State of	Statehouse	Topeka	66612	785	296-0111
Kentucky, Commonwealth of	State Capitol	Frankfort	40601	502	564-8100
Louisiana, State of	State Capitol	Baton Rouge	70804	225	324-6600
Maine, State of	State House Station	Augusta	04333	207	287-6826
Maryland, State of	State House	Annapolis	21401	410	946-5400
Massachusetts, Commonwealth of	State House	Boston	02133	617	722-2000
Michigan, State of	State Capitol	Lansing	48909	517	373-0184
Minnesota, State of	State Capitol	St. Paul	55155	651	296-3962
Mississippi, State of	State Capitol	Jackson	39215	601	359-3770
Missouri, State of	State Capitol	Jefferson City	65101	573	751-2000
Montana, State of	State Capitol	Helena	59620	406	444-2511
Nebraska, State of	State Capitol	Lincoln	68509	402	471-2311
Nevada, State of	State Capitol	Carson City	89701	775	684-5670
New Hampshire, State of	State House	Concord	03301	603	271-1110
New Jersey, State of	State House	Trenton	08625	609	292-6000
New Mexico, State of	State Capitol	Santa Fe	87501	505	986-4600
New York, State of	State Capitol	Albany	12224	518	455-7545
North Carolina, State of	State Capitol	Raleigh	27601	919	733-4111
North Dakota, State of	State Capitol	Bismarck	58505	701	328-2000
Ohio, State of	Statehouse	Columbus	43215	614	466-2000
Oklahoma, State of	State Capitol	Oklahoma City	73105	405	521-2011
Oregon, State of	State Capitol	Salem	97310	503	986-1848
Pennsylvania, Commonwealth of	Main Capitol Building	Harrisburg	17120	717	787-2121
Rhode Island and Providence Plantations, State of	State House	Providence	02903	401	222-2653
South Carolina, State of	State House	Columbia	29211	803	896-0000
South Dakota, State of	State Capitol	Pierre	57501	605	773-3011
Tennessee, State of	State Capitol	Nashville	37243	615	741-2001
Texas, State of	State Capitol	Austin	78701	512	463-4630
Utah, State of	State Capitol	Salt Lake City	84114	801	538-3000
Vermont, State of	State House	Montpelier	05633	802	828-2231
Virginia, Commonwealth of	State Capitol	Richmond	23219	804	698-7410
Washington, State of	Legislative Building	Olympia	98504	360	786-7579
West Virginia, State of	State Capitol	Charleston	25305	304	558-3456
Wisconsin, State of	State Capitol	Madison	53702	608	266-0382
Wyoming, State of	State Capitol	Cheyenne	82002	307	777-7434
District of Columbia	District Building	...	20004	202	724-8000
American Samoa, Territory of	Maota Fono	Pago Pago	96799	684	633-4116
Guam, Territory of	Congress Building	Hagatna	96932	671	472-8931
No. Mariana Islands, Commonwealth of	Civic Center Building	Saipan	96950	670	664-2286
Puerto Rico, Commonwealth of	The Capitol	San Juan	00902	787	721-7000
U.S. Virgin Islands, Territory of .... St. Thomas	Capitol Building	Charlotte Amalie,	00804	340	774-0001

(a) In some instances the name is not official.

TABLE 10.2
HISTORICAL DATA ON THE STATES

State or other jurisdiction	Source of state lands	Date organized as territory	Date admitted to Union	Chronological order of admission to Union
Alabama	Mississippi Territory, 1798 (a)	March 3, 1817	Dec. 14, 1819	22
Alaska	Purchased from Russia, 1867	Aug. 24, 1912	Jan. 3, 1959	49
Arizona	Ceded by Mexico, 1848 (b)	Feb. 24, 1863	Feb. 14, 1912	48
Arkansas	Louisiana Purchase, 1803	March 2, 1819	June 15, 1836	25
California	Ceded by Mexico, 1848	(c)	Sept. 9, 1850	31
Colorado	Louisiana Purchase, 1803 (d)	Feb. 28, 1861	Aug. 1, 1876	38
Connecticut	Fundamental Orders, Jan. 14, 1638; Royal charter, April 23, 1662	(e)	Jan. 9, 1788 (f)	5
Delaware	Swedish charter, 1638; English charter, 1638	(e)	Dec. 7, 1787 (f)	1
Florida	Ceded by Spain, 1819	March 30, 1822	March 3, 1845	27
Georgia	Charter, 1732, from George II to Trustees for Establishing the Colony of Georgia	(e)	Jan. 2, 1788 (f)	4
Hawaii	Annexed, 1898	June 14, 1900	Aug. 21, 1959	50
Idaho	Treaty with Britain, 1846	March 4, 1863	July 3, 1890	43
Illinois	Northwest Territory, 1787	Feb. 3, 1809	Dec. 3, 1818	21
Indiana	Northwest Territory, 1787	May 7, 1800	Dec. 11, 1816	19
Iowa	Louisiana Purchase, 1803	June 12, 1838	Dec. 28, 1846	29
Kansas	Louisiana Purchase, 1803 (d)	May 30, 1854	Jan. 29, 1861	34
Kentucky	Part of Virginia until admitted as state	(c)	June 1, 1792	15
Louisiana	Louisiana Purchase, 1803 (g)	March 26, 1804	April 30, 1812	18
Maine	Part of Massachusetts until admitted as state	(c)	March 15, 1820	23
Maryland	Charter, 1632, from Charles I to Calvert	(e)	April 28, 1788 (f)	7
Massachusetts	Charter to Massachusetts Bay Company, 1629	(e)	Feb. 6, 1788 (f)	6
Michigan	Northwest Territory, 1787	Jan. 11, 1805	Jan. 26, 1837	26
Minnesota	Northwest Territory, 1787 (h)	March 3, 1849	May 11, 1858	32
Mississippi	Mississippi Territory (i)	April 7, 1798	Dec. 10, 1817	20
Missouri	Louisiana Purchase, 1803	June 4, 1812	Aug. 10, 1821	24
Montana	Louisiana Purchase, 1803 (j)	May 26, 1864	Nov. 8, 1889	41
Nebraska	Louisiana Purchase, 1803	May 30, 1854	March 1, 1867	37
Nevada	Ceded by Mexico, 1848	March 2, 1861	Oct. 31, 1864	36
New Hampshire	Grants from Council for New England, 1622 and 1629; made Royal province, 1679	(e)	June 21, 1788 (f)	9
New Jersey	Dutch settlement, 1618; English charter, 1664	(e)	Dec. 18, 1787 (f)	3
New Mexico	Ceded by Mexico, 1848 (b)	Sept. 9, 1850	Jan. 6, 1912	47
New York	Dutch settlement, 1623; English control, 1664	(e)	July 26, 1788 (f)	11
North Carolina	Charter, 1663, from Charles II	(e)	Nov. 21, 1789 (f)	12
North Dakota	Louisiana Purchase, 1803 (k)	March 2, 1861	Nov. 2, 1889	39
Ohio	Northwest Territory, 1787	May 7, 1800	March 1, 1803	17
Oklahoma	Louisiana Purchase, 1803	May 2, 1890	Nov. 16, 1907	46
Oregon	Settlement and treaty with Britain, 1846	Aug. 14, 1848	Feb. 14, 1859	33
Pennsylvania	Grant from Charles II to William Penn, 1681	(e)	Dec. 12, 1787 (f)	2
Rhode Island	Charter, 1663, from Charles II	(e)	May 29, 1790 (f)	13
South Carolina	Charter, 1663, from Charles II	(e)	May 23, 1788 (f)	8
South Dakota	Louisiana Purchase, 1803	March 2, 1861	Nov. 2, 1889	40
Tennessee	Part of North Carolina until land ceded to U.S. in 1789	June 8, 1790 (l)	June 1, 1796	16
Texas	Republic of Texas, 1845	(c)	Dec. 29, 1845	28
Utah	Ceded by Mexico, 1848	Sept. 9, 1850	Jan. 4, 1896	45
Vermont	From lands of New Hampshire and New York	(c)	March 4, 1791	14
Virginia	Charter, 1609, from James I to London Company	(e)	June 25, 1788 (f)	10
Washington	Oregon Territory, 1848	March 2, 1853	Nov. 11, 1889	42
West Virginia	Part of Virginia until admitted as state	(c)	June 20, 1863	35
Wisconsin	Northwest Territory, 1787	April 20, 1836	May 29, 1848	30
Wyoming	Louisiana Purchase, 1803 (d)(j)	July 25, 1868	July 10, 1890	44
Dist. of Columbia	Maryland (m)	. . .	. . .	. . .
American Samoa	----------------------------------Became a territory, 1900----------------------------------			
Guam	Ceded by Spain, 1898	Aug. 1, 1950	. . .	. . .
No. Mariana Islands	. . .	March 24, 1976	. . .	. . .
Puerto Rico	Ceded by Spain, 1898	. . .	July 25, 1952 (n)	. . .
U.S. Virgin Islands	--------------------------------Purchased from Denmark, March 31, 1917--------------------------------			

See footnotes at end of table.

HISTORICAL DATA ON THE STATES—Continued

Key:

(a) By the *Treaty of Paris*, 1783, England gave up claim to the 13 original Colonies, and to all land within an area extending along the present Canadian to the Lake of the Woods, down the Mississippi River to the 31st parallel, east to the Chattahoochee, down that river to the mouth of the Flint, border east to the source of the St. Mary's down that river to the ocean. The major part of Alabama was acquired by the Treaty of Paris, and the lower portion from Spain in 1813.

(b) Portion of land obtained by Gadsden Purchase, 1853.

(c) No territorial status before admission to Union.

(d) Portion of land ceded by Mexico, 1848.

(e) One of the original 13 Colonies.

(f) Date of ratification of U.S. Constitution.

(g) West Feliciana District (Baton Rouge) acquired from Spain, 1810; added to Louisiana, 1812.

(h) Portion of land obtained by Louisiana Purchase, 1803.

(i) See footnote (a). The lower portion of Mississippi also was acquired from Spain in 1813.

(j) Portion of land obtained from Oregon Territory, 1848.

(k) The northern portion of the Red River Valley was acquired by treaty with Great Britain in 1818.

(l) Date Southwest Territory (identical boundary as Tennessee's) was created.

(m) Area was originally 100 square miles, taken from Virginia and Maryland. Virginia's portion south of the Potomac was given back to that state in 1846. Site chosen in 1790, city incorporated 1802.

(n) On this date, Puerto Rico became a self-governing commonwealth by compact approved by the U.S. Congress and the voters of Puerto Rico as provided in U.S. Public Law 600 of 1950.

TABLE 10.3
STATE STATISTICS

State or other jurisdiction	Land area: In square miles	Land area: Rank in nation	Population (e): Size	Population (e): Rank in nation	Percentage change 2004 to 2005	Density per square mile	Number of Representatives in Congress	Capital	Population (d)(f)	Rank in state	Largest city	Population (d)(f)
Alabama	50,744	28	4,599,030	23	1.1	90.6	7	Montgomery	200,127	2	Birmingham	231,483
Alaska	571,951	1	670,053	47	1.0	1.2	1	Juneau	30,987	2	Anchorage	275,043
Arizona	113,635	6	6,166,318	16	3.6	54.3	8	Phoenix	1,461,575	1	Phoenix	1,461,575
Arkansas	52,068	27	2,810,872	32	1.3	54.0	4	Little Rock	184,564	1	Little Rock	184,564
California	155,959	3	36,457,549	1	0.8	233.8	53	Sacramento	456,441	7	Los Angeles	3,844,829
Colorado	103,718	8	4,753,377	22	1.9	45.8	7	Denver	557,917	1	Denver	557,917
Connecticut	4,845	48	3,504,809	29	0.1	723.3	5	Hartford	124,397	3	Bridgeport	139,008
Delaware	1,954	49	853,476	45	1.4	436.8	1	Dover	34,288	2	Wilmington	72,786
Florida	53,927	26	18,089,888	4	1.8	335.5	25	Tallahassee	158,500	8	Jacksonville	782,623
Georgia	57,906	21	9,363,941	9	2.5	161.7	13	Atlanta	470,688	1	Atlanta	470,688
Hawaii	6,423	47	1,285,498	42	1.0	200.1	2	Honolulu	377,379	1	Honolulu	377,379
Idaho	82,747	11	1,466,465	39	2.6	17.7	2	Boise	193,161	1	Boise	193,161
Illinois	55,584	24	12,831,970	5	0.5	230.9	19	Springfield	115,668	6	Chicago	2,842,518
Indiana	35,867	38	6,313,520	15	0.8	176.0	9	Indianapolis	784,118	1	Indianapolis	784,118
Iowa	55,869	23	2,982,085	30	0.6	53.4	5	Des Moines	194,163	1	Des Moines	194,163
Kansas	81,815	13	2,764,075	33	0.6	33.8	4	Topeka	121,946	4	Wichita	354,865
Kentucky	39,728	36	4,206,074	26	0.8	105.9	6	Frankfort	27,210	7	Louisville	556,429
Louisiana	43,562	33	4,287,768	25	-4.9	98.4	7	Baton Rouge	222,064	2	New Orleans	454,863
Maine	30,862	39	1,321,574	40	0.3	42.8	2	Augusta	18,626	9	Portland	63,889
Maryland	9,774	42	5,615,727	19	0.5	574.5	8	Annapolis	36,300	7	Baltimore	635,815
Massachusetts	7,840	45	6,437,193	13	0.1	821.0	10	Boston	559,034	1	Boston	559,034
Michigan	56,804	22	10,095,643	8	-0.1	177.7	15	Lansing	115,518	6	Detroit	886,671
Minnesota	79,610	14	5,167,101	21	0.8	64.9	8	St. Paul	275,150	2	Minneapolis	372,811
Mississippi	46,907	31	2,910,540	31	0.1	62.0	4	Jackson	177,977	1	Jackson	177,977
Missouri	68,886	18	5,842,713	18	0.8	84.8	9	Jefferson City	39,062	15	Kansas City	444,965
Montana	145,552	4	944,632	44	1.1	6.5	1	Helena	27,383	6	Billings	98,721
Nebraska	76,872	15	1,768,331	38	0.6	23.0	3	Lincoln	239,213	2	Omaha	414,521
Nevada	109,826	7	2,495,529	35	3.5	22.7	3	Carson City	56,062	6	Las Vegas	545,147
New Hampshire	8,968	44	1,314,895	41	0.6	146.6	2	Concord	42,336	3	Manchester	109,691
New Jersey	7,417	46	8,724,560	11	0.2	1,176.2	13	Trenton	85,314	9	Newark	280,666
New Mexico	121,356	5	1,954,599	36	1.5	16.1	3	Santa Fe	70,631	3	Albuquerque	494,236
New York	47,214	30	19,306,183	3	0.0	408.9	29	Albany	93,523	6	New York City	8,143,197
North Carolina	48,711	29	8,856,505	10	2.1	181.8	13	Raleigh	341,530	2	Charlotte	610,949
North Dakota	68,976	17	635,867	48	0.2	9.2	1	Bismarck	57,377	2	Fargo	90,672
Ohio	40,948	35	11,478,006	7	0.1	280.3	18	Columbus	730,657	1	Columbus	730,657
Oklahoma	68,667	19	3,579,212	28	1.0	52.1	5	Oklahoma City	531,324	1	Oklahoma City	531,324
Oregon	95,997	10	3,700,758	27	1.7	38.5	5	Salem	148,751	3	Portland	533,427
Pennsylvania	44,817	32	12,440,621	6	0.3	277.5	19	Harrisburg	47,472	13	Philadelphia	1,463,281
Rhode Island	1,045	50	1,067,610	43	-0.6	1,021.6	2	Providence	176,862	1	Providence	176,862
South Carolina	30,109	40	4,321,249	24	1.7	143.5	6	Columbia	117,088	1	Columbia	117,088

See footnotes at end of table.

STATE STATISTICS — Continued

State or other jurisdiction	Land area		Population (e)		Percentage change 2004 to 2005	Density per square mile	Number of Representatives in Congress	Capital	Population (d)(f)	Rank in state	Largest city	Population (d)(f)
	In square miles	Rank in nation	Size	Rank in nation								
South Dakota............	75,885	16	781,919	46	0.9	10.3	1	Pierre	14,052	7	Sioux Falls	139,517
Tennessee................	41,217	34	6,038,803	17	1.4	146.5	9	Nashville	549,110 (c)	2	Memphis	672,277
Texas......................	261,797	2	23,507,783	2	2.5	89.8	32	Austin	690,252	4	Houston	2,016,582
Utah........................	82,144	12	2,550,063	34	2.4	31.0	3	Salt Lake City	178,097	1	Salt Lake City	178,097
Vermont...................	9,250	43	623,908	49	0.2	67.4	1	Montpelier	8,003	13	Burlington	38,531
Virginia...................	39,594	37	7,642,884	12	1.0	193.0	11	Richmond	193,777	4	Virginia Beach	438,415
Washington..............	66,544	20	6,395,798	14	1.7	96.1	9	Olympia	44,114	18	Seattle	573,911
West Virginia...........	24,078	41	1,818,470	37	0.2	75.5	3	Charleston	51,176	1	Charleston	51,176
Wisconsin................	54,310	25	5,556,506	20	0.5	102.3	8	Madison	221,551	2	Milwaukee	578,887
Wyoming..................	97,100	9	515,004	51	1.2	5.3	1	Cheyenne	55,731	1	Cheyenne	55,731
Dist. of Columbia.....	61	...	581,530	50	-0.1	9,533.3	1 (a)	...	...	...	...	...
American Samoa	77	...	57,291	...	22.0	744.0	1 (a)	Pago Pago	4,278	3	Tafuna	8,409
Guam	210	...	154,805	...	...	737.2	1 (a)	Hagatna	1,100	18	Dededo	42,980
No. Mariana Islands ...	179	...	69,221	...	...	386.7	...	Saipan	62,392	1	Saipan	62,392
Puerto Rico	3,425	...	3,927,776	...	0.4	1,146.8	1 (a)	San Juan	421,958	1	San Juan	421,958
U.S. Virgin Islands........	134	...	108,612	...	...	810.5	1 (a)	Charlotte Amalie, St. Thomas	11,004	1	Charlotte Amalie, St. Thomas	11,004

Source: U.S. Census Bureau, March 2007.
Key:
. . . — Not applicable
(a) 2006 Census Bureau estimate.
(b) 2005 Census Bureau estimate.
(c) This city is part of a consolidated city-county government and is coextensive with Davidson County.

Alabama

Nickname	The Heart of Dixie
Motto	*Aldemus Jura Nostra Defendere* (We Dare Defend Our Rights)
Flower	Camellia
Bird	Yellowhammer
Tree	Southern (Longleaf) Pine
Song	*Alabama*
Entered the Union	December 14, 1819
Capital	Montgomery

STATISTICS

Land Area (square miles)	50,744
Rank in Nation	28th
Population	4,599,030
Rank in Nation	23rd
Density per square mile	90.6
Capital City	Montgomery
Population	200,127
Rank in State	2nd
Largest City	Birmingham
Population	231,483
Number of Representatives in Congress	7
Number of Counties	67
Number of Municipal Governments	451
Number of 2008 Electoral Votes	9
Number of School Districts	130
Number of Special Districts	525

LEGISLATIVE BRANCH

Legislative Body	Legislature
President of the Senate	Jim Folsom Jr.
President Pro Tem of the Senate	Hinton Mitchem
Secretary of the Senate	McDowell Lee
Speaker of the House	Seth Hammett
Speaker Pro Tem of the House	Demetrius C. Newton
Clerk of the House	Greg Pappas
2007 Regular Session	March 6-June 18
Number of Senatorial Districts	35
Number of Representative Districts	105

EXECUTIVE BRANCH

Governor	Bob Riley
Lieutenant Governor	Jim Folsom Jr.
Secretary of State	Beth Chapman
Attorney General	Troy King
Treasurer	Kay Ivey
Auditor	Ronald L. Jones
Comptroller	Robert Childree
Governor's Present Term	1/03-1/11
Number of Elected Officials in the Executive Branch	7
Number of Members in the Cabinet	26

JUDICIAL BRANCH

Highest Court	Supreme Court
Supreme Court Chief Justice	Sue Bell Cobb
Number of Supreme Court Judges	9
Number of Intermediate Appellate Court Judges	10
Number of U.S. Court Districts	3
U.S. Circuit Court	11th Circuit

STATE INTERNET ADDRESSES

Official State Website	http://www.alabama.gov
Governor's Website	http://www.governor.state.al.us
State Legislative Website	http://www.legislature.state.al.us
State Judicial Website	http://www.judicial.state.al.us

Alaska

Nickname	The Last Frontier
Motto	*North to the Future*
Flower	Forget-Me-Not
Bird	Willow Ptarmigan
Tree	Sitka Spruce
Song	*Alaska's Flag*
Entered the Union	January 3, 1959
Capital	Juneau

STATISTICS

Land Area (square miles)	571,951
Rank in Nation	1st
Population	670,053
Rank in Nation	47th
Density per square mile	1.2
Capital City	Juneau
Population	30,987
Rank in State	2nd
Largest City	Anchorage
Population	275,043
Number of Representatives in Congress	1
Number of Counties	27
Number of Municipal Governments	149
Number of 2008 Electoral Votes	3
Number of School Districts	53
Number of Special Districts	14

LEGISLATIVE BRANCH

Legislative Body	Legislature
President of the Senate	Lyda Green
Secretary of the Senate	Kirsten Waid
Speaker of the House	John Harris
Chief Clerk of the House	Suzanne Lowell
2007 Regular Session	Jan. 16–May 16
Number of Senatorial Districts	20
Number of Representative Districts	40

EXECUTIVE BRANCH

Governor	Sarah H. Palin
Lieutenant Governor	Sean Parnell
Attorney General	Talis Colberg
Treasurer	Brian Andrews
Auditor	Pat Davidson
Comptroller	Kim Garnero
Governor's Present Term	12/06-12/10
Number of Elected Officials in the Executive Branch	2
Number of Members in the Cabinet	18

JUDICIAL BRANCH

Highest Court	Supreme Court
Supreme Court Chief Justice	Dana Fabe
Number of Supreme Court Judges	5
Number of Intermediate Appellate Court Judges	3
Number of U.S. Court Districts	1
U.S. Circuit Court	9th Circuit

STATE INTERNET ADDRESSES

Official State Website	http://www.state.ak.us
Governor's Website	http://www.gov.state.ak.us
State Legislative Website	http://www.legis.state.ak.us
State Judicial Website	http://www.state.ak.us/courts

Arizona

Nickname...The Grand Canyon State
Motto ....*Ditat Deus (God Enriches)*
Flower...Blossom of the Saguaro Cactus
Bird...Cactus Wren
Tree.. Palo Verde
Songs ....*Arizona March Song and Arizona*
Entered the Union..February 14, 1912
Capital ....Phoenix

STATISTICS

Land Area (square miles)...113,635
  Rank in Nation...6th
Population..6,166,318
  Rank in Nation..16th
  Density per square mile..54.3
Capital City..Phoenix
  Population 1,461,575
  Rank in State 1st
Largest City...Phoenix
Number Representatives in Congress.....................................8
Number of Counties...15
Number of Municipal Governments....................................87
Number of 2008 Electoral Votes 10
Number of School Districts 313
Number of Special Districts...305

LEGISLATIVE BRANCH

Legislative Body.. Legislature

President of the Senate.................................... Timothy S. Bee
President Pro Tem of the Senate ....Robert Blendu
Secretary of the Senate ....Jan Brewer

Speaker of the House ....James P. Weiers
Speaker Pro Tem of the House........................... Bob Robson
Chief Clerk of the House .... Norman L. Moore

2007 Regular Session ....Jan. 8, 2007 - TBD
Number of Senatorial Districts 30
Number of Representative Districts 30

EXECUTIVE BRANCH

Governor.. Janet Napolitano
Secretary of State ....Jan Brewer
Attorney General ....Terry Goddard
Treasurer.. Dean Martin
Auditor .... Debra K. Davenport
Comptroller .... D. Clark Partridge

Governor's Present Term 1/03-1/11
Number of Elected Officials in the Executive Branch.........11
Number of Members in the Cabinet.....................................38

JUDICIAL BRANCH

Highest Court .... Supreme Court
Supreme Court Chief Justice ....Ruth V. McGregor
Number of Supreme Court Judges 5
Number of Intermediate Appellate Court Judges 22
Number of U.S. Court Districts 1
U.S. Circuit Court...9th Circuit

STATE INTERNET ADDRESSES

Official State Website ....http://www.az.gov
Governor's Website ....http://www.governor.state.az.us
State Legislative Website...........................http://www.azleg.state.az.us
State Judicial Website ....http://www.supreme.state.az.us

Arkansas

Nickname...The Natural State
Motto ....*Regnat Populus (The People Rule)*
Flower..Apple Blossom
Bird...Mockingbird
Tree...Pine
Song...*Arkansas*
Entered the Union...June 15, 1836
Capital ....Little Rock

STATISTICS

Land Area (square miles)...52,068
  Rank in Nation...27th
Population.. 2,810,872
  Rank in Nation..32nd
  Density per square mile..54.0
Capital City..Little Rock
  Population 184,564
  Rank in State 1st
Largest City..Little Rock
Number of Representatives in Congress 4
Number of Counties...75
Number of Municipal Governments...................................499
Number of 2008 Electoral Votes 6
Number of School Districts 309
Number of Special Districts...704

LEGISLATIVE BRANCH

Legislative Body.......................................General Assembly

President of the Senate...................... Lt. Gov. Bill Halter
President Pro Tem of the Senate ....Jack Critcher
Secretary of the Senate .... Charlie Daniels

Speaker of the House ....Benny Petrus
Speaker Pro Tem of the House..........................Scott Sullivan
Chief Clerk of the House .... Jo Renshaw

2007 Regular Session ....Jan. 8–Mar. 8, 2007
Number of Senatorial Districts 35
Number of Representative Districts 100

EXECUTIVE BRANCH

Governor..Mike Beebe
Lieutenant Governor.. Bill Halter
Secretary of State.. Charlie Daniels
Attorney General ....Dustin McDaniel
Treasurer... Martha A. Shoffner
Auditor .... Charles L. Robinson
Comptroller .... Richard Weiss

Governor's Present Term 1/07-1/11
Number of Elected Officials in the Executive Branch............7
Number of Members in the Cabinet.....................................47

JUDICIAL BRANCH

Highest Court .... Supreme Court
Supreme Court Chief Justice ....Jim Hannah
Number of Supreme Court Judges 7
Number of Intermediate Appellate Court Judges 12
Number of U.S. Court Districts 2
U.S. Circuit Court...8th Circuit

STATE INTERNET ADDRESSES

Official State Website ....http://www.state.ar.us
Governor's Website ....http://www.state.ar.us/governor
State Legislative Website...........................http://www.arkleg.state.ar.us
State Judicial Website .... http://courts.state.ar.us

California

Nickname	The Golden State
Motto	*Eureka* (I Have Found It)
Flower	Golden Poppy
Bird	California Valley Quail
Tree	California Redwood
Song	*I Love You, California*
Entered the Union	September 9, 1850
Capital	Sacramento

STATISTICS

Land Area (square miles)	155,959
Rank in Nation	3rd
Population	36,457,549
Rank in Nation	1st
Density per square mile	233.8
Capital City	Sacramento
Population	456,441
Rank in State	7th
Largest City	Los Angeles
Population	3,844,829
Number of Representatives in Congress	53
Number of Counties	58
Number of Municipal Governments	475
Number of 2008 Electoral Votes	55
Number of School Districts	989
Number of Special Districts	2,830

LEGISLATIVE BRANCH

Legislative Body	Legislature
President of the Senate	Lt. Gov. John Garamendi
President Pro Tem of the Senate	Don Perata
Secretary of the Senate	Debra Bowen
Speaker of the Assembly	Fabian Nunez
Speaker Pro Tem of the Assembly	Sally J. Lieber
Chief Clerk of the Assembly	E. Dotson Wilson
2007 Regular Session	Dec. 4, 2006-Sept. 12, 2007
Number of Senatorial Districts	40
Number of Representative Districts	80

EXECUTIVE BRANCH

Governor	Arnold Schwarzenegger
Lieutenant Governor	John Garamendi
Secretary of State	Debra Bowen
Attorney General	Edmund Gerald Brown
Treasurer	Bill Lockyer
Auditor	Elaine M. Howle
Controller	John Chiang
Governor's Present Term	11/03-1/11
Number of Elected Officials in the Executive Branch	8
Number of Members in the Cabinet	11

JUDICIAL BRANCH

Highest Court	Supreme Court
Supreme Court Chief Justice	Ronald M. George
Number of Supreme Court Judges	7
Number of Intermediate Appellate Court Judges	88
Number of U.S. Court Districts	4
U.S. Circuit Court	9th Circuit

STATE INTERNET ADDRESSES

Official State Website	http://www.ca.gov
Governor's Website	http://www.governor.ca.gov
State Legislative Website	http://www.leginfo.ca.gov
State Judicial Website	http://www.courtinfo.ca.gov

Colorado

Nickname	The Centennial State
Motto	*Nil Sine Numine* (Nothing Without Providence)
Flower	Columbine
Bird	Lark Bunting
Tree	Blue Spruce
Song	*Where the Columbines Grow*
Entered the Union	August 1, 1876
Capital	Denver

STATISTICS

Land Area (square miles)	103,718
Rank in Nation	8th
Population	4,753,377
Rank in Nation	22nd
Density per square mile	45.8
Capital City	Denver
Population	557,917
Rank in State	1st
Largest City	Denver
Number of Representatives in Congress	7
Number of Counties	63
Number of Municipal Governments	270
Number of 2008 Electoral Votes	9
Number of School Districts	178
Number of Special Districts	1,414

LEGISLATIVE BRANCH

Legislative Body	General Assembly
President of the Senate	Joan Fitz-Gerald
President Pro Tem of the Senate	Peter C. Groff
Secretary of the Senate	Mike Coffman
Speaker of the House	Andrew Romanoff
Speaker Pro Tem of the House	Cheri Jahn
Chief Clerk of the House	Marilyn Eddins
2007 Regular Session	Jan. 10–May 9, 2007
Number of Senatorial Districts	35
Number of Representative Districts	65

EXECUTIVE BRANCH

Governor	Bill Ritter
Lieutenant Governor	Barbara O'Brien
Secretary of State	Mike Coffman
Attorney General	John W. Suthers
Treasurer	Cary Kennedy
Auditor	Sally Symanski
Controller	Leslie Shenefelt
Governor's Present Term	1/07-1/11
Number of Elected Officials in the Executive Branch	5
Number of Members in the Cabinet	21

JUDICIAL BRANCH

Highest Court	Supreme Court
Supreme Court Chief Justice	Mary Mullarkey
Number of Supreme Court Judges	7
Number of Intermediate Appellate Court Judges	16
Number of U.S. Court Districts	1
U.S. Circuit Court	10th Circuit

STATE INTERNET ADDRESSES

Official State Website	http://www.state.co.us
Governor's Website	http://www.state.co.us/gov_dir/governor_office.html
State Legislative Website	http://www.leg.state.co.us
State Judicial Website	http://www.courts.state.co.us

Connecticut

Nickname	The Constitution State
Motto	*Qui Transtulit Sustinet*
	(He Who Transplanted Still Sustains)
Flower	Mountain Laurel
Bird	American Robin
Tree	White Oak
Song	*Yankee Doodle*
Entered the Union	January 9, 1788
Capital	Hartford

STATISTICS

Land Area (square miles)	4,845
Rank in Nation	48th
Population	3,504,809
Rank in Nation	29th
Density per square mile	723.3
Capital City	Hartford
Population	124,397
Rank in State	3rd
Largest City	Bridgeport
Population	139,008
Number of Representatives in Congress	5
Number of Counties	8
Number of Municipal Governments	30
Number of 2008 Electoral Votes	7
Number of School Districts	166
Number of Special Districts	384

LEGISLATIVE BRANCH

Legislative Body	General Assembly
President of the Senate	Michael C. Fedele
President Pro Tem of the Senate	Donald E. Williams
Clerk of the Senate	Thomas P. Sheridan
Speaker of the House	James A. Amann
Deputy Speakers of the House	Emil Altobello, Mary G. Fritz, Bob Godfrey, Marie Kirkley-Bey
Clerk of the House	Garey E. Coleman
2007 Regular Session	January 3-June 6, 2007
Number of Senatorial Districts	36
Number of Representative Districts	151

EXECUTIVE BRANCH

Governor	M. Jodi Rell
Lieutenant Governor	Michael Fedele
Secretary of State	Susan Bysiewicz
Attorney General	Richard Blumenthal
Treasurer	Denise L. Nappier
Auditor	Robert Jaekle and Kevin P. Johnston
Comptroller	Nancy Wyman
Governor's Present Term	7/07-1/11
Number of Elected Officials in the Executive Branch	6
Number of Members in the Cabinet	27

JUDICIAL BRANCH

Highest Court	Supreme Court
Supreme Court Chief Justice	William J. Sullivan
Number of Supreme Court Judges	7
Number of Intermediate Appellate Court Judges	10
Number of U.S. Court Districts	1
U.S. Circuit Court	2nd Circuit

STATE INTERNET ADDRESSES

Official State Website	http://www.state.ct.us
Governor's Website	http://www.state.ct.us/governor
State Legislative Website	http://www.cga.state.ct.us
State Judicial Website	http://www.jud.state.ct.us

Delaware

Nickname	The First State
Motto	*Liberty and Independence*
Flower	Peach Blossom
Bird	Blue Hen Chicken
Tree	American Holly
Song	*Our Delaware*
Entered the Union	December 7, 1787
Capital	Dover

STATISTICS

Land Area (square miles)	1,954
Rank in Nation	49th
Population	853,476
Rank in Nation	45th
Density per square mile	436.8
Capital City	Dover
Population	34,288
Rank in State	2nd
Largest City	Wilmington
Population	72,786
Number of Representatives in Congress	1
Number of Counties	3
Number of Municipal Governments	57
Number of 2008 Electoral Votes	3
Number of School Districts	19
Number of Special Districts	260

LEGISLATIVE BRANCH

Legislative Body	General Assembly
President of the Senate	Lt. Gov. John Carney Jr.
President Pro Tem of the Senate	Thurman Adams Jr.
Secretary of the Senate	Harriet Smith Windsor
Speaker of the House	Terry R. Spence
Clerk of the House	JoAnn M. Hedrick
2007 Regular Session	Jan. 9–June 30, 2007
Number of Senatorial Districts	21
Number of Representative Districts	41

EXECUTIVE BRANCH

Governor	Ruth Ann Minner
Lieutenant Governor	John Carney Jr.
Secretary of State	Harriet Smith Windsor
Attorney General	Joseph R. Biden
Treasurer	Jack Markell
Auditor	R. Thomas Wagner
Comptroller	Richard S. Cordrey
Governor's Present Term	1/01–1/09
Number of Elected Officials in the Executive Branch	5
Number of Members in the Cabinet	19

JUDICIAL BRANCH

Highest Court	Supreme Court
Supreme Court Chief Justice	Myron T. Steele
Number of Supreme Court Judges	5
Number of Intermediate Appellate Court Judges	0
Number of U.S. Court Districts	1
U.S. Circuit Court	3rd Circuit

STATE INTERNET ADDRESSES

Official State Website	http://www.delaware.gov
Governor's Website	http://www.state.de.us/governor
State Legislative Website	http://www.legis.state.de.us
State Judicial Website	http://courts.state.de.us

Florida

Nickname..The Sunshine State
Motto .... *In God We Trust*
Flower..Orange Blossom
Bird..Mockingbird
Tree..Sabal Palmetto Palm
Song.........................*The Swannee River (Old Folks at Home)*
Entered the Union...March 3, 1845
Capital ....Tallahassee

STATISTICS

Land Area (square miles)......................................53,927
   Rank in Nation...26th
Population...18,089,888
   Rank in Nation...4th
   Density per square mile.....................................335.5
Capital City...Tallahassee
   Population...158,500
   Rank in State..8th
Largest City .... Jacksonville
   Population 782,623
Number of Representatives in Congress 25
Number of Counties..67
Number of Municipal Governments...404
Number of 2008 Electoral Votes 27
Number of School Districts 67
Number of Special Districts...626

LEGISLATIVE BRANCH

Legislative Body ....Legislature

President of the Senate...Ken Pruitt
President Pro Tem of the Senate .... Lisa Carlton
Secretary of the Senate ....Faye W. Blanton

Speaker of the House...................................... Marco Rubio
Speaker Pro Tem of the House ....Dennis K. Baxley
Clerk of the House...William S. Pittman III

2007 Regular Session ....March 6–May 4, 2007
Number of Senatorial Districts 40
Number of Representative Districts 120

EXECUTIVE BRANCH

Governor..Charlie Crist
Lieutenant Governor... Jeff Kottkamp
Secretary of State... Kurt Browning
Attorney General .... Bill McCollum
Chief Financial Officer .... Alex Sink
Auditor .... William O. Monroe

Governor's Present Term 1/07–1/11
Number of Elected Officials in the Executive Branch............................5
Number of Members in the Cabinet...4

JUDICIAL BRANCH

Highest Court.. Supreme Court
Supreme Court Chief Justice...R. Fred Lewis
Number of Supreme Court Judges 7
Number of Intermediate Appellate Court Judges 62
Number of U.S. Court Districts 3
U.S. Circuit Court.. 11th Circuit

STATE INTERNET ADDRESSES

Official State Website ....http://www.myflorida.com
Governor's Website ....http://www.state.fl.us/eog
State Legislative Website....................................http://www.leg.state.fl.us
State Judicial Website .... http://www.flcourts.org

Georgia

Nickname.................................. The Empire State of the South
Motto .... *Wisdom, Justice and Moderation*
Flower..Cherokee Rose
Bird... Brown Thrasher
Tree..Live Oak
Song..*Georgia on My Mind*
Entered the Union...January 2, 1788
Capital .... Atlanta

STATISTICS

Land Area (square miles)......................................57,906
   Rank in Nation...21st
Population... 9,363,941
   Rank in Nation...9th
   Density per square mile.....................................161.7
Capital City..Atlanta
   Population...470,688
   Rank in State..1st
Largest City .... Atlanta
Number of Representatives in Congress 13
Number of Counties..159
Number of Municipal Governments...531
Number of 2008 Electoral Votes 15
Number of School Districts 180
Number of Special Districts...581

LEGISLATIVE BRANCH

Legislative Body ....General Assembly

President of the Senate...Lt. Gov. Casey Cagle
President Pro Tem of the Senate ....Eric Johnson
Secretary of the Senate .... Bob Ewing

Speaker of the House...Glenn Richardson
Speaker Pro Tem of the House....................................Mark Burkhalter
Clerk of the House..Robert E. Rivers Jr.

2007 Regular Session .... Jan. 8–To be determined
Number of Senatorial Districts 56
Number of Representative Districts 180

EXECUTIVE BRANCH

Governor.. Sonny Perdue
Lieutenant Governor... Casey Cagle
Secretary of State... Karen Handel
Attorney General ....Thurbert E. Baker
Treasurer .... W. Daniel Ebersole
Auditor .... Russell W. Hinton

Governor's Present Term 1/03–1/11
Number of Elected Officials in the Executive Branch.........................13
Number of Members in the Cabinet.................No formal cabinet system

JUDICIAL BRANCH

Highest Court.. Supreme Court
Supreme Court Chief Justice....................................... Leah Ward Sears
Number of Supreme Court Judges 7
Number of Intermediate Appellate Court Judges 12
Number of U.S. Court Districts 3
U.S. Circuit Court.. 11th Circuit

STATE INTERNET ADDRESSES

Official State Website ....http://www.state.ga.us
Governor's Website .... http://gov.state.ga.us/
State Legislative Website............................http://www.legis.state.ga.us
State Judicial Website ....http://www.georgiacourts.org

Hawaii

Nickname...The Aloha State
Motto ....*Ua Mau Ke Ea O Ka Aina I Ka Pono*
   (The Life of the Land Is Perpetuated in Righteousness)
Flower...Native Yellow Hibiscus
Bird..Hawaiian Goose (Nene)
Tree ....*Kukue Tree (Candlenut)*
Song...*Hawaii Ponoi*
Entered the Union.......................................August 21, 1959
Capital .... Honolulu

STATISTICS

Land Area (square miles)...6,423
   Rank in Nation 47th
Population..1,285,498
   Rank in Nation 42nd
   Density per square mile...................................200.1
Capital City..Honolulu
   Population 377,379
   Rank in State 1st
Largest City ....Honolulu
Number of Representatives in Congress 2
Number of Counties...5
Number of Municipal Governments...............................1
Number of 2008 Electoral Votes 4
Number of School Districts 1
Number of Special Districts...15

LEGISLATIVE BRANCH

Legislative Body.. Legislature

President of the Senate..............................Colleen Hanabusa
Vice President of the Senate ....Donna Mercado Kim
Chief Clerk of the Senate ....Carol Taniguchi

Speaker of the House ....Calvin K.Y. Say
Vice Speaker of the House.......................Jon Riki Karamatsu
Chief Clerk of the House ....Patricia A. Mau-Shimizu

2007 Regular Session ....Jan. 17–May 3, 2007
Number of Senatorial Districts 25
Number of Representative Districts 51

EXECUTIVE BRANCH

Governor...Linda Lingle
Lieutenant Governor...James Aiona
Attorney General ....Mark J. Bennett
Treasurer..Georgina Kawamura
Auditor ....Marion M. Higa
Comptroller .... Russ K. Saito

Governor's Present Term 12/02–12/10
Number of Elected Officials in the Executive Branch............................2
Number of Members in the Cabinet..............................22

JUDICIAL BRANCH

Highest Court.. Supreme Court
Supreme Court Chief Justice.......................Ronald T.Y. Moon
Number of Supreme Court Judges 5
Number of Intermediate Appellate Court Judges 6
Number of U.S. Court Districts 1
U.S. Circuit Court...9th Circuit

STATE INTERNET ADDRESSES

Official State Website ....http://www.hawaii.gov
Governor's Website ....http://gov.state.hi.us
State Legislative Website .... http://www.capitol.hawaii.gov
State Judicial Website ....http://www.courts.hi.us

Idaho

Nickname.. The Gem State
Motto ....*Esto Perpetua* (Let It Be Perpetual)
Flower...Syringa
Bird...Mountain Bluebird
Tree ....Western White Pine
Song...*Here We Have Idaho*
Entered the Union...July 3, 1890
Capital ....Boise

STATISTICS

Land Area (square miles)..82,747
   Rank in Nation 11th
Population..1,466,465
   Rank in Nation 39th
Density per square mile 17.7
Capital City..Boise
   Population 193,161
   Rank in State 1st
Largest City ....Boise
Number of Representatives in Congress 2
Number of Counties...44
Number of Municipal Governments...............................200
Number of 2008 Electoral Votes 4
Number of School Districts 114
Number of Special Districts...798

LEGISLATIVE BRANCH

Legislative Body..Legislature

President of the Senate..............................Lt. Gov. Jim Risch
President Pro Tem of the Senate ....Robert L. Geddes
Secretary of the Senate ....Jeannine Wood

Speaker of the House ....Lawerence Denney
Chief Clerk of the House .... Pamm Juker

2007 Regular Session ....Jan. 8–TBD
Number of Senatorial Districts 35
Number of Representative Districts 35

EXECUTIVE BRANCH

Governor...C.L "Butch" Otter
Lieutenant Governor... Jim Risch
Secretary of State... Ben Ysursa
Attorney General ....Lawrence Wasden
Treasurer... Ron Crane
Controller ....Donna Jones

Governor's Present Term 1/07–1/11
Number of Elected Officials in the Executive Branch............................7
Number of Members in the Cabinet..............................22

JUDICIAL BRANCH

Highest Court.. Supreme Court
Supreme Court Chief Justice......................Gerald F. Schroeder
Number of Supreme Court Judges 5
Number of Intermediate Appellate Court Judges 3
Number of U.S. Court Districts 1
U.S. Circuit Court...9th Circuit

STATE INTERNET ADDRESSES

Official State Website.............. ....http://www.state.id.us
Governor's Website http://www2.state.id.us/gov
State Legislative Website http://www2.state.id.us/legislat
State Judicial Website http://www2.state.id.us/judicial

Illinois

Nickname...The Prairie State
Motto...*State Sovereignty-National Union*
Flower...Native Violet
Bird.. Cardinal
Tree .... White Oak
Song..*Illinois*
Entered the Union..December 3, 1818
Capital .... Springfield

STATISTICS

Land Area (square miles)..55,584
   Rank in Nation...24th
Population...12,831,970
   Rank in Nation..5th
   Density per square mile...230.9
Capital City.. Springfield
   Population 115,668
   Rank in State..6th
Largest City...Chicago
   Population 2,842,518
Number of Representatives in Congress 19
Number of Counties.. 102
Number of Municipal Governments.. 1,291
Number of 2008 Electoral Votes 21
Number of School Districts 887
Number of Special Districts..3,145

LEGISLATIVE BRANCH

Legislative Body ....General Assembly

President of the Senate.......................................Emil Jones Jr.
Secretary of the Senate .... Debra Shipley

Speaker of the House ....Michael J. Madigan
House Chief Clerk ....Mark Mahoney

2007 Regular Session ....Jan. 10–Dec. 31, 2007
Number of Senatorial Districts 59
Number of Representative Districts 118

EXECUTIVE BRANCH

Governor...Rod Blagojevich
Lieutenant Governor..Patrick Quinn
Secretary of State .... Jesse White
Attorney General .... Lisa Madigan
Treasurer.. Alexi Giannoulias
Auditor.. William G. Holland
Comptroller .... Daniel Hynes

Governor's Present Term 1/03–1/11
Number of Elected Officials in the Executive Branch............................6
Number of Members in the Cabinet 18

JUDICIAL BRANCH

Highest Court... Supreme Court
Supreme Court Chief Justice..Robert R. Thomas
Number of Supreme Court Judges 7
Number of Intermediate Appellate Court Judges 53
Number of U.S. Court Districts 3
U.S. Circuit Court...7th Circuit

STATE INTERNET ADDRESSES

Official State Website .... http://www.state.il.us
Governor's Website .... http://www.state.il.us/gov
State Legislative Website ....http://www.legis.state.il.us
State Judicial Website .... http://www.state.il.us/court

Indiana

Nickname...The Hoosier State
Motto ....*Crossroads of America*
Flower...Peony
Bird.. Cardinal
Tree .... Tulip Poplar
Song...*On the Banks of the Wabash, Far Away*
Entered the Union.. December 11, 1816
Capital .... Indianapolis

STATISTICS

Land Area (square miles)..35,867
   Rank in Nation...38th
Population...6,313,520
   Rank in Nation..15th
   Density per square mile...176.0
Capital City.. Indianapolis
   Population 784,118
   Rank in State..1st
Largest City... Indianapolis
Number of Representatives in Congress 9
Number of Counties..92
Number of Municipal Governments..567
Number of 2008 Electoral Votes 11
Number of School Districts 294
Number of Special Districts..1,125

LEGISLATIVE BRANCH

Legislative Body..General Assembly

President of the Senate......................................Lt. Gov. Becky Skillman
President Pro Tem of the Senate ....David C. Long
Principal Secretary of the Senate ....Mary C. Mendel

Speaker of the House .... B. Patrick Bauer
Speaker Pro Tem of the House... Chet Dobis
Principal Clerk of the House... Clinton Mckay

2007 Regular Session ....Jan. 8–April 29, 2007
Number of Senatorial Districts 50
Number of Representative Districts 100

EXECUTIVE BRANCH

Governor...Mitch Daniels
Lieutenant Governor..Becky Skillman
Secretary of State .... Todd Rokita
Attorney General .... Steve Carter
Treasurer..Richard E. Mourdock
Auditor.. Bruce Hartman

Governor's Present Term 1/05–1/09
Number of Elected Officials in the Executive Branch............................7
Number of Members in the Cabinet 16

JUDICIAL BRANCH

Highest Court... Supreme Court
Supreme Court Chief Justice......................................Randall T. Shepard
Number of Supreme Court Judges 5
Number of Intermediate Appellate Court Judges 15
Number of U.S. Court Districts 2
U.S. Circuit Court...7th Circuit

STATE INTERNET ADDRESSES

Official State Website ....http://www.state.in.us
Governor's Website .... http://www.in.gov/gov
State Legislative Website ....http://www.in.gov/legislative
State Judicial Website .... http://www.in.gov/judiciary

Iowa

Nickname	The Hawkeye State
Motto	*Our Liberties We Prize and Our Rights We Will Maintain*
Flower	Wild Rose
Bird	Eastern Goldfinch
Tree	Oak
Song	*The Song of Iowa*
Entered the Union	December 28, 1846
Capital	Des Moines

STATISTICS

Land Area (square mile)	55,869
Rank in Nation	23rd
Population	2,982,085
Rank in Nation	30th
Density per square mile	53.4
Capital City	Des Moines
Population	194,163
Rank in State	1st
Largest City	Des Moines
Number of Representatives in Congress	5
Number of Counties	99
Number of Municipal Governments	948
Number of 2008 Electoral Votes	7
Number of School Districts	370
Number of Special Districts	542

LEGISLATIVE BRANCH

Legislative Body	General Assembly
President of the Senate	John P. Kibbie
President Pro Tem of the Senate	Jeff Danielson
Secretary of the Senate	Michael E. Marshall
Speaker of the House	Pat Murphy
Speaker Pro Tem of the House	Polly Bukta
Chief Clerk of the House	Mark Brandsgard
2007 Regular Session	Jan. 8–April 28, 2007
Number of Senatorial Districts	50
Number of Representative Districts	100

EXECUTIVE BRANCH

Governor	Chet Culver
Lieutenant Governor	Patty Judge
Secretary of State	Michael Mauro
Attorney General	Thomas Miller
Treasurer	Michael Fitzgerald
Auditor	David A. Vaudt
Chief Operating Officer	Calvin McKelvogue
Governor's Present Term	1/07–1/11
Number of Elected Officials in the Executive Branch	7
Number of Members in the Cabinet	30

JUDICIAL BRANCH

Highest Court	Supreme Court
Supreme Court Chief Justice	Marsha K. Ternus
Number of Supreme Court Judges	7
Number of Intermediate Appellate Court Judges	9
Number of U.S. Court Districts	2
U.S. Circuit Court	8th Circuit

STATE INTERNET ADDRESSES

Official State Website	http://www.state.ia.us
Governor's Website	http://www.governor.state.ia.us/
State Legislative Website	http://www.legis.state.ia.us
State Judicial Website	http://www.judicial.state.ia.us

Kansas

Nickname	The Sunflower State
Motto	*Ad Astra per Aspera* (To the Stars through Difficulties)
Flower	Wild Native Sunflower
Bird	Western Meadowlark
Tree	Cottonwood
Song	*Home on the Range*
Entered the Union	January 29, 1861
Capital	Topeka

STATISTICS

Land Area (square miles)	81,815
Rank in Nation	13th
Population	2,764,075
Rank in Nation	33rd
Density per square mile	33.8
Capital City	Topeka
Population	121,946
Rank in State	4th
Largest City	Wichita
Population	354,865
Number of Representatives in Congress	4
Number of Counties	105
Number of Municipal Governments	627
Number of 2008 Electoral Votes	6
Number of School Districts	302
Number of Special Districts	1,533

LEGISLATIVE BRANCH

Legislative Body	Legislature
President of the Senate	Stephen Morris
Secretary of the Senate	Pat Saville
Speaker of the House	Melvin Neufield
Speaker Pro tem of the House	Donald Dahl
Chief Clerk of the House	Janet E. Jones
2007 Regular Session	Jan. 8–TBD
Number of Senatorial Districts	40
Number of Representative Districts	125

EXECUTIVE BRANCH

Governor	Kathleen Sebelius
Lieutenant Governor	Mark Parkinson
Secretary of State	Ron Thornburgh
Attorney General	Paul Morrison
Treasurer	Lynn Jenkins
Auditor	Barbara J. Hinton
Director, Division of Accounts & Reports	Robert Mackey
Governor's Present Term	1/03–1/11
Number of Elected Officials in the Executive Branch	6
Number of Members in the Cabinet	14

JUDICIAL BRANCH

Highest Court	Supreme Court
Supreme Court Chief Justice	Kay McFarland
Number of Supreme Court Judges	7
Number of Intermediate Appellate Court Judges	12
Number of U.S. Court Districts	1
U.S. Circuit Court	10th Circuit

STATE INTERNET ADDRESSES

Official State Website	http://www.accesskansas.org
Governor's Website	http://www.ksgovernor.org
State Legislative Website	http://www.kslegislature.org
State Judicial Website	http://www.kscourts.org

Kentucky

Nickname...The Bluegrass State
Motto...*United We Stand, Divided We Fall*
Flower..Goldenrod
Bird...Cardinal
Tree..Tulip Poplar
Song...*My Old Kentucky Home*
Entered the Union...June 1, 1792
Capital ....Frankfort

STATISTICS

Land Area (square miles)..39,728
  Rank in Nation..36th
Population..4,206,074
  Rank in Nation..26th
  Density per square mile...105.9
Capital City..Frankfort
  Population...27,210
  Rank in State...7th
Largest City..Louisville
  Population...556,429
Number of Representatives in Congress 6
Number of Counties..120
Number of Municipal Governments...424
Number of 2008 Electoral Votes 8
Number of School Districts...176
Number of Special Districts..720

LEGISLATIVE BRANCH

Legislative Body...General Assembly

President of the Senate...David L. Williams
President Pro Tem of the Senate ....Katie Stine
Secretary of the Senate ....Donna Holiday

Speaker of the House..Jody Richards
Speaker Pro Tem of the House..Larry Clark
Chief Clerk of the House ....Lois Pulliam

2007 Regular Session ....Jan. 2–March 30, 2007
Number of Senatorial Districts..38
Number of Representative Districts...100

EXECUTIVE BRANCH

Governor...Ernest L. Fletcher
Lieutenant Governor..Stephen Pence
Secretary of State..Trey Grayson
Attorney General ....Gregory D. Stumbo
Treasurer...Jonathan Miller
Auditor ....Crit Luallen
Controller ....Ed Ross

Governor's Present Term 12/03–12/07
Number of Elected Officials in the Executive Branch...........................7
Number of Members in the Cabinet..10

JUDICIAL BRANCH

Highest Court...Supreme Court
Supreme Court Chief Justice...Joseph E. Lambert
Number of Supreme Court Judges 7
Number of Intermediate Appellate Court Judges 14
Number of U.S. Court Districts 2
U.S. Circuit Court...6th Circuit

STATE INTERNET ADDRESSES

Official State Website ....http://kentucky.gov
Governor's Website ....http://governor.ky.gov/
Legislative Website...http://www.lrc.state.ky.us
Judicial Website...http://www.kycourts.net

Louisiana

Nickname..The Pelican State
Motto...*Union, Justice and Confidence*
Flower..Magnolia
Bird..Eastern Brown Pelican
Tree...Bald Cypress
Songs ....*Give Me Louisiana* and
                                                     You Are My Sunshine
Entered the Union...April 30, 1812
Capital ....Baton Rouge

STATISTICS

Land Area (square miles)..43,562
  Rank in Nation..33rd
Population..4,287,768
  Rank in Nation..25th
  Density per square mile...98.4
Capital City..Baton Rouge
  Population...222,064
  Rank in State...2nd
Largest City ....New Orleans
  Population...454,863
Number of Representatives in Congress 7
Number of Parishes..64
Number of Municipal Governments...302
Number of 2008 Electoral Votes 9
Number of School Districts..68
Number of Special Districts..45

LEGISLATIVE BRANCH

Legislative Body...Legislature

President of the Senate...Donald E. Hines
President Pro Tem of the Senate ....Diana E. Bajoie
Secretary of Senate ....Glenn Koepp

Speaker of the House...Joe R. Salter
Speaker Pro Tem of the House.......................................Yvonne Dorsey
Clerk of the House and Chief of Staff............................Alfred W. Speer

2007 Regular Session ....April 30–June 28, 2007
Number of Senatorial Districts..39
Number of Representative Districts...105

EXECUTIVE BRANCH

Governor...Kathleen B. Blanco
Lieutenant Governor..Mitch Landrieu
Secretary of State..Jay Gardenne
Attorney General ....Charles C. Foti
Treasurer...John Neely Kennedy
Comptroller ....Jerry Luke LeBlanc

Governor's Present Term 1/04–1/08
Number of Elected Officials in the Executive Branch...........................8
Number of Members in the Cabinet..16

JUDICIAL BRANCH

Highest Court...Supreme Court
Supreme Court Chief Justice...............................Pascal F. Calogero Jr.
Number of Supreme Court Judges 7
Number of Intermediate Appellate Court Judges 53
Number of U.S. Court Districts 3
U.S. Circuit Court...5th Circuit

STATE INTERNET ADDRESSES

Official State Website ....http://www.state.la.us
Governor's Website ....http://www.gov.state.la.us
Legislative Website..http://www.legis.state.la.us
Judicial Website........................http://www.state.la.us/gov_judicial.htm

Maine

Nickname...The Pine Tree State
Motto..*Dirigo* (I Direct or I Lead)
Flower...White Pine Cone and Tassel
Bird...Chickadee
Tree..White Pine
Song...*State of Maine Song*
Entered the Union...March 15, 1820
Capital ....Augusta

STATISTICS

Land Area (square miles)..30,862
   Rank in Nation...39th
Population..1,321,574
   Rank in Nation...40th
   Density per square mile...42.8
Capital City...Augusta
   Population...18,626
   Rank in State...9th
Largest City ....Portland
   Population...63,889
Number of Representatives in Congress 2
Number of Counties..16
Number of Municipal Governments...22
Number of 2008 Electoral Votes 4
Number of School Districts 283
Number of Special Districts...222

LEGISLATIVE BRANCH

Legislative Body..Legislature

President of the Senate..Beth Edmonds
Secretary of the Senate ....Joy J. O'Brien

Speaker of the House ....Glenn A. Cummings
Clerk of the House...Millicent M. MacFarland

2007 Regular Session ....Dec. 6, 2006–June 20, 2007
Number of Senatorial Districts 35
Number of Representative Districts 151

EXECUTIVE BRANCH

Governor..John E. Baldacci
Secretary of State...Matthew Dunlap
Attorney General ....G. Steven Rowe
Treasurer...David G. Lemoine
Auditor..Neria R. Douglas
Controller ....Edward Karass

Governor's Present Term 1/03–1/11
Number of Elected Officials in the Executive Branch...........................1
Number of Members in the Cabinet 21

JUDICIAL BRANCH

Highest Court...Supreme Judicial Court
Supreme Court Chief Justice..................................Leigh Ingalls Saufley
Number of Supreme Court Judges 7
Number of Intermediate Appellate Court Judges 0
Number of U.S. Court Districts 1
U.S. Circuit Court...1st Circuit

STATE INTERNET ADDRESSES

Official State Website ....http://www.state.me.us
Governor's Website ....http://www.state.me.us/governor
Legislative Website.....................................http://janus.state.me.us/legis
Judicial Website..http://www.courts.state.me.us

Maryland

Nicknames ....The Old Line State and Free State
Motto ....*Fatti Maschii, Parole Femine*
   (Manly Deeds, Womanly Words)
Flower..Black-eyed Susan
Bird...Baltimore Oriole
Tree...White Oak
Song...*Maryland, My Maryland*
Entered the Union...April 28, 1788
Capital ....Annapolis

STATISTICS

Land Area (square miles)..9,774
Rank in Nation...42nd
Population..5,615,727
   Rank in Nation...19th
   Density per square mile...574.5
Capital City...Annapolis
   Population...36,300
   Rank in State...7th
Largest City ....Baltimore
   Population...635,815
Number of Representatives in Congress 8
Number of Counties..24
Number of Municipal Governments...157
Number of 2008 Electoral Votes 10
Number of School Districts 24
Number of Special Districts...85

LEGISLATIVE BRANCH

Legislative Body..General Assembly

President of the Senate.................................Thomas V. Mike Miller Jr.
President Pro Tem of the Senate ....Nathaniel J. McFadden
Secretary of the Senate ....William B.C. Addison Jr.

Speaker of the House ....Michael Erin Busch
Speaker Pro Tem of the House ....Adrienne A. Jones
Clerk of the House...Mary Monahan

2007 Regular Session ....Jan. 10–April 9, 2007
Number of Senatorial Districts 47
Number of Representative Districts 47

EXECUTIVE BRANCH

Governor..Martin O'Malley
Lieutenant Governor...Anthony Brown
Secretary of State...Interim–Dennis Schnepfc
Attorney General ....Douglas Gansler
Treasurer...Nancy K. Kopp
Auditor..Bruce A. Myers
Comptroller ....Peter Franchot

Governor's Present Term 1/07–1/11
Number of Elected Officials in the Executive Branch...........................4
Number of Members in the Cabinet 28

JUDICIAL BRANCH

Highest Court...Court of Appeals
Court of Appeals Chief Judge ....Robert M. Bell
Number of Court of Appeals Judges 7
Number of Intermediate Appellate Court Judges 13
Number of U.S. Court Districts 1
U.S. Circuit Court...4th Circuit

STATE INTERNET ADDRESSES

Official State Website ....http://www.marlyand.gov
Governor's Website ....http://www.gov.state.md.us
Legislative Website.....................................http://www.mlis.state.md.us
Judicial Website..http://www.courts.state.md.us/

Massachusetts

Nickname...The Bay State
Motto ....*Ense Petit Placidam Sub Libertate Quietem*
(By the Sword We Seek Peace,
but Peace Only under Liberty)
Flower..Mayflower
Bird...Chickadee
Tree..American Elm
Song...*All Hail to Massachusetts*
Entered the Union..February 6, 1788
Capital ....Boston

STATISTICS

Land Area (square miles)..7,840
   Rank in Nation 45th
Population...6,437,193
   Rank in Nation 13th
   Density per square mile..821.0
Capital City...Boston
   Population..559,034
   Rank in State 1st
Largest City ....Boston
Number of Representatives in Congress 10
Number of Counties...14
Number of Municipal Governments......................................45
Number of 2008 Electoral Votes 12
Number of School Districts 350
Number of Special Districts..403

LEGISLATIVE BRANCH

Legislative Body...General Court

President of the Senate..........................Robert E. Travaglini
President Pro Tem of the Senate ....Stanley C. Rosenberg
Clerk of the Senate ....William F. Welch

Speaker of the House....................................Salvatore F. DiMasi
Clerk of the House...Steven T. James

2007 Regular Session ....Jan. 3–December 31, 2007
Number of Senatorial Districts 40
Number of Representative Districts 160

EXECUTIVE BRANCH

Governor.. Deval Patrick
Lieutenant Governor..Tim Murray
Secretary of the Commonwealth....................William F. Galvin
Attorney General ....Martha Coakley
Treasurer & Receiver General.......................Timothy Cahill
Auditor .... Joseph DeNucci
Comptroller .... Martin J. Benison

Governor's Present Term 1/07–1/11
Number of Elected Officials in the Executive Branch..........6
Number of Members in the Cabinet 10

JUDICIAL BRANCH

Highest Court.......................................Supreme Judicial Court
Supreme Judicial Court Chief Justice ....Margaret H. Marshall
Number of Supreme Judicial Court Judges 7
Number of Intermediate Appellate Court Judges 28
Number of U.S. Court Districts 1
U.S. Circuit Court... 1st Circuit

STATE INTERNET ADDRESSES

Official State Website ....http://www.mass.gov
Governor's Website ....http://www.state.ma.us/gov
Legislative Website.. http://www.state.ma.us/legis
Judicial Website.. http://www.state.ma.us/courts

Michigan

Nickname...The Wolverine State
Motto ....*Si Quaeris Peninsulam Amoenam Circumspice*
(If You Seek a Pleasant Peninsula, Look About You)
Flower..Apple Blossom
Bird... Robin
Tree .... White Pine
Song...*Michigan, My Michigan*
Entered the Union......................................January 26, 1837
Capital .... Lansing

STATISTICS

Land Area (square miles)...56,804
   Rank in Nation 22nd
Population..10,095,643
   Rank in Nation 8th
   Density per square mile... 177.7
Capital City.. Lansing
   Population..115,518
   Rank in State 6th
Largest City..Detroit
   Population..886,671
Number of Representatives in Congress 15
Number of Counties...83
Number of Municipal Governments....................................533
Number of 2008 Electoral Votes 17
Number of School Districts 553
Number of Special Districts..366

LEGISLATIVE BRANCH

Legislative Body.. Legislature

President of the Senate...............................Lt. Gov. John Cherry
President Pro Tem of the Senate .... Randy Richardville
Secretary of the Senate .... Carol Morey Viventi

Speaker of the House .... Andy Dillon

Speaker Pro Tem of the House....................... Michael Sak
Clerk of the House...Gary L. Randall

2007 Regular Session ....Jan. 10–Dec. 31, 2007
Number of Senatorial Districts 38
Number of Representative Districts 110

EXECUTIVE BRANCH

Governor... Jennifer Granholm
Lieutenant Governor...John Cherry
Secretary of State .... Terri Lynn Land
Attorney General .... Mike Cox
Treasurer.. Robert J. Kleine
Auditor .... Thomas McTavish
Director, Office of Financial Management................. Michael J. Moody

Governor's Present Term 1/03–1/11
Number of Elected Officials in the Executive Branch..........4
Number of Members in the Cabinet 24

JUDICIAL BRANCH

Highest Court... Supreme Court
Supreme Court Chief Justice..........................Clifford W. Taylor
Number of Supreme Court Judges 7
Number of Intermediate Appellate Court Judges 28
Number of U.S. Court Districts 2
U.S. Circuit Court...6th Circuit

STATE INTERNET ADDRESSES

Official State Website ....http://www.michigan.gov
Governor's Website ....http://www.michigan.gov/gov
Legislative Website........................ http://www.michiganlegislature.org
Judicial Website...................................... http://www.courts.michigan.gov

Minnesota

Nickname...The North Star State
Motto .... *L'Etoile du Nord* (The North Star)
Flower..Pink and White Lady-Slipper
Bird...Common Loon
Tree...Red Pine
Song..*Hail! Minnesota*
Entered the Union..May 11, 1858
Capital ....St. Paul

STATISTICS

Land Area (square miles)..79,610
    Rank in Nation...14th
Population...5,167,101
    Rank in Nation..21st
    Density per square mile..64.9
Capital City...St. Paul
    Population..275,150
    Rank in State..2nd
Largest City ....Minneapolis
    Population..372,811
Number of Representatives in Congress 8
Number of Counties..87
Number of Municipal Governments.................................854
Number of 2008 Electoral Votes..10
Number of School Districts 348
Number of Special Districts..403

LEGISLATIVE BRANCH

Legislative Body..Legislature

President of the Senate..James Metzen
Secretary of the Senate ....Patrick E. Flahaven

Speaker of the House ....Margaret Anderson Kelliher
Chief Clerk of the House ....Al Mathiowetz

2007 Regular Session ....Jan. 3–May 21, 2007
Number of Senatorial Districts 67
Number of Representative Districts 67

EXECUTIVE BRANCH

Governor..Tim Pawlenty
Lieutenant Governor...Carol Molnau
Secretary of State ....Mark Ritchie
Attorney General ....Lori Swanson
Commissioner of Finance ....Tom Hanson
Auditor ....Rebecca Otto

Governor's Present Term 1/03–1/11
Number of Elected Officials in the Executive Branch............5
Number of Members in the Cabinet....................................25

JUDICIAL BRANCH

Highest Court...Supreme Court
Supreme Court Chief Justice....................Russell A. Anderson
Number of Supreme Court Judges 7
Number of Intermediate Appellate Court Judges 16
Number of U.S. Court Districts 1
U.S. Circuit Court...8th Circuit

STATE INTERNET ADDRESSES

Official State Website ....http://www.state.mn.us
Governor's Website ....http://www.governor.state.mn.us
Legislative Website..http://www.leg.state.mn.us
Judicial Website ....http://www.courts.state.mn.us/home/

Mississippi

Nickname..The Magnolia State
Motto ....*Virtute et Armis* (By Valor and Arms)
Flower...Magnolia
Bird...Mockingbird
Tree...Magnolia
Song..*Go, Mississippi*
Entered the Union..December 10, 1817
Capital ....Jackson

STATISTICS

Land Area (square miles)..46,907
    Rank in Nation...31st
Population...2,910,540
    Rank in Nation..31st
    Density per square mile..62.0
Capital City..Jackson
    Population..177,977
    Rank in State..1st
Largest City ....Jackson
Number of Representatives in Congress 4
Number of Counties..82
Number of Municipal Governments.................................296
Number of 2008 Electoral Votes..6
Number of School Districts 152
Number of Special Districts..458

LEGISLATIVE BRANCH

Legislative Body..Legislature

President of the Senate.............................Lt. Gov. Amy Tuck
President Pro Tem of the Senate ....Travis Little
Secretary of the Senate ....John O. Gilbert

Speaker of the House ....William J. McCoy
Speaker Pro Tem of the House ........................J.P. Compretta
Clerk of the House ....Don Richardson

2007 Regular Session ....Jan. 2–April 1, 2007
Number of Senatorial Districts 52
Number of Representative Districts 122

EXECUTIVE BRANCH

Governor..Haley Barbour
Lieutenant Governor...Amy Tuck
Secretary of State..Eric Clark
Attorney General ....Jim Hood
Treasurer...Tate Reeves
Auditor ....Phil Bryant
State Fiscal Officer ....J.K. Stringer Jr.

Governor's Present Term 1/04–1/08
Number of Elected Officials in the Executive Branch............8
Number of Members in the Cabinet.................No formal cabinet system

JUDICIAL BRANCH

Highest Court...Supreme Court
Supreme Court Chief Justice....................James W. Smith Jr.
Number of Supreme Court Judges 9
Number of Intermediate Appellate Court Judges 10
Number of U.S. Court Districts 2
U.S. Circuit Court...5th Circuit

STATE INTERNET ADDRESSES

Official State Website ....http://www.ms.gov
Governor's Website ....http://www.governor.state.ms.us
Legislative Website..http://www.ls.state.ms.us
Judicial Website ....http://www.mssc.state.ms.us

Missouri

Nickname	The Show Me State
Motto	*Salus Populi Suprema Lex Esto*
	(The Welfare of the People Shall Be the Supreme Law)
Flower	White Hawthorn Blossom
Bird	Bluebird
Tree	Flowering Dogwood
Song	*Missouri Waltz*
Entered the Union	August 10, 1821
Capital	Jefferson City

STATISTICS

Land Area (square miles)	68,886
Rank in Nation	18th
Population	5,842,713
Rank in Nation	18th
Density per square mile	84.8
Capital City	Jefferson City
Population	39,062
Rank in State	15th
Largest City	Kansas City
Population	444,965
Number of Representatives in Congress	9
Number of Counties	115
Number of Municipal Governments	946
Number of 2008 Electoral Votes	11
Number of School Districts	524
Number of Special Districts	1,514

LEGISLATIVE BRANCH

Legislative Body	Legislative Assembly
President of the Senate	Lt. Gov. Peter Kinder
President Pro Tem of the Senate	Michael Gibbons
Secretary of the Senate	Terry L. Spieler
Speaker of the House	Rod Jetton
Speaker Pro Tem of the House	Carl Bearden
Clerk of the House	Adam Crumbliss
2007 Regular Session	Jan. 3–May 30, 2007
Number of Senatorial Districts	34
Number of Representative Districts	163

EXECUTIVE BRANCH

Governor	Matt Blunt
Lieutenant Governor	Peter Kinder
Secretary of State	Robin Carnahan
Attorney General	Jeremiah W. Nixon
Treasurer	Sarah Steelman
Auditor	Susan Montee
Director, Division of Accounting	Thomas Sadowski
Governor's Present Term	1/05–1/09
Number of Elected Officials in the Executive Branch	6
Number of Members in the Cabinet	17

JUDICIAL BRANCH

Highest Court	Supreme Court
Supreme Court Chief Justice	Michael A. Wolff
Number of Supreme Court Judges	7
Number of Intermediate Appellate Court Judges	32
Number of U.S. Court Districts	2
U.S. Circuit Court	8th Circuit

STATE INTERNET ADDRESSES

Official State Website	http://www.state.mo.us
Governor's Website	http://www.gov.state.mo.us
Legislative Website	http://www.moga.state.mo.us
Judicial Website	http://www.osca.state.mo.us

Montana

Nickname	The Treasure State
Motto	*Oro y Plata* (Gold and Silver)
Flower	Bitterroot
Bird	Western Meadowlark
Tree	Ponderosa Pine
Song	*Montana*
Entered the Union	November 8, 1889
Capital	Helena

STATISTICS

Land Area (square miles)	145,552
Rank in Nation	4th
Population	944,632
Rank in Nation	44th
Density per square mile	6.5
Capital City	Helena
Population	27,383
Rank in State	6th
Largest City	Billings
Population	98,721
Number of Representatives in Congress	1
Number of Counties	56
Number of Municipal Governments	129
Number of 2008 Electoral Votes	3
Number of School Districts	438
Number of Special Districts	592

LEGISLATIVE BRANCH

Legislative Body	Legislature
President of the Senate	Mike Cooney
President Pro Tem of the Senate	Dan W. Harrington
Secretary of the Senate	John Mudd
Speaker of the House	Scott Sales
Chief Clerk of the House	Marilyn Miller
2007 Regular Session	Jan. 3–April 24, 2007
Number of Senatorial Districts	50
Number of Representative Districts	100

EXECUTIVE BRANCH

Governor	Brian Schweitzer
Lieutenant Governor	John Bohlinger
Secretary of State	Brad Johnson
Attorney General	Mike McGrath
Treasurer	Janet Kelly
Auditor	Scott A. Seacat
Administrator, State Accounting	Paul Christoferson
Governor's Present Term	1/05–1/09
Number of Elected Officials in the Executive Branch	6
Number of Members in the Cabinet	22

JUDICIAL BRANCH

Highest Court	Supreme Court
Supreme Court Chief Justice	Karla M. Gray
Number of Supreme Court Judges	7
Number of Intermediate Appellate Court Judges	0
Number of U.S. Court Districts	1
U.S. Circuit Court	9th Circuit

STATE INTERNET ADDRESSES

Official State Website	http://www.state.mt.us
Governor's Website	http://www.discoveringmontana.com/gov2
Legislative Website	http://leg.state.mt.us
Judicial Website	http://www.lawlibrary.state.mt.us

Nebraska

Nickname...The Cornhusker State
Motto..*Equality Before the Law*
Flower...Goldenrod
Bird...Western Meadowlark
Tree...Western Cottonwood
Song..*Beautiful Nebraska*
Entered the Union...March 1, 1867
Capital..Lincoln

STATISTICS

Land Area (square miles)..76,872
    Rank in Nation..15th
Population...1,768,331
    Rank in Nation..38th
    Density per square mile...23.0
Capital City..Lincoln
    Population...239,213
    Rank in State..2nd
Largest City...Omaha
    Population...414,521
Number of Representatives in Congress.............................3
Number of Counties...93
Number of Municipal Governments................................531
Number of 2008 Electoral Votes...5
Number of School Districts..518
Number of Special Districts...1,146

LEGISLATIVE BRANCH

Legislative Body.................................Unicameral Legislature

President of the Legislature....................Lt. Gov. Rick Sheehy
Clerk of the Legislature..........................Patrick J. O'Donnell

2007 Regular Session..Jan.3–TBD
Number of Legislative Districts...49

EXECUTIVE BRANCH

Governor..David Heineman
Lieutenant Governor..Rick Sheehy
Secretary of State..John Gale
Attorney General..Jon Bruning
Treasurer...Shane Osborn
Auditor..Mike Foley
State Accounting Administrator.........................Paul Carlson

Governor's Present Term..1/05–1/11
Number of Elected Officials in the Executive Branch.............6
Number of Members in the Cabinet.......................................29

JUDICIAL BRANCH

Highest Court..Supreme Court
Supreme Court Chief Justice.....................Michael G. Heavican
Number of Supreme Court Judges...7
Number of Intermediate Appellate Court Judges....................6
Number of U.S. Court Districts..1
U.S. Circuit Court...8th Circuit

STATE INTERNET ADDRESSES

Official State Website.............................http://www.state.ne.us
Governor's Website...http://gov.nol.org
Legislative Website....................http://www.unicam.state.ne.us
Judicial Website..http://court.nol.org

Nevada

Nickname...The Silver State
Motto...*All for Our Country*
Flower..Sagebrush
Bird..Mountain Bluebird
Tree..Bristlecone Pine and Single-leaf Pinon
Song..*Home Means Nevada*
Entered the Union...................................October 31, 1864
Capital...Carson City

STATISTICS

Land Area (square miles)..109,826
    Rank in Nation...7th
Population...2,495,529
    Rank in Nation..35th
    Density per square mile...22.7
Capital City...Carson City
    Population...56,062
    Rank in State..6th
Largest City...Las Vegas
    Population...545,147
Number of Representatives in Congress.............................3
Number of Counties...17
Number of Municipal Governments..................................19
Number of 2008 Electoral Votes...5
Number of School Districts..17
Number of Special Districts..158

LEGISLATIVE BRANCH

Legislative Body...Legislature

President of the Senate....................................Lt. Gov. Brian K. Krolicki
President Pro Tem of the Senate........................Mark Amodei
Secretary of the Senate..Claire Clift

Speaker of the Assembly..Barbara Buckley
Speaker Pro Tem of the Assembly.................Bernie Anderson
Chief Clerk of the Assembly.....................Susan Furlong Reil

2007 Regular Session.............................Feb. 5–June 4, 2007
Number of Senatorial Districts...21
Number of Representative Districts.....................................42

EXECUTIVE BRANCH

Governor...James A. Gibbons
Lieutenant Governor...Brian Krolicki
Secretary of State...Ross Miller
Attorney General....................................Catherine Cortez Masto
Treasurer...Kate Marshall
Auditor..Paul V. Townsend
Controller...Kim Wallin

Governor's Present Term..1/07–1/11
Number of Elected Officials in the Executive Branch.............6
Number of Members in the Cabinet.......................................23

JUDICIAL BRANCH

Highest Court..Supreme Court
Supreme Court Chief Justice...........................A. William Maupin
Number of Supreme Court Judges...7
Number of Intermediate Appellate Court Judges....................0
Number of U.S. Court Districts..1
U.S. Circuit Court...9th Circuit

STATE INTERNET ADDRESSES

Official State Website.............................http://www.nv.gov
Governor's Website.........................http://www.gov.state.nv.us
Legislative Website.........................http://www.leg.state.nv.us
Judicial Website....................http://silver.state.nv.us/elec_judicial.htm

New Hampshire

Nickname.. The Granite State
Motto ....*Live Free or Die*
Flower...Purple Lilac
Bird...Purple Finch
Tree..White Birch
Song...*Old New Hampshire*
Entered the Union..June 21, 1788
Capital .... Concord

STATISTICS

Land Area (square miles).. 8,968
    Rank in Nation 44th
Population.. 1,314,895
    Rank in Nation 41st
    Density per square mile.. 146.6
Capital City.. Concord
    Population..42,336
    Rank in State..3rd
Largest City ....Manchester
    Population.. 109,691
Number of Representatives in Congress 2
Number of Counties... 10
Number of Municipal Governments.. 13
Number of 2008 Electoral Votes 4
Number of School Districts 178
Number of Special Districts.. 148

LEGISLATIVE BRANCH

Legislative Body ....General Court

President of the Senate...Sylvia B. Larsen
President Pro Tem of the Senate .... Margaret Wood Hassan
Clerk of the Senate ....Tammy L. Wright

Speaker of the House ....Terie N. Norelli
Clerk of the House..Karen O. Wadsworth

2007 Regular Session ....Jan. 3–July 1, 2007
Number of Senatorial Districts 24
Number of Representative Districts 103

EXECUTIVE BRANCH

Governor..John Lynch
Secretary of State...William M. Gardner
Attorney General ....Kelly Ayotte
Treasurer...Catherine Provencher
Auditor ....Michael Buckley
Comptroller .... Sheri Rockburn

Governor's Present Term 1/05–1/09
Number of Elected Officials in the Executive Branch............................1
Number of Members in the Cabinet.................No formal cabinet system

JUDICIAL BRANCH

Highest Court... Supreme Court
Supreme Court Chief Justice.................................John T. Broderick, Jr.
Number of Supreme Court Judges...5
Number of Intermediate Appellate Court Judges 0
Number of U.S. Court Districts 1
U.S. Circuit Court.. 1st Circuit

STATE INTERNET ADDRESSES

Official State Website ....http://www.state.nh.us
Governor's Website .... http://www.nh.gov/governor/
Legislative Website...............................http://www.gencourt.state.nh.us
Judicial Website .... http://www.courts.state.nh.us/

New Jersey

Nickname...The Garden State
Motto ....*Liberty and Prosperity*
Flower... Violet
Bird...Eastern Goldfinch
Tree.. Red Oak
Song...I'm From New Jersey
Entered the Union... December 18, 1787
Capital ....Trenton

STATISTICS

Land Area (square miles)..7,417
    Rank in Nation 46th
Population.. 8,724,560
    Rank in Nation 11th
    Density per square mile.. 1,176.2
Capital City..Trenton
    Population..85,314
    Rank in State..9th
Largest City ....Newark
    Population.. 280,666
Number of Representatives in Congress 13
Number of Counties... 21
Number of Municipal Governments.. 324
Number of 2008 Electoral Votes 15
Number of School Districts 598
Number of Special Districts.. 276

LEGISLATIVE BRANCH

Legislative Body ....Legislature

President of the Senate...Richard J. Codey
President Pro Tem of the Senate .... Shirley K. Turner
Secretary of the Senate ....Ellen M. Davenport

Speaker of the Assembly...Joseph J. Roberts Jr.
Speaker Pro Tem of the Assembly ....Wilfredo Caraballo
Clerk of the General Assembly ....Dana M. Burley

2007 Regular Session ....Jan. 9–Dec. 31, 2007
Number of Senatorial Districts 40
Number of Representative Districts 40

EXECUTIVE BRANCH

Governor..Jon Corzine
Secretary of State.. Nina Mitchell Wells
Attorney General .... Stuart Rabner
Treasurer... Bradley I. Abelow
Auditor .... Richard L. Fair
Controller .... Charlene Holzbaur

Governor's Present Term 1/06–1/10
Number of Elected Officials in the Executive Branch...........................1
Number of Members in the Cabinet.. 24

JUDICIAL BRANCH

Highest Court... Supreme Court
Supreme Court Chief Justice.................................James Zazzali
Number of Supreme Court Judges...7
Number of Intermediate Appellate Court Judges 35
Number of U.S. Court Districts 1
U.S. Circuit Court..3rd Circuit

STATE INTERNET ADDRESSES

Official State Website ....http://www.state.nj.us
Governor's Website .... http://www.state.nj.us/governor
Legislative Website.......................................http://www.njleg.state.nj.us
Judicial Website ....http://www.judiciary.state.nj.us

New Mexico

Nickname...The Land of Enchantment
Motto ....*Crescit Eundo* (It Grows As It Goes)
Flower...Yucca (Our Lord's Candles)
Bird...Chaparral Bird
Tree...Pinon
Songs...*Asi es Nuevo Mexico and*
O, Fair New Mexico
Entered the Union...January 6, 1912
Capital ....Santa Fe

STATISTICS

Land Area (square miles)...121,356
   Rank in Nation..5th
Population...1,954,599
   Rank in Nation...36th
   Density per square mile...16.1
Capital City...Santa Fe
   Population...70,631
   Rank in State 3rd
Largest City...Albuquerque
   Population..494,236
Number of Representatives in Congress 3
Number of Counties...33
Number of Municipal Governments......................................101
Number of 2008 Electoral Votes 5
Number of School Districts...89
Number of Special Districts..628

LEGISLATIVE BRANCH

Legislative Body.. Legislature

President of the Senate.........................Lt. Gov. Diane Denish
President Pro Tem of the Senate ....Ben D. Altamirano
Chief Clerk of the Senate........................ Margaret Larragoite

Speaker of the House .... Ben Lujan
Chief Clerk of the House .... Stephen R. Arias

2007 Regular Session ....Jan. 16–March 17, 2007
Number of Senatorial Districts 42
Number of Representative Districts 70

EXECUTIVE BRANCH

Governor.. Bill Richardson
Lieutenant Governor.......................................Diane Denish
Secretary of State...Mary Herrera
Attorney General .... Gary King
Treasurer..James Lewis
Auditor .... Hector Balderas
Controller .... Anthony Armijo

Governor's Present Term 1/03–1/11
Number of Elected Officials in the Executive Branch.............5
Number of Members in the Cabinet.....................................25

JUDICIAL BRANCH

Highest Court .... Supreme Court
Supreme Court Chief Justice .... Richard C. Bosson
Number of Supreme Court Judges 5
Number of Intermediate Appellate Court Judges 10
Number of U.S. Court Districts 1
U.S. Circuit Court... 10th Circuit

STATE INTERNET ADDRESSES

Official State Website ....http://www.state.nm.us
Governor's Website ....http://www.governor.state.nm.us
Legislative Website...............................http://legis.state.nm.us
Judicial Website ....http://www.nmcourts.com

New York

Nickname...The Empire State
Motto .... *Excelsior* (Ever Upward)
Flower..Rose
Bird..Bluebird
Tree..Sugar Maple
Song...*I Love New York*
Entered the Union...July 26, 1788
Capital .... Albany

STATISTICS

Land Area (square miles)...47,214
   Rank in Nation...30th
Population...19,306,183
   Rank in Nation...3rd
   Density per square mile...408.9
Capital City...Albany
   Population...93,523
   Rank in State 6th
Largest City .... New York City
   Population..8,143,197
Number of Representatives in Congress 29
Number of Counties...62
Number of Municipal Governments......................................616
Number of 2008 Electoral Votes 31
Number of School Districts...726
Number of Special Districts...1,135

LEGISLATIVE BRANCH

Legislative Body.. Legislature

President of the Senate.................................. Lt. Gov. David A. Paterson
President Pro Tem and Majority Leader of the Senate ...Joseph L. Bruno
Secretary of the Senate ....Steven M. Boggess

Speaker of the Assembly.............................Sheldon Silver
Speaker Pro Tem of the Assembly ....Aurelia Greene
Clerk of the Assembly.......................................June Egeland

2007 Regular Session ....Jan. 3–Dec. 31, 2007
Number of Senatorial Districts 62
Number of Representative Districts 150

EXECUTIVE BRANCH

Governor...Eliot Spitzer
Lieutenant Governor................................David A. Paterson
Secretary of State.........................Lorraine Cortes-Vazquez
Attorney General ....Andrew Cuomo
Treasurer...Aida Brewer
Comptroller .... Alan G. Hevesi

Governor's Present Term 1/07–1/11
Number of Elected Officials in the Executive Branch...........4
Number of Members in the Cabinet.....................................75

JUDICIAL BRANCH

Highest Court..Court of Appeals
Court of Appeals Chief Justice.........................Judith S. Kaye
Number of Court of Appeals Judges 7
Number of Intermediate Appellate Court Judges 57
Number of U.S. Court Districts 4
U.S. Circuit Court... 2nd Circuit

STATE INTERNET ADDRESSES

Official State Website ....http://www.state.ny.us
Governor's Website ....http://www.state.ny.us/governor
Senate Website.........................http://www.senate.state.ny.us
Assembly Website.........................http://assembly.state.ny.us
Judicial Website ....http://www.courts.state.ny.us

North Carolina

Nickname...................................The Tar Heel State and Old North State
Motto ....*Esse Quam Videri*
(To Be Rather Than to Seem)
Flower ....Dogwood
Bird..Cardinal
Tree...Long Leaf Pine
Song...*The Old North State*
Entered the United States..November 21, 1789
Capital ....Raleigh

STATISTICS

Land Area (square miles)...48,711
   Rank in Nation...29th
Population...8,856,505
   Rank in Nation...10th
   Density per square mile..181.8
Capital City..Raleigh
   Population...341,530
   Rank in State..2nd
Largest City ....Charlotte
   Population...610,949
Number of Representatives in Congress 13
Number of Counties...100
Number of Municipal Governments...........................541
Number of 2008 Electoral Votes 15
Number of School Districts 117
Number of Special Districts...319

LEGISLATIVE BRANCH

Legislative Body.......................................General Assembly

President of the Senate......................................Lt. Gov. Beverly Perdue
President Pro Tem of the Senate………………………………...
Marc Basnight
Principal Clerk of the Senate ....Janet Pruitt

Speaker of the House..Joe Hackney
Principal Clerk of the House................................Denise Weeks

2007 Regular Session ....Jan. 24–TBD
Number of Senatorial Districts 50
Number of Representative Districts 120

EXECUTIVE BRANCH

Governor...Michael Easley
Lieutenant Governor.....................................Beverly Perdue
Secretary of State...Elaine Marshall
Attorney General ....Roy A. Cooper III
Treasurer...Richard H. Moore
Auditor ....Leslie W. Merritt Jr.
Controller ....Robert Powell

Governor's Present Term 1/01–1/09
Number of Elected Officials in the Executive Branch.........................10

Number of Members in the Cabinet....................................10

JUDICIAL BRANCH

Highest Court...Supreme Court
Supreme Court Chief Justice................................Sarah Parker
Number of Supreme Court Judges 7
Number of Intermediate Appellate Court Judges 15
Number of U.S. Court Districts 3
U.S. Circuit Court...4th Circuit

STATE INTERNET ADDRESSES

Official State Website ....http://www.ncgov.com
Governor's Website ....http://www.governor.state.nc.us
Legislative Website.......................................http://www.ncleg.net
Judicial Website..http://www.nccourts.org

North Dakota

Nickname.. Peace Garden State
Motto ....*Liberty and Union, Now and Forever,*
One and Inseparable
Flower...Wild Prairie Rose
Bird...Western Meadowlark
Tree... American Elm
Song.......................................*North Dakota Hymn*
Entered the Union....................................November 2, 1889
Capital ....Bismarck

STATISTICS

Land Area (square miles)...68,976
   Rank in Nation...17th
Population...635,867
   Rank in Nation...48th
   Density per square mile...9.2
Capital City..Bismarck
   Population...57,377
   Rank in State..2nd
Largest City ....Fargo
   Population...90,672
Number of Representatives in Congress 1
Number of Counties...53
Number of Municipal Governments...........................360
Number of 2008 Electoral Votes 3
Number of School Districts 213
Number of Special Districts...764

LEGISLATIVE BRANCH

Legislative Body.......................................Legislative Assembly

President of the Senate.................................... Lt. Gov. Jack Dalrymple
President Pro Tem of the Senate .... Judy Lee
Secretary of the Senate ....William R. Horton

Speaker of the House...Jeff Delzer
Clerk of the House... Buell Reich

2007 Regular Session ....Jan. 9–March 30, 2007
Number of Senatorial Districts 47
Number of Representative Districts 47

EXECUTIVE BRANCH

Governor... John Hoeven
Lieutenant Governor...................................... Jack Dalrymple
Secretary of State..Alvin Jaeger
Attorney General .... Wayne Stenehjem
Treasurer.. Kelly Schmidt
Auditor .... Robert R. Peterson

Governor's Present Term 12/00–12/08
Number of Elected Officials in the Executive Branch.........................10
Number of Members in the Cabinet....................................18

JUDICIAL BRANCH

Highest Court.. Supreme Court
Supreme Court Chief Justice.............................. Gerald W. VandeWalle
Number of Supreme Court Judges 5
Number of Intermediate Appellate Court Judges 0
Number of U.S. Court Districts 1
U.S. Circuit Court...8th Circuit

STATE INTERNET ADDRESSES

Official State Website ....http://discovernd.com
Governor's Website ....http://www.governor.state.nd.us
Legislative Website.......................................http://www.state.nd.us/lr
Judicial Website..http://www.court.state.nd.us

Ohio

Nickname	The Buckeye State
Motto	*With God, All Things Are Possible*
Flower	Scarlet Carnation
Bird	Cardinal
Tree	Buckeye
Song	*Beautiful Ohio*
Entered the Union	March 1, 1803
Capital	Columbus

STATISTICS

Land Area (square miles)	40,948
Rank in Nation	35th
Population	11,478,006
Rank in Nation	7th
Density per square mile	280.3
Capital City	Columbus
Population	730,657
Rank in State	1st
Largest City	Columbus
Number of Representatives in Congress	18
Number of Counties	88
Number of Municipal Governments	942
Number of 2008 Electoral Votes	20
Number of School Districts	613
Number of Special Districts	631

LEGISLATIVE BRANCH

Legislative Body	General Assembly
President of the Senate	Bill Harris
President Pro Tem of the Senate	Jeff Jacobson
Clerk of the Senate	David Battocletti
Speaker of the House	Jon Husted
Speaker Pro Tem of the House	Kevin DeWine
Legislative Clerk of the House	Laura P. Clemens
2007 Regular Session	Jan. 2–Dec. 31, 2007
Number of Senatorial Districts	33
Number of Representative Districts	99

EXECUTIVE BRANCH

Governor	Ted Strickland
Lieutenant Governor	Lee Fisher
Secretary of State	Jennifer Brunner
Attorney General	Marc Dann
Treasurer	Richard Cordray
Auditor	Mary Taylor
Director, Office of Management & Budget	Timothy S. Keen
Governor's Present Term	1/07–1/11
Number of Elected Officials in the Executive Branch	6
Number of Members in the Cabinet	24

JUDICIAL BRANCH

Highest Court	Supreme Court
Supreme Court Chief Justice	Thomas J. Moyer
Number of Supreme Court Judges	7
Number of Intermediate Appellate Court Judges	68
Number of U.S. Court Districts	2
U.S. Circuit Court	6th Circuit

STATE INTERNET ADDRESSES

Official State Website	http://www.state.oh.us
Governor's Website	http://governor.ohio.gov/
Legislative Website	http://www.ohio.gov/ohio/GovState.stm#ohleg
Judicial Website	http://www.sconet.state.oh.us

Oklahoma

Nickname	The Sooner State
Motto	*Labor Omnia Vincit* (Labor Conquers All Things)
Flower	Mistletoe
Bird	Scissor-tailed Flycatcher
Tree	Redbud
Song	*Oklahoma*
Entered the Union	November 16, 1907
Capital	Oklahoma City

STATISTICS

Land Area (square miles)	68,667
Rank in Nation	19th
Population	3,579,212
Rank in Nation	28th
Density per square mile	52.1
Capital City	Oklahoma City
Population	531,324
Rank in State	1st
Largest City	Oklahoma City
Number of Representatives in Congress	5
Number of Counties	77
Number of Municipal Governments	590
Number of 2008 Electoral Votes	7
Number of School Districts	541
Number of Special Districts	560

LEGISLATIVE BRANCH

Legislative Body	Legislature
President of the Senate	Lt. Gov. Jari Askins
President Pro Tem of the Senate	Glenn Coffee
Secretary of the Senate	Michael Clingman
Speaker of the House	Lance Cargill
Speaker Pro Tem of the House	Gus Blackwell
Chief Clerk/Administrator of the House	Joel Kintsel
2007 Regular Session	Feb. 5–May 25, 2007
Number of Senatorial Districts	50
Number of Representative Districts	101

EXECUTIVE BRANCH

Governor	Brad Henry
Lieutenant Governor	Jari Askins
Secretary of State	Susan Savage
Attorney General	W. A. Drew Edmondson
Treasurer	Scott Meacham
Auditor	Jeff McMahan
Comptroller	Brenda Bolander
Governor's Present Term	1/03–1/11
Number of Elected Officials in the Executive Branch	8
Number of Members in the Cabinet	10–15

JUDICIAL BRANCH

Highest Court	Supreme Court
Supreme Court Chief Justice	James Winchester
Number of Supreme Court Judges	9
Number of Intermediate Appellate Court Judges	10
Number of U.S. Court Districts	3
U.S. Circuit Court	10th Circuit

STATE INTERNET ADDRESSES

Official State Website	http://www.state.ok.us
Governor's Website	http://www.governor.state.ok.us/
Legislative Website	http://www.lsb.state.ok.us
Judicial Website	http://www.oscn.net

Oregon

Nickname	The Beaver State
Motto	*She Flies with Her Own Wings*
Flower	Oregon Grape
Bird	Western Meadowlark
Tree	Douglas Fir
Song	*Oregon, My Oregon*
Entered the Union	February 14, 1859
Capital	Salem

STATISTICS

Land Area (square miles)	95,997
Rank in Nation	10th
Population	3,700,758
Rank in Nation	27th
Density per square mile	38.5
Capital City	Salem
Population	148,751
Rank in State	3rd
Largest City	Portland
Population	533,427
Number of Representatives in Congress	5
Number of Counties	36
Number of Municipal Governments	240
Number of 2008 Electoral Votes	7
Number of School Districts	199
Number of Special Districts	927

LEGISLATIVE BRANCH

Legislative Body	Legislative Assembly

President of the Senate	Peter Courtney
President Pro Tem of the Senate	Margaret Carter
Secretary of the Senate	Judy M. Hall

Speaker of the House	Jeff Merkley
Chief Clerk of the House	Ramona Kenady

2007 Regular Session	Jan.8–TBD
Number of Senatorial Districts	30
Number of Representative Districts	60

EXECUTIVE BRANCH

Governor	Ted Kulongoski
Secretary of State	Bill Bradbury
Attorney General	Hardy Myers
Treasurer	Randall Edwards
Auditor	Charles Hibner
Controller	John Radford

Governor's Present Term	1/03–1/11
Number of Elected Officials in the Executive Branch	6

Number of Members in the Cabinet	No formal cabinet system

JUDICIAL BRANCH

Highest Court	Supreme Court
Supreme Court Chief Justice	Paul J. De Muniz
Number of Supreme Court Judges	7
Number of Intermediate Appellate Court Judges	10
Number of U.S. Court Districts	1
U.S. Circuit Court	9th Circuit

STATE INTERNET ADDRESSES

Official State Website	http://www.oregon.gov
Governor's Website	http://www.governor.state.or.us
Legislative Website	http://www.leg.state.or.us
Judicial Website	http://www.ojd.state.or.us

Pennsylvania

Nickname	The Keystone State
Motto	*Virtue, Liberty and Independence*
Animal	White-tailed Deer
Flower	Mountain Laurel
Tree	Hemlock
Song	Pennsylvania
Entered the Union	December 12, 1787
Capital	Harrisburg

STATISTICS

Land Area (square miles)	44,817
Rank in Nation	32nd
Population	12,440,621
Rank in Nation	6th
Density per square mile	277.5
Capital City	Harrisburg
Population	47,472
Rank in State	13th
Largest City	Philadelphia
Population	1,463,281
Number of Representatives in Congress	19
Number of Counties	67
Number of Municipal Governments	1,018
Number of 2008 Electoral Votes	21
Number of School Districts	501
Number of Special Districts	1,885

LEGISLATIVE BRANCH

Legislative Body	General Assembly

President of the Senate	Lt. Gov. Catherine Baker Knoll
President Pro Tem of the Senate	Joseph B. Scarnati
Secretary-Parliamentarian of the Senate	Mark R. Corrigan

Speaker of the House	Dennis M. O'Brien
Chief Clerk of the House	Roger Nick

2007 Regular Session	Jan. 2–Dec. 31, 2007
Number of Senatorial Districts	50
Number of Representative Districts	203

EXECUTIVE BRANCH

Governor	Ed Rendell
Lieutenant Governor	Catherine Baker Knoll
Secretary of State	Pedro A. Cortes
Attorney General	Tom Corbett
Treasurer	Robin Wiessmann
Comptroller	Harvey Eckert

Governor's Present Term	1/03–1/11
Number of Elected Officials in the Executive Branch	5
Number of Members in the Cabinet	28

JUDICIAL BRANCH

Highest Court	Supreme Court
Supreme Court Chief Justice	Ralph J. Cappy
Number of Supreme Court Judges	7
Number of Intermediate Appellate Court Judges	23
Number of U.S. Court Districts	3
U.S. Circuit Court	3rd Circuit

STATE INTERNET ADDRESSES

Official State Website	http://www.state.pa.us
Governor's Website	http://www.governor.state.pa.us/
Legislative Website	http://www.legis.state.pa.us
Judicial Website	http://www.courts.state.pa.us

Rhode Island

Nicknames ....Little Rhody and Ocean State
Motto .... *Hope*
Flower .... Violet
Bird ....Rhode Island Red
Tree ....Red Maple
Song .... *Rhode Island*
Entered the Union .... May 29, 1790
Capital .... Providence

STATISTICS

Land Area (square mile) 1,045
   Rank in Nation 50th
Population... 1,067,610
   Rank in Nation 43rd
   Density per square mile.................................. 1,021.6
Capital City... Providence
Population... 176,862
   Rank in State 1st
Largest City .... Providence
Number of Representatives in Congress 2
Number of Counties 5
Number of Municipal Governments....................................8
Number of 2008 Electoral Votes 4
Number of School Districts...38
Number of Special Districts...75

LEGISLATIVE BRANCH

Legislative Body.. General Assembly

President of the Senate............................Lt. Gov. Joseph A. Montalbano
President Pro Tem of the Senate ....John C. Revens Jr.
Clerk of the Senate .... Raymond T. Hoyas Jr.

Speaker of the House .... William J. Murphy
Speaker Pro Tem of the House..........................Charlene Lima
Clerk of the House ....Frank McCabe

2007 Regular Session ....Jan. 2–TBD
Number of Senatorial Districts 38
Number of Representative Districts 75

EXECUTIVE BRANCH

Governor...Don Carcieri
Lieutenant Governor.....................................Elizabeth Roberts
Secretary of State... Ralph Mollis
Attorney General .... Patrick Lynch
Treasurer.. Frank T. Caprio
Auditor .... Ernest A. Almonte
Controller .... Lawrence Franklin

Governor's Present Term 1/03–1/11
Number of Elected Officials in the Executive Branch...........................5

Number of Members in the Cabinet....................................20

JUDICIAL BRANCH

Highest Court.. Supreme Court
Supreme Court Chief Justice........................Frank J. Williams
Number of Supreme Court Judges 5
Number of Intermediate Appellate Court Judges 0
Number of U.S. Court Districts 1
U.S. Circuit Court.. 1st Circuit

STATE INTERNET ADDRESSES

Official State Website .... http://www.state.ri.us
Governor's Website .... http://www.governor.state.ri.us
Legislative Website.....................................http://www.rilin.state.ri.us
Judicial Website ....http://www.courts.state.ri.us

South Carolina

Nickname..The Palmetto State
Motto...*Animis Opibusque Parati*
   (Prepared in Mind and Resources) and
   Dum Spiro Spero (While I breathe, I Hope)
Flower..Yellow Jessamine
Bird..Carolina Wren
Tree..Palmetto
Songs .... *Carolina* and *South Carolina on My Mind*
Entered the Union.. May 23, 1788
Capital .... Columbia

STATISTICS

Land Area (square miles)..30,109
   Rank in Nation 40th
Population... 4,321,249
   Rank in Nation 24th
   Density per square mile.................................. 143.5
Capital City... Columbia
Population... 117,088
   Rank in State 1st
Largest City .... Columbia
Number of Representatives in Congress 6
Number of Counties 46
Number of Municipal Governments....................................269
Number of 2008 Electoral Votes 8
Number of School Districts...89
Number of Special Districts...301

LEGISLATIVE BRANCH

Legislative Body.. General Assembly

President of the Senate....................................Lt. Gov. Andre Bauer
President Pro Tem of the Senate ....Glenn F. McConnell
Clerk and Director of Senate Research ....Jeffrey S. Gossett

Speaker of the House .... Robert W. Harrell Jr.
Speaker Pro Tem of the House....................W. Douglas Smith
Clerk of the House ....Charles Reid

2007 Regular Session ....Jan. 9–June 7, 2007
Number of Senatorial Districts 46
Number of Representative Districts 124

EXECUTIVE BRANCH

Governor...Mark Sanford
Lieutenant Governor..................................... R. Andre Bauer
Secretary of State... Mark Hammond
Attorney General .... Henry McMaster
Treasurer..Thomas Ravenel
Auditor .... Richard Gilbert
Comptroller .... Richard Eckstrom

Governor's Present Term 1/03–1/11
Number of Elected Officials in the Executive Branch...........................9

Number of Members in the Cabinet....................................15

JUDICIAL BRANCH

Highest Court.. Supreme Court
Supreme Court Chief Justice........................Jean Hoefer Toal
Number of Supreme Court Judges 5
Number of Intermediate Appellate Court Judges 10
Number of U.S. Court Districts 1
U.S. Circuit Court.. 4th Circuit

STATE INTERNET ADDRESSES

Official State Website ....http://www.myscgov.com
Governor's Website.............................. http://www.scgovernor.com
Legislative Website ....http://www.scstatehouse.net
Judicial Website ....http://www.judicial.state.sc.us

South Dakota

Nicknames	The Mt. Rushmore State
Motto	*Under God the People Rule*
Flower	American Pasque
Bird	Chinese ring-necked pheasant
Tree	Black Hills Spruce
Song	*Hail, South Dakota*
Entered the Union	November 2, 1889
Capital	Pierre

STATISTICS

Land Area (square miles)	75,885
Rank in Nation	16th
Population	781,919
Rank in Nation	46th
Density per square mile	10.3
Capital City	Pierre
Population	14,052
Rank in State	7th
Largest City	Sioux Falls
Population	139,517
Number of Representatives in Congress	1
Number of Counties	66
Number of Municipal Governments	308
Number of 2008 Electoral Votes	3
Number of School Districts	172
Number of Special Districts	376

LEGISLATIVE BRANCH

Legislative Body	Legislature
President of the Senate	Lt. Gov. Dennis Daugaard
President Pro Tem of the Senate	Bob Gray
Secretary of the Senate	Trudy Evenstad
Speaker of the House	Thomas J. Deadrick
Speaker Pro Tem of the House	Tim Rave
Chief Clerk of the House	Karen Gerdes
2007 Regular Session	Jan. 9–TBD
Number of Senatorial Districts	35
Number of Representative Districts	35

EXECUTIVE BRANCH

Governor	Mike Rounds
Lieutenant Governor	Dennis Daugaard
Secretary of State	Chris Nelson
Attorney General	Larry Long
Treasurer	Vernon L. Larson
Auditor	Martin Guindon
Governor's Present Term	1/03–1/11
Number of Elected Officials in the Executive Branch	7
Number of Members in the Cabinet	19

JUDICIAL BRANCH

Highest Court	Supreme Court
Supreme Court Chief Justice	David E. Gilbertson
Number of Supreme Court Judges	5
Number of Intermediate Appellate Court Judges	0
Number of U.S. Court Districts	1
U.S. Circuit Court	8th Circuit

STATE INTERNET ADDRESSES

Official State Website	http://www.state.sd.us
Governor's Website	http://www.state.sd.us/governor
Legislative Website	http://legis.state.sd.us
Judicial Website	http://www.sdjudicial.com

Tennessee

Nickname	The Volunteer State
Motto	*Agriculture and Commerce*
Flower	Iris
Bird	Mockingbird
Tree	Tulip Poplar
Songs	*When It's Iris Time in Tennessee; The Tennessee Waltz; My Homeland, Tennessee My Tennessee;* and *Rocky Top*
Entered the Union	June 1, 1796
Capital	Nashville

STATISTICS

Land Area (square miles)	41,217
Rank in Nation	34th
Population	6,038,803
Rank in Nation	17th
Density per square mile	146.5
Capital City	Nashville
Population	549,110
Rank in State	2nd
Largest City	Memphis
Population	672,277
Number of Representatives in Congress	9
Number of Counties	95
Number of Municipal Governments	349
Number of 2008 Electoral Votes	11
Number of School Districts	136
Number of Special Districts	475

LEGISLATIVE BRANCH

Legislative Body	General Assembly
Speaker of the Senate	Lt. Gov. Ron Ramsey
Speaker Pro Tem of the Senate	Rosalind Kurita
Chief Clerk of the Senate	Russell Humphrey
Speaker of the House	James O. Naifeh
Speaker Pro Tem of the House	Lois M. DeBerry
Chief Clerk of the House	Burney T. Durham
2007 Regular Session	Jan. 9–TBD
Number of Senatorial Districts	33
Number of Representative Districts	99

EXECUTIVE BRANCH

Governor	Phil Bredesen
Lieutenant Governor	Ron Ramsey
Secretary of State	Riley Darnell
Attorney General	Robert Cooper
Treasurer	Dale Sims
Auditor	John G. Morgan
Comptroller of the Treasury	Jan I. Sylvis
Governor's Present Term	1/03–1/11
Number of Elected Officials in the Executive Branch	1
Number of Members in the Cabinet	28

JUDICIAL BRANCH

Highest Court	Supreme Court
Supreme Court Chief Justice	William M. Barker
Number of Supreme Court Judges	5
Number of Intermediate Appellate Court Judges	24
Number of U.S. Court Districts	3
U.S. Circuit Court	6th Circuit

STATE INTERNET ADDRESSES

Official State Website	http://www.state.tn.us
Governor's Website	http://www.state.tn.us/governor
Legislative Website	http://www.legislature.state.tn.us
Judicial Website	http://www.tsc.state.tn.us

Texas

Nickname..The Lone Star State
Motto ....*Friendship*
Flower................................ Bluebonnet (Buffalo Clover, Wolf Flower)
Bird.. Mockingbird
Tree..Pecan
Song...*Texas, Our Texas*
Entered the Union .... December 29, 1845
Capital .... Austin

STATISTICS

Land Area (square miles).. 261,797
   Rank in Nation...2nd
Population...23,507,783
   Rank in Nation...2nd
   Density per square mile..89.8
Capital City... Austin
   Population..690,252
   Rank in State...4th
Largest City ....Houston
   Population..2,016,582
Number of Representatives in Congress 32
Number of Counties...254
Number of Municipal Governments... 1,196
Number of 2008 Electoral Votes 34
Number of School Districts 1,040
Number of Special Districts...2,245

LEGISLATIVE BRANCH

Legislative Body... Legislature

President of the Senate................................... Lt. Gov. David Dewhurst
President Pro Tem of the Senate .... Mario Gallegos
Secretary of the Senate ....Patsy Spaw

Speaker of the House...Tom Craddick
Speaker Pro Tem of the House ....Sylvester Turner
Chief Clerk of the House ....Robert Haney

2007 Regular Session ....Jan. 9–May 28, 2007
Number of Senatorial Districts 31
Number of Representative Districts 150

EXECUTIVE BRANCH

Governor...Rick Perry
Lieutenant Governor..David Dewhurst
Secretary of State..Roger Williams
Attorney General .... Greg Abbott
Comptroller of Public Accounts...Susan Combs
Auditor .... John Keel

Governor's Present Term 12/00–1/11
Number of Elected Officials in the Executive Branch..........................9

Number of Members in the Cabinet.................No formal cabinet system

JUDICIAL BRANCH

Highest Court.. Supreme Court
Supreme Court Chief Justice.....................................Wallace B. Jefferson
Number of Supreme Court Judges 9
Number of Intermediate Appellate Court Judges 80
Number of U.S. Court Districts 4
U.S. Circuit Court...5th Circuit

STATE INTERNET ADDRESSES

Official State Website ....http://www.state.tx.us
Governor's Website ....http://www.governor.state.tx.us
Legislative Website....................................http://www.capitol.state.tx.us
Judicial Website ....http://www.courts.state.tx.us

Utah

Nickname... The Beehive State
Motto ....*Industry*
Flower..Sego Lily
Bird.. California Seagull
Tree...Blue Spruce
Song... *Utah, We Love Thee*
Entered the Union..January 4, 1896
Capital .... Salt Lake City

STATISTICS

Land Area (square miles)... 82,144
   Rank in Nation..12th
Population...2,550,063
   Rank in Nation..34th
   Density per square mile..31.0
Capital City.. Salt Lake City
   Population... 178,097
   Rank in State...1st
Largest City .... Salt Lake City
Number of Representatives in Congress 3
Number of Counties...29
Number of Municipal Governments...236
Number of 2008 Electoral Votes 5
Number of School Districts 40
Number of Special Districts...300

LEGISLATIVE BRANCH

Legislative Body.. Legislature

President of the Senate... John L. Valentine
Secretary of the Senate ....Annette B. Moore

Speaker of the House .... Greg Curtis
Chief Clerk of the House ....Sandy Tenney

2007 Regular Session .... Jan. 15–Feb.28, 2007
Number of Senatorial Districts 29
Number of Representative Districts.....................................75

EXECUTIVE BRANCH

Governor.. Jon M Huntsman, Jr.
Lieutenant Governor .... Gary Herbert
Attorney General .... Mark L. Shurtleff
Treasurer...Edward T. Alter
Auditor .... Auston G. Johnson

Governor's Present Term 1/05–1/09
Number of Elected Officials in the Executive Branch..........................5

Number of Members in the Cabinet...21

JUDICIAL BRANCH

Highest Court.. Supreme Court
Supreme Court Chief Justice................................Christine M. Durham
Number of Supreme Court Judges 5
Number of Intermediate Appellate Court Judges 7
Number of U.S. Court Districts 1
U.S. Circuit Court .... 10th Circuit

STATE INTERNET ADDRESSES

Official State Website ....http://www.utah.gov
Governor's Website ....http://www.utah.gov/governor/
Legislative Website...http://www.le.state.ut.us
Judicial Website ....http://utcourts.gov

Vermont

Nickname...The Green Mountain State
Motto ....*Freedom and Unity*
Flower...Red Clover
Bird..Hermit Thrush
Tree ....Sugar Maple
Song..*Hail, Vermont!*
Entered the Union ....March 4, 1791
Capital ....Montpelier

STATISTICS

Land Area (square miles)..9,250
   Rank in Nation...43rd
Population...623,908
   Rank in Nation...49th
   Density per square mile.....................................67.4
Capital City...Montpelier
   Population...8,003
   Rank in State...13th
Largest City ....Burlington
Population...38,531
Number of Representatives in Congress 1
Number of Counties 14
Number of Municipal Governments....................47
Number of 2008 Electoral Votes 3
Number of School Districts...............................299
Number of Special Districts...............................152

LEGISLATIVE BRANCH

Legislative Body.......................................General Assembly

President of the Senate.........................Lt. Gov. Brian Dubie
President Pro Tem of the Senate ....Peter E. Shumlin
Secretary of the Senate.............................David A. Gibson

Speaker of the House................................Gaye R. Symington
Clerk of the House.....................................Donald G. Milne

2007 Regular Session ....Jan. 13–TBD
Number of Senatorial Districts 13
Number of Representative Districts...................106

EXECUTIVE BRANCH

Governor...James Douglas
Lieutenant Governor.......................................Brian Dubie
Secretary of State.................................Deborah Markowitz
Attorney General ....William H. Sorrell
Treasurer..Jeb Spaulding
Auditor ....Thomas M. Salmon

Governor's Present Term 1/03–1/09
Number of Elected Officials in the Executive Branch..........................6

Number of Members in the Cabinet....................................7

JUDICIAL BRANCH

Highest Court..Supreme Court
Supreme Court Chief Justice............................Paul L. Reiber
Number of Supreme Court Judges........................5
Total Number of Appellant Court Judges.............0
Number of U.S. Court Districts 1
U.S. Circuit Court..2nd Circuit

STATE INTERNET ADDRESSES

Official State Website ....http://vermont.gov
Governor's Website ....http://www.vermont.gov/governor/
Legislative Website...............................http://www.leg.state.vt.us
Judicial Website....................................http://www.vermontjudiciary.org

Virginia

Nickname..The Old Dominion
Motto ....*Sic Semper Tyrannis* (Thus Always to Tyrants)
Flower..Dogwood
Bird..Cardinal
Tree ....Dogwood
Song..............................*Carry Me Back to Old Virginia*
Entered the Union ....June 25, 1788
Capital ....Richmond

STATISTICS

Land Area (square miles)..39,594
   Rank in Nation...37th
Population...7,642,884
   Rank in Nation...12th
   Density per square miles.................................193.0
Capital City...Richmond
   Population...193,777
   Rank in State...4th
Largest City ....Virginia Beach
   Population...438,415
Number of Representatives in Congress 11
Number of Counties 135
Number of Municipal Governments....................229
Number of 2008 Electoral Votes 13
Number of School Districts...............................134
Number of Special Districts...............................196

LEGISLATIVE BRANCH

Legislative Body.......................................General Assembly

President of the Senate.........................Lt. Gov. Bill Bowling
President Pro Tem of the Senate ....John H. Chichester
Clerk of the Senate ....Susan Clarke Schaar

Speaker of the House................................William J. Howell
Clerk of the House.....................................Bruce F. Jamerson

2007 Regular Session Jan.10–Feb.24, 2007
Number of Senatorial Districts 40
Number of Representative Districts...................100

EXECUTIVE BRANCH

Governor...Tim Kaine
Lieutenant Governor.......................................William T. Bolling
Secretary of the Commonwealth....................Katherine Hanley
Attorney General ....Robert F. McDonnell
Treasurer..Braxton Powell
Auditor ....Walter J. Kucharski
Comptroller ....David Von Moll

Governor's Present Term 1/06–1/10
Number of Elected Officials in the Executive Branch..........................3

Number of Members in the Cabinet....................................14

JUDICIAL BRANCH

Highest Court..Supreme Court
Supreme Court Chief Justice............................Leroy R. Hassell Sr.
Number of Supreme Court Judges........................7
Total Number of Appellant Court Judges.............11
Number of U.S. Court Districts 2
U.S. Circuit Court..4th Circuit

STATE INTERNET ADDRESSES

Official State Website ....http://www.virginia.gov
Governor's Website ....http://www.governor.state.va.us
Legislative Website...............................http://legis.state.va.us
Judicial Website....................................http://www.courts.state.va.us

Washington

Nickname...The Evergreen State
Motto.........................*Alki* (Chinook Indian word meaning By and By)
Flower.. Coast Rhododendron
Bird...Willow Goldfinch
Tree ....Western Hemlock
Song .... *Washington, My Home*
Entered the Union......................................November 11, 1889
Capital .... Olympia

STATISTICS

Land Area (square miles)...............................66,544
  Rank in Nation...20th
Population..6,395,798
  Rank in Nation...14th
  Density per square mile...............................96.1
Capital City.. Olympia
  Population...44,114
  Rank in State...18th
Largest City ....Seattle
  Population...573,911
Number of Representatives in Congress 9
Number of Counties.......................................39
Number of Municipal Governments...............................279
Number of 2008 Electoral Votes 11
Number of School Districts 296
Number of Special Districts..............................1,173

LEGISLATIVE BRANCH

Legislative Body.. Legislature

President of the Senate.............................Lt. Gov. Brad Owen
President Pro Tem of the Senate ....Rosa Franklin
Secretary of the Senate ....Tom Hoemann.

Speaker of the House .... Frank Chopp
Speaker Pro Tem of the House............................. John Lovick
Chief Clerk of the House ....Rich Nafziger

2007 Regular Session ....Jan. 8–April 22, 2007
Number of Senatorial Districts 49
Number of Representative Districts 49

EXECUTIVE BRANCH

Governor..Christine O. Gregoire
Lieutenant Governor...Brad Owen
Secretary of State...Sam Reed
Attorney General .... Rob McKenna
Treasurer...Michael J. Murphy
Auditor .... Brian Sonntag
Director of Office of Financial Management ....Victor Moore

Governor's Present Term 1/05–1/09
Number of Elected Officials in the Executive Branch............................9

Number of Members in the Cabinet.....................................28

JUDICIAL BRANCH

Highest Court..Supreme Court
Supreme Court Chief Justice.....................................Gerry L. Alexander
Number of Supreme Court Judges 9
Total Number of Appellant Court Judges...22
Number of U.S. Court Districts 2
U.S. Circuit Court..9th Circuit

STATE INTERNET ADDRESSES

Official State Website ....http://access.wa.gov
Governor's Website ....http://www.governor.wa.gov
Legislative Website.....................................http://www.leg.wa.gov
Judicial Website .... http://www.courts.wa.gov

West Virginia

Nickname...The Mountain State
Motto .... *Montani Semper Liberi*
  (Mountaineers Are Always Free)
Flower... Rhododendron
Bird.. Cardinal
Tree..Sugar Maple
Songs .... *West Virginia, My Home Sweet Home;*
  The West Virginia Hills;
  and *This is My West Virginia*
Entered the Union ....June 20, 1863
Capital ....Charleston

STATISTICS

Land Area (square miles)... 24,078
  Rank in Nation 41st
Population... 1,818,470
  Rank in Nation 37th
  Density per square mile..................................75.5
Capital City...Charleston
  Population..51,176
  Rank in State 1st
Largest City ....Charleston
Number of Representatives in Congress 3
Number of Counties...55
Number of Municipal Governments........................234
Number of 2008 Electoral Votes 5
Number of School Districts 55
Number of Special Districts...............................342

LEGISLATIVE BRANCH

Legislative Body.. Legislature

President of the Senate...............................Earl Ray Tomblin
President Pro Tem of the Senate .... William R. Sharpe Jr.
Clerk of the Senate .... Darrell E. Holmes

Speaker of the House of Delegates ....Richard Thompson
Speaker Pro Tem of the House of Delegates ....Ron Fragale
Clerk of the House of Delegates ....Gregory M. Gray

2007 Regular Session ....Jan. 10–March 10, 2007
Number of Senatorial Districts 17
Number of Representative Districts 58

EXECUTIVE BRANCH

Governor..Joe Manchin III
Lieutenant Governor......................................Earl Ray Tomblin
Secretary of State.. Betty Ireland
Attorney General .... Darrell V. McGraw Jr.
Treasurer...John D. Perdue
Auditor .... Thedford L. Shanklin

Governor's Present Term 1/05–1/09
Number of Elected Officials in the Executive Branch............................6

Number of Members in the Cabinet......................................10

JUDICIAL BRANCH

Highest Court.. Supreme Court of Appeals
Supreme Court of Appeals Chief Justice............................. Robin Davis
Number of Supreme Court of Appeals Judges 5
Total Number of Appellant Court Judges...0
Number of U.S. Court Districts 2
U.S. Circuit Court..4th Circuit

STATE INTERNET ADDRESSES

Official State Website ....http://www.wv.gov/
Governor's Website ....http://www.state.wv.us/governor
Legislative Website................. http://www.legis.state.wv.us/legishp.html
Judicial Website .... http://www.state.wv.us/wvsca

Wisconsin

Nickname*	The Badger State
Motto	*Forward*
Flower	Wood Violet
Bird	Robin
Tree	Sugar Maple
Song	*On, Wisconsin!*
Entered the Union	May 29, 1848
Capitol	Madison

STATISTICS

Land Area (square miles)	54,310
Rank in Nation	25th
Population	5,556,506
Rank in Nation	20th
Density per square mile	102.3
Capital City	Madison
Population	221,551
Rank in State	2nd
Largest City	Milwaukee
Population	578,887
Number of Representatives in Congress	8
Number of Counties	72
Number of Municipal Governments	585
Number of 2008 Electoral Votes	10
Number of School Districts	437
Number of Special Districts	684

LEGISLATIVE BRANCH

Legislative Body	Legislature
President of the Senate	Fred Risser
President Pro Tem of the Senate	Tim Carpenter
Chief Clerk of the Senate	Robert J. Marchant
Speaker of the Assembly	Michael D Huebsch
Speaker Pro Tem of the Assembly	Mark Gottlieb
Chief Clerk of the Assembly	Patrick Fuller
2007 Regular Session	Jan. 3–TBD
Number of Senatorial Districts	33
Number of Representative Districts	99

EXECUTIVE BRANCH

Governor	James Doyle
Lieutenant Governor	Barbara Lawton
Secretary of State	Douglas LaFollette
Attorney General	J.B. Van Hollen
Treasurer	Dawn Marie Sass
Auditor	Janice L Mueller
Controller	William J. Rafferty
Governor's Present Term	1/03–1/11
Number of Elected Officials in the Executive Branch	6
Number of Members in the Cabinet	16

JUDICIAL BRANCH

Highest Court	Supreme Court
Supreme Court Chief Justice	Shirley S. Abrahamson
Number of Supreme Court Judges	7
Total Number of Appellant Court Judges	16
Number of U.S. Court Districts	2
U.S. Circuit Court	7th Circuit

STATE INTERNET ADDRESSES

Official State Website	http://www.wisconsin.gov
Governor's Website	http://www.wisgov.state.wi.us
Legislative Website	http://www.legis.state.wi.us
Judicial Website	http://www.courts.state.wi.us

*unofficial

Wyoming

Nicknames	The Equality State and The Cowboy State
Motto	*Equal Rights*
Flower	Indian Paintbrush
Bird	Western Meadowlark
Tree	Cottonwood
Song	*Wyoming*
Entered the Union	July 10, 1890
Capital	Cheyenne

STATISTICS

Land Area (square miles)	97,100
Rank in Nation	9th
Population	515,004
Rank in Nation	51st
Density per square mile	5.3
Capital City	Cheyenne
Population	55,731
Rank in State	1st
Largest City	Cheyenne
Number of Representatives in Congress	1
Number of Counties	23
Number of Municipal Governments	98
Number of 2008 Electoral Votes	3
Number of School Districts	48
Number of Special Districts	546

LEGISLATIVE BRANCH

Legislative Body	Legislature
President of the Senate	John C. Schiffer
Vice President of the Senate	Jim Anderson
Chief Clerk of the Senate	Diane Harvey
Speaker of the House	Roy Cohee
Speaker Pro Tem of the House	Thomas E. Lubnau II
Chief Clerk of the House	Patricia Benskin
2007 Regular Session	Jan. 9–March 14, 2007
Number of Senatorial Districts	30
Number of Representative Districts	60

EXECUTIVE BRANCH

Governor	Dave Freudenthal
Secretary of State	Max Maxfield
Attorney General	Pat Crank
Treasurer	Joseph B. Meyer
Auditor	Michael Geesey
Governor's Present Term	1/03–1/11
Number of Elected Officials in the Executive Branch	5
Number of Members in the Cabinet	20

JUDICIAL BRANCH

Highest Court	Supreme Court
Supreme Court Chief Justice	Barton R. Voigt
Number of Supreme Court Judges	5
Total Number of Appellant Court Judges	0
Number of U.S. Court Districts	1
U.S. Circuit Court	10th Circuit

STATE INTERNET ADDRESSES

Official State Website	http://www.state.wy.us
Governor's Website	http://www.state.wy.us/governor/governor_home.asp
Legislative Website	http://legisweb.state.wy.us
Judicial Website	http://www.courts.state.wy.us

District of Columbia

Motto .... *Justitia Omnibus* (Justice to All)
Flower .... American Beauty Rose
Bird .... Wood Thrush
Tree .... Scarlet Oak
Became U.S. Capital .... December 1, 1800

STATISTICS

Land Area (square miles) 61
Population 581,530
  Density per square mile 9533.3
Delegate to Congress* 1
Number of Municipal Governments 1
Number of 2008 Electoral Votes 3
Number of School Districts 2
Number of Special Districts 1

*Committee voting privileges only.

LEGISLATIVE BRANCH

Legislative Body .... Council of the District of Columbia

Chair .... Vincent C. Gray
Chair Pro Tem .... Jack Evans
Secretary to the Council .... Cynthia Brock Smith
2007 Regular Session .... Jan. 2–Dec.31, 2007

EXECUTIVE BRANCH

Mayor .... Adrian Fenty
Secretary of the District of Columbia .... Stephanie Scott
Corporation Counsel .... Linda Singer
Chief Financial Officer .... Lasana Mack
Auditor .... Deborah Nichols

Mayor's Present Term 1/07–1/11
Number of Elected Officials in the Executive Branch 10
Number of Members in the Cabinet 10

JUDICIAL BRANCH

Highest Court .... D.C. Court of Appeals
Court of Appeals Chief Justice .... Eric Washington
Number of Court of Appeals Judges 9
Number of U.S. Court Districts 1

INTERNET ADDRESSES

Official Website .... http://www.washingtondc.gov
Mayor's Website .... http://dc.gov/mayor/index.shtm
Legislative Website .... http://www.dccouncil.washington.dc.us
Judicial Website .... http://www.dcbar.org

American Samoa

Motto .... *Samoa-Maumua le Atua* (Samoa, God Is First)
Flower .... Paogo (Ula-fala)
Plant .... Ava
Song .... *Amerika Samoa*
Became a Territory of the United States 1900
Capital .... Pago Pago

STATISTICS

Land Area (square miles) 77
Population 57,291
  Density per square mile 744.0
Capital City .... Pago Pago
  Population 4,278
  Rank in Territory 3rd
Largest City .... Tafuna
Population 8,409
Delegate to Congress 1
Number of School Districts 1

LEGISLATIVE BRANCH

Legislative Body .... Legislature

President of the Senate .... Lola M. Moliga
President Pro Tem of the Senate .... Faiivae A. Galea'l
Secretary of the Senate .... Leo'o V. Ma'o

Speaker of the House .... Savali Talavou Ale
Chief Clerk of the House .... Fialupe Lutu

2007 Regular Session Jan.8–TBD
Number of Senatorial Districts 12
Number of Representative Districts 17

EXECUTIVE BRANCH

Governor .... Togiola T.A. Tulafono
Lieutenant Governor .... Ipulasi Aitofele Sunia
Attorney General .... Frederick O'Brien
Treasurer .... Velega Savali

Governor's Present Term 4/03–1/09
Number of Members in the Cabinet 16

JUDICIAL BRANCH

Highest Court .... High Court
High Court Chief Justice .... F. Michael Kruse
Number of High Court Judges 6

INTERNET ADDRESSES

Official Website .... http://www.asg-gov.com/
Governor's Website .... http://www.asg-/gov.com
 Legislative Website .... http://www.government.as/legislative.htm
Judicial Website .... http://www.government.as/highcourt.htm

Guam

Nickname...Hub of the Pacific
Flower .... Puti Tai Nobio (Bougainvillea)
Bird.. Toto (Fruit Dove)
Tree .... Ifit (Intsiabijuga)
Song.. *Stand Ye Guamanians*
Stone...Latte
Animal .... Iguana
Ceded to the United States
  by Spain... December 10, 1898
Became a Territory.. August 1, 1950
Request to become a
  Commonwealth Plebiscite...November 1987
Capital .... Hagatna

STATISTICS

Land Area (square miles)..210
Population..154,805
  Density per square mile..737.2
Capital .... Hagatna
  Population 1,100
  Rank in Territory...18th
Largest City ....Dededo
Population 42,980
Delegate to Congress 1
  Number of School Districts...1

LEGISLATIVE BRANCH

Legislative Body.. Legislature

Speaker...Mark Forbes
Vice Speaker... Edward J.B. Calvo
Clerk of the Legislature ....Patricia C. Santos

2007 Regular Session .... Jan. 9, 2007–TBD
Number of Senatorial Districts 15

EXECUTIVE BRANCH

Governor ....Felix Camacho
Lieutenant Governor...Michael Cruz
Attorney General .... Alicia Limtiaco
Treasurer .... Y'Asela A. Pereira
Auditor .... Doris Flores Brooks

Governor's Present Term 1/03–1/11
Number of Elected Officials in the Executive Branch..........................10

Number of Members in the Cabinet..55

JUDICIAL BRANCH

Highest Court... Supreme Court
Supreme Court Chief Justice...................................... F. Philip Cabullido
Number of Supreme Court Judges 3

INTERNET ADDRESSES

Official Website .... http://ns.gov.gu
Governor's Website ....http://ns.gov.gu/webtax/govoff.html
Legislative Website.............................. http://www.guam.net/gov/senate
Judicial Website..http://www.justice.gov.gu

Northern Mariana Islands

Flower...Plumeria
Bird.. Marianas Fruit Dove
Tree.. Flame Tree
Song.. *Gi TaloGi Halom Tasi*
Administered by the United States
  a trusteeship for the United Nations................................July 18, 1947
Voters approved a proposed constitution..............................June 1975
U.S. president signed covenant agreeing to
  commonwealth status for
  the islands.. March 24, 1976
Became a self-governing
  Commonwealth...January 9, 1978
Capital .... Saipan

STATISTICS

Land Area (square miles)..179
Population..69,221
  Density per square mile..386.7
Capital City.. Saipan
  Population 62,392
Largest City .... Saipan
Delegate to Congress 1
Number of School Districts 1

LEGISLATIVE BRANCH

Legislative Body.. Legislature

President of the Senate.. Joseph Mendiola
Vice President of the Senate ....Pete R. Reyes
Clerk of the Senate .... Doris Bermudes
Speaker of the House...Oscar M. Babauta
Vice Speaker of the House...Justo S. Quitugua
Clerk of the House... Evelyn C. Fleming

2007 Regular Session .... Not Available
Number of Senatorial Districts 9
Number of Representative Districts 18

EXECUTIVE BRANCH

Governor.. Benigno Fitial
Lieutenant Governor...Timothy Villagomez
Attorney General ....Matt Gregory
Treasurer..Antoinette S. Calvo

Governor's Present Term 1/06–1/10
Number of Elected Officials in the Executive Branch..........................10

Number of Members in the Cabinet..16

JUDICIAL BRANCH

Highest Court... Commonwealth Supreme Court
Commonwealth Supreme Court Chief Justice...........Miguel S. Demapan
Number of Commonwealth Supreme Court Judges.................................3

INTERNET ADDRESSES

Official Website ....http://www.saipan.com/gov
Governor's Website .... http://www.mariana-islands.gov.mp
Legislative Website............. http://www.saipan.com/gov/branches/senate
Judicial Website http://cnmilaw.org/htmlpage/hpg34.htm

Puerto Rico

Nickname.. Island of Enchantment
Motto .... *Joannes Est Nomen Ejus*
(John is Thy Name)
Flower..Maga
Bird...Reinita
Tree...Ceiba
Song.. *La Borinquena*
Became a Territory of the
United States... December 10, 1898
Became a self-governing Commonwealth...........................July 25, 1952
Capital ....San Juan

STATISTICS

Land Area (square miles)..3,425
Population..3,927,776
Density per square mile... 1,146.8
Capital City..San Juan
Population 421,958
Largest City ....San Juan
Delegate to Congress* 1
Number of School Districts 1
*Committee voting privileges only.

LEGISLATIVE BRANCH

Legislative Body..Legislative Assembly

President of the Senate...................................... Kenneth D. McClintock
Vice President
of the Senate .... Orlando Parga Figueroa
Secretary of the Senate ....Manuel A. Torres

Speaker of the House ....Jose Aponte Hernandez
Speaker Pro Tem..Epifanio Jimenez Cruz
Clerk of the House ....Nester Duprey-Salgado

2007 Regular Session ....Jan. 8–June 30, 2007

Governor..Anibal Acevedo-Vilá
Secretary of State..Fernando Bonilla
Attorney General ....Roberto J. Sanchez-Ramos
Treasurer...Juan Carlos Mendez Torres
Controller .... Manuel Diaz-Saldana

Governor's Present Term 1/05–1/09
Number of Elected Officials in the Executive Branch..........................10

Number of Members in the Cabinet..10

JUDICIAL BRANCH

Highest Court...Supreme Court
Supreme Court Chief Justice.................... Frederico Hernandez-Denton
Number of Supreme Court Judges 7

INTERNET ADDRESSES

Official State Website ....http://www.puertorico.pr
Governor's Website .... http://www.fortaleza.gobierno.pr
Senate Website................................ http://www.camaradepuertorico.org
House Website .... http://www.camaradepuertorico.org
Judicial Website...http://www.tribunalpr.org

U.S. Virgin Islands

Nickname...The American Paradise
Motto ....United in Pride and Hope
Flower...The Yellow Cedar
Bird.. Yellow Breast or Banana Quit
Song... *Virgin Islands March*
Purchased from Denmark...March 31, 1917
Capital .... Charlotte Amalie, St. Thomas

STATISTICS

Land Area (square miles)* 134
Population.. 108,612
Density per square mile... 810.5
Capital City.. Charlotte Amalie, St. Thomas
Population 11,004
Largest City .... Charlotte Amalie, St. Thomas
Delegate to Congress** 1
Number of School Districts 1

* The U.S. Virgin Islands is comprised of three large islands (St. Croix,
St. John, and St. Thomas) and 50 smaller islands and cays.
**Committee voting privileges only.

LEGISLATIVE BRANCH

Legislative Body.. Legislature

President .... Usie R. Richards
Vice President... Shawn-Michael Malone
Legislative Secretary of the Senate ....James A. Weber III

2007 Regular Session ....Jan. 9–Dec. 31, 2007

EXECUTIVE BRANCH

Governor ....John deJongh, Jr.
Lieutenant Governor...Greg Francis
Attorney General ....Vincent Frazer
(Acting) Commissioner of Finance ....Austin L. Nibbs

Governor's Present Term 1/07-1/11
Number of Elected Officials in the Executive Branch..........................10

Number of Members in the Cabinet...21

JUDICIAL BRANCH

Highest Court... Territorial Court
Territorial Court Chief Justice .... Darryl Dean Donohue
Number of Territorial Court Judges 3
U.S. Circuit Court..3rd

INTERNET ADDRESSES

Official Website ....http://www.usvi.org
Governor's Website ....http://www.usvi.org
Legislative Website...http://www.senate.gov.vi
Judicial Website .... http://www.vid.uscourts.gov

Index

—Q—

—R—